Facts About the 20th Century

Other titles in the Wilson Facts Series:

Titles in the Wilson Chronology Series:

Facts About the 20th Century

by George Ochoa and Melinda Corey

The H.W. Wilson Company
New York · Dublin
2001

Library of Congress Cataloging-in-Publication Data

Ochoa, George

Facts about the 20th century/by George Ochoa and
Melinda Corey

p.cm.

Includes bibliographical references and index.

ISBN 0-8242-0960-5 (alk. paper)

1. Twentieth century—Miscellanea—Dictionaries.

2. Civilization, Modern—20th century—Miscellanea—
Dictionaries. I. Title: Facts about the twentieth century.

II. Corey, Melinda. III. Title.

CB425 .O34 2000

909.82—dc21   99-045221

Cover Design and Page Composition: Resa Blatman
Production Editors: Denise M. Bonilla and Lynn M.
Messina

Printed in the United States of America

Once again, to Martha

TABLE OF CONTENTS

TABLE OF CHARTS

ACKNOWLEDGMENTS

Our thanks go to Michael Schulze of H.W. Wilson, who approached us with the idea of compiling a reference book on the 20th century, and our able and patient editors, Hilary Claggett and Lynn Messina. Our friend and frequent collaborator Tom Brown contributed some of the entries in "Events and Ideas of the Century." We also thank the librarians and staff at the Westchester Library System, particularly those in Ardsley and White Plains and their colleagues at the New York Public Library, especially those at the Center for the Humanities, who dug out antique almanacs and other materials from long ago. Finally, we thank Helen Chin for tackling and taming a monster index.

INTRODUCTION

What can you say about a century that brought us Gandhi and Hitler, antibiotics and nuclear weapons, Picasso and television? It seems to have been not one century but many. The 1920s saw flappers and bath-tub gin in the U.S. but warlords and anarchy in China; 1973 meant the Yom Kippur War to Israelis and *Roe v. Wade* to Americans. Will the 1990s be remembered more for the collapse of the Soviet Union or the first cloning of an adult mammal? To make sense of such a complex and tumultuous peri-od, the best way to begin is with the facts. In *Facts About the 20th Century*, we offer those facts: not just trivia but the essentials; not just the familiar but the little-known; not just the local but the global. It is not a record of any one country's 20th century, but of every country's, and of the great worldwide events and trends that affected them all.

Facts About the 20th Century is a comprehensive one-volume reference on the 20th century, combining the features of a chronology, encyclopedia, and almanac. It is organized around the time-honored principle of "who, what, where, and when." Chapter One, "Chronology of the Century," represents *when:* a year-by-year timeline from 1900 to 1999, display-ing the most important milestones in every area of human activity around the world, from culture to politics to science to sports. (To calendrical purists, of course, the 20th century ran from 1901 to 2000, but we follow the more common usage of beginning it with 1900 and ending it with 1999.) Chapter Two, "Events and Ideas of the Century," focuses on *what:* an A-to-Z listing of more than 300 selected events, movements, trends, and concepts that defined the century. Here you will find brief descriptions of topics as specific as the Beer Hall Putsch and the Vietnam War and as far-reaching as totalitarianism and globalization. Chapter Three, "People of the Century," represents *who:* concise biographies of 900 of the most important people of their times, including artists, philosophers, gen-erals, and presidents. Chapter Four, "Nations of the World," emphasizes *where:* a brief 20th-century history of every nation on earth from Afghanistan to Zimbabwe. The main text is supplemented with more than 40 charts, such as a list of all Nobel Prize winners (Chapter One) and battle and casualty tables for World Wars I and II (Chapter Two).

The world's dominant powers—including the U.S., the nations of western Europe, Russia, China, and Japan—had a disproportionate influence in shaping the 20th century, and they receive a corresponding emphasis in this book. But we include the achievements and struggles of people in all other regions as well. Chapter Four, "Nations of the World," contains tables of hard-to-find data on every independent nation's 20th-century history: a chronology of leaders; changes in population at 30-year-intervals; fluctuations in gross domestic product and other indicators over the last 20 years; and a "Historical Gazetteer" listing all major alterations in country names and sovereign status throughout the century. Combined with entries on people and topics as far-flung as Nigerian writer Wole Soyinka and South America's Chaco War, these features make *Facts About the 20th Century* genuinely global in scope.

Facts About the 20th Century contains chapters on "who, what, where, and when"—but not "why." In a sense, questions of "why" are woven throughout the text: the entry on World War II lists possible causes of the war; the entry on Sigmund Freud explains why he is important. But in another sense, we leave the "why" to the reader. The purpose of a reference book is not to reach conclusions about facts, but to present the facts as an aid to researchers seeking to reach their own conclusions. Whatever your question about the 20th century—whether it is as small as "When did the Wright Brothers fly their first plane?" or as large as "Why did the cold war end the way it did?"—we try to give you the information you need to find an answer. If you have no specific question in mind, by all means browse. Review the lives of Gandhi and Hitler; trace the histories of antibiotics and nuclear weapons, Picasso and television. Connections might begin to strike you; questions might arise. If the facts in this book help you make better sense of the 20th century, it will have served its purpose.

HOW TO USE THIS BOOK

Chapter One, "Chronology of the Century," is a time-line from 1900 to 1999. Within a year, entries are divided under seven alphabetically-listed topic headings: Arts and Entertainment, Ideas, Military, Politics, Science and Technology, Society, and Sports. Under each heading, entries are listed alphabetically by place (usually a country, though sometimes a territory or region). The country italicized at the start of each entry is normally the one in which the events took place; however, when the setting of the event differs from the nationality of the person named, the italicized country name refers to the latter. For example, Irish writer James Joyce's 1922 novel *Ulysses* can be found under "Ireland" even though it was first published in Paris. Such distinctions are usually noted in the text.

Chapter One is supplemented by table on all the Nobel Prizes; the years and locations of the Olympic Games; the Best Picture and Best Foreign Language Film Academy Awards; and 20th-century amendments to the U.S. Constitution.

Chapter Two, "Events and Ideas of the Century," is an alphabetical compendium of major events, movements, trends, catchphrases, and concepts. Each topic is briefly identified and discussed. Some entries are supplemented by tables of data, including AIDS Deaths in the U.S. 1981–96; Major Nuclear Arms Control Treaties; World Population Totals; and tables on World Wars I and II and the Korean and Vietnam Wars. If a phrase is **bolded** within an entry, it refers to a corresponding entry either in Chapter Two or Chapter Three.

Chapter Three, "People of the Century," is a biographical dictionary of major figures in politics, the military, culture, science, and society. All individuals are listed alphabetically by last name; nationality, profession, and birth and death dates are provided, along with an account of the individual's accomplishments. If a phrase is **bolded** within an entry, it refers to a corresponding entry either in Chapter Two or Chapter Three.

Chapter Four, "Nations of the World," lists every country on earth alphabetically by its current name. Each country entry includes a fact box listing vital data (such as area, population near century's end, capital, and form of government); a concise 20th-century history of the country; and a chronological table of leaders in the 20th century. In addition, this chapter includes a table showing population growth in every independent country throughout the 20th century (sampled at 30-year intervals); and tables showing changes in gross domestic product, infant mortality, and literacy in every country from the 1970s to the 1990s.

Following Chapter Four is "Historical Gazetteer: Geographic Changes 1900–present." It lists alphabetically the world territorial divisions of 1900, including nations, colonies, and imperial provinces, and shows how the names and status of these regions changed to become the place names of the present day. It allows you to trace the breakup of the Ottoman Empire and look up geographical terms no longer in use, such as "Basutoland" and "Ceylon."

At the end of the book are a bibliography and an index.

CHRONOLOGY OF THE CENTURY
1900-1999

1900

Arts and Entertainment

Austria—Gustav Mahler's Fourth Symphony premieres.

France—French painter Paul Gauguin paints in Tahiti (1891–93, 1895–1901); he will soon move to the Marquesas Islands (1901–03).

Henri Toulouse-Lautrec paints *La Modiste*.

Claude Debussy's *Nocturnes* is first performed.

Italy—Giacomo Puccini's opera *Tosca* opens.

Russia—Anton Chekhov's play *Uncle Vanya* has its premiere.

Spain—Painter Pablo Picasso begins his Blue Period (1900–14) while in Paris and Barcelona. Works include *La Vie* (1903).

U.K.—Edward Elgar's oratorio *The Dream of Gerontius* premieres.

U.S.—The cakewalk, a dance that originated among African-American slaves, becomes fashionable.

World—Novels include Joseph Conrad's *Lord Jim* (U.K.), Theodore Dreiser's *Sister Carrie* (U.S.), L. Frank Baum's *The Wonderful Wizard of Oz* (U.S.), Colette's *Claudine à l'école* (France), Gabriele D'Annunzio's *Il Fuoco* (Italy), and Joachim Maria Machado de Assis's *Don Casmurro* (Brazil).

Ideas

Uruguay—Philosopher José Enrique Rodó publishes the nonfiction book *Ariel*, in which he urges Latin America to retain its cultural values in the face of U.S. materialism.

U.S.—Political scientist Frank Goodnow publishes *Politics and Administration*.

Military

China—Continuing the Boxer Rebellion begun in 1899, an antiforeigner secret society called the *I ho ch'üan* ("Righteous Harmonious Fists"), or Boxers, occupies Peking and lays siege to foreign legations. An international force, with troops from Britain, France, Germany, Japan, and the U.S., is sent to stop the rebellion, which had been supported by the dowager empress.

Philippines—During the rebellion against U.S. rule (1899–1901), the U.S. military governor grants amnesty to insurgents.

South Africa—After several early Boer successes in the South African War (1899–1902), the British gain the edge, with victories at their besieged strongholds of Kimberley, Ladysmith, and Mafeking.

The British capture Johannesburg (May 31) and Pretoria (June 5) and annex the Orange Free State and the Transvaal. Boer forces fight back with guerrilla activity, while the British confine Boers in concentration camps.

Politics

Africa—France and Italy sign an agreement giving the former rights over Morocco and the latter rights over Libya. Britain assumes direct control of the Royal Niger Company's territories, as its protectorates of Southern Nigeria and Northern Nigeria take shape.

Ireland—A massive nationalist demonstration demanding Home Rule takes place in Phoenix Park, Dublin.

Italy—An anarchist murders King Umberto I; the king's son Victor Emmanuel III succeeds him.

Politician Giovanni Giolitti begins financial and social reforms.

Manchuria—Russia annexes Manchuria.

Spain—In the face of agitation by Carlists, supporters of a rival dynastic claim to the throne, the government suppresses Carlist journals and clubs and suspends the constitution.

Tonga—Britain establishes a protectorate over Savage Island and Friendly Islands (now Tonga), despite protest by the indigenous king.

U.K.—The Labour Representation Committee is founded by a coalition that includes the Independent Labour Party, the Fabian Society, and trade unions. In 1906 it will become the Labour Party.

U.S.—President William McKinley is reelected.

The Social Democratic Party is founded; it will become the Socialist Party in 1901.

Hawaii becomes a territory.

Science and Technology

France—Physicist Paul Ulrich Villard discovers gamma rays.

The first escalator is demonstrated at the Paris World Exhibition.

Germany—Physicist Max Planck founds quantum theory, introducing Planck's radiation law and the concept of quanta, or packets of energy.

Physicist Friedrich Ernst Dorn discovers the element radon.

Mathematician David Hilbert poses Hilbert's second problem: whether it can be proved that the axioms of arithmetic are consistent.

Ferdinand von Zeppelin flies the first of his rigid-frame airships, which will be known as zeppelins.

U.K.—Archaeologist Arthur John Evans excavates the palace of Knossos, Crete.

U.S.—Benjamin Holt invents the tractor.

Eastman Kodak introduces its one-dollar Brownie camera.

Walter Reed discovers the yellow fever virus and proves its link with mosquito bites.

World—German biologist Cal Correns, Dutch botanist Hugo de Vries, and Austrian botanist Erich Tachermak von Seysenegg independently rediscover the genetic laws of inheritance discovered by Austrian monk Gregor Mendel in 1866 and subsequently forgotten.

Society

France—The World Exhibition in Paris is held (April–November).

The Paris Metro, begun in 1898, opens.

Japan—Shintoism is reinstated in Japan as a native counter to Buddhist influence.

U.K.—In London, American civil rights activist W. E. B. DuBois and others hold the first Pan-African Congress.

U.S.—The deadliest hurricane in U.S. history kills more than 6,000 in Galveston, Texas, and the Texas Gulf Coast.

The dollar goes formally onto the gold standard.

In Connecticut, businessman Louis Lassen introduces the hamburger, a sandwich of ground lean beef on toast.

Railroad engineer John Luther "Casey" Jones (1863–1900) dies at the throttle slowing down the *Cannonball Express* train as it crashes into a stopped train. He will go down in legend for saving his passengers' lives.

The Automobile Club of America holds its first meeting and sponsors its first automobile show.

Sports

France—The first automobile race with international competitors is held; the course runs from Paris to Lyon.

U.S.—In baseball, the American League forms, but the existing National League will not recognize it as a major league until 1903.

Dwight Davis and Holcombe Ward win the first Davis Cup tennis tournament.

William Muldoon is the first professional wrestling champion.

World—Women compete for the first time at the second modern Olympic Games, Paris.

1901 Arts and Entertainment

Austro-Hungarian Empire—In Prague (now part of Czech Republic), Czech composer Antonín Dvořák's opera *Rusalka* premieres.

Germany—Thomas Mann publishes his first novel, *Buddenbrooks*.

Norway—Edvard Munch completes the painting *Girls on the Bridge*.

Russia—Anton Chekhov's play *The Three Sisters* is staged.

Sergey Rachmaninoff's Piano Concerto No. 2 in C Minor premieres.

U.K.—Rudyard Kipling publishes the novel *Kim*.

Edward Elgar composes the first of the five patriotic marches collectively titled *Pomp and Circumstance* (1901–30).

U.S.—Frank Norris publishes the muckraking novel *The Octopus*.

Ideas

U.K.—Philosopher Bertrand Russell states Russell's paradox, an apparent contradiction in Ludwig Gottlob Frege's theory of classes.

U.S.—Booker T. Washington, an influential educator of African-Americans, publishes the autobiography *Up from Slavery*.

Military

China—The Boxer Rebellion formally ends with the signing of a peace protocol, in which China is forced to pay an indemnity and permit the continuing presence of foreign troops.

North Somaliland—A British expedition routs forces of the "Mad Mullah" sect.

Philippines—U.S. forces take rebel leader Emilio Aguinaldo prisoner, putting a stop to major resistance against U.S. rule.

Venezuela—Colombian troops invade Venezuela; Venezuela responds by invading Colombia, with assistance from Ecuador and Nicaragua.

Politics

Australia—The Commonwealth of Australia is created.

Germany—An assassination attempt on Kaiser Wilhelm leaves him with only minor wounds.

Gold Coast—Britain annexes the Ashanti Kingdom to form part of the Gold Coast (now Ghana).

Japan—The militarist, imperialist Black Dragon Society is founded.

Russia—In St. Petersburg, an anticzarist riot, sparked by anger over the excommunication of writer Leo Tolstoy, is put down by force. Similar riots occur in Moscow, Odessa, and elsewhere.

Sudan—The border between British-controlled Sudan and Italian-controlled Eritrea is fixed by agreement.

U.K.—Edward VII succeeds to the throne upon Queen Victoria's death.

U.S.—As he begins his second term, President William McKinley is fatally shot by anarchist Leon Czolgosz; Vice President Theodore Roosevelt succeeds him.

Science and Technology

Africa—The okapi, a new species of mammal, is discovered.

Austria—Pathologist Karl Landsteiner discovers three of the four blood types and the basic principles governing safe blood transfusion. The fourth blood type, AB, will be discovered in 1902.

France—Chemist Victor Grignard discovers what will become known as Grignard reagents.

Italy—Italian electrical engineer Guglielmo Marconi broadcasts radio waves from England to Newfoundland, marking the invention of the radio.

Netherlands—Botanist Hugo de Vries uses the term *mutations* for the spontaneous genetic changes he describes.

U.S.—Thaddeus Cahill invents the electric typewriter.

Society

Germany—Gottlieb Daimler introduces a new automobile, the Mercedes. The Mercedes automobile company will be founded in 1906.

Sweden—The first Nobel Prizes are awarded.

U.S.—J. P. Morgan founds the U.S. Steel Corporation, then the world's largest company. It is formed in part from Andrew Carnegie's sale of his steel company to Morgan; Carnegie thereafter devotes his life to philanthropy. This year, he gives $5.2 million to the New York Public Library (founded 1895).

Oil is discovered at Spindletop near Beaumont, Texas, giving oil magnate John D. Rockefeller his first serious competition and sparking rapid growth in the Texas oil industry.

In the Oklahoma Land Rush, settlers flock to Oklahoma on a "first-come, first-claimed" basis after the U.S. acquires Indian treaty lands this year.

1902 Arts and Entertainment

Finland—Jean Sibelius's Second Symphony premieres.

France—Filmmaker Georges Méliès creates the pioneering *A Trip to the Moon*; Alice Guy-Blaché releases *Passion*. Both have been called the world's first feature film.

Claude Debussy's opera *Pelléas et Mélisande* premieres.

André Gide publishes the novel *L'Immoraliste*.

Claude Monet paints *Waterloo Bridge*.

Ireland—William Butler Yeats's and Lady Gregory's play *Cathleen ni Houlihan* premieres, with Yeats's beloved Maud Gonne in the title role.

Italy—Italian operatic tenor Enrico Caruso makes his first gramophone recordings for the Victor Company, a U.S. business.

Russia—Maxim Gorky's play *The Lower Depths* is produced.

U.K.—Joseph Conrad publishes the short novel *Heart of Darkness* and the novel *Youth*.

Arthur Conan Doyle publishes the Sherlock Holmes story "The Hound of the Baskervilles."

Beatrix Potter publishes the children's story "The Tale of Peter Rabbit."

U.S.—American-born Henry James, now living in Britain, publishes the novel *The Wings of the Dove*.

Edith Wharton publishes the novel *The Valley of Decision*.

In New York, photographers Alfred Stieglitz and Edward Steichen help found the Photo-Secession Group.

Ideas

Italy—Philosopher Benedetto Croce publishes *Estetica*.

Russia—Revolutionary leader V. I. Lenin outlines his program for Marxist revolution in *What Is to be Done?*

U.S.—Jane Addams publishes *Democracy and Social Action*.

Helen Keller publishes *The Story of My Life*.

Psychologist and philosopher William James publishes *The Varieties of Religious Experience*.

Sociologist Charles Horton Cooley publishes *Human Nature and the Social Order*, which introduces the phrase "the looking-glass self."

Military

Angola—Portugal defeats a major rebellion in this colony.

Arabia—The Arabian Civil War (1902–25) begins in the Nejd region.

Cuba—U.S. occupation following the Spanish-American War (1898) ends. Though nominally independent, the Platt Amendment (1901) makes the country a virtual protectorate of the U.S.

Macedonia, Ottoman Empire—Macedonian insurgents rebel against Ottoman rule. Great Power mediation averts a general war.

South Africa—The South African or Boer War (1899–1902) ends with the Boers acknowledging British sovereignty in the Treaty of Vereeniging.

Venezuela—Britain and Germany seize Venezuela's fleet and blockade the country, demanding payment of compensation for the 1899 seizure of their assets. The blockade, which is joined by Italy, will not end until 1903, after Venezuela agrees to submit European claims to American arbitration.

Politics

Finland—Russian czar Nicholas II abolishes Finnish autonomy.

Germany—The Triple Alliance between Germany, the Austro-Hungarian Empire, and Italy is renewed for 12 years from 1903.

Ireland—Twenty thousand people demonstrate against British rule in Phoenix Park, Dublin.

Japan/U.K.—The Anglo-Japanese Treaty is signed, strengthening ties between the two countries and marking an end to Britain's policy of "splendid isolation."

Persia—Russian influence in Persia (later Iran) grows with a 10 million–ruble Russian loan.

U.K.—A. J. Balfour becomes prime minister after the resignation of Lord Salisbury.

U.S.—President Theodore Roosevelt appoints Oliver Wendell Holmes to the Supreme Court.

Science and Technology

Denmark—Danish explorer Knud Rasmussen leads the first of several expeditions to study Greenland and its people.

France—Meteorologist Léon-Philippe Teisserenc de Bort proposes the distinction between the troposphere and stratosphere.

Physiologist Charles-Robert Richter identifies the allergic reaction anaphylaxis.

U.K.—Physicists Ernest Rutherford and Frederick Soddy explain radioactivity as the product of the disintegration of atoms.

William Bateson (1861–1926) publishes *Mendel's Principles of Heredity: A Defence*, which applies 19th-century Austrian botanist Gregor Mendel's laws to animals.

Scottish cardiologist James Mackenzie invents the polygraph.

James Edward Ransome introduces the lawn mower.

U.K./U.S.—British mathematician Oliver Heaviside and American electrical engineer Arthur Kennelly independently predict the existence of the ionosphere, which will not be detected until 1924.

U.S.—American geneticist Walter Sutton proposes that hereditary material is located in chromosomes (1902–03).

Society

China—Binding of women's feet ends in China as a period of military, economic, and social reform begins.

Martinique—The eruption of the volcano Mount Pelée kills 30,000 people.

U.S.—The Pepsi-Cola Company is founded.

The Texas Oil Company (Texaco) is founded.

World—Labor strikes occur in many countries, including France and Italy. In the U.S., a five-month strike by anthracite coal miners achieves some of the strikers' goals, including a nine-hour day and a wage increase. In Barcelona, Spain, a strike is suppressed with 500 strikers killed and a state of siege declared.

Sports

France—M. Serpollet sets an automobile speed record of 74.5 mph (120 kph).

U.S.—John J. McGraw, known as "Little Napoleon," becomes manager of the New York Giants. This National League baseball team will win 10 league pennants and three World Series over 30 years.

1903 Arts and Entertainment

Australia—The Marie Cowan–A. B. Patterson song "Waltzing Matilda" becomes an unofficial national anthem.

France—Sculptor Camille Claudel exhibits the work *Maturity*.

Germany—German composer Anton Bruckner's unfinished Symphony No. 9 in D Minor premieres posthumously in Vienna, Austria.

Ireland—William Butler Yeats publishes the poetry collection *In the Seven Woods*.

U.K.—Samuel Butler's novel *The Way of All Flesh* is published posthumously.

Thomas Hardy begins publishing the epic verse–drama *The Dynasts* (1903–08).

U.S.—Filmmaker Edwin S. Porter releases *The Great Train Robbery*, considered the first American feature film and the first western.

Henry James publishes the novel *The Ambassadors* and the short novel *The Beast in the Jungle*.

Jack London publishes the novel *The Call of the Wild*.

Scott Joplin composes *A Guest of Honor*, the first ragtime opera.

Victor Herbert's operetta *Babes in Toyland* premieres.

Ideas

U.K.—Philosopher George Edward Moore publishes *Principia Ethica*.

U.S.—Charlotte Perkins Gilman publishes *The Home: Its Work and Influence*.

W. E. B. DuBois publishes *The Souls of Black Folk: Essays and Sketches*.

Military

Morocco—French forces in Algeria attack Moroccan border forces as the French begin to penetrate Morocco.

Nigeria—The British conquest of Nigeria (begun in 1900) is completed with the capture of Kano and Sokoto.

Panama—With U.S. support, Panama revolts, winning independence from Colombia.

Tibet—Francis Younghusband leads British Indian forces to Lhasa, forcing Tibet to make border concessions.

Politics

Canada/U.S.—Outstanding boundary disputes between Canada and the U.S. territory of Alaska are settled by a British-American commission.

Hungary—Austro-Hungarian Emperor Franz Josef refuses Hungarian demands for greater recognition of ethnic differences within the Austro-Hungarian army, arousing protest in Hungary.

Persia—With Lord Curzon's tour of Persia and the signing of a new trade agreement, the British reassert supremacy in that country following recent advances in Russian influence (see 1902).

Russia—Meeting in London, the Russian Social-Democratic Workers' Party splits, with V. I. Lenin leading the extremist Bolsheviks against the more moderate Mensheviks.

Pogroms encouraged by the government result in the murder of about 50,000 Jews.

Serbia—Military conspirators murder King Alexander I and Queen Draga; Peter I becomes king.

Science and Technology

France—Physicist Marie Curie becomes the first woman to receive a Nobel Prize; for her research on radioactivity, she shares the Nobel Prize for physics with two other French scientists: her husband, Pierre Curie, and Antoine-Henri Becquerel.

Germany—Emil Hermann Fischer and Emil von Behring introduce barbiturates.

Norway—Explorer Roald Amundsen is the first to sail through the Northwest Passage, reaching the Pacific Ocean from the Atlantic.

Russia—Konstantin Tsiolkovsky publishes a seminal article on astronautics in which he suggests liquid oxygen for use as a propellant.

U.S.—At Kitty Hawk, North Carolina, Orville and Wilbur Wright invent the airplane as they achieve the first successful flight of an engine-powered, heavier-than-air machine.

Society

Ottoman Empire—In Constantinople, an earthquake kills 2,000.

Polynesia—A tidal wave kills thousands.

U.K.—Emmeline and Christabel Pankhurst found the Women's Social and Political Union, which will become the leading British woman suffrage group.

U.S.—An executive order of President Theodore Roosevelt creates the National Wildlife Refuge System.

Henry Ford founds the Ford Motor Company, introducing its first automobile, the Model A.

The Harley-Davidson motorcycle is developed.

In Chicago, a fire at the Iroquois Theater kills 602 people, sparking nationwide revisions in fire codes for theaters.

World—Child labor laws are enforced in Germany and begin to be enacted in the U.S.

Sports

France—Maurice Garin wins the first Tour de France cycling race.

U.K.—In tennis, Dorothea Douglass wins her first of seven singles titles at Wimbledon (1903, 1904, 1906, 1910, 1911, 1913, 1914).

U.S.—In baseball, the first World Series is held, as the American League's Boston Red Sox (Stockings) beat the National League's Pittsburgh Pirates by five to three games in an eight-game series. The two leagues form a national baseball commission.

1904 Arts and Entertainment

Czech Lands—Leos Janácek's opera *Jenufa* opens.

France—Henri Matisse paints *Luxe, calme et volupté* (1904–05).

Greece—Poet Constantine Cavafy publishes *Poems* (to be revised in 1910).

Hungary—Béla Bartók's *Kossuth* Symphony premieres.

Ireland—The Abbey Theatre is founded in Dublin.

Italy—Giacomo Puccini's opera *Madame Butterfly* premieres.

Russia—Anton Chekhov's *The Cherry Orchard* premieres.

U.K.—Joseph Conrad publishes the novel *Nostromo*.

The London Symphony Orchestra gives its first concert.

Scottish playwright James Barrie's children's play *Peter Pan* premieres.

U.S.—George M. Cohan's musical *Little Johnny Jones* premieres, introducing the songs "Give My Regards to Broadway" and "Yankee Doodle Boy."

Henry James publishes *The Golden Bowl*.

Uruguay—Florencio Sánchez's drama *La Gringa (The Foreign Girl)* premieres.

Ideas

U.S.—Ida Tarbell publishes the antitrust work *History of the Standard Oil Company*.

Lincoln Steffens publishes *The Shame of the Cities*.

Military

Russia/Japan—The Russo-Japanese War (1904–05) begins. Japanese forces besiege Port Arthur, Manchuria, and capture Korea and most of Manchuria.

German South-West Africa: In what is now Namibia, the Hereros and Hottentots rebel against Germany; the revolt will be crushed by 1908.

Politics

France/U.K.—The Anglo-French Entente Cordiale is signed, settling numerous disputes; among other things, it acknowledges British occupation of Egypt and French interests in Morocco.

U.K.—Nonviolent picketing during strikes is legalized.

U.S.—President Theodore Roosevelt, who wins reelection this year, states the Roosevelt Corollary to the Monroe Doctrine; the corollary asserts a U.S. right to act as international policeman in the Western Hemisphere.

In *Northern Securities v. United States,* the U.S. Supreme Court orders the breakup of the railroad holding company Northern Securities, giving a victory to President Roosevelt's antitrust policies.

Uruguay—President José Battle y Ordóñez, leading liberal Colorado forces, defeats the conservative Blanco rebellion led by Aparicio Sarava.

Science and Technology

Austria—Sigmund Freud publishes *The Psychopathology of Everyday Life*.

Germany—Mathematician Ernst Zermelo formulates Zermelo's axiom of choice.

U.K.—John Ambrose Fleming invents the diode, the first electron radio tube.

Physicist Joseph John Thomson suggests the "plum-pudding" model of atomic structure.

English chemist Frederic Stanley Kipping discovers silicones.

Society

China—The Bank of the Ministry of Finance is founded.

Germany—The chemical manufacturing giant IG Farben is formed.

Panama—The U.S. begins construction of the Panama Canal (1904–14) within the Panama Canal Zone, a strip of U.S.–administered land established by treaty with Panama this year.

Russia—The Trans-Siberian Railroad opens; then the longest line of track in the world, it links Moscow with Vladivostok across 3,200 miles.

U.K.—Charles Rolls and Henry Royce go into partnership to make cars; they will found the Rolls-Royce automobile company in 1906.

U.S.—The Louisiana Purchase Exposition, or St. Louis World's Fair, is held in St. Louis, Missouri. Among its highlights is reportedly the invention of the ice cream cone by Syrian immigrant pastry maker Ernest A. Hamwi (though there are rival claims to credit).

The first important New York City subway line opens. Stretching between the Brooklyn Bridge and 145th Street at Broadway, it inaugurates a period of growth that will make this rapid transit system the largest in the world.

The Flatiron Building, a 22-story early skyscraper, is completed in New York City.

A fire on the S.S. *General Slocum*, an excursion boat on the East River off Manhattan, kills 1,031 people.

Tea and coffee shop merchant Thomas Sullivan introduces the tea bag.

Sports

France—The Fédération Internationale de Football Associations is founded.

U.S.—In baseball, Cy Young of the Boston Red Sox pitches the first major league "perfect" game of the century.

In baseball, the World Series is cancelled because of New York Giants manager John McGraw's refusal to play against the Boston Red Sox.

1905 Arts and Entertainment

Austria—Gustav Mahler's *Kindertotenlieder*, a setting for soprano and orchestra of poems by Friedrich Rückert, is performed.

France—Claude Debussy's symphonic poem *La Mer* premieres.

The Salon d'Automne exhibits the paintings of the fauves, a group of artists led by Henri Matisse and also including Georges Braque and André Derain. Matisse's paintings this year include *The Joy of Life* (1905–06).

Germany—Poet Rainer Maria Rilke publishes the collection *Das Stunden-Buch (The Book of Hours)*.

Richard Strauss's opera *Salomé* premieres.

In painting, the German expressionist group Die Brücke (the Bridge) forms; it will last until 1913.

Nicaragua—Rubén Darío publishes the poetry collection *Songs of Life and Hope*.

Spain—Architect Antoni Gaudí designs the Casa Mila in Barcelona (1905–07).

Spanish painter Pablo Picasso, now living in Paris, begins his rose period.

U.K.—The Bloomsbury Group forms in London. The circle of writers, artists, and thinkers includes Virginia and Leonard Woolf, Vanessa and Clive Bell, Lytton Strachey, and E. M. Forster.

Oscar Wilde's extended prison letter *De Profundis* is published posthumously.

George Bernard Shaw's plays *Man and Superman* and *Major Barbara* premiere.

H. G. Wells publishes the novel *Kipps*.

U.S.—Edith Wharton publishes the novel *The House of Mirth*.

Winsor McCay develops the comic strip "Little Nemo in Slumberland."

Ideas

Germany—Theologian Leo Baeck publishes *The Essence of Judaism*.

Netherlands—Mathematician Luitzen Brouwer publishes *Life, Art, and Mysticism*.

U.S.—Spanish-born American philosopher George Santayana publishes *The Life of Reason* (1905–06).

Military

Japan/Russia—The Russo-Japanese War (1904–05) ends with Japanese victory, sealed in battles at Mukden and Tsushima. The Treaty of Portsmouth, New Hampshire, mediated by U.S. president Theodore Roosevelt, forces Russian withdrawal from Manchuria and makes Korea a Japanese sphere of influence.

Politics

Austria—Universal suffrage is granted.

China—Sun Yat-sen founds the T'ung Meng Hui, a union of secret societies working to overthrow the Manchu dynasty.

Crete—Crete gains independence from the Ottoman Empire.

Dominican Republic—The government agrees to U.S. administration of the Dominican customs department and control of Dominican debt repayment.

France—A new law separates church and state.

India—The unpopular Partition of Bengal stirs Indian nationalist feeling against British rule.

Ireland—The political party Sinn Fein is founded to pursue Irish independence.

Norway—Norway secedes from Sweden.

Persia—The Persian Revolution (1905–06) against Shah Muzaffar ad-Din begins. In 1906 it will force the shah to agree to a national assembly and consent to a liberal constitution.

Poland—In the face of growing agitation for Polish autonomy, Czar Nicholas II of Russia imposes martial law but permits the teaching of Polish in Polish schools for the first time in 15 years.

Russia—The Russian Revolution of 1905 takes place. A government massacre of more than 100 peaceful petitioners on Bloody Sunday, January 22 (January 9 Old Style), leads to a wave of demonstrations, insurrections, and mutinies, including a mutiny on the battleship *Potemkin* (June). By year's end, most rebel activity has been crushed; the czar agrees to establishment of a Duma, or parliament, and promises numerous reforms in the October Manifesto.

Government-supported pogroms against Jews continue in southern Russia, with more than a thousand Jews killed in Odessa.

Grand Duke Sergei Alexandrovich is assassinated in Moscow.

Science and Technology

Austria—Sigmund Freud publishes *Three Essays on the Theory of Sexuality*.

Denmark—Astronomer Ejnar Hertzsprung describes the relationship between brightness and star types (1905–07).

France—Psychologist Alfred Binet, with his student Théodore Simon, develops the first formal tests of human intelligence; Binet introduces the phrase "intelligence quotient," or I.Q.

Germany—Bacteriologists Fritz Schaudinn and P. Erich Hoffman discover the microbe that causes syphilis.

The U-boat, or submarine, is developed.

Switzerland—German-born physicist Albert Einstein (a Swiss citizen since 1901) proposes the special theory of relativity, introducing the equation $e = mc^2$. He also explains Brownian motion and the photoelectric effect, contributing thereby to the development of quantum theory.

U.S.—Geneticist Nettie Maria Stevens discovers that chromosomes are paired.

Almon Brown Strowger invents the dial telephone.

Society

Belgium / Germany—Miners strike, demanding reduced working hours.

Japan—Failure of the rice crop brings famine.

India—More than 10,000 die in an earthquake in Lahore.

Nationalist Gopal Krishna Gokhale founds the Servants of India Society.

U.K.—Suffragettes resort to hunger strikes and violence to promote their cause.

U.S.—The first Rotary Club, in Chicago, is founded.

The first nickelodeon opens, in Pittsburgh.

The syndicalist labor organization Industrial Workers of the World (IWW), or Wobblies, is founded.

World—Elastic rubber replaces whalebone and lacing as material for women's foundation garments.

Sports

U.S.—In football, rule changes allow the forward pass and prohibit certain dangerous plays.

American May G. Sutton becomes the first non-British tennis player to win a Wimbledon singles title.

1906 Arts and Entertainment

Austria—Arnold Schoenberg's First Chamber Symphony premieres.

The first Mozart Festival is held in Salzburg.

France—André Derain paints *London Bridge*.

Georges Braque paints *The St. Martin Canal*.

Japan—Toson Shimazaki publishes the novel *The Broken Commandment*.

Russia—Sergey Rachmaninoff's opera *Francesca da Rimini* premieres.

U.K.—Edward Elgar's oratorio *The Kingdom* premieres.

John Galsworthy publishes the novel *The Man of Property*, the first of the series of novels known as *The Forsyte Saga* (completed in 1922).

U.S.—Upton Sinclair publishes the novel *The Jungle*.

William Sydney Porter, known as O. Henry, publishes the short-story collection *The Four Million*, which contains the story "The Gift of the Magi."

Frank Lloyd Wright builds the Unity Temple, Oak Park, Illinois.

Vitagraph releases the first animated cartoon.

Ideas

Germany—Theologian and physician Albert Schweitzer publishes *The Quest of the Historical Jesus*.

U.K.—Anthropologist W. H. R. Rivers introduces the genealogical method of social science research in his work *The Todas*.

Military

Germany—As the naval arms race between Britain and Germany accelerates, the German Navy Bill passes, permitting larger battleships.

Guatemala—Guatemala fights a war (May–July) with El Salvador and Honduras.

Japan—Japan launches the world's largest battleship, the *Satsuma*.

U.K.—Britain launches the first of the Dreadnaught class of battleships.

Politics

Cuba—U.S. forces occupy the country in response to fighting between government and rebel forces.

Ethiopia—The Tripartite Pact (between Britain, France, and Italy) affirms Ethiopia's independence while dividing the country into British, French, and Italian spheres of influence.

France—Alfred Dreyfus is exonerated for treason and reinstated as an army captain. He had been convicted in 1894 and pardoned in 1900; his trial had exposed anti-Semitism in the military and polarized the country between Dreyfus's right-wing attackers and left-wing defenders.

Germany—Disagreement over military action in German South-West Africa (see 1904) sparks a parliamentary crisis, as the Reichstag is dissolved.

India—The Congress Party demands home rule.

The All-India Muslim League is founded.

Japan—Premier Katsura resigns in response to popular dissatisfaction with the results of the Treaty of Portsmouth (1905).

Morocco—At the Algeciras Conference, Germany recognizes French interests in Morocco. Control of the country is divided between France and Spain.

New Guinea—British New Guinea is put under Australian control and renamed Papua.

Russia—Premier Pyotr Stolypin leads a campaign to destroy the revolutionary movement through repression and terror. The new Duma meets for the first time in May and is dissolved by the czar in July.

The Octobrists, a political party, forms in Russia. It advocates the limited reforms named in the 1905 October Manifesto.

Transvaal—Local autonomy with white male suffrage is granted.

U.K.—The Labour Representation Committee (see 1900) becomes the Labour Party, one of Britain's two dominant political parties in the 20th century.

The Liberals under Henry Campbell-Bannerman come to power.

U.S.—Progressive legislation enacted this year includes the Pure Food and Drug Act, the Meat Inspection Act, and the Hepburn Act (expanding federal authority over interstate commerce).

Science and Technology

Austria/France—Austrian chemist Carl Auer von Welsbach and French chemist Georges Urbain discover the element lutetium.

France—Mathematician Maurice Fréchet develops functional calculus.

Germany—Physical chemist Walther H. Nernst states the third law of thermodynamics, that all bodies at absolute zero would have the same entropy.

Astronomer Karl Schwarzschild proposes that radiation is the principal cause of heat transmission within stars.

Russia—Botanist Mikhail Semenovich Tsvett develops the technique of chromatography.

Mathematician A. A. Markov introduces what will become known as Markov chains, or strings of linked probabilities.

U.K.—Biologist William Bateson coins the word *genetics*.

U.K./Germany—British physicist Ernest Rutherford and German physicist Hans Geiger discover that alpha particles are related to helium atoms.

U.S.—Lee De Forest contributes to the development of radio by inventing the Audion, or three-electrode vacuum-tube amplifier.

Society

South Africa—Indian attorney Mohandas Gandhi organizes his first satyagraha, or nonviolent resistance, campaign (1906–13), against discriminatory racial laws.

Switzerland/Italy—The Simplon tunnel, the longest tunnel in the world, opens. Joining Switzerland and Italy, it is 12.5 miles (20 km) long.

Tahiti—Thousands die in a typhoon.

U.S.—On April 18, San Francisco suffers an earthquake that destroys much of the city and kills more than 700 people. The quake is later estimated at 8.3 on the Richter scale.

In the first of several trials deemed in the U.S. the "trial of the century," wealthy Harry K. Thaw is found not guilty by reason of insanity for murdering architect Stanford White. Thaw killed White on June 25 for allegedly seducing Thaw's wife, Evelyn Nesbit, prior to their marriage.

Devil's Tower in Wyoming is named the country's first national monument.

William Kellogg founds the Battle Creek Toasted Cornflake Company.

Sports

Australia—The first Victorian Football League final, with Australian rules, is held at Melbourne.

France—The first international hot air balloon race is launched from Paris.

The first Grand Prix motor race is held near Le Mans. Hungarian Ferenc Seisz, driving a Renault, wins.

Greece—The "Interim Olympics" are held in Athens, celebrating the 10th anniversary of the modern Games, though some do not consider this an official Olympics. France leads in victories with 15 gold medals.

U.S.—The Intercollegiate Athletic Association (known as the National Collegiate Athletic Association from 1910) is established.

1907 Arts and Entertainment

Austria—Gustav Klimt paints *The Kiss* (1907–08).

France—The first exhibition of cubist works is held in Paris. Painters in the cubist movement, which will end with World War I, include Pablo Picasso, Georges Braque, Juan Gris, and Fernand Léger.

Georges Feydeau's farcical comedy *A Flea in Her Ear* premieres.

Germany—Gustav Mahler's Symphony no. 8 in E-flat Major *(The Symphony of a Thousand)* premieres.

Ireland—John M. Synge's comedy *The Playboy of the Western World* premieres.

James Joyce publishes the poetry collection *Chamber Music*.

Lithuania—Mikalojus Ciurlionis paints *Spring Sonata* and *Sun Sonata*.

Russia—Maxim Gorky publishes the novel *Mother*.

Spain—Pablo Picasso's painting *Les Demoiselles d'Avignon* is characteristic of his negro period, with its increasingly abstract forms. It has been called the first cubist painting.

U.K.—Joseph Conrad publishes the novel *The Secret Agent*.

The Fabian Arts Group begins publication of the modernist journal the *New Age*, which will include work by Ezra Pound, T. E. Hulme, and Katherine Mansfield.

U.S.—Rockwell Kent paints *Winter, Monhegan Island*.

Alfred Stieglitz produces the photograph *The Steerage*.

"Mr. Mutt," the first daily comic strip, appears in the *San Francisco Chronicle*. It is drawn by Bud Fisher and will later be called "Mutt and Jeff."

Uruguay—Poet Delmira Agustini publishes her first volume of poetry, *The White Book*.

Ideas

France—Philosopher Henri Louis Bergson publishes *Creative Evolution*.

Italy—Physician and educator Maria Montessori founds the Casa dei Bambini (Children's House) in Rome, the first Montessori school. Her innovative teaching approach will be popularized in her book *The Montessori Method* (1909).

In the encyclical *Pascendi*, Pope Pius X condemns religious modernism.

U.S.—Philosopher and psychologist William James publishes *Pragmatism*.

Sociologist William Graham Sumner publishes *Folkways*. In it, he originates the concept of ethnocentrism, the belief in the superiority of one's own culture.

Clergyman Walter Rauschenbusch reimagines Christian theology as a force for social change in *Christianity and the Social Crisis*.

Military

Morocco—French forces capture Casablanca and much of the coast, then advance inland.

U.S.—The U.S. sends its "Great White Fleet" of 16 battleships on a worldwide tour (1907–09) to demonstrate the country's status as a naval power.

Politics

Austria—Universal, equal, and direct suffrage for parliamentary elections is introduced.

Britain/Russia—The Anglo-Russian Entente is finalized, as Britain and Russia resolve most of their remaining disputes over Central Asia. Britain, France, and Russia become known as the Triple Entente.

Bulgaria—Prime Minister Nicholas Petkov is assassinated by an anarchist.

China—Sun Yat-sen establishes the Guomindang, or Nationalist Party.

Finland—The first women are elected to Parliament.

Korea—Japan takes over government administration, provoking a war of independence (1907–10) that will end with annexation by Japan.

Moldavia—In what is now Romania but was then part of the Ottoman Empire, Ottoman forces suppress an insurrection. Rebels carry out pogroms against Jews.

Netherlands—The Second Peace Conference is held at the Hague but fails to stop the arms race in Europe. A proposal to establish an International High Court of Justice is adopted.

Norway—Limited woman suffrage is introduced.

Orange River Colony—This British colony, formerly the Orange Free State and later part of the Union of South Africa, receives self-government.

Persia—Muhammad Ali Mirza is crowned shah.

Russia—A second Duma, more radical than the first, meets in March and is dissolved in June.

Siam—An Anglo-French convention confirms the independence of Siam (now Thailand).

U.K.—The status of the British dominions, with their significant degree of self-government, is clarified. New Zealand becomes a dominion.

U.S./Japan—The U.S. and Japan establish the informal "Gentlemen's Agreement," by which Japanese immigration to the U.S. is restricted in return for withdrawal of U.S. laws and regulations discriminating against Japanese immigrants.

Science and Technology

France—Physicist Pierre Weiss argues that ferromagnetic substances consist of small magnetized regions called domains, and that the poles of the domains are aligned in strongly magnetized pieces.

Netherlands—Botanist Hugo de Vries publishes *Plant Breeding*, in which he supports the importance of mutations in plant evolution.

Germany—Russian-born German mathematician Hermann Minkowski sets forth a mathematical treatment of time as the fourth dimension in his book *Time and Space*. Einstein will draw on Minkowski's work in his 1916 general theory of relativity.

A hominid mandible is discovered at Mauer, near Heidelberg, Germany.

Sweden—Engineer Sven Gustav Wingquist invents nearly frictionless chrome and manganese-alloy ball bearings.

Switzerland—Chemist Jean-Charles de Marignac discovers the element ytterbium.

U.S.—Zoologist Ross Granville Harrison is the first to culture tissues successfully.

The Hurley Machine Company of Chicago introduces the first all-in-one electric clothes washer, the Thor. The Maytag washer is introduced in Iowa later this year.

Society

France—The L'Oréal perfume and cosmetics company is founded.

U.K.—Shell Oil Trust is founded.

U.S.—In New York City, doctors trace recent outbreaks of typhoid fever to cook Mary Mallon, or "Typhoid Mary," who is a carrier of the disease though immune to it herself. Mary will refuse to stop handling food and will be institutionalized from 1915 until her death in 1938.

Immigration through the port of Ellis Island, New York City, reaches more than one million.

Defended by lawyer Clarence Darrow, Industrial Workers of the World leader William D. "Big Bill" Haywood is acquitted on charges that he hired an assassin to murder Idaho governor Frank Steunenberg.

Sports

U.S.—In baseball, the Chicago Cubs win the World Series; infielders Joe Tinker (1880–1948), Johnny Evers (1881–1947), and Frank Chance (1877–1924) become especially known for their double plays, spawning the phrase "Tinker to Evers to Chance" as a metaphor for precision teamwork.

1908 Arts and Entertainment

Austria-Hungary—Arnold Schoenberg's Second String Quartet, which contains the first instance of atonal music, premieres.

Anton Webern's *Passacaglia* is first performed.

Béla Bartók's First String Quartet premieres.

Belgium—The Musée Royal de l'Afrique Centrale is completed. It will contain an influential collection of Congolese artifacts.

Germany—Rainer Maria Rilke publishes the poetry collection *Neue Gedichte II.*

India—The Reliquary of Kanishka, dating from the Kushan Empire (78–144), is discovered.

Palestine—Polish-born writer Shmuel Yosef Agnon, later one of the most acclaimed Israeli novelists, publishes his first book, *Agunot (Forsaken Wives).*

Russia—Anna Pavlova and Vaslav Nijinsky dance the lead roles in Mikhail Fokine's ballet *Cleopatra.*

U.K.—Novelist Ford Madox Ford founds the journal the *English Review,* which will include work by Thomas Hardy, Henry James, D. H. Lawrence, and H. G. Wells.

E. M. Forster publishes the novel *A Room with a View.*

James Barrie's play *What Every Woman Knows* premieres.

U.S.—Henry James publishes the novel *The Princess Casamassima.*

The Ashcan school of artistic realism is founded in Philadelphia and will thrive until World War I. Its members include artists Robert Henri, George Bellows, William Glackens, John Sloan, and George Luks.

Columbia introduces 78 rpm disks recorded on both sides.

Florence Lawrence becomes known as the "Biograph Girl," for the studio she represents.

When her name is revealed in 1910, she will become the first American movie star to be known by name.

Ideas

France—Socialist Georges Sorel publishes *Reflections on Violence*.

Germany—Mathematician Ernst Zermelo axiomatizes set theory, which is central to 20th-century analytic philosophy.

Sociologist Georg Simmel publishes *Sociology: Investigations on the Forms of Sociation*.

U.K.—Political scientist Graham Wallas publishes *Human Nature in Politics*.

U.S.—Scholar Irving Babbitt publishes *Literature and the American College*, in which he presents principles of new humanism.

Political scientist Arthur Bentley publishes *The Process of Government*.

Military

Sumatra—Dutch forces complete their conquest of Atjeh (Achin) on the island of Sumatra, now part of Indonesia.

Politics

Belgian Congo—The Belgian Free State, a private possession of Belgium's King Leopold II, is annexed by the state as the Belgian Congo.

Bosnia and Herzegovina—The Austro-Hungarian Empire formally annexes this country, which it occupied in 1878.

China—The dowager empress Tz'u Hsi dies. As regent (1861–1908), she had long been de facto ruler of China. She is succeeded by the boy emperor P'u Yi.

Greece—Crete is united with Greece.

Ottoman Empire—Sultan Abdul Hamid II is forced to accept a new constitution containing liberal reforms.

Persia—The liberal constitution of 1906 is overthrown in a counterrevolution by Shah Muhammad Ali.

Portugal—King Carlos and Prince Manuel are assassinated by army dissenters. Manuel II succeeds as king.

South Africa—A constitutional convention is held in the British territory here, proposing a Union of South Africa, which will be realized in 1910.

U.K.—Liberal Party leader Herbert Asquith becomes prime minister.

The Old Age Pensions Act is passed; it will come into force in 1909.

U.S.—William Howard Taft is elected president.

Oklahoma becomes the 47th state.

The U.S. Supreme Court decision *Adair v. United States* outlaws the practice of requiring workers to sign yellow-dog contracts, agreements not to join unions.

The U.S. Supreme Court decision *Loewe v. Lawlor*, or the Danbury Hatters case, rules that workers who have boycotted nonunion manufacturers are unlawfully restraining trade.

The U.S. Bureau of Investigation is founded; it will develop into the Federal Bureau of Investigation (FBI).

Science and Technology

France—Physicist Jean Perrin uses Albert Einstein's equations on Brownian motion (see 1905) to calculate the approximate diameter of an atom.

Mathematician Maurice Fréchet introduces abstract spaces.

Germany—Physicist Hans Geiger invents the Geiger counter.

Netherlands—Physicist Heike Kamerlingh Onnes liquefies helium at 4° K.

Russia—A mysterious event (probably a meteorite impact) near Tunguska, Siberia, creates huge craters and levels trees for 20 miles.

U.K./Germany—Independently, British mathematician Godfrey Hardy and German obstetrician Wilhelm Weinberg formulate the Hardy-Weinberg law, used to predict gene distribution in large populations.

U.S.—Astronomer George Ellery Hale identifies magnetic fields in sunspots.

Paleontologists Charles H. Sternberg and his sons discover the first known fossilized dinosaur skin, that of a duck-billed dinosaur.

World—The International Conference on Electric Units and Standards adopts the international ampere as the basic unit of electric current.

Society

Germany—The Zeppelin airship company is founded.

Italy—Earthquakes in Sicily and mainland Italy kill 100,000 to 150,000 people.

Japan—More than 200 die when the Japanese cruiser *Matsushima* sinks off Pescadores Islands.

U.K.—The Hoover Company is founded to market the vacuum cleaner, invented in 1902.

Lord Baden Powell founds the Boy Scout movement.

U.S.—Henry Ford introduces the Model T, priced low enough to make driving accessible to a mass consumer public.

The General Motors Company is founded.

World—The universal Morse-code distress signal S.O.S. is adopted.

Sports

U.K.—Cricketer W. G. Grace, playing since 1865, retires. During his career, he scored 54,896 runs and took 2,876 wickets.

U.S.—American Jack Johnson defeats Canadian Tommy Burns for the world heavyweight boxing title in a bout in Sydney, Australia. Johnson is the first person of African descent to hold the title.

World—The International Swimming Federation (FINA) is formed.

1909 Arts and Entertainment

Austria-Hungary—Gustav Mahler's *Das Lied von der Erde (The Song of the Earth)* premieres.

Auguste Rodin completes *Bust of Gustav Mahler.*

France—Maurice Ravel's piano composition *Gaspard de la nuit* premieres in Paris.

Henri Matisse completes *The Dance.*

Sergey Diaghilev's Ballets Russes debuts, with principal choreography by Mikhail Fokine and featuring dancers Vaslav Nijinsky and Anna Pavlova.

Germany—Richard Strauss's opera *Elektra* premieres, with libretto by Hugo von Hofmannsthal.

Hungary—Ferenc Molnár completes the play *Liliom.*

Russia—Nikolay Rimsky-Korsakov's opera-ballet *The Golden Cockerel* is posthumously produced.

U.K.—Ezra Pound publishes the poetry collection *Exultations.*

Ralph Vaughan Williams's *Fantasia on a Theme by Thomas Tallis* premieres.

J. M. Synge completes the play *Deidre of the Sorrows.*

U.S.—W. C. Handy writes the campaign song "Mr. Crump," which in 1912 will be renamed "Memphis Blues" and become the first published blues song.

Architect Frank Lloyd Wright completes Robie House, Chicago.

World—Films include the first newsreels, the early animated film *Gertie the Dinosaur* (U.S.) and *Carmen* (France).

Novels include André Gide's *La Porte étroite* (France), Wladislaw Reyjont's *Peasants* (Russia, 4 vols. from 1902), Robert Walser's *Jacob of Gunten: A Diary* (Switzerland), and Jack London's *Martin Eden* (U.S.).

Ideas

Russia—Vladimir Lenin publishes *Materialism and Empiric Criticism.*

U.K.—William Beveridge publishes *A Problem for Industry.*

U.S.—Austrian-born psychiatrist Sigmund Freud lectures on psychoanalysis.

Military

Honduras—Civil war begins, continuing until 1911.

Korea—Japanese forces occupy Korea; the occupation will last 36 years.

Politics

Belgium—King Leopold II dies and is succeeded by Albert I.

Germany—Bethmann-Hollweg becomes chancellor.

Persia—Shah Mohammed Ali is deposed and succeeded by Sultan Ahmed Shah.

U.S.—William Howard Taft is inaugurated as president.

The Payne-Aldrich Act permits the free importation of sugar, tobacco, and hemp to the U.S. from the Philippines.

Science and Technology

Denmark—S. Sorensen develops the pH scale for testing acidity.

France—C. Nicole demonstrates that typhus is spread by the body louse.

U.S.—The synthetic resin Bakelite is developed by Belgian-born Leo H. Baekeland and becomes popular for its electrical resistance.

Society

Australia—Old-age pensions for those over 65 are instituted.

France—Public executions are resumed.

Aviator Louis Blériot becomes the first to cross the English Channel by air.

Italy—Medieval French heroine Joan of Arc is beatified by the Catholic Church.

Mexico—Floods in Monterey kill 1,500.

Palestine—The first kibbutz is held at Degania Aleph.

U.S.—Robert Peary is the first person to reach the North Pole.

Henry Ford's Model T, the "universal car," leads in sales.

20,000 garment workers hold a three-month strike.

The National Association for the Advancement of Colored People (NAACP) is formed in New York by W. E. B. DuBois and others.

Sports

U.K.—The Imperial Cricket Conference is founded, later the International Cricket Conference.

1910 Arts and Entertainment

Austria—Alban Berg's String Quartet premieres.

France—Jules Massenet's opera *Don Quichotte* premieres.

Henri Rousseau paints *The Dream*.

Robert Delaunay paints *The Eiffel Tower*.

Denmark—Karin Michaelis publishes the novel *The Dangerous Age*.

Germany—Franz Wedekind's play *Schloss Wetterstein* is produced.

Ireland—William Butler Yeats publishes the collection *The Green Helmet and Other Poems*.

Italy—Italian composer Puccini's opera *The Girl of the Golden West* premieres in New York.

Italian futurists led by Umberto Boccioni and Giacomo Balla publish *Technical Manifesto of the Futurist Painters*.

Sculptor Amedeo Modigliani creates *The Cellist*.

Russia—Wassily Kandinsky paints what may be the first entirely abstract or nonrepresentational painting, *First Abstract Watercolor*.

Russian composer Igor Stravinsky's ballet *The Firebird* opens in Paris.

U.K.—E. M. Forster publishes the novel *Howards End*.

U.S.—Victor Herbert's operetta *Naughty Marietta* premieres.

George Herriman creates the "Krazy Kat" comic strip.

The Metropolitan Opera, with tenor Enrico Caruso, is broadcast on radio for the first time.

Cartoonist John Randolph Bray patents the cel process of animation.

Ideas

France—Sociologist Lucien Lévy-Bruhl publishes *How Natives Think*; he will later publish *Primitive Mentality* (1922).

U.S.—Jane Addams publishes *Twenty Years at Hull House*.

W. E. B. DuBois becomes editor of "The Crisis" (1910–34), the journal of the National Association for the Advancement of Colored People.

Military

Albania—Albanians revolt against Ottoman rule; the major part of the insurrection is defeated, but a guerrilla war persists, weakening Ottoman control of the Balkans.

Politics

Africa—French Equatorial Africa is formed from several French colonies.

China—China abolishes slavery.

Egypt—Premier Butros Ghali is assassinated by a nationalist.

Greece—Eleutherios Venizelos becomes premier.

Korea—Japan formally annexes Korea.

Mexico—The Mexican Revolution (1910–40) begins when opposition candidate Francisco Madero rejects an election confirming the dictatorship of Porfirio Díaz; Madero calls for armed rebellion.

Montenegro—Montenegro is proclaimed a kingdom under Nicholas I.

Portugal—A revolution ousts King Manuel II and makes the nation a republic.

South Africa—The Union of South Africa is created as a dominion within the British Empire. Louis Botha, head of the South Africa Party he co-founds this year, is its first premier.

Spain—Freedom of belief is proclaimed by King Alfonso.

Switzerland—Railroads are nationalized.

U.K.—King Edward VII dies and is succeeded by George V.

A constitutional crisis continues, stemming from the House of Lords' veto of the 1909

"People's Budget."

U.S.—Congress passes the Mann or "White Slavery" Act, banning transportation of women across state lines for "immoral purposes."

Science and Technology

France—Physicist Marie Curie demonstrates conclusively that radium, which she co-discovered with husband and fellow physicist Pierre Curie in 1898, is an element.

Germany—Psychologists Max Wertheimer, Kurt Koffa, and Wolfgang Köhler found the school of Gestalt psychology.

Bacteriologist Paul Ehrlich produces the arsenical compound salvarsan, the first drug effective against syphilis. The discovery of this "magic bullet" marks the beginning of modern chemotherapy.

U.K.—Mathematicians Bertrand Russell and Alfred North Whitehead begin publication of their *Principia Mathematica* (1910–13).

U.S.—Physicist J. J. Thomson confirms the existence of isotypes through the use of positive cathode rays.

Society

France—Hairdresser Antoine creates bobbed hair.

U.K.—The nation now has 122,000 telephones in use.

Murderer Hawley Harvey Crippen is executed. This year, he became the first person apprehended by radio, when he tried to escape by ocean liner to Canada with his typist-lover after murdering his wife.

U.S.—The first significant militant woman suffrage parade in the country is held.

Andrew Carnegie founds the Carnegie Endowment for International Peace.

New York's Manhattan Bridge is completed (begun 1901).

In Spokane, Washington, Father's Day is celebrated for the first time.

Sports

U.S.—Driving a Benz automobile, Barney (Berna Eli) Oldfield sets a land speed record of over 131 miles per hour at Daytona Beach, Florida.

In boxing, world heavyweight champion Jack Johnson successfully defends his title against ex-champion Jim Jeffries.

In baseball, Philadelphia (American League) defeats Chicago (National League) four games to one in the World Series.

1911 Arts and Entertainment

France—Georges Braque paints the cubist work *The Portuguese*.

Henri Matisse paints *The Red Studio*.

Germany—Anton Webern composes *Five Orchestral Pieces*, Op. 10. (1911–13).

Richard Strauss's comic opera *Der Rosenkavalier* premieres.

The German expressionist group Der Blaue Reiter ("The Blue Horseman") is founded in Munich by Wassily Kandinsky, Franz Marc, Paul Klee, and August Macke. It will be dissolved by 1914.

Netherlands—Piet Mondrian paints the series *Flowering Apple Tree* (1911–12).

Russia—Russian composer Igor Stravinsky's ballet *Pétrouchka* opens in Paris.

U.K.—Joseph Conrad publishes the novel *Under Western Eyes*.

U.S.—Architect Frank Lloyd Wright builds Taliesin.

Edith Wharton publishes the novel *Ethan Frome*.

Theodore Dreiser publishes the novel *Jennie Gerhardt*.

Irving Berlin composes his first of many international song hits, "Alexander's Ragtime Band." His first published song was "Marie from Sunny Italy" (1907).

Ideas

Germany—Sociologist and economist Robert Michels introduces the "iron law of oligarchy" in *Political Parties: A Sociological Study of the Oligarchical Tendencies of Modern Democracy*.

Hungary—Philosopher György Lukács publishes *The Soul and Its Forms*.

U.S.—Anthropologist Franz Boas publishes *The Mind of Primitive Man*.

Historian James Robinson publishes the essay collection *The New History*, which argues that history should include not only political content but also social, cultural, economic, and other material.

Military

Libya—Battling Ottoman forces, Italy conquers Tripoli and much of Libya.

Morocco—The arrival of the German gunboat *Panther* in Agadir creates an international crisis.

Persia—Britain (in the south) and Russia (in the north) occupy much of the country.

Politics

China—Revolts at Wuchang initiate the Chinese Revolution; by 1912, the Manchu emperor will be deposed and China will become a republic.

France—Joseph Caillaux is named premier.

Mexico—Dictator Porfirio Díaz is overthrown; Francisco Madero succeeds him but is soon opposed by the forces of fellow revolutionaries Emiliano Zapata and Pancho Villa.

Portugal—A liberal constitution is promulgated. The First Republic will be extremely unstable, with 20 insurrections and 44 governments between 1911 and its demise in 1926.

Russia—Premier Peter Stolypin is assassinated.

U.K.—Winston Churchill becomes First Lord of the Admiralty.

J. Ramsay MacDonald is elected chairman of the British Labour Party.

David Lloyd George introduces the National Health Insurance Bill.

The first imperial conference, a meeting between prime ministers of the U.K. and its dominions, is held, in London.

U.S.—In *Standard Oil Company of New Jersey v. United States*, the Standard Oil trust is ordered dissolved.

Science and Technology

Denmark/U.S.—Working independently, Danish astronomer Ejnar Hertzsprung and, in 1913 American astronomer Henry Norris Russell develop the Hertzprung-Russell diagram, which plots magnitudes of stars against their colors and spectral classes.

Germany—Neurologist Alois Alzheimer discovers the presenile dementia that will be called Alzheimer's disease.

Netherlands—Physicist Heike Kamerlingh Onnes discovers superconductivity.

Norway—Norwegian explorer Roald Amundsen reaches the South Pole on December 16, ahead of British explorer Robert Falcon Scott, who will arrive on January 14, 1912.

U.K.—Physicist Ernest Rutherford proposes a model of the atom in which the atom is mostly empty space.

Scottish physicist C. T. R. Williams invents the cloud chamber.

U.S.—Geneticist Hermann J. Müller begins experimental breeding of the fruit fly (*Drosophil*).

Geneticists Thomas Hunt Morgan and Alfred Henry Sturtevant devise the first chromosome map.

Society

Japan—Raicho Hiratsuka organizes the Bluestocking Society and founds the magazine *Bluestocking (Seito)*.

U.S.—Automobile manufacturer W. C. Durant founds the Chevrolet Motor Company.

The electric self-starter on automobiles, invented in 1899, begins to be used on Cadillacs. In time, it will eliminate the hand crank.

Sports

U.K.—The first downhill ski race is organized by British skier Arnold Lunn.

U.S.—Nine-year-old golfer Robert T. Jones, later to be considered one of the game's greatest players, wins his first title, the Junior Championship of Atlanta, Georgia.

Cy Young retires from baseball after having set records for number of games won (511) and number of innings pitched (7,356); the annual award for best pitcher will be named for him.

Ray Harroun wins the first Indianapolis 500-mile auto race.

1912 Arts and Entertainment

Austria—Austrian composer Arnold Schoenberg's song cycle *Pierrot Lunaire* premieres in Berlin.

France—Composer Maurice Ravel's ballet *Daphnis and Chloe* premieres.

Marcel Duchamp paints *Nude Descending a Staircase No. 2.*

Germany—Richard Strauss's opera *Ariadne auf Naxos* premieres.

India—Rabindranath Tagore publishes the poetry collection *Gitanjali.*

Italy—Amedeo Modigliani sculpts *Stone Head.*

Russia—Marc Chagall paints *The Cattle Dealer.*

U.S.—Robinson Jeffers publishes his first collection of poems, *Flagons and Apples.*

The literary magazine *Poetry* is founded in Chicago.

Amy Lowell publishes her first book of poetry, *A Dome of Many-Coloured Glass.*

World—Synthetic cubism, typified by Spanish painter Juan Gris, supersedes analytic cubism, an earlier phase of this artistic movement.

Ideas

France—Sociologist Émile Durkheim publishes *Elementary Forms of Religious Life.*

India—Historian R. K. Mukherji publishes *Indian Shipping.*

U.K.—A separate chair of politics is established at Oxford.

Military

Central America—U.S. Marines take control of Honduras and Nicaragua.

Mediterranean Sea—Fighting the Ottoman Empire in Libya, Rhodes, and the Dodecanese Islands, Italy is the first country to use airplanes as bombers.

Morocco—France continues its conquest of Morocco and declares Morocco a protectorate.

Ottoman Empire—In the First Balkan War (1912–13), the Ottoman Empire is forced to cede most of its European possessions to Serbia, Bulgaria, Greece, and Montenegro.

Politics

China—On February 12, child emperor Hsüan T'ung (Henry P'u-i), the last emperor of China, abdicates; China becomes a republic. Provisional president Sun Yat-sen resigns in favor of General Yuan Shikai, who becomes first president of the Chinese republic (1912–16).

The Guomindang, or Nationalist Party, is formed. Led by Sun Yat-sen, it will govern China from 1927 to 1949.

Outer Mongolia—Outer Mongolia declares independence from China; full independence will not come until 1921.

Russia—Vladimir Ilich Lenin founds the Russian Social-Democratic Workers' Party (Bolshevik Party), formerly a faction of a larger party.

South Africa—The African National Congress is founded.

U.S.—The Republican Party splinters as former president Theodore Roosevelt leads the newly formed Progressive, or Bull Moose, Party in a challenge against incumbent president

William Howard Taft. The Republican split facilitates the election of Democrat Woodrow Wilson.

An assassination attempt on Theodore Roosevelt wounds but fails to kill him.

Science and Technology

Germany—Meteorologist and geophysicist Alfred Wegener proposes the theory of continental drift. At first rejected, it bears similarity to the later theory of plate tectonics.

Physicist Max von Laue discovers how to use crystals for X-ray diffraction, permitting measurement of the wavelength of X rays.

Chemist Friedrich Bergius develops a coal hydrogenation process in which coal and heavy oil are treated with hydrogen to produce gasoline.

Netherlands—Physical chemist Peter Debye develops equations describing the behavior of polar molecules or dipoles.

Peru/U.S.—American archaeologist Hiram Bingham discovers the Inca strongholds of Machu Picchu and Vitcos in Peru.

Poland/U.K.—Polish-born biochemist Casimir Funk, now working in England and later in the U.S., coins the term *vitamine*, which will be shortened to *vitamin* in 1920.

U.K.—Amateur archaeologist Charles Dawson claims to have discovered a fossil skull of Piltdown man, a purported "missing link" that will be shown to be a hoax in 1953.

British explorer Robert Falcon Scott leads the second party to reach the South Pole, but Scott and all the party die on the return trip.

U.S.—Astronomer Henrietta Leavitt discovers the period-luminosity curve of Cepheid variable stars; the discovery will be used to determine distances of stars and galaxies.

Society

France—Fashion designer Coco Chanel opens her first shop, a millinery, at Deauville. Her fashion house will be established in Paris in 1914.

Japan—The Japanese steamer *Kiche Maru* sinks off Japan (September 28), killing 1,000.

U.K.—In the early morning of April 15, the British liner *Titanic* sinks on her maiden voyage after colliding with an iceberg; 1,513 people die.

British aeronautical engineer Thomas Octave Murdoch Sopwith founds the Sopwith Aviation Company; its Camel airplane will be a widely used fighter plane in World War I.

U.S.—The Industrial Workers of the World lead the Lawrence, Massachusetts, textile strike.

The Alpha Beta Food Market and Ward's Groceteria, two self-service grocery stores that are forerunners of supermarkets, open independently in California.

The F. W. Woolworth Company is founded, merging Frank Winfield Woolworth's existing chains of five-and-ten-cent stores.

Mount Katmai in southern Alaska erupts, transforming the adjoining valley into the wasteland called the Valley of the Ten Thousand Smokes.

Sports

Finland—Runner Hannes Kolehmainen wins three gold medals at the Stockholm Olympics, setting a world record in one of the events, the 5,000 meters.

U.S.—Jim Thorpe, winner of the decathlon and pentathlon, is the outstanding athlete at the Stockholm Olympics, but he is stripped of his medals and his records are invalidated over a controversy concerning his amateur status.

1913 Arts and Entertainment

France—Novelist Marcel Proust publishes *Remembrance of Things Past* (1913–27).

Painter Georges Braque invents papier collé, a variety of collage.

India—Rabindranath Tagore's play *Dakaghan (The Post Office)* is produced; Tagore also publishes the philosophical work *Sadhana: The Realization of Life*.

Italy—Umberto Boccioni paints *Dynamism of a Cyclist*.

Russia—Russian composer Igor Stravinsky's ballet *The Rite of Spring* is produced in Paris.

U.K.—Joseph Conrad publishes the novel *Chance*.

D. H. Lawrence publishes the novel *Sons and Lovers*.

Jack Judge, a music hall comedian, composes the song "Tipperary."

U.S.—The Armory Show in New York City introduces postimpressionist and cubist works to the American audience.

Designed by architect Cass Gilbert, the Woolworth Building is erected, at the time the world's tallest building.

Joyce Kilmer publishes the poem "Trees."

Willa Cather publishes the novel *O Pioneers!*

Vachel Lindsay publishes the poetry collection *General William Booth Enters into Heaven and Other Poems*.

Cecil B. DeMille's film *The Squaw Man* is released.

Ideas

Austria—Sigmund Freud publishes *Totem and Taboo*.

Germany—Philosopher Edmund Husserl publishes *Phenomenology*.

Italy—Philosopher and historian Benedetto Croce publishes *Guide to Aesthetics*.

Spain—Philosopher Miguel de Unamuno y Jugo publishes *The Tragic Sense of Life*.

Switzerland—Psychiatrist Carl Gustav Jung breaks with his mentor Sigmund Freud and develops his own theories.

U.K.—Social reformers Sidney and Beatrice Webb found the political periodical the *New Statesman*.

U.S.—Psychologist John Broadus Watson explains his theory of behaviorism in the article "Psychology as the Behaviorist Views It."

Economist Wesley Clair Mitchell publishes *Business Cycles*.

American historian Henry Adams publishes the historical essay *Mont-Saint-Michel and Chartres*.

Editor Max Eastman founds and edits the radical periodical the *Masses* (through 1918).

Military

Bulgaria—In the Second Balkan War, Bulgaria is forced to cede territories to Serbia, Greece, Romania, and the Ottoman Empire.

Politics

Albania—As the First Balkan War (see 1912) ends, the new nation of Albania is founded.

Alsace-Lorraine—The Zabern affair threatens relations between France and Germany.

France—Raymond Poincaré is elected president; Aristide Briand becomes premier.

Greece—King George I is assassinated; Constantine I succeeds him.

Ireland—Patrick Pearse founds the Irish Volunteers, which will develop into the Irish Republican Army. In northern Ireland, the Protestant Ulster Volunteers is founded.

Mexico—Victoriano Huerta overthrows and assassinates President Francisco Madero.

Ottoman Empire—The Young Turks take power in a coup.

South Africa—James Hertzog founds the segregationist National Party.

U.S.—The 16th Amendment introduces federal income tax.

The Federal Reserve System is created.

Science and Technology

Denmark—Physicist Niels Bohr applies quantum theory to the structure of the atom, describing electron orbits and electron excitation.

France—Physicist Charles Fabry proves the existence of an ozone layer in the upper atmosphere.

Germany—Chemists Leonor Michaelis and Maud Leonora Menten formulate the Michaelis-Menten equation, describing the rate at which enzyme-catalyzed reactions take place.

Physicist Johannes Stark discovers the Stark effect, a spectral phenomenon.

Surgeon A. Saloman develops mammography.

Russia—Engineer Igor Ivan Sikorsky builds and flies the first multiengined aircraft.

U.K.—Chemist Frederick Soddy coins the term *isotopes*. He and Polish chemist Kasimir Fajans independently state the radioactive displacement law.

U.S.—Chemist Theodore William Richards discovers that lead varies in atomic weight.

Physicist Robert A. Millikan calculates the electric charge of a single electron.

Society

French Congo—Alsatian medical missionary Albert Schweitzer opens his hospital in Lambaréné, French Congo.

U.K.—Suffragette demonstrations lead to mass arrests.

U.S.—The Ford Motor Company begins using the assembly line system to build cars.

The Brillo Manufacturing Corp. introduces Brillo Pads, soap-laden steel wool pads.

Grand Central Terminal opens in New York.

The *New York World* introduces crossword puzzles.

Sports

U.S.—The U.S. team wins the Davis Cup tennis trophy.

1914 Arts and Entertainment

Chile—Gabriela Mistral publishes the poetry collection *Sonetos de la Muerte*.

Ireland—Literary works include William Butler Yeats's poetry collection *Responsibilities* and James Joyce's short story collection *Dubliners*.

Italy—Artistic works include Giorgio de Chirico's painting *The Mystery and Melancholy of a Street* and Giovanni Pastrone's film *Cabiria*.

Spain—Painter Juan Gris uses papier collé in *The Sunblind*.

U.K.—George Bernard Shaw's *Pygmalion* is produced.

Thomas Hardy publishes the poetry collection *Satires of Circumstance, Lyrics and Reveries*.

Ralph Vaughan Williams composes *A London Symphony* (Symphony No. 2).

U.S.—Poetry includes Robert Frost's collection *North of Boston* and Carl Sandburg's poem "Chicago."

Edgar Rice Burroughs publishes the novel *Tarzan of the Apes*.

Composer W. C. Handy publishes the song "The St. Louis Blues."

Ideas

U.K.—Anthropologist W. H. R. Rivers publishes *History of Melanesian Society*.

Critic Clive Bell publishes *Art*, in which he develops a highly formalist theory of art.

U.S.—Journalists Henry Louis Mencken and George Jean Nathan coedit the periodical the *Smart Set* (1914–23).

Military

Austro-Hungarian Empire—In Sarajevo, Bosnia, on June 28 the heir to the Austrian throne, Archduke Francis Ferdinand, is assassinated by Serbian nationalist Gavrilo Princip, triggering World War I (1914–18). Mutual declarations of war follow this year: on the one side, Germany, Austria-Hungary, and the Ottoman Empire form the Central Powers; on the other, the Allied Powers include Serbia, Russia, France, Britain, Belgium, Luxembourg, Montenegro, and Japan. Other nations will join the war in later years.

Belgium—German forces on their way to attack France invade neutral Belgium (and Luxembourg), prompting Britain to declare war. The First Battle of Ypres takes place October 19-November 22.

Central Europe—Austrian and Russian forces fight an inconclusive war.

France—Germany loses the First Battle of the Marne (September 5–9).

Germany—At Tannenberg and Masurian Lakes, Germany defeats Russia.

Mexico—U.S. forces capture Vera Cruz, blocking German arms shipments to Victoriano Huerta's government.

Venustiano Carranza captures Mexico City and battles Emiliano Zapata and Pancho Villa.

Poland—German forces capture Lodz.

Southwest Asia/North Africa—British and Russian forces fight against Ottoman forces.

World—German naval forces are unable to break British dominance, though German submarines and surface raiders will harry enemy shipping.

During World War I airplanes are used in combat on a significant scale for the first time.

Politics

France—Prominent socialist and pacifist Jean Jaurès is assassinated.

India—Lawyer Mohandas Gandhi returns home to India, where he will become the leader of the nationalist movement.

U.S.—The Federal Trade Commission is established.

Science and Technology

Canada—The Canadian Pacific liner *Empress of Ireland* sinks in the St. Lawrence River after colliding with a Norwegian coal ship; 1,024 people are killed.

France—Surgeon Alexis Carrel performs the first successful heart operation on a dog.

Germany—Geologist Beno Gutenberg proposes that the earth has a liquid core, separated from the mantle by what will be called the Gutenberg discontinuity.

U.K.—Physicist Ernest Rutherford discovers the proton.

Physicist Henry Gwyn Jeffreys Moseley proposes the concept of atomic number.

Biologist Henry Hallett Dale isolates acetylcholine.

Astronomer Arthur Eddington proposes that spiral nebulas are galaxies outside our own.

U.S.—Edward E. Kleinschmidt invents the teletype machine.

The last known passenger pigeon dies at Cincinnati Zoo on September 1.

Society

Italy—Pope Benedict XV (reigned 1914–22) succeeds Pope Pius X upon the latter's death.

Jamaica—Jamaican-born social reformer Marcus Garvey founds the Universal Negro Improvement Association (UNIA) in London. In the U.S. from 1916, he will be a leading black nationalist of the early 1920s, advocating a "back to Africa" movement.

Panama—The Panama Canal opens to traffic.

U.S.—Margaret Sanger, nurse and birth control advocate, coins the term *birth control* and begins publishing the pamphlet *Family Limitation* and the magazine *Woman Rebel*.

The Assemblies of God, the largest Pentecostal organization in the country, is founded.

The American Society of Composers, Authors, and Publishers (ASCAP) is founded.

Sports

U.S.—The country's first national figure skating tournament is held, in New Haven, Connecticut.

1915 Arts and Entertainment

Austria—Franz Kafka writes the story "The Metamorphosis."

Mexico—Mariano Azuela publishes the novel *The Underdogs*.

Romania—Constantin Brancusi sculpts *Le Nouveau-Né*.

Russia—Marc Chagall paints *The Birthday*.

Switzerland/U.S.—The Dada movement is founded by, among others, Romanian poet Tristan Tzara and French painters Hans Arp and Marcel Duchamp.

U.K.—Novels include Ford Madox Ford's *The Good Soldier*, Joseph Conrad's *Victory*, Somerset Maugham's *Of Human Bondage*, and Virginia Woolf's *The Voyage Out*.

Rupert Brooke publishes his five war sonnets, including "The Soldier."

U.S.—Film director D. W. Griffith releases *The Birth of a Nation*.

Theda Bara has her first starring role, in *A Fool There Was*.

Poetry includes Edgar Lee Masters's collection *Spoon River Anthology* and Robert Frost's poem "The Road Not Taken"; the latter will reappear in Frost's collection *Mountain Interval* (1916).

Ideas

Russia—Historian Mikhail Pokrovsky, the first Marxist interpreter of Russian history, publishes *An Outline History of Russian Culture* (1915–18).

Switzerland—Art historian Heinrich Wölfflin publishes *Principles of Art History*.

Military

Balkans—The First, Second, Third, and Fourth Battles of the Isonzo are fought.

Belgium—The first significant use of poison gas in warfare occurs when the Germans use chlorine gas against French troops at the Second Battle of Ypres (April 22).

France—French attempts to break through entrenched German battle lines, at the First Battle of Artois and at Champagne, fail with heavy casualties.

The first German submarine attack takes place near Le Havre.

Ireland—Off the Irish coast, a German submarine sinks the British liner *Lusitania* (May 7), killing 1,198 people, including 128 Americans. The event rouses American anger against Germany.

German South-West Africa—This colony, now Namibia, falls to South African troops.

Germany—At Gorlice, the Germans and Austrians drive the Russians back.

Ottoman Empire—The Gallipoli or Dardanelles campaign (1915–16), a major Allied offensive, fails to force the Ottoman Empire out of the war.

Serbia—The Central Powers capture Serbia.

Ukraine—At Lemberg (Lvov), the Russians defeat the Austrians.

U.S.—The U.S. Coast Guard is established.

Politics

Haiti—The country becomes a U.S. protectorate.

U.K.—The ministry of Herbert Henry Asquith becomes a coalition.

U.S.—Erich Muenter, a German instructor, bombs the U.S. Senate reception room, shoots J. Pierpont Morgan, and commits suicide.

Science and Technology

Canada—Bacteriologists Frederick William Twort and Felix Hubert d'Herelle separately discover bacteriophages (1915–17).

Germany—Physicist Arnold Sommerfeld proposes that electrons travel in elliptical orbits.

Japan—Scientists K. Yamagiwa and K. Ichikawa identify the first known carcinogen, coal tar.

U.K.—Scottish astronomer Robert Innes discovers the star Proxima Centauri.

U.S.—Geneticists Thomas Hunt Morgan, Calvin Bridges, Alfred Henry Sturtevant, and Hermann J. Müller publish *The Mechanism of Mendelian Heredity*, in which they argue that genes within chromosomes determine hereditary traits.

Physicist William Draper Harkins calculates that four hydrogen nuclei can fuse to form a helium nucleus, releasing a great deal of energy in the process.

Heat- and shock-resistant glass called Pyrex is developed by the Corning Glass Works.

Society

U.K.—The London *Daily Mail* reports on the "extraordinary short skirt" of the day, which falls above the ankles.

U.S.—The Ku Klux Klan, the racist terrorist organization that had not been a major force since the 1870s, is reorganized. It will gain great strength by the 1920s.

Labor leader Joe Hill is executed for murder based on circumstantial evidence. He will become a martyr of the labor movement.

Coast-to-coast long-distance telephone service is introduced.

Sports

U.S.—Jess Willard wins the heavyweight boxing title from Jack Johnson.

Gil Anderson, driving a Stutz, sets an automobile speed record of 102.6 mph.

1916 Arts and Entertainment

Argentina—Alfonsina Storni publishes the poetry collection *The Restless Rose Garden*.

Italy—Luigi Pirandello publishes the play *Six Characters in Search of an Author*.

U.K.—Edward Elgar completes the orchestral work *The Spirit of England*.

Robert Graves publishes his first poetry collection, *Over the Brazier*.

U.S.—*The Gulf Between* is the first film using the Technicolor process.

World—Poetry includes Edith and Osbert Sitwell's *20th Century Harlequinade* (U.K.), *The Spirit of Man*, a poetry and prose anthology edited by Robert Bridges; and Carl Sandburg's *Chicago Poems* (U.S.).

Novels include Henri Barbusse's *Feu* (France), Rabindranath Tagore's *The Home and the World* (India), James Joyce's *Portrait of the Artist as a Young Man* (Ireland), Soseki Natsume's *Light and Darkness* (Japan), and Vicente Blasco Ibáñez's *The Four Horsemen of the Apocalypse* (Spain).

Films include *Intolerance, War Brides* (U.S.), and *Perfido incanto* (Italy).

Ideas

U.S.—Stanford University psychologist Lewis M. Terman develops the Stanford-Binet Intelligence Scale by adapting the Binet-Simon Intelligence Scale (developed in 1911).

John Dewey publishes the antiauthoritarian educational tract *Democracy and Education*.

Military

Arabia—The Arab Revolt begins, led by Hussein Ibn Ali and his son Faisal; later they will be joined by British soldier T. E. Lawrence.

Egypt—Turkish forces advancing in the Sinai Peninsula are stopped by British and Indian forces.

France—Attacks on Verdun and the Somme generate enormous casualties: 1 million German casualties in Verdun, 1.25 million British and French casualties in the Somme.

Poland—Russia defeats Austria in the Brusilov Offensive (June 4–September 20).

Romania—The country becomes a member of the Allied forces.

U.K.—The first production model tank, the Mark I, or "Big Willie," is built by British engineers.

U.S.—Forces led by Mexican Pancho Villa raid Columbus, New Mexico.

Politics

Ireland—The Easter Uprising of Irish nationalists fails in Dublin; the group of up to 2,000 is defeated by British forces of 5,000.

Turkey—In what is now known as the Armenian Holocaust, Turkish forces murder up to 1.5 million Armenians, many in Armenian concentration camps.

U.S.—Democrat Woodrow Wilson is reelected president on the slogan "He kept us out of war!"

Science and Technology

Germany—Physicist Albert Einstein proposes his general theory of relativity, which extends his special theory of 1905 to systems moving at changing velocities relative to each other.

U.S.—Gilbert Newton Lewis publishes *The Atom and the Molecule*, in which he presents concepts of electron sharing and number of electrons in compounds.

Society

U.S.—Margaret Sanger opens the first birth control clinic in the country, in Brooklyn.

A poliomyelitis epidemic strikes, killing 6,000 and crippling thousands more; in all, over 28,000 are affected.

Sports

France—Olympic Stadium, designed by Tony Garnier, is built in Lyon.

U.S.—In the World Series the Boston Red Sox defeat the Brooklyn Dodgers, four games to one.

The first U.S. Professional Golfers' Association (PGA) tournament is held in Bronxville, N.Y.

1917 Arts and Entertainment

France—Symbolist poet Paul Valéry publishes *La Jeune Parque*.

Germany—Composer Hans Pfitzner's opera *Palestrina* premieres.

George Grosz completes *The Face of the Ruling Class*, a series of satirical drawings (1917–21).

Netherlands—Painters Piet Mondrian and Theo van Doesburg cofound the arts magazine and movement *De Stijl*.

Spain/France/Russia—Spanish painter Pablo Picasso, French writer and artist Jean Cocteau, and Russian impresario Sergey Diaghilev collaborate on the ballet *Parade*. French poet Guillaume Apollinaire coins the term *surrealism* in his review of the ballet.

Russia—Sergey Prokofiev composes *Classical Symphony no. 1 in D*.

U.S.—Edna St. Vincent Millay publishes the poetry collection *Renascence*.

Poet Ezra Pound publishes the first three cantos.

George M. Cohan composes the World War I anthem "Over There."

John Singer Sargent paints the *Portrait of John D. Rockefeller*.

U.S./U.K.—American-born British poet T. S. Eliot publishes the poem "The Love Song of J. Alfred Prufrock."

Ideas

Austria—Psychiatrist Sigmund Freud publishes *Introduction to Psychoanalysis*.

Military

Austro-Hungarian Empire—Austrian forces defeat Italian forces at the Battle of Caporetto (now part of Yugoslavia), October 24–November 12.

Belgium—The British try unsuccessfully to break the German line at the Third Battle of Ypres, Belgium, popularly called Passchendaele (June 21–November 4).

Cuba—A revolution is suppressed by U.S. troop landings.

France—At Cambrai, the British win the world's first tank victory (November 20–December 3).

From April to May, the First Battle of Aisne is fought.

Germany—Germany opens unrestricted submarine warfare on British and Allied shipping, a course that helps convince the United States to enter the war.

German forces withdraw to the Hindenburg Line and repel the French Nivelle Offensive (April 16–20).

Greece—Greece enters the war on the Allied side.

Romania—Romania, defeated, leaves the war.

U.K.—General Edmund Allenby takes over the British command in Palestine.

U.S.—On April 6 the U.S enters World War I. U.S. troops begin arriving in Europe in June.

Politics

Albania—Italy declares Albania a protectorate, though Albania declares itself independent.

Finland—Formerly part of Russia, Finland declares itself an independent republic (December 6).

Russia—In the Russian Revolution of March 1917 (also called the February Revolution; begun March 8, February 23 Old Style), Czar Nicholas II abdicates (March 15) in the face of strikes and mutinies. Radical workers' councils called Soviets form. The Duma forms a provisional government, headed by Aleksandr Kerensky.

On November 6 (October 24 Old Style) the Russian Revolution of November 1917 (October Revolution) begins. The Bolshevik Party, led by V. I. Lenin, overthrows Aleksandr Kerensky's provisional government and institutes the world's first Communist nation-state.

Following the Russian Revolution of November 1917, the Russian Civil War (1917–22) begins, between the Bolshevik Red Army and the counterrevolutionary White Armies.

The Cheka, the Soviet secret police, is founded.

U.K.—The British royal family renounces German names and titles.

The British government issues the Balfour Declaration, promising the establishment of a Jewish national homeland in Palestine.

U.S.—The Espionage Act is passed, making it illegal to speak, write, or demonstrate against the draft or U.S. participation in World War I. Thousands are prosecuted this year and the next for antiwar and antidraft activities.

The Senate rejects President Woodrow Wilson's woman suffrage bill.

Congress passes the Liberty Loan Act, authorizing the issuance of war bonds to fund the war.

The U.S. imposes literacy tests as a prerequisite for admission of immigrants.

Science and Technology

France—Physicist Paul Langevin develops sonar (sound navigation and ranging).

Germany—Astronomer Karl Schwarzschild predicts the existence of what will become known as black holes.

Physical chemist Otto Hahn and Austrian physicist Lise Meitner discover the element protactinium.

India/U.K.—At Cambridge, England, Indian mathematician Srinivasa Ramanujan collaborates with British mathematician G. H. Hardy on number theory.

Netherlands—Physicist Peter Debye develops a technique for determining crystal structure by diffracting X rays through powdered crystalline solids.

U.S.—Amplitude modulation for AM radio is pioneered by engineer Edwin H. Armstrong.

A 100-inch reflecting telescope, then the world's largest, is installed at Mount Wilson, California.

Society

Netherlands/France—In France, Dutch dancer Mata Hari is executed as a spy for Germany.

Russia—The Trans-Siberian Railroad, begun in 1891, is completed.

U.K.—The Imperial War Museum is founded.

Two new decorations, the Companion of Honour and the Order of the British Empire, are established.

U.K./U.S.—Bobbed hair is all the rage in Britain and the U.S.

France/Belgium—On December 6, in the harbor of Halifax, Nova Scotia, a collision between the French ammunition ship *Mont Blanc* and the Belgian steamer *Imo* kills 1,600 people.

France—On December 12, in the world's worst railroad disaster to date, a troop train derails in the Alps near Modane, France, killing 543 people.

Sports

U.S.—The first Sunday baseball game played in New York's Polo Grounds—between the New York Giants and Cincinnati Reds—results in arrests of the team managers for violating a New York blue law.

Ernie Shore of the Boston Red Sox pitches an unofficial perfect game against the Washington Senators. Shore relieved Babe Ruth and retired all 26 batters he faced.

1918 Arts and Entertainment

Bosnia—Ivo Andric publishes the prose poem *Ex Ponto*.

France—Erik Satie composes the symphonic drama *Socrate*.

Germany—Ernst Lubitsch's film *Carmen* premieres.

Hungary—Composer Béla Bartók's one-act opera *Bluebeard's Castle* opens in Budapest.

Russia—Kasimir Malevich paints the suprematist work *White on White*. Malevich founded the abstract-art movement suprematism in 1913.

U.K.—The works of neglected 19th-century poet Gerard Manley Hopkins are revived in a collection edited by his friend and fellow poet Robert Bridges.

U.S.—Architect Frank Lloyd Wright designs the Robie House in Chicago.

Willa Cather publishes the novel *My Antonia*.

Historian Henry Adams publishes the autobiography *The Education of Henry Adams* (privately printed in 1907).

The Yiddish Art Theatre opens in New York City.

Charlie Chaplin's film *A Dog's Life* premieres.

Ideas

Austria—Psychiatrist Alfred Adler publishes *The Theory and Practice of Individual Psychology*.

Germany—Historian Oswald Spengler publishes *The Decline of the West* (1918–22).

Philosopher Moritz Schlick publishes *General Epistemology*.

Sweden—Economist Gustav Cassel publishes *Theory of Social Economy*.

Switzerland/France—Swiss architect Le Corbusier and French painter Amédée Ozenfant publish *Après le cubisme*, which expounds their theory of purism.

U.K.—Lytton Strachey publishes the biographical collection *Eminent Victorians*.

U.S.—Economist Thorstein Veblen publishes *The Higher Learning in America*.

American philosopher Clarence Irving Lewis publishes *A Survey of Symbolic Logic*.

Military

Austro-Hungarian Empire—In the Battle of Vittorio Veneto, Italy (October 24–November 4), Allied forces destroy the Austrian army and force an armistice.

Bulgaria—Bulgaria, a Central Power, signs an armistice (September 30) removing it from the war.

Finland—With German help, Finland wins independence from Russia.

Germany—Baron Manfred von Richthofen (1892–1918), the German flying ace known as the "Red Baron" and credited with shooting down 80 aircraft, is killed in action (April 21).

In France, Germany mounts several failed offensives, including the Somme Offensive (March 21–April 6); the Aisne Offensive (May 27–June 6; including Battles of Chateau-Thierry, May 30–June 17, and Belleau Wood, May 30–June 17, 1918).

Germany is defeated at the Second Battle of the Marne, France (July 15–August 6).

The Battle of Argonne Forest (September 26–October 31) ends in Allied victory.

Germany concludes an armistice (November 11), ending the fighting in World War I.

Latvia—Latvia declares itself independent from Russia, beginning the Latvian War of Independence (1918–20).

Lithuania—Lithuania declares itself independent from Russia, beginning the Lithuanian War of Independence (1918–20).

Ottoman Empire—The Ottoman Empire signs an armistice removing it from the war (October 30).

Russia—Russia withdraws from World War I through the Treaty of Brest-Litovsk.

As the Russian Civil War rages, troops from the U.S., Britain, France, Germany, and Japan participate on the White side, capturing Murmansk, Odessa, and Archangel.

U.S.—In the Battle of St. Mihiel (September 12–13), an Allied victory, U.S. forces fight independently for the first time in World War I.

Politics

Austro-Hungarian Empire—The Empire begins to crumble into independent republics, including Austria, Hungary, and others.

Bulgaria—King Ferdinand abdicates in favor of his son Boris.

Czechoslovakia—Czechoslovakia, formerly part of the Austro-Hungarian Empire, is created.

Ethiopia—Ras Tafari, the future Emperor Haile Selassie, becomes regent and effective ruler.

Germany—Revolution forces Emperor William II to abdicate (November 9).

Hungary—Premier Count Tisza is assassinated.

Iceland—Iceland becomes an independent state.

India—The Indian National Congress demands full self-determination for India.

Ireland—The party Sinn Fein wins an electoral majority and forms a government.

Kingdom of Serbs, Croats, and Slovenes—This kingdom, which will later be renamed Yugoslavia, is created in December from Austro-Hungarian lands.

Mexico—Mexico nationalizes its oil fields.

Ottoman Empire—Sultan Mohammad VI accedes to the throne.

Poland—Poland is reconstituted as an independent nation from what had been Austrian, Prussian, and Russian sectors.

Russia—The former czar Nicholas II and his family are assassinated.

U.K.—Women over 30 win equal voting rights.

U.S.—President Woodrow Wilson presents the peace proposal the Fourteen Points.

Socialist leader Eugene V. Debs is sentenced to 10 years in prison for his opposition to World War I. The sentence will be commuted in 1921.

Science and Technology

Germany—Erythrocyte sedimentation is introduced as a medical laboratory test.

Mathematician Amalie (Emmy) Noether shows that every symmetry in physics implies a conservation law, and every conservation law a symmetry.

Hungary—Chemist Georg C. de Hevesy invents radioactive tracing.

U.K.—Scientists James Hopwood Jeans and Harold Jeffreys propose the tidal hypothesis as an explanation of the solar system's formation.

Society

Japan—Industrialist Konosuke Matsushita founds the Matsushita Electric Industrial Company.

The New Women's Association, a feminist activist group, is formed.

U.K.—A food shortage leads to the institution of national food kitchens and rationing.

U.S.—Daylight saving time is introduced.

Airmail, and the country's first airmail stamps, are introduced in the U.S.

Kimberly & Clark chemist Ernst Mahler invents a wood-cellulose bandage called Cellucotton for use with battle wounds. In 1921 it will be remarketed as the female sanitary napkin Kotex.

Inventor Charles Strite patents the pop-up toaster.

World—A worldwide pandemic of Spanish influenza kills an estimated 20million to 30 million people, including 675,000 in the United States.

Sports

U.S.—Knute Rockne (1888–1931) becomes head football coach at Notre Dame University (1918–31). His team, with such players as George "the Gipper" Gipp, will dominate college football during the period.

Exterminator wins the Kentucky Derby.

1919 Arts and Entertainment

Austria—Richard Strauss premieres *The Woman without a Shadow*.

Germany—The Bauhaus, a center for the teaching of architecture, painting, and sculpture, is founded in Weimar by Walter Gropius.

Italy—Artist Amedeo Modigliani completes *La Marchesa Casati*.

U.S.—James Branch Cabell's novel *Jurgen* is published and is the subject of an obscenity case in court.

World—Films include *Madame Dubarry (Passion)* (France), *The Cabinet of Dr. Caligari* (Germany), *Half-Caste* (Germany), *Broken Blossoms* (U.S.).

Literary works include André Gide's *La Symphonie pastorale* (France), Somerset Maugham's *The Moon and Sixpence* (U.K.), Thomas Hardy's *Collected Poems* (U.K.), Sherwood Anderson's story collection *Winesburg, Ohio* (U.S.), and H. L. Mencken's study *The American Language*.

Paintings include Claude Monet's *Nymphéas* (France), Edvard Munch's *The Murder* (Norway), Wassily Kandinsky's *Dreamy Improvisation* (Russia), and Paul Klee's *Dream Birds* (Switzerland).

Ideas

Austria—Social philosopher Rudolf Steiner publishes *The Essential Points of the Social Question*.

France—Philosopher Henri Bergson publishes *L'Energie spirituelle*.

Switzerland—Theologian Karl Barth publishes *The Epistle to the Romans*.

U.K.—Psychologist Havelock Ellis publishes *The Philosophy of Conflict*.

Economist John Maynard Keynes publishes *The Economic Consequences of the Peace*.

U.S.—Psychologist John Broadus Watson publishes *Psychology from the Standpoint of a Behaviorist*.

Military

Czechoslovakia—Hungarian troops invade but are forced out.

Russia—Troops take Omsk and Kharkov.

The country enters war with Finland.

The Third International, also known as Comintern (the association of national communist parties) is founded.

Syria—French and Syrian troops engage in battle.

Politics

China—On May 4, demonstrations in Beijing spark the student-led nationalist movement known as the May Fourth movement.

France—The first League of Nations meeting is held, presided over by U.S. President Woodrow Wilson.

The Peace Conference begins.

The Treaty of Versailles between Germany and the Allies is signed.

Germany—Socialist revolutionaries Rosa Luxembourg and Karl Liebknecht are killed by members of the German Freikorps.

Hungary—Béla Kun founds a Soviet regime that is overthrown within the year.

Italy—Benito Mussolini founds the Fasci del Combattimento.

U.S.—The 18th Amendment to the Constitution is passed, prohibiting the sale and distribution of alcoholic beverages; the period will be known as Prohibition.

Science and Technology

Germany—Physicist Arnold Sommerfeld publishes *Atombau und Spektrallinien*, a study of spectroscopy.

U.K.—The phenomena of isotopy is discovered by F. W. Aston.

Physicist Ernest Rutherford is the first to artificially disintegrate an element.

Society

Canada—A general strike occurs in Winnipeg.

Germany—The church and state are made separate.

U.S.—Radio Corporation of America (RCA) is founded.

The eight-hour workday is endorsed in Washington by the International Labor Conference.

Steelworkers go on strike; dock workers in New York go on strike.

Sports

France—Suzanne Lenglen wins the Wimbledon Lawn Tennis Championships, beginning a streak that will continue through 1923.

Spain—Matador Juan Belmonte kills 200 bulls in 109 corridas.

U.S.—Sir Barton is the first horse to win the Triple Crown: the Kentucky Derby, Preakness, and Belmont Stakes.

Jack Dempsey defeats Jess Willard for the boxing world championship.

Babe Ruth hits a 587-foot home run in Tampa, Florida.

1920 Arts and Entertainment

Europe—U.S. jazz musician Paul Whiteman tours Europe with his band.

France—Jean Cocteau and Darius Milhaud's ballet *The Ox on the Roof* premieres.

Igor Stravinsky's ballet *Pucinella* premieres.

Maurice Ravel's *La Valse* premieres.

Henri Matisse completes *L'Odalisque.*

Le Corbusier founds the magazine *L'Esprit nouveau.*

Piet Mondrian completes the painting *Composition I with Red, Black, Blue, Yellow, and Gray.*

Mexico—Public murals celebrating national history are commissioned by the state, with artists including Diego Rivera, David Alfaro Siqueiros, and José Vasconcelas.

U.K.—Katherine Mansfield publishes the story collection *Bliss and Other Stories.*

U.S.—Charles Demuth completes the painting *Machinery.*

Eugene O'Neill's *Beyond the Horizon* and *The Emperor Jones* premiere.

Jerome Kern's musical *Sally* premieres.

D. W. Griffith's film *Way Down East* premieres.

World—Notable poetic works include Paul Valéry's *Album des vers anciens* (France), Wilfred Owen's *Poems* (U.K.), W. B. Yeats's *The Wild Swans at Coole* (U.K.), A. A. Milne's *Mr. Pym Passes By* (U.K.), and Carl Sandburg's *Smoke and Steel* (U.S.).

Notable novels include Jaroslav Hasek's *The Good Soldier Schweik* (Czechoslovakia), Colette's *Chéri* (France), Marcel Proust's *The Guermantes Way*, part three of *Remembrance of Things Past* (France), Sigrid Undset's *Kristin Lavransdattar*, vol. 1 (Norway), D. H. Lawrence's *Women in Love* (U.K.), Edith Wharton's *The Age of Innocence* (U.S.), Sinclair Lewis's *Main Street* (U.S.), Ernest Hemingway's *A Farewell to Arms* (U.S.), F. Scott Fitzgerald's *This Side of Paradise* (U.S.).

Ideas

Austria—Alfred Adler publishes *The Theory and Practice of Individual Psychology*.

Italy—Spanish-born philosopher George Santayana publishes *Character and Opinion in the United States*.

Switzerland—C. G. Jung publishes *Psychological Types*.

U.S.—"Scientific management" theory for improved productivity is popularized, based on 19th-century theories of Frederick Taylor.

Military

Albania—Italian forces depart the country following occupation during World War I.

China—Civil war follows the death of President Yuan Shikai.

Russia—The Red Army captures Odessa.

U.K.—Following British-Irish warfare between "Black and Tans" and Sinn Fein forces, the Government of Ireland Act is passed, granting the establishment of parliaments in Southern and Northern Ireland.

Russia/Poland—The Russo-Polish War is fought; it will result in the redefinition of the territories through the 1921 Treaty of Riga.

Politics

Austria—Austria approves a new constitution.

Belgium—The Brussels Conference advises that Germany pay reparations of 13,450 gold marks over 42 years.

Czechoslovakia—Tomas Masaryk is elected the country's first president.

Czechoslovakia, Yugoslavia, and Romania form the Little Entente.

Germany—At the Spa Conference, Germany offers a reparations plan.

The German Workers Party is renamed the National Socialist German Workers Party.

Hungary—Hungary and the Allies sign the Treaty of Trianon, granting parts of Hungary to Czechoslovakia, Romania, and Yugoslavia.

India—Mohandas Gandhi generates support throughout India for a wide-ranging plan of noncooperation.

The Treaty of Rapallo is signed.

Japan—The Caroline, Marshall, and Marianas archipelagoes are granted to Japan through League of Nations mandate.

Kenya—British East Africa is renamed Kenya.

Mexico—President Carranza is assassinated and replaced by Adolfo de la Huerta.

Syria—Emir Faisal becomes king, but is not recognized by Britain and France and is later dethroned.

Turkey—The Treaty of Sèvres places unacceptable constraints on Turkey and is rejected.

U.S.—Republican Warren G. Harding is elected president, defeating Democrat James Cox.

Women gain the right to vote, with passage of the 19th Amendment to the Constitution.

World—The League of Nations is founded in January, with 32 Allied and Associative Powers as members; the first meeting is held in November.

Science and Technology

Germany—Chemist Hermann Staudinger discovers the molecular structure of polymers.

The structure of the Milky Way is determined by M. Wolf.

Switzerland—Hermann Rorschach develops the Rorschach inkblot test.

U.K.—*Space, Time, and Gravitation* is published by A. Eddington.

F. W. Aston determines that atomic numbers are integral multiples of the same number.

U.S.—The portable machine gun, or "tommy gun," is created by J. T. Thompson.

The star Betelgeuse is measured by A. A. Michelson.

Society

Austria—Unemployment insurance is introduced.

China—Earthquakes in Gansu take 150,000 to 200,000 lives.

France—Designer Coco Chanel introduces the chemise.

Italy—Earthquakes cause 500 deaths.

Food rationing begins, resulting in riots.

Joan of Arc is canonized by Pope Benedict XV.

Poland—A typhus epidemic strikes.

U.K.—The first public radio station in the U.K. is opened by inventor G. Marconi.

U.S.—The first public radio station in the U.S., KDKA in Pittsburgh, Pennsylvania, begins broadcasting by reporting U.S. presidential election results.

Transcontinental airmail service begins with a mail flight from New York to California.

Italian–American anarchists Nicola Sacco and Bartolomeo Vanzetti are arrested and charged with the murder of two workers in a Massachusetts shoe factory. For years the case will stir controversy.

Sports

Belgium—The Olympic Games open in Antwerp.

U.K.—The U.S. Open Golf Tournament is won by Ted Ray.

U.S.—Baseball player George Herman "Babe" Ruth is sold from the Boston Red Sox to the New York Yankees.

In the Chicago "Black Sox" baseball scandal, eight members of the Chicago White Sox are indicted on charges of having accepted bribes to throw the 1919 World Series. The team members will be acquitted in a 1921 trial.

The National Football League is created by Chicago Bears founder George Halas. At Wimbledon, tennis player William Tilden wins the men's singles title.

In tennis, the Davis Cup is won by the U.S.

In the World Series, the Cleveland Indians (AL) defeat the Brooklyn Dodgers (NL), five games to two.

1921 Arts and Entertainment

France—Georges Braque paints *Still Life with Guitar*.

Czechoslovakia—Karel Capek's play *R.U.R. (Rossum's Universal Robots)* premieres, coining the word "robot."

Germany—Max Ernst paints *The Elephant Célébes*.

Italy—Luigi Pirandello's play *Six Characters in Search of an Author* is produced.

Russia—Russian composer Sergey Prokofiev's farcical opera, *The Love for Three Oranges*, is produced in Chicago.

U.K.—Somerset Maugham's play *The Circle* is produced.

Actor John Gielgud makes his debut at the Old Vic.

William Butler Yeats publishes the poetry collection *Michael Robartes and the Dancer*, which includes the poems "The Second Coming" and "Easter 1916."

U.S.—*Shuffle Along*, the first all-black Broadway musical, is produced. The show helps usher in the period of African-American artistic flowering called the Harlem Renaissance.

Willa Cather publishes the novel *One of Ours*.

Eugene O'Neill's play *Anna Christie* is produced.

Films include Charlie Chaplin's *The Kid* and Rex Ingram's *Four Horsemen of the Apocalypse*.

Ideas

Switzerland—Carl Gustav Jung publishes *Psychological Types*.

Psychiatrist Hermann Rorschach introduces the inkblot test as an aid in diagnosing mental disorders.

U.K.—Mathematician and philosopher Bertrand Russell publishes *The Analysis of Mind*.

Military

Greece—Greece wins battles in its war with Turkey before being defeated at the Sakkaria River (August 24–September 16).

Ireland—A cease-fire ends the Irish War of Independence. Ireland is to be partitioned between the autonomous Irish Free State and British-ruled Northern Ireland. A civil war (1921–22) ensues in the Irish Free State, as elements of the Irish Republican Army refuse to accept the peace settlement.

Morocco—In the Rif War (1921–26), Abd el-Krim leads a rebellion against French and Spanish authorities.

Politics

Canada—Mackenzie King is elected prime minister.

China—The Communist Party of China holds its first Congress, in Shanghai.

Czechoslovakia—Eduard Benes is elected prime minister.

France—The Paris Peace Conference concludes.

Germany—Adolf Hitler becomes president of the National Socialist German Workers' Party, or Nazi Party. Nazi storm troopers begin terrorizing political opponents.

A clause in the Treaty of Versailles obligates Germany to pay 226 billion (later reduced to 132 billion) gold marks as reparations for material losses and suffering caused by World War I. The mark plummets in value as a period of severe inflation begins.

Finance minister Matthias Erzberger is assassinated.

India—The first Indian Parliament meets.

Iraq—Iraq becomes a British protectorate under King Faisal I.

Italy—Benito Mussolini forms the Fascist Party.

Japan—Prime minister Takashi Hara (1856–1921) is murdered by a right-wing assassin.

Crown Prince Hirohito (born 1901) is named prince regent; his father retires due to mental illness.

Kingdom of Serbs, Croats, and Slovenes—Alexander I becomes king.

Mongolia—Mongolia becomes a de facto protectorate of Bolshevik Russia.

Palestine—The British appoint Arab leader Haj Amin al Husseini as grand mufti of Jerusalem. Conflicts grow between Arabs and Jews.

Persia—General Reza Khan, later Reza Shah Pahlavi, leads a coup deposing the shah and establishes a military dictatorship under Ahmad Shah.

Portugal—António Machado Santos, the First Republic's founder, is killed in a revolution.

Russia—The Red Army suppresses a sailors' rebellion at Kronstadt naval base near St. Petersburg.

Sweden—Sweden abolishes capital punishment.

U.K.—The London Imperial Conference includes representatives from India.

Science and Technology

Canada—Surgeon Frederick C. Banting and physiologist Charles Best isolate insulin.

U.K.—Astronomer Edward Arthur Milne predicts the existence of the solar wind.

U.S.—Chemist Thomas Midgley Jr. discovers that tetraethyl lead, soon marketed as Ethyl, serves as an antiknock additive in gasoline.

Helium is first used as a lifting gas for dirigibles.

Society

Belgian Congo—Simon Kimbangu, founder of the nationalist religious movement Kimbanguism, begins preaching and healing. He will be arrested for sedition and imprisoned for life by colonial authorities.

U.K.—Lord Lee donates his estate of Chequers to the country; it will become the official country residence of the prime minister.

U.S.—Italian-American anarchists Nicola Sacco and Bartolomeo Vanzetti are found guilty of murder and sentenced to death. They will be executed in 1927.

The Unknown Soldier is interred at Arlington National Cemetery.

Sports

Australia—In cricket Australia wins the Ashes.

Cuba—Cuban chess player José Raoul Capablanca wins the world championship from Emanuel Lasker, holder of the title since 1894.

U.K.—Jockey Gordon Richards rides his first winner. When he retires in 1954, he will have won 4,870 races out of 21,834 mounts.

U.S.—From New York's Polo Grounds comes the first radio broadcast of a baseball game.

The U.S. tennis team defeats Japan 5–0 to retain the Davis Cup.

World—Table tennis is revived as a popular sport.

1922 Arts and Entertainment

France—An international Dadaist exhibition is held in Paris.

Paul Valéry publishes the poetry collection *Charmes*.

Germany—Bertolt Brecht's play *Drums in the Night* is produced.

F. W. Murnau's film *Nosferatu* is released.

Hermann Hesse publishes the novel *Siddhartha*.

Ireland—Irish writer James Joyce's *Ulysses* is published in Paris. It is banned as obscene in the U.K. and the U.S.

Italy—Luigi Pirandello's play *Henry IV* is produced.

Switzerland—Paul Klee paints *Twittering Machine*.

Rainer Maria Rilke publishes the poetry collections *Duino Elegies* and *Sonnets to Orpheus*.

U.K.—D. H. Lawrence publishes the short-story collection *England, My England*.

Virginia Woolf publishes the novel *Jacob's Room*.

Rebecca West publishes the novel *The Judge*.

20th-Century Amendments to the U.S. Constitution

Year Ratified	Amendment	Action
1913	XVI	authorizes federal income tax
1913	XVII	provides for direct popular election of senators
1919	XVIII	prohibits manufacture, sale, or transportation of intoxicating beverages (Prohibition)
1920	XIX	guarantees women the vote
1933	XX	changes starting dates for the terms of the president, vice president, and members of Congress; clarifies presidential succession
1933	XXI	repeals Amendment XVIII, ending Prohibition
1951	XXII	limits presidents to two terms
1961	XXIII	permits District of Columbia residents to vote for president and vice president
1964	XXIV	outlaws the poll tax in federal elections
1967	XXV	clarifies presidential succession and provides procedures for filling vacancies in the vice presidency
1971	XXVI	lowers the voting age to 18
1992	XXVII	forbids changes in congressional pay from taking effect until an election of representatives has intervened

U.S.—Sinclair Lewis publishes the novel *Babbitt*.

Edwin Arlington Robinson publishes *Collected Poems*.

Eugene O'Neill's play *The Hairy Ape* is produced.

Anne Nichols's long-running comedy *Abie's Irish Rose* (2,327 performances) premieres.

D. W. Griffith's film *Orphans of the Storm* and Robert Flaherty's documentary *Nanook of the North* are released.

Jazz trumpeter and singer Louis Armstrong joins King Oliver's Creole Jazz Band in Chicago. Having originated in the South, jazz becomes popular in Chicago, New York, and other northern cities.

Ideas

Germany—Philosopher Rudolf Carnap publishes *The Space*.

Sociologist Max Weber's *Methodology of the Social Sciences* is posthumously published.

U.K.—Anthropologist Bronislaw Malinowski publishes *Argonauts of the Western Pacific*.

U.S.—American philosopher Arthur Oncken Lovejoy and colleagues develop history of ideas as an interdisciplinary field of study (1922–23).

Journalist Walter Lippmann publishes *Public Opinion.*

U.S./U.K.—American-born British poet T. S. Eliot publishes *The Waste Land.*

Military

Greece/Turkey—Turkish troops drive back the Greeks and recapture Smyrna.

U.K./Turkey—A British force arrives at Chanakkale in Turkey to defend the straits against the Turks. A conference in October arranges for neutralization and internationalization of the straits.

Politics

Colombia/Venezuela—Swiss arbitration settles a boundary dispute between Colombia and Venezuela in favor of Colombia.

Egypt—Egypt declares independence as the British protectorate ends. Fu'ad I becomes king.

Germany—Nationalists assassinate Jewish cabinet minister Walther Rathenau.

India—An attack by nationalists on the police station at Chauri Chaura kills 22 policemen. Nationalist leader Mohandas Gandhi suspends the noncooperation and civil disobedience campaign; he is arrested and sentenced to six years in prison.

Iraq—Kurdish nationalists under Sheikh Mahmud mount an insurrection (1922–24).

Ireland—The Irish Free State is officially proclaimed.

Italy—In October, Benito Mussolini and his Fascists make the March on Rome. Mussolini is invited by King Victor Emmanuel III to form a cabinet. In November, Mussolini receives dictatorial powers, becoming known as *Il Duce* ("The Leader").

Southern Rhodesia—In a referendum, voters refuse to join the Union of South Africa.

Soviet Union—The Union of Soviet Socialist Republics is proclaimed in Russia and many former parts of the Russian Empire (December 30).

Turkey—Mustafa Kemal (later called Atatürk) abolishes the Ottoman sultanate, though the republic of Turkey will not be formally proclaimed until the following year. Abdul Mejid is proclaimed caliph.

U.K.—Prime minister David Lloyd George resigns and is replaced by Andrew Bonar Law. The Conservative Party wins the November elections.

World—The Genoa Conference convenes to discuss world economic problems. Talks break down over Russia's refusal to recognize debts from the czarist era.

Science and Technology

Poland—Mathematician Stefan Banach introduces the concept of normed linear spaces.

U.K.—Bacteriologist Alexander Fleming isolates the enzyme lysozyme from tears and mucus and finds it has bacteria-killing properties.

U.S./China—American paleontologist Roy Chapman Andrews begins a series of expeditions in the Gobi Desert of Mongolia. He uncovers fossils of the primitive horned dinosaur *Protoceratops*, including fossilized egg shells—the first dinosaur eggs ever found.

U.S.—Biochemist Elmer McCollum discovers Vitamin D. He had discovered Vitamin A in 1913 and will later contribute to the discovery of Vitamin E.

Physician James Herrick recognizes and names sickle-cell anemia.

U.K./Egypt—In Egypt, British archaeologists George Herbert, earl of Carnarvon, and Howard Carter discover the entrance to the tomb of the pharaoh Tutankhamen.

U.K./Iraq—In Iraq, British archaeologist Leonard Woolley excavates ancient Ur.

Society

Belgium—Flemish receives equal status with French as an official language.

Europe—The American cocktail becomes popular in Europe.

Italy—Pius XI becomes pope (1922–39).

U.K.—Unemployed workers in Glasgow stage a hunger march to London.

The British Broadcasting Company Ltd. is founded.

U.S.—The magazine *Reader's Digest* begins publication.

Writer Emily Post publishes the first edition of *Etiquette*.

Sports

France—Unofficial women's Olympics are held in Paris.

U.S.—Johnny Weissmuller is the first man to swim 100 meters in less than a minute.

1923 Arts and Entertainment

Austria—Arnold Schoenberg completes his first fully 12-note work, *Piano Suite*.

Finland—Jean Sibelius completes the Sixth Symphony.

France—Marcel Duchamp creates the sculpture *The Bride Stripped Bare by her Bachelors, Even* (unfinished).

Architect Le Corbusier publishes the theoretical work the *Vers une architecture*.

Germany—The first public exhibition of Bauhaus art is made, under the title, "Art and Technology—A New Unity."

Hungary—Béla Bartók completes the ballet *The Miraculous Mandarin*.

Soviet Union—The Blue Blouse Group forms, with aims to create film, dance, and art supporting Communist ideals.

U.S.—Architect Raymond Hood designs the Chicago Tribune Building, Chicago, Illinois.

Robert Frost publishes the poetry collection *New Hampshire*.

The New Orleans–style jazz of King Oliver and Jelly Roll Morton broaden the audience for jazz.

Jean Toomer publishes *Cane*, a collection of stories, play, and poetry.

Wallace Stevens publishes the poetry collection *Harmonium*, which includes the poem "Sunday Morning"; Vachel Lindsay publishes *Collected Poems*.

World—Novels include Italo Svevo's *Confessions of Zeno* (Italy), Willa Cather's *A Lost Lady*.

Ideas

Austria—Sigmund Freud publishes *The Ego and the Id*.

U.K.—Sidney and Beatrice Webb publish the political work *The Decay of Capitalist Civilization*.

U.S.—Economist John Maynard Keynes publishes *A Tract on Economic Reform*.

Military

Constantinople—After Allied evacuation (August 23), Turkey occupies Constantinople (October 6).

Greece—Following the assassination in Greece of five Italian diplomats, Italian forces occupy Crete (August 29). The event, known as the Corfu Incident, ends with the removal of Italian forces (September 27).

Politics

Bulgaria—Premier Stambolski is overthrown in a coup and replaced by Alexander Zankov.

Egypt—The Egyptian constitution is established and the first elections held, with Saad Zaghlul becoming premier (January 28).

Germany—The Ruhr District is occupied by French and Belgian forces following German default on coal deliveries, with a Franco-Belgian commission taking over mines and railroads until September 26.

The Beer Hall Putsch occurs in Munich (November 8–11). Led by Nazi Party leader Adolf Hitler and World War I general Erich von Ludendorff, it fails to overthrow the Bavarian government. Hitler is sentenced to five years in prison.

Lithuania—Following a Lithuanian-supported uprising, Memel is named an autonomous region within the Lithuanian state.

Persia—Reza Khan, minister of war and commander-in-chief, becomes premier.

Rhodesia—Southern Rhodesia is named a British crown colony (September 1).

Transjordania—Transjordania is set up as an autonomous state.

Turkey—Under the Treaty of Lausanne, Turkey gains eastern Thrace but gives up claims to non-Turkish territories lost in World War I.

The Turkish Republic is formed (October 29); Mustafa Kemal becomes president and Ismet Pasha prime minister. Ankara becomes its capital (October 29).

U.K.—Andrew Bonar Law resigns as prime minister and is replaced by Stanley Baldwin.

U.S.—Warren Harding dies suddenly (August 2); Calvin Coolidge is sworn in as president (August 3).

Science and Technology

Germany—O. H. Warburg establishes a method for studying respiration.

Spain—J. de la Cierva develops pioneering principle of the autogyro.

U.K.—Arthur Stanley Eddington explains the relationship between a star's mass and its luminosity.

H. Souttar conducts early cardiac surgery to widen the mitral valve.

U.S.—V. Zworykin invents the iconoscope, precursor to the cathode-ray tube, used for television.

Society

Germany—The government further inflates the mark, making it nearly worthless.

Anti-Semitic riots in Berlin result in the looting of over 1,000 shops.

Japan—A massive earthquake and resulting aftershocks and fires in Tokyo result in 200,000 deaths.

U.K.—Daily weather forecasts are broadcast for the first time on the BBC.

U.K. and U.S.—The McKenna Commission (U.K.) and Dawes Commission (U.S.) are appointed to establish reparations regulations for Germany.

Sports

Argentina—Enrique Tiriboschi establishes a record for swimming the English Channel: 16 hours, 33 minutes.

France—The first 24-hour Grand Prix auto race is held at Le Mans.

U.S.—In baseball, Yankee Stadium opens in New York.

In the World Series, the New York Yankees (American League) defeat the New York Giants (National League), four games to two.

1924 Arts and Entertainment

Chile—Pablo Neruda publishes the poetry collection *Twenty Love Poems and One Song of Despair*.

France—The surrealist artistic movement is officially founded, as writer André Breton publishes the first Surrealist Manifesto and the first surrealist exhibition is held.

Germany—Thomas Mann publishes the novel *The Magic Mountain*.

Erwin Piscator founds the Berlin Proletarian Theater.

Otto Dix creates the series of engravings *War*.

In Germany the Blue Four exhibit their works: Wassily Kandinsky, Paul Klee, Lyonel Feininger, and Alexej von Jawlensky.

Ireland—Sean O'Casey's play *Juno and the Paycock* premieres.

Italy—Rodolfo De Angelis founds the New Futurist Theater.

Nepal—Bhanu Bhakta Acharya, considered the founder of Nepali literature, completes his final poem, "Ramgeeta."

Netherlands—Architect Gerrit Rietveld, associated with the De Stijl movement, builds Schroeder House in Utrecht.

Soviet Union—Mikhail Bulgakov publishes the novel *The White Guard.*

U.K.—George Bernard Shaw's play *Saint Joan* premieres.

E. M. Forster publishes the novel *A Passage to India.*

U.S.—George Gershwin's *Rhapsody in Blue* for piano and jazz orchestra premieres.

The film studio Metro-Goldwyn-Mayer is formed.

John Ford's film *The Iron Horse* is released.

Ideas

Austria—Psychoanalyst Otto Rank publishes *The Trauma of Birth,* in which he departs from the views of his mentor Sigmund Freud.

Germany—Philosopher Moritz Schlick founds the Vienna Circle, a group of logical positivists that will last until his death in 1936. Other members will include Otto Neuurath, Rudolf Carnap, and Kurt Gödel.

Switzerland—Theologian Karl Barth publishes *The Word of God and the Word of Man.*

U.S.—From 1924 to 1933 journalist H. L. Mencken edits the *American Mercury*, cofounded with George Jean Nathan.

Scholar Irving Babbitt publishes *Democracy and Leadership.*

Sociologist Franklin Giddings publishes *The Scientific Study of Human Society.*

Non-voting, Causes and Methods of Control by political scientists Charles Merriam and Harold Gosnell is one of the first important works of political science to use survey data and sampling techniques.

Military

China—Military officer Chiang Kai-shek is given the influential post of running the Whampoa Military Academy.

Politics

Anglo-Egyptian Sudan—Sir Lee Stack, governor-general of the Sudan, is assassinated. The British demand and receive withdrawal of Egyptian troops from the Sudan, though not before Egyptian premier Saad Zaghul resigns in protest over the British demand.

China—The Guomindang allows Communists to join the party and accepts Soviet military advisers.

The Guomindang's "Three People's Principles"—Nationalism, People's Rights, and People's Livelihood—become a focus for Chinese allegiance.

Czechoslovakia/France—The two countries sign a treaty of alliance.

Ethiopia—Slavery is officially abolished.

Germany—The Dawes Plan provides for reorganization of the German Reichsbank under Allied direction.

The Reichsmark is introduced as a new currency.

Greece—A junta led by Eleutherios Venizelos forces King George II to abdicate. Greece is proclaimed a republic.

Hejaz—In what is now Saudi Arabia, Sherif Hussein of the Hejaz is forced to abdicate by rival Abd al-Aziz ibn Saud. Hussein's son Ali succeeds but is also forced to abdicate.

Iraq—A liberal constitution is enacted.

Italy—Philosopher Giovanni Gentile becomes first president of the National Fascist Institute of Culture.

Socialist deputy Giacomo Matteotti is assassinated by Fascist agents. Non-Fascist government members refuse to return to parliament, and Mussolini forces them to stay out.

Morocco—Tangier becomes an international city, governed by representatives from Britain, France, Spain, and other countries.

Soviet Union—The nation's founder and leader, V. I. Lenin, dies (January 21), setting off a power struggle between Joseph Stalin, supported at first by Lev Kamenev and Grigory Zinoviev, and Leon Trotsky.

Britain and France recognize the Soviet Union.

Spain—Manuel Azana founds the Republican Party.

U.K.—On January J. Ramsay MacDonald becomes the first prime minister to head a Labour government. Although the Labour Party has a minority of seats, it uses an alliance with the Liberty Party to take power.

On October the Labour government falls and Conservative leader Stanley Baldwin becomes prime minister. The outcome of the election is influenced by the discovery of the "Zinoviev letter," a document purportedly from Soviet official Zinoviev urging British Communists to engage in revolutionary activities. Though of questionable origin, the letter incites voters against the Labour government for its pro-Soviet policies.

U.S.—Republican Calvin Coolidge is reelected as president, defeating Democrat John W. Davis.

World—The League of Nations proposes the Geneva Protocol, which provides for the compulsory arbitration of all international disputes. Britain and its dominions reject the protocol.

Science and Technology

Czechoslovakia—Chemist Jaroslav Heyrovsky devises the polarograph, a device to analyze chemical solutions.

India/Germany—Indian physicist Satyendra Nath Bose and German physicist Albert Einstein develop the Bose-Einstein statistics, a method for handling the particles called bosons, for Bose.

South Africa—Australian-born South African anthropologist Raymond Arthur Dart discovers a fossil skull of the hominid *Australopithecus africanus*.

U.K.—Astronomer Edwin Powell Hubble discovers that the Andromeda "nebula" is a separate galaxy.

Biochemist David Keilin discovers cytochrome oxidase, an enzyme important in cell respiration.

U.S.—Harvard Observatory completes publication of the *Henry Draper* (or *Standard Draper*) *Catalogue* of stars, principally authored by astronomer Annie Jump Cannon.

Biochemist Harry Steenbock discovers how to irradiate food with sunlight to produce Vitamin D.

American Telephone & Telegraph and General Electric jointly found Bell Laboratories, for physics research.

Society

India—Plague is epidemic in the Punjab.

Mohandas Gandhi fasts for 21 days to protest violence between Hindus and Muslims. Gandhi is released from prison.

Political leader Bhimrao Ramji Ambedkar founds the Depressed Classes Institute, aimed at improving the lot of the "untouchables" caste to which he belongs. As India's first law minister (1947–51), he will help establish laws forbidding discrimination against untouchables.

U.K.—Hairdresser Antoine starts a fashion for dyeing gray hair blue.

U.S.—An immigration bill sets new limits on immigration and excludes Japanese immigration altogether.

Two Army biplanes, flown by Lowell Smith and Erik Nelson, complete the first round-the-world flight.

Sports

U.S.—Swimmer Johnny Weissmuller wins two gold medals at the Paris Olympic Games.

World—The first Winter Olympic Games are held, at Chamonix, France.

1925 Arts and Entertainment

Austria—Austrian composer Alban Berg's atonal opera *Wozzeck* is produced in Berlin.

Ireland—Liam O'Flaherty publishes the novel *The Informer*.

Japan—Kawabata Yasunari publishes the memoir *The Diary of a Sixteen-Year-Old* and the novel *The Izu Dancer.*

Russia—Sergey Eisenstein's film *The Battleship Potemkin* is released.

Soviet Union—Dmitry Shostakovich's Symphony no. 1 premieres.

U.K.—Virginia Woolf publishes the novel *Mrs. Dalloway* and the collection of essays *The Common Reader.*

Noel Coward's comedy *Hay Fever* is produced.

U.S.—Sculptor Gutzon Borglum is authorized by Congress to carve a colossal memorial of four U.S. presidents on the face of Mount Rushmore, South Dakota. The project will begin in 1927 and be finished in 1941 by Borglum's son Lincoln.

F. Scott Fitzgerald publishes the novel *The Great Gatsby*.

Theodore Dreiser publishes the novel *An American Tragedy*.

Sinclair Lewis publishes the novel *Arrowsmith*.

Countee Cullen publishes the poetry collection *Color*.

Films include Charlie Chaplin's *The Gold Rush*, King Vidor's *The Big Parade*, and Harold Lloyd's *The Freshman*.

George Luks paints *Boy with Baseball*.

U.S./France—American-born singer and dancer Josephine Baker, who will become a French citizen in 1937, performs in Paris in *La Revue Nègre*.

Ideas

Belgium—Historian Henri Pirenne publishes *Medieval Cities*.

France—Anthropologist Marcel Mauss publishes *The Gift*.

Germany—Nazi leader Adolf Hitler publishes the anti-Semitic manifesto *Mein Kampf (My Struggle)* (1925–27).

Russia—Historian Simon Dubnow publishes his 10-volume *World History of the Jewish People* (1925–29).

U.K.—Critic Ivor Armstrong Richards publishes *Principles of Literary Criticism*.

Philosopher Charles Dunbar Broad publishes *Mind and Its Place in Nature*.

Political scientist Harold Laski publishes *Grammar of Politics*.

Philosopher and educator John Dewey publishes *Experience and Nature*.

Political scientist Charles E. Merriam publishes *New Aspects of Politics*.

U.S.—Critic Alain Locke publishes *The New Negro*, an anthology of scholarship and creative writing from writers of the Harlem Renaissance.

Bruce Barton publishes the self-help book *The Man Nobody Knows*.

Military

Nicaragua—U.S. forces intervene in a civil war.

Syria—Druse rebels win early victories in the Druse Rebellion (1925–27).

Turkey—A Kurdish insurrection fails; the Kurds resort to low-level guerrilla warfare.

Politics

Albania—Ahmed Bey Zogu leads a republican revolution; he becomes head of the republic.

China—As antiforeign feeling grows, British troops fire on demonstrators in Shanghai, killing 12 (May 30) and sparking a wave of May 30th Movement demonstrations (1925–26).

Cyprus—Cyprus becomes a British crown colony.

Germany-Hans Luther becomes chancellor; Paul von Hindenburg is elected president. Adolf Hitler reorganizes the Nazi Party.

Greece—Following a coup, Theodore Pangalos becomes premier.

Japan—Universal suffrage for men is instituted.

Norway—Norway annexes Spitzbergen.

Persia—Reza Khan becomes shah.

U.K.—The Unemployment Insurance Act is passed.

The British Dominions Office is founded.

U.S.—Nellie Taylor Ross of Wyoming becomes the country's first woman governor.

World—The treaties of Locarno, Switzerland, settle boundary disputes and temporarily help to stabilize Europe. Germany, a participant in the Locarno Conference, is admitted to the League of Nations.

Science and Technology

Austria—Physicist Wolfgang Pauli states the Pauli exclusion principle, that no two electrons in an atom can have the same set of quantum numbers.

Germany—German chemist Walter Karl Noddack; his future wife, Ida Eva Tacke; and Otto C. Berg discover the element rhenium.

Oceanographers, using sonar, discover the undersea Mid-Atlantic Ridge.

Physicist Werner Heisenberg develops matrix mechanics, a mathematical technique for studying energy levels of electrons.

Netherlands—Physicists George Eugene Uhlenbeck and Samuel Abraham Goudsmit define particle spin as the fourth quantum number.

U.K.—Chemist Francis W. Aston discovers the packing fraction, which refers to the energy change produced by packing particles into a nucleus.

U.S.—In a confirmation of Albert Einstein's general theory of relativity, American astronomer Walter Sydney Adams discovers a red, or Einstein, shift in the spectral lines of white dwarf stars that is caused by the stars' massive gravity.

Society

Canada—The nation's Presbyterian, Congregational, and Methodist churches join together as the United Church of Canada.

Germany—The Leica, a new kind of 35-millimeter camera, is developed by Ernst Leitz GmbH.

Japan—The religious movement Reiyukai (Soul-Friend Association) grows out of the Nichiren Buddhist sect.

U.S.—Tennessee schoolteacher John Thomas Scopes goes on trial for violating a state law prohibiting the teaching of Darwin's theory of evolution. Defended by Clarence Darrow against prosecutor William Jennings Bryan, Scopes is convicted but later acquitted on a technicality.

Clarence Birdseye and Charles Seabrook develop a deep-freezing process for cooked foods; it will be patented in 1926.

Automobile manufacturer Walter Chrysler founds the Chrysler Corporation.

Crossword puzzles become fashionable.

Harold S. Vanderbilt invents contract bridge; auction bridge dates from 1904.

U.S./Europe—The Charleston becomes a popular dance.

World—Skirts climb above the knees. Straight dresses without waistlines and "cloche" hats are popular.

Factory ships begin to be used in whaling, increasing the pace at which whales are exploited.

Sports

U.S.—In golf, Willie Macfarlane wins the U.S. Open and Bobby Jones wins the U.S. Golf Association Amateur Championship.

Pittsburgh (National League) beats Washington (American League) in the World Series, four games to three.

1926 Arts and Entertainment

Argentina—Argentinian poet and novelist Ricardo Güiraldes publishes *Don Segundo Sombra*.

Belgium—René Magritte paints *The Menaced Assassin*.

Ireland—Sean O'Casey's play *The Plough and the Stars* is produced.

James Joyce's play *Exiles* premieres in London.

Italy—Giacomo Puccini's opera *Turandot* premieres posthumously.

Germany—Fritz Lang's film *Metropolis* is released.

Architect Walter Gropius designs the buildings of the Bauhaus at Dessau, early examples of the international style.

Hungary—Béla Bartók's ballet *The Miraculous Mandarin* premieres in Cologne.

Soviet Union—Isaac Babel publishes the short-story collection *Red Cavalry*.

Spain—Joan Miró paints *Dog Barking at the Moon* and *Person Throwing a Stone at a Bird*.

U.K.—A. A. Milne publishes the children's book *Winnie-the-Pooh*.

U.S.—Ernest Hemingway publishes *The Sun Also Rises*.

Langston Hughes publishes his first poetry collection, *The Weary Blues*.

The musical *Oh, Kay!* by George and Ira Gershwin premieres.

Jazz musician Jelly Roll Morton forms the Red Hot Peppers band.

Georgia O'Keeffe paints *Black Iris*.

Ideas

China—Political scientist Wang Shijie publishes *Bijiao Xienfa (Comparative Constitutions)*.

India—Poet and philosopher Sri Aurobindo Ghose, exponent of a philosophy of Integral Yoga, retires into seclusion until his death in 1950.

Soviet Union—Critic Osip Brik writes the essay "Photography Versus Painting."

Filmmaker Vsevolod Pudovkin publishes *Film Technique and Film Acting*.

U.S.—Carl Sandburg publishes *Abraham Lincoln: The Prairie Years*, the first part of his biography of the former president; the second, in 1939, will be *Abraham Lincoln: The War Years*.

Military

China—Chiang Kai-shek succeeds Sun Yat-sen as commander-in-chief of the National Revolutionary Army. Seeking to unify China, he launches from Canton the successful Northern Expedition (1926–28), which captures Hankow, Nanking, and Shanghai.

Morocco—The Rif War (1921–26) ends as Abd el-Krim's insurgents surrender to French and Spanish forces.

Politics

Germany—Joseph Goebbels becomes the leader of the Berlin Nazi Party organization.

Japan—Hirohito becomes emperor.

Mexico—The government pursues anti-Catholic policies, prompting an insurrection by Catholics called Cristeros (1926–29).

Poland—Jósef Pilsudski seizes power in a coup and becomes de facto dictator.

Portugal—A coup ends the First Republic.

Soviet Union—Joseph Stalin solidifies his hold on the country by removing rivals Grigori Zinoviev and Lev Kamenev from power.

Science and Technology

Austria—Physicist Erwin Schrödinger develops wave mechanics.

Germany—Physicist Max Born develops the concept of the wave packet.

Italy/U.K.—Italian physicist Enrico Fermi and British physicist P. A. M. Dirac develop the Fermi-Dirac statistics, which apply to the particles later called fermions, for Fermi.

Switzerland/Norway—Swiss-Norwegian geochemist Victor Goldschmidt codifies the isomorphism rule.

U.S.—On March 16 Robert H. Goddard launches the world's first liquid-fuel rocket, near Auburn, Massachusetts.

Astronomer Edwin Powell Hubble classifies galaxies by their structure, as elliptical, spiral, or irregular.

Bacteriologist Thomas Rivers establishes virology, the study of viruses, as a separate area from the study of bacteria.

Neurologist and physiologist Walter B. Cannon coins the term *homeostasis*.

Biochemist James Batcheller Sumner crystallizes the first pure enzyme, jack bean urease.

Society

China—On October 12 a troop ship in the Yangtze River explodes and sinks, killing 1,200 people.

India—English-born theosophist Annie Besant declares Indian mystic Jiddu Krishnamurti to be the new Messiah.

U.S.—The Book-of-the-Month Club is founded.

The Scholastic Aptitude Test (SAT) is administered to high school students applying to college.

David Sarnoff founds the National Broadcasting Company (NBC) as a network of nine radio stations.

Revivalist Aimee Semple McPherson disappears and, a month later, turns up in Mexico. To widespread skepticism, she claims to have been kidnapped.

Richard E. Byrd and Floyd Bennett make the first airplane flight over the North Pole.

World—International agreements are made assigning broadcasting wavelengths to each country's radio stations.

Sports

U.K.—Gertrude Ederle, the first woman to swim the English Channel, sets a new record time of 14 hours 39 minutes.

U.S.—In golf, Bobby Jones wins the British Open and the U.S. Open, becoming the first to hold both titles simultaneously.

Boxer Gene Tunney wins the world heavyweight title from Jack Dempsey.

In women's tennis, Helen Wills, later named Moody, begins her dominance of the sport. From 1926 to 1938, she wins 31 titles, including seven U.S. and a then-record eight Wimbledon singles titles.

1927 Arts and Entertainment

France—Igor Stravinsky's opera-oratorio *Oedipus Rex* (text additions by Jean Cocteau) is performed in concert in Paris.

Chaim Soutine completes the painting *Page Boy at Maxim's*.

American modern dancer Isadora Duncan is strangled by her scarf when it becomes entangled in her car wheels.

Antonin Artaud and Roger Vitrac introduce the "theater of cruelty" at their newly opened Théâtre Alfred Jarry.

Germany—The *Deutscher Werkbund* exhibition, organized by Mies van der Rohe, introduces the international style of architecture.

Kurt Weill's musical play *Royal Palace* debuts in Berlin.

Arnold Schoenberg's String Quartet no. 3 is performed.

The jazz-tinged opera *Jonny spielt auf* debuts.

Soviet Union—Dmitry Shostakovich's Symphony no. 2 ("To October") premieres.

U.S.—Alan Crosland's *The Jazz Singer,* the first full-length sound film, premieres.

Work begins on the monument at Mount Rushmore, South Dakota, which will represent presidents George Washington, Thomas Jefferson, Abraham Lincoln, and Theodore Roosevelt.

Jerome Kern's breakthrough musical *Show Boat* premieres.

Martha Graham opens her School of Modern Dance in New York City.

Duke Ellington's jazz compositions are broadcast from New York's Cotton Club.

World—Notable novels include Marcel Proust's *Le Temps retrouvé* (last volume of *A la recherche du temps perdu*, France), Franz Kafka's *Amerika* (Germany), Virginia Woolf's *To the Lighthouse* (U.K.), Willa Cather's *Death Comes for the Archbishop* (U.S.), William Faulkner's *Sartoris*, Sinclair Lewis's *Elmer Gantry*, and Thornton Wilder's *The Bridge of San Luis Rey* (U.S.).

Films include Abel Gance's *Napoleon* (France), Buster Keaton's *The General* (U.S), F. W. Murnau's *Sunrise* (U.S.).

Military

Portugal—A revolt of intellectuals against the military government is quashed.

Politics

Austria—A general strike follows the acquittal of Nationalists in the murder of two Socialists.

China—The Guomindang nationalist party is split into conservatives (led by Jiang Jieshi) and radicals.

The Communist Party in China has beginnings in Jiangxi and Fujian Districts.

Hejaz and Nejd—The independence of the kingdom later known as Saudi Arabia is recognized by the U.K.

Indonesia—The Indonesian Nationalist Party is founded.

India—Sikh and Muslim groups riot, resulting in 14 deaths and 100 injured.

Iraq—In a treaty between the two countries, Britain recognizes Iraq.

Mexico—Citizen rebellion against nationalization of church property is quashed.

Sierra Leone—Slavery is abolished.

Soviet Union—The 15th All-Union Congress of the Communist Party expels Leon Trotsky and others for not adhering to party tenets as decreed by Joseph Stalin.

U.K.—The U.K. severs relations with the Soviet Union.

U.S.—President Calvin Coolidge declines to run for reelection.

Science and Technology

Belgium—George Lemaitre develops the concept of the expanding universe.

France—Tetanus immunizations, developed by G. Ramon and C. Zoellar, are used for the first time on humans.

Germany—Niels Bohr presents the concept of complementarity.

Physicist Werner Heisenberg presents his uncertainty principle for quantum physics.

Soviet Union—I. P. Pavlov's *Conditioned Reflexes* is translated into English.

U.K.—Transatlantic telephone service begins, with the first transmission between New York City and London.

U.S.—The iron lung, an electric respirator created by physicians Philips Drinker and Louis A. Shaw, is put into operation in Bellevue Hospital, New York.

Television is demonstrated for the first time in New York.

The Ford Model A is introduced to replace the Model T.

Society

Germany—The German stock market collapses.

U.S.—Aviator Charles Lindbergh becomes the first person to fly nonstop across the Atlantic, flying the *Spirit of St. Louis* alone from New York to Paris.

Sports

U.S.—New York Yankee George Herman "Babe" Ruth hits a record-breaking 60 home runs during the 154-game season. His record will stand until 1961, when fellow Yankee Roger Maris hits 61.

Helen Wills dominates women's tennis, winning the U.S. Lawn Tennis Association singles and Wimbledon championships.

Walter Hagen wins the PGA golf tournament for a record-breaking fourth time.

1928 Arts and Entertainment

France—René Clair's film *The Italian Straw Hat* and Carl Dreyer's film *The Passion of Joan of Arc* premiere.

Germany—Bertolt Brecht's *The Threepenny Opera,* with music by Kurt Weill, is produced in Berlin.

G. W. Pabst's film *Pandora's Box* is released.

Ireland—William Butler Yeats's poetry collection *The Tower,* including "Leda and the Swan," is published.

Italy/U.S.—Italian conductor Arturo Toscanini leaves his post as musical director at La Scala, Milan, to become principal conductor of the New York Philharmonic Symphony Orchestra (1928–36).

Japan—Kobayashi Takiji publishes the novel *The Fifteenth of March.*

Soviet Union—Sergey Eisenstein's film *October* is released.

Mikhail Sholokhov publishes *And Quiet Flows the Don*, the first half of the novel *The Quiet Don*. The second half, *The Don Flows Home to the Sea,* will be published in 1940.

Spain—Federico García Lorca publishes the poetry collection *Romancero Gitano*.

U.K.—D. H. Lawrence publishes his last novel, *Lady Chatterley's Lover.*

Dorothy L. Sayers publishes *The Unpleasantness at the Bellona Club*, one of a series of novels featuring detective Lord Peter Wimsey.

Virginia Woolf publishes the novel *Orlando*.

U.S.—Eugene O'Neill's play *Strange Interlude* premieres.

Animator Walt Disney's first Mickey Mouse cartoons, including *Steamboat Willie* (the first Mickey Mouse cartoon with sound sequences), are released.

Ideas

Germany—Critic Walter Benjamin publishes *The Origin of German Tragic Drama*. He will become known for applying Marxist ideas to the analysis of literature, history, and culture.

Philosopher Rudolf Carnap publishes *The Logical Structure of the World*.

Philosopher Hans Reichenbach publishes *The Philosophy of Space and Time*.

India—Poet and philosopher Sir Muhammad Iqbal delivers the six lectures known as "The Reconstruction of Religious Thought in Islam" (1928–29).

U.S.—Ethnologist Franz Boas attacks theories of racial superiority in *Anthropology and Modern Life*.

Margaret Mead publishes *Coming of Age in Samoa*.

Military

China—As the Northern Expedition is completed, Chiang Kai-shek establishes the National Government in Nanjing (Nanking). It will last until 1937, uniting much of China under republican rule.

World—The Kellogg-Briand Pact, an international agreement banning war as an instrument of national policy, is signed by 15 nations (eventually, 62 will sign). It is named for its originators, U.S. secretary of state Frank Kellogg and French foreign minister Aristide Briand.

Politics

Egypt—King Fa'ud dissolves parliament until 1929.

Ethiopia—Ras Tafari, already wielding de facto power as regent, becomes King Haile Selassie I; he will become emperor in 1930, ruling until 1974.

Soviet Union—Joseph Stalin enacts his first Five-Year Plan, an economic program that entails forced collectivization of the property of *kulaks*, or landowning peasants, accompanied by famine and mass deportations.

U.K.—Women gain fully equal voting rights.

U.S.—In the presidential election, Republican Herbert Clark Hoover (1929–33) defeats

Democrat Alfred E. Smith.

Yugoslavia—Croatian People's Peasants' Party leader Stjepan Radic is assassinated. Croat deputies withdraw from parliament and set up a separatist parliament. King Alexander I dissolves parliament, establishes a dictatorship, and changes the country's name from the Kingdom of Serbs, Croats, and Slovenes to Yugoslavia ("Land of Southern Slavs").

Science and Technology

Germany—Physicist Arnold Sommerfeld discovers that in a conductor, electrons behave like a degenerate gas.

Hungary—Mathematician John von Neumann develops game theory.

Physicist Eugene P. Wigner develops the concept of parity of atomic states.

India—Physicist Venkata Raman discovers the Raman effect, an inelastic scattering of electromagnetic radiation.

Sweden—Astronomer Bertil Lindblad proposes that the Milky Way galaxy rotates.

U.K.—Bacteriologist Alexander Fleming isolates the mold *Penicillium natatum*; pure penicillin, an antibiotic, will not be produced until 1939.

Biologist Charles Elton publishes *Animal Ecology*.

U.S.—Neurosurgeons Harvey Cushing and W. T. Bowie introduce surgical diathermy, or blood vessel cauterization.

Greek-American pathologist George Papanicolaou develops the test for cervical cancer that will be called the Pap smear.

Society

France—Chef Georges Auguste Escoffier is the first chef to win the French Legion of Honor.

Japan—Holy man Taniguchi Masaharu founds Seicho no Ie (the House of Growth), which teaches that all religions are expressions of the one God.

U.S.—Station WGY in Schenectady, New York, makes the first ever scheduled television broadcasts.

Amelia Earhart flies from Newfoundland to Wales, becoming the first woman to pilot an airplane solo across the Atlantic Ocean.

Inventor Otto Frederick Rohwedder invents a commercial bread-slicing machine. Two years later the Continental Bakery will sell the first loaves of prepackaged sliced bread, labeled Wonder Bread.

Bakelite, the first major commercial plastic, comes into use.

A flood caused by a hurricane kills more than 2,000 people at Lake Okeechobee in central Florida (September 16–17).

Sports

Norway—Skater Sonja Henie wins the first of three consecutive Olympic gold medals for ice-skating (1928, 1932, 1936).

U.K.—Soccer player Dixie (William Ralph) Dean ends the 1927–28 season with a record 60 goals in 39 matches.

U.S.—Jack Dempsey fails in his attempt to regain the world heavyweight boxing title from Gene Tunney.

1929 Arts and Entertainment

France—Jean Cocteau publishes the novel *Les Enfants terribles*.

Painter Marc Chagall completes *Love Idyll*.

Germany—Franz Lehár's operetta *The Land of Smiles* premieres; Paul Hindemith's opera *Neues vom Tage* premieres.

Spain—Pablo Picasso completes the painting *Woman in Armchair*.

Switzerland—Painter Paul Klee completes *Fool in a Trance*.

U.K.—Noel Coward's operetta *Bitter Sweet* premieres; George Bernard Shaw's play *The Apple Cart* premieres.

Virginia Woolf publishes the essay collection *A Room of One's Own*.

Robert Graves publishes the memoir *Goodbye to All That*.

U.S.—Georgia O'Keefe paints *Black Flowers and Blue Larkspur*; Grant Wood paints *Woman with Plants*.

The Museum of Modern Art opens in New York City.

The first Academy Awards presentation is held: Best Picture—*Wings*; Best Actor—Emil Jannings; Best Actress—Janet Gaynor.

World—Novels include Richard Hughes's *A High Wind in Jamaica* (U.K.), William Faulkner's *Sartoris* (U.S.), Ernest Hemingway's *A Farewell to Arms* (U.S.), Oliver LaFarge's *Laughing Boy* (U.S.), Sinclair Lewis's *Dodsworth* (U.S.), Thomas Wolfe's *Look Homeward, Angel* (U.S.), Rómulo Gallegos's *Doña Bárbara* (Venezuela), and Ba Jin's *Mie-wang (Extinction)* (China).

Poetic works include Conrad Aiken's *Selected Poems* (U.S.), Robinson Jeffers's *Dear Judas and Other Poems* (U.S.).

Films include Alfred Hitchcock's *Blackmail* (U.K.), Ernst Lubitsch's *The Love Parade* (U.S.), King Vidor's *Hallelujah!* (U.S.), and Sergey Eisenstein's *The General Line* (Soviet Union).

Ideas

U.S.—Sociologists Robert S. and Helen M. Lynd publish *Middletown: A Study in American Culture*, a study of habits, beliefs, and practices of citizens in Muncie, Indiana.

Politics

Australia—The Labour Party wins elections.

Palestine—Arabs engage in attacks against Jews over the use of the Wailing Wall.

Soviet Union—Leon Trotsky is expelled from the country.

U.S.—The Senate approves the Kellogg-Briand Peace Pact.

In a Teapot Dome–related trial, Secretary of the Interior Albert B. Fall is found guilty of accepting a bribe and sentenced to a year in prison and $100,000 fine.

Science and Technology

Germany—The *Graf Zeppelin* airship flies around the world for the first time.

Albert Einstein publishes *Unified Field Theory*.

Germany/U.S.—Separately, German biologist A. F. Butenandt and U.S. biologist E. A. Doisy isolate the female hormone estrone.

U.S.—The first plane flight using only instruments is completed by Lt. James Doolittle.

Astronomer Edwin Hubble measures shifts in the spectra of extragalactic nebulae.

Society

South Africa—The term apartheid is used for the first time.

U.S.—In what will be known as the St. Valentine's Day Massacre, five gang members kill six members of rival "Bugs" Moran gang and one bystander in a Chicago garage. The massacre, possibly orchestrated by Al Capone, reflects the growth in bootlegging-related violence.

Stock prices reach their highest value on September 3.

On October 29, later known as Black Tuesday, the New York Stock Exchange trades a record 16,410,030 shares of stock in an attempt to bail out after several days of rapid market decline. The day will mark the beginning of the worldwide Great Depression.

Construction begins on the Empire State Building, New York City. It will be completed in 1931.

Lieutenant Commander Richard E. Byrd completes the first flight over the South Pole.

Sports

U.S.—The World Series is won by the Philadelphia Athletics (AL), who defeat the Chicago Cubs (NL), four games to one.

At the U.S. Lawn Tennis Association championships, the men's singles competition is won by William T. Tilden, the women's singles by Helen Wills.

The U.S. Open golf tournament is won by Robert "Bobby" Jones.

The PGA golf tournament is won by Leo Diegel.

1930 Arts and Entertainment

Cuba—Nicolás Guillén publishes his first book of poetry, *Motifs of Son*.

Czechoslovakia—Leos Janáček premieres the opera *From the House of the Dead*.

France—Igor Stravinsky's *Symphony of Psalms* premieres.

Designer Le Corbusier completes the Villa Savoye, Poissy.

Germany—Kurt Weill and Bertolt Brecht's opera *Rise and Fall of the City of Mahagonny* premieres.

U.S.—The Chrysler Building, an example of art deco architecture, is completed in New York City.

Martha Graham premieres her modern dance work *Lamentation*.

Paintings include Thomas Hart Benton's *City Scenes*, Edward Hopper's *Early Sunday*, and Grant Wood's *American Gothic*.

World—Poetry includes W. H. Auden's *Poems 1930* (U.K.), T. S. Eliot's *Ash Wednesday*, Hart Crane's *The Bridge* (U.S.).

Novels include Hermann Hesse's *Narziss und Goldmund* (Germany), Dashiell Hammett's *The Maltese Falcon* (U.S.), William Faulkner's *As I Lay Dying* (U.S.), and John Dos Passos's *The 42nd Parallel* (U.S.).

Films include Luis Buñuel's *L'Age d'or* (Spain), Aleksandr Dovzhenko's *The Earth* (Soviet Union), Mervyn LeRoy's *Little Caesar* (U.S.), Josef von Sternberg's *The Blue Angel* (Germany), Clarence Brown's *Anna Christie* (U.S.), Lewis Milestone's *All Quiet on the Western Front* (U.S.), Howard Hughes's *Hell's Angels* (U.S.), and George Hill's *The Big House* (U.S.).

Ideas

Austria—Sigmund Freud publishes *Civilization and Its Discontents*.

Germany—Nazi social critic Alfred Rosenberg publishes the pro-Aryan work *The Myth of the Twentieth Century*.

Spain—Philosopher José Ortega y Gasset publishes *The Revolt of the Masses*.

U.K.—Literary critic Sir William Empson publishes *Seven Types of Ambiguity*.

U.S.—Sinclair Lewis delivers the speech "The American Fear of Literature" at ceremonies marking his acceptance of the Nobel Prize in literature.

Military

Brazil—A military junta takes power, naming Dr. Gertuilo Vargas as president.

France—The final French troops leave the Rhineland.

André Maginot, France's minister of war, plans to build a military defense line against German attack during World War I along the France-Germany border. The line will be known as the Maginot line.

Politics

Belgium—With Scandinavia, Holland, and Luxembourg, the Oslo Agreement is signed, requiring consultation before the setting of tariffs.

China—The Nanjing government regains control after a threat by National Army vice commander-in-chief Gen. Yen Hsi-shan.

Dominican Republic—Rafael Leonidas Trujillo becomes dictator; his term will last 31 years.

Ethiopia—Haile Selassie (formerly Ras Tafari) becomes emperor of Abyssinia.

France—Minister of Foreign Affairs Aristide Brand writes a memorandum for establishment of United Nations of Europe.

Germany—The Young Plan is agreed to by the government, fixing reparation amounts and payment schedule (38 billion marks over 59 yearly installments).

In Reichstag elections, National Socialists increase representation from 12 to 107 seats.

India—Congress approves a boycott of the salt tax, beginning a campaign of civil disobedience.

Mohandas Gandhi conducts the Salt March, a civil disobedience campaign against the British monopoly on salt manufacture.

Japan—Fearing erosion of its market, Japan agrees to follow China's rules for tariffs.

Romania—The parliament elects exiled Crown Prince Carol as king.

Soviet Union—Under Joseph Stalin collectivization is extended throughout the republics, with the entire class of *kulaks*, or rich peasants, to be decimated.

Spain—King Alfonso requests the resignation of dictator Primo de Riviera; strikes occur throughout the year, with a general strike on December 16 supporting revolution.

Syria—France grants Syria a constitution.

Turkey—Constantinople is renamed Istanbul by Turkish nationalists.

U.K.—The government announces plans to permit limited self-government in Palestine and prohibit Jewish immigration and purchase of land in the region.

U.S.—Unemployment reaches 4.5 million; Congress authorizes $116 million for additional public works, and President Hoover establishes a Committee on Unemployment Relief.

The Hawley-Smoot Tariff Act is passed, imposing widespread duties worldwide.

Science and Technology

U.S.—The subatomic particle later known as the neutrino is devised by Austrian-American physicist Wolfgang Pauli; it will acquire its name in 1932 from Italian physicist Enrico Fermi.

The planet Pluto is discovered by scientist Clyde Tombaugh.

Frozen vegetables (peas) are sold for the first time, in Massachusetts. The quick-freezing process is developed by entrepreneur Clarence Birdseye.

Nylon, a synthetic fiber, is developed by scientist Wallace Carrothers and marketed by Du Pont.

Poly vinyl chloride (PVC), a plastic substitute for rubber, is discovered by W. L. Semon.

A vaccine for typhus is developed by Hans Zinnsser.

Society

France—The Workman's Insurance Law is passed, providing old age and disability insurance for much of the country.

Germany—Unemployment reaches three million.

South Africa—Caucasian women gain suffrage.

Soviet Union—Joseph Stalin requests international assistance to stave off national famine.

The Turkestan-Siberian railway is finished.

U.K.—The Church of England approves the use of birth control under certain circumstances.

U.S.—Richard Drew of the Minnesota Mining and Manufacturing Company (3M) invents Scotch tape.

Sports

Germany—German boxer Max Schmeling defeats U.S. boxer Jack Sharkey for world heavyweight boxing title.

Uruguay—Uruguay wins the first World Cup (football), beating Argentina 4–2.

U.S.—Hack Wilson of the Chicago Cubs drives in 190 runs, a record which stands for the entire century.

1931 Arts and Entertainment

Soviet Union—The music of composer Sergey Rachmaninoff is declared decadent by the government.

Spain—Salvador Dalí paints the surrealist work *The Persistence of Memory*.

U.K.—Frederick Ashton's ballet *Façade* premieres.

Hungarian-born British art historian Frederick Antal publishes *Florentine Painting and Its Social Background*, applying the study of social conditions to critical analysis.

U.S.—Composer and jazz musician Duke Ellington writes "Mood Indigo."

Martha Graham's modern dance work *Primi-Mysteries* premieres.

Composer Hoagy Carmichael publishes the song "Stardust."

The Group Theater is formed by Harold Clurman, Lee Strasberg, and Cheryl Crawford.

Musicals include George and Ira Gershwin's *Of Thee I Sing*.

Poet e. e. cummings publishes the collection *Viva*.

Nonfiction works include Edmund Wilson's *Axel's Castle*, Theodore Dreiser's *Newspaper Days*, and *The Autobiography of Lincoln Steffens*.

World—Novels include Antoine Saint-Exupéry's *Night Flight* (France), Hermann Broch's *The Sleepwalkers* (Germany), César Vallejo's *Tungsten* (Peru), Vita Sackville-West's *All Passion Spent* (U.K.), Pearl S. Buck's *The Good Earth* (U.S.), William Faulkner's *Sanctuary* (U.S.). Edna Ferber's *American Beauty* (U.S.), and T. S. Stribling's *The Forge* (U.S.).

Films include Fritz Lang's *M* (Germany), Tod Browning's *Dracula* (U.S.), Charles Chaplin's *City Lights* (U.S.), John Ford's *Arrowsmith* (U.S.), Victor Heerman's *Animal Crackers* (U.S.), and James Whale's *Frankenstein* (U.S.).

Ideas

Germany—Philosopher Edmund Husserl publishes *Cartesian Meditations*.

U.K.—Economic historian Richard Henry Tawney publishes *Equality*, on the baselessness for inequality.

U.S.—Elijah Muhammad founds the Black Muslim sect in Detroit.

Historian Frederick Lewis Allen publishes *Only Yesterday*, a chronicle of the 1920s.

Political commentator Walter Lippmann begins the column "Today and Tomorrow" in the New York *Herald Tribune*.

Military

Japan—Following the Mukden (China) Incident, the Kwangtung Army overtakes Mukden and Manchuria. Until the end of World War II, Manchuria is renamed Manchukuo.

Libya—The genocide of the Senussi by Italy is ended.

Soviet Union—The Kiangsi are attacked by China's Kuomintang armies.

Politics

Austria—The Credit-Anstalt fails, triggering financial breakdown in central Europe.

Bolivia—The country defaults on foreign debt; default by other South American countries follows.

Ceylon—Ceylon adopts universal suffrage.

Egypt/Iraq—The countries sign a friendship treaty.

India—Following the Salt March campaign in 1930, the British viceroy and Mahatma Gandhi agree to the Delhi Pact, allowing Indian citizens to make their own salt.

Japan—Prime Minister Hamaguchi Osachi is assassinated.

Spain—Alfonso XIII is overthrown in a revolution; he is succeeded by Alcalá Zamora, leader of a republican government.

U.K.—The Statute of Westminster establishes the British Commonwealth of Nations.

Following the resignation of the Labour government, a National Coalition government takes power, led by Prime Minister J. Ramsay MacDonald.

U.S.—Unemployment reaches between four million and five million.

Yugoslavia—A new constitution is adopted; royal dictator King Alexander is ousted.

Science and Technology

Austria—Mathematician Kurt Gödel generates Gödel's proof, the incompletability theorem. It posits that mathematical certainty can be neither proven nor disproven.

Germany—Chemist Adolf Butenandt isolates the male sex hormone androsterone.

Switzerland—Chemist Paul Karrer and others synthesize vitamin A.

U.S.—Chemist Harold Urey discovers deuterium, an isotope of hydrogen known as "heavy hydrogen," or U-2.

The cyclotron, or circular accelerator, is developed by physicist Ernest O. Lawrence.

Radio engineer Karl G. Jansky discovers radio radiation emanating from the sky, forming the basis for radio astronomy.

Chemist Linus Pauling develops the concept of resonance, which explains electron sharing in organic compounds through the application of quantum mechanics.

Pathologist Ernest William Goodpasture develops a technique for growing virus cultures in eggs.

The first flight around the world is completed by Wiley Post and Harold Gatty, in the plane *Winnie May.* Starting from Roosevelt Field, Long Island, they log a flying time of eight days, 15 hours, 51 minutes.

Society

Africa—The first trans-Africa railroad opens, the Benguela-Katanga railroad.

U.K.—The National Birth Control Council wins a battle for the government to grant birth control information and materials to married couples.

U.S.—A bank panic closes over 800 banks.

In Scottsboro, Alabama, nine African-American men are falsely tried and convicted of raping two Caucasian women. Known as the Scottsboro Case, it spurs a national uproar over the defendants' inadequate representation and a prejudiced court. Partial Supreme Court reversals will follow.

Hunger marchers demonstrate in Washington, D.C., requesting work.

Congress approves making "The Star Spangled Banner" the national anthem.

The Empire State Building is completed and at the time is the tallest building in the world, 1,250 feet high.

Alphonse "Al" Capone is convicted and sentenced to 11 years in prison for federal income tax evasion. He will be released in 1939.

Sports

U.K.—At the Wimbledon tennis championships, the men's singles title is won by Sidney B. Wood Jr., 20, the youngest player to win the event.

U.S.—In the World Series the St. Louis Cardinals (NL) defeat the Philadelphia Athletics (AL), four games to three.

The PGA golf tournament is won by Tom Creavy.

New York Yankee Lou Gehrig drives in 184 runs, setting an American League record for runs batted in during the season.

1932 Arts and Entertainment

Germany—Arnold Schoenberg's unfinished opera *Moses und Aron* premieres.

Painter Max Beckman completes *Seven Triptychs.*

India—Poet and philosopher Sir Muhammad Iqbal publishes *The Song of Eternity.*

Italy—The Venice Film Festival premieres.

Mexico—Painter Diego Riviera completes the fresco series *Detroit Industry* at the Detroit Institute of Arts.

U.K.—The London Philharmonic Orchestra is founded by Sir Thomas Beecham.

U.S.—Artist Ben Shahn completes works illusrating the Sacco and Vanzetti trials.

W. H. Auden publishes the poetry collection *The Orators.*

Artist Alexander Calder creates a new form of moving sculpture, given the name "mobile" by French painter Marcel Duchamp.

E.Y. ("Yip") Harburg and Jay Gorney write the song "Brother, Can You Spare a Dime?" which becomes a popular Great Depression lament.

World—Plays include Philip Barry's *The Animal Kingdom* (U.S.).

Novels include Sherwood Anderson's *Beyond Desire* (U.S.), Aldous Huxley's *Brave New World* (U.K.), Pearl S. Buck's *The Good Earth* (U.S.), Erskine Caldwell's *Tobacco Road* (U.S.), John Dos Passos's *1919* (U.S.), William Faulkner's *Light in August* (U.S.), Ernest Hemingway's *Death in the Afternoon* (U.S.), and T. S. Stribling's *The Store* (U.S.); story collections include Sean O'Faolain's *Midsummer Night Madness* (Ireland).

Films include René Clair's *Á Nous la Liberté* (France), Frank Borzage's *A Farewell to Arms* (U.S.), Edmund Goulding's *Grand Hotel* (U.S.), Howard Hawks's *Scarface* (U.S.), Mervyn LeRoy's *I Am a Fugitive from a Chain Gang* (U.S.), and W. S. Van Dyke's *Tarzan, the Ape Man* (U.S.).

Ideas

Austria—Psychoanalyst Melanie Klein publishes *The Psychoanalysis of Children.*

France—Philosopher Jacques Maritain publishes *The Degrees of Knowledge.*

Germany—Painter Hans Hoffman publishes the essay "On the Aims of Art."

Philosopher Karl Jaspers publishes the three-volume work *Philosophie.*

U.K.—Literary critic F. R. Leavis publishes *New Bearings in English Poetry* and edits the influential journal *Scrutiny.*

U.S.—Theologian Reinhold Niebuhr publishes *Moral Man and Immoral Society.*

Historian Charles Beard publishes *A Charter for the Social Sciences*, which will influence the teaching of history in the U.S.

Military

China—Japanese forces occupy Shanghai; forces supporting the Chinese are sent by the U.S., France, Italy, and the U.K. (January 28).

A Japan-China truce is signed, granting China a demilitarized zone and ending the western and Chinese boycott of Japanese goods (March–May).

Politics

France—At Lausanne, France and Great Britain sign a treaty of friendship.

Germany—Field Marshal Paul von Hindenberg is elected president, but fails to gain majority (March). Elections in April gain majority for von Hindenberg over Adolf Hitler, 19 million votes to 13 million votes.

Chancellor von Papen declares martial law on Berlin and Brandenburg.

In Reichstag elections, National Socialists take 233 seats and Social Democrats 133 seats (July 31).

President von Hindenberg offers vice chancellorship to Adolf Hitler, but is refused (August 13).

The Reichstag is dissolved.

India—Mahatma Gandhi begins a "fast unto death" after rejecting British plan for limited representation for "untouchables" (August 16); full representation under Poona Pact is granted and the fast ended (August 24).

At a conference in London on India, leaders allow the release of nearly 30,000 Indian prisoners, including Mahatma Gandhi (December 24).

Iraq—The country gains full independence from Great Britain and joins the League of Nations.

Japan—Premier Inukai Tsuyohi is assassinated by naval officers, ending party government. He is replaced by Viscount Makoto Saito.

Manchuria—Hsüan T'ung, former emperor of China (1908–12), is made puppet rule of Manchuria (Manchukuo) by Japan.

Portugal—Antonio de Oliviera Salazar is made premier; he will hold the position until 1968.

Soviet Union—The country concludes two nonaggression pacts: one with Estonia, Finland, and Latvia (July 25), one with France (November 29).

Spain—Catalonia gains autonomy and its own parliament.

Saudi Arabia—The country takes its name.

Turkey—The country joins the League of Nations.

U.S.—Promising "a new deal for the American people," Democratic candidate Franklin Delano Roosevelt defeats Republican President Herbert Hoover by a landslide and is elected president. The electoral college vote count is 472 to 59 (November 8).

Science and Technology

Germany—Physicist Werner Heisenberg develops a model of an atomic nucleus including neutrons and protons.

India—A jaw fragment from *Ramapithecus,* an ancient primate, is discovered by Edward Lewis.

U.K.—British physicist James Chadwick discovers the neutron.

U.K./Ireland—British physicist John Cockcroft and Irish physicist Ernest Walton produce helium by bombarding lithium with hydrogen nuclei, effecting the first nuclear reaction caused by bombarding an element with artificially accelerated particles.

U.S.—Hungarian-born physicist Leo Szilard develops the idea of a nuclear chain reaction.

Biochemist Charles King isolates vitamin C.

Physicist Carl D. Anderson discovers the anti-electron, which he calls a positron.

Inventor Edwin Land creates Polaroid film, the first synthetic light-polarizing film.

Society

Belgium—New regulations designate French the official language of the Wallon Provinces, Flemish the official language for Flanders.

Bulgaria—The country renounces its reparation payments.

China—An earthquake in Gansu results in 70,000 deaths.

Guatemala—The volcano Acatenago destroys three towns.

Scandinavia—The Oslo Convention, uniting Belgium, Holland, and Scandinavian states, promotes economic cooperation.

Soviet Union—Famine strikes throughout the region as the second Soviet Five-Year Plan is implemented. The plan stresses the growth of industry.

U.K.—At an economic conference attended by the U.K., Canada, Australia, New Zealand, South Africa, and Rhodesia, favorable regulations for British and dominion products are agreed upon.

U.S.—Unemployment reaches 13 million; business losses in 1932 range between five billion and six billion dollars.

The Reconstruction Finance Corporation is established, a government agency aimed at developing business and creating jobs.

The pro-labor Norris–La Guardia Anti-Injunction Act is passed.

The 20–month-old son of aviator Charles A. Lindbergh is kidnapped from the family home in New Jersey (March 12). After a highly publicized search and payment of a $50,000 ransom, the child is found dead (May 12). Suspect Bruno Richard Hauptmann is captured; he will be tried and convicted in 1936.

Aviatrix Amelia Earhart crosses the Atlantic Ocean in a solo flight, becoming the first woman to do so. Her flight begins in Newfoundland and ends in Ireland.

The Bonus Army of war veterans camps in Washington, D.C., requesting cash payment of their bonus certificates. Settlement for most is made but 2,000 who decline settlement and remain are forced from Washington, D.C., by troops led by General Douglas MacArthur (July 28).

Sports

U.S.—The Winter Olympics open in Lake Placid, N.Y. (February); the Summer Olympics open in Los Angeles (July).

British race car driver Sir Malcolm Campbell sets a land speed record of 253.958 mph (408.721 kph) in Daytona Beach, Florida.

1933 Arts and Entertainment

France—André Malraux publishes the novel *La Condition humaine*.

René Clair directs the film *Quatorze juillet*.

Germany—Kurt Weill's stage cantata *The Seven Deadly Sins*, with text by Bertolt Brecht, premieres.

Richard Strauss's opera *Arabella* premieres.

Spain—Federico García Lorca's play *Blood* premieres.

Switzerland—Alberto Giacometti creates the sculpture *The Palace at 4 am.*

U.K.—John Cowper Powys publishes the novel *A Glastonbury Romance.*

U.S.—Gertrude Stein publishes *The Autobiography of Alice B. Toklas.*

Poet Robinson Jeffers publishes *Give Your Heart to the Hawks, and Other Poems.*

Novels include Hervey Allen's *Anthony Adverse*; story collections include Sherwood Anderson's *Death in the Woods* and Ernest Hemingway's *Winner Take Nothing.*

Plays include Eugene O'Neill's *Ah, Wilderness!*

Films include George Cukor's *Little Women*, Lowell Sherman's *She Done Him Wrong*, and Merian C. Cooper's *King Kong.*

The U.S. ban on Irish writer James Joyce's novel *Ulysses* is lifted by a federal court judge.

Ideas

Germany—Psychologist and film critic Rudolf Arnheim publishes the essay "Film," which becomes the first of four essays constituting *Film as Art* (1957).

Philosopher Martin Heidegger presents the speech "The Role of the University in the New Reich," offering support of the Nazi Party.

U.K.—T. S. Eliot publishes *The Use of Poetry and the Use of Criticism.*

Economist Joan Violet Robinson publishes *The Economics of Imperfect Competition.*

U.S.—U.S. activist Dorothy Day and French philosopher Peter Maurin found the house of hospitality known as the Catholic Worker and the newspaper the *Catholic Worker.* The newspaper becomes a voice for Catholic social teachings.

Walter Piston publishes *Principles of Harmonic Analysis*, on modern music composition.

Politics

Austria—Engelbert Dollfuss dissolves the parliamentary government in response to growing Nazi power.

Germany—After Kurt von Schleicher is removed as prime minister, Adolf Hitler is appointed chancellor by Paul von Hindenberg (January 28).

A fire destroys the Reichstag building. It is tied to the Communist Party, resulting in the government's suspension of civil liberties and the free press.

The government orders the replacement of the German republic flag with the Nazi swastika flag and the imperial flag.

The Reichstag passes the Enabling Act, which grants Adolf Hitler increased powers.

Reichstag elections are held for Nazi candidates (November). Germans are able to express opposition only by casting invalid ballots.

The government's systematic persecution of European Jews known as the Holocaust begins. Early policies involve restrictions on movement and legal disenfranchisement.

At Dachau the first concentration camp is opened for political prisoners.

India—The All-India Congress votes to resume its campaign of civil disobedience. Mahatma Gandhi is sentenced to one year in prison but is released after a few days.

Japan—After the League of Nations condemns Japan's actions in Manchuria, Japan leaves the League of Nations.

Spain—Leader José Antonio Primo de Riviera founds the fascist political party, the Falange.

U.S.—Franklin Delano Roosevelt is inaugurated president (March 4). In his inaugural address, he tells the nation, "The only thing we have to fear is fear itself."

Following nationwide bank panics (March 1–4), banks are largely reopened (March 31).

Granted increased powers by Congress, President Roosevelt quickly establishes several federal programs and policies designed to generate jobs and regulate business. Among them are the Civilian Conservation Corps (CCC, March 31); the Agricultural Adjustment Act (AAA, May 12); Tennessee Valley Act, establishing the Tennessee Valley Authority (TVA, May 18), the National Industrial Recovery Act, establishing the National Recovery Administration (NRA) and the Public Works Administration (PWA, June 16); the Banking Act of 1933, establishing the Federal Bank Deposit Insurance Corporation (June 16); and the Civil Works Administration (November 8).

The 20th Amendment to the Constitution is passed, changing the inauguration date from March to January. It also eliminates the final session of Congress run after the election but before the congressional inauguration.

The 21st Amendment to the Constitution is passed, repealing Prohibition.

President Franklin Roosevelt makes his first radio "fireside chat," revealing his communication skills and the power of mass media (March 12).

Science and Technology

Germany—The Meissner effect, the condition that a magnetic field is excluded from the interior of a superconductor, is discovered by W. Meissner.

A synthetic rubber, styrene/butadiene, which will be used for tires, is developed at IG Farbenindustrie.

Italy—Physicist Enrico Fermi develops a theory of beta decay, discovering a particle he calls "neutrino".

North Africa—Rock paintings of prehistoric dwellers in the Sahara Desert are discovered

U.K.—A virus from flu victims that will be useful in developing vaccines is discovered by W. Smith, C. Andrewes, and P. Laidlaw.

U.S.—German physicist Albert Einstein immigrates to the U.S. and joins the Institute for Advanced Studies, Princeton University

The first U.S. aircraft carrier, the *USS Ranger,* is completed and christened for service in Virginia.

Society

Germany—The government proclaims a national boycott of German Jewish goods and services.

Jewish leaders Leo Baeck and Otto Hirsch found the National Agency of Jews in Germany, a social aid organization.

At a book burning in Berlin, thousands of students destroy 20,000 books deemed decadent by Nazi standards.

Spain—The government passes the Association Law, banning church schools and nationalizing church property.

U.K.—Britain makes its final payments of war debts to the U.S.

U.S.—President Roosevelt proclaims a four-day national closing of banks in response to ongoing bank panics.

Sports

Germany—The government bans German Jews from competing in the 1936 Olympics.

U.S.—The first baseball All-Star Game is held at Comiskey Field, Chicago, Illinois. The American League defeats the National League, four games to two.

In the World Series, the New York Giants (NL) defeat the Washington Senators (AL), 4 games to 1.

For the first National Football League championship, the Chicago Bears defeat the New York Giants, 23–21.

The PGA golf tournament is won by Gene Sarazen.

1934 Arts and Entertainment

Austria—Anton Webern's Concerto for Nine Instruments premieres.

Soviet Union—The aims of Soviet artistry to serve the proletariat are defined in the doctrine of "socialist realism," by government spokesman A. A. Zhdanov at the Congress of Soviet Writers.

Poet Osip Mandelstam is jailed for an antistate poem.

U.S.—Sergey Rachmaninoff's *Rhapsody on a Theme of Paganini* premieres.

Literary critic Malcolm Cowley publishes *Exile's Return*, a memoir of "lost generation" writers of the 1920s.

Humorist Alexander Woolcott publishes *While Rome Sleeps*.

World—Films include René Clair's *The Last Millionaire* (France) and Frank Capra's *It Happened One Night* (U.S.).

Paintings include René Magritte's *The Rape* (France), John Piper's *Rye Harbour* (U.K.), and Charles Sheeler's *American Interior* (U.S.).

Novels include Mikhail Sholokhov's *And Quiet Flows the Don* (Soviet Union); Robert Graves's *I, Claudius* (U.K.); Dashiell Hammett's *The Thin Man* (U.S.); F. Scott Fitzgerald's

Tender Is the Night (U.S.); James Hilton's *Goodbye, Mr. Chips* (U.S.); Henry Miller's *Tropic of Cancer* (U.S.), which is banned in the U.K. and U.S.; and John O'Hara's *Appointment in Samarra* (U.S.).

Short stories include William Saroyan's "The Daring Young Man on the Flying Trapeze" (U.S.).

Plays include Federico García Lorca's *Yerma* (Spain); musicals include Cole Porter's *Anything Goes* (U.S.).

Ideas

Austria—Martin Buber publishes *Tales of Angels, Ghosts, and Demons.*

Germany—Lazar Goldschmidt completes final volume of his translation of the Babylonian Talmud into German. Translation began in 1893.

U.K.—Historian Arnold Toynbee publishes first volume of 10-volume *History of the World.*

U.S.—Philosopher and educator John Dewey publishes *Art as Experience.*

Lithuanian-born American rabbi and founder of Reconstructionist Judaism Mordecai Menahem Kaplan publishes *Judaism as a Civilization.*

Psychiatrist Harry Stack Sullivan begins to develop his theory of interpersonal relations, which posits the importance of interpersonal interactions in the development of personality.

Anthropologist Ruth Benedict publishes *Patterns of Culture*, which influences the development of the field of cultural psychology.

German-born American philosopher Rudolf Carnap publishes *The Logical Syntax of Language.*

German-born American physicist Albert Einstein publishes *My Philosophy.*

Military

Austria—A leftist action against Chancellor Dollfuss and his government is stopped.

Bolivia/Paraguay—The Chaco War between the two countries begins again following the expiration of the League of Nations armistice.

Portugal—A leftist revolutionary action of Communists and the General Confederation of Labor is quashed.

Spain—Following a general strike by separatists and socialists, the government declares martial law and sets out to quash any revolt (October 6). Uprisings for independence in Catalonia and for Communist rule in Asturias are also crushed, with many deaths.

Politics

Austria—Nazi terrorists assassinate Chancellor Engelbert Dollfuss; he is replaced with Kurt von Schuschnigg.

China—Over the year, Mao Zedong leads followers in the 6,000–mile "Long March" across China, from the Jiangxi Province to the Shaanxi Province, where he establishes Communist headquarters.

India—The National Congress reaffirms complete independence as its aim at its annual meeting.

Latvia/Lithuania/Estonia—The three countries sign the Baltic Pact, confirming their aim of independence.

Libya—Cyrenaica, Fezia, and Tripolitania join to form the new country of Libya (January).

France—Premier Chautemps resigns following intimations of involvement in the Stavisky affair; Edouard Daladier becomes premier. Riots follow his establishment of a new government; Daladier resigns and is succeeded by Gaston Doumergue.

Germany—Adolf Hitler and the SS stage the Night of Long Knives (June 30). It results in the massacre of the leaders of the Storm Troopers' Association (Brownshirts), who are accused of attempting Hitler's overthrow. Also killed are 77 other members.

President von Hindenburg dies (August 2). Hitler succeeds him, combining the posts of chancellor and president and assuming the title Führer.

Soviet Union—The country signs treaties with Czechoslovakia and Romania in an attempt to counter growing Nazi influence.

Spain—In Catalonia elections, moderate-to-left candidates gain a majority.

U.S.—Congressional elections result in an increase in the Democratic Party majority, with the Senate gaining a 69–25 majority and the House gaining a 310–117 majority.

The National Housing Act provides for the establishment of the Federal Housing Administration; the Securities Exchange Act provides for the establishment of the Securities and Exchange Commission.

The Philippines is granted independence through passage of the Tydings-McDuffie Act. Independence will become effective on July 4, 1946.

Science and Technology

Austria—The presence of antiparticles in some subatomic particles is demonstrated by physicists Wolfgang Pauli and Victor F. Weisskopf.

France—Physicists Frédéric Joliot-Curie and Irène Joliot-Curie discover artificial radioactivity.

Germany—Radar is demonstrated by R. Kuenhold.

The female sex hormone progesterone is isolated by A. Butenandt.

Italy—Physicist Enrico Fermi examines the effects of bombarding uranium atoms with neutrons.

Soviet Union—Mathematician Aleksandr O. Gelfond publishes Gelfond's theorem.

Physicist Pavel Cherenkov discovers the phenomenon that will be known as Cherenkov radiation, the emission of light caused by particles moving faster than light in a medium other than a vacuum.

U.K.—British physicist James Chadwick and Austrian-American physicist Maurice Goldhaber determine the mass of the neutron.

Society

Canada—The Dionne Quintuplets are born, the first case of viable quintuplets.

France—A general strike protests the "Fascist peril" to the country.

India—Mahatma Gandhi leaves his position in the National Congress to improve the condition of the untouchables caste.

U.S.—The gold standard is abandoned (January).

Unemployment in the U.S. is 10.8 million.

A severe dust storm strikes several states, including Arkansas, Colorado, Kansas, Oklahoma, and Texas, leading thousands of families to migrate to western states, particularly California. Displaced citizens will be named by the epithet "Okie."

The nation's most wanted criminal, John Dillinger, is shot and killed by FBI agents in Chicago, Illinois; sweetheart criminals Bonnie Parker and Clyde Barrow are killed by Texas Rangers.

Sports

Germany—The world heavyweight boxing championship is won by Max Baer.

U.K.—Breaking a long U.S. streak, British golfer Henry Cotton wins the British Open.

U.S.—In the World Series, the St. Louis Cardinals (NL) defeat the Detroit Tigers (AL) in seven games.

For the NFL championship, the New York Giants defeat the Chicago Bears 30–13.

The yacht *Rainbow* defends the America's Cup against Britain's *Endeavour*.

1935 Arts and Entertainment

Peru—José María Arguedas publishes the story collection *Water*.

Soviet Union—Banned poet Anna Akhmatova writes the poem *Requiem* (1935–40); it will not be published in the Soviet Union until 1987.

U.K.—Paperback book publishing is introduced by Allen Lane, who founds Penguin Books.

U.S.—George Gershwin's folk-inspired opera *Porgy and Bess* premieres, featuring the songs "Summertime," "I Got Plenty of Nuttin'," and others.

Opening at the Palomar Ballroom in California, clarinetist Benny Goodman and his band popularize "swing" music, with Goodman hailed "King of Swing."

World—Notable plays include T. S. Eliot's *Murder in the Cathedral* (U.K.), Maxwell Anderson's *Winterset* (U.S.), and Clifford Odets's *Waiting for Lefty* (U.S.).

Notable films include Jean Renoir's *Toni* (France), Leni Riefenstahl's *The Triumph of the Will* (Germany), Alfred Hitchcock's *The 39 Steps* (U.K.), John Ford's *The Informer* (U.S.), Frank Lloyd's *Mutiny on the Bounty* (U.S.), Mark Sandrich's *Top Hat* (U.S.), and James Whale's *The Bride of Frankenstein* (U.S.).

Notable novels include Osami Dazai's *Gyakko* (Japan), Alberto Moravia's *Wheel of Fortune* (Italy), Ivy Compton-Burnett's *A House and its Head* (U.K.), Christopher Isherwood's *Mr. Norris Changes Trains* (U.K.), John Steinbeck's *Tortilla Flat* (U.S.), Sinclair Lewis's *It Can't Happen Here* (U.S.), Laura Ingalls Wilder's *Little House on the Prairie* (U.S.), and Thomas

Wolfe's *Of Time and the River* (U.S.).

Notable paintings include Max Ernst's *Lunar Asparagus* (France), and Salvador Dali's *Giraffe on Fire* (Spain).

Ideas

Austria—Konrad Lorenz describes the phenomenon of imprinting on animals.

U.S.—Economist John Maynard Keynes publishes *The General Theory of Employment, Interest and Money*.

Military

Italy—Repudiating League of Nations protests, Italy invades and captures Ethiopia (October 1935–May 1936).

U.S.—The American Neutrality Act restricts aid to Spain.

Politics

Brazil—Communist revolts break out in cities including Rio de Janiero, resulting in martial law.

Canada—Mackenzie King leads a Liberal Party government.

Bolivia—The Chaco War between Bolivia and Paraguay ends.

China—The Yenin Period of Chinese Communism begins.

Czechoslovakia—Foreign minister Eduard Benes succeeds Tomas Masaryk as president.

Ecuador—President Velasco Ibarra is overthrown by a military junta.

Egypt—The constitution is restored and elections planned.

France—Leftist groups form the Popular Front, meant to counter national Fascist and monarchist movements.

Germany—The Nuremberg Laws are passed, sanctioning anti-Jewish activities and making the swastika the national flag.

Japan—China is forced by Japan to follow the restrictive Ho-Umezu Agreement.

Persia—Persia changes its name to Iran.

Poland—Poland adopts a new constitution.

Soviet Union—The United Front against Fascism is ordered by the government and encouraged by Bulgarian Comintern leader Georgi Dimitrov.

Spain—The Revolutionary Marxist party POUM is founded.

U.K.—Clement Attlee becomes leader of Labor Party.

U.S.—Louisiana governor and national demagogue Huey Long is assassinated in Baton Rouge, Louisiana, by Dr. Carl Weiss Jr.

Science and Technology

Canada—The U-235 isotope of uranium is discovered by A. J. Dempster.

Denmark—Vitamin K is discovered by Henrik Dam.

Hong Kong—Fossil teeth of *Gigantopithecus*, the largest primate known, are discovered by R. von Koenigswald.

Scotland—Physicist Robert Alexander Watson-Watt refines radar to make it practical for detecting aircraft.

Switzerland—Swiss-Croatian chemist Leopold Ruzicka discovers structure of testosterone.

Chemist Paul Karrer synthesizes riboflavin (vitamin B_2).

U.S.—Biochemist Edward Calvin Kendall isolates the hormone cortisone.

The B-17, a four-engine, all-metal bomber, is introduced by Boeing.

Fluorescent lighting is demonstrated by General Electric.

The Richter scale, for rating earthquake magnitude, is developed by seismologist Charles F. Richter.

Society

U.S.—The Social Security Act is established, creating a national retirement benefits program.

The Works Progress Administration is founded, with programs including the Federal Arts Project and Federal Writers' Project, which commissions substantial writing and artwork. It is headed by Harry Hopkins.

The Rural Electrification Administration is created to bring electricity production to areas without power.

The Committee for Industrial Organization (CIO) is founded, led by John L. Lewis.

Alcoholics Anonymous (AA) is founded by Bill Wilson and Bob Smith.

Through the National Labor Relations Act (Wagner Act), the National Labor Relations Board (NLRB) is established to streamline labor-management activities and protect workers involved in labor organization.

Sports

U.K.—American Helen Wills Moody wins the women's singles championship for the seventh time.

U.S.—The first night major league baseball game is held, at Cincinnati's Crosley Field (Ohio) between the Philadelphia Phillies (NL) and Cincinnati Reds (NL). Final score is Reds 2, Phillies 1.

The World Series is won by the Detroit Tigers (AL), who defeat the Chicago Cubs (NL), four games to two.

Omaha becomes the third horse to win the Triple Crown.

James J. Braddock defeats Max Baer for the world heavyweight boxing championship.

Jesse Owens breaks five track-and-field records in one day of competition at Ohio State University.

1936 Arts and Entertainment

Netherlands—Piet Mondrian completes the painting *Composition in Red and Blue*.

Romania—Sculptor Constantin Brancusi completes the sculpture series *The Seal*.

Soviet Union—Sergey Prokofiev completes the symphonic story *Peter and the Wolf*.

Konstantin Stanislavsky publishes *An Actor Prepares*.

Turkey—Nazim Hikmet publishes the poem *The Epic of Sheikh Bedreddin*.

U.K.—T. S. Eliot begins publication of the four-part poem *Four Quartets*.

U.S.—Photographers Robert Capa and Dorothea Lange gain notice for works capturing the Spanish Civil War and the Great Depression, respectively.

The exhibition *Cubism and Abstract Art* is held at the Museum of Modern Art, New York.

Life magazine, founded by Henry Luce, begins publication November 23. It remains in publication as a weekly until 1972.

Lithuanian-born U.S. art historian Meyer Schapiro publishes the paper "The Social Bases of Art."

Samuel Barber composes *Adagio for Strings*.

Poetry includes Robert Frost's *A Further Range* and Carl Sandburg's *The People, Yes*.

Plays include Moss Hart and George S. Kaufman's *You Can't Take It with You*.

World—Books include André Malraux's *Man's Hope* (France), Margaret Mitchell's *Gone with the Wind* (U.S.), John Dos Passos's *The Big Money* (U.S.), and William Faulkner's *Absalom, Absalom!* (U.S.).

Films include Fritz Lang's *Fury* (Germany), Frank Capra's *Mr. Deeds Goes to Town* (U.S.), Charlie Chaplin's *Modern Times*, George Cukor's *Camille* (U.S.) Robert Z. Leonard's *The Great Ziegfeld* (U.S.). and William Wyler's *Dodsworth*.

Ideas

Austria—Psychoanalyst Anna Freud develops the theory of ego-defense mechanisms.

Switzerland—Theologian Karl Barth begins publication (through 1962) of *Church Dogmatics*.

U.K.—Philosopher Alfred Ayer publishes *Language, Truth, and Logic*.

U.S.—Motivational writer Dale Carnegie publishes *How to Win Friends and Influence People*.

Van Wyck Brooks publishes *Flowering of New England*, history of American literature.

Philosopher Arthur O. Lovejoy publishes *The Great Chain of Being*, on the natural hierarchy of actual things.

Military

Germany—Germany occupies the Rhineland.

Italy—Italy invades Addis Ababa and annexes Ethiopia.

Spain—The Spanish Civil War begins, with nationalist forces fighting republican Loyalists.

The war lasts until 1939 and involves world powers, with Fascist and Nazi powers supporting nationalists and Western, Communist, and Socialist forces supporting Loyalist troops.

Nationalist forces led by Francisco Franco invade Morocco and parts of Spain.

Nationalist forces enter Madrid and begin a three-year siege. The government flees to Valencia.

Palestine—The Arab Revolt begins following a Palestinian general strike. The war will last until 1939.

Politics

Belgium—Martial law is declared (October 22), following Belgium's secession from military alliance with France.

China—Chiang Kai-shek is kidnapped and held by Manchurian leader Chang Hsüeh-liang.

Germany—Germany invalidates the Versailles and Locarno Treaties.

Germany/Italy—The Berlin-Rome Axis is formed.

Greece—General Ioannis Metaxas becomes dictator and suspends civil liberties.

Japan—Several government officials are assassinated in Tokyo following an attempted military coup.

Nicaragua—In a military coup, General Anastasio Somoza replaces President Sacasa. Somoza becomes president and dictator.

Panama—A U.S.–Panama treaty ends Panama's place as a U.S. protectorate.

Peru—President Oscar Benavides becomes dictator, removing the constituent assembly.

U.K.—Edward VII is forced to abdicate as king (December 10) following his announcement of plans to marry U.S. citizen Wallis Simpson.

Soviet Union—The phase of Stalinist terror known as the Yezhovshchina or Great Purge begins and will continue until 1938.

U.S.—President Franklin Roosevelt is reelected president, defeating Republican candidate Alfred M. Landon in a landslide. Roosevelt carries 46 of 48 states; the electoral vote is 523 to 8.

Science and Technology

U.K.—The first electronic television system is established by the British Broadcasting Company.

Geologist Arthur Homes uses the uranium-lead absolute dating method on Precambrian minerals.

U.S.—French-American physician Alexis Carrel collaborates with U.S. aviator Charles Lindbergh to develop the first artificial heart.

Hungarian-born Eugene P. Wigner introduces the concept of the nuclear cross section in developing mathematics of neutron absorption by atomic nuclei.

Vitamin Plus, the first vitamin, to be marketed to consumers, debuts.

The 726–foot-high Boulder Dam is completed. Later (1947) known as the Hoover Dam, it provides low-cost electric power in the U.S. southwest.

The tampon is produced for commercial use by Tampax, Inc.

Society

France—The government's social reform program leads to rising costs and inflation; the franc is devalued.

Mexico—Peasants receive expropriated lands under a new government program.

U.S.—Unemployed in the U.S. number eight million.

The Federal Arts Project of the Works Progress Administration employs 5,000 artists, who create public murals and other artworks in 44 states.

The United Auto Workers, led by Walter Reuther, hold the first U.S. sit-down strike.

President Roosevelt signs the Soil Conservation and Domestic Allotment Act, a farmer support program that replaces the Agricultural Adjustment Act, which has been invalidated by the U.S. Supreme Court.

Sports

Germany—The Winter Olympic Games are held in Garmisch-Partenkirchen (February 5–16); the Summer Olympic Games are held in Berlin (August 5–16).

At the Summer Olympics, African-American Jesse Owens wins four gold medals. Adolf Hitler departs the stadium, refusing to acknowledge Owens's victory.

U.S.—In the World Series, the New York Yankees (AL) defeat the New York Giants (NL), four games to two.

For the NFL championship, the Green Bay Packers defeat the Boston Redskins, 21–6.

Tyrus Raymond (Ty) Cobb becomes the first player elected to the Baseball Hall of Fame.

Charles Goren publishes *Winning Bridge Made Easy*.

The U.S. Open golf tournament is won by Tony Manero, with a record-setting score of 282 for 72 holes.

1937 Arts and Entertainment

France—Pablo Picasso paints *Guernica*, which becomes a symbol of anti-Fascist action.

Germany—Carl Orff's *Carmina Burana*, a collection of settings of medieval poems, is first performed.

U.S.—The *Partisan Review* is reimagined from a Communist to a leftist journal and becomes an influential voice of leftist intellectual thinking.

Architect Frank Lloyd Wright completes Fallingwater, a residence in Bear Run, Pennsylvania.

World—Novels include J. R. R. Tolkien's *The Hobbit* (U.K.), John P. Marquand's *The Late George Apley* (U.S.), John Steinbeck's *Of Mice and Men* (U.S.), and Zora Neale Hurston's

Their Eyes Were Watching God (U.S.). Nonfiction works include *You Have Seen Their Faces*, with photos by Margaret Bourke-White and text by Erskine Caldwell (U.S.).

Films include Jean Renoir's *Grand Illusion* (France), Walt Disney's *Snow White and the Seven Dwarfs* (U.S.), and William Wyler's *Dead End*.

Ideas

France—Philosopher Gaston Bachelard publishes *The Psychoanalysis of Fire.*

Nigeria—Journalist and future Nigerian president Nnamadi Azikiwe founds a chain of nationalist newspapers.

Sweden—Political scientist Herbert Tingsten publishes *Political Behavior: Studies in Election Statistics.*

U.S.—Sociologist Talcott Parsons publishes *The Structure of Social Action.*

German-born U.S. psychoanalyst Karen Horney publishes *The Neurotic Personality of Our Time.*

Military

China—Following a battle near the Marco Polo Bridge in China between Japanese and Chinese forces, the Sino-Japanese War begins. It will continue until 1945. Over the year Japan takes Shanghai, Beijing, and Nanking, committing atrocities there that become known as the Rape of Nanking.

U.S.—Japanese forces sink the U.S. gunboat *Panay* in Chinese waters. Two Americans are killed.

Politics

Spain—In the Spanish Civil War, forces led by Francisco Franco push into northern Spain. Pro-Franco German air forces bomb Guernica (April 25).

U.K.—The Peel Commission recommends the partition of Palestine into Arab and Jewish areas.

Prime Minister Neville Chamberlain introduces the country's policy of appeasement toward Germany, which will eventually result in failure.

U.S.—President Franklin Roosevelt is inaugurated for a third term. Following passage of the 20th Amendment to the Constitution, the inauguration is held on January 20.

Science and Technology

Canada—Physicist James Hillier invents the first electron microscope.

Germany—Polyurethane is developed.

Italy—Physicists Emilio Segré and Carlo Perrier discover the element technetium.

Electroshock therapy is introduced by physicians Ugo Cerletti and Lucio Bini for treatment of symptoms of schizophrenia.

U.K.—Mathematician Alan Mathison Turing outlines the "Turing machine," which influences the development of digital computers.

Plant pathologist Frederick Charles Bawden discovers that the tobacco mosaic virus contains RNA (ribonucleic acid) in addition to protein.

German-born Hans Krebs discovers the citric acid cycle, later known as the Krebs cycle.

U.S.—Physician D. W. Gordon Murray develops heparin, an anti-clotting organic acid, for medical practice.

Physicists H. A. Jahn and Hungarian-born American Edward Teller develop what will be known as the Jahn-Teller effect, about the properties of nonlinear molecules.

Physicists Carl D. Anderson and Austrian-American Victor F. Hess discover the particle that will become known as a muon.

Society

France—Railroads are nationalized.

Germany—The first magnetic tape recorder is marketed by AEG/Telefunken.

Switzerland—Romansch is recognized as one of the country's national languages.

U.S.—The dirigible *Hindenburg* explodes into flames while landing at Lakehurst, New Jersey. The dramatic explosion largely ended the use of dirigibles as a mode of transportation.

Congress stymies the Supreme Court Bill, an attempt by President Roosevelt to alter the judicial branch of government, specifically the makeup of the Supreme Court, which he attempted to enlarge (or "pack") with supporters.

The National Housing Act or Wagner-Steagall Act is signed, providing loans to stimulate construction in small communities.

A stock market decline signals a nationwide recession.

The first coast-to-coast radio broadcast is conveyed, of Herbert Morrison announcing the explosion of the airship *Hindenburg*.

New York Supreme Court justice Joseph Force Carter disappears and will remain missing.

World—The first worldwide radio broadcast is conveyed, of the coronation of King George VI of England.

Sports

U.S.—In the World Series the New York Yankees (AL) defeat the New York Giants (NL) four games to one.

For the NFL championship the Washington Redskins defeat the Chicago Bears, 28–21.

The U.S. defeats Great Britain to win the Davis Cup.

War Admiral becomes the fourth horse to win the Triple Crown.

Joe Louis defeats James J. Braddock to win the world heavyweight boxing championship.

1938 Arts and Entertainment

Chile—María Luisa Bombal publishes the novella *The Shrouded Woman*.

France—Pablo Picasso paints *Woman in Easy Chair*; Raoul Dufy paints *Regatta*; Georges Rouault paints *Ecce Homo*.

Hungary—Béla Bartók completes Violin Concerto.

Puerto Rico—Julia de Burgos publishes her first volume of poetry, *Poem in Twenty Furrows*.

U.K.—George Orwell publishes *Homage to Catalonia*, about the Spanish Civil War.

Cyril Connolly publishes the nonfiction work *Enemies of Promise*.

U.S.—Aaron Copland's Wild West ballet *Billy the Kid* premieres.

Director Orson Welles produces a radio broadcast of H. G. Wells's *War of the Worlds* with such believability that listeners fear Martian invasion.

Bandleader Benny Goodman presents the first jazz concert at Carnegie Hall, New York.

Singer Frank Sinatra makes his first appearance on a national radio program.

Poetry collections include Robinson Jeffers's *The Selected Poetry of Robinson Jeffers* and Archibald MacLeish's *Land of the Free*.

World—Films include Leni Riefenstahl's *Olympische Spiele* (Germany), Sergey Eisenstein's *Alexander Nevsky* (Soviet Union), George Cukor's *Holiday* (U.S.), and Howard Hawks's *Bringing up Baby* (U.S.).

Plays include Ernest Hemingway's *The Fifth Column* (U.S.), Thornton Wilder's *Our Town* (U.S.), and Robert Sherwood's *Abe Lincoln in Illinois*.

Novels include Samuel Beckett's *Murphy* (France), Jean-Paul Sartre's *La Nausée* (France), Shiga Naoya's *A Dark Night Passing* (Japan), Graham Greene's *Brighton Rock* (U.K.), Evelyn Waugh's *Scoop* (U.K.), James Branch Cabell's *The King Was in His Counting House* (U.S.), William Faulkner's *The Unvanquished* (U.S.), and Elizabeth Madox Roberts's *Black Is My Truelove's Hair*. Story collections include Richard Wright's *Uncle Tom's Children* (U.S.).

Ideas

Japan—The Nichiren Buddhist movement Risshokoseikai is founded by religious leaders Niwano Nikkyo and Naganuma Myoko.

U.S.—Psychologist B. F. Skinner publishes the results of his study with the Skinner Box, on behaviorism.

Educator John Dewey publishes *Logic: The Theory of Inquiry*.

Military

Austria—The Anschluss is realized, as German forces invade Austria (March 12). There is little opposition, and Austria is declared a province of Germany (March 13). Attacks on Austrian Jews begin.

China—Japanese forces capture Qingdao (January 10) and install a puppet government (March). The Japanese press forward, capturing Guangzhou (October 12) and Wuhan (October 25). Western nations and the League of Nations issue protests.

Germany—Germany occupies Sudetenland (October 1–10).

Soviet Union—Soviet and Japanese forces fight at the border of Siberia and Manchuria.

Spain—Francisco Franco leads forces to capture Teruel and Vinaroz (February–April)

Francisco Franco leads an offensive against Catalonia.

Politics

Austria—Following an ultimatum from Adolf Hitler, Premier Von Schuschnigg resigns and is replaced by Arthur Seyss-Inquart, a Nazi.

Bulgaria/Greece—The two countries sign a nonaggression pact.

Czechoslovakia—Slovakia gains full autonomy (October 6); Ruthenia gains autonomy as Carpatho-Ukraine (October 8).

Following the signing of the Munich Pact, leader Edvard Benes resigns and flees to the U.S.

France—Following the resignation of Popular Front leader Léon Blum, Edouard Daladier becomes leader. The Popular Front is dissolved (October) after the Munich Agreement.

France/Germany—The two countries sign a friendship pact.

Germany—Adolf Hitler proclaims the right of self-determination for Sudeten Czechs.

At the Munich Conference the Munich Pact is signed, granting Germany the Sudetenland portions of Czechoslovakia and fulfilling the British and French policy of appeasement. The conference is attended by Adolf Hitler (Germany), Neville Chamberlain (U.K.), Benito Mussolini (Italy), and Edouard Daladier (France); Czechoslovakia is not represented. Following the pact's signing, British prime minister Neville Chamberlain proclaims "peace in our time" (September 29).

The pogrom against Jews known as Kristallnacht occurs. The assassination of a French embassy official by a Jewish refugee leads German forces to kill 100 Jews and deport 20,000 to concentration camps.

Italy—Benito Mussolini begins a persecution campaign against Italian Jews.

Libya—Libya is claimed as part of Italy.

Palestine—The Woodhead Commission, established in Britain, determines that partitioning into Arab and Jewish territories is unfeasible (November 9). Throughout the year, Arab-Jewish terrorist attacks continue.

Poland/Soviet Union—The two countries renew a nonaggression pact.

Soviet Union—Political purges continue, including the trial and killing of Nikolai Bukharin (March).

Turkey—Turkish Republic president Kemal Ataturk dies; elected to succeed him is Ismet Inonu.

U.K.—Foreign secretary Anthony Eden resigns in protest of Prime Minister Chamberlain's policy on Italy. He is replaced by Lord Halifax.

U.S.—President Roosevelt signs the second Agricultural Adjustment Act (February 16).

President Roosevelt signs the Wage and Hours Act, raising the minimum wage for interstate commerce workers from 25 to 40 cents per hour (June 25).

The stock market recession continues into the spring, leading Congress to pass the Revenue Bill of 1938, which reduces taxes on corporations.

In congressional elections Democrats lose 7 Senate seats but retain a 69–23 majority. In

House elections, Democrats lose 70 seats but retain a 261–164 majority.

Science and Technology

Germany—The uranium atom is split for the first time by physicist Otto Hahn.

The Volkswagen beetle car is introduced by Ferdinand Porsche.

Vitamin B$_6$ is isolated by R. Kuhn.

Hungary—The ballpoint pen is developed and patented by Lazslo Biró.

South Africa—The *coelacanth*, an ancient fish believed to have been extinct for 70 million years, is discovered near South Africa.

Switzerland—Vitamin E is synthesized by Paul Karrer.

U.K.—Engineer G. S. Callendar develops the theory of the warming of the earth's atmosphere due to an increase of carbon dioxide through human actions. The process will be known as the greenhouse effect.

The stainless steel artificial hip is developed by Philip Wiles.

U.S.—A machine able to learn through feedback is developed by engineer T. Ross.

A vaccine for typhus is developed by Harold Cox.

Du Pont begins manufacturing nylon for consumer use. Toothbrushes with nylon bristles are introduced to the consumer market.

Chester Floyd Carlson discovers the dry copying process, xerography.

Society

China—To fight the Japanese invasion, the Chinese divert the Yellow River, with resulting floods killing hundreds of thousands of people.

France—Following a series of government edicts aimed at stimulating the economy, several strikes occur, including a one-day general strike.

The number of Americans receiving federal relief aid is reduced in number by nearly one-third since 1937, from 3,184,000 to 2,122,960.

Departing from New York, aviator Douglas "Wrong Way" Corrigan aims for California but lands in Dublin, Ireland. His antics gain him fame.

Sports

Italy—Italy defeats Hungary to win the World Cup football title.

U.S.—In the World Series the New York Yankees (AL) defeat the Chicago Cubs (NL) in four games. It is the Yankees' third straight World Series championship.

New York Yankee Lou Gehrig sets a record up to that time for consecutive games played (2,122).

For the NFL championship the New York Giants defeat the Green Bay Packers, 23–17.

At the Wimbledon tennis championships, J. Donald Budge wins the men's singles title; Helen Wills Moody wins the women's singles title.

1939 Arts and Entertainment

Europe/U.S.—The fast-stepping jitterbug dominates as a popular dance.

Ireland—James Joyce's *Finnegans Wake* is published in complete form.

Spain—Pablo Picasso paints *Night Fishing at Antibes.*

Musician Pablo Casals leaves Spain in protest of the policies of dictator Francisco Franco.

Painter Joan Miró begins the *Constellation* series, which will be completed in 1941

U.S.—Carl Sandburg publishes the four-volume biography *Abraham Lincoln: The War Years.*

Henry Moore completes the sculpture *Reclining Figure.*

Composer Irving Berlin's "God Bless America" (sung by Kate Smith) becomes popular.

World—Novels include Patrick White's *Happy Valley* (Australia), Richard Llewellyn's *How Green Was My Valley* (U.K.), William Faulkner's *The Wild Palms* (U.S.), C. S. Forester's *Captain Horatio Hornblower* (U.S.), and John Steinbeck's *The Grapes of Wrath* (U.S.). Story collections include Christopher Isherwood's *Goodbye to Berlin* (U.K.) and Katherine Anne Porter's *Pale Horse, Pale Rider* (U.S.).

Plays produced include Jean Giraudoux's *Ondine* (France), Russel Crouse and Howard Lindsay's *Life with Father* (U.S.), Lillian Hellman's *The Little Foxes* (U.S.), George S. Kaufman and Moss Hart's *The Man Who Came to Dinner* (U.S.), Cole Porter's musical *Du Barry Was a Lady* (U.S.), and Rodgers and Hart's musical *Pal Joey* (U.S.).

Poetic works include William Butler Yeats's *Last Poems and Two Plays* (Ireland), Robert Frost's *Collected Poems* (U.S.), and Mark Van Doren's *Collected Poems* (U.S.).

Films include Jean Renoir's *Rules of the Game* (France), Marcel Carné's *Daybreak* (France), Carol Reed's *The Stars Look Down* (U.K.), Zoltán Korda's *The Four Feathers* (U.K.), Frank Capra's *Mr. Smith Goes to Washington* (U.S.), Victor Fleming's *Gone with the Wind* (U.S.) and *The Wizard of Oz* (U.S.), John Ford's *Stagecoach* (U.S.) and *Young Mr. Lincoln* (U.S.), and Ernst Lubitsch's *Ninotchka* (U.S.). The year will be remembered as marking the peak of the Hollywood studio system.

Ideas

Germany—*Mein Kampf* is published in English translation.

Army officer Karl Ernst Haushofer publishes *German Cultural Policy in the Indo-Pacific Area.*

U.K.—Astronomer Arthur Eddington publishes *The Philosophy of Physical Science.*

Physiologist Charles Sherrington publishes *Man and His Nature.*

U.S.—Educator/philosopher John Dewey publishes *Freedom and Culture.*

Military

Germany—Germany invades Poland (September 1) and annexes Danzig, marking the start of World War II (1939–45).

Germany occupies Bohemia and Moravia and places Slovakia under protection.

Italy—Italy invades Albania.

Soviet Union—The Soviet Union invades Poland from the east.

U.K.—The HMS Royal Oak is sunk.

The British Expeditionary Force of nearly 160,000 soldiers is sent to France.

U.S.—President Roosevelt requests of Congress $552 million for defense costs.

Politics

France/U.K.—France and U.K. declare war on Germany (September 3).

France and U.K. recognize the Spanish dictatorship of Francisco Franco.

Germany—Germany dissolves its nonaggression pact with Poland and ends its nonaggression pact with the Soviet Union.

Germany ends its decade-long alliance with Italy.

Peru—Military government gives way to civilian rule under Presidents Manuel Prado (1939–45) and José Luis Bustamente (1945–48). Military rule will return in 1948.

U.K.—King George VI and Queen Elizabeth visit the U.S., becoming the first British king and queen to do so.

U.K./Poland—The two countries sign a mutual cooperation treaty.

U.S.—Congress passes the Neutrality Act of 1939, repealing the prohibitions on arms sales to belligerents outlined in the Neutrality Act of 1937.

Science and Technology

Germany—Barium isotopes are obtained through neutron bombardment of uranium by Hahn and Strassman.

U.S.—The first helicopter is built by Russian-American scientist Igor Sikorsky.

Transatlantic air service is begun, on the flight of the *Dixie Clipper* from New York to Portugal.

The radio transmission and reception method known as frequency modulation (FM) is developed by Edwin H. Armstrong.

Society

U.K.—Conscription begins; women and children start being evacuated from London.

U.S.—World Fairs are held in New York, New York, and San Francisco, California

The U.S. Supreme Court rules that sit-down strikes are illegal.

The Methodist Church is reunited after more than a century of separation involving branches of the church.

Sports

Australia—The Davis Cup is won by Australia.

U.K.—At the Wimbledon tennis championships, Robert Riggs (U.S.) wins the men's singles championship; Alice Marble (U.S.) wins the women's singles.

U.S.—In the World Series the New York Yankees (AL) defeat the Cincinnati Reds (NL), in a four-game sweep.

The U.S. Open golf tournament is won by Byron Nelson.

In the NFL championship, the Green Bay Packers defeat the New York Giants, 27–0.

New York Yankee Lou Gehrig sits out a game for the first time in 14 years after having played in 2,130 straight games. This record would stand until 1995, when it was broken by Cal Ripken, Jr.

1940 Arts and Entertainment

China—Ba Jin completes the trilogy of autobiographical novels known as the *Torrent Trilogy*, consisting of *The Family, Spring,* and *Autumn.*

Romania—Constantin Brancusi completes *Bird in Flight*, an abstract sculpture.

Soviet Union—Sergey Prokofiev's *Romeo and Juliet* premieres.

U.K.—Potter Bernard Howell Leach publishes the influential *A Potter's Book.*

U.S.—The *Billboard* chart of popular hit songs begins; the first number-one song is "I'll Never Smile Again," sung by Frank Sinatra and the Tommy Dorsey Band.

World—Films include Veidt Harlan's anti-Semitic *Jew Suess* (Germany), Humphrey Jennings and Harry Watt's *London Can Take It* (U.K.), and Charlie Chaplin's *The Great Dictator*, George Cukor's *The Philadelphia Story*, Walt Disney's *Fantasia*, and John Ford's *The Grapes of Wrath* (all U.S.).

Novels include Arthur Koestler's *Darkness at Noon* (U.K.), C. P. Snow's *Strangers and Brothers* (U.K.), Ernest Hemingway's *For Whom the Bell Tolls* (U.S.), and Richard Wright's *Native Son* (U.S.).

Ideas

U.K.—Anthropologist Edward Evans-Pritchard publishes *The Nuer.*

Mathematician and philosopher Bertrand Russell publishes *An Inquiry into Truth and Meaning.*

U.S.—German-American psychoanalyst Erich Fromm writes *Escape from Freedom*, on the place of the modern individual.

Art critic Clement Greenberg publishes the essay "Towards a Newer Laocoön," on the importance of abstract art.

Critic Harold Rosenberg publishes the essay "The Fall of Paris."

Military

Belgium—Belgium surrenders to Germany (May 28).

France—France falls to German troops and is occupied; the Vichy government is established, led by General Henri Pétain.

British and French soldiers evacuate Dunkirk (May 28–June 4).

Locations of Olympic Games

The Modern Olympic Games were instituted in 1896. A separate series of Winter Games was begun in 1924.

Summer		Winter	
1896	Athens, Greece	1924	Chamonix, France
1900	Paris, France	1928	St. Moritz, Switzerland
1904	Saint Louis, Missouri, U.S.	1932	Lake Placid, New York, U.S.
1908	London, England	1936	Garmisch-Partenkirchen, Germany
1912	Stockholm, Sweden	1948	St. Moritz, Switzerland
1920	Antwerp, Belgium	1952	Oslo, Norway
1924	Paris, France	1956	Cortina d'Ampezzo, Italy
1928	Amsterdam, Netherlands	1960	Squaw Valley, California, U.S.
1932	Los Angeles, California, U.S.	1964	Innsbruck, Austria
1936	Berlin, Germany	1968	Grenoble, France
1948	London, England	1972	Sapporo, Japan
1952	Helsinki, Finland	1976	Innsbruck, Austria
1956	Melbourne, Australia	1980	Lake Placid, New York, U.S.
1960	Rome, Italy	1984	Sarajevo, Yugoslavia
1964	Tokyo, Japan	1988	Calgary, Alberta
1968	Mexico City, Mexico	1992	Albertville, France
1972	Munich, West Germany	1994	Lillehammer, Norway
1976	Montreal, Canada	1998	Nagano, Japan
1980	Moscow, Soviet Union	2002	Salt Lake City, Utah, U.S.
1984	Los Angeles, California, U.S.		
1988	Seoul, South Korea		
1992	Barcelona, Spain		
1996	Atlanta, Georgia, U.S.		
2000	Sydney, Australia		

Germany—German troops begin the Battle of Britain, a massive air attack on the country in preparation for invasion.

Germany invades Norway.

German troops invade and conquer Denmark and Norway (April 9).

Germany overruns Luxembourg and Netherlands.

German planes and submarines cause substantial damage to British ships in the Battle of the Atlantic.

Italy—Italy declares war against the Allies on June 10.

Italian forces attack Malta; they invade Greece but are repelled after one month of battle (October–November).

Italian forces invade North Africa in the Western Desert Campaign but are defeated by British troops.

Japan—Japanese forces capture Indochina.

Romania—Monarch Carol II is deposed in a coup; Romania enters the war.

Soviet Union—Troops cross the Mannerheim Line (February).

U.K.—British forces sink three Italian battleships at Taranto (November 11).

British Royal Air Force troops defeat the German Luftwaffe air corps in the Battle of Britain (August–October).

U.S.—The Selective Service Act is passed by Congress, the nation's first peacetime draft. It requires one year of service.

Politics

India—The Muslim League parts from the Congress Party and calls for the independent country of Pakistan.

U.K.—Winston Churchill succeeds Neville Chamberlain as prime minister.

From London, Charles de Gaulle organizes the Free French movement, a resistance arm.

U.S.—President Franklin Roosevelt is reelected for a record third term, defeating Republican candidate Wendell Willkie.

Science and Technology

France—The Lascaux Cave, source of paintings dating from the Cro-Magnon era, is discovered by children while playing.

Italy—Physicists Emilio Segré, Dale Corson, and K. R. Mackenzie discover the element astatine.

U.K.—Reconstructive surgery for burn victims is developed and practiced by New Zealand–born plastic surgeon Archibald McIndoe.

Penicillin is refined and isolated for clinical trials by German-British biochemist Ernst Boris Chain and Australian-British pathologist Howard Florey.

U.S.—The element plutonium is discovered by Glenn T. Seaborg and others.

Physicists Edwin McMillan and Philip Hauge Abelson discover neptunium, the first known transuranium element (element with a number greater than 92, the number of uranium).

The Rh factor in human blood is discovered by scientists at Rockefeller University, including Austrian-American pathologist Karl Landsteiner.

The first electron microscope is presented at the Radio Corporation of America laboratories, Camden, New Jersey. It was developed by scientists working under Dr. Vladimir Zworykin.

DES (diethylstilbestrol) is prescribed for pregnant women with morning sickness. It will be banned by the Food and Drug Administration in 1971.

A version of color television is developed by Peter Goldmark for CBS (Columbia Broadcasting System).

The jeep, a four-cylinder general purpose field vehicle, is developed by U.S. engineer Karl Pabst. The vehicle proves useful in World War II transport.

A process for enriching uranium by accumulating the isotope uranium-235 for use in an atomic bomb is presented by American physicist Philip Hauge Abelson.

The Advisory Committee on Uranium houses the first work on the development of the atomic bomb; research is led by Hungarian-born American physicist Leo Szilard and Italian physicist Enrico Fermi.

Society

Canada—The Canadian ship *St. Roch* becomes the first ship to sail west to east on the Northwest Passage.

U.S.—Radios are found in 30 million homes, according to a national survey.

The hamburger stand that will become the basis of the McDonald's chain is opened by Maurice and Richard McDonald in southern California (*see* **1954**).

The 40–hour work week is instituted at workplaces, following passage of the 1938 Fair Labor Standards Act.

Passage of the Alien Registration Act (also known as the Smith Act) forces the registration and fingerprinting of about five million aliens and forbids membership in organizations advising overthrow of the U.S. government.

Nylon stockings are sold for the first time.

Sports

U.S.—In the World Series, the Cincinnati Reds (NL) defeat the Detroit Tigers (AL), four games to three.

For the NFL championship, the Chicago Bears defeat the Washington Redskins, 73–0.

Joe Louis retains his crown as world heavyweight boxing champion in two matches against Chilean Arturo Godoy.

The PGA golf tournament is won by Byron Nelson.

World—The Olympic Games are suspended due to the world war. Games will resume in 1948.

1941 Arts and Entertainment

France—Olivier Messiaen composes *Quatuor pour la fin du temps.*

Soviet Union—Dmitry Shostakovich premieres Seventh Symphony, also known as Leningrad Symphony.

U.K.—War-related artistic works include Henry Moore's drawings of families during the Blitz, Feliks Topolski's drawings and paintings of naval troops, Paul Nash's painting *Bombers over Berlin*, and Stanley Spencer's painting *Shipbuilding in the Clyde.*

U.S.—Notable films include Orson Welles's *Citizen Kane,* John Huston's *The Maltese Falcon,* Raoul Walsh's *High Sierra,* William Wyler's *The Little Foxes,* Frank Capra's *Meet John Doe,* and John Ford's *How Green Was My Valley.*

World—Notable nonfiction works include William Shirer's *Berlin Diary* (U.S.); novels include Virginia Woolf's *Between the Acts* (U.K.), F. Scott Fitzgerald's *The Last Tycoon* (U.S.), James Hilton's *Random Harvest* (U.S.), John P. Marquand's *H. M. Pullman, Esq.* (U.S.), Mary

O'Hara's *My Friend Flicka* (U.S.), Franz Wurfel's *The Song of Bernadette*, and Ilya Ehrenburg's *The Fall of Paris* (Soviet Union).

Notable works of poetry include Louis Aragon's *Le Crève-Coeur* (France), Alice Duer Miller's *The White Cliffs of Dover* (U.S.), and W. H. Auden's *New Year Letter* (U.S.).

Notable plays premiered include Noël Coward's *Blithe Spirit* (U.K.), and Bertolt Brecht's *Mother Courage and Her Children* (U.S.).

Ideas

U.K.—The BBC popularizes the slogan "V for Victory," which becomes an Allied rallying cry in Europe.

U.S.—Henry Luce introduces the idea of the "American Century" in a *Time* editorial.

Poet and critic John Crowe Ransom publishes *The New Criticism*, giving a name to a developing movement in literary criticism.

Literary critic Francis Otto Matthiessen publishes *American Renaissance*.

President Roosevelt introduces the concept of the Four Freedoms—freedom of speech and expression, freedom of worship, freedom from fear, freedom from want—in a speech to the U.S. Congress.

Coined by a chaplain at the attack on Pearl Harbor, "Praise the Lord and pass the ammunition" becomes a U.S. war rallying cry.

Military

Egypt—As part of the German North African campaign, German troops led by Rommel invade Egypt.

Ethiopia—Following British and Ethiopian troop advances, Italian troops surrender (July 3).

Germany—Germany sinks the U.S. destroyer *Reuben James* and damages the U.S. destroyer *Kearny*.

Germany and Italy declare war on the U.S. (December 11).

Hong Kong—Britain surrenders Hong Kong to Japanese forces.

Indochina—Japanese forces invade and occupy Indochina.

Philippines—Japanese forces invade the islands at Luzon.

Soviet Union—German troops invade Russia, beginning the Siege of Leningrad (September 13). Germany captures Kiev on September 19; U.S./U.K. support is pledged on October 1. The siege will continue until January 1944.

U.K.—The British Navy sinks the German battleship *Bismarck* in the Pacific.

Britain declares war on Finland, Hungary, and Romania.

Russian troops force Germany to evacuate Rostov-on-Don (November 27).

British troops clash with German troops and force a German withdrawal from Tobruk, with much damage to Afrika Corps (November).

U.S.—Japanese forces attack Pearl Harbor, Hawaii, on December 7, killing approximately

3,000 soldiers and sinking four battleships. Japanese forces also attack Guam, Wake Island, the Philippines, and other Pacific sites. Twenty-eight Japanese airplanes and three submarines were lost in the attack.

U.S./U.K.—The countries declare war against Japan on December 8.

Wake Island—Japanese forces capture the island in fighting against U.S. forces.

Yugoslavia/Greece—German forces invade Yugoslavia and Greece (April 6). Yugoslavia signs an armistice with Germany (April 17); Greece surrenders to Germany (April 22).

Politics

Germany/Italy—The two countries agree to relax trade restraints over the course of the war.

Iran—Tehran is occupied by Allied forces. The shah abdicates and is replaced by Crown Prince Mohammad Reza Pahlavi.

Japan—General Hideki Tojo becomes prime minister.

Japan/Soviet Union—The two countries sign a neutrality pact.

Lebanon—Lebanon declares itself an independent state.

U.S.—President Franklin Roosevelt is inaugurated for a record-breaking third term. Vice president is Henry A. Wallace.

The Lend-Lease Bill is signed by President Roosevelt, granting a system for exchange of U.S. munitions for foreign goods and services.

President Roosevelt freezes German and Italian assets in the U.S.

U.S./U.K.—President Roosevelt and Prime Minister Winston Churchill formulate the Atlantic Charter, which outlines the governments' roles during and after World War II.

Yugoslavia—Yugoslavia joins the Tripartite Pact.

Science and Technology

Austria—A link between rubella and congenital infant abnormalities is detected by Norman Gregg.

Germany—Polyurethanes are manufactured by IG Farbenindustrie.

Soviet Union—The spontaneous fission of uranium is discovered by G. N. Flerov.

U.S.—The Manhattan Project begins in Oak Ridge, Tennessee, and Los Alamos, New Mexico, to research development of the atomic bomb.

Penicillin production is increased, making it widely available.

Grand Coulee Dam, Washington, is put into operation.

The word *antibiotic* is coined by scientist S. A. Wakeman.

The artificial element plutonium is discovered by Glenn T. Seaborg and E. McMillan.

Society

U.K.—Rationing of clothing begins.

U.S.—President Roosevelt establishes the Office of Price Administration.

The American Red Cross blood donor service is created.

President Roosevelt resets Thanksgiving as the last Thursday of November.

The first contract between a U.S. company and a U.S. trade union is signed, by the Ford Motor Company and the Congress of Industrial Organizations.

Rubber rationing is instituted.

Sports

U.S.—New York Yankee Joe DiMaggio hits in a major league record-setting 56 consecutive games, from May 15 through July 16.

Whirlaway becomes the fifth horse to win the Triple Crown; the jockey in all three races is Eddie Arcaro.

In the World Series, the New York Yankees (AL) defeat the Brooklyn Dodgers (NL), four games to one.

For the NFL championship, the Chicago Bears defeat the New York Giants, 37–9.

New York Yankee first baseman Lou Gehrig dies at age 37 of the muscle disorder (ALS) that will later bear his name.

The U.S. Open golf tournament is won by Craig Wood. The tournament will be suspended until after World War II.

Ted Williams of the Boston Red Sox hits .406, holding a record for a player to hit over .400 for a season that lasts until the end of the century.

1942 Arts and Entertainment

China—Mao Zedong issues the essay "Talks at the Yenan Forum on Art and Literature," which posits the utilitarian use of the arts.

France—Henri Matisse completes *The Idol*; Pablo Picasso completes *Woman with an Artichoke;* Georges Braque completes *The Kitchen Table,* all paintings.

U.K.—T. S. Eliot publishes the poem *Little Gidding,* which completes the poetry collection *Four Quartets* (1936–42).

U.S.—Edward Hopper completes the painting *Nighthawks.*

Aaron Copland's ballet *Rodeo* premieres, with choreography by Agnes de Mille.

The first gold record (representing sales of one million) is awarded to "Chattanooga Choo-Choo" by Glenn Miller and His Orchestra.

Irving Berlin presents the army show *This Is the Army.*

In the film *Holiday Inn,* singer Bing Crosby introduces Irving Berlin's "White Christmas." It becomes a holiday standard.

World—Novels include Jean Genet's *Our Lady of the Flowers* (France), Evelyn Waugh's *Put out More Flags* (U.K.), James Gould Cozzens's *The Just and Unjust* (U.S.), Lloyd C. Douglas's *The Robe* (U.S.), William Faulkner's *Go Down, Moses,* and John Steinbeck's *The Moon Is Down* (U.S.).

Films include Luchino Visconti's *Obsession* (Italy), Walt Disney's *Bambi* (U.S.), Michael Curtiz's *Casablanca*, George Stevens's *Woman of the Year* (U.S.), Orson Welles's *The Magnificent Ambersons* (U.S.), and William Wyler's *Mrs. Miniver* (U.S.).

Plays include Sean O'Casey's *Red Roses for Me* (Ireland) and Thornton Wilder's *The Skin of Our Teeth* (U.S.).

Ideas

France—Philosopher Albert Camus publishes the essay "The Myth of Sisyphus," on existentialism and the absurd.

Military

Bataan—Japanese forces capture Bataan after battle with U.S. forces. General Jonathan M. Wainwright withdraws with troops to Corregidor (April 9). U.S. troops and Filipinos captured by the Japanese are forced on a six-day march of 85 miles that will be known as the Bataan Death March. The march results in over 5,000 Allied deaths (April 10).

Brazil—Brazil declares war on Germany and Italy (August 22).

Burma—Japanese forces invade Burma in January, capturing Lashio in April and Mandalay in May.

Canada—Full conscription begins throughout the country.

Coral Sea—U.S. and Japanese air forces engage in the Battle of the Coral Sea. Seven Japanese warships are lost; three U.S. warships are destroyed (May 4–8). Throughout the battle, the fleets remained out of sight from one another.

Corregidor—Japanese forces under the command of General Tomoyuki Yamashita capture Corregidor after battle with U.S. forces (May 6).

France—Massive U.S. bombing raids begin (September).

Gilbert Islands—U.S. troop guerrilla unit called Carlson's Raiders take out the Japanese radio station on Makin Island. All 350 Japanese soldiers on the island are killed (August 18).

Guadalcanal—U.S. Marines invade Guadalcanal, Solomon Islands, to claim it from Japanese forces (August 7). The first major U.S. amphibious attack in the Pacific will continue until February 1943 and result in massive losses. A U.S. naval victory (November 12–15) prevents Japanese reinforcements from entering the island.

Japan—U.S. carriers led by Major General James H. Doolittle conduct an air raid on Tokyo that marks the first U.S. success in the Pacific (April 18).

Java Sea—Japanese naval forces defeat the U.S. Navy in the Battle of the Java Sea (February 27–March 1). Commander is Admiral Thomas C. Hart.

Malaya—Japanese forces capture Malaya.

Manila—Japanese forces take the island after battle with U.S. and Philippine troops (January 2). Commander U.S. General Douglas MacArthur leads withdrawal to the Battan peninsula, vowing "I shall return."

Midway Island—U.S. troops gain a major naval victory over Japanese troops in the Battle of Midway (June 4–6) and mark a turning point in the war. The Japanese lose four of their primary aircraft carriers and 4,800 soldiers. U.S. losses include one aircraft carrier and 300 deaths.

New Guinea—Japanese forces attack New Guinea in January and capture regions including New Britain and the Solomon Islands over the ensuing weeks.

North Africa—German and Italian forces defeat British troops at Bir Hacheim (May 28–June 13) and capture Tobruk (June 21). In November German troops defeat the British at El Alamein. U.S. troops under Lieutenant General Dwight Eisenhower join British naval and air units.

Singapore—Japanese troops overtake the British outpost in Singapore (February 8–15).

Soviet Union—German forces take Russian cities in July: Sevastopol, Veronezh, and Rostov.

The Battle of Stalingrad begins (August 23, 1942–February 2, 1943), resulting in Russian capture of the German Sixth Army.

Politics

Germany—The final solution *(Endlsüng)* to the "Jewish Problem" is discussed at the Wannsee Conference (January 20), with German leaders systematizing the mass murder of Jews, Gypsies, Poles, and other groups. The death camps where this genocide, known as the Holocaust, takes place will include Auschwitz and Treblinka in Poland and Buchenwald and Dachau in Germany.

India—The Congress Party requests withdrawal of the British presence in India. Party leaders are imprisoned for their action.

U.S.—In Congressional elections the Democratic Party loses seats in the Senate and House of Representatives but retains a majority.

Internment of 110,000 Japanese-Americans is ordered by President Roosevelt's Executive Order 9066.

Science and Technology

Canada—Curare is used as a muscle relaxant in operations by H. R. Griffith and Enid Johnson.

Germany—The first successful guided missile is launched by a team headed by German scientist Wernher Von Braun. It attains an altitude of 60 miles.

The first jet fighter, the Messerschmidt Me262, has its first flight (July).

U.S.—Under an approach developed by Italian physicist Enrico Fermi, the Manhattan Project generates the first sustained nuclear reaction at the University of Chicago. The process requires the piling of a critical mass of fuel, uranium-235 (December 2).

The country's first jet airplane, XP-59, is tested at Muroc Army Base, Calif.

Napalm, an incendiary material for bombs, is developed by American chemist Louis Fieser.

The Atanasoff-Berry Computer is completed by physicist John Atanasoff and Cliford Berry. Though not fully operational, it will become a prototype for future electronic computer designs.

A decade-long series of poliomyelitis epidemics begins.

Society

France—Germany orders that Jews above age six are required to wear a yellow Star of David.

Holland—Removal of Jews to German factories begins (May).

India—A cyclone and tidal wave decimate part of Bengal (October).

Norway—The deportation of Jews by German forces begins.

Poland—A half million Poles are killed in purges by German troops.

U.S.—Coffee, gasoline, and sugar rationing begin.

The Office of War Information is established to control the dissemination of materials; the Office of Price Administration is granted price-setting powers with passage of the Price Control Bill.

With hundreds of thousands of men serving in the war, women enter the workforce in large numbers, manufacturing war material.

Sports

U.S.—In the World Series, the St. Louis Cardinals (NL) defeat the New York Yankees (AL) four games to one.

For the NFL championship, the Washington Redskins defeat the Chicago Bears 14–6.

Joe Louis retains the world heavyweight boxing championship by defeating Buddy Baer. It is Louis's 20th defense of the title.

Sam Snead wins the PGA golf tournament.

1943 Arts and Entertainment

Austria—Arnold Schöenberg premieres *Ode to Napoleon*.

Cuba—Wilfredo Lam paints *The Jungle*.

Germany—Thomas Mann completes the four-part work *Joseph and His Brothers*.

Mexico—Rodolfo Usigli's historical drama *Crown of Shadow* is produced.

U.K.—American-born poet T. S. Eliot publishes *Four Quartets*.

U.S.—Richard Rodgers and Oscar Hammerstein II's influential musical *Oklahoma!* premieres on Broadway.

In the U.S. during the war, French-born artist Marc Chagall completes *The Juggler* and Dutch painter Piet Mondrian completes *Broadway Boogie-Woogie* (1942–43).

Artist Jackson Pollock holds his first solo show.

Jive music, a swinging form of jazz, gains popularity.

Nat "King" Cole (Nathaniel Adams Cole) releases his first Top-40 song hit.

World War II–related books include Ernie Pyle's *Here Is Your War*, Ted Lawson's *Thirty Seconds over Tokyo*, and Richard Tregaskis's *Guadalcanal Diary*.

World—Films include Vittorio de Sica's *Children Look at You* (Italy), Akira Kurosawa's

Sanshio Sugata, Emilio Fernandez's *Maria Candelaria* (Mexico), Sergey Eisenstein's *Ivan the Terrible, Part 1* (Soviet Union), Michael Powell and Emeric Pressburger's *The Life and Death of Colonel Blimp* (U.K.), Alfred Hitchcock's *Shadow of a Doubt* (U.S.), and Sam Wood's *For Whom the Bell Tolls* (U.S.).

Notable novels include Antoine de St. Exupéry's *The Little Prince* (France), Ayn Rand's *The Fountainhead* (U.S.), Betty Smith's *A Tree Grows in Brooklyn* (U.S.), and William Saroyan's *The Human Comedy* (U.S.).

Ideas

France—Existentialist philosopher Jean-Paul Sartre publishes *Being and Nothingness*.

U.S.—Walter Lippmann publishes *U.S. Foreign Policy*.

John Maynard Keynes presents ideas for an international currency union.

Former presidential candidate Wendell Willkie publishes *One World*.

Military

England—Axis forces begin round-the-clock bombing in England.

Germany—German air forces continue widespread bombing.

German forces surrender in Tunisia.

Italy—Allied forces invade Italy.

The U.S. Fifth Army captures Naples.

Italy surrenders to Allied forces (September).

Italy declares war on Germany (December).

Japan—The Battle of the Bismarck Sea results in the destruction of a 22–ship Japanese convoy.

New Guinea—U.S. forces land in New Guinea.

Poland—German forces perpetrate a massacre in the Warsaw ghetto.

Solomon Islands—Allied forces drive the Japanese Army from Guadalcanal, marking a turning point in the war.

Soviet Union—The Russian Army destroys German forces southwest of Stalingrad.

The Russian Army takes Smolensk and Kiev.

Politics

Canada—The Quebec Conference is held, attended by Churchill, Roosevelt, and Mackenzie King.

Egypt—At the Cairo Conference General and Mme. Chiang Kai-shek pledge to Churchill and Roosevelt to relinquish control of Korea following the defeat of Japan.

Morocco—The Casablanca Conference is held, attended by Winston Churchill and Franklin Roosevelt.

Soviet Union—The Soviet Union and Czechoslovakia sign a treaty on postwar cooperation.

Science and Technology

Austria—Psychiatrist Leo Kanner is the first to write about infantile autism.

Switzerland—Chemist Albert Hoffman synthesizes lysergic acid diethylamide (LSD). Chemists produce xylocaine (lidocaine), a local anesthetic.

U.S.—Chinese-born biochemist Choh Hao Li isolates the adrenocorticotropic hormone (ACTH), which stimulates the adrenal cortex to produce and release cortical hormones.

Society

India—Famine strikes Bengal.

U.S.—Income taxes are withdrawn from paychecks for the first time.

Race riots occur in Detroit, Michigan, Los Angeles, California, and Harlem in New York City, among other cities.

Rationing of meat, fat, cheese, canned goods, and shoes begins, and a minimum 48-hour work week for war goods factories is instituted.

A polio epidemic kills nearly 1,200.

The Supreme Court rules that schoolchildren may refuse to salute the flag if it runs counter to their religion.

Sports

U.S.—Count Fleet wins the Triple Crown.

1944   Arts and Entertainment

Argentina—Jorge Luis Borges publishes the short-story collection *Ficciones*.

France—Pablo Picasso completes *Seated Woman in Blue*, painting; Georges Rouault completes *Homo Homini*, painting; Henri Matisse completes *The White Dress*, painting.

New Zealand—Poet James Kier Baxter (1926–72) publishes his first poetry collection, *Beyond the Palisade*.

Soviet Union—Sergei Prokofiev's Fifth Symphony premieres; Dmitry Shostakovich's Eighth Symphony premieres.

Painter Francis Bacon completes *Three Figures at the Base of a Crucifixion*.

U.S.—Popular wartime cartoonists include Bill Mauldin, creator of "Up Front with Mauldin," and George Baker, creator of the "Sad Sack."

Poet Karl Shapiro publishes the collection *V-Letter and Other Poems*.

Béla Bartók's *Sonata for Unaccompanied Violin* premieres.

Bandleader Major Glenn Miller is reported lost at sea.

Photographer Ansel Adams publishes *Born Free and Equal*, a portrait of a Japanese-American internment camp.

Aaron Copland's folk ballet *Appalachian Spring* premieres, with choreography by Martha Graham.

Jerome Robbins's ballet *Fancy Free* premieres; later this year, it is the basis for the Broadway musical *On the Town*.

Novels include Saul Bellow's *Dangling Man*, Kathleen Winsor's *Forever Amber*, John Hersey's *A Bell for Adano*, and Lillian Smith's *Strange Fruit*.

World—Films include Alf Sjoberg's *Frenzy* (Sweden), Laurence Olivier's *Henry V* (U.K.), George Cukor's *Gaslight* (U.S.), Edward Dmytryk's *Murder My Sweet* (U.S.), Howard Hawks's *To Have and Have Not* (U.S.), Leo McCarey's *Going My Way* (U.S.), Robert Stevenson's *Jane Eyre* (U.S.), and Billy Wilder's *Double Indemnity* (U.S.).

Plays include Jean Anouilh's *Antigone* (France), Jean-Paul Sartre's *No Exit* (France), Mary Chase's *Harvey* (U.S.), and Philip Yordan's *Anna Lucasta* (U.S.).

Ideas

Austria—Psychoanalyst Helene Deutsch publishes *The Psychology of Women*.

Germany—Economist Friedrich Hayek publishes *The Road to Serfdom*, which will influence conservative political thinking.

U.S.—Mathematicians Oskar Morganstern and John von Neumann publish *The Theory of Games and Economic Behavior*, which will influence the development of game theory.

American Southern Baptist clergyman William Franklin (Billy) Graham begins his religious crusades.

Artist Robert Motherwell publishes "The Modern Painter's World," on forces leading to an artist's isolation from society.

World—The word *genocide* is coined to refer to the systematic elimination by the Nazis of the Jews and other groups. It will come to refer to the systematic elimination of any ethnic or racial group.

Military

Baltic States—Soviet troops complete their march through the Baltic States with the capture of Latvia from German troops (October 1944–May 1945).

France—On D-Day (June 6, 1944) Allied air and ground forces led by General Dwight Eisenhower land in Normandy on five invasion beachheads. Allied forces take Cherbourg (June 27) and liberate Paris (August 25). They take Brussels (September 3) and Antwerp (September 4) and battle German forces up to the Siegfried Line. There (October 20), they are met by the U.S. First Army, which takes Aachen. By sea, Allied forces land in southern France (August 15) and take Marseilles and Toulon.

The Battle of the Bulge (December 1944–January 1945) begins in the Ardennes as German forces attempt to crack the Allied line. German forces are defeated, with Allied forces forcing the Germans to the Rhine River.

French Resistance forces capture much of Paris (August 24); General Charles de Gaulle follows the U.S. Fourth Army into Paris (August 25), with the provisional government established on August 30. The Allies will recognize the government in October.

Italy—At Anzio (January–May), Allied naval forces take the site and capture Rome (June).

Leyte—U.S. forces recapture Leyte (October–December); a U.S. naval armada destroys many pieces of Japanese warcraft—airplanes, battleships, and aircraft carriers.

Pacific Islands—Allied forces led by U.S. General Douglas MacArthur take several islands including Kwajalein (February 1), Eniwetok and the Parry Islands (February 17–21), New Guinea (April–July), Saipan (June 15–July 9), and Guam (July–August).

Poland—Soviet troops capture the bulk of eastern Poland; German forces capture Warsaw (October 2).

Romania—Soviet forces capture Romania (August 23).

Soviet Union—German forces are repulsed by advancing Soviet troops. Sites retaken by Soviets include Leningrad (January 15–19), Odessa (April 10), Sevastopol (May 19), Minsk (July 3), the Ukraine, and western Russia. One-half million German prisoners-of-war are taken.

Yugoslavia/Hungary—Soviet forces take Belgrade (October 20) and capture Budapest (November).

Politics

Canada—At the Quebec Conference, President Roosevelt and Prime Minister Churchill discuss the invasion of Japan and other matters (September 12–16).

France—The Brazzaville Declaration outlines postwar colonial policy for Africa. Plans for independence and self-rule are dismissed.

Women gain the right to vote.

Germany—At the Potsdam Conference (July–August), Allied representatives discuss post-war plans and war crimes trials.

An officers' plot to kill Adolf Hitler fails (July 20).

India—Mahatma Gandhi is set free by the government.

U.S.—President Franklin Roosevelt defeats Republican Thomas Dewey to gain a record fourth term.

At the Dumbarton Oaks Conference (August–October) in Washington, D.C., several countries discuss the formation of the United Nations.

Science and Technology

Germany—The first V-2 rockets (designed by Wernher von Braun) are fired at London (September 7).

Astronomer Carl F. von Weizsäcker reexamines the nebula postulation of the solar system.

U.K.—Biochemists Archer Martin and Richard Synge invent paper chromatography.

U.S.—Physicist Glenn T. Seaborg and colleagues discover two elements, americium and curium.

Chemists R. B. Woodward and William E. Doering synthesize quinine, which will be used to treat malaria.

The Harvard-IBM Automatic Sequence Controlled Calculator is developed at Harvard University under the supervision of Howard Hathaway Aiken.

German-American astronomer Walter Baade postulates two populations of stars, distinguished by age and site in the galaxies.

Kodacolor negative film for consumer use is developed by Eastman Kodak.

Society

U.S.—Congress passes a federal highways act establishing the U.S. National System of Interstate Highways, which results in the construction of 40,000 miles of highway nationwide.

Congress passes the G.I. Bill, which fully subsidizes college education for World War II veterans.

Sports

U.S.—In the World Series, the St. Louis Cardinals defeat the St. Louis Browns, four games to two.

For the NFL championship, the Green Bay Packers defeat the New York Giants, 14–7.

1945 Arts and Entertainment

Italy—British author Ezra Pound writes *Pisan Cantos* while in prison for pro-fascist activities.

Soviet Union—Dmitry Shostakovich's Ninth Symphony premieres.

U.K.—Benjamin Britten's opera *Peter Grimes* premieres.

Henry Moore completes *Family Group*, sculpture.

U.S.—Jazz musician Charlie "Bird" Parker records for the first time with his own band.

Carousel, a musical by Richard Rodgers and Oscar Hammerstein, premieres on Broadway.

Alexander Calder completes *Red Pyramid*, sculpture.

Arthur Schlesinger Jr. publishes *The Age of Jackson*.

World—Novels include Jean-Paul Sartre's *The Age of Reason* (France), Carlo Levi's *Christ Stopped at Eboli* (Italy), George Orwell's *Animal Farm* (U.K.), Evelyn Waugh's *Brideshead Revisited* (U.K.), Sinclair Lewis's *Cass Timberlane* (U.S.), Richard Wright's *Black Boy* (U.S.), and Richard Schellabarger's *Captain from Castile* (U.S.).

Films include Marcel Carné's *Children of Paradise* (France).

Ideas

U.K.—Austrian-born philosopher Karl Popper publishes *The Open Society and its Enemies*.

Military

Burma—The Burmese army and civilians revolt against Japanese occupation troops and join Allies.

Ecuador—Ecuador declares war on Germany in February, followed by other South American countries including Argentina, Chile, Paraguay, Peru, Uruguay, and Venezuela.

Europe—V-E (Victory over Europe) Day is proclaimed following ratification of German unconditional surrender (May 8).

Finland—Finland declares war on Germany (March 3).

Germany—U.S. forces cross the Rhine River and capture the Remagen Bridge.

Adolf Hitler orders "scorched earth" policy on Allied forces.

Allied forces firebomb city of Dresden, resulting in 135,000 deaths.

Germany surrenders unconditionally (May 8).

Germany is partitioned into occupation zones by Britain, France, and the U.S. (June 22).

Germany/Poland—Concentration camps at Bergen-Belsen and Buchenwald are liberated by Allied troops (April 30).

Iwo Jima—U.S. troops place a flag on Mt. Suribachi (February 23). Following weeks of combat between Japanese and U.S. forces, the U.S. captures the island (March 16).

Japan—Japan surrenders unconditionally to the Allies following the dropping of two American atomic bombs (*see* **U.S.**). V-J (Victory over Japan) Day on August 15 signifies the end of war in the Pacific.

Okinawa—U.S. troops invade Okinawa (April 1). Japanese forces surrender to the U.S. on June 21.

Philippines—The U.S. Sixth Army invades Luzon on January 9. Following months of fighting between U.S. and Japanese forces, General Douglas MacArthur and his troops liberate the Philippines.

Soviet Union—The Soviet Union declares war on Japan (August 9).

U.S.—The first atomic bomb is detonated in a trial explosion, Alamogordo, New Mexico.

For the first time in war, an atomic bomb is used, on Hiroshima, Japan, on August 6.

A second atomic bomb is used, on Nagasaki, Japan, on August 9.

Politics

Algeria—Algerian riots against French colonial occupation result in thousands of deaths. British troops occupy Lebanon and Syria (May).

Cambodia—Cambodia, Vietnam, and Indonesia declare independence.

Egypt—The Arab League is inaugurated in Cairo in March.

Germany—Adolf Hitler commits suicide (April 30).

At the Potsdam Conference, Allied leaders discuss Japanese surrender and postwar plans for demilitarizing Japan.

Hungary—Martial law is instituted (October 19).

Indonesia—Indonesia is declared a republic in August, with status lagging until British and Dutch troops reinstate colonial regime in December.

Italy—Fascist ex-dictator Benito Mussolini and mistress Clara Petacci are shot by Italian partisans.

Ukraine—The secret Yalta Conference is held in February, attended by Winston Churchill, Franklin Roosevelt, and Joseph Stalin. Its central purpose is to discuss postwar policy.

U.S.—President Franklin Roosevelt dies in Warm Springs, Georgia, on April 12. Vice President Harry S Truman is sworn in as president.

The first United Nations conference is held in San Francisco, California, with 50 countries represented.

President Truman presents his Fair Deal domestic program.

Yugoslavia—The Republic of Yugoslavia is proclaimed by Marshal Tito.

Science and Technology

Hungary—Cosmic radiation is studied by L. Janossy.

The first radar signals as reflected by the moon are discovered by astronomer Z. Bay.

Soviet Union—The synocyclotron, a particle accelerator, is developed by Vladimir Veksler.

U.S.—ENIAC (Electronic Numerical Integrator and Computer), the first fully successful electronic computer, is developed by scientists J. Presper Eckert Jr. and Dr. John W. Mauchly. The 30–ton, 18,000 vacuum-tube computer will be presented in 1946 at the Moore School of Electrical Engineering, Philadelphia, Penna.

The endoplasmic reticulum and mitochondria are detailed in electron microscope studies by cytologist Albert Claude.

Folic acid is discovered.

Fluoridated water is used in public systems to decrease cavities.

The herbicide 2,4–D is put into general use.

Society

Austria—Renaissance and other artworks looted by Nazis are discovered in a mine.

Germany—Monetary and banking systems collapse in May and June.

Food riots break out early in the year.

In Nuremberg in November, war trials of Nazi criminals are begun.

New Zealand—Bank nationalization and social welfare laws are passed.

U.S.—The New York State Commission Against Discrimination, the first U.S. antidiscrimination agency, is founded.

Written on any edifice, "Kilroy Was Here" becomes a popular international phrase to mark any place visited by the U.S. military. The name Kilroy represents the average U.S. soldier.

World—The International Monetary Fund (IMF) and International Bank of Reconstruction and Development (World Bank) are established as UN agencies.

Sports

U.S.—In the World Series, the Detroit Tigers (AL) defeat the Chicago Cubs (NL), four games to three.

For the NFL championship, the Cleveland Rams defeat the Washington Redskins 14–14.

1946 Arts and Entertainment

France—The Cannes Film Festival premieres.

Guatemala—Miguel Angel Asturias publishes the novel *Mr. President*.

New Zealand—Keith Douglas publishes *Almaden to Zem Zem*, based on war experiences.

Soviet Union—Sergey Prokofiev's opera *The Duenna* premieres in New York.

U.K.—Dylan Thomas completes poetry collection *Deaths and Entrances*.

Benjamin Britten's opera *The Rape of Lucretia* premieres.

U.S.—Gian Carlo Menotti's opera *The Medium* premieres.

William Carlos Williams completes part of the poem cycle *Paterson*.

Mark Rothko completes the painting *Prehistoric Memories*.

Willem de Kooning begins a series of black-and-white abstract expressionist paintings.

Journalist John Hersey publishes *Hiroshima*, about the effects of atomic bombing.

Buckminster Fuller designs Dymaxion House.

Edmund Wilson's story collection *Memoirs of Hecate County* is published to calls for censorship for its treatment of sex.

World—Novels include Simone de Beauvoir's *All Men Are Mortal* (France), Nikos Kazantzakis's *Zorba the Greek* (Greece), Elias Canetti's *Auto da fé* (U.K.), Thomas Heggen's *Mister Roberts* (U.S.), John P. Marquand's *B. F.'s Daughter* (U.S.), Robert Penn Warren's *All the King's Men* (U.S.), and Eudora Welty's *Delta Wedding* (U.S.).

Plays include Christopher Fry's *A Phoenix Too Frequent* (U.K.), Terrence Rattigan's *The Winslow Boy* (U.K.), Arthur Miller's *All My Sons*, Eugene O'Neill's *The Iceman Cometh* (U.S.); musicals include Irving Berlin's *Annie Get Your Gun* (U.S.), and Alan Jay Lerner and Frederick Loewe's *Brigadoon* (U.S.).

Films include Jean Cocteau's *Beauty and the Beast* (France), Roberto Rossellini's *Paisá*(Italy), David Lean's *Great Expectations* (U.K.), Frank Capra's *It's a Wonderful Life* (U.S.), Alfred Hitchcock's *Notorious* (U.S.), Charles Vidor's *Gilda* (U.S.), and William Wyler's *The Best Years of Our Lives* (U.S.).

The United Nations Educational, Scientific, and Cultural Organization (UNESCO) is founded.

Ideas

U.K.—In a U.S. speech Winston Churchill introduces the term iron curtain to mark the schism between Communist and non-Communist countries.

U.S.—The Revised Standard Version of the Bible is completed by biblical scholars.

Dr. Benjamin Spock publishes *Baby and Child Care*, which will influence childrearing for decades.

Military

China—A National Army is founded.

Egypt—British troops are withdrawn.

France—France declares martial law on Indochina.

Greece—Civil war begins after monarchy is restored.

Politics

Albania—Albania becomes a people's republic.

Algeria—Riots occur after France offers citizenship to colonial inhabitants.

Argentina—Juan Perón becomes president.

Bikini Islands—The U.S. detonates an atomic bomb on Bikini Atoll in testing. The bomb is approximately the size of that used on Nagasaki.

France—Charles de Gaulle resigns as president.

A new constitution for the Fourth Republic is approved.

Germany—Free elections are held in Berlin, the first since the election of Adolf Hitler in 1933.

Hungary— Hungary names itself a republic.

India—The British plan for Indian independence is rejected by the Congress party.

Italy—In a referendum, Italy decides to end monarchy, forcing the abdication of Victor Emmanuel III.

Japan—A new constitution declaring the emperor a constitutional monarch is approved.

Jordan—Transjordan becomes independent of Britain and is renamed Jordan.

Philippines—U.S. president Truman proclaims independence for the Philippines, adhering to the 1898 agreement made on the U.S. acquisition of the islands.

Vietnam—Ho Chi Minh becomes president. France recognizes the Democratic Republic of Vietnam as autonomous.

World—The League of Nations is formally dissolved.

Science and Technology

Germany—A V-2 rocket is launched to study the sun.

Germany/U.S.—German scientist Max Delbrück and U.S. scientist Alfred Hershey; each determine that a new virus can be formed from the combination of two separate viruses.

Soviet Union—The country's first nuclear reactor is set into operation.

Switzerland/U.S.—Swiss scientist F. Bloch and U.S. scientist E.W. Purcell each develop nuclear magnetic resonance.

U.K.—The Atomic Energy Commission is established in London.

U.S.—Xerography is developed by scientist Chester Carlson.

Carbon dating with radioactive isotope carbon-14 is determined by scientist Willard Libby.

The word *lepton* is presented by scientists Abraham Pais and C. Moller as a term for certain particles not subject to strong nuclear force.

The synchro-cyclotron is developed at the University of California, Berkeley.

Society

Argentina—Banks and telecommunication services are nationalized.

France—Riots break out over food shortages in Paris and elsewhere.

Germany—At the Nuremberg war crimes trials, 12 Nazis are sentenced to death and five to prison terms, including a life term for Rudolf Hess. Hermann Göring is sentenced to death; he kills himself before execution.

Italy—U.S. nun Mother Frances Xavier Cabrini becomes the first American to be canonized.

Women are granted the right to vote.

U.K.—The Bank of England is nationalized.

U.S.—Philanthropist John D. Rockefeller Jr. grants $8,500,000 to the United Nations to buy a site for permanent headquarters in New York.

U.S./Europe—The ballpoint pen, developed by Hungarian inventor Lazlo Biró, is sold to the public.

Sports

U.S.—The PGA golf tournament is won by Ben Hogan.

In the World Series, the St. Louis Cardinals (NL) defeat the Boston Red Sox (AL), four games to three.

For the NFL championship, the Chicago Bears defeat the New York Giants, 24–14.

1947 Arts and Entertainment

Australia—A. D. Hope publishes the poem "Conquistador."

France—Henri Matisse completes the painting *Young English Girl*.

Germany—Poet Nelly Sachs publishes a collection about the Holocaust, *Dwellings of Death*.

Spain—Musician Pablo Casals vows not to return to Spain until Franscisco Franco ceases being leader of Spain.

Switzerland—Sculptor Max Bill completes *Continuity*, a monument based on the structure of the Möbius strip.

U.K.—Sculptor Henry Moore completes *Three Standing Figures*

U.S.—Mahalia Jackson releases the album *Move on up a Little Higher*, which establishes her as a major gospel singer.

Opera singer Maria Callas debuts in Ponchielli's *Gioconda*, in Vienna.

World—Plays include Jean Anouilh's *Ring around the Moon* (France), Jean Genet's *The Maids* (France), Arthur Miller's *All My Sons* (U.S.), and Tennessee Williams's *A Streetcar Named Desire* (U.S.).

Books include Thomas Mann's *Doctor Faustus* (Germany), Malcolm Lowry's *Under the Volcano* (U.K.), A. B. Guthrie's *The Big Sky* (U.S.), Laura Z. Hobson's *Gentleman's Agreement* (U.S.), James Michener's *Tales of the South Pacific* (U.S.), Mickey Spillane's *I, the Jury* (U.S.), and John Steinbeck's *The Pearl* (U.S.).

Films include Michael Powell and Emeric Pressburger's *Black Narcissus* (U.K.), Charlie Chaplin's *Monsieur Verdoux* (U.S.), Elia Kazan's *Gentleman's Agreement* (U.S.), and George

Seaton's *Miracle on 34th Street* (U.S.).

Ideas

Germany—Philosopher Theodor Adorno publishes *Dialectic of Enlightenment*, on the Western desire to dominate nature.

Netherlands—*The Diary of a Young Girl* by German-born Dutch writer Anne Frank, a young victim of the Holocaust, is published posthumously by her father, Otto Frank.

U.S.—Critic Yvor Winters publishes *In Defense of Reason*.

Critic Cleanth Brooks publishes *The Well Wrought Urn*, on the New Criticism.

Historian Allan Nevins publishes *Ordeal of the Union*, an eight-volume history of the U.S. Civil War.

Pilot Kenneth Arnold becomes the first to report viewing "flying saucers," or unidentified flying objects (UFOs).

Politics

Belgium—Belgium, Luxembourg, and Netherlands ratify the Benelux Customs Union.

Burma—Burma proclaims itself an independent republic.

Ceylon—Ceylon becomes a self-governing dominion within the British Commonwealth through the Ceylon Independence Act.

France—Robert Schuman becomes prime minister.

India—India gains independence from Great Britain (August 15) and is partitioned into India and Pakistan.

Palestine—The United Nations votes to establish a Jewish state through a partitioning of Palestine. Arab protests and fighting between Arabs and Jews follow.

U.K.—Princess Elizabeth marries Philip Mountbatten, duke of Edinburgh.

The British coal industry is nationalized.

U.S.—While requesting passage of the Greek-Turkish Aid Bill, President Truman cites the U.S. position that will become known as the Truman Doctrine: "to support free peoples who are resisting attempted subjugation by armed minorities or by outside pressures."

President Truman establishes the Central Intelligence Agency (CIA).

President Truman signs the Greek-Turkish Aid Bill, authorizing approximately $400 million to the two countries.

At Harvard University, Secretary of State George C. Marshall presents the idea of the Marshall Plan to aid in the postwar reconstruction of Europe (June 5).

The Taft-Hartley Act, which prohibits closed shops and restricts a wide range of other labor practices, is passed by Congress despite being vetoed by President Truman.

Several peace treaties with the U.S. are ratified; countries involved include Bulgaria, Hungary, Italy, and Romania.

President Truman signs the Presidential Succession Act.

Science and Technology

Dead Sea—The Dead Sea Scrolls, religious texts on Judaism and Christianity, are discovered in pottery jars in a cave near the Dead Sea shore.

U.K.—The subatomic particle known as a pion or pimeson is discovered by physicist Cecil F. Powell.

Hungarian-British physicist Dennis Gabor develops the theory of holography.

Austrian-born psychoanalyst Anna Freud (daughter of Sigmund Freud) opens the London Hampstead Child-Therapy Clinic.

U.S.—Dr. Alfred C. Kinsey founds the Institute for Sex Research.

The antibiotic chloramphenicol is isolated by U.S. biochemists.

The element promethium is identified by chemists J. A. Marinsky, L. E. Glendenin, and C. C. Coryell.

Pan American Airways flies the first passenger airplane to travel around the world. The trip begins at LaGuardia Airport, New York, and is completed in Gander, Newfoundland.

Society

France—The feminine "New Look" is introduced to great success by designer Christian Dior.

U.S.—Funded by the G.I. Bill of Rights (the Servicemen's Readjustment Act of 1944), over 1 million veterans attend college.

Levittown, the first mass-produced suburban housing development, is built on Long Island, New York., by designer Abraham Levitt and his sons.

In California, Captain Charles E. Yeager completes the first manned supersonic airplane flight, taking the *Glamorous Glynnis*, a Bell X-1 rocket-powered plane, to a speed higher than the speed of sound.

An explosion on the French freighter *Grandcamp* and subsequent fires and explosions result in the decimation of the town of Texas City, Texas, and 500 deaths.

A snowstorm in the northeast results in record-breaking snowfalls of over two feet; 80 deaths result.

Sports

U.S.—Baseball player Jackie Robinson is signed to the Brooklyn Dodgers (NL) and becomes the first African-American player in the major leagues.

In the World Series, the New York Yankees (AL) defeat the Brooklyn Dodgers (NL) in seven games.

For the NFL championship the Chicago Cardinals defeat the Philadelphia Eagles, 28–21.

The world heavyweight boxing title is defended by Joe Louis, who defeats Jersey Joe Walcott.

1948 Arts and Entertainment

France—Olivier Messiaen's *Turangalila Symphony* premieres.

Germany—Richard Strauss's *Four Last Songs* premieres.

Soviet Union—Government oppression of cultural expression intensifies. Among works disparaged is Dmitry Shostakovich's Ninth Symphony.

U.K.—Ralph Vaughan Williams's Sixth Symphony premieres.

U.S.—Andrew Wyeth completes the painting *Christina's World*.

Television series premieres include *Texaco Star Theater*, starring Milton Berle (NBC, 1948–53; 1954–55) and *Toast of the Town*, starring Ed Sullivan (CBS, 1948–55; 1955–1971 as the *Ed Sullivan Show*).

World—Books include Nikos Kazantzakis's *Christ Recrucified* (Greece), Alan Paton's *Cry, the Beloved Country* (South Africa), Graham Greene's *The Heart of the Matter* (U.K.), Willam Faulkner's *Intruder in the Dust* (U.S.), Ross Lockridge's *Raintree County* (U.S.), Norman Mailer's *The Naked and the Dead* (U.S.), and Irwin Shaw's *The Young Lions* (U.S.).

Plays include Jean-Paul Sartre's *Dirty Hands* (France), Christopher Fry's *The Lady's Not for Burning* (U.K.), Bertolt Brecht's *The Caucasian Chalk Circle* (U.S.), and Tennessee Williams's *Summer and Smoke* (U.S.). Musicals include Cole Porter's *Kiss Me, Kate* (U.S.).

Films include Vittorio de Sica's *The Bicycle Thief* (Italy), Michael Powell and Emeric Pressburger's *The Red Shoes* (U.K.), John Ford's *Fort Apache* (U.S.), and John Huston's *The Treasure of the Sierra Madre* (U.S.).

Ideas

U.K.—Winston Churchill publishes *The Gathering Storm*, the first volume of his history of World War II.

Literary critic F. R. Leavis publishes *The Great Tradition*.

The World Council of Churches is founded.

U.S.—Keynesian economist Paul Samuelson publishes *Economics*.

Anthropologist Margaret Mead publishes *Male and Female: A Study of Sexes in a Changing World*, in which she discusses the effects of culture on gender identity.

The term "cold war" is introduced nationally by businessman Bernard M. Baruch.

Military

China—Chinese Communists capture Nan.

India—The rebel Hindu state of Hyderabad fights Indian forces for independence but announces defeat after five days of battle.

Indonesia—Dutch forces occupy Jakarta, eventually overtaking the entire country.

Israel—Upon the creation of the state of Israel (May 14–15), the country is attacked by forces of Arab League nations, including Egypt, Iraq, Lebanon, Syria, and Jordan). Jordan occupies the old city of Jerusalem and the West Bank, but Israel prevails and extends its borders.

Politics

Czechoslovakia—Communist forces overtake the country (February 25–27) and introduce a Soviet-style government (May–June). President Benes resigns and is replaced by Klement Gottwald. Anti-Communist foreign minister Jan Masaryk dies mysteriously (June 7).

Germany—Following the Soviet blockade of goods between Berlin and West Germany, an Allied airlift to Berlin begins.

India—Mahatma Gandhi is assassinated by Hindu extremist Nathuram Godre.

Israel—The British mandate on Palestine ends and the state of Israel is proclaimed (May 14–15). Leader of the provisional government is David Ben-Gurion; named first president is Chaim Weizmann (May 16).

Japan—General Tojo and seven others are sentenced to death for World War II crimes.

Kenya—The Mau-Mau, a secret society protesting white settlement in Kikuyu, is formed.

Korea—South Korea is proclaimed a republic (September 9); Syngman Rhee is named president. Communist North Korea announces its independence under the name the Democratic People's Republic of Korea (September 9); Kim Il Sung is named leader.

Malaya—Following the killings of British planters, a state of emergency is called, and Communist forces hunted and killed.

Netherlands—Queen Wilhelmina grants the throne to daughter Julianna.

U.K.—The British Commonwealth is renamed the British Commonwealth of Nations.

U.S.—President Truman signs the Foreign Assistance Act, which provides for the European Recovery Program (also known as the Marshall Plan) and military aid to China, Greece, and Turkey.

The Displaced Persons Act is passed, allowing for over 200,000 European persons displaced by World War II.

The House Un-American Activities Committee begins hearings on the presence of Communists in the U.S. government.

In a political upset, Democratic candidate President Harry Truman is elected president, defeating Republican candidate Thomas E. Dewey. Democrats retain control of the House and Senate.

Former U.S. State Department official Alger Hiss is indicted by a grand jury for two counts of perjury. The indictment stems from questions resulting from his denial of giving government documents to Communist courier Whittaker Chambers.

Science and Technology

Switzerland—Physicist Auguste Piccard builds the bathyscaphe.

U.S.—Physicist Richard P. Feynman develops the theory of quantum electronics.

The concept of the ferrite core memory for computers is developed by Chinese-American computer scientist An Wang.

A monkey is launched in a V-2 rocket's nose cone.

The fifth known moon of Uranus is discovered by astronomer Gerard P. Kuiper.

U.S.—A method for studying viruses within living cells is developed by microbiologist John Enders, virologist Thomas Weller, and physician Frederick Robbins.

Starch chromatography is developed by biochemists Stanford Moore and William H. Stein.

Mathematician Norbert Weiner publishes *Cybernetics*.

CBS engineer Peter Goldmark develops and demonstrates the long-playing vinyl phonograph 33 ⅓ record.

The transistor is developed at Bell Laboratories by physicists William Shockley, John Bardeen, and Walter H. Brattain.

U.S./Germany—Separately, German-born American physicist Maria Goeppert Mayer and German physicist J. Hans D. Jensen promote the shell model of the nucleus and introduce the concept of magic numbers.

Society

U.S.—Kansas repeals its 68-year-old ban on alcoholic beverages.

The Supreme Court declares religious education in public schools a violation of the First Amendment.

World—The UN adopts a statement of human rights.

The UN establishes the World Health Organization.

Sports

Sweden—The Winter Olympic Games open in St. Moritz.

U.K.—The Summer Olympic Games open in London.

U.S.—In the World Series, the Cleveland Indians (AL) defeat the Boston Braves (NL), four games to two.

Citation becomes the eighth horse to win the Triple Crown; jockey Eddie Arcaro wins the Triple Crown for the second time.

1949 Arts and Entertainment

France—Jean Genet's play *Deathwatch* and Jean Cocteau's film *Orphée* premiere.

Olivier Messiaen's composition *Mode de valeurs et d'intensités* for piano premieres.

Henri Matisse creates artwork, including tile murals and stained-glass windows, for the Chapel of the Rosary of Venice.

U.K.—George Orwell (pseudonym of Eric Arthur Blair) publishes the novel *1984*.

Nancy Mitford publishes the novel *Love in a Cold Climate*.

U.S.—Shirley Jackson publishes the short story "The Lottery."

Gwendolyn Brooks publishes the poetry collection *Annie Allen*.

The musical *South Pacific*, by Oscar Hammerstein II, Richard Rodgers, and Joshua Logan, premieres.

Arthur Miller's drama *Death of a Salesman* premieres.

Acting teacher Lee Strasberg becomes artistic director of the Actors Studio, a New York City institution that will train generations of "Method" actors.

Ideas

France—Philosopher Simone de Beauvoir publishes *The Second Sex*.

Anthropologist Claude Lévi-Strauss publishes *Elementary Structures of Kinship*.

U.K.—Philosopher Gilbert Ryle publishes *Concept of Mind*, which introduces the term *ghost in the machine*.

U.S.—Critics René Wellek and Austin Warren publish *Theory of Literature*.

Philosopher Wilfrid Sellars publishes *Readings in Philosophical Analysis*.

Mythologist Joseph Campbell publishes *The Hero with a Thousand Faces*.

Military

Algeria—Algerian guerrilla actions begin against French colonial forces.

China—The Communists win the Chinese Civil War and establish the People's Republic of China (October 1).

Greece—Government forces defeat Communist insurgents, though a low-level guerrilla war continues.

India/Pakistan—The Kashmir War between India and Pakistan ends with a UN-mediated ceasefire.

Indonesia—A ceasefire in May ends the Indonesian War of Independence; the Netherlands concedes independence on December 27. Sukarno becomes the new nation's first president.

Soviet Union—The Soviet Union detonates its first atomic bomb.

World—A UN convention defines *genocide* and specifies rules for international punishment of perpetrators.

Politics

Europe—The Council of Europe is formed, an international association focusing on human rights.

Germany—The Federal Republic of Germany (West Germany) and the German Democratic Republic (East Germany) come into existence.

Gold Coast—In what is now Ghana, Kwame Nkrumah founds the Convention People's Party.

India—The "untouchable" caste is officially abolished, though de facto discrimination will continue.

South Africa—The Citizenship Act tightens racial restrictions, outlawing racially mixed marriages.

Soviet Union—The government reduces the prices of food and clothing.

U.K.—The government nationalizes the gas industry.

U.S.—President Harry Truman puts forth the "Fair Deal" slogan to describe his domestic program.

World—On April 4 the North Atlantic Treaty is signed, creating the North Atlantic Treaty Organization (NATO).

Science and Technology

China—Engineer J. S. Lee becomes known for his work as the founder of geomechanics.

U.K.—Anatomist P. B. Medawar develops a technique that will help reduce problems associated with tissue transplants.

Chemist Derek H. R. Barton begins to study complex organic molecules; he will eventually demonstrate the high dependence chemical properties have on molecular shape.

U.S.—As a consequence of Big Bang theory, Russian-born American physicist George Gamow predicts the existence of a homogeneous background of radio-wave radiation; that evidence will be found in 1964.

Astronomer Fred L. Whipple theorizes that comets are "dirty snowballs" composed of ice and dust.

A rocket-testing site is founded at Cape Canaveral, Florida, future site of U.S. space launches.

Engineers build and launch the first multistage rocket, made up of a smaller rocket on top of a V-2.

Society

China—On September 2 a fire spreading from river docks in Chungking kills 1,700 people.

Czechoslovakia—Bishops in Prague denounce persecution when the police seize the Archbishop of Prague's residence.

Ecuador—An earthquake kills about 6,000 people and leaves 100,000 homeless.

Poland—An express train derails near Nowy Dwor, killing more than 200 people.

U.K.—Clothes rationing comes to an end.

U.S.—A six-week, nationwide steel strike ends in victory for the United Steelworkers of America.

One million television sets are in use.

World—The Latin American dance the samba becomes popular in the U.S. and Europe.

Sports

Czechoslovakia—Czech tennis player Jaroslav Drobny applies for political asylum in the West.

Italy—Italy's national soccer team is killed in an air crash in Turin.

U.S.—The National Basketball Association (NBA) is formed, with Maurice Podoloff as its first president (1949–63).

Joe Louis retires from boxing, having successfully defended his world heavyweight championship title against a record 25 challenges (1937–49).

In golf, Sam Snead wins the U.S. Masters and PGA tournaments.

1950 Arts and Entertainment

France—Marc Chagall creates *King David*.

Italy—Giacometti completes the sculpture *Seven Figures and a Head*.

U.K.—Austrian-born art historian Ernst Gombrich publishes *The Story of Art*.

U.S.—Journalist John Hersey publishes *The Wall*, about the Warsaw ghetto.

The United Nations building, New York City, is completed.

Caroline Gordon and Allen Tate edit the anthology *The House of Fiction*.

The television series *Your Show of Shows*, starring Sid Caesar, premieres (NBC, 1950–54).

Notable novels include Robert Penn Warren's *World Enough and Time* and Budd Schulberg's *The Disinherited*.

Notable plays include Clifford Odets's *The Country Girl* and Tennessee Williams's *The Roman Spring of Mrs. Stone*; musicals include Frank Loesser's *Guys and Dolls*.

Notable poetry includes Gwendolyn Brooks's *Annie Allen* and Ezra Pound's *Seventy Cantos*.

World—Films include Max Ophuls's *La Ronde* (France), Akira Kurosawa's *Rashomon* (Japan), Joseph Mankiewicz's *All about Eve* (U.S.), and Billy Wilder's *Sunset Boulevard* (U.S.).

Ideas

China—Historians begin to rewrite Chinese history to reflect the current Marxist government.

Germany—Philosopher Rudolph Carnap publishes *Logical Foundations of Probability*.

Italy—Pope Pius XII defines the dogma of the Assumption of Mary.

U.S.—German-born political philosopher Leo Straus publishes *Natural Right and History*.

German-born psychoanalyst Erik Erikson publishes *Childhood and Society*, about stages of life.

L. Ron Hubbard publishes *Dianetics*.

Literary critic Lionel Trilling publishes *The Liberal Imagination*.

Psychologist James J. Gibson publishes *The Perception of the Visual World*, presenting the theory later known as psychophysical correspondence.

Military

China—Communist Chinese forces occupy Tibet.

Korea—On June 25 North Korean troops cross the 38th parallel and invade South Korea, beginning the Korean War (1950–53).

Authorized by U.S. president Truman, U.S. forces set up a naval blockade (June); U.S. troops invade Korea (July), with General Douglas MacArthur named commander of UN forces.

U.S. forces recapture Seoul, the capital of South Korea (September).

At the Yalu River, Chinese Communist troops (allied with North Korea) hold off U.S. troops.

U.S.—The United Nations orders a cease-fire (June) on the Korean invasion (June).

A state of emergency is declared by President Truman following defeats in Korea.

Politics

China—Chiang Kai-shek resumes leadership of nationalist China.

U.S.—FBI director J. Edgar Hoover announces the presence of 55,000 Communist Party members and 500,000 sympathizers in the country.

President Truman allows the development of the hydrogen bomb by the U.S. Atomic Commission.

Science and Technology

Belgium—Cytologist Albert Claude discovers the endoplasmic reticulum.

China—The Chinese Academy of Sciences is founded.

Holland—Astronomer Jan Hendrik Oort posits the idea that comets begin in material revolving around the sun lying beyond Pluto, a region that becomes known as the Oort Cloud.

U.S.—Biochemist William Cumming Rose determines the role of essential amino acids in building protein.

The element californium is discovered by physicist Glenn Seaborg and others; berkelium is also discovered.

The first Xerox machine is built by the Haloid Company, New York.

Society

South Africa—Anti-apartheid riots occur in Johannesburg.

U.K.—Klaus Fuch is convicted of betraying British atomic secrets.

U.S.—U.S. State Department official Alger Hiss is convicted of two counts of perjury and sentenced to two concurrent five-year prison terms. In this, his second trial, he is found guilty of lying to a grand jury. The trial follows charges of espionage by Whittaker Chambers.

A minimum wage of 75 cents per hour is set under an amendment to the Fair Labor Standards Act.

The Columbia Broadcasting System gains a license to begin color transmission broadcast.

World—World population is approximately 2.3 billion.

Sports

Australia—The Australian team wins the Davis Cup against the American team.

U.S.—The first National Basketball Association championship is played between the Minneapolis Lakers and Syracuse Nationals. The Lakers win, four games to two.

The U.S. Open ends in a three-way tie among Ben Hogan, George Fazio, and Lloyd Mangrum. Hogan becomes champion in an 18–hole playoff.

The World Series is won by the New York Yankees (AL), who defeat the Philadelphia Phillies (NL) in four games.

The NFL championship is won by the Cleveland Browns, defeating the Los Angeles Rams (NL) 30–28.

1951 Arts and Entertainment

Canada—In Toronto Celia Franca founds the National Ballet of Canada.

Finland—Architect Alvar Aalto designs Town Hall in Saynatsalo, Finland.

France—Eugene Ionesco's play *The Chairs* premieres.

Greece—Nikos Kazantzakis publishes *The Last Temptation of Christ*.

Ireland—Irish writer Samuel Beckett, writing in French, publishes *Molloy* and *Malone Dies*, the first two novels of the trilogy that will conclude with *The Unnamable* (1953).

U.K.—New operas include Benjamin Britten's *Billy Budd* and Ralph Vaughan Williams's *The Pilgrim's Progress*.

Welsh poet Dylan Thomas publishes the poem "Do Not Go Gentle into That Good Night" (revised 1952).

U.S.—John Cage composes *Imaginary Landscape No. 4* for 12 radios, 24 musicians, and a conductor.

Rhythm-and-blues singer, composer, and pianist Ray Charles records his first hit, "Baby Let Me Hold Your Hand." Other hits will include 1959's "What'd I Say."

Photographer Aaron Siskind creates the photo *New York 2*.

Novels include J. D. Salinger's *The Catcher in the Rye*, James Jones's *From Here to Eternity*, and, from 1951 to 1953, Isaac Asimov's *Foundation* trilogy.

The situation comedy *I Love Lucy* (1951–57) premieres, making a television star out of Lucille Ball.

U.S./Italy—American soprano Maria Callas joins La Scala in Milan (1951–58, 1960–62).

World—Films include John Huston's *The African Queen* and Vincente Minnelli's *An American in Paris* (both U.S.), Jean Renoir's *The River* (India), and Charles Crichton's *The Lavender Hill Mob* (U.K.).

Ideas

France—Critic André Bazin and director Jacques Doniol-Valcroze found the film journal *Les Cahiers du cinéma*. The magazine will help shape *auteur* theory and the French New Wave filmmaking movement.

Philosopher Gabriel Marcel publishes *The Mystery of Being*.

The notebooks of French mystic Simone Weil are published posthumously (1951–56).

U.S.—Historian C. Vann Woodward publishes *Origins of the New South, 1877–1913*.

Sociologist Talcott Parsons publishes *The Social System*.

German-born American political scientist Hannah Arendt publishes *The Origins of Totalitarianism*.

German-born American theologian Paul Tillich publishes *Systematic Theology*.

Minister Norman Vincent Peale publishes *The Power of Positive Thinking*.

Military

Korea—Chinese and North Korean forces capture Seoul; Allied forces recapture it. Peace negotiations begin in July.

U.S.—General Douglas MacArthur is dismissed by President Harry Truman for insubordination.

Vietnam—Ho Chi Minh's Communist guerrillas capture much of the Indochinese countryside.

Politics

Bolivia—General Hugo Ballívian leads a coup blocking the installation of elected president Victor Paz Estenssoro.

China—China annexes Tibet, which it invaded the year before.

Iran—Mohammed Mossadeq is named prime minister.

Libya—Libya becomes independent.

U.K.—Winston Churchill is reinstated as prime minister.

U.S.—The 22nd Amendment to the Constitution, limiting U.S. presidents to two terms, is ratified.

World—The Organization of American States (OAS) is founded.

The UN establishes the office of the UN High Commissioner for Refugees.

Science and Technology

China—Following a major locust outbreak this year, China organizes what may be the most extensive pest management program in history.

Germany—Biochemist Feodor Lynen is the first to isolate acetyl coenzyme A.

U.S.—Astronomer Harold Irving Ewen and physicist Edward M. Purcell discover radio emissions from interstellar hydrogen clouds.

Physicist John Bardeen develops an explanation of superconductivity.

Remington Rand introduces the Univac computer for business use.

An experimental nuclear reactor in Idaho is the first nuclear reactor to generate electricity.

Society

India—Religious leader Vinoba Bhave, seen by many as the spiritual successor to Mohandas Gandhi, founds the Bhudan, or land-gift, movement, which seeks voluntary redistribution of land.

U.K.—Soviet spies Guy Burgess and Donald MacLean flee to the Soviet Union.

U.S.—The number of television sets in use reaches 10 million. The TV networks begin coast-to-coast broadcasting.

Direct coast-to-coast long-distance dialing is introduced.

Chrysler Corporation introduces power steering in its high-end automobiles.

Chinese-American scientist An Wang founds Wang Laboratories, which will introduce a desktop calculator in 1964 and word processor in 1971.

Color television programming is transmitted for the first time, by CBS. Color TV sets will not be marketed commercially until 1954.

Sports

Argentina—Auto racer Juan Manuel Fangio becomes world driving champion; he will regain the title in 1954 and hold it through 1957.

U.S.—Althea Gibson is the first African-American tennis player to play at Wimbledon.

Boxer Sugar Ray Robinson defeats Jake Lamotta to become world middleweight champion for the first of five times.

1952 Arts and Entertainment

Germany—Hans Werner Henze's first opera, *Boulevard Solitude*, is performed.

Mexico—Amalia Hernández founds the ballet Folklórico de México.

Nigeria—Amos Tutuola publishes the novel *The Palm Wine Drinkard*.

Soviet Union—Dmitry Shostakovich's *Twenty-Four Preludes and Fugues* premieres.

U.K.—Doris Lessing publishes the novel *Martha Quest*.

Agatha Christie's play *The Mousetrap* opens in London; it will become the longest-running play in theater history.

U.S.—Finnish-American architect Eero Saarinen designs the General Motors Technical Center in Warren, Michigan.

The theater Circle-in-the-Square opens in New York City.

Novels include Ralph Ellison's *Invisible Man*, John Steinbeck's *East of Eden*, Bernard Malamud's *The Natural*, Ernest Hemingway's short novel *The Old Man and the Sea*, and E. B. White's novel for children *Charlotte's Web*.

The television series *Today*, the first national morning television program, premieres (NBC, 1952–)

World—Films include Gene Kelly and Stanley Donen's *Singin' in the Rain* and Fred Zinnemann's *High Noon* (both U.S.) and Vittorio De Sica's *Umberto D* (Italy).

Ideas

Martinique—Martinique-born psychiatrist Frantz Fanon publishes *Black Skin, White Masks*.

U.K.—Anthropologist Alfred Reginald Radcliffe-Brown publishes *Structure and Function in Primitive Society*.

Philosopher Mervyn Hare publishes *The Language of Morals*.

U.S.—German-born American philosopher of science Carl Gustav Hempel publishes *Fundamentals of Concept Formation in Empirical Science.*

Military

Bolivia—An insurrection against the military regime allows elected president Victor Paz Estenssoro to take office.

Cyprus—Greek Cypriots calling for union (*enosis*) with Greece mount a guerrilla insurgency (1952–59) against the British and launch attacks on Turkish Cypriots.

Kenya—The Mau Mau rebellion (1952–59) against British rule begins.

Tunisia—Habib Bourguiba leads independence forces in a guerrilla war against France (1952–55).

U.K.—Britain explodes its first atomic bomb.

Politics

Cuba—Fulgencio Batista y Zaldívar leads a coup that establishes him as dictator (1952–58).

Ecuador—José Maria Velasco Ibarra, out of the presidency since 1947, returns as president for a third term (1952–56). His other terms are 1934–35, 1944–47, 1960–61, and 1968–72.

Egypt—Gamal Abdel Nasser leads a coup that deposes King Farouk I. General Mohammed Naguib is the first premier of the Egyptian republic.

Europe—The European Coal and Steel Community, precursor to the European Community, is formed.

Jordan—Hussein becomes king (1952–99) when his father, Tallal, is declared mentally incompetent.

Lebanon—Maronite Christian forces led by Camille Chamoun take power in a coup.

South Africa—Demonstrations against apartheid mount. The government bans meetings of more than 10 blacks while the UN begins a policy of condemning apartheid.

U.K.—King George VI dies; his daughter Elizabeth II succeeds him as monarch.

U.S.—The Republican Party regains control of the White House for the first time in 20 years when Dwight D. Eisenhower defeats Democrat Adlai Stevenson to win the presidency.

Science and Technology

Germany/U.S.—German-American astronomer Walter Baade revises the Cepheid luminosity scale to show that the galaxies are twice as far away as previously thought.

Poland—Physicists Marian Danysz and Jerzy Pniewski discover the K meson, or kaon, and the lambda particle.

U.K.—Archaeologist Michael Ventris deciphers the ancient Cretan language Linear B.

Biochemist Arthur J. P. Martin develops gas chromatography.

U.S.—Physicist Albert Ghiorso and colleagues discover the element einsteinium.

Archaeologists discover signs of human settlement near Clovis, New Mexico, dating from 11,500 years ago. For decades, these remains will be the earliest undisputed evidence of human settlement in the Americas.

On November 1 the U.S. detonates the world's first hydrogen bomb, at Eniwetok Atoll in the South Pacific.

Physician Jonas Salk develops the world's first poliomyelitis vaccine. He will begin testing it in 1953; it will be approved for general distribution in 1955.

The American Psychiatric Association publishes its first *Diagnostic and Statistical Manual of Mental Disorders* (DSM-1).

The antibiotic erythromycin is isolated.

Society

Brazil—Two passenger trains collide in Rio de Janeiro, killing 119 people.

Europe—The U.S. founds Radio Free Europe, which broadcasts to Eastern Europe.

Japan—Sony produces the first pocket-sized transistor radio.

U.K.—Using a De Havilland Comet, British Overseas Airways (BOAC) institutes the first jetliner service, between London, England, and Johannesburg, South Africa.

U.S.—Eleven people die in an earthquake at Tehachapi in Kern County, California. At 7.7 on the Richter scale, it is the largest earthquake in the state since the 1906 San Francisco earthquake.

The Eisenhower presidential campaign is the first to be reported on live television.

Writer L. Ron Hubbard founds the Church of Scientology.

Sports

Czechoslovakia—At the Summer Olympics in Helsinki, Finland, long-distance runner Emil Zátopek wins three gold medals and breaks three Olympic records.

U.S.—At the Helsinki Olympics pole-vaulter Bob Richards wins the first of a record two successive gold medals in the sport.

At the Oslo, Norway, Winter Olympics, Dick Button wins his second men's figure skating gold medal.

Tennis player Maureen Connolly wins the first of three consecutive singles titles at Wimbledon (1952–54).

Golfer Ben Hogan wins the Masters tournament and U.S. Open.

1953 Arts and Entertainment

Cuba—Alejo Carpentier publishes the novel *The Lost Steps*.

France—Jean Anouilh's plays *The Lark* and *Becket* are produced.

Germany/Mexico—German sculptor Mathias Golritz establishes the Echo, an experimental museum in Mexico City for the display of massive geometric steel structures.

Ireland—Samuel Beckett's play *Waiting for Godot*, written in French, premieres.

Mexico—Juan Rulfo's short-story collection *The Burning Plain and Other Stories* is published.

New Zealand—Poet James Kier Baxter publishes the poetry collection *The Fallen House.*

U.S.—Arthur Miller's play *The Crucible* premieres.

Novels include James Baldwin's *Go Tell It on the Mountain* and Arthur C. Clarke's *Childhood's End.*

Country singer and songwriter Hank Williams dies at age 29. His songs include "Your Cheatin' Heart."

Abstract expressionist painter Larry Rivers completes *Washington Crossing the Delaware.*

Henry Koster's *The Robe* is the first film to be released in the widescreen process CinemaScope; Arch Oboler's *Bwana Devil* is the first 3-D, or three-dimensional, film.

World—Films include Fred Zinnemann's *From Here to Eternity* and George Stevens's *Shane* (both U.S.), Ozu Yasujiro's *Tokyo Story* (Japan), and Federico Fellini's *I Vitelloni* (Italy).

Ideas

France—Critic Roland Barthes publishes *Writing Degree Zero.*

U.K.—*Philosophical Investigations*, by Austrian-born British philosopher Ludwig Wittgenstein, is published posthumously.

Latvian-born British political philosopher Isaiah Berlin publishes *The Hedgehog and the Fox: An Essay on Tolstoy's View of History.*

U.S.—Critic M. H. Abrams publishes *The Mirror and the Lamp.*

Economist Robert Heilbroner publishes *The Worldly Philosophers.*

Historian Bruce Catton publishes *A Stillness at Appomattox.*

Philosopher Willard Quine publishes *From a Logical Point of View.*

Political scientist David Easton publishes *The Political System.*

Military

Cuba—On July 26 rebel Fidel Castro leads an unsuccessful raid on Cuba's Moncada barracks. He is captured but later released in an amnesty (1955).

Italy—At the disputed Trieste, Yugoslav forces fight against Italian, British, and American forces. A settlement is reached in December.

Korea—Peace talks break down; hostilities resume in June. On July 27 an armistice ends the war, establishing a demilitarized zone between North and South Korea.

Soviet Union—The Soviet Union becomes the second nation (after the U.S. in 1952) to explode a hydrogen bomb.

Syria—Syria defeats a Druze insurrection.

Politics

British Guiana—In the colony that is now Guyana, Britain grants a constitution that provides for home rule. Left-leaning Cheddi Jagan wins the general elections and becomes prime minister.

Colombia—General Gustavo Rojas Pinilla takes power in a coup and becomes dictator.

East Germany—Soviet forces suppress antigovernment riots that began in East Berlin and spread nationwide.

India—Mohammed Abdullah, known as the "Lion of Kashmir" for his leadership of the Kashmiri independence movement, is imprisoned (1953–73).

Iran—Mohammed Mossadeq's government defeats an American- and British-backed coup. Shah Mohammed Reza Pahlavi flees into exile, but is reinstated in another coup, this one successfully deposing Mossadeq.

Morocco—France deports Sultan Muhammad Ibn Yusuf to Madagascar for his ostensible support of independence for Morocco.

Philippines—Ramón Magsaysay becomes president (1953–57).

Soviet Union—Shortly before his death on March 5, dictator Joseph Stalin begins a new purge, attacking those allegedly involved in the "doctors' plot."

In the struggle for power that follows dictator Joseph Stalin's death, Nikita Khrushchev emerges as first secretary and Soviet leader. Rival Lavrentii Beria, formerly security chief under Stalin, is executed.

Sweden—Swedish diplomat Dag Hammarskjöld becomes the UN's second secretary-general (1953–61).

U.S.—Senator Joseph McCarthy conducts televised hearings in which he mercilessly grills suspected Communists.

President Dwight D. Eisenhower appoints Earl Warren as chief justice of the Supreme Court; Warren's tenure (1953–69) will be one of the Court's most liberal and activist periods.

Science and Technology

Germany—Chemist Karl W. Ziegler develops the Ziegler process, used in making plastics.

Germany/Italy—German chemist Karl W. Ziegler and Italian chemist Giulio Natta develop isotactic polymers.

Soviet Union—Soviet physicists Aleksandr Prokhorov and Nikolai Basov and, independently, Charles H. Townes, invent the maser.

U.K./U.S.—British molecular biologist Francis Crick, American molecular biologist James D. Watson, and British biophysicist Maurice H. F. Wilkins discover the double-helix structure of the DNA molecule.

U.S.—Physicist Albert Ghiorso discovers the element fermium.

Physicist Donald A. Glaser invents the bubble chamber.

Physicist Murray Gell-Mann investigates the particle property called strangeness.

The first successful open-heart surgery is performed, using surgeon John Gibbon Jr.'s heart-lung machine.

IBM introduces the IBM 701, its first computer for scientific and business use.

Society

Nepal/New Zealand—On May 29, New Zealander Edmund P. Hillary and his Nepalese guide Tenzing Norgay are the first to reach the summit of Mount Everest. The world's tallest mountain, it is located on the Tibet-Nepal border.

Netherlands—More than 1,000 people die from burst dykes and floods.

New Zealand—A train derails near Wairoa, killing 166 people.

U.K.—The National Health Service makes smog masks available to people in polluted areas or with respiratory diseases.

U.S.—Julius and Ethel Rosenberg, convicted of spying for the Soviet Union, are executed, despite widespread doubts about their guilt.

Anti-Communism is a powerful force in the culture at large, with libraries, movie theaters, and other institutions under fire from anti-Communist groups for allegedly promulgating subversion.

Sports

Australia—In tennis, 19-year-old Australian Kenneth Rosewall is the youngest player to win both the Australian and French men's singles titles.

U.S.—In baseball the New York Yankees win their fifth consecutive World Series, this time against the Brooklyn Dodgers, four games to two.

In golf Ben Hogan wins three tournaments: the U.S. Open, the Masters, and the British Open.

Rocky Marciano defeats "Jersey Joe" Walcott to become the world heavyweight champion. When he retires undefeated in 1956, he will be the only heavyweight champion never to have lost a professional fight.

1954 Arts and Entertainment

Cameroon—Mongo Beti (1932–) publishes the novel *Mission terminée.*

Europe—Eurovision, the European television community, begins experimental transmissions; countries involved include Belgium, Denmark, France, Italy, the Netherlands, Switzerland, the U.K., and West Germany.

France—Jean Dubuffet paints *Vagabonds.*

Impresario Maurice Béjart becomes director of the Ballets de l'Étoile.

Italy—Luigi Nono's *La Victoire de Guernica* for voices and orchestra premieres.

Spain—Pablo Picasso paints *Sylvette.*

Switzerland—Rolf Liebermann's Concerto for Jazz Band and Symphony Orchestra premieres.

U.K.—Paintings include John Bratby's *Dustbins* and Francis Bacon's *Head Surrounded by Sides of Beef.*

Barbara Hepworth sculpts *Two Figures, Menhirs.*

Kingsley Amis publishes his first novel, *Lucky Jim.*

J. R. R. Tolkien publishes his fantasy trilogy *The Lord of the Rings* (1954–55).

Cecil Day-Lewis publishes his *Collected Poems.*

U.S.—Dancer Robert Joffrey founds the Joffrey Ballet.

Thornton Wilder's play *The Matchmaker* premieres.

Eudora Welty publishes the short novel *The Ponder Heart.*

The Newport Jazz Festival in Newport, Rhode Island, is held for the first time.

Rock singer Elvis Presley records his first hit single, coupling "That's All Right, Mama" and "Blue Moon of Kentucky."

Bill Haley and the Comets release a cover of Joe Turner's "Shake, Rattle and Roll"; next year they will release "Rock Around the Clock."

The television series *The Tonight Show* premieres on NBC. Hosts will include Steve Allen (1954–57); Jack Paar (1957–62); Johnny Carson (1962–92), Jay Leno (1992–).

World—Films include Elia Kazan's *On the Waterfront* and Alfred Hitchcock's *Rear Window* (both U.S.), Akira Kurosawa's *The Seven Samurai* (Japan), Federico Fellini's *La Strada* (Italy), Henri-Georges Clouzot's *Diabolique* (France), and Andrzej Wajda's *A Generation* (Poland).

Ideas

U.S.—Philosopher Nelson Goodman publishes *Fact, Fiction, and Forecast.*

Political scientists Angus Campbell, Gerald Gurin, and Warren Miller publish *The Voter Decides.*

Journalist Edward R. Murrow attacks Communist-hunting Senator Joseph McCarthy on the television program *See It Now.*

Military

Algeria—On November 1 the Algerian War of Independence (1954–62) begins. In December France sends 20,000 troops to Algeria.

Italy—An international treaty ends the Allied occupation of Trieste.

Vietnam—In May the besieged French fortress at Dien Bien Phu falls to the Communist Vietminh. In July an armistice is signed, dividing Vietnam along the 17th parallel, with a Communist government in the north and a nationalist government in the south.

Taiwan—Taiwan sinks Chinese gunboats; China attacks nationalist targets on the island of Quemoy. The U.S. and Taiwan sign a mutual security pact.

Politics

British Guiana—In what is now Guyana, Prime Minister Cheddi Jagan's government falls; moderate socialist Forbes Burnham becomes prime minister.

Burma—Burma's government and three oil companies form Burmah Oil.

Egypt—President and Premier Mohammed Naguib is forced to resign by Gamal Abdel Nasser. Nasser assumes power as president. Britain agrees to leave the Suez Canal Zone by the end of 1956.

Europe—Sweden, Norway, Denmark, and Finland form a common labor market giving equal employment opportunities to each other's nationals.

France—Pierre Mendès-France becomes premier.

Guatemala—A U.S.–backed coup deposes President Jacobo Arbenz Guzmán and installs military rule.

Morocco—Riots occur in Morocco, as nationalist demonstrators demand the return of their deposed sultan (*see* **1953**) and France sends in the Foreign Legion.

Paraguay—General Alfredo Stroessner takes power, beginning his dictatorship (1954–89).

U.S.—In *Brown v. Board of Education*, the Supreme Court declares racial segregation in public schools to be unconstitutional.

The Durham Rule, named for defendant Monte Durham, becomes law. It states that a criminal is not guilty if his unlawful behavior is the result of "mental defect or disease."

President Dwight Eisenhower signs the St. Lawrence Seaway Bill, authorizing construction of the new U.S./Canada waterway.

In August, the Communist Party in the U.S. is outlawed.

In December the Senate censures Senator Joseph McCarthy for his unfair tactics in investigating Communist infiltration in the army and government.

Science and Technology

Egypt—Kamal el-Malakh discovers two previously unknown chambers near the base of the Great Pyramid of Cheops, or Khufu, at Giza; one contains a 142-foot boat meant to transport the deceased pharaoh to the next world.

Switzerland—CERN, the European Organization for Nuclear Research, is founded in Geneva.

U.S.—Chinese-American physicist Chen Ning Yang and American physicist Robert Mills develop the mathematics of Yang-Mills gauge-invariant fields.

Scientists at the University of California build the bevatron, a new kind of particle accelerator.

Under the trade name Thorazine, chlorpromazine is approved for use as an antipsychotic.

Biochemist Vincent du Vigneaud synthesizes the hormone oxytocin, the first naturally occurring protein to be synthesized in the exact form it takes in the body.

Texas Instruments introduces silicon transistors.

Society

Canada—In Toronto Canada's first subway line opens.

Iran—The British Petroleum Company is created, which owns 40 percent of the newly established National Iranian Oil Company.

Japan—On September 26 the ferry *Toya Maru* sinks in Tsugaru Strait off Japan, killing 1,172 people.

South Korea—Sun Myung Moon founds the Unification Church, which will later be widely characterized as a cult, with its converts known as "Moonies."

Soviet Union—The country's first nuclear power plant begins production.

U.K.—The London gold market opens for the first time since 1939.

U.S.—The frozen food industry now exceeds $1 billion in sales.

Salesman Raymond Kroc purchases the franchise rights to the California-based McDonald brothers' hamburger chain (*see* **1940**). Kroc begins to build McDonald's into the world's largest fast-food restaurant chain.

BHA, butylated hydroxyanisole, is approved for use as a food preservative.

RCA markets the first color television set. Televisions are now in 29 million American homes.

U.S./Canada—Hurricanes Carol, Edna, and Hazel strike North America's Atlantic coast, killing 300 in the U.S. and Canada.

Sports

U.K.—Roger Bannister is the first person to run the mile in under four minutes (3 minutes, 59.4 seconds).

In golf Peter Thomson wins the British Open for the first of three consecutive times (1954–56); he will win again in 1958 and 1965.

Flat-racing jockey Lester Keith Pigott wins his first of a record nine Derbys and 29 Classics.

U.S.—In baseball's World Series, the New York Giants (NL) sweep the Cleveland Indians (AL) in four games.

West Germany—West Germany wins the World Cup for the first time.

1955 Arts and Entertainment

France—Pierre Boulez's work for contralto and six instruments, *Le Marteau sans maitre*, premieres.

Germany—Oskar Kokoschka completes *Thermopylae*, a triptych for the University of Hamburg.

Italy—Artist Pietro Annigoni's portrait of Queen Elizabeth, *H.M. The Queen,* is exhibited in London at the Royal Academy's Summer Exhibition.

Spain—Salvador Dalí completes *The Lord's Supper*, painting.

U.S.—U.S. artists including Willem de Kooning, Robert Motherwell, and Jackson Pollock are part of a major show at the Museum of Modern Art, New York.

Jasper Johns completes *Flags, Targets, and Numbers*, a series of paintings begun in 1954; Robert Rauschenberg completes *Red*, painting; Larry Rivers completes *Double Portrait of Birdie*, painting.

Actor James Dean is killed in an auto accident; he will become a cult hero.

The television series *Gunsmoke* premieres (CBS, 1955–75). It will be U.S. television's longest-running western series.

The television series *The Honeymooners* premieres (NBC, 1955–56).

World—Novels include Patrick White's *The Tree of Man* (Australia), Alain Robbe-Grillet's *The Voyeur* (France), Graham Greene's *The Quiet American* (U.K.), and Iris Murdoch's *The Flight from the Enchanter* (U.K.). American novels include MacKinlay Kantor's *Andersonville*, Robert Penn Warren's *Band of Angels*, Sloan Wilson's *The Man in the Gray Flannel Suit*, Herman Wouk's *Marjorie Morningstar*, and Vladimir Nabokov's *Lolita*. Story collections include Jorge Luis Borges's *Extraordinary Tales* (Argentina) and Flannery O'Connor's *A Good Man Is Hard to Find and Other Stories* (U.S.).

Plays include Samuel Beckett's *Waiting for Godot* (U.K.), and Arthur Miller's *A View from the Bridge* (U.S.).

Films include René Clair's *Les Grandes manoeuvres* (France), Alain Resnais's *Night and Fog* (France), Satyajit Ray's *Pather Panchali* (India), Michelangelo Antonioni's *The Girlfriends* (Italy), Ingmar Bergman's *Smiles of a Summer Night* (Sweden), Delbert Mann's *Marty* (U.S.), and Billy Wilder's *The Seven Year Itch* (U.S.).

Ideas

U.S.—German-born American political philosopher Herbert Marcuse publishes *Eros and Civilization*, which joins Freudianism and Marxism.

Austrian-born critic René Wellek publishes *History of Modern Criticism* (8 vols.).

Psychologist Albert Ellis develops rational-emotive therapy.

Editor William F. Buckley founds the *National Review*, which will become a leading voice of conservatism.

Military

Argentina—President Perón is ousted in a revolt led by General Eduardo Lonardi (September 16). Provisional President Lonardi is ousted in a bloodless coup by General Pedro Aramburo (November 13).

Cyprus—A state of emergency is proclaimed.

Politics

Algeria/Morocco—Following acts of violence and protest, French and Moroccan leaders negotiate a peace agreement and the removal of the sultan.

Argentina—President Juan Perón flees after being ousted; he remains in exile until 1971.

China—China petitions the UN to request U.S. withdrawal from China.

Egypt/Syria—The two countries sign a defense agreement.

Germany—West Germany approves the Hallstein Doctrine, dissolving relations with states acknowledging East Germany.

India—A five-year plan for economic development is put into effect.

Indonesia—Leaders of 29 countries at the Bandung Conference call for an end to colonialism and independence.

Iraq/Turkey—The two countries sign the Baghdad Pact, a treaty of alliance against Soviet expansion in the Middle East. Also joining the alliance are Iran, Pakistan, and the U.K.

Kenya—British action against the Mau Mau in Kenya continues.

Philippines—The Southeast Asia Treaty Organization (SEATO) is established by treaty in Manila. Signing the treaty are Australia, France, Great Britain, New Zealand, Pakistan, the Philippines, Thailand, and the U.S.

Soviet Union—The country plans to share nuclear knowledge with China, Czechoslovakia, East Germany, Poland, and Romania.

Switzerland—The Geneva Conference, aimed at narrowing conflicts among major countries, is attended by leaders from France, Great Britain, the Soviet Union, and the U.S.

U.K.—Prime Minister Winston Churchill resigns and is replaced by Anthony Eden.

U.S.—President Eisenhower is granted emergency powers to defend Formosa from potential invasion by Communist Chinese forces.

Voting 84–0, the Senate approves continuing its investigation of Communism in the U.S.

A foreign policy of "massive retaliation" is proposed by Secretary of State John Foster Dulles.

South Vietnam—Emperor Bao Dai is deposed in a referendum; a republic is proclaimed, with Ngo Dinh Diem named its leader.

Science and Technology

U.K.—Dorothy Hodgkin determines the composition of Vitamin B_{12}.

Optical fibers are made for the first time by Narinder Kapary.

U.S.—A polio vaccine developed by Dr. Jonas Salk is successfully tested in 44 states.

The subatomic particle known as the antiproton is discovered at the University of California by Owen Chamberlain and Emilio Segré.

Physicists Clyde Cowan and Frederick Reines observe neutrinos for the first time.

Spanish-born American biochemist Severo Ochoa develops enzymes that cause nucleic acid bases to form RNA.

Through experiments with protein synthesis, M. B. Hoagland discovers that transfer DNA combines with certain amino acids that are combined with messenger RNA.

A presidential press conference is filmed for television for the first time.

The U.S. grants $216 million in aid to South Vietnam.

Society

Australia—Floods leave nearly 45,000 people homeless.

India—Social reforms are passed permitting equal inheritance for women and relaxed laws for divorce.

South Africa—Following a nonviolent protest of several days, the government moves 600,000 blacks from Johannesburg to a nearby town.

Soviet Union—An agricultural plan emphasizing independence and decentralization is effected.

U.S.—The American Federation of Labor (AFL) and Congress of Industrial Organizations (CIO) merges. George Meany is the first president.

African-American citizen Rosa Parks defies a local segregation law on a bus in Montgomery, Alabama Civil rights activists led by Martin Luther King Jr. mount a year-long bus boycott in Montgomery that will integrate the buses and grow into a nationwide civil rights movement.

The General Assembly of the Presbyterian Church approves the ordination of women ministers.

Sports

U.S.—The World Series is won by the Brooklyn Dodgers (NL), defeating the New York Yankees (AL) in seven games.

For the NFL championship, the Cleveland Browns defeat the Los Angeles Rams 38–14.

U.S. boxer Rocky Marciano defends the world heavyweight title against British boxer Don Cockell.

1956 Arts and Entertainment

Brazil—Construction begins on the country's new capital, Brasília, laid out on barren land in east central Brazil by architect Lúcio Costa, with ultramodern buildings by architect Oscar Niemeyer. It will replace Rio de Janeiro as capital in 1960.

U.K.—Lynn Chadwick sculpts *Teddy Boy and Girl*.

Richard Hamilton's collage *Just What Is It That Makes Today's Homes So Different, So Appealing?* is exhibited. It is often considered the first pop art object.

John Osborne's play *Look Back in Anger* premieres.

U.S.—Architects Ludwig Mies van der Rohe and Philip Johnson design the Seagram Building in New York City, an exemplar of the international style.

Alan Jay Lerner and Frederick Loewe's musical *My Fair Lady* opens on Broadway.

Eugene O'Neill's play *Long Day's Journey into Night*, written in 1941, premieres posthumously.

Literary works include Grace Metalious's novel *Peyton Place*, Saul Bellow's fiction and drama collection *Seize the Day*, and Allen Ginsberg's poem "Howl."

Country singer and songwriter Johnny Cash records the song "I Walk the Line."

Ellsworth Kelly paints *Atlantic*.

World—Films include Cecil B. DeMille's *The Ten Commandments* and George Stevens's *Giant* (U.S.), Jean Renoir's *Paris Does Strange Things* and Alain Resnais's *Night and Fog* (both France), and Ingmar Bergman's *The Seventh Seal* (Sweden).

Ideas

U.S.—Polish-born American mathematician and philosopher Alfred Tarski publishes *Logic, Semantics, and Metamathematics*.

Sociologist C. Wright Mills publishes *The Power Elite*.

Editor William Hollingsworth Whyte publishes *The Organization Man.*

Military

Cuba—Rebel leader Fidel Castro, exiled in 1955, returns to Cuba to lead a new insurrection, the "26th of July Movement" (*see* **1953**).

Egypt—On July 26 President Gamal Abdel Nasser nationalizes the Suez Canal, initiating the Suez Crisis. With British and French collusion, Israel invades Egypt's Sinai Peninsula on October 29. Britain and France intervene; under U.S. pressure, they accept a cease-fire and withdraw their forces.

Politics

China—Leader Mao Zedong launches the Hundred Flowers period (1956–57), in which he encourages freedom of thought. Criticism of the government runs unexpectedly high and will prompt a crackdown in 1957, ending the experiment.

Cyprus—Archbishop Makarios, Greek Cypriot leader, is arrested and deported as a terrorist.

France/U.K.—The Suez Crisis (*see* **Military**) forces France and the U.K. to adopt gasoline rationing.

Guinea—Amílcar Cabral founds the African Party for the Independence of Guinea and Cape Verde.

Hungary—On October 23 an anti-Soviet revolt occurs in Budapest.

Imre Nagy's government withdraws from the Warsaw Pact and declares itself neutral between East and West. János Kádár forms a countergovernment, which calls in Soviet military support that crushes the rebellion.

India—India inaugurates its second five-year plan, which includes widespread nationalization of industry.

Morocco—Morocco becomes independent from France and Spain.

Pakistan—Pakistan becomes a republic.

Poland—Workers at an industrial fair in Poznán riot against the government; more than 100 are killed.

Wladyslaw Gomulka becomes premier (1956–70).

Soviet Union—At the 20th Party Congress on February 25, Premier Nikita Khrushchev denounces the late dictator Joseph Stalin. Khrushchev pursues a de-Stalinization policy aimed at reversing his predecessor's worst excesses.

Sudan—Sudan becomes independent.

Tunisia—Tunisia becomes independent.

U.K.—Republican incumbent Dwight Eisenhower defeats Democratic challenger Adlai Stevenson to win a second term as president.

Science and Technology

U.S.—Dutch-born American physicist Nicolaas Bloembergen invents the continuous maser.

Physicists Frederick Reines and Clyde Lorrain Cowan Jr. discover proof of the existence of neutrinos.

Chinese-American physicists Chen Ning Yang and Tsung-dao Lee show that the property called parity is conserved in the strong and electromagnetic interactions but not in the weak interaction between elementary particles.

Geologists Maurice Ewing and Bruce Charles Heezen propose the existence of the world-girdling Mid-Oceanic Ridge and Great Global Rift.

The Dartmouth Summer Research Project on Artificial Intelligence (AI) is a pioneering event in the field of AI. Attendees Marvin Minsky and John McCarthy will found the AI lab at the Massachusetts Institute of Technology (MIT).

Chinese-born American biochemist Choh Hao Li isolates human growth hormone from the pituitary gland.

Physiologist George E. Palade discovers that microsomes contain ribonucleic acid (RNA) and renames them ribosomes.

Biochemist Earl W. Sutherland Jr. isolates cyclic adenosine monophosphate (AMP), a molecule that stimulates enzymatic activity.

FORTRAN, the first computer programming language, is developed.

Society

Colombia—A dynamite blast in seven parked army trucks kills at least 1,000 people and destroys the center of Cali.

Monaco—Prince Rainier (1923–) marries American actress Grace Kelly (1928–82).

Spain—Couturier Cristóbal Balenciaga creates the "Sac," a loose chemise dress.

U.K.—Anti-nuclear-weapons protesters march from Aldermaston, site of a nuclear weapons research facility, to London.

A videotape recording machine is exhibited by Ampex Corporation.

The Ringling Brothers and Barnum and Bailey Circus performs its last show under canvas. With tent costs high, the circus will now perform only in permanent structures.

West Germany—West Germany becomes integrated into the world capital market.

Sports

Soviet Union—At this year's Summer Olympics in Melbourne, Australia, the Soviet Union wins the most medals.

U.S.—The U.S. wins two gold medals at the Winter Olympics in Cortina d'Ampezzo, Italy.

The Philadelphia Warriors defeat the Fort Wayne Pistons, four games to one, to win the National Basketball Association championship.

In baseball's World Series, the New York Yankees(AL) defeat the Brooklyn Dodgers (NL), four games to three.

Floyd Patterson defeats Archie Moore to become world heavyweight boxing champion.

1957 Arts and Entertainment

Mexico—Poet Octavio Paz publishes *Sun Stone*.

U.K.—Poet Ted Hughes publishes his first collection, *The Hawk in the Rain*.

Fin de partie (*Endgame*) by Samuel Beckett premieres in London.

The Entertainer, a play by John Osborne, opens in London.

U.S.—The musical *West Side Story* by Leonard Bernstein and Stephen Sondheim opens on Broadway, inspired by Shakespeare's *Romeo and Juliet*.

The Seagram Building in New York City is completed.

World—Notable novels include Max Frisch's *Homo Faber* (Switzerland), John Braine's *A Room at the Top* (U.K.), Iris Murdoch's *The Sandcastle* (UK), Lawrence Durrell's *Justine* (U.K.), V. S. Naipaul's *The Mystic Masseur* (U.K.), James Agee's *A Death in the Family* (U.S.), John Cheever's *The Wapshot Chronicle* (U.S.), Langston Hughes's *Simple Stakes a Claim*, William Faulkner's *The Town*, James Gould Cozzens's *By Love Possessed* (U.S.), Jack Kerouac's *On the Road* (U.S.), and Vladimir Nabokov's *Pnin* (U.S.).

Notable musical works include Benjamin Britten's *The Prince of the Pagodas* (U.K.), Dmitry Shostakovich's Eleventh Symphony (Soviet Union), Elliott Carter's *Variations for Orchestra* (U.S.), and Igor Stravinsky's ballet *Agon* (U.S.).

Notable films include Akira Kurasawa's *Throne of Blood* (Japan), Ingmar Bergman's *Wild Strawberries* (Sweden), David Lean's *The Bridge on the River Kwai* (U.K.), Charlie Chaplin's *A King in New York* (U.S.), and Nunnally Johnson's *The Three Faces of Eve* (U.S.).

Ideas

Norway—Albert Schweitzer advises the Nobel Committee to promote international opinion against nuclear testing.

U.S.—Noam Chomsky publishes *Syntactic Structures*, which explores the sources of human grammar and language.

Military

Soviet Union—Long-range intercontinental ballistic missiles (ICBMs) are developed.

Politics

Albania—Albanian Communist leader Enver Hoxha separates from the Khrushchev Soviet government.

Canada—The Conservative Party gains power for the first time in 22 years, with John Diefenbaker becoming prime minister.

Ghana—Ghana becomes an independent state.

Haiti—Papa Doc Duvalier is elected president.

Malaya—Malaya gains independence and becomes a member of the British Commonwealth.

Soviet Union—Nikita Khrushchev expels three high-ranking members of the Central Committee of the Soviet Communist Party.

U.S.—President Eisenhower presents the Eisenhower Doctrine, a policy offering support and armed intervention to Middle Eastern countries seeking aid against a Communist threat.

Soviet intelligence agent Rudlof Abel is imprisoned for espionage; he will be exchanged for U.S. spy plane pilot Gary Powers in 1962.

Science and Technology

Soviet Union—*Sputnik I*, the first Earth satellite, is launched in October; *Sputnik II*, with a dog (named Laika), is launched in November.

Sweden—Nobelium, element number 102, is discovered.

U.K.—Interferon, a virus fighting protein, is discovered by Alick Isaacs and Jean Lindenmann.

U.K./Germany—Thalidomide, which will later be banned for causing birth defects, is prescribed as a sleeping agent.

U.S.—Stereo records are marketed for the first time.

Surgeon General Leroy Burney reports a direct relationship between cigarette smoking and lung cancer.

The first underground atomic explosion is conducted near Las Vegas, Nevada.

The concept of the ecological niche is developed by G. E. Hutchinson.

Albert Sabin develops a workable live vaccine against poliomylitis.

The tranquilizer meprobamate is discovered by Czech-born chemist Frank Berger.

World—The International Geophysical Year begins. Scientists from 67 nations will study Earth and the Sun (July 1, 1957–December 31, 1958).

Society

Iran—The Trans-Iranian pipeline is finished.

Soviet Union—An explosion at a plutonium-producing facility near Kyshtym kills an unknown number and releases contamination over several hundred miles.

U.K.—A fire in the Windscale plutonium plant (later known as Sellafield) releases radioactive materials into the environment.

U.S.—President Eisenhower orders 1,000 Army paratroopers to enforce desegregation of Central High School in Little Rock, Arkansas, following violent protests.

The Southern Christian Leadership Conference (SCLC) is founded.

The Teamsters Union is expelled from the AFL–CIO under charges that Teamsters international vice president James R. Hoffa harbors criminals in the union.

The Mackinac Straits Bridge in Michigan, the world's longest suspension bridge, opens.

Sports

U.K.—At Wimbledon U.S. player Althea Gibson wins the women's singles title, the first black champion there.

U.S.—Carmen Basilio defeats Sugar Ray Robinson for the middleweight boxing championship.

Floyd Patterson defeats Tommy "Hurricane" Jackson for the heavyweight boxing championship.

In the World Series, the Milwaukee Braves (NL) defeat the New York Yankees (AL), four games to three.

Two New York baseball teams depart the city: the New York Giants for San Francisco, the Brooklyn Dodgers for Los Angeles.

The Boston Celtics defeat the St. Louis Hawks for the NBA Championship, four games to three.

The PGA golf tournament is won by Lionel Hebert.

The Detroit Lions defeat the Cleveland Browns, 59–14, to win the NFL championship.

1958 Arts and Entertainment

France—Jean Genet publishes the play *The Blacks*.

Italy—The ballet *Ondine* by Hans Werner Henze, choreographed by Frederick Ashton, premieres.

South Africa—Folk singer Miriam Makeba gains international attention for her performance in the film *Come Back, Africa*.

Soviet Union—U.S. pianist Van Cliburn wins the Tchaikovsky International Piano and Violin Festival.

U.K.—Ralph Vaughan Williams composes Symphony no. 9 in E minor.

U.S.—Rock musician Elvis Presley enters the army.

John Cage's Concert for Piano and Orchestra premieres.

The collection *95 Poems* by e. e. cummings is published.

World—Notable films include Jacques Tati's *Mon Oncle* (France), Andrej Wajda's *Ashes and Diamonds* (Poland), Luis Buñuel's *Nazarin* (Spain), Alfred Hitchcock's *Vertigo* (U.S.), and Vincente Minnelli's *Gigi* (U.S.).

Notable literary works include Chinua Achebe's *Things Fall Apart* (Nigeria), Truman Capote's *Breakfast at Tiffany's* (U.S.), Archibald MacLeish's *J. B.* (U.S.), William Humphrey's *Home from the Hill* (U.S.), Graham Greene's *Our Man in Havana* (U.K.), Alan Sillitoe's *Saturday Night and Sunday Morning* (U.K.), J. P. Donleavy's *The Ginger Man* (U.K.), T. H. White's *The Once and Future King* (U.K.), and Boris Pasternak's *Dr. Zhivago* (Soviet Union, first published in Italy).

Notable plays include Brendan Behan's *The Hostage* (Ireland), Peter Shaffer's *Five Finger Exercise* (U.K.), and Harold Pinter's *The Birthday Party*.

Ideas

China—The Great Leap Forward, a program of national economic change, is instituted.

Europe—The beatnik movement, born in the U.S., moves to Europe.

Italy—Pope Pius XII dies and is replaced by Pope John XXIII.

U.S.—Economist John Kenneth Galbraith publishes *The Affluent Society.*

Military

China—Nationalist leaders attempt to maintain the Quemoy and Little Quemoy Islands, despite bombardment from Chinese Communist forces.

Cuba—Fidel Castro and followers begin "total war" against the Batista government, and after several confrontations over the year, the Castro forces are victorious.

Pakistan—President Mirza proclaims martial law.

Politics

Belgium—Belgium, Luxembourg, and the Netherlands establish the Benelux Economic Union.

Egypt and Sudan—The two countries form the United Arab Republic.

Europe—The European Common Market is formed.

France—With France near civil war over the war in Algeria, a new constitution is established granting the president greater powers; Charles de Gaulle is elected president by overwhelming numbers.

Guinea—Refusing to accept France's invitation to become part of the French community, Guinea declares itself an independent republic.

Haiti—Papa Doc Duvalier represses an attempted coup.

Iraq—King Faisal and his heir and premier, Nuri-es-Said, are assassinated; successor Brigadier General Abdul Karim Kassem institutes anti-Western regime.

Palestine—The Palestinian independence movement al-Fatah is founded.

Poland—Premier Gomulka places limits on workers' groups and makes strikes illegal.

Soviet Union—Nikita Khrushchev becomes chairman of Council of Ministers.

West Indies—The West Indies Federation is organized.

Science and Technology

U.K.—The use of ultrasound (high-frequency sound waves) to evaluate human fetuses is begun by I. Donald.

U.S.—The Van Allen Belt, a highly powerful radiation zone surrounding Earth, is noted by U.S. satellites and named for project leader James Van Allen.

The National Aeronautics and Space Administration (NASA) is established.

Two satellites, *Explorer I* and *Vanguard 1*, are launched.

A Pioneer rocket is launched in a lunar exploration, but it fails to circle the Moon.

John Enders develops a vaccine against measles.

Lycra, a manmade elastic fiber, is marketed by Du Pont.

Society

U.S.—Arkansas governor Orval Faubus defies the Supreme Court school integration ruling, closing four high schools and chartering a private school corporation.

A major recession occurs for much of the year.

Sports

Brazil—Brazil wins the World Cup, with team member Pelé becoming a star for his performance.

U.K.—American Althea Gibson wins the women's singles Wimbledon tennis championship.

Members of the highly successful U.K. Manchester United football team are killed in an air disaster in Yugoslavia.

U.S.—The PGA golf tournament is won by Dow Finsterwald.

The Baltimore Colts defeat the New York Giants, 23–17, to win the NFL championship.

The New York Yankees (AL) defeat the Milwaukee Braves (NL), four games to three, to win the World Series.

The St. Louis Hawks defeat the Boston Celtics, four games to two, to win the NBA championship.

Sugar Ray Robinson wins the world middleweight boxing championship for a record fifth time, beating Carmen Basilio.

Arnold Palmer wins his first Masters golf tournament.

1959 Arts and Entertainment

France—Eugène Ionesco's play *Rhinocéros* is produced.

Jean Genet's play *The Blacks* opens.

U.K.—Peter Maxwell Davies's orchestral work *Prolation* premieres.

U.S.—On February 2, rock musician Buddy Holly (Charles Harden Holley) dies at age 22 in a plane crash. Songs recorded with his band, the Crickets, include "That'll Be the Day."

American playwright Edward Albee's first play, *The Zoo Story*, premieres in Berlin.

Lorraine Hansberry's drama *A Raisin in the Sun* is produced.

Tennessee Williams's play *Sweet Bird of Youth* premieres.

The musical *Gypsy*, by Arthur Laurents, Stephen Sondheim, and Jule Styne, premieres.

The television series *Bonanza* premieres (NBC, 1959–73).

Novels include William S. Burroughs's *Naked Lunch*, Saul Bellow's *Henderson the Rain King*, and Walter M. Miller Jr.'s *A Canticle for Liebowitz*.

Grace Paley publishes her first short-story collection, *The Little Disturbances of Man*.

Robert Frank publishes the photography collection *The Americans*.

Academy Awards 1927–28 to 1999
Best Picture and Best Foreign Language Film

The Academy of Motion Picture Arts and Sciences, which annually presents the Academy Awards, or Oscars, was founded in the U.S. in 1927. Foreign Language Film became an official category in 1956.

Best Picture

1927–1928	*Wings*	1966	*A Man for All Seasons*
1928–1929	*The Broadway Melody*	1967	*In the Heat of the Night*
1929–1930	*All Quiet on the Western Front*	1968	*Oliver!*
1930–1931	*Cimarron*	1969	*Midnight Cowboy*
1931–1932	*Grand Hotel*	1970	*Patton*
1932–1933	*Cavalcade*	1971	*The French Connection*
1934	*It Happened One Night*	1972	*The Godfather*
1935	*Mutiny on the Bounty*	1973	*The Sting*
1936	*The Great Ziegfeld*	1974	*The Godfather, Part II*
1937	*The Life of Emile Zola*	1975	*One Flew over the Cuckoo's Nest*
1938	*You Can't Take It with You*	1976	*Rocky*
1939	*Gone with the Wind*	1977	*Annie Hall*
1940	*Rebecca*	1978	*The Deer Hunter*
1941	*How Green Was My Valley*	1979	*Kramer vs. Kramer*
1942	*Mrs. Miniver*	1980	*Ordinary People*
1943	*Casablanca*	1981	*Chariots of Fire*
1944	*Going My Way*	1982	*Gandhi*
1945	*The Lost Weekend*	1983	*Terms of Endearment*
1946	*The Best Years of Our Lives*	1984	*Amadeus*
1947	*Gentleman's Agreement*	1985	*Out of Africa*
1948	*Hamlet*	1986	*Platoon*
1949	*All the King's Men*	1987	*The Last Emperor*
1950	*All about Eve*	1988	*Rain Man*
1951	*An American in Paris*	1989	*Driving Miss Daisy*
1952	*The Greatest Show on Earth*	1990	*Dances with Wolves*
1953	*From Here to Eternity*	1991	*The Silence of the Lambs*
1954	*On the Waterfront*	1992	*Unforgiven*
1955	*Marty*	1993	*Schindler's List*
1956	*Around the World in 80 Days*	1994	*Forrest Gump*
1957	*The Bridge on the River Kwai*	1995	*Braveheart*
1958	*Gigi*	1996	*The English Patient*
1959	*Ben-Hur*	1997	*Titanic*
1960	*The Apartment*	1998	*Shakespeare in Love*
1961	*West Side Story*	1999	*American Beauty*
1962	*Lawrence of Arabia*		
1963	*Tom Jones*		
1964	*My Fair Lady*		
1965	*The Sound of Music*		

Academy Awards, continued

Best Foreign Language Film

1956	*La Strada* (Italy)		1976	*Black and White in Color* (Ivory Coast/France)
1957	*Nights of Cabiria* (Italy)		1977	*Madame Rosa* (France)
1958	*My Uncle* (France)		1978	*Get out Your Handkerchiefs* (France)
1959	*Black Orpheus* (France, filmed in Brazil)		1979	*The Tin Drum* (West Germany)
1960	*The Virgin Spring* (Sweden)		1980	*Moscow Does Not Believe in Tears* (Soviet Union)
1961	*Through a Glass Darkly* (Sweden)		1981	*Mephisto* (Hungary)
1962	*Sundays and Cybele* (France)		1982	*To Begin Again* (Spain)
1963	*8 1/2* (Italy)		1983	*Fanny and Alexander* (Sweden)
1964	*Yesterday, Today, and Tomorrow* (Italy)		1984	*Dangerous Moves* (Switzerland)
1965	*The Shop on Main Street* (Czechoslovakia)		1985	*The Official Story* (Argentina)
			1986	*The Assault* (Netherlands)
1966	*A Man and a Woman* (France)		1987	*Babette's Feast* (Denmark)
1967	*Closely Watched Trains* (Czechoslovakia)		1988	*Pelle the Conqueror* (Denmark)
			1989	*Cinema Paradiso* (Italy)
1968	*War and Peace* (Soviet Union)		1990	*Journey of Hope* (Switzerland)
1969	*Z* (France/Algeria)		1991	*Mediterraneo* (Italy)
1970	*Investigation of a Citizen above Suspicion* (Italy)		1992	*Indochine* (France)
			1993	*Belle Epoque* (Spain)
1971	*The Garden of the Finzi-Continis* (Italy)		1994	*Burnt by the Sun* (Russia)
			1995	*Antonia's Line* (Netherlands)
1972	*The Discreet Charm of the Bourgeoisie* (France)		1996	*Kolya* (Czech Republic)
			1997	*Character* (Netherlands)
1973	*Day for Night* (France)		1998	*Life Is Beautiful* (Italy)
1974	*Amarcord* (Italy)		1999	*All About My Mother* (Spain)
1975	*Dersu Uzala* (Japan/Soviet Union)			

West Germany—Novels include Günter Grass's *The Tin Drum* and Heinrich Böll's *Billiards at Half-Past Nine.*

World—Films include William Wyler's *Ben-Hur* and Billy Wilder's *Some Like It Hot* (both U.S.), Federico Fellini's *La Dolce Vita* (Italy), and Alain Resnais's *Hiroshima, mon amour* (France).

Ideas

Germany—Philosopher Theodor Adorno publishes *Theory of Modern Music.*

Sociologist Ralf Dahrendorf publishes *Class and Class Conflict in Industrial Society.*

U.K.—Physicist C. P. Snow delivers the lecture "The Two Cultures," in which he analyzes the gulf between the scientific and humanistic cultures in England.

U.S.—German-born American psychiatrist Viktor Frankl publishes *Man's Search for Meaning.*

Anthropologist Elizabeth Thomas publishes *The Harmless People.*

French-born American economist Gerard Debreu publishes *Theory of Value*.

Philosopher Saul Aaron Kripke publishes the paper "A Completeness Theorem in Modal Logic."

Military

Indochina—North Vietnamese forces open the Ho Chi Minh Trail, a guerrilla supply route, through Laos and Cambodia to South Vietnam.

Politics

Ceylon—A Buddhist monk assassinates the prime minister of Ceylon.

Cuba—On January 8 Fidel Castro's forces enter Havana unopposed. Castro becomes dictator.

Cyprus—Greek Cypriot leader Archbishop Makarios is allowed to return to Cyprus and become president, in preparation for independence next year.

France—Charles de Gaulle becomes the first president (1959–69) of the Fifth Republic.

Ireland—Eamon de Valera resigns as premier and becomes president.

Iraq—Two insurrections—a military one in Mosul in March and a broad-based one in the Kirkuk region in July—fail to topple the government.

Iraq withdraws from the Baghdad Pact, which is renamed the Central Treaty Organization (CENTO).

Rwanda—In a Hutu uprising thousands of Tutsi are massacred, and the Tutsi monopoly on power is effectively ended.

Singapore—Singapore achieves internal self-government.

Southwest Africa—The Southwest Africa People's Organization (SWAPO) is founded, to advocate independence for Southwest Africa (Namibia).

Soviet Union/U.S.—Soviet premier Nikita Khrushchev and U.S. vice president Richard Nixon engage in the informal "kitchen debate" in the kitchen of an American model home at a Moscow trade show.

Tibet—China crushes a revolt. The Dalai Lama and 100,000 followers go into exile in India.

U.S.—A federal court rules against an Arkansas state law that had closed Little Rock public schools in an attempt to block segregation; the schools are reopened and integrated.

Alaska becomes the 49th state.

Hawaii becomes the 50th state.

Science and Technology

Japan—Physicists Saburo Fukui and Shotaro Miyamoto invent the spark chamber.

Soviet Union—The unmanned spacecraft *Luna 1* makes the first flyby of the Moon; a second craft, *Luna 2*, is the first vehicle to reach the Moon, where it crashes on September 14.

U.K.—Anthropologists Louis and Mary Leakey discover fossil remains of the australopithecine they call *Zinjanthropus boisei* in Olduvai Gorge in present-day Tanzania.

U.S.—Engineers Jack Kilby of Texas Instruments and Robert Noyce of Fairchild Semiconductors invent the microchip.

The antipsychotic drug haloperidol, or Haldol, is first synthesized.

World—Twelve nations sign the Antarctic Treaty, freezing territorial claims and establishing freedom of scientific activity.

Society

Canada/U.S.—The St. Lawrence Seaway is opened, connecting the Atlantic Ocean and the Great Lakes.

India—Indian guru Maharishi Mahesh Yogi introduces transcendental meditation to the West.

Japan—Hurricane Vera kills 4,500 on Honshu Island.

Sony introduces the first transistorized television set.

U.S.—Strikes by the United Steelworkers of America (July–November) and the International Longshoremen's Association (October) are stopped by federal injunctions.

In the quiz show scandal, grand jury and congressional investigations uncover the fixing of many television game shows; Charles Van Doren, winner of *The $64,000 Question*, admits to participating in one of these schemes.

The Xerox Corporation introduces the first xerographic copier for commercial use.

Glen Raven Mills, a North Carolina company, develops the first pantyhose.

Sports

Canada—In hockey Montreal Canadiens player Jacques Plante introduces regular use of the face mask to protect goalkeepers.

Sweden—Ingemaar Johansson defeats Floyd Patterson to become Sweden's first world heavyweight boxing champion.

U.S.—The American Football League is founded.

The Boston Celtics, coached by Red Auerbach, defeat the Los Angeles Lakers to win the National Basketball Association championship; the Celtics will win a record eight consecutive titles (1959–66) and, shortly afterward, two more titles (1968–69).

Jockey Willie Shoemaker wins both the Kentucky Derby and the Belmont Stakes.

1960 Arts and Entertainment

Greece—Jules Dassin directs the film *Never on Sunday*.

Italy—Films include Luchino Visconti's *Rocco and His Brothers*.

Netherlands—Karel Appel wins the Guggenheim Award for abstract painting for *Woman with Ostrich*.

Sweden—Ingmar Bergman releases the film *The Virgin Spring*.

Switzerland—Swiss architect Le Corbusier designs the Monastery La Tourette at Eveux, near Lyons, France.

Uruguay—Mario Benedetti publishes the novel *The Truce* and the essay collection *The Country with the Straw Tail*.

U.S.—Alvin Ailey choreographs *Revelations*.

Chubby Checker starts a dance craze with his recording of "The Twist."

Roy Orbison writes and records his first hit, "Only the Lonely."

The musical *The Fantasticks* by Tom Jones and Harvey Schmidt premieres in New York. Its run will continue to the present.

Films include Billy Wilder's *The Apartment*, Stanley Kubrick's *Spartacus*, and Alfred Hitchcock's *Psycho*.

Novels include John Barth's *The Sot-Weed Factor*, John Updike's *Rabbit, Run*, and Harper Lee's *To Kill a Mockingbird*.

Elliott Carter's String Quartet no. 2 wins a Pulitzer Prize.

Jazz musician John Coltrane debuts at New York's Jazz Gallery.

Ideas

France—The journal *Tel Quel* is founded. It will become a principal vehicle for French theory, which includes philosophical, critical, social, and other strands.

Germany—Film historian Siegfried Kracauer publishes *Theory of Film*.

Philosopher Hans-Georg Gadamer publishes *Truth and Method*.

U.S.—Philosopher Willard Quine publishes *Word and Object*.

Economist Walt Whitman Rostow publishes *The Stages of Economic Growth*.

Journalist William L. Shirer publishes the history *The Rise and Fall of the Third Reich*.

Military

Algeria—The French army suppresses an uprising of French colonists.

Congo, Democratic Republic of—In what will later be called Zaire, civil war erupts (1960–67) as Moise Tshombe leads the Katanga secession. UN peacekeepers arrive and stay until 1964. Joseph Mobutu takes power in a coup.

Iraq—Kurdish forces led by Mustafa al-Barzani begin an insurrection that will last until 1970, resuming in 1974 and continuing to the present.

Laos—A three-way civil war erupts as the government struggles against both the Pathet Lao and the forces of General Phoumi Nosavan. Phoumi captures the capital, Vientiane, in December.

Politics

Africa—Many former European colonies gain independence, including Cameroon (1960–61), Central African Republic, Chad, Democratic Republic of Congo, Republic of Congo, Côte d'Ivoire, Dahomey (now Benin), Gabon, Madagascar, Mali, Mauritania, Niger, Nigeria, Senegal, Somalia, Togo, and Upper Volta (now Burkina Faso).

Ceylon—In what is now Sri Lanka, Sirimavo Bandaranaike becomes the world's first woman prime minister (1960–65; 1970–77), succeeding her assassinated husband, Solomon Bandaranaike.

China—Aid from the Soviet Union to China is stopped as an ideological rift develops between the two countries.

Cuba—Fidel Castro takes power. Relations with the U.S. deteriorate as Castro institutes socialist policies, including nationalization of banks and industries.

El Salvador—President José Maria Lemus is overthrown in a coup and replaced by Colonel Cesar Yanes Urias.

Israel/Argentina—Israeli agents in Argentina capture German Nazi official Adolf Eichmann, who will be tried and executed for war crimes (1962).

Pakistan—Mohammad Ayub Khan becomes dictator (1960–69) in a coup.

South Africa—Police kill 67 and wound 200 unarmed demonstrators in the Sharpeville Massacre, prompting worldwide condemnation and convincing the previously nonviolent African National Congress to turn to guerrilla war.

Soviet Union/U.S.—An American U-2 spy plane is shot down over Soviet territory and its pilot, Francis Gary Powers, captured, raising tensions between the two countries.

U.S.—Democrat John Fitzgerald Kennedy is elected president (1961–63), the first Roman Catholic to attain that office.

The Civil Rights Act of 1960 is passed.

World—The Organization of Petroleum Exporting Countries (OPEC) is founded.

Science and Technology

Canada—At L'anse aux Meadows in Newfoundland, Helge Instad and George Decker discover remains of a Viking settlement dating to the 11th century, indicating that Vikings settled in North America before Columbus.

U.S.—Physicist Luis W. Alvarez discovers resonance particles.

Zoologists Kenneth Norris and John Prescott show that marine mammals (in this case dolphins) use echolocation.

Tiros I, the first weather satellite, is launched.

Physicist Theodore Harold Maiman invents the laser.

Geologist Harry H. Hess proposes the concept of sea-floor spreading, an important idea in plate tectonics.

Polish-American chemist Leo Sternback discovers the antianxiety drug that will be marketed as Librium.

World—The General Conference on Weights and Measures sets a new standard for the meter, based on the spectral line of a krypton isotope.

Society

Japan—Tokyo, with nearly 10 million people, becomes the world's largest city.

U.K.—Enovid 10 becomes the first commercially available contraceptive. Birth control pills, invented by American biologist Gregory Pincus in 1955, contribute to a revolution in sexual mores in many countries.

U.S.—Presidential candidates Vice President Richard Nixon and Senator John Kennedy appear in the first televised presidential debate.

Lunch counter sit-ins protesting racial segregation begin in the South.

Around this time, the "new math," which constructs mathematical relationships from set theory, is introduced in public schools.

Aluminum cans come into use as containers for soft drinks and food products.

The nuclear-powered submarine *USS Nautilus* is the first to travel around the world underwater.

World—The planet's population passes three billion.

Sports

Ethiopia—Barefoot runner Abebe Bikila wins the marathon at the Rome Olympics; he will be the first man ever to win two Olympic marathons (1960, 1964).

U.S.—Rafer Lewis Johnson wins a gold medal in the Olympic decathlon, after receiving a world record 8,683 points in the pre-Olympics decathlon trials.

Track star Wilma Rudolph is the first American woman to win three Olympic gold medals (in her case, the 100 meters, 200 meters, and 400–meter relay).

The Dallas Cowboys football team, coached by Tom Landry, is founded.

Wilt Chamberlain wins the first of four National Basketball Association Most Valuable Player Awards (1960, 1966–68).

1961 Arts and Entertainment

France—Films include François Truffaut's *Jules and Jim* and Alain Resnais's *Last Year at Marienbad.*

U.K.—The Shakespeare Memorial Theatre Company becomes the Royal Shakespeare Company.

Painter Allen Jones exhibits his work in the *Young Contemporaries* pop art exhibition in London.

U.S.—Films include Robert Wise and Jerome Robbins's *West Side Story* and Anthony Mann's *El Cid.*

Folk singer and songwriter Bob Dylan makes his first concert appearance at Gerde's Folk City in Greenwich Village, New York City.

World—Novels include Joseph Heller's *Catch-22* and Walker Percy's *The Moviegoer* (U.S.), Muriel Spark's *The Prime of Miss Jean Brodie* (U.K.), and V. S. Naipaul's *A House for Mr. Biswas* (West Indies).

Ideas

France—Philosopher Michel Foucault publishes *Madness and Civilization: A History of Insanity in the Age of Reason.*

Martinique—Frantz Fanon publishes *The Wretched of the Earth*, which advocates the use of violence in overthrowing colonial domination.

U.K.—Philosopher of law Herbert Lionel Hart publishes *The Concept of Law*.

U.S.—Critic Wayne C. Booth publishes *The Rhetoric of Fiction*.

Historian John Hope Franklin publishes *Reconstruction after the Civil War*.

Sociologist George Homans publishes *Social Behavior: Its Elementary Forms*.

Vatican City—Pope John XXIII issues the encyclicals *Mater et Magistra* and *Pacem in Terris*, in which he calls for social reform, workers' rights, and world peace.

Military

Algeria—French general Raoul Salan leads an army mutiny that fails. Salan then becomes the leader of the Secret Army Organization (OAS), which conducts terrorism in France and Algeria.

Angola—A war of independence (1961–75) begins against Portugal.

Cuba—On April 7, 1,600 Cuban exiles trained by the U.S. Central Intelligence Agency land at the Bay of Pigs. Their attempt to overthrow Castro's government is a disaster and embarrasses President John F. Kennedy, who failed to provide the rebels with expected military support.

A cease-fire halts the civil war in Laos, as the heads of the three rival forces agree to a coalition government headed by Souvanna Phouma.

India—Indian forces capture Goa, ending Portuguese rule.

Nicaragua—Cuban-backed Sandinista guerrillas begin their long insurgency against the U.S.-backed Somoza dynasty's government.

South Vietnam—U.S. aid to South Vietnam expands as President John F. Kennedy increases the number of American military advisers.

Politics

Africa—Rwanda, Sierra Leone, and Tanganyika gain independence.

Congo, Democratic Republic of—On January 17, Prime Minister Patrice Lumumba is assassinated by Katangese secessionist forces.

Dominican Republic—On May 30, dictator Rafael Léonidas Trujillo Molinas (1891–1961) is assassinated.

East Germany—From August 15 to August 17 East Germany builds a wall to separate East Berlin from West German–controlled West Berlin. The Berlin Wall, built to stop the flow of refugees from Communist East Germany, becomes a symbol of the cold war.

Kuwait—The British protectorate ends, but British troops soon arrive to defend the newly independent nation from an Iraqi claim to possession of Kuwait.

South Africa—South Africa leaves the Commonwealth of Nations and becomes a republic.

South Korea—General Park Chung Hee takes power in a coup.

U.S.—The Peace Corps is founded.

World—Burmese diplomat U Thant becomes secretary-general, replacing Dag Hammarskjöld, killed in an air crash.

Yugoslavia—President Tito convenes a meeting of nonaligned nations in Belgrade.

Science and Technology

China—Mathematician Hua Luogeng applies operations research to wheat-harvesting problems.

Soviet Union—On April 12 cosmonaut Yuri Gagarin becomes the first human to reach outer space and orbit Earth.

U.K.—Physicist Jeffrey Goldstone formulates Goldstone's theorem, which predicts the existence of a particle called a Goldstone boson.

U.S.—On May 5, astronaut Alan B. Shepard Jr. becomes the first American in space, in a suborbital flight.

Physicist Albert Ghiorso and colleagues discover the element lawrencium.

Meteorologist Edward N. Lorenz begins to develop the mathematics that will become chaos theory.

The first industrial robot, built by the firm Unimation, is installed in a General Motors plant in New Jersey.

U.S./Israel—Physicist Murray Gell-Mann develops a classification system for the particles called hadrons. He calls the system the Eightfold Way. Israeli physicist Yuval Ne'emen independently develops a similar system around this time.

Society

China—The Museum of the Chinese Revolution opens in Beijing.

France—In Paris designer André Courrèges founds his fashion house. He will make trousers for women popular, as well as knee-length skirts accompanied by high boots.

U.S.—The Congress of Racial Equality (CORE) organizes nonviolent "freedom rides" to oppose segregation in the South; freedom riders meet with racist violence.

World—The human rights organization Amnesty International is founded.

Sports

U.S.—In baseball Yankees outfielder Roger Maris hits 61 home runs, breaking Babe Ruth's 1927 record. Maris's record would be broken by Mark McGwire (70) and Sammy Sosa (66) in 1998.

Auto racer A. J. Foyt wins his first of four victories in the Indianapolis 500 (1961, 1964, 1967, 1977).

1962 Arts and Entertainment

France—Jean-Luc Godard's film *My Life to Live* is released.

Italy—Vittorio De Sica's film *The Condemned of Altona* is released.

Russia—Aleksandr Solzhenitsyn publishes his first novel, *One Day in the Life of Ivan Denisovich*.

U.K.—Novels include Anthony Burgess's *A Clockwork Orange* and Doris Lessing's *The Golden Notebook*.

Sean Connery becomes a star playing James Bond in *Dr. No*, first in a long-running series about the suave superspy.

Michael Tippett's opera *King Priam* premieres.

Benjamin Britten composes *War Requiem*.

U.S.—Novels include Katherine Anne Porter's *Ship of Fools*; Ken Kesey's *One Flew over the Cuckoo's Nest*; and Vladimir Nabokov's *Pale Fire*.

Films include David Lean's *Lawrence of Arabia*, John Ford's *The Man Who Shot Liberty Valance*, Robert Mulligan's *To Kill a Mockingbird*, and John Frankenheimer's *The Manchurian Candidate*.

Edward Albee's first full-length play, *Who's Afraid of Virginia Woolf?*, premieres.

Folk-singing group Peter, Paul, and Mary (Peter Yarrow, Paul Stookey, and Mary Travers) spur interest in folk music, with renditions of songs like Pete Seeger's *If I Had a Hammer*.

Sam Cooke's dance tune "Twistin' the Night Away" promotes mainstream acceptance of soul music.

Ideas

France—Anthropologist Claude Lévi-Strauss publishes *The Savage Mind*.

Nigeria—Critic Obiajunwa Wali publishes the article "The Dead End of African Literature?" in which he denounces domination of African letters by the West.

U.K.—Linguistic philosopher John Langshaw Austin's books *Sense and Sensibilia* and *How to Do Things with Words* are published posthumously.

Anthropologist Victor Turner publishes *Forest of Symbols*.

U.S.—Film critic Andrew Sarris publishes the essay "Notes on the *Auteur* Theory in 1962," in which he outlines his criteria for judging film directors as *auteurs*.

Philosopher of science Thomas Kuhn publishes *The Structure of Scientific Revolutions*.

Psychologist Abraham Maslow publishes *Toward a Psychology of Being*.

American sociologist Neil Smelser publishes *Theory of Collective Behavior*.

American political activist Michael Harrington publishes *The Other America*.

Environmentalist Rachel Carson publishes *Silent Spring*.

Military

Burma—General Ne Win (Maung Shu Maung) takes power in a coup.

China/India—China and India go to war (October–November) over a boundary dispute; China wins.

New Guinea—An Indonesian-backed guerrilla war in West New Guinea forces the Dutch to relinquish the colony, which will become part of Indonesia as West Irian.

Peru—Victor Haya de la Torre wins the presidential election but is prevented from taking office by the military.

Rwanda—Civil war begins as Tutsi military forces try to wrest control from the government elected by the majority Hutus.

South Vietnam—The civil war intensifies, as does U.S. involvement.

Yemen—Civil war begins (1962–70) between the Saudi- and British-backed Imam Muhammad al-Badr and the Egypt- and Syria-backed republican forces of General Abdullah al-Sallah.

Politics

Algeria—On July 3 Algeria wins independence from France.

Burundi—Burundi becomes independent.

Ethiopia—Ethiopia makes Eritrea a province rather than a federal state, prompting a long civil war (1962–91).

Mozambique—FRELIMO, the Mozambique National Liberation Front, is founded by Eduardo Mondlane.

South Africa—Nelson Mandela, head of the guerrilla arm of the African National Congress, is convicted of sabotage; he will remain in prison until 1990.

Soviet Union/U.S./Cuba—The Soviet Union constructs nuclear missile sites in Cuba, prompting a showdown in October with U.S. president John F. Kennedy. A U.S. naval blockade around Cuba and the threat of full-scale nuclear war persuade Soviet leader Nikita Khrushchev to dismantle the missile sites.

Uganda—Uganda becomes independent.

U.S.—A Supreme Court ruling upholds the ban on prayer in public schools.

West Indies—Jamaica and Trinidad become independent.

Western Samoa—Western Samoa becomes independent.

Science and Technology

Japan—Physicians introduce the first flexible fiber-optic endoscope.

Soviet Union—Ukrainian academician Victor M. Glushkov becomes director of the Institute of Cybernetics of the Ukrainian Academy of Sciences. He and the institute contribute to developing the theory and application of computers and informatics in the Soviet Union.

U.K.—Physicist Brian D. Josephson predicts the group of low-temperature electrical results that will become known as the Josephson effects.

German-born British physicist Heinz London develops a technique for inducing very low temperatures with a mixture of helium-3 and helium-4.

U.S./France—American chemist Linus Pauling and Austrian-born French biochemist Émile Zuckerkandl suggest that changes in genetic material can be used as a biological clock to date the time one species separated from another.

U.S.—American physicists Leon Max Lederman, Melvin Schwartz, and Jack Steinberger confirm the existence of two types of neutrino.

Telstar I is launched.

The unmanned spacecraft *Mariner 2* completes the first flyby of Venus.

In February John Glenn becomes the first American to orbit Earth.

Society

Iran—An earthquake kills 10,000.

U.S.—The Students for a Democratic Society (SDS), meeting in Port Huron, Michigan, issues the Port Huron Statement, a manifesto for left-wing revolution.

Walter Cronkite becomes chief television news anchor for CBS (1962–81).

Diet-Rite Cola becomes the first low-calorie soda with a sugar substitute, in this case cyclamate, to be sold nationally.

The Aluminum Corp. of America develops a can with a discardable pull tab.

Color television grows in popularity (1962–66).

Vatican City—The Second Vatican Council (Vatican II) is convened by Pope John XXIII. Completed in 1965 under Pope Paul VI, it institutes many reforms aimed at renewal of the Roman Catholic Church.

Sports

Australia—Rod Laver wins the Grand Slam of tennis as he sweeps all four major championships.

Canada—In hockey, the Toronto Maple Leafs win the Stanley Cup championship.

U.S.—The New York Yankees win their 17th World Series in 27 years as they defeat the San Francisco Giants, four games to three. The next World Series victory for the Yankees will be in 1977.

Wilt Chamberlain is the first professional basketball player to score 100 points in a game (March 2).

The Boston Celtics beat the Los Angeles Lakers four games to three in the National Basketball Association championship. The Celtics will defeat the Lakers for the title seven times in nine years.

1963 Arts and Entertainment

Iran—Forugh Farrokhzad publishes the poetic work *Another Birth*.

U.K.—The Beatles release the song "I Want to Hold Your Hand" to international success; during the year the group will have several songs on the record charts, many simultaneously.

U.S.—On loan from the Louvre, the *Mona Lisa* by Leonardo da Vinci is exhibited in Washington, D.C., and New York. Viewers number nearly one million.

The first large-scale exhibition of pop art is held at the Guggenheim Museum, New York.

World—Notable musical compositions include Hans Werner Henze's Symphony no. 5 (Italy), Benjamin Britten's Cello Symphony (U.K.), Michael Tippett's Concerto for Orchestra (U.K.), Leonard Bernstein's Symphony no. 3 (U.S.).

Notable novels and literary works include Julio Cortázar's *Hopscotch*.(Argentina), Gunter Grass's *Dog Years* (Germany), Yukio Mishima's *The Sailor Who Fell from Grace with the Sea* (Japan), John Le Carré's *The Spy Who Came in from the Cold*, Sylvia Plath's *The Bell Jar* (U.S.), Mary McCarthy's *The Group* (U.S.), Kurt Vonnegut's *Cat's Cradle* (U.S.), and J. D. Salinger's story collection *Raise High the Roof Beam, Carpenters* (U.S.).

Notable films include Federico Fellini's *8 ½* (Italy), Joseph Losey's *The Servant* (U.K.), and Alfred Hitchcock's *The Birds* (U.S.).

Ideas

U.K.—Jessica Mitford publishes *The American Way of Death*.

U.S.—Hannah Arendt publishes *Eichmann in Jerusalem: A Report on the Banality of Evil*.

Military

Algeria—Despite continuing border skirmishes, Algeria and Morocco begin a cease-fire (November 2).

Iraq—Arab-Kurd civil war resumes.

The government is overthrown by the army and is replaced by the All-Military Revolutionary Council.

Politics

Germany—In West Berlin U.S. president Kennedy attacks Communism, pronouncing, "Ich bin ein Berliner."

Greece—Prime Minister Constantine Karamanlis resigns following parliamentary opposition and refusal to recognize 1961 elections.

Malaysia—The country of Malaysia is created from the Federation of Malaya, Singapore, Sarawak, and North Borneo.

Nigeria—Nigeria becomes an independent republic.

Nyasaland—Nyasaland gains self-rule.

South Africa—Black nationalist leader Nelson Mandela is brought to trial.

South Vietnam—President Ngo Dinh Diem is assassinated in U.S.–supported action.

U.K.—Harold Wilson becomes leader of the Labor Party.

U.S.—On November 22, on a trip to Dallas, Texas, president John Fitzgerald Kennedy is assassinated. Vice President Lyndon Baines Johnson is immediately sworn in as president. Presidential assailant Lee Harvey Oswald is shot and killed by businessman Jack Ruby.

World—The U.K., U.S., and Soviet Union sign a nuclear test ban treaty in Moscow.

Science and Technology

Soviet Union—Cosmonaut Valery Bykovsky orbits Earth 82 times.

Lunik IV launch for the Moon misses target by over 5,000 miles (8,500 km.).

U.K.—Scientists develop a radiation-based method for preserving food.

U.S.—Dutch-American astronomer Maarteen Schmidt discovers the first quasar.

Communications satellite *Synacom 1* is launched but soon loses radio contact with Earth.

The tranquilizer Valium (diazepam) by Roche Laboratories is marketed and gains widespread acceptance, eventually becoming the most widely used tranquilizer in the world.

Dr. Michael DeBakey uses an artificial heart in surgery.

Astronaut L. Gordon Cooper circles Earth 22 times in *Mercury* capsule.

The phenomenon of periodic magnetic reversal is discovered, leading to support for the theory of plate tectonics and sea-floor spreading.

Society

India—In Punjab the Bhakra dam is completed after 15 years in construction.

Vatican City—Elizabeth Ann Seton is beatified by Pope John XXIII, the first native-born American to be so honored. She will be canonized in 1975.

U.S.—Civil rights leader Martin Luther King Jr. presents the "I have a dream" speech at a massive demonstration in Washington, D.C.

School segregation ends when South Carolina becomes the final state to admit blacks to the state system. Alabama governor George Wallace ends attempts to block desegregation when, under the presence of National Guard troops, he permits the entry of two African-American students to the University of Alabama.

English replaces Latin as the language of the mass and sacraments following a ruling by the Roman Catholic Ecumenical Council.

World—The word *psychedelic* is first used.

Yugoslavia—An earthquake decimates the city of Skopje.

Sports

U.S.—Jack Nicklaus wins the PGA golf tournament.

The Boston Celtics defeat the Los Angeles Lakers for the NBA basketball championship.

The Los Angeles Dodgers (NL) defeat the New York Yankees (AL) to win the World Series.

1964 Arts and Entertainment

China—The government restricts performances of classical Peking opera.

Italy—Vittorio De Sica's film *Marriage Italian-Style* is released.

Japan—Masaki Kobayashi's film *Kwaidan* is released.

Nicaragua—Ernesto Cardenal publishes the poetry collection *Psalms of Struggle and Liberation*.

U.K.—Joe Orton's first play, *Entertaining Mr. Sloane*, is produced.

Films include American-born director Stanley Kubrick's *Dr. Strangelove* and Guy Hamilton's *Goldfinger*.

U.K./U.S.—Beatlemania crosses from Britain to the U.S., as the British rock band the

Beatles releases six number-one hits, more than any other new act in rock history. The Rolling Stones and other British bands also contribute to the pop music "British invasion."

U.S.—Paintings include Helen Frankenthaler's *Interior Landscape* and Ellsworth Kelly's *Red/Blue*.

Jazz musician John Coltrane releases the album *A Love Supreme*.

Theatrical musicals include Michael Stewart and Jerry Herman's *Hello, Dolly!* and *Fiddler on the Roof*, by Joseph Stein, Sheldon Harnick, and Jerry Bock.

Films include Robert Stevenson's *Mary Poppins*, George Cukor's *My Fair Lady*, and Blake Edwards's *The Pink Panther*.

World—Popular go-go dances in discotheques include the monkey, the watusi, and the frug.

Op art, a nonrepresentational style relying on optical illusions, comes into fashion.

Ideas

Canada—Marshall McLuhan publishes *Understanding Media*.

Psychologist Eric Berne publishes *Games People Play*.

France—Critic Roland Barthes publishes *Elements of Semiology*.

U.S.—Malcolm X, with Alex Haley, publishes *The Autobiography of Malcolm X*.

Critic Leo Marx publishes *The Machine in the Garden: Technology and the Pastoral Ideal in America*.

Historian Richard Hofstadter publishes *Anti-Intellectualism in American Life*.

German-born American political philosopher Herbert Marcuse publishes *One-Dimensional Man*.

Military

Vietnam/U.S.—Spurred by alleged North Vietnamese attacks on the U.S. destroyer *Maddox* in the Gulf of Tonkin, Congress passes the Tonkin Gulf Resolution (August 7), giving President Lyndon Johnson broad powers to conduct war in Vietnam. The resolution permits Johnson to commit large numbers of troops, marking a new, stepped-up phase of the Vietnam War.

Politics

Africa—Malawi and Zambia win independence.

Bolivia—A coup deposes elected president Victor Paz Estenssoro.

Brazil—A coup deposes elected president João Goulart.

Haiti—Dictator François "Papa Doc" Duvalier declares himself president for life.

India—Jawaharlal Nehru, prime minister since independence in 1947, dies; his daughter Indira Gandhi will carry on the family tradition of rule beginning in 1966.

Malta—Malta gains independence.

Kenya—Kenya becomes a republic, with Jomo Kenyatta its first president.

Middle East—The Palestine Liberation Organization (PLO) is founded.

Mozambique—A guerrilla war of independence begins against Portugal (1964–74).

Soviet Union—Nikita Khrushchev loses power and is succeeded by Leonid Brezhnev as party leader and Aleksey Kosygin as premier.

Tanzania—Tanganyika and Zanzibar merge into the United Republic of Tanzania.

U.K.—Labour Party leader Harold Wilson becomes prime minister.

U.S.—Democrat Lyndon Johnson, campaigning on a "Great Society" platform, wins his reelection bid for president against Republican Barry Goldwater. He launches what he calls a "War on Poverty."

Congress passes the Civil Rights Act of 1964, the most sweeping civil rights legislation to date.

Congress passes the Wilderness Act and the Land and Water Conservation Fund Act.

The Supreme Court rules that congressional districts should be roughly equal in population.

The 24th Amendment to the Constitution outlaws the Poll Tax as a requirement for voting.

The President's Commission on the Assassination of President Kennedy issues the Warren Report, finding that assassin Lee Harvey Oswald acted alone. Conspiracy theorists will long doubt the report.

Science and Technology

Australia/Germany—Australian geneticist Pamela Abel and German geneticist T. A. Trautner report evidence that shows the genetic code is universally the same in all living things.

U.K.—Anthopologist Louis Leakey and colleagues announce the discovery of fossils of *Homo habilis* in the Olduvai Gorge of what will become Tanzania.

Physicist Peter Higgs predicts the existence of the particle later called the Higgs boson.

U.S.—The unmanned spacecraft *Mariner 4* completes the first flyby of Mars.

Physicist Arno A. Penzias and astronomer Robert W. Wilson detect cosmic radio-wave background radiation that corroborates the Big Bang theory.

Physicist Murray Gell-Mann proposes the existence of quarks, the most fundamental particles of matter.

Physicists Val L. Fitch and James W. Cronin disprove CP conservation, a previously accepted law related to particles; the more complex CPT theorem results.

Society

China—By now more than 2,000 characters of Chinese script have been simplified by the government, in an effort to reform the complex system of writing.

Japan—The Sacred Hall in Tokyo is opened by members of Risshokoseikai, a Nichiren Buddhist movement.

U.S.—Three civil rights workers—Michael Schwerner, Andrew Goodman, and James Cheney—are murdered in Mississippi; seven Ku Klux Klan members are later convicted for the crime on federal charges.

Students at the University of California at Berkeley launch the free speech movement

(1964–65), which will merge into a larger wave of national student protest against the Vietnam War.

On March 13, Kitty Genovese is killed on the streets of New York City, but none of the people who heard her screaming for 35 minutes assist her or call the police.

A World's Fair is held in New York City.

Sports

U.S.—John Wooden coaches the University of California at Los Angeles (UCLA) basketball team to victory against Duke University for the National Collegiate Athletic Association (NCAA) Division I title. UCLA teams coached by Wooden will win nine more such national championships in the 11 years that follow.

At the Tokyo Olympics American swimmer Don Schollander is the first swimmer ever to win four Olympic gold medals.

Cassius Clay defeats Sonny Liston to become world heavyweight boxing champion. Clay joins the Black Muslims and changes his name to Muhammad Ali.

1965 Arts and Entertainment

China—Historian Wu Han's historical drama *The Dismissal of Hai Rui* receives government condemnation for its covert criticism of Chinese leader Mao Zedong.

France/Italy—Films include Jean-Luc Godard's *Alphaville* (France), Federico Fellini's *Juliet of the Spirits* (Italy), and Michelangelo Antonioni's *Red Desert* (France/Italy).

Italy—Italo Calvino publishes the short-story collection *Cosmicomics*.

U.K.—Films include Roman Polanski's *Repulsion*.

John Fowles publishes the novel *The Magus*.

U.S.—Frank Stella paints *Empress of India*.

Randall Jarrell publishes the poetry collection *The Lost World*.

Polish-born American novelist Jerzy Kosinski publishes his first novel, *The Painted Bird*.

Films include Robert Wise's *The Sound of Music*, then the top-grossing film of all time, and David Lean's *Doctor Zhivago*.

New pop music groups include the Jefferson Airplane, exemplifying the San Francisco sound, and the Supremes, avatar of the Motown sound.

Ideas

Argentina—Argentinean-born leftist revolutionary Ernesto "Che" Guevara publishes *Guerrilla Warfare*, a manual for rebels; he will be executed as a rebel in Bolivia in 1967.

Austria—Psychoanalyst Anna Freud publishes *Normality and Pathology in Childhood*.

China—A trial edition of a comprehensive dictionary, the *Xiandai hanyu cidian*, is published.

France—Marxist philosopher Louis Althusser publishes *For Marx* and *Reading Capital*.

Soviet Union—M. M. Bakhtin publishes *Rabelais and His World*.

U.S.—Sociologist Daniel Patrick Moynihan publishes *The Negro Family*, with his controversial claim that impaired family structures have caused many of the difficulties besetting African-Americans.

Consumer advocate Ralph Nader publishes *Unsafe at Any Speed*, an exposé of the auto industry.

Military

Dominican Republic—U.S. Marines arrive to intervene in a rebellion.

India/Pakistan—India and Pakistan fight a war over rival claims to Kashmir. UN mediation brings a cease-fire.

Vietnam/U.S.—U.S. bombing of North Vietnam fails to bring a quick end to the war. U.S. forces in Vietnam climb to 150,000 by the end of the year.

Politics

Algeria—Houari Boumedienne seizes power in a coup and imprisons former leader Ahmed Ben Bella.

Gambia—Gambia becomes independent.

Indonesia—The government is overthrown in an army revolt. Hundreds of thousands of suspected Communists, some guilty only of being ethnic Chinese, are massacred.

Laos—General Mobutu Sese Seko (Joseph Mobutu) deposes President Joseph Kasavubu in a coup and seizes power.

Maldives—The Maldives become independent.

Rhodesia—Led by Ian Douglas Smith as prime minister, Rhodesia unilaterally declares independence from Britain (November 11) to preserve the white minority's monopoly on power.

Romania—Upon the death of national leader Gheorghe Gheorghiu-Dej, Nicolae Ceausescu succeeds him, becoming general secretary of the Romanian Communist Party.

Singapore—Singapore becomes independent.

U.S.—The Medicare and Medicaid programs, providing government medical insurance for senior citizens and the poor, are instituted.

Science and Technology

China—Mathematician Feng Kang publishes a general convergence theory justifying the finite element method.

Japan—Physicist Yoichiro Nambu and colleagues develop the concept of color charge, a property of quarks.

Soviet Union/U.S.—In March cosmonaut Alexei A. Leonov becomes the first human to walk in space. In June astronaut Edward H. White II will become the first American to walk in space.

U.S.—Paleontologist Elso Sterrenberg Barghoorn discovers the first micro-fossils, remains of prehistoric single-celled organisms.

Psychologists Ronald Melzack and Patrick Ward develop the gate control theory of pain.

Society

Bay of Bengal—From June 1 to June 2 cyclones in the Bay of Bengal kill 40,000 to 45,000 people.

Canada/U.S.—On November 9, a faulty relay in a Canadian power plant leads to one of the biggest electrical blackouts in history, affecting much of southern Canada and the northeastern U.S., including New York City.

Sahel—A period of famines and epidemics begins in the Sahel region, aggravated by civil wars and desertification caused by destructive land use.

U.S.—Muslim minister and black nationalist Malcolm X is assassinated in New York City.

Students liable to the draft begin to show discontent at the increasing pace of the Vietnam War.

Civil rights demonstrations continue, including one led in Selma by Martin Luther King Jr. to secure voting rights for African-Americans.

Cesar Chavez leads the United Farm Workers of America in a strike against table grape growers (1965–70). Supported by a national boycott, "La Huelga" (The Strike) succeeds in forcing change.

African-Americans riot in the Watts section of Los Angeles, leaving 34 dead and more than 1,000 injured (August 11–16).

The National Organization for Women (NOW) is founded.

Hindu teacher Swami Pradhupada founds the International Society of Krishna Consciousness.

World—The Roman Catholic and Eastern Orthodox churches officially remove their anathemas of excommunication from one another.

Sports

U.S.—At about age 59 Cleveland Indian Satchel (Leroy Robert) Paige plays his final major league baseball game, becoming the oldest man to play in a major league professional game.

1966 Arts and Entertainment

Brazil—Jorge Amado publishes the novel *Dona Flor and Her Two Husbands*.

China—Writer Lao She (1899–1966) dies during the Cultural Revolution, reportedly killed for writing works opposed by the state.

France/U.S.—French-born American writer Anaïs Nin publishes her diaries (1966–83), some of them posthumously.

Ireland—Seamus (Justin) Heaney publishes the poetry collection *Death of a Naturalist*.

Israel—Amos Oz publishes the novel *Elsewhere, Perhaps*.

U.K.—The British rock band Cream, which includes guitarist Eric Clapton, is formed.

U.S.—Edward Albee's play *A Delicate Balance* is produced.

Novels include Bernard Malamud's *The Fixer* and John Barth's *Giles Goat-Boy*.

Anne Sexton publishes the poetry collection *Live or Die*.

Samuel Barber's opera *Antony and Cleopatra* premieres.

The television series *Star Trek* premieres (NBC, 1966–69).

World—Films include Billy Wilder's *The Fortune Cookie* (U.S.), Michelangelo Antonioni's *Blow-up* (U.K./Italy), Fred Zinnemann's *A Man for All Seasons* (U.K.), Claude Lelouch's *A Man and a Woman* (France), and Ingmar Bergman's *Persona* (Sweden).

Ideas

Austria—Ethologist Konrad Lorenz publishes *On Aggression*. Lorenz, who pioneered the study of ethology, or animal behavior, links human aggression to animal roots.

France—Psychoanalyst Jacques Lacan publishes *Écrits*, his collected lectures (1966–71).

Germany—Philosopher Theodor Adorno publishes *Negative Dialectics*.

U.S.—Writer Susan Sontag publishes the essay collection *Against Interpretation*.

Gynecologist William Howell Masters and psychologist Virginia Johnson publish *Human Sexual Response*.

Sociologists Peter Berger and Thomas Luckmann publish *The Social Construction of Reality*.

Robert Ardrey publishes *The Territorial Imperative*, which argues that humans, like animals, are driven by territoriality.

Military

Cambodia—The U.S. launches air attacks on Vietcong supply lines through Cambodia.

Namibia—The Namibian War of Independence (1966–88) begins.

Vietnam—More than 400,000 U.S. troops are in Vietnam by year's end.

Politics

Africa—Botswana and Lesotho become independent.

Central African Republic—Jean Bédel Bokassa seizes power in a coup.

China—Mao Zedong leads the Cultural Revolution, a violent movement to restore Communist purity by purging the country of cultural influences considered bourgeois (1966–69).

Dominican Republic—Joaquin Balaguer takes office as the elected president as the civil war ends.

France—Charles de Gaulle, inaugurated for a second seven-year term as president, requests removal of NATO forces from France.

Ghana—A military coup deposes President Kwame Nkrumah.

Guyana—Guyana gains independence.

India—Indira Gandhi, daughter of the late prime minister Jawaharlal Nehru, becomes prime minister.

Indonesia—Suharto succeeds Sukarno as president.

Iraq—Abdul Rahman Arif is elected president.

Israel/Jordan—Israeli and Jordanian forces clash in the Hebron region.

Soviet Union—The Soviet Union receives visits from the leaders of both France and the U.K.

U.K.—Prime minister Harold Wilson announces a "standstill" in wages and prices.

U.S.—Congress passes the Freedom of Information Act.

West Germany—Kurt Georg Kiesinger is elected chancellor.

Science and Technology

China—Seismologists forecast the Xingtai earthquake based on a study of tilt and crustal deformation.

Mathematician Chen Jingrun makes progress on proving the Goldbach conjecture.

Soviet Union—On February 3 the unmanned spacecraft *Luna 9* makes the first soft landing on the Moon.

Society

Italy—Floods rage through northern Italy.

Lebanon—The financial institution Intra Bank fails.

U.K.—The *Times* of London changes its format, putting news rather than advertisements on the front page.

Designer Mary Quant introduces the miniskirt, which becomes a leading fashion.

U.S.—Civil rights activists in the Student Nonviolent Coordinating Committee (SNCC) and Congress of Racial Equality (CORE) begin to abandon their commitment to nonviolence, calling instead for violent separatism under the banner of "Black Power."

Stokely Carmichael becomes head of SNCC.

The Black Panther Party is founded by Huey Newton and Bobby Seale.

World—International Days of Protest are held against U.S. involvement in the Vietnam War.

Supermarket retailing becomes more commonplace in Europe and Asia.

Sports

Australia—In tennis Australia wins the Davis Cup against India, 4–1.

Soviet Union—Wrestler Ivanitski wins the world heavyweight wrestling championship.

Spain—Manuel Santana wins the men's tennis singles title at Wimbledon.

U.K.—England defeats West Germany to win the World Cup in soccer.

U.S.—In baseball the Baltimore Orioles (A.L.) win the World Series in a four-game sweep over the Los Angeles Dodgers (N.L.).

In tennis Billie Jean King wins her first of six women's singles titles at Wimbledon; she will gather a record 20 Wimbledon titles altogether.

1967 Arts and Entertainment

Colombia—Gabriel García Márquez publishes the novel *One Hundred Years of Solitude*.

Nigeria—Musician King Sunny Adé has his first hit song, sung in tribute to the winner of soccer's World Cup.

U.K.—Czech-born British playwright Tom Stoppard's play *Rosencrantz and Guildenstern Are Dead* premieres.

Alan Ayckbourn's play *Relatively Speaking* premieres.

U.S.—*Hair*, one of the first rock musicals, premieres. Book and lyrics are by Gerome Ragni and James Rado, music by Galt MacDermott.

Novels include Richard Brautigan's cult favorite *Trout Fishing in America*.

Aretha Franklin records Otis Redding's song "Respect."

The Monterey Pop Festival in Monterey, California, is held, making stars of Janis Joplin, Jimi Hendrix, and others. Joplin and Hendrix will both die in 1970.

The first "Human Be-In" is held at Golden Gate Park in San Francisco, featuring the music of Jefferson Airplane and the Grateful Dead.

Singer Barbra Streisand holds a concert in Central Park, New York City.

Richard Diebenkorn begins painting the *Ocean Park* series, which he will continue for decades.

Romare Bearden creates the collage *Three Folk Musicians*.

World—Films include Arthur Penn's *Bonnie and Clyde* and Mike Nichols's *The Graduate* (both U.S.), Joseph Strick's *Ulysses* (U.K.), Luis Buñuel's *Belle de jour* (France/Italy), Jacques Tati's *Playtime* (France), and Philippe de Broca's *King of Hearts* (France/U.K.).

Ideas

China—*Quotations from Chairman Mao Zedong* is published. Known as the "little red book," it inspires leftists worldwide.

France—Philosopher Jacques Derrida publishes *Of Grammatology*, in which he introduces the critical approach called deconstructionism.

U.S.—Critic Stanley Fish initiates reader-response criticism with his book *Surprised by Sin: The Reader in "Paradise Lost."*

Philosopher Richard Rorty edits *The Linguistic Turn*.

Sociologist Robert N. Bellah publishes *Civil Religion*.

Military

France—France launches its first nuclear-powered submarine.

Israel—Moshe Dayan is appointed defense minister.

Israel fights the Six-Day War (June 5–11) against Arab neighbors Egypt, Syria, and Jordan. Israel defeats them and occupies the West Bank, East Jerusalem, the Gaza Strip, and the Sinai Peninsula.

Nigeria—Civil war breaks out as Biafra declares its independence. Famine and war will kill about a million Ibo people before the rebels surrender in 1970.

North Vietnam—U.S. bombers attack Hanoi.

Politics

Canada—Queen Elizabeth II visits for Canada's centennial celebration.

French president Charles de Gaulle visits Canada and calls for an independent Quebec.

Greece—An army coup overthrows King Constantine and establishes a ruling junta known as the Greek Colonels.

St. Christopher and Nevis—The British colony becomes independent.

Anguilla breaks away to retain ties with Britain.

U.K.—Harold Wilson reduces the British cabinet from 23 to 21 members.

Thurgood Marshall is the first African-American to be appointed to the Supreme Court.

The 25th Amendment to the Constitution is ratified; it includes a provision for presidential appointment of the vice president should that position be vacated.

Science and Technology

South Africa—Surgeon Christiaan Barnard performs the first human heart transplant.

Soviet Union—The unmanned spacecraft *Venera 4* is the first to enter the atmosphere of Venus.

U.K.—Astronomer Jocelyn Bell discovers the first pulsar, in the constellation Vulpecula.

Biologist John B. Gurden is the first to clone a vertebrate, a South African clawed frog, using the technique of nuclear transplantation.

U.S.—The first deaths of U.S. astronauts in the line of duty occurs on January 27, in a test at Cape Kennedy, Florida. Astronauts Virgil I. Grissom, Edward H. White II, and Roger Chaffee are killed.

Biochemists at the Roswell Park Memorial Institute, in Buffalo, New York, discover the structure of the protein enzyme ribonuclease.

Molecular biologists Walter Gilbert, Benno Müller-Hill, and Mark Ptashne isolate two of the cell substances believed to control the process of making genes either operational or dormant.

Psychologist Aaron T. Beck designs the Beck Depression Inventory, a test measuring the depth of the disorder.

Neurophysiologist Roger W. Sperry, studying split brains, reports on specialization in brain hemispheres.

Society

Brazil—Eastern Brazil is flooded by tropical rains.

Canada—Expo 67 opens in Montreal.

Sweden—Sweden changes from left-side to right-side driving.

U.S.—Tens of thousands of people demonstrate against the Vietnam War at the Lincoln Memorial in Washington, D.C.

Race riots take place in Cleveland, Newark, and Detroit.

Fluoridation, the addition of fluoride to the water supply with the aim of combating tooth decay, has been widely adopted.

The Amana Refrigeration Company introduces the country's first small microwave oven for home use.

Former Harvard professor Timothy Leary inspires students to try mind-altering substances. A comment of his will be adapted to become the counterculture slogan, "Turn on, tune in, and drop out."

World—The UN World Health Organization (WHO) begins a worldwide vaccination campaign to eradicate smallpox. In 1980, after several years with no known cases, the disease will be declared vanquished.

Sports

Australia—Tennis player John Newcombe wins the Wimbledon and U.S. Open singles titles.

Canada—In hockey the Toronto Maple Leafs win the Stanley Cup.

U.S.—Boxer Muhammad Ali is indicted for refusing the draft; he will be forced to stay out of boxing for three years.

Mickey Mantle hits his 500th career home run.

The American Basketball Association (ABA), a second professional basketball league, is formed. It will disband in 1976, with four of its teams merging into the preexisting National Basketball Association (NBA).

In football the first Super Bowl is held, with the Green Bay Packers (National Football League) defeating the Kansas City Chiefs (American Football League), 35–10, at Memorial Coliseum, Los Angeles.

1968 Arts and Entertainment

Czechoslovakia—Václav Havel's play *The Increased Difficulty of Concentration* is produced.

Germany—Karlheinz Stockhausen composes the experimental musical work *Spiral* for soloist with short-wave radio receiver.

Ghana—Ayi Kwei Armah publishes the novel *The Beautyful Ones Are Not Yet Born.*

Poland—Stage director Jerzy Grotowski publishes *Towards a Poor Theatre*, in which he presents his concept of actor-based theater.

U.K.—Rock group Led Zeppelin is formed.

U.S.—Photorealist Chuck Close paints *Self-Portrait.*

The Gateway Arch in St. Louis, Missouri, designed by architect Eero Saarinen, is completed.

Actor James Earl Jones opens on Broadway in the play *The Great White Hope.*

The band Santana, combining Latin sounds with blues, debuts at the Fillmore West in San Francisco.

Joan Didion publishes the essay collection *Slouching Toward Bethlehem.*

World—Films include Mel Brooks's *The Producers* (U.S.), Stanley Kubrick's *2001: A Space*

Odyssey (U.K.), Sergei Bondarchuk's *War and Peace* (Soviet Union), Franco Zeffirelli's *Romeo and Juliet* (U.K./Italy), and Andrej Wajda's *Gates to Paradise* (U.K./West Germany).

Ideas

Brazil—Educator Paolo Freire publishes *Pedagogy of the Oppressed*.

France—Anthropologist Napoléon Chagnon publishes *The Fierce People*.

Philosopher Gaston Bachelard publishes *The Psychoanalysis of Fire*.

Semiotician Christian Metz publishes *Film Language: A Semiotics of the Cinema*.

Italy—Semiotician Umberto Eco publishes *La Struttura assente*, which he will revise and translate into English in 1976 as *A Theory of Semiotics*.

U.S.—Critic Mary Ellmann publishes *Thinking About Women*.

The television series *60 Minutes* premieres (CBS, 1968–).

Vatican City—Pope Paul VI issues the encyclical *Humanae Vitae*, in which he reaffirms the church's condemnation of artificial contraceptives.

Military

North Korea—The U.S. Navy intelligence ship *Pueblo* is captured by North Korea; the crew is eventually released.

South Vietnam—From January 29 to February 25, during the Tet holiday season (the lunar New Year), Vietcong guerrillas and North Vietnamese army units conduct the Tet Offensive, a coordinated assault throughout South Vietnam. The U.S. repulses the offensive, but only with difficulty, convincing many Americans of the need to end U.S. involvement.

On March 16 American troops under William L. Calley Jr. massacre more than a hundred unarmed civilians in the village of My Lai. Calley will be convicted of responsibility for the atrocity in 1971.

Politics

Canada—The Parti Québécois is formed to promote Quebec independence.

Czechoslovakia—Alexander Dubcek is named First Secretary of the Communist Party. His anti-Soviet stance, embodied in the period of democratic renewal known as the "Prague Spring," results in a Soviet crackdown: on August 20 Soviet troops invade Czechoslovakia to crush the democracy movement and reassert control. Hard-liner Gustav Husák replaces Dubcek as first secretary.

Mauritius—Mauritius becomes an independent state.

U.K.—The government restricts immigration from India, Pakistan, and the West Indies.

U.S.—Senator Robert F. Kennedy, then running for the Democratic presidential nomination, is assassinated in Los Angeles. Sirhan Sirhan, a Jordanian, is later convicted of the crime.

President Lyndon Johnson, a Democrat, declines to run for reelection. Republican Richard Nixon defeats Democrat Hubert Humphrey in the presidential election.

Science and Technology

Iran—Scholar Seyyed Hossein Nasr publishes *Science and Civilization in Islam*, which stimulates a renewed interest in science in Muslim countries.

Japan—The first research institute opens in Tsukuba Science City, a planned center for scientific research.

Pakistan/U.S.—Pakistani physicist Abdus Salam, with American physicists Steven Weinberg and Sheldon L. Glashow, propose the electroweak theory.

U.S.—Astronomers discover a pulsar or neutron star in the Crab Nebula, corroborating the theory that neutron stars form in the aftermath of supernovae.

During the *Apollo 8* mission, astronauts Frank Borman, James A. Lovell Jr., and William A. Anders are the first humans to orbit the Moon and the first to see its dark side.

Chemical geneticist Sol Speigelman announces the first method of observing, in a test tube, molecular events associated with evolutionary change.

Surgeons Charles Dotter and Melvin Judkins introduce the surgical technique angioplasty.

Paleontologist Robert Bakker proposes that dinosaurs were warm-blooded.

Physicists trap neutrinos emanating from the Sun in an underground tank in South Dakota.

Society

Poland—Protests are staged against government interference in cultural affairs.

U.K.—The government drops a plan to build London's third airport at Stansted.

U.S.—On April 4 Martin Luther King Jr. is assassinated in Memphis, Tennessee, inciting riots in many cities.

The Kerner Commission, organized to report on recent urban riots, states that racial divisions are producing in effect two nations within the U.S.

Large-scale protests are launched nationwide, particularly on college campuses, against the Vietnam War. At the Democratic National Convention in Chicago, violence results when police confront demonstrators. (*see* **1969**).

Jacuzzi Bros., a farm pump manufacturer, demonstrates the Jacuzzi whirling bath.

The emergency telephone number 911 is first used, in New York State. It will become widespread across the country.

Former First Lady Jacqueline Kennedy marries Greek tycoon Aristotle Onassis.

World—The midiskirt, an attempt to replace the miniskirt, flops.

Sports

Mexico—Mexico City hosts the Summer Olympics. The U.S. takes 45 gold medals and the Soviet Union takes 29.

U.K.—In cricket England's team under M. C. Cowdrey wins the West Indies series.

U.S.—Peggy Fleming wins the only U.S. gold medal at the Winter Olympics.

Forward Pass wins the Kentucky Derby and the Preakness Stakes.

Southern California defeats Indiana, 14–3, in college football's Rose Bowl game.

1969 Arts and Entertainment

Canada—Singer and songwriter Joni Mitchell (Roberta Joan Anderson) releases the album *Clouds*, containing her own version of her composition "Both Sides Now"; the song was also released the previous year, when it was sung by American Judy Collins.

U.K.—The absurdist television comedy series *Monty Python's Flying Circus* (1969–74) premieres.

U.S.—The Dance Theater of Harlem is founded in New York City.

John Berryman publishes the poetry collection *The Dream Songs*.

Novels include Kurt Vonnegut's *Slaughterhouse Five* and Philip Roth's *Portnoy's Complaint*.

The rock band Creedence Clearwater Revival releases "Proud Mary."

The television series **Sesame Street** (PBS, 1969–) premiers.

World—Films include George Roy Hill's *Butch Cassidy and the Sundance Kid*, Dennis Hopper's *Easy Rider*, and John Schlesinger's *Midnight Cowboy* (all U.S.); Karel Reisz's *Isadora* (U.K.); Eric Rohmer's *My Night at Maud's* and François Truffaut's *The Wild Child* (both France); and Federico Fellini's *Fellini Satyricon* (Italy).

Ideas

France—Bulgarian-born French linguist Julia Kristeva publishes *Semeiotike: Recherches pour une semanalysis*.

Algerian-born French feminist scholar Hélène Cixous publishes *Dedans*.

Critic Tzvetan Todorov introduces the term *narratology* in *Grammaire du Décaméron*.

U.K.—Latvian-born political philosopher Isaiah Berlin publishes *Four Essays on Liberty*.

U.S.—Philosopher Stanley Cavell publishes *Must We Mean What We Say?*

Philosopher Willard Quine publishes *Philosophy of Logic*.

Military

South Vietnam—The first U.S. troops withdraw from Vietnam; 75,000 will leave by year's end.

Politics

Czechoslovakia—A new federal government is initiated.

France—Georges Pompidou is elected president.

Japan/U.S.—The U.S. agrees to return the Ryukyu Islands, including Okinawa, in 1972.

Northern Ireland—Fighting breaks out between Roman Catholics and Protestants; Britain sends troops to attempt to quell the disorders.

Pakistan—President Ayub Khan resigns and is replaced by Aga Muhammad Yahya Khan.

Palestine—Yasir Arafat is elected chairman of the Executive Committee of the Palestine

Liberation Organization (PLO). Arafat shifts the main PLO guerrilla forces to Jordan.

Science and Technology

Japan—Japanese geologists discover meteorites on the Antarctic ice cap.

Soviet Union—The *Soyuz 4* and *Soyuz 5* spacecraft are the first manned vehicles to dock in space.

U.S.—On July 20 astronaut Neil Armstrong, commander of the *Apollo 11* mission, becomes the first human to set foot on the Moon.

Physicist Albert Ghiorso and colleagues discover element 104, rutherfordium.

The first precursor of the Internet is the Advanced Research Project Agency Net (ARPANET), a computer communications network initiated by the Department of Defense.

Society

Norway—Norwegian explorer Thor Heyerdahl sails from Morocco to Barbados in the *Ra II*, a reed boat made in ancient Egyptian fashion, to show that such a voyage was possible in antiquity.

U.K.—Student uprisings force the closing of the London School of Economics.

U.S.—The *Saturday Evening Post*, founded in 1821, suspends publication.

The Woodstock rock music festival is held near Bethel, New York (August 15–19). Drawing about 300,000 people, the event becomes a symbol of the 1960s youth counterculture.

Gays and lesbians violently resist a police raid at the Stonewall Tavern in New York City, marking the birth of the country's gay liberation movement.

The Chicago Eight, eight radical leaders accused of conspiracy to incite riots at the 1968 Democratic convention in Chicago, go on trial. Reduced to the Chicago Seven when Bobby Seale's case is treated separately, they will be acquitted of the conspiracy charges in 1970, though some are convicted on other charges.

Pantsuits for women come into vogue.

World—The inflation rate begins to grow worldwide.

Sports

Soviet Union—The Soviet Union wins World and European amateur hockey titles in Stockholm, Sweden.

U.S.—The U.S. tennis team keeps the Davis Cup, defeating Romania, 5–0.

Lew Alcindor (later Kareem Abdul-Jabbar), playing for the University of California at Los Angeles, emerges as one of basketball's greatest players.

The New York Mets win their first World Series, defeating the Baltimore Orioles five games to three.

1970 Arts and Entertainment

Chile—José Donoso publishes the novel *The Obscene Bird of Night*.

U.K.—The heavy-metal band Black Sabbath releases the album *Paranoid*.

U.S.—The folk singing duo Paul Simon and Art Garfunkel release the song and album "Bridge Over Troubled Water."

The band Crosby, Stills, Nash & Young releases its first album, *Deja Vu*.

Philip Pearlstein creates paintings of nude, minutely realistic figures in domestic surroundings.

Eliot Porter publishes the photograph collection *Appalachian Wilderness*.

Artist Robert Smithson completes his earthwork piece *Spiral Jetty*.

The television series *The Mary Tyler Moore Show* premieres (CBS, 1970–77).

World—Films include Robert Altman's *M*A*S*H* (U.S.); François Truffaut's *Bed and Board* (France); Elio Petri's *Investigation of a Citizen beyond Suspicion* (Italy); and Akira Kurosawa's *Dodeskaden* (Japan).

Ideas

Australia—Feminist writer Germaine Greer publishes *The Female Eunuch*.

India—Mystic and poet Sri Chinmoy Ghose publishes *Yoga and the Spiritual Life*.

U.S.—Philosopher Thomas Nagel publishes *The Possibility of Altruism*. He will also be known for his paper "What Is It Like to Be a Bat?"

Social critic Alvin Toffler publishes *Future Shock*.

Swiss-born American psychiatrist Elisabeth Kübler-Ross publishes *On Death and Dying*.

Feminist writer Kate Millett publishes *Sexual Politics*.

Military

Cambodia—The Khmer Rouge, Communist guerrillas, wage civil war against the government (1970–75).

Jordan—In a civil war, Jordan expels the Palestine Liberation Organization (PLO), which relocates in Lebanon.

Nigeria—The Biafran Civil War ends with secessionist Biafra surrendering.

Politics

Albania—Albania forms a trade agreement with China.

Cambodia—Prince Sihanouk is deposed in a U.S.–backed coup by Lon Nol, who will be president from 1972 to 1975.

Chile—Salvador Allende is elected president, becoming the world's first Marxist head of state to win office by democratic means. He will be overthrown in 1973.

Gambia—Gambia becomes a republic.

Jordan—An assassination attempt on King Hussein fails.

Poland—Riots result when First Secretary Wladyslaw Gomulka raises prices on foodstuffs; he is replaced as first secretary by Edward Gierek.

U.K.—In national elections, Conservative Edward Heath defeats Harold Wilson to become prime minister.

U.S.—Harry A. Blackmun is appointed to the Supreme Court.

Science and Technology

China/Japan—China and Japan launch their first artificial satellites.

U.K.—Physicist Stephen Hawking suggests that black holes may evaporate over long periods.

U.S.—Large reflecting telescopes are completed at Kitt Peak, Arizona, and Mauna Kea, Hawaii.

Archaeologist J. M. Adovasio claims to have discovered 19,000-year-old human remains at Meadowcroft, Pennsylvania, much earlier than previously known sites. The claim will remain controversial.

Sri Lanka–born American biochemist Cyril Ponnamperuma discovers several kinds of amino acids in a meteorite, showing amino acids have arisen beyond the earth.

Physicist Albert Ghiorso and colleagues discover element 105, hahnium.

The *Apollo 13* lunar mission (April 11–17) is aborted when an oxygen tank malfunctions; the crew returns to Earth safely.

Intel scientist Ted Hoff invents the microprocessor.

Society

Bangladesh—Cyclones kill up to 500,000 people.

France—The Concorde supersonic passenger jet reaches speeds of up to twice the speed of sound.

Japan—Expo 70, a world exhibition, opens in Osaka.

Peru—Earthquakes, landslides, and floods kill 30,000.

U.S.—In May four students are killed by U.S. National Guard troops during an antiwar demonstration at Kent State University in Ohio.

Unemployment rises, growing to 5.8 percent by the end of the year.

The first Earth Day, promoting environmental awareness, is celebrated (on April 22 in most places).

Vatican City—An assassination attempt on Pope Paul VI in the Philippines fails.

Sports

Australia—Tennis player Margaret Smith Court wins the Grand Slam.

U.S.—The Boston Bruins win the Stanley Cup hockey championship.

Joe Frazier becomes the official world heavyweight boxing champion.

The American Football League becomes the American Football Conference of the National Football League (NFL); the old NFL roster becomes the National Football Conference.

1971 Arts and Entertainment

U.K.—Rock singer Rod Stewart releases the song "Maggie May."

British television contributes many dramatic programs to the U.S. public television series *Masterpiece Theatre*.

U.S.—Robb Pendleton and Jonathan Wolken found the Pilobolus Dance Theater.

David Rabe's plays *The Basic Training of Pavlo Hummel* and *Sticks and Bones* premiere.

Willem de Kooning paints *Amityville*.

Artist Chris Burden has himself shot in the left arm by a friend for the artwork called *Shoot*.

Singer and songwriter Carole King releases the album *Tapestry*.

American singer and songwriter Jim Morrison, leader of the rock band the Doors, is found dead in Paris.

The Philly Sound, a variety of soul music, develops in Philadelphia; groups include the Spinners and the Stylistics.

Films include William Friedkin's *The French Connection* and Peter Bogdanovich's *The Last Picture Show* (both U.S.), Sam Peckinpah's *Straw Dogs* (U.K.), Louis Malle's *Murmur of the Heart* (France), Nicolas Roeg's *Walkabout* (Australia), and Bernardo Bertolucci's *The Conformist* (France/Italy/West Germany).

The TV situation comedy *All in the Family* (CBS, 1971–79) premieres.

Ideas

France—Philosopher Jean-François Lyotard publishes *Discours, figure*.

U.S.—Belgian-born American deconstructionist critic Paul de Man publishes his first book, *Blindness and Insight*.

Behaviorist psychologist B. F. Skinner publishes *Beyond Freedom and Dignity*.

Feminist scholars Vivian Gornick and Barbara K. Moran edit *Woman in Sexist Society: Studies in Power and Powerlessness*.

Military

Indochina—Fighting in the Vietnam War spreads from Vietnam to Laos and Cambodia. The U.S. bombs Vietcong supply lines in Cambodia and conducts large-scale bombing of North Vietnam.

Politics

Australia—Algeria seizes majority control of French oil and gas interests in the country.

Neville Thomas Bonner is the first Aboriginal Australian elected to his country's parliament.

Bangladesh—East Pakistan wins independence from Pakistan as Bangladesh, with military help from India.

China—The UN votes to allow the mainland People's Republic of China into the UN, while expelling Taiwan (the Republic of China).

Minister of Defense Lin Baio (Piao) reputedly makes a coup attempt on Chinese leader Mao Zedong; fleeing China, Lin is killed in an air crash.

Haiti—Jean-Claude "Baby Doc" Duvalier succeeds as dictator upon the death of his father, François Duvalier.

Switzerland—Women win the right to vote.

U.S.—The 26th Amendment to the Constitution, lowering the voting age to 18, is ratified.

Congress appoints the National Railroad Passenger Corporation, or Amtrak, to assume all U.S. passenger train business.

President Richard Nixon orders a 90-day freeze on wages and prices to curb inflation.

Uganda—Idi Amin leads a coup against President Milton Obote and becomes Uganda's dictator (1971–80).

Science and Technology

China—Chinese plant breeders are the first to apply the haploid breeding procedure to wheat.

Soviet Union—*Salyut I*, the first Earth-orbiting space station, is launched.

U.K.—Paleontologist Harry Whittington begins a major revision of Charles Walcott's interpretation of the Cambrian fossils of the Burgess Shale. Colleagues Simon Conway Morris and Derek Briggs will contribute to the revision.

Physicist Stephen Hawking proposes the existence of mini black holes formed when the universe was created.

Ethologist Jane Goodall publishes *In the Shadow of Man*.

U.S.—Entomologist Edward O. Wilson publishes *The Insect Societies*.

Society

U.K.—A postal strike leaves the public without mail for 47 days.

U.S.—Psychiatrist Daniel Ellsberg leaks the "Pentagon Papers" to the press. The classified documents on early U.S. involvement in the Vietnam War intensify popular opposition to the war and earn Ellsberg criminal charges (to be dropped in 1973).

An uprising in New York's Attica prison results in the deaths of 10 guards and 32 prisoners.

Television commercials for cigarettes are banned, though print advertisements remains legal.

Chicago's Union Stockyards close, ending the city's century-old role in the meat business.

The insecticide DDT (dichloro-diphenyltrichloroethane) is banned nationwide for all but essential uses.

Dioxin waste from a herbicide factory spills in Times Beach, Missouri. The toxic chemical disaster forces complete evacuation of the town by 1983.

Texas Instruments markets the first portable calculator, which weighs 2 $1/2$ pounds and costs $150.

Look magazine ceases publication.

Sports

Brazil—Soccer star Pelé retires from international competition, having played in four World Cup finals and scored 97 goals in 110 games.

Canada—In hockey, the Montreal Canadiens defeat the Chicago Blackhawks to win the Stanley Cup.

China—China hosts the American table-tennis team, beginning a new era of warmer relations with the U.S.

U.S.—In football, the Baltimore Colts defeat the Dallas Cowboys, 16–2, to win the Super Bowl.

Joe Frazier defeats challenger Muhammad Ali to retain the world heavyweight boxing championship.

In baseball's World Series, the Pittsburgh Pirates beat the Baltimore Orioles, four games to three.

1972 Arts and Entertainment

U.K.—Margaret Drabble publishes *The Needle's Eye*.

U.S.—The World Trade Center, designed by architect Minoru Yamasaki, opens in New York City. It is the world's tallest building until next year, when the Sears Tower in Chicago displaces it.

The musical *Grease* opens on Broadway, spawning a 1950s nostalgia craze.

The rock group the Eagles releases its self-titled debut album.

Sam Shepard's play *The Tooth of Crime* premieres.

Andy Warhol paints *Mao*, in silkscreen and paint on canvas.

Films include Francis Ford Coppola's *The Godfather* (U.S.), Peter Medak's *The Ruling Class* (U.K.), Robert Bresson's *Four Nights of a Dreamer* (France), Werner Herzog's *Aguirre, the Wrath of God* (West Germany), and Ingmar Bergman's *Cries and Whispers* (Sweden).

Ideas

Cameroon—Writer Mongo Beti publishes the political essay *The Plundering of Cameroon*.

France—Critic René Girard publishes *Violence and the Sacred*.

Philosopher Simone de Beauvoir publishes *The Coming of Age*.

U.S.—Political scientists Sidney Verba and Norman Nie publish *Participation in America: Political Democracy and Social Equality*.

Military

U.S.—The military draft is phased out, with the armed forces becoming all-volunteer.

Vietnam—The U.S. mines North Vietnamese ports.

Politics

Australia—Gough Whitlam leads the Australian Labour Party to victory in national elections, ending 23 years of Liberal-Country Party government.

Canada—The government moves to institute limited control over foreign investments in the nation's economy and resources.

China/U.S.—U.S. President Richard Nixon visits Chinese leader Mao Zedong in Beijing, marking a warming of relations between the two nations.

East Germany—Erich Honecker succeeds Walter Ulbricht as head of the country's Communist Party.

Europe—Ireland, the U.K., and Denmark agree to full membership in the European Economic Community, while Norway rejects entry.

Japan—Kakuei Tanaka is elected premier.

New Zealand—Norman E. Kirk leads the Labour Party to victory over the National Party, which had been in power for 12 years.

Northern Ireland—On Bloody Sunday, January 30, British troops fire on Catholic demonstrators in Londonderry, killing several. The British government suspends Northern Ireland's constitution and assumes direct rule.

Philippines—Ferdinand Marcos assumes near-dictatorial powers, in part in response to a growing Communist insurgency.

Soviet Union/U.S.—The SALT I treaty (for Strategic Arms Limitation Talks) is signed between the Soviet Union and U.S.

Sri Lanka—Ceylon changes its name to Sri Lanka and becomes a republic.

U.S.—On June 17 burglars affiliated with Republican President Richard Nixon's reelection committee break into Democratic Party headquarters at the Watergate complex in Washington, D.C. Investigation of the crime escalates into a scandal that will force Nixon to resign in 1974.

Alabama governor George Wallace, a candidate for the Democratic presidential nomination, is shot by attempted assassin Arthur Bremer and paralyzed.

Richard Nixon is reelected president over Democratic opponent George McGovern.

Congress passes the Equal Rights Amendment (ERA), forbidding sex discrimination, but the ERA will fail to be ratified and expire in 1982.

Science and Technology

U.K./U.S.—The first computerized axial tomography (CAT or CT) scanner goes into operation. The inventors are British engineer Godfrey Hounsfield and American physicist Allan Cormack.

U.S.—Physicist Murray Gell-Mann establishes the theory of quantum chromodynamics (QCD).

ARPANET developers (*see* **1969**) introduce electronic mail, or e-mail.

Apollo 17, launched December 7, is the last manned mission to the Moon.

Paleontologists Niles Eldredge and Stephen Jay Gould publish their evolutionary theory of punctuated equilibrium.

Society

Nicaragua—An earthquake in Managua kills at least 5,000 people.

Sierra Leone—The largest diamond (969.8 carats) in history, the Star of Sierra Leone, is discovered.

U.K.—Coal industry workers stage a national strike.

U.S.—The Dow Jones industrial stock market index closes above the 1,000 mark for the first time.

Life magazine ceases publication.

Journalist Gloria Steinem and others found *Ms.* magazine.

Militant activist Angela Davis is acquitted of murder-conspiracy charges.

Sports

Germany—The Munich Summer Olympics are put in turmoil when Palestinian terrorists kill two Israeli Olympic athletes and take nine other athletes hostage, all of them killed in a shoot-out with West German soldiers and police.

Japan—The Winter Olympics are held at Sapporo. The Soviet team wins eight gold medals.

U.S.—Professional baseball players strike, delaying the season opening by 13 days.

Baseball player Roberto Clemente, who this year becomes the 11th player to reach 3,000 base hits, dies in a plane crash while aiding victims of the earthquake in Managua, Nicaragua.

American chess player Bobby Fischer defeats Soviet champion Boris Spassky for the world title.

1973 Arts and Entertainment

Soviet Union—Publication of Soviet writer Aleksandr Solzhenitsyn's nonfiction work *The Gulag Archipeligo* (1973–75) begins outside the Soviet Union.

U.K.—Composer Benjamin Britten's *Death in Venice* premieres.

The rock band Pink Floyd releases the album *Dark Side of the Moon*.

U.S.—The Sears Tower, then the tallest building in the world, opens in Chicago. Its designers are Skidmore, Owings & Merrill.

Novels include Thomas Pynchon's *Gravity's Rainbow* and Erica Jong's *Fear of Flying*.

Adrienne Rich publishes the poetry collection *Diving into the Wreck*.

Singer-songwriter Jim Croce (b. 1943) dies in a plane crash at the height of his fame for such songs as "Time in a Bottle."

World—Plays include Peter Shaffer's *Equus* (U.K.), Alan Ayckbourn's *Absurd Person Singular* (U.K.), and Lanford Wilson's *Hot l Baltimore* (U.S.).

Films include George Roy Hill's *The Sting* and William Friedkin's *The Exorcist* (U.S.), Bernardo Bertolucci's *Last Tango in Paris* (France/Italy), François Truffaut's *Day for Night* (France), Djibril Diop Mambety's *Touki-Bouki* (Senegal), and Ingmar Bergman's *Scenes from a Marriage* (Sweden).

Ideas

Peru—Catholic theologian Gustavo Gutierrez coins the term *liberation theology*.

U.S.—Anthropologist Clifford Geertz publishes *The Interpretation of Cultures*.

Critic Harold Bloom publishes *The Anxiety of Influence*.

Philosopher David Lewis publishes *Counterfactuals*.

Military

Middle East—The Yom Kippur War, pitting Israel against Egypt, Syria, Iraq, Jordan, and Libya, begins and ends.

U.S.—A cease-fire ends direct involvement of U.S. ground forces in the Vietnam War.

Politics

Afghanistan—The last king, Muhammad Zahir Shah, is overthrown in a coup led by Muhammad Daoud Khan, who proclaims a republic.

Argentina—Former dictator Juan D. Perón is elected president, with wife Isabel as vice president.

Bahamas—Independence from Britain is achieved.

Chile—Marxist president Salvador Allende is overthrown by a military junta aided by the CIA; right-wing leader General Augusto Pinochet becomes president.

Europe—Great Britain, Ireland, and Denmark join European Common Market.

Germany—East and West Germany establish diplomatic relations.

Greece—The ruling military junta officially abolishes the monarchy and proclaims a republic.

Iran—Mohammad Reza Shah Pahlavi nationalizes the oil industry.

U.S.—Spiro Agnew resigns as vice president and pleads no contest to a charge of income tax evasion; Gerald Ford replaces him.

In *Roe v. Wade*, the Supreme Court establishes women's constitutional right to abortion.

Science and Technology

Pakistan—Physicist Abdus Salam suggests some of the implications of a Grand Unified Theory (GUT) uniting the strong, weak, and electromagnetic interactions. The first GUT will be presented in 1974.

Soviet Union—The unmanned spacecraft *Mars 2* and *3* are the first to enter the atmosphere of Mars.

U.K.—Scottish scientists isolate endorphins, the brain's natural painkillers.

U.S.—Biochemists Stanley Cohen and Ernest Boyer begin the age of genetic engineering by recombining genes within bacteria.

Skylab, the first American space station, is launched into Earth's orbit on May 14.

The unmanned spacecraft *Pioneer 10* is the first to fly past Jupiter.

Paleontologist John Ostrom argues that birds are direct descendants of dinosaurs.

Society

U.S.—Chicago Board Options Exchange (CBOE) opens.

Tom Bradley is elected the first African-American mayor of Los Angeles.

A committee of grocers and manufacturers recommends a Universal Product Code (UPC) for all supermarket items, to permit electronic scanning of prices.

Militant Native Americans occupy Wounded Knee, South Dakota.

World—Spearheaded by Arab nations angry at Western support for Israel in the Yom Kippur War, the Organization of Petroleum Exporting Countries (OPEC) imposes an oil embargo that leads to an energy crisis in the industrialized world.

Sports

U.S.—Baseball's American League introduces the designated hitter.

Outfielder Willie Mays retires from baseball with 660 home runs, placing him 3rd on the all-time list behind Babe Ruth (714) and Hank Aaron (713 at the end of the 1973 season).

In a "Battle of the Sexes" tennis match, Billie Jean King beats Bobby Riggs.

In boxing, George Foreman wins the world heavyweight championship from Joe Frazier.

Halfback O. J. Simpson sets a one-year rushing mark of 2,003 yards.

1974 Arts and Entertainment

Cuba—Alejo Carpentier publishes the novel *Reasons of State*.

France—Oliver Messaien's *Des canyons aux étoiles...* for orchestra is performed.

Hungary—Hungarian-born composer György Ligeti's *San Francisco Polyphony* for orchestra premieres in West Germany.

South Africa—Athol Fugard's play *Sizwe Bansi Is Dead* is produced.

Soviet Union—Dmitry Shostakovich's String Quartet no. 15 is performed.

Ballet dancer Mikhail Baryshnikov defects to the West.

U.K.—Tom Stoppard's play *Travesties* is produced.

Norman Foster designs the Willis, Faber and Dumas Building, Ipswich.

Alan Ayckbourn's comedy trilogy *The Norman Conquests* premieres.

U.S.—Ed Paschke paints *Minnie*.

John de Andrea creates the superrealist sculpture *Freckled Woman*.

Jasper Johns creates the oil, encaustic, and collage work *Corpse and Mirror*.

Dance works include George Balanchine's *Coppelia* and Eliot Feld's *Sephardic Songs*.

Annie Dillard publishes the essay collection *Pilgrim at Tinker Creek*.

Stephen King publishes his first novel, *Carrie*.

World—Films include Francis Ford Coppola's *The Godfather, Part II* and Roman Polanski's *Chinatown* (both U.S.), Rainer Werner Fassbinder's *Effi Briest* (West Germany) and Federico Fellini's *Amarcord* (Italy).

Ideas

Belgium—Feminist theorist Luce Irigaray publishes *Speculum of the Other Woman*.

France—Bulgarian-born French linguist Julia Kristeva publishes *Revolution in Poetic Language*.

U.S.—Political theorist Robert Nozick publishes *Anarchy, State, and Utopia*.

French-born American writer Jacques Barzun publishes *Clio and the Doctors* and *The Use and Abuse of Art*.

Military

Cyprus—Turkey invades and establishes the Turkish Republic of Northern Cyprus.

Israel—Palestinian guerrilla raids are met with Israeli military attacks on their reputed bases. In May three Palestinian guerrillas take 190 Israeli children hostage; in fighting with Israeli troops, 20 children and the guerrillas die. Israel retaliates with bombing raids on Palestinian refugee camps in Lebanon.

Politics

Cyprus—Archbishop Makarios is overthrown in a Greece-backed coup but soon returns from exile.

Ethiopia—Mengistu Haile Mariam leads a coup deposing Emperor Haile Selassie I; Mengistu takes power as dictator.

France—Valéry Giscard d'Estaing becomes president.

Greece—The military regime known as the Greek Colonels resigns. Constantine Karamanlis becomes prime minister.

Grenada—Grenada gains independence from Britain.

Guinea-Bissau—Guinea-Bissau, formerly Portuguese Guinea, gains independence from Portugal.

Israel—In April Golda Meir resigns as prime minister and is succeeded by Yitzhak Rabin.

In November the government imposes austerity measures and devalues the pound by 43 percent in an attempt to fight inflation.

Japan—Prime Minister Kakuei Tanaka resigns under suspicion of corruption.

Middle East—The Arab countries introduce the currency unit Arcru to recycle oil income.

Portugal—An almost bloodless coup overthrows Prime Minister Marcello Caetano and establishes military junta rule.

U.K.—Labour Party leader Harold Wilson becomes prime minister at the head of a Labour-Liberal coalition.

U.S.—On March 1 seven White House officials are indicted in the Watergate scandal. On July 24 the Supreme Court orders the White House to hand over presidential tapes. On July 30, the House Judiciary Committee votes three articles of impeachment against President Richard Nixon.

On August 9, under pressure from the Watergate scandal, President Richard Nixon becomes the first president in the nation's history to resign. Vice president Gerald Ford succeeds and, on September 8, pardons him.

President Gerald Ford puts forward his economic program to "Whip Inflation Now" (WIN); it proves unsuccessful.

West Germany—Social Democrat Helmut Schmidt becomes chancellor.

Science and Technology

Africa—Ministers of 32 African nations participate at the CASTAFRICA conference, where they frame recommendations to stimulate research in science and technology.

Australia/U.K.—The Anglo-Australian telescope, located on Sliding Spring Mountain in Australia and owned jointly by Britain and Australia, is commissioned.

Belgium—Mathematician Pierre Deligne proves the last of French mathematician André Weil's conjectures concerning algebraic topology.

China—Mathematician Hou Zhending contributes to the study of Markov processes.

India—India detonates its first nuclear bomb.

Soviet Union/U.S.—Scientists in both countries discover element 106, unnil-hexium.

U.S.—Astronomer Charles Kowal discovers Leda, the 13th known satellite of Jupiter. In 1975 he will find a 14th satellite.

Scientists F. Sherwood Rowland and Mario Molina show that release of chlorofluorocarbons (CFCs), such as Freon, degrades the atmosphere's ozone layer and permits a greater amount of harmful ultraviolet radiation to reach Earth.

Paleontologist Donald Johanson discovers the partial skeleton of Lucy, an australopithecine dating back more than 3 million years.

Physicists Samuel C. C. Ting and Burton Richter independently discover the J-Psi particle.

Physicists Sheldon L. Glashow and Howard Georgi set forth the first grand unified theory (GUT), uniting the strong, weak, and electromagnetic interactions.

Society

Australia—A cyclone destroys 90 percent of Darwin in northern Australia.

India—A smallpox epidemic kills up to 30,000 people.

Soviet Union—Writer Aleksandr Solzhenitsyn is deported and stripped of his citizenship for his criticisms of the Soviet system.

U.K.—Strikes in the coal, power, and transport industries, begun last year, continue. From January to March, a three-day work week is instituted to cope with power shortages brought on by the strikes.

U.S.—Mrs. Alberta King, the mother of slain civil rights leader Martin Luther King Jr. is assassinated.

In February heiress Patty Hearst is kidnapped by the terrorist group the Symbionese Liberation Army. She joins them in a bank robbery before being captured with them. She will be sentenced in 1976 and released by executive clemency in 1979.

Citizens are allowed to buy and sell gold for the first time since 1963.

West Germany—Bankhaus I.D. Herstatt KG, a large private bank, collapses.

Sports

South Africa—In golf Gary Player wins his third British Open and second Masters championship.

U.S.—Muhammad Ali defeats George Foreman to win back the world heavyweight boxing title.

On April 8 Hank Aaron hits his 715th home run, breaking Babe Ruth's career record. Aaron will raise his record to 755 by his retirement in 1976.

Frank Robinson is named manager of the Cleveland Indians, becoming the first African-American manager in major league baseball.

Chris Evert wins her first of six tennis titles at the French Open and her first of three titles at Wimbledon. Jimmy Connors wins men's singles tennis championships at Wimbledon and the Australian and U.S. Opens.

West Germany—West Germany wins the World Cup soccer championship.

1975 Arts and Entertainment

Czechoslovakia—Václav Havel's play *Audience* premieres.

Finland—Aulis Sallinen's opera *Ratsumies* premieres.

France—Pierre Boulez's *Rituel* for orchestra premieres.

Mexico—Carlos Fuentes's novel *Terra Nostra* is published.

Nigeria—Wole Soyinka's play *Death and the King's Horseman* premieres.

Nigerian-born British writer Buchi Emecheta publishes the novel *Second-Class Citizen*

Switzerland—Heinz Holliger's Quartet for Strings premieres.

U.K.—Harold Pinter's play *No Man's Land* premieres.

Ruth Prawer Jhabvala's novel *Heat and Dust* wins the Booker Prize.

Paul Scott publishes *A Division of the Spoils*, completing his series of novels the Raj Quartet.

U.S.—Saul Bellow publishes the novel *Humboldt's Gift*.

Musician and songwriter Bruce Springsteen records the album and title song *Born to Run*, which establish him as a rock icon.

Van McCoy's song "The Hustle" ushers in a dance craze, as disco music becomes popular.

Opera singer Beverly Sills makes her Metropolitan Opera debut in Rossini's *The Siege of Corinth*.

The musical *A Chorus Line* premieres on Broadway. It will run until 1990 and rank as Broadway's second longest-running show (behind *Cats*, 1982–present).

Roy Lichtenstein paints *Cubist Still Life with Lemons*.

West Germany—Karlheinz Stockhausen's *Tierkreis*, a set of 12 melodies, premieres.

World—Films include Steven Spielberg's blockbuster hit *Jaws* and Robert Altman's *Nashville* (both U.S.), Akira Kurosawa's *Dersu Uzala* (Japan), Peter Weir's *Picnic at Hanging Rock* (Australia), and Michelangelo Antonioni's *The Passenger* (Italy).

Ideas

France—Michel Foucault publishes *Discipline and Punish: The Birth of the Prison.*

U.K.—Critic Laura Mulvey publishes the essay "Visual Pleasure and Narrative Cinema."

U.S.—Critic Norman Holland publishes *Five Readers Reading.*

Entomologist Edward O. Wilson publishes *Sociobiology: The New Synthesis*, which controversially applies evolutionary theory to human behavior.

Writer Susan Brownmiller publishes *Against Our Will: Men, Women, and Rape.*

Military

Cambodia—The Khmer Rouge overthrows President Lon Nol and restores Prince Sihanouk as head of state.

Cambodian naval forces seize the U.S. merchant ship *Mayaguez*, which is recovered by U.S. forces.

Ethiopia—The civil war over Eritrean secession (*see* **1962**) heats up.

Laos—The Communist-led Pathet Lao takes over the country.

Lebanon—Fighting breaks out between Christians and Muslims in Beirut.

South Vietnam—President Nguyen Van Thieu resigns on April 21. U.S. forces and personnel are evacuated. On April 30 the Saigon government surrenders to Communist forces, ending the Vietnam War.

Politics

Africa—Portugal grants independence to its remaining African colonies: Angola, Mozambique, Cape Verde, and São Tomé and Principe.

Australia—Malcolm Fraser becomes prime minister.

Chad—President Françoise Tombalbaye is killed in a coup and succeeded by General Félix Malloum; civil war breaks out (*see* **1979, 1987**).

Egypt—The Suez Canal is reopened; it had been closed since the Six-Day War in 1967.

India—Sikkim abolishes its monarchy and becomes a state of India.

Italy—Socialists and Communists show large electoral gains at the local, provincial, and regional levels.

Northern Mariana Islands—In the first U.S. territorial acquisition in decades, the people of the Northern Mariana Islands vote to become U.S. citizens and make their land a U.S. commonwealth.

Peru—President Juan Velasco Alvarado is ousted in a coup.

Portugal—The military government institutes a constitution that legitimizes its regime.

Saudi Arabia—King Faisal is assassinated; he is succeeded by his brother Khalid.

Spain—Dictator Francisco Franco dies; King Juan Carlos I succeeds him as leader and moves swiftly toward democratization.

U.S.—Several former Nixon administration officials are convicted of Watergate-related crimes, including John Mitchell, John Erlichman, and H. R. Haldeman.

Two assassination attempts on President Gerald Ford fail.

World—At the Helsinki Conference in Finland, leaders of 35 nations accept international conventions on human rights.

Nations gaining independence this year include Comoros, Papua New Guinea, and Suriname.

Science and Technology

China—The tomb of Emperor Ch'in Shih Huang Ti (d. 210 b.c.) is uncovered. It contains 7,500 life-sized terra-cotta statues of guards.

Japan—Japan introduces its first launch vehicle, the N-1 rocket, and its first engineering test satellites.

Soviet Union/U.S.—On July 17 the first space docking between U.S. and Soviet spacecraft occurs as the *Soyuz 19* performs a rendezvous with an *Apollo* spacecraft.

U.K.—Argentinean-born British geneticist César Milstein announces the use of genetic cloning to create monoclonal antibodies (MABs).

U.S.—Inventor Ed Roberts puts the Altair, the first personal computer, on the market.

Mathematician Benoit Mandelbrot coins the term *fractals* to describe a class of irregular patterns and structures.

Society

Burma—An earthquake destroys the Great Temples of Pagan.

Canada—Mirabel International Airport, then the world's largest airport, opens in Montreal.

The Anglican Church in Canada approves ordination of women to the priesthood.

Japan—Sony introduces the Betamax, the first practical home video recorder.

The first woman to climb Mount Everest is Mrs. Junko Tabei.

U.K.—Inflation rises 25 percent.

The public school Rugby, 408 years old, accepts coeds for the first time.

U.S.—William Henry Gates III and Paul Gardner Allen found Microsoft, which will grow into the world's most successful manufacturer of computer software.

The unemployment rate reaches 9.2 percent, the highest since 1941.

Physicians go on strike in New York City in the country's first such labor action by doctors.

Mauna Loa erupts in Hawaii for the first time since 1950.

In the country's worst domestic air crash to date, 113 die when an Eastern Airlines jet crashes at Kennedy Airport.

World—Terrorist kidnappings plague several countries, including Argentina, Italy, Tanzania, and West Germany.

Sports

New Zealand—John Walker sets a new world's record for the mile, running it in 3 minutes, 49.4 seconds.

Soviet Union—Anatoly Karpov becomes chess champion by default when U.S. player Bobby Fischer gives up the title over a dispute concerning match rules.

U.S.—In football, the Pittsburgh Steelers beat the Minnesota Vikings, 16–6, to win the Super Bowl.

In golf Jack Nicklaus wins his fifth Masters and his fourth Professional Golfers' Association championship.

1976 Arts and Entertainment

Argentina—Manuel Puig publishes the novel *The Kiss of the Spider Woman*.

Japan—Kisho Kurokawa designs the Sony Tower in Osaka.

Mexico—Oscar Villegas's play *Atlantida* is produced.

Soviet Union—Alfred Shnitke's Piano Quintet premieres.

U.K.—The National Theatre in London, designed by architect Denys Lasdun, opens.

Benjamin Britten's Third String Quartet premieres a few days before his death.

Punk music emerges, typified by such bands as The Buzzcocks and The Sex Pistols, who released their first single, "Anarchy in the U.K."

U.S.—Ntozake Shange's play *For Colored Girls Who Have Considered Suicide When the Rainbow is Enuf* is produced.

Philip Glass and Robert Wilson's opera *Einstein on the Beach* premieres.

Jake Berthot paints *Walken's Ridge*.

Elizabeth Murray paints *Beginner*.

Bulgarian-born American artist Christo installs *Running Fence*, a 25-mile-long ribbon strung through Califronia.

Books include Raymond Carver's short-story collection *Will You Please Be Quiet, Please* and Maxine Hong Kingston's memoir *The Woman Warrior: Memoirs of a Girlhood Among Ghosts*.

World—Films include Martin Scorsese's *Taxi Driver* and Sidney Lumet's *Network* (both U.S.); Wim Wenders's *Kings of the Road* (West Germany), and Eric Rohmer's *The Marquise of O* (France).

Ideas

Austria—Psychologist Bruno Bettelheim publishes *The Uses of Enchantment*.

France—Philosopher and critic Paul Ricoeur publishes *Interpretation Theory: Discourse and the Surplus of Meaning*.

Germany—Philosopher Hans-Georg Gadamer publishes the essay collection *Philosophical Hermeneutics*.

Nigeria—Writer Wole Soyinka publishes *Myth, Literature, and the African World*.

U.K.—Zoologist Richard Dawkins publishes *The Selfish Gene*.

U.S.—Poet Adrienne Rich publishes the essay collection *Of Woman Born: Motherhood as Experience and Institution*.

Military

Israel/Uganda—Israeli commandos rescue 103 Israeli hostages held by pro-Palestinian hijackers at Entebbe Airport, Uganda.

Lebanon—Civil war rages. Syrian troops intervene, taking control of Beirut, Tripoli, and Sarda. Syrians and Lebanese Christians battle Lebanese Muslims and Palestinians.

U.S.—The Air Force Academy admits 155 women, putting an end to exclusion of women at U.S. military academies.

Politics

Argentina—President Isabel Perón is overthrown and a junta headed by Jorge Videla takes power.

Argentina devalues the peso 70 percent.

Cambodia—Prince Sihanouk is deposed as head of state. Premier Pol Pot becomes the effective leader of Cambodia, better known as Kampuchea during his tenure.

China—Chairman Mao Zedong dies; Hua Kuo-feng is appointed premier and chairman.

Shortly after Mao Zedong's death, four radical leaders of the Cultural Revolution—the "Gang of Four," which includes Mao's widow, Jian Qing—are arrested for plotting to overthrow the government. They will be convicted in 1981.

Mexico—José Lopez Portillo succeeds Luis Echeverría Alvarez as president.

Seychelles—The Seychelles become independent.

South Africa—A demonstration in Soweto, a black township, is brutally suppressed, prompting riots and international outrage.

South Africa grants nominal independence to black homeland Transkei, in an effort to buttress its apartheid system. Most foreign countries will not recognize the homelands as real nations.

Spanish Sahara—Spain gives up control of Spanish Sahara, now Western Sahara; Morocco and Mauritania divide it. Saharawi insurgents begin fighting for independence.

Sweden—The Social Democratic Party suffers its first defeat in national elections in 44 years, prompting party leader and premier Olof Palme to resign.

Thailand—A military coup topples the government.

U.K.—Prime minister Harold Wilson resigns and is succeeded by James Callaghan.

U.S.—The first televised debates since the Nixon-Kennedy debates in 1960 are held between Republican incumbent Gerald Ford and Democratic challenger Jimmy Carter. The latter wins the presidency.

A few years after striking down state death penalty statutes as unconstitutional (1972), the Supreme Court upholds several state death penalty laws, permitting the return of capital punishment.

Venezuela—Venezuela nationalizes the petroleum industry.

Vietnam—North and South Vietnam reunite as one country, the Socialist Republic of Vietnam. Saigon is renamed Ho Chi Minh City.

Science and Technology

Cameroon—A national commission is formed to study the role of traditional African medicine in modern health care.

China—Researchers perform clinical studies on traditional herbal pharmacology.

U.S.—Astronomers discover rings around Uranus.

The unmanned spacecraft *Viking 1* and *2* are the first to complete successful landings on Mars.

Society

France/U.K.—Air France and British Airways begin the first regularly scheduled commercial flights of supersonic transports (SSTs).

U.S.—On July 4, the country celebrates its bicentennial with nationwide festivities, including an international parade of "tall ships" up the Hudson River.

A previously unknown bacterial infection, Legionnaires' disease, kills 29 American Legion convention attendees.

A handwritten will attributed to late millionaire Howard Hughes and naming gas station operator Melvin Dummar as a substantial beneficiary is contested.

World—Facsimile, or fax, machines gain in popularity for office use.

Earthquakes roil Beijing and Tientsin, China; Mindanao, the Philippines; northern Italy; Guatemala; Bali; and eastern Turkey.

Yugoslavia—Two airliners collide over Yugoslavia. All 176 passengers are killed in what ranks as aviation's worst midair collision.

Zaire/Sudan—The filovirus Ebola, named for Zaire's Ebola River, emerges for the first time, killing hundreds of people in Zaire and the Sudan.

Sports

Canada—In hockey the Montreal Canadiens defeat the Philadelphia Flyers to win the Stanley Cup.

France/Turkey—The Orient Express railroad passenger line ends its Istanbul-to-Paris run.

U.S.—In football's Super Bowl, the Pittsburgh Steelers defeat the Dallas Cowboys, 21–17.

The Cincinnati Reds win a second consecutive World Series, this time against the New York Yankees, in a four game sweep. The previous year they had defeated the Boston Red Sox, four games to three.

World—The Winter Olympics are held at Innsbruck, Austria; the Soviet team wins 13 gold medals. The Summer Olympics are held in Montreal; the Soviet team leads with 47 gold medals. Thirty-two African and Asian countries withdraw from the summer Games over political differences.

1977 Arts and Entertainment

U.K.—Barbara Pym publishes the novel *Quartet in Autumn*.

Elvis Costello releases the album *My Aim Is True*.

U.K./U.S.—British-American band Fleetwood Mac releases the album *Rumours*.

U.S.—New plays include David Mamet's drama *American Buffalo* and the musical *Annie*, by Thomas Meehan, Martin Charnin, and Charles Strouse.

The Citicorp Center, designed by Hugh Stubbins & Associates, opens in New York City.

New music includes Elliott Carter's *A Symphony of Three Orchestras*, Ned Rorem's organ suite *A Quaker Reader*, and Roger Sessions's *Five Pieces for Piano*.

On August 16 rock musician Elvis Presley dies. Graceland, his home in Memphis, Tennessee, will become a pilgrimage site for fans.

Artist Cindy Sherman creates *Untitled Film Stills*, a photographic series.

For eight consecutive nights, the ABC television miniseries *Roots* is broadcast to record-breaking ratings.

John Badham's film *Saturday Night Fever* makes a star of John Travolta and epitomizes the era's disco craze. The soundtrack album, featuring British-Australian band the Bee Gees, becomes the biggest-selling soundtrack album ever.

World—Paintings include David Hockney's *Looking at Pictures on a Screen* (U.K.); Robert Moskowitz's *The Swimmer* (U.S.); and Balthus's (Count Balthasaiklossowski) *Nude in Profile* (France).

Films include George Lucas's *Star Wars* and Woody Allen's *Annie Hall* (both U.S), Luis Buñuel's *That Obscure Object of Desire* (Spain/France), and Bernardo Bertolucci's *1900* (Italy/France/West Germany).

Ideas

U.S.—Anthropologist Marvin Harris publishes *Cannibals and Kings*.

Critic Elaine Showalter publishes *A Literature of Their Own*.

Military

Ethiopia—Government forces stop a Somali-backed rebellion in the Ogaden region. Fighting continues in Eritrea.

Politics

Central African Empire—President Jean Bédel Bokassa crowns himself Emperor Bokassa I.

Djibouti—Djibouti becomes independent from France.

India—Prime Minister Indira Gandhi resigns when her ruling Congress party suffers its first defeat in national elections. Morarji Desai, head of the Janata Party, becomes prime minister.

Israel—Yitzhak Rabin resigns as prime minister and is replaced by Menachem Begin.

Israel/Egypt—Israel receives a visit from Egyptian president Anwar Sadat, the first Arab leader to do so since Israel's founding.

Pakistan—The military seizes power and institutes martial law.

Panama/U.S.—The U.S. agrees to give Panama full sovereignty over the Panama Canal by the year 2000.

Soviet Union—Leonid Brezhnev, head of the Communist Party, is elected president, becoming the first leader to hold both positions.

U.S.—President Jimmy Carter pardons most Vietnam-era draft resisters.

A scandal called Koreagate rocks Congress, when allegations surface of influence-peddling masterminded by South Korean businessman Tongsun Park.

Barnes v. Costle, an appeals court decision, is the first ruling in which sexual harassment is found to be a form of discrimination.

Science and Technology

China—Astronomers studying ancient data provide data on comet durability and sunspot cycles.

U.S.—Physicist Alan Guth postulates an inflationary universe, one that expanded exponentially after the Big Bang.

Physicist Leon Lederman discovers a particle called the upsilon.

At a Yale University conference, behavioral medicine, an area of medicine that includes biofeedback, comes into existence.

Researchers aboard the submersible *Alvin* discover deep ocean vents that sustain an ecology of sulfur-eating bacteria and other life forms.

The Apple II computer is marketed by inventors Stephen Wozniak and Steve Jobs. It is the first personal computer accessible not just to hobbyists but to the public at large.

Society

Canada—French becomes the official language of Quebec.

Canary Islands—A KLM Royal Dutch Airlines Boeing 747 crashes into a Pan American World Airways Boeing 747 on the runway in Tenerife. More than 580 people die in what is still the world's worst aviation disaster.

India—A cyclone kills 20,000 people.

Trinidad and Tobago—Janelle Penny Commissiong is the first black woman to win the Miss Universe title.

U.S.—The first successful human-powered aircraft, the *Gossamer Condor*, is flown three miles. The inventor is Paul MacCready, the pilot Bryan Allen.

Capital punishment, reinstated last year as an option by the Supreme Court (*see* **1976**), returns when Utah murderer Gary Gilmore is executed.

David Berkowitz is arrested for the "Son of Sam" serial murders in New York City; he will be convicted next year.

Lightning at local power plants causes a major New York City blackout, which leaves 9 million people without electricity and spawns looting and vandalism. About 3,700 people are arrested.

Colorado mother Ann Moore patents the Snugli baby carrier. The idea came from carriers she had seen while serving with the Peace Corps in West Africa.

Sports

Canada—Hockey player Gordie Howe (1928–) becomes the first to score 1,000 professional career goals.

Japan—First baseman Sadaharu Oh hits his 756th home run, becoming worldwide professional baseball's most prolific home-run hitter.

Sweden—Bjorn Borg wins his second consecutive Wimbledon men's singles tennis title.

U.S.—In baseball St. Louis Cardinal outfielder Lou Brock breaks Ty Cobb's record for stolen bases (892).

In baseball the New York Yankees win their first of two consecutive World Series, both times against the Los Angeles Dodgers and both times four games to two.

1978 Arts and Entertainment

Belgium—Choreographer Maurice Béjart creates the dance work *Gaité Parisienne*.

Hungary—Hungarian-born composer György Ligeti's opera *Le Grand macabre* premieres in Sweden.

Poland—Polish-born composer Krzysztof Penderecki's opera *Paradise Lost* and Concerto for Violin premiere in the U.S.

U.S.—Chinese-born American architect I. M. Pei designs the east wing of the National Gallery of Art, Washington, D.C.

Choreographer Martha Graham creates the dance works *The Owl and the Pussycat* and *The Flute of Pan*.

New music includes Samuel Barber's *Third Essay for Orchestra* and Charles Wuorinen's *Percussion Symphony* and *Two-Part Symphony*.

John Irving publishes the novel *The World According to Garp*.

World—Films include Michael Cimino's *The Deer Hunter* (*U.S.*); Claude Chabrol's *Violette* (France); and Rainer Werner Fassbinder's *The Marriage of Maria Braun* (West Germany).

Neo-expressionism, a new form of representational art, is launched in New York. Painters in the movement include American Joan Brown and German Anselm Kiefer.

Ideas

Germany—Critic Wolfgang Iser publishes *The Act of Reading: A Theory of Aesthetic Response*.

U.K.—Philosopher Michael Dummett publishes the essay collection *Truth and Other Enigmas*.

U.S.—Writer Susan Sontag publishes *Illness as Metaphor*.

Psychiatrist M. Scott Peck publishes *The Road Less Traveled*.

Critic Edward Said publishes *Orientalism*.

Feminist scholar Nancy Chodorow publishes *The Reproduction of Mothering: Psychoanalysis and the Sociology of Gender.*

Philosopher Nelson Goodman publishes *Ways of Worldmaking.*

Military

Nicaragua—Sandinista guerrillas make gains in their campaign to overthrow dictator Anastasio Somoza.

U.S.—Brigadier General Margaret A. Brewer becomes the first female general in the U.S. Marine Corps.

Zaire—Secessionist rebels in Katanga Province wage war. Angola, Cuba, the Soviet Union are reportedly involved on the rebel side. The U.S. airlifts in troops from Morocco and other countries to support the government.

Politics

Afghanistan—A military junta takes power.

China/U.S.—China and the U.S. announce the establishment of full diplomatic relations.

Dominican Republic—In the first peaceful transfer of power between constitutionally elected governments in the nation's history, Antonio Guzmán is elected president, defeating opponent Joaquin Balaguer.

Honduras—A military junta takes power.

Iran—As antigovernment demonstrations rock the country, Shah Mohammad Reza Pahlavi institutes martial law.

Israel/Egypt/U.S.—Meeting at Camp David, Maryland, with the assistance of U.S. president Jimmy Carter, Israeli prime minister Menachem Begin and Egyptian President Anwar Sadat agree on a framework for peace between the two countries. It is the first such agreement between Israel and its Arab neighbors since Israel's independence.

North Yemen—Ali Abdullah Saleh establishes a new military government.

South Africa—Pieter Willem Botha succeeds John Vorster as prime minister.

South Yemen—A pro-Soviet group seizes control, deposing and executing the president.

Sri Lanka—A presidential governing system adopted in 1977 takes effect, with Prime Minister Junius Richard Jayawardene becoming president.

Taiwan—Premier Chiang Ching-kuo is elected president.

Turkey—Bulent Ecevit becomes premier.

U.S.—The Supreme Court affirms a decision requiring the University of California to admit Allan P. Bakke, who had claimed himself a victim of "reverse discrimination."

Science and Technology

China—A National Science Conference marks the beginnings of a resurgence of scientific research in China. At the event, China introduces a "four modernizations" policy, including modernization in science and technology.

Czechoslovakia—Czechoslovakian Vladimir Remek, flying aboard the Soviet *Soyuz 28*, becomes the first person in space who is not from the U.S. or Soviet Union.

U.K.—The world's first successful human pregnancy by in vitro (test tube) fertilization comes to fruition when baby Louise Brown is delivered by doctors Patrick Steptoe and Robert Edwards.

The laparoscope, a type of endoscope, is invented.

U.S.—Astronomer James Christy discovers Charon, Pluto's only satellite.

Paleontologists John Horner and Bob Makela discover the first known nest of baby dinosaurs, indicating that dinosaurs cared for their infants. The new species is called the *Maiasaura* ("good mother lizard").

The Princeton Large Torus nuclear fusion reactor attains a temperature of 60 million° F., higher than any other fusion reactor so far.

Society

France—Off the Brittany coast of France, the supertanker *Amoco Cadiz* spills 68 million gallons of oil, causing damage along 100 miles of coastline in what will remain the world's largest tanker disaster.

Guyana—Nine hundred and seventeen members of the U.S.–based cult the People's Temple commit murder-suicide at their commune in the Guyana jungle. The dead include their leader, Jim Jones. Previously that year, U.S. Representative Leo J. Ryan and four other Americans had been killed by members of the cult.

India—In India's worst air disaster up to that time, 213 people die in an Air India Boeing 747 crash.

Italy—Former premier Aldo Moro is kidnapped and murdered by the terrorist group the Red Brigades.

Jordan—King Hussein marries Elizabeth Halaby.

U.K.—Naomi James is the first woman to sail around the world alone.

U.K./U.S.—Strikes of newspaper employees temporarily shut down London's *Times* and *Sunday Times* and New York City's *New York Post*, *New York Times*, and *Daily News*.

U.S.—Max Anderson, Ben Abruzzo, and Larry Newman are the first to cross the Atlantic Ocean by balloon.

Vatican City—Pope John Paul I succeeds Paul VI, then dies after a month. He is succeeded by John Paul II, the first non-Italian pope in more than four centuries.

Sports

Argentina—In soccer Argentina wins the World Cup.

Canada—In hockey the Montreal Canadiens beat the Boston Bruins to win their 21st Stanley Cup.

Soviet Union—In chess Anatoly Karpov successfully defends his world championship title against challenger Viktor Korchnoi.

U.S.—The Dallas Cowboys defeat the Denver Broncos, 27–10, to win the Super Bowl.

Leon Spinks defeats Muhammad Ali for the world heavyweight boxing championship. In a rematch later this year, Ali defeats Spinks and regains the title.

1979 Arts and Entertainment

France—Samuel Beckett publishes *Company*, a prose work.

Israel—Artist Jim Dine paints *Jerusalem Nights*.

U.K.—Peter Shaffer's play *Amadeus* premieres, directed by Peter Hall.

U.S.—The first theft ever at the 110–year–old Metropolitan Museum of Art results in the loss of an ancient Greek marble bust.

John Cage premieres his musical work *Roaratorio, an Irish Circus on Finnegans Wake*.

Ernest Thompson's play *On Golden Pond* premieres on Broadway; musicals on Broadway include Stephen Sondheim's *Sweeney Todd* and Andrew Lloyd Webber and Tim Rice's *Evita*.

Norman Mailer publishes *The Executioner's Song*, about the life and death of convicted killer Gary Gilmore.

Artist Judy Chicago completes *The Dinner Party* (1974–79), a celebration of women.

Architect I. M. Pei designs the John F. Kennedy Library, in Dorchester, Massachusetts.

World—Notable poetic works include Ted Hughes's *Moortown* (U.K.) and *The Poems of Stanley Kunitz* (U.S.).

Novels include Nuruddin Farah's *Sweet and Sour Milk* (Somalia), V. S. Naipaul's *A Bend in the River* (U.K.), Philip Roth's *The Ghost Writer* (U.S.), and William Styron's *Sophie's Choice* (U.S.).

Films include Woody Allen's *Manhattan*, Francis Ford Coppola's *Apocalypse Now*, and Robert Benton's *Kramer vs. Kramer* (all U.S.); Bruce Beresford's *Breaker Morant* (Australia); Luchino Visconti's *The Innocent* (Italy); and Rainer Werner Fassbinder's *Despair* (West Germany).

Ideas

Switzerland—Theologian Hans Küng is prohibited from officially teaching Roman Catholic doctrine, following years of questioning papal authority.

U.S.—Philosopher Richard Rorty publishes *Philosophy and the Mirror of Nature*.

The use of affirmative action to lessen discrimination in hiring is upheld by the Supreme Court in *United Steelworkers of America v. Weber*.

Military

Afghanistan—Soviet troops invade and take control of Afghanistan.

Chad—The civil war ends (*see* **1975**); a coalition government is established.

El Salvador—Civil war breaks out between guerrilla forces and U.S.–supported government troops.

Nicaragua—Sandinista forces take control of Nicaragua; dictator Anastasio Somoza Debayle flees the country.

Western Sahara—A three-year-old civil war ends when Mauritania concludes peace with rebels in the southern half of Western Sahara. Morocco, already governing the north, occupies the south, with rebel activity continuing.

Politics

Afghanistan—The U.S. ambassador is kidnapped and killed.

Central African Republic—Emperor Bokassa I is overthrown in a coup; former president David Dacko returns to power and restores the country's name to Central African Republic (from Central African Empire).

Ecuador—Ecuador returns to democracy after seven years of military rule.

Egypt/Israel—A peace treaty is signed in Washington, D.C., by Egyptian president Anwar Sadat and Israeli prime minister Menachem Begin.

Germany—The West German Green Party is formed.

Iran—The government of Shah Mohammad Reza Pahlavi is overthrown by Islamic fundamentalist forces led by Ayatollah Ruhollah Khomeini. Ayatollah Ruhollah Khomeini is installed as dictator.

The U.S. embassy in Tehran is overthrown by Islamic revolutionaries, with 66 U.S. hostages seized under demands that the Shah, living in the U.S., be returned to Iran for trial. The U.S. refuses the demands, and 52 hostages will be held for 444 days until 1981, after the inauguration of U.S. president Ronald Reagan.

Kiribati—The Republic of Kiribati becomes an independent state and member of the British Commonwealth.

Libya—A mob attacks the U.S. embassy in Tripoli, causing moderate damage but no injuries.

Middle East—Beginning with the installation of a Shiite Muslim fundamentalist government in Iran, Islamic fundamentalism becomes a powerful force in the region's politics and society.

Nicaragua—With the accession of the leftist Sandinista government, U.S. military aid is ended and economic aid reduced.

Pakistan—The U.S. embassy in Islamabad is attacked; one U.S. Marine is killed.

Panama—Panama takes control of the Canal Zone after 70 years of U.S. control.

Saint Lucia—Saint Lucia becomes an independent state and member of the British Commonwealth.

Saint Vincent and the Grenadines—Saint Vincent and the Grenadines become an independent state and member of the British Commonwealth.

South Korea—President Park Chung Hee is assassinated by the director of intelligence; Prime Minister Kyu Ha Choi becomes president.

Uganda—Dictator Idi Amin is overthrown by Tanzanian troops; he is replaced by former president Milton Obote.

U.K.—Conservative Party member Margaret Thatcher becomes the first female prime minister in Britain.

U.S./Soviet Union—President Carter and President Leonid Brezhnev sign a SALT II strategic arms limitation treaty in Vienna, Austria.

Science and Technology

Europe—*Ariane*, the first European Space Agency rocket, is launched from French Guiana.

Germany—Subatomic particles known as gluons are first observed.

Japan—The Sony Walkman is introduced to the public.

Soviet Union—The unmanned *Soyuz 34* is launched and docks with the space station *Salyut 6*.

U.K.—*Gaia: A New Look at Life on Earth* by scientist James Lovelock is published, outlining theories of a global ecosystem.

U.S.—A study suggests even low levels of lead in the blood of children results in lower intelligence test results. In 1980 the sale of lead-based paint will be banned.

Voyager 1 and *2*, launched in 1977, fly by Jupiter.

Space laboratory *Skylab* returns to Earth's atmosphere and breaks into shards.

Society

Mexico—The largest oil spill to date occurs when the *Ixtoc I* releases some 600,000 tons of crude oil into the Bay of Campeche, causing great damage to the ecosystem.

New Zealand—A DC-10 crashes into Mount Erebus, in Antarctica, causing 257 deaths.

U.S.—At Pennsylvania nuclear power plant Three Mile Island, a malfunction causes the release of radioactive gases.

High inflation, rising foreign trade deficit, and increasing losses in industrial jobs erode national morale.

Both Pope John Paul II and the Dalai Lama make visits to the U.S, Pope John Paul becoming the first pope to visit the White House.

The surgeon general proclaims cigarette smoking the "single most important environmental factor contributing to early death."

An American Airlines crash in Chicago, Illinois, kills all 272 passengers and three people on the ground.

Sports

U.S.—In the NBA championship, the Seattle Supersonics defeat the Washington Bullets, four games to one.

In Super Bowl XIII the Pittsburgh Steelers (AFC) defeat the Dallas Cowboys (NFC), 35–31.

In the World Series the Pittsburgh Pirates (NL) defeat the Baltimore Orioles (AL), four games to three.

In the U.S. Open tennis singles, the men's singles' championship is won by John McEnroe; the women's singles' championship by Tracy Austin. At 16, she is the youngest player to win women's singles at the Open.

1980 Arts and Entertainment

Germany—Anselm Kiefer paints *To the Unknown Painter*.

India—Anita Desai publishes the novel *Clear Light of Day*.

Ireland—The new-wave band U2 releases its debut album, *Boy*.

Italy—Umberto Eco publishes the novel *The Name of the Rose*.

Kenya—Ngugi Wa Thiong'o (James T. Ngugi) publishes the novel *Devil on the Cross*.

South Africa—J. M. Coetzee publishes the novel *Waiting for the Barbarians*; Andre Brink publishes the novel *A Dry White Season*.

U.K.—P. D. James publishes the novel *Innocent Blood*.

The rock band the Clash releases the double album *London Calling*.

U.S.—Architects Philip Johnson and John Burgee design the Crystal Cathedral in Garden Grove, California.

Choreographer Laura Dean presents her first ballet, *Night*.

Jazz trumpeter Wynton Marsalis joins Art Blakey's Jazz Messengers.

Laurie Anderson's *United States Parts 1 and 2*, combining electronic music and film, premieres.

A few months before his death this year, Clyfford Still's abstract paintings are exhibited at the Metropolitan Museum of Art in its largest one-man show to date of work by a living artist.

Jeff Koons begins the sculptural program "The New," centering on vacuum cleaners encased in Plexiglas.

John Kennedy Toole's novel *A Confederacy of Dunces* is published posthumously.

Businessman Ted Turner founds the Cable News Network (CNN). Cable stations will proliferate over the next several years.

World—Films include Martin Scorsese's *Raging Bull* (U.S.); Gillian Armstrong's *My Brilliant Career* (Australia); Vladimir Menshov's *Moscow Does Not Believe in Tears* (Soviet Union); and Jamie Uys's *The Gods Must Be Crazy* (Botswana).

Ideas

Canada—Philosopher of science Bas van Fraassen publishes *The Scientific Image*.

U.S.—Philosopher Saul Aaron Kripke publishes *Naming and Necessity*.

Historian John Boswell publishes *Christianity, Social Tolerance, and Homosexuality: Gay People in Western Europe from the Beginning of the Christian Era to the Fourteenth Century*.

Critic Stanley Fish publishes *Is There a Text in This Class? The Authority of Interpretive Communities*.

Critic Geoffrey Hartman publishes *Criticism in the Wilderness: The Study of Literature Today*.

Critic Stephen Greenblatt publishes *Renaissance Self-Fashioning*, one of the earliest works in the critical movement known as new historicism.

Military

Chad—Libyan forces invade Chad but will leave the following year.

El Salvador—Civil war heats up, with right-wing paramilitary groups known as "death squads" using terror and murder to support the government's efforts against left-wing guerrillas.

Iran—An attempted commando raid to free U.S. hostages is disastrously aborted.

Iraq/Iran—War breaks out between Iraq and Iran over disputed territory (1980–88). The war will end with over 500,000 dead and no substantial territorial gains for either country.

Politics

Afghanistan—Martial law is imposed in response to a general strike in protest against the Soviet invasion.

China—Hua Guofeng and Deng Xiaoping resign from the state council. Zhao Ziyang replaces Hua as prime minister.

El Salvador—In March Archbishop Oscar Romero, a critic of the government, is shot dead. In December three American nuns and a lay worker are killed. Forces allied to the government are suspected in both cases.

José Napoleon Duarte becomes the country's first civilian president in 49 years.

Iceland—Vigdis Finnbogadottir becomes the first democratically elected female head of state in Europe.

India—Indira Gandhi dissolves legislative assemblies in nine states and brings the states under direct rule.

Israel—The Knesset approves a bill making united Jerusalem the country's capital. The UN General Assembly calls for founding of a Palestinian state and Israeli withdrawal from all occupied territories.

Netherlands—Princess Beatrix becomes queen upon the abdication of her mother, Juliana.

Peru—After more than a decade of military rule, the country returns to democracy, with Fernando Belaunde Terry elected president.

Poland—In August strikes break out at the Lenin shipyard in Gdansk. The national labor union Solidarnosc (Solidarity) is formed. In November the government recognizes its legality, even though the union challenges its monopoly on political power. First Secretary Edward Gierek is dismissed.

Spain—Voters in the Basque region elect their first regional parliament, ending four decades of direct rule from Madrid.

Turkey—General Kenan Evren becomes head of state after a military coup.

U.S.—Republican candidate Ronald Reagan wins the presidency from Democratic incumbent Jimmy Carter.

Yugoslavia—Communist founder Tito dies; a collective rotating presidency is established.

Zimbabwe—The Zimbabwe African National Union (ZANU), led by Robert Mugabe, wins elections. Mugabe becomes Zimbabwe's leader when it gains independence on April 18.

Science and Technology

Germany—Physicist Klaus von Klitzing discovers the quantum Hall effect, named for 19th century American physicist Edwin H. Hall.

Soviet Union/U.S.—Soviet and U.S. scientists suggest that neutrinos, previously thought to be massless, do have mass.

U.K.—Research psychiatrist T. J. Crow distinguishes between Type I and Type II schizophrenia.

U.S.—The Very Large Array (VLA) radio telescope in Socorro, New Mexico, begins operations.

The scanning tunneling microscope, which can produce images of individual atoms, is invinted.

Dietary guidelines recommend avoiding excessive cholesterol, fats, sugar, salt, and alcohol.

Society

Canada—Hockey player Scott Olsen patents rollerblades.

China—In a move toward greater toleration of religion, China permits the renovation of some historic Buddhist and Taoist temples and monasteries.

Tibet—China permits the opening of the Potala Palace to pilgrimage by exiled Tibetan Buddhists.

U.K.—The Church of England introduces the Alternative Service Book, an alternative to the Book of Common Prayer.

U.S.—On May 18 the volcano Mount St. Helens in Washington State erupts, killing dozens.

In the first long-distance solar-powered flight, Janice Brown flies six miles in the aircraft *Solar Challenger*.

Bernardine Dohrn and Cathlyn Wilkerson, leaders of the terrorist movement the Weather Underground, surrender to the law after years in hiding.

U.S./U.K.—On December 8 in New York City, British musician John Lennon is shot dead by a deranged fan.

Sports

Sweden—Bjorn Borg is the first to win five successive men's singles tennis titles at Wimbledon.

U.S.—At the Winter Olympics in Lake Placid, New York, speed-skater Eric Heiden wins all five gold medals for his sport, a Winter Olympic record.

In basketball, Earvin "Magic" Johnson leads the Los Angeles Lakers to the first of five National Basketball Association championships (1980, 1982, 1985, 1987, 1988).

World—More than 45 nations, including the U.S., decline to participate in the Summer Olympics in Moscow, to protest the Soviet invasion of Afghanistan.

1981 Arts and Entertainment

Colombia—Gabriel García Márquez publishes the novella *Chronicle of a Death Foretold.*

Italy—Francesco Clemente paints *Toothache.*

Jamaica—Reggae musician Bob Marley dies one month after receiving Jamaica's Order of Merit for his work.

U.K.—Punk rocker Billy Idol, formerly of the band Generation X, moves to New York City and releases the solo single "Dancing with Myself."

U.S.—Artist Robert Moskowitz creates the pastel on paper work *Red Mill.*

Robert Ryman paints *Paramount.*

Claes Oldenburg creates the sculpture *Flashlight* for the University of Nevada at Reno.

The rock band R.E.M., led by Michael Stipe, makes its debut.

Philip Glass's operas *The Panther* and *Satyagraha* premiere.

Roger Session's Concerto for Orchestra premieres.

The cable channel MTV (Music Television) premieres, ushering in the age of the music video.

World—Novels include Toni Morrison's *Tar Baby* and John Updike's *Rabbit Is Rich* (both U.S.), Mario Vargas Llosa's *War of the End of the World* (Peru), Janet Frame's *Living in the Maniototo* (New Zealand), and D. M. Thomas's *The White Hotel* and Salman Rushdie's *Midnight's Children* (U.K.).

Films include Steven Spielberg's *Raiders of the Lost Ark* and Warren Beatty's *Reds* (both U.S.), Hugh Hudson's *Chariots of Fire* and Karel Reisz's *The French Lieutenant's Woman* (both U.K.), Rainer Werner Fassbinder's *Lili Marleen* (West Germany), and Bill Forsyth's *Gregory's Girl* (U.K.).

Ideas

Germany—Marxist philosopher Jürgen Habermas publishes *The Theory of Communicative Action.*

U.K.—Philosopher Richard Mervyn Hare publishes *Moral Thinking: Its Levels, Method, and Point.*

U.S.—Philosopher Hilary Putnam publishes *Reason, Truth, and History.*

Economists Robert Heilbroner and Lester Thurow publish *Five Economic Challenges.*

Economist Milton Friedman publishes *Free to Choose.*

Military

Afghanistan—A stalemate develops in the war between Soviet forces and U.S.–backed Mujaheddin guerrilla forces.

Bangladesh—President Ziaur Rahman is assassinated in a coup attempt that fails to topple the government.

Canada—The international nuclear freeze movement, calling for a halt to further expansion of nuclear weapons arsenals, begins at the 31st Pugwash anti–nuclear weapons meeting.

Chad—Peacekeeping forces from the Organization of African Unity replace Libyan forces in Chad. Civil war in Chad is temporarily stopped.

France—François Mitterrand, a Socialist, is elected president.

Iran—Prime minister Bahomar and president Rajaj are among 15 people killed in a terrorist bombing.

Iraq/Israel—Israeli bombers destroy a nuclear power plant being built in Iraq.

Libya—Two Libyan warplanes are shot down by U.S. warplanes.

Sri Lanka—Civil war (1981–) breaks out as the Tamil United Liberation Front rebels against the government.

Politics

Antigua and Barbuda—Antigua and Barbuda become independent from Britain.

Belize—Belize, formerly British Honduras, becomes independent from Britain.

Central African Republic—The regime of David Dacko is overthrown in a coup led by General André Kolingba.

Cuba—Barriers to emigration are temporarily lifted to permit more than 100,000 people to flee Cuba for the U.S.; embarking from Mariel, they are known as the Marielitos.

Egypt—Islamic fundamentalists assassinate President Anwar al-Sadat. Hosni Mubarak succeeds him.

Greece—Greece joins the European Economic Community.

Poland—In October General Wojciech Jaruzelski, backed by the Soviet Union, becomes first secretary. In December he declares martial law and arrests Lech Walesa and other opponents of the regime.

U.S.—President Ronald Reagan survives an assassination attempt by deranged gunman John W. Hinckley Jr.

Sandra Day O'Connor is the first woman to be appointed to the Supreme Court.

Science and Technology

China—Geneticists in China are the first to successfully clone a fish, the golden carp.

Ethiopia—Hominid fossil bones are found dating to four million years ago.

Soviet Union—Scientists discover element 107, unnilseptium.

Spain—Archaeologists discover the remains of a Neanderthal religious sanctuary.

U.K.—Scientists introduce magnetic resonance imaging (MRI), a diagnostic imaging technique.

U.S.—The space shuttle *Columbia*, the first reusable manned space vehicle, is launched.

The entire sequence of nucleotides in the DNA of a mitochondrion, a constituent of cells, is determined.

Psychologist Eleanor Rosch expands her theory of prototypes and basic level categories.

On August 12 the first IBM personal computer, with the Microsoft operating system MS-DOS, is introduced.

Society

Australia—Australian communications magnate Rupert Murdoch buys the *Times* of London.

Indonesia—In the Java Sea off Indonesia, the ferry *Tampomas 2* catches fire and sinks, killing 580 people.

Northern Ireland—Irish Republican Army hunger striker Robert Sands is permitted to die of hunger in prison, prompting riots in Northern Ireland.

U.K.—Prince Charles marries Lady Diana Spencer, henceforth known as Princess Diana.

Race riots break out in Brixton in south London.

Jack Sutcliffe, known as the Yorkshire Ripper, is sentenced to life in prison for his murders of alleged prostitutes.

U.S.—A wave of unusual cases of pneumocystis pneumonia are reported among homosexual men. The cases will lead to diagnosis of the new and deadly disease AIDS (Acquired Immune Deficiency Syndrome) in 1982.

One hundred and thirteen people die in the collapse of two interior walkways in the Hyatt Regency Hotel in Kansas City, Missouri.

Vatican City—Pope John Paul II survives an assassination attempt by Turkish terrorist Mehmet Ali Agca.

Sports

Canada—Wayne Gretzky of the Edmonton Oilers is the top scorer in the National Hockey League, a distinction he will maintain for seven straight years (1981–87).

U.K.—Snooker player Steve Davis wins the world championship at age 23.

Jayne Torvill and Christopher Dean win the first of three consecutive European and World ice-dance championships (1981–83).

U.S.—John McEnroe wins the men's singles championship at Wimbledon for the first time and wins the U.S. Open for the third consecutive time.

1982 Arts and Entertainment

Australia—Thomas Keneally publishes the novel *Schindler's Ark*.

Italy—Luciano Berio's opera *La Vera storia* premieres.

Trinidad and Tobago—Derek Walcott publishes the poetry collection *The Unfortunate Traveller*.

U.K.—Bruce Chatwin publishes the novel *On the Black Hill*.

Frank Auerbach paints *Primrose Hill, Early Summer*.

U.S.—Rap music, which began in the 1970s among African-American and Hispanic youth in New York City, increases in mainstream popularity.

Michael Jackson becomes a superstar with the album *Thriller.*

Sculptor Maya Lin designs the Vietnam Veterans Memorial in Washington, D.C.

Robert Arneson sculpts *Californian Artist.*

Artist Jean-Michel Basquiat, former graffiti painter, holds eight one-man shows.

The television series *Cheers* premieres (NBC, 1982–93).

West Germany—Artist Joseph Beuys creates the installation *Dernier espace avec introspecteur.*

World—Films include Steven Spielberg's *E. T. The Extra-Terrestrial* and Sydney Pollack's *Tootsie* (U.S.), Daniel Vigne's *The Return of Martin Guerre* and Adrzej Wajda's *The Danton Affair* (France), and Richard Attenborough's *Gandhi* (U.K./India).

Ideas

France/U.S.—Postmodernism becomes a buzzword in intellectual circles. French philosopher Jean-François Lyotard publishes the essay "What Is Postmodernism?," while American critic Frederic Jameson gives a talk entitled "Postmodernism and Consumer Society."

U.S.—Anthropologist Melvin Konner publishes *The Tangled Wing.*

Military

Argentina/U.K.—In the Falklands War (April–June), Argentina seizes the Falkland Islands (Malvinas) from Britain but is forced to return them.

Iraq—Iran lends support to Kurdish insurrection in northern Iraq.

Lebanon—In June Israel invades Lebanon. Israeli troops force the withdrawal of Palestine Liberation Organization (PLO) and Syrian forces from West Beirut. UN peacekeeping forces, including American troops, arrive.

Lebanese president-elect Bashir Gemayel is assassinated in September, prompting his supporters in the Christian militia to massacre more than 400 people in Beirut's Sabra and Shatilla Palestinian refugee camps. Israel, which had responsibility for the camps, is accused of complicity in the massacre.

Syria—The government defeats an insurrection of the Muslim Brotherhood at Hama.

Politics

Argentina—The military government collapses in the wake of defeat in the Falklands War (*see* **Military**).

Bangladesh—General Hossein Mohammed Ershad comes to power in a coup.

France—Led by Socialist President François Mitterrand, France nationalizes five groups of industries and 39 banks and begins a four-month wage and price freeze.

Gambia/Senegal—Gambia and Senegal join in the confederation of Senegambia (1982–89).

Jamaica—Jamaica becomes independent from Britain.

Japan—Liberal Democratic Party leader Yasuhiro Nakasone becomes prime minister.

Mexico—With inflation at 70 percent, Mexico nationalizes private banks.

New Zealand—New Zealand announces a 12–month freeze on wages and prices.

Panama—Manuel Noriega becomes de facto dictator of Panama.

Peru—Peruvian diplomat Javier Pérez de Cuéllar becomes secretary-general of the UN.

Soviet Union—On the death of Leonid Brezhnev, Yuri Andropov becomes general secretary of the Communist Party, effectively the leader of the country.

West Germany—Christian Democrat Helmut Kohl succeeds Helmut Schmidt as chancellor.

World—The Convention on the Law of the Sea is adopted at Montego Bay, Jamaica.

The International Whaling Comission adopts a worldwide ban on whaling, to be made fully effective by 1986.

Science and Technology

Japan—Compact disc (CD) players becomes commercially available.

U.K.—Physician Michael Epstein identifies the herpeslike microbe called the Epstein-Barr virus.

U.S.—The Cray supercomputer is introduced.

Physicist Blas Cabrera reports the unconfirmed discovery of a magnetic monopole.

Psychologist Carol Gilligan publishes *In a Different Voice: Psychological Theory and Women's Development.*

Pharmaceutical company Eli Lilly markets the first genetically engineered human insulin.

The first artificial heart is implanted, but the patient dies 92 days after the surgery.

Society

U.S.—Acquired Immune Deficiency Syndrome (AIDS) is first diagnosed.

The first national news daily, *USA Today*, begins publication.

American Telephone and Telegraph (AT&T) settles a federal antitrust suit by agreeing to divest itself of its local telephone systems. The breakup ends AT&T's American telephone monopoly.

A demonstration in favor of a nuclear freeze involves 500,000 to a million people.

World—Pope John Paul II, head of the Roman Catholic Church, meets with Anglican Church leaders, including Archbishop of Canterbury Robert Runcie, in a step toward reconciliation of the denominations.

Sports

U.K.—In cricket Ian Botham becomes the first to score 3,000 runs and take 250 wickets in test matches.

U.S.—In football quarterback Joe Montana leads the San Francisco 49ers to the first of four Super Bowl victories (1982, 1985, 1989, 1990).

In tennis Jimmy Connors defeats John McEnroe to win his second Wimbledon men's singles championship.

1983 Arts and Entertainment

France—Russian-born dancer Rudolf Nureyev becomes director of the Paris Opera Ballet.

U.K.—Bridget Riley paints *Midi*.

Fay Weldon publishes the novel *The Life and Loves of a She-Devil*.

The rock group the Police releases the album *Synchronicity*.

U.S.—Merce Cunningham's dance pieces *Quartets* premiere.

Architect Frank Gehry designs the Norton house in Venice, California.

Architects Philip Johnson and John Burgee design the AT&T Building in New York City.

David Mamet's play *Glengarry Glen Ross* premieres.

Alice Walker publishes the novel *The Color Purple*.

Brice Marden paints *Elements IV*.

West Germany—Hans Werner Henze's opera *The English Cat* premieres.

Jorg Immendorf paints *Café Deutschland Hörerwunsch*.

World—Films include James L. Brooks's *Terms of Endearment* (U.S.), Ingmar Bergman's *Fanny and Alexander* (Sweden), Ettore Scola's *La Nuit de Varennes*, and Andrei Tarkovsky's *Nostalgia* (Soviet Union).

Ideas

Guatemala—Human rights activist Rigoberta Menchú publishes her autobiography, *I, Rigoberta Menchú*, a personal report of human rights abuses by her country's government.

U.K.—Critic Terry Eagleton publishes *Literary Theory: An Introduction*.

U.S.—Anthropologist Clifford Geertz publishes *Local Knowledge*.

Philosopher Saul Aaron Kripke publishes *Wittgenstein on Rules and Private Language*.

Military

Israel/Lebenon—Israeli forces withdraw from Beirut. Lebanon descends into a chaotic civil war. Palestine Liberation Organization forces are evacuated from Tripoli. Terrorists kill 241 Americans and 58 French in suicide-bombings of U.S. and French military barracks.

Sudan—Christian and animist forces in the south step up a guerrilla war against the Muslim-dominated north, in protest against nationwide imposition of Islamic law.

U.S.—In October U.S. forces, with nominal assistance from other countries, invade and capture Grenada, ousting its Marxist government.

Politics

Australia—Labour Party leader Bob Hawke becomes prime minister.

Israel—Yitzhak Shamir succeeds Menachem Begin as prime minister.

Philippines—Benigno Aquino is assassinated, allegedly with government complicity, while returning from exile. Corazon Aquino replaces him as leader of the Liberal Party.

Saint Kitts and Nevis—Saint Kitts and Nevis gains independence from Britain.

South Korea—While visiting Burma, President Chun Doo Hwan, four cabinet members, and 13 other South Koreans are assassinated in a bombing by North Korean agents.

U.K.—Irish Republican Army (IRA) forces increase terrorist attacks, bombing Harrod's department store in London and killing six.

Neil Gordon Kinnock becomes leader of the Labour Party, moving it in a more centrist direction.

U.S.—President Ronald Reagan proposes the Strategic Defense Initiative, commonly known as "Star Wars," a program for defense against a nuclear attack.

Science and Technology

France—Neurologist A. Roch-Lecours discovers that humans are born with two language areas in the brain.

Italy/Netherlands—Italian physicist Carlo Rubbia and Dutch physicist Simon van der Meer discover the two W bosons and neutral Z boson predicted by electroweak theory.

U.S.—Sally Ride becomes the first American woman in space, and Guion Bluford Jr. the first African-American in space. The two fly, in separate missions, aboard the space shuttle *Challenger*.

The first artificially made chromosome is synthesized at Harvard University.

Astronomer Carl Sagan and others theorize that a nuclear war could trigger a nuclear winter.

Society

France—Chanel's new design director, Karl Lagerfeld, begins to modernize the house's style.

Germany—More than 600,000 demonstrators protest against installation of U.S. medium-range nuclear missiles in Europe. Antinuclear protests take place elsewhere in Europe as well.

Iran—Iraqi attacks on Iranian installations during the Iran-Iraq War contribute to the world's worst oil spill, as 225,000 barrels of crude oil spill from the Nowruz and Kharg Island oil facilities.

South Korea—On September 1 Soviet warplanes shoot down Korean Air Lines Flight 007 after the airliner strays into Soviet airspace off Sakhalin Island; all 269 people aboard are killed.

Spain—Near the Madrid airport, a Colombian 747 crashes, killing 183 people.

U.S.—Martin Luther King Day becomes a federal holiday.

A federal government report on education, *A Nation at Risk*, argues that the country's educational system has fallen behind that of other industrialized countries.

The United Presbyterian Church of North America and the Presbyterian Church in the United States merge to form the Presbyterian Church (U.S.A.).

Cellular telephones, made by Motorola, are first test-marketed in Chicago.

Aspartame-based Nutrasweet is used for the first time to sweeten beverages.

Vanessa Williams becomes the first African-American to win the Miss America pageant but is forced to give up the title in a scandal over nude photographs.

West Germany—The "Hitler diaries," acquired by the magazine *Stern* for $3.7 million, are uncovered as a hoax.

Sports

Australia—The *Australia II* is the first Australian vessel to win yachting's America's Cup.

U.S.—Czechoslovakian-born American tennis player Martina Navratilova wins the sport's grand slam.

1984 Arts and Entertainment

Czechoslovakia—Milan Kundera publishes the novel *The Unbearable Lightness of Being*.

Ireland—Seamus Heaney publishes the poetry collection *Station Island*.

New Zealand—Keri Hulme's novel *The Bone People* wins the Booker Prize.

U.K.—Julian Barnes publishes the novel *Flaubert's Parrot*.

J. G. Ballard publishes the novel *Empire of the Sun*.

U.S.—August Wilson's play *Ma Rainey's Black Bottom* premieres.

Novels include Jay McInerney's *Bright Lights, Big City* and Louise Erdrich's *Love Medicine*.

Philip Levine publishes *Selected Poems*.

New albums include Bruce Springsteen's *Born in the USA*, Madonna's *Like a Virgin*, Prince's *Purple Rain*, and Cyndi Lauper's *She's So Unusual*.

Artists Andy Warhol, Jean-Michel Basquiat, and Francesco Clemente paint *Polestar*.

The television series *The Cosby Show* premieres (NBC, 1984–92).

World—Films include Milos Forman's *Amadeus* and Jim Jarmusch's *Stranger Than Paradise* (both U.S.), David Lean's *A Passage to India* and Roland Joffe's *The Killing Fields* (both U.K.), and Krzysztof Kieslowski's *No End* (Poland).

Ideas

Belgium—Feminist theorist Luce Irigaray publishes *Éthiques de la différence sexuelle*.

France—Philosopher Jean-François Lyotard publishes *The Postmodern Condition*.

Germany—Psychoanalyst Adolf Grünbaum publishes *Foundations of Psychoanalysis*, which questions the scientific basis of psychoanalysis.

U.K.—Philosopher Derek Parfit publishes *Reasons and Persons*.

U.S.—Critic Henry Louis Gates Jr. publishes the essay "Criticism in the Jungle."

Military

Iraq—Government forces use poison gas against Kurdish rebels in northern Iraq and on the front lines against Iran; Iran also uses poison gas against Iraq.

Lebanon—The civil war continues as peacekeeping forces are withdrawn.

Sri Lanka—Several hundred die in two weeks of violence instigated by Tamil separatists in December.

Politics

Brunei—Brunei becomes independent from Britain.

Canada—Progressive Conservative Party leader Martin Brian Mulroney becomes prime minister.

India—Militant Sikhs demanding independence for the Punjab State occupy the Golden Temple in Amritsar. Hundreds are killed when Prime Minister Indira Gandhi sends in troops to remove them. Gandhi is assassinated later this year by Sikh extremists; anti-Sikh riots follow.

Lebanon—Terrorists begin taking Western hostages, including William Buckley, Central Intelligence Agency (CIA) station chief in Beirut.

New Zealand—Labour Party leader David Russell Lange becomes prime minister.

Poland—The police abduct Father Jerzy Popieluszko, a supporter of the Solidarity movement who is later found murdered. His funeral on November 3 is attended by more than 200,000 people.

Soviet Union—General secretary Yuri Andropov dies; he is succeeded by Konstantin Chernenko.

U.S.—President Ronald Reagan is reelected, defeating Democratic challenger Walter Mondale. Mondale's choice for vice president, Geraldine Ferraro, is the first woman to run on a major party's presidential ticket.

Science and Technology

Chile—Scientists at the European Southern Observatory near Santiago, Chile, confirm the existence of a partial ring around Neptune (first suggested in 1981).

France/U.S.—French scientist Luc Montagnier and American physician Robert Gallo announce their discovery of a virus believed to cause AIDS.

India—Astronomer J. C. Bhattacharyya discovers two more rings of Saturn.

Ireland—Lindow man, the 2,200-year-old body of what is probably a victim of Druid human sacrifice, is found preserved in a peat bog.

Kenya/U.K.—Near Lake Turkana, Kenya, British paleontologist Richard Leakey discovers the skeleton of Turkana boy, a hominid who lived 1.6 million years ago.

U.K.—A chimera, a cross between a sheep and a goat, is created through manipulation of embryos.

U.S.—Astronauts aboard the space shuttle *Challenger* use jet-propelled backpacks in the first untethered space walks.

The Monsanto Life Sciences Research Center is founded in Missouri to develop biotechnological drugs and agricultural products, marking the beginning of large-scale biological research in private industry.

Scientists find that chimpanzees differ from humans by only one percent of their DNA, and that the two species are more closely related to each other than either are to other apes. It is hypothesized that humans and chimpanzees diverged from a common ancestor five million to six million years ago.

Scientist Allan Wilson is the first to clone gene fragments from an extinct species (a quagga).

The first one-megabit random access memory (RAM) chip is developed by Bell Laboratories.

West Germany—West German scientists discover element 108, unniloctium.

Society

Bolivia—Unions carry out a week-long general strike.

Ethiopia—Severe drought, aggravated by civil war, leads to famine (1984–85). More than a million people die.

India—In Bhopal on December 3, a leak of lethal gas from a Union Carbide plant kills more than 3,500 people and injures at least 200,000 more.

U.S.—On December 22 Bernhard Goetz, the "subway vigilante," shoots four alleged robbers on a New York City subway. Goetz, who is white while the shooting victims are black, added a racial component to the case. He will be acquitted of major charges (1987) but convicted of carrying a concealed weapon (1989).

The Macintosh computer is introduced by Apple, with a mouse, icons, and pull-down menus.

Laptop computers are introduced.

The CD-ROM (compact disc, read-only memory) is introduced.

Sports

U.K.—At the Winter Olympics in Sarajevo, Yugoslavia, ice dancers Jayne Torvill and Christopher Dean win the gold medal.

U.S.—At Daytona, stock car racer Richard Lee Petty wins his last championship, a record 200th.

Track athlete Carl Lewis wins four gold medals at the Summer Olympics in Los Angeles.

Kareem Abdul-Jabbar becomes the all-time leading scorer in professional basketball.

In basketball Larry Bird wins his first of three Most Valuable Player Awards (1984–86).

In football Walter Payton breaks Jim Brown's records for career rushing yards, total career yards, and total games rushing for 100 yards or more.

World—The Los Angeles Summer Olympics are boycotted by the Soviet Union and all Eastern bloc countries except Romania.

1985 Arts and Entertainment

Canada—The Vancouver Jazz Festival is founded.

U.S.—Artist Red Grooms's work from 1956 to 1984 is exhibited at the Pennsylvania Academy of Fine Arts.

Sculptor Louise Bourgeois has her first large-scale exhibition at the Museum of Modern Art.

More than 30 singers participate in recording the Michael Jackson–Lionel Richie anthem "We Are the World." The recording is arranged by composer Quincy Jones to benefit famine victims in Africa.

Composer Stephen Albert's *Symphony, Riverrun* premieres in Washington, D.C.

World—Novels include Anne Tyler's *The Accidental Tourist* and Larry McMurtry's *Lonesome Dove* (U.S.), Italo Calvino's *Mr. Palomar* (Italy), Carlos Fuentes's *The Old Gringo* (Mexico), and Isabel Allende's *The House of the Spirits* (Chile).

Films include Sydney Pollack's *Out of Africa* (U.S.), Agnès Varda's *Vagabond* (France), Dorris Dorrie's *Men* (West Germany), Akira Kurosawa's *Ran* (Japan), and Stephen Frears's *My Beautiful Laundrette* (U.K.).

Ideas

Brazil—Theologian Leonardo Boff is censured by the Roman Catholic Church for his promulgation of liberation theology.

U.K.—Philosopher Bernard Williams publishes *Ethics and the Limits of Philosophy*.

U.S.—Critic Robert Scholes publishes *Textual Power*.

Critic J. Hillis Miller publishes *The Linguistic Moment*.

Computer scientist Marvin Minsky publishes *The Society of Mind*, in which he offers a theory of human intelligence based on studies of artificial intelligence (AI).

Military

Burma—The Karen insurgency bombs a train, killing more than 60 people.

Colombia—The military storms the Palace of Justice in Bogota in an attempt to free 300 hostages held by guerrillas. Ninety-five hostages die, including 11 Supreme Court justices.

Politics

Brazil—President-elect Tancredo de Almeida Neves dies; Vice President José Sarney becomes president.

France—French agents bomb and sink the Greenpeace ship *Rainbow Warrior* in the harbor at Auckland, New Zealand. Greenpeace, an environmental group, had been protesting French nuclear tests. Relations between France and New Zealand are strained.

Nicaragua—Daniel Ortega Saavedra becomes president.

Nigeria—General Ibrahim Babangida takes power in a coup.

South Africa—International pressure to end apartheid increases as the U.S. imposes economic sanctions. The government imposes a state of emergency in response to growing domestic unrest (1985–86).

Soviet Union—General Secretary Konstantin Chernenko dies; he is succeeded by Mikhail Gorbachev.

Sudan—General Abdar-Rahman Siwar el-Dahab seizes power in a coup and steps up the civil war against southern rebels.

Uganda—A coup led by General Tito Okello deposes President Milton Obote.

U.S.—White House officials, including Oliver North, Robert McFarlane, and John Poindexter, conspire secretly and illegally to sell arms to Iran in return for the release of Western hostages in Lebanon, and to funnel the profits from the sale to the Contras, rebels against the Sandinista government of Nicaragua. Senate investigation will begin to expose the plot in 1986.

Science and Technology

Japan—The JT-60 tokamak, an experimental nuclear fusion reactor, begins operation.

Tanzania—By now the Traditional Medicine Research Unit, founded in 1974, has identified 2,300 plant specimens used in treating more than 1,000 diseases.

U.K.—The British Antarctic Expedition detects a hole that forms annually in the ozone layer above Antarctica.

U.S./Rwanda—American primatologist Dian Fossey is murdered in Rwanda, probably by enemies she made while protecting mountain gorillas from poaching. Her book *Gorillas in the Mist* was published in 1983.

U.S./U.K.—American chemists Richard Smalley and Robert F. Curl Jr. and British chemist Harry W. Kroto discover buckminsterfullerene, a form of pure carbon.

U.S.—Construction begins on the Keck telescope, the world's largest, on Mauna Kea in Hawaii. The reflecting telescope will be finished in 1990.

Positron emission tomography (PET) scans are developed.

Researchers at the University of California–San Francisco announce that condoms block the passage of the AIDS virus.

The National Science Foundation forms the NSFNET, one of several academic computer networks established in the 1970s and 1980s. As they become linked to each other, they will be known collectively as the Internet, which, by the 1990s, will include commercial and recreational users as well.

Society

Bangladesh—A cyclone kills more than 10,000 people.

France/U.S.—French and American oceanographers locate the liner *Titanic*, sunk in 1912, on the bottom of the North Atlantic Ocean.

Japan—A Japan Air 747 crashes into Mount Ogura, killing 520 people in the world's worst single-plane air disaster.

Mexico—Earthquakes destroy part of Mexico City and devastate southern Mexico.

U.S.—In Philadelphia, police trying to evict the radical group MOVE drop a bomb that sets the neighborhood ablaze and kills 11 people.

Paperback-sized video cameras are produced for home use.

World—Conservative Judaism approves ordination of women as rabbis.

In June the terrorist group Islamic Jihad hijacks an Athens-to-Rome TWA airliner, murdering U.S. Navy diver Robert Stethem. In October Palestinian terrorists hijack the Italian ship *Achille Lauro* and murder American passenger Leon Klinghoffer.

Sports

Germany—In tennis 17-year-old German athlete Boris Becker is the youngest player and the first unseeded player to win the men's singles title at Wimbledon. He will win the title again in 1986 and 1989.

Soviet Union—Gary Kasparov becomes the youngest world chess champion ever, taking the title from fellow Soviet player Anatoly Karpov. Kasparov will defend the title against challenges from Karpov in 1986, 1987, and 1990.

U.S.—In baseball Pete Rose of the Cincinnati Reds breaks the major league record for most career hits, 4,191, set by Ty Cobb in 1928; Rose will tally 4,256 hits by his retirement in 1987.

1986 Arts and Entertainment

U.K.—Frank Auerbach paints *Head of Catherine Lampert*.

Martin Amis publishes the short-story collection *Einstein's Monsters*.

U.S.—Art Spiegelman publishes the two-part graphic novel *Maus: A Survivor's Tale* (1986–91).

Anthony Davis's opera *X (The Life and Times of Malcolm X)* premieres.

Run-D.M.C.'s album *Raisin' Hell* is the first rap album to go platinum.

Jeff Koons sculpts *Rabbit*.

Paul Auster publishes *Ghosts* and *The Locked Room*, the second and third novels in his series *The New York Trilogy*; the first installment, *City of Glass*, was published in 1985.

West Indies—Derek Walcott publishes *Collected Poems 1948–1984*.

World—Novels include Margaret Atwood's *The Handmaid's Tale* (Canada), Kazuo Ishiguro's *An Artist of the Floating World* (Japan), Kingsley Amis's *The Old Devils* (U.K.), and Patrick White's *Memoirs of Many in One* (Australia).

Films include Woody Allen's *Hannah and Her Sisters* and Oliver Stone's *Platoon* (U.S.), James Ivory's *A Room with a View* (U.K.), Chen Kaige's *Yellow Earth* (China), Jovan Acin's *Hey Babu Riba* (Yugoslavia), and Claude Berri's *Manon of the Spring* (France).

Ideas

U.S.—Philosopher David Lewis publishes *The Plurality of Worlds*.

Philosopher Ronald Dworkin publishes *Law's Empire*.

Physician Oliver Sacks publishes the study of neurological patients *The Man Who Mistook His Wife for a Hat*.

Military

Libya/U.S.—In March and April U.S. warplanes bomb Libya in retaliation for alleged Libyan missile attacks on U.S. aircraft and alleged involvement in terrorist acts.

South Yemen—Rebels take power after a six-day civil war.

Politics

Australia—Australia's constitutional ties to the U.K. are formally severed.

Chile—An assassination attempt on President Augusto Pinochet prompts declaration of a state of siege.

China/Taiwan—China and Taiwan talk face-to-face for the first time since 1949.

France—The Socialists lose control of the government in a general election. Socialist president François Mitterrand must share power (or "cohabit") with Conservative prime minister Jacques Chirac.

Haiti—President-for-life Jean-Claude "Baby Doc" Duvalier is overthrown and forced to flee. General Henri Namphy forms a new government.

Kuwait—The emir dissolves the National Assembly.

Liberia—Samuel K. Doe, head of Liberia since he seized power in 1980, becomes president of a new civilian state.

Philippines—In February Ferdinand Marcos is overthrown after allegations of having rigged a victory in this month's presidential election. Opposition leader Corazon Aquino becomes president.

South Africa—The government rescinds the pass laws, which were a symbol of apartheid. A new state of emergency is declared in June as antiapartheid protests continue.

Soviet Union—General Secretary Mikhail Gorbachev institutes the policies of glasnost (openness) and perestroika (restructuring), marking a shift toward a more democratic and liberal Soviet Union.

Soviet Union/U.S.—A summit meeting between leaders of the two countries at Reykjavík, Iceland, fails to produce an arms control agreement.

Sweden—Prime minister Olof Palme is assassinated; Ingvar Carlson succeeds him.

Uganda—Yoweri Museveni leads the military overthrow of the government.

U.S.—Senate investigation begins into the Iran-Contra scandal (*see* **1985**).

A major tax reform bill is passed.

The Senate rejects the nomination of arch-conservative Robert Bork to the Supreme Court.

Science and Technology

Germany/U.S.—German and American researchers, working independently, observe individual quantum jumps in single atoms for the first time.

Soviet Union—The *Mir* space station is launched, in which cosmonauts will set new space endurance records.

Switzerland/Germany—Swiss physicist Karl Alexander Müller and German physicist Johannes George Bednorz discover superconductivity in certain ceramics at temperatures higher (and therefore more practical) than any results obtained previously.

U.S.—On January 28, in history's worst space flight disaster, the space shuttle *Challenger* explodes shortly after takeoff, killing its crew of seven, including teacher Christa McAuliffe.

Linguist Joseph H. Greenberg uses the technique of mass comparisons of Native American languages to classify them into three groups; he claims these groups represent successive waves of migration from Asia.

Physicist Arthur Ashkin develops a technique of using a laser's radiation pressure to observe and manipulate biological particles.

World—Several spacecraft make close approaches to Halley's comet, including the Japanese probes *Suisei* and *Sakigake* and the European Space Agency's probe *Giotto*.

Society

Cameroon—A toxic cloud rises from the volcanic crater in Lake Nios, killing 1,700 people.

Japan/U.S.—The Japanese company Nintendo introduces its video games to the U.S.

South Africa—Antiapartheid leader Desmond Tutu becomes archbishop of Johannesburg, the first black leader of South Africa's Anglican Church.

Soviet Union—On April 26 the Chernobyl 4 reactor in the Ukraine undergoes a meltdown, killing 31 people and spreading radioactive fallout over a wide region.

Anatoly Scharansky and three other imprisoned dissidents are set free in exchange for five alleged Eastern European spies held prisoner in the West. Dissident Andrey Sakharov is permitted to return to Moscow from internal exile.

U.S.—The Supreme Court decision *Meritor Savings Bank v. Vinson* widens the scope of sexual harassment cases.

A stock market scandal involving the illegal use of inside information breaks; Ivan Boesky, Dennis Levine, Michael Milken, and others will be implicated, and some will serve prison terms.

In Oklahoma, disgruntled post office worker Patrick Sherrill kills 14 coworkers and wounds seven others before killing himself.

Dick Rutan and Jeana Yeager complete the first nonstop around-the-world flight without refueling, aboard their airplane *Voyager*.

Sports

U.S.—In boxing, 22-year-old Mike Tyson becomes the youngest person to be the undisputed world heavyweight champion.

American cyclist Greg LeMond wins the Tour de France; he will win again in 1989 and 1990.

The New York Mets defeat the Boston Red Sox to win the World Series, four games to three.

1987 Arts and Entertainment

Africa—African music gains in international popularity, with Youssou n'Dour among the world's widely known musicians.

Belgium/Switzerland—Belgian choreographer Maurice Béjart moves his Ballet of the Twentieth Century from Brussels, Belgium, to Lausanne, Switzerland.

France—Architect Jean Nouvel designs the Institut du Monde Arabe, Paris.

Japan—Architect Kenzo Tange wins the Pritzker Architecture Prize.

U.K.—Lucian Freud paints *Painter and Model*.

Architect Quinlan Terry designs the Howard Building, Downing College, Cambridge.

U.S.—Paintings include Brice Marden's *Diptych* and Robert Ryman's *Constant*.

West Germany—Rainer Fetting paints *Embrace at the Pier*.

World—Films include Norman Jewison's *Moonstruck* (U.S.), Louis Malle's *Au revoir lLes enfants* (France), Juzo Itami's *A Taxing Woman* (Japan), and Bernardo Bertolucci's *The Last Emperor* (Italy/U.K./China).

Novels include Toni Morrison's *Beloved* and Tom Wolfe's *The Bonfire of the Vanities* (U.S.); Friedrich Dürrenmatt's *Der Auftrag* (West Germany), Brian Moore's *The Colour of Blood* (U.K.), and Mario Vargas Llosa's *The Storyteller* (Peru).

Musical compositions include Steven Paulus's *Construction Symphony* and John Adams's opera *Nixon in China* (both U.S.), Olivier Messiaen's *Bird Sketches* for piano (France), and Robert Saxton's choral work *I Will Awake the Dawn* (U.K.).

Ideas

Austria—Philosopher of science Paul Feyerabend publishes *Farewell to Reason*.

Belgium/U.S.—The late Belgian-born American deconstructionist critic Paul De Man (1919–83), becomes a center of controversy upon the discovery of his collaborationist and anti-Semitic writings during the Nazi occupation of Belgium.

U.S.—Scholar Allan Bloom publishes *The Closing of the American Mind*.

Philosopher Jerry Fodor publishes *Psychosemantics*.

Military

Chad—In the civil war that has raged intermittently since 1975, southern Chadian forces capture Libyan bases at Faya-Largeau and Ouadi Doum, then invade Libya, forcing negotiation of a truce.

Iraq—In what is considered an accident, Iraqi missiles kill 37 sailors aboard the U.S.S. *Stark*.

Politics

China—Li Peng succeeds Zhao Ziyang as prime minister.

Costa Rica—Costa Rican president Oscar Arias Sánchez proposes the Arias Plan, which will help end the Nicaraguan Civil War.

Czechoslovakia—President Gustav Husák announces liberalizing political and economic reforms.

Fiji—After two bloodless coups, Fiji becomes a republic.

India—India imposes direct rule on the Punjab in response to terrorism by Sikh separatists.

Israel—The Intifada, a Palestinian uprising, begins (1987–94).

Italy—Prime Minister Bettino Craxi resigns. His Socialist government, three and a half years old, was the longest-lived government in Italy since World War II.

New Zealand—New Zealand declares its waters a nuclear-free zone.

South Korea—Roh Tae Woo wins the first direct presidential election since the early 1970s.

Soviet Union—Voters in some local elections are able to choose from among several candidates for the first time.

Soviet Union/U.S.—The Intermediate-Range Nuclear Forces (INF) Treaty is signed, the first agreement to destroy a category of nuclear weapons.

U.K.—Voters in a general election retain Margaret Thatcher as prime minister, making her the first British prime minister in 160 years to be reelected for a third term.

U.S.—Economist Alan Greenspan becomes chairman of the Federal Reserve Board.

Vatican City—The Vatican expresses opposition to in vitro fertilization, artificial insemination, and other medical practices that involve manipulation of conception.

Science and Technology

Canada—Astronomer Ian Shelter discovers Supernova 1987A in the Large Magellanic Cloud.

Czechoslovakia—Ceramics are developed that are superconductive at temperatures as high as 170 degrees Kelvin.

Soviet Union—Cosmonaut Yuri Romanenko, traveling aboard the space station *Mir*, sets a new endurance record for a single space flight: 326.5 days.

U.S.—Astronomer R. Brent Tully reports the discovery of the Pisces-Cetus supercluster complex, the largest-known structure in the universe.

Genetically engineered bacteria are released into the environment for the first time, when a microbe is tested for its ability to retard frost formation on plants. The plant pathologists who developed the microbe were American Steve Lindow and Greek Nickolas Panopoulos.

The anti-AIDS drug AZT (azidothymidine, or zidovudine) receives approval from the Food and Drug Administration.

Scientists produce a standing wave called a dark pulse soliton.

The pharmaceutical company Eli Lilly introduces the antidepressant Prozac (fluoxetine).

Society

Israel/U.S.—U.S. Navy employee Jonathan J. Pollard is convicted of having spied for Israel and sentenced to life in prison.

Philippines—The ferry *Dona Paz* collides with an oil tanker and sinks, killing up to 3,000 people in the century's worst peacetime marine disaster.

Saudi Arabia—Police clash with Iranian fundamentalist pilgrims at Mecca's Grand Mosque, killing hundreds.

South Korea—A Korean Air jet crashes near the Thailand-Burma border, killing 115 people, probably as a result of a North Korean bomb.

U.K./Lebanon—Terry Waite, the Archbishop of Canterbury's envoy, is taken hostage in Beirut, Lebanon.

U.K.—Genetic identification is used to convict a criminal for the first time anywhere.

U.S.—On Black Monday, October 19, the Dow Jones industrial average drops a record 508.32 points (22.6 percent). The Crash of 87 is costly to many investors but does not trigger a recession or depression.

Televangelist Jim Bakker resigns from his Praise the Lord (PTL) network over a sex and corruption scandal. He will later be convicted on federal charges and imprisoned.

Michael Deaver, a former aide to President Ronald Reagan, is convicted of perjury regarding his lobbying efforts after leaving the White House.

In Howard Beach, Brooklyn, African-American Michael Griffith is killed in a racial confrontation with white youths. Four of his attackers will receive criminal convictions.

The Patent and Trademark Office rules that genetically engineered animals can be patented.

Sports

Canada—In track Ben Johnson sets a new 100–meter world record at 9.83 seconds.

U.K.—Golfer Nick Faldo wins his first of three British Opens (1987, 1990, 1992).

West Germany—In tennis West German player Steffi Graf wins the French Open. She will dominate women's tennis in the late 1980s.

1988 Arts and Entertainment

Spain—Roberto Marquez paints *Mirrors Have No Mercy.*

U.K.—Indian-born British writer Salman Rushdie publishes the novel *The Satanic Verses*; its alleged blasphemy against Islam will prompt Iran to issue a death edict against the author the following year.

U.S.—Elliott Carter's Oboe Concerto premieres.

Heavy metal bands like Guns 'N' Roses, Def Leppard, Metallica, and Van Halen gain popularity.

Singer Whitney Houston is the first to release seven consecutive chart-topping songs in the U.S.

Wendy Wasserstein's play *The Heidi Chronicles* premieres.

U.S./France—Chinese-born American architect I. M. Pei remodels France's Louvre Museum, adding a 65-foot glass pyramid.

West Germany—Karlheinz Stockhausen's opera *Montag aus Licht* premieres.

World—Novels include Don DeLillo's *Libra* (U.S.), Iris Murdoch's *The Book and the Brotherhood* (U.K.), Peter Carey's *Oscar and Lucinda* (Australia), Gabriel García Márquez's *Love in the Time of Cholera* (Colombia), and Chinua Achebe's *Anthills of the Savannah* (Nigeria).

Poetry collections include Richard Wilbur's *New and Collected Poems* and Joseph Brodsky's *To Urania* (U.S.), Czeslaw Milosz's *The Collected Poems: 1931–87* (Poland), and Wole Soyinka's *Mandela's Earth and Other Poems* (Nigeria).

Films include Barry Levinson's *Rain Man* (U.S.), David Cronenberg's *Dead Ringers* (Canada), Zhang Yimou's *Red Sorghum* (China), Giuseppe Tornatore's *Cinema Paradiso* (Italy/France), and Wim Wenders's *Wings of Desire* (West Germany/France).

Ideas

Ghana—Critic Kwame Anthony Appiah publishes the essay "Out of Africa: Typologies of Nativism."

U.S.—Philosopher Richard Rorty publishes *Contingency, Irony, and Solidarity.*

Legal scholar Robert Unger publishes *Politics, a Work in Constructive Social Theory.*

Critic Catharine R. Stimpson publishes *Where the Meanings Are.*

Military

Afghanistan/Soviet Union—The Afghan-Soviet War ends when the Soviet Union, in the Geneva Agreement, commits to withdrawal of its forces. Soviet troop withdrawals begin while the Afghan Civil War continues.

Angola—An Angolan peace agreement is signed by Angola, Cuba, and South Africa; foreign intervention ends and agreement is made for a free Namibia. But the civil war continues.

Azerbaijan/Armenia—The Soviet republics of Azerbaijan and Armenia go to war over the disputed region of Nagorny-Kharabach.

Burundi—Thousands die in fighting between Hutu and Tutsi peoples.

India/Sri Lanka—Indian forces intervene in Sri Lanka, but their attacks on Tamil separatists are unsuccessful.

Iran/Iraq—The Iran-Iraq War ends with a UN-mediated cease-fire and Geneva peace negotiations. Afterward, Iraq attacks Kurdish insurgents in the north.

Nicaragua—The Nicaraguan Civil War ends with a cease-fire.

U.S.—The U.S. warship *Vincennes* mistakenly shoots down an Iranian civilian airliner, killing 290 people.

Politics

Burma—Dictator Ne Win resigns in the wake of "Burmese Spring" antigovernment demonstrations. The democratic government of U Nu is established but overthrown in September by General Saw Maung. Dissident Daw Aung San Suu Kyi is put under house arrest.

Chile—Voters in a referendum reject dictator Augusto Pinochet's continued rule; he will step down in 1990.

France—Jacques Chirac resigns as prime minister; he is succeeded by Michel Rocard.

Hungary—János Kádár, dictator since 1956, is deposed as general secretary amid a wave of pressure for democratic reform.

Pakistan—President Mohammed Zia-ul-Haq is killed in an air crash.

He is succeeded by the Muslim world's first female leader, Prime Minister Benazir Bhutto.

U.S.—Attorney General Ed Meese III resigns under pressure from corruption investigators.

Democratic senator and presidential aspirant Gary Hart is forced out of the primary race when he is accused of having an adulterous affair.

Republican George Bush defeats Democrat Michael Dukakis in the presidential election.

Science and Technology

Israel—Fossils of hominids bearing many characteristics of modern humans are found that date back 90,000 to 100,000 years, more than twice as old as previously known specimens of modern humans.

U.S.—The space shuttle *Discovery* is launched in the first U.S. manned space mission since the *Challenger* disaster of 1986.

Psychiatrist Richard Haier reports that high intelligence may be the result of an efficiently organized brain.

Biochemist Sidney Fox develops proteinlike substances called proteinoids.

World—Scientists will determine that 1988 was the warmest year to date for average temperatures worldwide. Global warming linked to an atmospheric greenhouse effect is suspected, though some scientists dispute it.

Society

Bangladesh—Floods kill hundreds of people and leave millions homeless.

Brazil—Labor leader and environmentalist Chico Mendez is killed; three ranchers opposed to his attempts to halt rain forest clearing are convicted of the crime.

Soviet Union—An earthquake devastates Soviet Armenia, killing 55,000 people.

U.S./Lebanon—U.S. Colonel William Higgins is murdered in Lebanon by Islamic terrorists.

U.S./U.K.—An Islamic terrorist bomb causes Pan Am Flight 103 to explode over Lockerbie, Scotland, killing 270 people in the U.K.'s worst air disaster.

U.S.—The fax, or facsimile machine, becomes standard office equipment as the price drops below $1,000.

Sports

Canada—Findings of drug use disqualify Canadian sprinter Ben Johnson from accepting his gold medal at the Summer Olympics in Seoul, Korea.

West Germany—Steffi Graf wins the grand slam of tennis.

Violence among fans at the soccer championships is quelled by riot police.

1989 Arts and Entertainment

Ivory Coast—Architect Pierre Fakhoury designs the Basilica of Our Lady of Peace in Yamoussoukro, Ivory Coast, the tallest church in Christendom.

U.S.—Congress prohibits the National Endowment for the Arts (NEA) from funding artworks deemed obscene. Grants to several artists will be revoked, including performance artist Karen Finley.

Janet Jackson releases the number-one album *Janet Jackson's Rhythm Nation 1814*.

A retrospective on painter Helen Frankenthaler opens at the Museum of Modern Art in

New York City.

John Berryman's *Collected Poems, 1937–1971* is published posthumously.

Novels include E.L. Doctorow's *Billy Bathgate* and Amy Tan's *The Joy Luck Club.*

The television series *The Seinfeld Chronicles* premieres. It will become the weekly series *Seinfeld* in 1991 (NBC, 1989–98).

World—Films include Steven Soderbergh's *Sex, Lies and Videotape,* Spike Lee's *Do the Right Thing,* and Gus Van Sant's *Drugstore Cowboy* (U.S.), Peter Greenaway's *The Cook, the Thief, His Wife and Her Lover* (France/Netherlands), Wayne Wang's *Life Is Cheap. . . But Toilet Paper is Expensive* (Hong Kong), Percy Adlon's *Rosalie Goes Shopping* (West Germany), and Jim Sheridan's *My Left Foot* (Ireland).

Ideas

Australia—Critics Bill Ashcroft, Gareth Griffiths, and Helen Tiffin publish *The Empire Writes Back: Theory and Practice in Post-Colonial Literatures.*

U.S.—Anthropologist Marvin Harris publishes *Our Kind.*

Social scientist Francis Fukuyama publishes the essay "The End of History."

Political scientist Roger Masters publishes *The Nature of Politics.*

Military

Afghanistan—Soviet forces complete their withdrawal from Afghanistan.

Lebanon—Civil war becomes more intense, with Michel Aoun's Lebanese army forces failing to vanquish Muslim forces in Beirut.

Liberia—Charles Taylor launches a rebellion against the government of Samuel K. Doe. The resulting civil war will devastate the country (*see* **1997**).

Nicaragua—The civil war formally ends with the signing of the Tesoro Beach Accords on February 14.

Panama—The U.S. invades Panama and deposes the government. On January 3, 1990, U.S. forces will arrest Panama's leader, Manuel Noriega, taking him to the U.S. to face drug trafficking charges.

Soviet Union—Regional conflicts get worse in various parts of the nation: Armenia and Azerbaijan intensify their war; conflict breaks out between Sunni and Shi'ite Muslims in Uzbekistan; in Kirghizia, Uzbeks and Kirghiz clash.

Politics

China—Beginning in April students, workers, and others demonstrate in Tiananmen Square in Beijing, demanding democratic reform. On June 3 and 4 the military invades the square, killing thousands and ending the movement.

Czechoslovakia—In the Velvet Revolution the Communist government collapses in the wake of a general strike. In December, a new government composed mostly of non-Communists is formed, with one-time imprisoned dissident Václav Havel as president and Alexander Dubcek, former leader of the Prague Spring (1968), as parliament chairman.

East Germany—The Communist government falls. In November the Berlin Wall, a symbol of the cold war since its erection in 1961, begins to be dismantled.

Hungary—Parliament votes to legalize opposition parties, ending four decades of one-party Communist rule.

Iran—Ayatollah Ruhollah Khomeini dies and is succeeded as leader by Ali Akbar Hashemi Rafsanjani.

Japan—Prime minister Noboru Takeshita and several cabinet members resign over their involvement in the Recruit stock scandal.

Paraguay—General Andres Rodriguez takes power in a coup, ending the long dictatorship (1954–89) of Alfredo Stroessner (1912–).

Poland—The trade union Solidarity is legalized. As the Communist monopoly on power ends, Poland's first non-Communist prime minister since 1945, Tadeusz Mazowiecki, is elected.

Romania—In the Romanian Revolution, dictator Nicolae Ceausescu and his wife, Elena, (1918–89) are deposed and executed (December 25).

South Africa—F.W. deKlerk becomes acting president upon the resignation of P.W. Botha.

Soviet Union—Under Mikhail Gorbachev the Soviet Union effectively ceases its long-standing policy of propping up Eastern Europe's Communist governments. As a result, a wave of democratic change sweeps through the region (*see* **individual countries**).

The first democratic Soviet national elections take place, to elect the Congress of People's Deputies.

In Latvia, Lithuania, and Estonia, independence movements grow.

Science and Technology

Canada/U.S.—Canadian researcher La-Chee Tsui and American Francis Collins discover the gene that causes cystic fibrosis.

Japan—Physicists report the first experimental confirmation that the sun generates neutrinos.

U.S.—The spacecraft *Voyager 2* is the first probe to fly past Neptune.

Biologist Stephen Jay Gould publishes *Wonderful Life*, a popular account of fossil findings from Canada's Burgess Shale (*see* **1971**).

Geneticists at the National Institutes of Health are the first to inject genetically engineered nonhuman cells into a human patient. The cells will be used to mark and trace other cells in an experimental therapy for skin cancer.

University of Utah researchers claim to have discovered "cold" fusion of atomic nuclei at room temperature. Further investigation will discredit the claim.

Congress approves funding for construction of the Superconducting Super Collider, but will vote to terminate the project in 1993.

Researchers James W. Tetrud and J. William Langstrom develop Deprenyl, an anti–Parkinson's disease drug that is the first shown to delay symptoms of the neurological disorder.

World—More than 80 nations, including the U.S. and the members of the European Community, agree to plans to phase out ozone-destroying chlorofluorocarbons by the year 2000.

Society

Africa—To try to save the African elephant, the Convention on International Trade in Endangered Species (CITES) declares a worldwide ban on the ivory trade.

U.S.—On October 17, in the San Francisco Bay area, an earthquake measuring 7. 1 on the Richter scale kills 67 people and injures more than 3,000.

On March 24 the tanker *Exxon Valdez* spills 250,000 barrels of oil into Prince William Sound off the Alaskan coast.

In Stockton, California, on January 17, Patrick Edward Purdy kills five children and wounds 30 children and adults when he opens fire with an AK-47 assault rifle before killing himself. In March the federal government bans the import of such rifles.

Vinyl records are phased out of music stores, replaced by compact discs.

Barbara Clementine Harris becomes the first woman bishop, and the first African-American woman bishop, of the Episcopal Church and of the worldwide Anglican Communion.

West Indies/U.S.—Hurricane Hugo sweeps across the Caribbean and causes severe damage in Charleston, South Carolina, where it leaves tens of thousands homeless.

Sports

U.K.—On April 15 at Hillsborough, near Sheffield, England, 95 people are killed and hundreds injured in a stampede at a soccer stadium.

U.S.—In the World Series Oakland (American League) defeats San Francisco (National League) in four games.

1990 Arts and Entertainment

Ireland—Edna O'Brien publishes the fiction collection *Lantern Slides.*

Singer Sinead O'Connor has a hit with her cover of Prince's ballad "Nothing Compares 2 U," from her second album, *I Do Not Want What I Haven't Got.*

Japan—Architect Kenzo Tange designs the twin tower City Hall in Tokyo.

Spain/Italy—Operatic tenors Placido Domingo and José Carreras of Spain and Luciano Pavarotti of Italy team up in Rome for an internationally televised concert celebrating the World Cup. In addition to having solo careers, the singers will record together as the Three Tenors.

U.S.—Choreographer Martha Graham's dance *Maple Leaf Rag* premieres.

Mark Strand publishes the poetry collection *The Continuous Life.*

Mel Powell's concerto *Duplicates* premieres.

Guitarist and vocalist Bonnie Raitt wins four Grammy Awards, including album of the year for *Nick of Time.*

An exhibition of sexually suggestive photographs by Robert Mapplethorpe in Cincinnati,

Ohio, triggers public protests and an obscenity trial.

World—Novels include Thomas Pynchon's *Vineland* (U.S.), A. S. Byatt's *Possession* (U.K.), and J. M. Coetzee's *Age of Iron* (South Africa).

Films include Martin Scorsese's *GoodFellas* (U.S.), Pedro Almodóvar's *Tie Me Up! Tie Me Down!* (Spain), and Jim Sheridan's *The Field* (Ireland).

Ideas

U.S.—Critic Henry Louis Gates Jr. publishes *Reading Black, Reading Feminist.*

Critic Camille Paglia publishes *Sexual Personae.*

Economist David M. Kreps publishes *Game Theory and Economic Modeling.*

Military

Kuwait—On August 2 Iraq invades Kuwait and soon annexes it. The UN condemns the invasion and U.S. and allied forces mass in the region in preparation for a counterattack (*see* **1991, the Persian Gulf War**).

Liberia—An internally mediated cease-fire fails to stop the Liberian Civil War.

Politics

Bulgaria—One-party Communist rule ends, though the new government is dominated by former Communists, now calling themselves the Bulgarian Socialist Party.

Chile—The dictatorship of Augusto Pinochet ends.

Germany—On October 3 East Germany is absorbed into the Federal Republic of Germany (formerly known as West Germany). In December Helmut Kohl's Christian Democrats win the first national elections in a unified Germany since 1933.

Haiti—Jean-Bertrand Aristide is elected president.

India—India takes over direct rule of the province of Assam, site of a growing insurrection.

Namibia—Namibia becomes independent, with South West Africa People's Organization (SWAPO) leader Sam Nujoma elected to be its first president.

Nepal—Confronted by large-scale demonstrations, King Birenda Bir Bikram Shah Deva agrees to end autocracy and accept democratic elections.

Nicaragua—Violeta Chamorro is elected president, ending 11 years of Sandinista rule.

Pakistan—President Ghulam Ishaq Khan removes Prime Minister Benazir Bhutto from office.

Poland—Lech Walesa is elected president of newly non-Communist Poland.

South Africa—On February 11 longtime prisoner and African National Congress (ANC) leader Nelson Mandela is set free. A cease-fire between South Africa and the ANC follows; other political prisoners are released; and negotiations begin to end apartheid and make South Africa a multiracial democracy.

Soviet Union—Mikhail Gorbachev's reforms fail to reverse the country's economic decline.

Boris Yeltsin becomes the first popularly elected leader of the Russian Federation. He is a vocal critic of Soviet leader Mikhail Gorbachev.

Several constituent republics declare independence, including Armenia, Estonia, Lithuania, and Latvia.

U.K.—Margaret Thatcher, the century's longest-serving British prime minister, is succeeded by John Major.

U.S.—President George Bush breaks a "no new taxes" campaign pledge when he agrees to tax increases as part of a deficit reduction plan. The broken promise will plague him during his 1992 reelection bid.

World—In November the cold war officially ends with the international signing of the Treaty on Conventional Armed Forces in Europe (CFE Treaty), drastically reducing NATO and Warsaw Pact conventional arsenals.

Science and Technology

Soviet Union/U.S.—American and Soviet scientists discover the first known fresh water geothermal vents, in the floor of Lake Baikal, Russia.

U.K.—Physicians Norman Winston and Alan Handyside are the first to implant embryos screened in a test tube for genetic defects.

U.S./Europe—The Hubble Space Telescope, the first intended for permanent Earth orbit, is launched on April 25 aboard the U.S. space shuttle *Discovery*. A joint *U.S./European* project, it will prove to have technical flaws that will be repaired in 1993.

U.S.—The space probe *Magellan* (launched 1989) reaches Venus and begins to send back detailed radar maps of the planet's surface.

Controversy about the origins of homosexuality is stirred by studies suggesting that genes may have an effect on sexual orientation.

The first U.S.–government-approved infusion of genetically engineered cells into a human for therapeutic purposes is successfully performed, to treat a girl with an inherited immune disorder.

The government approves the first significantly new contraceptive in 25 years, Norplant, a hormone-releasing system to be implanted in a woman's arm.

Rheumatologist Lawrence E. Shellman discovers the gene that causes osteoarthritis.

Researchers argue that a high-fiber diet can help protect against colon cancer.

Psychologists discover that faces usually found to be attractive have features that approximate the mathematical average of all faces in the area's population.

Society

Bangladesh—A cyclone kills 125,000 to 150,000 people.

Iran—An earthquake measuring 7. 7 on the Richter scale strikes the northwest, killing more than 40,000 people, injuring 60,000, and leaving more than 400,000 homeless.

Peru—A cholera epidemic begins in Lima, killing more than 8,000 Peruvians.

Philippines—An earthquake measuring 7. 7 on the Richter scale occurs near Manila, killing up to 2,000 people, injuring 3,000, and leaving more than 100,000 homeless.

Saudi Arabia—In Mecca during the annual pilgrimage, 1,426 people die in a stampede in a pedestrian tunnel.

U.S.—The renovated main building at Ellis Island in New York harbor is opened to the public as a museum of immigration.

World—The UN calls for a moratorium on drift net use, to preserve dolphins that would otherwise be caught in nets intended for tuna. American tuna canners agree to the ban, responding in part to a tuna boycott, but the practice continues in other countries.

Sports

Canada—In hockey Wayne Gretzky scores his 2,000th point.

U.S.—Quarterback Joe Montana throws a record five touchdowns, with no interceptions, in leading the San Francisco 49ers to victory over the Denver Broncos in the Super Bowl.

1991 Arts and Entertainment

Canada—Fiction writer Douglas Copeland popularizes a catchphrase with the title of his book *Generation X: Tales for an Accelerated Culture*.

Norway—Jostein Gaarder (1952–) publishes the novel *Sophie's World*, a fictional treatment of the history of philosophy that becomes an international bestseller.

U.S.—Bulgarian-born American artist Christo sets up thousands of umbrellas in Japan and California, but the project is dismantled when two people are injured.

Choreographer Merce Cunningham creates the dance *Trackers*.

John Adams and Alice Goodman's opera *The Death of Klinghoffer* premieres.

The first annual musical tour Lollapalooza begins its run at Irvine Meadows Amphitheater near Los Angeles. The tour features such alternative rock groups as Nine Inch Nails and the Butthole Surfers. Alternative rock becomes mainstream during the decade, with "grunge" groups such as Nirvana, Pearl Jam, and Stone Temple Pilots gaining broad popularity.

World—Films include Jonathan Demme's *The Silence of the Lambs* and Ridley Scott's *Thelma and Louise* (both U.S.), Carlos Saura's *Ay, Carmela!* (Spain), Zhang Yimou's *Raise the Red Lantern* (China/Taiwan/Hong Kong), Gabriele Salvatore's *Mediterraneo* (Italy), and Sven Nykvist's *The Ox* (Sweden).

Ideas

U.K.—Critic Anthony Easthope publishes *Literary into Cultural Studies*.

Philosopher of language Paul Grice publishes *The Conception of Value*.

U.S.—Philosopher Daniel C. Dennett publishes *Consciousness Explained*.

Critic Harold Bloom publishes *The Book of J*.

Philosopher Allen Gibbard publishes *Wise Choices, Apt Feelings*.

Military

Cambodia—Civil war ends with the Treaty of Paris on October 23. The treaty provides for a cease-fire and the introduction of democracy.

Ethiopia—Eritrean and rebel Ethiopian forces overthrow the government, forcing dictator Mengistu Haile Mariam to flee and ending the Ethiopian-Eritrean War.

Iraq—Following the Persian Gulf War, Kurds in the north and Iranian-supported Shi'ites in the south unsuccessfully rebel against Saddam Hussein's government. UN-enforced no-fly zones are instituted in both regions.

Iraq/Kuwait—In the Persian Gulf War (January 17–February 28), the U.S. and allied forces launch Operation Desert Storm. A massive bombing campaign strikes Iraqi targets and troops and is followed by a ground assault (February 24–28) that liberates Kuwait and captures southern Iraq. Iraqi leader Saddam Hussein remains in power, though UN international economic sanctions continue due to his noncooperation with UN arms control and inspection demands. Casualties of the war include 343 allied soldiers, about 110,000 Iraqi soldiers, 10,000 Iraqi civilians, and up to 5,000 Kuwaiti civilians.

Somalia—Rebel forces overthrow dictator Mohammed Siad Barre. The country descends into anarchy as various factions clash; famine and disease begin to take a large toll.

South Africa—A low-level civil war grows between the Inkatha Freedom Party, founded in 1990 to represent the Zulus, and the African National Congress.

U.S.—Sexual harassment in the Navy is spotlighted by the Tailhook scandal, in which women at the Navy's annual Tailhook convention in Las Vegas report mistreatment by Navy aviators.

Yugoslavia—Serbia and Croatia go to war when Croatia declares its independence (*see* **Yugoslavia** in **Politics**, below).

Politics

Haiti—President Jean-Bertrand Aristide is deposed in a coup and flees the country.

India—Former prime minister Rajiv Gandhi is assassinated while campaigning.

Lebanon—The last Western hostages held in Lebanon are freed (1991–92).

Soviet Union—From August 19 to 21 a hardline Communist coup attempts to overthrow Soviet leader Mikhail Gorbachev. Russian president Boris Yeltsin rallies popular support to resist the coup, which collapses.

Mikhail Gorbachev resigns as head of the Soviet Union on December 25. On December 31 the Soviet Union is dissolved. It is replaced by numerous independent states, including Russia.

The Commonwealth of Independent States is created, a loose association of many former republics of the Soviet Union.

U.K.—Irish Republican Army terrorism increases, including a mortar attack on the British prime minister's quarters at 10 Downing Street in London.

U.S.—Supreme Court nominee Clarence Thomas is confirmed only after controversial Senate hearings on charges that he sexually harassed former employee Anita Hill.

World—The Warsaw Pact is formally dissolved.

Yugoslavia—Yugoslavia breaks apart as Croatia and Slovenia declare their independence.

Science and Technology

Austria/Italy—The 5,000-year-old body of a man preserved in ice and dubbed the "ice-man" is discovered in the Alps between Austria and Italy.

Europe—CERN, the European Organization for Nuclear Research, releases the World Wide Web. Developed by Tim Berners-Lee, the Web begins as a networked information project and will become the most widely used way of accessing the Internet.

France—Diver Henri Cosquer discovers prehistoric paintings and engravings in an undersea cave in the Calanque region of France. The artwork dates to 27,000 years ago and 19,000 years ago.

U.K.—Astronomers report indirect evidence for a planet orbiting a distant pulsar.

U.S.—Astronomers discover a quasar 12 billion light-years away, the most distant object ever identified.

The space probe *Galileo* takes the first close-up photograph of an asteroid in space when it captures the image of 951 Gaspra from a distance of 10,000 miles.

The privately financed *Biosphere 2* project begins. Its attempt to establish a closed "bubble" ecology will fail, though the structure will be rehabilitated for other scientific uses.

Neurobiologist Simon LeVay announces that the hypothalamus, a part of the brain, is different in homosexual men than in heterosexual men.

Each year in the 1990s, new disease-linked gene mutations are discovered, including, this year, a gene mutation linked to colon cancer.

Society

Germany—Neo-Nazis commit acts of violence against foreigners; large anti-Nazi demonstrations are held in response, prompting the government to act more vigorously to stop the racist acts.

Kuwait—During the Persian Gulf War, retreating Iraqi troops set hundreds of Kuwaiti oil wells on fire, blanketing the area in smoke and sending soot as far west as Egypt and as far east as China.

U.K.—Publishing mogul Robert Maxwell (1923–91) dies mysteriously in a fall off a yacht near the Canary Islands. His publishing empire, heavily in debt, collapses.

U.S.—The eruption of Mount Pinatubo on Luzon Island in the Philippines, which kills more than 400 people, is the largest volcanic eruption in the 20th century. The pyroclastic density current it emits will lead to increased global temperatures and accelerate erosion of the ozone layer.

Banker Charles Keating is convicted in California on state charges of criminal fraud in the Lincoln Savings and Loan Association case.

World—Civil wars and regional wars raise the number of refugees worldwide to about 17 million.

Sports

U.S.—The Chicago Bulls, led by Michael Jordan, win their first of three consecutive

National Basketball Association championships, this time over the Los Angeles Lakers.

The Los Angeles Lakers' Earvin "Magic" Johnson retires from basketball after learning he is HIV-positive.

In baseball Nolan Ryan, age 44, of the Texas Rangers pitches his seventh career no-hitter.

1992 Arts and Entertainment

U.S.—Philip Glass and David Henry Hwang's opera *The Voyage* premieres.

Country music rises in popularity, with performers like Garth Brooks, Reba McEntire, Clint Black, and Wynonna and Naomi Judd.

Poetic works include Tess Gallagher's *Moon Crossing Bridge* and John Ashbery's *Hotel Lautréamont*.

August Wilson's play *Two Trains Running* premieres.

In May comedian Johnny Carson retires from his 30-year position as host of *The Tonight Show* (NBC); he is replaced by Jay Leno.

World—Literary works include Terry McMillan's *Waiting to Exhale* (U.S.), Ben Okri's *The Famished Road* (Nigeria), Peter Ackroyd's *English Music* (U.K.), and Martinican-born Patrick Chamoiseau's *Texaco* (published in France).

Films include Clint Eastwood's *Unforgiven* and Robert Altman's *The Player* (U.S.), Neil Jordan's *The Crying Game* and James Ivory's *Howards End* (U.K.), and Alfonso Arau's *Like Water for Chocolate* (Mexico).

Ideas

Mexico—Writer Carlos Fuentes publishes *The Buried Mirror: Reflections on Spain and the New World*.

U.K.—Philosopher and novelist Iris Murdoch publishes *Metaphysics and Morals*.

Writer Naomi Wolf publishes *The Beauty Myth*, in which she investigates women's obsession with beauty.

Military

Bosnia and Herzegovina—Bosnia and Herzegovina secede from Yugoslavia. Civil war breaks out between Bosnian Muslims and Bosnian Serbs, the latter aided by Serb-controlled Yugoslavia. Sarajevo is placed under siege; Croatian forces intervene. By year's end, the Serbs hold 65 to 70 percent of the country. UN peacekeeping forces are unable to stop Serbian "ethnic cleansing," a euphemism for genocide and mass deportation of Muslims.

Georgia—The government fights a rebellion by separatists in Abkhazia (1992–93). The government is also engaged in fighting a separatist insurgency in South Ossetia (1990–96).

Mozambique—The Mozambican Civil War, in progress since 1975, ends with a cease-fire and peace treaty providing for establishment of democratic rule.

Philippines—U.S. forces leave the Philippines, ending nearly a century of military presence.

Somalia—In December U.S. troops arrive to protect famine relief efforts.

Politics

Angola—Elections are held, but Jonas Savimbi refuses to accept the victory of incumbent president José Eduardo dos Santos. Civil war, temporarily halted, resumes.

Canada—In *R. v. Butler*, the Canadian Supreme Court includes in its definition of obscenity materials deemed to degrade, dehumanize, or subordinate women.

Georgia—Eduard Shevardnadze becomes president.

Israel—Yitzhak Rabin becomes prime minister at the head of a Labor-dominated coalition government.

Peru—Alberto Fujimori, president since 1990, dissolves Congress and assumes dictatorial powers, ostensibly to better cope with guerrilla insurgency, drug trafficking, and corruption.

Russia—Russia institutes drastic economic reforms, removing controls on most prices. An economic downturn results.

U.S.—Democratic challenger Bill Clinton defeats Republican incumbent George Bush and independent candidate Ross Perot to win the presidency.

In *Planned Parenthood v. Casey*, the Supreme Court affirms the legality of abortion but permits state restrictions on the procedure.

President George Bush pardons former Reagan administration officials involved in the Iran-Contra scandal.

World—A UN Conference on Environment and Development, known as the Earth Summit, is held in Rio de Janeiro, Brazil. Among other topics discussed are conventions on forest conservation, climate change, and biodiversity.

Science and Technology

Japan—NEC Corporation scientists synthesize buckytubes, hollow cylinders of carbon atoms.

Mexico—In the Yucatán Peninsula geologists find evidence of a crater from the crash of a meteorite or comet 65 million years ago, an event hypothesized by physicist Luis W. Alvarez in 1979.

U.K.—Using a Cray supercomputer, scientist David Slowinski discovers the largest prime number to date, which is 227,832 digits long.

U.S./France—Scientists in the U.S., France, and elsewhere complete the first comprehensive maps of two human chromosomes, the Y chromosome and chromosome 21. These maps are a major advance for the Human Genome Project, a multiyear effort to determine the entire human genome.

U.S.—Scientists discover what may be the oldest and largest living organism, a giant mold called *Armillaria bulbosa* found in Crystal Falls, Michigan.

The Cosmic Background Explorer (COBE) satellite, launched in 1989, uncovers temperature variations in the universe's microwave background radiation that support the Big Bang theory.

Public protest spurs the National Institutes of Health to withdraw funds from an academic conference searching for a genetic basis for criminal behavior.

Researchers extract DNA fragments from an extinct termite embedded in amber for 30 million years.

Society

Australia/U.K.—The Anglican Churches of Australia and England vote to allow the ordination of women as priests; such ordinations will begin in 1994.

Bahamas/U.S.—Hurricane Andrew devastates the Bahamas, South Florida, and Louisiana. The storm kills more than 40 people and causes about $20 billion in damage.

Canada—Olympia and York Developments, Ltd., a large real estate concern, goes into bankruptcy.

U.K.—Prince Charles and Princess Diana agree to separate.

U.S.—Race riots erupt in Los Angeles following the acquittal of white police officers accused of beating black motorist Rodney King.

Mafia kingpin John Gotti is convicted of murder and other crimes and sentenced to life in prison without parole.

Sports

Canada—In baseball the Toronto Blue Jays win the World Series; they will do so again in 1993, becoming the first back-to-back winners since the New York Yankees in 1977–78.

France—The Winter Olympics are held in Albertville, France.

U.S.—At the Summer Olympics in Barcelona, Spain, the American basketball team, known as the "Dream Team," includes professional players for the first time.

Boxer Mike Tyson, who lost the world heavyweight title in 1990, is convicted of the 1991 rape of a Miss Black America contestant.

1993 Arts and Entertainment

Australia—Poet and novelist David Malouf publishes the novel *Remembering Babylon*.

Japan—Sculptor Osami Tamaka creates constructions drawn from Asian and minimalist sources.

U.S.—Artist Chuck Hoberman completes *Iris Dome* and *Expanding Geodesic Sphere*, works that combine architecture, robotics, and sculpture.

The U.S. Holocaust Memorial Museum, designed by architect James I. Freed, opens in Washington, D.C.

Terrence McNally's play *A Perfect Ganesh* is produced.

Tony Kushner's play *Angels in America: A Gay Fantasia on National Themes, Part I: Millennium Approaches* opens on Broadway. *Part II: Perestroika* will be produced later in the year.

Donald Hall publishes the poetry collection *The Museum of Clear Ideas*.

Maya Angelou composes the poem "On the Pulse of Morning" for President Bill Clinton's inauguration.

The science-fiction thriller *The X-Files* premieres on the fledgling Fox network. This drama chronicles the investigations of FBI Special Agents Dana Scully and Fox Mulder into paranormal phenomena and a government conspiracy to hide the truth about alien life on Earth. The first science-fiction series to be a ratings success, it will become an international hit and continue airing into the next century.

World—Literary works include Roddy Doyle's *Paddy Clarke Ha Ha Ha* (Ireland), Vikram

Seth's *A Suitable Boy* (India), E. Annie Proulx's *The Shipping News* (U.S.), and Banana Yoshimoto's *Kitchen* (Japan).

Films include Steven Spielberg's *Schindler's List* (U.S.); Chen Kaige's *Farewell, My Concubine* (China), Ang Lee's *The Wedding Banquet* (U.S./Taiwan); and Jane Campion's *The Piano* (Australia/France).

Operas premiering at the Vienna Festival include Russian composer Alfred Schnittke's *Homage to Zhivago* and American composer Steve Reich's *The Cave*.

Ideas

U.K.—Philosopher Bernard Williams publishes *Shame and Necessity*.

U.S.—Former secretary of education William Bennett edits the collection *The Book of Virtues*.

Linguist Deborah Tannen examines miscommunication between the sexes in *You Just Don't Understand*.

Philosopher of law Ronald Dworkin publishes *Life's Dominion: An Argument about Abortion, Euthanasia, and Individual Freedom*.

Military

Angola—Jonas Savimbi's rebel National Union for the Total Independence of Angola (UNITA) captures several major cities.

Bosnia and Herzegovina—The civil war continues; the U.S. and other powers threaten military intervention.

Israel—Israel responds with air and artillery attacks to Hezbollah assaults from Lebanon.

Russia—In October, led by Vice President Aleksandr Rutskoy, parliamentary opponents of President Boris Yeltsin launch an insurrection. Government forces bombard and storm opposition headquarters in the White House, ending the rebellion.

Somalia—In May the UN takes over for the U.S. in providing military security for famine relief efforts. Somali warlord Mohammed Farah Aidid ambushes UN troops and drags American bodies through the streets. The anarchic civil war continues.

Politics

Canada—Liberal Party leader Jean Chrétien succeeds Tory (Progressive Conservative) Party leader Kim Campbell as prime minister.

Georgia—In return for Russian support in its civil war, Georgia agrees to join the Russian-dominated Commonwealth of Independent States.

Israel—In a peace agreement signed in Washington, D.C., on September 13, Israeli prime minister Yitzhak Rabin and Palestine Liberation Organization (PLO) leader Yasir Arafat concur on principles for establishing Palestinian autonomy.

Pakistan—A general election restores Benazir Bhutto, ousted in 1990, as prime minister.

Russia—In April public confidence in President Boris Yeltsin is affirmed in a national referendum; Yeltsin also wins a December referendum on a new constitution.

South Africa—A new constitution establishing majority rule is adopted.

Turkey—Tansu Çiller becomes Turkey's first female prime minister.

U.K.—Peace talks concerning Northern Ireland begin between Britain and the Irish Republican Army, though fighting continues.

U.S.—President Bill Clinton wins ratification of the North American Free Trade Agreement.

President Bill Clinton appoints Ruth Bader Ginsburg to the Supreme Court.

The Brady Handgun Control Law is passed.

Science and Technology

U.K.—Mathematician Andrew Wiles and his former student Richard Taylor prove Fermat's last theorem, perhaps the most famous unsolved mathematical problem.

Geneticists find the gene whose mutation is believed to cause amyotrophic lateral sclerosis, or Lou Gehrig's Disease.

U.S.—Physicists run a computer calculation that appears to confirm the theory of quantum chromodynamics.

Astronomer Douglas Lin presents evidence that the Milky Way is much larger than previously believed and is surrounded by a halo of "dark matter" invisible to telescopes.

Researchers at the National Cancer Institute claim to have linked a genetic marker on the X chromosome to homosexual orientation.

A deadly disease linked to a virus in rodent droppings afflicts Navajos in New Mexico and Arizona.

Paleontologist John Horner reports the discovery of red blood cells in the fossilized leg bone of a 65-million-year-old *Tyrannosaurus rex*.

Society

Colombia—The military captures and kills escaped Medellin drug cartel leader Pablo Escobar.

India—An earthquake in Maharashtra State, measuring 6.4 on the Richter scale, kills about 10,000 people.

U.S.—On February 26 Islamic terrorists bomb the World Trade Center in New York City, killing six and injuring more than 1,000.

Near Waco, Texas, on April 19, federal law-enforcement officers attack the compound of the Branch Davidian sect, killing 86 members, including 17 children and leader David Koresh.

A flood that may be the worst in U.S. history ravages the Mississippi and Missouri River basins, killing 50 and leaving at least 70,000 people homeless.

Sports

U.S.—Michael Jordan retires from basketball, a game he has dominated since 1991, to pursue a baseball career. He will return to basketball in 1995.

In football's Super Bowl the Dallas Cowboys defeat the Buffalo Bills; they will do so again in 1994.

1994 Arts and Entertainment

France—Architect Christian de Portzamparc wins the Pritzker Prize. His works include the City of Music Center in Paris.

Switzerland—The Museum of Modern and Contemporary Art opens.

U.S.—Edward Albee's play *Three Tall Women* premieres.

Composer Morton Gould's *Stringmusic* debuts.

After a decades-long absence from the concert stage, singer Barbra Streisand mounts an international concert tour.

Singer and songwriter Kurt Cobain, leader of the rock group Nirvana, commits suicide at age 27.

Photographer Lee Friedlander's work is exhibited at the Museum of Modern Art.

Artists exhibited in New York galleries this year include Pat Adams, Robert Gober, Jenny Holzer, John Baldessari, Julian Schnabel, and Ann Agee.

The television series *E.R.* premieres (NBC, 1994–).

World—Works of fiction include V. S. Naipaul's *A Way in the World* (West Indies), Grace Paley's *Collected Stories* and Cormac McCarthy's *The Crossing* (U.S.), and Nadine Gordimer's *None to Accompany Me* (South Africa).

Films include Quentin Tarantino's *Pulp Fiction* (U.S.), Atom Egoyan's *Exotica* (Canada), Abbas Kiarostami's *Through the Olive Trees* (Iran), Ang Lee's *Eat Drink Man Woman* (Taiwan), and Cheik Boukouré's *Le Ballon d'or* (Guinea).

Ideas

U.K.—Philosopher Michael Dummett publishes *The Seas of Language*.

U.S.—Philosopher Jerry Fodor publishes *The Elm and the Expert*.

Critic Harold Bloom publishes *The Western Canon*.

Sociologists Charles Murray and Richard J. Herrnstein publish *The Bell Curve*, which controversially links race and intelligence.

Sociologist John Gagnon and colleagues publish a comprehensive study of sexuality.

Economist Nancy Folbre publishes *Who Pays for the Kids?: Gender and the Structures of Constraint*.

Military

Haiti—With the U.S. poised to invade, Haitian military ruler Raoul Cedras surrenders power peacefully. U.S. forces occupy Haiti; exiled president Jean-Bertrand Aristide returns to his country and forms a new government.

Mexico—In January Native Americans in the state of Chiapas rebel, calling themselves the Zapatista National Liberation Army. Mexico brings the rebellion under control this year, but peace will not be concluded until 1996.

Russia—On December 11 Russian forces invade the breakaway republic of Chechnya, which had declared independence in 1991. The ensuing war (1994–96) will cost 80,000 lives, reveal Russian military weakness, and end with an agreement for almst total autonomy for Chechnya.

Rwanda—Rwanda's president Juvénal Habyarimana and Burundi's president Cyprien Ntaryamira, both Hutus, die when their plane is shot down in Rwanda. The majority Hutus respond with genocidal attacks on the Tutsi minority, killing up to a million people and driving hundreds of thousands more into exile. In the ensuing civil war, the Tutsi Rwandan Patriotic Front defeats the Rwandan military and takes control of the country. Up to two million Hutus flee into exile.

U.K.—A cease-fire is declared in Northern Ireland, and formal peace negotiations begin.

Politics

Brazil—Sociologist and political scientist Fernando Cardoso wins the presidency. Once left-leaning, he now advocates free-market policies to combat inflation.

Israel—The Gaza Strip and Jericho are the first areas to gain limited autonomy under the terms of Israeli-Palestinian peace agreements.

Israel/Jordan—Israel and Jordan sign a peace treaty, bringing a formal end to their 46-year state of war.

Mexico—Luis Donaldo Colosio Murrieta, presidential candidate of the ruling Institutional Revolutionary Party (PRI), is assassinated. Economist Ernesto Zedillo Ponce de Leon is elected president.

North Korea—Dictator Kim Il Sung dies. During the ensuing period of uncertainty, his son Kim Jong-Il emerges as leader.

South Africa—In April Nelson Mandela and his African National Congress win South Africa's first fully free elections. In May he becomes president at the head of a government of national unity.

U.S.—President Bill Clinton's proposed health care reform proposals are defeated in Congress.

In November midterm elections the Democratic Party loses control of both houses of Congress to the Republican Party. In December Republican Newt Gingrich is voted the next Speaker of the House.

Science and Technology

New Zealand—Physicist Daniel F. Walls and colleagues advance the theoretical understanding of the relationship between complementarity and uncertainty principles in quantum experiments.

Pakistan—In Pakistan paleontologist J. G. M. Thewissen discovers fossil remains of a 50-million-year-old whale, *Ambulocetus natans*, that was intermediate between land- and sea-dwelling mammals.

U.K.—Researchers discover a "deep biosphere" of bacteria living 1,700 feet or more below the ocean floor.

Eleven people are killed by a rare Group A streptococcus infection known as necrotizing fasciitis, or flesh-eating disease.

U.S.—The unmanned spacecraft *Clementine* maps the Moon, 22 years after the last American lunar mission in 1972.

Using the world's largest radio telescope, Astronomer Alexander Wolszczan discovers indirect evidence of at least three planets outside the solar system.

American brain researchers Hanna and Antonio Damasio discover evidence that the ventromedial region of the brain governs social behavior.

Vietnam—The first live specimen of *Pseudoryx nghetinhensis*, or *sao la*, a wild Vietnamese cow relative, is captured.

World—Fragments of Comet Shoemaker-Levy 9 smash into Jupiter, providing astronomers worldwide with a torrent of data about the planet's atmosphere.

An international team of physicists at Fermilab in Illinois, U.S., discovers evidence for the top quark, a hitherto elusive fundamental particle.

Society

Finland—On September 28 the ferry *Estonia* capsizes off the Finnish coast; about 900 people die.

Russia—Russia suffers two large oil spills, one near Ursinsk and the other into the Kolva River tributary.

U.S.—Former football player O. J. Simpson is accused of the murders of his wife, Nicole Brown Simpson, and her friend Ronald Goldman. The controversial and highly publicized case will conclude with his acquittal on criminal charges in 1995 but a finding of liability in a civil suit in 1997.

Central Intelligence Agency officer Aldrich Ames is exposed as having been a Soviet spy. He is sentenced to life in prison, while his wife, Rosario Ames, also found guilty of espionage, is sentenced to a lesser term.

Acts of terrorism against clinics and physicians providing abortions are on the rise. Antiabortionist John Salvi kills two people at a Massachusetts Planned Parenthood clinic; another antiabortionist, Paul J. Hill, kills two in Pensacola, Florida.

On January 17, a magnitude 6.7 earthquake centered in Northridge, California, strikes the Los Angeles area; the disaster kills 61 people and costs $15 billion in damages.

Sports

Norway/Ukraine—The Winter Olympics are held in Lillehammer, Norway. Ukrainian figure skater Oksana Baiul wins a gold medal.

U.S.—Major league baseball players go on strike on August 11; the rest of the season is canceled and the World Series is canceled for the first time 90 years. The strike will be settled in 1995.

Boxer George Foreman, aged 45, defeats Michael Moorer for the world heavyweight championship, becoming the oldest fighter at any weight to win a title.

Figure skater Nancy Kerrigan is injured in an attack later traced to associates of rival skater Tonya Harding. Harding is fined, put on probation, stripped of her championship title, and banned from future events of the U.S. Figure Skating Association.

1995 Arts and Entertainment

Bulgaria/U.S.—Bulgarian-born American artist Christo wraps the Reichstag in silver fabric.

Canada—French-Canadian director Robert Lepage debuts the experimental theatrical work *The Seven Streams of the River Ota.*

Ireland/U.S.—Michael Flatley, an American-born dancer of Irish descent, popularizes Irish step-dancing by starring in and choreographing *Riverdance—The Show.*

Nigeria—Exiled Nigerian writer Wole Soyinka's play *The Beatification of Area Boy*, banned at home, premieres in Britain.

Russia—Yury Grigorovich, longtime artistic director of the Bolshoi Ballet, resigns and is replaced by Vladimir Vasilyev.

U.K.— "Britpop" sweeps the international popular music scene. New guitar-based British bands include Bush, Oasis, Blur, Pulp, and Suede.

The first "new" Beatles song since the band's 1970 demise is released. Titled "Free as a Bird," it is based on a recording by the late John Lennon newly accompanied by the surviving ex-Beatles.

Artist Damien Hirst wins the Turner Prize.

U.S.—Terrence McNally's *Love! Valour! Compassion!* wins the Tony for best play; Horton Foote's *The Young Man from Atlanta* wins the Pulitzer Prize for drama.

New operas include *Harvey Milk* by Stewart Wallace and Michael Korie and *Modern Painters* by David Lang and Manuela Hoelterhoff.

Popular music performers include Hootie and the Blowfish, Elastica, Alanis Morissette, and Courtney Love's band Hole.

Tejano singer Selena (Selena Quintanilla Perez) is murdered by a disgruntled employee.

The Grateful Dead disbands following the August 9th death of lead member Jerry Garcia.

World—Fiction includes Richard Ford's *Independence Day* (U.S.), Pat Barker's *The Ghost Road* (U.K.), Tim Winton's *The Riders* (Australia), Nathalie Serraute's *Ici* (France), Mikhail Kurayev's *Blokada* (Russia), and Baba Tahir's *Love in Exile* (Egypt).

Nonfiction includes Mary Karr's *The Liars' Club* (U.S.), Jerzy Giedroyé's *Autobiography for Four Hands* (Poland), and Hermo Vianna's *O mistério do samba* (Brazil).

Works of poetry include William Matthews's *Time & Music* (U.S.), David Malouf's *Selected Poems* (Australia), and Sachiko Yoshihara's *Hakko.*

Films include Mel Gibson's *Braveheart* and Mike Figgis's *Leaving Las Vegas* (both U.S.), Chris Noonan's *Babe* (Australia), Claude Sautet's *Nelly et Monsieur Arnaud* (France), Zhang Yimou's *Shanghai Triad* (China), Idrissa Ouedraogo's *Africa, My Africa* (Burkina Faso), and Tran Anh Hung's *Cyclo* (Vietnam).

Orchestral works include Joseph Schwantner's *Evening Land*; Christopher Rouse's Second Symphony; Toru Takemitsu's *Family Tree* and Karlheinz Stockhausen's *Helicopter Quartet.*

Ideas

U.K.—At Oxford University scraps of a mid-first-century manuscript are unearthed that may reveal the oldest reference to Jesus as a divine being.

U.S.—Historian Gertrude Himmelfarb publishes *The De-Moralization of Society: From Victorian Virtues to Modern Values*.

Economist Paul Krugman publishes *Development, Geography, and Economic Theory*.

Military

Bosnia and Herzegovina—The Dayton Agreement (signed in Dayton, Ohio, U.S.) ends the Bosnian Civil War. Bosnia and Herzegovina is divided into two largely autonomous parts: a Muslim-Croat federation and a Serb republic.

Politics

Armenia—A new constitution expanding presidential powers is approved in a referendum alleged to be corrupt.

Bolivia—Facing a general strike, the government declares a state of siege and suspends civil liberties.

Brazil—Fernando Henrique Cardoso becomes president.

Egypt—An assassination attempt on president Hosni Mubarak, in Ethiopia, fails. The Sudan is suspected of sponsoring the attack.

Ethiopia—Meles Zenawi is elected prime minister.

Europe—Austria, Finland, and Sweden join the European Union.

France—Jacques Chirac is elected president.

Ireland—Voters approve an end to a constitutional ban on divorce.

Israel—Prime Minister Yitzhak Rabin is assassinated by an Israeli for his efforts at promoting peace with Palestinians. Shimon Peres succeeds him as prime minister.

Peace talks with Syria are suspended.

Liberia—Elections scheduled for November are prevented by a resumption of civil war (1995–96).

Mexico/U.S.—Mexico's economy is rescued by a $20 billion U.S. aid package.

Poland—Communist candidate Aleksander Kwasniewski is elected president in the face of economic instability.

Somalia—UN forces withdraw from Somalia, leaving the country in anarchy amid continuing factional warfare.

Turkey—The Justice Party government of Tansu Çiller falls amid corruption scandals. The Welfare Party, a pro-Islamic group, wins the largest share of the vote in national elections.

U.S.—Senator Robert Packwood (Republican of Oregon) resigns under pressure under charges of sexual and official misconduct.

A budget stalemate between the president and Congress shuts down the government.

Vietnam/U.S.—Full diplomatic relations are established between the two former enemies.

Science and Technology

Argentina—Paleontologists discover a carnivorous dinosaur called *Giganotosaurus* at least as large as *Tyrannosaurus rex*, previously believed to be the largest land predator ever.

U.S.—The U.S. spacecraft *Galileo* reaches Jupiter and launches a probe into the planet's atmosphere.

Researchers led by Craig Venter are the first to decipher the complete genome of an organism: the bacterium *Haemophilus influenzae*.

Scientists discover a protein called leptin that regulates body weight in mice.

Medical researchers Byron Caughey and Peter Lansbury present evidence that scrapie and mad cow disease are caused by protein crystals called prions.

Physicists Carl Weiman and Eric Cornell are the first to produce a Bose-Einstein condensate.

Society

Japan—An earthquake (7.2 on the Richter scale) in Kobe kills 5,100 people and injures 26,800.

Zaire—An outbreak of Ebola virus infects 315 people, killing 244 of them.

U.K.—For the first time the Church of England ordains women as priests.

U.S.—On April 19 the Alfred P. Murrah federal building in Oklahoma City, Oklahoma, is destroyed by a far-right terrorist bomb, killing 167 people.

Bill Gates, founder and head of Microsoft, buys the 16 million–image Bettman Archive, in part for use in the company's multimedia products.

Sports

U.S.—By playing in his 2,131st straight game, Baltimore Oriole infielder Cal Ripken Jr. breaks Lou Gehrig's record of 2,130 for consecutive games played. He will play in 2,632 games before taking a game off in 1999.

In basketball the Houston Rockets win the National Basketball Association championship.

In football San Francisco beats San Diego in Super Bowl XXIX, 49–26.

In baseball's World Series, Atlanta beats Cleveland, four games to two.

1996 Arts and Entertainment

Asia—Chinese sculptor Cai Guo Qiang and Japanese photo artist Yasumasa Morimura exhibit their works in New York. Other acclaimed contemporary Asian artists include Marikuo Mori, Hiroshi Sugimoto, and Chen Yifei.

Austria—Eight thousand pieces of art stolen by Nazis from Jews who died in the Holocaust are auctioned in Vienna, with the proceeds to go to Holocaust survivors. The art had been hoarded by the Austrian government since World War II.

Netherlands—South African–born Dutch artist Marlene Dumas paints *Pink Puff*.

Poland—Poet Wislawa Szymborska is the first Slavic woman to win the Nobel Prize for literature.

Spain—Architect José Rafael Moneo is the first Spaniard to win the Pritzker Architecture Prize. His works include the National Museum of Roman Art in Merida.

U.K.—Harold Pinter's play *Ashes to Ashes* and Stephen Poliakoff's *Blinded by the Sun* have their premieres.

U.S.—Ellsworth Kelly creates an installation composed of seven four-sided panels, each a different color.

"Gangsta rap" musician Tupac Shakur is killed in a drive-by shooting in Las Vegas. Rival rapper the Notorious B.I.G. (Christopher G. Wallace) will be shot dead the following year.

The musical *Rent* wins the Pulitzer Prize for drama and the Tony for best musical in the same year as the death of its young author, Jonathan Larson. Terrence McNally's *Master Class* wins the Tony for best play.

Plays opening this year include Christopher Durang's *Sex and Longing*, Cynthia Ozick's *The Shawl*, and David Hare's *Skylight*.

Two nonfiction works gain wide popularity: Frank McCourt's *Angela's Ashes* and Jonathan Harr's *A Civil Action*.

World—Novels include David Foster Wallace's *Infinite Jest* (U.S.) and Graham Smith's *Last Orders* (U.K.). Short story collections include Andrea Barrett's *Ship Fever and Other Stories* (U.S.). Other writers producing new works this year include Swedish poet Tomas Tranströmer, Colombian novelist Gabriel García Márquez, Egyptian novelist Naguib Mahfouz, Canadian novelist Margaret Atwood, South African novelist J.M. Coetzee, Nigerian poet Wole Soyinka, and Australian poet and novelist David Malouf.

New films include Anthony Minghella's Oscar-winning *The English Patient* (U.S.), Roland Emmerich's top-grossing *Independence Day* (U.S.), Danny Boyle's *Trainspotting* (U.K.), Scott Hicks's *Shine* (Australia), Jan Sverák's *Kolya* (Czech Republic), and Lars von Trier's *Breaking the Waves* (Denmark/Netherlands/Sweden/France).

Ideas

U.S.—Historian Daniel Jonah Goldhagen publishes *Hitler's Willing Executioners*, which argues that ordinary Germans share responsibility for the Holocaust.

Economists Lester Thurow, in *The Future of Capitalism*, and Paul Krugman, in *Pop Internationalism*, take contrary positions on issues related to global competition and economic growth.

Philosopher David J. Chalmers publishes *The Conscious Mind: In Search of a Fundamental Theory*.

Spiritual writer Neale Donald Walsch publishes *Conversations with God: An Uncommon Dialogue*.

Military

Afghanistan—The Taliban, a group of Islamic fundamentalists, captures Kabul, the capital.

Guatemala—The government and rebels sign a peace accord to end the 35-year-old civil war, the longest guerrilla conflict in the Western Hemisphere.

Iraq—Iraq attacks a Kurdish enclave, prompting a *U.S.* attack on Iraqi air defenses.

Russia—A peace treaty ends the civil war in Chechnya.

Zaire—Rebel forces led by Laurent Kabila threaten the government of Mobutu Sese Seko. Ethnic violence erupts in refugee camps, prompting refugees from Rwanda and Burundi to flee the camps.

Politics

Ghana—Ghanaian diplomat Kofi Annan is named the UN secretary-general.

Israel—Yasir Arafat is elected president of the Palestinian Authority.

After Palestinian suicide bombers opposed to the peace process kill 59 people, hard-line candidate Benjamin Netanyahu is elected prime minister.

Russia—Boris Yeltsin wins reelection as president.

Saudi Arabia—Two separate terrorist bombings aimed at U.S. military installations kill a total of 26 people.

South Africa—A new constitution is adopted.

Sri Lanka—At least 73 people are killed in a suicide bombing.

U.K.—Relations with the European Union (EU) are strained when the EU bans imports of British beef because of fears of "mad cow" disease.

U.S.—Congress grants the president a line-item veto.

With the president's support, Congress passes a welfare reform bill that ends decades in which welfare was viewed as a federal entitlement.

Congress makes it a crime to display indecent material on an interactive computer network in a way accessible to minors. The Supreme Court will overturn the law the following year.

Soon after winning reelection, President Clinton appoints Madeleine Albright the country's first female secretary of state.

Yugoslavia—Serbian president Slobodan Milosevic annuls local elections that would have given opposition candidates control of Belgrade; more than 100,000 people march in protest.

Science and Technology

Canada—Paleontologist Philip Currie discovers that at least one dinosaur species, dating to 120 million years ago, had feathers.

China—American and Chinese paleontologists discover evidence that the primate *Eosimias*, dating to 45 million years ago, was the common ancestor of monkeys, apes, and humans.

Greenland—A team of British, American, and Australian scientists discovers evidence that life originated on earth more than 3.85 billion years ago, 350 million years earlier than previously believed.

Romania—In a cave, biologists discover the first known land ecosystem that derives energy not from sunlight but from the breakdown of hydrogen sulfide by bacteria.

U.S.—Based on meteorite studies, National Aeronautics and Space Administration scientists report that microbial life may once have existed on Mars; many colleagues are skeptical of the claim.

A study of a group of American nuns over a 60-year period reveals that an individual's writing style in youth may indicate the likelihood of developing Alzheimer's in later life.

Treatment with drug combinations that include protease inhibitors is found to be effective in postponing and possibly preventing the onset of AIDS in HIV-infected patients.

Intel Corporation reports the development of the world's fastest computer, capable of performing one trillion operations per second.

Society

South Africa—President Nelson Mandela is divorced from his wife of 38 years, Winnie Mandela.

U.K.—Prince Charles and Princess Diana agree on their divorce.

U.S.—Falling crime rates bring relief and spark debate as to the causes of the decline, including changing demographics and improved police work.

More than 200 people die when TWA Flight 800 crashes into the Atlantic off Long Island. Though the disaster is originally suspected to be an act of terrorism, a lengthy investigation fails to uncover evidence for that scenario.

The Food and Drug Administration approves Olestra, a fat substitute for snack foods.

Sports

U.S.—With the return of Michael Jordan to professional basketball, the Chicago Bulls resume their dominance of the sport, winning each National Basketball Association championship from 1996 to 1998.

A bomb disrupts the Summer Olympics in Atlanta, Georgia. The U.S. wins the most gold medals (44) and the most medals overall (101).

1997 Arts and Entertainment

Asia—New York's Asia Society presents "Contemporary Art in Asia: Traditions/Tensions," featuring works by 27 artists, including Bali's I Wayan Bendi, Korea's Soo-Ja Kim, Thailand's Chatchai Puipia, Indonesia's Heri Dono, and India's Ravinder G. Reddy.

Cuba—Recording artists spotlighted at the Cuban Record Fair include NG la Banda and Lucretia.

Spain—The Guggenheim Museum in Bilbao opens, designed by American architect Frank O. Gehry.

U.K.—Elton John's new version of his earlier release "Candle in the Wind," revised to honor the late Princess Diana, sells nearly 32 million copies in 37 days, becoming the best-selling single of all time.

Plays include Tom Stoppard's *The Invention of Love* and Patrick Marber's *The Closer*.

U.S.—New musicals include *Titanic*, *The Life*, *Steel Pier*, and *Jekyll & Hyde*; musical revivals include *Chicago*.

New plays include William Luce's *Barrymore* and Wendy Wasserstein's *An American Daughter.*

The rap album *Life after Death* by the Notorious B.I.G., who is shot to death this year (*see also* **1996, Tupac Shakur**), rises to the top of the charts. Folk singer and songwriter John Denver (1943–97) also dies this year.

Best-selling albums include the British-based Spice Girls' *Spice*, Mary J. Blige's *Share My World*, George Strait's *Carrying Your Love with Me*, and Bob Dylan's *Time out of Mind.*

Lilith Fair, an all-female-artist touring music festival, showcases such performers as Fiona Apple, Tracy Chapman, Sheryl Crow, and Jewel.

New musical compositions include Myron Fink's opera *The Conquistador* and Elliott Carter's orchestral work *Allegro Scorrerole.*

In an episode of the comedy *Ellen*, the character played by Ellen DeGeneres becomes the first leading character in a prime-time television series to "come out" as gay.

New TV series include the Fox comedy-drama *Ally McBeal* (1997–).

World—Novels include Charles Frazier's *Cold Mountain*, Don De Lillo's *Underworld*, and Cynthia Ozick's *The Puttermesser Papers* (all U.S.), Martin Amis's *Night Train* (U.K.), Arundhati Roy's *The God of Small Things* (India), Marie Darrieussecq's *Pig Tales (La Truismes)* (France), and Peter Carey's *Jack Maggs* (Australia).

Films include James Cameron's *Titanic* and Curtis Hanson's *L. A. Confidential* (both U.S.), Peter Cattaneo's *The Full Monty* and John Madden's *Mrs. Brown* (both U.K.), Roberto Benigni's *Life is Beautiful* (Italy), and Mike Van Diem's *Character* (The Netherlands).

Dance companies visiting the U.S. include the Ballet Gulbenkian (Portugal), the Shobana Jeyasingh Dance Company (U.K.), the Sydney Dance Company (Australia), and Pina Bausch's Tanztheater Wuppertal (Germany).

Afropop music gains in international popularity as the Afropop band Zap Mama, led by Zairian-Belgian Marie Daulne, releases its album 7.

Visual artists receiving attention in exhibitions this year include photographer Jeff Wall (Canada); sculptors Jake and Dinos Chapman (U.S.); installation artist Kara Walker (U.S.); ephemeral artist Lita Albuquerque (U.S.); photographer Marikuo Mori (Japan); and sculptor Joep van Lieshout (Netherlands).

Ideas

France—Philosophical discussions led by moderators such as philosopher Marc Sautet become popular events at cafes.

Japan—Historian Takanori Irie publishes *The Rise and Fall of the Pacific Civilization.*

U.K.—Historian Hugh Thomas publishes *The Slave Trade: The Story of the Atlantic Slave Trade, 1440–1870.*

U.S.—Anthropologist Jared Diamond publishes *Guns, Germs, and Steel: The Fates of Human Societies.*

Journalists Richard Bernstein and Ross H. Munro publish *The Coming Conflict with China.*

Sociologists Kathryn Edin and Laura Lein document the lives of women on welfare in *Making Ends Meet.*

Military

Afghanistan—Taliban rebels seize Kabul, the capital, instituting Islamic fundamentalist rule, though an opposition alliance continues to fight against them.

Russia—President Boris Yeltsin signs a treaty ending the Chechnyan Civil War.

Politics

Albania—Anarchy results when a third of the population loses their savings in pyramid schemes. Riots and rebellions are quelled by a multinational force; in elections, Rexhep Mejdani becomes president.

Cambodia—Khmer Rouge leader Pol Pot is arrested by his own troops and convicted of war crimes in a show trial.

China—Paramount leader Deng Xiaoping dies, sealing the authority of the younger generation of leaders, including President Jiang Zemin.

Hong Kong reverts from British to Chinese rule.

France—A Socialist coalition headed by Lionel Jospin as prime minister wins national elections.

India—Kocheril Raman Narayanan becomes the first president of India to come from the "untouchables" caste.

Israel—Israel agrees to give up control of a large part of the West Bank city of Hebron.

Liberia—After a long civil war that began in 1989, former rebel leader Charles Taylor is elected president and begins trying to reconstruct the country.

Sierra Leone—A coup deposes President Ahmad Tejan Kabbah. He will be restored to power next year by West African peacekeeping forces.

South Korea—Corruption scandals and a currency devaluation destabilize the government; in December elections, former dissident Kim Dae Jung is voted in as president.

Thailand—The economy collapses under the burden of foreign debt. The shockwaves will ripple throughout Asia in 1998, causing widespread financial downturns.

U.K.—Labour Party leader Tony Blair is elected prime minister, ending 18 years of Conservative rule.

Science and Technology

China—The first fossilized inner organs of dinosaurs ever seen are discovered near Beipiao.

Peru—Government commandos rescue 72 hostages held for four months by Túpac Amaru rebels, all of whom are killed.

Russia/U.S.—A U.S. space shuttle docks with the Russian space station *Mir*.

Spain—Paleontologists report the discovery of 800,000-year-old hominid fossils near Burgos that represent the earliest known Europeans.

U.K.—Scientists at the National Physical Laboratory in Teddington, England, report discovery of an unusually long-lasting "excited" state of an atom.

In the first cloning ever of an adult mammal, Scottish embryologist Ian Wilmut announces his 1996 replication of a lamb from a ewe's DNA.

U.S.—On July 4 the unmanned spacecraft *Mars Pathfinder* lands on Mars, releasing a robotic vehicle, the Mars Sojourner Rover.

The most distant galaxy ever seen, 13 billion light-years from Earth, is discovered.

Comet Hale-Bopp, intrinsically the brightest comet to pass inside Earth's orbit in more than 400 years, is visible to the naked eye.

Neurobiologist Evan Balaban shows that the unique songs of birds are genetically programmed.

U.S./Chile—American and Chilean archaeologists conclude that Monte Verde, Chile, was settled by a population of human hunter-gatherers 12,500 years ago, at least 1,000 years earlier than the Clovis culture of New Mexico (*see* **1952**).

Society

Egypt—Islamic militants kill 62 people at Luxor.

France—In Paris international terrorist "Carlos the Jackal" is convicted of murder.

On December 31 riots break out over unemployment.

India—Albanian-born nun Mother Teresa, known for her charitable work in India and worldwide, dies on September 5.

Indonesia/Malaysia—Smoke from jungle fires in Indonesia creates thick smog in the Malaysian state of Sarawak.

Russia—In Terekhovo, one woman is murdered and others assaulted for allegedly practicing witchcraft. The crimes are a sign of increasing belief in the occult since the fall of Communism.

Saudi Arabia—Three hundred pilgrims die in a fire outside Mecca.

U.K.—On August 31 Britain's Princess Diana, age 36, dies in a car crash in Paris, inspiring worldwide mourning.

U.S.—In California 39 members of the Heaven's Gate cult, led by Marshall Herff Applewhite, kill themselves in the worst mass suicide on American soil.

Drifter Andrew Cunanan murders fashion designer Gianni Versace.

Floods plague the West; in April thousands of people in North Dakota are driven from their homes by flooding.

World—The heads of three UN agencies join in the growing international appeal to end female genital mutilation, common in Africa and parts of the Middle East.

Sports

U.S.—Tiger Woods wins the Masters golf tournament. At age 21 he is the youngest player ever to win the Masters; he does so with the lowest score (270) and the greatest margin of victory (12 strokes).

The Florida Marlins defeat the Cleveland Indians, four games to three, in their first World Series win.

1998 Arts and Entertainment

Italy—Italian architect Renzo Piano wins the Pritzker Architecture Prize. His works include the Kansai International Airport in Japan's Osaka harbor.

Portugal—José Saramago becomes the first Portuguese writer to win the Nobel Prize in literature.

U.K.—The Spice Girls, a pop band that rocketed to fame the year before, become one fewer with the departure of Geri Halliwell (a.k.a. Ginger Spice).

U.S.—Among winners of this year's MacArthur Fellowships are artist Janine Antoni, painter Ida Applebroog, video artist Gary Hill, and poets Linda Bierds and Edward Hirsch.

Choreographer Jaques d'Amboise and visual artist Agnes Martin are among the recipients of the National Medal of Arts.

New musicals in the 1997–98 Broadway season include *Ragtime*, by Terrence McNally, Stephen Flaherty, and Lynn Ahrens and *The Lion King*, by Roger Allers, Irene Mecchi, Elton John, and Tim Rice.

Best-selling albums include *Backstreet Boys*, Shania Twain's *Come on Over*, Lauryn Hill's *The Miseducation of Lauryn Hill*, Alanis Morissette's *Supposed Former Infatuation Junkie*, Snoop Dogg's *Da Game Is to Be Sold*, and Barenaked Ladies' *Stunt*.

Novels include Tom Wolfe's *A Man in Full*, Barbara Kingsolver's *The Poisonwood Bible*, and Alice McDermott's *Charming Billy*.

World—Movies include Steven Spielberg's *Saving Private Ryan* (U.S.), John Madden's *Shakespeare in Love* (U.S./U.K.), Shekhar Kapur's *Elizabeth* (U.K./India), Thomas Vinterberg's *The Celebration* (Denmark), and Kirk Jones's *Waking Ned Divine* (Ireland).

Ideas

France—Critic and sociologist Pierre Bourdieu publishes *On Television*.

India—Economist Amartya Sen wins the Nobel Prize in Economics for his contributions to welfare economics.

U.K.—Physicist and priest John C. Polkinghorne publishes *Belief in God in an Age of Science*.

U.S.—Entomologist Edward O. Wilson publishes *Consilience: The Unity of Knowledge*, a proposal for unifying the sciences and humanities.

Vatican City—Pope John Paul II issues the encyclical *Fides et Ratio (Faith and Reason)*.

Military

Congo—Civil war breaks out in August as rebels attack President Laurent Kabila's government. Other African countries intervene, including Rwanda and Uganda on the rebel side and Angola, Zimbabwe, Namibia, Chad, and some Rwandan Hutus on the government side.

India/Pakistan—India and Pakistan conduct a series of underground nuclear tests, raising fears of a South Asian arms race.

Iraq—From December 16 to 19 the U.S. and U.K. bomb Iraq to punish it for noncompliance with UN weapons inspectors. Bombing will continue the following year.

Spain—The Basque separatist group ETA calls its first open-ended ceasefire.

U.S.—In August terrorist bombs explode at U.S. embassies in Tanzania and Kenya, killing hundreds. Islamic fundamentalist leader Osama bin Laden is accused of masterminding the attacks. The U.S. retaliates with missile strikes on alleged terrorist bases in Afghanistan and Sudan.

Yugoslavia—Civil war breaks out between the Serb-controlled government and the break-away province of Kosovo. Serbian massacres of ethnic Albanians in Kosovo prompt threats of NATO air strikes; under that pressure, President Slobodan Milosevic agrees to with-drawal of military forces and to future elections in Kosovo.

Politics

Brazil—The International Monetary Fund announces a $42 billion aid package to stave off Brazilian economic collapse.

Cambodia—Former Khmer Rouge leader Pol Pot dies in April. Current Khmer Rouge leaders Khieu Samphan and Nuon Chea surrender in December to Prime Minister Hun Sen.

Chile—Former Chilean dictator Augusto Pinochet is detained in Britain based on a Spanish warrant charging him with human-rights offenses.

Germany—Chancellor Helmut Kohl is voted out of office; Gerhard Schroeder succeeds him, heading a coalition of the Social Democratic Party and the Green Party.

Indonesia—Public outrage over the economy's collapse forces President Suharto to resign after 32 years of rule; B. J. Habibie replaces him.

Iran—Gholamhossein Karbaschi, the reformist mayor of Tehran, is sentenced to prison on charges that indicate growing tensions between conservatives and moderates.

Israel—Meeting in October in Maryland, Israeli and Palestinian representatives sign the Wye Memorandum, outlining steps for an Israeli military withdrawal from parts of the West Bank.

In December parliament dissolves Prime Minister Benjamin Netanyahu's government.

Italy—Premier Romano Prodi resigns after his government loses a confidence vote; leftist Massimo D'Alema becomes premier.

Japan—Japan experiences its worst recession since World War II. Prime Minister Ryutaro Hashimoto resigns in July.

Malaysia—In the midst of an economic downturn, Prime Minister Mahathir bin Mohamad imprisons his heir apparent, Anwar Ibrahim.

Nigeria—The death in prison of Moshood K. O. Abiola, apparent winner of the cancelled elections of 1993, causes riots.

Russia—In August, the ruble is devalued, taking its worst fall in four years. President Boris Yeltsin dismisses his government, while the economic emergency roils financial markets around the world.

Slovakia—Premier Vladimir Meciar is removed in national elections.

Turkey—Premier Mesut Yilmaz's government loses a parliamentary confidence vote, prompting his resignation.

U.K.—On April 10 a Northern Ireland peace accord is signed by representatives of Britain, Ireland, and Northern Ireland's main political parties.

Trade Secretary Peter Mandelson and Paymaster General Geoffrey Robinson resign in a loan scandal.

U.S.—On December 19 the House of Representatives impeaches President Bill Clinton for lying under oath and obstructing justice in trying to cover up his sexual affair with former White House intern Monica Lewinsky. Throughout the year-long scandal, public opinion polls have shown support for Clinton and not for his accusers.

World—Economies around the world are affected by the economic turmoil in Russia, Brazil, and such Asian countries as Indonesia, Japan, and Malaysia (*see* **individual entries**).

Science and Technology

U.S.—Astronomers report that the universe will expand forever.

Scientists isolate and cultivate human embryonic stem cells for the first time.

The field of behavioral genetics continues to grow; books on the subject include this year's *Living With Our Genes* by American molecular geneticist Dean Hamer and writer Peter Copeland.

The anti-impotence drug Viagra, or sildenafil citrate, is approved.

Society

Canada/Switzerland—Swissair Flight 111 crashes into the Atlantic Ocean off Nova Scotia, Canada, killing 229 people.

Central America—From October 26 to 31 Hurricane Mitch becomes the deadliest Atlantic hurricane of the 20th century as it strikes Central America, particularly Honduras and Nicaragua. About 11,000 people die; one million are left homeless.

Germany/U.S.—Germany's Daimler-Benz AG and Chrysler Corporation merge in the largest foreign takeover of a U.S. firm.

Switzerland—The country's two largest banks agree to compensate victims of the Nazi Holocaust for lost deposits from that period.

U.S.—In April the jobless rate falls to 4.3 percent, the lowest since 1970.

Montana recluse Theodore J. Kaczynski pleads guilty to being the Unabomber, the mysterious antitechnology activist whose package bombs had terrorized the country for 17 years. He is sentenced to four life terms with no possibility of parole.

The U.S. files two antitrust lawsuits against Microsoft Corporation.

Oil company Exxon acquires its rival Mobil, forming the largest corporate combination ever.

The United Auto Workers stage a 54-day strike against General Motors.

Gunman Russell E. Weston Jr. kills two Capitol Police officers in an attack in the U.S. Capitol.

Assisted-suicide advocate Dr. Jack Kevorkian is charged with murder for aiding the suicide of a terminally ill man.

Sports

Brazil—Brazilian runner Ronaldo da Costa sets a world marathon record, running the Berlin Marathon in 2 hours, 6 minutes, and 5 seconds.

Japan—The Winter Olympics are held in Nagano.

U.S.—In baseball, on September 8, Mark McGwire of the St. Louis Cardinals hits his 62nd home run of the season, breaking the record set by Roger Maris in 1961. Sammy Sosa of the Chicago Cubs hits his 62nd home run of the season on September 13. McGwire finishes the season with 70 home runs, Sosa with 66.

The New York Yankees defeat the San Diego Padres to win the World Series, four games to zero.

In basketball the National Basketball Association owners lockout the players in a labor dispute, resulting in a two-month delay in opening the 1998–99 season.

In football's Super Bowl the Denver Broncos defeat the defending champion Green Bay Packers 31–24.

1999 Arts and Entertainment

U.S.—Novels include Thomas Harris's *Hannibal*, Ha Jin's *Waiting*, Jonathan Lethem's *Motherless Brooklyn*, Nathan Englander's *For the Relief of Unbearable Urges*, Elizabeth Strout's *Amy and Isabelle*, and Oscar Hijuelos's *Empress of the Splendid Season*.

Theatrical musicals include Michael John LaChiusa's *Marie Christine*, Ann Reinking and Chet Walker's *Fosse!*, Cole Porter and Sam and Bella Spewack's *Kiss Me, Kate* (revival), Irving Berlin's *Annie Get Your Gun* (revival), and Clark Gesner and Andrew Lippa's *You're a Good Man, Charlie Brown* (revival).

World—Films include Sam Mendes's *American Beauty* (U.S.), Harold Ramis's *Analyze This* (U.S.), Spike Jonze's *Being John Malkovich* (U.S.), Stanley Kubrick's *Eyes Wide Shut* (U.S./U.K.), Guy Ritchie's *Lock, Stock, and Two Smoking Barrels* (U.K.), M. Night Shyamalan's *The Sixth Sense* (U.S.), Kimberly Peirce's *Boys Don't Cry* (U.S.), Mike Leigh's *Topsy-Turvy* (U.K.), and Pedro Almodóvar's *All About My Mother* (Spain/France).

Notable albums include Santana's *Supernatural*, Mary J. Blige's *Mary*, TLC's *Fanmail*, Backstreet Boys's *Millennium*, Christina Aguilera's *Christina Aguilera*, Dixie Chicks's *Fly*, Sting's *Brand New Day* (U.K.), Britney Spears's *...Baby One More Time*, Eminem's *The Slim Shady LP*.

Ideas

U.S.—Works of history include John W. Dower's *Embracing Defeat: Japan in the Wake of World War II*, David M. Kennedy's *Freedom From Fear: The American People in Depression and War, 1929–1945*, Dava Sobel's *Galileo's Daughter: A Historical Memoir of Science, Faith, and Love*, and Nicholas Lehman's *The Big Test: The Secret History of the American Meritocracy*.

The how and why of the increasing speed of day-to-day living is explored in James Gleick's *Faster: The Acceleration of Just About Everything*.

A little-explored subset of society is revealed in Lawrence Otis Graham's *Our Kind of People: Inside America's Black Upper Class*.

Law and ethics professor Martha C. Nussbaum publishes *Sex and Social Justice*.

Military

India—In May India launches attacks on what it believes to be Pakistan-supported Islamic militants located in Kashmir. Peace talks follow later in the month.

Israel—Following deadly guerilla attacks resulting in Israeli deaths, Israel begins aerial bombing over southern Lebanon.

Russia—Hundreds of Chechens die and thousands are displaced after weeks of bombing by Russia, including the October bombing of the Chechen capital of Grozny.

Sierra Leone—Opposing factions that have fought an eight-year civil war sign an agreement granting some power to the rebel forces.

Yugoslavia—On March 24, NATO forces begin bomb and cruise missile attacks on Serbia over its treatment of ethnic Albanians in Yugoslavia's Kosovo region. The next day, Serbian forces increase attacks on Kosovo. Attacks on both sides continue, with many refugees fleeing Kosovo. In June the Serbs capitulate, agreeing to greater autonomy for Kosovo and permitting NATO peacekeeping forces to enter Kosovo.

Politics

Argentina—Buenos Aires Mayor Fernando de la Rúa is elected president, defeating Governor Eduardo Duhalde of the Buenos Aires province.

Armenia—Prime Minister Vazgen Sargissian, the Speaker of the Parliament, and six others are assassinated by gunmen who invade the Parliament building. The prime minister is replaced by Aram Sargissian, brother of the prime minister.

Australia—On November 6, Australians reject a proposal to abandon the British monarch as head of state and to establish a republic instead.

China—On December 19, Portugal grants China sovereignty over the territory of Macao, which had been under colonial rule for 442 years. It was the last vestige of European control in Asia.

India—In April, Prime Minister Atal Behari Vajpayee resigns.

Indonesia—Abdurrahman Wahid is elected president by the People's Consultative Assembly. He defeats Megawati Sukarnoputri, daughter of former Indonesian president Sukarno.

Israel—Ehud Barak is elected Prime Minister, defeating Benjamin Netanyahu.

Nigeria—On May 29 sixteen years of uninterrupted military rule end when the military grants power to the civilian government. Elected as president is former general Olusegun Obasanjo.

Pakistan—For only the third time in 50 years, an Indian Prime Minister (Atal Behari Vajpayee) visits with a Pakistani prime minister (Nawaz Sharif). The meeting takes place in Pakistan.

Russia—A Communist-led move to impeach Boris Yeltsin fails, but on December 31 Yeltsin resigns of his own accord. He appoints Russian prime minister Vladimir Putin as acting president.

South Africa—Thabo Mkebi, deputy of President Nelson Mandela, is elected president.

He is the second black president in the country's history.

Turkey—In February, Turkish commandos arrest Kurdish rebel leader Abdullah Öcalan in the Greek embassy in Nairobi, Kenya. The arrest sparks a coordinated wave of riots by Kurds in Paris, Frankfurt, Milan, London, Moscow, and other European cities. Öcalan is convicted on charges of treason and sentenced to die.

U.K.—Britain denies the Chilean government's petition to free former Chilean dictator Augusto Pinochet for reasons of age and failing health. Pinochet is facing torture charges and is to be put on trial in Spain.

For the first time since 1707, Scottish citizens vote to elect their own Parliament.

For the first time, Welsh voters elect a Welsh assembly.

U.S.—On January 7, the first presidential impeachment trial since 1868 opens. On February 12, the Senate acquits President Bill Clinton on charges of perjury, 55–45, and obstruction of justice, 50–50, in the Monica Lewinsky scandal.

In March, President Clinton is held in contempt of court by a Federal judge in Little Rock, Arkansas, for false testimony about his interactions with Monica Lewinsky.

The U.S. Senate, powered largely by Republican forces, votes not to sign the Comprehensive Test Ban Treaty, prompting President Clinton to accuse the Senate of isolationism. The treaty had already been signed by 150 nations.

On October 18 the independent counsel Kenneth Starr resigns. Over the past five years, his investigations of President Bill Clinton and his associates have totaled over $47 million.

On November 25, a five-year-old Cuban boy, Elían González, is rescued off the coast of Florida. His mother, divorced from father Juan Miguel González, drowned in the escape from Cuba, as did 9 of the group of 13 who attempted to escape from Cuba. The custody battle between Elían's Miami relatives and his father in Cuba will rage into 2000, when American courts will rule that the boy should return to his father.

In fall presidential election campaigning, Arizona Senator John McCain and Texas Governor George W. Bush emerge as Republican front runners; Vice-President Al Gore and former Senator Bill Bradley are Democratic front runners. In a hotly contested election in 2000, Bush will emerge victorious over Gore.

World—On January 1, the euro begins to be phased in. The European Union's new unified currency becomes available for currency trading and some retail transactions in eleven participating countries.

Poland, Hungary, and the Czech Republic become the first former Soviet-bloc nations to join the North Atlantic Treaty Organization (NATO).

Science

U.S.—In February physicists at Massachusetts's Rowland Institute for Science announce that they have created a system that lowers the speed of light to 38 miles per hour.

Record-setting heat occurs in the eastern U.S., part of a general warming trend over the northern hemisphere.

Mars Polar Lander, an unmanned U.S. spacecraft en route to Mars, ceases communication with earth.

World—Two groups of astronomers announce the discovery of three large planets located around the star Upsilon Andromedae.

Society

China—The largest group protest since Tiananmen Square occurs in Bejing, when 10,000 adherents of the religious cult Falun Gong meet to call for recognition. China bans the cult.

Egypt—EgyptAir 990, an Egyptian airliner, dives into the Atlantic Ocean, causing the deaths of all 217 people aboard.

Israel—Rana Raslan is the first Arab to win the Miss Israel beauty pageant, earning her the job of representing Israel in the Miss World pageant.

Romania—Pope John Paul II meets with Patriarch Teoctist of the Romanian Orthodox Church, marking the first visit to an Orthodox Christian country by a pope since 1054.

Russia—In September, a bomb explodes in Moscow, resulting in at least 95 deaths. It is the third bombing of the past month in Russia and is believed by authorities to be the work of Islamic militants.

Turkey—On August 17, a massive earthquake kills more than 17,000 people and leaves hundreds of thousands displaced.

U.S.—In April the deadliest school act of violence in the nation occurs in Littleton, Colorado's Columbine High School, where two male students kill 12 other students and a teacher.

In July a plane piloted by John Kennedy Jr., the son of former president John F. Kennedy, crashes near the Massachusetts coast, resulting in the deaths of Kennedy Jr., his wife, and her sister.

In Seattle, pro-labor and pro-environment groups disrupt meetings of the World Trade Organization, leading Mayor Paul Schell to declare a state of emergency.

In an antitrust case ruling, the U.S. District Court decides that Microsoft Corp. used "monopoly power" to undercut rivals.

In March Philip Morris is told to pay an Oregon family $81 million in tobacco smoking-related damages, the largest award of its kind.

In a highly successful year for the stock market, the Dow Jones Industrial Average advances 25.2% by year's end; the Nasdaq index increases 85.5 percent.

Venezuela—In December, heavy rains cause floods and mudslides that result in over 9,000 deaths.

World—Fears that computer technology will be unable to handle configurations using the date 2000 (a.k.a. Y2K) lead businesses and governments to establish safeguards in computer systems. Fearing that the Y2K bug will lead to the collapse of civilization, some people worldwide prepare by stockpiling survival foods and products. Y2K-related problems will turn out to be minor.

Spectacular celebrations are held worldwide to celebrate the end of the millennium on December 31, 1999, though calendrical purists point out that the millennium will technically not come to an end until December 31, 2000.

AIDS becomes the leading cause of death in Africa, according to the United Nations AIDS Program.

Sports

U.S—Chicago Bulls player Michael Jordan, widely considered the greatest player in the history of the National Basketball Association, retires.

On October 25, U.S. golfer and 1999 U.S. Open winner Payne Stewart and five others are killed in a plane crash in South Dakota.

Super Bowl XXXIII is won by the Denver Broncos over the Atlanta Falcons, 34-19. The game is played at Pro Player Stadium, Miami, Florida.

The 1998–1999 NBA Championship Series is won by the San Antonio Spurs over the New York Knicks, 4-1.

The American League's New York Yankees win the World Series against the National League's Atlanta Braves, in four games. It is the 25th world championship for the Yankees.

The 1999 Stanley Cup Championship is won by the Dallas Stars over the Buffalo Sabres, 4–2.

World—U.S. cancer survivor Lance Armstrong wins cycling's Tour De France.

Nobel Prize Winners
1901–99

Endowed by the will of Swedish chemist and inventor Alfred Nobel (1833–96), the Nobel Prizes (in Peace, Chemistry, Physics, Physiology or Medicine, and Literature) were instituted in 1901. A prize in Economic Science was added in 1969.

1901

Peace: Jean-Henri Dunant (Switzerland); Frédéric Passy (France)
Chemistry: Jacobus van't Hoff (Netherlands)
Physics: Wilhelm Roentgen (Germany)
Physiology or Medicine: Emil von Behring (Germany)
Literature: René F. A. Sully Prudhomme (France)

1902

Peace: Elie Ducommun (Switzerland); Charles-Albert Gobat (Switzerland)
Chemistry: Emil Fischer (Germany)
Physics: Hendrik Antoon Lorentz (Netherlands); Pieter Zeeman (Netherlands)
Physiology or Medicine: Ronald Ross (U.K.)
Literature: Theodor Mommsen (Germany)

1903

Peace: William R. Cremer (U.K.)
Chemistry: Svante Arrhenius (Sweden)
Physics: Antoine-Henri Becquerel (France); Pierre Curie (France); Marie Curie (France)
Physiology or Medicine: Niels R. Finsen (Denmark)
Literature: Björnstjerne Björnson (Norway)

1904

Peace: Institute of International Law (Belgium)
Chemistry: Sir William Ramsay (U.K.)
Physics: John William Strutt, Lord Rayleigh (U.K.)
Physiology or Medicine: Ivan Pavlov (Russia)
Literature: Frédéric Mistral (France); José Echegaray (Spain)

1905

Peace: Bertha von Suttner (Austria)
Chemistry: Adolf von Baeyer (Germany)
Physics: Philipp Lenard (Germany)
Physiology or Medicine: Robert Koch (Germany)
Literature: Henryk Sienkiewicz (Poland)

1906

Peace: Theodore Roosevelt (U.S.)
Chemistry: Henri Moissan (France)
Physics: J. J. Thomson (U.K.)
Physiology or Medicine: Camillo Golgi (Italy); Santiago Ramón y Cajal (Spain)
Literature: Giosuè Carducci (Italy)

1907

Peace: Ernesto Teodoro Moneta (Italy); Louis Renault (France)
Chemistry: Eduard Buchner (Germany)
Physics: A. A. Michelson (U.S.)
Physiology or Medicine: Alphonse Laveran (France)
Literature: Rudyard Kipling (U.K.)

1908

Peace: Klas Pontus Arnoldson (Sweden); Fredrik Bajer (Denmark)
Chemistry: Ernest Rutherford (U.K.)
Physics: Gabriel Lippmann (France)
Physiology or Medicine: Paul Ehrlich (Germany); Élie Metchnikoff (Russia)
Literature: Rudolf Eucken (Germany)

1909

Peace: Auguste Beernaert (Belgium); P. H. B. d'Estournelles de Constant (France)
Chemistry: Wilhelm Ostwald (Germany)
Physics: Guglielmo Marconi (Italy); Ferdinand Braun (Germany)
Physiology or Medicine: Emil Kocher (Switzerland)
Literature: Selma Lagerlöf (Sweden)

1910

Peace: Permanent International Peace Bureau (Switzerland)
Chemistry: Otto Wallach (Germany)
Physics: Johannes van der Waals (Netherlands)
Physiology or Medicine: Albrecht Kossel (Germany)
Literature: Paul von Heyse (Germany)

1911
Peace: Tobias Asser (Netherlands); Alfred Fried (Austria)
Chemistry: Marie Curie (France)
Physics: Wilhelm Wien (Germany)
Physiology or Medicine: Allvar Gullstrand (Sweden)
Literature: Maurice Maeterlinck (Belgium)

1912
Peace: Elihu Root (U.S.)
Chemistry: Victor Grignard (France); Paul Sabatier (France)
Physics: Nils Gustaf Dalen (Sweden)
Physiology or Medicine: Alexis Carrel (France)
Literature: Gerhart Hauptmann (Germany)

1913
Peace: Henri-Marie Lafontaine (Belgium)
Chemistry: Alfred Werner (Switzerland)
Physics: Heike Kamerlingh Onnes (Netherlands)
Physiology or Medicine: Charles Richet (France)
Literature: Rabindranath Tagore (India)

1914
Peace: no award
Chemistry: Theodore Richards (U.S.)
Physics: Max von Laue (Germany)
Physiology or Medicine: Robert Barany (Austria)
Literature: no award

1915
Peace: no award
Chemistry: Richard Willstätter (Germany)
Physics: William Bragg (U.K.); Lawrence Bragg (U.K.)
Physiology or Medicine: no award
Literature: Romain Rolland (France)

1916
Peace: no award
Chemistry: no award
Physics: no award
Physiology or Medicine: no award
Literature: Verner von Heidenstam (Sweden)

1917
Peace: International Red Cross
Chemistry: no award
Physics: Charles Barkla (U.K.)
Physiology or Medicine: no award

Literature: Karl Gjellerup (Denmark); Henrik Pontoppidan (Denmark)

1918
Peace: no award
Chemistry: Fritz Haber (Germany)
Physics: Max Planck (Germany)
Physiology or Medicine: no award
Literature: no award

1919
Peace: Woodrow Wilson (U.S.)
Chemistry: no award
Physics: Johannes Stark (Germany)
Physiology or Medicine: Jules Bordet (Belgium)
Literature: Carl Spitteler (Switzerland)

1920
Peace: Léon Bourgeois (France)
Chemistry: Walther Nernst (Germany)
Physics: Charles Guillaume (Switzerland)
Physiology or Medicine: August Krogh (Denmark)
Literature: Knut Hamsun (Norway)

1921
Peace: Hjalmar Branting (Sweden); Christian L. Lange (Norway)
Chemistry: Frederick Soddy (U.K.)
Physics: Albert Einstein (Switzerland)
Physiology or Medicine: no award
Literature: Anatole France (France)

1922
Peace: Fridtjof Nansen (Norway)
Chemistry: Francis Aston (U.K.)
Physics: Niels Bohr (Denmark)
Physiology or Medicine: A. V. Hill (U.K.); Otto Meyerhof (Germany)
Literature: Jacinto Benavente y Martínez (Spain)

1923
Peace: no award
Chemistry: Fritz Pregl (Austria)
Physics: Robert Millikan (U.S.)
Physiology or Medicine: F. G. Banting (Canada); J. J. R. Macleod (U.K.)
Literature: William Butler Yeats (Ireland)

1924
Peace: no award
Chemistry: no award

Nobel prize winners, continued

Physics: Manne Siegbahn (Sweden)
Physiology or Medicine: Willem Einthoven
    (Netherlands)
Literature: Wladyslaw Reymont (Poland)

1925
Peace: Sir Austen Chamberlain (U.K.); Charles G.
    Dawes (U.S.)
Chemistry: Richard Zsigmondy (Austria)
Physics: James Franck (Germany); Gustav Hertz
    (Germany)
Physiology or Medicine: no award
Literature: George Bernard Shaw (Ireland)

1926
Peace: Aristide Briand (France); Gustav
    Stresemann (Germany)
Chemistry: Theodor Svedberg (Sweden)
Physics: Jean Perrin (France)
Physiology or Medicine: Johannes Fibiger
    (Denmark)
Literature: Grazia Deledda (Italy)

1927
Peace: Ferdinand Buisson (France); Ludwig
    Quidde (Germany)
Chemistry: Heinrich Wieland (Germany)
Physics: Arthur Holly Compton (U.S.); C. T. R.
    Wilson (U.K.)
Physiology or Medicine: Julius Wagner-Jauregg
    (Austria)
Literature: Henri Bergson (France)

1928
Peace: no award
Chemistry: Adolf Windaus (Germany)
Physics: Owen Richardson (U.K.)
Physiology or Medicine: Charles Nicolle (France)
Literature: Sigrid Undset (Norway)

1929
Peace: Frank B. Kellogg (U.S.)
Chemistry: Arthur Harden (U.K.); Hans von
    Euler-Chelpin (Sweden)
Physics: Louis-Victor de Broglie (France)
Physiology or Medicine: Christiaan Eijkman
    (Netherlands); Sir Frederick Hopkins (U.K.)
Literature: Thomas Mann (Germany)

1930
Peace: Nathan Soderblom (Sweden)
Chemistry: Hans Fischer (Germany)
Physics: Sir Chandrasekhara Raman (India)
Physiology or Medicine: Karl Landsteiner (U.S.)
Literature: Sinclair Lewis (U.S.)

1931
Peace: Jane Addams (U.S.); Nicholas Murray
Butler (U.S.)
Chemistry: Carl Bosch (Germany); Friedrich
    Bergius (Germany)
Physics: no award
Physiology or Medicine: Otto Warburg (Germany)
Literature: Erik Axel Karlfeldt (Sweden)

1932
Peace: no award
Chemistry: Irving Langmuir (U.S.)
Physics: Werner Heisenberg (Germany)
Physiology or Medicine: Edgar D. Adrian (U.K.);
    Sir Charles Sherrington (U.K.)
Literature: John Galsworthy (U.K.)

1933
Peace: Sir Norman Angell (U.K.)
Chemistry: no award
Physics: P. A. M. Dirac (U.K.); Erwin Schrödinger
    (Austria)
Physiology or Medicine: Thomas Hunt Morgan
    (U.S.)
Literature: Ivan Bunin (Soviet Union)

1934
Peace: Arthur Henderson (U.K.)
Chemistry: Harold Urey (U.S.)
Physics: no award
Physiology or Medicine: George H. Whipple
    (U.S.); George R. Minot (U.S.); William P.
    Murphy (U.S.)
Literature: Luigi Pirandello (Italy)

1935
Peace: Carl von Ossietzky (Germany)
Chemistry: Frédéric Joliot-Curie (France); Irène
    Joliot-Curie (France)
Physics: James Chadwick (U.K.)
Physiology or Medicine: Hans Spemann
    (Germany)
Literature: no award

1936
Peace: Carlos Saavedra Lamas (Argentina)
Chemistry: Peter Debye (Netherlands)
Physics: Carl Anderson (U.S.); Victor Hess (Austria)
Physiology or Medicine: Sir Henry Dale (U.K.); Eugene O'Neill (U.S.)
Literature: Otto Loewi (Germany)

1937
Peace: Viscount Cecil of Chelwood (U.K.)
Chemistry: Norman Haworth (U.K.); Paul Karrer (Switzerland)
Physics: Clinton Davisson (U.S.); George Paget Thomson (U.K.)
Physiology or Medicine: Albert Szent-Gyorgyi (Hungary)
Literature: Roger Martin du Gard (France)

1938
Peace: Nansen International Office for Refugees (Switzerland)
Chemistry: Richard Kuhn (Germany) (declined)
Physics: Enrico Fermi (Italy)
Physiology or Medicine: Corneille Heymans (Belgium)
Literature: Pearl Buck (U.S.)

1939
Peace: no award
Chemistry: Adolf Butenandt (Germany) (declined); Leopold Ruzicka (Switzerland)
Physics: Ernest Lawrence (U.S.)
Physiology or Medicine: Gerhard Domagk (Germany)
Literature: Frans Eemil Sillanpää (Finland)

1940–42: no prizes awarded

1943
Peace: no award
Chemistry: George de Hevesy (Hungary)
Physics: Otto Stern (U.S.)
Physiology or Medicine: Edward A. Doisy (U.S.); Henrik Dam (Denmark)
Literature: no award

1944
Peace: International Red Cross
Chemistry: Otto Hahn (Germany)

Physics: Isidor Rabi (U.S.)
Physiology or Medicine: Joseph Erlanger (U.S.); Herbert S. Gasser (U.S.)
Literature: Johannes V. Jensen (Denmark)

1945
Peace: Cordell Hull (U.S.)
Chemistry: Artturi Virtanen (Finland)
Physics: Wolfgang Pauli (Austria)
Physiology or Medicine: Sir Alexander Fleming (U.K.); Ernst Boris Chain (U.K.); Sir Howard Florey (Australia)
Literature: Gabriela Mistral (Chile)

1946
Peace: John R. Mott (U.S.); Emily Greene Balch (U.S.)
Chemistry: James Sumner (U.S.); John Northrop (U.S.); Wendell Stanley (U.S.)
Physics: P. W. Bridgman (U.S.)
Physiology or Medicine: Hermann J. Muller (U.S.)
Literature: Hermann Hesse (Switzerland)

1947
Peace: American Friends Service Committee (U.S.); Friends Service Council (U.K.)
Chemistry: Sir Robert Robinson (U.K.)
Physics: Sir Edward Appleton (U.K.)
Physiology or Medicine: Carl F. Cori (U.S.); Gerty T. Cori (U.S.); Bernardo Houssay (Argentina)
Literature: André Gide (France)

1948
Peace: no award
Chemistry: Arne Tiselius (Sweden)
Physics: Patrick Blackett (U.K.)
Physiology or Medicine: Paul Mueller (Switzerland)
Literature: T. S. Eliot (U.K.)

1949
Peace: Lord Boyd-Orr (U.K.)
Chemistry: William Giauque (U.S.)
Physics: Yukawa Hideki (Japan)
Physiology or Medicine: Walter Rudolf Hess (Switzerland); Antonio Egas Moniz (Portugal)
Literature: William Faulkner (U.S.)

Nobel prize winners, continued

1950

Peace: Ralph Bunche (U.S.)

Chemistry: Otto Diels (Germany); Kurt Alder (Germany)

Physics: Cecil Powell (U.K.)

Physiology or Medicine: Philip S. Hench (U.S.); Edward C. Kendall (U.S.); Tadeus Reichstein (Switzerland)

Literature: Bertrand Russell (U.K.)

1951

Peace: Léon Jouhaux (France)

Chemistry: Edwin McMillan (U.S.); Glenn Seaborg (U.S.)

Physics: Sir John Cockcroft (U.K.); E. T. S. Walton (Ireland)

Physiology or Medicine: Max Theiler (South Africa)

Literature: Pär Lagerkvist (Sweden)

1952

Peace: Albert Schweitzer (France)

Chemistry: A. J. P. Martin (U.K.); R. L. M. Synge (U.K.)

Physics: Felix Bloch (U.S.); E. M. Purcell (U.S.)

Physiology or Medicine: Selman A. Waksman (U.S.)

Literature: François Mauriac (France)

1953

Peace: George C. Marshall (U.S.)

Chemistry: Hermann Staudinger (Germany)

Physics: Frits Zernike (Netherlands)

Physiology or Medicine: Fritz A. Lipmann (U.S.); Hans A. Krebs (U.K.)

Literature: Sir Winston Churchill (U.K.)

1954

Peace: Office of the United Nations High Commissioner for Refugees

Chemistry: Linus Pauling (U.S.)

Physics: Max Born (U.K.); Walther Bothe (Germany)

Physiology or Medicine: John F. Enders (U.S.); Thomas H. Weller (U.S.); Frederick Robbins (U.S.)

Literature: Ernest Hemingway (U.S.)

1955

Peace: no award

Chemistry: Vincent Du Vigneaud (U.S.)

Physics: Willis Lamb Jr. (U.S.); Polykarp Kusch (U.S.)

Physiology or Medicine: Axel Hugo Theorell (Sweden)

Literature: Halldór Laxness (Iceland)

1956

Peace: no award

Chemistry: Sir Cyril Hinshelwood (U.K.); Nikolay Semyonov (Soviet Union)

Physics: William Shockley (U.S.); Walter H. Brattain (U.S.); John Bardeen (U.S.)

Physiology or Medicine: Dickinson Richards (U.S.); André F. Cournand (U.S.); Werner Forssmann (Germany)

Literature: Juan Ramón Jiménez (Spain)

1957

Peace: Lester B. Pearson (Canada)

Chemistry: Sir Alexander Todd (U.K.)

Physics: Tsung-Dao Lee (China); Chen Ning Yang (China)

Physiology or Medicine: Daniel Bovet (Italy)

Literature: Albert Camus (France)

1958

Peace: Dominique Georges Pire (Belgium)

Chemistry: Frederick Sanger (U.K.)

Physics: Pavel A. Cherenkov (Soviet Union); Igor Y. Tamm (Soviet Union); Ilya M. Frank (Soviet Union)

Physiology or Medicine: Joshua Lederberg (U.S.); George W. Beadle (U.S.); Edward L. Tatum (U.S.)

Literature: Boris Pasternak (Soviet Union) (declined)

1959

Peace: Philip Noël-Baker (U.K.)

Chemistry: Jaroslav Heyrovsky (Czechoslovakia)

Physics: Emilio Segrè (U.S.); Owen Chamberlain (U.S.)

Physiology or Medicine: Severo Ochoa (U.S.); Arthur Kornberg (U.S.)

Literature: Salvatore Quasimodo (Italy)

1960
Peace: Albert Luthuli (South Africa)
Chemistry: Willard Libby (U.S.)
Nobel prize winners, continued

Physics: Donald Glaser (U.S.)
Physiology or Medicine: Sir Macfarlane Burnet
(Australia); Peter B. Medawar (U.K.)
Literature: Saint-John Perse (France)

1961
Peace: Dag Hammarskjöld (Sweden)
Chemistry: Melvin Calvin (U.S.)
Physics: Robert Hofstadter (U.S.); Rudolf
Moessbauer (Germany)
Physiology or Medicine: Georg von Békésy (U.S.)
Literature: Ivo Andric (Yugoslavia)

1962
Peace: Linus Pauling (U.S.)
Chemistry: Max F. Perutz (U.K.); John C.
Kendrew (U.K.)
Physics: Lev D. Landau (Soviet Union)
Physiology or Medicine: James D. Watson (U.S.);
Francis H. C. Crick (U.K.); Maurice Wilkins
(U.K.)
Literature: John Steinbeck (U.S.)

1963
Peace: International Red Cross Committee;
League of Red Cross Societies
Chemistry: Giulio Natta (Italy); Karl Ziegler
(Germany)
Physics: Eugene Paul Wigner (U.S.); Maria
Goeppert Mayer (U.S.); J. Hans D. Jensen
(Germany)
Physiology or Medicine: Sir John Eccles (Australia);
Alan Lloyd Hodgkin (U.K.); Andrew Huxley
(U.K.)
Literature: George Seferis (Greece)

1964
Peace: Martin Luther King Jr. (U.S.)
Chemistry: Dorothy M. C. Hodgkin (U.K.)
Physics: Charles H. Townes (U.S.); Nikolay G.
Basov (Soviet Union); Aleksandr M. Prokhorov
(Soviet Union)
Physiology or Medicine: Konrad Bloch (U.S.);
Feodor Lynen (Germany)

Literature: Jean-Paul Sartre (France) (declined)

1965
Peace: United Nations International Children's
Emergency Fund (UNICEF)
Chemistry: R. B. Woodward (U.S.)
Physics: Richard P. Feynman (U.S.); Tomonaga
Shin'ichiro (Japan); Julian S. Schwinger (U.S.)
Physiology or Medicine: François Jacob (France);
André Lwoff (France); Jacques Monod (France)
Literature: Mikhail Sholokhov (Soviet Union)

1966
Peace: no award
Chemistry: Robert S. Mulliken (U.S.)
Physics: Alfred Kastler (France)
Physiology or Medicine: Francis Peyton Rous
(U.S.); Charles B. Huggins (U.S.)
Literature: Shmuel Yosef Agnon (Israel); Nelly
Sachspoet (Sweden)

1967
Peace: no award
Chemistry: Manfred Eigen (Germany); Ronald G.
W. Norrish (U.K.); George Porter (U.K.)
Physics: Hans A. Bethe (U.S.)
Physiology or Medicine: Haldan Keffer Hartline
(U.S.); George Wald (U.S.); Ragnar A. Granit
(Sweden)
Literature: Miguel Angel Asturias (Guatemala)

1968
Peace: René Cassin (France)
Chemistry: Lars Onsager (U.S.)
Physics: Luis W. Alvarez (U.S.)
Physiology or Medicine: Robert W. Holley (U.S.);
Har Gobind Khorana (U.S.); Marshall W.
Nirenberg (U.S.)
Literature: Kawabata Yasunari (Japan)

1969
Peace: International Labour Organisation
Chemistry: Derek H. R. Barton (U.K.); Odd
Hassel (Norway)
Physics: Murray Gell-Mann (U.S.)
Physiology or Medicine: Max Delbrück (U.S.);
Alfred D. Hershey (U.S.); Salvador E. Luria
(U.S.)
Literature: Samuel Beckett (Ireland)

Nobel prize winners, continued

Economic Science: Ragnar Frisch (Norway); Jan Tinbergen (Netherlands)

1970
Peace: Norman E. Borlaug (U.S.)
Chemistry: Luis F. Leloir (Argentina)
Physics: Louis Néel (France); Hannes Alfvén (Sweden)
Physiology or Medicine: Julius Axelrod (U.S.); Sir Bernard Katz (U.K.); Ulf von Euler (Sweden)
Literature: Aleksandr Solzhenitsyn (Soviet Union)
Economic Science: Paul A. Samuelson (U.S.)

1971
Peace: Willy Brandt (Germany)
Chemistry: Gerhard Herzberg (Canada)
Physics: Dennis Gabor (U.K.)
Physiology or Medicine: Earl W. Sutherland (U.S.)
Literature: Pablo Neruda (Chile)
Economic Science: Simon Kuznets (U.S.)

1972
Peace: no award
Chemistry: Stanford Moore (U.S.); William H. Stein (U.S.); Christian B. Anfinsen (U.S.)
Physics: John Bardeen (U.S.); Leon N. Cooper (U.S.); John R. Schrieffer (U.S.)
Physiology or Medicine: Gerald M. Edelman (U.S.); Rodney Porter (U.K.)
Literature: Heinrich Böll (Germany)
Economic Science: Sir John Hicks (U.K.); Kenneth J. Arrow (U.S.)

1973
Peace: Henry Kissinger (U.S.); Le Duc Tho (North Vietnam) (Tho declined)
Chemistry: Ernst Fischer (Germany); Geoffrey Wilkinson (U.K.)
Physics: Leo Esaki (Japan); Ivar Giaever (U.S.); Brian D. Josephson (U.K.)
Physiology or Medicine: Konrad Lorenz (Austria); Nikolaas Tinbergen (U.K.); Karl von Frisch (Austria)
Literature: Patrick White (Australia)
Economic Science: Wassily Leontief (U.S.)

1974
Peace: Sean MacBride (Ireland); Sato Eisaku (Japan)
Chemistry: Paul J. Flory (U.S.)
Physics: Sir Martin Ryle (U.K.); Antony Hewish (U.K.)
Physiology or Medicine: Albert Claude (U.S.); George E. Palade (U.S.); Christian R. de Duve (Belgium)
Literature: Eyvind Johnson (Sweden); Harry Martinson (Sweden)
Economic Science: Gunnar Myrdal (Sweden); Friedrich von Hayek (U.K.)

1975
Peace: Andrey D. Sakharov (Soviet Union)
Chemistry: John W. Cornforth (U.K.); Vladimir Prelog (Switzerland)
Physics: Aage N. Bohr (Denmark); Ben R. Mottelson (Denmark); L. James Rainwater (U.S.)
Physiology or Medicine: David Baltimore (U.S.); Renato Dulbecco (U.S.); Howard M. Temin (U.S.)
Literature: Eugenio Montale (Italy)
Economic Science: Leonid V. Kantorovich (Soviet Union); Tjalling C. Koopmans (U.S.)

1976
Peace: Mairead Corrigan (N. Ireland); Betty Williams (N. Ireland) Chemistry: William N. Lipscomb (U.S.)
Physics: Burton Richter (U.S.); Samuel C. C. Ting (U.S.)
Physiology or Medicine: Baruch S. Blumberg (U.S.); D. Carleton Gajdusek (U.S.)
Literature: Saul Bellow (U.S.)
Economic Science: Milton Friedman (U.S.)

1977
Peace: Amnesty International
Chemistry: Ilya Prigogine (Belgium); Physics: Philip W. Anderson (U.S.); Sir Nevill F. Mott (U.K.); John H. Van Vleck (U.S.)
Physiology or Medicine: Rosalyn S. Yalow (U.S.); Roger Guillemin (U.S.); Andrew Schally (U.S.)
Literature: Vicente Aleixandre (Spain)
Economic Science: James Meade (U.K.); Bertil Ohlin (Sweden)

1978

Peace: Menachem Begin (Israel); Anwar el-Sadat (Egypt)

Chemistry: Peter D. Mitchell (U.K.)

Physics: Pyotr L. Kapitsa (Soviet Union); Arno A. Penzias (U.S.); Robert W. Wilson (U.S.)

Nobel prize winners, continnued

Physiology or Medicine: Werner Arber (Switzerland); Daniel Nathans (U.S.); Hamilton O. Smith (U.S.)

Literature: Isaac Bashevis Singer (U.S.)

Economic Science: Herbert A. Simon (U.S.)

1979

Peace: Mother Teresa of Calcutta (India)

Chemistry: Herbert C. Brown (U.S.); Georg Wittig (W. Germany)

Physics: Steven Weinberg (U.S.); Sheldon Glashow (U.S.); Abdus Salam (Pakistan)

Physiology or Medicine: Allan M. Cormack (U.S.); Godfrey N. Hounsfield (U.K.)

Literature: Odysseus Elytis (Greece)

Economic Science: Sir W. Arthur Lewis (U.K.); Theodore W. Schultz (U.S.)

1980

Peace: Adolfo Pérez Esquivel (Argentina)

Chemistry: Paul Berg (U.S.); Walter Gilbert (U.S.); Frederick Sanger (U.K.)

Physics: James W. Cronin (U.S.); Val Logsdon Fitch (U.S.)

Physiology or Medicine: Baruj Benacerraf (U.S.); George D. Snell (U.S.); Jean Dausset (France)

Literature: Czeslaw Milosz (U.S.)

Economic Science: Lawrence R. Klein (U.S.)

1981

Peace: Office of the United Nations High Commissioner for Refugees

Chemistry: Fukui Kenichi (Japan); Roald Hoffmann (U.S.)

Physics: Nicolaas Bloembergen (U.S.); Arthur L. Schawlow (U.S.); Kai M. Siegbahn (Sweden)

Physiology or Medicine: Roger W. Sperry (U.S.); David H. Hubel (U.S.); Torsten N. Wiesel (Sweden)

Literature: Elias Canetti (Bulgaria)

Economic Science: James Tobin (U.S.)

1982

Peace: Alfonso García Robles (Mexico); Alva Myrdal (Sweden)

Chemistry: Aaron Klug (U.K.)

Physics: Kenneth G. Wilson (U.S.)

Physiology or Medicine: Sune K. Bergström (Sweden); Bengt I. Samuelsson (Sweden); John R. Vane (U.K.)

Literature: Gabriel García Márquez (Colombia)

Economic Science: George Stigler (U.S.)

1983

Peace: Lech Woelsa (Poland)

Chemistry: Henry Taube (U.S.)

Physics: Subrahmanyan Chandrasekhar (U.S.); William A. Fowler (U.S.)

Physiology or Medicine: Barbara McClintock (U.S.)

Literature: William Golding (U.K.)

Economic Science: Gerard Debreu (U.S.)

1984

Peace: Desmond Tutu (South Africa)

Chemistry: Bruce Merrifield (U.S.)

Physics: Carlo Rubbia (Italy); Simon van der Meer (Netherlands)

Physiology or Medicine: César Milstein (Argentina); Georges J. F. Köhler (W. Germany); Niels K. Jerne (U.K.–Denmark)

Literature: Jaroslav Seifert (Czechoslovakia)

Economic Science: Sir Richard Stone (U.K.)

1985

Peace: International Physicians for the Prevention of Nuclear War

Chemistry: Herbert A. Hauptman (U.S.); Jerome Karle (U.S.)

Physics: Klaus von Klitzing (W. Germany)

Physiology or Medicine: Michael S. Brown (U.S.); Joseph L. Goldstein (U.S.)

Literature: Claude Simon (France)

Economic Science: Franco Modigliani (U.S.)

1986

Peace: Elie Wiesel (U.S.)

Chemistry: Dudley R. Herschbach (U.S.); Yuan T. Lee (U.S.); John C. Polanyi (Canada)

Physics: Ernst Ruska (W. Germany); Gerd Binnig (W. Germany); Heinrich Rohrer (Switzerland)

Nobel prize winners, continued

Physiology or Medicine: Rita Levi-Montalcini (Italy); Stanley Cohen (U.S.)
Literature: Wole Soyinka (Nigeria)
Economic Science: James M. Buchanan (U.S.)

1987
Peace: Oscar Arias Sánchez (Costa Rica)
Chemistry: Donald J. Cram (U.S.); Charles J. Pedersen (U.S.); Jean-Marie Lehn (France)
Physics: K. Alex Müller (Switzerland); J. Georg Bednorz (W. Germany)
Physiology or Medicine: Tonegawa Susumu (Japan)
Literature: Joseph Brodsky (U.S.)
Economic Science: Robert M. Solow (U.S.)

1988
Peace: United Nations Peacekeeping Forces
Chemistry: Johann Deisenhofer (W. Germany); Robert Huber W.Germany); Hartmut Michel (W. Germany)
Physics: Leon M. Lederman (U.S.); Melvin Schwartz (U.S.); Jack Steinberger (U.S.)
Physiology or Medicine: Gertrude B. Elion (U.S.); George H. Hitchings (U.S.); Sir James W. Black (U.K.)
Literature: Naguib Mahfouz (Egypt)
Economic Science: Maurice Allais (France)

1989
Peace: Dalai Lama (Tibet)
Chemistry: Thomas R. Cech (U.S.); Sidney Altman (U.S.)
Physics: Norman F. Ramsey (U.S.); Hans G. Dehmelt (U.S.); Wolfgang Paul (W. Germany)
Physiology or Medicine: J. Michael Bishop (U.S.); Harold E. Varmus (U.S.)
Literature: Camilo José Cela (Spain)
Economic Science: Trygve Haavelmo (Norway)

1990
Peace: Mikhail Sergeyevich Gorbachev (Soviet Union)
Chemistry: Elias James Corey (U.S.)
Physics: Richard E. Taylor (Canada); Jerome I. Friedman (U.S.); Henry W. Kendall (U.S.)
Physiology or Medicine: Joseph E. Murray (U.S.); E. Donnall Thomas (U.S.)

Literature: Octavio Paz (Mexico)
Economic Science: Harry M. Markowitz (U.S.); William F. Sharpe (U.S.); Merton H. Miller (U.S.)

1991
Peace: Daw Aung San Suu Kyi (Myanmar)
Chemistry: Richard R. Ernst (Switzerland)
Physics: Pierre-Gilles de Gennes (France)
Physiology or Medicine: Erwin Neher (Germany); Bert Sakmann (Germany)
Literature: Nadine Gordimer (South Africa)
Economic Science: Ronald H. Coase (U.S.)

1992
Peace: Rigoberta Menchú (Guatemala)
Chemistry: Rudolph A. Marcus (U.S.)
Physics: Georges Charpak (France)
Physiology or Medicine: Edmond H. Fischer (U.S.); Edwin G. Krebs (U.S.)
Literature: Derek Walcott (St. Lucia)
Economic Science: Gary S. Becker (U.S.)

1993
Peace: F. W. de Klerk (South Africa); Nelson Mandela (South Africa)
Chemistry: Kary B. Mullis (U.S.); Michael Smith (Canada)
Physics: Joseph H. Taylor Jr. (U.S.); Russell A. Hulse (U.S.)
Physiology or Medicine: Phillip A. Sharp (U.S.); Richard J. Roberts (U.K.)
Literature: Toni Morrison (U.S.)
Economic Science: Robert W. Fogel (U.S.); Douglass C. North (U.S.)

1994
Peace: Yasir Arafat (Palestine); Yitzhak Rabin (Israel); Shimon Peres (Israel)
Chemistry: George A. Olah (U.S.)
Physics: Clifford G. Shull (U.S.); Bertram N. Brockhouse (Canada)
Physiology or Medicine: Alfred G. Gilman (U.S.); Martin Rodbell (U.S.)
Literature: Oe Kenzaburo (Japan)
Economic Science: John F. Nash (U.S.); John C. Harsanyi (U.S.); Reinhard Selten (Germany)
1995
Peace: Joseph Rotblat and Pugwash Conference

on Science and World Affairs (U.K.)
Chemistry: F. Sherwood Rowland (U.S.); Mario
   Molina (U.S.); Paul Crutzen (Netherlands)
Physics: Martin L. Perl (U.S.); Frederick Reines
   (U.S.)
Physiology or Medicine: Edward B. Lewis (U.S.);
   Eric F. Wieschaus (U.S.); Christiane
   Nüsslein-Volhard (Germany)
Literature: Seamus Heaney (Ireland)
Economic Science: Robert E. Lucas Jr. (U.S.)

1996
Peace: Carlos Ximenes Belo (Timorese); José
   Ramos-Horta (Timorese)
Chemistry: Richard E. Smalley (U.S.); Robert F.
   Curl Jr. (U.S.); Sir Harold W. Kroto (U.K.)
Physics: David M. Lee (U.S.); Robert C.
Richardson (U.S.); Douglas D. Osheroff (U.S.)
Physiology or Medicine: Peter C. Doherty
   (Australia); Rolf M. Zinkernagel (Switzerland)
Literature: Wislawa Szymborska (Poland)
Economic Science: James A. Mirrlees (U.K.);
   William Vickrey (U.S.)

1997
Peace: Jody Williams (U.S.); International
   Campaign to Ban Landmines
Chemistry: Paul D. Boyer (U.S.); Jens C. Skou
   (Denmark); John E. Walker (U.K.)
Physics: Steven Chu (U.S.); William D. Phillips
   (U.S.); Claude Cohen-Tannoudji (France)
Physiology or Medicine: Stanley B. Prusiner (U.S.)
Literature: Dario Fo (Italy)
Economic Science: Robert C. Merton (U.S.);
   Myron S. Scholes (U.S.)

1998
Peace: John Hume (U.K.); David Trimble (U.K.)
Chemistry: Walter Kohn (U.S.); John Pople (U.K.)
Physics: Daniel Tsui (U.S.); Horst Stoermer (U.S.);
   Robert Laughlin (U.S.)
Physiology or Medicine: Robert Furchgott (U.S.);
   Louis Ignarro (U.S.); Ferid Murad (U.S.)
Literature: Jose Saramago (Portugal)
Economic Science: Amartya Sen (India)

1999
Peace: Doctors Without Borders (*Médecins Sans
   Frontiéres*) (France)

Chemistry: Ahmed H. Zewail (U. S.)
Physics: Gerardus 't Hooft (Hetherlands);
   Martinus J.G. Veltman (Netherlands)
Physiology or Medicine: Günter Blobel (U. S.)
Literature: Günter Grass (Germany)
Economic Science: Robert A. Mundell (Canada)

CHAPTER TWO

EVENTS AND IDEAS OF THE CENTURY

A

Abdication Crisis (1936) British constitutional emergency that ensued on November 16, 1936, when King **Edward VIII** announced his intention to marry divorced American Wallis Simpson (1896–1986). Prime Minister **Stanley Baldwin** and senior government and church officials opposed the marriage, arguing that Edward could not marry a divorcée and remain head of the Church of England. Edward abdicated on December 10 and went ahead with the marriage; his brother succeeded him as **George VI**.

Abortion *See* **Birth Control**.

Acquired Immune Deficiency Syndrome *See* **AIDS**.

Action Française French nationalist political movement. Founded in 1899, the extreme right-wing movement was led by writer Charles Maurras (1868–1952), who expressed its views in the journal *L'Action Française*. Anti-Socialist and anti-Semitic, the movement advocated a restored monarchy and emphasized the greatness of French culture. Banned in the 1930s, the movement was revived in the 1940s for its support of the **Vichy regime**. After **World War II**, Maurras was imprisoned (1945–52) as a collaborationist.

Action Squad *See* **Blackshirts**.

Affirmative Action Government policy of discriminating in favor of minority ethnic groups and women in such areas as employment, education, and housing in an attempt to correct patterns of historical discrimination against members of such groups. In the U.S., the federal government began implementing the policy in the late 1960s; it prompted charges of "reverse discrimination" that several times came to the attention of the Supreme Court, notably in *Regents of the University of California v. Bakke* (1978). Despite the controversy, affirmative action remained an element of American public policy. Similar programs were enacted in such European countries as the Netherlands, Sweden, and Belgium.

AFL–CIO (American Federation of Labor–Congress of Industrial Organizations) Multinational labor union formed (1955) with the merger of the American Federation of Labor and the Congress of Industrial Organizations. Member countries include Canada, Mexico, Panama, and the U.S. with its territories. The American Federation of Labor (AFL) was founded in 1886 by British-born American labor leader **Samuel Gompers** as an association of craft unions, representing skilled trades. In the 1930s an internal rift developed over whether the union should be organized by craft or industry, resulting in the expulsion of rebel members. Under **John L. Lewis**, the industry-oriented faction, which included semiskilled workers, reorganized (1937) into a new union, the Congress of Industrial Organizations. Facing antiunion sentiment in the 1950s, the two unions merged. The AFL–CIO's first leader was George Meany (1894–1980). The dominant labor union in the U.S. and elsewhere, it has lobbied successfully for shorter hours, increased pay, and other benefits.

AFL–CIO Membership, 1897–1995

	AFL membership			AFL–CIO membership
1897	264,800		1955	12,622,000
1904	1,676,200		1965	12,919,000
1912	1,770,100		1975	14,066,000
1920	4,078,700		1987	15,000,000
1924	2,865,800		1995	13,000,000
1930	2,961,100			
1939	3,878,000			
1945	6,890,400			

Source: Gary M. Fink, Labor Unions; AFL–CIO Web site

African National Congress (ANC) South African multiracial political organization. Founded in 1912 as the South African Native National Congress, it was renamed the African National Congress in 1923. Until the 1940s, it relied on peaceful lobbying to oppose discrimination against blacks, but leaders **Nelson Mandela** and Oliver Tambo (1917–93), who founded the ANC Youth League in 1944, turned the group in a more militant direction. In the 1950s the ANC conducted nonviolent resistance campaigns against apartheid. After the organization was banned in 1960, it moved into exile in Mozambique, where Mandela and others founded a military wing, Umkhonto we Sizwe (Spear of the Nation), which carried out sabotage and guerrilla warfare. Mandela was imprisoned from 1962 to 1990; during that time, Tambo became president-general of the ANC (1977–90) and made it the nucleus of an international antiapartheid campaign. South African president **F. W. de Klerk** legalized the ANC in 1990 and released Mandela, who resumed leadership of the ANC. Apartheid was dismantled, Mandela renounced violence, and the ANC won victory in the 1994 multiracial elections, with Mandela assuming the presidency of South Africa shortly thereafter.

AIDS Acronym for Acquired Immune Deficiency Syndrome, which is caused by a retrovirus that attacks the human immune system, making it susceptible to life-threatening infection and illness. Caused by HIV (human immuno-deficiency virus), a.k.a. HTLV (human T-lymphrotropic virus), AIDS follows a period of incubation possibly lasting years and presents through infections such as pneumonia or Kaposi's sarcoma, a cancer. Possibly introduced from Africa, AIDS was first noted in Denmark in 1977 and in the U.S. in 1979. The AIDS virus was discovered in 1983 in the U.S. and in Paris. During the 1980s it was discovered that the disease spreads through the intermingling of blood or blood products, not through casual contact.

In Western nations, AIDS has disproportionately affected homosexual men, hemophiliacs, and drug users, with its occurrence in heterosexuals increasing during and after the 1980s. Worldwide, AIDS is most commonly spread by unprotected heterosexual sexual intercourse. About 75–85 percent of infections worldwide have been sexually transmitted. From the 1990s in the U.S., HIV transmission to women increased markedly. Up to 30 percent of children born to HIV/AIDS infected parents contract the virus.

Social advocacy in Western countries has popularized early detection of the disease; medical research has brought the development of drugs to extend the lives of AIDS patients. Estimated deaths due to AIDS through 1999 totaled 18.8 million: 15 million adults and 3.8 million children. Estimated deaths in 1999 alone totaled 2.8 million. Since the start of the pandemic, more than 50 million people have been infected with the HIV virus.

AIDS Deaths in the U.S., 1981–96

Year	Known deaths	Cumulative deaths	
Pre-1981	31	31	
1981	128	159	
1982	460	619	
1983	1,504	2,123	
1984	3,500	5,623	
1985	6,971	2,594	
1986	12,096	24,690	
1987	16,360	41,050	
1988	21,086	62,136	
1989	27,731	89,867	
1990	31,466	21,333	
1991	36,458	57,791	
1992	40,807	98,598	Source: U.S. Dept. of
1993	43,889	242,487	Health and Human
1994	47,636	290,123	Services, Centers for
1995	45,765	335,888	Disease Control and
1996	25,695	361,583	Prevention

HIV/AIDS Estimates Worldwide by Region (as of December 1996)

Region	Adults and children living with HIV/AIDS	
Sub-Saharan Africa	14 million	
South and South-East Asia	5.2 million	
Latin America, North America, and Western Europe	1.3 million	
Australia/New Zealand	1.3 million	
Caribbean	270,000	
North Africa, Middle East	200,000	
East Asia, Pacific	100,000	Source: United Nations/
Central/Eastern Europe, Central Asia	50,000	World Health Organization

Airplane Winged, flying, engine-powered, heavier-than-air vehicle. Until the 20th century, air transportation was limited to lighter-than-air balloons and their close cousins, airships or dirigibles (*see* **Hindenburg**). In 1903 American inventors **Wilbur and Orville Wright** flew the first airplane, a biplane with two sets of wings. Monoplanes with one set of wings were not widely used until mid-century. At first exhibited mostly as a novelty in county fairs, airplanes soon proved their usefulness for many functions: combat, beginning with **World War I**; mail delivery; and commercial passenger service.

The first modern passenger airliner was the Boeing Model 247, unveiled in 1933. However, commercial air travel did not become commonplace until after **World War II**, which brought about many technological advances to meet the need for large numbers of efficient fighter and bomber planes. With the introduction of the Boeing 707 in 1958, propeller-driven planes gave way to jets, with faster flying speeds due to their propulsion by high-velocity gases.

World's 10 Busiest Airports (as of 1996)

	Total passengers
1. Chicago O'Hare International	69,153,528
2. Hartsfield Atlanta International	63,303,171
3. Dallas/Ft. Worth International	58,034,503
4. Los Angeles International	57,974,559
5. Heathrow Airport, London	56,037,798
6. Tokyo-Haneda International	46,631,475
7. San Francisco International	39,251,942
8. Frankfurt/Main, Germany	38,761,174
9. Kimpo International, Seoul	34,706,158
10. Miami International	33,504,579

	Total cargo (metric tons)
1. Memphis International Tenn.	1,933,846
2. Los Angeles International	1,719,449
3. Miami International	1,709,906
4. J.F. Kennedy International, N.Y.	1,636,497
5. New Tokyo International-Narita	1,626,661
6. Hong Kong International	1,590,773
7. Frankfurt/Main, Germany	1,497,245
8. Standiford, Louisville, Ky.	1,368,520
9. Kimpo International, Seoul	1,361,497
10. Chicago O'Hare International	1,259,858

Source: Airports Association Council International

Supersonic or faster-than-sound flight became a reality with the breaking of the sound barrier by U.S. military pilot Chuck Yeager (1923–) in 1947. Aside from the Anglo-French Concorde, however, which began commercial service in 1976, supersonic travel mostly remained a military enterprise. The ease and relative cheapness of air travel contributed to **globalization**, the shrinking of the world into one interconnected community.

Alcoholics Anonymous (AA) Worldwide alcohol abuse self-help and advocacy organization. Founded in the U.S. in 1935 by two former alcoholics, AA aims to help drinkers to stop drinking through a 12-step program that is reinforced by local AA groups. The program involves abstinence, communal support, and reordering of one's personality and principles. Alcoholics Anonymous reflects the 20th-century social and scientific determination that alcohol is a drug that may be abused and that alcoholism is a disease requiring treatment. As of 1997, AA membership was near 1,800,000, with 87,000 local AA groups in the U.S.

Allied Powers In **World War I**, the alliance that opposed the **Central Powers**. The principal members of the formal alliance were the British Empire and France, but more than 20 other nations cooperated with them in a grouping called the Allied and Associated Powers. These ultimately included the United States, Russia, Serbia, Belgium, Luxembourg, Montenegro, Japan, Italy, Romania, Portugal, and Greece.

In **World War II**, the Allied Powers opposed the **Axis Powers**. The dominant members, known as the Big Three, were the United States, Britain, and the Soviet Union, but the alliance comprised nearly 50 countries, including the British Commonwealth countries (such as Australia), France, China, Poland, and Yugoslavia. In both conflicts, the Allied Powers were victorious.

Alsace-Lorraine Provinces of northeastern France, west of the Rhine River. A center of industry and mining, the region also had strategic military importance. Germany annexed Alsace and Lorraine after the Franco-Prussian War (1870–71) but was forced to return them to France in 1919, after **World War I**. In **World War II**, Germany again annexed Alsace-Lorraine (1940), only to return the provinces after the war (1945).

American Expeditionary Force Name given to the U.S. army in France during **World War I**.

Anarchism Political philosophy rejecting the state and all forms of government control in favor of free, egalitarian cooperation among individuals. Though many anarchists, such as Russian activist Piotr Kropotkin (1842–1921), believed in nonviolence, others—following in the tradition of Russian revolutionary Mikhail Bakunin (1814–76)—advocated violent overthrow of the state. To many, the assassination of U.S. president **William McKinley** by an anarchist in 1901 made anarchism synonymous with terrorism; antianarchist sentiment contributed to the guilty verdicts in the **Sacco-Vanzetti trial** (1921). Anarchism had more peaceful incarnations in, for example, the pacifist Catholic Worker movement, founded by **Dorothy Day** in the 1930s. Anarchism became linked with **syndicalism** as anarcho-syndicalism, a trade-union philosophy practiced by the **Industrial Workers of the World** and by labor unions in Spain, France, and Latin America into the 1930s. Anarchism also informed the actions of the New Left in the 1960s and of the protesters against the Worl Trade Organization in Seattle in 1999.

Animal Rights Social and political advocacy movement to prevent perceived abuse to animals. Although interest in animal protection dates to the 19th-century U.S. antivivisection movement, increased concern in the 20th century sprang from the environmental movement in the 1970s, particularly in North America and Europe. Practices targeted for reform or elimination include the use of laboratory animals for medical and cosmetic testing, inhumane conditions for the raising of livestock, and the killing of animals for fur outerwear. Political lobbying and acts of civil disobedience have brought attention to the animal rights movement, with active organizations including Greenpeace and People for the Ethical Treatment of Animals (PETA).

Anschluss (German, "union" [1938]) German annexation of Austria. The 1919 Treaty of **St. Germain** forbade union of Austria with Germany, even though it was desired by many German-speaking Austrians. On March 12, 1938, after having made sure of the compliance of Italian leader **Benito Mussolini**, German dictator **Adolf Hitler** sent troops into Austria. Austrians did not resist the annexation, nor did other world powers contest it.

Anti-Comintern Pact or **Anti-Communist Pact** (November 25, 1936) Agreement signed between Germany and Japan opposing the Communist activities of the **Comintern**. Italy joined the pact in 1937; Hungary, Spain, and the Japanese puppet state of Manchukuo (a.k.a. Manchuria) signed in 1939. The agreement was followed by the **Tripartite Pact**.

Apartheid Policy of racial segregation and economic inequity practiced in South Africa against nonwhites. After its electoral victory in 1948, the National Party strengthened the country's racial laws and formally named the policy apartheid (Afrikaans for "apartness").

All South Africans were classified as white, nonwhite of African descent (Bantu), or non-white (of mixed descent). A fourth category, Asian, was added later. Laws passed in the 1950s reserved 80 percent of the land for whites, banned nonwhites from living or doing business in certain areas, prohibited social relations between races, and forced nonwhites to carry identification documents. Nonwhites were denied most political and civil rights. From 1951 the government instituted a policy of "separate development" that relegated blacks to Bantustans, or "homelands," within South Africa. Blacks, led by the **African National Congress** and **Nelson Mandela**, resisted these policies, and increasing unrest in the 1970s forced the government to modify some apartheid laws. Continuing resistance and interna-tional economic sanctions led to the end of apartheid in 1993 and the country's first mul-tiracial national elections in 1994. Apartheid's legacy remains in the continuing social and economic disparities between the races.

Appeasement Foreign policy of placating an aggressive nation to avoid war. The term applies particularly to the policy of **World War I**–devastated Britain and France with respect to Italy, Japan, and Nazi Germany (*see* **Nazi Party**) in the 1930s. Under this poli-cy as practiced by British prime minister **Neville Chamberlain**, among others, German dictator Adolf Hitler rearmed the country, stopped reparations payments, and annexed Austria (1938). In the Munich Agreement (1938), Chamberlain accepted the Nazi rationale for taking the **Sudetenland**. Appeasement was abandoned following the full Nazi invasion of Czechoslovakia in 1939.

Arab-Israeli Wars Series of wars between Israel and Arab states. The First Arab-Israeli War (1948–49), also known as the Israeli War of Independence, was caused by the refusal of Arab states to accept the creation of Israel. On May 15, 1948, the day after Israel came into being, Arab armed forces from Egypt, Syria, Transjordan (Jordan), Lebanon, and Iraq invaded Israel and captured territory in southern and eastern Palestine. The Israelis not only wrested away these gains but also expanded their territory by about one-half. Some 400,000 Palestinian Arabs fled to refugee camps in neighboring Arab countries.

Second Arab-Israeli War (1956) *See* **Suez Crisis.**

Third Arab-Israeli War (1967) *See* **Six-Day War.**

Fourth Arab-Israeli War (1973) *See* **Yom Kippur War.**

Arab League Organization of Arab states, founded in Cairo in 1945. Its founding mem-bers were Egypt, Syria, Iraq, Lebanon, Transjordan (now Jordan), Saudi Arabia, and Yemen; later members included Libya, Sudan, Tunisia, Kuwait, and the **PLO**. In the spirit of **pan-Arabism**, the league aimed to promote Arab political unity, usually in opposition to Israel. Egypt was suspended in 1979 for making peace with Israel but was readmitted in 1989. Often contentious, the league suffered a serious split in the **Gulf War** (1991), when a majority of members joined the fighting against Iraq.

Architecture The design and erection of buildings. Moving from the Gothic and classic revival movements of the 19th century, architecture styles adapted to the urbanization of society and the availability of new elements including steel, reinforced concrete, and elec-tricity. The combination of new tools and a rapidly changing way of life led to a century of architecture marked by eclecticism and experimentation.

Active and still developing in the early 20th century was Victorian architecture, which included eclectic works informed by the Ecole des Beaux Arts. Classically-inspired buildings include American architectural firm McKim, Mead, and White's Pennsylvania Station (New York City, N.Y., 1906–10).

Beginning in the 1920s and for many decades afterward, the German art and architectural school known as the Bauhaus was highly influential. Founded in 1919 by **Walter Gropius**, the Bauhaus embodied a geometric, economical style that was respectful of modern materials. Controversial upon its debut, the Bauhaus school of architecture provided early examples of the architectural movement known as the International Style. Notable Bauhaus architects include **Mïes Van Der Rohe**. Early examples of Bauhaus architecture include the Bauhaus (Dessau, Germany, 1926) by Walter Gropius and the Barcelona pavilion (Mïes Van Der Rohe, 1929).

After the closing of the Bauhaus by the Nazi government in 1933, which led to an exodus of Bauhaus members to other countries in Europe and the U.S., the International Style proliferated throughout western countries. Important to its growth was the rise of American architecture. Major American practitioners of the International Style were Richard Neutra (1892–1970) and Philip C. Johnson (1906–). Coauthor of *The International Style* (1932), Johnson created several seminal examples of the streamlined style, including his glass house (New Canaan, Conn., 1949) and the New York State Theater at Lincoln Center (New York City, N.Y., 1964). He and Mïes Van Der Rohe collaborated on the Seagram Building (New York City, N.Y., 1958). These later works marked the period of full flowering of the International Style, and the most characteristic use of its elements: regularized structure, minimal ornamentation, and light, streamlined framework. A trademark International Style element is the expansive, dramatic use of glass.

Perhaps the most influential American designer in 20th-century modern architecture is **Frank Lloyd Wright**, who integrated design with the landscape (as in his prairie-style houses such as Robie House, Chicago, Ill., 1909) and reimagined interior house design to open the space to create fluid movement. Notable designs include Falling Water (Bear Run, Pa., 1936–37) and the Guggenheim Museum (New York City, N.Y., 1946–59).

Beginning in the 1950s, architects began to incorporate more playful and sculptural elements, in response to the longstanding dominance of the International Style. **Eero Saarinen** integrated sculpture into such designs as the Trans World Airlines terminal at John F. Kennedy Airport (New York City, N.Y., 1962). Other notable modern architects include American architect Robert Venturi (1925–), who has integrated commercial elements into his designs and made architecture more inclusive of the trappings of society, and American architect Louis Kahn (1901–74), who revived the use of Beaux Arts elements.

Increased eclecticism and expansion of the boundaries of architectural design have been hallmarks of postmodern architecture, which closed the century. Major practitioners have included American architects Michael Grave (1934–) and Philip C. Johnson (1906–).

Arms Control *See* **Nuclear Weapon.**

Art In the 20th century, the visual arts were marked by at least two types of expression: nonrepresentational art and varieties of realism. Beginning early in the century, many painters and sculptors abandoned the European tradition of imitating nature through representation.

Early in the century, fauvist artists including **Henri Matisse** and French painters Raoul Dufy (1877–1953) and André Derain (1880–1954) abandoned descriptive uses of color for experimentation with nonnaturalistic hues. Fauvism continued only until **World War I**, but was key to the development of the highly exaggerated movement of German expressionism. Notable expressionist artists include **George Grosz** and German painter Otto Dix (1891–1969). Cubism, practiced by such artists as **Pablo Picasso** and **Georges Braque** around 1907, marked a transition to abstract art in its attempt to represent objects through geometrical planes. The first fully abstract paintings were those of **Wassily Kandinsky** in about 1910; other abstract painters included **Piet Mondrian** and **Joan Miro**.

During the 1920s, the movement of surrealism developed and became the major modern aesthetic through the 1930s. As defined by French critic Andre Breton, surrealism aimed to revolutionize art through its adherence to the antirational, the poetic, and the fantastic. Along with Miro, major surrealist artists included Max Ernst and **Salvador Dalí**.

Other artistic movements originated in part from political and social beliefs. Suprematism, an abstract art movement based on primary geometrical shapes, was founded by Russian painter and designer Kasimir Malevich (1878–1935) in 1915. Malevich's aim was to achieve spiritual and artistic truth through the abandonment of objective representation. In 1909 Italian poet Filippo Marinetti (1876–1944) presented his manifestos of futurism, an artistic movement aimed at bringing Italy into the modern age by championing what Marinetti called "a new form of beauty—the beauty of speed." Lasting until World War I, futurism was important in the development of dadaism. The Dada (French for "hobbyhorse") movement, founded in 1915 in Switzerland by Tristan Tzara and other artists, was a revolution of anti-art that reflected despair over **World War I** as well as Continental European and U.S artistic stasis. Practitioners in the U.S. and Europe included U.S. painter Man Ray (1890–1977) and **Marcel Duchamp**.

In design, Art Nouveau (or Modern Style, for its English origins), which flourished from about 1890 to about 1920 in Europe and the U.S., countered the strictures of historicism with a more organic style based on nature. Also relying on characteristic shapes was Art Deco, which in the 1920s and 1930s in the west succeeded Art Nouveau. Rather than the liquid shapes of nature, it relied on geometric or formalized shapes.

After **World War II**, abstract expressionism, more radical and spontaneous than earlier varieties of abstraction, became a leading artistic movement. It originated in New York City and was associated with such artists as **Jackson Pollock**. Later movements included post-painterly abstraction (1960s), which emphasized impersonal formal elements. Major innovators include Americans Morris Louis (1912–62) and Ellsworth Kelly (1923–), the latter also a practitioner of hard edge painting.

In the 1950s pop art developed in Britain and the U.S. as a counter to abstract expressionism. Using commonplace, often commercial imagery as bases, it revived figurative representation while providing commentary on modern, transient society. Major practitioners included Jasper Johns, American artist Robert Rauschenberg, and **Andy Warhol**.

Beginning in the 1960s, superrealism (also known as photo-realism, photographic realism or hyperrealism) gained vogue. Practiced by American painter Chuck Close (1940–), American sculptor Duane Hanson (1925–), and others, it involves immersion in minutiae and rendering of precise detail in works that may be derived from life or photographs.

In the last 25 years of the decade, electronic and environmental installations gained popularity. As practiced by Bulgarian-American sculptor and designer Christo (Christo Javacheff,

1935–) and others, these works may include the repackaging of ordinary objects such as a car or statue for closer study of its forms.

Atlantic Charter Joint statement issued by U.S. president **Franklin Delano Roosevelt** and British prime minister **Winston Churchill** in August 1941, after their **World War II** conference on a British battleship off Newfoundland. Outlining the countries' war aims, the declaration rejected territorial gains by either nation. It affirmed the right of nations to choose their own form of government, freedom of the seas, and the construction of a peace that would make all people "free from fear and want." The Charter signaled the increasingly close relationship between the U.S., which was not yet officially at war, and Britain. It was approved by all Allied nations in 1942 and would become the ideological cornerstone of the **United Nations**.

Automation Automatic operation and control of equipment or processes. The assembly line was a precursor of contemporary automation. Developed by U.S. industrialist **Henry Ford** for automobile production about 1913, automation moved the product down a conveyor belt to stations where each worker performed a specific operation. As computer technology developed after World War II, it became increasingly possible for robots (computer-controlled machines) to take the place of workers in assembly-line settings. Feedback loops allowed the robots to monitor and correct their own operations. Automation is now widely employed in manufacturing, as well as in information processing—everything from automatic billing to the UPC scanners in supermarkets. Though industrialists are fond of the low-cost accuracy and tirelessness of robots, automation has been criticized for causing unemployment. It also creates new jobs—such as automation software design—and has transformed many factories from low-skill settings to ones where skilled workers tend sophisticated machines.

Axis Powers The **World War II** alliance comprising Germany, Japan, Italy, Hungary, Bulgaria, Romania, and the puppet states of Slovakia and Croatia. The association began with the formation of the Rome-Berlin Axis in 1936, linking Germany and Italy. This became a full military and political alliance in 1939. The **Tripartite Pact** of September 1940 created the Rome-Berlin-Tokyo Axis by adding Japan to the alliance; other countries joined later. The term originated in **Benito Mussolini**'s description of Rome-Berlin as the axis around which like-minded powers could revolve.

B

Ba'ath Party (Arab Socialist Renaissance Party) Arab political party, dominant in Syria and Iraq. Founded in Syria in the 1940s, it advocated pan-Arab unity, **socialism**, and secularism. The party's commitment to **pan-Arabism** led to the merger of Egypt and Syria as the United Arab Republic (1958–61). That union fell apart, but Ba'athists continued to thrive in Syria, where a 1963 coup made them the ruling party. A 1970 coup put General Hafiz al-Assad (1928–) in charge of the one-party state. In Iraq a 1968 revolution put the Ba'ath Party in control, with Iraqi leader **Saddam Hussein** becoming president in 1979.

Baby Boomers *See* **Youth Culture**.

Balfour Declaration (November 2, 1917) Pledge of British support for a Jewish national homeland in Palestine, as stated in a letter issued by British foreign secretary Arthur James Balfour. Though it conflicted with promises made to Arab leaders guaranteeing their right to rule Palestine, the declaration became the basis for the British mandate over Palestine following **World War I**.

Balkan Wars (1912, 1913) Wars fought over the territories of the Balkan Peninsula, a region of southeast Europe long held by the declining Ottoman Empire. In the First Balkan War (1912–13), Serbia, Montenegro, Bulgaria, and Greece expelled the Ottoman Empire from all its European possessions, except for a small area around Constantinople (now Istanbul). The victors increased their territory, with Greece gaining much of Macedonia. Albania became an independent state.

The Second Balkan War (1913) arose from Bulgaria's dissatisfaction with its territorial gains in the first war. Bulgaria attacked Serbia, which retaliated. Aided by Greece, Montenegro, Romania, and the Ottoman Empire, Serbia won. Bulgaria was forced to cede territory to the victors, losing its gains from the first war. The nationalist ambitions and resentments stoked by the Balkan Wars were among the causes of **World War I**. (*See also* **Bosnian Civil War** and **Kosovo Crisis**.)

Balkanization The division of a region, nation, or community into small, antagonistic states or camps. The term originated in the splitting of eastern Europe's Balkan Peninsula into contentious nation-states early in the 20th century (*see* **Balkan Wars**). In the 1990s the term was used to describe the process of division along ethnic or national lines within the Soviet Union and the former Eastern bloc countries. *Balkanization* has also been used to describe the tendency of ethnic or tribal rivalries to cause civil strife in regions such as sub-Saharan Africa. Some see balkanization in movements, such as **multiculturalism** in the United States, that heighten ethnic identity at the expense of cultural uniformity.

Bandung Conference (1955) First conference of independent nations of Africa and Asia. Held in Bandung, Indonesia, the conference launched the nonaligned movement. The participants called for peaceful coexistence, an end to colonialism, and neutrality with respect to the superpowers.

Bauhaus *See* **Architecture**.

Bay of Pigs Invasion (April 17, 1961) Military fiasco that resulted when about 1,500 Cuban exiles landed in the Bahía de Cochinos (Bay of Pigs), Cuba, with the aim of overthrowing Cuban leader **Fidel Castro**'s regime. Though backed by the CIA, they were decimated by Castro's armed forces when U.S. president **John F. Kennedy** canceled plans for military support and an expected popular rebellion failed to materialize. Approximately 120 invaders were killed and 1,200 taken prisoner, the latter to be traded later for food and medicine. The failed invasion embarrassed the United States, boosted Castro's popularity, and convinced Soviet leader **Nikita Khrushchev** of Kennedy's weakness, setting the stage for the **Cuban Missile Crisis**.

Beer Hall Putsch (November 8–9, 1923) An abortive attempt by German leader **Adolf Hitler** and his fledgling **Nazi Party** to incite a right-wing revolt against Germany's Weimar Republic. On November 8, Hitler and his stormtroopers captured several leading Bavarian officials at a Munich beer hall, forcing them to swear loyalty to the Nazi cause. The next day some 3,000 Nazis, accompanied by one of Germany's most prestigious World War heroes, General **Erich Ludendorff**, marched from the beer hall to the center of Munich. Police opened fire, killing 16 marchers and scattering the rest. Ludendorff was released but Hitler served nine months of a five-year sentence for treason, during which time he wrote *Mein Kampf*. The incident brought him international attention.

Berlin Airlift (1948–49) Supply of necessities to West Berlin during the Soviet blockade.

The **Soviet Union** initiated a land and water blockade of the German city in June 1948, in an effort to force the **Allies** to abandon West Berlin. In the first direct confrontation of the **cold war**, the West responded vigorously. From June 1948 to September 1949, the Allies, led by the U.S., made about 277,000 flights, bearing more than 2 million tons of food and fuel to West Berlin to keep its people alive. The blockade ended in May, but flights continued until West Berlin had a sufficient stockpile of supplies.

Berlin Wall Wall between the former countries of East and West Germany. The Communist government of East Germany, to stop the flight of its citizens to democratic-capitalist West Germany, raised the wall overnight in August 1961 along the border between East and West Berlin. The wall was later extended along the entire frontier between the two countries. The barrier was manned by guards with orders to shoot to kill. A symbol of the cold war, the wall came down in November 1989, unifying Germany and marking the demise of Soviet power in Eastern Europe.

Biafran War *See* Nigeria-Biafra Civil War.

Biological Weapon Device that causes mass fatalities through the use of harmful microorganisms. Though used sporadically throughout history (notably in the 18th-century French and Indian Wars, when the British tried to infect Native Americans with smallpox), biological warfare became fully practical only with 20th-century advances in microbiology. The 1925 Geneva Protocol banned use of biological and **chemical weapons**; the protocol was not ratified by the U.S. Senate until 1974. Many nations stockpiled biological weapons, including anthrax and plague, as a deterrent but did not use them for fear of retaliation. The development of **genetic engineering** in the 1970s increased the potential effectiveness of biological weapons, leading to a greater desire on the part of the world community to prevent their use. The 1972 **Geneva Convention** banned development and use of biological weapons, but nations such as Iraq nevertheless pursued vigorous research programs. After the **Gulf War** (1990–91), Iraq was required to destroy its capability for chemical, biological, and **nuclear** warfare and to allow **UN** inspections. Its refusal to comply led to continuing UN economic sanctions.

Biotechnology *See* Genetic Engineering.

Birth Control The practice of avoiding pregnancy, planning births, and choosing family size. While the first family planning clinic on record appeared in Amsterdam, Holland, in the 19th century, the practice of controlling pregnancy developed widely in the 20th century. It has been marked by improved methods of avoiding pregnancy, increased awareness and acceptance of family planning, and social and government efforts to legislate aspects of childbirth. Coining the phrase "birth control" in 1914 was American social activist Margaret Sanger (1883–1966), a social health nurse who founded the first American birth control clinic in 1916 in Brooklyn, New York. In 1917 her clinic was closed by police, and she was arrested. Her court case led to a landmark decision permitting U.S. doctors to provide contraceptive information. A separate 1936 ruling permitted U.S. doctors to prescribe contraceptives. The first British birth control clinic opened in 1921.

As availability of birth control information increased, several contraceptive devices were developed. In the 1920s intrauterine devices were refined, and in Britain, spermicides were developed (1927). The first oral contraceptive was developed in 1955 and introduced to public approval in the U.S. in the 1960s. A combination of hormones—chiefly synthesized estrogen—"the pill" stops monthly ovulation, preventing pregnancy. In the 1980s scientists in France developed a morning-after pill known as RU-486, which is taken following intercourse to end pregnancy.

Worldwide, abortion became more widely practiced as a form of birth control, sometimes illegally and other times with government legalization. In the U.S. some but not all states permitted abortion until the U.S. Supreme Court made abortion legal nationally with its 1973 decision *Roe v. Wade*. The decision generated ongoing protests against government approval of abortion, notably in the U.S. through the Right-to-Life movement. Worldwide, the Roman Catholic Church has been an outspoken opponent of both abortion and artificial contraception.

In China, various forms of birth control are sanctioned by the government to promote population control. Late marriages are encouraged, abortion is legal, and couples are encouraged to pledge to have only one child. By the late 1990s, 24 million couples had so pledged.

Black and Tans Nickname of auxiliary force of the Royal Irish Constabulary employed by the British in 1920–21 to combat republican rebels. Composed of British ex-soldiers uniformed in khaki with black hats and belts, the force was notorious for its harshness, notably in the 1920 incidents of **Bloody Sunday** and the burning down of the County Hall in Cork.

Black Consciousness General term for social and political movements emphasizing the unique identity and experience of people of African origin. The term encompasses such separatist, black nationalist movements as that of Jamaican-American activist **Marcus Garvey** in the 1920s and the **Black Muslims** beginning in the 1930s. It includes such cultural movements as that led by Martinican poet Aimé Césaire (1913–) and Senegalese poet **Léopold Senghor** in the 1930s, who argued for reaffirmation of African cultural traditions in the name of preserving *négritude* (French, "blackness"). Another manifestation was Pan-Africanism, which stressed the unity of African peoples and helped spur independence movements in the 1950s and 1960s.

Black consciousness was promoted by the Black Power movement, which originated in the U.S. in the 1960s and espoused militant black separatism. At odds with more moderate elements in the **civil rights movement**, it was embodied most visibly in the Black Panther Party, founded by American activists Huey Newton (1942–89) and Bobby Seale (1937–89) in 1966. Greater awareness of African heritage was also fostered through such routes as the establishment of black studies departments in universities (*see* **Multiculturalism**) and the observance of Kwanzaa, an African-American holiday (celebrated December 26–January 1) that originated in the U.S. in 1966.

Black Muslims American black nationalist movement, also known as the Nation of Islam. African-American activist Wali Farad (or Wallace D. Fard; c. 1877–1934?) founded the movement in Detroit in 1930; **Elijah Muhammad** was its leader from 1934 to his death in 1975. Blending Muslim religious teaching with black separatism, the movement grew swiftly in the 1950s and 1960s, thanks largely to the preaching of **Malcolm X**. He was killed in 1965, reportedly by some of Muhammad's followers. The Black Muslims split in 1976 into the American Muslim Mission, an integrationist movement led by Muhammad's son, African-American activist Wallace D. Muhammad, and the steadfastly separatist Nation of Islam, led by African-American activist Louis Farrakhan (1933–). The Black Muslims contributed to the rise of **black consciousness** in the U.S.

Black Tuesday The day of the largest decline in value of stocks on the U.S. stock market that precipitated the **Great Depression**. After reaching a peak in late September 1929, largely on highly inflated stocks, the market began a decline. A major loss occurred on

October 24, Black Thursday, when 13 million shares (a then-huge sum) were sold off. The most damaging day was Tuesday, October 29, when 16,410,030 shares were sold off. Over its weeks-long decline, the stock market lost 30 billion dollars, twice the U.S. national debt. The decline triggered the Depression: a nearly decade-long period of international economic struggle and failure.

Blackshirts Colloquial name, based on the color of their uniform shirts, for members of **Benito Mussolini's** paramilitary "Action Squad." The group was founded in 1919 to harass and intimidate leftists. The term was loosely extended to mean **Fascists** in general.

Blitzkrieg ("lightning war") In **World War II**, swift, fierce German military campaigns using tanks and air support, notably in the invasions of Poland and France. The abbreviated *Blitz* refers to the German bombing of London and other English cities (1940–41).

Bloody Sunday (Russia, January 22, 1905; Old-Style Calendar, January 9) Massacre of protesters in St. Petersburg. After a series of strikes, thousands of peaceful and well-organized workers marched toward the Winter Palace to present their petitions and grievances to Czar **Nicholas II.** The czar was away from the city. The head of the security police tried to halt the demonstration, then gave the order to fire on the crowd. Over 100 marchers died and hundreds more were wounded. The incident triggered the **Russian Revolution of 1905** and ignited work stoppages in other cities, peasant uprisings, and mutinies in the army.

Bloody Sunday (Ireland, November 21, 1920) One of the worst single incidents of the Irish struggle for independence from Great Britain (the Anglo-Irish War, 1919–21). On this day, the **Irish Republican Army** executed 11 Englishmen believed to be spies. That afternoon, members of the **Black and Tans** auxiliary police force retaliated by shooting into a large crowd at a football (soccer) game in Dublin. They killed 12 people and wounded about 60 more. Hours later, two suspected Irish Republican Army members held by the British were executed.

Bloody Sunday (Northern Ireland, January 30, 1972) Massacre of unarmed Catholic demonstrators in Londonderry by British troops. Thousands of marchers were protesting internment without trial, imposed by Britain, which had sent troops to Northern Ireland to stop violence between Protestants and Catholics. The soldiers opened fire on the demonstrators, killing 14. The British lord chief justice's investigation exonerated the soldiers despite strong evidence that the marchers were unarmed and peaceful. The incident outraged Catholics and intensified sectarian violence. The British government announced in 1998 that it was reopening the inquiry.

Boer War *See* **South African War.**

Bolsheviks ("members of the majority") Russian revolutionary party. Led by **V. I. Lenin,** the Bolsheviks began as the left-wing faction of the Russian Social Democratic Workers' Party, following that party's split in 1903. Unlike the rival **Mensheviks,** the Bolsheviks argued that the party should be small and centralized and that a revolution should take place swiftly. From 1912, the Bolsheviks were a separate party. They took power in the **Russian Revolution** of November 1917 and became formally known as the Communist Party (*see* **Communism**), with the term *Bolshevik* continuing in use as a synonym for *Communist.*

Bosnian Civil War (1992–95) Internal conflict in Bosnia-Hercegovina. In 1992 Muslim-dominated Bosnia-Hercegovina declared its independence from Serb-dominated Yugoslavia. Bosnia's Serbs rebelled, declaring the formation of the Serb Republic of Bosnia-

Hercegovina. With heavy military assistance from Serbia (the dominant part of Yugoslavia), the Bosnian Serbs took control of 70 percent of the country and kept the capital, Sarajevo, under siege. The Bosnian Serbs were internationally condemned for their policy of "ethnic cleansing," or expelling Muslims and Croats from areas deemed Serb; the policy produced many refugees and was enforced by murder, rape, and concentration camps. **UN** mediation and U.S. pressure persuaded the warring parties to make peace with the Dayton Agreement (1995). The agreement divided the country between two largely autonomous areas, one Muslim-Croat, one Serb. The inability of the global community to stop the bloodshed in Europe was a stark symbol of how uncertain and violent the post–**cold war** world could be.

Boxer Rebellion (1899–1900) Uprising in China. In 1899 a Chinese secret society called the *I ho ch'üan* ("Righteous Harmonious Fists"), or Boxers, rebelled against increasing foreign control of China by attacking foreigners and Chinese Christians. With support from the dowager empress, Cixi or Tz'u-Hsi (1835–1908), they occupied Peking in 1900 and laid seige to foreign legations. An international force, with troops from Britain, France, Germany, Japan, and the U.S., stopped the rebellion. China was forced to pay a large indemnity and permit the continuing presence of foreign troops.

Brain Trust Informal group of experts who, from 1932, advised U.S. president **Franklin Delano Roosevelt** on the development of his **New Deal** policies addressing the **Great Depression**. They included Columbia legal scholars Raymond Moley (1886–1975) and Adolfe Berle (1895–1971), Columbia economist Rexford Tugwell (1891–1979), one-time law partner Basil O'Connor (1892–1972), and Harvard legal scholar **Felix Frankfurter**. Representing a variety of ideological positions, they contributed to the eclectic nature of the New Deal. Many were appointed to official posts during Roosevelt's presidency.

Brest-Litovsk, Treaty of (March 3, 1918) The first peace agreement of **World War I**, it was signed in Brest-Litovsk, Poland, between Russia and the **Central Powers**. In return for peace, Russia gave up the Ukraine, Poland, Finland, the Baltic States (Estonia, Latvia, and Lithuania), and parts of Belorussia and the Caucasus. The treaty, with its harsh terms for Russia, was repudiated after Germany's defeat by the **Allies**.

Bretton Woods Conference Meeting attended by 44 nations in July 1944 at Bretton Woods, New Hampshire. The gathering, officially named the **UN** Monetary and Financial Conference, outlined a financial plan for the postwar world and established two institutions to carry it out. The International Bank for Reconstruction and Development—commonly known as the **World Bank**—was formed to furnish credit for development enterprises and international commerce. The **International Monetary Fund** was established to maintain strong currencies among member nations. The conference also founded a system of fixed exchange rates that prevailed in modified form until the 1970s.

Brinkmanship Term coined by U.S. secretary of state **John Foster Dulles** for the confrontational tactics of the United States and the **Soviet Union** in an age of **nuclear weapons**. To "go to the brink" was to risk nuclear war rather than surrender on matters of national interest. Brinkmanship reached its peak in the **Cuban Missile Crisis** (1962), when Soviet premier **Nikita Khrushchev** was the first to concede. Neither superpower again risked such a confrontation.

British Expeditionary Force Name given to British forces fighting in continental Europe in **World Wars I** and **II**.

Brownshirts Colloquial name for the SA, or Nazi storm troops (*see* **Nazi Party**).

C

Cambodian Civil War (1970–75) The **Khmer Rouge**, a Communist organization, launched a guerrilla insurgency, first against Prince **Sihanouk** and then against General Lon Nol (1913–85), who overthrew Sihanouk in 1970. The Khmer Rouge was aided by North Vietnam, while Lon Nol was aided by the U.S., which attacked with massive bombing raids (North Vietnam and the U.S. were locked at the time in the **Vietnam War**). The Khmer Rouge won in 1975, forcing Lon Nol into exile and renaming the country Kampuchea. Headed by **Pol Pot**, the new government carried out a campaign of mass murder that killed more than a million people. Kampuchea fell to Vietnamese invasion in 1979, after which the Khmer Rouge waged guerrilla war against the Vietnam-backed government. This new civil war continued into the 1990s.

Camp David Accords (September 1978) Peace agreements made between Israel and Egypt at the U.S. presidential retreat of Camp David, Maryland. U.S. president **Jimmy Carter** sponsored the accords between Israel's **Menachem Begin** and Egypt's **Anwar-el Sadat**. A resolution to work toward greater Palestinian autonomy did not come to fruition, but the accords did lead to a peace treaty (March 26, 1979) normalizing relations between the two countries and effecting the return of the Sinai Peninsula to Egypt. The accords were denounced by other Arab countries.

Capitalism Economic system in which property and the means of production are privately owned. In a capitalist society, profit motivates production and prices are competitively set in a free market, according to laws of supply and demand. First outlined by 18th-century British philosopher Adam Smith (1723–90), capitalism became one of the two main economic systems of the 20th century, the other being **socialism**. Though often criticized for creating unconscionable extremes of wealth and poverty, capitalism has been the engine of economic growth for many nations, particularly those of western Europe and the United States. In practice, its excesses were often restrained by organized **labor** and by socialist institutions such as nationalized industries in what were called mixed economies. **Communism**, a form of socialism, posed a challenge to capitalism during the **cold war**, but that challenge was widely considered defeated with the fall of the **Soviet Union** in 1991. Though not all capitalist societies have been democratic, many are, providing an argument for the view that free enterprise is linked to personal and political liberty (*see* **Liberalism**).

Carter Doctrine (1980) Foreign policy statement by U.S. president **Jimmy Carter** that the United States would protect its vital interest in the Persian Gulf region with military force if necessary. The assertion was prompted by the Soviet invasion of Afghanistan and by instability in Iran.

Casablanca Conference (January 14–24, 1943) **World War II** meeting at Casablanca, Morocco, between U.S. president **Franklin Delano Roosevelt** and British prime minister **Winston Churchill**. The leaders made plans for the invasion of Sicily and agreed to demand unconditional surrender from the **Axis Powers**.

Central Intelligence Agency (CIA) U.S. federal agency founded in 1947 to collect and analyze foreign intelligence. It grew out of the **World War II**–era Office of Strategic Services (OSS). Beginning in the 1950s, the CIA's purview included covert action, as it intervened clandestinely to influence foreign governments and, at times, depose or install leaders (as in Guatemala in 1954 and Chile in 1973). The CIA's involvement in the

Watergate and **Iran-Contra** scandals, as well as evidence of serious intelligence failures, led to increasing legislative controls on the agency. Since the end of the **cold war,** the CIA has undergone budget cuts.

Central Powers In **World War I**, the alliance comprising Germany, Austria-Hungary, Ottoman Empire, and Bulgaria.

Chaco War (1932–35) Conflict between Bolivia and Paraguay over possession of the Gran Chaco, a lowland plain that had been occupied by Paraguay. The region had an outlet to the sea (desired by the landlocked Bolivia) and was suspected to have oil reserves. Though the Bolivians were numerically superior, the Paraguayans outfought them, and the war ended in truce. The Treaty of Buenos Aires (1938) awarded Paraguay most of the disputed land, but Bolivia was granted a corridor to and port on the Paraguay River. About 50,000 Bolivians and 35,000 Paraguayans died in the war.

Cheka (All-Russian Extraordinary Commission for the Suppression of Counter-Revolution and Sabotage) Soviet secret police organization founded by **V. I. Lenin** in 1917. It used terror to enforce Soviet rule. In 1922 it became GPU, and later OGPU. It was succeeded in 1934 by **NKVD**.

Chemical Weapon Device that causes mass fatalities through the use of harmful chemicals. Though crude chemical weapons, such as burning oil, have been used since antiquity, 20th-century technology was required to develop sophisticated poison gases. The first of these were used by the Germans in **World War I**: chlorine at Ypres, Belgium, in 1915; and later, mustard gas (a lethal compound that causes blistering on body surfaces), also at Ypres, in 1917. In **World War II**, chemical weapons were not used in combat, but the Germans did use nerve gas (which kills by inhibiting nerve function) for mass murder in the **Holocaust**. Herbicides such as Agent Orange, used by the U.S. to destroy vegetation in the **Vietnam War**, are also chemical weapons, as is tear gas, a nonlethal substance used in riot control. Except in World War I, most countries have been reluctant to use chemical weapons for fear of retribution, though major powers developed and stockpiled them as a deterrent. The 1925 Geneva Protocol banned use of chemical and **biological weapons** but was not ratified by the U.S. Senate until 1974. Toward the end of the century, the world's leading nations increasingly tried to restrict proliferation of chemical, biological, and **nuclear weapons**. Iraq used chemical weapons in the **Iran-Iraq War** (1980–88). After the **Gulf War** (1990–91), Iraq was required to destroy its chemical, biological, and nuclear warfare capabilities and to allow **UN** inspection to confirm that it had done so. Its refusal to comply led to continuing UN economic sanctions.

Chernobyl (April–May 1986) The worst peacetime nuclear disaster in history. The accident occurred at the nuclear power plant at Chernobyl near Kiev, Ukraine. A meltdown, explosion, and fire resulted in 31 immediate deaths; radioactive contamination affected hundreds of thousands of people in the region. Radiation from Chernobyl was detected as far away as Scandinavia and other parts of Europe. The **Soviet Union**'s slow bureaucratic response to the disaster contributed to the country's image as an ailing superpower.

Chetniks Serbian nationalist guerrillas during the German occupation of Yugoslavia in **World War II**. They were pushed aside by their rivals—the Communist partisans led by **Josip Tito**—in the underground. During the Yugoslav Civil War of the 1990s, the term *Chetniks* was applied to Serbian guerrilla forces.

Chinese Civil War (1946–49) **Guomindang** (Nationalist) and Communist forces had been at odds since they split in 1927. The Communists established a state called the Jiangxi Soviet Republic (1931), but it collapsed under attack from the Nationalists in 1934, forcing the Communists to escape in the **Long March**. Nationalists and Communists formed a united front to fight Japan in the **Sino-Japanese War** (1937–45), but soon after that war ended they resumed fighting in the Chinese Civil War. In the conflict with Japan, the Communists had grown stronger, expanding their bases and influence among peasants in the north, including those in Manchuria. The Nationalists, by contrast, had been weakened by heavy losses in battles with the Japanese. The U.S. aided the Nationalists, but to no avail. In the crucial Huai-Hai campaign (November 1948–January 1949), the Nationalists lost over half a million men. By the end of 1949, the Communists had captured Shanghai, Canton, and Chungking. The Nationalist government collapsed and was evacuated to Taiwan (Formosa) in December 1949. There its leader, **Chiang Kai-shek**, formed a new Republic of China (1950). On the Chinese mainland, **Mao Zedong** led the formation of the new People's Republic of China on October 1, 1949.

Chinese Revolution (1911) Uprising that overthrew the Qing (Ch'ing or Manchu) Dynasty and ended a tradition of imperial rule dating to the 3rd century B.C. Led by **Sun Yat-sen** and supported by provincial assemblies and army commanders, the revolution began with an army mutiny at Wuchang on October 10. In February 1912 boy-emperor P'u-i (Hsüan T'ung, 1906–67) abdicated, and China became a republic. **Yuan Shikai**, a prominent Qing military leader who had switched sides, became president (*see also* **Guomindang** [Kuomintang]).

CIA *See* **Central Intelligence Agency.**

Civil Rights Movement (c. 1955–c. 1965) Movement of African-Americans to attain rights and opportunities equal to those of white Americans. The movement began soon after **World War II**, prompted in part by the experience of African-American soldiers who faced the paradox of fighting in a segregated army to preserve their country's freedom. (U.S. president **Harry S Truman** desegregated the armed forces in 1948.) The Supreme Court decision of *Brown v. Board of Education of Topeka, Kansas* (1954) declared public school segregation unconstitutional, giving a boost to civil rights advocates, such as those associated with the **NAACP**. A mass civil rights movement began with the Montgomery, Ala., bus boycott (1955), in which African-Americans led by **Martin Luther King Jr.** won desegregation of public transportation through nonviolent protests. From then until the early 1960s, blacks and supportive whites practiced nonviolent civil disobedience throughout the south, drawing on the **satyagraha** principles of **Mohandas Gandhi**. About 250,000 rallied around King to express their commitment in the peaceful March on Washington (1963). The federal government responded with a series of Civil Rights Acts (1957, 1960, 1964, 1968) and a Voting Rights Act (1965), and the protesters largely succeeded in ending the system of de jure segregation then prevalent in the South. However, African-Americans still faced serious problems related to racism—most notably poverty and lack of opportunities. The civil rights movement splintered in the mid-1960s, as moderate or nonviolent groups, such as the NAACP and King's Southern Christian Leadership Council, disputed methods and goals with more militant ones, such as the Black Panthers (*see* **black consciousness**). Some African-Americans showed their rage in race riots, most notably the riot in the Watts section of Los Angeles (1965). The Los Angeles race riots of 1992, stemming from the acquittal of white policemen in the beating of black motorist Rodney King, indicated the precarious state of race relations nearly 40 years after the start of the civil rights movement.

Poverty Status for U. S. Blacks and Whites, 1959–90

Year	Blacks*	%	Whites*	%	Black/white ratio
1959	9.9	55.1	28.5	18.1	3.0
1970	7.5	33.5	17.5	9.9	3.4
1975	7.5	31.3	17.7	9.7	3.2
1980	8.6	32.5	19.7	10.2	3.2
1985	8.9	31.3	22.9	11.4	2.8
1990	9.8	31.9	22.3	10.7	3.0

* number in millions
Source: L. Mpho Mabunda, ed., *The African-American Almanac*

Cloning *See* **Genetic Engineering.**

Cold War (1945–91) Period of tension and rivalry between the U.S. and its allies on one side and the **Soviet Union** and its allies on the other. **World War II** transformed the world from one with many centers of power to one with two: the democratic–capitalist U.S. in the West and the Communist **Soviet Union** in the East, opposed by ideology and national interest. Separated by what British politician **Winston Churchill** called an **iron curtain**, both of these superpowers had vast military might and industrial bases; both were armed with **nuclear weapons** (the U.S. from 1945, the Soviet Union from 1949); and both were the dominant members of European military alliances (**NATO** on the Western side, the **Warsaw Pact** on the Eastern side). Unwilling to risk open war and nuclear annihilation, the superpowers promoted the spread of their influence through aid to sympathetic governments and political parties and, sometimes, military intervention to establish proxy regimes. "Hot" regional clashes—most notably the **Korean War** and the **Vietnam War**—became a chronic symptom of the cold war. In the U.S., military intervention was justified by **containment** doctrine, while the principles of **deterrence** and **brinkmanship** guided the nuclear arms strategy. Locked in an arms race, the two sides tried to best each other in nuclear and conventional weapons and in the effectiveness of covert intelligence programs. **Space exploration** began in the context of a cold war "space race." After the **Cuban Missile Crisis** in 1962, there ensued a period of **détente**, or easing of tensions, which ended with the Soviet invasion of Afghanistan (1979). The cold war heated up again in the 1980s with a renewal of the arms race, including the U.S. military research program called the **Strategic Defense Initiative**, and with proxy wars in El Salvador and Nicaragua. The cold war ended with the collapse of Communist governments in eastern Europe in 1989 and the dissolution of the Soviet Union in 1991.

Colombo Plan Cooperative program to develop the economies of Southeast Asia and the Pacific. Conceived in Colombo, Sri Lanka, in 1950, the organization has 26 member nations. Though the original members were British Commonwealth countries, others—including the United States and Japan—later joined. Richer members provide aid to poorer ones in the form of training, grants, loans, food, equipment, and technical support.

Cominform *See* **Comintern.**

Comintern (Communist International [1919–43]) International organization of the world's Communist Parties. Also known as the Third International, it was founded in Moscow by Soviet leader **V. I. Lenin** in 1919. It was a successor to the Second International (1889–1914), an organization of the world's socialist parties that had broken up over the issue of entry into World War I; that group, in turn, had been a successor to the First International (1864–76). The Comintern coordinated the actions of Communist Parties worldwide, requiring conformity to the policies of the Soviet Communist Party. Soviet leader **Joseph Stalin** abolished it in 1943 as a concession to the **Allies** in **World War II**. Some of its functions were reassigned to the Cominform (Communist Information Bureau) from 1947 to 1956.

Commonwealth of Independent States (CIS) Association of independent republics conceived as a successor to the **Soviet Union**. It was established on December 8, 1991, by Russia, Belorussia, and Ukraine, as a forum of consultation on economic and foreign policy matters. Other former components of the Soviet Union soon joined: Armenia, Azerbaijan, Kazakhstan, Kyrgyzstan, Moldova, Tajikistan, Turkmenistan, and Uzbekistan.

Commonwealth of Nations Voluntary association of Great Britain, certain sovereign states that formerly belonged to the British Empire, and the dependencies of Britain or other sovereign members. Founded in 1931 and headquartered in London, the Commonwealth was created for consultation and cooperation. No decisions made collectively are binding on individual members. All members recognize the British monarch as the Commonwealth's symbolic head.

Communications Revolution Rapid growth in pace of information exchange and diversity of media. For most of human history, the potential reach of a message was limited by the slow pace of transmission over long distances. The 19th century introduced new communications technologies—the telegraph (1837) and telephone (1876)—that made possible instantaneous transmission by wire over any distance; the phonograph (1877) and motion picture (1895) allowed quick dissemination of sounds and images to large audiences. In the 20th century, these technologies evolved and proliferated while two "wireless" machines—radio (1901) and television (1926)—expanded communications still more. Communications satellites (1960) allowed relaying of messages around the earth; computer networks, most notably the worldwide Internet which had its origins in 1969 and gained broad popularity in the 1990s, created yet another new medium. Facsimile (fax) machines and audio and videotape further expanded and accelerated communications. Coupled with innovations in **transportation** and information processing, the communications revolution has created worldwide mass audiences united by shared messages and served by powerful industries. It has contributed to **globalization** of tastes and ideas.

Communism Political and economic system in which property and the means of production are owned communally. Though an ancient concept, Communism was developed by 19th-century German philosophers Karl Marx (1818–83) and Friedrich Engels (1820–95) into the modern system of Marxism, which promoted revolution of the proletariat in expectation of establishing a classless society. Russian revolutionary **Vladimir Ilych Lenin** modified Marxism by arguing that a Communist Party elite should lead the revolution and manage the state through central economic planning and political control. Following the establishment of the **Soviet Union** in 1917, Marxist-Leninist Communism became a form of **totalitarianism**, with tight controls on speech, education, and political activity. It was also expansionist, attempting to export revolution and control foreign Communist Parties through such means as the **Comintern**. After **World**

War II, Communism spread into the **Warsaw Pact** nations of eastern Europe, which were dominated by the Soviet Union, and into China, which pursued a separate path. During the **cold war,** Communism was seen as the great enemy of the liberal-democratic, capitalist nations of the West, even as Marxist-Leninism was adopted by nations in Asia, Africa, and Latin America and Eurocommunist parties flourished in Europe. The fall of the Soviet Union and the end of the cold war in 1991 seemed to mark the defeat of Communism, though several nations—including China, Cuba, and North Korea—continued to practice it, and it continued to influence the thinking of scholars in some academic disciplines.

Communist International *See* **Comintern.**

Computer Programmable electronic device for processing information. Mechanical adding machines had existed since the 17th century, but the modern electronic digital computer, which processes data in numerical form by controlling the flow of electrons through circuits, did not exist until the 20th century. In the 1930s analog computers were developed, and researchers such as **Alan Turing** and **John von Neumann** developed computer theory. The first successful electronic digital computer was the U.S.–based ENIAC (1946), which relied on vacuum tubes.

Until the 1970s, computers were mainly large machines used for science, government, and business purposes, assisting on projects from guiding spaceflight to predicting weather. The miniaturizing of components—through the development of transistors, integrated circuits, and microprocessors—made it possible for computers to grow much smaller in relation to their computing power.

In the 1980s the personal computer became a mainstay of most businesses and many homes. Business and industry became dependent on computers for everything from managing accounts to automating factories. By the end of the century, computers themselves were big business: American entrepreneur **William H. (Bill) Gates III,** head of the software company Microsoft (founded 1975), was one of the world's richest people. Computer microchips were incorporated into automobiles, answering machines, and a host of other everyday technologies. Computer technology was the basis for video games and for virtual reality (V.R.), a type of simulation in which the subject interacts with an apparently real environment; V.R. became a new medium for entertainment, training, and other uses. Computer-aided design became a basic tool of engineering, while computer-generated special effects became a common feature of motion pictures.

Computers vastly increased the amount of available data, contributing to the information explosion of the 20th century. Linked globally through the **Internet,** computers contributed to the **communications revolution** and to the **globalization** of cultural and

U.S. Households with One or More Computers	
No. of households with computer	*Percent of households with computer*
1984 6,980,000	8.2
1989 13,683,000	15.0
1993 22,605,000	22.8
1998 43,200,000	42.1
Source: U.S. Bureau of the Census, U.S. Dept. of Commerce	

economic life (*see also* **information revolution**).

Concentration Camp Prison or forced-labor camp in wartime or in totalitarian states. Employed by the British to intern Afrikaners in the **South African War** (1899–1902), concentration camps were used on a much larger scale by the Nazis in Germany before and during **World War II** (1933–45). During the **Holocaust**, camps such as Auschwitz were used to imprison, enslave, and systematically murder all those deemed undesirable, particularly Jews but also political dissenters, homosexuals, gypsies, and the mentally ill. The term *concentration camps* was also applied to the Soviet gulag system of forced labor camps and prisons, used to silence political opponents of the ruling party.

Conscientious Objection *See* **Pacifism.**

Conservative Party British political party. It descended from the Tory Party but took the name "Conservative" in about 1830. Though historically the party of empire, patriotism, and established social order, it acted pragmatically throughout much of the 20th century, often taking reformist positions. In the 1930s, under British prime minister **Neville Chamberlain**, it pursued the foreign policy of **appeasement**, but during World War II it provided a powerful war leader in British prime minister **Winston Churchill**. In the 1950s the party helped install socialist institutions; from 1979, under the highly conservative British prime minister **Margaret Thatcher**, it dismantled many of these.

Containment Cold war U.S. policy of confining **Communism** to countries already under its control. Its first major articulation was the **Truman Doctrine** of 1947. Containment was effected by regional alliances, aid to sympathetic governments, and military and clandestine intervention.

Corporatism Economic system in which economic sectors, such as banking, industry, and labor, are organized as corporate entities representing their members' interests. Decisions are made by the government in consultation with these entities. Italian leader **Benito Mussolini**'s Italy was the first corporatist state.

Council of Europe Association of European states, founded in London in 1949. Dedicated to human rights and the rule of law, it has a Committee of Foreign Ministers, a Parliamentary Assembly, a European Court of Human Rights, and a European Commission of Human Rights. As of 1995, it included 36 states.

Cuban Missile Crisis (1962) Confrontation between the United States and **Soviet Union**. In October 1962, U.S. spy planes revealed that the Soviet Union was assembling nuclear missile launching sites in Cuba. U.S. president **John F. Kennedy** ordered a naval blockade of Cuba and prepared to invade unless the Soviet Union accepted his demand to dismantle the missile sites. For two weeks, the world hovered on the brink of nuclear war. Then Soviet premier **Nikita Khrushchev** accepted Kennedy's demand, while the United States agreed not to sponsor further invasions of Cuba (*see* **Bay of Pigs Invasion**).

Cuban Revolution (1956–59) Revolt in Cuba that overthrew U.S.–backed dictator **Fulgencio Batista** and established the first Communist regime in the Western Hemisphere. On July 26, 1953, Cuban guerrilla leader **Fidel Castro** launched an unsuccessful attack on the Batista government at the Moncada army base. Arrested, Castro was sent into exile in Mexico, but he soon returned to lead a revolutionary force called the 26th of July Movement. From 1956 Castro and his troops, who included **Che Guevara**, waged guerrilla warfare from their base in the Sierra Maestra. In the early hours of January 1, 1959,

Batista fled Cuba by plane. On January 8 Castro's forces marched victoriously into Havana.

Cultural Revolution (1966–69) Chinese political movement. Chinese Communist Party chairman **Mao Zedong** led this mass movement to restore Communist purity by purging the nation of influences deemed bourgeois. The principal targets—zealously pursued by unofficial bands of young **Red Guards**—were the upper middle class, including Communist Party officials, bureaucrats, academics, and artists, all of whom were "purified" through imprisonment, humiliation, reeducation, and sometimes, execution. About 500,000 people died in the Cultural Revolution, which left Mao in absolute control of the purged ranks of the Communist Party.

Curragh Incident (1914) British army incident in Ireland, considered a mutiny by some. The British government feared that Protestants in Ulster, Northern Ireland, would rebel violently against incorporation into an Ireland ruled by a Catholic majority, as required by the Home Rule Bill of 1912. British troops were expected to suppress such a rebellion, but some expressed unwillingness to do so. Brigadier General Sir Hubert Gough (1870–1963) and 58 other British officers in the Curragh Camp near Dublin were allowed to resign rather than serve in Ulster, where they might have had to fight against Protestants. Sir John French (1852–1925), chief of the Imperial General Staff, without the knowledge of British prime minister **Herbert Asquith**, gave assurances that troops would not be used to enforce Home Rule, and the officers were reinstated. Asquith disavowed that pledge and dismissed French, but the event suggested that the British government might not have the will to enforce its Irish policies.

Curzon Line The border between Poland and the **Soviet Union**, established at the Versailles conference in 1919. It was based on the eastward limit of areas that were predominantly Polish in population. Named for British foreign secretary **Lord Curzon**, it was contested by the Poles, who gained more territory in the Russo-Polish War (1919–21). The frontier established after **World War II** generally followed the Curzon line.

D

Dance Rhythmic movement, usually in time to music. Dance in the 20th century is in part marked by the integration of the informality of the street with the formality of the stage in its intermixing of a variety of dance styles. At the beginning of the 20th century, formal dance in the theater was dominated by classical ballet. Notable companies included Denmark's Royal Danish Ballet and Russia's Bolshoi Ballet and the Imperial Russian Ballet (later the Kirov Ballet). Dance as popular entertainment was offered in musical comedies, vaudeville, or music halls.

The influence of African-American culture extended from the 19th century with the integration of tap dancing into popular entertainment. Similarly, jazz dance, which developed with jazz music and affected stage and social dancing, grew from African-American influences.

Social dance in the 20th century moved from the waltz to more playful, sensual pacing reflecting an increasingly urbanized culture, like the cake walk and fox trot (U.S.), both early examples. Fast-changing dance styles continued over the decades, including the Charleston (1920s), Lindy Hop (1930s), Jitterbug (1940s), Rhumba (1950s), Rock 'n' Roll (1950s–70s), Twist (1960s), Cha-Cha (1960s), Disco (1970s), and Hip-Hop (1990s).

The advent of modern dance early in the century introduced a new style separate from ballet and music hall dance. Created by **Isadora Duncan**, Ruth St. Denis (1877–1968), and others, modern dance was experimental and emotionally expressive. Beginning in the 1920s, **Martha Graham** and others developed streamlined choreography that contrasted with modern dance's initial styles. By mid-century, modern dance revealed its broad influence, linking itself to such areas as musical theatre, through Agnes De Mille's (1909–93) choreography (*Oklahoma!*), and ballet, through **Alvin Ailey** (American Dance Theater). Later modern dance innovators include Merce Cunningham (1922–) and Twyla Tharp (1941–).

By mid-century, a number of new major ballet companies had formed, extending the presence of ballet worldwide. Establishing a position in ballet for the U.S. were the New York City Ballet (1946), the American Ballet Theatre (1937–40), and the Robert Joffrey Ballet (1954). Other newly established ballet companies included the Australian Ballet (1940), the National Ballet of Canada (1951), and the Stuttgart (Germany) Ballet. Notable ballet innovators of the postwar years include **Mikhail Baryshnikov** and Rudolf Nureyev (1938–93). American Jerome Robbins (1918–97) linked ballet to the musical theater in *West Side Story* (1957) and other works.

Tap dancing maintained popularity throughout the century, through film and stage. From the 1930s through the 1950s, tap dancing figured prominently in musical films starring **Fred Astaire**, Gene Kelly (1912–96), and others. From the 1970s through the 1990s tap dancing has been championed by performers including Americans Gregory Hines (1946–) and Savion Glover. In the 1990s a highly stylized form of tap dancing was used in the Irish folk dance–based performance work *Riverdance*.

D-Day (June 6, 1944) Day of Allied military invasion of Nazi-occupied Normandy, France, which led to the liberation of western Europe during **World War II**. Led by U.S. general Dwight D. Eisenhower over several beaches on the Cotentin peninsula (Gold, Juno, Omaha, Sword, and Utah), the Normandy invasion was the largest amphibious landing in history. Two U.S. airborne battalions also arrived behind German lines; involved forces totaled more than 325,000. Allied-built artificial harbors called mulberries permitted delivery of military equipment; within a week, over 50,000 vehicles and 100,000 tons of materiel were engaged. D-Day was part of a three-month long Normandy Campaign, code-named Operation Overlord (June–August 1944), resulting in the liberation of Paris (August 26) and Belgium (September 3).

Decolonization The process by which former colonies of imperial powers achieved independence in the 20th century. Following **World War I**, Germany and the Ottoman Empire were forced to give up their imperial possessions, which were assigned to other powers (mainly Britain, France, and South Africa) as League of Nations mandates, with the long-term goal of converting the nations to self-government. Within the British Empire, decolonization involved the transformation in 1907 of several states (Australia, Canada, New Zealand, South Africa, Newfoundland, and later Ireland) into self-governing Dominions, which gained full autonomy as members of the **Commonwealth of Nations** in 1931. After World War II, European powers granted independence to many former colonies and mandates, including India and Palestine. However, in some cases, particularly in Africa, independence struggles continued into the 1960s and 1970s. Portugal, for example, only relinquished its hold on Angola and Mozambique in 1975.

Timeline of Decolonization
(not including the breakup of the Austro-Hungarian, Ottoman, and Soviet Empires)

Year of independence	Country decolonized	Colonizer
1941	Ethiopia	Italy
1946	Philippines	U.S.
1947	India	U.K.
1947	Pakistan	U.K.
1948	Myanmar	U.K.
1948	Sri Lanka	U.K.
1949	Indonesia	Netherlands
1951	Libya	Italy
1953	Cambodia	France
1954	Laos	France
1954	Vietnam	France
1956	Sudan	U.K./Egypt
1956	Tunisia	France
1957	Ghana	U.K.
1960	Burkina Faso	France
1960	Cameroon	Germany; U.K./France from 1916
1960	Central African Republic	France
1960	Chad	France
1960	Congo, Republic of the	France
1960	Congo, Democratic Republic of (formerly Zaire)	Belgium
1960	Côte d'Ivoire	France
1960	Gabon	France
1960	Madagascar	France
1960	Mali	France
1960	Niger	France
1960	Nigeria	U.K.
1960	Somalia	Italy
1960	Togo	Germany; France from 1914
1961	Sierra Leone	U.K.
1961	Tanzania	Germany; U.K. from 1919
1962	Algeria	France
1962	Burundi	Belgium
1962	Jamaica	U.K.
1962	Rwanda	Belgium
1962	Trinidad and Tobago	U.K.
1962	Uganda	U.K.
1963	Kenya	U.K.
1963	Malaysia	U.K.
1964	Malawi	U.K.
1964	Malta	U.K.
1964	Zambia	U.K.
1965	Gambia	U.K.

Timeline of decolonization, continued

Year of independence	Country decolonized	Colonizer
1965	Singapore	Formerly part of Malaysia
1966	Botswana	U.K.
1966	Guyana	U.K.
1966	Lesotho	U.K.
1968	Swaziland	U.K.
1971	Bangladesh	Formerly East Pakistan
1975	Angola	Portugal
1975	Mozambique	Portugal
1975	Papua New Guinea	Germany; Australia/U.K. from 1914
1975	Suriname	Netherlands
1980	Zimbabwe	U.K.
1981	Belize	U.K.
1984	Brunei	U.K.
1990	Namibia	Germany; S. Africa from 1920
1997	Hong Kong	U.K.
1999	Macao	Portugal

Source: Jan Palmowski, A Dictionary of Twentieth Century World History

Democratic Party American political party. Rooted in the political thinking of founding father Thomas Jefferson (1743–1826), the Democratic Party took shape in the early 19th century. By the 20th century it had split into two wings: an agrarian-rural faction based in the south and west, and an urban-business faction. This division kept it out of the White House until 1912 when **Woodrow Wilson** defeated a divided **Republican Party**. Republicans recaptured the presidency in 1920 and held it until 1932, when **Franklin Delano Roosevelt** won the first of his four terms, based on a coalition of urban workers, western farmers, and small businessmen. The party also dominated Congress from 1933 to 1981. Roosevelt's **New Deal** associated Democrats with government intervention in the economy and social programs such as Social Security. Republican **Dwight D. Eisenhower**'s two terms (1952–60) broke the Democrats' hold on the Oval Office, but **John F. Kennedy** recaptured the office in 1960, and Democrat **Lyndon Baines Johnson** won a landslide victory in 1964. The party's commitment to civil rights and programs for the poor, coupled with its internal splits over the **Vietnam War** and social values, alienated enough white southern supporters and northern ethnic voters to elect Republican **Richard Nixon** in 1968. Democrat **Jimmy Carter** retook the presidency in 1976, but 1980 ushered in the 12-year Republican **Ronald Reagan–George Bush** era. Democrat **Bill Clinton** won two elections (1992 and 1996), but the Republicans captured control of Congress in 1994.

Depression *See* **Great Depression.**

Détente A French word meaning "easing of tensions," an improvement in relations between antagonistic powers, most notably the U.S. and **Soviet Union** from 1962 to 1979. During that period, cultural and commercial exchange was promoted and diplomatic relations progressed.

Deterrence Cold war doctrine arguing that nuclear war could best be avoided by possessing a nuclear arsenal so powerful that it would make nuclear war unacceptably devastating to the opponent. In the 1960s the doctrine was tied to the concept of Mutual Assured Destruction, the idea that neither the U.S. nor the **Soviet Union** would launch a first strike if nuclear war would inevitably result in the destruction of both superpowers.

Developing World *See* **Third World.**

Dien Bien Phu *See* **Indochina War.**

Dollar Diplomacy U.S. foreign policy, associated with U.S. president **William Howard Taft**, of promoting U.S. influence in Latin America and Asia by encouraging private investment. The phrase referred particularly to investments by U.S. banks in China, Honduras, Nicaragua, and Haiti from 1909 to 1913.

Domino Theory The **cold war** proposition, articulated by U.S. president **Dwight D. Eisenhower** in 1954, that if one country in Southeast Asia fell to Communist rule, neighboring countries were likely to fall as well. The belief was used to justify American involvement in the **Vietnam War.**

Dreyfus Affair Late-19th-century crisis that divided France and influenced its politics into the 20th century. Alfred Dreyfus (1859–1935), a Jewish army captain, was sentenced to life imprisonment in 1894 on trumped-up espionage charges. The proceedings engulfed France in a bitter, sometimes violent controversy that revealed deep divisions in the French political system and stirred up anti-Semitic passions. Liberal and socialist groups demanded a retrial. The army, the Roman Catholic Church, and reactionary political groups opposed reopening the case and argued that French national security was being undermined by disloyal Jews and socialists. In 1906 a third trial exonerated Dreyfus, who later fought in World War I. The controversy prompted legislation that officially separated church and state in 1905. The military's prestige plummeted; sharp divisions between left and right were created by the affair and polarized French politics for decades.

Drugs, Illegal Chemical substances used for prohibited nonmedicinal purposes. Such drugs include narcotics (e.g., codeine, opium, cocaine, morphine, and heroin, a morphine derivative), amphetamines, barbiturates, hallucinogenic drugs, and marijuana. Some are derived from organic sources, some are created within the laboratory. Many cause physical or psychological addiction. As of 1995 over 34 percent of the U.S. population had used illegal drugs.

In the early 20th century, few of these drugs had been developed for medicinal purposes (morphine, opium) and regulation on them was limited. Some now heavily regulated substances were used as ingredients in patent medicines. Some medicines contained high qualities of alcohol, and Coca-Cola, created in 1883 as a health drink, was derived from extracts of the coca leaf, the source of cocaine. To regulate the manufacture of drugs and other comestibles, the U.S. passed the Pure Food and Drug Act (1906). Over the next few decades, drug regulation became more widespread, with some countries establishing drug-related programs and agencies.

Heroin trafficking has been subject to stringent national and international laws for most of the 20th century. Developed in Germany in 1898 as an analgesic, heroin was made illegal in most countries early in the 20th century when its severe side effects as a highly habit-forming drug were discovered. For decades afterward it had limited use, but greater availability increased consumption in industrialized nations in the 1960s. After some decline in the 1980s, its popularity rose again in the 1990s, due in part to the availability of purer heroin (greater than the standard 2 percent to 5 percent purity). Heroin can be sniffed, inhaled, or (in solution) injected under the skin or intravenously.

Cocaine, which for most of the 20th century has been illegal, is also habit-forming. While it was available in several forms, for sniffing, injecting, and smoking (as freebase), it remained a limited problem for most of the century. Cocaine gained a glamorous position in western countries during the 1970s, with usage and drug-related deaths greatly increasing. In the 1980s a more powerful and addictive version of cocaine called crack appeared. This relatively less expensive, smokable cocaine further increased cocaine use.

Hallucinogenic drugs, which comprise a wide range of organic and inorganic substances, grew in popularity after the development of LSD (lysergic acid diethylamide) in 1954. Beginning in the 1960s, LSD was an accepted drug of members of the **youth culture**. It has been under regulation as a controlled substance since its development.

Similarly, marijuana has been illegal under international law since the early 20th century. In 1925 the International Opium Convention placed marijuana and hashish trade under its jurisdiction. In response, stringent trading and possession laws were instituted in several countries worldwide by the 1960s. In the U.S., marijuana was made illegal in 1937. Although research after **World War II** revealed the efficacy of marijuana for reducing nausea in cancer patients undergoing chemotherapy, it has not been legalized for medicinal use.

Drug-related regulatory agencies in the U.S. include the Drug Enforcement Administration (DEA), a division of the Department of Justice (1973), and the Office of National Drug Control Policy, a result of the passage of the National Narcotics Leadership Act (1998).

Dumbarton Oaks Conference Meetings held from August to October 1944 at the Dumbarton Oaks estate, Washington, D.C., to plan the rules and procedures for the **United Nations**. Attending were representatives of China, Great Britain, the **Soviet Union**, and the U.S.; topics discussed included the place of the Security Council.

E

Easter Rising (April 24–29, 1916) Insurrection in Ireland against British rule. Led by Patrick Pearse (1879–1916) of the Irish Volunteers and James Connolly (1868–1916) of the Irish Citizen Army, it began on Easter Monday, when about 1,600 Irish rebels captured several buildings in Dublin, including the General Post Office. The rebellion stayed confined to Dublin, and British artillery forced the rebels to surrender within the week. Fifteen rebel leaders, including Pearse and Connolly, were court-martialed and executed. Though the Easter Rising was a failure, the execution of its leaders made them martyrs, inspiring widespread outrage against Britain that would soon lead to Irish independence.

Energy Crisis (oil-price shock [October 1973–March 1974]) Worldwide oil shortage. To express disapproval for Western support of Israel in the **Yom Kippur War** (1973), the **OPEC** nations enacted an oil embargo. This caused crude oil prices to quadruple and touched off energy shortages in many industrialized countries. The energy crisis shook economies throughout the world, causing inflation and unemployment. Western countries grew alarmed at their dependence on foreign oil. They pursued greater development of domestic oil reserves and alternative sources of energy, including nuclear power. In the **Third World**, the energy crisis increased political unrest and reliance on foreign loans. Arab countries became more aware of their global economic power. After the **Iranian**

Revolution (1979), a second energy crisis caused uncertainty about regional stability in the Persian Gulf and led to a renewed tightening of the oil supply, with similar economic implications.

Entente Cordiale (1904) British–French agreement in which Britain recognized French interests in Morocco and France recognized British interests in Egypt. It laid the foundation for Anglo-French cooperation before **World War I**.

Ethnic Cleansing *See* **Bosnian Civil War; Kosovo Crisis.**

Environmentalism Movement to protect the environment from pollution and degradation. From the late 19th century, conservation of natural resources and wilderness areas became a popular movement and, in the U.S., a matter of government policy. This was especially so during the presidency of dedicated conservationist **Theodore Roosevelt**, who created the National Park Service in 1916. While this movement continued throughout the century, a new concern became widespread by the 1960s: the pollution of air, water, and soil as a result of industrial wastes, engine emissions, and other products of modern technology. This was coupled with ecological awareness of the connectedness of living things and concern about the imminent extinction of a number of species as a result of human activity. American biologist Rachel Carson's *Silent Spring* (1962), an account of how pesticides, especially DDT, damage ecosystems, led to federal restrictions on pesticides and helped launch the contemporary environmental or "green" movement. The apex of that movement came on the first Earth Day in 1970 (observed by some on March 21, by others on April 22). Similar annual events were held internationally in subsequent years.

Throughout the 1970s, various groups kept environmental issues alive—most notably Greenpeace, founded in Canada in 1971, which led high-publicity nonviolent resistance campaigns. The U.S. government enacted environmental legislation, such as the Endangered Species Act (1973). In Germany, the **Green Party**, founded in 1980 with a focus on environmental issues, became an important political force. Nevertheless, the worldwide environmental movement suffered from declining popular interest until the mid-1980s, when it was revived with new evidence about two phenomena: the greenhouse effect, or suspected global warming produced by concentration of carbon dioxide and other substances in the atmosphere; and damage to the ozone layer (which protects living things from ultraviolet radiation) as a result of chlorofluorocarbons, used in aerosol sprays and air-conditioning equipment. In 1987, 24 nations at a conference in Montreal agreed to limit production of chlorofluorocarbons. International efforts were also made to control emission of greenhouse gases.

Eurocommunism The policy of Western European Communist Parties, notably in Italy and France, to seek power within existing national political frameworks rather than through revolution. Eurocommunist parties acted independently from the **Soviet Union**.

European Economic Community (EEC) Association of European states that encouraged among its member states free trade and tariff reform, and that became a base for the European Community and European Union. With roots in post–**World War II** Western European restructuring, the EEC was created in 1957 under the terms of the Treaties of Rome. It included six members: Belgium, France, Germany, Italy, Luxembourg, and the Netherlands. On July 1, 1967, the EEC and two other European federations—the European Coal and Steel Community (ECSC) and the European Atomic Energy Commission (Euratom)—were merged into a bureaucratic organization later named the European

Community. In the 1970s and 1980s, new members included Denmark, Ireland, and the United Kingdom (all 1973); Greece (1981); and Portugal and Spain (1986). Under the 1991 Treaty of Maastricht, the European Union (EU) was formed, with the expanded aims or pillars of common currency, shared foreign and security policies, and interaction in domestic and justice matters. In 1995 it admitted new members Austria, Finland, Norway, and Sweden.

Existentialism Philosophical movement emphasizing human isolation in an indifferent or hostile universe. While positing that human experience is largely incomprehensible, it stresses the importance of individual choice. The movement had its roots in the 19th century, with the writings of Danish philosopher Søren Kierkegaard (1813–55), but flourished in the 20th century, most prominently in the works of **Martin Heidegger, Karl Jaspers, Jean-Paul Sartre,** and **Albert Camus**. It informed theology (e.g., **Karl Barth** and **Paul Tillich**) and literature (e.g., **Samuel Beckett**).

F

Fair Deal A program of domestic policies outlined by Democratic president **Harry S Truman** in January 1949. He called for aid to education, a medical insurance program, a civil rights act, government housing subsidies, and a repeal of the Taft-Hartley Act. The 81st Congress, dominated by conservative Southern Democrats and northern Republicans, approved only a few of Truman's measures. The Fair Deal expanded Social Security coverage to 10 million more people, raised the minimum wage, and helped cities rebuild slum housing. The outbreak of the **Korean War** in 1950 doomed any further major spending on domestic programs.

Falange (Falange Española) Spanish Fascist party. Founded in 1933, it resembled the Italian Fascist and German Nazi Parties (*see* **Nazi Party**) in structure and ideology. **Francisco Franco** was its leader from 1937, when, as the Falange Española Tradicionalista, it was declared the only legal party. After **World War II**, the party renounced some of its more extreme positions, while continuing to emphasize such elements as a strong link to the Roman Catholic Church. It was dissolved in 1977, soon after Franco's death.

Falklands War (1982) War between Argentina and Britain over the Falkland Islands (Islas Malvinas in Spanish). Since the 19th century, Argentina had disputed British sovereignty over the island group off Argentina's east coast. On April 2, 1982, Argentina invaded and occupied the islands. The **UN** Security Council called for Argentina to withdraw. Britain dispatched a large naval task force, supported by U.S. bases. Warships on both sides were sunk as British ground forces invaded, forcing Argentine surrender on June 14. About 750 Argentine and 256 British troops were killed. The defeat prompted the collapse of Argentina's president Leopoldo Galtieri (1926–) and boosted the renown of British prime minister **Margaret Thatcher**.

Fascism Right-wing political philosophy calling for subordination of the individual to a **totalitarian** nation-state. It is characterized by nationalism, militarism, anti-Communism, and belief in the mystical authority of a ruling dictator. The term was first used in Italy c. 1919 to describe **Benito Mussolini**'s movement; Fascism was also practiced by the **Nazi Party** in Germany (where it was linked to anti-Semitism) and the **Falange** in Spain. It achieved its greatest popularity in the **Great Depression** with working people threatened by economic hardship and wealthy interests threatened by social disorder. Most of the prominent Fascist movements were defeated in **World War II**.

Federal Bureau of Investigation (FBI) Agency of U.S. Department of Justice that investigates all violations of federal law not specifically assigned to other agencies. Crimes investigated include sabotage, espionage, civil rights violations, bank robbery, and kidnapping. Established in 1908, it grew in size and power during the directorship (1924–72) of J[ohn] Edgar Hoover (1895–1972). In the decades following **World War II**, the FBI's harassment of left-wing dissenters led to controversy; reforms began to be instituted in the 1970s.

Federal Reserve System American monetary regulation system. Established in 1913, it sets national banking policies and controls the amount of available credit and currency in circulation. The Fed, as it is popularly known, consists of a seven-member Board of Governors appointed by the president, 12 Federal Reserve banks and thousands of member branches. In the midst of the **Great Depression** of the 1930s, Congress reorganized the Fed to make it a stronger weapon against economic turmoil. When the Fed buys U.S. government securities, it increases the bank deposits that make up most of the money supply. Selling securities lowers the money supply. The Fed can also determine the amount of reserves that banks must maintain. To influence credit markets, the Fed manipulates the interest rate it charges to member banks (the discount rate). In times of slow economic growth, lower rates make it easier for member banks to borrow money and make it available to consumers and businesses. To fight inflation, the Fed raises the discount rate to tighten credit.

Feminism *See* **Women's Movement.**

Fianna Fáil (Gaelic, "Soldiers of Destiny") Irish political party. It was founded in 1926 by opponents of the Anglo-Irish Treaty, which established the Irish Free State. Its founder and leader, **Eamon De Valera,** was elected prime minister in 1932. The party dominated elections in the 1930s and 1940s, during which time it severed Ireland's remaining legal ties with Britain. Voted out of power in 1948, the party again governed Ireland—sometimes in coalition with smaller parties—from 1957 to 1973. During this period it tried to cultivate Ireland's sluggish economy. During the 1980s and 1990s, Fianna Fáil and Ireland's other major party, Fine Gael, exchanged power several times and often depended on minor parties for their majorities in the Irish assembly.

Fifth Column Term for subversive forces, attributed to two men during the **Spanish Civil War**—Spanish Fascist general Queipo de Llano and Spanish nationalist general Emilio Mola (1887–1937). The term refers to the four military columns advancing on Madrid and the "fifth column" of nationalist supporters in the city that would aid the four. During **World War II** the term was used more generally to denote enemy sympathizers.

Film *See* **Motion Pictures.**

Four Freedoms Basic ideals outlined by U.S. president **Franklin Delano Roosevelt** in his January 6, 1941, State of the Union speech. They are: freedom of speech and expression, freedom of worship, freedom from want, and freedom from fear of war. The expression was meaningful in the U.S. during and after **World War II**; it was incorporated into the Atlantic Charter and inspired the series of paintings *Four Freedoms* (1943) by **Norman Rockwell.**

Fourteen Points Peace program for ending **World War I**, proposed by U.S. president **Woodrow Wilson** in an address to Congress on January 8, 1918. The first five of the 14 articles called for open rather than secret diplomacy, freedom of the seas, removal of trade barriers, disarmament, and impartial settlement of colonial claims. The next eight dealt with specific territorial questions, including evacuation and restoration of conquered territory in Russia, Belgium, and France; self-determination for the peoples of the Austro-Hungarian and Ottoman Empires; and the creation of an independent Poland. The final point called for the creation of a **League of Nations** dedicated to keeping the peace (as did occur, though without U.S. involvement). Overall, the Fourteen Points exhibited a high-minded intent to seek a peace that would be just and lasting, not punitive. Aimed partly at persuading the **Central Powers** to surrender, it may have helped shorten the war. At the **Paris Peace Conference**, some but not all of the Fourteen Points were followed. Many Germans cried betrayal when forced to accept the decidedly more punitive Treaty of **Versailles**.

Freikorps ("Free Corps") In Germany, independent paramilitary units active from 1918 to 1921. Right-wing in orientation, they were useful to the government in crushing left-wing uprisings, such as the **Spartaçist Revolt** (1919), but were also a destabilizing force, as when they themselves revolted in the **Kapp Putsch** (1920). Though the units were officially disbanded by 1921, many members remained unofficially active in murder squads or in the SA.

FRELIMO (Front for the Liberation of Mozambique) Nationalist resistance group formed in 1962 to gain independence for Mozambique from Portugal. A Marxist group, it was armed by the **Soviet Union**, China, and other Communist countries. In 1975, it won independence and became the nation's single party. In the 1980s, a dissident guerrilla group, RENAMO or Mozambique National Resistance, used support from South Africa to wage civil war against the FRELIMO government. Multiparty elections in 1994 confirmed FRELIMO as the ruling party.

Fundamentalism Strict adherence to basic religious principles, in opposition to modernizing or liberalizing trends.

In the U.S., Christian fundamentalists—most of them Evangelical Protestants—emerged as an organized movement in the 1920s. They espoused literal faith in the Bible, opposing the teaching of biological evolution (*see* **Scopes Trial**). In the 1980s, they became a powerful conservative force, pushing the Republican Party to the right on issues such as public school prayer and abortion.

In the Arab world, Islamic fundamentalists opposed secular and western influences and pushed for theocratic rule based on the Shariah, or Islamic law. In 1979, the Iranian Revolution established the Islamic fundamentalist regime of **Ayatollah Khomeini**. Since then, Islamic fundamentalist terrorists and guerrillas increasingly destabilized the Arab world, striking, for example, against governments in Algeria and Egypt. In the 1990s, the fundamentalist group Hezbollah used terror to combat the Israeli-Palestinian peace process, while the fundamentalist Taliban took control of post-Soviet Afghanistan.

Futurism *See* **Art.**

G

Gang of Four Radical Maoist group accused of trying to take power in China in 1976. Leaders of the **Cultural Revolution** (1966–69), they included **Mao Zedong** widow Jian Qing (1914–), Zhang Chunqiao, Wang Hungwen, and Yao Wenyuan. Following Mao's death in 1976, they were arrested and convicted (1981) of treason, leaving China under the more moderate rule of leaders like **Deng Xiaoping**.

GATT *See* **General Agreement on Tariffs and Trade**.

Gay Liberation Social movement to promote group identity, tolerance, and civil rights for homosexuals. The movement saw its origins in the June 1969 riot following the police raid of the Stonewall Inn, a gay bar in New York City; this was the first public protest against police harassment of homosexuals. In following decades, gay people have received more acceptance, though discrimination persists. Several public interest organizations have formed, including the Gay and Lesbian Task Force, a civil rights group; the Lambda Legal Defense and Education Fund, to provide legal assistance; and the Human Rights Campaign Fund, a lobbying group. Since the 1970s, the **AIDS** epidemic has generated medical advocacy programs among gay and lesbian groups.

Gaza Strip Section of Mediterranean coast in southwestern Palestine around the town of Gaza. Assigned by the **UN** to the Arabs in 1947, it was fought over in several **Arab–Israeli Wars**. The Gaza strip was successively occupied by Egypt (1948–56, 1957–67) and Israel (1956–57, 1967–). The poverty of its Palestinian inhabitants made it a focus of rebellion in the **Intifada**. It received limited autonomy in 1994.

General Agreement on Tariffs and Trade (GATT) International organization founded in 1948 to encourage free trade. Since its establishment, GATT has organized eight major rounds of trade and tariff negotiations. These included the Uruguay Round, which resulted in a 1994 GATT agreement, signed by 110 member states, to reduce national subsidies and trade tariffs. Nations have pursued free trade by other means, also, most commonly by forming regional trade zones, such as the **European Economic Community**, originating in the 1950s, and the North American Free Trade Agreement (NAFTA), created in the 1990s.

General Strike British Work stoppage from May 4 to 12, 1926, by British coal miners over low wages and poor working conditions. Discontent arose when the British government suspended **World War I** subsidies to the industry, which workers feared would lead to lower wages. In addition, a March 1926 report, *Samuel's Royal Commission of the Coal Industry*, recommended modernization and restructuring but also decreased wages and increased hours. Several weeks of negotiations between the government and the Trades Union Congress failed, and the strike began. Government troops and volunteer workers undercut the strike's power, and on May 12 the strike ended. Miners were forced to accept lower wages, and the passage of the Trade Disputes Act (1927) made general strikes illegal.

Generation X *See* **Youth Culture**.

Genetic Engineering Manipulation of genetic structure in living organisms. In 1953 **James Watson** and **Francis Crick** discovered the double-helix structure of the DNA molecule, unlocking for the first time the genetic code that governs heredity. In 1973 the age of genetic engineering began when American biochemists Stanley Cohen (1922–) and Herbert Boyer succeeded in splicing genes from different organisms into one strain of bacteria. Despite warnings from some quarters about moral and environmental dangers, the 1980s and 1990s brought rapid development of genetic engineering techniques. Numerous genetically engineered products came to market, particularly in agriculture, medicine, and scientific research. With associated technologies, genetic engineering became part of the burgeoning biotechnology industry. In the 1990s scientists around the world labored to map the entire human genome, in part to prepare for further research in biotechnology. The developments coincided with advances in manipulating reproduction, such as in vitro, or test tube, fertilization (first achieved with humans in 1978), and the first cloning of an adult mammal (a sheep) announced in 1997.

Geneva Conventions Series of treaties signed in Geneva, Switzerland, to establish civilized standards for treatment of combatants and civilians in wartime. The scope of the conventions expanded from an original focus on wounded soldiers (1864) to cover naval warfare (1906), prisoners of war (1929), civilians (1949), refugees (1951), and biological weapons (1972). Though accepted in principle by many countries, the conventions are often ignored in practice.

Genocide Systematic destruction of a racial, ethnic, or religious group. The term was first used in the 1940s to describe the **Holocaust**, in which the **Nazi Party** tried to eradicate European Jewry. Some acts of genocide predated the Holocaust (notably the massacres of Armenians by Ottoman Turks from the late 19th to early 20th centuries); others have occurred since, such as the mass murder of the Tutsi by the Hutu in Rwanda in 1994. A 1948 **UN** convention defines genocide as a crime and provides for international or national prosecution. The United States has never ratified the convention.

Gentlemen's Agreement (1907) Informal agreement between the United States and Japan that Japan should restrict emigration to the United States, while the United States should rescind laws discriminating against Japanese. The agreement ended with a 1924 act of Congress excluding immigration from Japan.

Glasnost (Russian, "openness") Soviet policy of liberal reform. It allowed greater freedom of expression, including criticism of the government, and promoted better relations with Western nations. With *perestroika*, it was instituted by Soviet leader **Mikhail Gorbachev** in 1986.

Global Warming *See* **Environmentalism.**

Globalization The unification of the world through trends, organizations, and products with worldwide impact. The European colonial empires formed from the 15th to the 19th centuries helped to link the disparate regions of the world, as did such 19th-century technological innovations as the telegraph, telephone, steamship, and railroad. But the 20th century saw significant advances in the connectedness of human activity around the world.

The **communications revolution** linked the world via satellite, allowing instant communication almost anywhere; **airplanes** and other forms of **transportation** reduced travel times and encouraged immigration from one country or region to another; and the development of the **computer** and the **Internet** facilitated the easy spread of ideas. Multinational corporations—companies with operations in more than two countries— hired employees and marketed products in many parts of the globe, fostering homogeneity in brandname recognition and consumer buying habits. After **World War II**, many nations increasingly pursued free trade; institutions such as **GATT** and regional trade zones such as the **European Economic Community** helped to reduce tariffs and other trade barriers.

Wars in the 20th century tended to have global repercussions, particularly **World Wars I** and **II** and the **cold war**; peacemaking also became a global issue, with the rise of the **League of Nations** and the **United Nations**. International conferences sought to address problems of global concern, including **environmentalism** and control of **nuclear, chemical,** and **biological weapons**. At the same time, there were forces that kept the world from becoming a single "global village" (a term coined by **Marshall McLuhan** in the 1960s). Through the process of **decolonization**, old colonial empires broke apart, with many new nations declaring independence. The end of the cold war in 1991 left the world with only one superpower—the U.S.—but gave free reign to **balkanization** tendencies in many countries, particularly in Eastern Europe and the former **Soviet Union**. The result was often civil war based on ethnic and tribal rivalries. Forces such as anarchism and Islamic **fundamentalism** also bespoke an unwillingness on the part of many to join the trend toward one modern, secular, technologically advanced world.

Great Depression International economic crisis begun by the collapse of the U.S. stock market in 1929. The U.S. economy, the most influential of the day, had enjoyed years of growing wealth, much of it due to wild speculation on a largely unregulated stock market. This shaky economic source, combined with inequality in distribution of wealth (5 percent of all people held one-third of the wealth), constituted a volatile economy with a relatively small consumer base for the vast quantities of goods being manufactured.

Unemployment Rate in the U.S. Civilian Labor Force, 1920–50

Year	Unemployment rate
1920	5.2
1922	6.7
1924	5.0
1926	1.8
1928	4.2
1930	8.7
1932	23.6
1934	21.7
1936	16.9
1938	19.0
1940	14.6
1942	4.7
1944	1.2
1946	3.9
1948	3.8
1950	5.3

Source: Dept. of Labor, Bureau of Labor Statistics

In fall 1929 the stock market experienced weeks of turmoil, marked first by a steep decline on **Black Thursday** (October 24, 1929), when almost 13 million shares of stock were sold in panic. Five days later, on Black Tuesday (October 29, 1929), the stock market crashed, with market values sustaining their greatest decline in history.

With profits and consumer base evaporated, record numbers of banks and businesses closed, creating mass unemployment throughout the U.S. A similar disaster struck Europe as U.S. investors called in loans made to Europe to purchase American goods. The loss of assets generated financial panic (1931) in Great Britain, central Europe, and Germany, where its deficit led U.S. president **Herbert Hoover** to suspend reparations payments for a year (1931). Emergency U.S. measures to regulate trade, such as the Hawley-Smoot Tariff Act (1930), which raised tariffs to decrease foreign trade, did substantially lessen international trade in manufactured goods (e.g., up to a 50 percent drop in Great Britain), but its effect on world economies was limited. By the early 1930s worldwide unemployment approached 20 percent. The hard economic and social climate proved receptive to right-wing authoritarian political leaders in Europe and South America, such as **Benito Mussolini** in Italy and **Adolf Hitler** in Germany.

For its solution, the U.S. turned to government intervention. In the 1932 presidential election, the country of 13 million unemployed rejected the moderating efforts of Republican president Herbert Hoover and elected Democrat **Franklin Delano Roosevelt**. Taking office in 1933 amidst a 33 percent unemployment rate, he immediately effected a broad range of emergency regulations and government job programs known as the **New Deal**.

Employing eight million Americans in public works projects, he improved economic conditions and raised public morale with his forceful optimism.

By the end of the 1930s, many countries' economies were recovering. However, the U.S. achieved full economic recovery only with entry into **World War II** and the resulting defense boom.

Great Leap Forward (1958–60) Chinese economic program. It aimed to transform China rapidly into a major industrial power by organizing large agricultural communes that freed laborers for industry. It resulted in crop shortages and a flood of unwanted shoddy products, such as steel made in backyard furnaces. The economic fiasco, coupled with natural disasters, resulted in famines that killed about 20 million people. China's leaders were forced to focus again on agricultural production.

Great Purge (1934–39) Campaign of terror and mass execution to solidify the power of Soviet dictator **Joseph Stalin**. In 1934 Communist official Sergei Kirov (1886–1934) was murdered, possibly on Stalin's orders. Stalin used the murder as a pretext for rounding up his opponents in the Communist Party, including such senior revolutionaries as **Grigory Zinoviev** (1883–1936), **Lev Kamenev** (1883–1936), and Nikolay Bukharin (1888–1938). These and many others were tried, forced to confess, and executed; others were sentenced to likely death in labor camps. The ranks of government and military were drastically thinned and restocked with Stalin supporters. The height of the terror came in the *Yezhovschchina* (1937–38), when N. I. Yezhov ran the secret police. Between 1 million and 10 million people are estimated to have died in the Great Purge.

Great Society A phrase that U.S. president **Lyndon B. Johnson** introduced in 1965 to describe an ambitious legislative program that he hoped would wage a war on poverty and reduce racial inequities. Johnson won passage of most of his agenda after his landslide victory over Barry Goldwater (1909–98) in the 1964 presidential election. The Great Society included the Voting Rights Act, Medicare, and federal support of education housing, and job training. The increasing involvement of the U.S. in the **Vietnam War** soon diverted money and attention away from these programs.

Green Party Political party active in Western Europe from the 1970s and in Eastern Europe from the 1980s. General aims focus on stemming unchecked, potentially destructive economic growth and conserving the environment. In Germany, the Green Party has been a national organization since 1980 and has been part of several national governments from 1983, increasing in voter popularity and influence over environmental policies. It merged with the East German Greens and Bündnis 90 groups in 1993.

Green Revolution Agricultural term referring to a change in farming methods to increase and improve yield. Introduced to developing countries during the 1940s and 1950s, it was complicated by the overuse of chemicals and unfamiliar machinery, with some countries discontinuing the methods.

Gulf War (Persian Gulf War) (1990–91) Conflict between Iraq and an international coalition led by the U.S. Iraq invaded Kuwait in August 1990 and ignored **UN** resolutions to withdraw. The U.S., France, Great Britain, Syria, Saudi Arabia, and Egypt deployed over 700,000 troops in the region while Iraqi leader **Saddam Hussein** reinforced his troops in Kuwait. The coalition launched an air campaign in January 1991 that devastated Iraq's transportation and communications systems and crippled its units in Kuwait. The allies mounted a ground offensive on February 24 that quickly liberated Kuwait. Iraqi resistance crumbled in three days and U.S. president **George Bush** declared a cease-fire. Hussein agreed to pay reparations and to allow the UN to supervise destruction of Iraqi chemical and biological weapons. As a result of Hussein's refusal to comply with UN inspection requirements, most of the economic sanctions initiated in 1990 remained in force years after the war.

Guomindang (Kuomintang, Chinese Nationalist Party) Chinese political party. It was founded in 1912 by **Sun Yat-sen** and Sung Chiao-jen (1882–1913). Banned in 1913, the nationalist, moderately socialist party (*see* **socialism**) fought a civil war for control of China. From 1922, it was aided by the **Soviet Union** and reorganized along **Bolshevik** lines. In 1927 the party's right-wing, led by **Chiang Kai-shek**, expelled the Communists and took control of the party. Through the campaign called the Northern Expedition (1926–28), the Guomindang captured the existing capital at Beijing and established its own internationally recognized capital at Nanjing (1928). The Guomindang, or Nationalists, joined forces with the Communists to fight Japan in the **Sino-Japanese War** (1937–45), but afterward, in the **Chinese Civil War** (1946–49), the Communists won control of mainland China. The Guomindang fled to Taiwan, where they established a rival government claiming to be China's legitimate ruling body.

H

Haganah (Hebrew, "Defense") Zionist military organization in Palestine. Originating in 1920 as a paramilitary group to defend Jewish settlements, it grew in size in the 1920s and 1930s. It waged guerrilla war with Palestinian Arab forces from 1937. It supplied troops to British forces in **World War II** and opposed the terrorist actions of the **Irgun** and **Stern Gang**. In 1948, it formed the nucleus of the army of the new state of Israel.

Helsinki Conference (1975) Meeting aimed at reducing **cold war** political tensions and increasing international cooperation. Attended by representatives of 35 countries, including the U.S. and the **Soviet Union**, it established the Conference on Security and Cooperation in Europe (CSCE), a vehicle for East-West dialogue that was later reorganized into a **UN** agency (1992). The conference resulted in the Helsinki accords, in which the participants accepted international conventions for human rights, though these had no binding power.

Hindenburg German airship or dirigible. It exploded on May 6, 1937, on reaching the mooring mast in Lakehurst, N.J. The explosion was caused by the use of highly flammable hydrogen gas to lift the craft, which contained a rigid steel framework. The disaster killed 36 people and sped the demise of zeppelins, or rigid airships, as a form of transportation. Helium-inflated blimps, the nonrigid cousin of zeppelins, are still in use.

Hiroshima Industrial city on Honshu Island, Japan, that was the site of the first atomic bomb attack, by the U.S. on August 6, 1945. The bomb decimated four square miles, or approximately 90 percent, of the city and caused 137,000 deaths, over one-third of the city's population of 343,000. Extensive damage also occurred in neighboring areas. On August 9, 1945, a second bomb was detonated on the city of Nagasaki, killing approximately 75,000 people and destroying over one-third of the area. The Japanese issued an unconditional surrender on August 14, 1945. A portion of Hiroshima has been preserved as a memorial (*see also* **nuclear weapons**).

Estimated Number of Jews Killed in the Holocaust

Country	Estimated pre-Holocaust population	Estimated Jewish population killed	Percent killed
Poland	3,300,000	3,000,000	90
Baltic countries	253,000	228,000	90
Germany/Austria	240,000	210,000	90
Protectorate	90,000	80,000	89
Slovakia	90,000	75,000	83
Greece	70,000	54,000	77
The Netherlands	140,000	105,000	75
Hungary	650,000	450,000	70
S.S.R. White Russia	375,000	245,000	65
S.S.R. Ukraine*	1,500,000	900,000	60
Belgium	65,000	40,000	60
Yugoslavia	43,000	26,000	60
Rumania	600,000	300,000	50
Norway	1,800	900	50
France	350,000	90,000	26
Bulgaria	64,000	14,000	22
Italy	40,000	8,000	20
Luxembourg	5,000	1,000	20
Russia (R.S.F.S.R.)*	975,000	107,000	11
Denmark	8,000		
Finland	2,000		
Total	8,861,800	5,933,900	67

*The Germans did not occupy all the territory of this republic.

Source: Lucy S. Dawidowicz, *The War Against the Jews 1933–1945*

Holocaust (1933–45) Nazi attempt to exterminate European Jews through mass murder (*see* **Nazi Party**). Slavs, socialists, and other "defectives" were targeted by the Nazis, but Jews were the special object of Nazi hatred. Beginning in 1933 German chancellor **Adolf Hitler** oversaw the increasing social persecution of German Jews, through job exclusion, revoking of citizenship through the Nuremberg Laws (1935), and the organized property destruction of **Kristallnacht** (1938). The genocide began with the June 1941 invasion of Russia, where over the course of six months 500,000 Jews and Communists were killed. Systematic extinction was devised at the Wannsee Conference in January 1942, where the "final solution" of deporting Jews and undesirables to concentration camps was planned. Deportation of German Jews began in 1941 and of other European Jews in 1942. At **concentration camps** including Auschwitz and Treblinka in Poland and Buchenwald and Dachau in Germany, victims were killed in gas chambers, hanged, or shot. Some were tortured or made subjects of forced medical experiments. By the end of **World War II**, more than 67 percent of European Jews had been exterminated. In all, about 6 million Jews were killed.

Hukbalahap (Huk) Movement Filipino left-wing guerrilla movement. Established to fight Japanese occupation of the Philippines during **World War II**, it was based in central Luzon. After the war, from 1946, it fought for peasant land reform against wealthy landowners. With U.S. military aid, the Filipino government defeated the insurgency in 1954.

Human Rights Rights and freedoms to which all human beings are entitled. The concept of individual rights and liberties had been a mainstay of **liberalism** since the 18th century, but in practice it was enacted on a country-by-country basis. The first general international statement of human rights came in 1948, when the **UN** passed the Universal Declaration of Human Rights, including the rights to life, liberty, security, freedom of speech and thought, and due process of law. Several countries abstained, including the **Soviet Union**, Saudi Arabia, and South Africa. Though not legally binding, the declaration became the basis of future agreements on human rights, including the 1975 **Helsinki** accords. The late 20th century saw several victories for the international human rights movement, including the end of **apartheid** in South Africa and the collapse of Soviet-bloc Communism, with its restrictions on individual liberty. However, in many nations, human rights remained under assault, whether from genocide, political repression, torture, discrimination, or inescapable poverty.

Hundred Flowers Campaign (1956–57) Chinese government-sponsored movement to open political and intellectual debate. Named for the proverb "Let a hundred flowers bloom, let a hundred schools of thought contend," it resulted in an unexpected deluge of criticism of the government, triggering a crackdown on the dissenters.

Hungarian Revolution (October 23–November 14, 1956) National rebellion against Soviet domination. The revolt began in Budapest when Hungarian armed forces attacked demonstrators celebrating Polish reform and protesting the Soviet presence in Hungary. Overnight the revolt became national, and on October 24, former premier **Imre Nagy** was restored to power. He demanded Soviet withdrawal from Hungary and petitioned the **United Nations** for a neutral presence. Countering Nagy was Hungarian politician János Kádár (1912–89). who was named head of the Communist Party and formed an opposition government. Soviet troops invaded Hungary and by November 14 had quelled the revolt, placing Kádár in charge. Nagy was removed and executed.

I

India-Pakistan (Indo-Pakistani) Wars (1947–49, 1965, 1971) Series of conflicts between the neighboring countries of India and Pakistan. On August 15, 1947, British India was partitioned into the new nations of India and Pakistan. Mass migrations took place, as Hindus in Muslim-controlled Pakistan fled to Hindu-controlled India while Muslims in India fled to Pakistan. Rioting between the two communities had been increasing since 1946; it now became worse, with up to a million refugees killed. In the midst of this conflict (known as the Indian Civil War of 1947–48), the first war between the new states took place.

In the India-Pakistan War of 1947–49 (or Kashmir War), the autocratic Hindu ruler of Kashmir, an independent state bordering West Pakistan, tried to cede the state to India, over the violent protests of Muslim insurgents aided by Pakistani invaders (October 1947). Indian troops entered Kashmir and clashed with Pakistan. A **UN** cease-fire (1948) and truce (1949) ended the war, with Kashmir informally partitioned along the battlefront.

In the India-Pakistan War of 1965, the two countries again went to war over Kashmir but soon accepted another UN cease-fire. The two sides agreed at Tashkent to resolve the issue peacefully, but within a few years they clashed again. In 1971 East Pakistan declared independence as Bangladesh. Pakistan suppressed the revolt, driving millions of refugees into India, which assisted the Bangladeshi insurgents.

In the India-Pakistan War of (December) 1971, Pakistan attacked India, prompting India to invade East Pakistan. There India captured Dhaka and forced the surrender of Pakistani forces. With India's help, Bangladesh had won independence.

Indian National Congress Indian political party, also known as the Congress Party. Founded in 1885 to press for Indian political representation within the British Empire, it demanded home rule in 1906 and full self-determination in 1918. Led by **Mohandas Gandhi** and associated with his **satyagraha** campaigns, it became the central institutional vehicle of India's independence movement. Many party leaders were imprisoned during **World War II**. When independence was achieved in 1947, the Congress Party, headed by **Jawaharlal Nehru**, became the party of government; it advocated nationalism, **socialism**, and a breakdown of the caste system. After Nehru's death (1964), the party was long headed by his daughter **Indira Gandhi**. It suffered splits in the 1960s and 1970s and briefly lost power to the Janata Alliance Party (1977–80) before resuming its dominant role.

Indochina War (First Indochina War) (1945–54) Struggle of Vietnamese nationalists to end French rule of their country. The Communist revolutionary **Ho Chi Minh** led the Vietminh (League for the Independence of Vietnam) against Japanese occupation forces during **World War II**. In September 1945 he declared Vietnam's independence. France initially accepted the new state, but failure to negotiate a political settlement sparked the outbreak of guerrilla warfare by the Vietminh in 1946. The French formed a rival government in 1949, which became South Vietnam. The military struggle ended in 1954 when the French surrendered the besieged fortress of Dien Bien Phu. An international conference called for a temporary division of Vietnam along the 17th parallel, which would divide Communist North Vietnam from South Vietnam. Elections to reunite the country were planned for 1956 but South Vietnam refused to participate; with help from the U.S., South Vietnam began to strengthen its army. The Communists began guerrilla warfare against the south in 1959, a conflict that came to be known as the **Second Indochina War** or the **Vietnam War**.

Industrial Revolution Transformation of an agricultural society to one emphasizing large-scale, mechanized factory production. Societies in the midst of industrializing commonly exhibit such features as urbanization, rapid economic growth, population growth, improving living standards, the rise of a professional class, and strained relations between capital and labor.

The first industrial revolution took place in Great Britain from the mid-18th to mid-19th centuries; by the late 19th century, it had spread to France, Germany, and the U.S. In the 20th century, other countries, particularly Japan and the **Soviet Union**, went through the pangs of industrialization and reaped its benefits. Some Asian countries, such as China and Singapore, became significant industrial producers in the second half of the 20th century.

In the **Third World**, many countries remained at heart agrarian, but tried hard to develop domestic industry—conscious of the fact that economies based on exporting agricultural commodities are usually weaker than those based on exporting manufactured goods. Governments sought to foster industrial development by introducing electric power, rail-

Production of World Manufacturing Industries, 1900–80 (1900 = 100)		
	Total production	Annual growth rate
1900	100.0	2.6
1913	172.4	4.3
1928	250.8	2.5
1938	311.4	2.2
1953	567.7	4.1
1963	950.1	5.3
1973	1730.6	6.2
1980	3041.6	2.4

Source: Paul Kennedy, *The Rise and Fall of the Great Powers*, Table 39

roads, highways, and other infrastructure necessary to industrial production. Even with half-completed industrial revolutions, these developing countries experienced such common side effects as industrial pollution, urban slums, and rising unemployment.

Industrialized countries themselves underwent changes in the last quarter of the century. With the spread of computers and automation, heavy industries such as steel production became less important to economic growth and job creation than high technology and information industries (*see* **Information Revolution**).

Industrial Workers of the World (IWW) U.S.–based industrial union encompassing 43 labor associations and promoting direct action rather than collective bargaining to achieve its labor goals. Founded in Chicago in 1905, it originally included skilled and unskilled laborers as members, but by 1910, unskilled workers dominated, with membership of about 60,000 at its pre–**World War I** peak. Under the direction of American labor leaders **Eugene Debs**, Daniel De Leon (1852–1914) and William Dudley ("Big Bill") Haywood (1869–1928), the union (also called the Wobblies) followed syndicalist ideals and aimed to refashion a capitalist society into a socialist one. Unsuccessful strikes, federal suppression, and antilabor sentiment brought about the union's decline by the 1920s. Expelled from the union in 1905, De Leon formed the Workers' International Industrial Union in 1908.

Intifada ("shaking off") (1987–94) Uprising of Palestinians in the Israeli-occupied territories of the **West Bank** and the **Gaza Strip**. In sporadic attacks, Palestinians fought Israeli troops with stone throwing and bombing. Although many more Palestinians than Israelis were killed or wounded, the Intifada successfully drew attention to the Palestinian cause. Unable to suppress the uprising militarily, Israel decided to negotiate a settlement with the **Palestine Liberation Organization**. The occupied territories received limited autonomy beginning in 1994.

Influenza Pandemic *See* **Spanish Influenza Pandemic.**

Information Revolution The transformation of a society by new methods of creating and disseminating data. Some historians place the first information revolution in the 15th century, with German printer Johannes Gutenberg's development of the printing press.

Others date it from the invention of the telegraph in 1837, making the term virtually synonymous with **communications revolution**, the rapid growth in the pace of information exchange in the modern world. The term, however, is most often used to describe the transforming effects of the **computer** and associated information technologies in the last 50 years, particularly the last 20 years. These technologies include robotics, which are used in **automation**, and the compact disc (CD), a laser-based system for storing and retrieving digital information that was introduced in 1982. The CD is used for, among other things, recording music and presenting multimedia games and reference works (the latter is often in a format called CD–ROM, for Compact Disc–Read Only Memory).

The information revolution is sometimes considered to encompass the rapid development of telecommunications in the last 20 years, including cable and satellite television; teleconferencing and telecommuting (methods of meeting with and working with people at a distance); and the global linkage of computer networks called the **Internet**. Once the preserve of scientists and other specialists, the Internet became accessible to millions through the World Wide Web (1991), a system that allows for interactive "browsing" of text, images, and sound. Hypertext, text linked electronically to enable jumping from one passage to another, and hypermedia, computer-based media that permit jumping between related pieces of content, became familiar catchphrases.

Toward the end of the decade, the Web became a way of bypassing traditional news outlets to share information more directly. That function became prominent during the Monica Lewinsky scandal (see **Bill Clinton**), when many Americans first read the report of Independent Counsel Kenneth Starr on the Web (1998), rather than waiting for journalistic accounts.

As the 1990s progressed, information and telecommunications technologies were viewed as converging, with the various media and delivery vehicles increasingly being integrated. Television programmers and newspaper publishers supplemented their offerings with "on-line editions"; a new generation of equipment was developed that might integrate the computer, the television, and the telephone.

The term *information revolution* is associated with *information age*, a phrase most often used to describe the data-heavy world of the late 20th century. The information age is sometimes considered part of the postindustrial age, marked by **globalization** and a surge in the wealth and power of information industries (see also **Industrial Revolution**). Other related terms are the *information explosion,* which refers to the exponential growth of available data during this period, *and information overload,* the feeling of bombardment by more information than one can use, with corresponding scarcity of the selected information one needs.

International Brigades Volunteer military units that traveled from 53 countries to fight for the Republican cause in the **Spanish Civil War**. Active from 1936 to 1938, they were organized by the **Comintern**, though only about 60 percent of brigade members were Communists. About 60,000 volunteers participated, aiding in such clashes as the siege of Madrid (1936), the Battle of Jaroma (1937), and the Battle of the Ebro (1938). The brigades included the 2,800 Americans who formed the Abraham Lincoln Battalion. The brigades were withdrawn in 1938.

International Monetary Fund (IMF) Specialized agency of the **United Nations** aimed at promoting economic cooperation, world trade, and balance of payment programs within countries. Established in 1945 after the **Bretton Woods Conference** in New Hampshire (1944), it became an agency of the United Nations in 1947 and is headquartered in Washington, D.C. For several years, it has granted loans to developing countries to ensure their economic restructuring, administered with the countries' promises to enact strict corrective practices. Although a United Nations arm, it is independent of the agencies constituting the **World Bank**.

International Style *See* **Architecture**.

Internet Global linkage of **computer** networks, through which the computers can share information electronically. It originated in the U.S. Department of Defense network ARPANET in 1969. Electronic communication was aided by the introduction of electronic mail, or e-mail (1972), and the development of a standard protocol, TCP/IP (1974). In the 1970s and 1980s an increasing number of scientists and universities joined the Internet to communicate electronically. By the 1990s millions of commercial and recreational users joined the Internet as well, many of them accessing it through the system called the World Wide Web. That system, released by CERN, the European Organization for Nuclear Research, in 1991, permits the interactive dissemination of text, images, and sound, and allows users to jump from one Web site or Web page to another through the use of hyperlinks. The Internet contributed to the **communications revolution** and to the **globalization** of cultural and economic life. *also* **information revolution.**

Iran–Contra Affair U.S. political scandal during the presidency of **Ronald Reagan**. In 1985 and 1986 the National Security Council sold arms to Iran in an attempt to free American hostages in Lebanon, a violation of official American policy. A Council aide, Oliver North (1943–), then illegally diverted some of the sales money to Contra rebels who were trying to overthrow the Nicaraguan government. When news broke about the plot, it caused an uproar that damaged Reagan's credibility and prestige. North was found guilty of obstructing Congress but his conviction was later reversed. In 1992 President **George Bush**, implicated but not charged in the scandal, pardoned many officials involved in the affair. In 1994 an independent prosecutor's investigation found no proof that Reagan violated the law but left open the possibility that he may have condoned or abetted a cover-up.

Iran–Iraq War (First Gulf War, 1980–88) Conflict between Iran and Iraq. It was sparked by a border dispute over the Shatt-al-Arab waterway, Iraq's only access to the Persian Gulf. A contributing cause was Iraqi leader **Saddam Hussein's** desire to strengthen his absolute control of Iraq in the face of dissent from Kurdish and Shi'ite populations. An Iraqi offensive in 1980 was followed by an Iranian counteroffensive in 1982; the war developed into one of attrition, in which neither country gained any territory and Iraq resorted to chemical weapons. More than 500,000 people died in the war, with one million wounded.

Iranian Revolution (1979) Iranian overthrow of **Mohammad Reza Shah Pahlavi**. A series of riots and strikes against the autocratic, U.S.–supported shah forced him to flee to Egypt on January 16, 1979. He left a regency council to rule in his absence, but Islamic fundamentalist leader **Ayatollah Khomeini**, exiled in France, sensed its weakness. At the head of a growing movement, Khomeini returned to Iran, where, on February 11, his forces seized power. Khomeini established a theocratic state based on Islamic law, consolidating his power through a reign of terror. He broke relations with the West, showing his contempt for the U.S. by supporting the seizure of hostages at the U.S. embassy at Tehran (November 4, 1979); the hostage-taking militants demanded the return of the shah and his assets to Iran.

The hostage crisis did not end until, with Algerian mediation and U.S. concessions, the hostages were released on January 20, 1981.

Irgun Zionist guerrilla group in Palestine. Known formally as the Irgun Zvai Leumi (National Military Society), it sought to drive both British and Arabs out of Palestine through terrorist acts, such as the bombing of the King David Hotel in Jerusalem (July 22, 1946), which killed 91 people. It was founded in 1931 to fight Palestinian Arabs, but from 1939 it focused on the British. **Menachem Begin** was its leader from 1944 to 1948, when it was incorporated into the Israeli army.

Irish Republican Army Army organized in 1919 to end British rule of Ireland. Its guerrilla campaign resulted in the formation of the Irish Free State in 1922. Many members rejected this settlement, which kept the province of Ulster under British rule, but the new government defeated the IRA "diehards" in 1923. The IRA continued sporadic acts of violence and was outlawed in Ireland in 1931. It continued intermittent bombings and raids but with little success. Support for it grew in the late 1960s, when Catholic civil rights campaigns provoked violent responses from Protestant extremists and British troops were dispatched to Ulster. The group split in 1969, with a faction called the Provisional IRA, or Provos, waging a campaign of bombings and other attacks up until 1994 when it declared a cease-fire. Part of the Provisional IRA resumed bombings and assassinations in England and Northern Ireland in 1996. **Sinn Féin**, the political arm of the IRA, participated in a peace plan approved in an all-Ireland vote in 1998, but implementation of the agreement proved difficult. A faction called the Real IRA continued violent attacks, as did some Protestant paramilitary groups.

Iron Curtain During the **cold war**, the symbolic border between the Democratic-capitalist West and the Communist East. The term was coined by **Winston Churchill** in 1946.

Israeli War of Independence See **Arab–Israeli Wars**.

J

July Plot or **July Conspiracy** (1944) In Germany, unsuccessful attempt by senior military officers to assassinate dictator **Adolf Hitler** and overthrow the Nazi government (*see* **Nazi Party**). On July 20, 1944, a bomb planted under a conference table at Hitler's headquarters at Rastenburg, East Prussia, injured but did not kill Hitler. The planned coup was crushed; 5,000 alleged conspirators—including the bomber, Colonel Claus Schenk von Stauffenberg (1907–44)—were executed. Some, like **Erwin Rommel**, were forced to commit suicide.

K

Kapp Putsch (March 13–17, 1920) Attempted coup against Germany's Weimar Republic. Angered by reductions in the size of the army made in compliance with the Treaty of **Versailles**, paramilitary troops of the **Freikorps** marched on Berlin and established a new government headed by right-wing activist Wolfgang Kapp (1858–1922). The regular army refused to defend the Weimar Republic against the takeover, but a general strike by workers forced the rebels to surrender. The coup showed the reluctance of the army to put down right-wing insurrection.

Katyn Massacre (1940) Mass murder of about 10,000 Polish soldiers at Katyn Forest. The Nazis blamed the Soviet occupation force for the massacre; the Soviets blamed the Nazis. In 1991 Russian president **Boris Yeltsin** verified the widespread belief that the Soviets, under orders from **Joseph Stalin,** had perpetrated the massacre.

Kellogg–Briand Pact (August 27, 1928) Treaty proposed initially between the United States and France but ultimately signed by many nations, agreeing to renounce war and submit international disputes to peaceful arbitration. It was named for its sponsors, U.S. secretary of state Frank B. Kellogg (1856–1937) and French foreign minister **Aristide Briand.** Because the pact included no sanctions for violators, it was useless in controlling Fascist aggression in the 1930s.

KGB Abbreviation of Komitet Gosudarstvennoi Bezopasnosti, Committee of State Security, the Soviet Security Service. Founded in 1954, it was responsible for eliminating internal resistance, conducting espionage, and controlling internal security. It was dissolved in 1991 and replaced by a more modest, streamlined security force.

Khmer Rouge ("Red Khmer") Cambodian political and military organization. Named for the Khmer, Cambodia's dominant ethnic group, it was founded in the 1960s as an outgrowth of Cambodia's Communist Party. Led by **Pol Pot,** it mounted a guerrilla insurgency and took power in 1975. The Khmer Rouge slaughtered more than a million people before being driven out of power by the Vietnamese invasion of 1979. It waged guerrilla war in the 1980s and gained a share of power in the 1990s.

Korean War (1950–53) Conflict between Communist North Korea and U.S.–supported South Korea that developed into a war fought by 20 nations. North Korean troops invaded the South in June 1950; South Korea appealed to the U.S. and the **UN** for help. A predominantly American international force under the command of General Douglas MacArthur did not stop the invaders until September, when an amphibious counterattack at Inchon pushed them back into North Korea. The UN forces invaded the North and neared the Yalu River, which formed the border with Communist China. The Chinese mounted a huge attack that drove the UN forces back into the South. A UN advance in the spring of 1951 reestablished control of South Korea and inaugurated a military stalemate that dragged on until peace talks ended the war in 1953. The Panmunjon armistice established a demilitarized zone between the two Koreas. About 3.5 million people were killed or wounded in the war. This number included, for the U.S., 54,000 killed and 103,000 wounded.

Korean War Deaths	
U.S.[1]	54,246
Other UN allies	3,094
South Korea	415,004
North Korea	700,000
China[2]	900,000

[1] Includes 33,269 battle deaths and 20,617 other deaths.

[2] Includes both killed and wounded. Figures for North Korea and China are estimates.

Kosovo Crisis Conflict between Serbian forces and ethnic Albanians. Since the late 1980s the Serbian-led government of Yugoslavia has controlled the largely ethnic Albanian region of Kosovo. In 1992, when Kosovo voted to secede from Serbia and Yugoslavia, the Serbian government intensified its rule over the area. Western-led efforts at normalization between Yugoslavia and Kosovo resulted in the signing of a normalization agreement in the late 1990s. However, in 1998 Yugoslavian president Slobodan Milosevic broke the agreement and intensified his ongoing program of "ethnic cleansing" of the region. Deportation, widespread killing, and elimination of villages by Serbian forces resulted in the deaths of 1,500 Kosovar Albanians and the exile of 400,000 more. In October 1998 **NATO** (North

American Treaty Organization) representatives attempted diplomatic initiatives and withdrew threats of air strikes. In 1999 Milosevic's intensified acts of ethnic cleansing led NATO to launch its first uninvited offensive against a sovereign nation, a massive bombing campaign against Serbia. A peace accord followed in June 1999, under which NATO peacekeeping forces were permitted to enter Kosovo.

Kristallnacht (Crystal Night or Night of Broken Glass, November 9–10, 1938) Nazi pogrom against Jews in Germany (*see* **Nazi Party**). It was the brainchild of German Nazi politician **Joseph Goebbels,** who conceived it as supposed retaliation against the assassination in Paris of a German Embassy member by a Polish Jew. Kristallnacht was a sustained attack against German Jews that prefigured the **Holocaust.** In one night Nazi-backed German and Austrian SA (Sturmabteilung) forces damaged or destroyed over 7,000 shops and synagogues. More than 90 Jews died and about 30,000 were sent to **concentration camps.** The name refers to the smashed glass of Jewish-owned buildings.

Ku Klux Klan Secret U.S. white supremacist organization aimed at denying rights to nonwhites. The first Klan (1866–69) countered post–Civil War Reconstruction practices through lynchings and other practices in the southern U.S. The second was founded in 1915 in response to increased immigration and reduction in discriminatory political and social laws. Racist, anti-Semitic, and anti-Catholic, it claimed four million to five million members in the 1920s, its rise was aided by a heroic representation in **D. W. Griffith's** *The Birth of a Nation* (1915). Known for their white-hooded garb and practice of cross burning, they spread into the northern U.S. and remained active into the 1960s, fighting civil rights activities. By the end of the century the Klan became largely a fringe organization, associated with far right-wing and neo-Nazi groups.

Kulak In Russia, a peasant with the means to hire labor and lend money. Because they resisted Stalin's collectivization program in the 1920s, the kulaks were eliminated, with between five million and ten million killed or deported to Siberia.

Kuomintang *See* **Guomindang.**

Kurdistan Region of southwest Asia inhabited by the Kurds, a non-Arab, mostly Sunni Muslim people. At the end of **World War I,** the Treaty of Sèvres (1920) promised autonomy for Kurdistan, formerly part of the Ottoman Empire. The Kurds saw that promise vanish when the Treaty of Lausanne (1923) superseded Sèvres. Kurdistan was divided among Turkey, Iraq, and Iran, with smaller sections going to Syria and Armenia. The presence of oil in Kurdistan has made the region's governments loath to part with any of the land. Throughout the 20th century, Kurds seeking autonomy have frequently rebelled: against Turkey, Iraq, and Iran in the 1920s and 1930s; and against Iraq in the 1960s. In 1970 Iraq promised local autonomy for Kurds but soon broke the promise. Kurds rebelled against Iraq during the **Iran-Iraq War** (1980–88), but the rebellion was crushed, partly through the use of **chemical weapons.** After the **Gulf War** (1990–91), northern Iraq was declared a **UN** "safe haven" for Kurds, allowing them de facto autonomy there, with parliamentary elections held in 1992. However, Iraqi leader **Saddam Hussein** soon reasserted some control over the region.

L

Labor Movement Organizations and actions of workers throughout the world aimed at improving working conditions, benefits, and payment for services. After forming in large numbers during the 19th century, labor unions sought ways to increase their influence during the early 20th century.

With that aim the first international labor union federation was formed in 1901, the International Federation of Trade Unions (IFTU). Founded by the Communist-led Second Socialist International, it represented nearly half of the world's union members by 1920. Beginning in 1921 with the formation of a splinter Communist union association, the IFTU was weakened by lost membership and internal dissention and disbanded in 1945. Replacing it in 1945 was the World Federation of Trade Unions (WFTU), an association of Communist and non-Communist unions. In 1949 non-Communist unions broke ranks to form the International Confederation of Free Trade Unions (ICFTU). Among other aims, both have worked to increase union membership in **Third World** countries.

From the 19th century U.S. labor unions were united through several national federations, with the Knights of Labor (founded 1869) and the American Federation of Labor (AFL, founded 1886) active after 1900. The Knights of Labor, an umbrella association organized by industry, had declined greatly since its blame for the Haymarket Square Riot (1886) and several strikes, and disbanded in 1917. Its place was taken primarily by the American Federation of Labor (AFL), which was organized by craft rather than industry. Under the leadership of **Samuel Gompers** and others, the AFL gained improvements on issues of child labor, hours, and benefits, while avoiding socialist involvement and acquiring respect for organized labor. Following years of internal conflict over organization by craft, AFL member **John L. Lewis** formed a splinter organization, the Committee for Industrial Organization. After being dropped from the AFL it became the Congress of Industrial Organizations (CIO) in 1938. Although both groups achieved success through the 1940s, they faced antilabor sentiment in the 1950s and merged in 1955, forming the **AFL–CIO**. Its first president was American activist and AFL president George Meany (1894–1980).

While other unions have been more long-lived, the **Industrial Workers of the World** (IWW) gained lasting notoriety in the U.S. during the early century for its radical stance and militant actions in support of **syndicalism**. Founded in 1905, it was composed largely of unskilled workers and staged many dozens of strikes before facing government prosecution and loss of power during the 1920s.

In 20th-century Europe, unions became better organized than they had in the 19th century and achieved greater influence. Among them are the Confédération Générale du Travail (GCT) in France and Christian trade unions in Belgium, the Netherlands, and elsewhere. Unions have also seen their goals represented through political parties, such as the Labour Party in Britain and Australia and the Social Democratic Party (SPD) in Germany. In Poland the Solidarnosc (Solidarity) trade union movement became a strong opponent of the Communist government, taking power once open elections were held in 1989.

Labour Party British political party with socialist tenets. The party had its origins in the Labour Representation Committee, founded in 1900, which was organized to gain government representation for the newly enfranchised working class. Active in its creation was British politician **James Ramsay MacDonald**, who was elected to the House of Commons in 1906. From 1906, the committee was renamed the Labour Party; it elected its first members of Parliament in 1924.

During the 1920s Labour became the official opposition party to the **Conservative Party** and lobbied throughout **World War II** for increased nationalization. When the Labour Party first established a Parliament majority (1945–51) under **Clement Attlee** it instituted several social reforms, including increases in social security and national health insurance

(National Health Service). Since then, the party gained majority rule from 1964 to 1970 and from 1974 to 1976, under **James Harold Wilson**.

Facing ideological differences in 1981, right-leaning members left the party to begin the Social Democratic Party. This split the party and prevented it from winning majority rule in the 1980s. The party regained majority rule in 1994 under the leadership of **Tony Blair**, who updated the party by decreasing focus on social welfare programs and increasing concern for the middle class. He renamed it New Labour.

Lateran Treaties Agreement signed February 11, 1929, between **Benito Mussolini** and Pope **Pius XI** that resolved territorial issues active since the unification of Italy (1860–70), which made papal-run territories part of the Italian state. The treaty set up the independent state of Vatican City and restored to the papacy many churches and the papal summer residence. For its part the Catholic Church abandoned its opposition to the secular Italian state. In related treaties, Italy agreed to pay the pope 1.75 billion liras for the loss of the Papal States and declared Roman Catholicism the state religion.

Lausanne, Treaty of (July 24, 1923) Agreement between Turkey and the Allied countries in **World War I**. It allowed Turkey to become the only defeated country to negotiate terms for itself that differed from the peace terms dictated by the Allies. Under the agreement, Turkey was relieved of reparations payments. In addition, some elements of the Treaty of Sèvres were modified in Turkey's favor, including the recovery of Greek-controlled eastern Thrace, the Dardanelles, and portions of Smyrna. Also, populations were transferred between Greece and Turkey, with one million Greeks moved from Turkey and 350,000 Turks from Greece (*see also* **Paris Peace Conference**).

League of Nations International organization. It was formed in 1919 to settle international disputes, protect member nations against aggression, and end the system of secret alliances that helped start **World War I**. It also administered the mandate system through which the former colonies of Germany and Turkey were ruled by member nations. The League was weakened when the American Senate refused to allow the U.S. to join even though President **Woodrow Wilson** was one of the organization's main architects. During the 1920s the League mediated some minor disputes, but in the 1930s it could not stop the aggressions of the **Soviet Union**, Italy, Japan, and Germany. The League entered a limbo state during **World War II** and was replaced by the **UN** in 1945.

Lebensraum (German, "living space") Nazi theory (*see* **Nazi Party**). It justified annexation of other countries, particularly to the east, on the basis of the "need" of the Aryan, or German, people for more space in which to dwell and prosper.

Lend-Lease Program through which the U.S. provided over $50 billion worth of arms, food, and other materials to countries fighting Germany, Japan, and Italy during **World War II**. The plan was prompted by Great Britain's need for help against Nazi Germany after the fall of France in 1940. Convoys began delivering materials in April 1941, eight months before the U.S. entered the war. Britain received about half of all Lend-Lease aid while the **Soviet Union** received one-fifth. France, China, and over 38 other countries also benefited. Recipient nations partially repaid the U.S. by supplying American armed forces with bases and materials overseas and by opening up their markets to American trade.

Liberalism Political theory founded on the rights of the individual. Rooted in the thinking of 17th-century English philosopher John Locke (1632–1704), it argues for civil and political liberties and for government by law with the consent of the governed. During the

cold war, liberal democracies, such as those of the U.S. and Western Europe, were the principal adversaries of **Communism**, which they saw as a threat to liberal principles. Communism was also considered a threat to the economic system of **capitalism**—though in practice many 20th-century liberal democracies combined capitalist private enterprise with **socialist** institutions. In the U.S. *liberal* acquired the additional meaning of being politically and socially progressive and favoring government intervention to promote social welfare. In these senses it was opposed to *conservative* and became a somewhat pejorative term with the ascent of the Republican right wing in the 1980s and 1990s.

Likud (Union) Party Israeli political party. The hard-line nationalist party was founded in 1973 as an alliance of right-wing parties. Led by **Menachem Begin**, it came to power in 1977, ending the domination of Israeli politics by socialist parties such as Labor. Despite Begin's role in concluding peace with Egypt in the **Camp David accords**, the party generally regarded Arab states and Palestinians with distrust and antagonism and encouraged Jewish settlement in occupied lands.

Literature   Naturalism, **modernism**, and social realism dominated the written word in the first decades of the century. **Joseph Conrad**, U.S. writer Jack London (1876–1916), and **Rudyard Kipling** used the adventure story to explore society or the human psyche. Authors commenting on western **capitalism** included U.S. writer Frank Norris (1870–1902), **Theodore Dreiser, Upton Sinclair**, and **Sinclair Lewis**. Frontier experiences were captured in the works of **Willa Cather**, while established society was studied by **Edith Wharton**. British writers included **E. M. Forster, Ford Madox Ford, D. H. Lawrence**, and **Virginia Woolf**, who exemplified modernism and commented on the post-Victorian era. Irish literature gained importance through the poetry of **William Butler Yeats** and the short stories and novels of **James Joyce**. Joyce's use of autobiography and stream-of-consciousness influenced literary writing throughout the century. German writers included **Thomas Mann** and **Franz Kafka**. The poetry and fiction of Indian writer **Rabindranath Tagore** was prized in his country and influenced western writers including Yeats and **Ezra Pound**. Nonfiction was marked by the investigative works of U.S. **muckrakers** including **Ida Tarbell** and **Lincoln Steffens** and U.S. journalists including **H. L. Mencken**. A central U.S. social and literary critic was **Edmund Wilson**.

World War I, the excesses of the 1920s, and the **Great Depression** yielded literature marked by disillusionment and soul searching. In the forefront were U.S. novelists and short story writers **Ernest Hemingway, F. Scott Fitzgerald**, and **William Faulkner**. U.S. authors commenting on society included **John Dos Passos, John Steinbeck**, and others. Bringing academic sensibility to poetry was **T. S. Eliot**. Latin American writers included avant-garde storytellers such as **Jorge Luis Borges**, realists like Brazilian novelist Jorge Amado (1912–), and surrealists such as Chilean poet Pablo Neruda (1904–73). Yet despite this international experimentation, the best-selling novel in North America between the two world wars was the Civil War saga *Gone with the Wind* (1936) by an unknown writer named **Margaret Mitchell**.

Darkness and irony characterized much of post–**World War II** English language writing. Notable U.S. post–World War II fiction writers included Saul Bellow (1915–), John Cheever (1912–82), **Norman Mailer, Mary McCarthy**, and **John Updike**. British writers of the era included **Kingsley Amis, Doris Lessing**, and **Graham Greene**. Latin American writers gained prominence, popularizing the literary form of magic realism. Among these writers were **Gabriel García Márquez** and Peruvian writer Mario Vargas

Llosa (1936–). African writers, often addressing social injustices, included **Chinua Achebe**, **Wole Soyinka**, and others. Postwar nonfiction writers dealing with the problem of evil as demonstrated by the **Holocaust**, were **Hannah Arendt**, **Primo Levi**, **Elie Wiesel**, and others. Writing about the philosophy of **existentialism** were **Jean-Paul Sartre**, **Simone De Beauvoir**, and **Albert Camus**. Major poets of the era included **Robert Frost**, and **Wallace Stevens**.

In the 1980s and 1990s fiction writers continued to explore the experience of the outsider or observer in society. Notable British authors included **Martin Amis** and A. S. Byatt (1936–). Canadian authors included Robertson Davies (1913–). U.S. writers included Richard Ford (1944–), Don DeLillo, and **Philip Roth**. Strong representation of the African-American experience was provided by **Toni Morrison** and **Alice Walker**. South African writers included **Nadine Gordimer** and J. M. Coetzee (1940–). Mexican writers included **Carlos Fuentes**. In nonfiction, memoirs and essays gained popularity, with notable authors including U.S. writers Annie Dillard (1945–) and Cynthia Ozick (1928–). English-language poets included U.S. writers Galway Kinnell (1927–), Richard Wilbur (1921–) and Philip Levine (1928–).

Little Entente Alliance system among Yugoslavia, Czechoslovakia, and Romania. It was built by a series of treaties in the early 1920s and consolidated by the Treaty of Belgrade in 1929. The name echoed the **Triple Entente** of pre–**World War I** Europe. The members pledged mutual aid in deterring Hungary and Austria from reclaiming territory lost in World War I. France supported the alliance because of Czechoslovakia's long border with Germany. In 1937 Czechoslovakia, menaced by Germany, tried unsuccessfully to obtain pledges of mutual military support against aggression. The alliance dissolved when France and Britain failed to stop Germany from annexing the **Sudetenland** region of Czechoslovakia in 1938.

Locarno, Pact of Agreements discussed in October 1925 and signed in December 1925 in Locarno, Switzerland, by Belgium, Czechoslovakia, France, Germany, Great Britain, Italy, and Poland to set common borders and the status of the Rhineland. Under the agreement the borders for Belgium, France, and Germany mandated by the Treaty of **Versailles** (1919) were maintained. Also, although borders between Czechoslovakia, Germany, and Poland were not made final, the countries agreed not to seek to change them by force. In addition, the Rhineland region was assured its demilitarized status.

Germany's signing of the pact allowed its entry into the **League of Nations** as a permanent member, and the pact itself generated hope for a period of international peace. However, the "spirit of Locarno" remained only until 1936, when Germany remilitarized the Rhineland, prefiguring **World War II**.

London, Treaty of (1915) Secret agreement in which Russia, Britain, and France promised territorial gains to Italy if it entered **World War I** on the Allied side. The promised awards included Trentino, Trieste, Istria, a portion of the Dalmatian coast, control of Albania, colonies in Africa, and Turkish areas, including the Dodecanese Islands. After the war several of these promises were broken; Italy failed to gain Albania, the Dalmatian coast, or any African territory. **Benito Mussolini** made use of Italian outrage over the treaty violations in his rise to power.

Long March (1934–35) Military retreat by Chinese Communist troops. Defeated by **Guomindang** forces at Juangxi in 1934, Mao Zedong and his Communist forces marched

6,000 miles northwest to Shensi. Along the way they repeatedly battled Guomindang forces. Of about 100,000 who started the march, only 30,000 survived. Many future leaders of the Communist government, including **Mao Zedong** and **Zhou Enlai**, took part.

Lusitania British ocean liner sunk by a German submarine on May 7, 1915. Nearly 1,200 people died, including 128 U.S. citizens. The disaster eliminated most of the sympathy for Germany that had existed in the United States, helping to prepare the U.S. for entry into **World War I**.

M

Magic Realism *See* **Literature.**

Maginot Line System of fortifications on France's border with Germany, extending from Switzerland to Belgium. Named for its principal instigator, French minister of war André Maginot (1877–1932), and erected in 1929–32, it was considered impregnable. However, in 1940, during **World War II**, it proved useless as the Germans outflanked it, invading France instead through the Ardennes Mountains of southern Belgium.

Manhattan Project Name for the U.S. plan to develop a nuclear bomb. U.S. interest in developing a nuclear bomb arose in 1939 with reports that German scientists had achieved atomic fission. Upon the suggestion of **Albert Einstein** and others, President **Franklin Delano Roosevelt** sanctioned a research program, which was expanded in 1941 by the Office of Scientific Research and Development. In 1942, after American physicist Ernest Lawrence (1901–58) discovered that atomic fission could be more relatively achieved through some radioactive materiel, President Roosevelt approved the creation of the atomic bomb. From then on the program was known as the Manhattan Project, after the army section—the Manhattan District— that coordinated it.

Within months the Manhattan Project expanded nationwide. In December 1942 at the University of Chicago, the first chain reaction in uranium was successfully completed. In 1943 a research site was established in Los Alamos, N.Mex., headed by American physicist **J. Robert Oppenheimer**. Materials were produced at plants in Oak Ridge, Tenn.

On July 16, 1945, the first test explosion (a plutonium device) successfully took place at Alamogordo, N.Mex. On August 6, 1945, two months after the death of President Roosevelt (April 12) and the swearing in of President **Harry S Truman**, Truman ordered the atomic bomb to be dropped on **Hiroshima**, Japan. The second bomb was dropped on Nagasaki, Japan, on August 9, 1945.

Mapai (Mifleget Poalei Eretz Yisrael, or Israel Workers' Party) Israeli democratic socialist party founded in 1930 and led until the early 1960s by David Ben-Gurion (1886–1973). In 1968 it allied with two other like-minded parties to form the Labor Party. From independence until 1977, Mapai and its successor, Labor, were Israel's ruling party.

March on Rome (October 1922) Means used by Fascist leader **Benito Mussolini** to take power in Italy. Mussolini mobilized his **blackshirt** supporters for a march on Rome to seize power in a coup. Instead of opposing him, King Victor Emmanuel III (1869–1947; reigned 1900–46) offered Mussolini the premiership rather than risk civil war. Mussolini's supporters marched on Rome to celebrate his acquisition of power.

Marshall Plan U.S. economic relief program for European countries ravaged in **World War II**, implemented from 1948 to 1952. Officially called the European Recovery

Program, it was popularly named for U.S. General **George Catlett Marshall**, who introduced the program at Harvard in 1947. The plan was conceived and administered by American politician **Dean Acheson** and the U.S. State Department. The U.S. aim was to avoid Communist domination of an economically distressed Europe by rebuilding the European economies. In all the U.S. provided 13 billion dollars in aid.

Mau Mau Uprising (1952–56) Kenyan guerrilla war. The Mau Mau Society was a Kenyan guerrilla organization associated with the Kikuyu people and dedicated to ending British colonial rule. In 1952 it began a large-scale campaign against British settlements and plantations. British troops defeated the uprising in 1956, but it prompted Britain to increase black African representation and speed progress toward Kenyan independence, which came in 1963.

May Fourth Movement (1919) Chinese nationalist movement. It began in Beijing on May 4, 1919, when university students protested provisions of the **Versailles** Treaty that awarded German territory in China to Japan. A wave of demonstrations, boycotts, and intensive discussion followed. Activists urged government reform and social modernization; different camps urged the adoption of Western liberal and Communist ideas. The movement resulted in the birth of China's **Guomindang** (Nationalist) and Communist Parties.

Media *See* **Information Revolution.**

Medicine Science and art of preventing and treating disease and promoting health. At the dawn of the 20th century, few effective cures for specific diseases were known, but the new century brought many such therapies. Armed with the germ theory of disease (discovered in the 19th century), scientists and physicians determined the microbes responsible for many diseases and developed ways to combat them. Virology, the study of viruses, became an established science by the 1930s, the decade when the electron microscope made it possible to see these tiny microorganisms for the first time. Vaccines were introduced for such diseases as influenza, polio, measles, and mumps. Antibiotics were invented to combat bacterial infection, with sulfa drugs and pure penicillin both discovered in the 1930s. Public health officials used the knowledge of the causes of disease to mount effective campaigns to improve sanitation and change unhealthy behavior.

The discovery of X rays in 1895 led to a new age in which physicians could peer inside the

---

Infant Mortality Worldwide

The benefits of modern medicine have not been equally distributed around the world. Below are six world regions, listed by infant mortality rate.

Region	Infant mortality rate (per 1,000 live births)	
Northern America	7	
Europe	12	
Oceania	24	
Latin America and Caribbean	35	
Asia	56	*Source:* United Nations Population Fund,
Africa	86	*The State of World Population 1997*
World	57	(1997)

Annual Death Rates in the U.S., 1900–90

One indicator of the success of 20th-century medicine is the decline in mortality since 1900. Below is the annual death rate (per 100,000 population) in the U.S. by decade from 1900 to 1990.

Year	Rate
1900	17.2
1910	14.7
1920	13.0
1930	11.3
1940	10.8
1950	9.6
1960	9.5
1970	9.5
1980	8.7
1990	8.6

Sources: Dept. of Health and Human Services, National Center for Health Statistics

bodies of patients to diagnose maladies and plan surgery. Later imaging techniques included ultrasound, CAT (computerized axial tomography) scanning, PET (positron emission tomography) scanning, and MRI (magnetic resonance imaging); all but ultrasound (1950s) were introduced in the 1970s and 1980s.

Surgical advances were made: organ transplants became possible through new research in immunology and the phenomenon of tissue rejection. The discovery of blood types, beginning in 1901 with Austrian pathologist Karl Landsteiner (1868–1943), made blood transfusions safe. Nutritional diseases could be treated thanks to the new theory of vitamins (1912). Hormone therapy was developed for conditions such as diabetes and thyroid disease. Psychotropic drugs were used to treat mental disorders, while new understanding developed of the functioning of the brain and nervous system. The discovery of DNA (1953) and the development of genetic engineering (1973) gave medical science new tools in fighting disease. These tools included gene therapy, genetic screening, and therapy with human hormones grown in bulk in genetically engineered organisms.

The century's advances in medical science were a boon for humanity, but they did not come without costs. Increases in longevity and decreases in infant mortality contributed to the **population explosion.** Cancer and heart disease became more common causes of fatality as deaths from infectious disease declined. At the close of the century, new infectious diseases appeared, most notably **AIDS**, that were difficult to combat; old diseases, such as tuberculosis, mounted a comeback, with increased resistance to antibiotics. Reliant on high technology and costly drugs, Western medicine became exorbitantly expensive, raising the price of good health beyond the means of many people. The issue of whether the government should provide universal health insurance, and how it could afford to do so, became a pressing matter in the U.S. and other countries. The benefits of Western medicine remained out of the reach of many in the **Third World**. Even in the West, some people felt that modern medicine was too cold, expensive, and focused on disease rather than health. Sentiments like these spurred the growth of holistic and alternative medicine movements.

Mensheviks ("members of the minority") Russian revolutionary party. When the Russian Social Democratic Workers' Party split in 1903, this faction was in the majority but was deemed the "minority" by **V. I. Lenin** and the **Bolsheviks**, who won some key votes. More moderate than the Bolsheviks, the Mensheviks believed in a loosely organized mass party and argued that Russia must pass through a bourgeois-democratic stage before proceeding to socialist revolution. The Mensheviks, led by **Georgy Plekhanov**, took part in the **Aleksandr Kerensky** provisional government of 1917. After the November **Revolution of 1917**, they were suppressed by the Bolsheviks.

Mexican Revolution (1910–40) Rebellion and armed conflict between national troops and antigovernment peasants and workers. In 1910 a challenge to longstanding dictator **Porfirio Díaz** (from 1876) by Mexican politician Francisco I. Madero (1873–1913) sparked an armed rebellion among peasants that spread nationwide. The rebellion, fueled by economic iniquities and state-encouraged dispossession of peasants and workers, brought about Diaz's resignation in 1911. Madero, his successor, was unable to quell the rebellion, which was led in the southwest part of the country by **Emiliano Zapata** and in the north by **Pancho Villa**. A resistance movement arose, and its leader, Venustiano Carranza (1859–1920), proclaimed himself president of Mexico in 1913. Following the overthrow and murder (1913) of Madero by his military chief of staff, Victoriano Huerta (1854–1916), and Huerta's resignation in 1914, Carranza took full power. From 1914 to 1919 Villa and Zapata joined forces and led peasant armies against Carranza for control of the country and the implementation of agrarian reforms. In 1917 Carranza (elected provisional president, 1917–20) supervised the writing of a new constitution favoring workers' rights and redistribution of land.

Revolutionary unrest continued, with Zapata, Carranza, and Villa all assassinated by 1923. By then, the revolution's most violent phase was over. The last leader to commit himself fully to the promises of the revolution was **Lázaro Cárdenas**, president from 1934 to 1940.

Modernism Collective term for innovative movements in the arts and literature of the late 19th and early 20th century. Modernist artists and writers rebelled against traditional forms and invented new ones. In literature, modernists included such stylistic innovators as **Joseph Conrad, Virginia Woolf, James Joyce, Gertrude Stein, Ezra Pound**, and **T. S. Eliot**. In Spanish-speaking countries, a literary movement called *modernismo* emphasized finely wrought language and imagery; its leading practitioner was Nicaraguan poet and essayist Rubén Darío, 1867–1916.

In the visual arts, modernism produced abstract art, new uses of color, and the varied works of **Pablo Picasso, Alexander Calder, Piet Mondrian**, and **Joan Miró**. In music, **Arnold Schoenberg**'s atonality and **Igor Stravinsky**'s narrative experimentation were aspects of modernism. Modernism also affected dance, architecture, and other artistic forms.

Various intellectual trends influenced modernism, including **psychoanalysis, relativity**, and religious skepticism. Modernism is often considered to have given way to postmodernism after **World War II**, though the influence of modernist styles and presuppositions remained strong.

The term *modernism* also refers to a late 19th or early 20th century religious movement to interpret Christian texts and principles in the context of contemporary criticism, science, and philosophy. The result was often declining belief in the literal truth of dogma and rising emphasis on humanistic aspects of religion. A related Roman Catholic theological movement called Modernism was condemned by Pope **Pius X** as heretical (1907).

Moroccan Crises Two international confrontations that occurred when Germany challenged French colonial interests in Morocco by publicly supporting Moroccan independence. The first crisis (1905) led to the Algeciras Conference (1906), in which France, with British support, effectively retained its control of Morocco. The second crisis (1911) arose when the German gunboat *Panther* was sent to the Moroccan port of Agadir. This conflict was resolved when Germany recognized French hegemony in Morocco in return for French territorial concessions in the Congo. Both crises contributed to the tensions that erupted in **World War I**.

Motion Pictures The art form of recording movement on film, usually to tell a story, and the industry involved in creating and distributing completed works. Motion pictures were pioneered in the late 19th century by French chemists Louis (1864–1948) and Auguste (1862–1954) Lumière, among others. The first narrative film is generally credited as the work of American director Edwin S. Porter (1870–1941) in his eight-minute *The Great Train Robbery* (1903), which introduced film editing and launched movies as popular entertainment. American filmmakers soon took pre-eminence in filmmaking. Major studios were situated in New York, and the medium's most influential director was American **D. W. Griffith**. He pioneered the use of lighting, variety of composition, and filters to evoke emotion. His highly successful *The Birth of a Nation* (1915) introduced the idea of film as an art form.

Between 1910 and 1920, American filmmaking shifted to Hollywood, where hundreds of films were made by American filmmakers such as Thomas Harper Ince (1882–1924), **Cecil B. De Mille**, and **Mack Sennett**. Sennett pioneered film slapstick comedy with the Keystone Cops and introduced English comic Charlie Chaplin, who, as the forlorn Tramp, became film's first international star.

During the 1920s, filmmaking became a major American business and an increasingly sophisticated art form. Leading directors such as **Ernst Lubitsch** and **John Ford** offered a variety of films marked by technical proficiency and a popular sensibility. German filmmaking was marked by expressionist works by Fritz Lang and others. Russian directors **Sergey Eisenstein** and Vsevolod Pudovkin (1893–1953) developed the idea of *montage*, used in Eisenstein's *Potemkin* (1925). French directors included René Clair (1898–1981) and Abel Gance (1889–1981).

The 1927 U.S. film *The Jazz Singer* introduced sound to movies and revolutionized the industry worldwide. Wit- and action-oriented films like screwball comedies and gangster movies were popular fare, as were spectacles such as musicals and literary adaptations. American studios built the industry through their efficient studio system of film production. The system reached its apex in 1939 with the Civil War epic *Gone with the Wind* (1939). Notable pre–**World War II** European directors included Jean Renoir and Leni Riefenstahl (1902–).

World War II and afterward was marked by the international movement of neorealism, introduced by Italian directors Roberto Rossellini (1906–77) and **Vittorio De Sica**. American social realist films included *On the Waterfront* (1953). Countering realism were idiosyncratic stylists, including Italian director **Federico Fellini**, Swedish director **Ingmar Bergman**, and Spanish director Luis Buñuel.

In the 1950s and 1960s a group of French directors introduced the *nouvelle vague* (new wave) of French cinema, capturing modern French life. Directors included François

Most Popular Films in the U.S., by Decade (as of March 9, 1998)

Title (year)	Director	$ in millions
pre-1930		
The Birth of a Nation (1915)	D. W. Griffith	$10.0
1930–39		
Gone with the Wind (1939)	V. Fleming	$77.6
1940–49		
Cinderella (1949)	(Animated)	$38.5
1950–59		
The Ten Commandments (1956)	C. B. DeMille	$43.0
1960–69		
The Sound of Music (1965)	R. Wise	$79.98
1970–79		
Star Wars (1977)	G. Lucas	$460.94
1980–89		
E.T.: The Extra-Terrestrial (1982)	S. Spielberg	$228.17
1990–99		
Titanic (1997)	J. Cameron	$449.16

Sources: *The New York Times Almanac*; Internet Movie Database; *Variety* Web site

Truffaut (1932–84) and **Jean-Luc Godard**. Postwar German cinema offered the social critiques of directors Werner Herzog (1942–) and **Rainer Werner Fassbinder**. Postwar non-Western cinema gained an international following the works of Japanese directors **Akira Kurosawa** and **Yasujiro Ozu** and Indian filmmaker **Satyajit Ray**.

In the U.S., changing tastes and business takeovers ended the American studio system by the end of the 1960s. In its wake came increased experimentation and independence in films by Robert Altman (1925–), **Francis Ford Coppola**, and **Martin Scorsese**. In recent years, independent studios have become known for original filmmaking and wide industry influence. Since the 1970s American cinema has also been known for big-budget blockbusters, which rely heavily on special effects and often aim at young audiences. These include many of the films of **George Lucas** and **Steven Spielberg**, along with 1997's *Titanic*, written and directed by James Cameron (1954–).

Muckrakers Term applied to a group of American journalists during the early 20th century whose reform-minded, investigative works exposed corruption in big business and public policy. In magazines such as *McClure's* and *Collier's*, exposés included **Lincoln Steffens** on corruption in city governments; **Ida S. Tarbell** on **John D. Rockefeller's** monopolistic Standard Oil; and **Upton Sinclair** on the unsanitary practices of the meat-packing business. The works, often later published in book form, influenced U.S. regulatory acts, such as the Pure Food and Drug Act and the Hepburn Act of 1906, for railroad regulation. The term *muckraker* derives from 17th-century British writer **John Bunyan's** *Pilgrim's*

Progress. Its modern usage was inspired by U.S. president **Theodore Roosevelt**, who considered the reporters' goals germane but their practices little more than "raking the muck."

Mujahidin (Arabic, "holy warriors") Islamic groups who formed a coalition in response to the Soviet invasion of Afghanistan. With military aid from the U.S., they mounted a guerrilla war that forced Soviet armed forces out of Afghanistan in 1989 and toppled the Communist government in 1992. The Mujahidin who won the war soon split into factions; by 1996, most of the country was under the control of the disciplined, fundamentalist Islamic group the Taliban.

Multiculturalism In the United States, movement to increase awareness of other cultures besides those originating in western Europe. Begun in the 1960s, the movement has resulted in such curriculum reforms as the creation of ethnic studies departments at many universities. Multiculturalism is associated with the tendency to identify oneself not solely as an American but as a hyphenated American (e.g., an African-American or Hispanic-American), with traditions and interests not necessarily held in common with other Americans.

Munich Agreement (July 29, 1938) Pact granting the **Sudetenland** districts of Czechoslovakia to Germany. Signed by British prime minister **Neville Chamberlain**, French prime minister **Édouard Daladier**, German head of state **Adolf Hitler**, and Italian prime minister **Benito Mussolini**, it was meant to restore peaceful relations to Europe. Less than a year later (March 1939), Hitler invaded and seized Czechoslovakia.

Music At the beginning of the 20th century, classical composers were challenging the formal ideal set by German composer Ludwig van Beethoven (1770–1827) and the romanticism of Russian composer Peter Ilich Tchaikovsky (1840–93) and others. Composers experimenting with harmony and form during the first few decades of the century included **Gustav Mahler**, **Jean Sibelius**, **Igor Stravinsky**, **Arnold Schoenberg**, and others.

Popular music in the early century was played in music halls as well as in more casual gatherings. The musical, which originated in England in the late 19th century, and particularly, the **radio**, offered huge possibilities for popularizing songs on a mass level. Notable early composers of the musical included **George M. Cohan**, **Irving Berlin**, **Jerome Kern**, and **George** and Ira **Gershwin**.

Jazz music saw its beginnings in the work songs and spirituals of African-Americans during the late 19th century. By the 1920s its African rhythms and harmonies were popularized in major northern U.S. cities by **Louis Armstrong** and others. At the same time, the emotionally direct form known as the blues arose through the works of U.S. composer W. C. Handy (1873–1958) and performers including **Bessie Smith**. Syncopated ragtime music was widely popular in the U.S. before **World War I**, with its leading composer Scott Joplin (1868–1917). Borrowing from all the new musical styles were the composers of Louisiana-based Dixieland jazz, who included U.S. musician Jelly Roll Morton (1885–1941).

In the 1930s a fast-paced music called swing dominated popular tastes. Played by large ensembles led by U.S. musician Count Basie (1904–84), **Duke Ellington**, **Benny Goodman**, and others, the music ushered in the big-band era. The big-band sound, smoother than swing, was popularized by the bands of **Glenn Miller** and U.S. musician Tommy Dorsey (1905–56). In the 1950s the big-band was eclipsed by the individual pop singer, a trend begun by **Frank Sinatra**, a former big-band singer himself.

In the 1940s a new harmonic jazz style known as bop evolved. Also known as bebop, its major innovators included **Charlie Parker** and **Dizzy Gillespie**. In its later incarnation as hard bop, it was represented by **John Coltrane**. Progressive jazz, a cooler incarnation of bop, was developed by U.S. musician Lester Young (1909–59) and others.

Classical music during the mid to late century was marked in part by experimentation in sources and musicality. Innovators included British composer Benjamin Britten (1913–76), **Gian Carlo Menotti**, U.S. composer Elliott Carter (1908–), and **Philip Glass**.

With his 1956 songs "Heartbreak Hotel," "Hound Dog," and others, **Elvis Presley** introduced the musical form called rock 'n' roll. Through Presley, who dominated the genre for several years, rock 'n' roll displayed its roots in country-and-western and, particularly, the rhythm-and-blues music of Chuck Berry (1926–) and Little Richard (1932–), among others. In 1963 the Beatles, a British rock group, began its dominance in popular music with three U.K. number one hit songs including "She Loves You," "From Me to You," and "I Want to Hold Your Hand." Already hugely popular in Europe in 1963, the Beatles gained North American prominence after their appearance on U.S. television and the release of their records in the U.S. Led by songwriters **John Lennon** and Paul McCartney, the Beatles commanded the rock 'n' roll audience until the group's demise in 1970, with songs including "Yesterday" and "Hey Jude."

Also popular during the 1960s was folk music, by practitioners often reflecting views of political protest, including **Bob Dylan** and Simon and Garfunkel. From Detroit, Mich., in the 1960s came a polished pop-soul music called the Motown Sound. It featured performers including the Supremes and the Temptations. In the 1970s a dance-inspired music known as disco gained some foothold in popular music, while punk rock began to express the anger and alienation of contemporary youth.

By the end of the century, many types of music have become popular, each representing different social and ethnic interests. The mass representation associated with Tin Pan Alley and rock 'n' roll has diminished. In the 1990s music known as grunge gained vogue, with groups including Nirvana and Pearl Jam. Country music broadened an already expanding audience, with artists such as U.S musician Garth Brooks (1962–). World music, reflecting various musical cultures, also gained popularity. Examples include Afro-pop and Latin music. African-American–based music styles known as rap and hip-hop also gained considerable influence, with innovators including U.S. musicians Tupac Shakur (1971–96) and Lauryn Hill (1975–).

Muslim Brotherhood Muslim religious and political movement. It was founded in Egypt in 1928 by schoolteacher Hasan al-Banna (1906–49) to revive Islamic faith and to press for a theocracy based on Islamic law. In the 1930s and 1940s it turned to paramilitary activity and terrorism, violently opposing Western influence. In 1948 a member of the group killed Egyptian prime minister Mahmoud Fahmy el-Nokrachy (1882–1948), leading to Hasan's assassination. The movement survived him and became active in other Arab countries.

Muslim League Indian Muslim political organization. It was founded as the All India Muslim League in 1906. It cooperated with the Indian National Congress and its leader **Mohandas Gandhi** in opposing British rule. But in 1940, the Muslim League's leader, **Mohammed Ali Jinnah**, split with the congress by demanding the establishment of an independent Muslim state. The league's efforts helped bring about the creation of Pakistan (1947), but the organization did not long survive, splintering into different groups in the 1950s.

My Lai Massacre (March 16, 1968) Slaughter of 200 to 400 unarmed Vietnamese civilians, many of them women and children, by American troops in the village of My Lai, Vietnam, during the **Vietnam War**. The American public did not learn of the incident until late 1969. Thirteen soldiers were charged with war crimes; 12 were indicted for trying to cover up the atrocities. Lieutenant William L. Calley Jr. (1943–), the only soldier found guilty of any crime, was convicted of murdering 22 people. He was sentenced to life at hard labor but after several appeals was released in 1974. The incident led to increased demands for an American withdrawal from Vietnam.

N

NAACP (National Association for the Advancement of Colored People) American civil rights organization. It was established in 1909 by African-American and white activists to fight racial discrimination, improve economic opportunities for black Americans, and protect black Americans' civil rights. Its main publication, the *Crisis*, featured articles on cultural, economic, and legal issues related to civil rights. In its early years the NAACP campaigned against lynching and lobbied to secure voting rights for African-Americans. Its most noted triumph was the 1954 Supreme Court decision *Brown v. the Board of Education of Topeka*, which abolished legal segregation in public schools. The NAACP helped organize the famous March on Washington in 1963, and helped win passage of the Civil Rights Acts of 1957 and 1964 and the Voting Rights Act of 1965. In later years it pressured corporations to revise their hiring and promotion policies and started programs to fight drug abuse and other social ills.

Nanjing (Nanking), Rape of (1937) Massacre in China during the **Sino-Japanese War**. In December 1937 Japanese troops captured Nanjing. Over the next six weeks they raped, murdered, and looted at will, killing 200,000 or more Chinese civilians and prisoners-of-war. Japanese military leaders encouraged the atrocities.

Nation of Islam *See* **Black Muslims**.

NATO Abbreviation for North Atlantic Treaty Organization, an association formed in 1949 among North American and Western European countries to defend against the **Soviet Union** and its allies. Active bodies include the Council of Foreign Ministers and the Military Committee. There is also an International Secretariat in Brussels, Belgium. Following the 1991 disbanding of the Warsaw Pact, an affiliate organization, the North Atlantic Cooperation Council, was created to promote European security.

As of May 1999 there were 19 member nations of NATO: Belgium, Canada, the Czech Republic, Denmark, France, Germany, Greece, Hungary, Iceland, Italy, Luxembourg, Netherlands, Norway, Poland, Portugal, Spain, Turkey, the United Kingdom, and the United States.

Since 1998 NATO has been actively involved in the conflict between the Serbian military and police forces against Kosovar Albanians. On June 12, 1998, following escalation of the months-long conflict in Kosovo (*see* **Kosovo Crisis**), the NATO Council authorized military action, but diplomacy temporarily prevented the attack. Further escalation of the Serbian aggression against ethnic Albanians led NATO to order the beginning of air strikes on March 23, 1999.

Naturalism *See* **Literature.**

Nazi Party German political party, known in full as the National Socialist German Workers' Party (NSDAP). Founded in 1919 as the German Worker's Party, it was led from 1921 by **Adolf Hitler,** who capitalized on post–**World War I** sentiment through a combination of anti–Semitism, anti–Communism, and super-nationalism and was elected chancellor in 1933. Amassing 6.5 million members in Germany at its peak (1943), the Nazi Party ruled in Germany until the country's defeat in **World War II** (1945). The word *Nazi* comes from the combination of the first syllable of *National* and the second of *Sozialist*.

New Deal The term for the program for U.S. economic and social recovery instituted by President **Franklin Delano Roosevelt** in his first term (1933–36) and lasting throughout the decade. The most extensive government recovery program instituted by and for the U.S., the New Deal first aimed at ameliorating the economic disarray of the **Great Depression,** in which 14 million Americans were unemployed. During his first hundred days, Roosevelt launched a variety of emergency programs and regulations. Among them were the Emergency Banking Act (March 1933), the Economy Act (March 1933), and the establishment of the Federal Emergency Relief Administration (March 1933). Additionally, the National Recovery Administration (NRA, June 1933) was created to deal with work-related issues, and the Agricultural Adjustment Administration (AAA, May 1933) was established to monitor subsidies and crop production. Although the latter two programs were later rendered invalid by the U.S. Supreme Court, the entire package of programs addressed the immediate problems.

Other elements of the New Deal during Roosevelt's first term included a multipronged public works program that employed millions. It consisted of the Public Works Administration (PWA), a $3.3 billion project funding public building; the Tennessee Valley Authority (TVA), the government-subsidized independent entity that provided electrification and built dams and hydroelectric facilities in underserved regions; the Civilian

U.S. Federal Programs Established During the New Deal	
Name	*Year etablished*
Agricultural Adjustment Administration (AAA)	1933; ended 1936
Bureau of Investigation (later Federal Bureau of Investigation, or FBI)	1935
Civil Works Administration (CWA)	1934
Civilian Conservation Corps (CCC)	1933
Federal Communications Commission (FCC)	1934
Federal Deposit Insurance Corporation (FDIC)	1933
Federal Emergency Relief Administration (FERA)	1933
Federal Housing Administration (FHA)	1934
Federal Power Commission	1935
National Recovery Administration (NRA)	1933; ended 1935
Public Works Administration (PWA)	1933
Securities and Exchange Commission (SEC)	1934
Social Security	1935
Tennessee Valley Authority (TVA)	1933
Works Progress Administration (WPA)	1935

Conservation Corps (CCC, November 1933), which employed over two million through 1941 in surveying and reforestation projects; and the Civil Works Administration (February 1934), which employed millions of Americans in public works projects.

Beginning in 1935 second-phase New Deal legislation included the creation of the Works Progress Administration, a public employment program that supplanted some emergency plans. Other New Deal–related projects included the 1935 Social Security Act, an old-age pension program, and the 1935 Wealth Tax Act, which increased tax rates and taxes on profits. In addition, the Federal Reserve System was created to regulate savings institutions and prohibit future total collapse.

In its eight years the New Deal cost over $11 billion and employed over eight million Americans. It is generally credited with initiating economic growth and fostering social stability. Yet its effectiveness was undercut by a 1937 recession, and complete recovery occurred only with the defense growth of **World War II**. Over several decades, long-term effects of the New Deal have included the increased role of government in daily life and the broadened power of the presidency.

New Economic Policy (NEP, 1921–28) Soviet economic program instituted by **V. I. Lenin**. It followed the failure of War Communism, the 1918–21 policy in which the government nationalized most industries and tried to control every aspect of economic life. The results were famine and civil unrest. Under the NEP, private enterprise and free-market trading were reinstated in limited fashion, with peasants permitted to sell some produce for profit. The NEP was followed by the first Five-Year Plan.

Nigeria-Biafra Civil War (1967–70) Conflict that began with the secession of eastern Nigeria on May 30, 1967. The region was dominated by Ibos, who had been persecuted elsewhere in the country by other ethnic groups. The rebels proclaimed their region the republic of Biafra, with military governor Chukwuemeka Odumegwu Ojukwu (1933–) as its president. The Nigerian government fought the secession in a civil war that killed nearly two million people, many of them noncombatants felled by starvation and disease in the famine that accompanied the war. Worldwide relief efforts were hampered by the Nigerian government's reluctance to accept aid shipments. On January 15, 1970, Biafra surrendered, ending the war.

NKVD (Soviet People's Commissariat for Internal Affairs) Soviet secret police organization, established in 1934. Feared as an instrument of state repression, it carried out **Stalin's Great Purge** (1936–38). In 1943 the NKVD was broken into two parts, the NKVD and the NKGB (Soviet People's Commissariat for State Security). In 1946 the NKVD was renamed the MVD (Ministry of Interior), and the NKGB was renamed the MGB (Ministry of State Security). The two groups were linked in a newly formed MGB in 1953, and in 1954 became the KGB.

Nonaligned Movement International movement of countries expressing neutrality in the **cold war**. The movement was launched at the **Bandung Conference** (1955) in Indonesia; many members were **Third World** nations, including India and several countries from Southeast Asia and Africa. Shared goals included peaceful coexistence and **decolonization**.

North Atlantic Treaty Organization (*see* NATO)

Northern Ireland Civil War (1969–) Sectarian conflict between Protestants wishing to remain in the United Kingdom and Roman Catholic groups wanting to end British rule of the area. Civil rights demonstrations by Catholics in 1968 against the rule of the Protestant majority triggered violent confrontations between a resurgent **Irish Republican Army** (IRA) and Protestant police and paramilitary groups. Great Britain sent troops in the early 1970s to restore order but bombings, ambushes, and assassinations continued. More than 3,200 people have been killed since 1969. The IRA declared a cease-fire in 1994 but negotiations between Britain, Ireland, and both sides in the north failed to resolve the conflict immediately. On Good Friday, April 10, 1998, a peace agreement was reached, giving Northern Ireland greater autonomy, but the peace proved shaky.

Nuclear Power The development and use of energy gained from atoms through nuclear fission or nuclear fusion; only the former has so far proved commercially viable. After the first wartime atomic bombs were dropped on **Hiroshima** and Nagasaki, Japan, in August 1945, hastening the end of **World War II**, the awesomeness of nuclear power was demonstrated.

After the war, scientists and policy planners attempted to use nuclear power as an energy source for peacetime use. In 1946 the Atomic Energy Act mandated the replacement of the **Manhattan Project** by the Atomic Energy Commission (AEC), which was to monitor the use of nuclear power in the U.S. In 1954 the U.S. government sanctioned private companies to research and develop atomic production. By the mid–1950s U.S. facilities were generating electric power from nuclear energy, and by the end of the decade it was available commercially. As of 1997 the U.S. had 109 operable nuclear reactors in 32 states.

In 1974 the AEC was replaced by two agencies, the Energy Research and Development Administration (ERDA) and the Nuclear Regulatory Commission (NRC).

Immediately after World War II, many industrialized countries—such as the **Soviet Union** (1949), Great Britian (1957), China (1962), and France (1968)—gained knowledge of nuclear technology. Many of these countries became huge producers of nuclear electric power. In 1995 the top five producers were the United States, France, Japan, Germany, and Russia.

By the 1970s the hazards of nuclear power and the difficulties of containing nuclear waste were demonstrated by serious nuclear accidents worldwide. Two of the most serious occurred at **Three Mile Island** in the U.S. (March 28, 1979) and at **Chernobyl** in the Ukraine (April 26, 1986), the latter being the world's worst peacetime nuclear disaster to date.

Nonetheless, nuclear power remains a huge source of primary energy throughout the world, with world output of nuclear electric power at least tripling since 1980. Among all countries in 1995, nuclear electric power was the fifth greatest source of primary energy production (behind petroleum, natural gas, coal, and hydroelectric power).

Nuclear Weapon Device that causes mass destruction through the release of nuclear energy. The first nuclear weapon was the atomic bomb, developed in the U.S. through the **Manhattan Project**. Two of these fission devices, which drew their energy from the splitting of atomic nuclei, were dropped on **Hiroshima** and Nagasaki in August 1945, marking the first and only combat uses of nuclear weapons. The U.S. monopoly on nuclear weapons ended in 1949 with the detonation of a Soviet atomic bomb. The "club" of nuclear-armed nations grew larger in 1952, as Britain exploded its first atomic bomb. Other countries, such as France and China, followed suit beginning in 1960. In 1952 the U.S. developed the far more powerful hydrogen bomb, a fusion or thermonuclear weapon that

Major Nuclear Arms Control Treaties

1963	Nuclear Test Ban Treaty	U.S., Soviet Union, U.K.
1968	Nuclear Non-proliferation Treaty	U.S., Soviet Union, U.K.; later ratified by more than 150 nations
1972	SALT I (Strategic Arms Limitation Talks)	U.S., Soviet Union
1979	SALT II	U.S., Soviet Union; signed but never ratified by U.S. Senate
1987	INF (Intermediate-range Nuclear Forces) Treaty	U.S., Soviet Union
1991	START I (Strategic Arms Reduction Talks)	U.S., Soviet Union
1992	START II	U.S., Soviet Union

works by fusing atomic nuclei rather than splitting them. The **Soviet Union** detonated its first hydrogen bomb in 1953. Throughout the **cold war** the existence of nuclear weapons shaped the antagonistic relationship between the superpowers. Both sides amassed arsenals of bombs and nuclear-tipped missiles (including intercontinental ballistic missiles, or ICBMs) that could destroy the world many times over. Both feared using them but were convinced that the arsenals were necessary to deter the other side from attacking (*see* **Deterrence**). In several instances, most notably the **Cuban Missile Crisis** (1962), nuclear weapons were the ultimate bargaining tool, the art of threatening nuclear war to influence the other side's behavior was known as **brinkmanship**. The Cuban Missile Crisis, which nearly resulted in nuclear war, persuaded the two sides to begin serious pursuit of arms control and disarmament; the Nuclear Test Ban Treaty of 1963, which banned all but underground nuclear tests, was the first result. The spread of nuclear weapons to other nations was also a subject of concern. In 1968 the U.S., the Soviet Union, and Britain signed the Nuclear Nonproliferation Treaty, committing them not to assist other countries in developing nuclear weapons. Under the first Strategic Arms Limitations Talks (SALT, 1969–72), the U.S. and the Soviet Union signed the SALT I agreement, which limited the deployment of antiballistic missiles and froze the number of intercontinental ballistic missiles. SALT II (1973–79) resulted in the SALT II treaty, which called for modest reductions in the number of missile launchers and other weapons.

In 1982 the U.S. and Soviet Union began the Strategic Arms Reduction Talks (START), which, after a hiatus, resulted in the first START treaty (1991), which reduced launchers and warheads. In 1992 **George Bush** and **Boris Yeltsin** signed the second START treaty. The two countries also reduced their numbers of nuclear arms with the signing of the INF (Intermediate-range Nuclear Forces) Treaty in 1987.

The century neared its close with the signing of a multinational Nuclear Test-Ban Treaty in 1996. Those signing the disarmament agreement (which was to be effected in 1999) were China, France, Russia, the United Kingdom, and the U.S.

Throughout the century, the pace of arms control was too slow for many people. Protests against nuclear weapons began in the 1950s, leading to the nuclear freeze movement of the 1980s, which sought to freeze nuclear arsenals at current levels. The collapse of the Soviet Union in 1991, which ended the cold war, reduced worldwide fear of nuclear annihilation without bringing about the abolition of nuclear weapons. It increased fears that these weapons, like **chemical** and **biological weapons**, would spread to other nations and to terrorists.

Nuremberg Laws Anti-Semitic laws in Nazi Germany. Continuing its persecution against the Jews in Germany, the Nazi government passed legislation (September 15, 1935) that revoked German citizenship for Jews, and severely curtailed economic and social rights. Along with rescinding citizenship, provisions included prohibiting marriage between Jews and Germans.

Nuremberg Trials (1945–56) Legal proceedings against major Nazi war criminals. The best-known trial is the first, lasting from November 1945 to October 1946, and resulting in 12 Nazi leaders being sentenced to death and seven being sentenced to long prison terms. Three were acquitted. Nazi organizations, including the **SS** (Schutzstaffel) and the Gestapo, were pronounced criminal. Members of the military tribunal included four judges and four prosecutors, representing the Allied Powers of France, Britain, the U.S., and the **Soviet Union**. Twelve additional war trials occurred over the next decade, with 24 persons being sentenced to death. The city of Nuremberg is notable for being the site of annual Nazi rallies from 1933 to 1938.

O

OAS (Organization of American States) International political association of American and Caribbean states formed to promote interaction among its members. Founded on April 30, 1948, in Colombia, it originally included Argentina, Bolivia, Brazil, Chile, Colombia, Costa Rica, Cuba, the Dominican Republic, Ecuador, El Salvador, Guatemala, Haiti, Honduras, Mexico, Nicaragua, Panama, Paraguay, Peru, the United States, Uruguay, and Venezuela. In 1967 Barbados and Trinidad and Tobago were admitted; Jamaica joined in 1969. Canada, France, Guyana, Israel, and Spain received Permanent Observer status in 1970, with France becoming a full voting member in 1990. Other Caribbean nations have also been added. In 1962 Cuba was expelled as a member, but many countries have since resumed trade and diplomatic relations with that country.

OPEC (Organization of Petroleum Exporting Countries) Multinational association founded in 1960 to organize actions and protect interests of oil-producing nations. Members include Algeria, Ecuador, Gabon, Indonesia, Iran, Iraq, Kuwait, Libya, Nigeria, Qatar, Saudi Arabia, the United Arab Emirates, and Venezuela. In the 1970s it engineered price increases, which brought about international shortages and rationing.

Open-Door Policy Agreement between the United States and other world powers (Britain, France, Germany, Japan, Italy, and Russia) that guaranteed American trading rights in China. Secretary of State John Hay (1838–1905) negotiated the policy after European powers attempted to stake out spheres of influence in China that would have severely restricted the commerce of other nations. The Open Door Policy also pledged U.S. support of China's territorial integrity. Japan violated the policy in the 1930s, and the Communist takeover of China in 1948 ended it.

Organization of African Unity (OAU) International association of African states intended to foster cooperation and oppose colonialism. Founded in 1963 and headquartered in Addis Ababa, Ethiopia, it includes more than 50 countries. It fought against apartheid in South Africa until that system ended in the 1990s; it also has attempted to improve the continent's economic conditions.

P

Pacifism Opposition to war or violence as a means of resolving conflicts. The movement entered the 20th century with the teachings of such thinkers as French economist Frédéric Passy (1822–1912), founder of the International League for Permanent Peace (1867) and cowinner of the first Nobel Peace Prize (1901). The massive casualties of **World War I** led to efforts to establish an international peacekeeping organization, which resulted in the founding of the League of Nations (1920, dissolved in 1946 following the charter of the **United Nations** in 1945). **Mohandas Gandhi** with his doctrine of **satyagraha,** or non-violent resistance, was perhaps the century's most influential pacifist.

During World War I and **World War II**, some recruits petitioned for exemption from service as conscientious objectors. Reasons for being conscientious objectors often derived from religious beliefs, as with the Religious Society of Friends, or Quakers, and the Catholic Workers. Political beliefs in opposition to a particular war were also cited, as in petitions for conscientious objector status during the **Vietnam War**.

Palestine Liberation Organization (PLO) Palestinian Arab political organization. It was founded in 1964 to unite Palestinian Arab groups around the goal of eliminating Israel and establishing a Palestinian Arab state. After the Arab defeat in the **Six-Day War** (1967), the PLO increasingly waged guerrilla warfare. Al-Fatah, the guerrilla Palestine National Liberation Movement founded in 1958, became the leading group in the PLO in 1969 when its leader, **Yasir Arafat**, was named PLO chairman. Expelled from Jordan in 1970–71, the PLO was headquartered in Lebanon until the 1982 Israeli invasion of Lebanon, after which it was forced to move to Tunisia. Becoming more moderate, it came to be seen internationally as a government in exile. In 1993 Israel and the PLO signed peace accords in which the two sides mutually recognized each other's legitimacy and set a path for establishing Palestinian autonomy. In 1996 elections, the PLO won control of the autonomous government in Israel's occupied territories.

Panama Canal Engineered waterway across the isthmus of Panama, connecting the Atlantic to the Pacific Ocean. The isthmus was part of Colombia at the start of the 20th century, but Colombia was unwilling to cooperate with U.S. president **Theodore Roosevelt**'s plans for a canal. Roosevelt solved the problem by giving military support to Panama's successful war of independence against Colombia (1903). U.S. military engineers under Chief Engineer George Washington Goethals (1858–1928) built the canal between 1904 and 1914 across land leased in perpetuity from Panama. The 40-mile-wide canal became an important shipping facility. The Panama Canal Treaty of 1977 ended the Canal Zone's status as being politically independent, while continuing U.S. upkeep of the Canal until 1999. It also allowed for the canal to be turned over to Panama on January 1, 2000.

Pan-Arabism Movement for Arab unity based on common culture, history, and language. It became a mass movement following **World War I** and resulted in the formation of the **Arab League** (1945) and the **Ba'ath Party**. Shared opposition to Israel and common oil interests supported Pan-Arabism in the decades after **World War II**, but competing national interests tended to undermine it, as did Egypt's decision to seek peace with Israel in the **Camp David Accords**. The rise of Islamic **fundamentalism** further helped divide Arab states from each other.

Paris Peace Accords (January 1973) An agreement between the U.S., South Vietnam, North Vietnam, and Communist guerrillas in the south of Vietnam to end the Vietnam War.

The parties agreed to a cease-fire policed by an international force, the withdrawal of American forces, and a release of prisoners. North Vietnam was allowed to keep its troops in South Vietnam but could not reinforce them. The 17th parallel would continue to divide the two nations. Both sides routinely violated the cease-fire, and in March 1975 North Vietnam invaded the south. By the end of April the North had toppled the South Vietnamese government; the two countries were officially united in 1976.

Paris Peace Conference (1919–20) Congress in Paris of representatives of Allied and Associated Powers at the end of **World War I**. It redrew the map of Europe and produced several treaties that were imposed on the defeated **Central Powers: Versailles** (1919) with Germany; **St. Germain** (1919) with Austria; Neuilly (1919) with Bulgaria; **Trianon** (1920) with Hungary; and Sèvres (1920) with the Ottoman Empire (superseded in 1923 by the Treaty of **Lausanne** with Turkey). The conference was dominated by **Georges Clemenceau** of France, **David Lloyd George** of Britain, **Woodrow Wilson** of the U.S., and Italian prime minister Vittorio Emanuele Orlando (1860–1952), who made up the Big Four. Wilson's **Fourteen Points**, calling for national self-determination and a just peace, were only partly heeded, as punitive measures were imposed on Germany and national communities were stranded in states ruled by other peoples. The resentment and instability that resulted were among the principal causes of **World War II**.

Peace Corps American government agency established by President **John Fitzgerald Kennedy** in 1961. The agency assigns volunteers to countries that need skilled personnel in education, public health, technology, and agriculture. Volunteers serve two years for a modest stipend. The number of recruits peaked in 1966 with some 15,500 Americans working in 52 countries. Budget cuts in the 1980s reduced this number to about 5,000 volunteers per year working in about 90 countries. The Corps' success inspired the creation of Volunteers in Service to America (VISTA), which enlists volunteers to work in poor areas of the U.S.

Pearl Harbor U.S. (Oahu Island, Hawaii) military base that was attacked by Japanese air forces on December 7, 1941, precipitating U.S. entry into **World War II**. Beginning at 7:55 A.M., the approximately two-hour attack caused about 3,000 American enlisted and civilian casualties and destroyed 19 U.S. ships and 150 planes. On December 8, President **Franklin Delano Roosevelt** spoke before Congress and requested a declaration of war on Japan, citing December 7 as a "day which will live in infamy." Upon near-unanimous votes (100–0, Senate; 388–1, House), war was declared.

Pentagon Papers A 47-volume history of the U.S. involvement in Vietnam, commissioned by Secretary of Defense Robert McNamara (1916–) in 1967. Daniel Ellsberg (1931–), a former Pentagon consultant who had turned against the **Vietnam War**, leaked the history to the press in 1971, and in June of that year the *New York Times* and the *Washington Post* published articles based on the documents. The government obtained a court order to stop publication of more stories, but the Supreme Court lifted the ban. Discrepancies between the official policy of four administrations and their actual plans to wage war in Indochina intensified antiwar sentiments. A treason charge against Ellsberg was dismissed when it was learned that White House agents had burglarized his psychiatrist's office in 1971 in an attempt to discredit Ellsberg.

Perestroika (Russian, "restructuring") Soviet policy of reforming the Soviet economy and society. It included development of a more market-oriented economy, with increased private ownership, and reform of the Communist Party to include more progressive members in top posts. With **glasnost** it was instituted by Soviet leader **Mikhail Gorbachev** in 1986.

Phony War The period of **World War II** between September 1939, when the Germans occupied Poland, and April 1940, when Denmark and Norway were invaded. Despite multiple declarations of war, there was little military activity, as Germany regrouped its forces and the Allies waited for Germany to attack.

Persian Gulf War (*see* **Gulf War**)

PLO *See* **Palestine Liberation Organization.**

Pollution *See* **Environmentalism.**

Population Explosion The massive expansion in human population in the 19th and 20th centuries. The **industrial revolution,** with its improved food distribution systems and advances in medicine and public health, had the effect of lengthening lives and lowering infant mortality. The result was an increase in global population from about 1 billion in the mid–19th century to 2 billion by 1930. By the 1990s the world population was nearly 6 billion. Population growth was proportionately greater in developing countries than in developed ones, where families were likely to be smaller. The result was often that the countries with the most mouths to feed had the fewest resources to do so. To curb inordinate population growth, many governments—including those of Japan, India, China, Kenya, and Chile—introduced family planning policies. Some international organizations, such as the International Planned Parenthood Federation, also addressed the issue. **Birth control** and abortion were increasingly offered as means to contain population growth, sometimes over vigorous moral objections from the Roman Catholic Church and other groups.

World Population Totals, 1900–96
1900—1.57 billion
1914—1.81 billion
1920—1.81 billion
1939—2.23 billion
1950—2.513 billion
1960—3.027 billion
1970—3.678 billion
1980—4.478 billion
1990—5.292 billion
1996—5.772 billion

Postmodernism Movement in arts, literature, criticism, and philosophy that followed **modernism.** Originating after **World War II**, postmodernism represented an attitude of playful detachment, often associated with irony and parody. Postmodernists were skeptical about the possibility of absolute knowledge, even questioning the objective reality of scientific conclusions. In the field of literary criticism, **Jacques Derrida** developed deconstructionism (post-structuralism), a movement that denies the possibility of fixed or coherent meaning while claiming to discern the social power structures that determine texts. In philosophy, postmodernists such as American Richard Rorty (1931–) were skeptically detached even about their own beliefs. Postmodernist fiction writers, such as **Vladimir Nabokov** and American Thomas Pynchon (1937–), reacted against modernist and traditional styles while borrowing freely from them.

Potsdam Conference (July 17–August 2, 1945) Meeting held among Allied countries in **World War II**. Representatives attending included President **Harry S Truman**, Premier **Joseph Stalin**, and Prime Minister **Winston Churchill**, replaced by Prime Minister

Clement Attlee following British elections. The purpose of the conference was to solidify agreements discussed at the **Yalta Conference** earlier in the year. Among its conclusions were an ultimatum to Japan, which had to choose between total, unconditional surrender and annihilation, and the establishment of postwar German occupation zones and economic restructuring plans. Soviet noncompliance with portions of the agreement was significant in the growth of the **cold war**.

Prague Spring Period of reform in Czechoslovakia (January–August 1968) instituted by first secretary of the Communist Party and Czech de facto leader **Alexander Dubcek** (1921–92). Changes included the pardon or release of unjustly jailed political prisoners and a suspension of press censorship. Foreseeing the reforms' power to break the Communist system, leaders of East Germany, Poland, and the **Soviet Union** ordered troops to invade Czechoslovakia on August 20, 1968. Dubcek was arrested and replaced; most reforms were ended.

Profumo Affair British political scandal in 1963 involving Conservative minister of war John Profumo (1915–) and British call girl Christine Keeler. When their affair and her simultaneous liaison with Soviet assistant naval attaché Lieutenant Commander Yevgeny Ivanov were made known, Profumo was forced to resign from Parliament. A national inquiry concluded that the affairs resulted in no state security damage. However, the tawdry goings-on damaged Prime Minister **Harold Macmillan** and the Conservative government.

Progressive Party Three United States political parties organized to counter existing parties and promote liberal social reform. They were present in three presidential elections: those of 1912, 1924, and 1948.

In 1912 American politician Robert M. La Follette (1855–1925) and others helped found the party (also known as the Bull Moose Party) in opposition to Republican president **William Howard Taft**. Its platform included women's suffrage and various social reforms; in its ideals, it recalled 19th-century Republicanism. Its 1912 presidential candidate, former president **Theodore Roosevelt**, received four million votes and 88 electoral votes. The party divided the Republican vote, however, causing the election of Democrat **Woodrow Wilson**.

In the 1924 presidential election, La Follette was the nominee of the second Progressive Party. Its aims included the preservation of national resources and support for labor unions. La Follette won six million votes but only 13 electoral votes.

In 1948 a third Progressive Party nominated Henry A. Wallace (1888–1965), Cabinet member to Democratic presidents **Franklin Delano Roosevelt** and **Harry S Truman**. In his campaign he charged the Truman administration with generating the **cold war**. Wallace received 2 percent of the popular vote (over one million) and no electoral college votes.

Prohibition A government ban on the production and sale of alcoholic beverages. In the U.S. it refers to the national period of Prohibition that began in 1920 after the enactment (1919) of the 18th Amendment to the Constitution. Prior to 1920, various temperance movements had passed prohibition legislation in 33 states and had lobbied for a nationwide ban. National Prohibition proved impossible to enforce as enterprising criminals—the most famous among them **Al Capone**—built huge empires based on smuggling, brewing illegal spirits, and running speakeasies. By the late 1920s many recognized that prohibition had failed and the 21st Amendment, passed in 1933, repealed the 18th Amendment. Some states remained dry after the repeal, but by 1966 statewide prohibition laws had ended.

Psychoanalysis System of understanding the mind and treating its disorders. It was developed by Austrian psychiatrist **Sigmund Freud** and described in such works as *The Interpretation of Dreams* (1899). Freud believed that conscious life is influenced by the unconscious mind. Neurosis, he argued, is caused by repressed feelings, which could be brought to light through "talk therapy," in which a neurotic patient undergoes regular private talking sessions with the therapist over long periods, often years. The psychoanalyst's tools include dream interpretation, free association, and transference. Psychoanalytic theory (sometimes called Freudianism) influenced many areas of scholarship, including philosophy and literary criticism, and became common intellectual currency after **World War II**. However, Freud's theories of the mind had competitors, including those of behaviorism (*see* **John Broadus Watson**) and of Freud's former followers **C. G. Jung** and **Alfred Adler**. By the 1990s Freudian theory was widely criticized as unscientific and inaccurate, while other views gained prominence, including cognitive neuroscience. As a method, psychoanalysis fell in importance compared with the many other competing schools of psychotherapy. Still, psychoanalysis was the crucial model for all the varieties of "talk therapy" that followed and for such common notions as the ego, id, and superego.

Q

Quantum Theory or **Quantum Mechanics** Physical theory that electromagnetic radiation is emitted and absorbed by matter in discrete units known as *quanta*. Originated in 1900 by **Max Planck**, the theory was elaborated by many of the 20th-century's great physicists, including **Albert Einstein, Niels Bohr, Werner Heisenberg, Erwin Schrödinger**, and **Richard Feynman**. It developed in conjunction with the growing understanding of the structure and behavior of the atom and of elementary particles, including the constituents called quarks (first proposed in 1963 by **Murray Gell-Mann**). Quantum theory describes light as both wavelike and particlelike. Limits on the accuracy of quantum measurements are set by Heisenberg's **uncertainty principle**.

R

Radio Communications system employing electromagnetic radiation in the radio frequency range. Although radio waves were first detected by German physicist Heinrich Hertz (1857–94) in 1888, practical radio communication did not become a reality until the early 20th century. Italian engineer **Guglielmo Marconi** sent the first transatlantic message (a letter S in Morse code) via radio in 1901. By 1905 ships were using "wireless" telegraphy to communicate with shore stations. British engineer John A. Fleming (1849–1945) invented the vacuum electron tube in 1904 and American inventor Lee De Forest (1873–1961) invented the triode, a three-element tube, in 1906. Further technical refinements improved sound transmission, permitting commercial broadcasts; station KDKA in Pittsburgh became the first commercial radio broadcasting station in 1920. By the 1930s radio receivers were standard household equipment, especially in the U.S., with listeners enjoying a cornucopia of entertainment and news programming. Frequency Modulation (FM) radios were sold commercially from 1939; transistors, invented in 1948, allowed radios to become smaller, with pocket-sized transistor radios introduced in 1952. Radio technology was employed in the 1930s in the development of radar—a system for detecting objects by reflecting radio waves from their surfaces—with many military and civilian applications.

As an entertainment form radio lost popularity to **television** beginning in the 1950s. As a system of communications (employed, for example, in cellular phones), radio has contributed to the continued shrinking of distances around the globe (*see also* **Communications Revolution, Globalization**).

Red Brigades Italian leftist terrorist group active mainly in the 1970s, when it committed several murders aimed at undermining the Italian government. In 1978 it abducted and assassinated former Italian prime minister Aldo Moro (1916–78).

Red Cross International aid organization. Founded in 1863 by Swiss philanthropist Jean-Henri Dunant (1828–1910), the politically and commercially neutral International Red Cross was aimed at aiding wounded soldiers, with its precepts becoming the bases for the **Geneva Convention** (1864). Its insignia of the red cross against a white background is the reverse of the Swiss flag. In the 20th century, the Red Cross expanded its services to cover natural and human disasters of all kinds. Membership widened, including Muslim countries, which operate as the Red Crescent. To reflect inclusion of Arab members, the International Red Cross was renamed the International Movement of the Red Cross and the Red Crescent in 1986. From its international headquarters in Geneva, Switzerland, it oversees 150 national Red Cross and Red Crescent organizations.

Red Guards 1) Maoist activists in China's **Cultural Revolution**. In 1966 and 1967, these marauding bands of school and college students, adorned with red armbands, sought to root out suspected enemies of Maoism. Encouraged by the government at first, they got out of control and were suppressed militarily. 2) **Bolshevik** workers' militias in the **Russian Revolution** of November 6–7, 1917. These armed workers helped the revolution to victory and contributed to the formation of the Red Army.

Red Scare (1919–20) In the U.S., a period of mass panic about Communist subversion. Following **World War I**, a wave of labor strikes and bomb incidents engendered fear that a Communist revolution was imminent. Immigrants, labor leaders, and radicals were suspect. U.S. attorney general Alexander Mitchell Palmer (1872–1936) authorized mass arrests, known as the Palmer Raids, placing 6,000 people in custody and deporting 500. The red scare laid the basis for the immigration restrictions of 1924 and succeeded in preventing the Left from wielding much influence in the 1920s. The term *red scare* is also used for the period of government-sponsored anti-Communist activity in the United States from 1946 to the early 1950s; it was associated with Senator **Joseph McCarthy** from 1950 to 1954, when it was known as McCarthyism.

Reichstag Fire (February 27, 1933) Fire that destroyed part of the German parliament, or Reichstag, building. Although most scholars today believe the fire to have been the work of a lone arsonist, then-chancellor **Adolf Hitler** blamed it on the Communists. The accusation allowed him to imprison political opponents, demand elections, and, in March, assume dictatorial powers.

Relativity Physical theory. Proposed by German-born physicist **Albert Einstein** in 1905 (the special theory) and 1916 (the general theory), it rejected the concept of absolute points in space and time, arguing that motion is always relative to the observer. It revised the system of classical mechanics that had prevailed since it was developed by English mathematician Isaac Newton (1642–1727). While accepting that Newtonian mechanics is accurate in most ordinary situations, Einstein accurately predicted different results at velocities close to the speed of light. Relativity declared the speed of light to be a maximum velocity, set forth that space and time are parts of the same four-dimensional continuum, claimed that gravitational fields curve space-time, and proposed that mass and energy are mutually convertible according to the equation $E = mc^2$ (where e is energy, m is mass, and c is the velocity of light). The last proposition was the basis for the invention of **nuclear weapons**. Tested and confirmed many times, relativity became a transforming theory in 20th-century physics. It was applied in such disparate fields as astronomy, cosmology, and nuclear physics. It also influenced philosophy and, more loosely, encouraged the **postmodernist** notion of a universe without absolutes.

RENAMO *See* **FRELIMO**.

Reparations Compensation for war damages. Following **World War I** the Allies demanded $33 billion from Germany, which submitted only after the victors threatened to occupy the Ruhr Valley. After 1921 Germany requested several reschedulings of payments, and the delays prompted the French to occupy the Ruhr in 1923. U.S. vice president Charles Dawes (1865–1951) brokered a plan that stretched out payments and provided American loans to stabilize the German economy. Owen Young (1874–1962), an American lawyer, negotiated another extension in 1929. In 1932 the **Great Depression** prompted the Allies to reduce substantially the remaining payments. Germany was also forced to pay reparations after **World War II**.

Republican Party American political party. Established in 1854 to oppose the spread of slavery, the Republican Party became the majority party in the U.S. by 1900. Republicans drew support from big business, rural areas, and small towns, often appealing to the legacy of 19th-century president Abraham Lincoln (1809–1965) and the Union's victory over the predominantly Democratic South. The party held the White House from 1900 to 1912, despite a split in ranks caused by reform Republicans who objected to the party's allegiance to business trusts and who wanted increased government regulation of business. This split cost the party the presidency, but it recovered and occupied the White House again from 1920 until 1932, when the Republicans, held responsible for the **Great Depression**, lost the election to **Franklin Delano Roosevelt**. His victory signaled the end of the Republican Party's majority status; Republicans failed to win again until **Dwight D. Eisenhower** was elected in 1952. The Republican Party has had control of both houses of Congress in only two periods since 1932: from 1947 to 1949 and from 1997 to the present. The party became increasingly conservative in the 1960s and attracted the allegiance of many white male voters, especially in the south, who felt threatened by the civil rights movement and opposition to the **Vietnam War**. Republican **Richard Nixon** was elected president in 1968 but was forced to resign in 1974 (*see* **Watergate**). **Ronald Reagan** won two presidential terms (1980 and 1984) running on a platform of tax cuts, increased military spending, strong anti-Communism and a return to "traditional" social values. The Republicans' hold on the presidency was broken in 1992 with the election of **Bill Clinton**, but the party won control of Congress in the 1994 elections.

Resistance Groups of underground forces active against Axis Powers during **World War II**. Best known is the French resistance, which operated during the Nazi occupation of France and included Gaullist Free French, Communist, and independent forces. Its activities included escape planning, intelligence gathering, and sabotage. Also active were resistance forces in eastern Europe, particularly in Poland, Russia, and Yugoslavia. Forces included the Polish Home Army and Communist Partisan forces led by **Josip Tito**. Communist-run anti-Japanese resistance forces also existed in China and Vietnam. In recent years, the term has referred to a range of actions against political or social injustice.

Roosevelt Corollary U.S. foreign policy articulated by President **Theodore Roosevelt** in 1904. Amending the 19th-century Monroe Doctrine, Roosevelt argued that the U.S. had the right to intervene in the affairs of any nation in the Western Hemisphere deemed guilty of "chronic wrong-doing" or "impotence." Roosevelt's assumption of international police power was used to justify military interventions in Cuba and other Latin American countries during the early decades of the 20th century.

Russian Civil War (1918–21) Russian internal conflict. The October Revolution, the second of the **Russian Revolutions of 1917**, established the world's first Communist state, which almost immediately found itself fighting for survival. In December 1917, counterrevolutionary armies, known as the Whites, organized against the **Bolsheviks**. In 1918, fighting broke out between the Whites and the Red Army organized by Bolshevik military leader **Leon Trotsky**. The Whites were supported by foreign expeditionary forces, including Japanese troops who took Vladivostok in southeast Russia, and British and American troops who helped establish a provisional government in Archangel in northwest Russia. Cossacks and Ukrainians aided the White cause; a legion of released Czech prisoners of war fought for the Whites in Siberia. White armies nearly captured Moscow and Petrograd (St. Petersburg), but were repelled. Most of the foreign troops were withdrawn in 1919, leaving the White armies to be suppressed by the Red Army. At the same time several nations won freedom from Russian control, including Finland (in the Finnish War of Independence, 1918–20), Poland (in the Russo-Polish War, 1919–20), Latvia, Lithuania, and Estonia. By 1921, the Bolsheviks were firmly in control of Russia, and the civil war was over.

Russian Revolution of 1905 Uprisings against economic inequities and the increasingly repressive practices of Czar **Nicholas II** that resulted in the establishment of a constitutional monarchy. For years peasants faced high taxes and poor working conditions under the industrialization of minister of finance Count Sergei Witte (1845–1915) and from 1905 they were discontented with losses in the **Russo-Japanese War**. While revolts began in the Ukraine in 1902, the spark for the revolution occurred on **Bloody Sunday** (January 1905), when police fired on a crowd of demonstrators.

Hundreds of strikes and protests in urban areas followed, lasting into October and joining together workers, professionals, the intelligentsia, and the armed forces, which staged a mutiny on the *Potemkin* (June 1905). The effectiveness of the protests led Czar Nicholas II to issue the October Manifesto (October 1905), which brought the first change to the Russian political system since the rule of Peter the Great (1672–1725). The manifesto mandated constitutional rule and a lawmaking body. Although protests continued, his proposals helped end the uprising.

Russian Revolutions of 1917 Russian political upheavals in January through March 1917 and November 1917 (October in Old-Style Calendar). 1) *February Revolution* (January–March 1917). Russians were frustrated by years of war (*see* **World War I**) and unsatisfied by the reforms that resulted from the **Russian Revolution of 1905**. In January 1917 a wave of strikes, demonstrations, and mutinies began. Russian troops refused orders to quell the rebellion. By February Czar **Nicholas II** could no longer govern. He abdicated on March 15. A provisional government took over, headed at first by Prince Georgy Lvov (1861–1925) and later by **Aleksandr Kerensky**. Socialist workers' councils, or soviets, were founded in Petrograd (formerly St. Petersburg) and elsewhere. By that fall the

Petrograd and other key soviets were under the control of the **Bolsheviks,** who promised peace, bread, and power to the soviets. 2) *October Revolution* (November 1917). The provisional government made the unpopular decision to keep Russia in World War I. The government proved helpless in the face of food shortages and continuing strikes and demonstrations. On November 6 and 7, Bolshevik forces led by **Leon Trotsky** occupied strategic sites in Petrograd, including government offices, newspaper offices, and telegraph and telephone offices. The government headquarters in the Winter Palace was captured on November 7 (October 25, Old Style). A Communist state was proclaimed. In December 1917 the Bolsheviks withdrew Russia from World War I with the armistice of Brest-Litovsk (broken in February, then formalized [with harsher terms for the Russians] with the Treaty of **Brest-Litovsk,** March 3, 1918), founded the **Cheka** secret police to suppress dissent, and fought the **Russian Civil War** to confirm their position. The Union of Soviet Socialist Republics (USSR, or **Soviet Union**) was formally constituted in 1922.

Russo-Japanese War (1904–05) Conflict between Russia and Japan over rival imperial ambitions. Responding to Russian penetration of Manchuria and Korea, Japan launched a surprise attack on Port Arthur (February 1904), defeated the Russian army at the Battle of Mukden (February–March 1904), and destroyed the Russian fleet at the Battle of Tsushima (May 27, 1905). U.S. president **Theodore Roosevelt** mediated the Treaty of Portsmouth, New Hampshire (September 5, 1905), ending the war. Japan emerged as an imperial power, while Russia was forced to give up its interests in Manchuria. With Russia's government revealed as incompetent and corrupt, the war helped spark the **1905 Russian Revolution.**

S

Sacco-Vanzetti Trial U.S. murder trial of two Italian immigrants in 1921 that has come to demonstrate difficulties in receiving a fair trial. Foreign-born anarchists Nicola Sacco (1891–1927) and Bartolomeo Vanzetti (1888–1927) were tried and convicted of being part of a group that killed two men during an armed robbery in Braintree, Mass. Amidst anti-immigrant fervor and with circumstantial evidence, the two were convicted on July 4, 1921. Widespread international support for the two, who were perceived as martyrs, postponed execution until August 23, 1927. Interest in the case continued for decades, and the two were posthumously exonerated by Massachusetts governor Michael Dukakis (1933–) in 1977.

St. Germain, Treaty of (September 10, 1919) Agreement, at the end of **World War I,** between the **Allied Powers** and Austria. Signed at Saint-Germain-en-Laye near Paris, it recognized the dissolution of the Austro-Hungarian monarchy and the creation of the independent states of Austria, Hungary, Czechoslovakia, Poland, and Yugoslavia (known then as the Kingdom of the Serbs, Croats, and Slovenes). Austria lost other territories to Italy and Romania. Austria was forbidden to unite with Germany. Reparations payments were required but never paid.

Satyagraha ("truth-force") Philosophy and method of nonviolent resistance against British rule in India. The term was coined by its developer and chief practitioner, **Mohandas Gandhi.** Rooted in Hinduism and informed by Christianity, satyagraha required the resister to oppose evil actively but without resort to violence, through such means as civil disobedience and noncooperation. Gandhi first applied it in South Africa (1907–14), then brought it to India, where he led such memorable satyagraha campaigns as the Salt March of 1930, a disciplined mass protest against the British salt tax.

Schlieffen Plan Military strategy devised in 1905 by German soldier Alfred Graf von Schlieffen (1833–1913), chief of general staff (1891–1905). Designed to handle a two-front war with France and Russia, it proposed that German forces defeat France quickly by striking through Belgium and the Netherlands, thus circumventing French defense lines. German forces could then be concentrated on the Eastern Front against Russia. The plan was unsuccessfully implemented at the start of **World War I** and informed **Adolf Hitler's** strategy in **World War II**.

Scopes Trial U.S. trial in 1925 that tested the teaching of evolution in the public schools. On trial in Dayton, Tenn., was biology teacher John T. Scopes (1900–70), who taught evolution rather than the biblical interpretation of creation, which was mandated by state law. The highly publicized trial featured two noted lawyers: **William Jennings Bryan** for the prosecution and **Clarence Darrow** for the defense. Among leading journalists present was **H. L. Mencken**. Scopes was found guilty and charged a small fine, but the conviction was later overturned by a higher court and in 1967 the creationist law was repealed. Bryan died five days after the trial ended.

Scottsboro Case A 1931 U.S. legal case that continued for years and demonstrated long-standing American racial prejudice. In Scottsboro, Ala., in 1931, nine young African-American males were charged with raping two Caucasian women. Despite inconclusive evidence, the "Scottsboro boys" were found guilty at trial and sentenced to death. In 1932 the U.S. Supreme Court reversed the convictions on procedural grounds concerning right to counsel and ordered a new trial. At the 1933 second trial, one of the women involved recanted her testimony. The defendants were again convicted and the judgment was again overturned and a new trial ordered. In a third trial (1936–37), five defendants were found guilty and charges against four defendants were dropped. Two defendants were paroled in 1944, and another was paroled in 1951. A fourth defendant escaped to Michigan, and the state refused to extradite him to Alabama. The final surviving defendant, Clarence Norris, was pardoned in Alabama in 1976.

Second International *See* **Comintern**.

Second Vatican Council *See* **Vatican II**.

Sharpeville Massacre Attack by South African police on black demonstrators in Sharpeville Township (near the Transvaal) on March 21, 1960, resulting in the deaths of 69 and injuries to 186 blacks. The demonstrators were members of the militant anti-apartheid Pan Africanist Congress (PAC). The massacre led to further demonstrations by the PAC and the **African National Congress** (ANC). In response, the apartheid government tightened security and banned the ANC and PAC.

Sian Incident or **Xian Incident** (December 1936) Event that brought a truce between nationalist and Communist forces in China. With Japan threatening China, Chinese nationalist leader **Chiang Kai-shek** was kidnapped in Sian (Xian), China, by his own troops. One of his generals, Chang Hsueh-liang (c. 1901–), demanded that Chiang negotiate a truce with the Communists to create a united front against the Japanese. Chiang complied and was released. In retaliation, Chiang arrested the rebellious Chang and placed him under long-term house arrest.

Sinn Féin (Gaelic, "We Ourselves") Irish nationalist organization formed in 1902 to fight for independence from Great Britain. Its leaders helped organize the 1916 Easter Rebellion, and after that the organization, led by **Eamon De Valera**, won a majority of the Irish seats in the British Parliament. They boycotted Parliament and pronounced themselves the legitimate government of an independent Ireland. Many of them refused to recognize the Irish Free State after its establishment in 1922 and waged an unsuccessful civil war against the new government. De Valera then formed **Fianna Fáil**, a political party that enlisted most of the Sinn Féin adherents, in 1926. Sinn Féin continued to field candidates but rarely won any seats. Its primary importance rests in its link with the **Irish Republican Army**, which it has represented since 1994 in peace talks concerning the civil war in Northern Ireland.

Sino-Indian Border War (Indo-Chinese War; Chinese-Indian Border War)

(1962) Conflict between China and India over disputed territory in the Aksai-Chin Plateau and along the McMahon Line dividing Tibet and India. Soon after China annexed Tibet in 1950, disputes with India over the legitimate boundary began. In 1962 India crossed the line claimed by China, prompting China to attack. China won handily, revealing India's military weakness and leading India to build up its armaments.

Sino-Japanese War

(1937–45) Conflict between China and Japan. In 1931 Japan occupied Manchuria—a region in China—and there established the puppet state of Manchukuo. Chinese nationalist leader Chiang Kai-shek was too occupied with fighting the Communists to repel the invasion, but in the **Sian Incident** (1936) he was forced by his own generals to create a united front with the Communists to oppose Japan. Hostilities began with the Marco Polo Bridge Incident (July 7, 1937), an armed clash between Chinese and Japanese troops at the Marco Polo Bridge near Beijing. By year's end, Japan had captured Beijing, Tientsin, Shanghai, Nanjing (*see* **Rape of Nanjing**), and much of the north China plain. The Chinese moved their capital to Hankow. In 1938 Japan continued to expand, capturing such cities as Hankow and Canton, as the Chinese moved their capital to Chungking. In 1939 the Japanese advance stalled. The nationalists engaged the Japanese in open warfare while the Communists fought a guerrilla war in the north, expanding their bases and influence. After 1941 the war merged with **World War II**, as U.S. forces gave air support to the Chinese. The Sino-Japanese War ended with the Japanese defeat in World War II; it was soon followed by the **Chinese Civil War**.

Six-Day War

(Third Arab-Israeli War) (June 5–10, 1967) Military conflict between Israel and the Arab nations of Egypt, Jordan, and Syria. In May 1967, Egypt demanded and obtained the removal of **UN** peacekeeping forces from the Sinai Peninsula. Egypt massed its forces in the Sinai while blockading the Israeli port of Eilat. On June 5 Israel struck preemptively against Egypt and its allies Jordan and Syria, disabling their air forces in surprise attacks. Israeli ground forces swiftly captured the **Gaza Strip** and the Sinai Peninsula from Egypt, eastern Jerusalem and the **West Bank** from Jordan, and the Golan Heights from Syria. The war ended with a UN cease-fire but no peace treaty. Israel's occupation of the captured lands became a new source of international tension, much of it focused on the situation of Palestinian Arabs living in the West Bank and Gaza.

Soccer War or Football War

(July 14–18, 1969) Brief conflict between El Salvador and Honduras. It was caused by Honduran resentment over heavy immigration from El Salvador, and Salvadoran resentment over treatment of the immigrants. Riots against the immigrants broke out in Honduras when El Salvador defeated that country in a three-game soccer series. Salvadoran air and ground forces attacked, and Honduras retaliated. By the time the **OAS** arranged an armistice, more than 2,000 people had been killed.

Social Realism *See* **Literature.**

Socialism Economic theory advocating collective or state ownership of the means of production. There have been many varieties of socialism, from the gradualist, reform-minded views of the Fabian Society (founded in 1884 in Britain and influencing the **Labour Party**) to the revolutionary doctrines of Marxist-Leninist **Communism.** While the latter is associated with totalitarian rule, there are many democratic socialists, who work within liberal political systems to push for some degree of public ownership, central planning, and social welfare legislation. Socialists of this stripe came to power after **World War II** in most Western European countries, nationalizing key industries and establishing welfare states in which health, education, and unemployment benefits were guaranteed. Socialism was also widespread in **Third World** countries. Though government intervention in the economy was supported by British economist **John Maynard Keynes** and his followers (known as Keynesians), more conservative economists considered socialist measures a drain on the economy; these included the monetarists who joined American economist Milton Friedman (1912–) in opposing government spending and advocating tight government control of a country's money supply. In the 1980s and 1990s socialism became less popular in many countries as governments tried to shake off debt and encourage economic growth through private enterprise.

Solidarity ("Solidarnosc" in Polish) Polish trade union confederation. Led by **Lech Walesa,** it was founded in September 1980 following the successful Gdansk Lenin shipyard strike (August 1980). Solidarity grew to include 10 million workers and won important political concessions, but was outlawed by martial law decrees in December 1981. It continued as an underground movement and gained force as the **Soviet Union** under **Mikhail Gorbachev** withdrew its support from the Polish government. In 1989 Solidarity was legalized, and its candidates won the national elections. Afterward the union's political strength declined.

South African War (Boer War) Armed military conflict (1899–1902) between the Boers of the Orange Free State and the Transvaal (South African Republic) against Great Britain. From the late 19th century, Boer and British settlements had faced territorial conflicts, particularly after the 1886 discovery of gold in the Transvaal, which brought additional settlers.

Tensions culminated in the 1895 Jameson Raid, in which the British attempted to overthrow the Boer government. The attack prompted a military alliance between Transvaal and the Orange Free State in 1896. The Boers declared war on October 12, 1899, and gained early victories. Reinforcements led by British field marshal Horatio Kitchener stemmed Boer forces, leading to British annexation of the Transvaal in September 1901.

Sporadic fighting continued until 1902, when the Treaty of Vereeniging was signed on May 31. The agreement reinstituted British rule within a representative government and also mandated reparations.

Soviet Union (Union of Soviet Socialist Republics, or USSR) (1922–1991) The world's first Communist state. Formerly spanning parts of eastern Europe and northern Asia, it was centered in Russia. As a result of the **Russian Revolutions of 1917, V. I. Lenin,** leader of the Communist Party, reconstituted Russia on Marxist principles. In 1922 the Soviet Union was formally established, placing Russia at the head of several other constituent republics. Its fundamental unit of government was the soviet, or council; national legislative power resided in the Supreme Soviet, which appointed a council of ministers headed by a premier. In practice, however, the Communist Party controlled government at all levels. The most powerful individual in the Soviet Union was the party's general secretary, and the most powerful group was the Politburo—a small "political bureau" elected by the party's Central Committee.

Under the dictatorship of Lenin's successor, **Joseph Stalin**, which lasted from 1924 to 1953, the Soviet Union emerged as a **totalitarian** state and one of the world's two superpowers. Following **World War II** it engaged in a protracted struggle known as the **cold war** with the U.S., the other superpower and leader of the liberal-democratic, capitalist West. Following World War II the Soviet Union controlled most of the Communist nations of Eastern Europe, including Poland, Czechoslovakia, and East Germany (*see* **Warsaw Pact**). It also supplied aid to Communist insurgents and governments around the world, assisting at various times China, Cuba, and Vietnam. The economic failure of the Communist system, coupled with internal ethnic tensions and other factors, had severely weakened the country by the 1980s. Soviet leader **Mikhail Gorbachev**, who came to power in 1985, attempted to reform his government's version of the Communist system but succeeded only in presiding over its collapse. In 1991, the Soviet Union ceased to exist. Many of its former constituent republics joined the **Commonwealth of Independent States**.

Constituent Republics of the Soviet Union

Armenia
Azerbaijan
Belorussia
Estonia
Georgia
Kazakhstan
Kirghizia
Latvia
Lithuania
Moldavia
Russia (Russian Soviet Federated Socialist Republic)
Tadzhikistan
Turkmenistan
Ukraine
Uzbekistan

Space Exploration Investigation of outer space through the use of manned and unmanned spacecraft. As early as 1903 Russian inventor Konstantin Tsiolkovsky (1857–1935) argued for the use of rockets in exploring space. American **Robert H. Goddard** tested the first liquid-fuel rocket in the 1920s, but no rockets powerful enough for space travel existed until after **Wernher von Braun** developed V-2 rockets for Germany in **World War II**. Following the war the U.S. and the Soviet Union developed rockets capable of launching spacecraft. The Soviets were the first into space, launching the artificial satellite *Sputnik I* into Earth orbit in 1957. A space race ensued between the superpowers, with the U.S. hurriedly establishing NASA (the National Aeronautics and Space Administration) in 1958 to manage the space program. The Soviets sent the first man into space (Yuri Gagarin [1934–68], April 12, 1961); the first American in space, Alan Shepard (1923–98), followed on May 5, 1961. By the end of the decade, U.S. astronaut Neil Armstrong (1930–), heading the *Apollo 11* mission, became the first person to set foot on the Moon (July 20, 1969).

In the 1970s and 1980s, the Soviet manned space program focused on establishing space stations, with cosmonauts on the *Mir* (launched 1986) setting records for continuous habitation in space. After the glory days of its Apollo lunar missions (1968–72), NASA pursued less glamorous research with its reusable space shuttle, first launched in 1981. Hopes of an international space station, the return of humans to the Moon, and manned missions to Mars remained just hopes at century's close. However, unmanned missions sent back a wealth of data about the solar system and its planets; these included the NASA *Mariner* probes to Venus, Mercury, and Mars (1960s–70s), the NASA *Voyager* probes to Jupiter and the outer planets (1970s–80s), the European Space Agency (ESA) probe *Giotto* to Halley's Comet (1986), and NASA's *Mars Pathfinder* (1997). NASA and ESA jointly launched the Hubble Space Telescope into orbit in 1990 to make observations impossible to obtain under Earth's atmosphere. Other countries, such as Japan, have also developed space programs.

Despite the glamour of space exploration, many of the most important space-related discoveries of the 20th century were done from Earth, using optical telescopes of increasing refinement and radio telescopes (invented in the 1930s). These discoveries included the finding that the universe is expanding; evidence of the Big Bang theory of the universe's origin; and the detection of quasars, black holes, and planets around distant stars.

Spanish Civil War (1936–39) Spanish internal conflict. In 1936 the election of a leftist Popular Front government in Spain coalesced conservative opposition to the Spanish Second Republic. This nationalist movement was led by the Dascist **Falange** Party, headed by General **Francisco Franco**. On July 17 and 18, 1936, right-wing military officers in Morocco and Spain staged revolts against the republic. Full-scale civil war broke out, with nationalist forces taking control of southern and western Spain by August. Their opponents, the Loyalists or Republicans, remained strong in Catalonia and the Basque provinces, but Madrid, the capital, was placed under nationalist siege (November 1936–March 1939) and Barcelona became the seat of the Loyalist government. Fascist Germany and Italy supported Franco with arms and advisers, thereby testing armaments (including tanks and airplanes) and techniques that would be used in **World War II**. The **Soviet Union** sent aid to the Republicans, and volunteers from around the world were organized by the **Comintern** to fight for the Republican cause in **International Brigades**. Nationalist forces wore down the Republicans, who were divided ideologically among liberals, anarchists, socialists, and Communists. In 1939 the nationalists conquered Barcelona (January) and Madrid (March). About one million people died in the Spanish Civil War, many as a result of aerial bombing raids, such as the one that destroyed Guernica in April 1937. The war ushered in Franco's long dictatorship (1939–75).

Spanish Influenza Pandemic (1918–19) Worldwide epidemic of Spanish influenza, an unusually lethal form of influenza. It killed at least 21 million people around the world, including 550,000 in the U.S., making it perhaps the deadliest pandemic in human history. Troop movements in **World War I** helped to spread the disease to most inhabited parts of the globe. Despite its name, it was first identified in Kansas in the U.S. Unlike most flu viruses, the Spanish influenza virus was especially dangerous to young, otherwise healthy adults. Fear of a recurrence of the disease spurred influenza and viral research throughout the century.

Spartacist [or Spartakist] Revolt Communist uprising against the German socialist government in Berlin (January 1919). It was named for the revolutionary Spartacist League, founded in 1916 to counter traditional socialism, including that of the German government. Volunteer troops known as the **Freikorps** ended the revolt by mid-January, killing

100 people, including revolt leaders Karl Liebknecht (1871–1919) and **Rosa Luxemburg.**

SS (Schutzstaffel) German Nazi police organization. Founded in 1925, it became an independent force in 1934 under German Nazi leader **Heinrich Himmler.** From 1936 its internal security force fought internal dissent. During **World War II** it was responsible for killing millions of Eastern European Jews and directing concentration camps. At its peak it included 900,000 members.

Stavisky Affair French political scandal in 1934 involving Russian-born Frenchman Serge Alexandre Stavisky (1886–1934) and his illegal sale of forged French bonds. Upon public discovery of his crime, he committed suicide. Delayed inquiries into the death revealed his connection to and support from deputies and ministers of the Third Republic. Fostering the suspicious nature of events was the murder of a member of the public prosecutor's office. Rightist factions protested against government corruption and threatened overthrow, with one demonstration causing 14 deaths. Tensions resulted in the resignations of French prime minister **Édouard Daladier.**

Stern Gang Zionist guerrilla group founded in Palestine in 1940 by Abraham Stern (1907–42). Known formally as Lohamei Herut Yisrael (Fighters for the Freedom of Israel), it fought against British rule through attacks on individuals and installations. Though the British killed Stern in 1942, the group fought on until 1948, when it was outlawed with the establishment of Israel.

Strategic Defense Initiative (SDI) U.S. military research program to develop an antiballistic missile defense system. First proposed by President **Ronald Reagan** in 1983, it was derisively known as Star Wars for its planned use of space-based lasers to destroy nuclear missiles in flight. Critics contended that SDI represented an escalation of the arms race and that the nuclear shield could never be more than partially effective. After expenditures of about $30 billion, SDI was phased out in 1993, but the question of whether to build some kind of missile defense system remained a live one.

Sudetenland Name for mountainous region in northern Czechoslovakia annexed to Germany with the 1938 **Munich Agreement.** For centuries the area had become widely populated by Germans, yet the 1919 **Paris Peace Conference** made it part of Czechoslovakia, causing much conflict between Czechs and Germans. The land was returned to Czechoslovakia in 1945.

Suez Crisis (1956) International conflict over the Suez Canal in Egypt. In July 1956, after Britain and the U.S. canceled plans to bankroll the building of the Aswan High Dam, Egyptian president **Gamal Abdel Nasser** took over the Suez Canal Company, which was dominated by English and French interests. Britain and France secretly enlisted the aid of Israel to take back the canal and possibly overthrow Nasser. In what was known as the Second **Arab-Israeli War,** Israel invaded Egypt in October, easily pushing back Nasser's armies and capturing the **Gaza Strip** and other territory. France and Britain occupied the canal zone, ostensibly to separate the warring armies and keep the canal open. Egypt then blocked the canal with scuttled ships. Domestic opposition and denunciations by the U.S. and the **Soviet Union** eventually forced the invaders to leave. Israel and Egypt accepted a **UN** cease-fire in November, with Israel returning captured territory. The canal reopened in 1957, and a UN emergency force replaced British and French troops by March of that year. The canal remained nationalized, but Egypt reimbursed the owners of the Suez Canal Company by 1963.

Surrealism *See* **Art.**

Syndicalism Political philosophy arguing that political power should reside in federated trade unions, and that the unions should take power through direct action against government and industry, including general strikes and sabotage. Originating in the 19th century, syndicalism was often linked with **anarchism** in a doctrinal brew called anarcho-syndicalism. In the U.S. the **Industrial Workers of the World** practiced anarcho-syndicalism; in Spain, France, Italy, and Latin America, the philosophy influenced labor movements into the 1930s.

T

Taliban *See* **Mujahidin.**

Teapot Dome American cabinet-level scandal that began in 1922 when President **Warren Harding**'s secretary of the interior, Albert B. Fall (1861–1944) improperly leased two naval oil reserve sites, including one at Teapot Dome, Wyoming, to private oil companies in exchange for bribes. A Senate investigation exposed the wrongdoing, leading to Fall's bribery conviction in 1929.

Tehran Conference Meeting in Tehran, Iran, of Allied leaders **Winston Churchill, Franklin Delano Roosevelt,** and, as a member of the Allies, **Joseph Stalin,** from November 28 to December 1, 1943, in the Iran capital. Issues discussed included the formation of the **United Nations**; Soviet plans for a 1944 European offensive and that country's potential entry into the war against Japan; and future Soviet influence in the Baltic States and Eastern Europe.

Television System for sending and receiving visual images and sound via electromagnetic waves. Television had no single inventor but developed gradually in the first half of the 20th century. Among the pioneers were British inventor J. L. Baird (1888–1946) and American inventor C. F. Jenkins, who demonstrated early television systems in 1926. After **World War II**, television sets began to reach the consumer market, particularly in industrialized countries. In the 1950s television supplanted **radio** as the principal home entertainment medium; it also posed a competitive threat to **motion pictures**. It had numerous industrial, research, and communication uses, from security video surveillance to communication with spacecraft.

Later innovations included home videocassette recorders (VCRs, 1970s) and the widespread availability of cable systems (1980s), with the potential for many more stations than were available through broadcast

First Countries to Have Television (high-definition regular public broadcasting service)	
Country	Year
U.K.	1936
U.S.	1939
Soviet Union	1939
France	1948
Brazil	1950
Cuba	1950
Mexico	1950
Argentina	1951
Denmark	1951
Netherlands	1951

Source: Russell Ash, *The Top Ten of Everything*

channels. With its capacity for live transmission of events, television became a force for **globalization**, unifying the world around moments like the funeral of Princess **Diana** (1997). This trend was accentuated by the rise of all-news stations, such as the Cable News Network (CNN). *See also* **Communications Revolution**.

Temperance *See* **Prohibition**.

Terrorism Illegal use of violence by individuals or organized groups to intimidate governments and communities for political reasons. Terrorist tactics in the 20th century included murder, bombing, sabotage, destruction of property, abduction, torture, hijacking, and hostage taking. Many paramilitary revolutionary groups—including the **Irish Republican Army**, the Zionist **Irgun**, and the **PLO**—were called terrorists by their opponents, but guerrillas or freedom-fighters by their friends. Other groups— such as the **Red Brigades** in Italy and the U.S.'s Weathermen (founded in 1969)—did not obviously represent a constituency and could be more neatly described as terrorists.

Terrorism was widespread in many countries in the 1970s and afterward. Governments sometimes sponsored terrorism against opponents within their own borders—for example, the death squads that preyed on the citizens of such Latin American countries as Argentina, El Salvador, Guatemala, and Chile during periods of military rule in the 1970s and 1980s. Governments also sponsored terrorism abroad, as Iran has supported the Islamic fundamentalist group Hezbollah, responsible for terrorist attacks in Lebanon and Israel since the early 1980s. The worst terrorist attack in U.S. history came from right-wing, antigovernment activists who bombed a federal building in Oklahoma City, Okla., on April 19, 1995, killing 168 people.

Theater On-stage dramatic performances. In the early 20th century serious dramatic works, old and new, were performed at several major theater companies, such as the Comédie Française or Théâtre Français (1680, France), the Old Vic (1914, London), the Abbey Theatre (1902, Ireland), and the Moscow Art Theater (1897, Russia). Prominent playwrights of the first quarter century included **George Bernard Shaw**, **John Millington Synge**, **Arthur Wing Pinero**, **Eugene O'Neill**, and **Luigi Pirandello**. Notable performers included British actors Mrs. Patrick Campbell (1865–1940) and Ellen Terry (1848–1928).

Popular theater was often performed on the road by dramatic or vaudeville troupes. Starting in the 1880s, vaudeville, consisting of a string of musical, comedy, and novelty acts provided, mass entertainment across the U.S. until the rise of **radio**. Notable vaudeville performers included Eddie Cantor (1892–1964), **George M. Cohan**, and W. C. Fields (1880–1946). Acts traveled along a circuit of theaters of varying levels of status.

By the 1910s large-scale musical galas competed with serious drama for Broadway dominance. Under producers such as **Florenz Ziegfeld**, spectacular revues (e.g., Ziegfeld's *Follies*) featured musical and comedic performers including **Will Rogers** and Fanny Brice (1891–1951). The rise of book-based musical theater, along with radio and **motion pictures** curtailed the revue's popularity.

Elements of musical theater included a book with a sometimes contrived, sometimes serious plot, and a melodic score. Major pre–**World War II** composers included **Jerome Kern**, **George** and Ira **Gershwin**, **Cole Porter**, and **Richard Rodgers** and Lorenz Hart. Notable prewar works included Kern's *Show Boat*, the Gershwins' folk opera *Porgy and Bess*, and Porter's *Anything Goes*. In *Oklahoma!* (1943), Rodgers and Oscar Hammerstein (1895–1960) changed the musical form with a score that furthered plot and character development. Other major postwar works included Rodgers and Hammerstein's *South Pacific* and *The King and I* and Stephen Sondheim's *West Side Story* and *Gypsy*. Late-century musical theater, as seen in the works of **Andrew Lloyd Webber**, is marked by more elements of spectacle. His works include *Jesus Christ Superstar* and *Evita*. Major musical theater actors include **Mary Martin** and **Ethel Merman**.

Much drama in the U.S. during the 1930s centered on social realism and protest, reflecting the conditions of the **Great Depression**. Notable works include *Waiting for Lefty*, *Awake and Sing!*, and *Golden Boy*, all by **Clifford Odets**. By mid-century, playwrights aimed at greater naturalism and/or psychological development of character. Dominant postwar U.S. playwrights included **Arthur Miller** (*Death of a Salesman*, *All My Sons*) and **Tennessee Williams** (*The Glass Menagerie*, *A Streetcar Named Desire*).

In France, the new philosophy of existentialism was presented in the plays of **Jean-Paul Sartre** (*No Exit*, *The Flies*). In postwar France, the theater of the absurd was epitomized by the works of **Eugène Ionesco** (*The Bald Soprano*, *Rhinoceros*) and **Samuel Beckett** (*Waiting for Godot*, *Endgame*). Defining the theater of cruelty were the works of **Jean Genet** (*The Balcony*, *The Blacks*).

British drama was defined in part by the witty, worldly works of **Noël Coward** (*Private Lives*, *Blithe Spirit*). Imagination and realism marked the varieties of postwar British dramatists. Tom Stoppard (1937–) combined humor and high emotion in *Rosencrantz and Gildenstern Are Dead*, *The Real Inspector Hound*, and others. **Harold Pinter** explored everyday life through his "comedies of menace," which include *The Birthday Party* and *The Homecoming*. The "angry young man" as hero was introduced in *Look Back in Anger* by **John Osborne**. Other plays by Osborne include *The Entertainer* and *Luther*. Also noteworthy for commentary on postwar Britain is David Hare (1947–), whose works include *Plenty*.

In the 1980s and 1990s U.S. plays—such as *Angels in America* and *Rent*—concerning current social problems have flourished. The boundaries of art and theater have also been broken down through the many varieties of performance art. This wide category includes monologists such as U.S. performer Spalding Gray (1941–).

The theater of nonwestern nations in the 20th century is marked by variety. In China, the realistic drama that developed after **World War I** has largely served propagandistic purposes. In Japan, the centuries-old puppet theater and Kabuki remain popular. Popular throughout much of Asia are shadow shows, employing flat, jointed figures playing across a translucent screen.

Third International *See* **Comintern**.

Third Reich Nazi term referring to Germany from the 1933 election of **Adolf Hitler** as chancellor to the end of **World War II** in 1945. Also known as the third empire, it refers to the Reich's place as successor to two earlier German empires: the federation of lands created during the Holy Roman Empire (lasting until 1806) and the second empire (1871–1918).

Third World Developing or underdeveloped nations of Asia, Africa, and Latin America. The term came into use in the 1950s to designate nonaligned nations, those not affiliated with the First World of the U.S. and its allies, nor with the Second World of the **Soviet Union** and its allies. Third World came to connote poverty and a low level of industrialization, often associated with recent emergence from colonial status.

Three Mile Island (March 28, 1979) The site of the worst nuclear power mishap in American history. The accident occurred at the Three Mile Island reactor near Harrisburg, Pa., when the emergency cooling system failed after the regular cooling system malfunctioned. About half of the core of Unit 2 melted down and small amounts of radioactive gas were released into the air. The degree of impact on the area's residents was disputed, but the accident cost the industry billions of dollars, as design and construction standards were tightened and public opposition to nuclear power increased.

Tiananmen Square Public meeting place in the center of Beijing, China, which has been the site of notable national demonstrations. On April 5, 1976, 100,000 citizens mounted a memorial to the recently deceased **Zhou Enlai** and a protest against **Mao Zedong**. Beginning on April 22, 1989, human rights demonstrators gathered to mourn the death of reform leader Hu Yaobang (1915–79) and promote continued political openness. Within a month, demonstrators numbered one million, their presence symbolized by their erection of a 30-foot statue, the *Goddess of Liberty*. The state imposed martial law on May 20. Troops entered the square, killing between 3,000 and 5,000, injuring 10,000, and destroying the statue. While the massacre generated public disapproval, it allowed the state to regain its authority.

Titanic British ocean liner that sank in the early hours of April 15, 1912. Billed as unsinkable, the ship went down on its maiden voyage after hitting an iceberg in the North Atlantic. More than 1,500 of the 2,200 people aboard died, most of them because of a shortage of lifeboats. The disaster prompted strict regulations concerning lifeboats and safety drills and led to the creation of an international iceberg patrol. The wreck of the *Titanic* was located in 1985.

Tokyo Trials (1946–48) War crimes trials held in Japan's capital, an Asian counterpart to the **Nuremberg Trials**. An international tribunal tried 28 Japanese military and civilian leaders for crimes committed during **World War II**. The most famous defendant was General **Hideki Tojo**, who led the Japanese war effort until 1944. Among the indicted were 13 generals, three admirals, and five diplomats. Twenty-six defendants were found guilty of waging "aggressive war." Tojo and six others were hung. Sixteen defendants were given life sentences and two others received lesser judgments. Two died during the trial; one was deemed unfit to stand trial because of insanity.

Tonkin Gulf Resolution (August 1964) U.S. congressional resolution that became the legal basis for increased American involvement in the **Vietnam War**. The resolution, introduced by President **Lyndon Baines Johnson**, was approved by the U.S. Congress after North Vietnamese boats allegedly attacked American warships in the Tonkin Gulf off North Vietnam. The resolution approved presidential action to protect American troops and deter aggression against South Vietnam. Johnson used it to justify the bombing of North Vietnam and a vast increase in the number of American troops in Vietnam. In 1968 a Senate inquiry cast doubts on Johnson's account of the attacks; Congress repealed the resolution in 1971.

Totalitarianism Political system in which a single-party government strives for absolute control of all aspects of life. Political dissent is suppressed, cultural expression is regulated, and individual liberties are denied. The term was first applied to the Fascist regimes of **Benito Mussolini** in Italy and **Adolf Hitler** in Germany, as well as to the Communist rule of **Joseph Stalin** in the **Soviet Union**, indicating that totalitarianism can exist in concert with either right-wing or left-wing ideology. However, in the West during the **cold war**, Communist states were usually tarred with the pejorative *totalitarian*, while states friendly to the West but politically repressive were assigned the milder term *authoritarian*.

Transportation The conveying of people or goods. At the beginning of the 20th century, steam-driven railroads, steamships, and horse-drawn conveyances were the principal means of transportation. The internal combustion engine, perfected in the 1880s and 1890s, changed that situation. Gasoline-powered automobiles, also invented in the 1880s and 1890s, became commonplace in the 20th century with the advent of mass-production techniques that lowered their cost and broadened their availability. The leading pioneer in mass

World Motor Vehicle Ownership
(including both cars and commercial vehicles)

Ratio of motor vehicles owned		Ration of People to vehicles
1960	126,954,817	23.0
1993	595,306,648	8.8

Source: Russell Ash, *The Top Ten of Everything*

Top Vehicle-owning Countries
(including both cars and commercial vehicles, as of 1993)

Total vehicles owned

Country	In millions	Country	In millions
U.S.	188.4	Former Soviet Union	24.5
Japan	59.9	Canada	16.8
Germany	40.7	Spain	15.2
Italy	30.7	Brazil	13.2
France	28.8		
U.K.	26.4		

Source: Russell Ash, *The Top Ten of Everything*

The Decline of American Railroads

In the 20th century, use of railroads decreased as use of motor vehicles and air transportation increased. Below are two indicators of change in the U.S. railroad industry from 1900 to the late 1980s: mileage and number of employees.

	Mileage	Railroad employees
1900	193,000	1,018,000
1916	254,000	1,701,000
1920	253,000	2,076,000
1933	246,000	991,000
1945	227,000	1,439,000
1965	212,000	655,000
1987	163,000	247,000

Source: Eric Foner and John A. Garraty, *The Reader's Companion to American History*

production was American industrialist **Henry Ford**, who introduced the assembly-line method in about 1913 to build his Model T. Cars, which made distances seem magically shorter, soon became indispensable to many people, who came to rely on them for commuting and daily errands. Highways sprang up to serve people with cars; residential areas, such as suburbs, were reorganized to accommodate them. Yet many people complained about the pollution, traffic congestion, safety problems, and suburban isolation the automobile caused.

Diesel fuel replaced steam as the preferred energy source for trains and ships, as well as trucks and buses. Electrically powered streetcars or trolleys—a late 19th-century innovation—lost favor to buses after **World War I**, though electric power remained important for rapid transit systems and heavily traveled railroad corridors. **Airplanes**—an early 20th-century invention—opened the skies for the first time to heavy traffic for commercial, passenger, and military uses. By century's end, airplanes were the preferred means of swift long-distance travel, making it possible to go from virtually any place on earth to any other within a single day. By seeming to decrease distances across the globe, the transportation revolution joined with the **communications revolution** to foster **globalization**.

Trench warfare Mode of combat most notably employed in **World War I**. Thousands of miles of opposing trenches, fronted by barbed wire, were dug along the Western Front. Artillery bombardment, trench mortars, hand grenades, **chemical weapons**, and tanks were all used to try to budge the enemy out of the trenches, with little success. To attack, infantry went "over the top" and across no-man's land to the enemy trenches, but soldiers were cut down in large numbers by machine gunners. As a result, trench warfare represented stalemate, with the front line not moving more than ten miles in either direction from 1914 to 1918. The development of superior tanks and air support for mechanized attacks reduced the usefulness of trench warfare in **World War II**.

Trianon, Treaty of (June 4, 1920) Agreement at the end of **World War I** between the **Allied Powers** and Hungary. Signed at the Grand Trianon Palace at Versailles, France, it drastically reduced Hungary's size and population, taking away outlying areas that were not predominantly Magyar. Czechoslovakia received Slovakia and Ruthenia, Yugoslavia received Croatia, and Romania received Transylvania. Resentment in Hungary over the treaty led it to side with Germany in **World War II**.

Tripartite Pact (September 27, 1940) Treaty that formally created the **World War II** military alliance among Germany, Japan, and Italy, the most prominent **Axis Powers**. It was an extension of the **Anti-Comintern Pact**.

Triple Alliance Military compact between Germany, Austria-Hungary, and Italy, formed in 1882 and renewed every five years until 1915. The alliance ended when Italy declined to enter **World War I** on the side of Germany and Austria-Hungary, joining the Allied side instead.

Triple Entente Alliance of Britain, France, and Russia, formed in 1907 to supplement the **Entente Cordiale** between Britain and France. It was transformed into a military alliance after the outbreak of **World War I** in 1914.

Truman Doctrine U.S. foreign policy articulated by President **Harry S Truman** in 1947. Epitomizing the principle of **containment**, it stated that the U.S. would support countries opposing Communism throughout the world. It was used immediately to justify sending military and economic aid to Greece and Turkey, which were then faced with Communist insurgents; later, it provided the rationale for involving U.S. troops in the **Korean War** and the **Vietnam War**.

Tupac Amaru *See* **Tupamaros**.

Tupamaros (National Liberation Movement) Uruguayan political organization. Founded as a socialist urban guerrilla movement in 1963, it was named for 18th-century Peruvian Inca revolutionary Tupac Amaru II (1740–81) (who also supplied the name for Tupac Amaru, the Peruvian guerrilla group of the 1980s). The tactics of Tupamaros included bombing, assassination, and kidnapping. In 1973, as Uruguay settled into military government, the army crushed the movement and drove many members into exile. In 1985, one year after the restoration of constitutional government, Tupamaros reconvened as a legal political party and renounced violence.

U

U-2 incident (1960) International imbroglio caused by the downing of an American U-2 spy plane over the **Soviet Union** on May 1, 1960, just prior to an East-West summit meeting. Initially the U.S. claimed that the captured pilot, Gary Francis Powers (1929–77), lacked authorization for the flight, but it later acknowledged responsibility. Soviet premier **Nikita Khrushchev** threatened to cancel the summit unless the U.S. apologized and ended the flights. President **Dwight D. Eisenhower**'s promise to stop reconnaissance flights for the rest of his term did not satisfy Khrushchev, who suspended the conference. Powers received a 10-year prison sentence, but he was exchanged for a Soviet spy in February 1962. The U-2 incident severely strained Soviet-American relations.

Uncertainty Principle Physical principle, stated by German physicist **Werner Heisenberg** in 1927, that it is impossible to know both the position and the momentum of a subatomic particle with complete precision. Also known as the principle of indeterminism, this rule makes it impossible in theory to predict the future states of a system of elementary particles. The uncertainty principle had philosophical implications, notably in raising doubt about causality and undermining deterministic worldviews.

Union of Soviet Socialist Republics *See* **Soviet Union**.

United Nations (UN) International organization conceived during **World War II** and chartered in 1945 to act on problems affecting world peace. Under a name coined by **Franklin Delano Roosevelt**, it developed at the **Dumbarton Oaks** and **Yalta Conferences** to counter **Axis Powers** in 1944 and 1945. In 1945 the United Nations charter was signed and ratified, with the first meeting held in London in 1946, attended by 51 member states.

As outlined in the charter, major divisions of the UN include the General Assembly, Security Council, International Court of Justice (World Court), Economic and Social Council, and Secretariat. The General Assembly, which is open to all nations willing to accept the obligations of membership, addresses administrative, economic, and political matters. The Security Council, which deals with international security problems, has 15 members, including five permanent ones: China, France, Great Britain, Russia, and the U.S. The Secretariat is responsible for administrative concerns.

Following the establishment of the United Nations Truce Supervision Organization (UNTSO) in 1948, the UN has allowed the use of multinational peacekeeping observers and, from 1956, peacekeeping forces. United Nations programs include the United Nations

---

Specialized Agencies within the UN

Food and Agriculture Organization of the United Nations (FAO)
International Atomic Energy Agency (IAEA)
International Civil Aviation Organization (ICAO)
International Fund for Agricultural Development (IFAD)
International Labor Organization (ILO)
International Maritime Organization (IMO)
International Telecommunication Union (ITU)
United Nations Educational, Scientific, and Cultural Organization (UNESCO)
United Nations Industrial Development Organization (UNIDO)
United Nations Relief and Works Agency for Palestine Refugees in the Near East (UNRWA)
Universal Postal Union (UPU)
World Bank Group, comprising International Bank for Reconstruction and Development (IBRD, World Bank):

    International Finance Corporation (IFC),

    International Development Association (IDA),

    International Monetary Fund (IMF), and Multilateral Investment Guarantee Agency (MIGA)
World Health Organization (WHO)
World Intellectual Property Organization (WIPO)
World Meteorological Organization (WMO)

Children's Fund (UNICEF); agencies include the World Health Organization (WHO) and United Nations Educational, Scientific, and Cultural Organization (UNESCO).

The first UN Secretary-General was Norwegian diplomat Trygve Lie (1896–1968), who served from 1946 to 1952. UN headquarters has been in New York City since 1952, on land donated by John D. Rockefeller, Jr., and New York City. As of 1997, there are 185 member states.

V

Vatican II or **Second Vatican Council** (1962–65) Ecumenical council of the Roman Catholic Church. Pope **John XXIII** convened the council (called the second in memory of the first Vatican Council in 1869–70) to pursue renewal of the church in the modern world; it was concluded under his successor, Pope **Paul VI**. The participants decided on numerous reforms, including greater lay participation in the church and use of the vernacular rather than Latin in the liturgy. The council denounced anti-Semitism and encouraged ecumenism; observers were included from Protestant and Eastern Orthodox denominations. Though some of its decisions met with controversy and resistance, the council did much to modernize and revitalize the church.

Versailles Treaty (June 28, 1919) Treaty imposed on Germany by the victorious **Allied Powers** after **World War I**. Germany ceded territory to France, Poland, Belgium and Denmark. Britain, France, and other victors took control of German colonies under a mandate system. The treaty contained a "war guilt" clause that blamed Germany for starting the

Secretaries-General of the United Nations

Name	Country of origin	Birth & death dates	Period of service
Trygve Lie	Norway	1896–1968	Feb. 1, 1946–April 10, 1953
Dag Hammarskjöld	Sweden	1905–61	April 10, 1953–Sept. 18, 1961
U Thant*	Myanmar (Burma)	1909–74	Nov. 30, 1962–Dec. 31, 1971
Kurt Waldheim	Austria	1918–	Jan. 1, 1972–Dec. 31, 1981
Javier Pérez de Cuellar	Peru	1920–	Jan. 1, 1982–Dec. 31, 1991
Boutros Boutros-Ghali	Egypt	1922–	Jan. 1, 1992–Dec. 31, 1996
Kofi Annan	Ghana	1938–	Jan. 1, 1997–

*Acting secretary-general from Nov. 3, 1961.

United Nations Principal Organs

General Assembly
Security Council
Secretariat
Economic and Social Council (ECOSOC)
International Court of Justice (World Court)
Trusteeship Council (inactive)

United Nations Programs

International Research and Training Institute for the Advancement of Women (INSTRAW)
United Nations Center for Human Settlements (UNCHS, Habitat)
United Nations Children's Fund (UNICEF)
United Nations Conference on Trade and Development (UNCTAD)
United Nations Development Program (UNDP)
United Nations Environment Program (UNEP)
United Nations Fund for Population Activities (UNFPA)
Office of the United Nations High Commissioner for Refugees (UNHCR)
United Nations Institute for Training and Research (UNITAR)
United Nations University (UNU)
World Food Council (WFC)
World Food Program (WFP)

war. It established a reparations commission, which determined that Germany owed $33 billion in war damages. Other provisions limited the German army to 100,000 men, abolished the General Staff, and demilitarized the Rhine River valley. The treaty also established the **League of Nations**. Many Germans bitterly resented the treaty, and it contributed to the economic problems and political instability of postwar Germany.

Vichy Regime Government established by Nazi Germany (*see* **Nazi Party**) in the unoccupied southeastern two-fifths of France after the French defeat in 1940. Marshal **Philippe Pétain** and politician Pierre Laval (1883–1945) molded the provisional government into an authoritarian, reactionary regime. Vichy retained control of the French navy and French troops in its overseas colonies. The government leaders differed over how far to collaborate with Germany in military matters. It refused to join Germany in joint actions in the Middle East and was split over helping the Allied invasion of North Africa in 1942. After the Germans occupied Vichy in November 1942, the regime cooperated fully with the Nazis. The Free French government abolished Vichy in September 1944.

Vietnam War (Second Indochina War) (1959–1975) Successful war waged by Communist North Vietnam to topple the South Vietnam government and reunify the country. North Vietnam began waging guerrilla warfare after South Vietnam refused in 1956 to participate in elections to reunite the country, which had been divided by an international conference (*see* **Indochina War**). South Vietnamese Communist troops—Viet Cong—began attacking military and government installations with aid from the North. The U.S. supported South Vietnam and began sending troops in 1961. By 1962 over 11,000 U.S. troops were stationed there. The South Vietnamese government, beset by numerous coups and riddled with corruption, could not stop the insurgency. North Vietnam, led by **Ho Chi Minh** and aided by the **Soviet Union** and China, started infiltrating regular troops into the South to help the Viet Cong.

Vietnam War Deaths	
U.S.[1]	58,167
South Vietnam	400,000
North Vietnam[2]	900,000

[1]Includes 47,366 battle deaths and 10,801 other deaths.

[2]Includes both Viet Cong and North Vietnamese. Figures for South and North Vietnam are estimates.

In August 1964, citing an alleged North Vietnamese attack on American ships in the Gulf of Tonkin, President **Lyndon Baines Johnson** persuaded Congress to give him authority to escalate the war (*see* **Tonkin Gulf Resolution**). American planes began bombing the North in early 1965; by the end of that year, almost 200,000 American troops were in Vietnam. Despite their superior weaponry and command of the air, the Americans and South Vietnamese could not uproot the Viet Cong from the countryside nor stop more North Vietnamese from crossing into the South. American policy makers—committed to **containment** of Communist expansion and fearing the U.S. would lose credibility by backing down—sent more troops to Vietnam.

In January 1968 Communist forces launched a formidable offensive during the lunar new year festival (Tet). They suffered enormous casualties in fierce struggles in Saigon, Hue, and other major cities. Known as the Tet offensive, the campaign failed, but its initial success and potency convinced many more Americans that the war was a hopeless mistake. Shortly afterward Johnson announced he would not run for reelection in 1968, and **Richard Nixon** was elected in November. Nixon announced a policy of *Vietnamization* whereby South Vietnam would assume more responsibility for fighting the war and ultimately stand on its own.

American troops attacked Communist staging areas inside Cambodia in 1970, a decision that increased domestic opposition to the war in America. A powerful antiwar movement had already been growing, led by such groups as Students for a Democratic Society (SDS, founded in 1960) and spurred by events like the release of the **Pentagon Papers** (1967) and the **My Lai Massacre** (1968). Peace talks had begun in 1968, but petered out in 1972, after which the war intensified with increased bombing of the North and a major Communist offensive. An agreement was finally hammered out in 1973 (*see* **Paris Peace Conference**), and the last American combat soldier withdrew that year. In December 1974

North Vietnam invaded the South and by April 1975 had won complete victory. On April 21 President Thien resigned, and Saigon was surrendered to North Vietnamese forces on April 30. At the time of surrender, the more than 1,300 Americans remaining were evacuated by U.S. helicopters. It is estimated that 1.3 million Vietnamese soldiers and civilians died in the war; another 3 million were wounded. About 58,000 Americans lost their lives in the conflict while another 153,000 were wounded.

W

Warsaw Pact (Warsaw Treaty Organization) Mutual defense alliance between the Soviet Union and its Eastern European client states. The pact was established in Warsaw, Poland, on May 14, 1955, as a counterbalance to **NATO**. The signatories were Albania (a member until 1968), Bulgaria, Czechoslovakia, East Germany, Hungary, Poland, Romania, and the **Soviet Union**. The alliance was formally dissolved in 1991, following the collapse of the Communist governments of Eastern Europe.

Warsaw Rising Rebellion from August to October 1944 during which the Polish underground army recaptured and then lost the German-held city. After seizing parts of the city on August 1, the anti-Communist Polish Home Army received no reinforcements from the nearby Red Army, and British and U.S. planes were prohibited by **Joseph Stalin** from using Soviet airfields to deliver supplies. Well-equipped German troops forced surrender on October 4. By the siege's end, the city was decimated and 200,000 Poles had died. Previously inactive Russian troops invaded Warsaw on January 17, 1945, raising speculation that Russia withheld support in order to assure Communist takeover of the city.

Watergate (1972–74) U.S. political scandal that forced President **Richard Nixon** to resign. Criminal and congressional investigation of a bungled 1972 burglary at the Democratic National Committee's headquarters in the Watergate Apartment Complex in Washington, D.C., led to charges that the Republican administration was engaged in a complex web of wrongdoing. Evidence accumulated of espionage and sabotage against political opponents, acceptance of illegal campaign contributions, and obstruction of justice. After the House Judiciary Committee adopted three articles of impeachment, Nixon resigned on August 9, 1974; shortly afterward, his successor, **Gerald Ford**, pardoned him.

Weimar Republic German republic established in 1919 after the collapse of the German Empire in **World War I**. The government suffered from high postwar inflation and the burden of reparations payments imposed by the **Versailles Treaty**. It also faced violent opposition from reactionary military and political elites and from left-wing radicals. Despite these handicaps it stabilized its currency in the 1920s and benefited from a global economic boom. However, the **Great Depression** triggered a political crisis that enabled **Adolf Hitler**'s **Nazi Party** to become the majority party in the German parliament by 1932. After he was appointed chancellor in 1933, Hitler suppressed all political opposition and abolished the Weimar government.

West Bank Section of Palestine on the west bank of the river Jordan. Though deemed by the **UN** partition plan of 1947 a separate Arab state, it was captured by Jordan in the first **Arab-Israeli War** (1948). It was taken by Israel in the **Six-Day War** (1967). Israeli occupation and settlement of the West Bank stoked tensions with Palestinian Arabs, resulting in frequent bloodshed. In 1994 the West Bank, starting with Jericho, began to receive limited autonomy under **PLO** rule.

Women's Movement The effort by women to achieve social, political, and economic equality. Building on efforts begun by U.S. reformers Susan B. Anthony (1820–1906) and Elizabeth Cady Stanton (1815–1902), 20th-century U.S. reformers such as Carrie Chapman Catt (1859–1947) campaigned for women's suffrage, becoming known as suffragists. In 1920 the 19th Amendment to the U.S. Constitution granted women the right to vote. In Great Britain, British reformer **Emmeline Pankhurst** (1858–1928) founded the Women's Social and Political Union in 1903 and organized radical action to support women's suffrage and social equality. British women were granted partial enfranchisement in 1918 and full equality with men in 1928. Other industrialized democratic countries granting voting rights to women near or during the 20th century include New Zealand (1893), Australia (1902), and Switzerland (1971). Revolutions sometimes sparked women's voting rights, as in Russia (after 1917), Eastern Europe (after 1945), Germany (1918–19), Turkey (1922–23), and Communist China (after 1945).

After **World War II**, the Western women's movement for social and legal equality became known as feminism. Influential writers of the period included **Simone de Beauvoir** (*The Second Sex*, 1949) and American author **Betty Friedan**, whose book *The Feminine Mystique* (1963) crystallized middle-class women's discontent and sparked the women's liberation movement. In 1966 she and others founded the National Organization for Women (NOW), whose stated goals included working for "true equality for all women in America, and toward a fully equal partnership of the sexes."

The organization and other feminists including American activist and writer Gloria Steinem (1936–) successfully raised consciousness about equal pay, shared child care, and reproductive rights, effecting some long-term change, including the 1973 U.S. Supreme Court decision on abortion, *Roe v. Wade*, which has been challenged ever since by groups styling themselves as a "right-to-life" movement or "pro-life." (Feminists prefer to refer to these activists as "anti-choice" and to themselves as "pro-choice.") In addition to the setbacks the movement has faced regarding state and local restrictions on the availability of abortion, its leaders failed to secure adoption of the Equal Rights Amendment (ERA) to the U.S. Constitution. Drafted in 1921 and first introduced to the U.S. Congress in 1923, the ERA was finally passed by Congress in 1972. It then went to the states for ratification,

Achievement of Women's Suffrage in Selected Countries	
1893	New Zealand (first nation)
1902	Australia
1906	Finland (first European nation)
1915	Denmark
1917	Soviet Russia
1919	Austria
1919	Germany
1920	U.S. (19th Amendment ratified)
1928	U.K.
1932	Brazil
1934	Turkey
1944	France
1945	Italy
1947	Argentina
1947	China
1948	Israel
1953	Mexico
1956	Egypt
1963	Iran
1964	Iraq
1971	Switzerland
1975	Portugal

Source: Joni Seager and Ann Olson, *Women in the World*

needing two-thirds of the states, or 38, to ratify within seven years. Despite a three-year extension of the deadline to 1982, the ERA missed the mark by three states. It has continued to be reintroduced to Congress ever since.

From the 1970s, the movement has continued to act on such issues as pay equity and child care while developing further in other areas, including sex discrimination, sexual harassment, women's role in the military, women's leadership in elective offices, the rights and experiences of lesbians, domestic violence, rape, pornography, and artists' representations of the female form and of the female experience. It has also worked to introduce gender-neutral language into all forms of discourse. The diversity of the theories and positions espoused by third-wave activists and thinkers has been considered both a strength and a weakness of the women's movement at the end of the century.

Woodstock Festival (August 1969) Rock music festival near Bethel, N.Y. Known formally as the Woodstock Music and Arts Fair, it was attended by about 400,000 young people. It symbolized the height of the 1960s youth counterculture in the U.S., with its rejection of authority and belief in love, peace, sexual freedom, and—for many—the power of mind-bending drugs. The youth counterculture encompassed such disparate movements as those of hippies, who tried to retreat from modern industrial life into rural communes, and the New Left, a collection of radical individuals and groups (such as Students for a Democratic Society) opposed to the **Vietnam War** and the status quo. Musicians who performed at Woodstock included Jimi Hendrix (1943–70), Janis Joplin (1943–70), the Grateful Dead, Joan Baez (1941–), and Joe Cocker (1944–).

World Bank Common name for the International Bank for Reconstruction and Development, a specialized agency of the UN. Founded in 1945 in keeping with the 1944 **Bretton Woods Conference**, it borrows money in the commercial market and offers development loans on commercial terms to developing countries. Most of the world's nations belong to the bank; all members must also belong to the **International Monetary Fund**. Its goals varied over the decades. Post–**World War II** it administered loans to rebuild war-damaged European economies. From the 1950s, it concentrated on building underdeveloped nations. In the 1990s it focused on reconfiguring economies of former Communist nations.

World War I (1914–18) Global military conflict. Known also as the Great War and centered in Europe, it was caused by territorial and economic rivalry among the world's great powers. The rivalry had grown since the late 19th century, when Germany emerged as an imperialist nation, acquiring colonies and building a fleet that threatened Britain's naval supremacy. Contributing to the war were nationalist fervor, particularly in France and Germany, and nationalist yearnings in the weakened Austro-Hungarian and Ottoman Empires.

The war's worldwide scale arose from alliances, such as the **Triple Alliance** and **Triple Entente**, that committed nations to mutual defense; colonial empires that provided far-flung stages for battles; and the ability of modern ships and railroads to move armies rapidly into place. The unprecedented deadliness of the war was due to a massive arms race in the decades prior to the war; the mass-production capabilities of 20th-century industry; and advances in the machinery of killing—artillery, tanks, submarines, airplanes, and chemical weapons. Nearly 10 million combatants were killed, including 8.5 million known deaths from all causes and about 1 million missing. An additional 21 million were wounded. Millions of civilians died, many through starvation and epidemics, most lethally the

```
┌─────────────────────────────────────────────────────────────────────────┐
│                        World War I Major Battles                          │
│                                                                           │
│  1914                                                                     │
│  Aug. 14–25              Frontiers, Battles of (including Mons, Aug. 22–23, 1914; and │
│                             Ardennes, Aug. 20–25, 1914)                   │
│  Aug. 26–31              Tannenberg, Battle of                            │
│  Sept. 5–9               Marne, First Battle of                           │
│  Sept. 9–14              Masurian Lakes, Battle of                        │
│  Oct. 19–Nov. 22         Ypres, First Battle of                           │
│  Nov. 1                  Coronel, Battle of                               │
│                                                                           │
│  1915                                                                     │
│  Feb.                    Masurian Lakes, Second Battle of                 │
│  Apr. 22–May 25          Ypres, Second Battle of                          │
│  Apr. 25, 1915–Jan. 9, 1916   Gallipoli (Dardanelles) Campaign            │
│  May 9–June 18           Artois, First Battle of                          │
│  May–Dec.                Gorlice, Battle of                               │
│                                                                           │
│  1916                                                                     │
│  Feb. 21–Dec. 18         Verdun, Battle of                                │
│  May 31–June 1           Jutland, Battle of                               │
│  July 1–Nov. 18          Somme, Battle of                                 │
│                                                                           │
│  1917                                                                     │
│  Apr.–May                Aisne, First Battle of                           │
│  June 21–Nov. 4          Ypres, Third Battle of (Passchendaele)           │
│  Oct. 24–Nov. 12         Caporetto, Battle of                             │
│  Nov. 20–Dec. 4          Cambrai, Battle of                               │
│                                                                           │
│  1918                                                                     │
│  Mar. 21–Apr. 6          Somme Offensive                                  │
│  May 27–June 6           Aisne Offensive (including Battles of Chateau-Thierry, May │
│                             30–June 17, 1918; and Belleau Wood, May 30–June 17, 1918) │
│  July 15–Aug. 6          Marne, Second Battle of                          │
│  Sept. 12–13             St. Mihiel, Battle of                            │
│  Sept. 26–Oct. 31        Argonne Forest, Battle of                        │
│  Oct. 24–Nov. 4          Vittorio Veneto, Battle of                       │
│                                                                           │
│  Source: Erik Goldstein, Wars and Peace Treaties 1816-1991                │
└─────────────────────────────────────────────────────────────────────────┘
```

Spanish influenza pandemic of 1918–19.

The war was triggered on June 28, 1914, when Serbian nationalist Gavrilo Princip (1894–1918) assassinated the Austrian heir apparent, Archduke Francis Ferdinand (1863–1914), and his wife Sophie Chotek, duchess of Hohenberg (1868–1914). The murders took place in Sarajevo, Bosnia, which was then part of the Austro-Hungarian Empire. One month later, Austria declared war on Serbia (July 28), causing the tangle of prewar alliances to come into play. Serbia's ally Russia mobilized for war on Austria; Austria's ally

Germany declared war on Russia and France. On August 3, German forces set out to attack France, invading neutral Luxembourg and Belgium along the way, prompting Britain (with its dominions, such as Australia) to declare war on Germany. Within weeks, Montenegro and Japan joined Britain and the other Allies; the Ottoman Empire joined the opposing **Central Powers**. Later, Bulgaria joined the Central Powers, while more than 20 nations, including Italy, Romania, Portugal, Greece, and the United States, joined the **Allied** and Associated **Powers**.

Germany's strategy, known as the **Schlieffen Plan**, was to capture France quickly, allowing time to concentrate forces on the Eastern Front against Russia. France's counterattacks in Alsace-Lorraine and the Ardennes were unsuccessful (*see* page 364 for battle dates), but the French were boosted by the arrival in August 1914 of the British Expeditionary Force. Before the Germans could reach Paris, Allied victories at the First Battles of the Marne and Ypres drove them back to the Aisne River, where the opposing lines settled into the stalemate of **trench warfare**. The front lines hardly budged until just before war's end; attempts to break through, such as those of France at Artois and Champagne in 1915, failed with heavy casualties. The Germans tried poison gas at the Second Battle of Ypres in 1915 and major offensives at Verdun (1916) and the Second Battle of the Marne (1918), but none of these attacks succeeded. The British tried to break the German line at the Somme (1916) and the Third Battle of Ypres, popularly called Passchendaele (1917), but these too were unsuccessful. At Cambrai (1915), the British smashed through the line with tanks, winning the world's first tank victory. They were forced back soon afterward by a German counterattack.

On the Eastern Front, Russian forces invaded East Prussia in Germany but were repulsed at Tannenberg and Mazurian Lakes (1914). The Russians enjoyed victories against the Austrians at Lemberg (1915) and elsewhere. But the Germans and Austrians, in such victories as Gorlice (1915), succeeded in driving the Russians back and forcing them out of most of Poland. A Russian offensive in 1916 foundered, and, in 1917, under the strain of war, Russia's czarist regime was overthrown. The **Bolsheviks**, who came to power in the second of the **Russian Revolutions of 1917,** signed the armistice of Brest-Litovsk (December 15, 1917, a precursor to the Treaty of **Brest-Litovsk,** March 3, 1918), withdrawing Russia from the war. This allowed Germany to concentrate its forces on the Western Front.

The war was fought outside Europe as well. At sea, the only major battle was Jutland (1916), between the navies of Britain and Germany; it was indecisive but succeeded in confirming British naval supremacy. The Germans adopted unrestricted submarine warfare on British and Allied shipping (1917), a course that helped convince the United States to enter the war (April 1917).

The Gallipoli or Dardanelles campaign (1915), a major Allied offensive against the Ottoman Empire, failed to force the Turks out of the war. But the Arab Revolt (1916–18) ended Ottoman control of the Arabian peninsula. By 1918, the British had captured Palestine and most of Mesopotamia (now Iraq); the French captured Lebanon and Syria.

Persuaded by the territorial promises in the Treaty of **London,** Italy entered the war in 1915, opening a new Southern Front against the Austrians. The Austrians won at the Battle of Caporetto (1917) but were defeated at Vittorio Veneto (1918).

In the Balkans, the Central Powers captured Serbia (1915) and Romania (1916), but were unable to conquer Greece. In the Pacific region, German Oceania, German New Guinea,

World War I Armed Forces and Casualties by Country

Country	Total mobilized forces	Killed	Wounded	Prisoners or casualties	Total missing
Allied and associated powers					
Belgium	267,000	13,716	44,686	34,659	93,061
British Empire	8,904,467	908,371	2,090,212	191,652	3,190,235
France	8,410,000	1,357,800	4,266,000	537,000	6,160,800
Greece	230,000	5,000	21,000	1,000	27,000
Italy	5,615,000	650,000	947,000	600,000	2,197,000
Japan	800,000	300	907	3	1,210
Montenegro	50,000	3,000	10,000	7,000	20,000
Portugal	100,000	7,222	13,751	12,318	33,291
Romania	750,000	335,706	120,000	80,000	535,706
Russia	12,000,000	1,700,000	4,950,000	2,500,000	9,150,000
Serbia	707,343	45,000	133,148	152,958	331,106
United States	4,355,000	116,516	204,002	4,500	325,018
Total	42,188,810	5,142,631	12,800,706	4,121,090	22,066,427
Central powers					
Austria-Hungary	7,800,000	1,200,000	3,620,000	7,020,000	
Bulgaria	1,200,000	87,500	152,390	266,919	
Germany	11,000,000	1,773,700	4,216,058	7,142,558	
Turkey	2,850,000	325,000	400,000	975,000	
Total	22,850,000	3,386,200	8,388,448	15,404,477	
Grand total	65,038,810	8,528,831	21,189,154	37,470,904	

Sources: Britannica Online; Encarta 97; Otto Johnson, ed., Information Please Almanac

World War I Combatants (with year of entry into war)

Central powers
Austria-Hungary (1914)
Germany (1914)
Ottoman Empire(1914)
Bulgaria (1915)
Turkey

Allied and associated powers (principal members)
Serbia (1914)
Russia (1914)
Luxembourg (1914)
France (1914)
Belgium (1914)
British Empire (1914)
Japan (1914)
Montenegro (1914)
Russia (1914)
Luxembourg (1914)
France (1914)
San Marino (1915)

Italy (1915)
Romania (1916)
Siam (now Thialand) (1917)
Liberia (1917)
China (1917)
Brazil (1917)
Guatemala (1917)
Nicaragua (1918)
Costa Rica (1918)
Haiti (1918)
Honduras (1918)

Source: Erik Goldstein, Wars and Peace Treaties 1816–1991

and Togo fell to the Allies in 1914. In Africa, most German colonies were captured by the Allies: German South-West Africa (now Namibia) fell to South African troops in 1915; Cameroon surrendered in 1916. German East Africa held out against Allied attacks until after Germany's surrender.

The arrival of U.S. troops in Europe in 1917 changed the course of the war. While the other powers were economically exhausted and drained of manpower and morale, the American forces were fresh. In 1918 the Germans were forced to retreat behind the Hindenburg Line, their western line of fortifications built in 1916–17. The Allies won victories at Amiens and Argonne Forest (1918). Still, there was no single decisive battle that ended the war. Rather, the Central Powers collapsed under the strain of so many costly years. Bulgaria signed an armistice on September 30; the Ottoman Empire on October 30. As it crumbled into independent republics, the Austro-Hungarian Empire signed its armistice on November 3. In Germany, revolution forced Emperor William II to abdicate (November 9). Germany concluded an armistice on November 11, ending the fighting.

At the **Paris Peace Conference** (1919–20), the victorious Allies dictated a harsh peace to the defeated Central Powers. The Ottoman and Austro-Hungarian Empires were dissolved; heavy **reparations** were required of the defeated countries; the maps of Europe, the Middle East, and Africa were redrawn to provide self-determination to some national communities and to benefit the Allies. The treaties produced at the conference included **Versailles** (1919) with Germany, **St. Germain** (1919) with Austria, and **Trianon** (1920) with Hungary. Though the **Fourteen Points** of U.S. president **Woodrow Wilson**'s peace program were only partly followed, one point was put into effect: the formation of a **League of Nations**, an international organization meant to keep the peace. But the League proved incapable of handling the resentments and tensions left over by the war, particularly in Germany, which had been forced to acknowledge guilt for the war. Just 20 years after the **Paris Peace Conference**, most of the combatants were fighting again, in the even more massive conflict of **World War II**.

World War II (1939–45) Global military conflict. The two principal theaters were Europe and the Pacific Ocean, but fighting also took place in East Asia, North Africa, the Middle East, and the North Atlantic. On one side were the **Axis Powers**—principally Germany, Japan, and Italy, but also including Hungary, Bulgaria, and Romania. On the other were the **Allied Powers**—principally the United States, Britain, and the Soviet Union, but eventually including nearly 50 nations, such as the British Commonwealth countries (e.g., Australia and Canada), France, China, Poland, and Yugoslavia. The war was the largest in history, involving more troops and costing more lives than any that had come before. To the greatest extent yet seen, it was an example of total war, in which civilians were highly involved and the belligerents' industrial base was of vital importance. The war succeeded in destroying Fascism as a threat to world peace while reordering the world into one dominated by two superpowers locked in a **cold war**.

Preying on economic hardship and German resentment over the harsh terms of the Treaty of **Versailles**, **Adolf Hitler** and his **Nazi Party** came to power in Germany in 1933. The German dictator espoused a Fascist ideology similar to that of **Benito Mussolini** in Italy and the military regime in Japan, but he combined it with a bizarre racial theory that exalted Germans (whom he called Aryans), discounted Slavs, and scapegoated Jews. On the basis of that theory, Hitler began a campaign to increase the *lebensraum*, or living space, of Germans through territorial expansion. He did so with the consent of Mussolini, with

World War II Combatants (with year of entry into war)

Axis powers	Axis states that subsequently declared war against
Germany (1939)	Italy (1943)
Italy (1940)	Romania (1944)
Hungary (1941)	Bulgaria (1944)
Bulgaria (1941)	Finland (1944)
Romania (1941)	San Marino (1944)
Finland (1941)	Hungary (1945)
Japan (1941)	
Manchukuo (1941)	
Slovakia (1941)	
Croatia (1941)	
Albania (occupied by Italy; 1941)	
Thailand (1942)	
China (Nanking government; 1943)	

Allied powers

Poland (1939)	El Salvador (1941)	Chile (1945)
Great Britain (1939)	Haiti (1941)	Venezuela (1945)
France (1939)	Honduras (1941)	Uruguay (1945)
Australia (1939)	Nicaragua (1941)	Turkey (1945)
New Zealand (1939)	Czechoslovakia (1941)	Egypt (1945)
South Africa (1939)	China (1941)	Syria (1945)
Canada (1939)	Cuba (1941)	Lebanon (1945)
Denmark (1940)	Guatemala (1941)	Saudi Arabia (1945)
Norway (1940)	Mexico (1942)	Argentina (1945)
Belgium (1940)	Brazil (1942)	Mongolia (1945)
Luxembourg (1940)	Ethiopia (1942)	
Netherlands (1940)	Iraq (1943)	
Greece (1940)	Iran (1943)	
Yugoslavia (1941)	Colombia (1943)	
Soviet Union (1941)	Bolivia (1943)	
United States (1941)	Liberia (1944)	
Panama (1941)	Ecuador (1945)	
Costa Rica (1941)	Paraguay (1945)	Source: Erik Goldstein, *Wars*
Dominican Republic (1941)	Peru (1945)	*and Peace Treaties 1816–1991*

whom he formed the Rome-Berlin Axis in 1936, and, initially, without opposition from Britain or France, who pursued a policy of **appeasement**. Contravening agreements made at the **Paris Peace Conference**, Hitler rearmed Germany; reoccupied and remilitarized the Rhineland, the territory bordering the Rhine River (1936); and annexed Austria (in the **Anschluss**, 1938). In 1938 he annexed the **Sudetenland**, a part of Czechoslovakia, then broke the **Munich Agreement** (1938) by capturing the remainder. A nonaggression pact (August 1939) with the **Soviet Union**, persuading him that he would not face war on two fronts, emboldened him to continue.

On September 1, 1939, German armies invaded Poland in the form of a rapid, mobilized attack known as **blitzkrieg**. The invasion brought declarations of war from Britain and France and the start of World War II. Later that month, the Soviet Union invaded Poland from the east, capturing part of the country in accord with partition terms in the German-Soviet nonaggression pact.

At first there followed a period known as the **Phony War** for its lack of military activity. That ended in April 1940 when Germany invaded and occupied Denmark and Norway. In May Hitler invaded France, striking through Belgium, Luxembourg, and the Netherlands (*see* **Schlieffen Plan**), thus avoiding the fortifications of the **Maginot line**. The **British Expeditionary Force** in France was forced to retreat across the English Channel in the evacuation at Dunkirk (1940). Germany occupied northern and central France; in southern France, it installed the puppet government of the **Vichy regime**. In September 1940 the **Tripartite Pact** was signed, creating the formal military alliance among Germany, Italy, and Japan, the most prominent Axis Powers.

Hitler attacked Britain with air raids in the Battle of Britain (1940). The bombing campaign damaged many cities but did not establish air superiority, forcing Hitler to abandon a planned invasion, while British prime minister **Winston Churchill** emerged as an indomitable war leader. Churchill received support from U.S. president **Franklin Delano Roosevelt**, who with him issued the **Atlantic Charter** (1941), a statement of war aims, and who provided military assistance through the **Lend-Lease** Act (1941).

By then Italy had expanded the war to North Africa. Prior to World War II, Italy had invaded and annexed Ethiopia in the Abyssinian or Ethiopian-Italian War (1935–36). In September 1940 Italy invaded Egypt. British forces repelled the advance; Germany intervened in 1941, sending forces under General **Erwin Rommel**. Rommel's troops won victories at Bir Hacheim and Tobruk (1942) but were defeated at El Alamein (October–November 1942) by the British, led by General **Bernard Montgomery**. That victory, with an Allied North African invasion on November 8, led to the securing of North Africa by spring 1943. Previously, British and Free French forces had secured Iraq, Iran, Syria, and Lebanon from German control (1941).

In April 1941, Germany conquered Yugoslavia and Greece. In June, Hitler broke his nonaggression pact by invading the Soviet Union. The campaign, code-named Barbarossa, caused tremendous casualties on both sides. Germany rapidly captured much of the western U.S.S.R., besieging Leningrad and threatening Moscow. But in the winter of 1941–42, the Soviets, under General **Georgi Zhukov**, launched a counteroffensive that saved Moscow. Germany's offensives in spring and summer 1942 failed to defeat the Soviets. The decisive Battle of Stalingrad (August 23, 1942–February 2, 1943) was the turning point of the war in Europe. As German forces, commanded by General Friedrich Paulus (1890–1957), fought house-to-house for control of Stalingrad, Soviet forces barraged and encircled them in November. Trapped and forbidden by Hitler to surrender, the German army slowly froze and starved before the remnants surrendered in February. From then on, Soviet forces went on the offensive, with Germany at last on the defensive.

By this time, a new theater had opened in the Pacific and East Asia. Since the start of the **Great Depression** in 1929, Japan had been rocked by economic and political turmoil. In this climate, a group of military officers, including **Hideki Tojo** (prime minister, 1941–44), came to control the government in the 1930s. They espoused Fascist views, advocated a military buildup and territorial expansion, and regarded war with the Western powers as inevitable. Japan conquered the Chinese region of Manchuria (1931) and fought China in the **Sino-Japanese War** (1937–45). The U.S. responded with trade sanctions (1939–40), which prompted Japan to establish bases in Indochina and Thailand (1940-41) in preparation for a war of expansion to increase its economic self-sufficiency. Determined to strike the U.S. before it could develop further naval strength, the Japanese attacked the U.S. naval base at **Pearl Harbor**, Hawaii, on December 7, 1941. Roused by the surprise attack, the country declared war on the Axis Powers and mobilized rapidly, converting its large industrial capacity to war production and ultimately recruiting 16 million troops.

From December 1941 to early 1942, Japan invaded and occupied Malaya (now Malaysia), Singapore, the Philippines, Burma, the Dutch East Indies (now Indonesia), northern New Guinea, and much of the South Pacific. In the Philippines many U.S. and Philippine troops died in the Bataan Death March (April 1942) following their surrender. Japan tried to occupy Australian New Guinea but was stopped by a U.S. naval victory at the Battle of the Coral Sea (May 4–8, 1942). A decisive victory in defense of the U.S. base at Midway Island (June 4, 1942) turned the tide against the Japanese. U.S. forces now took the offensive, capturing the Japanese-held Solomon Islands (1942–43)—where a fierce battle took place at Guadalcanal (1942–43)—and the Kiribati (Gilbert) Islands (1943).

In 1944 the U.S. enjoyed victories at Philippines Sea, Leyte Gulf, and the Mariana Islands. These prepared the way for General **Douglas MacArthur**'s recapture of the Philippines (1945), the conquest of Okinawa (1945), and a planned invasion of Japan. In Southeast Asia, Japan was also on the defensive. An attempted Japanese invasion of Imphal in north India was repelled in 1944. By May 1945, British and other Allied troops had recaptured Burma.

Allied offensives were aided by underground **resistance** movements in many Axis-occupied countries, including France, China, and Yugoslavia. Fighting also took place at sea and in the air. In the Battle of the Atlantic (1939–45), German U-boats or submarines harried Allied shipping but were gradually defeated by the Allied fleets, which used radar to detect and sink submarines. German air raids on Britain (known as the Blitz, 1940–41) were followed by bombing with V1 and V2 rockets (1944–45). The Allied bombing campaign in Europe focused at first on strategic military targets, but came to include "area bombing" of civilian centers; the best-known case was Dresden, a historic German city destroyed by a British-led force in 1945, with about 100,000 people killed. The U.S. capture of Iwo Jima (February–March 1945) provided a crucial air base for U.S. bombing raids on Japan, in preparation for an invasion. Incendiary raids against Japanese cities resulted in massive casualties: Tokyo was firebombed by U.S. planes in March 1945, killing about 100,000.

The carnage of World War II was increased by Hitler's determination to murder the Jews of Europe. They had been persecuted since the start of the **Third Reich** in 1933, but, with the Wannsee Conference of January 1942, **SS** leaders decided to carry out the "final solution" to what they called the Jewish question: the extermination of European Jewry in **concentration camps** such as Auschwitz, Dachau, and Treblinka. In the **genocide** known as the **Holocaust**, the Nazis killed 6 million Jews.

The Allies invaded Italy in summer 1943. By year's end, Italy was divided into Allied- and German-controlled areas. Through victories at Anzio, Monte Cassino, and elsewhere, the Allies advanced north, liberating Rome (June 4, 1944) and all of Italy by May 1945.

World War II Major Military Actions

1939

Sept. 1	German invasion of Poland
Sept. 17	Soviet invasion of Poland
Sept. 27	Warsaw, fall of
1939-1945	Atlantic, Battle of the
Nov. 30, 1939–Mar. 12, 1940	Winter War (Russo-Finnish War)

1940

Apr.–June	German conquest of Denmark and Norway
May–June	German conquest of France
May	German conquest of the Netherlands
May 29–June 4	Dunkirk, evacuation at
June 14	Paris, fall of
June–Sept.	Britain, Battle of
Aug.	Italian conquest of British Somaliland
Sept. 13–15	Italian invasion of Egypt
Sept.	Japanese conquest of French Indochina
Oct.	German conquest of Romania
1940–41	Blitz (German bombing of Britain)

1941

Mar.–Apr.	German conquest of Greece and Yugoslavia
Apr. 1941–June 1942	Tobruk, siege of
June	Allied conquest of Iraq
June 22-Dec.	Barbarossa campaign (German invasion of the Soviet Union)
July	Allied conquest of Syria
Aug.–Sept.	Allied conquest of Iran
Sept. 8, 1941–Jan. 27, 1944	Leningrad, siege of
Dec. 7	Pearl Harbor, attack on
Dec. 1941–Feb. 1942	Japanese conquest of Malaya and Singapore
Dec. 1941	Japanese invasion of Philippines

1942

Jan. 1942–May 1945	Burma campaigns
Apr.	Bataan Death March
Apr. 18	Tokyo, first Allied bombing of
May 4–8	Coral Sea, Battle of
June 4	Midway Island, Battle of
Aug. 7, 1942–Feb. 1943	Guadalcanal, Battle of
Sept. 1942–Feb. 2, 1943	Stalingrad, Battle of
Oct. 23–Nov. 4	El Alamein
Nov. 8, 1942–May 1943	Operation Torch (Allied invasion of North Africa)

1943

July–Aug.	Allied invasion of Sicily
Sept. 3	Allied invasion of Italy
Nov. 24	U.S. invasion of Kiribati (Gilbert) Islands

World War II major military actions, continued

1944

Jan. 22	Anzio, first landings at
Feb. 1–22	U.S. invasion of Marshall Islands
May 18	Monte Cassino, capture of
June 4	Rome, fall of

1944

June 6	D-Day (start of Normandy campaign)
June 19–21	Philippines Sea, First Battle of
Aug. 25	Paris, liberation of
Sept. 17–26	Arnhem, Battle of
Oct.	Leyte Gulf, Battle of
Oct.	Aachen, fall of
Oct. 21–22	Philippines Sea, Second Battle of
Dec. 16–24	Bulge, Battle of the (Ardennes Offensive)
1944–5	German V1 and V2 bombing campaigns in Britain

1945

Jan. 17	Warsaw, Soviet capture of
Feb. 13–14	Dresden, Allied bombing of
Feb. 19–Mar. 17	Iwo Jima, Battle of
Feb. 23	Manila, liberation of
Mar. 7	Remagen Bridge, capture of
March	Tokyo, Allied bombing of
Apr. 1–June 21	Okinawa, Battle of
Apr. 16–May 2	Berlin, Battle of
Apr. 29	Italy, surrender of
May 2	Berlin, fall of
May 8	V-E (Victory in Europe) Day
Aug. 6	Hiroshima, destruction of
Aug. 9	Nagasaki, destruction of
Aug. 15	V-J (Victory in Japan) Day

World War II Battle Deaths

Estimates of World War II casualties vary widely. This is one estimate of deaths in battle for principal combatants. *Italicized* figures indicate deaths from all causes.

	Men in war	Battle deaths
Australia	1,000,000	29,976
Austria	800,000	*280,000*
Belgium	625,000	8,460
Bulgaria	339,760	6,671
Canada	1,086,343	42,042
China[1]	17,250,521	1,324,516
Czechoslovakia	—	6,683

World War II battle deaths, continued

	Men in war	Battle deaths
Denmark	—	4,339
Finland	500,000	79,047
France	—	201,568
Germany	20,000,000	3,250,000
Greece	—	17,024
Hungary	—	147,435
India	2,393,891	32,121
Italy	3,100,000	149,496
Japan	9,700,000	1,270,000
Netherlands	280,000	6,500
New Zealand	194,000	11,625
Norway	75,000	2,000
Poland	—	664,000
Romania[2]	650,000	350,000
South Africa	410,056	2,473
U.S.S.R.	—	6,115,000
U.K.	5,896,000	357,116
U.S.[3]	16,112,566	291,557
Yugoslavia	3,741,000	305,000

[1]Chinese regular troops only, 1937-45; guerrillas and local military corps not included.

[2]Includes only forces mobilized against Soviet Russia; in addition, of 385,847 mobilized against Nazi Germany, there were 169,822 battle deaths.

[3]In addition, U.S. forces suffered 113,842 deaths from other causes, for a total of 405,399 deaths from all causes. There were 670,846 cases of wounds not mortal, for a total of 1,076,245 dead and wounded.

Source: Otto Johnson, ed., Information Please Almanac

On June 6, 1944, known as **D-Day**, the Allies landed at Normandy to invade France. After fierce fighting in northwest Normandy, Allied troops swept through France, liberating Paris on August 26. The Allies crossed through northwest Europe into Germany, taking Aachen in October 1944. Germany launched a desperate counteroffensive in the Battle of the Bulge (or Ardennes Offensive, December 16–24, 1944), but it failed. Soviet forces invaded from the east, capturing Berlin on May 2, 1945. Hitler committed suicide on April 30. Germany surrendered unconditionally on May 7, 1945; the Allies announced the surrender the next day, known as V-E (Victory in Europe) Day.

By that summer, U.S. scientists in the **Manhattan Project** had developed the atomic bomb, the world's first **nuclear weapon**. On August 6, 1945, this weapon of mass destruction was dropped on **Hiroshima**, wiping out the city. Nagasaki was destroyed three days later. The need for an Allied invasion of Japan was obviated. Faced with nuclear obliteration, Japan surrendered unconditionally on August 14; the Allies announced it the next day, known as V-J (Victory in Japan) Day.

The war was followed by prosecution of German leaders for war crimes in the **Nuremberg Trials** and of Japanese leaders in the **Tokyo Trials**. The **League of Nations**, which had proved incapable of preventing a world war, was scrapped, and the **United**

Nations was established in its place (1945).

The map of the world was altered. Some of the changes were decided during the war by the U.S., Britain, and the Soviet Union at conferences at **Tehran** (1943), **Yalta** (1945), and **Potsdam** (1945). Germany, Italy, and Japan were reconstituted and forced to give up their wartime conquests. Germany was divided between the U.S.–backed Federal Republic of Germany in the West and the Soviet-backed German Democratic Republic in the East (1949). The UN created the state of Israel as a Jewish homeland in Palestine (1948). Southeast Asians proved unwilling to accept the return of Western colonizers after the Japanese had nearly routed them permanently. **Decolonization** came quickly: the Philippines in 1946, India in 1947, Indonesia in 1949.

As a result of World War II, the nations of Western Europe were no longer the dominant powers in the world. That role now went to the U.S. and the Soviet Union, the nations that had contributed the most to Allied victory and had emerged with the strongest armed forces. Its mainland unscathed by war, its economy boosted by war production, the U.S. became the leader of the capitalist West. Through the **Marshall Plan** and other means, it poured money into reconstructing Western Europe and Japan. Through the G. I. Bill (1944), it rewarded its victorious troops with such benefits as free higher education and low-interest housing loans, supporting the nation's continued prosperity.

The Soviet Union became the leader of the Communist East. By virtue of the position of its forces at war's end, the Soviet Union established hegemony over Eastern Europe and, in 1948, installed a Communist regime in North Korea. The Soviets turned captured Japanese armaments over to China's Communists, who used them to win the **Chinese Civil War** (1946–49) and turn mainland China into a Communist state. By 1947 the Soviet Union possessed the atomic bomb. In Churchill's terms, an **iron curtain** fell between the two superpower blocs. The **cold war** that followed did not end until 1991, with the Soviet Union's collapse.

In all, about 25 million troops died in World War II, out of a total mobilized force of 110 million. About 35 million civilians were killed, including the victims of the Holocaust.

X

Xian Incident *See* **Sian Incident**

Y

Yalta Conference (Feb. 4–11, 1945) Meeting between Allied leaders **Winston Churchill** of Britain, **Franklin Delano Roosevelt** of the U.S., and **Joseph Stalin** of the **Soviet Union.** Issues discussed included late-stage strategies, including postwar occupation of Germany. Germany and Austria were to be divided into four occupation zones governed by the four Allied powers (France being the fourth Allied power). Stalin pledged Soviet involvement in the war with Japan, to occur shortly after German surrender. The border between Poland and the Soviet Union was also redrawn, favoring the latter. Gravely ill, President Roosevelt died shortly after the conference, on April 12.

Yom Kippur War (Fourth Arab-Israeli War) (October 6–24, 1973) Military conflict between Israel and an Arab alliance headed by Egypt and Syria. Also called the October War, it began with a surprise attack on Israel on October 6, Yom Kippur (the Day of Atonement), the holiest day of the Jewish year. In the first days, Egypt advanced over the Suez Canal into the Sinai Peninsula, while Syria reached the Golan Heights. Forces from

Iraq, Jordan, and Libya also participated, inflicting heavy casualties on the Israelis. Israel recaptured the territories (which it had occupied since the 1967 **Six-Day War**) and advanced further into Egypt and Syria. A cease-fire ended the fighting, with the forces disengaging along the Suez Canal and a **UN** peacekeeping force established on the Golan Heights. Israel won the war, but with the image of its invincibility tarnished.

Young Turks Turkish political movement founded by disaffected young army officers in the Ottoman Empire in 1889. Advocating secular reform and modernization, they led a rebellion against Sultan Abdulhamid II (1842–1918) in 1908, forcing him to restore the 1876 constitution, which he had abrogated in 1878. One year later (1909), the Young Turks deposed the sultan; a 1913 coup, led by army officer Enver Pasha (1881–1922), put them firmly in power. At the start of **World War I**, the Young Turks steered the empire into war as an ally of Germany; the defeat of the **Central Powers** in **World War I** ended their period of sway. The term *Young Turks* now refers to any rebellious faction of young people within an organization.

Youth Culture The practices of human beings from childhood through adolescence. Growing from a 19th-century interest (largely within industrialized countries) in the perceived innocence of children, the study and codification of childhood and adolescence expanded greatly during the 20th century. Adolescence became a fruitful topic of inquiry for psychologists and anthropologists. In his influential writings on child psychology, American psychologist G. Stanley Hall (1844–1924) determined that adolescence was a period fraught with psycho-sexual tension and emotional stress brought on by social and physiological changes. The term *teenager*, used to mark ages 13 through 18, was first used in 1933. More generally, the child and all his or her phases—psychological, social, and intellectual—became central to family life. Flexible, humanistic childrearing (rather than the more regimented practices of the 19th century) became practiced widely in Western society, due largely to the publication of *Baby and Child Care* by Dr. **Benjamin Spock**.

As youth came to dominate culture, terms arose to distinguish various generations, with each moniker assuming its own connotation. The more than 50 million children born in the decades after **World War II** (roughly between 1945 and 1963) were named baby boomers. Children born after 1963 are often referred to as members of generation X. Although the subsequent generation is sometimes referred to as Generation Y, no lasting term was fixed by century's end for the fin de siècle group.

Particularly in capitalist markets, teenagers in the 20th century became important sources of revenue. Objects and celebrities appealing to youths were marketed widely by manufacturers and the media. Enduring objects of 20th-century youth culture have included comic books, records, **motion pictures**, and video games. Popular celebrities of youth culture have included **Frank Sinatra**, **Elvis Presley**, the Beatles, and **Michael Jordan**, among many others. Mass-attended youth events such as the **Woodstock Festival** reflected the younger generation's numbers and cultural force.

In the post–World War II years and afterward, political beliefs and practices of the younger generation became more influential. In the 1950s and 1960s youths demonstrated for the **civil rights movement** and against the **Vietnam War**, among other causes, on college campuses and at seats of government. Radical youth political parties included the Youth International Party, or YIPPIES.

At the beginning of the 20th century, children's rights (largely in Western society) centered on child welfare. Legislation such as the Children's Charter Act of 1908 and the Ohio Children's Code Commission of 1911 (U.S.) mandated a government role in childcare for children without parents or with parents unable to raise children properly, both of which led to legislation providing foster care, child medical coverage, and various school services. Similarly, child labor laws were aimed at protecting children by limiting the number of hours they could legally work. In the late 20th century, children's rights law has also focused on the child's legal rights in bringing cases against adults (including parents).

Children's aid organizations include the Children's Defense Fund, Child Welfare League of America, National Child Labor Committee, and the **United Nations** International Children's Fund (UNICEF).

Z

ZANU *See* **ZAPU.**

ZAPU (Zimbabwe African People's Union) Zimbabwean political party founded by politician Joshua Nkomo (1917–) in 1961. Calling for black political representation, it was banned by the white Rhodesian government in 1962. It waged guerrilla warfare against that regime until 1979. From 1976, it fought as part of the Patriotic Front coalition with the Zimbabwe African National Union (ZANU), a party that had broken away from ZAPU in 1963. In the 1980 elections, ZAPU, the older of the two parties, won only a minority of the vote, mostly from the minority Matabele people. ZANU, led by **Robert Mugabe** and representing the majority Shona people, became the party of government. Marginalized, ZAPU fought a sporadic guerrilla war against the new govrnment until 1987, when it merged with ZANU, making Zimbabwe a one-party state.

Zimbabwe African National Union *See* **ZAPU.**

Zimbabwe African People's Union *See* **ZAPU.**

Zimmermann Note or **Zimmermann Telegram** Sent in secret in January 1917 by German foreign secretary Arthur Zimmermann (1864–1940), it contained a coded message to the German minister in Mexico. The message instructed the minister to propose an alliance with Mexico should the United States enter **World War I**. Mexico would receive aid in recovering its lost territories in Texas, New Mexico, and Arizona. The British intercepted and decoded the message and passed it to the U.S. government, which made it public in March. The note provoked widespread outrage and helped prompt the United States to declare war on Germany on April 6.

Zionism Political movement advocating the establishment of a Jewish national homeland in Palestine. The movement formally began in 1897 at Basel, Switzerland, with the convening of the first World Zionist Congress; there the World Zionist Organization was founded, led by Hungarian journalist Theodor Herzl (1860–1904). The organization sponsored Jewish emigration to Palestine in preparation for statehood. In 1917, Russian Zionist leader **Chaim Weizmann** persuaded Britain to pledge its support for the Zionist cause with the **Balfour Declaration**, which became the basis for the British mandate over Palestine following **World War I**. The genocide of Jews in the **Holocaust** gave renewed impetus to the cause. In 1948 the **UN** plan for the partition of Palestine led to the establishment of Israel.

CHAPTER THREE

A

Abbas, Ferhat (1899–1985) Algerian politician. Calling for an autonomous Algerian state from 1943, he at first cooperated with the French. Discouraged by slow progress, he joined the revolutionary National Liberation Front (FLN) in 1956. He was elected first president of the Algerian provisional government (1958–61). When Algeria won independence from France in 1962, he became president of the constituent assembly, but he resigned in 1963 to protest the FLN's proposed constitution. He was ousted from the FLN and placed under house arrest (1964–65).

Abd el-Krim or **Muhammad ibn 'Abd al-Karim al-Khattabi** (1882–1963) Berber chieftain. In the Rif war of 1920–26, he led a rebellion of the Rif, or Muslim Berber tribes, against Spanish rule. After defeating Spain at Anual in 1921, he served as president of the Republic of the Rif from 1921 to 1926. In 1925, Abd el-Krim led a force against the French portion of Morocco but was defeated by a French-Spanish alliance in 1926. He was exiled to the island of Réunion, and French and Spanish rule of Morocco was restored.

Abdul Rahman, Tunku (1903–90) Malaysian politician. The son of the sultan of Kedah (the epithet "tunku" means "prince"), he was educated at Cambridge University and cofounded the United Malays National Organization. He helped negotiate Malaya's independence (1957) and became its first prime minister (1957–63). Forging alliances with Singapore, Sarawak, and Sabah, he helped create the Federation of Malaysia and served as its first prime minister (1963–70).

Achebe, Chinua (1930–) Nigerian writer. In novels, poems, and essays, he wrote of the interplay between traditional African tribal life and Western culture and explored the impact of colonialism. Novels include *Things Fall Apart* (1958) and *A Man of the People* (1966); poetry collections include *Beware, Soul Brother* (1972).

Acheson, Dean [Gooderham] (1893–1971) American diplomat. He became a member of the U.S. Department of State in 1941, serving as undersecretary (1945–47) and secretary of state (1949–53). Highly influential in American postwar foreign policy, he shaped such initiatives as the **Truman Doctrine** (1947) and the **Marshall Plan** (1947–48). He also actively promoted the development of the **North Atlantic Treaty Organization** (1949). Among his books is *Present at the Creation* (1969), which won the Pulitzer Prize.

Adams, Ansel [Easton] (1902–84) American photographer. Born in San Francisco, he began taking photographs at age 14 and published his first book, *Parmelian Prints of the High Sierras*, in 1927. Influenced by the work of American photographer Paul Strand (1890–1976) he refined his photographic style to convey sharpness, detail, and great depth of field. In 1936 he held his first New York one-man show and wrote the influential book *Making a Photograph*, which outlined his techniques. From 1937 he lived in the Yosemite Valley, Calif., the site of many of his works. He aided in the founding of the department of photography at the Museum of Modern Art, New York City.

Addams, Jane (1860–1935) American social worker. In 1889, with American social worker Ellen Gates Starr (1860–1940), she founded Hull House, a Chicago settlement house serving the poor and serving as a center for social reform. As resident head of Hull House from 1889 to 1935, Addams was the leader of the American settlement house movement. She founded the National Federation of Settlements and was its first president (1911–35). A prominent woman suffragist and pacifist, she was a cofounder of the American Civil Liberties Union (1920). In 1931 she shared the Nobel Peace Prize with American educator Nicholas Murray Butler (1862–1947). Books include *Twenty Years at Hull House* (1910).

Adenauer, Konrad (1876–1967) West German politician. He was imprisoned by the Nazis during **World War II**; after the war, he cofounded the Christian Democratic Union, a political party (1945). As chancellor (1949–63) of West Germany, he guided the nation's postwar economic recovery and its integration with the West.

Adler, Alfred (1870–1937) Austrian psychiatrist. He received his medical degree from the University of Vienna (1895). An associate of **Sigmund Freud** from 1902 to 1911, he turned away from Freud's emphasis on sex to found his own school, individual psychology. He argued that inferiority feelings, resulting from a frustrated need for self-assertion, are the root of neurosis. He founded the first child guidance clinic in Vienna (1921). He taught in the U.S. from 1927 to 1937. Works include *The Practice and Theory of Individual Psychology* (1923).

Aguinaldo, Emilio (1869–1964) Philippine revolutionary. He led an unsuccessful rebellion against Spanish rule in 1896 and a successful one, with U.S. help, in 1898, during the Spanish-American War. He became the first president of the independent Philippines in 1899. He then fought against American domination but was captured and forced to swear allegiance to the U.S. During **World War II**, he cooperated with the Japanese occupiers, for which he was briefly imprisoned by U.S. forces.

Ailey, Alvin (1931–90) American choreographer and dancer. Born in Rogers, Tex., he debuted professionally with the Lester Horton Dance Theater and became its director in 1953. In New York from 1954, he studied with **Martha Graham** and others, and was a Broadway dancer and choreographer. In 1958, he founded the Alvin Ailey Dance Theatre, performing the modern works of others as well as his own. His works, including *Blues Suite* (1958) and *Revelations* (1960), employ a mix of modern dance, classical ballet, and jazz and gospel music, often to explore the African-American experience. He founded a dance school in 1971.

Aleichem, Sholem See **Sholem Aleichem**.

Alfonso XIII (1886–1941) Spanish king (1886–1931). Son of Alfonso XII and Maria Cristina. During the first years (1886–1902) of his reign his mother acted as regent. A critic of the parliamentary system, he supported the military dictatorship of Primo de Rivera (1870–1930) from 1923 to 1930. With the founding of the Second Republic, the king was forced into exile in 1931.

Ali, Muhammad (1942–) American athlete. Born Cassius Marcellus Clay, he won a gold medal in the light-heavyweight division at the 1960 Olympics. Turning professional, he defeated American boxer Sonny Liston (c. 1917–70) for the world heavyweight championship in 1964, beginning a career as a playful, arrogant, peerless fighter. After his victory, he joined the Nation of Islam and changed his name to Muhammad Ali. He defended his title successfully until 1967, when his license to box was withdrawn after he was drafted during the **Vietnam War** and claimed exemption as a conscientious objector. He did not box again until 1971, when he lost to American boxer Joe Frazier (1944–). In 1974 Ali defeated **George Foreman** and regained the title. He became the only boxer to hold the heavyweight title three separate times when he lost and regained the title in two 1978 bouts with American boxer Leon Spinks (1953–). He retired in 1981 and was later afflicted by Parkinson's disease, most likely boxing-related.

Allen, Woody (1935–) American filmmaker, actor, and writer. Born Allen Stewart Konigsberg in Brooklyn, N.Y., he began his career as a comedy writer and stand-up comic before beginning to write, direct, and act in films. The anarchic hilarity of his early movies, such as *Sleeper* (1973), was followed by more serious works beginning with *Annie Hall* (1977), which won a best picture Oscar. This and later films, including *Zelig* (1983) and *Hannah and Her Sisters* (1986), are marked by cinematic inventiveness and philosophical searching. Allen has also written essays and plays and is a jazz clarinetist.

Allende Gossens, Salvador (1908–73) Chilean politician. In 1933 he cofounded the Chilean Socialist Party. He was elected president in 1970, the first Marxist to win a presidential election in Latin America. He launched such initiatives as nationalization of industries and redistribution of land. In 1973, in the midst of economic crisis, General **Augusto Pinochet** overthrew and killed him in a U.S.–supported military coup.

Amin Dada, Idi (1925–) Ugandan dictator. Deposing Ugandan president **Milton Obote** in a coup, he became president and chief of armed forces (1971–79). In 1976 he proclaimed himself president for life, ordered death to Obote supporters, and expelled Uganda's Asian minority. Overthrown in 1979 by Tanzanian forces, he fled first to Libya and, in 1980, Saudi Arabia.

Amis, Sir Kingsley (1922–1995) British writer. Author of novels, many of which satirize English life. He was associated with the 1950's Angry Young Men, who also included British playwright **John Osborne** (1929–) and who attacked British pretensions and hypocrisy. Amis's novels include *Lucky Jim* (1953), *Take a Girl Like You* (1960), *Jake's Thing* (1978), and *The Old Devils* (1986), which won the Booker Prize. He also published poetry and short stories. He was knighted in 1990. His son, Martin Amis (1949–), is the author of *London Fields* (1989) and *Time's Arrow* (1991), among other novels.

Anderson, Marian (1902–1993) American singer. Singing first in hometown Philadelphia, Pa., church choirs, she gained fame in Europe for her concert mix of opera and spirituals. When in 1939 the African-American contralto was barred by the Daughters of the American Revolution from singing at Constitution Hall, Washington, D.C., First Lady **Eleanor Roosevelt** and others arranged a hugely attended concert at the Lincoln Memorial. In 1955 she became the first black permanent member of the Metropolitan Opera Company. She was an alternate delegate to the **UN** (1958).

Anderson, Sherwood (1876–1941) American writer. Born in Camden, Ohio, he is best known for his short-story collection *Winesburg, Ohio* (1919), a series of naturalistic, psychological studies of small-town inhabitants. The work's sensitivity to its subject matter influenced the American short story for decades. Among Anderson's novels are *Windy McPherson's Son* (1916), *Poor White* (1920), and *Dark Laughter* (1925). Among his other short-story collections are *The Triumph of the Egg* (1921), *Horses and Men* (1923), and *Death in the Woods* (1933). Autobiographical works include *Story Teller's Story* (1924) and *Tar: A Midwest Childhood* (1926).

Andretti, Mario (1940–) Italian-born American automobile racer. A versatile racer, he won the United States Auto Club championship in 1965 and 1966. He is the only person to have won the Daytona 500 (1967), the Indianapolis 500 (1969), and the Grand Prix world driving championship (1978). His sons Michael and Jeff also became automobile racers.

Andrews, Julie (1935–) British actress. Born Julia Elizabeth Wells, she became a Broadway star in 1956 as Eliza Doolittle in *My Fair Lady* and gained fame in Hollywood in lead roles in two hugely popular films, *Mary Poppins* (1965) and *The Sound of Music* (1965). Andrews wrote the children's books *Mandy* (1971) and *Last of the Really Freat Wangdoodles* (1974) under the pseudunym Julie Edwards.

Andropov, Yuri Vladimirovich (1914–84) Soviet politician. Active in the Communist Party since the 1930s, he rose through a series of posts to become head of the **KGB** (1967–82); in that role, he pursued a hard-line policy against dissidents. Upon the death of **Leonid Brezhnev** in 1982, Andropov succeeded him as the country's leader, being named general secretary of the Communist Party (1982–84) and president of the **Soviet Union** (1983–84). Andropov died after little more than a year in office.

Angelou, Maya (1928–) American writer and performer. Born Marguerite Johnson. An African-American civil rights activist who worked in Africa for several years, she was also an actress and singer, primarily on stage. She wrote such autobiographical works as *I Know Why the Caged Bird Sings* (1970) and such poetry collections as *And I Still Rise* (1987). She recited a poem at the inauguration of President **Bill Clinton** in 1993.

Antonioni, Michelangelo (1912–) Italian film director. He assisted Italian filmmaker Roberto Rossellini (1906–77) and French filmmaker Marcel Carné (1909–) before directing his first film, *Gente del Po* (1943–47). He became a major force in postwar Italian cinema with his stylized meditations on life's emptiness, including *L'Avventura* (1960), *Red Desert* (1964), *Blow-Up* (1966), and *The Passenger* (1975). His films are noted for using place to convey states of being.

Aquino, [Maria] Corazon (1933–) Philippine politician. Her surname was Cojuangco before she married journalist and politician Benigno Aquino Jr. (1932–83) in 1954. After agents of President **Ferdinand Marcos** assassinated her husband because of his opposition to Marcos, Corazon Aquino became the leader of the anti-Marcos "people power" movement. In 1986 both Aquino and Marcos claimed victory in a presidential election, but popular opposition forced Marcos to flee the country. Aquino governed as president from 1986 to 1992, introducing a new democratic constitution. Her term of office was plagued by coup attempts, civil war with Communist guerrillas, a weak economy, and dissatisfaction with her leadership.

Arafat, Yasir (1929–) Palestinian leader. Known as Abu Ammar ("the Builder"). Born in Jerusalem, he was an anti-Zionist who fled his native land after the creation of Israel in 1948. He studied engineering at Cairo University and was an engineer in Kuwait (1957–65). In 1956 he served with the Egyptian army in the **Suez Crisis** and cofounded the guerrilla movement Al Fatah, which pursued the cause of Palestinian independence through commando raids on Israeli territory. In 1964, Al Fatah became linked with similar groups in the **Palestine Liberation Organization (PLO).** Arafat has served as PLO chairman since 1968. Though widely denounced as a terrorist, he became, in 1974, the first representative of a nongovernmental organization to address the **UN** General Assembly. A pragmatic survivor, he retained PLO leadership despite much factional infighting and a forced departure from Beirut, Lebanon, in 1982. Gradually, he modified his more extreme positions. At first committed to the destruction of Israel, he renounced that commitment in 1988, accepting Israel's right to exist and denouncing **terrorism**. He seemed to backtrack when he supported Iraq in the **Gulf War** in 1991. But in 1993, he signed a peace agreement with Israeli prime minister **Yitzhak Rabin**. Through this agreement, Israel and the PLO recognized each other, and limited Palestinian self-rule was mandated in the **Gaza Strip** and the **West Bank** town of Jericho. Arafat became interim president of the Palestinian Authority; 1996 elections confirmed him as president. For their efforts, Arafat, Rabin, and Israeli foreign minister **Shimon Peres** shared the 1994 Nobel Peace Prize. The peace process was shaken by Rabin's assassination in 1995, though it continued to move ahead, with limited autonomy coming to other Palestinian areas in the West Bank. However, the election of right-wing prime minister **Benjamin Netanyahu** in 1996 stalled peace negotiations, as did Arafat's inability to prevent radical factions from conducting suicide bombing raids in Israel. Arafat's own people criticized him for the PLO's corruption and brutality. In 1998, Arafat reached a new agreement with Israel, but the peace process stalled completely in 2000, leading to a new wave of violence.

Arendt, Hannah (1906–75) German-born American political theorist. Born in Hanover, she immigrated to the U.S. in 1940 to escape Nazi rule. Until 1952, she worked as a research director and book editor; she later taught at Princeton (1959), Columbia (1960), the University of Chicago (1963–67), and the New School for Social Research (1967–75). Her first book, *The Origins of Totalitarianism* (1951), which traced the beginnings of Nazism and **Communism**, influenced mid-century political thought. Among her other works are *The Human Condition* (1958); *On Revolution* (1963); and *Eichmann in Jerusalem* (1963), in which she developed the idea of the "banality of evil."

Aristide, Jean-Bertrand (1953–) Haitian politician. Ordained a Catholic priest in 1982, he was expelled from the Salesian order in 1988 for his leftist revolutionary teachings; he later left the priesthood entirely. He was a harsh critic of the dictatorship of Jean-Claude "Baby Doc" Duvalier (1951–) and the military regimes that followed its fall in 1986. Supported by a leftist coalition, Aristide won election as president in 1990, but in September 1991, seven months after his inauguration, he was forced into exile by a military coup. Backed by the threat of a U.S. invasion, Aristide was restored to office in 1994. He took steps to curb the army's power and stepped down in 1996 in accordance with Haiti's constitution. His handpicked successor, René Préval (1943–), was elected to take his place.

Armstrong, Louis [Daniel] (1900–71) American jazz musician. Known as "Satchmo." Born in New Orleans, he played trumpet there and, after 1922, in Chicago and New York City. He became a solo performer, band leader, and film performer. He is credited with inventing the scat singing style and elevating the role of the soloist in jazz. Compositions include "Dipper Mouth Blues."

Armstrong, Neil [Alden] (1930–) American astronaut. Born in Wapakoneta, Ohio, he served as a navy pilot (1949–52) in the **Korean War**. Afterward, he became a civilian test pilot and, from 1962, an astronaut. In 1966 he was command pilot of *Gemini 8*, which accomplished the first successful docking of two spacecraft. On July 20, 1969, during the *Apollo 11* flight, which he commanded, Armstrong became the first person to walk on the Moon. He was followed onto the Moon's surface by lunar module pilot Edwin "Buzz" Aldrin Jr. (1930–); command module pilot Michael Collins (1930–) remained in lunar orbit. Armstrong has since lived inconspicuously as an administrator at the National Aeronautics and Space Administration (1970–71), professor of engineering at the University of Cincinnati (1971–79), and businessman.

Asquith, Herbert Henry, first earl of Oxford and Asquith (1852–1928) British politician. A Liberal M.P. from 1886 to 1918 and from 1920 to 1924, he became prime minister in 1908. His government instituted old-age pensions (1908) and unemployment insurance (1911) and won passage of the Parliament Act of 1911, which abolished the veto power of the House of Lords. Military setbacks during **World War I** led to his resignation in 1916.

Assad, Hafiz al- (1928–) Syrian politician. An air force officer and **Ba'ath Party** member, he became minister of defense in 1966, after the Ba'athists seized power. In a 1970 coup, he came to power as the country's leader, enjoying the title president from 1971. Under his rule, dissent was repressed, the economy improved, and Syria formed ties to the **Soviet Union**. Beginning with a 1976 military intervention, Syria gained control over much of Lebanon. An implacable foe of Israel, Assad was accused of sponsoring international **terrorism**. His relations with the West improved during the **Gulf War** (1991), when he sided with U.S.–led coalition forces.

Astaire, Fred (1899–1987) American dancer, actor, and singer. Born in Omaha, Ne., he debuted on Broadway with sister and partner Adele in *Over the Top* (1917), afterward enjoying a string of hits on Broadway and in London. After the partnership dissolved in the early 1930s with his sister's marriage, Astaire turned to Hollywood. Appearing in ten titles with American dancer Ginger Rogers (1911–1995), he transformed the film musical with his easygoing sophistication, flawless dancing, and relaxed song styling. Beginning with *Flying down to Rio* (1933), notable Astaire-Rogers titles include *The Gay Divorcee* (1934), *Top Hat* (1935), *Swing Time* (1936), and *Shall We Dance* (1937). Paired with other leading actresses throughout the 1940s and beyond, he made several popular films, such as *Easter Parade* (1948), *The Band Wagon* (1953), and *Funny Face* (1957). He won a special Academy Award in 1949.

Atatürk, Kemal (1881–1938) Turkish soldier and politician. Born Mustafa in Salonika (now Thessalonika, Greece), he adopted the name Kemal ("Perfect One") in school. He graduated from the military academy in Constantinople (now Istanbul) in 1905. Briefly imprisoned for opposing Ottoman sultan Abdulhamid II (1842–1918), he was a rival of Enver Pasha (1881–1922), who led the "**Young Turk** Revolution" against that ruler in 1908. During **World War I**, he fought heroically at Gallipoli (1915) and became a general (1916). In 1919, after the war, he launched a revolution from Anatolia against the last Ottoman sultan, Mohammed VI (1861–1926), and the Allied forces (see **Allied Powers**) that had imposed a harsh peace. He successfully repelled Greek occupation forces (1921–22), and, as head of the Grand National Assembly (from 1920), he negotiated the Lausanne Treaty of 1923 (see **Lausanne, Treaty of**), establishing Turkey's present borders. In 1923, Kemal became first president of the new republic of Turkey. He abolished the Ottoman sultanate and expelled the last caliph, titular head of Islam, in 1924, making Turkey a secular state. He introduced a parliamentary government, though with only one party, which supported his despotic tendencies. Other modernizing steps included European-style law codes, state schools, woman suffrage (1934), and a ban on the veil and fez, two symbols of the Ottoman days. Regarded as the founder of modern Turkey, he received the name Atatürk ("Father of the Turks") from parliament in 1935.

Attlee, Clement Richard, first Earl Attlee and Viscount Prestwood (1883–1967) British politician. He was a social worker and lecturer at the London School of Economics (1913–23) before entering Parliament (1922–55). As leader of the **Labour Party** from 1935, he served in **Winston Churchill**'s coalition government during **World War II**. As prime minister (1945–51), he put his socialist views into practice, nationalizing the Bank of England and numerous industries, founding the National Health Service, and overseeing the transition to independence of India, Pakistan, Burma (now Myanmar), Palestine, and Ceylon (now Sri Lanka). He led the Labour opposition until 1955.

Auden W[ystan] H[ugh] (1907–73) British-born American poet. Oxford-educated, he published his first collection, *Poems*, in 1930. Among other notable poetic works are *The Double Man* (1941), *Collected Poetry* (1945), and *The Age of Anxiety* (1947, Pulitzer Prize). With British writer Christopher Isherwood (1904–86), he collaborated on plays including *The Dog beneath the Skin* (1935) and *The Ascent of F6* (1936). He also wrote critical essays and opera librettos, including *The Rake's Progress* (1951), written with Chester Kallman (1921–1975), and edited *The Oxford Book of Light Verse* (1938). In the U.S. from 1939, he became a citizen in 1944 but returned to England in 1972.

Ayer, Sir Alfred Jules (1910–89) British philosopher. Educated at Oxford and the University of Vienna, he introduced to Britain the logical positivism of the Vienna Circle. His *Language, Truth, and Logic* (1936) influenced the development of analytic philosophy; in it, he used his verification principle to demonstrate that traditional metaphysical, religious, and ethical statements are nonsensical. He later modified some of his early claims. Other works include *The Problem of Knowledge* (1956).

Azaña y Díaz, Manuel (1880–1940) Spanish politician. One of the leaders of the Republican revolution of 1930, he served as prime minister in the Second Republic (1931–33). He took measures to secularize and modernize the country, such as instituting Catalan autonomy, curbing church influence, and expanding the educational system. During the **Spanish Civil War**, he was president of the Loyalist government (1936–39); his attempts to negotiate an end to the war failed. **Francisco Franco**'s victory in 1939 forced him into exile in France. For his biography of Spanish novelist Juan Valera (1824–1905), Azaña won the national prize for literature in 1926.

Azikiwe, Benjamin Nnamdi (1904–96) Nigerian politician. Considered the father of modern Nigeria, he studied in the United States and returned to Africa as a newspaper editor. He founded the *West African Pilot*, which promoted nationalism and, in 1944, helped to found the National Council of Nigeria and the Cameroons. He was premier of the eastern region (1954–59) and, in 1959, became Nigeria's first indigenous governor-general. When the newly independent nation became a republic, Azikiwe was its first president (1963–66), but a military coup deposed him. He supported the attempt to create an independent Biafra and, as leader of the Nigerian People's Party, ran unsuccessfully for the presidency in 1979.

B

Babel, Isaac [Emmanuelovich] (1894–1941) Russian writer. He gained an international reputation as a stylist with his fiction works *Odessa Tales* (1916) and *Red Cavalry* (1926). Affiliated with the **Bolsheviks** from 1917, he was arrested in 1939 during the

Stalinist purges and died two years later in a labor camp.

Baden-Powell, Robert Stephenson Smyth, first baron Baden-Powell of Gilwell (1857–1941) British soldier. A lieutenant general who fought in the **Boer War**, he retired in 1910. He founded the Boy Scouts in 1908, the year of the publication of his *Scouting for Boys*. He founded the Girl Guides in 1909. Both movements sought to build character and fitness among the young. The Boy Scouts organization was incorporated in the U.S. in 1910, and the Girl Guides inspired the creation in the U.S. of the Girl Scouts in 1912. At the first Boy Scout Jamboree in 1920, he was made Chief Scout of the World. He was made a peer in 1929.

Baker, Josephine (1906–75) American entertainer. Born Freda Josephine McDonald, she became a musical star of Broadway and Paris in the 1920s. In such shows as *La Revue nègre* (1925), she was noted for her exotic costumes and electric jazz singing and dancing. She became a naturalized French citizen in 1937 and worked with the **resistance** during **World War II**.

Balanchine, George (1904–83) Russian-born American choreographer. The leading neoclassicist of 20th-century ballet, he was born Georg Melitonovich Balanchivadze in St. Petersburg and began his career with the Diaghilev Company in 1925. With American patron Lincoln Kirstein (1907–1996) he cofounded the School of the American Ballet in 1934 (American Ballet Company from 1935) and the Ballet Society in 1946 (New York City Ballet from 1948), becoming the latter's artistic director. His streamlined ballets include *The Four Temperaments* (1946) and *Jewels* (1967); he also choreographed the works of classical composers, notably those of **Igor Stravinsky** (*Agon*, 1957). Choreography for *On Your Toes* (1936) and other musicals encouraged the use of ballet in the form.

Baldwin, James (1924–87) American writer. Born in New York City, he lived in France from age 24 and established himself as a leading writer on the place of African-Americans in U.S. society. Among his novels are *Go Tell It on the Mountain* (1953), *Another Country* (1962), *If Beale Street Could Talk* (1974), and *Just above My Head* (1979). His highly esteemed essay collections include *Notes of a Native Son* (1955), *Nobody Knows My Name* (1961), and *The Fire Next Time* (1963). His plays include *The Amen Corner* (1955) and *Blues for Mister Charlie* (1964); he has also published short stories. He returned to the U.S. in 1977.

Baldwin, Stanley, first earl Baldwin of Bewdley (1867–1947) British politician. A Conservative M.P. from 1908 to 1937, he served three times as prime minister (1923–24, 1924–29, 1935–37). He broke a **general strike** in 1926 and won passage of the Trade Disputes Act (1927) limiting the power of unions. He secured the abdication of **Edward VIII** in 1936. Baldwin opposed British rearmament despite the mounting threat of **Fascism** in Europe.

Balfour, Arthur James, first earl (1848–1930) British politician. Born in Scotland, he became a Conservative M.P. in 1874. He held posts in the government of his uncle, Robert Gascoigne-Cecil, third marquess of Salisbury (1830–1903), and succeeded him as prime minister (1902–05). A Conservative split over tariff reform led to Balfour's resignation. As foreign secretary (1916–19), he issued the **Balfour Declaration** (1917), promising British support for a Jewish homeland in Palestine. He was made an earl in 1922.

Bao Dai (1913–97) Vietnamese emperor. The last emperor of Vietnam (1926–45), he ruled as a puppet of French colonial authorities and, during **World War II**, of the Japanese occupation force. **Ho Chi Minh**'s Vietminh forced his abdication in 1945, but Bao Dai returned as chief of state in 1949, again with French support. He became president of South Vietnam in 1954 but was deposed by **Ngo Dinh Diem** in 1955.

Bardeen, John (1908–91) American physicist. Born in Madison, Wisc., he was educated at the University of Wisconsin and at Princeton University. He became the first scientist to win two Nobel Prizes in the same category. He shared his first prize for physics, in 1956, for his codevelopment of the transistor; his co-recipients were American physicists Walter Brattain (1902–87) and William Shockley (1910–89). He shared the second, in 1972, for his codevelopment of a theory to explain superconductivity; his co-recipients were American physicists Leon Cooper (1930–) and John Schrieffer (1931–).

Barnard, Christiaan Neething (1922–) South African surgeon. As director of surgical research at Groote Schuur Hospital, Cape Town, he performed the first human heart transplant in 1967. In addition, he designed artificial heart valves and procedures for other organ transplants.

Barrymore American family of actors. Lionel (1878–1954), Ethel (1879–1959), and John (1882–1942) were the Philadelphia-born children of British actor Maurice Barrymore (born Herbert Blythe, 1847–1905) and his American wife, Georgiana, née Drew (1854–93), also an actor. Through the 1930s and into the 1940s, the three children reigned as stars of American stage and screen. John, known as "the Great Profile," was a matinee idol and a serious actor known for his stage *Hamlet* (1922). His films include *Grand Hotel* (1932), in which his brother Lionel also appeared. A character actor, Lionel appeared in such plays as *Peter Ibbetson* (1917) and such films as *A Free Soul* (1931; Academy Award) and *You Can't Take It with You* (1938). Ethel won an Academy Award for *None but the Lonely Heart* (1944); her stage credits include *Captain Jinks of the Horse Marines* (1901). The actress Drew Barrymore (1975–) is the granddaughter of John.

Barth, Karl (1886–1968) Swiss Protestant theologian. A Swiss minister, he became a professor (1921–35) at several German universities. For his refusal to swear allegiance to **Adolf Hitler**, he was deported to Switzerland, where he taught at Basel University. He developed dialectical theology, or theology of the word, which emphasizes God's revelation in Christ as communicated in the Bible. This "neo-orthodox" or "theocentric" approach emphasizes the discontinuity between humanity and God and influenced many other theologians. His works include *The Epistle to the Romans* (1933) and *Church Dogmatics* (four vols., 1932–62).

Bartók, Béla (1881–1945) Hungarian composer. Blending atonality and elements of folk music, he gained acclaim for compositions for piano (including *Mikrokosmos*, 1926–39), violin, string quartets, and orchestra (including Concerto for Orchestra, 1943). From 1907 to 1940, he was a professor at the Academy of Music, Budapest. In 1940 he immigrated to the U.S., where he translated Yugoslavian folk music for Columbia University. He published collections of over 6,000 Hungarian, Romanian, and Arabic folk songs throughout his life.

Baryshnikov, Mikhail Nikolayevich (1948–) Latvian-born American dancer. After graduating from the Riga Choreographic School, he joined the Kirov Ballet in 1966, creating ballet roles such as *Hamlet* and becoming a star. While touring with the Bolshoi Ballet in 1974, he defected to Canada and joined the American Ballet Theatre (ABT). From 1978 to 1979 he danced with the New York City Ballet. From 1980 to 1989 he served as artistic director for the American Ballet Theatre. He became known for his technical prowess, flamboyance, and ability to dance in both classical and modern modes. Although he has made few films, he was nominated for the Best Supporting Actor Academy Award for his debut, *The Turning Point* (1977). In 1990 he and American choreographer Mark Morris (1956–) formed the White Oak Dance Project.

Basie, Count (1904–84) American jazz musician. Born William Basie, he was a pianist who studied informally with fellow musician Fats (Thomas Wright) Waller (1904–43). Performances at Harlem's Savoy ballroom, beginning in 1938, made the Count Basie Orchestra one of the best-known big bands of the swing era. He recorded with such vocalists as **Ella Fitzgerald** and **Frank Sinatra**.

Batista [y Zaldívar], Fulgencio (1901–73) Cuban dictator. A soldier, he led a 1933 coup against President Carlos Manuel de Céspedes y Quesada (1871–1939). As head of the army from 1933 to 1959, he used U.S. support to dominate Cuban politics. He was president from 1940 to 1944 and dictator from 1952 to 1959. His regime's corruption and brutal repressiveness antagonized both the poor and the middle class. Under his tenure, Havana became a center for prostitution, drugs, and gambling, controlled by organized criminals from the United States. Batista was unable to defeat **Fidel Castro's** rebel army. In the early hours of January 1, 1959, Batista fled Cuba by plane, allowing Castro to take power.

Beauvoir, Simone [Bertrand] de (1908–86). French writer and philosopher. She influenced the feminist movement with *The Second Sex* (1949), a study of the oppression of women in Western society. Also influential is her study of aging, *The Coming of Age* (1970). Her best-known novel, *The Mandarins*, was published in 1954; among other novels are *She Came to Stay* (1943) and *The Blood of Others* (1945). From 1929 she maintained a relationship with philosopher **Jean-Paul Sartre** and helped him to develop existentialist theory; her memoir of their union is *Adieux: A Farewell to Sartre* (1984).

Beaverbrook, William Maxwell Aitken, first baron (1879–1964). Canadian-born British businessman and politician. A successful Canadian stockbroker, he immigrated to Britain in 1910 and soon began building a newspaper empire that would support his conservative, isolationist views. In 1916, he gained control of the *Daily Express* (1916); two years later he launched the *Sunday Express*. In 1923, he bought a competing paper, the *Evening Standard*. Throughout, he also served widely in British government. He was elected local M.P. in 1910 and appointed to ministerial posts in both world wars. Nicknamed "the Beaver," he was knighted in 1911 and made a baron in 1917. His memoirs include *Politicians and the War* (1928–32, 2 vols.) and *The Decline and Fall of Lloyd George* (1963).

Beckett, Samuel (1906–89) Irish-born French writer. Writing mostly in French (and translating his own works into English), he presented a bleak vision of cosmic absurdity and futility, alleviated by humor and wordplay. As a novelist, he wrote the trilogy *Molloy* (1951), *Malone Dies* (1952), and *The Unnamable* (1960); as a playwright, he wrote *Waiting for Godot* (1952) and *Endgame* (1957). A veteran of the French **resistance** during **World War II**, he received the 1969 Nobel Prize for literature.

Begin, Menachem (1913–92) Israeli politician. Born in Brest-Litovsk, Russia (later Poland), and educated as a lawyer, he came in 1942 to Palestine, where he headed the **Irgun**, a militant Zionist organization. From 1949 he was a Knesset member. His right-wing **Likud Party** took power for the first time in 1977, with Begin as prime minister (1977–83). He signed the **Camp David Accords** with Egyptian president **Anwar el-Sádát** in 1978; the two leaders shared that year's Nobel Peace Prize. In 1982, Begin ordered the invasion of Lebanon, which failed in its objective to destroy the **Palestine Liberation Organization** and received international condemnation. Begin resigned in 1983.

Benchley, Robert [Charles] (1889–1945) American writer and actor. He displayed sophisticated wit in writing drama criticism, humorous essays, and short, satirical films. In addition to writing and acting in his own short films, he acted in such feature films as *The Major and the Minor* (1942). He was associated with the magazine the *New Yorker* from 1929 to 1940. Books include *The Treasurer's Report* (1930), *From Bed to Worse* (1934), and *My Ten Years in a Quandary* (1936). His short film *How to Sleep* (1935) won an Academy Award.

Benedict XV (1854–1922) Pope (1914–22). Born Giacomo della Chiesa in Italy, he maintained neutrality and pursued peace efforts during **World War I**.

Benes, Edvard (1884–1948) Czechoslovak politician. A nationalist follower of **Tomás Masaryk**, he was a founder of the **Little Entente** and served as Czech president from 1935 to 1938; he resigned after Germany annexed the **Sudetenland**. In England until 1945, he headed the Czech government in exile. Returning home after the war, he served again as president until 1948, when a Communist coup ended his government.

Benét, Stephen Vincent (1898–1943) American writer. Principally a poet, he also wrote fiction, including the short story "The Devil and Daniel Webster" (1937). He frequently drew subjects from American folklore and history. Poetry volumes include *John Brown's Body* (1928) and *Western Star* (1943, unfinished), both of which won Pulitzer Prizes. His brother, William Rose Benét (1886–1950), was a poet, novelist, and editor, for whom *Benét's Reader's Encyclopedia* (first ed., 1948) is named.

Benjamin, Walter (1892–1940) German critic. A leader of the Frankfurt School whose other members have included German philosopher Max Horkheimer (1895–1973), Theodor Adorno (1903–1969), Herbert Marcuse, and Jürgen Hubermas (1929–), he took a Marxist approach to understanding literary and artistic production. Works include *The Origin of German Tragic Drama* (1928).

Bergman, Ingmar (1918–) Swedish filmmaker. Influenced by his father, a Lutheran pastor, he wrote and directed films that explore religious and philosophical themes, particularly the silence of God. He was adept at portraying human relationships and the inner life of women. *Smiles of a Summer Night* (1955) and *The Seventh Seal* (1957), both of which won prizes at the Cannes Film Festival, made him internationally renowned. Other works include *Wild Strawberries* (1957), *Cries and Whispers* (1972), and *Fanny and Alexander* (1983).

Bergman, Ingrid (1915–82) Swedish actress. Appearing in Swedish films from the 1930s, she became a Hollywood star in such films as *Casablanca* (1942) and *Notorious* (1946). When she abandoned her husband, Peter Lindstrom, for Italian film director Roberto Rossellini (1906–77), scandal nearly wrecked her career, but she rebounded; actress Isabella Rossellini (1952–) is their daughter. Bergman won three Oscars—for *Gaslight* (1944), *Anastasia* (1956), and *Murder on the Orient Express* (1974). She also appeared on stage and **television**. Her final feature film role was in **Ingmar Bergman**'s *Autumn Sonata* (1978).

Berle, Milton (1908–) American comedian. Born Milton Berlinger, he was a vaudeville, film, and **radio** comic before becoming famous as host of **television's** "Texaco Star Theatre" (1948–56). Known as "Mr. Television," he was a pioneer of the medium whose immense popularity helped establish the television set as a fixture of the average American household. After the show's demise, he continued to act and perform comedy on television, on stage, and in films.

Bergson, Henri Louis (1859–1941) French philosopher. Opposed to scientific materialism, he posited an *élan vital*, or "vital spirit," in the world and argued that evolution was driven by a life force. He distinguished the experiential phenomenon of duration from merely abstract time. He received the 1927 Nobel Prize for literature. Works include *Time and Free Will* (1889) and *Creative Evolution* (1911).

Berlin, Irving (1888–1989) Russian-born American songwriter. Born Irving Baline, he immigrated to the U.S. in 1893 and gained his first success in 1911 with "Alexander's Ragtime Band." Though unable to read music, he wrote over 1,500 songs in his lifetime, including "Always," "God Bless America," and "White Christmas," the best-selling record in history. Broadway scores include *Annie Get Your Gun* (1946), and films include *Top Hat* (1935).

Berlin, Sir Isaiah (1909–97) Latvian-born British philosopher and historian of ideas. He was educated at Oxford, where he became professor of social and political theory (1957–67) and president of Wolfson College (1966–75). A dedicated opponent of historical determinism, he explored the genesis of such modern ideas as nationalism and romanticism. His works include *Karl Marx* (1939), *Historical Inevitability* (1954), and *Four Essays on Liberty* (1969). He was knighted in 1957.

Bernhardt, Sarah (1844–1923) French actress. Born Rosine Bernard and known as the "Divine Sarah," she was the reigning queen of French tragedy. She starred in *Phèdre* (1874), *Ruy Blas* (1872), and *L'Aiglon* (1901) and continued touring Europe and the United States even after her leg was amputated in 1915. Silent film appearances included *Queen Elizabeth* (1912). She was also a theater manager and playwright.

Bernstein, Eduard (1850–1932) German politician. A Social Democrat from 1872, he lived in exile in England for a time, returning to Germany in 1901. In his book *Evolutionary Socialism* (1898) and other writings, he propounded his controversial doctrine of revisionism, a modified Marxism that embraces evolutionary socialist change. A member of the Reichstag (1902–06, 1912–18, 1920–28), he split from his party to protest its support for **World War I** but rejoined it after the war.

Bernstein, Leonard (1918–90) American composer. Named assistant conductor of the New York Philharmonic after graduating from Harvard, he gained national fame in 1943 when he substituted for German-born American conductor Bruno Walter (1876–1962). From 1945 to 1948 he conducted the New York City Symphony Orchestra. He became known for his facility with popular and classical forms in his compositions. Among his Broadway musicals are *On the Town* (1944), *Wonderful Town* (1953), *Candide* (1956, with **Stephen Sondheim**), and the renowned *West Side Story* (1959, also with Sondheim). Film scores include *On the Waterfront* (1954). As music director of the New York Philharmonic from 1958 to 1969, he used **television** to widen the audience for classical music in the *Omnibus* and *Young People's Concerts* series.

Besant, Annie (1847–1933) British reformer and theosophist. Née Annie Wood. From the 1870s, she crusaded for **birth control**, women's rights, free thought, and **socialism**. In 1889, she became a theosophist and moved to India. There she preached theosophy and advocated Indian home rule, becoming president of the **Indian National Congress** (1917). She was associated with British freethinker Charles Bradlaugh (1833–91) and was a member of the Fabian Society. Works include *Wisdom of the Upanishads* (1906).

Bettelheim, Bruno (1903–90) Austrian-born American psychotherapist. A student of **Sigmund Freud**, he survived imprisonment in the **concentration camps** of Dachau and Buchenwald (1938–39). He came to the United States, where he joined the University of Chicago (1939–42, 1944–73). He was known for his treatment of severely disturbed children and his popular books on raising normal children. Works include *Love Is Not Enough* (1950), *The Uses of Enchantment* (1976), and *Freud and Man's Soul* (1983).

Bhutto, Zulfikar Ali (1928–79) Pakistani politician. In 1967, he formed the People's Party, which opposed President Ayub Khan (1907–1974). Following the loss of East Pakistan (which became Bangladesh) in 1971, Bhutto became president (1971–77) and prime minister (1973–77). Overthrown in a 1977 coup by General Zia-ul Haq (1924–88), he was executed two years later, rousing international protest. His daughter, Benazir Bhutto (1953–), became prime minister (1988–90) soon after Zia's death in a plane crash.

Binet, Alfred (1857–1911) French psychologist. Director of the psychology laboratory at the Sorbonne (1897–1911), he pioneered projective intelligence testing. With Théodore Simon, he developed the standardized Binet, or Binet-Simon, test for measuring intelligence (1905–11). Binet founded the journal *Année psychologique* in 1895, in which many of his findings appeared.

Bishop, Elizabeth (1911–79) American poet. Esteemed for her clear eye and poetic detachment, she won a Pulitzer Prize for *Poems: North and South—A Cold Spring* (1955). Other works include *Complete Poems* (1969) and *Geography III* (1976).

Blair, Tony (1953–) British politician. Born Anthony Charles Lynton Blair, he was educated at Oxford and became a lawyer in 1976. A Labour M.P. from 1983, he rose through a succession of party offices, including Shadow Home Secretary (1992–94), to become party leader in 1994. A youthful, telegenic moderate with populist appeal, he helped revitalize the party at a time when it had lost power to the Conservatives. He persuaded the party to give up its commitment to nationalization and emphasize personal responsibility and law and order. The result was a victory for his party in 1997, making Blair the first Labour prime minister in 18 years.

Blum, Léon (1872–1950) French politician. As leader of the Socialist Party, he headed the Popular Front government (1936–37). This left-wing coalition instituted such reforms as the 40-hour week, collective bargaining, compulsory arbitration, and bank nationalization. Blum served again as premier in 1938 and 1946–47; during **World War II**, he was imprisoned by the **Vichy** government (1940–45).

Boas, Franz (1858–1942) German-born American anthropologist. He taught at Columbia University from 1896, where he greatly influenced 20th-century anthropology. A specialist in North American Indian societies, he emphasized the role of culture and language on human behavior and relied on precise methodology. His works include *The Mind of Primitive Man* (1911).

Bogart, Humphrey [DeForest] (1899–1957) American actor. Born in New York City to a physician and a magazine illustrator, he shuttled between stage and film roles during the 1920s and 1930s before gaining public attention as a gangster in the stage (1935) and film (1936) versions of *The Petrified Forest*. The 1941 mystery *The Maltese Falcon* established him as Hollywood's definitive tough-guy antihero, a persona he evoked in other major films such as *Casablanca* (1943), *The Big Sleep* (1946), *Key Largo* (1948), and *The Treasure of the Sierra Madre* (1948). While filming *To Have and Have Not* (1944), he fell in love with costar and future fourth wife Lauren Bacall (1924–); they married in 1944. He won an Academy Award for *The African Queen* (1951).

Bohr, Niels [Henrik David] (1885–1962) Danish physicist. One of the leading scientists of the century, he studied at Copenhagen University (Ph.D., 1911) and Cambridge. He worked at Manchester University (1912–16), then returned to Denmark to serve as professor of physics at Copenhagen University from 1916 and as founding director for the Institute for Theoretical Physics from 1920. His 1913 model of atomic structure, known as the "Bohr atom," explained the spectral lines of hydrogen. Drawing on **quantum theory**, it postulated that electrons move in restricted orbits around a central nucleus. For his work on atomic structure, Bohr received the 1922 Nobel Prize for physics. He also developed the concept of complementarity, or the Copenhagen interpretation. In the late 1930s he introduced the liquid-drop model of the nucleus, important to the development of nuclear fission and nuclear weapons. During **World War II**, he came to the United States to work on the atomic bomb; he returned to Denmark afterward. A champion of nuclear arms control, he organized the first Atoms for Peace conference in 1955. His son, Danish physicist Aage Bohr (1922–), shared the 1975 Nobel Prize for physics (with Ben R. Moltelson and James Rainwater) for his work on atomic structure. Niels's brother, Danish mathematician Harald August Bohr (1887–1951), coformulated the Bohr-Landau theorem in 1914.

Böll, Heinrich Theodor (1917–85) German writer. His early works, such as the novel *Adam, Where Art Thou?* (1951), reflect his experience as a soldier during **World War II**; they are antimilitarist in theme and realist in technique. Later novels exhibit symbolic and structural innovation in critiquing postwar German society; these include *Billiards at Half Past Nine* (1959) and *Group Portrait with Lady* (1971). He received the 1972 Nobel Prize for literature.

Bonhoeffer, Dietrich (1906–45) German Protestant theologian. A leader of the anti-Nazi **resistance**, he was imprisoned and hanged for his role in a plot to assassinate **Adolf Hitler**. His writings, notably *The Cost of Discipleship* (1937), emphasize Christlike commitment to others and concern for social and political problems. Influenced by **Karl Barth**, his thought in turn influenced secularization of Protestant theology.

Borges, Jorge Luis (1899–1986) Argentine writer. Director of the National Library, he wrote short stories that cunningly combined metaphysical allegory, erudition, and wit. Fiction works include *Ficciones* (1944) and *El Aleph* (1949). He also wrote essays, including those collected in *Other Inquisitions* (1952). As a poet, he was a leader of the ultraist movement, which sought to create pure poems. His poems are collected in *Fervor of Buenos Aires* (1923) and elsewhere.

Botha, Louis (1862–1919) South African soldier and politician. A farmer in the Orange Free State, he commanded Afrikaner forces in the **Boer War** (1899–1902). He became the first prime minister of the Transvaal (1907–10) and, as leader of the Unionist Party, assisted the creation of the Union of South Africa, of which he became the first prime minister (1910–19). Supporting the Allies (see **Allied Powers**) in **World War I**, he annexed German Southwest Africa in 1915.

Bradley, Omar N[elson] (1893–1981) American soldier. Born in Clark, Missouri, he graduated from West Point and led the U.S. 1st Army in the invasion of Normandy (1944). Made commander of the 12th Army, he led an advance across France and into Germany (1944–45) that led to the liberation of the two countries. He served as army chief of staff (1948–49) and chairman of the Joint Chiefs of Staff (1949–53); in 1950 he was named general of the Army.

Brancusi, Constantin (1876–1957) Romanian sculptor. Central to the development of

20th-century sculpture, he aimed his abstract, geometric works to capture essential, rather than external, meaning. Notable works include *The Kiss* (1908) and *Fish* (1922). He often explored themes for years, as with *Sleeping Muse* (1910–12) and *Bird in Space* (1919–40). He became a French citizen in 1957.

Brandeis, Louis [Dembitz] (1856–1941) American jurist. With a degree from Harvard Law School (1877), he practiced public interest law in Boston, Mass., influencing modern legal practice with his development of the "Brandeis Brief," which incorporated sociological and specialized data. Associate justice of the Supreme Court (1916–39), he became known for promoting judicial **liberalism** and defending free speech.

Brando, Marlon (1924–) American actor. Born in Omaha, Ne., he studied at the Actors' Studio, where he learned the techniques that would make him the epitome of the "Method" actor. He became a Broadway star with his intense portrayal of Stanley Kowalski in **Tennessee Williams**'s *A Streetcar Named Desire* (1947; reprised on film, 1951) and made his film debut in *The Men* (1950). Controversial throughout his career, he won two best actor Oscars, for *On the Waterfront* (1954) and *The Godfather* (1972), but refused to accept the latter to protest U.S. treatment of Native Americans.

Brandt, Willy (1913–92) West German politician. Born Herbert Ernst Karl Frahm, he fled to Norway (1933) in opposition to **Adolf Hitler** and participated in the Norwegian and German **resistance** during **World War II** (1940-45). After the war he returned and was elected mayor of West Berlin, representing the Social Democratic Party. Chancellor of the Federal Republic of Germany from 1969 to 1974, he established peace talks among Eastern European countries; for his efforts he was awarded the Nobel Peace Prize (1971). Upon the discovery that a personal aide in his administration was an East German spy, he resigned. He was a member of the European Parliament (1979–83).

Braque, Georges (1882–1963) French painter. Though at first a fauvist (1905), he later developed, with **Pablo Picasso**, the movement called cubism (c. 1907), emphasizing geometrical analysis. Braque is credited with the first *papier collé* picture (1912). Gravely wounded in **World War I**, he later developed a more curvilinear style of painting, mainly still lifes. Works include *Nude* (1907–8), *The Portuguese* (1911), and *The Studio* (1950s).

Braun, Wernher von (1912–77) German-born American rocket engineer. Born in Wirsitz, Germany (now Poland), he was a pioneer rocket experimenter who became technical director of Germany's Peenemünde test facility (1936–45), where he developed the world's first ballistic missiles, including the V-2 rockets (1944) used to bomb Britain in **World War II**. At the end of the war, Von Braun surrendered to the U.S., where he lived from 1945, working on missiles for the army and rockets for the space program. As director of the National Aeronautic and Space Administration's (NASA) Marshall Space Flight Center (1960–70), he led the development of the Saturn rockets that landed *Apollo* astronauts on the moon. He was also deputy administrator of NASA (1970–72).

Brecht, Bertolt (1898–1956) German playwright and poet. Born Berthold Brecht, he was long a Marxist. In the 1920s, he developed his radical "epic" theater of color, signs, and lighting to reflect political sensibility in works such as *The Threepenny Opera* (1928, music by **Kurt Weill**). With the advent of Nazi rule in Germany, he moved to Denmark in 1933, then to Sweden and the U.S., creating such works as *Mother Courage and Her Children* (1939) and *The Good Woman of Setzuan* (1943). Called before the U.S. House Committee on Un-American Activities in 1947, he resettled in Switzerland and later East Berlin, directing the

Berliner Ensemble. Among later works is *The Caucasian Chalk Circle* (1955).

Breton, André (1896–1966) French poet and critic. A member of the dadaists, he founded the magazine *Littérature* in 1919. In 1924 he originated the artistic movement known as surrealism and wrote tracts on it: *Manifeste du surréalisme* (1924) and two others in 1930 and 1942. Other works include the novel *Nadja* (1928) and poetry collections *Fata Morgana* (1942) and *Arcane 17* (1945).

Breuer, Marcel Lajos (1902–81) Hungarian-born American architect and designer. He studied at the Bauhaus (1920–25), gaining fame for his tubular-steel chair (1925). Moving to London in 1935 to escape Nazi rule, he immigrated to the U.S. in 1937 and designed houses with American architect **Walter Gropius**. He became a U.S. citizen in 1944. After the war, he designed widely in the U.S. and Europe, often in concrete. Notable buildings include the United Nations Educational, Scientific, and Cultural Organization Secretariat, Paris (1953), and the Whitney Museum of American Art, New York City (1966).

Brezhnev, Leonid Ilyich (1906–82) Soviet politician. He joined the Communist Party in 1931 and was a major general in **World War II**. He was elected to the party's Central Committee in 1952; in 1957, as a protege of **Nikita Khrushchev**, he became a full member of the Politburo. From 1960 to 1964, as chairman of the Presidium of the Supreme Soviet, he was the titular head of state, but real power came in 1964, when Khrushchev was ousted from power and Brezhnev became first secretary of the party, dominating Premier **Alexsey Kosygin**. In 1968, Brezhnev ordered the Soviet invasion of Czechoslovakia and defended this action with the Brezhnev doctrine, which entitled his nation to intervene in the affairs of Soviet bloc countries when Communist rule was threatened. He promoted détente, or closer ties with the West (1972–74), but his invasion of Afghanistan in 1979 renewed **cold war** tensions. Having regained the post of chairman of the Presidium in 1977, he led the **Soviet Union** until his death.

Briand, Aristide (1862–1932) French politician. Initially a socialist, he was a member of the chamber of deputies from 1902 and helped draft the law separating church and state (1905). He held several ministerial posts and was elected prime minister numerous times (1909–10, 1910–11, 1913, 1915–17, 1921–22, 1925–26, and 1929). He headed a coalition cabinet during **World War I**. After the war, he advocated international peace and cooperation, supporting the **League of Nations**, urging rapprochement with Germany, and proposing a "United States of Europe." As foreign minister (1925–32), he was the major force behind the **Locarno Pact** (1925) and the **Kellogg-Briand Pact** (1928). The Nobel Peace Prize was awarded to him and **Gustav Stresemann** in 1926.

Bridges, Robert [Seymour] (1844–1930) British poet and critic. Educated at Oxford, he gave up medical practice in the 1880s to dedicate himself to literary interests. Poetic works include the sonnet-sequence *The Growth of Love* (1876) and the long philosophical poem *The Testament of Beauty* (1929). He edited the popular wartime anthology *The Spirit of Man* (1916) and championed the work of Gerard Manley Hopkins (1844–89), whose poetry he edited (1918). He was named his country's poet laureate in 1913.

Brooke, Rupert [Chawner] (1887–1915) British poet. In romantic, patriotic poems, he extolled the idealism of war. He himself died of disease en route to service in **World War I**. He was renowned for his personal charm and wit. Works include *1914 and Other Poems* (1915).

Bryan, William Jennings (1860–1925) American politician; known as "the Commoner."

Born in Salem, Ill., he was elected congressman from Nebraska (1891–95) and advocated free coinage of silver as a means for rural debt relief. He was famed for his oratory, exemplified in the "Cross of Gold" speech that won him the **Democratic Party**'s presidential nomination (1896). It was the first of his three unsuccessful bids for the presidency; the others occurred in 1900 and 1908. He continued to wield influence in the party and advocate populist reforms, notably in his weekly the *Commoner* (founded 1901). He served as **Woodrow Wilson**'s secretary of state from 1913 to 1915 but resigned in protest of Wilson's drift toward war after the sinking of the *Lusitania*. In later years, Bryan became a leading defender of religious fundamentalism, particularly in his 1925 prosecution of American schoolteacher John Scopes (1900–1970) for breaking Tennessee's law against teaching evolution.

Buber, Martin (1878–1965) German philosopher. Born in Vienna and educated at German universities, he became a Zionist, founding and editing the periodical *Der Jude* (1916–24). He taught at the University of Frankfurt-am-Main until the Nazis dismissed him in 1933. In 1938, he fled to Palestine, where he was professor at Hebrew University (1938–51). Influenced by Hasidism and 19th-century Danish philosopher Søren Kierkegaard, he described man's relationship with God as a dialogue, notably in *I and Thou* (1923). Other works include *Kingship of God* (1932) and a cotranslation of the Hebrew Bible. He worked tirelessly to promote Arab-Israeli understanding. Though rooted in Judaism, his humanist views influenced both Jewish and Christian theology.

Budge, [John] Donald (1915–) American athlete. Born in Oakland, Calif., he became the first tennis player to win the Grand Slam of four singles titles—Wimbledon and the French, U.S., and Australian championships—in one year (1938). A left-hander known for his backhand, he also won Wimbledon and U.S. singles titles in 1937. He turned professional in 1939.

Bukharin, Nikolai Ivanovich (1888–1938) Soviet politician. Imprisoned and banished several times for his socialist activities from 1906 to 1917, he became a leading government figure after the **Russian Revolution**: editor of *Pravda* (1917–29), member of the Politburo (1924–29), and head of the Third International (1926–29). He supported **Joseph Stalin** against **Leon Trotsky, Lev Kamenev,** and **Grigori Zinoviev,** but was ousted from power for opposing Stalin's agricultural policy. A target of Stalin's purge trials, he was executed for treason.

Bulganin, Nikolai Aleksandrovich (1895–1975) Soviet politician. Member of the Communist Party from 1917, he proved himself an able administrator in many positions under **Joseph Stalin** and **Georgi Malenkov,** including mayor of Moscow (1931–37), chairman of the state bank (1937–41), defense minister (1953–55), member of the Politburo (1948–58), and deputy premier (1937–41, 1953–55). Becoming premier in 1955, he was removed by **Nikita Khrushchev** in 1958 and expelled from the party's Central Committee in 1961 after having served on it since 1939.

Buñuel, Luis (1900–1983). Spanish film director. Living in Paris in the 1920s, he made groundbreaking films including *Un Chien andalou* (1928, with **Salvador Dalí**), which introduced his sometimes disturbing surrealist imagery. His films' combination of shocking visuals and criticism of church and society made them critically praised and controversial, sometimes banned. Notable works include *L'Age d'or* (1930), *Los Olvidados* (1950), *The Exterminating Angel* (1962), *Belle de jour* (1967), and *That Obscure Object of Desire* (1977).

Burger, Warren [Earl] (1907–95) American jurist. President **Richard Nixon** named him 15th chief justice of the U.S. Supreme Court (1969–86). Generally a conservative, he sometimes joined with liberal majorities in controversial cases, most notably *Roe v. Wade* (1973), which established a woman's right to an abortion.

Burgos, Julia de (1917–53). Puerto Rican writer. Her verse works *Poema en veinte surcos* (1938) and *Canción de la verdad sencilla* (1939), both self-published, explore the sociopolitical and emotional barriers to women's self-realization. Her third collection, *El Mar y tú: Otros poemas* (1954), was published posthumously.

Burton, Richard (1925–84) British actor. Born in Wales as Richard Jenkins, he was acclaimed for his golden-voiced stage and screen performances. He was also notorious for his rocky romance with **Elizabeth Taylor,** to whom he was twice married (1964–70, 1975–76). Stage roles include Prince Hal in *Henry IV* (1951) and King Arthur in the musical *Camelot* (1960 and 1980); films include *The Robe* (1953) and *Becket* (1964).

Bush, George [Herbert Walker] (1925–) Forty-first U.S. president (1989–93). Born in Milton, Mass., the son of Senator Prescott Bush (1895–1972), he was a navy combat pilot in **World War II.** Shot down in the Pacific, he won the Distinguished Flying Cross. After the war, he studied at Yale and moved to Texas, where he cofounded an oil company. He served as a Republican congressman from Houston (1967–71) but lost two senatorial campaigns (1964 and 1970). He was **UN** ambassador (1971–73), chairman of the Republican National Committee (1973–74), and **CIA** director (1976–77). After his failed bid for the 1980 Republican presidential nomination, he joined **Ronald Reagan**'s winning ticket, serving as Reagan's vice president (1981–89). With Dan Quayle (1947–) as his running mate, Bush won the Republican nomination in 1988 and defeated Democratic candidate Michael Dukakis (1933–). As president, Bush continued his predecessor's conservative policies at home while enjoying several foreign policy triumphs. He presided over the end of the **Cold War** as the Communist governments of the **Soviet Union** and Eastern Europe fell. He invaded Panama in 1989, ousting dictator Manuel Noriega (1938–) and bringing him to the United States to be tried and convicted on drug trafficking charges. He responded to Iraq's invasion of Kuwait in 1990 by marshaling international support for a U.S.–led military force, which, in the **Gulf War** (1991), quickly liberated Kuwait. However, Bush received the blame for an economic recession and was derided for abandoning his pledge not to raise taxes. He was defeated by **Bill Clinton** in the 1992 election, but had the satisfaction of seeing his son, Texas governor George W. Bush (1946–), defeat Clinton's vice president Al Gore (1948–) in the closely contested presidential election of 2000. John Ellis "Jeb" Bush (1953–) was elected governor of Florida in 1998.

Byrd, Richard Evelyn (1888–1957) American aviator and explorer. A naval aviator who reached the rank of rear admiral, he made the first flight over the North Pole on May 9, 1926, with American copilot Floyd Bennett (1890–1928). He commanded the first flight over the South Pole on November 29, 1929. He led several expeditions to Antarctica, including one in which he established the Antarctic base "Little America."

C

Cagney, James (1899–1986) American actor. He was the quintessential tough guy, starring in such films as *The Public Enemy* (1931), *Angels with Dirty Faces* (1938), and *White Heat* (1949). A talented dancer, he also appeared in such musicals as *Yankee Doodle Dandy* (1942), for which he won a best actor Oscar.

Calder, Alexander (1898–1976) American sculptor. In the 1930s, he introduced abstract constructions made of suspended, moving shapes, which were given the name "mobiles" by **Marcel Duchamp**. Calder also created wire portraits and immobile sculptures called stabiles.

Callaghan, Leonard James, Baron Callaghan of Cardiff (1912–) British politician. He was a Labour M.P. from 1945. Under **Harold Wilson**, he held the posts of chancellor of the exchequer (1964–67), home secretary (1967–70), and foreign secretary (1974–76) before succeeding Wilson as prime minister (1976–79). He was hampered by economic recession and an inability to overcome trade-union opposition to his austerity measures. In 1979 he had the dubious distinction of being the first prime minister to receive a vote of no confidence in the House of Commons since Ramsay MacDonald in 1924. His government fell to Conservative **Margaret Thatcher** in 1979. Callaghan resigned as **Labour Party** leader in 1980.

Callas, Maria (1923–77) American-born Greek singer. Born Maria Anna Sofia Cecilia Kalogeropoulos in New York City, she moved to Athens at 13. An operatic soprano, she was the preeminent prima donna of the 1950s and 1960s. She helped revive the *bel canto* repertoire and was praised for her acting ability and the distinctive color of her voice. She sang mainly at La Scala, the Rome and Paris Operas, Covent Garden, and the Metropolitan Opera.

Calvino, Italo (1923–85) Italian writer. At first a neorealist, he turned in the 1950s to fantastic, allegorical tales that won an international following. Works include *The Baron in the Trees* (1957), *Cosmicomics* (1965), and *If on a Winter's Night a Traveller* (1979).

Campbell-Bannerman, Sir Henry (1836–1908) British politician. An M.P. from 1868, he became Liberal leader (1899) and prime minister (1905–08). His ministry gave self-government to the Transvaal and Orange River Colony (1907) and passed such reforms as the Trade Disputes Act (1906) and Merchant Shipping Act (1907).

Camus, Albert (1913–60) French writer. Born in Algeria, he organized an avant-garde theater group in the 1930s and worked as a journalist in North Africa and Paris until the start of **World War II**. In novels such as *The Stranger* (1942) and *The Plague* (1947), essays such as *The Myth of Sisyphus* (1942), and plays such as *Caligula* (1945), he presented his philosophy, which was informed by (but not identical to) **existentialism** and focused on commitment to human values in an uncaring universe. During the German occupation of France, he was an intellectual leader of the **resistance**, founding and editing the underground newspaper *Combat*. He was awarded the Nobel Prize for literature in 1957. He died in an automobile crash.

Canetti, Elias (1905–94) Bulgarian-born British writer. He wrote in German but lived in England from 1939. His works, which shed light on dark obsessions, include the horrific novel *Auto da fé* (1935); *Crowds and Power* (1960), a nonfiction study of mass psychology; and *Kafka's Other Trial* (1969), a literary study. He was the first Bulgarian to win the Nobel Prize for literature (1981).

Capa, Robert (1913–54) Hungarian-born American photographer. Born Andrei Friedmann in Budapest, he became known for his vivid, immediate war photography covering the **Spanish Civil War**, **World War II** (notably the Normandy invasion), and Palestine. With French photographer Henri Cartier-Bresson (1908–) and others, he helped found the Magnum Photos agency (1947). He was killed by a land mine in French

Indochina.

Capek, Karel (1890–1938) Czech writer. Staff member at *Národni Listy* in Prague (1919–23) and from 1923 at *Lidové Noviny*, he was a popular and prolific playwright, short-story writer, and novelist who often satirized modern science, industry, and **totalitarianism**. His internationally successful science fiction play, *R.U.R.* = *Rossum's Universal Robots* (1921) established him in the genre and introduced the word *robot*; the science fiction novel *Krakatit* (1924) involved the creation of an atomic bomb. Aside from science fiction, notable works include the novel trilogy *Hordubal* (1933), *Meteor* (1934), and *An Ordinary Life* (1934). Nonfiction works include *President Masaryk Tells His Story* (1928). Early short-story collections, including *The Life of Insects* (1922), were cowritten with painter brother Josef.

Capone, Al[phonse] (1899–1947) Italian-born American gangster. Born in Naples, he immigrated to the U.S. and began his criminal career in 1920 with Italian-born American bootlegger Johnny Torrio (1882–1957). Defeating Chicago's O'Banion gang (1924–26), he gained control of the bootlegging business and soon controlled city law enforcement, labor, and political officials. In 1929 he ordered the St. Valentine's Day Massacre of the Bugs Moran gang. In 1931 he was convicted for income tax evasion and served time in prison from 1931 to 1939; he was released for health complications due to syphilis. Known as "Scarface," he epitomized **Prohibition**-era gangsterism.

Capra, Frank (1897–1991) Italian-born American film director. Immigrating to the U.S. at age six, he gained early film experience in the 1920s directing **Mack Sennett** silent comedies. His 1934 *It Happened One Night*, which helped introduce the screwball comedy, won five Academy Awards and established Capra as a major director. Signature films *Mr. Deeds Goes to Town* (1936) and *Mr. Smith Goes to Washington* (1939) championed the idealism and courage of an average Joe fighting business or government tyranny, an appealing sentiment during the **Great Depression**. With post–**World War II** taste growing darker, Capra lost favor; his last film was *Pocketful of Miracles* (1961). Perhaps his most enduring film is the 1946 comedy-drama *It's a Wonderful Life*, which has been a U.S. **television** Christmas staple since the 1970s.

Cárdenas, Lázaro (1895–1970) Mexican soldier and politician. In the revolutionary army during the **Mexican Revolution** (1913–17), he became a general in 1923 and held several government posts before serving as president from 1934 to 1940. His Six-Year Plan instituted social reforms that redistributed wealth and public policy programs and further marked him as a revolutionary leader for the poor. In 1938 he expropriated foreign-owned oil lands, apportioning them to peasants. During **World War II** he was minister of defense (1943–45) and in 1945 commander of the army.

Carmichael, Hoagy (1899–1981) American songwriter. Born Hoagland Howard Carmichael, he was a popular composer, pianist, and arranger who also acted in films, notably *To Have and Have Not* (1944). His songs included "Stardust," "Am I Blue," "Two Sleepy People," and "In the Cool, Cool, Cool of the Evening" (Academy Award, 1951).

Carnap, Rudolf (1891–1970) German-born American philosopher. After teaching in Vienna and Prague, he came to the U.S., where he taught at the University of Chicago (1936–52) and the University of California, Los Angeles (1954–70). A founder of logical positivism, he argued that the only legitimate task for philosophy was describing and criticizing scientific language. He was opposed to metaphysics, though in later years he modified his extreme reductionism. Works include *The Logical Structure of the World* (1928), *The*

Logical Syntax of Language (1934), and *Logical Foundations of Probability* (1950).

Carnegie, Andrew (1835–1919) American industrialist and philanthropist. Of Scottish background, he immigrated to the U.S. in 1848. While superintendent for the Pennsylvania Railroad (1859–65), he invested heavily in iron manufacturing. From 1873 he turned to steel, acquiring companies that in 1899 became the Carnegie Steel Co. He also controlled much iron and ore manufacturing and many railroads. After selling his interests in 1901, he retired and practiced philanthropic beliefs outlined in his 1889 article "Wealth." Donations of about $350 million resulted in over 2,800 libraries and philanthropic organizations such as the Carnegie Corp. of New York and the Carnegie Endowment for International Peace.

Carson, Johnny (1925–) American **television** entertainer. He was born in Iowa and raised in Nebraska. As the genial and witty host of *The Tonight Show* from 1962 to 1992, he dominated late-night television and set the pattern for numerous talk shows to come.

Carter, Jimmy (1924–) Thirty-ninth U.S. president (1977–81). Born James Earl Carter Jr. in Plains, Georgia, he graduated from the U.S. Naval Academy at Annapolis (1946) and served in the navy until 1953, reaching the rank of lieutenant commander before rejoining the family's peanut business. He served in the Georgia state senate (1963–66) and was elected governor (1971–75). A Democrat who appealed to voters disgusted with the scandals of **Richard Nixon's** administration, he defeated **Gerald Ford**, Nixon's successor, in the 1976 presidential election. Despite his efforts to run an open and accountable administration, he received much public blame for persistent high inflation, the **Iranian hostage crisis**, and the Soviet invasion of Afghanistan. His major success was his negotiation of the **Camp David Accords** that led to a 1979 peace treaty between Egypt and Israel; he also effected a treaty transferring control of the **Panama Canal** to Panama. **Ronald Reagan** defeated Carter's reelection bid in 1980. In recent years, Carter has been active in building homes for the poor and mediating foreign conflicts, notably in Haiti.

Caruso, Enrico (1873–1921) Italian singer. Born in Naples, Italy; he became one of the world's greatest operatic tenors, known especially for performing Verdi, Puccini, and Massenet. He was engaged by the Metropolitan Opera, New York City, from 1902 to his death.

Casals, Pablo or **Pau** (1876–1973) Spanish cellist, conductor, and composer. Professor (from 1897) at the conservatory of music in Barcelona, he debuted as a cellist in 1898 and began touring in 1901. He gained fame for his virtuoso performances and interpretations of major composers, particularly Bach. In 1919 he established the Orquesta Pau Casals in Barcelona and in 1950 the Casals Festival in France. Compositions include works for cello and piano, violin and piano, and orchestra. Through his performances, he raised the stature of solo cello works.

Casement, Sir Roger David (1864–1916) Irish revolutionary. Born near Dublin, he gained fame as a British consul (1892–1911) who reported on mistreatment of native workers in the Belgian Congo (1903) and Peru (1910). Knighted for his efforts, he retired to Ireland and joined the nationalist cause. During **World War I**, he sought German help in gaining Irish independence. He was hanged as a traitor.

Castro, Fidel (1926–) Cuban dictator. Dedicated to overthrowing dictator **Fulgencio Batista**, he led two revolts that failed, in 1953 and 1956, and founded the revolutionary 26th of July movement. After years of guerrilla fighting from their base in the Sierra Maestra mountains, Castro's forces, including his brother Raúl and **Che Guevara**, overthrew Batista on January 1, 1959. Proclaiming himself a Marxist-Leninist, Castro established a Communist government allied to the **Soviet Union**. Despite long-standing U.S. opposition to Castro, including economic sanctions and a failed U.S.–backed invasion at **Bay of Pigs** (1961), Castro has remained premier from 1959. His totalitarian rule has been marked by political repression and exporting of revolution as well as economic and social reforms, including nationalization of industry and collectivization of agriculture.

Cather, Willa [Sibert] (1873–1947) American writer. Born in Winchester, Va., she grew up in Red Cloud, Ne., and attended the University of Nebraska. Her adopted state provided the setting for *O Pioneers!* (1913) and life among European immigrants the background for *My Ántonia* (1918), which established her as a voice of the American prairie. The novel *One of Ours* (1922), about the decline of the pioneer spirit, won the Pulitzer Prize. Another work, *Death Comes to the Archbishop* (1927), blends history and religion; *Lucy Gayheart* (1935) explores the creative confinement of country life.

Ceausescu, Nicolae (1918–89) Romanian politician. A peasant's son, he joined the Communist Party in 1936. He survived imprisonment and **World War II** to become the protegé of Gheorghe Gheorghiu-Dej (1901–65), the party leader who led the Communist Romanian Republic from its establishment in 1948. Ceausescu succeeded Gheorghiu-Dej as the party's first secretary in 1965, adding the office of president two years later (1967–89). He continued his predecessor's policy of distancing himself from the **Soviet Union**. He promoted closer ties with China and the West. A conservative Marxist, he embarked on economic reforms that proved disastrous. He ruled tyrannically and repressively, staffing his government with relatives, including his wife, Elena. His drive to expand the country's population, in part by outlawing abortion, resulted in a vast increase of children raised in underfunded orphanages. In 1989, he was deposed by revolution. He and his wife, both widely hated, were executed.

Chadwick, Sir James (1891–1974) British physicist. Educated at Manchester University, he worked at Cambridge and the University of Liverpool. He discovered the neutron in 1932, an achievement that earned him the 1935 Nobel Prize for physics. A veteran of the **Manhattan Project**, he was knighted in 1945.

Chagall, Marc (1887–1985) Russian-born French painter and designer. Born in Vitebsk, he studied painting in St. Petersburg and first came to Paris in 1910. After returning to Russia, he was made a Soviet commissar of fine arts, but disagreements with the authorities led him to settle in France in the 1920s. He lived in the U.S. from 1941 to 1947. Considered a forerunner of the surrealists, he produced many works, such as *I and the Village* and *The Rabbi of Vitebsk*, that drew on Jewish life and folklore and displayed a naive, fairytale style. He also designed sets and costumes for **Igor Stravinsky's** ballet *The Firebird* (1945) and created stained-glass windows, murals, and book illustrations. A Chagall museum opened in Nice in 1973.

Chamberlain, [Arthur] Neville (1869–1940) British politician. The son of politician Joseph Chamberlain (1836–1914), he was a Conservative member of Parliament from 1918. He rose to chancellor of exchequer (1923–24, 1931–37) before succeeding **Stanley Baldwin** as prime minister (1937–40). Believing **Adolf Hitler** to be a reasonable leader, Chamberlain pursued a policy of **appeasement** toward the **Axis Powers**, recognizing Italy's conquest of Ethiopia (1938) and making concessions to Germany in the **Munich Agreement** (1938). However, he increased the pace of British rearmament and declared war on Germany when Hitler invaded Poland (1939). Britain's disastrous defeat in Norway forced Chamberlain to resign.

Chandler, Raymond [Thornton] (1888–1959) American writer. Born in Chicago but educated in England, he was a master of hard-boiled detective fiction. His private eye Philip Marlowe was featured in such novels as *The Big Sleep* (1939) and *Farewell, My Lovely* (1940). He also wrote such screenplays as *Double Indemnity* (1944).

Chanel, Coco (1883–1971) French fashion designer. Born Gabrielle Chanel, she established her Paris fashion house in 1914. By the 1920s, the Chanel style was well known, shaping modern fashion with clothing design stressing comfort and simple lines in wearable fabrics of knits and jersey. She pioneered women's wearing of trousers and the use of costume jewelry as an accessory. Among her most influential creations are the Chanel suit (1954) and Chanel No. 5 perfume (1922).

Chaplin, Sir Charles [Spencer] (1889–1977) British film director and screenwriter. Born in London, Charlie Chaplin first appeared on stage at age five and appeared in his first silent film in 1914 (*Making a Living*). Shortly he began directing and developing his "Tramp" character in films like *The Tramp* (1915) and *The Kid* (1921). In 1919 he cofounded the film studio United Artists with **D.W. Griffith** and American film stars **Mary Pickford** and Douglas Fairbanks (1883–1939). There he directed some of his finest works: *The Gold Rush* (1925), *City Lights* (1931), and *Modern Times* (1936). He received a special Oscar in 1927–28. His increasingly serious sound films include *The Great Dictator* (1940), *Monsieur Verdoux* (1947), and *Limelight* (1952). After the war he was accused of having Communist affiliations, and in 1952 he was denied reentry to the U.S. He returned only to receive another special Oscar in 1972. He was knighted in 1975.

Chávez, César Estrada (1927–93) American labor leader. Born in Yuma, Ariz., the son of migrant farm workers, he founded the union that would become the United Farm Workers, a member of the American Federation of Labor and Congress of Industrial Organizations. From 1965 to 1970, the union waged a strike demanding higher wages from growers of California table grapes. Carried out according to principles of Gandhian non-violence, *La Huelga*, or "the Strike," drew national attention to the plight of Chicano farm workers. Supported by a national grape boycott, the strike ended with a union victory. Later boycotts were not as successful, as Chávez struggled over jurisdictional issues with the Teamsters Union and with growers who failed to honor agreements. Chávez, who went on several hunger strikes, was respected for helping Mexican-Americans achieve a new level of community awareness.

Chen Kaige (1952–) Chinese film director. He became known as a leading director of post–Cultural Revolution China with such highly dramatic works as *Yellow Earth* (1984), *King of Children* (1987), and *Farewell My Concubine* (1993).

Chernenko, Konstantin Ustinovich (1911–85) Soviet politician. A Communist Party member since 1931, he was a protegé of **Leonid Brezhnev** since the late 1940s. He became a full member of the Central Committee in 1971. Upon the death of **Yuri Andropov** in 1984, Chernenko became general secretary of the Communist Party and president of the **Soviet Union** (1984–85). Like Andropov, his time in office was cut short by death after little more than a year.

Chiang Kai-shek or **Jiang Jie-shi** (1887–1975) Chinese soldier and politician. He took part in the **Chinese Revolution** of 1911 and the rebellions establishing the Chinese Republic; from 1918, he served in **Sun Yat-sen's Guomindang (Nationalist)** government. Made generalissimo of the Guomindang army in 1925 following Sun's death, he led the Northern Expedition (1926–28). In 1927 Chiang broke with the Communists, sparking the **Chinese Civil War**. He was president of the Nationalist government at Nanjing from 1928 until the civil war ended with Communist victory in 1949. The struggle was interrupted by the **Sian Incident** (1936), in which Chiang was arrested by his own troops and forced to agree to form the United Front against the Japanese. Chiang then led a Nationalist-Communist alliance against Japan in the second **Sino-Japanese** War (1937–45) and **World War II**. In 1949, Chiang and his Nationalist regime were driven into exile in Taiwan. As president of Nationalist China (1950–75), he received backing from the U.S., but lost international standing in 1972 when his government was expelled from the **UN** in favor of mainland Communist China.

Chiang Tse-min See **Jiang Zemin**.

Chirico, Giorgio de (1888–1978) Italian painter. Around 1913, he founded metaphysical painting, a precursor of surrealism characterized by hallucinatory images with peculiar iconography, such as tailor's dummies in place of human figures. After **World War I**, he repudiated the movement and painted in an increasingly academic style. Works include *Melancholy of a Beautiful Day* (1913).

Chisholm, Shirley (1924–) American politician. Born Anita St. Hill in New York, N.Y., she was a teacher and educational consultant before becoming the first African-American woman in the U.S. House of Representatives (1969–83). An energetic supporter of minority education, she was a Democratic candidate for president in 1972.

Chomsky, Noam (1928–) American linguist and political theorist. He began teaching at Massachusetts Institute of Technology in 1955, the same year he received his Ph.D. from the University of Pennsylvania. In 1957, he became a central founder of transformational-generative grammar with his landmark book *Syntactic Structures*, which argued that innate structures in the mind are the basis for language. A radical activist, he has expressed his political views in such works as *American Power and the New Mandarins* (1969).

Christian X (1870–1947) King of Denmark (1912–47) and Iceland (1912–44). He succeeded his father Frederick VIII (1843–1912; reigned 1906–12). Christian granted women the right to vote (1915) and presided over the granting of independence of Iceland (1944). While his country was under German occupation (1940–45) in **World War II**, he became a hero of the **resistance** by refusing to flee Denmark and opposing anti-Semitism; he was imprisoned for his efforts (1943–45). His son Frederick IX (1899–1972) succeeded him.

Chu Teh (1886–1976) Chinese soldier. In 1911 he participated in the overthrow of the Ch'ing dynasty; a decade later, while a student in Europe, he joined the Chinese Communist Party (1922). Returning to China, he became part of the **Guomindang** army in 1927. After the split of the Nationalist and Communist forces, Chu joined **Mao Zedong** and helped found the Fourth Red Army in 1928. As the army's commander, Chu led forces in the **second Sino-Japanese War** (1937–45). He was commander of the People's Liberation Army for the People's Republic of China from 1949 to 1954 and later served as chairman of the Standing Committee, National People's Congress (1959–76).

Churchill, Sir Winston [Leonard Spencer] (1874–1965) British politician and writer. Born at Blenheim Palace, he was the son of politician Lord Randolph Churchill (1849–95) and educated at Harrow and Sandhurst. Entering the army, he served as soldier and some-time war correspondent in Cuba (1895), India (1897), the Sudan (1898), and South Africa

(1899). Returning to England, he was elected M.P. (1900–22 and 1924–64). Initially a Conservative, he broke with the party over its adoption of tariffs, joining the Liberals in 1904. As president of the Board of Trade (1908–10), he set up labor exchanges and carried the Trade Boards Act (1909). He was also home secretary (1910–11) and first lord of the admiralty (1911–15). In the latter post, he built up the navy in preparation for **World War I**, but was blamed for the failure of the Dardanelles campaign and demoted. He joined the army in France (1916), then was called back by **David Lloyd George** to serve as minister of munitions (1917). Between the world wars, he rejoined the **Conservative Party** (1924) and served as secretary for war and air (1919–21), colonial secretary (1921–22), chancellor of the exchequer (1924–29), and again as first lord of the admiralty (1939–40). Stubborn and outspoken in his views—which included opposition to **Communism**, **Fascism**, colonial independence, and organized labor—Churchill made many enemies. But as prime minister (1940–45) in a coalition government during **World War II**, he rallied Britain with his stirring oratory and his determination to fight through to victory. "I have nothing to offer," he said, "but blood, toil, tears, and sweat." He forged an alliance with U.S. president **Franklin Roosevelt**, cosigning with him the statement of war aims known as the **Atlantic Charter** (1941). Churchill participated in the Allied (see **Allied Powers**) conferences at Tehran (1943), **Yalta** (1945, see **Yalta Conference**), and **Potsdam** (1945, see **Potsdam Conference**). Defeated at the polls at war's end, Churchill returned as prime minister in 1951–55. He coined the phrase "**iron curtain**" in a speech at Fulton, Mo. (1946). He was knighted in 1953. A writer of biography and history, he won the 1953 Nobel Prize for literature; his works include *The Second World War* (6 vols., 1948–53).

Ciurlionis, Mikalojus [Konstantinas] (1875–1911) Lithuanian painter and composer. Painting from 1905, he drew on Lithuanian folklore, mysticism, and a belief in the link between visual arts and music. Works include *Spring Sonata* and *Sun Sonata* (both 1907). Musical compositions include symphonic poems, chamber music, and folk song adaptations.

Clemenceau, Georges (1841–1929) French politician. As a prominent left-wing journalist, he supported Dreyfus in the **Dreyfus affair** in the 1890s. From 1906 to 1909 and 1917 to 1920, he served as premier; during the latter term, he reinvigorated France's will to victory in the last months of **World War I** and led the French delegation at the **Paris Peace Conference** (1919), where he pushed for draconian punishment of Germany.

Clinton, Bill (1946–) Forty-second U.S. president (1993–2001). Born William Jefferson Blythe IV in Hope, Ark., he adopted his stepfather's surname after his father's death, becoming William Jefferson Clinton. Raised in humble circumstances in Hot Springs, Ark., he attended Georgetown University, studied at Oxford as a Rhodes scholar, and earned a law degree from Yale, where he met Hillary Rodham (1947–), who, as his wife, would be known as Hillary Rodham Clinton. After working as a law professor and Arkansas state attorney general, he was elected to the governorship in 1978, voted out of office in 1980, and voted back into office in 1982, 1984, and 1988. As chair of the pragmatic Democratic Leadership Council, he positioned himself as a moderate "new Democrat" to win his party's nomination and the general election in the 1992 presidential race, defeating Republican incumbent **George Bush** and third-party candidate **Ross Perot**. His vice president was Al Gore (1948–), a former senator from Tennessee. In his first term, Clinton suffered a major setback when his proposal for comprehensive health care, developed under the first lady's leadership, was defeated in Congress. He was criticized for vacillation and dishonesty and for the liberal tendencies exhibited in his unsuccessful move to lift the ban on gays in the military. Also during his first term, he was investigated for his role in the Whitewater affair, a web of alleged financial misconduct while he was governor of Arkansas, and accused of sexual improprieties. He had the misfortune of losing his party's control of both houses of Congress in 1994. By the 1996 elections, Clinton was able to rebuild his popularity due to a growing economy and his own determined turn to the center. Notably, he supported welfare reform legislation that abolished guarantees of aid to the poor, while striving to curb what he characterized as the excesses of the Republican Right. Before his first term ended, he succeeded in reducing the federal deficit, passing the Brady Bill (gun control legislation), and winning ratification of the North American Free Trade Agreement. In foreign affairs, he used military intervention to bring democracy to Haiti and helped mediate peace agreements in the **Bosnian Civil War** and between the **Palestine Liberation Organization** and Israel.

Following his reelection in 1996, in which he defeated Republican candidate Bob Dole (1923–), Clinton negotiated with Congress an agreement to balance the federal budget by 2002. In the meantime, Clinton faced new scandals. Some were related to campaign finance, but it was one scandal related to sexual misconduct that nearly toppled his presidency. In January 1998 Independent Counsel Kenneth Starr began investigating Clinton on charges that he had made a false deposition in a sexual misconduct lawsuit brought by former Arkansas state employee Paula Jones (a suit later dismissed). The alleged falsehoods concerned Clinton's sexual affair with former White House intern Monica Lewinsky. Although Clinton at first denied the affair, overwhelming evidence forced him to admit to a relationship with Lewinsky before a grand jury in August while denying that he had lied in his January deposition. Clinton refused to resign, buoyed by public opinion polls that showed strong support for him, in large part because of the strong economy and his success in achieving the first budget surplus since 1969. On December 19, the House of Representatives impeached Clinton on perjury and obstruction of justice before a grand jury, thereby making him the first U.S. president since Andrew Johnson in 1868 to be impeached. On January 7, 1999, the first presidential impeachment trial since Johnson's 1868 trial opened. On February 12 the Senate acquitted Clinton on both charges: perjury 55–45, and obstruction of justice 50–50. Shortly after, a federal judge found Clinton in contempt of court for his false testimony in the Paula Jones case, making him the first president to be held in contempt of court.

The Lewinsky scandal dominated the domestic headlines in 1998, but the Clinton administration also kept an eye on foreign policy, brokering a peace agreement in Northern Ireland; bombing Sudan and Afghanistan over their alleged support of terrorists responsible for two U.S. embassy bombings in Africa; and bombing Iraq over its refusal to comply with **UN** inspection requirements. Clinton was faulted by some for not acting more vigorously in response to the discovery during his administration of China's past theft of nuclear secrets. In 1999, with Clinton's approval, the **North Atlantic Treaty Organization** **(NATO)** launched its first uninvited offensive against a sovereign nation when it initiated a massive bombing campaign against Serbian targets in Yugoslavia. At issue was Yugoslav President **Slobodan Milosevic's** policy of "ethnic cleansing" against ethnic Albanians in the separatist province of Kosovo, a policy carried out through massacres and destruction of villages.

In the 2000 presidential election, Clinton's vice-president Gore was defeated by George W. Bush (1946–), son of the former president, in a bitterly contested vote. But his wife Hillary provided some consolation that year: elected to the Senate from New York, she became the first wife of a president to be elected to political office.

Cocteau, Jean (1889–1963) French writer and filmmaker. A leader of the French avant-garde in the 1920s, he created experimental, surrealist works that span nearly all art forms. Notable works include films *The Blood of a Poet* (1932) and *Beauty and the Beast* (1945); novel *Les Enfants terribles* (1929, film 1950); plays *Orphée* (1926; film 1949) and *The Infernal Machine* (1934); and the autobiographical work *Opium* (1930). He also wrote ballets and produced frescoes and other visual works. He is considered one of the most inventive creative forces of the century.

Cohan, George M[ichael] (1878–1942) American playwright and actor. A prolific performer, producer and playwright, he dominated Broadway for decades with rousing, patriotic musicals including *Little Johnny Jones* (1904), *Forty-five Minutes from Broadway* (1905), *George Washington, Jr.* (1906), and *The Man Who Owns Broadway* (1908). Notable songs include "Give My Regards to Broadway," "Yankee Doodle Dandy," and "Over There." He also acted in *Ah, Wilderness!* (1934).

Colette (1873–1954) French writer. Pen name of Sidonie-Gabrielle Colette. She wrote sensual, sensitive novels centered on female characters. Her first novels—the "Claudine" series beginning with *Claudine at School* (1900)—were published under the name "Willy," a pseudonym of her first husband, writer Henri Gauthier-Villars. Later works included *Cheri* (1920), *Sido* (1929), and *Gigi* (1944). She also wrote memoirs, criticism, and sketches of animal life.

Collins, Michael (1890–1922) Irish revolutionary. A leader of the Irish nationalist movement **Sinn Féin**, he participated in the Easter Rebellion (1916) and organized guerrilla warfare against British rule. With Irish revolutionary Arthur Griffith (1872–1922), he negotiated peace with Britain (1921) and helped found the Irish Free State. In the midst of civil war with republican insurgents, Collins was assassinated.

Coltrane, John [William] (1926–67) American jazz musician. A saxophonist, he played in the bands of **Dizzy Gillespie**, **Miles Davis**, Thelonius Monk (1917–82), and others. As leader of his own quartet from 1960, he was an influential figure in the transition from the dense jazz of the 1950s to the free jazz of the 1960s. Eastern music and philosophy influenced his style in such recordings as *A Love Supreme* (1964).

Conrad, Joseph (1857–1924) Polish-born British writer. Born Józef Teodor Konrad Korzeniowski, he became a British subject while serving as a merchant seaman (1874–94). He left the sea to settle in England and write novels, starting with *Almayer's Folly* (1895). Although he learned English late in life, Conrad was a recognized master of English prose style and modernist technique. Often drawing on his maritime adventures, his novels probe the nature of moral corruption, European imperialism, and human isolation. Works include the short novel *Heart of Darkness* (1902) and the longer works *The Nigger of the "Narcissus"* (1897), *Lord Jim* (1900), *Nostromo* (1904), *The Secret Agent* (1907), *Under Western Eyes* (1911), and *Victory* (1915).

Constantine I (1868–1923) Greek king (1913–17, 1920–22). Forced to abdicate in 1917 for opposing the Allies (see **Allied Powers**) in **World War I**, he was succeeded by his second son, Alexander (1893–1920; reigned 1917–20), who died soon thereafter. Constantine was restored to the throne but was forced out again by a military revolt. His eldest son **George II** succeeded him.

Coolidge, [John] Calvin (1872–1933) Thirtieth U.S. president (1923–29). Born in Plymouth, Vt., he attended Amherst College and practiced law in Massachusetts before becoming state senator in 1911. As governor of Massachusetts (1919–20), he gained national attention for using military force to end the 1919 Boston police strike. Vice president of the U.S. from 1921, he became president in 1923 following the death of Republican president **Warren G. Harding**. Coolidge was elected president in 1924. His positions reflected the national mood: noninterference in business and foreign affairs, government streamlining, and support for stock market growth. Famously terse, he declined a chance for reelection by announcing, "I do not choose to run."

Copland, Aaron (1900–90) American composer. Born in Brooklyn, N.Y., he studied in Paris with French conductor and teacher Nadia Boulanger (1887–1979) and began writing in the 1920s, eventually fusing varieties of American music into works that reached wide audiences and reflected a national character. Well-known works include the ballets *Billy the Kid* (1940), *Rodeo* (1942), and *Appalachian Spring* (1944); the orchestral work *El Salón México* (1936); and a concerto for clarinet and string orchestra (1948) for **Benny Goodman**.

Coppola, Francis Ford (1939–) American film director and screenwriter. Born in Detroit, Mich., he received an M.F.A. in film at the University of California, Los Angeles, with his thesis film *You're a Big Boy Now* (1967). After sharing a screenwriting Oscar for *Patton* (1970), he rose to directorial prominence with the gangster epics *The Godfather* (1972) and *The Godfather, Part II* (1974), both of which won best picture Oscars. Other equally ambitious but less successful films include *The Conversation* (1974), *Apocalypse Now* (1979), *Peggy Sue Got Married* (1986), and *The Godfather, Part III* (1990).

Cortázar, Julio (1914–84) Argentine writer. Born in Belgium, he was raised in Argentina but left in 1951 in opposition to the rule of **Juan Perón**. He settled in France, becoming a citizen in 1981. His fiction features surrealistic imagery, labyrinthine plots, and metaphysical themes. His works include the novels *The Winners* (1960) and *Hopscotch* (1963) and the short-story collection *End of the Game* (1956).

Cousteau, Jacques Yves (1910–1997) French oceanographer. With Émil Gagnan in 1943, he developed the aqualung or scuba (self-contained underwater breathing apparatus). He started the underwater research team for the French Navy (1945) and helped to develop the bathyscaphe. From 1951 he led ocean explorations, the book, film, and **television** records of which introduced generations to oceanography and ocean ecology. Among his books are *The Silent World* (1953, with Frédéric Dumas) and *Life and Death in a Coral Sea* (1970, with Philippe Diolé); his films include *World without Sun* (1954) and *Tragedy of Red Salmon* (1970).

Coward, Sir Nöel Peirce (1899–1973) British playwright and actor. A child actor from 1910, he began writing plays after **World War I**, with his witty social comedies appearing widely on Broadway and London stages from the 1920s. Among his many plays are *Hay Fever* (1925), *Private Lives* (1930), *Cavalcade* (1931), *Words and Music* (1932), *Design for Living* (1933), *Tonight at 8:30* (1936), *Blithe Spirit* (1942), and *Present Laughter* (1943), a musical. Films include *In Which We Serve* (1942) and *Brief Encounter* (1946). Among his well-known songs are "Mad Dogs and Englishmen." Autobiographies include *Present Indicative* (1937) and *Future Indefinite* (1954). He was knighted in 1970.

Crick, Francis [Harry Compton] (1916–) British molecular biologist. In 1953, while at the Cavendish Laboratory in Cambridge, England, he and **James Dewey Watson** collaborated to codiscover the double helix structure of the DNA molecule. With Irish biophysicist Maurice Wilkins (1916–), they shared the 1962 Nobel Prize for physiology or **medicine**. Crick went on to research in detail how DNA carries genetic information and to study the brain. In 1977 he joined the Salk Institute in La Jolla, California. Books include *Of Molecules and Men* (1966).

Croce, Benedetto (1866–1952) Italian philosopher, critic, historian, and politician. His works include the four-volume idealist treatise *Philosophy of the Spirit* (1902–17). The leader of the intellectual opposition to **Benito Mussolini**, he served in several government posts and was the founder and president of the reconstituted Liberal Party (1943–52).

Cronkite, Walter [Leland, Jr.] (1916–) American broadcast journalist. Possibly the most famous television journalist of all time, he helped initiate the Columbia Broadcasting System (CBS) evening news in 1962 and anchored it until 1981. Widely trusted even in times of national turmoil, he was known for his nightly sign-off line: "And that's the way it is."

Crosby, Bing (1904–77) American singer and film actor. Born Harry Lillis Crosby, he became America's most popular singer of the 1930s with an easygoing crooning style and signature songs that included his radio show theme *Where the Blue of the Night* and *White Christmas*. In films he paired with **Bob Hope** in the successful *Road* series (e.g., *Road to Morocco*, 1942) and won an Academy Award for his performance as a priest in *Going My Way* (1944).

cummings, e[dward] e[stlin] (1894–1962) American writer. Graduating from Harvard, he became known for his original, fanciful poetry, in collections including *Tulips and Chimneys* (1923), *XLI Poems* (1925), *50 Poems (1958)*, and *73 Poems* (1962). His work is characterized by its idiosyncratic use of punctuation and typography, as in the use of lowercase lettering for his name for part of his career. Prose works include the novel *The Enormous Room* (1922).

Curie, Marie (1867–1934) Polish-born French scientist. Born in Warsaw as Manya Sklodowska, she married French physicist Pierre Curie (1859–1906) in 1895. In 1898, with French physicist Antoine-Henri Becquerel (1852–1908), the Curies investigated radioactivity (a term Marie coined); the Curies also isolated the elements radium and polonium. For their work, the three scientists were awarded the 1903 Nobel Prize for physics. Following Pierre's death in 1906, Marie continued studying radium and received a second Nobel Prize, this time for chemistry, in 1911. She succeeded her husband as professor at the Sorbonne in 1906 and directed research at the Radium Institute of the University of Paris (1918–34). Her daughter, Irène Joliot-Curie (1897–1956), also became a Nobel Prize–winning scientist (1935, chemistry). Marie Curie died of leukemia caused by her work with radioactivity.

Curzon, George Nathaniel, first baron and marquess Curzon of Kedleston (1859–1925) British politician. As viceroy of India (1898–1905), he ordered the Partition of Bengal in 1905, an administrative division that sparked nationalist protest and was rescinded in 1911. During **World War I**, he served in the cabinets of **Herbert Henry Asquith** and **David Lloyd George**. As foreign secretary (1919–24), he condemned French occupation of the Ruhr and presided over the Conference of Lausanne, which yielded a peace treaty with Turkey (see **Lausanne, Treaty of**).

D

Daladier, Édouard (1884–1970) French politician. Active in the radical Socialist Party from 1919, he was premier of France in 1933, 1934, and from 1938 to 1940. In 1938 he signed the **Munich Agreement** but declared war on Germany in 1939 after the invasion of Poland. He was arrested after the fall of France (1940), tried for war-guilt crimes, and deported to Germany until liberated in 1945. Postwar he served in the national assembly of the Fourth Republic 1946 to 1958.

Dalai Lama (1935–) Tibetan religious and political leader. Born Tenzin Gyatso, he was declared the 14th Dalai Lama, the incarnation of the bodhisattva Avalokiteshvara, in 1940. As such, he was to be Tibet's secular and spiritual ruler, but he was prevented from fulfilling his destiny by China's invasion and occupation of Tibet in 1950. In 1959 he fled, following an unsuccessful revolt by Tibetans, with many of his followers to India, where he has since headed the Tibetan exile community. He received the 1989 Nobel Peace Prize for his efforts to inform the world of his country's plight and for his emphasis on nonviolence.

Dalí, Salvador (1904–89) Spanish painter. The man who became an eccentric leader of the surrealist movement began by being expelled from the Madrid School of Fine Arts for outrageous behavior in 1926. Influenced by futurism and **Sigmund Freud**'s writings on dreams, he developed a dazzling surrealist style and created a series of paintings of precisely executed dream "photographs" that include *The Persistence of Memory* (1931), with its drooping watch faces. Before moving to New York in 1940, he worked with Spanish film director **Luis Buñuel** on *Un Chien andalou* (1928) and *L'Age d'or* (1931). Back in Spain from 1955, he turned in part to religious themes, with *The Crucifixion of St. John of the Cross* (1951) a representative work.

Darrow, Clarence [Seward] (1857–1938) American lawyer. Originally a corporate lawyer, he became known for representing controversial long-shot clients, including American socialist **Eugene Debs** and American teacher John Scopes (1900–1970) in the **Scopes trial** on teaching evolution in public schools (1925). He was a founding member of the American Civil Liberties Union (1920). An opponent of the death penalty, he had no clients who were condemned to death.

Davis, Bette (1908–89) American film actress. Born Ruth Elizabeth Davis, she became a leading actress with her performance in *Of Human Bondage* (1934) and sustained decades of renown for fiery portrayals of independent women in works including *Dangerous* (1935, Academy Award), *Jezebel* (1938, Academy Award), *Dark Victory* (1939), *The Little Foxes* (1941), *Now, Voyager* (1942), and *All about Eve* (1950).

Davis, Miles [Dewey] (1926–91) American jazz musician. A trumpeter, he played with **Charlie Parker** in the 1940s and went on to pioneer several styles and trends, including cool jazz, hard bop, modal jazz, and jazz-rock fusion. His recordings included *Birth of the Cool* (1949) and *Kind of Blue* (1959).

Day, Dorothy (1897–1980) American reformer and journalist. With Peter Maurin, she founded the Catholic Worker (1933), a Catholic movement dedicated to social justice, pacifism, and the works of mercy. She also edited its monthly, the *Catholic Worker*.

Dayan, Moshe (1915–81) Israeli soldier and politician. Born in Palestine, he joined the Haganah, the Jewish militia, and was jailed by British mandate authorities (1939–41). He served with the British in **World War II**, losing his left eye and necessitating the well-known eyepatch. He served in the Israeli army after independence in 1948. Appointed chief of staff (1953–58), Dayan distinguished himself as a brilliant military strategist when he directed the 1956 Sinai campaign against Egypt. He achieve similar success when, as defense minister (1967, 1969–74), he directed the **Six-Day War** (1967). He was a member of the Knesset (1958–81) and minister of agriculture (1959–64). Blamed for Israel's unpreparedness in the **Yom Kippur War** (1973), he resigned with **Golda Meir** in 1974. He later became foreign minister (1977–79).

Deakin, Alfred (1856–1919) Australian politician. Champion of Australian federation, he wrote constitutional legislation creating the commonwealth and promoted its passage through the British Parliament in 1900. The commonwealth's first attorney general, he served as prime minister for three terms in fusion governments (1903–04, 1905–08, 1909–10) and was known for his socially progressive legislation.

Dean, Dixie (1906–80) British athlete. Born William Ralph Dean, he became one of the British Association's top-scoring footballers (soccer players). He made a record 60 goals in 39 matches during the 1927–28 season, with five in one match. Over his career he scored 37 hat tricks.

Dean, James [Byron] (1931–55) American actor. Born in Marion, Ind., he appeared in a few stage and **television** roles before rocketing to fame as the brooding young star of *East of Eden, Rebel without a Cause* (1955), and *Giant* (1956). His premature death in a car crash secured his lasting status as a pop icon of troubled youth.

Debs, Eugene [Victor] (1855–1926) American labor leader. Born in Terre Haute, Ind., he was founder and first president of the American Railway Union (1893). During the Pullman strike (1895), he was sentenced to six months in jail for contempt of court; he was sentenced again to 10 years in 1918 for breaching the Espionage Act but was released in 1921 by U.S. president **Warren Harding**. A cofounder of the Social Democratic Party of America, he was its presidential candidate in five elections between 1900 and 1920. He also cofounded the Industrial Workers of the World in 1905.

Debussy, Claude [Achille] (1862–1918) French composer. Born near Paris, he won the Grand Prix de Rome in 1884 for *L'Enfant prodigue*. In later works he experimented further with harmony, tone, color, and atmosphere and was highly influenced by impressionism and symbolist poetry. Some major works include *Suite bermanesque* (for piano, including "Clair de Lune," 1890–1905), *Prélude à l'après-midi d'un faune* (1894, illustrating Mallarmé's poem), *Pelléas and Mélisande* (opera, 1902), and *La Mer* (tone poem, 1905).

de Gaulle, Charles[-André-Marie-Joseph] (1890–1970) French soldier and politician. A veteran of **World War I**, he wrote *The Army of the Future* (1934), in which he argued in vain for a mechanized, mobile army, and was made brigadier general in 1940. During the German occupation of France in **World War II**, he organized the Free French forces in London (1940). He became joint president, with French soldier Henri Giraud (1879–1949), of the French Committee of National Liberation at Algiers (1943) but forced Giraud out by 1944. Returning to liberated France in August 1944, he became president of the provisional French government (1945–46). He opposed the Fourth Republic, and, in 1958, helped to frame and became first president of the Fifth Republic. He granted independence to several African territories, including Algeria (1962), thereby ending the Algerian war. Seeking to restore France's international status, he withdrew French troops from the **North Atlantic Treaty Organization** in 1966, developed French nuclear weapons, and supported French membership in the Common Market while opposing British participation. He pursued an independent foreign policy, including closer ties to China and Russia. His administration weakened by student and labor protests in 1968, he resigned in 1969 after defeat of his referendum on constitutional reform.

de Klerk, F[rederik] W[illem] (1936–) South African politician. He was elected a National Party member of the House of Assembly in 1972. He held several posts, including minister of internal justice, before becoming National Party leader and president in 1989, following the resignation of President P. W. Botha (1916–). Surprising those who viewed him as a cautious reformer, de Klerk acted swiftly in 1990 to legalize the **African National Congress** and release its imprisoned leader, **Nelson Mandela**. He lifted the state of emergency in effect since 1985, repealed **apartheid** laws, and, in 1991, proposed a new constitution abolishing black homelands and extending the vote to black South Africans. In a 1992 referendum, white voters approved the end of white-only rule, and a transitional constitution was approved in 1993. In the country's first multiracial elections held in 1994, de Klerk was voted out of office and Mandela succeeded him as president.

de Kooning, Willem (1904–97) Dutch-born American painter. He held his first one-man show in 1948 and became known as a major practitioner (along with **Jackson Pollock**) of abstract expressionism in creating paintings of furious color and movement. Works include the 1950s series *Woman*, notably the shocking *Woman 1* (1950–2). From the 1970s, he also created sculptures.

De Mille, Cecil B[lount] (1881–1959) American film director. Producing his own films since the silent era, he specialized in modern narratives laced with sex before becoming known as the master of religious and historical epics. His movies were often criticized for sentimentality and vulgarity but almost always drew large audiences. He is credited with helping to establish Hollywood as a film capital. Works include *The Ten Commandments* (1923; remade 1956), *The Sign of the Cross* (1932), *Samson and Delilah* (1949), and *The Greatest Show on Earth* (1952).

Dempsey, Jack (1895–1983) American athlete. Born William Harrison Dempsey, in Manassa, Colo., he was known as the "Manassa Mauler," holding the heavyweight boxing title from 1919 to 1926, when he was defeated by American boxer Gene Tunney (1898–1978). He also lost a controversial 1927 "long count" rematch marked by his refusal to return to his corner of the ring. In 1921 he fought in the first match to gross more than $1 million.

Deng Xiaoping or **Teng Hsiao-p'ing** (1904–97) Chinese leader. Born in Sichuan Province, he joined the Chinese Communist Party while studying in France in the 1920s. Serving with the Red Army in the **Chinese Civil War** and **World War II**, he participated in the **Long March** (1934–35) with **Mao Zedong**. After the People's Republic of China was established (1949), he became the party's general secretary (1956–67). A non-comformist in his interpretation of Marxism, he was ousted from power during the **Cultural Revolution**. He was made vice premier in 1973 but forced out of power again in 1976 by the "**Gang of Four**." Returning to government a year later, he became vice premier (1977–80), vice chairman of the party's central committee (1977–80), and chief of the armed forces general staff. He was chairman of the state and party military commissions (1982–89) and remained on the Politburo Standing Committee until 1987. Whatever his specific posts, he was the dominant Chinese leader in the 1980s and remained influential to his death. He spurred economic growth by incorporating elements of free enterprise and decentralized management into the Chinese Communist system. He supported improved relations with the West, but cracked down on political dissent at home by suppressing the **Tiananmen Square** demonstrations (1989).

De Niro, Robert (1943–) American film actor. Born in New York City., he gained attention for his intense, edgy performances as urban misfits in *Mean Streets* (1973) and *Taxi Driver* (1976), both directed by longtime collaborator **Martin Scorsese**. He won two Academy Awards: best supporting actor for *The Godfather, Part II* (1974) and best actor for *Raging Bull* (1980).

Derrida, Jacques (1930–) Algerian-born French philosopher. In the 1960s he founded deconstructionism, a critical movement that shows how contradictions uncovered within a text subvert its surface meaning. Derrida's thought is associated with **postmodernism** and poststructuralism. Works include *Of Grammatology* (1967) and *Margins of Philosophy* (1972).

Desai, Morarji (1896–1995) Indian politician. A member of the Indian National Congress, or Congress Party, from 1931, he opposed British rule, participating in **Mohandas Gandhi**'s civil disobedience movement in the 1930s and 1940s. After independence in 1947, he held several posts between 1956 and 1969 in **Jawaharlal Nehru**'s government and **Indira Gandhi**'s government but broke with the Congress Party in 1969. He was later imprisoned by Indira Gandhi, but defeated her at the polls in 1977 as leader of the Janata ("People's") Party. He was prime minister from 1977 until 1979, when weaknesses in his political coalition led to Indira Gandhi's return to power.

De Sica, Vittorio (1902–74) Italian film director. A stage and screen actor from young adulthood, he began directing in the 1940s, becoming known for humanistic works of Italian neorealism like *Sciuscia* (*Shoeshine*, 1946) and *The Bicycle Thief* (1948). Both won best foreign film Academy Awards. Other notable works include *Umberto D.* (1952), *Yesterday, Today and Tomorrow* (1963), and *The Garden of the Finzi-Continis* (1971), the latter two winning foreign film Academy Awards.

De Valera, Eamon (1882–1975) Irish politician. Born in New York City to a Spanish father and Irish mother, he participated in the Easter Rebellion of 1916 and was imprisoned (1916–17 and 1918–19) before escaping to the U.S. The president of **Sinn Féin** (1918–26) and of the provisional Republican government (1918–22), he raised funds for his cause in the U.S. and returned to Ireland in 1920. He left the government over his rejection of the Anglo-Irish treaty (1921), which established the Irish Free State but required an oath of loyalty to the British crown. In 1932 he returned to lead the Free State parliament with his party, **Fianna Fáil**. As prime minister (1932–48, 1951–54, and 1957–59), he made Ireland a fully sovereign nation and maintained neutrality during **World War II**. He was president of Ireland from 1959 to 1973.

Dewey, John (1859–1952) American philosopher and educator. Born in Burlington, Vt., he helped develop, with American philosophers Charles Peirce (1839–1914) and **William James** the philosophy of pragmatism. His pedagogical views integrating democratic principles and pragmatism helped define progressive education and made him the leading educator of the era. His works include *How We Think* (1910), *Democracy and Education* (1916), and *Art as Experience* (1934). He taught at the Universities of Minnesota (1888–89), Michigan (1889–94), and Chicago (1894–1904) and at Columbia University (1904–34), and helped found the New School for Social Research, New York City (1919).

Diaghilev, Sergey Pavlovich (1872–1929) Russian dance impresario and art critic. From 1899 until 1906, when he moved to Paris, he was a member of the staff of the Imperial Russian Theater. In 1909, he cofounded the Ballets Russes in Paris, which revolutionized the form with its use of motion and assymetry and attracted choreographers such as American Michel Fokine (1880–1942) and dancers **Varlav Nijinsky** and **Anna Pavlova**. Productions included **Igor Stravinsky**'s *Firebird* (1910). Diaghilev's 1913 production of *Sacre du printemps* (*The Rite of Spring*) caused a riot.

Diana, Princess (1961–97) British princess. Born Lady Diana Spencer, she taught school before marrying His Royal Highness Charles, Prince of Wales (1948–) in 1981. Amidst much media attention, the couple was divorced in 1996; they had two sons, Prince William (1982–) and Prince Harry (1984–). She, her companion Saudi Arabian businessman Dodi al-Fayed (1954–), and their driver were killed in an auto accident in France while pursued by photographers. Internationally beloved for her charm and devotion to humanitarian causes, she was widely mourned.

Díaz, [José de la Cruz] Porfirio (1830–1915) Mexican soldier and politician. A distinguished soldier since the Mexican War (1846–48), he seized power in 1876, beginning nearly four decades in which he dominated Mexican politics. As president (1877–80 and 1884–1911), he invited foreign investment and technological progress, but his dictatorial methods and neglect of the poor forced him to resign in the revolt led by Mexican revolutionary Francisco Madero (1873–1913). He died in exile in Paris.

Didrikson, Babe See **Zaharias, Babe Didrikson**.

Dietrich, Marlene (1901–1992) American actress. Born Maria Magdalene Dietrich in Berlin, she became internationally known for her portrayal of seductress Lola Lola in *The Blue Angel* (1930). In 1930 she settled in the U.S., becoming a citizen in 1939. Notable prewar films include *Blonde Venus* (1932) and *Destry Rides Again* (1939). Fiercely anti-Nazi, she appeared widely overseas for Allied (see **Allied Powers**) troops during **World War II**, reviving a Medal of Freedom in the U.S for her efforts. *Witness for the Prosecution* (1958) and *Touch of Evil* (1958) were among later film efforts. From the 1950s, she was a popular club and cabaret performer.

Dinesen, Isak (1885–1962) Danish writer. Pen name of Baroness Karen Blixen-Finecke. She is known for her imaginative story collections, written primarily in English, including *Seven Gothic Tales* (1934), *Winter's Tales* (1942), and *Last Tales* (1957). Her memoir of life on a coffee plantation in Kenya (1914–31) is *Out of Africa* (1937).

Dior, Christian (1905–57) French fashion designer. An international trendsetter, he is known for his feminine creations, including the short sack dresses (early 1950s) and the A-line shape (1956), which made a major comeback in the skirts and dresses of the 1990s. He is perhaps best known for his elegant post–**World War II** line, the "New Look." He founded the house of Dior in 1947.

Dirac, Paul [Adrien Maurice] (1902–84) British physicist. In 1928, he developed the theoretical framework for **quantum mechanics**, presenting it in *The Principles of Quantum Mechanics* (1930). He modified the theories of **Erwin Schrödinger** by integrating the theory of **relativity**. His work suggested the possibility of antimatter, leading to the theory of positrons. Professor of mathematics at the University of Cambridge (1932–69), he and Schrödinger shared the Nobel Prize for physics in 1933.

Disney, Walt[er Elias] (1901–66) American film producer. Born in Chicago, he revealed his inventiveness with animated film in 1928, introducing his character Mickey Mouse in the cartoon *Steamboat Willie*. He followed with the first feature-length animated film, *Snow White and the Seven Dwarfs* (1937), and several others, including *Fantasia* (1940), *Dumbo*

(1941), and *Bambi* (1942). From the 1950s he also produced nature and live action features such as *The Incredible Journey* (1963). In 1955 he opened his first amusement park, Disneyland, in Los Angeles, Calif.; Disney World, near Orlando, Fl., opened in 1971.

Divine, Father (1877–1965) American religious leader. Born George Baker near Savannah, Ga., he began preaching in the rural South around 1900 and moved to New York City around 1915. Naming himself Father Divine and gaining strong support among African-Americans in New York City and Philadelphia, he established the Peace Mission movement in 1919, a religious society preaching communal living, racial equality, and abstemiousness. Over 170 settlements were established before his death.

Doenitz, Karl (1891–1980) German naval officer. Having served with a U-boat fleet during **World War I**, he was chosen by **Adolf Hitler** to build up and lead a new U-boat fleet in 1935. A grand admiral, he led decisive battles during **World War II**, becoming supreme commander of the German navy in 1943. Following Hitler's death in 1945, he led the German government at the time of the country's surrender. Convicted for war crimes at Nuremberg, he was imprisoned from 1946 to 1956.

Dollfuss, Engelbert (1892–1934) Austrian politician. As chancellor from 1932 to 1934, at the head of the Christian Social coalition, he formed an alliance with Italy and supported **Fascism** but opposed union with Germany. In 1934 he established a new authoritarian constitution but was assassinated by Austrian Nazi rebels, whose revolt was later suppressed.

Dos Passos, John [Roderigo] (1896–1970) American writer. Born in Chicago, he is best known for his *U.S.A.* trilogy of novels: *The 42nd Parallel* (1930), *1919* (1932), and *The Big Money* (1936). They interweave fictional and real characters, newsreel techniques, and "camera eye" views, in a panorama of a disillusioned early-20th-century America. Other notable works include novels *Three Soldiers* (1921), *Manhattan Transfer* (1925), and *Midcentury* (1961), the 12th book in a series of novels begun in the 1950s called "Contemporary Chronicles."

Douglas, William O[rville] (1898–1980) American jurist. After serving as chairman of the Securities and Exchange Commission (1937–39), he became an associate justice of the U.S. Supreme Court (1939–75). During his tenure, the longest in the court's history, he interpreted the court's powers broadly, championing civil rights, free speech, and conservation.

Douglas-Home, Sir Alexander Frederick See **Home, Sir Alexander Frederick Douglas-Home, 14th earl of**

Dreiser, Theodore [Herman Albert] (1871–1945) American writer. Born in Indiana to German immigrants, he attended Indiana University for a year before becoming a journalist in New York City. After the publication of his first novel, *Sister Carrie* (1900), was suppressed, he ceased writing for years. His second novel, *Jennie Gerhardt* (1911), finally brought success; it, like his first, concerned a "fallen" woman. His novels grew in complexity and deterministic outlook over the years, notably his best-known work, *An American Tragedy* (1925), based on the true-life Chester Gillette/Grace Brown murder case. Posthumously published was *The Stoic* (1947), which, with *The Financier* (1912) and *The Titan* (1914), completed his trilogy of an American industrialist. He is remembered for being a voice of American naturalism and for presenting the underside of the new century.

Dubcek, Alexander (1921–92) Czechoslovak politician. A member of the Slovak **resistance** in **World War II**, he became first secretary of the Czechoslovak Communist Party (1968–69). He led the liberalization campaign known as the **Prague Spring**, which was crushed by the Soviet invasion of 1968. He was expelled from the party in 1970. He took part in the prodemocracy movement that toppled the Communist regime. Afterward, he was made speaker of the federal assembly (1989–92).

Du Bois, W[illiam] E[dward] B[urghardt] (1868–1963) American civil rights leader and writer. Born in Great Barrington, Mass., he earned a Ph.D. at Harvard in 1895 and was professor of economics and history at Atlanta University (1897–1910). Among the earliest advocates of complete racial equality, he cofounded the National Negro Committee in 1909, which in 1910 became the **National Association for the Advancement of Colored People**, and from 1910 to 1934 edited its journal, *Crisis*. In later years, he promoted worldwide black liberation and pan-Africanism. From 1961 to 1963 he lived in Ghana, where he joined the Communist Party and edited an *African Encyclopedia for Africans*. His best-known work was *The Souls of Black Folk* (1903); other titles include *John Brown* (1909) and *The World and Africa* (1947).

Duchamp, Marcel (1887–1968) French painter and sculptor. A seminal force in early modern art, he cofounded the dada movement and aimed to redefine concepts of aesthetic beauty through the use of ready-made objects as art and other anti-art practices. Influential works include the cubist-futurist painting *Nude Descending a Staircase* (1912) and the unfinished construction *The Large Glass, or the Bride Stripped Bare by her Bachelors, Even* (in process 1915–23). His brother was French sculptor Raymond Duchamp-Villon (1876–1918) and his half-brother was French painter Jacques Villon (1875–1963).

Dulles, John Foster (1888–1959) American diplomat. A lawyer, he attended the Versailles Peace Conference as legal adviser in 1919. He helped prepare the **UN** Charter (1945) and was U.S. delegate to the UN (1946–49). He negotiated the 1951 peace treaty with Japan that formally ended **World War II**. As secretary of state (1953–59) under President **Dwight D. Eisenhower**, he was a dedicated anti-Communist and the principal architect of the Eisenhower Doctrine and the Southeast Asia Treaty Organization pact. He emphasized collective security through economic and military aid to allies. Encouraging development of a powerful nuclear deterrent force to support confrontations with the **Soviet Union** and China, he coined the terms **brinkmanship** and **massive retaliation**. His brother Allen Welsh Dulles (1893–1969), was director of the **CIA** (1953–61), but resigned in the wake of the **Bay of Pigs invasion**.

Duncan, Isadora (1877–1927) American dancer. A magnetic performer and personality, she influenced modern dance with her natural, expressive choreography and presentation informed by Greek classical art and clothing. Her trademark stage attire included flowing gowns and scarves, and bare feet. Influential appearances included a tour of Europe (1905) and appearances in New York City (1908). Dogged by tragedy, Duncan lost her two children in a 1913 auto accident; she died 14 years later when her scarf caught in a car wheel.

Durkheim, Émile (1858–1917) French sociologist. He was a founder of modern sociology who applied the empirical methods of natural science to the study of society. He argued that collective social bonds underlie religion and morality, and that anomie, or the absence of such bonds, results in social disorder and suicide. Works include *Suicide* (1897) and *The Elementary Forms of the Religious Life* (1912).

Duvalier, François (1907–71) Haitian dictator. A physician, he was elected president in 1957. In 1964 he declared himself president for life. Known as "Papa Doc," he ruled by terror; his *Tontons macoutes*, a paramilitary and secret police force, crushed dissent mercilessly. His son Jean-Claude Duvalier (1951–), "Baby Doc," succeeded him in 1971. A popular uprising forced Jean-Claude to flee in 1986, ending the Duvalier regime.

Dylan, Bob (1941–) American singer and songwriter. Born Robert Allen Zimmerman in Duluth, Minn., he moved to New York City in 1960, where he inspired a generation with his folk and folk-rock songs, many of them anthems of social protest. His hits included "Blowin' in the Wind" and "The Times They Are A-Changin'." After becoming a born-again Christian in the 1970s, he continued to record songs; his evolving style is reflected in such albums as *Time out of Mind* (1997).

E

Earhart, Amelia (1897–1937). American aviator. Born in Achison, Kan., she gained fame in 1932 as the first woman to fly solo across the Atlantic, from Harbour Grace, Newfoundland, to Londonderry, Ireland. In September 1932 she also became the first woman to fly solo nonstop across the U.S. On a round-the-world flight in July 1937, she and navigator Fred Noonan disappeared and were never found. She was married to American publisher George P. Putnam (1887–1950).

Eastwood, Clint[on, Jr.] (1930–) American film director and actor. A **television** actor in the 1950s, he became internationally known as a screen hero in westerns, such as *A Fistful of Dollars* (1964) and *The Good, the Bad and the Ugly* (1966), and action films, including *Dirty Harry* (1971). From the 1970s he directed numerous films, noted for their visual spareness and strong story elements. Among them are *Bird* (1988), *The Bridges of Madison County* (1995), and the best picture Academy Award–winning dark western *Unforgiven* (1992).

Eden, Sir [Robert] Anthony, first earl of Avon (1897–1977) British politician. He served in **World War I** and became an M.P. in 1923. He resigned as foreign secretary (1935–38) in opposition to **Neville Chamberlain's appeasement** policy. In **Winston Churchill's** cabinet, he served as dominions secretary and war secretary (both 1940); as foreign secretary (1940–45, 1951–55), he helped establish the **UN** and resolve the Indochina conflict. He was prime minister (1955–57) but resigned after controversy over his military intervention in Egypt during the **Suez** Canal **crisis** (1956). He was made a life peer in 1961.

Edward VII [Albert Edward] (1841–1910) British king (1901–10). Succeeding his mother Queen Victoria (born 1819; reigned 1837–1901), he was a popular king who helped forge alliances with France and Russia and supported renewal of British military strength. He was succeeded by his son **George V**.

Edward VIII [Edward Albert Christian George Andrew Patrick David] (1894–1972) British king (1936). Succeeding his father, **George V,** in January 1936, he aroused controversy by proposing to marry Mrs. Wallis Warfield Simpson (1896–1986), an American then pursuing her second divorce. Faced with a constitutional crisis when Prime Minister **Stanley Baldwin** refused to permit the marriage, Edward abdicated in December, the only British monarch ever to do so voluntarily. He married Simpson the following year. His brother and successor, George VI, made him duke of Windsor. Later appointed governor of the Bahamas (1940–45), Edward lived most of his remaining years in France.

Eichmann, [Karl] Adolf (1906–62) German Nazi official. Born in the Rhineland, he joined the Austrian **Nazi Party** in 1932 and quickly rose in the ranks. After the Nazi annexation of Austria and Bohemia (1938–39), he was responsible for expelling Jews from the two countries. From 1942, he executed the Nazi "final solution" of mass murder of European Jews by overseeing the death camps. After the war he lived in Argentina until his capture by Israeli agents in 1960. He was then tried and killed for war crimes.

Einstein, Albert (1879–1955) German-born American physicist. Born in Ulm, Germany, he was working in the Swiss patent office in 1905 when he received his Ph.D. and published his first three important papers: one explaining Brownian movement; one explaining the photoelectric effect by postulating light quanta or photons (a discovery that won him the 1921 Nobel Prize for physics); and one expounding his special theory of **relativity**, which rejected the concept of absolute space and time and related matter and energy in the equation $E = mc^2$. His general theory of relativity (1916) displaced Newtonian mechanics, arguing that gravitation curves the space-time continuum. Fleeing Nazi persecution of Jews, he immigrated to the U.S. in 1933, becoming a U.S. citizen in 1940. He held a post at the Institute for Advanced Study in Princeton from 1933 to 1945. A pacifist, he nevertheless urged President **Franklin Delano Roosevelt** in 1939 to develop an atomic bomb, a device made possible by Einstein's discoveries. In his later years, he tried unsuccessfully to develop a unified field theory. Einstein was renowned internationally as a humanitarian, philosopher of science, and symbol of genius.

Eisenhower, Dwight D[avid] (1890–1969) Thirty-fourth U.S. president (1953–61), known as "Ike." Born in Denison, Tex., he graduated from West Point in 1915 and held various military positions until **World War II**. From 1942 to 1943 he was Allied (see **Allied Powers**) commander in North Africa and Italy, becoming supreme commander of Allied forces in Europe in 1943. He led the **D-Day** invasion of Normandy on June 6, 1944, and the Allied drive across Europe leading to V-E Day (May 2, 1945). From 1945 to 1948 he served as army chief of staff, and from 1951 to 1952 as supreme commander of **NATO** forces in Europe. He was also president of Columbia University (1948–1953). A Republican and an immensely popular war hero, he was elected U.S. president in 1952 and again in 1956, both times soundly defeating Democratic candidate **Adlai Stevenson**. A military statesman, he oversaw the truce ending the **Korean War** in 1953 and avoided involvement in the 1956 Hungarian uprising. A strong anti-Communist, he promoted a policy of "**containment**" of **Communism**. Under his Eisenhower Doctrine (1957), he offered economic and military aid to Mideast countries as a counter to Communist incursions. Late in his administration, he faced the **U-2 incident** with the **Soviet Union** (1960). In the U.S., he instigated reforms to stimulate the economy and dispatched troops to oversee school desegregation in Little Rock, Ark. (1957).

Eisenstein, Sergey Mikhailovich (1898–1948) Russian filmmaker. A film pioneer, he introduced montage and other now-standard film techniques. A student at the Petrograd Institute, he abandoned a theater career for the greater artistic possibilities of film and made his first feature, *Strike*, in 1925. His most influential work, *Potemkin* (1925), tested the effects possible through montage. Other notable works include *October* (1928) and *Alexander Nevsky* (1938).

Elgar, Sir Edward William (1857–1934) British composer. With no formal musical training, he became one of the principal composers of the century. Often inspired by his Catholicism, his works were romantic and colorful. Compositions include *Enigma Variations*

(1899), the oratorio *Dream of Gerontius* (1900), the *Pomp and Circumstance* marches (1903–30), the violin concerto (1910), and the cello concerto (1919). He was knighted in 1904.

Eliade, Mircea (1907–86) Romanian-born American scholar of religion. He left Romania in 1940, teaching in Western Europe before settling at the University of Chicago (1957–85). He pioneered the systematic, comparative study of religion. Works include *The Myth of the Eternal Return* (1949) and *A History of Religious Ideas* (3 vols., 1978–85).

Eliot, Charles William (1834–1926) American educator. As president of Harvard University (1869–1909), he transformed the college into a modern university by expanding the faculty and restructuring curriculum and entrance requirements. He encouraged uniformity in high school curricula and college entrance requirements. He edited the *Harvard Classics.*

Eliot, T[homas] S[tearns] (1888–1965) American-born British poet. One of the most significant poetic voices of the 20th century, he was born in St. Louis, Mo., graduated from Harvard (B.A.; 1909, M.A., 1910) and did additional graduate work at the Sorbonne (1910–11) and Oxford (1914–15). In Britain from 1914 (and a citizen from 1927), he became friends with **Ezra Pound**, who aided in the publication of Eliot's "The Love Song of J. Alfred Prufrock" (1915) and celebrated first poetry collection, *Prufrock and Other Observations* (1917). His reputation established, Eliot followed with other seminal verse works of poetic experimentation and commentary on a materialistic, spiritually bereft society. Among them are "The Waste Land" (1922), "Gerontion" (1920), "The Hollow Men" (1925), "Ash Wednesday" (1930), and the *Four Quartets* (1935–42), the latter two works informed by his conversion to Anglicanism in the 1920s. An influential essayist as well, the conservative, antisecular thinker shaped modern literary attitudes through his collection *The Sacred Wood* (1920); other critical works include *The Use of Poetry and the Use of Criticism* (1933) and *Man of Letters* (1942). Collections of cultural criticism include *The Idea of a Christian Society* (1939) and *Notes toward the Definition of Culture* (1940). Among his plays are *Murder in the Cathedral* (1935) and *The Cocktail Party* (1950). As editor at British publishing firm Faber and Faber from 1926 to 1965, he supported much new talent. He won the Nobel Prize for literature in 1948. His light verse work *Old Possum's Book of Practical Cats* (1939) inspired the stage musical *Cats* (1981).

Elizabeth II (1926–) Queen of Britain and Northern Ireland. Daughter of Elizabeth (1900–), she succeeded her father, **George VI**, in 1952. Married to Philip Mountbatten (1921–), duke of Edinburgh, from 1947, she has four children: Prince Charles (1948–), Princess Anne (1950–), Prince Andrew (1960–), and Prince Edward (1964–). Some have gained notoriety through marital discord.

Ellington, Duke (1899–1974) American jazz musician. Born Edward Kennedy Ellington in Washington, D.C., he became known by the 1920s as a singular jazz composer and tone painter. For decades he maintained a big band and toured widely. Among his compositions were "Mood Indigo," "Sophisticated Lady," and "Caravan."

Ellis, [Henry] Havelock (1859–1939) British physician and writer. Although qualified in **medicine**, he devoted himself to writing and study rather than practice. He pioneered investigation and open discussion of human sexual behavior in the seven-volume *Studies in the Psychology of Sex* (1897–1928), which was banned for obscenity in his own country. An advocate of women's rights and sex education, he also wrote essays and edited English

Renaissance drama. Other works include *The New Spirit* (1890) and *The Erotic Rights of Women* (1918).

Ellison, Ralph [Waldo] (1914–94) American writer. Born in Oklahoma City, he wrote the classic novel *Invisible Man* (1952), an intense depiction of an African-American man's search for identity in a hostile society. He has also written essays (some collected in *Shadow and Act*, 1964) and short stories.

Éluard, Paul (1895–1952) French poet. Pen name of Eugène Grindel. A founder of surrealism, he broke with the movement in 1938 to write politically militant poetry. He served in **World War I** and was active in the French **resistance** during **World War II**. He joined the Communist Party in 1942. Works include *Capital de la douleur* (1926), *Poésie et vérité* (1942), *Au rendez-vous allemand* (1944), and *Poèmes politiques* (1948).

Escher, M[aurits] C[ornelis] (1898–1972) Dutch artist. From the 1940s he was known for his surreal, geometric prints and woodcuts incorporating visual illusion and mathematical concepts.

Evans, Walker (1903–75) American photographer. Born in St. Louis, Mo., he is known for his evocative portraits and architectural views, notably of Depression-era tenant farmers and their world in *Let Us Now Praise Famous Men* (1941), with American author James Agee (1909-55). Other works include *American Photographs* (1938).

F

Faisal I (1885–1933) King of Syria (1920) and Iraq (1921–33). With **T. E. Lawrence**, he united the Arabs in the Arab Revolt against the Ottoman Empire (1916–18). The Syrian national congress proclaimed him king, but the French quickly deposed him. The British made him king of Iraq. He negotiated a 1930 treaty of independence with Britain and was succeeded by his son Ghazi I (1912–39).

Faisal ibn Abd al-Aziz (c. 1906–75) Saudi king (1964–75). The son of Ibn Saud, he waged a successful campaign against Yemen (1934) and served as prime minister (1953–60) and defense minister (1958–64). His brother, King Saud ibn Abd (1902–69; reigned 1953–64), succeeded their father as king but was considered incompetent. Faisal concentrated power during his reign and deposed him, becoming king in his place. Though culturally conservative, Faisal promoted economic and educational progress. As a leader of the **Organization of Petroleum Exporting Countries** and the main provider of U.S. oil, he exercised much influence in international affairs. Upon his assassination by a nephew, he was succeeded by his brother Khalid (1913–82; reigned 1975–82).

Fanon, Frantz Omar (1925–61) French West Indian philosopher. Born in Martinique and educated in France as a psychiatrist, he was radicalized by his experiences of racism in Algeria; he joined the Algerian liberation movement in 1954. In his book *The Wretched of the Earth* (1961), he analyzed the political and socioeconomic dimensions of racism, advocating the use of violence in overthrowing colonial domination. His work influenced many **Third World** nationalists.

Farouk I [Faruq al-Awwal] (1920–65) King of Egypt (1936–52). He succeeded his father **Fuad I**, but his regime's corruption and ineffectiveness made him unpopular. Following Egypt's defeat by Israel in 1948, the army withdrew its support from Farouk. In 1952, **Gamal Abdel Nasser** led a military coup overthrowing Farouk and ending the monarchy.

Fassbinder, Rainer Werner (1946–82) German film director. A prominent voice in postwar German cinema, he was born in Bad Wörshofen, Bavaria, and made his first feature-length film in 1969. A feverishly fast worker (making up to four films per year), he earned international respect for his iconoclastic studies of the misuse of power, including *The Merchant of Four Seasons* (1972), *The Bitter Tears of Petra von Kant* (1972), *Mother Kuster Goes to Heaven* (1975), *The Marriage of Maria Braun* (1979), *Berlin Alexanderplatz* (1980, originally for **television**), and *Veronika Voss* (1982). Living a life of professional and personal excess, he died of a drug overdose.

Faulkner, William (1897–1962) American writer. Born in Oxford, Miss., he was a child of rural gentry (great-grandfather Colonel William C. Falkner was a Civil War hero), a background that influenced his writing. After briefly attending the University of Mississippi, he traveled to Paris. Befriended by **Sherwood Anderson**, he published his first work, *Soldiers' Pay* (1926). With *Sartoris* (1929), he introduced the imaginary Yoknapatawpha County, which embodied themes of identity, alienation, and the weight of Southern history. *The Sound and the Fury* (1929) brought critical acclaim; *Sanctuary* (1931) brought commercial success. *Light in August* (1932), *Absolom, Absolom!* (1936), *Go Down, Moses* (1942), *Intruder in the Dust* (1948), and *Requiem for a Nun* (1951) are among his most praised works. He was awarded the Nobel Prize for literature in 1949 and won the Pulitzer Prize for literature for *A Fable* (1954) and *The Reivers* (1962).

Fellini, Federico (1920–93) Italian film director. Italy's most revered and beloved filmmaker held many arts-related odd jobs before meeting Italian director Roberto Rossellini (1906–1977) and collaborating with him on the scripts for *Open City* (1945) and *Paisan* (1946). A director from 1951, he gained international fame with his lively, well-observed third feature *I Vitelloni* (1953). His next film, *La Strada* (1954), won the Oscar for best foreign film, as did *The Nights of Cabiria* (1957) and *8 ½* (1963). Other notable works include *La Dolce vita* (1960) and *Juliet of the Spirits* (1965).

Fermi, Enrico (1901–54) Italian-born American physicist. In the United States from 1938, he discovered the element neptunium and created the first self-sustaining nuclear chain reaction, using uranium, on a converted squash court at the University of Chicago (1942). He received the 1938 Nobel Prize for physics for his discovery of neutron-induced nuclear reactions. He helped develop the first atomic bomb and hydrogen bomb.

Feynman, Richard P[hillips] (1918–88) American physicist. Receiving his Ph.D. from Princeton in 1942, he helped develop the first atomic bomb. He taught at Cornell University (1945–50) and afterward at the California Institute of Technology. With **Murray Gell-Mann**, he proposed the theory of the weak nuclear force and the existence of quarks. He invented the Feynman diagram and shared the 1965 Nobel Prize for physics for helping to develop quantum electrodynamics.

Fitzgerald, Ella (1918–1996) American jazz singer. Born in Virginia, she was discovered at New York's Apollo Theater in the 1930s by American bandleader Chick Webb (1902–1939), with whom she toured. In 1938 she recorded her first hit, "A-Tisket, A-Tasket." For six decades she toured worldwide and recorded with **Louis Armstrong** and **Duke Ellington**, among others. Known to fans as "The First Lady of Jazz," she was renowned for the suppleness of her voice and the boldness of her jazz phrasing, epitomized in her legendary "scat" singing.

Fitzgerald, F[rancis] Scott [Key] (1896–1940) American writer. Born in St. Paul,

Minn., he attended Princeton University. In 1920 he published his first work, *This Side of Paradise*, which established him as the voice of the 1920s Jazz Age. He married southern belle Zelda Sayre; with their equally extravagant ways, they lived in New York City and France as the representative couple of the times. In 1925 came *The Great Gatsby*; acknowledged even in its day as a masterpiece, it evoked powerful imagery of the elusive American dream. Other novels include *The Beautiful and Damned* (1922), *Tender Is the Night* (1934), and the unfinished *The Last Tycoon* (1941). Facing financial problems and Zelda's mental instability in the 1930s, Fitzgerald moved to Hollywood and turned to screenwriting. A prolific short-story writer, his works are noted for dazzling prose and keen observation. He was killed by a heart attack.

Fleming, Sir Alexander (1881–1955) British bacteriologist. Born in Scotland, he qualified in **medicine** in 1906 at St. Mary's Hospital, University of London, where he was later professor (1928–48). In 1921 he discovered lysozyme, an antibacterial substance found in body secretions. In 1928 he discovered penicillin, which later became the first antibiotic used to treat human infections. For his work with penicillin, he was awarded the Nobel Prize in physiology or **medicine** in 1945 with British scientists Sir Ernst Chain (1906–1979) and Sir Howard Florey (1898–1968). He was knighted in 1944.

Foch, Ferdinand (1851–1929) French soldier. He became general of brigade in 1908 and served as director of the École de Guerre (1908–11). In **World War I** he helped plan the victory at the Battle of the Marne (1914), by which the German advance on Paris was stopped; he also fought at Ypres (1915) and the Somme (1916). Appointed chief of the French general staff in 1917 and supreme commander of Allied armies and marshal of France in 1918, he earned much of the credit for Germany's final defeat.

Fonda American family of actors. Henry (1905–82) was primarily a film star, though he also appeared on Broadway and **television**. His many movies, in which he typically projected self-effacing decency, included *The Grapes of Wrath* (1940), *My Darling Clementine* (1946), and *Mister Roberts* (1955); for *On Golden Pond* (1981), his final film, he won a best actor Academy Award. He served in the Navy in World War II. His daughter Jane (1937–) is known not only for her film performances, including those that netted her two best actress Oscars (for *Klute*, 1971, and *Coming Home*, 1978), but also for her left-wing political activism, particularly against the **Vietnam War**. Henry's son Peter (1939–) produced, co-wrote, and starred in the '60s counterculture favorite *Easy Rider* (1969), among other films. Peter's daughter Bridget (1964–) has continued the family acting tradition.

Ford, Ford Madox (1873–1939) British writer. Born Ford Hermann Hueffer (and also known as Ford Madox Hueffer), he is known for prose, verse, and fiction. Novels include *The Good Soldier* (1915) and the tetralogy *Parade's End*, comprising *Some Do Not* (1924), *No More Parades* (1925), *A Man Could Stand Up* (1926), and *The Last Post* (1928). A noted editor, he founded and worked on the *English Review* (1908–11) and *Transatlantic Review* (1924).

Ford, Gerald R[udolph, Jr.] (1913–) Thirty-eighth U.S. president (1974–77). Born in Omaha, Nebr., as Leslie Lynch King Jr., he served in the Navy in **World War II**. A Republican, he was elected to the U.S. Congress from Michigan (1949–73) and was House minority leader from 1965. Following the resignation of Spiro Agnew (1918–96) in 1973, Ford was appointed **Richard Nixon's** vice president in Agnew's place. Upon Nixon's resignation in 1974 due to the **Watergate** scandal, Ford succeeded to the office, becoming the first person to hold the nation's top two posts without having been elected to either. Ford's pardon of Nixon was widely criticized, and his economic initiatives during a time of recession and high inflation received little support. He lost the 1976 election to **Jimmy Carter**.

Ford, Henry (1863–1947) American industrialist. Born near Dearborn, Mich., he worked as an engineer and machinist before becoming an organizer of the Detroit Automobile Company in 1899. In 1903 he founded and became president of the Ford Motor Company (1903–19, 1943–45), which pioneered several manufacturing refinements that made him the world's largest automobile manufacturer. Foremost was the use from 1913 of the assembly-line method for building the Model T, which was designed in 1908 as an inexpensive, standardized car. In addition he introduced the Model A in 1928 and the V-8 engine in 1932. His business practices included the then–shockingly high wage of five dollars per 40-hour week. His innovations extended to many types of factory manufacture. Among his philanthropic endeavors was the Ford Foundation. His son Edsel Bryant Ford (1893–1943) and grandson Henry Ford II (1917–1987) both served as Ford presidents.

Ford, John (1895–1973) American film director. Born Sean Aloysius O'Feeney (O'Fearna) in Cape Elizabeth, Maine, he followed actor brother Francis Ford to Hollywood and directed his first feature, *Straight Shooting*, in 1917. Though successful in silents (*The Iron Horse*, 1924), he left his legacy in sound films, becoming the era's most honored and long-lived American director. In dramas and westerns, he combined strong narrative skills and a classical visual style in explorations of frontier versus civilization. Influential works include *Stagecoach* (1939), *My Darling Clementine* (1946), and *The Searchers* (1956). He won the Academy Award for best director for three films: *The Grapes of Wrath* (1940), *How Green Was My Valley* (1941), and *The Quiet Man* (1952).

Foreman, George (1949–) American athlete. Born in Marshall, Tex., he won the heavyweight boxing gold medal at the 1968 Olympics. As a professional (from 1969), Foreman won 40 consecutive fights and was world heavyweight champion (1973–74) until his defeat by **Muhammad Ali**. He retired in 1977, becoming an ordained minister and devoting himself to community service, but he returned to heavyweight boxing in 1987. A popular personality who made frequent **television** appearances, he knocked out Michael Moorer in 1994 to become the oldest heavyweight champion in history. The title was later rescinded for his refusal to fight Moorer in a rematch.

Forster, E[dward] M[organ] (1879–1970) British novelist. Raised by his doting, widowed mother, he graduated from King's College, Cambridge (1901) and wrote seriously from 1905. Beginning with *Where Angels Fear to Tread* (1905), his sensitive, ironic social novels revealed English upper-class failings and revitalized the novel of manners in the early century. Other notable titles include *A Room with a View* (1908), *Howard's End* (1910), and *A Passage to India* (1924). He also wrote short stories and literary essays, including *Aspects of the Novel* (1927).

Foucault, Michel [Paul] (1929–84) French philosopher. From 1970 he was a professor at the Collège de France. He was noted for his historical studies of Western attitudes toward insanity, punishment, and sexuality, beginning with *Madness and Civilization* (1961). His idea that all social relations are rooted in power influenced many academic fields. Other works include *The Order of Things* (1966).

Foyt, A[nthony] J[oseph] (1935–) American automobile racer. A former mechanic, he became the first four-time winner of the Indianapolis 500 (1961, 1964, 1967, and 1977). He also won seven United States Auto Club championships (1960, 1961, 1963, 1964, 1967,

1975, and 1979); the Daytona 500 (1972); and, with American automobile racer Dan Gurney, the 24 Hours of Le Mans (1967). He retired in 1993.

Franco [Bahamonde], Francisco [Paulino Hermenegildo Teódulo] (1892–1975) Spanish soldier and dictator. Entering the army in 1910, he was a war hero in Morocco (1920–26) and rose to major general by 1934. In 1935 he was named chief of army general staff. In 1936 he joined the Nationalist rebellion against the Spanish Second Republic, being named *caudillo* (leader) of the rebel government and *generalissimo* (commander in chief) of its forces. In 1937 he reorganized the **Falange**, the Spanish Fascist Party, making it the rebel government's official political movement. The **Spanish Civil War** that he helped instigate in 1936 ended in Fascist victory in 1939. Though sympathetic to **Adolf Hitler**, Franco kept Spain neutral during **World War II**, allowing himself to remain in power after the war. In 1947 he arranged for succession by proclaiming Spain a monarchy, with himself as a dictatorial regent for life. He remained to his death an authoritarian, anti-Communist ruler, though somewhat more liberal as of the 1960s. He was succeeded by King **Juan Carlos**, whom he had named as successor in 1969.

Frank, Anne (1929–45) German writer. In Amsterdam, Holland, from 1933 to escape Nazi Jewish persecution, she and her family went into hiding there on July 9, 1942, to evade German occupation troops. She kept a diary of her existence until they were discovered (August 4, 1944) and sent to **concentration camps**. She died at Bergen-Belsen. Her father, Otto Frank, published the diary *Het Achterhuis* in 1947 (*The Diary of a Young Girl*, 1953); it has been translated into over 30 languages and inspired a play and film.

Frankfurter, Felix (1882–1965) Austrian-born American jurist. After coming to the United States in 1894, he became a Harvard law professor and U.S. Supreme Court associate justice (1939–62). His decisions combined **liberalism** with judicial restraint.

Frazer, Sir James George (1854–1941) British anthropologist and classical scholar. Born in Glasgow, Scotland, he entered Trinity College, Cambridge, in 1874, becoming a fellow in 1879. His major work, *The Golden Bough*, was a comprehensive study of comparative religion and mythology. First published in two volumes in 1890, it expanded to 13 volumes by 1915; the author issued a single-volume condensation in 1923. It influenced not only anthropologists but also such writers as **James Joyce** and such psychologists as **Carl Jung**. Other works included *Folk-Lore in the Old Testament* (1918). He was knighted in 1914.

Freud, Sigmund (1856–1939) Austrian neurologist, psychiatrist, and founder of psychoanalysis. Born in Freiberg, Moravia (now Pribor, Czech Republic), he received his medical degree from the University of Vienna (1881), where he later served as professor of neuropathology (1902–38). In 1895, he and Josef Breuer published *Studies in Hysteria*, the founding work of psychoanalysis, but he split with Breuer to develop his own theories. (In turn, Freud's associates **Carl Jung** and **Alfred Adler** later broke from him to establish their own psychoanalytic schools.) Freud held that repression of childhood sexuality is the principal cause of neurosis, which can be treated through talk therapy based on free association of ideas. He introduced the Oedipus complex and extended his theories to cultural interpretation. In 1938 he fled from Vienna to England to escape Nazi persecution of Jews. Though Freud's theories have never ceased to be controversial, they laid the basis for modern schools of psychoanalysis and provided inspiration to writers, artists, and thinkers in many fields. Works include *The Interpretation of Dreams* (1900), *Totem and Taboo* (1913), *Introduction to Psychoanalysis* (1917), and *Civilization and Its Discontents* (1930).

Friedan, Betty (1921–) American writer. Born Naomi Goldstein, she graduated from Smith College (1942) and after two decades of suburban housewifery wrote *The Feminine Mystique* (1963), about the social and emotional constraints on modern middle-class women. A best-seller, her book influenced the development of the postwar feminist movement. In 1966 she helped found the National Organization for Women (NOW). Later works include *The Second Stage* (1982) and *The Fountain of Age* (1993).

Frost, Robert [Lee] (1874–1963) American poet. A major 20th-century poet and literary celebrity, he was born in San Francisco, Calif., but was recognized for his lyrical, colloquial work on the land and people of New England. Poetry collections include *A Boy's Will* (1913), *North of Boston* (1914), *New Hampshire* (1923), *A Witness Tree* (1942), *Steeple Bush* (1947), and *In the Clearing* (1962). From 1939 to 1943 he was professor of poetry at Harvard; he also taught at Amherst College and Dartmouth. He was awarded the Pulitzer Prize for literature in 1924, 1931, 1937, and 1941.

Frye, Northrop (1912–91) Canadian critic. His *Anatomy of Criticism* (1957) focused on the mythic archetypes underlying world literature. Other works include *Fearful Symmetry* (1947), a study of 18th-century British poet William Blake.

Fu'ad I [Ahmed Fuad Pasha] (1868–1936) King of Egypt (1922–36). Sultan from 1917 to 1922, he became the first king to reign in Egypt after it was nominally declared independent of Britain in 1922. Opposed by the ultranationalist Wafd Party, he dissolved parliament twice (in 1928 and 1930).

Fuentes, Carlos (1928–) Mexican writer. Also a lawyer and statesman, he is known for his experimental works exploring Mexican history and ideals, including novels *Where the Air is Clear* (1958), *The Death of Artemio Cruz* (1962), *Terra Nostra* (1975), *Distant Relations* (1980), and *The Old Gringo* (1985).

G

Gabin, Jean (1904–76) French actor. Born Jean-Alexis Moncorgé, he gained international fame for his performances—often as a strong, taciturn loner—in such films as *Grand Illusion* (1937), *Port of Shadows* (1938), *French Cancan* (1955), and *Les Misérables* (1957).

Galbraith, John Kenneth (1908–) Canadian-born American economist. In the United States from 1931, he became a Harvard professor (1949–75), adviser to President **John F. Kennedy**, and ambassador to India (1961–63). A Keynesian whose bestselling works made economics accessible to a broad audience, he analyzed the interaction of power and market forces. Works include *The Affluent Society* (1958).

Gallup, George [Horace] (1900–84) American statistician. Born in Jefferson, Iowa, he founded the American Institute of Public Opinion in 1935 and began the Gallup Poll to mark national concerns. From 1936 Gallup polls have been used during U.S. presidential campaigns and in other measures of social mood. Generally correct, the poll erred in the 1948 presidential campaign between New York governor Thomas Dewey (1902–1971) and **Harry S Truman**. Gallup founded the Audience Research Institute in 1939.

Gandhi, Indira [Priyadarshini Nehru] (1917–84) Indian politician. Daughter of Prime Minister Jawaharlal Nehru, she attended the University of Bengal and Somerville College, Oxford, and married Feroze Gandhi in 1942. Learning about Indian politics as an aide to her father, she was elected president of the All-India Congress Party (1959–60) and prime minister in 1966. A decisive ruler, she implemented a strong population control program and supported the Bengalis against West Pakistan in the 1971 Pakistani civil war. After declaring a government emergency to stem opposition in 1975, she was forced from office in 1977 and imprisoned for in-office offenses. Her reelection in 1980 marked her impressive comeback. She was assassinated by her own Sikh bodyguard months after she ordered the storming of the Sikh base at Amritsar.

Gandhi, Mohandas [Karamchand] (1869–1948) Indian political and spiritual leader, called Mahatma ("Great Soul"). Born in Porbandar, he studied law in England (1888–91). He traveled to Natal, South Africa (1893), where, in 1906, he launched his first campaign of nonviolent civil disobedience and noncooperation. Calling his movement *satyagraha* ("firmness in truth"), he struggled for better treatment of the Indian minority by the white government. He won some concessions before returning to India in 1914. In 1919 he organized a new *satyagraha* movement demanding political independence. Outrage at the Amritsar massacre (1919) mobilized support for Gandhi, who became leader of the Indian National Congress. By 1920 a general boycott of British goods was underway; other campaigns followed over the next two decades. Dedicated to nonviolence, Gandhi was willing to call off civil disobedience campaigns when his followers turned violent. He campaigned against mistreatment of "untouchables" and in favor of village-centered production and Hindu-Muslim unity. His 1930 march from Ahmedabad to the sea, to distill salt from seawater in protest of the government's salt monopoly, resulted in one of many imprisonments. During **World War II**, he was jailed again (1942–44) for refusing to cooperate in Britain's war effort. He led the postwar negotiation for India's independence, which was achieved in 1947, and reluctantly agreed to the partition creating Pakistan. He was assassinated by a Hindu fanatic who opposed his conciliatory attitude toward Muslims. Revered for his personal austerity, Gandhi dressed in loincloth and shawl and, despite being married, was celibate. His actions and writings, such as his autobiography *The Story of My Experiments with Truth* (1927–29), influenced protest movements in many nations, including the American **civil rights movement**.

Garbo, Greta (1905–90) Swedish-born American film actress. Born Greta Loisa Gustafsson, she appeared in *The Story of Gosta Berling* (1924) and was brought to Hollywood, where she became a legendary star. Mysterious and aloof onscreen, she is best known for silent films *Flesh and the Devil* (1927) and *Love* (1927); sound films include *Grand Hotel* (1932), *Camille* (1937), and *Ninotchka* (1939). From 1941 she lived in near seclusion. She won a special Academy Award in 1956.

García Lorca, Federico (1898–1936) Spanish writer. Born in Andalusia to a wealthy family, he attended law school but instead turned to writing. His first collection, *Book of Poems*, was published in 1921. His poetry was marked by imagistic experimentation, use of traditional forms, and exploration of the weight of convention. Other notable poetic works include *Poem of the Deep Song* (1933); the surrealistic *Poet in New York* (1940), which comments on his homosexuality; and *Llanto por Ignacio Sánchez Mejías* (1935), about a gored bullfighter. Plays include the trilogy *Blood Oranges* (1933), *Yerma* (1933), and *The House of Bernarda Alba* (1936). He is considered the most influential Spanish writer of the 20th century. During the **Spanish Civil War**, he was shot and killed by Nationalists.

García Márquez, Gabriel (1928–) Colombian writer. Born in the village of Aracataca, he worked as a reporter in Europe, the U.S., and Cuba before gaining acclaim for the novel *La Mala Hora* (1962; *In Evil Hour*, 1979), which introduced the imaginary town of Macando. The village was the setting of his masterpiece of magic realism, the novel *One*

Hundred Years of Solitude (1967), which charted seven generations of Macando's founding family. Later novels include *The Autumn of the Patriarch* (1975) and *Chronicle of a Death Foretold* (1981). He has also written short-story collections. He won the Nobel Prize for literature in 1982. Leftist political views led him to self-exile for much of his life.

Garland, Judy (1922–69) American singer and actress. Born Frances Gumm in Grand Rapids, Minn., she was a stage performer from age three and became a teenaged Hollywood film star in 1939 as Dorothy in *The Wizard of Oz* (special Oscar for juvenile performer). The leading Hollywood female musical star of the 1940s, she appeared in *Meet Me in St. Louis* (1944) and *Easter Parade* (1948), among others. She received Academy Award nominations for her dramatic performances in *A Star Is Born* (1954) and *Judgment at Nuremberg* (1961). Encountering problems with alcohol and drugs from her early career, she came to symbolize the price for some of Hollywood fame. Married five times, her husbands included American film director Vincente Minnelli (1903–86); her children include American singer and actress Liza Minnelli (1946–). Garland died of an accidental drug overdose.

Garvey, Marcus [Moziah] (1887–1940) Jamaican-born American political thinker. A leading black nationalist, he founded the Universal Negro Improvement Association in 1914, before coming to the U.S. in 1916. He advocated black pride and self-sufficiency, opposed integration, and called for a "Back to Africa" movement. Convicted of fraud, he was deported to Jamaica in 1927. He influenced later "Black Power" movements.

Gates, Bill (1955–) American businessman. Born William Henry Gates III in Seattle, Wash., he cofounded the software company Microsoft in 1975. He dropped out of Harvard to develop the company, which became wildly successful for its operating system MS-DOS, adopted by IBM for its personal **computers** in 1981. Microsoft products, including the Windows operating system, became industry standards, making Gates one of the world's richest men. In the 1990s, he faced federal antitrust charges for monopolistic practices, the trial ended in 2000 with a U.S. District Court ruling requiring Microsoft to bhe divided into two separate companies.

Geiger, Johannes Hans Wilhelm (1882–1945) German physicist. Involved in radium studies, he and Walther Müller created the first device for counting radioactive particles. Called the Geiger counter, it was invented in 1928.

Gell-Mann, Murray (1929–) American physicist. His discoveries in subatomic physics included the concepts of "strangeness" (1953), the "eightfold way" (1961), and quarks (1963). He taught at the University of Chicago (1952–55) and the California Institute of Technology (from 1955). He won the 1969 Nobel Prize for physics.

Genet, Jean (1910–86) French writer. The Paris-born son of a prostitute was a spokesman for the antibourgeois life, writing plays and confessional poems and novels, beginning during his incarceration for thievery. His identity as a homosexual and his experiences as a prostitute and pimp gave him ample material with which to shock conventional sensibilities and explore erotic themes. Verse works and novels include *Notre Dame des Fleurs* (1943) and *Journal du voleur* (1949); plays include *Les Bonnes* (1947), *Le Balcon* (1956), and *Les Nègres* (1959).

George II (1890–1947) Greek King (1922–23 and 1935–47). He succeeded his father **Constantine I**, but rebellion forced him to leave Greece the next year. A republic was proclaimed, but George returned in 1935 to reign over the dictatorship of **Ioannis Metaxas**.

German invasion forced him into exile (1941–46) until after **World War II**. He was succeeded by his brother Paul I (1901–64).

George V [George Frederick Ernest Albert] (1865–1936) British king (1910–36). Succeeding his father, **Edward VII**, he was a popular monarch who exerted a moderating influence during a tumultuous time. During **World War I**, he gave up all German titles and changed the family name from Saxe-Coburg-Gotha to Windsor.

George VI [Albert Frederick Arthur George] (1895–1952) British king (1936–52). He became king when his brother **Edward VIII** abdicated. He contributed to public morale in **World War II**, particularly during the bombing of Britain. He was succeeded by his daughter **Elizabeth II**.

Gershwin, George (1898–1937) American composer. Born Jakob Gershvin in Brooklyn, he combined jazz and folk elements in such compositions as *Rhapsody in Blue* (1923) and *An American in Paris* (1928). His music for the folk opera *Porgy and Bess* (1935) mixed popular and classical musical styles. Among his Broadway musicals are *Lady, Be Good!* (1923) and *Of Thee I Sing* (1931), which won a Pulitzer Prize; he also composed for films. His brother Ira Gershwin (1896–1983) was his frequent lyricist. Well-known songs include "Swanee" (1919), "Embraceable You" (1930), and "Summertime" (1935).

Giap, Vo Nguyen (1912–) Vietnamese soldier and politician. A member of the Vietnamese Communist Party from the 1930s, he helped organize the Viet Minh military force, becoming its commander in 1946. As a master of guerrilla fighting, he helped drive out the Japanese in **World War II** and the French afterward, and directed North Vietnam's winning strategy in the **Vietnam War**. Among his military achievements were the overthrow of the French at Dien Bien Phu (1954) and the Tet Offensive (1968) against the U.S. His posts included commander in chief, deputy prime minister, and minister of defense. He retired in 1982.

Gibran, Kahlil (1883–1931) Syrian-born American writer and artist. Born Jubran Khalil Jubran in Bechari, Lebanon (now Syria), he immigrated with his family to the U.S. in 1895. He attended college in Beirut, and later studied art in Paris with Rodin. He settled in New York City in 1912. While painting and sculpting, he concentrated on novels and especially prose poems, the form in which he wrote his greatest success, *The Prophet* (1923). The meditations joining mysticism, love, and redemption have remained popular for decades. Among other works are *The Madman* (1918), *The Forerunner* (1920), and *Broken Wings* (1922). He wrote in both Arabic and English.

Gide, André[-Paul-Guillaume] (1869–1951) French writer. Born in Paris to a university professor and Norman heiress, he published over 80 works across several genres, including stories, satires, and fables. His works touched on many subjects but were driven by the search for self, as with the 1897 prose-and-verse work *Les Nourritures terrestres*, which concerns his awakening to his homosexuality. Among his narratives are *L'Immoraliste* (1902), *La Porte étroite* (1907), *La Symphonie pastorale* (1919), and *Les Faux-Monnayeurs* (1926), which he considered his one true novel. Poetic works include *Le Retour de l'enfant prodigue* (1907) and *Les Nouvelles nourritures* (1935); plays include *Le Roi candaule* (1901) and *Oedipe* (1931). His *Journal* (1939–50) reflects his lifetime in thought. He was awarded the Nobel Prize for literature in 1947.

Gielgud, Sir [Arthur] John (1904–2000) British actor. Grandnephew of British actress Ellen Terry (1948–1928), he was educated at the Royal Academy of Dramatic Art and debuted at the Old Vic in *Henry V* (1921). A leading Shakespearean actor of his generation, he is noted for his many *Hamlet* performances. Films include *Becket* (1964) and *Arthur* (1981, supporting actor Academy Award). He was knighted in 1977. Autobiography: *An Actor and His Times* (1979).

Gillespie, Dizzy (1917–93) American musician. Born John Birks Gillespie, he was a leader of the bop movement in jazz as it emerged in the 1940s. A trumpeter and composer, he was known for his mode of scat singing and his performances with **Charlie Parker**. From the 1940's, he frequently toured with his own big band and incorporated Afro-Cuban rhythms.

Ginsberg, Allen (1926–97) American writer. Born in Paterson, N.J., he attended Columbia University, where he became acquainted with American writers William Burroughs (1914–1997) and Jack Kerouac (1922–1969). In 1956 Ginsberg published the long, expansive poem *Howl*, which (along with Kerouac's 1957 novel *On the Road*) would define the countercultural movement of the Beats. Ginsberg's other collections include *Kaddish and Other Poems* (1961), *Reality Sandwiches* (1963), and *Mind Breaths* (1978).

Giolitti, Giovanni (1842–1928) Italian politician. A parliament deputy from 1882 to 1928, he was elected prime minister five times (1892–93, 1903–05, 1906–1909, 1911–14, and 1920–21). His terms were marked by his political corruption as well as his progressive positions such as universal male suffrage. In his final years, he opposed Italy's entry into **World War I** and abetted the growth of **Fascism** in Italy by permitting Fascists to appear as government-sponsored candidates (and win 35 seats) in 1921 elections.

Giscard d'Estaing, Valéry (1926–) French politician. In the French Army during **World War II**, he entered public service in 1952, serving as finance minister under **Charles de Gaulle** and **Georges Pompidou**. In 1965 he founded and led the conservative faction Républicans Indépendants. After Pompidou's death, he was elected president in 1974. His term was marked by programs aimed at economic stability. He was defeated by Socialist **François Mitterand**.

Glass, Philip (1937–) American composer. He incorporated electronics and Eastern influences into long, repetitive, minimalist works, including the operas *Einstein on the Beach* (1976) and *Satyagraha* (1980).

Godard, Jean-Luc (1930–) French film director. A major figure of the French New Wave, he was born in Paris and became a film devoteé while attending the Sorbonne. He wrote for *Cahiers du Cinéma* and other journals before gaining fame with his first feature, *Breathless* (1960). It and subsequent films influenced New Wave filmmakers with their improvised look and original compositions. Other films include *The Little Soldier* (1963), *Masculine Feminine* (1966), *Weekend* (1968), and *Hail Mary!* (1986).

Goddard, Robert Hutchings (1882–1945) American rocket scientist. In 1926 he launched the first liquid-fuel rocket. His theories of rocketry and his patented rocket devices were instrumental in the development of the U.S. space program.

Gödel, Kurt (1906–78) Czech-born American mathematician and logician. Born in Brünn, Austria (now Brno, Czech Republic), he was educated at the University of Vienna. In 1931 he proved the impossibility of rigorously self-consistent mathematical systems, demonstrating that such projects as those embodied in **Bertand Russell** and **Alfred North Whitehead**'s *Principia Mathematica* (1910–13) could never be completed. He achieved other important results in mathematical logic, such as demonstrating that the continuum hypothesis is consistent with the axioms of set theory (1938). Gödel came to the United States in 1940, joining the Institute for Advanced Studies as professor of mathematics (1953–76).

Goebbels, Paul Josef (1897–1945) German politician. Rejected for military service in **World War I**, he received a doctorate in German philology from Heidelberg University in 1922, the same year he joined the **Nazi Party**. In 1926 he became district leader of the Nazi Party in Berlin, then held increasingly influential positions until being named minister for Propaganda and National Enlightenment in 1933. In addition to controlling the German media, he built the image of the *Führer*, supported the Final Solution, and promoted the idea of total war. In August 1944 he was named reich plenipotentiary for Total War. Fiercely loyal to **Adolf Hitler,** he followed Hitler's suicide in 1945 with the deaths of his six children, his wife, and himself.

Goldman, Emma (1869–1940) Lithuanian-born American anarchist. After coming to the U.S. in 1885, she worked in clothing factories and became active as an anarchist. Widely known for her lectures and known as "Red Emma," she was frequently jailed—notably in 1893 on charges of inciting the unemployed to riot and in 1917–19 for agitating against conscription. Her long association with anarchist Alexander Berkman (1870–1936) included cofounding and co-editing *Mother Earth* (1906–17). Deported with Berkman to the **Soviet Union** in 1919, she later lived in France and Canada. Her works include the autobiography *Living My Life* (1931).

Gompers, Samuel (1850–1924) American labor leader. Born in London, England, he immigrated to the U.S. in 1863 and worked as a cigar maker. In 1881 he helped found the organization that in 1886 became the American Federation of Labor (AFL). He remained AFL president until his death (except in 1895), gaining better wages and hours for workers and greater acceptance of organized labor. He battled the Knights of Labor to keep its radical tendencies from the AFL, instead championing a "pure and simple" unionism. Becoming the leading voice of American labor, he was a member of the Council of National Defense (1917) and the Commission on International Labor Legislation at the **Paris Peace Conference** (1919). In 1955 the AFL would merge with the Congress of Industrial Organizations (CIO) to form the **AFL–CIO.**

Gomulka, Wladyslaw (1905–82) Polish politician. Member of the Communist Party from 1926, he helped found the Polish Workers' (Communist) Party and was secretary (1943–49). Criticism of **Joseph Stalin** and the **Soviet Union** led to his party dismissal and imprisonment (1951–56). In 1956 he was reinstated in the party and re-elected secretary (1956–70). During his tenure, he attempted a moderate **socialism**, with increased private ownership and decreased religious opposition. He resigned during the 1970 food riots.

Goodman, Benny (1909–86) American musician. Born Benjamin David Goodman in Chicago, he formed his first band in 1934. He became a national sensation during a 1935 stint at the Palomar Ballroom, Los Angeles, Calif., introducing the Swing Era and acquiring the moniker "King of Swing." In 1936 he formed a racially mixed quartet including American musicians Lionel Hampton (1909–) and Teddy Wilson (1912–86). Goodman's 1938 Carnegie Hall jazz concert included appearances by members of the **Count Basie** and **Duke Ellington** Orchestras. He disbanded his groups in 1944, but resumed national and international touring from the 1950s to the 1970s, including a U.S. State Department–sponsored tour of the **Soviet Union.**

Gorbachev, Mikhail Sergeyevich (1931–) Soviet politician. Born in Privolnoye near Stavropol, he studied to become a lawyer at Moscow University and joined the Communist Party in 1952. He rose steadily, becoming a protégé of **Yuri Andropov**, who secured him membership in the Politburo in 1980. Following **Constantin Chernenko**'s death in 1985, Gorbachev became the party's general secretary (1985–91). In 1988 he also became head of state, replacing Andrei Gromyko (1909–89) as president of the Supreme Soviet (1988–91). In economic, political, and social life, he introduced liberal reforms known as *perestroika* (restructuring) and *glasnost* (openness). He eased travel restrictions, established religious toleration, and expanded artistic freedom. Proposing a multiparty democracy, he founded a Congress of People's Deputies (1989) permitting dissident views. To the post of foreign minister (1985–90) he appointed the reformist Eduard Shevardnadze (1928–), who later became president of the independent republic of Georgia (1992–). Gorbachev withdrew Soviet troops from Afghanistan, allowed Communist regimes in Eastern Europe to fall (1989), and signed major new arms control agreements, effectively ending the **cold war**. In 1990 he won the Nobel Peace Prize. Though praised in the West, he was distrusted at home, both by conservatives and more radical reformers. He was blamed domestically for his country's economic woes and internationally criticized for refusing to accept independence movements in the Baltic states; he tried unsuccessfully to keep those republics in the **Soviet Union**. An attempted coup by hard-liners in August 1991 nearly toppled him. After a few days of house arrest, he returned to power, but with his political base severely weakened in favor of Russian president **Boris Yeltsin**, who had led resistance to the coup. On December 25, 1991, Gorbachev resigned and was not replaced. One week later, at midnight on December 31, the **Soviet Union** officially ceased to exist.

Gordimer, Nadine (1923–) South African writer. She has expressed the conflicts and injustice of her native country's **apartheid** in many of her works, such as *Burger's Daughter* (1979), which was banned for a time in South Africa. Other novels include *The Voice of the Serpent* (1953), *A Guest of Honour* (1970), and *July's People* (1981). Among short-story collections are *Face to Face* (1949), *The Soft Voice of the Serpent* (1952), and *Something out There* (1984). She was awarded the Nobel Prize for literature in 1991.

Göring, Hermann [Wilhelm] (1893–1946) German politician and soldier. Born in Rosenheim, Bavaria, Göring led the Richtofen squadron during **World War I** and studied at the University of Munich before joining the **Nazi Party** in 1922. He led the SA (stormtroopers) in the unsuccessful 1923 Munich putsch, was exiled in Austria (1923–1927), and joined the Reichstag in 1928. President of the Reichstag in 1932, he was named Prussian prime minister, minister of the interior, and air minister after **Adolf Hitler** assumed power in 1933. He built up the Luftwaffe (German Air Force) and through the Prussian secret police established the first **concentration camps**. In 1940 he was named reischmarshall, a position created for him. Following defeats, he lost favor with Hitler and in 1945 was expelled from the Nazi Party. He was convicted of war crimes and condemned to death at the **Nuremberg Trials** in 1946. He committed suicide in jail.

Gorky, Maxim (1868–1936) Russian writer. Born Aleksey Maximovich Pyeshkov into great poverty, he adopted the pen name *Gorky*, "the bitter one." His works, which combine realism and poetry in championing locals and peasants, are central examples of Socialist Realism. They include the play *The Lower Depths* (1902), the novel *Mother* (1907), and his three-volume autobiography *Childhood* (1913–14), made up of *In the World* (1916), and *My Universities* (1923).

Graham, Billy [William Franklin Jr.] (1918–) American evangelist. Ordained a Southern Baptist minister in 1939, he has been a traveling evangelist from 1944. His 1949 Los Angeles, Calif., crusade marked him a major religious leader, known for fiery, compelling preaching. Active on **radio** and **television**, he has also met with U.S. presidents, beginning with **Harry S Truman**. The Billy Graham Evangelical Association publishes *Decision* magazine.

Graham, Martha (1895–1991) American dancer and choreographer. After dancing with the Denishawn School, she formed her own troupe in 1929, the Martha Graham School of Contemporary Dance. Her bare works, which infused dance with psychological depth, were highly influential in the maturation of modern dance. Works include *Primitive Mysteries* (1931), *Appalachian Spring* (1944), and *Archaic Hours* (1969). She retired as a dancer in 1970 but continued teaching.

Gramsci, Antonio (1891–1937) Italian politician. Educated at the University of Turin, he became a member of the Socialist Party in 1914, developing key policy and becoming a major theoretician for the Italian Left. He established the influential leftist newspaper *L'Ordine nuovo* (1919). Severing ties with the Socialists, he cofounded the Italian Communist Party in 1921, becoming its leader in 1924. He was imprisoned by Italy's Fascist government for leftist views from 1926 until the end of his life.

Grange, Red (1903–91) American athlete. Born Harold Edward Grange in Forksville, Pa., he was a three-time All-American halfback at the University of Illinois (1923–25). With the Chicago Bears in 1925 and from 1928 to 1935, he promoted the game and solidified his place as the era's finest football player. From 1926 to 1927 he also played professional baseball with the New York Yankees. In retirement, he was a **radio** and **television** broadcaster.

Grant, Cary (1904–86) British-born American actor. Born Archibald Alexander Leach in Bristol, England, he worked as an acrobat and stage actor before becoming a Hollywood film star during the 1930s. He was a prototypically suave, witty presence in such films as *Bringing up Baby* (1938), *His Girl Friday* (1940), *The Philadelphia Story* (1940), *Notorious* (1946), *To Catch a Thief* (1955), and *North by Northwest* (1959). He was awarded an honorary Academy Award in 1970.

Grass, Günter [Wilhelm] (1927–) Polish-born German writer. Born in Danzig (Gdánsk), he gained international success with his imaginative first novel *The Tin Drum* (1959), about childhood in Nazi Germany. Other novels, known for their social criticism, include *Dog Years* (1963) and *The Flounder* (1977). Among his plays is *Plebians Rehearse the Uprising* (1966). He won the Nobel Prize for Literature in 1999.

Greene, [Henry] Graham (1904–91) British writer. A convert to Catholicism (1926), he explored problems of faith and morality in light adventure novels he called "entertainments" and in serious novels. His novels include *The Power and the Glory* (1940) and *The Heart of the Matter* (1948). He also wrote short stories, plays, essays, and journalism. His screenplays include *The Third Man* (1949).

Gretzky, Wayne (1961–) Canadian athlete. On the Edmonton Oilers (1978–88), Los Angeles Kings (1988–96), St. Louis Blues (1996), and New York Rangers (1996–99) ice hockey teams, he set several single-season and lifetime records, notably surpassing **Gordie Howe** as the leading career goal scorer in 1994. During the 1981–82 season he became the first player to total over 200 points (212) and set records for goals (92) and assists (120). He also holds the lifetime record for assists. He is considered by many to be the greatest player in the history of the National Hockey League (N.H.L).

Griffith, Arthur (1872–1922) Irish politician. In 1899 he founded and in 1901 was editor of the newspaper the *United Irishman*, in which he promoted the establishment of an Irish parliament. In 1905 he founded the Irish nationalist party **Sinn Féin** and was imprisoned repeatedly for activism (1916–21). Vice president of the Irish Republic (1919), he also served as acting president (1919–20). After aiding in the negotiation of the Anglo-Irish Treaty admitting the Irish Free State, he served as the state's first president (1922).

Griffith, D[avid] [Lewelyn] W[ark] (1875–1948) American film director. Born in Kentucky, he is considered one of the most important filmmakers in American cinema. With cameraman G. W. Bitzer, he pioneered many techniques that became essential to film grammar, including cross-cutting, close-ups, pan shots, flashbacks, and fade-in and fade-out. He introduced such stars as **Mary Pickford**, Dorothy Gish (1898–1968), and Lillian Gish (1893–1993). His epic *The Birth of a Nation* (1915), on the Civil War and Reconstruction, influenced many filmmakers and helped established **motion pictures** as a serious art form while inciting controversy for its racist content. Other films include *Judith of Bethulia* (1914), *Intolerance* (1916), *Broken Blossoms* (1919), and *Orphans of the Storm* (1921). He usually produced his own films and often scripted or coscripted them. He cofounded United Artists in 1919. Unable to cope with the advent of talkies and the increasingly tight controls of the studio system, he made no films after 1931 but received an honorary Oscar in 1935.

Gris, Juan (1887–1927) Spanish painter. Born José Victoriano González, he came to Paris in 1906, where he was associated with **Pablo Picasso** and **Georges Braque**. He was the principal developer of synthetic cubism. He also illustrated books and designed sets and costumes for **Sergey Diaghilev**.

Gropius, Walter (1883–1969) German-born American architect. Born in Berlin, he first gained notice with his Fagus shoe factory at Alfeld (1911) and the Machinery Hall at the 1914 Cologne Exhibition. After service in **World War I**, he founded the Bauhaus at Weimar (1919), a school of **art** and **architecture** that sought to unify the arts in the service of mass-production needs, with an emphasis on functional, formalistic shapes and modern industrial materials. His ideas were expressed in the design of the buildings of the Bauhaus at Dessau, where the school moved in 1925. Gropius left the Bauhaus in 1928; fleeing the Nazis, he came to England in 1934 and to the U.S. in 1937, where he taught at Harvard until 1952. Later buildings include the Harvard Graduate Center (1950) and the U.S. Embassy, Athens (1960). His influence is felt in all areas of architecture and design, including the International Style of building.

Grosz, George (1893–1959) German-born American artist. Born in Berlin, he is known for his stylized caricature expressing disgust at bourgeois post–**World War I** society. Originally a dadaist, he was later associated with the *Neue Sachlichkeit* (New Objectivity). Immigrating to the U.S. in 1932 (and becoming a citizen in 1938), he developed a more romantic style, concentrating on landscapes and still lifes. His **World War II** studies of figures reflected his horror at the war.

Guevara, Che (1928–67) Argentine revolutionary. Born Ernesto Guevara de la Serna, he originally trained as a medical doctor (1953). Traveling widely throughout Latin America, he became convinced of the need for violent revolution to combat poverty. He was **Fidel Castro's** chief lieutenant in the Cuban revolution (1956–59) and minister of industry afterward (1961–65). A master of guerrilla warfare, he later fought in leftist military operations in Africa and Latin America. He was executed in Bolivia. The author of such works as *Guerrilla Warfare* (1961), he was an inspiration to leftists and revolutionaries throughout the world.

Guinness, Sir Alec (1914–2000) British actor. He performed with the Old Vic in Shakespearean and other roles. During **World War II**, he served in the Royal Navy; afterward, he became known for subtle character portrayals in many films, including *Oliver Twist* (1948), *Kind Hearts and Coronets* (1949), and *Lawrence of Arabia* (1962). He won a best actor Oscar for *The Bridge on the River Kwai* (1957). He was knighted in 1959.

Guthrie, Woody (1912–67) American folk singer and composer. Born Woodrow Wilson Guthrie, he wrote over 1,000 songs, many with populist and left-wing themes. Songs included "So Long (It's Been Good to Know Ya)" and "This Land Is Your Land." His son is singer and composer Arlo Guthrie (1947–).

H

Haig, Douglas Haig, first earl (1861–1928) British soldier leader. Serving under **Horatio Herbert Kitchener** in the **Boer War**, he was named colonel. At the start of **World War I** in 1914 he was named commander of First Army corps in France; from 1915 he was commander in chief of expeditionary forces in France. Encountering huge losses in the battles of the Somme (1916) and at Arras and Ypres in the Passchendaele campaign (1917), he attracted criticism from Prime Minister **David Lloyd George** and eventually took joint command (1918) with French general Ferdinand Foch (1851–1929). After the war he cofounded the soldiers' aid service, the British Legion (1921). He was named Earl Haig of Bemersyde in 1919.

Haile Selassie (1892–1975) Ethiopian emperor (1930–36). Born Lij Tafari; also known as Ras (Prince) Tafari. Crowned king in 1928, he became Emperor Haile Selassie ("Might of the Trinity") in 1930, succeeding Empress Zaudita. From 1935 to 1936, he led troops against invaders from Italy but was forced into exile in England until 1941, when, with British help, he was restored to the throne. Despite a record of modernization and social and political reforms, he was deposed by a military coup in 1974 and died in prison.

Hammarskjöld, Dag [Hjalmar Agne Carl] (1905–61) Swedish statesman. Son of politician Hjalmar Hammarskjöld (1862–1953), he served in the ministry of finance (1936–47) and ministry of foreign affairs (1947–53) before joining the Swedish delegation to the **United Nations**. From 1953 to 1961, he was UN security general; during his tenure, he led the UN through crises in the Suez, Lebanon, and the Congo. He died in an **airplane** crash near the Congo.

Hammerstein, Oscar See **Richard Rodgers**.

Hamsun, Knut (1859–1952) Norwegian writer. Pseudonym of Knut Pederson. He worked many jobs, some in the U.S., including streetcar conductor, dairyman, and fisherman. His novels, including *Sult* (1890), *Mysterier* (1892), and *Markens Grode* (1917), express a neo-Romantic love of nature and belief in the individual. He was awarded the Nobel Prize for literature in 1920. His support of the Nazi occupation of Norway in **World War II** hurt his reputation. He also wrote poems, plays, and a memoir, *On Overgrown Paths* (1949).

Hanks, Tom (1956–) American actor. Following a career in **television**, he established his comedic film talent with *Splash* (1984) and *Big* (1988) and followed with Academy

Award–winning dramatic performances in *Philadelphia* (1993) and *Forrest Gump* (1994). The latter two films made him one of only two men (the other being Spencer Tracy) to win the Oscar for best actor in two consecutive years. Widely acclaimed for his persona of every-man decency, he is often said to recall the generation of Hollywood stars that included **James Stewart** and **Henry Fonda**. Other films include *Sleepless in Seattle* (1993), *Apollo 13* (1995), *Saving Private Ryan* (1998), and *Cast Away* (2000).

Harding, Warren G[amaliel] (1865–1923) Twenty-ninth U.S. president (1921–23). Born in Blooming Grove, Ohio, he became publisher of the Marion, Ohio, *Star* and was elected to the U.S. Senate as a Republican in 1914. In 1920 he was elected president; a highlight of his term was the calling of the Washington Naval Conference in 1921. He died in office in 1923, as rumors of government corruption were surfacing. The **Teapot Dome** scandal, which brought charges against cabinet appointees Albert B. Fall and Harry M. Daugherty, branded the Harding administration as deeply corrupt. He was the first presi-dent to broadcast over the **radio**, with a speech in Baltimore in 1922.

Hari, Mata (1876–1917) Dutch dancer and spy. Born Margaretha Geertruida Zelle; mar-ried name MacLeod, from 1895. She was a dancer in Paris from 1905 and worked as a spy for Germany during **World War I**, with many Allied (see **Allied Powers**) officers as lovers and information sources. She was tried and executed by firing squad in France.

Harriman, W[illiam] Averell (1896–1986) American politician. Son of American busi-nessman Edward Henry Harriman (1848–1909), he was born in New York City and became known for his diplomacy with the **Soviet Union** during the **cold war**. His diplo-matic career over four Democratic presidencies began in 1941 as a negotiator with the Soviet Union and Britain on **lend–lease** aid. From 1943 to 1946 he was U.S. ambassador to the Soviet Union and in 1946 ambassador to Great Britain. In 1963 he also was the chief U.S. negotiator for the Nuclear Test-Ban Treaty. During the Vietnam conflict, he was U.S. representative during the **Paris Peace Talks**. He also served as U.S. secretary of commerce (1946–48) and governor of New York (1955–59).

Hart, Lorenz See **Richard Rodgers**

Hasek, Jaroslav (1883–1923) Czech writer. He was a journalist and satirist before join-ing the Austrian army in **World War I** and being captured by the Russians. He later became a political commissar in the Red Army. His fame rests on one long, unfinished, satirical novel, *The Good Soldier Schweik* (1921–23). The book was finished by his friend Karel Vanek.

Havel, Vaclav (1936–) Czech playwright and politician. His avant-garde plays, including *The Garden Party* (1963), were banned by the Czech government from the late 1960s. Active in the struggle for **human rights**, he was sentenced twice to prison, in 1979 and 1989. Released from prison, he led an opposition movement resulting in the establishment of a non-Communist government. From 1989 until his resignation in December 1992, he served as president of Czechosolvakia; from January 1993, he was president of the Czech Republic.

Hawking, Stephen [William] (1943–) British physicist. Despite his confinement to a wheelchair as a result of amyotrophic lateral sclerosis, his mind remained potent and he developed influential theories of black holes and quantum gravity. His book *A Brief History of Time* (1988) made him known to a wide audience.

Hawks, Howard (1896–1977) American film director. Born in Goshen, Ind., he attended Cornell University and was a **World War I** pilot before directing his first film (*The Road to Glory*, 1926). Over four decades of filmmaking, he was increasingly esteemed for his economical narrative skills and facility across genres. Noteworthy works include gangster dramas (*Scarface*, 1932), screwball comedies (*Bringing up Baby*, 1938; *His Girl Friday*, 1940), action films (*Only Angels Have Wings*, 1939), musicals (*Gentlemen Prefer Blondes*, 1953), and westerns (*Red River*, 1948). He introduced American film actress Lauren Bacall (1924–) in *To Have and Have Not* (1944). He won an honorary Oscar (1974).

Hayes, Helen (1900–93) American actress. Born Helen Hayes Brown, she made her stage debut at age five. She was celebrated for her performances in George Bernard Shaw's *Caesar and Cleopatra* (1925) and British playwright Laurence Housman's (1865–1959) *Victoria Regina* (1935), among other plays. Her films included *The Sin of Madelon Claudet* (1932) and *Airport* (1969), for both of which she won Academy Awards. She retired in 1970. She married American playwright Charles MacArthur (1895–1956) in 1928.

Hearst, William Randolph (1863–1951) American businessman. Son of American industrialist George Hearst (1820–91), he took charge of his father's newspaper, the *San Francisco Examiner*, in 1887. By the early 20th century, the Hearst empire owned 18 newspapers in nine states, and nine magazines, including *Good Housekeeping*. His newspapers, distinguished by flashy design and sensational writing, epitomized "yellow journalism"; their coverage of Cuba's fight for independence spurred the Spanish-American War. His lush residence San Simeon became a museum; his life was fictionalized in American director **Orson Welles**'s film *Citizen Kane* (1941).

Heath, Sir Edward Richard George (1916–) British politician. An M.P. since 1950, he held several government posts, including secretary of state for trade and industry (1963–64), before becoming Conservative prime minister (1970–74). During his ministry, he negotiated Britain's entry into the European Community (1973), but his government was plagued by high inflation and poor relations with labor, including a miners' strike that forced the nation to adopt a three-day work week. He lost party leadership to **Margaret Thatcher** in 1975.

Heidegger, Martin (1889–1976) German philosopher. He succeeded his teacher **Edmund Husserl** as professor of philosophy at Freiburg in 1928. A supporter of the Nazis, he was removed from his post by the victorious Allies (*see* **Allied Powers**) in 1945. Emphasizing the quest for being and the importance of authenticity, he was a founder of **existentialism**, though he rejected the title himself. Works include *Being and Time* (1927).

Heifetz, Jascha (1901–87) Lithuanian-born American violinist. He was a child prodigy in Lithuania before settling in the U.S. in 1917 and becoming a citizen in 1923. Touring internationally from age 12, he became a renowned musician, delivering performances noted for their robustness and maturity.

Heisenberg, Werner Karl (1901–76) German physicist. In 1927 he stated the **uncertainty principle**, or principle of indeterminism; that it is impossible to know both the position and momentum of a subatomic particle with complete precision. A developer of **quantum theory**, he introduced matrix mechanics, a mathematical technique for studying energy levels of electrons, and proposed the model of an atomic nucleus containing both protons and neutrons. He was awarded the 1932 Nobel Prize for physics.

Hellman, Lillian (1905–84) American playwright. Born in New Orleans, she attended New York University and Columbia, gaining success with her first play, *The Children's Hour*

(1934). Other notable plays include *The Little Foxes* (1939) and *Watch on the Rhine* (1941). Her refusal to testify before the House Un-American Activities Committee is described in *Scoundrel Time* (1976), which, along with her other autobiographical works—*An Unfinished Woman* (1969) and *Pentimento* (1973) —earned her wide recognition. She had a lengthy relationship with American mystery writer Dashiell Hammett (1896–1961).

Hemingway, Ernest [Miller] (1899–1961) Born in Oak Park, Ill., he was wounded at age 18 in ambulance corps service during **World War I**. After the war he became a foreign correspondent for the *Toronto Star* and settled in Paris. Among the many American expatriates he met there was Gertrude Stein, who influenced his early writing. In 1923 he published his first collection, *Three Stories and Ten Poems*, containing the important early stories "Up in Michigan" and "My Old Man." Other notable collections include *In Our Time* (1924), which introduces the semi-autobiographical character Nick Adams; *Men without Women* (1927), containing "The Killers"; *Winner Take Nothing* (1932); and *The First Forty-Nine Hours and Other Stories* (1937), with "The Snows of Kilimanjaro" and "The Short Happy Life of Francis Macomber." Novels include *A Farewell to Arms* (1929), *To Have and Have Not* (1937), *For Whom the Bell Tolls* (1940), and *Islands in the Stream* (1970, posthumously published). Among nonfiction works are *Death in the Afternoon* (1932), *Green Hills of Africa* (1935), and the posthumously published *A Moveable Feast* (1964). A hard-drinking, oft-married adventurer, Hemingway the public celebrity was a fit adjunct to his muscular, restrained works and danger-worshiping heroes. His pared-down prose and dramatic dialogue influenced many writers. He won the Pulitzer Prize in 1952 for the novella *The Old Man and the Sea* and the Nobel Prize for literature in 1954. He committed suicide in 1961.

Henderson, Arthur (1863–1935) British labor leader and politician. An iron molder, union leader, and Methodist lay-preacher, he was elected to Parliament as a Labour member in 1903. He was chief party whip in 1914, from 1921 to 1923, and from 1925 to 1927. As secretary of the **Labour Party** (1911–34), he led its reorganization as one of the two major government parties; in 1918 he helped draft the party constitution, making Labour an openly Socialist organization influenced by **Sidney Webb**. Henderson supported British participation in **World War I**; during the war, he served in several posts, including president of the Board of Education (1915) and minister without portfolio (1916). For his efforts on behalf of world peace, including chairmanship of the International Disarmament Conference (1932), he was awarded the Nobel Peace Prize in 1934.

Henie, Sonja (1912–1969) Norwegian ice skater. Ten-time winner of the world women's amateur figure skating championship (1927–1936), she earned gold medals in three Olympics (1928, 1932, and 1936). Her dramatic skating with elements of ballet influenced women's professional skating.

Henry, O. (1862–1910) American writer. Pen name of William Sydney Porter. Born in North Carolina, he was imprisoned for three years for embezzling funds while working as a bank teller. While in prison in 1899, he began his career as "O. Henry," a popular author of humorous, sentimental short stories, often ending with a twist. Collections include *Cabbages and Kings* (1904), *The Four Million* (1906), and *The Voice of the City* (1908).

Hepburn, Audrey (1929–93) British actress. Born Audrey Hepburn-Ruston in Belgium of Dutch-British parents and educated in Holland and London, she brought a continental bearing to plays and film. Requested by **Colette** to play the title role in the stage adaptation of *Gigi*, she then appeared in films including *Roman Holiday* (1953), *Sabrina* (1954), *Funny Face* (1956), *Love in the Afternoon* (1956), *Breakfast at Tiffany's* (1961), and *My Fair Lady*

(1964). In later years she was a special ambassador for UNICEF and worked to fight famine in Somalia.

Hepburn, Katharine (1909–) American actress. Born in Hartford, Conn., to a noted surgeon and social crusader, she attended Bryn Mawr. She appeared widely in summer stock and on the Broadway stage before making a memorable film debut in *A Bill of Divorcement* (1932). Although she won her first Academy Award for her performance in the 1933 *Morning Glory* and starred in successes including *Holiday* and *Bringing up Baby* (both 1938), the strong-minded actress was labeled by a major exhibitor "box-office poison." She regained her place in Hollywood with *The Philadelphia Story* (1940) and followed with four decades of much-honored acting, notably in nine movies with **Spencer Tracy**, with whom she had a legendary 25-year affair. Among her films with Tracy are *Woman of the Year* (1942), *Adam's Rib* (1949), *Pat and Mike* (1952), and *Guess Who's Coming to Dinner* (1967), for which she won a second Academy Award. Other notable films include *The African Queen* (1951) and *The Lion in Winter* (1968), which brought her third Academy Award, and *On Golden Pond* (1981), which brought her fourth. Her second and third Oscar wins made her the first person since Austrian-born American actress Luise Rainer (1910–) in 1936 and 1937 to be awarded the best actress Oscar in two consecutive years. Following Tracy's death in 1967, Hepburn also appeared on Broadway (*Coco*, *A Delicate Balance*) and wrote books, including the memoir *Me* (1991). She is remembered for her regal, mannered acting style and her personal independence.

Herbert, Victor (1859–1924) Irish-born American composer and conductor. The conductor of his own orchestra in New York from 1904, he composed light operas, including *Babes in Toyland* (1903) and *Naughty Marietta* (1910), as well as scores for the Ziegfeld Follies (beginning in 1917).

Hess, [Walther Richard] Rudolph (1894–1987) Egyptian-born German politician. He served in the German army during **World War I** and became **Adolf Hitler**'s personal secretary in 1920. While he and Hitler were imprisoned after participating in the 1923 Munich putsch, Hitler dictated *Mein Kampf* (1924, *My Struggle*, 1940) to him. Active in the **Nazi Party** through the 1920s, he became deputy leader of the Nazi Party in 1934. Interned in England from 1941 to 1945 following attempted peace negotiations, he was tried in 1946 for war crimes in Nuremberg. Sentenced to life imprisonment at Spandau (in Germany), he served 41 years before committing suicide.

Hesse, Hermann (1877–1962) German-born Swiss writer. He is known for his deeply felt novels of the search for spiritual satisfaction, which interweave elements of psychoanalysis and Eastern mysticism. Notable works include *Demian* (1919), *Siddhartha* (1922), *Steppenwolf* (1927), and *Magister Ludi: The Glass-Bead Game* (1943). He was awarded the Nobel Prize for literature in 1946. In Switzerland from 1914 as a pacifist, he became a citizen in 1923.

Hillary, Sir Edmund [Percival] (1919–) New Zealand explorer. On May 29, 1953, he and Nepalese guide Tenzing Norgay (c. 1914–86) became the first people to reach the summit of Mt. Everest, the world's tallest mountain. Hillary was knighted that year. He later led an overland expedition to the South Pole (1958).

Himmler, Heinrich (1900–1945) German official. He participated in the Munich putsch (1923) and became a member of the **Nazi Party** (1925). Chosen chief of police in Munich in 1933, he also served as head of the Gestapo (secret police) from 1936 to 1945. Gaining vast power during **World War II**, he directed the operation of the **concentration camps**, authorizing medical experimentation on and mass extermination of prisoners, largely Jews. He was named minister of the interior in 1943. After capture by the British, he committed suicide.

Hindenburg, Paul von (1847–1934) German soldier and politician. Full name Paul Ludwig Hans Anton von Beneckendorff und Hindenburg. After an unremarkable military career, he retired from service as a general in 1911 but was recalled to duty in **World War I**. Though dependent on his chief of staff **Erich von Ludendorff**, Hindenburg received much credit for victories at Tannenberg and Masurian Lakes (1914) that repelled a Russian invasion. Promoted to field marshal, he introduced unrestricted submarine warfare, which drew the U.S. into the war. After Germany's defeat, he retired from public life until 1925, when, despite his monarchist views, he became the second president (1925-34) of the **Weimar Republic**. He defeated **Adolf Hitler** in the election of 1932, but in 1933, under continuing Nazi pressure, he appointed Hitler as chancellor. Hitler quickly took dictatorial power, with Hindenburg a figurehead until his death the next year.

Hirohito (1901–89) Japanese emperor (1926–1989). His reign was named Showa ("Enlightened Peace"). Regent from 1921, he succeeded his father, Taisho, in 1926. During his reign, Japan participated in **World War II**. He helped persuade Japan's government to accept unconditional surrender, marking the end of the war. In 1946 he renounced the idea of imperial divinity, and a new constitution made him a constitutional monarch.

Hiss, Alger (1904–96) American public servant. In 1948, after years of exemplary service in the Department of State (1936–47), he was accused by U.S. journalist Whittaker Chambers (1901–61) of conveying State Department material to the Russians. A first trial for perjury in 1949 resulted in a hung jury, but the second in 1950 brought a five-year sentence. He was released in 1954 and for the rest of his life maintained his innocence.

Hitchcock, Sir Alfred [Joseph] (1899–1980) British film director. Born in London, he had early success with the thriller *The Lodger* (*The Case of Jonathan Drew*, 1926). In the 1930s he gained international repute with thrillers *The Man Who Knew Too Much* (1934, remade 1956), *The 39 Steps* (1935), and *The Lady Vanishes* (1938). In 1939 he came to Hollywood for American producer David O. Selznick (1902–1965); there his works became more opulent and he became a household name. Notable works include *Rebecca* (1940, best director Academy Award), *Notorious* (1946), *Rear Window* (1954), *Vertigo* (1958), *North by Northwest* (1959), and *Psycho* (1960). His U.S. **television** mystery series (1955–65) and appearance in nearly all films made his rotund shape known.

Hitler, Adolf (1889–1945) German dictator. Born in Braunau, Upper Austria, he served in a Bavarian regiment in **World War I**, winning the Iron Cross. In 1919 he joined the German Workers' Party, which he reorganized in 1920 as the National Socialist German Workers' Party, or the **Nazi Party**. In 1923, with **Erich von Ludendorff**, he launched an unsuccessful revolt in Munich known as the "**Beer Hall Putsch**." While imprisoned for nine months because of his part in the revolt, Hitler wrote *Mein Kampf* (*My Struggle*), a vitriolic testament of his anti-Semitic, Fascist views. Following his release, he rebuilt the Nazi Party, gathering support from conservative industrialists and preying on widespread economic hardship and anti-Semitism to attract a mass following. Hitler lost the 1932 presidential election to **Paul von Hindenburg** but was named chancellor in 1933. He soon acquired dictatorial powers, and upon Hindenburg's death in 1934 united the offices of president and chancellor to become *Der Führer* (Leader). Political opponents were murdered, as in the 1934 "night of the long knives," or intimidated into silence. Propaganda and mass meetings encouraged a cult of adoration of Hitler and faith in his ideology of the Aryan (German) master race. Jews were systematically persecuted through legal disenfranchisement, ghettoization, and ultimately, in the **Holocaust**, the **genocide** of six million in **concentration camps**. The camps also claimed the lives of hundreds of thousands of others, including Slavs, homosexuals, alleged Communist sympathizers, and Gypsies. Rearming massively over the next few years, Hitler reoccupied the Rhineland (1936) and annexed Austria and the **Sudetenland** (1938) and Czechoslovakia (1939). He formed alliances with Italy and Japan (1936) and made a nonaggression pact with the **Soviet Union** (1939). Britain and France condoned his aggressions through the policy of **appeasement**, but they balked at his invasion of Poland (1939), which inaugurated **World War II**. Hitler went on to capture France (1940), but his fortunes turned after his invasion of the **Soviet Union** resulted in the disastrous defeat at Stalingrad (1943). Injured in an assassination attempt (1944), he committed suicide in a bunker in Berlin as Allied armies (see **Allied Powers**) advanced on the city. Accompanying him in suicide was his mistress, Eva Braun (1912–1945), whom he had married shortly beforehand. Many regard him as the 20th century's greatest incarnation of evil.

Ho Chi Minh (1890–69) Vietnamese soldier and politician. Born Nguyen That Thanh, he traveled widely in his early years, from England (1915) to France (1917) to the **Soviet Union** (1923) to China (1924). Blending anticolonial nationalism with Marxist revolution, he was a founding member of the French Communist Party (1920) and founded the Indochinese Communist Party (1930). Living mostly in Moscow and China throughout the 1930s, he returned to Vietnam in 1941 to found the Viet Minh, a Vietnamese independence movement, and formed a guerrilla army to fight the Japanese invaders. In 1945, at the end of **World War II**, he captured Hanoi and declared Vietnam independent, with himself as president. He fought the French from 1946 until the final French defeat at Dien Bien Phu in 1954. Agreeing to a partition of the country, he became president of North Vietnam in 1954; in 1959 he began supporting the Viet Cong guerrilla movement in South Vietnam, leading to the **Vietnam War** with the U.S. He died before the North Vietnamese victory in that war, but Saigon in South Vietnam was renamed Ho Chi Minh City in his honor (1975).

Hoffman, Dustin [Lee] (1937–) American actor. On stage from the mid-1960s, he became a film star with *The Graduate* (1967). He was known for his meticulous characterizations, often as antiheroes. He won two best actor Oscars, for *Kramer vs. Kramer* (1979) and *Rain Man* (1989).

Holiday, Billie (1915–59) American singer. Born Eleanora Fagan, she was also known as Lady Day. Born in Baltimore Md., she began singing professionally in the 1930s. With her distinctive phrasing and style, she gained a reputation as the greatest jazz singer of her time. She performed with the bands of **Benny Goodman**, Teddy Wilson (1912–1986), **Count Basie**, and others before embarking on a solo career. Her death was hastened by drug addiction.

Holmes, Oliver Wendell, Jr. (1841–1935) American jurist and writer. Son of American physician and author Oliver Wendell Holmes (1809–1894), he graduated from Harvard Law School (1866), where he taught from 1870, becoming a professor of law in 1882. His influential book *The Common Law* (1881) questioned standing legal positions. From 1902 to 1932 he served on the U.S. Supreme Court, where he wrote lasting opinions on free speech and promoted the concept of "judicial restraint." His frequent dissenting opinions from those of the more conservative justices earned him the moniker "the Great Dissenter."

Home, Sir Alexander Frederick Douglas-Home, 14th earl of Home (1903–92) British politician. A Conservative M.P. from 1931, he was private secretary to **Neville Chamberlain** (1937–39) and foreign secretary (1960–63) before becoming prime minister (1963–64). To take office, he renounced his Scottish title for life but was later made a life peer (1974).

Hoover, Herbert Clark (1874–1964) Thirty-first U.S. president (1929–33). Born in West Branch, Iowa, he worked as an engineer and began government service in **World War I** as head of food and relief bureaus in Europe and the U.S. As secretary of commerce from 1921 to 1928, he oversaw the development of the Hoover Dam and St. Lawrence Waterway. A Republican, he was elected president in 1928, having run against Democratic nominee Alfred Smith (1873–1944). Following the October 1929 stock market crash, he believed the economy would regenerate itself and opposed government intervention to stimulate it. The continuing effects of the **Great Depression** led to his defeat by Democrat **Franklin D. Roosevelt** in 1932. That year Hoover also ordered the removal of **World War I** Bonus war veterans from their encampment in Washington, D.C. In later years, Hoover administered postwar food delivery programs (1946) and led the Hoover Commission (1947–49).

Hoover, J[ohn] Edgar (1895–1972) United States government official. Named director of the **Federal Bureau of Investigation (FBI)** in 1924, he remained its head until his death nearly 50 years later. Under Hoover, the FBI was enlarged and its powers increased to face the rise of organized crime. During World War II, Hoover and the FBI were in control of U.S. espionage activities. After the war he began operations against the radical Left in America, compiling detailed files on numerous individuals ranging from popular entertainers to presidents. He has been criticized for his authoritarian control and his lack of respect for civil liberties.

Hope, Bob (1903–) British-born American comedian. Born Leslie Townes Hope, he became a leading comedian in vaudeville, **radio**, and film, notably in seven *"Road"* features (1940–62), such as *The Road to Singapore* (1940) with U.S. singer and actor **Bing Crosby**. For five decades beginning in **World War II** he toured worldwide, entertaining U.S. troops in shows sponsored by the United Service Organizations (USO). Self-effacing and nationally esteemed, he won five special Academy Awards (1940, 1944, 1952, 1959, and 1965) and a Kennedy Center award (1985).

Hopkins, Sir Anthony (1937–) British actor. Acting on the stage from 1960 and in films from 1967, he won a best actor Oscar for his portrayal of serial killer Hannibal Lecter in *The Silence of the Lambs* (1991). Other films include *The Lion in Winter* (1968), *The Elephant Man* (1980), and *The Remains of the Day* (1993).

Hopper, Edward (1882–1967) American artist. Born in Nyack, N.Y., he exhibited his paintings at the Armory Show in New York City (1913) and abandoned painting for 10 years afterward to work as a commercial illustrator. He returned to painting, capturing in works such as *Early Sunday Morning* (1930) and *Nighthawks* (1942) a haunting sense of loneliness and distance.

Horowitz, Vladimir (1904–89) Russian-born American pianist. Studying piano at the Kiev Conservatory, he made his debut at age 17 and his first New York City and London appearances in 1928. His technical expertise and distinctive interpretation made him renowned by critics and appreciated by the public. Married to Wanda Toscanini (daughter of Italian conductor **Arturo Toscanini**) in 1933, he settled in New York City in 1940. He returned to the **Soviet Union** to perform in 1986.

Horthy de Nagybánya, Miklós [Nicholas] (1868–1957) Hungarian soldier and politician. Aide-de-camp to Emperor Franz-Joseph (1909–14), he was appointed admiral and commander-in-chief of the Austro-Hungarian fleet during **World War I** (1918). Chief of the national army from 1919, he led the counterrevolutionary forces against Communist Béla Kun and occupied Budapest (1919). Regent from 1920 to 1944, he appeased **Adolf Hitler** before **World War II**, but after attempting peace negotiations with the **Soviet Union** during the war, he was taken by Nazi forces in 1944. From 1945 he lived in Portugal.

Houdini, Harry (1874–1926) Hungarian-born American magician. Born Ehrich Weiss, he immigrated to the U.S. in 1874 and joined the circus in his youth, taking the name Houdini from French magician Jean-Eugène Robert-Houdin (1805–1871). From adulthood he was internationally renowned as a conjurer, able to escape handcuffs, locked vaults, underwater bondage, and other barriers. He also inveighed against false mediums and mind-readers. Books include *Miracle Mongers and Their Methods* (1920) and *A Magician among the Spirits* (1924).

Howe, Gordie [Gordon] (1928–) Canadian athlete. Over a remarkably long-lived career (1946–80) as a hockey forward, he set National Hockey League records for most seasons (26), most games (1,767), most goals (801; surpassed by **Wayne Gretzky** in 1994), and assists (1,049, also surpassed by Gretzky). Teams include the Detroit Red Wings (1946–71), marking his first retirement; and the Houston Aeros (1973), New England Whalers (1977), and Hartford Whalers (1980), marking his second.

Hoxha, Enver (1908–85) Albanian soldier and politician. He cofounded the Albanian Communist Party in 1941 and led the radical **resistance** against Italian occupation in **World War II**. In 1944 Hoxha gained control over Albania; proclaiming the country a republic in 1946, he was premier to 1954 and the country's leader until his death. A Stalinist, he broke with the **Soviet Union** in 1961, instead forming an alliance with China that ended in 1978. His policies kept Albania one of the poorest and most isolated countries in Europe.

Hu Shih (1891–1962) Chinese philosopher. He was an intellectual leader of liberals in the **May Fourth Movement** (1917–23). Influenced by **John Dewey**, with whom he studied at Columbia University, he advocated pragmatic evolutionary change, opposed **Communism**, and promoted vernacular literature. He was a professor and chancellor at Peking University and Nationalist ambassador to the United States (1938–42) and the **UN** (1957).

Hua Guofeng or **Hua Kuo-feng** (1920–) Chinese politician. He took part in the **Long March**, fought in **World War II** and the **Chinese Civil War**, and became deputy governor of Hunan Province (1958–67). A pragmatic Maoist and member of the Politburo from 1973, he succeeded **Zhou Enlai** as premier (1976–80). After defeating the **Gang of Four**, he became chairman of the Central Committee (1976–81) but was forced out of power by **Deng Xiaoping**, one of whose protégés, Hu Yaobang (1915–89), replaced Hua as chairman.

Hughes, [James] Langston (1902–67) American writer. A major figure of the Harlem

Renaissance and highly influential in the growth of black literature, he is known for his musical, idiomatic poetry of the black American experience. Collections include *Weary Blues* (1926), *The Dream Keeper* (1932), *Shakespeare in Harlem* (1942), and *One-Way Ticket* (1949). Fiction includes the novel *Not without Laughter* (1930) and story collection *The Ways of White Folks* (1934). He also wrote children's books and two autobiographies.

Huidobro, Vicente (1893–1948) Chilean writer. He was a leading experimental avant garde poet. His verse collections include *Las Pagodas ocultas* (1914), *Adán* (1916), and *Saisons choisies* (1921). Novels include *Mio Cid Campeador* (1929).

Hurston, Zora Neale (1901–60) American writer. A pioneer female voice of African-American fiction and nonfiction, she attended Barnard and studied with Columbia anthropologist **Franz Boas**, which proved influential to her writing. Her nonfiction includes *Mules and Men* (1935) and *Tell My Horse* (1938), both studies of black culture. Among her novels are *Jonah's Gourd Vine* (1934) and her most respected work, *Their Eyes Were Watching God* (1937), both about blacks in the American South.

Hussein I [Hussein Ibn Talal] (1935–) Jordanian king. In 1953 he succeeded his father, Talal, to the throne. Generally pursuing a moderate, pro-Western policy, he nevertheless joined other Arab nations in the 1967 war against Israel. The loss of Jordanian territory in that conflict was followed by a Palestinian revolt (1970), which Hussein suppressed. His support of Iraq in the Persian **Gulf War** (1991) strained relations with the U.S., but relations improved after Hussein agreed to join Middle East peace talks. In 1994 Hussein agreed to a formal peace between Jordan and Israel.

Hussein, Saddam (1937–) Iraqi dictator. A member of the nationalist, socialist **Ba'ath Party** from 1957, he took part in the 1968 revolution that placed it in power. Even before becoming president (1979–), he gathered dictatorial powers and was effectively the country's ruler. His rule has been marked by nepotism, a personality cult, and ruthless suppression of dissent. He used U.S. aid to wage war with Iran (1980–88), suppress a Kurdish independence movement, and develop **chemical weapons**. In 1990 he annexed Kuwait, but was driven out by a U.S.–led coalition force in the **Gulf War** (1991). Soon afterward, he suppressed another Kurdish rebellion and bombarded Shi'ites in southern Iraq, causing the **UN** to impose "no-fly" zones. Despite the Gulf War defeat and the UN sanctions and economic distress that followed, Saddam Hussein remained in power. Charged with attempting to develop chemical, biological, and **nuclear weapons**, he has repeatedly refused to comply with UN arms inspection requirements. As a result, he faced new rounds of air raids by the United States and Britian in the winter of 1998 and on into 1999.

Husserl, Edmund (1859–1938) German philosopher. He was the founder of phenomenology, which seeks to analyze consciousness, and moved in later works toward an idealist position. Teaching at Halle, Göttingen, and Freiberg, he influenced the existentialists. Works include *Logical Investigations* (1900-01), *Ideas* (1913), and *Cartesian Meditations* (1931).

Huston, John (1906–87) American film director. The son of Canadian-born American actor Walter Huston (1884–1950), he was born in Nevada, Mo., and was an actor, writer, and cavalryman in Mexico before directing his first film, *The Maltese Falcon* (1941), now considered a classic *noir* mystery. During **World War II**, he served in the U.S. Army and directed documentaries. Returning to Hollywood after the war, he directed several lauded films, including *The Treasure of Sierra Madre* (1948, Academy Award for best director); *The African Queen* (1952), *The Misfits* (1961), *The Man Who Would Be King* (1975), and *Prizzi's*

Honor (1985). He is remembered for his ability to convey moral ambiguity and the conflict and cameraderie of adventure. His daughter is actress Anjelica Huston (1952–).

Huxley, Aldous [Leonard] (1894–1963) British writer. The grandson of 19th century British biologist T. H. Huxley, he published his first novel, *Crome Yellow*, in 1923. His best-known novel is *Brave New World*, a dark, satirical vision of 25th-century life. The author of several other works, including the novel *Point Counter Point* (1928), he also wrote widely in the genres of short stories and essays.

I

Ibn Saud or **Abd al-Aziz ibn Saud** (c. 1880–1953) Saudi king (1932–53). The founder of Saudi Arabia, he was the son of the sultan of Najd, who was driven into exile by rivals. Beginning in 1902 with the capture of Riyadh, Ibn Saud reconquered the lands to which he laid ancestral claim. He proclaimed himself leader of the Wahabi, a puritanical Islamic sect, and conquered the Hejaz (1924–26). In 1929 he defeated the Ikhwan, an ascetic warrior group he had founded but that had gotten out of his control. In 1932 he unified Najd and Hejaz as Saudi Arabia. In 1933 he granted a prospecting concession to a U.S. oil company; the discovery of oil in 1936 guaranteed his country a longterm source of wealth. Ibn Saud put in place a nationalistic, stable form of government based on the *sharia*, or Islamic law.

Ionesco, Eugène (1909–94) Romanian-born French dramatist. Settling in Paris after **World War II**, he pioneered the Theater of the Absurd with his first play, *The Bald Soprano* (1950). This and subsequent works, including *The Lesson* (1951) and *Amédée* (1954), emphasized alienation and the meaninglessness of language; *Rhinoceros* (1959) was a political satire. Other plays include *Exit the King* (1962) and *Man with Bags* (1975). He became a chevalier of the Legion of Honor in 1970.

Iqbal, Sir Muhammad (1877–1938) Indian poet, philosopher, politician, and lawyer. Born in Sialkot, Punjab, India (now Pakistan), he studied at Government College, Lahore (where he later taught), Cambridge, and the University of Munich. He was elected to the Punjab provincial legislature in 1927 and was president of the **Muslim League** in 1930. He outlined his views on Islamic renewal and reconciliation with the modern world in the lecture series *The Reconstruction of Religious Thought in Islam* (1928–29). In 1930, he called for the creation of a homeland for Indian Muslims, a vision realized as Pakistan after his death. Influential as a thinker, he was also widely read as a poet in Urdu and Persian; his poems include "Secrets of the Self" (1915) and "The Song of Eternity" (1932). He was knighted in 1922.

J

Jackson, Jesse [Louis] (1941–) American civil rights activist. Born in Greenville, N.C., he attended the Agricultural and Technical College of North Carolina and Chicago Theological Seminary. In the Southern Christian Leadership Conference (SCLC) and his own organization People United to Save Humanity (PUSH), he has led drives for equal housing and education for African-Americans. Notable for his controversial oratory and relentless pursuit of racial equality, he ran in the Democratic presidential primaries of 1984 and 1988, gaining enough votes to exercise strong influence in the party.

Jackson, Michael (1958–) American singer and songwriter. In the 1970s he performed with his brothers as the youngest member of the pop group the Jackson Five. Working solo, he became the best-selling pop artist of the 1980s: his album *Thriller* won an unprecedented eight Grammy Awards and became the best-selling album in history up to that time. His popularity was accompanied by media interest in his private eccentricities, notably his use of cosmetic surgery to change his appearance.

James, Henry (1843–1916) American writer. Born to a distinguished family, brother of American philosopher **William James**, he was a dominant writer across two centuries, renowned for dense, well-observed works. In 1876 he moved to England where he lived for the rest of his life. Among notable 19th-century titles are *The Portrait of a Lady* (1881), *What Maisie Knew* (1897), and *The Turn of the Screw* (1898). To some critics, he created his most mature, accomplished works in the 20th century. Notable later titles include novels *The Wings of the Dove* (1902), *The Ambassadors* (1903), and *The Golden Bowl* (1904) and short stories "The Beast in the Jungle" (1903) and "The Jolly Corner" (1908). In 1904 to 1905 he visited the U.S., setting up publication of the New York editions of his works (1907–09). Prefaces to these editions, which present his principal literary theories, are collected in *The Art of the Novel* (1934). He became a British subject in 1915.

James, William (1842–1910) American philosopher and psychologist. The brother of novelist **Henry James**, he earned his M.D. at Harvard (1869), where he taught from 1872. In philosophy, he was a founder of pragmatism; he also contributed to the disciplines of psychology and the study of religion. Works include *The Varieties of Religious Experience* (1902) and *Pragmatism* (1907).

Jaspers, Karl [Theodor] (1883–1969) German psychiatrist and philosopher. A founder of **existentialism**, he moved from psychiatry to philosophy in his book *Psychology of World Views* (1919). His emphasis on human freedom and transcendence and opposition to despotism, as in *Philosophie* (1932) and *Man and the Modern World* (1933), prompted the Nazis to bar him from teaching after 1937. Following the war, he joined the University of Basel, Switzerland (1948).

Jaurès, Jean[-Joseph-Marie-Auguste] (1859–1914) French politician and writer. He entered the chamber of deputies in 1885 and became an outspoken Socialist, communicating through such journals as *L'Humanité*, which he co-founded (with **Aristide Briand**, 1904) and edited (until 1914). An opponent of nationalism, he advocated world peace and peaceful revolution toward economic equality. He sought to reconcile Marxist materialism and his own individualism in such works as *Histoire socialiste de la révolution française* (1901–07). He was a founder of the unified French Socialist Party (1905). On the eve of **World War I**, he urged arbitration rather than war and was assassinated.

Jiang Jie-shi See **Chiang Kai-shek**.

Jiang Zemin or **Chiang Tse-min** (1926–) Chinese politician. He joined the Chinese Communist Party in 1946. An electrical engineer and government official, he was purged in the **Cultural Revolution** but rehabilitated as a protégé of **Deng Xiaoping**. Rising to power after **Mao Zedong**'s death, he served as minister for electronic industries and mayor of Shanghai during the 1980s. In 1989, following the **Tiananmen Square** massacre, he was elected general secretary as a compromise candidate acceptable to the party's different factions. He was then chosen chairman of the Central Military Commission (1989) and president (1993). As holder of the country's three most powerful positions, he became China's preeminent leader upon Deng's death in 1997. As such, he presided over the return of Hong Kong from Britain to China (1997) and moved to privatize state-owned industries.

Jinnah, Mohammed Ali (1876–1948) Indian politician, known as Quaid-i-Azam ("Great Leader"). Born in Karachi, India (now Pakistan), he studied law in England and began participating in the Indian National Congress in 1906. He later negotiated the Lucknow Pact between the Congress and the Muslim League (1916) and was a member of the Imperial Legislative Council (1910–19). Dedicated to independence from Britain, he nonetheless opposed the noncooperation movement of **Mohandas Gandhi**. His early belief in Hindu-Muslim unity changed to a demand for a separate Muslim nation, a stance articulated in the Lahore Resolution of 1940. He headed the Muslim League from 1934 to 1948 and is regarded as the founder of Pakistan. He was Pakistan's first governor-general (1947–48).

Joffre, Joseph-Jacques-Césaire (1852–1931) French soldier. A general since 1902, he became the commander in chief of French armies in 1914, at the start of **World War I**; later his command expanded to Allied armies (see **Allied Powers**) in France. He helped achieve the victory in the Battle of the Marne (1914), which stopped the German advance on Paris, but was forced out of command after the Germans nearly captured Verdun (1916).

John XXIII (1881–1963) Pope (1958–63). Born Angelo Giuseppe Roncalli in Italy, he was ordained in 1904 and became a papal diplomat (1925–44) and papal nuncio to France (1944–53). He was named cardinal and patriarch of Venice in 1953. As pope, he was beloved for his humanity, vision, and willingness to consider new approaches. He revitalized the church by convening **Vatican II** (1962), which modernized age-old traditions. He promoted peace and social welfare, notably in the encyclicals *Pacem in Terris* and *Mater et Magistra*, and encouraged ecumenical dialogue.

John Paul I (1912–78) Pope (1978). Born Albino Luciani in Italy, he was patriarch of Venice (1969–78) and was made a cardinal in 1973. He died just one month into his papacy.

John Paul II (1920–) Pope (1978–). Born Karol Jozef Wojtyla in Wadowice, Poland, he was an underground resister during the German occupation in **World War II**. He was ordained in 1946, made a bishop in 1958, and appointed archbishop (later cardinal) of Krakow in 1964. In 1978 John Paul II became the first non-Italian to be elected pope since the Dutch Adrian VI (1522–23). John Paul II emphasized the international aspect of Catholicism through his numerous trips, visiting 50 countries in his first 10 years as pope. Although committed to the mandates of the **Second Vatican Council** (which he attended from 1962 to 1965), he took conservative stands on many issues of theology and morality. His appointments to the College of Cardinals favored conservatives but expanded international representation. He survived an assassination attempt in 1981.

Johnson, James Weldon (1871–1938) American writer and lawyer. A leading advocate for African-Americans, he cofounded the **National Association for the Advancement of Colored People** and was secretary from 1916 to 1930. His works celebrating black life include the anonymously published novel *The Autobiography of an Ex-Colored Man* (1912) and poetry collection *God's Trombones* (1927). He also edited *The Book of Negro Poetry* (1922) and wrote an autobiography, *Along This Way* (1933). From 1906 to 1912 he served as American consul in Venezuela and Nicaragua.

Johnson, Lyndon Baines (1908–73) Thirty-sixth U.S. president (1963–69). Born near Stonewall, Tex., he taught school before serving in the U.S. House of Representatives (1937–49), his terms marked by his strong support of **New Deal** programs. He also served in the navy (1941–42) during **World War II**, until congressmen were recalled to the U.S. by President **Franklin D. Roosevelt**. Elected to the U.S. Senate (1949–61), he became Democratic whip (1951) and minority leader (1953). As majority leader from 1955, he championed passage of the civil rights acts of 1957 and 1960. Elected vice president under President **John F. Kennedy** in 1960, he was named president after Kennedy's assassination in 1963 and re-elected by a landslide in 1964 against Republican Barry Goldwater (1909–98). Johnson's administration, called the "**Great Society**," was marked by landmark domestic programs, including Medicare, national health care for the elderly, and passage of social welfare legislation, including the Civil Rights Act (1964) and Voting Rights Act (1965). Concurrently he escalated the conflict in Vietnam into a war so divisive to the country that he declined to run for reelection in 1968. Retiring to Texas, he spent his last years writing his memoirs.

Jordan, Barbara [Charline] (1936–96) American politician. Born in Houston, Tex., she attended Boston University Law School and served in the Texas Senate from 1967 to 1972, the first African-American woman to win a seat in the Texas Senate. In the U.S. House of Representatives from 1973 to 1979, she was a member of the Judiciary Committee investigating President **Richard Nixon**, gaining national attention for her eloquent oratory.

Jordan, Michael [Jeffrey] (1963–) American athlete. Widely considered the greatest all-around basketball player in the history of the game, he led the University of North Carolina to a National Collegiate Athletic Association Division I championship in 1982. Playing with the Chicago Bulls from the start of his National Basketball Association (NBA) career (1984), he led his team to six championships and was named Most Valuable Player five times. He set numerous scoring records, including most points in a playoff game (63 points against the Boston Celtics, 1986). He played for U.S. teams in two Olympics competitions (1984, 1992), both times taking the gold medal. He retired from basketball in 1993 to become a minor-league baseball player, only to return to the Bulls in 1995 to reenergize the sport with his scoring and defense. Jordan retired from basketball for good in 1999.

Joyce, James [Augustine] (1882–1941) Irish writer. Born in Dublin, he was educated at Jesuit schools and University College, Dublin. He left Ireland in 1902, living afterward in Italy, Switzerland, and France but writing all his life on Irish themes. His first book of fiction was the short-story collection *Dubliners* (1914), followed by the autobiographical novel *A Portrait of the Artist as a Young Man* (1916). With his masterpiece *Ulysses* (1922), he combined stream-of-consciousness techniques with inventive wordplay and allusion; its account of an ordinary day in Dublin resonates with themes and imagery from Homer's *Odyssey*. Controversial for its profanity and sexual content, *Ulysses* was banned from publication in the U.S. until 1933. Joyce's *Finnegans Wake* (1939) was an even more daring, seemingly incomprehensible, stream-of-consciousness narrative. Joyce also wrote plays (notably *Exiles*, 1918) and poetry (*Chamber Music*, 1907). He married Nora Barnacle, whom he met on June 16, 1904, the day on which the action of *Ulysses* is set (known as "Bloomsday" for the novel's hero, Leopold Bloom). He died in Zürich. One of the century's greatest novelists, he has elicited endless critical interpretation.

Juan Carlos (1938–) Spanish king (1975–). The grandson of King Alfonso XIII, he was born in Rome and was named by Franco as his successor. He received commissions in all three Spanish armed forces and married Princess Sophia (1938–) of Greece. Juan Carlos presided skillfully over Spain's transition from dictatorship to democracy. He opposed an attempted coup in 1981.

Jung, Carl Gustav (1875–1961) Swiss psychiatrist. He qualified in **medicine** at the University of Basle (1900) and later taught at the Universities of Zürich (1905–13) and Basle (1943–61). The founder of analytical psychology, he was at first a friend and associate of **Sigmund Freud**, whom he met in 1907. Jung became first president of the International Psychoanalytic Association (1911–12). In 1912 Jung and Freud split over Jung's denial of the sexual basis of neuroses. Jung began to describe his own theories in *Psychology of the Unconscious* (1913). Jung proposed the existence of a collective unconscious containing archetypes and introduced the concepts of extroversion and introversion. Other works include *Psychological Types* (1923).

K

Kafka, Franz (1883–1924) Austrian writer. Born in Prague, he worked for an insurance company there (1908–22) while writing his strange, nightmarish fiction, rife with absurdity and themes of modern alienation, anxiety, and guilt. He published little during his lifetime, but after his death from tuberculosis, his friend and fellow writer Max Brod (1884–1968) published his manuscripts, ignoring Kafka's instructions to destroy them. By the 1950s, Kafka's reputation as a major German writer had been established. Works include the story "The Metamorphosis" (1915), and the novels *The Trial* (1925) and *The Castle* (1926).

Kahlo, Frida (1907–54) Mexican artist. Born Magdalena Carmen Frida Kahlo Calderónin Coyoacán, she began painting as a teenager, while recuperating from a motor vehicle accident, and exhibited seriously from 1938. Her vivid, stylized paintings include *Frame* (1938), *The Two Fridas* (1939), and *The Broken Column* (1944). She was twice married to painter **Diego Rivera**, subject of her *Portrait of Diego* (1937).

Kaige, Chen See **Chen Kaige**.

Kaiser Wilhelm See **William II**.

Kamenev, Lev Borisovich (1883–1936) Russian politician. His original surname was Rosenfeld. Banished to Siberia (1915–17) for agitating against **World War I**, he returned after the **Russian Revolution of 1917** to join the first Politburo of the Communist Party. After **V. I. Lenin**'s death in 1924, he joined in the triumvirate with **Joseph Stalin** and **Grigory Zinoviev**, but Stalin's growing power forced him and Zinoviev into the Left Opposition. In 1927 Kamenev was expelled from the Central Committee. In the first show trial of the **Great Purges** in 1936, he was convicted of treason and shot.

Kandinsky, Wassily (1866–1944) Russian painter and theorist. He was considered a pioneering force behind **abstract art**. Encountering French impressionist works exhibited in Moscow, he left an academic career teaching law to study painting. Early in the 20th century, he developed theories on pure color and nonrepresentational painting; his work *Concerning the Spiritual in Art* (1912) discussed psychological effects of color. From 1911 to 1914, he and others led the German expressionist movement Blaue Reiter. He was a member of the Bauhaus faculty from 1922 to 1933. From the 1920s he employed more geographical representation in his works; his Bauhaus pamphlet *Point, Line and Surface* (1926) discusses abstract pictorial composition.

Kaunda, Kenneth David (1924–) Zambian politician. Born in Northern Rhodesia (now Zambia), he led the nationalist movement there from the 1950s, when he created the Zambian African National Congress. His practice of civil disobedience against the British resulted in imprisonment, but after he was freed in 1960, the government negotiated independence terms with him and his United National Independence Party. In 1964 he became the first president of independent Zambia. He was an influential international leader, supporting the Zimbabwean independence movement in Rhodesia. He grew increasingly authoritarian in the 1970s but eventually accepted multiparty elections, one of which his party lost in 1991, forcing him out of office.

Kazantzakis, Nikos (1883–1957) Greek writer. Born in Crete and trained in law, he explored the basic human struggle of body and spirit in novels *Zorba the Greek* (1946, later the basis for the Broadway play), *The Greek Passion* (1951), *The Last Temptation of Christ* (1951), and the epic poem *The Odyssey: A Modern Sequel* (1938). His autobiography is *Report to Greco* (1961).

Keaton, Buster (1895–1966) American actor, director, and producer. Born in Piqua, Kans., to a family of medicine show players, he led the act to vaudeville success with his acrobatic and comedic talents. From 1917 he appeared in films, first with American comedian Roscoe "Fatty" Arbuckle (1887–1933) and later on his own. He developed his "stone face" persona in several films in the 1920s, notably *One Week* (1920), *Cops* (1922), *Sherlock, Jr.* (1924), *The General* (1927), *College* (1927), and *Steamboat Bill, Jr.* (1928). After leaving his production company, his career diminished. He was married to American film actress Natalie Talmadge (1898-1969).

Keller, Helen [Adams] (1880–1968) American author and lecturer. Born in Tuscumbia, Ala., she was rendered blind and deaf by scarlet fever at 19 months. From 1887 she was educated by Anne Sullivan Macy, who taught her to communicate through the manual alphabet and lip-touch reading. Keller graduated from Radcliffe College with honors in 1904 and devoted her life to increasing awareness of blindness and to raising funds, notably for the American Foundation for the Blind. Macy became a lifelong companion until her death in 1936.

Kelly, Gene (1912–96) American dancer. Born Eugene Curran Kelly, he was a star of Hollywood musicals who helped shape the genre with innovative dance numbers that he performed and choreographed. He is best known for *Singin' in the Rain* (1952), one of three films he co-directed with American director Stanley Donen (1924–). Other films include *Cover Girl* (1944), *On the Town* (1949), and *An American in Paris* (1951). He acted in and directed several non-musical films as well. He received an honorary Academy Award in 1951.

Kemal, Mustafa See **Atatürk, Kemal.**

Kennedy, John Fitzgerald (1917–63) Thirty-fifth U.S. president (1961–63). Son of banker and tycoon Joseph P. Kennedy (1888–1969), he graduated from Harvard in 1940 and served in the U.S. Navy as a PT boat commander during **World War II**. He was decorated for saving his crew following an attack in 1943. After the war, he was elected as a Democrat to the U.S. House of Representatives for Massachusetts (1947–53), and later to the U.S. Senate (1953–61). His book *Profiles in Courage* (1956) won the Pulitzer Prize. In a narrow election in 1960, he defeated Republican candidate **Richard Nixon**, becoming the youngest man and first Roman Catholic elected president. His domestic policy, the New Frontier, called for federal funds for education, medical care for the elderly, and support of civil rights, advanced in part by brother and attorney general Robert Kennedy (1925-68, also assassinated). International events included the calamitous **Bay of Pigs Invasion** in

Cuba (1961) and the **Cuban Missile Crisis,** in which he ordered the blockade of Cuba to force removal of Soviet missiles (1962). The latter crisis precipitated the signing of a U.S.–**Soviet** limited nuclear test-ban treaty in 1963. He also increased the number of advisers to South Vietnam, stepping up the **Vietnam War.** Adding style and luster to the White House was his wife Jackie (Jacqueline Kennedy Onassis, 1929–94). On November 22, 1963, Kennedy was assassinated in a motorcade in Dallas, Tex. Suspect Lee Harvey Oswald (1939–63) was apprehended but killed two days later by Jack Ruby (1911–67). The president's death was marked by a period of national mourning in the U.S. He is remembered for the youthful energy and promise he brought to the presidency, a time informally known as the Camelot years.

Kenyatta, Jomo (c. 1894–1978) Kenyan politician. A member of the Kikuyu people of the former British East Africa, he was born Johnstone Kamau but changed his name to Jomo Kenyatta in the 1920s. He studied anthropology at the London School of Economics, using scholarship to support his nationalist views. He was active in pan-Africanist and Kenyan nationalist movements, becoming president of the Kenya African Union in 1947. He was imprisoned (1953–61) on charges of leading the **Mau Mau Uprising** but went on to negotiate Kenya's independence, which was realized in 1963. As Kenya's first prime minister (1963-64) and first president (1964–78), he became increasingly authoritarian, imprisoning most opponents. He died in office.

Kerensky, Aleksandr Fyodorovich (1881–1970) Russian revolutionary. A member of the Socialist Revolutionary Party from about 1905, he became part of the provisional government that followed the **Russian Revolution of February 1917.** He was made prime minister in July, but was overthrown by the **Bolsheviks** in November for his failure to improve economic conditions or end Russian involvement in **World War I.** He fled to France and, in 1940, the U.S.

Kern, Jerome [David] (1885–1945) American composer. Born in New York City, he shaped the modern stage musical through works including *Show Boat* (1927, with Oscar Hammerstein II) and *Roberta* (1933). He also composed film scores. Well-known songs include "Ol' Man River," "A Fine Romance," and "Smoke Gets in Your Eyes."

Keynes, John Maynard, first baron Keynes of Tilton (1883–1946) British economist. He was educated at Cambridge, where he later taught. In 1919 he represented the Treasury at the **Paris Peace Conference** and argued against imposing high **reparations** on Germany in *Economic Consequences of the Peace* (1919). A government adviser during the **Great Depression,** he influenced several nations, including the U.S., to create jobs through spending on public works. His major work, *The General Theory of Employment, Interest, and Money* (1936), counters classical free-market economics by advocating government intervention and deficit spending as remedies for recession. He was the chief British representative at the **Bretton Woods Conference** in 1944, which established the **International Monetary Fund.** He was made a peer in 1942.

Khadafy, Muammar See **Qaddafi, Muammar al-**

Khomeini, Ayatollah Ruholla (1900–89) Iranian political and religious leader. Born in Khomein as Ruhollah Musawi, he took the name Khomeini, from his hometown, Khomein, in 1930. Becoming an ayatollah (a Shi'ite Muslim religious leader) like his father, he taught in the theological school in Qom. Following arrest in 1963 for criticizing **Mohammad Reza Pahlavi,** he was forced into exile in Iraq and France until 1979, when he returned to lead the Islamic Revolution following the shah's overthrow. Until his death, Khomeini exercised autocratic power over the Islamic Republic. He led a repressive, intolerant regime rooted in Islamic fundamentalism. He received international criticism for supporting the taking of hostages at the U.S. Embassy in Tehran in 1979. In 1989 he called for the killing of British author **Salman Rushdie** for alleged blasphemy. A long war with Iraq (1980–88) ended shortly before Khomeini's death.

Khrushchev, Nikita Sergeyevich (1894–1971) Soviet politician. Of Ukrainian background, he joined the Communist Party in 1918 and was elected a full member of its Central Committee in 1934. He served **Joseph Stalin** in purging the Ukrainian Communist Party and was a lieutenant general in **World War II**. He won the power struggle after Stalin's death in 1953, becoming first secretary of the party (1953–64) and premier (1958–64). In 1956 he denounced Stalin and launched the destalinization program, attempting to ease domestic and international tensions. He also crushed an uprising in Hungary (1956) and, in 1960, cancelled a summit conference with U.S. president **Dwight D. Eisenhower** after the **U-2 incident**. In 1962 U.S. president **John Fitzgerald Kennedy** forced him to back down in the **Cuban Missile Crisis**; that perceived failure of nerve, coupled with agricultural problems and a rift with China, led to his ouster in 1964.

Kim Il Sung (1912–94) Korean political leader. Born Kim Song Ju, he adopted a heroic Korean name while fighting Japanese control of Korea in the 1930s. A staunch Communist closely tied to Soviet powers, he served as first premier of North Korea, or the Democratic People's Republic of Korea (1948–72). During his tenure he triggered the **Korean War** through a 1950 invasion of South Korea. In 1972 he became North Korea's first president.

Kimbangu, Simon (1889–1951) Congolese religious leader. A migrant laborer educated by the Baptists, he declared himself the *Gounza* (Swahili for *Messiah*) in 1921 and began preaching and healing. Later that year, he was arrested for sedition by the colonial Belgian government and imprisoned for life. He is revered as the founder of the nationalist, Christian separatist movement called Kimbanguism or Gounzism, which was the first African church to attain full membership in the World Council of Churches (1969).

King, Billie Jean [Moffitt] (1943–) American athlete. Born in Long Beach, Calif., she competed professionally from 1968 and won multiple championships, including 20 Wimbledon titles (six singles, 10 doubles, and four mixed doubles between 1966 and 1975). Her abilities and advocacy, including a 1973 "battle of the sexes" victory over American tennis champion Bobby Riggs (1918–95), improved the status of women's sports. She retired in 1983.

King, Martin Luther, Jr. (1929–68) American civil rights leader and clergyman. Born in Atlanta, Ga., he was ordained a Baptist minister in 1947 and in 1955 received a Ph.D. from Boston University. As pastor of a Baptist church in Montgomery, Ala., he became the leader of a bus boycott demanding desegregation of blacks and whites on city bus lines (1955–56). After achieving victory in that campaign, King organized the Southern Christian Leadership Conference (1957), becoming the national leader of the African-American **civil rights movement**. An eloquent orator, he firmly advocated nonviolent resistance, combining ideas from **Mohandas Gandhi** and Christian teaching. Frequently jailed, his home bombed, he led demonstrations and marches in such cities as Birmingham, Ala., and outlined his views in such works as "Letter from Birmingham Jail" (1963). He helped to organize the 1963 March on Washington, at which event he delivered his "I Have a Dream" speech. At the peak of his influence in 1964, he received the Nobel Peace Prize, but King's nonviolence was increasingly criticized at home by militant African-American leaders who felt the pace of change was too slow. King expanded his range of issues to include protests against poverty and the **Vietnam War**. He was assassinated in Memphis, Tenn.; James Earl Ray (1928–98) was convicted of the crime. King's birthday was later made a national holiday.

King, Stephen (1947–) American writer. Spectacularly popular author of horror novels, including *Carrie* (1974) and *The Shining* (1977), and short fiction, as in the collection *Skeleton Crew* (1985). Sometimes writing under the name Richard Bachman, he has been a pioneeer in publishing books electronically.

King, William Lyon Mackenzie (1874–1950) Canadian politician. Educated at Harvard and the University of Chicago, he was leader of the Liberal Party from 1919 to 1948, and served in Parliament (1908–11, 1919–48), much of that time as prime minister (1921–30, 1935–48). His tenure was marked by his support of national independence and harmony between French and English peoples in the country.

Kipling, Rudyard (1865–1936) British writer. Born in India of English parents, he established himself in several genres through poetry collections *Departmental Ditties* (1886) and *Barrack-Room Ballads* (which included "Gunga Din" and "Mandalay," 1892); short-story collections such as *Soldiers Three* (1888); the novel *The Light That Failed* (1890); and children's books *The Jungle Book* (1894), *Captains Courageous* (1897), and *Kim* (1901). In many works, he romanticized British colonial life; his 1899 poem "The White Man's Burden" reflected then-popular beliefs toward heathen nonwhites. In 1907 he became the first English writer to receive the Nobel Prize for literature. His later works included the children's book *Just So Stories* (1902) and his unfinished autobiography *Something of Myself* (1937).

Kirov, Sergey Mironovich (1888–1934) Russian politician. His original surname was Kostrikov. He helped wage war on counterrevolutionary forces after the **Russian Revolution** (1917–20) and became a top aide to **Joseph Stalin**. His assassination sparked Stalin's **Great Purges** (1934–38).

Kissinger, Henry A[lfred] (1923–) American diplomat. Born in Germany, he immigrated to the U.S. with his family in 1938 to escape Nazi persecution (citizen in 1943) and attended City College, New York City, and Harvard, where he became a professor in 1962. As national security adviser (1969–75) and U.S. secretary of state (1973–77) under Presidents **Richard Nixon** and **Gerald Ford**, he directed foreign policy, overseeing the U.S. visit to China and helping negotiate the end of the 1973 **Arab-Israeli War**. He was awarded the Nobel Peace Prize in 1973 (with North Vietnamese politician Le Duc Tho) for efforts to end the **Vietnam War**. In 1977 he was named professor at Georgetown University.

Kitchener, Horatio Herbert, first earl Kitchener of Khartoum and of Broome (1850–1916) British soldier and statesman. Serving in the mideast from 1874, he led British and Egyptian forces to victory at Omdurman (1898), leading to the reoccupation of Khartoum. Commander in chief (1900) during the **Boer War**, he engaged in a harsh two-year campaign against Boer forces, resulting in Boer capitulation in 1902. His measures, including civilian internment and destruction of homesteads, were widely criticized. Commander in chief in India (1902–29), and secretary of state for war and later field marshal (1914) during **World War I**, he oversaw the massive growth of the British army. He was named an earl in 1914. He died by drowning when his ship was struck by a German mine.

Klee, Paul (1879–1940) Swiss artist. Living in Germany from 1906, he cofounded the Blaue Reiter group (1912) and taught at the Bauhaus (1921–31). Nazi opposition forced him to flee to Switzerland in 1933. His witty, whimsical paintings embodied his theories on abstraction and color use; he also executed drawings and prints. Works include *Twittering Machine* (1922) and *Revolutions of the Viaducts* (1937). He published *Pedagogical Sketchbooks* (1925).

Klimt, Gustav (1862–1918) Austrian artist. Klimt's earliest works were mainly architectural decorations, but he became famed for his ornate, highly detailed, sensual paintings, which are seen as some of the best examples of art noveau. His elaborate murals, *Philosophy*, *Medicine*, and *Jurisprudence* (1900–02) prompted many critics of the time to condem his work for being pornographic and too vague. Other important work includes *Frau Frista Reidler* (1906) and *The Kiss* (1907–08).

Knopf, Alfred A. (1892–1984) American publisher. Born in New York, he cofounded Alfred A. Knopf, Inc. in 1915. Known for literary excellence, Knopf has published works by over 15 Nobel Prize winners and over 25 Pulitzer Prize winners. It was acquired by Random House in 1960 but retained independence.

Kobayashi Takiji (1903–33) Japanese writer. A leader of the proletarian literary movement, he wrote the novels *The Fifteenth of March* (1928) and *Kanikosen* (*The Factory Ship*, 1929), both of which urge collective action against Japan's oppressive capitalist rulers. He was arrested and tortured to death.

Koestler, Arthur (1905–83) Hungarian-born British writer. A Communist in the 1930s, he grew disillusioned with Joseph Stalin's Russia and became a spokesperson for the non-Communist Left. He is known for journalism, novels (such as *Darkness at Noon*, 1941), and essays (such as "The Ghost in the Machine," 1968).

Kohl, Helmut (1930–) German politician. A member of the Christian Democratic Party from 1947, he served on the state legislature of Rhineland-Palatinate from 1959 to 1976. Leading opposition forces in the Bundestag, he replaced Social Democrat **Helmut Schmidt** as chancellor of West Germany in 1982. He served as chancellor until 1990, when he became chancellor of the reunified Germany. Absorption of the weak eastern German economy proved a strain on the nation as a whole. After several years of high unemployment, Kohl's party was defeated in the 1998 elections, ending his 16 years in office.

Kokoschka, Oskar (1886–1980) Austrian artist and writer. Influenced by Austrian art nouveau painter **Gustav Klimt**, he is known for his revealing expressionist portraits, landscapes, and allegorical compositions. Works include *Portrait of Auguste Forrel* (1910) and *Jerusalem* (1929–30), and the *Prometheus* ceiling at Princes Gate in London (1950). His work condemned by the Nazis, he fled to London in 1938, resettling in Switzerland in 1953. He also wrote plays and an autobiography (1971).

Kollontay, Aleksandra Mikhaylovna (1872–1952) Soviet revolutionary and politician. Her maiden name was Domontovich. She joined the Bolshevik Party (see **Bolshekviks**) in 1915 and, with the **Russian Revolution** of November 1917, became the only woman in **V. I. Lenin**'s government. As commissar of public welfare and director of the Women's Department of the party, she urged radical social changes, including communal living and free love, and introduced laws to permit easy divorce and abortion. Her disagreements with Lenin, as a member of the Workers' Opposition group within the Bolshevik Party, got her banished from domestic politics, and she became minister to Norway (1923–25, 1927–30) and Mexico (1926–27) and minister (1930–43) and ambassador (1943–45) to Sweden. She was the first woman to hold the diplomatic ranks of minister and ambassador. Her ideas and accomplishments inspired many Western feminists.

Kosygin, Aleksey Nikolayevich (1904–80) Soviet politician. Born in St. Petersburg, he joined the Communist Party in 1927, became a member of the Central Committee (1939), and was named first deputy chairman of the **U.S.S.R.** Council of Ministers (1960). In 1964 he followed **Nikita Khrushchev** as premier, serving until ill health forced his retirement (1980). During his tenure, he shared power with **Leonid Brezhnev.**

Krupp, Gustav von Bohlen und Halbach (1870–1950) and **Krupp, Alfried Krupp von Bohlen und Halbach** (1907–67) German businessmen. Son-in-law of 19th-century armament manufacturer Friedrich Alfred Krupp (1854–1902), Gustav Krupp (who took the family name) built the conglomerate into the center of the Nazi defense arsenal during the 1930s and into **World War II**. He also helped fund the Nazis' 1933 election. From 1943, son Alfried ran the business until war's end, seizing factories in German-occupied lands and using **concentration camp** prisoners as laborers. Convicted of war crimes in 1948, Alfried was released from prison in 1951 and retook control of the business, which remained in family control until 1968.

Kubrick, Stanley (1928–99) American film director. Born in the Bronx, N.Y., he turned from a career as a still photographer to become an austere, meticulous creator of visually stunning films. Living and working in Britain since the 1960s, he usually produced and wrote his own films, which express a sardonic, often pessimistic view of human nature. Works include *Paths of Glory* (1957), *Dr. Strangelove* (1964), *2001: A Space Odyssey* (1968), *A Clockwork Orange* (1971), *Full Metal Jacket* (1987) and *Eyes Wide Shut* (1999).

Kun, Béla (1886–1937) Hungarian politician. In 1919 he succeeded Hungarian Count Karolyi and led the new government of Communists and Social Democrats, forming a Red Army that overtook Slovakia. A counterrevolution ensued and he was defeated with the aid of a Romanian army. Fleeing to **Russia** in 1920, he became a leader of the Third International, attempted further political foment in Western Europe, and died in the Stalinist purges.

Kundera, Milan (1929–) Czech writer. Born in Brno, he published several volumes of poetry but was barred by the government from further publication following his first novel *The Joke* (1967), about life in Czechoslovakia during the Stalinist era. Moving to France in 1975, he published widely, with works including the short-story collection *Laughable Loves* (1963) and novels *The Book of Laughter and Forgetting* (1980) and *The Unbearable Lightness of Being* (1984).

Kurosawa, Akira (1910–98) Japanese film director. Born in Tokyo, he worked with Japanese director Kajiro Yamamoto (1902–74) before directing his first film, *Judo Saga* (1943). His ability to convey universal themes beginning with *Drunken Angel* (1948) and *Rashomon* (1950, best foreign film Academy Award) brought international renown. His *Seven Samurai* (1954, best foreign film Academy Award) inspired the U.S. film *The Magnificent Seven* (1960). Other notable films include *Yojimbo* (1961), Shakespeare adaptations *Throne of Blood* (1957) and *Ran* (1985), and *Dersu Uzala* (1975, best foreign film Academy Award).

L

La Guardia, Fiorello H[enry] (1882–1947) American politician. Born in New York City, he served as a Republican member of the House of Representatives (1917–21 and 1923–33) but is best known for his three terms as mayor of New York (1934–45). Nicknamed "Little Flower," he was a spirited leader who fought city corruption, oversaw the 1938 revision of the city charter, and promoted slum clearance and urban planning programs. A New York City airport is named for him.

Laver, Rodney George (1938–) Australian athlete. He became the first two-time winner of the grand slam of tennis (Australian, British, French, and U.S. championships), with titles in 1962 and 1969. A four-time winner at Wimbledon, he is also known for becoming the first professional tennis player to make more than $1 million.

Law, Andrew Bonar (1858–1923) British politician. Born in Canada and raised in Scotland, he was an M.P. from 1900. As chancellor of the exchequer (1916–19), he introduced National Savings. Succeeding **Arthur Balfour** as **Conservative Party** leader in 1911, he tried to unite the party around opposition to Irish home rule. He briefly became prime minister (1922–23).

Lawrence, D[avid] H[erbert] (1885–1930) British writer. He became known for works attacking the mechanistic modern age and celebrating nature and sexual union, including *Sons and Lovers* (1913), *The Rainbow* (1915), and *Women in Love* (1920). Sexually explicit, the works were often banned, the most long-lived ban for *Lady Chatterly's Lover* (1928). Later novels such as *The Plumed Serpent* (1926) reflect his interest in the ideas of Friedrich Nietzsche. He is also noted for his plays (*David*, 1926), poetry (*Amores*, 1916), short-story collections (*England, My England*, 1922), and idiosyncratic literary criticism (*Studies in Classic American Literature*, 1923).

Lawrence, T[homas] E[dward] (1888–1935) British soldier and writer. Known as Lawrence of Arabia. During **World War I**, he turned from archaeology to serve with British military intelligence in Egypt. In 1916 he became an adviser to Prince Faisal (later **Faisal I**), who was uniting the Arabs in a revolt against the Ottoman Empire (1916). Famed for adopting the customs and dress of the Arabs, Lawrence became a leader of the revolt. His exploits, including the capture of Aqaba (1917) and the occupation of Damascus (1918), earned him promotion to lieutenant colonel in 1918. At the **Paris Peace Conference** and as a Colonial Office adviser (1921–22), he tried unsuccessfully to gain a fair settlement for the Arabs. Fleeing his celebrity status, he served as an enlisted man in the Royal Air Force (1922–35) under the assumed names J. H. Ross and T. E. Shaw. His major work, *The Seven Pillars of Wisdom* (1935; abbreviated edition *Revolt in the Desert*, 1925), recounts his Arabian experiences. He was killed in a motorcycle accident.

Leakey, Louis [Seymour Bazett] (1903–72) British anthropologist. Born in Kenya, the son of missionaries, he was educated at Cambridge University in England and became curator of Coryndon Museum, Nairobi, Kenya (1945–61). From 1959 to 1961, he and his wife, Mary Leakey (1913–) discovered hominid fossils at Olduvai Gorge, in what is now Tanzania, dating back 1.75 million years and establishing Africa as the birthplace of humanity. Their son Richard Leakey (1944–) has also made important discoveries in paleoanthropology and is an advocate of wildlife conservation.

Lean, Sir David (1908–91) British film director. Joining Gaumont Pictures in 1927, he worked his way up from teaboy to editor and director. He made film adaptations of works by **Noel Coward** (*Brief Encounter*, 1945) and 19th century British writer Charles Dickens (*Great Expectations*, 1946) but is best known for epics that balance human drama and momentous events in 20th-century history. These include *The Bridge on the River Kwai* (best picture Oscar, 1957), *Lawrence of Arabia* (best picture Oscar, 1962), and *Doctor Zhivago* (1965). His last film, *A Passage to India*, was an adaptation of the **E. M. Forster** novel. He coscripted and produced some of his films. He was knighted in 1984.

Le Corbusier (1887–1965) Swiss-born French architect, painter, and writer. Born Charles-Édouard Jeanneret-Gris, he was a major force in modern architecture and theory and urban planning. Notable designs include the villa in Vaucresson, France (1923), the chapel at Ronchamp (1950–55), and the Visual Arts Center, Harvard University (1961–62). Books include *Towards a New Architecture* (1923). His works were influenced by industrial design and experiments with glass, steel, and concrete.

Lee Kwan Yew (1923–) Singapore politician. A Cambridge-educated lawyer, he was the founder of the moderately leftist People's Action Party (1954). He became Singapore's first prime minister, a post he maintained for three decades (1959–90), even during Singapore's period as part of the Malaysian Federation (1963–65) and during its transition to republican government (1965). Blending welfare state policies with free enterprise, he encouraged foreign investment. Though criticized for repressing political dissent, he was respected for making Singapore's economy one of the strongest in Asia. After resigning from office, he became a senior minister.

Lenin, V[ladimir] I[lich] (1870–1924) Soviet revolutionary and politician. Born Vladimir Ilich Ulyanov in Simbirsk, he became a follower of German political philosopher Karl Marx (1818–83) in 1889, before graduating from the University of St. Petersburg with a degree in law (1891). In St. Petersburg from 1893, he was arrested for his Socialist activities (1895) and exiled to Siberia (1897–1900). During his exile, he adopted the name Lenin (from the Lena River) and wrote his economic study, *The Development of Capitalism in Russia* (1899). From 1900 to 1917, he lived principally in Western Europe. During this period, his pamphlets, including *What Is to Be Done?* (1902), and periodicals, including *Iskra* (The *Spark*), *Vperyod* (*Forward*), and *Pravda* (*Truth*), made him the major interpreter of the works of Marx for 20th-century Communists; his approach, emphasizing the role of a strong central party, became known as Marxism-Leninism. When the Socialists split at the Second Socialist Congress (1903), Lenin became the leader of the **Bolshevik** (as opposed to **Menshevik**) Party. In Russia briefly for the failed **1905 Revolution**, he returned for the successful **Russian Revolution in November 1917**, leading the **Bolsheviks** to overthrow **Aleksandr Kerensky**'s government (November 7–8). As chairman of the Council of People's Commissars, he exercised dictatorial power and established the Bolshevik Party's authority. He ended Russian involvement in **World War I** (1918), won a civil war with the White Army and fought off foreign intervention (1918–21), and founded the Communist **(Third) International** (1919). His radical Socialist reforms were modified by the New Economic Policy (1921). His body was preserved for decades in Red Square as an object of veneration.

Lennon, John [Winston] (1940–80) British musician and composer. Born in Liverpool, the singer, songwriter, and guitarist founded the Quarrymen, a skiffle group, in 1956, while still in high school. Singer, songwriter, and guitarist Paul McCartney (1942–) soon joined the band, which by 1962 had evolved into the rock group the Beatles. Its two other members were guitarist George Harrison (1943–) and drummer Ringo Starr (born Richard

Starkey, 1940); Stuart Sutcliffe (1940–) and Pete Best (1941–) had left the band. In 1963 the "Fab Four," as the group was popularly known, had a string of No. 1 hits in Britain, including "I Wanna Hold Your Hand"; in 1964 success came in the United States. Throughout the 1960s, the Beatles were phenomenally popular, dominating rock music worldwide and becoming symbols of the youth counterculture. Influenced by **Elvis Presley** and rhythm and blues, their music—most of it credited jointly to Lennon and McCartney—was marked by wit, lyricism, and a synthesis of styles. In addition to recording albums, they went on concert tours and made such films as *A Hard Day's Night* (1964). By the time the Beatles disbanded in 1970, they had created such hits as "Can't Buy Me Love," "Yesterday," and "Let It Be." Following the group's demise, credited in part to Lennon's well-publicized marriage to Yoko Ono (1933–), all four singers embarked on solo careers, with McCartney knighted in 1997. Lennon's post-Beatles music included the album *Imagine* (1971). Lennon was murdered by a deranged fan outside his residence in New York City.

Lessing, Doris [May] (1919–) Iranian-born British writer. Since the 1950s she has been acclaimed for her explorations of women's lives and world concerns. Her "Children of Violence" series, including *Martha Quest* (1952), *A Proper Marriage* (1954), *A Ripple from the Storm* (1958), and *The Four-Gated City* (1969), established her as a serious realistic novelist. Her 1962 novel *The Golden Notebook* (1962) became a feminist standard. Other notable works include *The Habit of Loving* (1958), *The Stories of Doris Lessing* (1978), and *The Sirian Experiments* (1981).

Levi, Primo (1919–87) Italian writer. Following internment as a Jew at the Nazi **concentration camp** Auschwitz, he published *If This Is a Man* (1947), about the experience. Other works further established him a spokesman of the Holocaust: *The Truce* (1963) and *The Drowned and the Saved* (1986), both about the moral struggle wrought by sustained dehumanization. *The Periodic Table* (1975), a series of philosophical explorations linking science and art, gained wide success. Haunted throughout his life by memories of Auschwitz, he died after a possibly suicidal fall.

Lévi-Strauss, Claude [Gustave] (1908–) Belgian-born French anthropologist. A major voice of structuralism, his works *The Elementary Structures of Kinship* (1949) and *Structural Anthropology* (2 vols., 1958, 1973) explore the relationships between elements of a cultural system built upon language (including art, religion, kinship, and myths), uncovering similarities among all human societies. Other notable works include *Tristes tropiques* (1955) and *The Savage Mind* (1962). His ideas have influenced linguistics and literary criticism.

Lewis, C[live] S[taples] (1898–1963) British scholar and writer. He taught English at Oxford (1925–54) and Cambridge (1954–63). His works included literary scholarship (e.g., *The Allegory of Love*, 1936), Christian apologetics (e.g., *Mere Christianity*, 1952), and science fiction and fantasy (e.g., the children's book series *The Chronicles of Narnia*, 1950–56).

Lewis, John Llewellyn (1880–1969) American labor leader. Beginning as a coal miner, he ascended to the position of president of the United Mine Workers (UMW) in 1920. Citing disagreements with the American Federation of Labor, he founded the Committee for Industrial Organization, renamed in 1938 the Congress of Industrial Organizations (CIO). He served as its president from 1938 to 1940. During the 1940s he led miners in several important strikes, remaining as president until resigning in 1960. He removed the UMW from the CIO in 1942.

Lewis, [Harry] Sinclair (1885–1951) American writer. Born in Sauk Centre, Minn., and a graduate of Yale (1908), he satirized small-town American mores in popular novels including *Main Street* (1920), *Babbitt* (1922), *Elmer Gantry* (1927), and *Dodsworth* (1929). He became the first American to win the Nobel Prize for literature (1930); he refused the Pulitzer Prize for *Arrowsmith* (1925). Other works include *It Can't Happen Here* (1935) and *Cass Timberlane* (1945). From 1928 to 1942 he was married to American journalist Dorothy Thompson (1894–1961).

Li Peng (1928–) Chinese politician. Orphaned when his father was executed by the **Guomindang**, he was adopted by **Zhou Enlai**. He joined the Communist Party in 1945. An engineer, he became minister for electricity supply in 1981. He joined the party's central committee (1982) and the Politburo (1985) and became prime minister in 1987. A conservative Maoist, he supported **Deng Xiaoping** in the **Tiananmen Square** massacre.

Lichtenstein, Roy (1923-97) American artist. Born in New York City, he held his first one-man New York show in 1962 and soon became a major force in the pop art movement. Known for his seemingly playful, ironic paintings inspired by comic strips and other commercial sources, he also created sculptures, often in brass. Notable works include *Wham!* (1963).

Lin Yutang (1895–1976) Chinese writer. Educated at Harvard and Leipzig Universities (Ph.D., Leipzig, 1923), he taught at Beijing National University and lived in the U.S. from 1936 to 1966. He popularized Chinese culture for Western readers in such books as *My Country and My People* (1935) and *The Chinese Way of Life* (1959). He also wrote novels, including *Moment in Peking* (1939), and translated and edited Chinese works.

Lindbergh, Charles [Augustus] (1902–74) American aviator. Born in Detroit, he was an airmail pilot before becoming the first person to make a solo transatlantic flight on May 20 and 21, 1927. The 33 ½-hour flight from Roosevelt Field, New York City, to Le Bourget Field, Paris, took place in the **airplane** *Spirit of St. Louis* (a monoplane) and made him a national hero. In 1929 he married Anne Morrow (1906–), later an author; in 1932 his son was kidnapped and found dead, resulting in a highly publicized trial. In several speeches, he promoted U.S. neutrality in **World War II**. He won a Pulitzer Prize for his 1953 autobiography, *The Spirit of St. Louis*.

Lippmann, Walter (1889–1974) American journalist. A graduate of Harvard (1910), he participated in the **Paris Peace Talks** (1918–19). He became a staff member of the New York City *World* (1921–31), then moved to the New York City *Herald Tribune* to write the highly influential column "Today and Tomorrow" (1931–1962). Read widely and respected by politicians for his astute analysis and restraint, he was one of the century's leading journalists. From 1962 to 1967, he continued his column at the *Washington Post*. Books include *Public Opinion* (1922) and *The Good Society* (1937). He was twice awarded the Pulitzer Prize (1958, 1962).

Litvinov, Maxim Maximovich (1876–1951) Russian revolutionary and diplomat. Born Meir Wallach. A **Bolshevik** since the 1903 Russian Socialist schism, he became commissar for foreign affairs (1930–39). In that role, he gained U.S. recognition of the **Soviet Union** and urged united action against the **Axis Powers**. He was ambassador to the U.S. (1941–43).

Liu Shaoqi or **Liu Shao-ch'i** (c. 1898–1974) Chinese politician. A member of the Chinese Communist Party from the 1920s, when he studied in Moscow, he became the party's secretary general (1943–54). He was vice chairman (1949–59) and chairman of the People's Republic of China (1959–68). A leading party theoretician, he was denounced as "number one capitalist-roader" during the **Cultural Revolution** and ousted from power (1968).

Lloyd George, David, first earl of Dwyfor (1863–1945) British politician. Born in Manchester to Welsh parents, he was a Liberal M.P. from 1890 until his death. As chancellor of the exchequer (1908–15), he showed his commitment to social reform in a "People's Budget" (1909) raising taxes on the wealthy; controversy over the bill led to the Parliament Act of 1911 diminishing the power of the House of Lords. Lloyd George also designed Britain's first health and unemployment insurance programs (1911). Following **Herbert Henry Asquith**'s resignation in 1916, Lloyd George became prime minister (1916–22). Exerting dictatorial control through a coalition cabinet, he led Britain to victory in **World War I** and advocated moderate peace terms at the **Paris Peace Conference**. Organizing a conference with Irish leaders in 1921, he began the negotiations that led to the founding of the Irish Free State. The withdrawal of the Conservatives from his coalition led to the collapse of his government.

Lloyd Webber, Lord Andrew (1948–) British composer. One of the few successful authors of stage musicals in the late century, he composed such works as *Joseph and the Amazing Technicolor Dreamcoat* (1968, with Tim Rice), *Jesus Christ Superstar* (1970), *Cats* (1976), *Evita* (1981), and *Phantom of the Opera* (1986). His works invigorated the London stage and became long-running Broadway successes. He was knighted in 1992 and became a life peer in 1996.

Lodge, Henry Cabot (1850–1924) American politician and writer. A Harvard historian and Republican, he was elected to the U.S. Congress as a representative (1887–93) and senator (1893–1924). A close associate of President **Theodore Roosevelt**, he led the successful opposition to the peace treaty and U.S. entry into the **League of Nations** (1919) following **World War I**. His grandson Henry Cabot Lodge (1902–85) was a Republican senator from Massachusetts (1937–44 and 1947–53), an unsuccessful vice-presidential candidate (1960), and a diplomat.

Lorenz, Konrad Zacharias (1903–89) Austrian ethnologist. He received an M.D. (1928) and Ph.D. (1933) in zoology from Vienna University and began a lifelong interest in behavior patterns. Studies of birds led to the discovery of the early learning process known as imprinting. In the controversial book *On Aggression* (1966), he suggested that aggressive tendencies are partly inborn and that humans may not be able to control them. He was awarded the 1973 Nobel Prize for physiology or **medicine**, with Anglo-Dutch zoologist Nikolaas Tinbergen (1907–88) and Austrian zoologist Karl von Frisch (1887–1982). His book *King Solomon's Ring* (1949) was a popular success.

Louis, Joe (1914–81) American athlete. Born Joseph Louis Barrow in Lafayette, Ala., the boxer later known as the "Brown Bomber" turned professional in 1934. After defeating American boxer James J. Braddock (1905–74) for the world heavyweight championship in 1937, he held the title until 1949, a record duration. He defended his title 25 times, with 21 knockouts. In 1938 he scored a first-round knockout of German boxer Max Schmeling (1905–), who had defeated him earlier. Louis's autobiography, *Joe Louis: My Life*, was published in 1978.

Lowell, Amy (1874–1925) American poet and critic. Cousin of poet **Robert Lowell**, she was a leader of the imagist movement in poetry. She wrote many poems in free verse and "polyphonic prose." Poetic works include *A Dome of Many-Coloured Glass* (1912) and *Sword Blades and Poppy Seed* (1914); critical works include *Six French Poets* (1915).

Lowell, Robert [Traill Spence, Jr.] (1917–77) American poet. Born in Boston, he was the great-grandnephew of 19th-century poet James Russell Lowell and cousin of poet **Amy Lowell.** With John Berryman (1914–72), he was considered a confessional poet, treating the minutiae of his family and personal life intensely but with artful control. His works include the Pulitzer Prize–winning *Lord Weary's Castle* (1946), *Life Studies* (1959; revised 1968), and the verse translations in *Imitations* (1961). He was married to writers Jean Stafford (1915–1979) and Elizabeth Hardwick (1916–).

Lu Xun or **Lu Hsün** (1881–1936) Chinese writer. Pseudonym of Chou Shu-jen (Zhou Shuren). Often considered the most important Chinese fiction writer and critic of the 20th century, he first became known for short stories such as "A Madman's Diary" (1918) and "The True Story of Ah Q" (1921), using dark humor to criticize traditional Chinese society. Active in the **May Fourth Movement** (1919), he became a supporter of the Communist Party. He also wrote essays and translations. His "Outline History of Chinese Fiction" is a standard work.

Lubitsch, Ernst (1892–1947) German-born American film director. Born in Berlin, he began directing in 1918, developing the witty "Lubitsch Touch" in films including *Madame Dubarry (Passion)* (1919). In 1922 he settled in the U.S., gaining huge success with dramas, musicals, and especially sophisticated comedies that poked fun at American mores. Notable films include *The Marriage Circle* (1924), *The Love Parade* (1929), *Monte Carlo* (1930), *Trouble in Paradise* (1932), *Ninotchka* (1939), and *To Be or Not to Be* (1942). He received an honorary Academy Award in 1937. He became an American citizen in 1933.

Lucas, George (1944–) American film director and producer. Born in Modesto, Calif., he studied at the Cinema School of the University of Southern California. His first feature-length film was *THX-1138* (1971), but it was his second film, the nostalgic *American Graffiti* (1973), that gained him broad commercial success. His third film, *Star Wars* (1977), was an even bigger hit, becoming the greatest box-office success up to its time and influencing many future productions. Lucas went on to produce (but not direct) other films that followed the *Star Wars* pattern of high-speed adventure laden with special effects. He also founded a special effects company, Industrial Light & Magic, which pioneered digital effects and helped develop **television** programming and multimedia software.

Luce, Clare Boothe (1903–87) American writer and politician. Born Anne Clare Boothe, she wrote for *Vogue* and *Vanity Fair* and became managing editor of the latter. Soon after marrying **Henry Robinson Luce** in 1935, she embarked on a successful career as a playwright, with Broadway hits that included *The Women* (1936). A conservative, she was a Republican member of the House of Representatives (1943–47) and ambassador to Italy (1953–57).

Luce, Henry [Robinson] (1898–1967) Chinese-born American editor and publisher. He graduated from Yale and in 1923 cofounded the weekly newsmagazine *Time*. Other Luce magazines soon followed: business magazine *Fortune* (1930), photo magazine *Life* (1936), and *Sports Illustrated* (1954). He also acquired and rejuvenated *Architectural Digest* (1932). His magazines were often a platform for his conservative Republican views. They, along with **radio** stations and Time-Life Books, formed the communications giant, Time,

Inc. His second wife was **Clare Boothe Luce** (1903-87).

Ludendorff, Erich von [Friedrich Wilhelm] (1865–1937) German soldier. During **World War I** he was named general and chief of staff under Field Marshal **Paul von Hindenburg** (1847–1934). A masterful strategist, he was responsible for the 1914 victory against the Russians at Tannenberg; he and Hindenburg directed the German war effort from 1916 to 1918. In the 1920s he supported the Nazis and wrote pro-Nazi pamphlets and led group events. In his final years he became a pacifist.

Lumumba, Patrice Hemery (1925–61) Congolese politician. A member of the Batatele tribe, he became active as a nationalist in 1955 and founded the Congolese National Movement, Congo's first nationwide political party, in 1958. He advocated immediate independence from Belgium and survived arrest in 1959 to become the first prime minister of the Republic of the Congo in June 1960. In September President Joseph Kasavubu (1910–69), a rival for power, dismissed him. He was captured by supporters of Kasavubu and Colonel **Joseph Mobutu** and transported to the secessionist province of Katanga, where he was murdered.

Luxemburg, Rosa (1871–1919) Polish revolutionary. Born in Russian Poland, she helped found the Polish Social Democratic Party in 1892. Settling in Germany in 1898, she became active in the German Social Democratic Party, advocating working-class revolution. After spending much of **World War I** in prison for her opposition to the war, she and German revolutionary Karl Liebknecht (1871–1919) co-founded the Spartacus Party in 1918, precursor of the German Communist Party. She led the 1919 **Spartacist** uprising against the **Weimar Republic**, and she and Liebknecht were arrested and killed.

Lyons, Joseph Aloysius (1879–1939) Australian politician. Becoming a Labour Party member of the House of Representatives in 1929, he resigned in 1931 and helped found the coalition United Australia Party. Prime minister from 1931 to 1939, he aided in building economic stability. Wife Dame Enid Lyons was the first female member of the House of Representatives.

M

MacArthur, Douglas (1880–1964) American soldier. Born in Little Rock, Ark., he was the son of a Civil War military hero and graduated from West Point in 1903. He commanded a brigade in France during **World War I** and became West Point's youngest superintendent (1919–22). As U.S. Army chief of staff (1930–35) he led the purge of Bonus Army veterans from Washington, D.C. From 1942 to 1945, he was commander of the Southwest Pacific area and became supreme commander of the **Allied Powers**, administering the Japanese surrender in September 1945. During the **Korean War** he was commander of the **United Nations** forces in Korea, leading the Inchon offensive and later publicly advocating a second push into North Korea. His dissent led President Harry S Truman to dismiss him from command in April 1951. Returning to the U.S., he spoke to Congress, concluding with a quote from a military song, "Old soldiers never die, they just fade away." He ran unsuccessfully for the Republican presidential nomination in 1948 and 1952.

McCarthy, Joseph [Raymond] (1909–57) U.S. senator. Born in Grand Chute, Wisc., he received a law degree from Marquette University and served in **World War II** before being elected to the Senate (1947–57). In February 1950 he gained fame by claiming that the U.S. State Department was infiltrated by Communists. As chairman of the Senate's Government Operations Committee, he continued the Communist "witchhunt" of government agencies and nongovernment businesses, at times forcing loyalty oaths and damaging careers. Following a televised confrontation with U.S. Army officials, he was censured by the U.S. Congress in 1954 and faded from public view. "McCarthyism" now refers to his inquisitorial tactics.

McCarthy, Mary [Therese] (1912–89) American writer. A major 20th-century woman of letters, she is known for her sharp, erudite works in several genres. Novels include *The Groves of Academe* (1952), *The Group* (1963), and *Birds of America* (1971). Nonfiction works include *Venice Observed* (1956), *Vietnam* (1967), and her memoir *Memories of a Catholic Girlhood* (1957), which recalls her parents' death during the 1918 influenza epidemic and her difficult early years. Her criticism also appeared in *Partisan Review*, the *Nation*, and other periodicals. She was married to the American writer **Edmund Wilson**.

McCartney, Paul *See* **John Lennon**

MacDonald, James Ramsay (1866–1937) British politician. Born in Scotland to a servant girl and a farm worker, he joined the **Labour Party** in 1894 and served as its leader from 1911 to 1914. In 1906 he was elected to the House of Commons and served until a 1918 defeat, due largely to his pacifist stance during **World War I**. He was reelected in 1922 and, from January to December 1924, became prime minister in Britain's first Labour government. His government fell under charges that the party was pro-Communist. In 1929 he again became prime minister and in 1931 formed the coalition National government, which included members of the Liberal and **Conservative** Parties. He served on it as prime minister until 1935.

McKinley, William (1843–1901). Twenty-fifth U.S. president (1897–1901). Born in Niles, Ohio, he served as Republican U.S. congressman from Ohio (1877–90) and Ohio governor in 1891 and 1893. Elected president in 1896 against Democratic candidate **William Jennings Bryan** and reelected in 1900, he helped establish the U.S. as a 20th-century global power through the Spanish-American War, the annexation of Cuba and the Philippines, and the **Open-Door Policy** with China. Economically, he supported high tariffs and the Gold Standard Act of 1900. Shot by anarchist Leon Czolgosz (1873–1901) in Buffalo, N.Y., on Sept. 6, 1901, he died on Sept. 14.

McLuhan, [Herbert] Marshall (1911–80) Canadian commentator and sociologist. At the University of Toronto (1946–66) and U.S. universities, he became known for commentary on the effects of the media on society. He contended that "the medium is the message," meaning that the medium (e.g., **radio, television**) influences audiences more than the material it presents. Works include *The Gutenberg Galaxy* (1962), *Understanding Media* (1964), and *War and Peace in the Global Village* (1968), referring to the "global village" of electronic communication.

Macmillan, [Maurice] Harold, earl of Stockton (1894–1986) British politician. He entered Parliament as a Conservative in 1924. After serving in several postwar cabinet positions, including chancellor of the exchequer (1955–57), he became prime minister (1957–63). He restored good relations with the U.S. (damaged by the **Suez Crisis**) and worked for better East-West relations. He also sought unsuccessfully to gain British entry into the Common Market. In 1963 his government fell, partly over a scandal linking his minister of war, John Profumo, to prostitute Christine Keeler and a Soviet official (see **Profumo Affair**). Macmillan was made an earl in 1984.

Madonna (1958–) American singer and actress. Born Madonna Louise Veronica Ciccone, she rose to rock stardom with albums such as *Like a Virgin* (1984), promoted through her skillful use of the emerging medium of music videos. Stoking controversy through performances some considered indecent or blasphemous, she has sold more records worldwide than any other female performer. She is a popular concert artist and has starred in such films as *Evita* (1996).

Maeterlinck, Maurice [Polydore-Marie-Bernard] (1862–1949) Belgian writer. In Paris from 1896, he became a widely published Symbolist writer, with poetic works about the mystery of life including *Serres chaudes* (1889) and plays *Pelléas et Mélisande* (1892), *The Blue Bird* (1909), and others. Meditations on nature include *The Life of the Bee* (1901) and *Life and Flowers* (1907). In 1911 he won the Nobel Prize for literature.

Magritte, René[-François-Ghislain] (1898–1967) Belgian painter. A leading surrealist, his witty paintings incongruously juxtaposed the ordinary and the strange. Influenced by **Giorgio de Chirico**, he influenced other artists such as **Claes Oldenburg**. Works include *Threatening Weather* (1928), *Human Condition* (1935), and *The Red Model* (1935).

Mahfouz, Naguib (1911–) Egyptian writer. His Cairo Trilogy, comprising *Palace Walk*, *Palace of Desire*, and *Sugar Street* (1956–57), is famed for its realist historical sweep in telling a multigenerational story of Egypt that spans the 1910s to the 1950s. His novel *The Children of Gebelawi* (1959) was long banned in Egypt for its treatment of Islam. In 1988 Mahfouz became the first Arabic writer to receive the Nobel Prize for literature.

Mahler, Gustav (1860–1911) Austrian composer and conductor. Born in Bohemia, he was first recognized as a brilliant, tempestuous conductor, notably as director of the Imperial Opera in Vienna (1897–1907) and in the U.S. (1907–10). His compositions are considered important links between 19th and 20th-century classical music. Influenced by Austrian composer Anton Bruckner (1824–96), they incorporate folk music and a broad range of emotion. Notable works include 10 symphonies (no. 10 unfinished), six songs with orchestra, and song cycles including *Kindertotenlieder* (1901–04) and *Das Lied von der Erde* (1907–10), which marked a daughter's death.

Mailer, Norman [Kingsley] (1923–) American writer. He graduated from Harvard and served in **World War II** before establishing himself as a serious postwar writer with his dark **World War II** novel *The Naked and the Dead* (1948). Later works explored the American scene, notably a memoiristic recounting of a 1967 peace march on Washington, *The Armies of the Night* (1968), and a study of a young killer, *The Executioner's Song* (1979). Both won the Pulitzer Prize.

Major, John (1943–) British politician. In local government from the 1960s, he served in Parliament and state positions including Exchequer (1989) before being named successor to Conservative prime minister **Margaret Thatcher** in 1990. He served a second term following 1992 general elections, but was defeated by Liberal candidate **Tony Blair** in 1996. Major's tenure was marked by a tempered relations with European nations and abolition of the poll tax.

Malcolm X (1925–65) African-American nationalist leader. Born Malcolm Little in Omaha, Nebr., he was imprisoned for burglary (1946–52). In prison, he joined the Nation of Islam and took the Muslim name El-Hajj Malik El-Shabazz and the public name Malcolm X. He traveled widely around the country, advocating black separatism and denouncing white racism. Personal and ideological differences led him to break with the Nation of Islam in 1963. In 1964, following a pilgrimage to Mecca and conversion to orthodox Islam, he founded the Organization of Afro-American Unity and espoused greater hope for racial coexistence. He was assassinated by **Black Muslims** while addressing a rally in New York City. He was the coauthor (with Alex Haley) of *The Autobiography of Malcolm X* (1964).

Malenkov, Georgi Maksimilianovich (1902–88) Soviet politician. Active in the Soviet Communist Party from 1920, he became aide to **Joseph Stalin**. During **World War II** he sat on the Committee of State Defense (1942–44), and in 1946 was named deputy premier and Politburo member. Following Stalin's death, he served as premier (1953–55), his tenure marked by domestic problems and attempts at improving foreign relations. Forced to retire in 1955, he lost all government appointments in 1957 and was expelled from the Communist Party in 1961.

Mandela, Nelson [Rolihlahla] (1918–) South African revolutionary and politician. Born near Umtata, the son of a Tembu tribal chief, he was the country's first black lawyer. A member of the **African National Congress (ANC)** from 1944, he helped form the organization's Youth League. He was accused of treason in 1956 but acquitted in 1961. He married Winnie Mandela (born Nkosikazi Nomzamo Madikizela, 1934–) in 1958. Abandoning nonviolent resistance, he founded the ANC's armed wing, the Spear of the Nation, to conduct sabotage and guerrilla warfare. He was arrested in 1962 and sentenced in 1964 to life imprisonment. During the next three decades, the imprisoned ANC leader became an international symbol of resistance to **apartheid**. Believing white rule to be no longer tenable, President **F. W. de Klerk** legalized the ANC and released Mandela in 1990. A transitional constitution was approved in 1993, and Mandela and de Klerk shared that year's Nobel Peace Prize. In 1994, after the country's first multiracial elections, Mandela became president. In 1996, a permanent constitution was approved. While facing opposition from the Inkatha Freedom Party, Mandela remained a popular and charismatic leader. He and his wife, Winnie Mandela, separated in 1992 and divorced in 1996. A leader of the ANC during his long imprisonment, Winnie Mandela was tarred by scandals, including her 1991 conviction for her role in the kidnapping and beating of four youths. Mandela stepped down from the presidency in 1999.

Mandelstam, Osip Emilyevich (1891–1938) Russian poet. A member of the acmeists, he wrote classically influenced, concrete poetry that countered less precise symbolist works. His collections include *Stone* (1913) and *Tristia* (1922); he also wrote novellas and translations. Imprisoned for insufficient support of the Stalinist regime, he died in a labor camp.

Mann, Thomas (1875–1955) German novelist. Brother of novelist Heinrich Mann (1871–1950), he is esteemed for novels and short stories capturing the emotional and cultural effects of Germany in transition, and the place of the artist in society. He gained fame with first novel *Buddenbrooks* (1901); other novels include his masterwork *The Magic Mountain* (1924) and *Doctor Faustus* (1947). Stories and novellas include *Tonio Kroger* (1903) and *Death in Venice* (1912); among anti-Nazi essays is *Appeal to Reason* (1930). Exiled by Nazis, he lived in Switzerland from 1933 to 1938 and from 1952 to 1955; he was in the U.S. from 1938 to 1952, becoming a citizen in 1944. He was awarded the Nobel Prize for Literature in 1929. Son Klaus Mann (1906–49) was a novelist; daughter Erika (1905–69) was an actress and was married to American poet **W. H. Auden**.

Mao Zedong or **Mao Tse-tung** (1893–1976) Chinese revolutionary and politician. Born in Hunan Province, he participated in the **Chinese Revolution** of 1911 and the **May Fourth Movement** (1919). He cofounded the Chinese Communist Party (1921). He organized peasant unions for the **Guomindang (Nationalist Party)**, but Mao and the Communists split with the Guomindang in 1927, igniting the **Chinese Civil War**. In 1934 and 1935, Mao led his Red Army on the **Long March**, a 6,000-mile trek from Jiangxi Province to Shaanxi Province. As a theoretician, he adapted Marxism to Chinese conditions, emphasizing the peasantry rather than the urban proletariat. In 1949 the Communists succeeded in driving the Nationalist government into exile in Taiwan. Mao became chairman of the Communist Party and of the People's Republic of China. During the **Hundred Flowers** period (1956–57), Mao briefly encouraged independent thought and criticism of his regime before becoming more repressive. In the Great Leap Forward (1958–60), he unsuccessfully tried to transform the country into a major industrial power; the failure led to his removal as chairman of the republic (1959), though he remained party chairman. Repression worsened during the **Cultural Revolution** (1966–69), a violent movement to purge the nation of bourgeois influences. Initially a close ally of the **Soviet Union**, China under Mao moved toward a more independent international position. Many in the **Third World** looked to him for inspiration, and Mao developed closer ties with the West by meeting U.S. president **Richard Nixon** in Beijing in 1972. Mao's works include *Strategic Problems of China's Revolutionary War* (1936) and *Quotations from Chairman Mao Zedong* (1967).

Marconi, Guglielmo, Marchese (1874–1937) Italian physicist. He pioneered wireless telegraphy in 1895. In December 1901 he became the first to transmit radio waves across the Atlantic, from England to Newfoundland. In later years he worked on developing shortwave wireless communication. He shared the 1909 Nobel Prize for physics. He was given the title Marchese in 1929.

Marcos, Ferdinand [Edralin] (1917–89) Philippine politician. In **World War II** he fought as a guerrilla against the Japanese. After the war, he served in the House of Representatives (1949–59) and Senate (1959–66) before gaining the presidency (1966–86) as the Nationalist candidate. A staunch U.S. ally and anti-Communist, he declared martial law in 1972 in the face of Communist and Muslim separatist insurgencies. A new constitution (1973) made him virtual dictator. Economic woes roused widespread opposition, as did his corruption and extravagance, symbolized after his fall by the discovery of his wife Imelda Marcos's (1930–) vast shoe collection. After opposition leader Benigno Aquino (1932–83) was assassinated, the growing "people power" movement forced Marcos to hold elections (1986). Both Marcos and Aquino's widow, **Corazon Aquino**, claimed victory, but Marcos was accused of fraud and forced to flee the country. Marcos died in Hawaii while awaiting trial in the U.S. for racketeering and embezzlement.

Marcuse, Herbert (1898–1979) German-born American philosopher. Born in Berlin, he was associated with the Frankfurt School. He fled Nazi Germany for the U.S. (1934), where he became known as the "Father of the New Left" for the influence that his book *One-Dimensional Man* (1964) exerted on student radicals. He argued that revolution must come from alienated elites, such as students, rather than from workers stupefied by the capitalist system. Other works include *Eros and Civilization* (1955).

Maritain, Jacques (1882–1973) French philosopher. Educated at the Sorbonne and converted to Catholicism in 1906, he sought to revitalize Thomist thought. He taught in France and North America and was French ambassador to the Vatican (1945–48). Works include *Art and Scholasticism* (1920) and *Degrees of Knowledge* (1932).

Marshall, George C[atlett] (1890–1959) American soldier and politician. A U.S. Army officer during **World War I**, he was an aide to General John Pershing (1919–24) and chief of staff during **World War II** (1939–45). He became Army general from 1944. After the war, he served as U.S. secretary of state (1945–47), during which time he developed and led the European Recovery Program or **Marshall Plan** (1947). For his efforts he won the Nobel Peace Prize (1953). From 1950 to 1951 he was U.S. secretary of defense.

Marshall, Thurgood (1908–1993) American jurist. Born in Baltimore, Md., he graduated from Howard University Law School (1933). A civil rights advocate from the 1930s, he successfully argued *Brown v. Board of Education* to the Supreme Court in 1954, which overturned *Plessy v. Ferguson* (1896) and prohibited public-school segregation. He became the first African-American associate justice of the Supreme Court in 1967, serving until 1991. His concerns often focused on civil and economic rights.

Martin, Mary [Virginia] (1913–90) American stage actress. After debuting memorably in *Leave It to Me* (1938) with a saucy rendition of "My Heart Belongs to Daddy," she starred in several musicals, including *South Pacific* (1949), *Peter Pan* (1954), and *The Sound of Music* (1959). Her son is American actor Larry Hagman (1931–).

Marx Brothers American comedy team. Born in New York City, the brothers went from vaudeville (c. 1904) to Broadway (with *I'll Say She Is*, 1924) to film (with *The Cocoanuts*, 1929). They became famous for their anarchic humor, particularly in films such as *Duck Soup* (1933) and *A Night at the Opera* (1935). Their best-known members were Chico (born Leonard, 1886-1961), Harpo (born Adolph, known as Arthur, 1888–1964), and Groucho (born Julius Henry, 1890–1977). Gummo (born Milton, 1893–1977) left the act before 1920; Zeppo (born Herbert, 1901–79) left in the mid-1930s. After the team's last film (*Love Happy*, 1949), Groucho went on to a solo career as a wisecracking wit on **television** and in print.

Masaryk, Tomás Garrigue (1850–1937) and **Jan Garrigue Masaryk** (1886–1948) Born in Moravia, Tomás was a professor of philosophy at the University of Prague (1882–1914) and served as member of the Hapsburg Parliament (1891–93 and 1907–14), beginning his campaign with **Eduard Benes** for Czechoslovak independence in 1907. Upon the creation of the Czechoslovak Republic in 1918, he became its first president. Highly popular, he was reelected three times, resigning for health reasons in 1935. His son Jan served as foreign minister (1940–1948), first in exile in London, then in Czechoslovakia after the war. He also served as vice premier (1941–45) of the government in exile. Shortly after the 1948 Communist takeover he died, officially by suicide, though the particulars remain unresolved.

Matisse, Henri (1869–1954) French artist, painter, sculptor, and lithographer, he is considered (with **Pablo Picasso**) one of the foremost painters of his time. Trained as a lawyer, he turned instead to art and soon came to experiment with various artistic styles, including impressionism and postimpressionism, notably in *Luxe, calme et voluptè* (1905). That year he and others exhibited the first fauvist works. Throughout the early 20th century, he developed influential new uses of pure color and shape to construct works of art, such as *The Blue Nude* (1907). Late in life, he made joyous paper cutouts that included *Jazz*, and windows and murals for the Dominican chapel in Vence, France.

Mauriac, François (1885–1970) French writer. A Catholic, he explored desire, sin, suffering, and possibilities for redemption in novels, essays, and plays. Among his works are the novels *The Kiss to the Leper* (1922), *The Desert of Love* (1925), *Thérèse Desqueyroux* (1927), and *Vipers' Tangle* (1933); the play *Asmodée* (1937); and the prose works *Life of Jesus* (1936) and *The Son of Man* (1958). He was active in the **resistance** during **World War II**. His son is new wave novelist and critic Claude Mauriac (1914–).

Mayakovsky, Vladimir Vladimirovich (1893–1930) Russian poet. Leading proponent of the futurist artistic movement, he experimented with untraditional, coarse language and imagery he felt more akin to the modern age. Notable works before the **Russian Revolution** include *A Cloud in Trousers* (1914–5) and *The Backbone Flute* (1915). **Bolshevik party** member from 1908, he focused works written after the Russian Revolution on his cause, including the poem *150,000,000* (1919–20) and the play *Misteriya-buff* (1918). Possibly influenced by decreased Soviet approval of his work, he committed suicide by shotgun.

Mead, Margaret (1901–78) American anthropologist. Born in Philadelphia, she graduated from Barnard (1923) and received a Ph.D. at Columbia University (1929), studying with **Franz Boas**. From a lifetime of field work among the peoples of the South Pacific, she wrote widely read works on children and culture that opened the field of anthropology to a broader audience. Among her books are *Coming of Age in Samoa* (1928), *Growing up in New Guinea* (1930), *Male and Female* (1949), *Culture and Commitment* (1970), and her autobiographical work *Blackberry Winter* (1972). From 1926 she was affiliated with the American Museum of Natural History; from 1954 she was adjunct professor at Columbia.

Mei Lanfang (1894–1961) Chinese actor. The son and grandson of actors, he studied at the Peking Opera as a child and made his first public appearance at 14. He specialized in female roles and developed his own style, particularly in dance. Internationally known, he retired from the stage during the **Chinese Civil War**. He returned to Beijing in 1949, performing again and becoming president of the Research Institute of Chinese Drama.

Meir, Golda (1898–1978) Israeli politician. Born Goldie Mabovitch in Kiev, Russia, she immigrated to the U.S. in 1906. A **Zionist**, she emigrated from the U.S. with her husband, Morris Meyerson (Meir), to Palestine in 1921 and was a founder of Israel in 1948. A member of the Knesset from 1949 to 1974, she served as minister of labor (1949–56) and foreign minister (1956–66) and helped form Israel's Labor Party. In 1969 she became Israel's first female prime minister, inspiring women around the world. Attempts to achieve a diplomatic peace with Arab neighbors failed when the **Yom Kippur War** erupted in October 1973. Blamed for the nation's unpreparedness, she resigned in 1974.

Mencken, H[enry] L[ouis] (1880–1956) American writer. Born in Baltimore, Md., he wrote for the *Baltimore Sun*, from 1906 to his death, in the strident, clever style that became a trademark. With George Jean Nathan he edited the *Smart Set* (1914–23), and cofounded (with Nathan) and edited the highly influential *the American Mercury* (1925–33). Among his many books were The *American Language* (1919; revised and supplemented to 1948) and *Prejudices* (6 vol., 1919–27), a collection of his essays. He is remembered as a groundbreaking journalist and tireless critic of the self-satisfied bourgeoisie.

Mendès-France, Pierre (1907–82) French politician. A Radical-Socialist, he was first elected deputy in 1932. He fought with the Free French in **World War II**. As prime minister (1954–55), he ended French involvement in Indochina and maintained a liberal policy toward Algeria.

Menotti, Gian Carlo (1911–) Italian composer. His operas have been highly popular in the U.S., where he immigrated to in 1928. Works include *The Old Maid and the Thief* (1939),

The Medium (1945), and *Amahl and the Night Visitors* (1951).

Menzies, Sir Robert Gordon (1894–1978) Australian politician. As head of the United Australia Party, his period as prime minister lasted only two years (1939–41). However, after **World War II**, Menzies founded and led a new Liberal Party, thereby becoming his country's longest-serving prime minister (1949–66). Presiding over a time of prosperity, he pursued an anti-Communist, pro-American policy. He was knighted in 1963.

Merman, Ethel (1908–84) American stage actress. Born Ethel Zimmerman in Astoria, N.Y., she became known for her singularly roaring voice in several Broadway musicals, notably *Annie Get Your Gun* (1946), *Call Me Madam* (1950), and *Gypsy* (1958). Many of her roles were written especially for her.

Merton, Thomas [James] (1915–68) French-born American monk and writer. After studies at Columbia, he converted from agnosticism to Catholicism and, in 1941, entered a Trappist monastery at Gethsemani, Kentucky. He was ordained a priest in 1949. His memoir *The Seven Storey Mountain* (1948) is a classic of spiritual autobiography. He also wrote poetry and, in later years, pursued an interest in Eastern mysticism and agitated against the **Vietnam War**.

Metaxas, Ioannis or **John** (1871–1941) Greek soldier and politician. After serving in the Turkish War (1897) and **Balkan War** (1912–13), he became Greek army chief of staff. A monarchist supporter, he became prime minister in 1936, after the monarchy was restored (1935) under **George II**. In August 1936 Metaxas established a dictatorship but joined Allied forces (see **Allied Powers**) when Italy invaded Greece in 1940.

Mïes van der Rohe, Ludwig (1886–1969) German-born American architect. A shaper of modern architecture, he was director of the Bauhaus (1930–33). Born in Aachen, he immigrated to the U.S. in 1937 to become director of the School of Architecture at the Illinois Institute of Technology (formerly Armour Institute). His use of glass walls, exposed supports, and uncluttered design is evident in the Seagram Building, New York City (1956–58, with Phillip Johnson) and New National Gallery, Berlin (1968).

Mifune, Toshiro (1920–97) Japanese actor. Born in Tsingtao, China, to Japanese parents, he was in the Japanese Army during **World War II**. He gained international fame through powerful performances in several films by **Akira Kurosawa**, including *Rashomon* (1950), *Seven Samurai* (1954), *Throne of Blood* (1957), *The Lower Depths* (1957), and *Yojimbo* (1961).

Milhaud, Darius (1892–1974) French composer. Influenced by jazz, he pioneered polytonal music. Works include the dance suites *Saudades do Brasil* (1920-21), the ballet *La Création du monde* (1923), and the opera *Christophe Colomb* (1928).

Miller, Arthur (1915–) American playwright. His masterpiece *Death of a Salesman* (1949) was a contemporary tragedy centered on the common man. Other plays include *All My Sons* (1947), *The Crucible* (1953), and *After the Fall* (1964). He also wrote the screenplay for *The Misfits* (1961), a film based on his short story and starring his second wife, **Marilyn Monroe**.

Miller, Glenn (1904–44). American musician. After stints as a trombonist with other dance bands, he formed his own in 1938 and became a leader in the big-band swing sound. Hit songs include "Moonlight Serenade" and "Chattanooga Choo-Choo." Head of the U.S. Army Air Force band (1944) in Europe during **World War II**, he was reported lost in flight over Europe.

Miller, Henry (1890–1980) American writer. While in Paris from 1930 to 1940, he published his best-known works, *Tropic of Cancer* (1934) and *Tropic of Capricorn* (1939). They were distinguished by their liberal use of autobiography, philosophical digression, and sexual explicitness, the latter of which prohibited U.S. publication until 1961. Other works include the trilogy *The Rosy Crucifixion* (1941) and the autobiography *My Life and Times* (1972).

Millikan, Robert Andrews (1868–1953) American physicist. He received the 1923 Nobel Prize for physics for measuring the electron's charge and researching the photoelectric effect. He also studied and named cosmic rays (1925).

Milne, A[lan] A[lexander] (1882–1956) British writer. Popular in the 1920s and 1930s for plays including *Mr. Pym Passes By* (1919) and *Toad of Toad Hall* (1929), he is best remembered for juvenile works written for his young son Christopher Robin: the poetry collections *When We Were Very Young* (1924) and *Now We Are Six* (1927), and the stories *Winnie-the-Pooh* (1926) and *The House at Pooh Corner* (1928). He also wrote essays and mystery novels.

Milosevic, Slobodan (1941–) Serbian politician. Prior to entering into the field of politics, Milosevic was president of the state-owned gas company, Tehnogas, and later the United Bank of Belgrade. In 1984 he became chief of the local Communist Party organization in Belgrade. Over the next few years he rose up through party ranks becoming head of the Communist Party in Yugoslavia. Milosevic deposed his mentor, Serbian president Ivan Stambolic, in 1987 and took over as president two years later. He fostered Serb nationalism in the province of Kosovo, and deprived the area of its autonomy. Milosevic's attempts to stop the succession of the Yugoslavian republics of Croatia and Bosnia ignited years of violence and ethnic cleansing in those states. However, with sanctions in force, and air threats looming, Milosevic accepted the independence of both in 1995. A Separatist movement in Kosovo erupted in violence in February 1998. Despite denials from Milosevic, reports surfaced of massacres of ethnic Albanians by Serb police forces. Milosevic's refusal to sign a peace treaty over Kosovo resulted in the **NATO** bombing of Serbia and Kosovo in the spring of 1999. Meanwhile, 750,000 ethnic Albanians fled or were forced out of Kosovo into Albania and Macedonia. Milosevic fell from power in 2000, unseated by popular demonstrations prompted by his refusal to concede an election defeat that year.

Milosz, Czeslaw (1911–) Lithuanian-born American poet and novelist. Avant-garde poet in the 1930s in Poland, he fled to Paris in opposition to Communist rule in 1951. He immigrated to the U.S. in 1960. Influenced by politics, memory, and morality, his poetry has gained notice in the U.S. and abroad. Collections include *Selected Poems* (1973) and *Bells in Winter* (1978). Prose works include the essay collections *The Captive Mind* (1953) and *Native Realm* (1981). He was awarded the Nobel Prize for literature in 1980.

Miró, Joan (1893–1983) Spanish painter and graphic artist. Moving to Paris in 1919 and meeting **Pablo Picasso**, he created works influenced by cubism and later surrealism, taking part in the first surrealist exhibition in 1926. He settled in Barcelona from 1932 to 1936, during which time he developed a growing interest in collage and graphics. In 1940 he returned to Barcelona and thereafter split his time between that city and Paris. His paintings radiate gaiety and show original use of bright color, geometric shape, and representations of the unconscious; they influenced abstract expressionists. From the 1940s he experimented in ceramics and also created several public sculptures, mosaics, and other public artworks.

Mishima Yukio (1925–70) Japanese writer. Pseudonym of Kimitake Hiraoka, he is known for his complex, psychological novels finely exploring problems of postwar Japan. Titles include *The Temple of the Golden Pavilion* (1950), *The Sound of Waves*, (1954), and *The Sea of Fertility* (1965–70), He committed public hara-kiri to protest Japanese Westernization and the loss of traditional Japanese military power.

Mitchell, Margaret (1900–49) American novelist. Born in Atlanta, she wrote the novel *Gone with the Wind* (1936), a saga of Georgia during the Civil War and its aftermath. It was awarded the Pulitzer Prize in 1937 and made into a highly successful film in 1939.

Mitterrand, François [Maurice Marie] (1916–96) French politician. **Resistance** fighter and escaped prisoner-of-war during **World War II**, he entered government in 1946 as deputy and served in various cabinet posts from 1948 to 1957. First secretary of the Socialist Party in 1971, he helped build the party's power in the 1970s. Although defeated in his 1974 attempt at the presidency (by French politician Valéry Giscard d'Estaing), he was elected in 1981, becoming the first Socialist president of the French Fifth Republic. He was reelected in 1988.

Mobutu Sese Seko (1930–97) Congolese soldier and politician. Born Joseph Désiré Mobutu, he led an army coup against Congo prime minister **Patrice Lumumba** in 1960 and became army chief of staff. A second coup (1965) led to his becoming prime minister (1966) and president (1967–97). As part of a campaign of "national authenticity," he changed the Congo's name to Zaire (1971) and ordered all Zairians with European names to replace them with African names (1972). He ruled dictatorially at the head of a one-party state whose corruption was legendary; Mobutu himself was said to have amassed a fortune of $3 billion. As the economy declined and demands for multiparty elections went unheeded, civil war broke out. In 1997 Mobutu was driven from office by rebel leader Laurent Kabila (1939–), who changed the country's name back to Congo.

Modigliani, Amedeo (1884–1920) Italian painter and sculptor. In Paris from 1906, he combined elements of cubism and African and Italian art in simple, sweeping sculptures. His life was marked by poor health and poverty; his work became known after his death.

Mohammad Reza Pahlavi (1919–80) Shah of Iran (1941–79). He succeeded his father, **Reza Shah Pahlavi**, who was deposed by Great Britain and the **Soviet Union**. Overthrown by Mohammad Mosaddeq's (1880–1967) nationalist forces in 1953, Mohammad Reza Pahlavi lived in exile until Mosaddeq's defeat allowed him to return the following year. Using oil revenues, Mohammad Reza Pahlavi developed the nation's economy and pursued pro-Western policies. He governed repressively with the help of Savak, his secret police force. The fundamentalist-led Islamic Revolution cost him his throne in 1979. He fled the country in January; later that year, Iranian students took hostages at the U.S. Embassy in Tehran, demanding the former shah's extradition. He died in exile in Egypt.

Moholy-Nagy, Lázló (1895–1946) Hungarian painter, designer, and photographer. Influential in the development of modern design, he was a founder of constructivism and professor at the Bahaus (1923–28), where he furthered experiments with industrial design and photography, among other forms. From 1928 to 1937 he lived in Berlin, Amsterdam, and London, immigrating to the U.S. in 1937. In Chicago, Ill., he was director of the New Bauhaus, or American School of Design, and founded the Chicago Institute of Design in 1939 (later Illinois Institute of Technology). Books include *The New Vision* (1928) and *Vision in Motion* (1947).

Molotov, Vyacheslav Mikhailovich (1890–1986) Soviet politician. Born Vyacheslav Mikhailovich Skyrabin, he changed his surname to Molotov (Russian for hammer) as a student in 1906. From the 1920s he was a staunch supporter of **Joseph Stalin** and helped purge the Communist Party of anti-Stalinists. Prime minister (1930–41) and commissar of foreign affairs (1939–49), he negotiated the German-Soviet Nonagression Pact in 1939, but after the German invasion of the **Soviet Union** in 1941 he built ties with Allied forces (see **Allied Powers**) for the duration of **World War II**. During the war he authorized the use of incendiary liquid bombs known as Molotov cocktails. After Stalin's death, he was foreign minister from 1953 to 1956, when he was dismissed by **Nikita Khrushchev**. He was removed from the party completely in 1962 and reinstated in 1984.

Mondrian, Piet (1872–1944) Dutch painter. Influenced by cubism and a Calvinist upbringing, he developed a geometric, nonrepresentational style of painting called neoplasticism that informed architectural design and Bauhaus artists. His work is often identified by its blocks of primary colors and black or gray horizontal and vertical lines. Notable works include his *Boogie Woogie* series (1940-44). He cofounded the De Stijl group, which detailed its austere aestheticism in books and the magazine *De Stijl.* His work influenced architecture and the Bauhaus.

Monet, Claude (1840–1926) French painter and founder of impressionism. A caricaturist, he turned to landscape painting under study with French painter Eugène Boudin (1824–98). With French painters Pierre Auguste Renoir (1841–1919), Alfred Sisley (1839–99), and Jean-Frèdèric Bazille (1841–70), he formed the core of the impressionist group. So integral was he to the form's development that an early work, *Impression: Sunrise* (1872), inspired the movement's name. In his experiments with color, he eliminated black and gray from his palette to render color like a prism. Beginning in 1890, he worked to capture changes in hour and season by returning to sites and subjects, as with his studies of water lilies (1899 and 1904–25), and his water garden at Giverny.

Monroe, Marilyn (1926–62) American actress. Born Norma Jean Baker, she became a leading Hollywood star and sexual icon. Films include *Gentlemen Prefer Blondes* (1953) and *Some Like It Hot* (1959). She was married three times; her husbands included American baseball player Joe DiMaggio (1914–1999) and American playwright **Arthur Miller**. She died of a drug overdose.

Montessori, Maria (1870–1952) Italian educator and physician. The first woman in Italy to receive a medical degree (1894), she developed her theories of game-oriented, self-motivating education while working as a psychiatrist with retarded children at the Orthoprenic School in Rome. In 1907 she opened her first school (*Casa de Bambini*) for preschool slum children in Rome; by the 1930s, Montessori schools opened throughout western Europe. Books include *The Montessori Method* (1912) and *The Secret of Childhood* (1938).

Montgomery, Bernard Law, first viscount Montgomery of Alamein] (1887–1976). British soldier. Platoon leader during **World War I**, he was field marshal during **World War II**, becoming a national hero for his important Allied (see **Allied Powers**) victory in El Alamein (1942). In 1943 he led the Eighth Army in the invasion of Sicily and led troops throughout Italy. In 1944 he led ground troops in the Normandy invasion. After the war he led the British occupation forces in Germany (1945–46) and was deputy commander of Allied powers in Europe (1951–58). Though his military record was mixed, he inspired loyalty from his troops, who commonly knew him as "Monty."

Moore, Henry Spencer (1898–1986) British sculptor. Born in Yorkshire, he became known for his large-scale abstract works that integrate elements of primitive art, often in bronze, stone, and cement. Notable sculptures include pieces for Lincoln Center, New York City (1963–65), the University of Chicago (1964–66), and the National Gallery of Art (1978). He is also known for his drawings and watercolors, many done during **World War II**.

Moreau, Jeanne (1928–) French actress. Projecting feminine sophistication and sensuality, she has been a star of French and international films since the 1950s notably in *The Lovers* (1958), *Jules and Jim* (1961), *La Notte* (*The Night*, 1961), and *Until the End of the World* (1991).

Morgan, J[ohn] P[ierpont] (1837–1913) American financier and philanthropist. Born in Hartford, Conn., he established the banking house Drexel, Morgan & Co. in 1871, which in 1895 became known as J. P. Morgan Co. The leading force in American finance by century's end, he purchased the steel companies of **Andrew Carnegie** and others to form the United States Steel Corporation in 1901. He was a noted art collector and benefactor to the Metropolitan Museum of Art. His manuscripts and art collection were the basis for the Morgan Library, New York City.

Morrison, Toni (1931–) American novelist. Born Chloe Anthony Wofford, she is known for her intense, poetic novels of the African-American experience, including *The Bluest Eye* (1970), *Sula* (1973), *Song of Solomon* (1977, National Book Award), *Tar Baby* (1981), *Beloved* (1987, Pulitzer Prize), and *Paradise* (1998). Formerly a book editor, she is professor of English at Princeton.

Mosley, Sir Oswald Ernald, sixth baronet (1896–1980) British politician. As a member of Parliament (1918–24 and 1926–31), he successively identified himself as a Conservative, Independent, and member of the Labour Party. In 1932 he founded the British Union of Fascists, known as "Blackshirts" for their black uniforms. The organization was suppressed by the Public Order Act of 1936. Interned (1940–43) during **World War II**, Mosley later founded the right-wing Union Movement (1948).

Mountbatten, Louis Francis Albert Victor Nicholas, first earl Mountbatten of Burma (1900–79) British naval officer and administrator. He was born Prince Louis Battenberg, a great-grandson of Queen Victoria, but his family changed its name from "Battenberg" to "Mountbatten" in 1917, reflecting anti-German sentiment in Britain during **World War I**. He entered the navy in 1913 and, during **World War II**, directed the recapture of Burma as supreme allied (see **Allied Powers**) commander in Southeast Asia (1943–45). As the last viceroy of India (1947), he negotiated the rapid independence of the colony and its partition into India and Pakistan. He was later governor-general of India (1947–48), first sea lord (1955–59), and chairman of the United Kingdom Defense Staff (1959–65). He was made an earl in 1947 and admiral of the fleet in 1956. He was killed by an **Irish Republican Army** bomb while vacationing in Ireland.

Mubarak, Muhammad Hosni Said (1928–) Egyptian politician. He graduated from Cairo Air Force Academy in 1950. He was air force chief of staff (1969–72) and air force commander-in-chief (1972–75); his performance in the latter role during the 1973 **Yom Kippur War** won him promotion to air marshal in 1974. He was named vice president in 1975 and became president (1981–) upon the assassination of **Anwar el-Sadat**. He has maintained the peace treaty with Israel that Sadat signed, though he protested the Israeli invasion of Lebanon (1982). His efforts to strengthen ties with other Arab states won Egypt readmission to the **Arab League** in 1989. Domestically, he has tried to build the country's technological base and struggled to preserve his regime against growing Islamic fundamentalism.

Mugabe, Robert [Gabriel] (1924–) Zimbabwean revolutionary and politician. In 1963 he co-founded the militant Zimbabwe African National Union and led guerrilla resistance to British rule in Rhodesia. A member of the majority Shona people, he joined forces with Joshua Nkomo (1917–), who led the **ZAPU**, which represented the minority Matabele. Jointly heading the Patriotic Front, the two negotiated independence in 1979. Mugabe was elected prime minister (1980–87) and president (1987–). He split with Nkomo in 1982, but later reestablished the alliance. A respected leader, he was able to keep the trust of many white settlers.

Muhammad ibn 'Abd al-Karim al-hattbi See **Abd el-Krim**

Muhammad, Elijah (1897–1975) American religious leader. Born Elijah Poole, he greatly expanded the Nation of Islam, also known as the **Black Muslims**, during his leadership (1934–75) of the movement. Founded in 1930, the movement preached separatist black nationalism.

Murdoch, Dame [Jean] Iris (1919–99) Irish-born British writer. Her novels, which blend realism and symbolism, include *The Bell* (1958), the Booker Prize–winning *The Sea, The Sea* (1978), and *The Good Apprentice* (1986). Her nonfiction works as a philosopher include *The Sovereignty of Good* (1970). She received the title dame in 1987.

Murnau, F[rederick] W[ilhelm] (1888–1931) German film director. Born Friedrich Wilhelm Plumpe, he began directing in 1919 and developed his fluid cinematography and visual grace in *Nosferatu the Vampire* (1922) and *The Last Laugh* (1924). His first U.S. work, *Sunrise* (*Sunrise: The Story of Two Humans*, 1927), is highly prized for its beauty. Other U.S. films include *City Girl/Our Daily Bread* (1930) and *Tabu* (1931, codirected with Robert Flaherty).

Murrow, Edward R[oscoe] (1908–65) American broadcast journalist. Born Egbert Roscoe Murrow in Greensboro, N.C., he gained early notice for his firsthand Columbia Broadcasting System (CBS) **radio** reporting from London rooftops during **World War II**. After the war he hosted the influential CBS **television** programs *Person to Person* (1953–59) and *See It Now* (1951–58). On *See It Now* he challenged Senator **Joseph McCarthy** and hastened his political downfall. From 1961 to 1964 Murrow was director of the U.S. Information Agency.

Mussolini, Benito [Amilcare Andrea] (1883–1945) Italian dictator. Born in Dovia, he was a left-wing journalist and labor leader before splitting with the Socialist Party over his support of Italy's (1914) entry into **World War I**. He founded a Fascist paper, *Il Popolo d'Italia* (1914), and was wounded while serving in the war (1915–17). In 1919 he organized a violent Fascist party known as the **Blackshirts** for their uniforms. In 1921 he was elected to parliament as the head of the National Fascist Party; he became known as *il duce* (the leader). In 1922 Mussolini led the Fascist **March on Rome**, which persuaded King Victor Emmanuel III (1869–1947) to name him as government leader. Within a few years, he was ruling openly as a dictator, supported by secret police and presiding over a state economy he characterized as a "corporate state." In 1929 he signed the **Lateran Treaty,** ending a long-standing sovereignty dispute with the Vatican. As a Fascist, Mussolini had much in common with German dictator **Adolf Hitler**, with whom he formed the Rome-Berlin

Axis in 1937. But after some military successes—notably the annexation of Ethiopia in 1936–37 and of Albania in 1939—Mussolini proved an incompetent conqueror. Declaring war on the Allies (**Allied Powers**) in 1940, he went on to suffer serious defeats in Greece and North Africa. Forced to resign (July 1943), he was arrested and held prisoner for two months. Rescued by the Germans, he was made a puppet ruler by the Nazis in northern Italy. Mussolini and his mistress, Clara Petacci, were arrested and killed by Communist partisans upon the fall of his puppet state in April 1945.

Myrdal, [Karl] Gunnar (1898–1987) Swedish economist and sociologist. Professor of economics at Stockholm University, he wrote *Monetary Equilibrium* (1932), about the operation of macroeconomic forces. From 1947 to 1957 he was executive secretary of the **UN** Economic Commission for Europe. He was awarded the Nobel Prize for economics in 1974 (with British economist Friedrich August von Hayek, (1899–1992). Other works include *Crisis of the Population Question* (1934), cowritten with his wife, the Swedish sociologist Alva Myrdal (1902-86). Ambassador to India (1956–61), she won the Nobel Peace Prize (1982) for her work on nuclear disarmament.

N

Nabokov, Vladimir [Vladimirovich] (1899–1977) Russian-born American writer. Born in St. Petersburg, he and his aristocratic family left Russia after the **Russian Revolution of November 1917**. After living in England, Germany, and France, he moved to the United States in 1940; he was naturalized in 1945. He taught literature at Wellesley College (1941–48) and Cornell University (1948–58) and lived in Switzerland thereafter. He was a critic, memoirist, short-story writer, poet, and lepidopterist but is best known for his novels: allusive, witty constructions of complex imagery and word play. He wrote his novels in Russian at first—including *The Defense* (1930) and *The Gift* (1937)—but in English from the 1940s. His masterpiece is *Lolita* (1955), the story of a man obsessed with a young girl. Other English-language novels include *Pnin* (1957) and *Pale Fire* (1962).

Nader, Ralph (1934–) American consumer activist. Graduating from Princeton and Harvard Law School, he became known for his study of automotive safety, *Unsafe at Any Speed* (1965), which led to federal legislation regulating vehicle design. In 1969 he founded the Study of Responsive Law; other agencies he launched include the Public Interest Research Group and the Tax Reform Group. His efforts fostered passage of the Wholesale Meat Act (1967) and the Occupational Safety and Health Act (1970). Nader was the candidate of the Green Party for president in 1996, when he won less than 1 percent of the vote, and in 2000, when he won less than 3 percent. In the 2000 race, he was widely considered to have helped defeat Democratic candidate Al Gore by siphoning away liberal Democrats who might otherwise have voted for Gore.

Nagy, Imre (1896–1958) Hungarian politician. Russian Red Army member during **World War I**, he also participated in the **Bolshevik revolution** (1917). Named to several Hungarian government positions in the 1940s, he served as premier from 1953–1955, his years marked by liberal domestic practices and criticism of Soviet control. Removed from office during the Soviet invasion of Hungary (1956), he was reinstated to stem the national revolt against it. Abducted while seeking Western assistance, he was later tried and executed.

Nasser, Gamal Abdel or **Gamâl 'Abd al-Nâsir** (1918–70) Egyptian politician. In 1952 he led a military coup to depose King **Farouk**. The first ethnically Egyptian leader since antiquity, he headed the revolutionary council (1952–56) and became president (1954–70) and prime minister (1954–62). In 1956 he nationalized the Suez Canal, prompting military intervention from Britain, France, and Israel until Egypt's claim was upheld by the **UN**. In 1958 he joined Egypt with Syria in the United Arab Republic, which broke apart in 1961. As Egypt's president until his death, he ruthlessly suppressed political opponents. He also instituted land reforms, social programs, and public works such as the construction of the Aswan Dam (completed 1968). In 1967 Egypt was defeated in the **Six-Day War** with Israel. Throughout his career, Nasser inspired Arabs with the spirit of Arab nationalism and unity. As a cofounder of the **nonaligned movement**, he was respected throughout the **Third World** for his efforts to stay independent of Western and Eastern blocs.

Nehru, [Pandit] Jawaharlal (1889–1964) Indian politician. He was the son of lawyer and Indian nationalist Motilal Nehru (1861–1931). Educated in England at Harrow and Cambridge, the younger Nehru returned to India in 1912 to practice law. After the Amritsar massacre (1919), Nehru became deeply involved in the fight for Indian independence. He joined the Indian National Congress and became a close follower of nationalist leader **Mohandas Gandhi**, who helped arrange for his election as Congress president in 1929. Nehru spent a total of nine years in prison for his civil disobedience campaigns. After **World War II**, he participated in negotiations for Indian independence and in 1947 was elected India's first prime minister; he remained in office until his death. Unlike Gandhi, he was not committed absolutely to nonviolence and used military force in a border dispute with China (1962), among other instances. Nehru pursued a foreign policy of nonalignment; at home, he developed India's industries, instituted liberalizing social reforms, and encouraged cultural and religious pluralism. He was the founder of the political dynasty that also included his daughter **Indira Gandhi** and grandson Rajiv Gandhi, each of whom would also serve as prime minister.

Neruda, Pablo (1904–73) Chilean poet and diplomat. Pen name of Neftalí Ricardo Reyes Basoalto. His evocative, anguished, sometimes surrealistic poetry often expressed social and political concerns, particularly in his works since **World War II**. Volumes include *Twenty Love Poems and One Song of Despair* (1924), *Residence on Earth* (1933), *Canto general* (1950), and *Estravagario* (1959). He fulfilled several diplomatic assignments, including consul in Buenos Aires (1933–34) and in Barcelona and Madrid (1934–36) and ambassador to Mexico (1940–42) and France (1971–72). His support for the Loyalists in the **Spanish Civil War** led to his recall from Spain. He was a senator (1945–48) until his Communist affiliation led to his expulsion from the Senate and temporary exile. He won the 1971 Nobel Prize for literature. Considered one of the greatest Latin American poets, he died just days after the right-wing coup of 1973.

Netanyahu, Benjamin (1949–) Israeli politician. Born in Tel Aviv, he grew up in the United States and Israel. He studied at the Massachusetts Institute of Technology and was an officer in an Israeli antiterror unit (1967–72). Considered an expert on **terrorism**, he became Israeli ambassador to the **UN** (1984–88), deputy foreign minister (1988–91), and deputy minister in the Prime Minister's Office (1991–92). As head of the **Likud Party** from 1993, he strongly opposed that year's Israeli-Palestinian peace accords. Charismatic and telegenic, he became prime minister in 1996, presenting himself to voters as the protector of Israeli security. He slowly continued the peace process while placating right-wing supporters by continuing to build new Jewish settlements on the **West Bank**. In 1997 the peace process all but ground to a halt, as new Palestinian terrorist attacks were met with new Israeli restrictions. Netanyahu survived an influence-peddling investigation but faced-dissension from many in his religious-nationalist coalition. His government toppled in 1996.

Neumann, John von (1903-57) Hungarian-born American mathematician. Immigrating to the U.S. in 1930, he joined the faculty at Princeton and, later, the Institute for Advanced Study (1933–57). He contributed to game theory, **quantum theory**, and **computer** theory and helped develop the first atomic bomb. He established a theoretical basis for building self-replicating machines. He was appointed to the Atomic Energy Commission in 1954. With Oskar Morgenstern (1902–77), he published *The Theory of Games and Economic Behavior* (1944).

Newman, Paul (1925–) American actor. A star since the 1950s, he has exhibited humor and intelligence in such films as *The Hustler* (1961), *Hud* (1963), and two movies with **Robert Redford**, *Butch Cassidy and the Sundance Kid* (1969) and *The Sting* (1973). He won a best actor Oscar for *The Color of Money* (1986). He has also directed and produced films. He has campaigned for liberal causes and been active as a philanthropist. His wife (since 1958) is American actress Joanne Woodward (1930–).

Ngo Dinh Diem (1901–63) South Vietnamese politician. A minister of Emperor Bao Dai, he was exiled (1945–54) but returned as prime minister (1954) under U.S. sponsorship. Overthrowing the monarchy and declaring South Vietnam a republic, he became president (1955–63). In 1956 he refused to allow scheduled elections on the question of reunification with Communist North Vietnam, sparking the **Vietnam War**. With heavy U.S. aid, he resisted the Communist guerrilla forces, the Vietcong. However, the corruption and repressiveness of his dictatorial regime made him unpopular, as did his persecution of Buddhists in favor of his fellow Catholics. He was overthrown and assassinated in a coup apparently supported by the U.S.

Nguyen Cao Ky (1930–) South Vietnamese soldier and politician. An air force officer, he participated in the 1963 coup overthrowing President **Ngo Dinh Diem**. He became premier (1965–67) and vice president (1967–71) under **Nguyen Van Thieu**. He ran against Thieu for the presidency in 1971 but was defeated in a controversial election. After South Vietnam fell to the North, he lived in exile in the U.S.

Nguyen Van Thieu (1923–) South Vietnamese soldier and politician. He led the 1963 coup overthrowing President **Ngo Dinh Diem**. He was president (1967–75) of the Republic of South Vietnam at the time of the heaviest U.S. involvement in the **Vietnam War**. When South Vietnam fell to the North, he resigned and fled into exile.

Nicholas II (1868–1918) Russian czar (1894–1917). He continued the repressive tactics of his father and predecessor, Alexander III (1845–94), but revolutionary fervor continued to spread. He proved ineffective as a war leader in the **Russo-Japanese War** (1904–05), which Russia lost. On **Bloody Sunday**, January 22, 1905, his troops fired on protesters outside the Winter Palace, igniting the **Revolution of 1905**. He agreed to establish a constitutional government but soon dissolved the Duma (assembly). During **World War I** he took command of Russian forces, leaving Czarina Alexandra (1872–1918) and her adviser **Grigory Rasputin** to govern at home. Popular discontent with their administration and frustration with the miseries of war contributed to the **Russian Revolution of November 1917**. Nicholas abdicated in March 1917; in July 1918 he and his family were shot by the victorious **Bolsheviks** at Ekaterinburg.

Nicholson, Jack (1937–) American actor. He is known for his sardonic smile and powerful performances in four decades of films, including *Chinatown* (1974). He won two best actor Oscars, for *One Flew Over the Cuckoo's Nest* (1975) and *As Good as It Gets* (1997), and a best supporting actor Oscar for *Terms of Endearment* (1983). He has also directed and co-scripted films.

Nicklaus, Jack [William] (1940–) American athlete. Considered history's greatest golfer, he won 20 championship titles, setting a record for most major golf tournament victories in a career. He won his first professional tournament in 1962, at the U.S Open. Nicknamed the "Golden Bear," he won five Professional Golfers' Association (PGA) tournaments, four U.S. Opens, three British Opens, and six Masters tournaments, including a 1986 win that made him the oldest Masters winner in history. The PGA named him Golfer of the Century in 1988. He designed many noted golf courses.

Niebuhr, Reinhold (1892–1971) American theologian. Born in Wright City, Mo., he was a socially conscious pastor of Bethel Evangelical Church in Detroit, Mich., for 13 years before joining the faculty of Union Theological Seminary, New York City (1928–60). A socialist and political activist from the 1930s, he explored political morality and Christianity in *Moral Man and Immoral Society* (1932) and *Christianity and Power Politics* (1940). After the war he developed a view he called conservative realism, applied in works including *Christian Realism and Political Problems* (1953). His brother was American theologian Helmut Richard Niebuhr (1894–1964).

Nijinsky, Vaslav Formich (1890–1950) Russian dancer and choreographer. One of the finest dancers of the century, he began his career with the Imperial Ballet but became known for roles with Sergey Diaghilev's Ballet Russes. In roles including *Petrouchka* and *The Afternoon of a Faun* (1912) he demonstrated his strong presence and free expression. He often choreographed and starred in works, e.g., *Till Eulenspiegel* (1916). Mental illness ended his career in 1919, with much of his later life spent in asylums.

Nin, Anaïs (1903–77) French-born American writer. Born in Paris, she is known for her far-reaching diaries (6 volumes, 1966–80), which begin in 1914 and explore her artistic development and psychology. Her works include the novel *Seduction of the Minotaur* (1961), the short-story collection *Under a Glass Bell* (1944), and a work of criticism, *The Future of the Novel* (1968).

Nixon, Richard Milhous (1913–94) Thirty-seventh U.S. president (1968–74). Born in Yorba Linda, Calif., he was educated at Whittier College (B.A., 1934) and Duke University Law School (graduated 1937). He served in the Navy (1942–46) during **World War II**. A devoted anti-Communist, he gained national attention when, as a Republican congressman from California (1947–51), he investigated **Alger Hiss** on espionage charges. His subsequent Senate term (1951–53) was cut short when he was elected to the vice presidency (1953–61) on the Republican ticket with **Dwight D. Eisenhower**. Running for the presidency in 1960, Nixon lost to **John F. Kennedy**; he later lost a California gubernatorial campaign (1962). In 1968, appealing to conservatives tired of the **Vietnam War** and antiwar protest, Nixon defeated **Democrat** Hubert Humphrey (1911–78) in the race for the White House. He was reelected in 1972, defeating George McGovern (1922–). He accomplished a cease-fire in the **Vietnam War** (1973) that permitted complete withdrawal of U.S. ground forces, though not victory. Before the cease-fire, he escalated bombing and invaded Cambodia (1970) and Laos (1971). He improved relations with the **Soviet Union** and opened up relations with China, which he visited in 1972. Trying to combat inflation, he instituted wage and price controls in 1971. His second term was dominated by scandal.

Charges of tax evasion and corruption forced his vice president, Spiro Agnew (1918–96), to resign in 1973; Nixon replaced him with **Gerald Ford**. In the **Watergate** scandal, Nixon and his top aides were accused of employing illegal tactics to win the 1972 election as part of a persistent pattern of abusing federal power. After the House Judiciary Committee adopted three articles of impeachment in July 1974, Nixon became the first president to resign from office (August 9, 1974). Shortly afterward, his successor, Ford, granted him an unconditional pardon. Nixon wrote several books, including *Memoirs* (1978).

Nkrumah, Kwame (1909–72) Ghanaian politician. Born in what was then the British colony of the Gold Coast, he was educated as a teacher. From 1935 to 1947 he lived in the U.S. and England, becoming a committed anticolonialist. In 1945 he organized the fifth Pan-African Congress in Manchester, England. He returned to the Gold Coast in 1947, where he broke with the United Gold Coast Convention (UGCC) to form the more radically anticolonialist Convention People's Party (CPP). After his party won the first national elections in 1951, he became prime minister (1952–60). In 1957 the Gold Coast became Ghana, the first sub-Saharan African nation to gain independence from colonial rule, with Nkrumah continuing as its first prime minister. Ghana became a republic in 1960, with Nkrumah as its first president. An increasingly autocratic ruler, he pursued African socialist and Pan-Africanist policies while in office but lost support because of corruption and economic woes. Overthrown in a coup in 1966, he lived his last years in exile in Guinea. Works include *Towards Colonial Freedom* (1946) and *Handbook of Revolutionary Warfare* (1968).

Nureyev, Rudolf Hametovich (1938–93) Russian dancer and choreographer. One of the principal ballet dancers of his age, he was born in Siberia and became a soloist dancer in 1958, with the Kirov Ballet. In 1961 he defected to Paris, and in 1962 he joined London's Royal Ballet. There he entered a memorable partnership with British ballerina Dame Margot Fonteyn (1919–91), performing in *Giselle* and *Swan Lake,* among other works. Known as the "Boss," he was noted for his athletic dancing and strong stage presence.

Nyerere, Julius Kambarage (1922–1993) African politician. Born in the former Tanganyika, he was educated in Uganda and at the University of Edinburgh. He returned home to become a leader of his country's independence movement, founding the Tanganyika African National Union in 1954. When Britain granted Tanganyika independence in 1961, Nyerere became its first prime minister. In 1962 he helped make the country a republic, with him as its first president. In 1964 he united Tanganyika and Zanzibar as the republic of Tanzania, with him as president (1964–85). His one-party form of government, led by the Revolutionary Party (CCM), emphasized a form of **socialism** based on *ujamaa,* Swahili for "familyhood": its measures included rural collectivization and mass literacy campaigns. He retired from the presidency in 1985.

O

Oates, Joyce Carol (1938–) American writer. She is a prolific and respected author of fiction, drama, poetry, and criticism. Her novels, often intense and violent, include *I Lock My Door upon Myself* (1990) and the trilogy *A Garden of Earthly Delights* (1967), *Expensive People* (1968), and *them* (1969; winner of the National Book Award).

Obote, [Apollo] Milton (1924–) Ugandan politician. Becoming prime minister in 1962, he guided the country to independent rule that year. After directing the Ugandan revolution in 1966, he served as president from 1966 to 1971. Forced from office by **Idi Amin**

in 1971, he regained his position (1980–84) after Amin's forced exile in 1979 and established a democracy. He was unseated by a military coup.

O'Casey, Sean (1880–1964) Irish playwright. Born John Casey, he wrote several sinewy, socially conscious plays for Dublin's Abbey Theatre, including *The Shadow of a Gunman* (1923), *Juno and the Paycock* (1924) and *The Plough and the Stars* (1926), which provoked local riots. In 1928 he broke with the theater over its rejection of his expressionist play *The Silver Tassie* (1928), later produced in London. Subsequent, more doctrinaire plays include *Within the Gates* (1933) and *The Star Turns Red* (1940). His six-volume autobiography was published from 1939 to 1954.

O'Connor, [Mary] Flannery (1925–64) American writer. Born in Savannah, Georgia, she set most of her short stories and novels in the South. Her emphasis on brutal violence and grotesque comedy was known as Southern Gothic. Central to her work were themes of faith and redemption, informed by her own Catholicism. Works include the novels *Wise Blood* (1952) and *The Violent Bear It Away* (1960) and the short-story collection *A Good Man Is Hard to Find* (1955).

O'Connor, Frank (1903–66) Irish writer. Born Michael O'Donovan, he was a member of the **Irish Republican Army** (1921–22) and gained immediate fame with his first short-story collection, *Guests of the Nation* (1931). Other collections, also known for their incisiveness, include *The Wild Bird's Nest* (1932) and *Crab Apple Jelly* (1944). He has written poetry, autobiographies, and criticism and was director of Dublin's Abbey Theatre (1936–39).

O'Connor, Sandra Day (1930–) American jurist. The first female justice of the U.S. Supreme Court, she was born in El Paso, Tex., and received a law degree from Stanford University in 1952. She served as Republican state senator from Arizona (1969–75). On the state court of appeals from 1979, she was nominated an associate justice of the U.S. Supreme Court in 1981. Her tenure has been marked by temperate conservatism.

Odets, Clifford (1906–63) American writer. Born in Philadelphia, Pa., he cofounded the experimental Group Theater and in the early 1930s established himself as the foremost playwright of left-leaning social realism. His plays include *Waiting for Lefty* (1935), *Awake and Sing!* (1935), *Golden Boy* (1937), *They Clash by Night* (1941), and *The Country Girl* (1950). In 1934 he joined the Communist Party. From the mid-1930s he wrote film scripts in Hollywood.

Oe, Kenzaburo (1935–) Japanese writer. Often characterized by intense emotion and violence, his novels and short fiction have expressed much about Japan's cultural and political searching after the country's defeat in **World War II**. Works include *Shiiku* (1958), *A Personal Matter* (1964), and *Teach Us to Outgrow Our Madness* (1969). He won the Nobel Prize for literature in 1994.

Oldenburg, Claes [Thure] (1929–) Swedish-born American artist. A U.S. citizen from 1953, he was a leader of the pop art movement. He worked principally in sculpture and graphic arts; he also created happenings, such as "The Store" (1961), at which he sold plaster replicas of food and other common items. Works include giant sculptures of ordinary objects, such as *Lipstick* (1969), and soft sculptures, such as *Soft Typewriter* (1963).

Olivier, Laurence Kerr, baron (1907–89) British actor and director. Widely considered the greatest Shakespearean actor of the century, he appeared on the professional stage from

1924 and joined the Old Vic in 1937, giving a notable title performance in *Hamlet*. In Hollywood he appeared in *Wuthering Heights* (1939), *Rebecca* (1939), and *Pride and Prejudice* (1940), among other films. Following **World War II** service, he became codirector (with British actor Ralph Richardson, 1902–83) of England's the Old Vic theater, and he directed and starred in films *Henry V* (1945) and *Hamlet* (1948). Other memorable films in which he appeared include *The Entertainer* (1960). From 1962 to 1973 he was founder-director of the Royal National Theatre. He was knighted in 1947 and became Baron Olivier of Brighton in 1970, the first stage actor so honored. His second wife was British actress Vivien Leigh (1913–67), to whom he was married from 1940 to 1961; his third wife, whom he married in 1961, was British actress Joan Plowright (1929–).

O'Neill, Eugene [Gladstone] (1888–1953) American writer. Born in New York City to a pair of actors, he created several one-act plays before writing the full-length *Beyond the Horizon* (1920), which won a Pulitzer Prize. From the 1920s through the 1940s, he established himself as the nation's preeminent playwright with a string of psychological works that experimented with theme and technique. They include *The Emperor Jones* (1920); *Anna Christie* (1921, Pulitzer); *The Hairy Ape* (1922); *Desire under the Elms* (1924); *All God's Chillun Got Wings* (1924); *The Great God Brown* (1926); *Strange Interlude* (1928, Pulitzer); the trilogy *Mourning Becomes Electra* (1931); *Ah, Wilderness!* (1933); *The Iceman Cometh* (1946); and *A Moon for the Misbegotten* (1947). His autobiographical Pulitzer Prize–winner masterwork, *Long Day's Journey into Night* (1941), was produced posthumously in 1956. He was awarded the Nobel Prize for literature in 1936.

Ophüls, Max (1902–57) German film director. Born Maximilian Oppenheimer, he was a stage director before turning to film in 1930. With films like *Liebelei* (1933) he began to develop his intricate, fluid cinematic style. In France and Switzerland from 1933, he settled in the U.S. in 1941; notable films of the period include *Letter from an Unknown Woman* (1948). Back in France in the 1950s, he directed his finest works: *La Ronde* (1950), *The Earrings of Madame De* (1953), and *Lola Montez* (1955). His son is American filmmaker Marcel Ophüls (1927–).

Oppenheimer, [Julius] Robert (1904–67) American physicist. While at the University of California (1929–47), he was recruited to direct the **Manhattan Project** (1942–45), the top-secret government program to build the first atomic bomb. Though Oppenheimer succeeded—with the first bomb detonated near Los Alamos, N.M., in 1945—and remained a government adviser after the war, his left-wing views cast him under suspicion of espionage and his security clearance was withdrawn in 1953. He was director of the Institute for Advanced Study at Princeton (1947–66).

Orozoco, José Clemente (1883–1949) Mexican painter. Working in fresco, he pioneered modern murals with his works of social conscience rendered in a bold, expressionistic style. Early murals include a controversial series for the Escuela Nacional Prepatoria, Mexico City (1923–24), notably *The Rich Banquet While the Workers Quarrel*. While in the U.S. (1927–34), he painted murals for colleges, including *Quetzalcoatl* (Dartmouth, N.H.), and *Mankind's Struggle* (New School for Social Research, N.Y.). Paintings include *Zapatistas* (1931).

Ortega y Gasset, José (1883–1955) Spanish philosopher. Professor of metaphysics at the University of Madrid, he influenced Western thinking with his metaphysical works on the human power to understand and transcend limitations of history, reason, and other forces. Works include *Meditations on Quixote* (1914) and the essay volume *The Modern Theme*

(1923). Most well-known is *The Revolt of the Masses* (1929), which posits elite intellectual leadership for the masses.

Orwell, George (1903–50) Indian-born British writer. Pen name of Eric Arthur Blair. He expressed his antitotalitarian views throughout his works, notably in his political novels *Animal Farm* (1946) and *1984* (1949). Other works include the autobiographical *Down and out in Paris and London* (1933), *The Road to Wigan Pier* (1937), and *Homage to Catalonia* (1938), influenced by his participation in the **Spanish Civil War**. His essays are respected for their lucidity and unaffected style.

Osborne, John James (1929-94) British playwright. Originally an actor, he came to prominence with his play *Look back in Anger* (1956), which captured postwar working-class disaffection and defined the writers known as the Angry Young Men. Other notable works include *The Entertainer* (1957), *Luther* (1961), and *Time Present* (1968). He won an Academy Award for his screenplay for *Tom Jones* (1964).

Owens, Jesse (1913–80) American athlete. Born James Cleveland Owens in Danville, Ala., he set three track-and-field world records and tied another at an event in Michigan on May 25, 1935. At the Olympic Games in Berlin in 1936, the African-American athlete epitomized defiance of Nazi views as he won four gold medals—in the 100 meters, 200 meters, long jump, and 400 meters relay.

Oz, Amos (1939–) Israeli writer. Born Amos Klausner, he writes novels and short stories in Hebrew. His works explore contemporary Israeli society. Novels include *My Michael* (1968) and *A Perfect Peace* (1982).

Ozu, Yasujiro (1903–63) Japanese film director. Born in Tokyo, he worked as a scriptwriter and assistant editor before becoming known for his films, traditionally cinematic studies of middle-class family relationships. Among his works are *The Story of Floating Weeds* (1934), *Tokyo Story* (1953), *Early Spring* (1956), and *Late Autumn* (1960).

P

Pacino, Al (1940–) American actor. Though he has won two Tony Awards on stage, he is best known for his intense, brooding performances in such films as *The Godfather* (1972), *The Godfather Part II* (1974), and *Dog Day Afternoon* (1975). He won a best actor Oscar for *Scent of a Woman* (1992).

Paderewski, Ignacy Jan (1860–1941) Polish composer and politician. Famed for his piano performances, he was a Polish patriot who served as prime minister in 1919 and briefly headed the government in exile during **World War II**. Compositions included the Minuet in G for piano and the opera *Manru* (1901).

Paley, William S[amuel] (1901–90) American broadcasting executive. He bought a small local **radio** network in 1928 and built it into the Columbia Broadcasting System (CBS), one of the nation's most powerful radio, and later **television**, networks. As head of CBS, first as president and then as chairman, until 1990, he built a respected news organization and founded Columbia Records. An avid art collector, he was president of the Museum of Modern Art.

Pandit, Vijaya Lakshmi (1900–90) Indian diplomat. The sister of **Jawaharlal Nehru**, she was a member of the Indian National Congress and was imprisoned several times for agitating for independence. She led the Indian delegation to the **UN** (1946–51) and served as ambassador to the **Soviet Union** (1947–49) and the United States (1949–51). She was later president of the UN General Assembly (1953–54), India's high commissioner to the United Kingdom (1955–61), and governor of Maharashtra (1962–64).

Pankhurst, Emmeline [Goulden] (1858–1928) British suffragist. A fervent activist for women's rights, she founded the Women's Franchise League in 1889 and the Women's Social and Political Union in 1903. From 1912 the union employed extreme militancy to further its goals, resulting in Pankhurst's frequent arrest and imprisonment. During **World War I**, she shifted her focus from women's rights to her country's war effort. She was married to Richard Marsden Pankhurst, a barrister who wrote the first British woman suffrage bill in the 1860s.

Papen, Franz von (1879–1969) German soldier and politician. He was military attaché in Mexico City (1913–15) and Washington, D.C. (1915) until being recalled at the request of the U.S. on suspicion of espionage. After serving and being deposed as German chancellor in 1932, he aided in the election of **Adolf Hitler** as chancellor in 1933. He became vice chancellor under Hitler (1933–34) and ambassador to Austria (1934–38) and Turkey (1939–44). In 1946 he was acquitted of war crimes at Nuremberg.

Parker, Charlie (1920–55) American jazz musician. Born Charles Christopher Parker Jr., he was known as "Bird." He was a chief force in the development of modern jazz, as swing was being replaced by bop. An alto saxophonist, he was noted for intricate, quicksilver improvisation.

Parker, Dorothy (1893–1967) American writer. Born Dorothy Rothschild in West End, N.Y., she acquired her professional name from Edwin P. Parker, to whom she was married from 1917 until their divorce in 1928. She worked for *Vogue* (1916) and *Vanity Fair* (1917–20) before becoming a book reviewer for the *New Yorker* (1927–33). In the 1920s she was a leading member of the Algonquin Round Table, a circle of wits that included James Thurber and Alexander Woolcott. Her short stories, noted for their mordant, wrenching observations of the world, are collected in *Laments for the Living* (1930), *After Such Pleasures* (1933), and *Here Lies* (1939); one of the best-known is "Big Blonde." Among her verse collections is *Enough Rope* (1926). She collaborated on the screenplays for *A Star Is Born* (1937, 1954), among other titles.

Pasternak, Boris [Leonidovich] (1890–1960) Soviet writer. Following study at Moscow University and the University of Marburg in Germany, he began publishing poetry and established himself as a major poet with two collections, *My Sister, Life* (1922) and *Themes and Variations* (1923). In light of 1930s intellectual repression, he turned to translations of major Western writers. In 1955 he completed the novel *Doctor Zhivago*, but the Soviet government prohibited publication. After the novel's 1957 publication in Italy, the book gained worldwide praise and its author won the 1958 Nobel Prize for literature, which the government forced him to refuse. Despite being expelled from the Union of Soviet Writers and enduring calls for deportation, he remained in Russia until his death.

Patton, George [Smith], Jr. (1885–1945) American soldier. Born in San Gabriel, Calif., he was an aide-to-camp to General John Pershing during **World War I**. During **World War II** he commanded various divisions and armies, fighting victoriously in Tunisia (1943), leading the Seventh Army in the invasion of Sicily (1943), and leading the Third Army in its advance across France and Germany (1944–45). Stern and flamboyant, and a masterful leader of tank warfare, he was known as "Old Blood and Guts."

Paul VI (1897–1978) Pope (1963–78). Born Giovanni Battista Montini in Italy, he presided over much of **Vatican II** following the death of its convener, **John XXIII**, and implemented many of the reforms it called for, including liturgical renewal and vernacular Masses. He traveled widely and promoted ecumenism. His encyclical *Humanae Vitae* (1968) ignited controversy by reaffirming the church's ban on artificial contraception.

Pauling, Linus Carl (1901–94) American chemist. Receiving a Ph.D. at the California Institute of Technology (1925), he was professor of chemistry there (1931–64), doing research in molecular biology and chemical bonds. For his work he was awarded the Nobel Prize for chemistry (1954). In 1962 he won the Nobel Peace Prize for efforts to ban nuclear testing. He is popularly known for promoting the use of vitamin C to treat colds. Books include *The Nature of the Chemical Bond and the Structure of Molecules and Crystals* (1939) and *Vitamin C and the Common Cold* (1970).

Pavarotti, Luciano (1935–) Italian singer. An operatic tenor, he debuted at the Teatro Municipale in Reggio Emilia in 1961 as Rodolfo in *La Bohème*, one of his best-known roles. His full and open voice won him wide acclaim as he performed in opera houses around the world. In the 1990s, his albums as part of the "Three Tenors," with Spanish tenors Placido Domingo (1941–) and Jose Carreras (1946–), became the best-selling classical recordings of all time.

Pavlov, Ivan Petrovich (1849–1936) Russian physiologist. Through experiments with dogs as described in *Conditioned Reflexes* (1926), he established the existence of conditioned reflexes, an important contribution to the psychological school of behaviorism. He received the 1904 Nobel Prize for physiology or **medicine** for his research on the physiology of the digestive system.

Pavlova, Anna (1882–1931) Russian dancer. Considered the finest ballerina of the age, she danced with the Russian Imperial Ballet and briefly with the Ballets Russes before forming her own company in 1914 and touring widely. She was renowned for her classical technique in such ballets as *Giselle* and *The Dying Swan* and for popularizing ballet throughout the world.

Paz, Octavio (1914–98) Mexican writer. Born to an intellectually distinguished family, he is known for his stately, nuanced poetry and prose influenced by Mexican history and social conscience. Essay collections include his influential study of the roots of the Mexican character *The Labyrinth of Solitude* (1950), and *The Bow and the Lyre* (1956) and *The Other Mexico* (1972). Poetry collections include *Eagle or Sun* (1951) and *Sunstone* (1957). He translated the works of Japanese poet Basho. For 25 years he served in the diplomatic corps, retiring from his position as ambassador to India in 1968 in political protest. He was awarded the Nobel Prize for literature (1990).

Pearson, Lester Bowles (1897–1972) Canadian politician. Born in Toronto, he worked in diplomatic service from 1928. Instrumental in the founding of the **United Nations** (1944), he was president of the UN General Assembly (1952–53). Member of Canada's Liberal Party, he served as minister of Canada's external affairs (1948–57) and from 1963 to 1968 was prime minister. He was awarded the Nobel Peace Prize in 1957 for his mediation of the 1956 **Suez Crisis** of the **Arab–Israeli War**.

Peary, Robert Edwin (1856–1920) American explorer. A U.S. Navy engineer from 1881, he led several arctic expeditions to Greenland. He claimed to be the first to reach the North Pole on April 6, 1909, accompanied by African-American dogsled driver Matthew Henson

(1866–1955) and several Eskimos. His claim was disputed by Frederick Albert Cook (1865–1940), who claimed to have reached the Pole a year earlier, but the U.S. Congress recognized Peary's claim in 1911; Peary retired from the navy as a rear admiral that year. Controversy over Peary's claim has continued since. In 1997 historian Robert M. Bryce asserted that neither Peary nor Cook had reached the North Pole's latitude of 90 degrees north. Bryce credited a Joseph Otis Fletcher of Shawnee, Okla., with being the first person to reach the Pole, on May 3, 1952.

Pei, I[eoh] M[ing] (1917–) Chinese-born American architect. After studying at the University of Pennsylvania and MIT, he opened his own architectural firm in 1955. Specializing in public buildings, he is renowned for his simple, stunning, geometric designs. Notable buildings include the John Hancock Tower (1973, Boston, Mass.) and the East Wing of the National Gallery of Art (1971–78, Washington, D.C.). He became a U.S. citizen in 1954.

Pelé (1940–) Brazilian soccer player. Born Edson Arantes do Nascimento, he led Brazil's national team to their first World Cup title in 1958, and again in 1962 and 1970. He retired from international play in 1971. From 1975 to his 1977 full retirement, he played with the New York Cosmos, helping to popularize soccer in the U.S. He is considered the game's greatest inside forward, scoring more than 1,200 goals in his three-decade career.

Peres, Shimon (1923–) Israeli politician. Born Shimon Peresky in Poland, he immigrated to Palestine in 1934 but was educated in the United States. Elected to the Knesset in 1959, he held several government posts, including minister of defense (1974–77). He was Labor prime minister in 1977, 1984 to 1986, and 1995 to 1996. In 1992 he became foreign minister in the cabinet of his rival, **Yitzhak Rabin**. In that role, Peres spearheaded the negotiations that led to peace agreements between Israel and the **Palestine Liberation Organization (PLO)** in 1993. He shared the 1994 Nobel Peace Prize with Rabin and PLO leader **Yasir Arafat**.

Perón, Juan [Domingo] (1895–1974) Argentine soldier and politician. An army officer, he participated in a 1943 coup and was elected president (1946–55). As president, he spurred industrialization, nationalized railroads, and supported laborers; he also suppressed political dissent. His popular wife, **Evita Perón,** was unofficial copresident and de facto minister of health and labor. Though he was deposed in a coup and exiled in Madrid, his Peróniste movement kept his name alive and backed his return to power in 1973, when he was reelected president. He died in office in 1974, to be succeeded by his third wife and vice president, Isabel Perón (1930–), who was deposed by a coup in 1976.

Perón, Maria Eva Duarte (1919–52) Argentine politician. Known as Evita, she was a **radio** and film actress before becoming the second wife of Juan Perón in 1945. From the time he came to power as president (1946) until her early death from cancer, she was his unofficial copresident. She was enormously popular with workers, women, and the poor. She secured the vote for women, instituted social welfare programs, and was de facto minister of health and labor. Though she was nominated for the vice presidency in 1951, the army forced her to withdraw.

Perot, Ross (1930–) American businessman and politician. Born Henry Ross Perot in Texarkana, Tex., he served in the navy (1953–57) and founded Electronic Data Systems (1962). The data processing business, which he took public in 1968 and sold in 1984, made him a billionaire; he later founded another data processing company, Perot Systems (1988).

In 1992 he was a third-party candidate for president. Spending his own money lavishly and appealing to discontented voters with his populist themes, he won 19 percent of the popular vote but carried no states. His appeal had declined by 1996, when he ran for president on the Reform Party ticket and carried only 8 percent of the popular vote.

Pershing, John Joseph (1860–1948) American general. Known as "Black Jack." Born near Laclede, Mo., he graduated from West Point in 1886 and served in the frontier cavalry before fighting in Cuba in the Spanish-American War (1898) and in the Philippines from 1899. He became a brigadier general in 1906, a major general in 1916, and general of the armies in 1919. From 1916 to 1917 he led the expeditionary force into Mexico in pursuit of **Pancho Villa**. From 1917 to 1919, he was commander in chief of the **American Expeditionary Force** in **World War I**, cooperating in the Meuse-Argonne offensive that led to the collapse of German forces. He was chief of staff from 1921 until his retirement in 1924. His memoir, *My Experiences in the World War* (1931), won the Pulitzer Prize for history.

Pétain, Henri Philippe Omer (1856–1951) French soldier and politician. Son of a farmer, he was born in Cauchy-la-Tour and became an instructor at the *Ecole de Guerre* (Staff College) in 1888. Named general during **World War I**, he led a successful command against the Germans at Verdun (1916) and was named French commander in chief. In 1939 he became ambassador to Spain, and in 1940 premier of France. He soon signed an armistice with Germany and became head of the **Vichy** collaboration government, until he fled for Switzerland after the Allied (see **Allied Powers**) invasion in 1944. In 1945 postwar trials he was convicted of treason and sentenced to death, but **Charles de Gaulle** commuted his sentence to life imprisonment. He died alone on the Ile d'Yeux.

Petty, Richard Lee (1937–) American automobile racer. The most successful stock car driver in history, he won the Daytona 500 and the national championship of the National Association for Stock Car Auto Racing each seven times between 1964 and 1981. Known as "King Richard," he notched over 200 victories before his retirement in 1992.

Philby, Kim (1912–88) British spy. Byname of Harold Adrian Russell Philby. The son of British explorer Harry St. John Bridger Philby (1885–1960), he was recruited by Soviet intelligence in 1933. From 1937 to 1940 he was a journalist and Soviet agent in Spain and Europe. During **World War II** he was in British secret intelligence, providing material for Soviet contacts. After the war, he was named liaison for U.S. and British intelligence services until he defected to the **Soviet Union** in 1951. In 1963 the British government pronounced him a spy.

Piaf, Edith (1915–63) French singer. Born Edith Giovanna Gassion, she was a street singer before being discovered and renamed la môme piaf (little sparrow) by a French cabaret impresario in 1930. She was beloved worldwide for her dramatically rendered love songs, such as "L'Hymme a l'amour" and "La Vie en rose."

Piaget, Jean (1896–1980) Swiss psychologist. He received his Ph.D. at the University of Neuchâtel (1918), working afterward with psychologist Théodore Simon in Paris. Beginning in 1921, he researched the intellectual processes of children at the Institut Jean-Jacques Rousseau in Geneva; he was codirector of that institute from 1933 to 1971. His theory of children's mental development, emphasizing the effects of human interactions, influenced educational philosophy around the world. Works include *The Language and Thought of the Child* (1926).

Picasso, Pablo (1881–1973) Spanish artist. Born Pablo Ruiz y Picasso, he attended the Royal Academy of Barcelona, then moved to Paris and began working as a painter. Following a period of early experimentation influenced by 19th-century French painter Henri de Toulouse-Lautrec (*Old Woman*, 1901), he entered his "blue period," with often melancholy paintings of blue tones (*The Old Guitarist*, 1903), followed by his "rose period," of light tones and circus subject matter. His 1907 *Les Demoiselles d'Avignon* was crucial to the development of cubism. Into the 1920s, his figures became larger and more representational (*The Three Musicians*, 1921). His most famous painting, *Guernica* (1937), expressed outrage at Fascist atrocities in the **Spanish Civil War**. In 1947 he moved from Paris and concentrated in sculpture, ceramics, and the graphic arts, often in works of fantasy and comic invention. He is remembered as perhaps the most important figure in 20th-century art.

Pickford, Mary (1893–1979) Canadian-born American film actress. Born Gladys Mary Smith, she gained fame as "America's Sweetheart" by starring in many films including *The Poor Little Rich Girl* (1917), *Rebecca of Sunnybrook Farm* (1917), and *Pollyanna* (1920). From 1920 to 1935 she was married to swashbuckling American film actor Douglas Fairbanks (1883–1939). Together with **Charlie Chaplin** and **D. W. Griffith** they formed the U.S. film studio United Artists (1919).

Pilsudski, Józef Klemens (1867–1935) Polish soldier and politician. Son of a poor nobleman serving under the czar, he worked for Polish independence throughout his life. Several times during the early 20th century he was imprisoned and exiled by Russian officials. He founded the Polish Socialist Party and led a bloody uprising that failed to achieve his goal of Polish revolution. On Poland's independence after the Allied (see **Allied Powers**) victory in **World War I**, Pilsudski became head of state (until 1923) and army chief of staff. Among his accomplishments was the Treaty of Riga (1921), which extended Poland's eastern border. In 1926 he led a coup and established a military dictatorship. One of his final acts was to sign nonaggression pacts with Germany and the **Soviet Union** in 1934.

Pinero, Sir Arthur Wing (1855–1934) British playwright. Although he gained fame with his farces and romantic comedies, he is best remembered for his social dramas, particularly *The Profligate* (1889) and *The Second Mrs. Tanqueray* (1893).

Pinochet [Ugarte], Augusto (1915–) Chilean dictator. He was a professional soldier who rose to become commander-in-chief. With **CIA** support, he led the right-wing military coup that deposed and killed leftist president **Salvador Allende** in 1973. As head of a military junta and president of Chile, Pinochet ruled through bloody repression, imprisoning, killing, and torturing thousands. Many opponents "disappeared" and are presumed dead. His free-market reforms boosted the economy but widened the gap between rich and poor. His dictatorship lasted from 1973 to 1990, when he accepted the verdict of a plebiscite calling on him to step down. He remained commander of the army until 1998, when he took the post of senator-for-life. That year, he was arrested in Great Britain at the request of a Spanish magistrate, who sought Pinochet's extradition to face charges of murdering Spanish citizens in Chile during his dictatorship. In 2000, upon his release by British authorities who declared him unfit to stand trial, he returned to Chile, where he faced more charges of kidnapping and murder.

Pinter, Harold (1930–) British playwright. Originally an actor, he gained his first success as a playwright with *The Caretaker* (1960), which introduced his enduring preoccupation with the erosion of human relationships. Among his other plays are *The Birthday Party* (1958), *The Homecoming* (1964), and *No Man's Land* (1975). His screenplays include *The*

Servant (1962), *The Go-Between* (1969), and *The French Lieutenant's Woman* (1981).

Pirandello, Luigi (1867–1936) Italian writer. An author of wide range, he began writing poetry in the 1890s, then published seven novels, notably *The Late Mattia Pascal* (1904). He began writing plays around **World War I**, experimenting with the "theater within the theater" in over 43 titles. His best-known works include *Right You Are, If You Think You Are* (1917), *Six Characters in Search of an Author* (1921), *Henry IV* (1922), *Lazzaro* (1929), and *Tonight We Improvise* (1930). His work influenced the development of absurdist theater and such playwrights as **Eugène Ionesco** and **Samuel Beckett**. In 1934 Pirandello was awarded the Nobel Prize for literature.

Pius XI (1857–1939) Pope (1922–39). Born Achille Ratti in Italy, he spoke out on many social and political questions of the day. He opposed **Fascism**, racism, and anti-Semitism. Criticizing both **Communism** and laissez-faire **capitalism**, he called for social reform and greater lay participation in religion. During his papacy, the **Lateran Treaty** (1929) resolved the conflict between the church and Italy by creating the independent state of Vatican City and establishing papal recognition of Italy.

Pius XII (1876–1958) Pope (1939–58). Born Eugenio Pacelli in Italy, he became papal secretary of state in 1930, negotiating the concordat with Nazi Germany in 1933. As pope, he maintained the church's neutrality during **World War II**, and he was later criticized for not speaking out against the **Holocaust** or striving to protect Italian Jews. After the war, he was a vigorous opponent of **Communism**, particularly in Italy. In 1950 he defined the dogma of the Assumption of the Virgin Mary.

Pius X, Saint (1835–1914) Pope (1903–14). Born Giuseppe Melchiorre Sarto in Italy, he condemned religious modernism as heretical (1907) and opposed anticlerical laws in France and Portugal. He initiated recodification of canon law and established a new breviary. He was concerned with the condition of the poor and was widely venerated during his life. He was canonized in 1954.

Planck, Max [Karl Ernst Ludwig] (1858–1947) German physicist. After studies at the Universities of Munich and Berlin (Ph.D., 1879), he taught at those institutions and the University of Kiel. In 1900 he founded **quantum theory** with his discovery that radiant energy is absorbed or emitted in discrete amounts called quanta. He also formulated Planck's constant. He won the Nobel Prize for physics in 1918.

Plekhanov, Georgy Valentinovich (1857–1918) Russian revolutionary and political philosopher. In exile from Russia from 1880 to 1917, living mainly in Geneva, Switzerland, he founded the first Russian Marxist revolutionary group, the Liberation of Labor (1883), which later became the Russian Social Democratic Workers' Party (1898). He influenced **V. I. Lenin's** thought but split with Lenin in 1903, becoming the leader of the **Menshevik** ("minority") wing as opposed to **Bolshevik** ("majority") wing of the divided Social Democratic Party. Unlike Lenin, he supported Russian involvement in **World War I**. Returning to Russia after the **Russian Revolution of February 1917**, he fruitlessly opposed the Bolsheviks. Works include *Socialism and Anarchism*.

Poincaré, Raymond (1860–1934) French politician. Cousin of French mathematician [Jules] Henri Poincaré (1854–1912), he was a Republican senator (1903–12) and was president (1913–20) and premier of France (1912–13, 1922–23, 1926–29). During **World War I**, he increased national defenses and sustained morale; postwar, he sent French troops to occupy the Ruhr to demand German payment of **reparations** (1923). As premier and minister of finance (1926–29), he stabilized the franc and stemmed a financial crisis.

Pol Pot (c. 1925–1998) Cambodian dictator. Born Saloth Sar to a peasant family and educated in a monastery and in France, he joined the Communist Party in 1946. In the 1960s he became leader of the **Khmer Rouge** guerrillas seeking to overthrow Prince **Sihanouk**. In 1975 he succeeded in establishing the Democratic Republic of Kampuchea, of which he became prime minister (1976–79). In pursuit of his vision of an agrarian society, he systematically wiped out the middle class and drove urban dwellers into rural labor camps, killing between 2 million and 3 million people. A Vietnamese invasion in December 1978 overthrew Pol Pot in January 1979, but, in exile, he remained in command of the Khmer Rouge. In 1982 the Khmer Rouge joined in a coalition government recognized by the **UN**; Pol Pot nominally withdrew from leadership in 1985. In 1997, a year before his death, his own troops convicted him of crimes against his country and sentenced him in a jungle show trial to life imprisonment.

Pollock, [Paul] Jackson (1912–56) American painter. Born in Cody, Wyo., he went as a young man to New York City, where he became a leading abstract expressionist. In 1947 he developed action painting, a style characterized by "drip and splash" technique. He died in a car crash. Works include *Full Fathom Five* (1947), *Autumn Rhythm* (1950), and *White Light* (1954).

Pompidou, Georges [Jean-Raymond] (1911–74) French politician. Adviser to **Charles de Gaulle** from 1944, he became chief of cabinet in 1958 after de Gaulle returned from exile. Named premier in 1962, he resigned in 1968 following national student-worker demonstrations. He was elected president in 1969 and until his death in office worked to improve the economy and foreign relations.

Popper, Sir Karl [Raimund] (1902–94) Austrian-born British philosopher. Born in Vienna, he became a British citizen in 1945 and taught at the London School of Economics (1949–69). As a philosopher of science, he argued against positivism, claiming that scientific statements are falsifiable products of imagination that have withstood repeated attempts at refutation. His position was accepted by many scientists. A champion of democracy, he argued against the totalitarian idea that there are laws of history. Works include *The Logic of Scientific Discovery* (1935), *The Open Society and Its Enemies* (1945), and *Objective Knowledge* (1972). He was knighted in 1965.

Porter, Cole [Albert] (1891–1964) American songwriter. He was born in Peru, Ind., to a wealthy family and educated at Yale. His sophisticated, witty songs graced numerous stage and film musicals and became popular standards. Songs include "Let's Do It," "Begin the Beguine," "Night and Day," "Anything Goes," "You're the Top," and "I've Got You under My Skin." Stage musicals include *The Gay Divorce* (1932) and *Kiss Me, Kate* (1948). He was seriously injured by a riding accident in 1937.

Porter, Katherine Anne (1890–1980) American writer. Born in Indian Creek, Tex., she became known with her short-story collection *Flowering Judas* (1930), which distinguished her as a writer of psychological depth and symbolism. Other notable works include *Pale Horse, Pale Rider* (1939), a collection of three short novels, and the allegorical novel *Ship of Fools* (1962). She won a Pulitzer Prize and National Book Award for *Collected Stories* (1965).

Pound, Ezra [Weston Loomis] (1885–1972) American poet. Born in Hailey, Idaho, he emigrated from the U.S. to Europe in 1907, where he lived variously in England, France, and Italy. As a poet he was a leader of imagism, publishing his first book of poems, *A Lume*

Spento, in 1908. An influential editor and critic, he found publishers for such writers as **T. S. Eliot, James Joyce, William Carlos Williams,** and British author Wyndham Lewis (1882–1957). He also was a translator, notably of Chinese and Japanese works, which influenced his poetry. A Fascist and anti-Semite, he broadcast Axis propaganda from Rome during **World War II.** Arrested and charged with treason, he was judged insane and confined to a mental hospital in Washington, D.C. (1946–58). Upon his release, he returned to Italy. Among his works of poetry, famed for their erudition and originality, are *Homage to Sextus Propertius* (1917), *Hugh Selwyn Mauberley* (1920), and the never completed *The Cantos* (1925–68).

Powell, Colin [Luther] (1937–) American soldier. A decorated **Vietnam War** veteran, he was national security adviser to President **Ronald Reagan** (1987–89) and was the first African-American to hold the nation's highest military post, chairman of the Joint Chiefs of Staff (1989–93). He was praised for his oversight of the Allied victory in the **Gulf War** (1991). President George W. Bush (1946–) named him as secretary of state (2001–).

Powell, Michael [Latham] (1905–90) British film director. He is best known for his collaborations with Hungarian-born British filmmaker Emeric Pressburger (1902–88). Under the aegis of their production company, the Archers, the two men collaborated as director-writer-producers on several literate, beautiful dramas, including *The Life and Death of Colonel Blimp* (1943), *I Know Where I'm Going* (1945), *A Matter of Life and Death* (U.S. title, *Stairway to Heaven,* 1946), *Black Narcissus* (1947), and the ballet film *The Red Shoes* (1948). Powell also directed numerous films on his own, such as *Peeping Tom* (1960), sometimes producing and co-scripting them as well.

Presley, Elvis [Aaron] (1935–77) American singer. Born in Tupelo, Miss., he appeared at local country and western shows before gaining national fame with the song "Heartbreak Hotel" (1956). Through the early 1960s he dominated rock-'n'-roll music with hit songs including "Don't Be Cruel," "Hound Dog," and "Love Me Tender," performed with an earthy sexuality that influenced generations of musicians. His nicknames were "Elvis the Pelvis" and the "King of Rock 'n' Roll." From the 1960s he appeared often in Las Vegas and, between 1956 and 1969, in 33 films. His death was caused by an accidental drug overdose. Graceland, his home in Memphis, Tenn., remains an international tourist attraction.

Pressburger, Emeric See **Michael Powell.**

Priestley, J[ohn] B[oynton] (1894–1984) British writer. He was a prolific author of novels, plays (experimental and traditional), and essays. Works include the comic novel *The Good Companions* (1929), the experimental drama *I Have Been Here Before* (1937), the critical work *The English Novel* (1927), and the autobiographical work *Midnight on the Desert* (1937).

Proust, Marcel (1871–1922) French novelist. A member of Parisian society, he retired in 1905 following severe asthma attacks and his parents' deaths. Living quietly, often in a cork-lined bedroom, he wrote the seven-volume work *Remembrance of Things Past* (1913–27). The work, which presents varieties of reality through its rendering of time, sense, and memory, is a major 20th-century literary work.

Puccini, Giacomo [Antonio Domenico Michele Secondo Maria] (1858–1924) Italian composer. Born at Lucca, he studied at Milan Conservatory. His major operas *La Bohème* (1896), *Tosca* (1900), and *Madame Butterfly* (1904)—all tragic love stories with female protagonists—are among the world's most popular. His last opera, *Turandot,* left unfinished at his death, was completed by Italian composer Franco Alfano (1875–1954) and premiered in 1926.

Q

Qaddafi, Muammar al- (1942–) Libyan dictator. An army officer, he led a coup against King Idris I (1890–1983) in 1969, proclaiming the Libyan Arab Republic. He has ruled the country since, with the title president from 1977. He improved economic conditions and espoused Arab unity, but efforts to federate with other countries were short-lived. He intervened militarily in Chad in the 1980s. His support for international **terrorism** led to the U.S. bombing of Libya in 1986.

Quine, W[illard] V[an] O[rman] (1908–2000) American philosopher. He received his Ph.D. from Harvard (1932), where he has taught since 1936. Systematically studying language as a logical system, he drew attention to the ontic commitments of language users and rejected the distinction between analytic and synthetic statements. He contributed to set theory. Works include *Mathematical Logic* (1940), *Word and Object* (1960), and *Theories and Things* (1981).

Quiroga, Horacio (1878–1937) Uruguayan writer. Though he wrote novels and poetry, he is best known for his short stories. Many of these imaginatively depict the forces of nature, sometimes via animal protagonists. His short-story collections include *South American Jungle Tales* (1918), *Anaconda* (1921), and *The Desert* (1924).

Quisling, Vidkun Abraham Lauritz Jonsson (1887–1945) Norwegian politician. Son of a Lutheran pastor, he was minister of defense from 1931 to 1933 and founded the Fascist Nasjonal Samling (National Unity) Party. During **World War II**, he collaborated with Germany during its invasion of Norway in 1940 and acted as Norwegian political head until 1945. After the war, he was convicted of treason and executed, his name entering the vocabulary as a synonym for traitor.

R

Rabin, Yitzhak (1922–95) Israeli politician. Born in Jerusalem, he became Israel's first native-born prime minister (1974–77, 1992–95). In 1940 he joined the Haganah, the Jewish militia. A brigade commander in the 1948 **Arab-Israeli War**, he was named chief of staff in 1964, in which capacity he led the Israeli military to victory in the **Six-Day War** (1967). He was Israeli ambassador to Washington, D.C. (1968–73), then was elected a Labor representative to the Knesset. He was **Golda Meir's** labor minister (1974) and succeeded her as prime minister (1974–77). In 1976 he authorized the Entebbe raid, which rescued more than 100 Jewish hostages. He was succeeded as prime minister by **Shimon Peres**, his chief rival within the party, and went on to serve as minister of defense (1984–90). He again became prime minister in 1992. Although he had been a military hard-liner, Israel's inability to overcome the **Intifada** uprising that began in 1987 convinced him of the need to negotiate peace with the Palestinians. In 1993 he signed agreements with **PLO** leader **Yasir Arafat** in which Israel and the PLO recognized each other and limited Palestinian self-rule was mandated in the **Gaza Strip** and the **West Bank** town of Jericho. For their efforts, Arafat, Rabin, and Peres, who had become foreign minister in 1992, shared the 1994 Nobel Peace Prize. The accords led to a peace treaty with Jordan in 1994, but an Israeli extremist assassinated Rabin before the peace process could be completed.

Rachmaninoff, Sergey Vasilyevich (1873–1943) Russian composer. His early works were influenced by Russian composer Pyotr Ilich Tchaikovsky, notably his first two (of four) symphonies (1895, 1907). From 1904 to 1906 he was conductor of the Bolshoi Theater, and over the next decade he conducted and performed widely in the U.S. and Europe, gaining particular fame as a pianist. In 1917 he left Russia and lived in Switzerland until moving to the U.S. in 1935. Other compositions include Prelude in C-sharp Minor for Piano (1892), four piano concertos (most notably no. 2, 1901, and no. 3, 1909), the symphonic poem *The Island of Death* (1907), the choral symphony *The Bells* (1913), and the orchestral work *Rhapsody on a Theme of Paganini* (1934). He became a U.S. citizen shortly before his death.

Rand, Ayn (1905–82) Russian-born American writer. A U.S. resident from 1926, she became a citizen in 1931 and published her first novel, *We the Living,* in 1936. Like many of her works, notably novels *The Fountainhead* (1943) and *Atlas Shrugged* (1957), *We the Living* was a polemical piece promoting her philosophy of objectivism or "rational selfishness." Nonfiction works include *For the New Intellectual: The Philosophy of Ayn Rand* (1961) and *The Virtue of Selfishness* (1965).

Rankin, Jeannette (1880–1973) American politician. Née Pickering. Born in Missoula, Mont., she led the fight to obtain women's suffrage in her home state, a struggle that succeeded in 1914. She was the first woman elected to the U.S. Congress, as a representative from Montana (1917–19, 1941–43). A pacifist, she voted against U.S. entry into **World War I**. Following the Japanese attack on **Pearl Harbor,** she was the only member of Congress to vote against U.S. entry into **World War II**. She worked for peace during the **Korean** and **Vietnam Wars** as well.

Rasputin, Grigory Yefimovich (1872–1916) Russian religious and political leader. Original surname Novykh; the given name Rasputin means "the Dissolute." A farmer's son with little education, he became known as a holy man and healer among the peasantry, though some considered him a charlatan. From 1905 he gained influence over Czarina Alexandra for his apparent ability to improve her son's hemophilia. He was hated for his debauchery as well as for his interference in state and church politics. Dubbed the "mad monk," he was assassinated by a group of nobles.

Rauschenberg, Robert (1925–) American artist. He produced "combine paintings," which blend painting, collage, and assemblage of objects. He also created prints and environmental pieces. Works include *Bed* (1955), *Gloria* (1956), and *Soundings* (1968).

Ravel, Maurice [Joseph] (1875–1937) French composer. He created impressionistic works infused with fantasy and the exotic, most notably the ballets *Daphnis et Chloé* (1908) and *Ma mère d'oye* (1915). His prolific output included the orchestral works *Bolero* (1928) and *Rhapsodie espagnole* (1908), such piano works as *Valses nobles et sentimentales* (1911), and such songs as "Shéhérazade" (1903). Three times he lost the Prix de Rome, possibly due to his modern musical sensibilities.

Ray, Satyajit (1921–92) Indian film director. Born in Calcutta, he worked as an art director and book illustrator before directing his first film, *Father Panchali* (1955). The first of his Apu Trilogy, about a Bengali child, it was followed by *The Unvanquished* (1957) and *The World of Apu* (1959). His works, prized for their delicacy and human understanding, also include *The Lonely Wife* (1964), *Distant Thunder* (1973), and *The Home and the World* (1984). In 1992 Ray won an honorary Academy Award.

Reagan, Ronald Wilson (1911–) Fortieth U.S. president (1981–89). Born in Tampico,

Ill., he graduated from Eureka College (1932). He was a radio sports announcer before becoming a movie actor, appearing in such films as *Knute Rockne—All American* (1940) and *Kings Row* (1942). He was president of the Screen Actors Guild (1947–52, 1959–60) and a **television** performer. Changing his early liberal beliefs to become a conservative Republican, he was elected governor of California (1967–75). After two failed bids for the Republican presidential nomination (1968, 1976), he not only won the nomination but also defeated incumbent **Jimmy Carter** in a landslide (1980). In a time of high inflation and unemployment, Reagan's optimistic personality and folksy anecdotes charmed the public, though his supply-side economics, conservative social policies, and harsh anti-Soviet rhetoric aroused controversy. After surviving an assassination attempt (March 1981) by drifter John W. Hinckley Jr. (1955–) shortly after taking office, Reagan carried out his economic plan of cutting taxes and social spending while greatly raising military expenditures. The result was large budget deficits, with the national debt doubling from $998 billion in 1981 to $2.1 trillion in 1986. However, after a recession in 1982, the economy boomed and inflation fell, ensuring Reagan's landslide reelection in 1984, when he defeated former Carter vice president Walter Mondale (1928–). In military matters, Reagan conducted the largest peacetime defense escalation in U.S. history, launching the **Strategic Defense Initiative**, an expensive project, derisively known as Star Wars, aimed at developing an anti-nuclear-missile system. In October 1983 Reagan suffered a setback in Lebanon, where 239 U.S. Marines and 21 other U.S. military personnel were killed by a suicide bomber, but he won a victory in Grenada, where U.S. troops ousted a Communist government. He freely supported anti-Communist forces in Latin America, including the authoritarian government of El Salvador and the right-wing Contra rebels in Nicaragua. Relations with the **Soviet Union** were chilly until 1988, when Reagan and Soviet leader **Mikhail Gorbachev** signed the Intermediate-Range Nuclear Forces (INF) Treaty. Reagan's last few years in office were marred by the **Iran-Contra affair**, which concerned the sale of U.S. arms to Iran and the illegal diversion of proceeds to the Nicaraguan Contras.

Redford, Robert (1937–) American actor and director. Born Charles Robert Redford Jr. The good looks and easy-going heroism he embodied in such films as *Butch Cassidy and the Sundance Kid* (1969) and *All the President's Men* (1976) made him a star. As a director, he won an Academy Award for *Ordinary People* (1980). He founded the Sundance Institute in 1980, a training ground for young filmmakers; its Sundance Film Festival has promoted the growth of independent film.

Redgrave British family of actors. The son of stage actors, Sir Michael Redgrave (1908–95) appeared in many Shakespearean roles and in such films as *Dead of Night* (1945). His children Lynn (1943–), Corin (1939–), and Vanessa (1937–) are also actors, as are Vanessa's daughters Joely Richardson (1965–) and Natasha Richardson (1963–). Vanessa, who won a best supporting actress Oscar for her performance in *Julia* (1977), is a prominent spokesperson for left-wing causes. Natasha won a Tony Award for best actress in a musical in 1998 for her performance in *Cabaret*.

Rehnquist, William [Hubbs] (1986–) American jurist. He was named an associate justice of the U.S Supreme Court in 1971 and 16th chief justice in 1986. Decisions of his Court often reflected his conservative views and his support for the doctrine of judicial restraint.

Remarque, Erich Maria (1897–1970) German-born American novelist. He used his experiences serving in **World War I** to produce the classic antiwar novel *All Quiet on the*

Western Front (1929). Subsequent works dealt with postwar Germany. From 1939 he lived in the U.S.

Renoir, Jean (1894–1979) French-born American film director. Born in Paris, the son of French painter Pierre Auguste Renoir (1841–1919), he directed his first film, *La Fille de l'Eau,* in 1925. Through the 1930s he developed his fluid, humanistic filmmaking style (*La Chienne,* 1931; *Toni,* 1935), reaching an apex in his antiwar masterwork, *Grand Illusion* (1937), and in his poetic drama *The Rules of the Game* (1939), the latter a critical failure in its day. In America from 1941, he directed works including *The Southerner* (1945) and *The Woman on the Beach* (1947). In India and Europe after **World War II**, he made *The River* (1951) and *The Golden Coach* (1953). An American citizen from the 1940s, he retained French citizenship.

Reza Shah Pahlavi (1877–1944) Shah of Iran (1925–41). Born Reza Khan, he was a general when he led a successful coup in 1921. He became minister of war (1921–23) and prime minister (1923–25). Parliament elected him shah after the deposition of Ahmad Shah (1925). He modernized the country, rebuilding its infrastructure and emancipating women. His German sympathies led to the occupation of Iran by British and Soviet forces in 1941. Upon his forced abdication, his son **Mohammad Reza Pahlavi** succeeded him.

Rhee, Syngman (1875–1965) South Korean politician. Educated in the United States, he was the leader of the Korean independence movement from 1911. Following the U.S. occupation after **World War II**, he became the first president (1948–60) of the Republic of Korea. Ruling as a dictator, he was forced from office in 1960 and went into exile in Hawaii.

Ribbentrop, Joachim von (1893–1946) German politician. Active in Nazi programs from 1930, including service as ambassador at large (1935), he was named foreign minister (1938–45). He was instrumental in effecting the Russo-German nonaggression pact (1939) and the Italo-German-Japanese alliance (1940). He was sentenced at the **Nuremberg Trials** and hanged for war crimes.

Rilke, Rainer Maria (1875–1926) German poet. Born in Prague as René Karl Wilhelm Josef Maria Rilke, he is considered the greatest lyric poet of 20th-century Germany. He traveled extensively, visiting Russia (1899–1900) and living in Paris (1903–09), where he worked for a time as secretary to sculptor Auguste Rodin (1840–1917). Influenced by Russian mysticism, Rilke wrote *Poems from the Book of Hours* (1905). He broke from the effusive subjectivity of his early works, pursuing precise objectivity in works such as *New Poems* (1907–08). His last works, *The Duino Elegies* (1923) and *Sonnets to Orpheus* (1936), are concerned with death and the meaning of life. Throughout his work, Rilke exhibits spiritual and emotional sensitivity and rich poetic style. His marriage (1901) to German artist Clara Westhoff produced one daughter but soon ended in separation.

Rivera, Diego (1886–1957) Mexican artist. Born Diego Maria Conception Juan Nepomuceno Estanislao de la Riviera y Barrientos Acosta y Rodríguez. After studying in Madrid and traveling through Europe, he returned to Mexico influenced by cubism but compelled to create art for the Mexican people. Interweaving native folklore and Aztec and Mayan art, he created public murals conveying social, historical, and political themes from a Marxist stance. Mural sites include the National Palace, Mexico City (1929–35) and the Hotel del Prado, Mexico City (1947–48). Because a character in his *Man at the Crossroads* (1933), commissioned for New York's Rockefeller Center, resembles **V. I. Lenin**, the work was moved to the Palace of Fine Arts, Mexico City. He was an active member of the Communist Party. He was twice married to the artist **Frida Kahlo**.

Rivera, José Eustasio (1889–1928) Colombian writer. His single novel, *La vorágine* (*The Vortex*, 1924), about the exploitation of Amazon rubber gatherers, was highly influential in Latin America. He also wrote the sonnet collection *Tierra de promisión* (1921).

Robbe-Grillet, Alain (1922–) French writer and filmmaker. He originated the French "new novel," characterized by experiments with structure and time rather than traditional character or plot development. Works include the novels *The Erasers* (1953) and *Jealousy* (1957) and the critical treatise *Towards a New Novel* (1963). His nontraditional screenplays include *Last Year at Marienbad* (1961); experimental films include *Trans-Europe Express* (1967).

Robinson, Jackie (1919–72) American athlete. Born John Roosevelt Robinson in Cairo, Ga., he joined baseball's Brooklyn Dodgers in 1947 and became the first black player in the major leagues. Among his accolades were Rookie of the Year (1947) and Most Valuable Player (1949). He retired from baseball in 1956 and was elected to the Baseball Hall of Fame in 1962. He is remembered for opening previously segregated American professional sports to African-Americans and all minorities.

Rockefeller, John D[avison] (1837–1937) American businessman and philanthropist. A leading industrialist, he founded the Standard Oil Company of Ohio in 1870 (dissolved in 1892) and the Standard Oil Company of New Jersey in 1899. He dominated the U.S. oil industry until the company was dissolved by the Supreme Court on antitrust grounds in 1911. A major philanthropist, he founded the Rockefeller Institute for Medical Research (1901, now Rockefeller University) the Laura Spelman Rockefeller Memorial Foundation (1913), and the University of Chicago (1891). His son John Davison Rockefeller Jr. (1874–1960) continued the Rockefeller business and philanthropic practices, including the restoration of colonial Williamsburg, Va., and the founding of Rockefeller Center, New York City (1931). His grandson Nelson Aldrich Rockefeller (1908–79) served widely in government, attaining such posts as undersecretary of health, education, and welfare (1953–54), governor of New York (1958–73), and vice president (1974–77) of the United States.

Rockwell, Norman [Perceval] (1894–1978) American artist and illustrator. Through decades of illustrating covers for the *Saturday Evening Post* (1916–63) and other magazines, he became hugely popular for his idealized evocations of American small-town life. Paintings include *Four Freedoms* (1943) and *Triple Self-Portrait* (1960).

Rodgers, [Charles] Richard (1902–79) American composer. Beginning in the 1920s he collaborated with leading American lyricists on stage musical comedies that defined the genre during the century. With American lyricist **Jerome Kern**, he wrote *Show Boat* (1927); its songs included "Ol' Man River." With American lyricist Lorenz Hart (1895–1943), he wrote *Babes in Arms* (1937), *The Boys from Syracuse* (1938), *Pal Joey* (1940), and others. Their songs include "The Lady Is a Tramp" and "My Funny Valentine." With American lyricist Oscar Hammerstein II (1895–1960), he wrote *Oklahoma!* (1943, Pulitzer Prize), *Carousel* (1945), *South Pacific* (1949, Pulitzer Prize), *The King and I* (1951), and *The Sound of Music* (1959). Their songs include "Oh, What a Beautiful Morning," "Hello Young Lovers," and "My Favorite Things." In his final years he collaborated with others and composed on his own.

Rogers, Ginger See **Fred Astaire**.

Rogers, Will[iam Penn Adair] (1879–1935) American humorist. A vaudeville rope twirler, he joined the Ziegfeld Follies in 1915, and his acute homespun social commentary gained international appeal. His books include *The Cowboy Philosopher on Prohibition* (1919) and *The Illiterate Digest* (1924); he wrote a syndicated column for the *New York Times* (weekly from 1922, daily from 1926). He was killed in a plane crash with American aviator Wiley Post (1899–1935).

Rommel, Erwin [Johannes Eugen] (1891–1944) German soldier. A teacher's son, he rose quickly in the German army and served valiantly in **World War I**. During **World War II**, he headed the seventh panzer division in 1940 and was instrumental in the invasion of France. In the North Africa campaign (1941–43), he won the moniker "Desert Fox," commanding the Afrika Korps to victories until defeat by British forces at El Alamein. He was commander in northern France during the 1944 Allied (see **Allied Powers**) invasion. In July 1944, after he supported a plot to overthrow Hitler, two Nazi generals compelled him to poison himself.

Roosevelt, [Anna] Eleanor (1884–1962) American first lady (1932–45) and humanitarian. A niece of Theodore Roosevelt, she was born in New York City and married her distant cousin **Franklin Delano Roosevelt** in 1905. She was active in his campaigns for governor of New York and for president of the U.S. During his presidency, she traveled widely and made **radio** appearances to promote the New Deal; her nationally syndicated newspaper column, "My Day," began in 1936. A lifelong liberal, she fought for causes such as women's issues and civil rights and encouraged her husband to increase his commitment to social issues. After her husband's death, she served as delegate to the **United Nations** (1945–53, 1961) and chaired the UN Commission on **Human Rights** (1946–51). She is remembered as the most active first lady in American history and as a role model for women.

Roosevelt, Franklin Delano (1882–1945) Thirty-second U.S. president (1933–45). The only president elected for four terms was born in Hyde Park, N.Y., to a distinguished family that included his fifth cousin **Theodore Roosevelt**, who would become president of the U.S. in 1901. Franklin Delano Roosevelt graduated from Harvard (1904) and Columbia University Law School (1907). In 1905 he married his distant cousin **Eleanor Roosevelt**. He served in the New York State Senate (1910–13) and as assistant secretary of the U.S. Navy (1913–20) before being nominated for vice president with Democratic presidential candidate James Cox (1870–1957). (The Cox-Roosevelt ticket lost the 1920 election to the Republican team of Warren Harding and his running mate, Calvin Coolidge.) In 1921 Roosevelt contracted polio, which rendered him partially paralyzed. Resuming public life, he was elected governor of New York (1929–33). In the 1932 presidential election, he defeated Republican incumbent Herbert Hoover, who was perceived as ineffectual against the national economic collapse triggered by the 1929 stock market crash. After announcing in his March 1933 first inaugural address, "The only thing we have to fear is fear itself," Roosevelt assembled a **brain trust** of advisers and implemented his ambitious first hundred days of the **New Deal**. During this period he secured passage of legislation that instituted several programs aimed at creating jobs and reviving the economy, including the Agricultural Adjustment Administration, Civilian Conservation Corps, National Recovery Administration, Public Works Administration, and Tennessee Valley Authority. He also repealed **Prohibition** and reformed banking laws, eventually establishing the Securities and Exchange Commission (1934). An effective communicator, he pioneered the regular use of **radio** speeches, called fireside chats, generating public support. His wife, Eleanor Roosevelt, traveled widely to rally for the **New Deal** and meet with constituents. In 1935 he passed the Social Security Act, implementing compulsory old-age insurance and unemployment compensation programs. Roosevelt was reelected for three additional terms, defeating Republicans Alf Landon (1887–1987) in 1936, Wendell Willkie (1892–1944) in 1940, and Thomas Dewey (1902–71) in 1944. To aid Allied (see **Allied Powers**) countries in **World War II**, he championed passage of the **Lend-Lease** Act (1941) and with **Winston Churchill** established the **Atlantic Charter** (August 1941). On December 8, 1941, he procured a declaration of war on Japan following its December 7 attack on **Pearl Harbor**, Hawaii. From 1942 he used emergency powers granted him by Congress to institute war-related agencies and programs. He met with leaders of Allied countries, notably at **Yalta** in February 1945 (see **Yalta Conference**). He died of a cerebral hemorrhage on April 12, 1945, four weeks before the German surrender to the Allies. Despite detractors, Roosevelt is remembered for guiding the U.S. through the **Great Depression** and **World War II** by broadening presidential powers, employing flexible leadership, and projecting infectious confidence about the country's ability to prevail.

Roosevelt, Theodore (1858–1919) Twenty-sixth U.S. president (1901–09). Born in New York City, he graduated from Harvard (1880) and served in New York state government and civil service positions until he became assistant secretary of the U.S. Navy (1897–98). During the Spanish-American War, he cofounded the Rough Riders and fought in Cuba, becoming a hero during the Battle of San Juan Hill. In 1900 he was elected vice president under **William McKinley** and became president following McKinley's 1901 assassination. Roosevelt's terms were marked by activism and attention to what he called the "little man." Among his accomplishments were conservation legislation, creation of the Department of Commerce and Labor, passage of the Pure Food and Drug Act (1906), and lawsuits against the business trusts (trust-busting). He actively involved the U.S. in foreign policy initiatives, including intervention in a Panamanian civil war (1903) to hasten the building of the **Panama Canal**. His mediation at the Portsmouth Conference to end the **Russo-Japanese War** (1904–05) resulted in his winning the Nobel Peace Prize in 1906. Unsatisfied with his successor, Republican president **William Howard Taft**, he ran for president in 1912 on the **Progressive** (Bull Moose) **Party** ticket, but succeeded only in effecting the election of Democratic candidate **Woodrow Wilson**.

Rorschach, Hermann (1884–1922) Swiss psychiatrist. In 1921 he devised the Rorschach inkblot test for diagnosing psychiatric disorder and assessing personality.

Rosenberg, Julius (1918–53) and **Ethel Greenglass Rosenberg** (1915–53). American-born spies. An electrical engineer and his wife, the two were convicted of delivering military secrets on **nuclear weapons** to the **Soviet Union**, the U.S.'s chief adversary in the **cold war**. Supplying evidence against the couple was David Greenglass, brother of Ethel Rosenberg. Amid much controversy over the guilty verdict and the severity of the sentence, the Rosenbergs were executed on June 19, 1953, becoming the first American civilians executed for espionage.

Roth, Philip [Milton] (1933–) American writer. Educated at Bucknell University and the University of Chicago, he published the critically acclaimed novella and short-story collection *Goodbye, Columbus* (1959, National Book Award) and has continued with several witty, ironic works exploring modern Jewish identity. Among them are novels *Letting Go* (1962), *When She Was Good* (1967), *Portnoy's Complaint* (1969), *My Life as a Man* (1974), *The Professor of Desire* (1977), *The Ghost Writer* (1979), *Zuckerman Unbound* (1985), *Zuckerman*

Bound (1985), *The Counterlife* (1986, National Book Critics Circle Award), *Sabbath's Theater* (1990, National Book Award) and *American Pastoral* (1997, Pulitzer Prize).

Rothko, Mark (1903–70) Russian-born American painter. He immigrated to the U.S. in 1913. A leading member of the New York school and abstract expressionist movement, he pioneered color field painting. Works include *No. 10* (1950) and the *Blacks on Maroon* and *Red on Maroon* series (1958–59).

Rubinstein, Arthur (1887–1982) Polish-born American pianist. A pupil of **Ignacy Jan Paderewski**, he became a U.S. citizen in 1946. He was one of the century's greatest concert pianists, known particularly for his interpretations of Polish composer Frédéric-François Chopin (1810–49).

Rushdie, [Ahmed] Salman (1947–) Indian-born British writer. He has been recognized from early novels *Midnight's Children* (1981) and *Shame* (1983) for presenting an original voice of modern India, with intricate narration and a keen understanding of contemporary problems. His novel *The Satanic Verses* (1988) was considered blasphemous in some Muslim countries and generated a death order in 1989 from Iranian leader **Ayatollah Khomeini**. In response, Rushdie went into hiding for nine years, until Iran formally dissociated itself from the death order in 1998. Subsequent works include the children's fable *Haroun and the Sea of Stories* (1990) and the essay collection *Imaginary Homelands* (1991).

Russell, Bertrand [Arthur William], third earl (1872–1970) British philosopher and mathematician. He won the Nobel Prize for literature in 1949. Born in Wales, the grandson of 19th-century British prime minister Lord John Russell, he succeeded to the earldom in 1931. He was educated at Cambridge University, where he later taught. He wrote *Principles of Mathematics* (1903) and, with **Alfred North Whitehead**, *Principia Mathematica* (1910–13), two works that attempted to deduce the laws of mathematics from purely logical principles. Russell's thought influenced symbolic logic, set theory, and logical positivism. He freely espoused controversial views, including rationalist opposition to religion, a liberal attitude toward sexuality, and pacifism. He was a leader of the "ban the bomb" movement against **nuclear weapons** and, with **Jean-Paul Sartre**, organized European opposition to the **Vietnam War**. His other works include *Introduction to Mathematical Philosophy* (1919) and *Marriage and Morals* (1929).

Ruth, Babe (1895–1948). American athlete. Born George Herman Ruth in Baltimore, he began his career in 1914 with the minor-league Baltimore Orioles (where he also gained the nickname Babe). From 1914 to 1919 he was an exceptional pitcher for the Boston Red Sox, but when purchased by the New York Yankees in 1920, he was placed in the outfield to maximize his hitting. Between 1920 and 1935, his playing was unparalleled: He led the league in home runs for 12 years and hit a then-record 60 home runs in one season (1927) and 714 home runs over his career. During his career, the Yankees won seven pennants and five World Series. In 1935 he played for the Boston Braves. Still the most famous player of the game, the "Bambino" made Yankee Stadium known as "the house that Ruth built."

Rutherford, Ernest, first baron (1871–1937) New Zealand–born British physicist. Known as the father of nuclear physics, he taught at McGill University, Montreal (1898–1907), and the University of Manchester (1907–19); from 1919 he was director of the Cavendish Laboratory, Cambridge. He discovered and named alpha and beta radiation and helped propose a theory of radioactive transformation of elements. He received the 1908 Nobel Prize for chemistry. He discovered the atomic nucleus (1911) and was the first to split atomic nuclei artificially. He was made a baron in 1931.

S

Saarinen, Eero (1910–61) Finnish-born American architect. He is known for his modern,innovative design in buildings including the General Motors Technical Center, Mich., the chapel and auditorium at the Massachusetts Institute of Technology, and the Trans World Airlines terminal, New York City. His father was Finnish architect Eliel Saarinen (1873–1950).

Sabin, Albert Bruce (1906–93) Polish-born American immunologist. Born in Bialystok, Russia (now Poland), he immigrated with his family to the U.S. in 1921. He received his M.D. from New York University in 1931 and was later affiliated with the University of Cincinnati (1939–69). He did basic research on polio and, during **World War II**, developed vaccines for encephalitis and dengue fever. Unlike rival **Jonas Salk**, who used killed viruses to develop the first polio vaccine (1953), Sabin used live viruses in his polio vaccine, first tested on humans in 1955. Judged simpler and more effective, Sabin's vaccine became preferred in most countries. Sabin served as a consultant to the World Health Organization (1969–86).

Sadat, [Mohammed] Anwar el- (1918–81) Egyptian politician. He graduated from Cairo Military Academy in 1938. A foe of British domination, he was imprisoned during **World War II** for conspiring with the Germans. He joined **Gamal Abdel Nasser**'s Free Officers Movement, which overthrew King **Farouk** in 1952, and was rewarded with a series of government posts, including minister of state (1955–56) and chairman of the national assembly (1960–68). He was vice president (1964–66; 1969–70) and succeeded Nasser as president (1970–81). He turned the country away from reliance on the **Soviet Union**, introducing free-market reforms and developing ties to the United States instead. He launched the **Yom Kippur War** (1973) but afterward began working for peace with Israel, despite the protests of other Arab states. In 1977 he flew to Jerusalem to start peace negotiations. The resulting **Camp David Accords** (1978) and peace treaty with Israel (1979) earned him and his Israeli counterpart, **Menachem Begin**, the 1978 Nobel Peace Prize. While reviewing a military parade, Sadat was assassinated by Muslim extremists. His vice president, **Hosni Mubarak**, succeeded him.

Sakharov, Andrey Dmitriyevich (1921–89) Soviet physicist and dissident. He was a principal developer of the **Soviet Union**'s hydrogen bomb (1947–54) and proposed the tokamak process for achieving controlled nuclear fusion, later realized experimentally by others. In the 1960s he denounced the arms race and criticized Soviet political repression. He won the Nobel Peace Prize (1975), an award that embarrassed the **Soviet Union**. Banished to the closed town of Gorki in 1980, Sakharov continued to speak out on **human rights** and disarmament issues, sometimes staging hunger strikes. He was released in 1986. In 1989, shortly before his death, he became a member of the newly established Congress of People's Deputies.

Saki (1870–1916) Burmese-born British writer. Pen name of Hector Hugh Munro. He wrote witty, paradoxical stories, often very short, collected in such volumes as *Reginald* (1904) and *The Chronicles of Clovis* (1911). He also wrote novels, such as *The Unbearable Bassington* (1912), plays, and journalism. He was killed in action in **World War I**.

Salazar, António de Oliveira (1889–1970) Portuguese politician. His background as an economics professor at the University of Coimbra led to his appointment as minister of finance (1926, 1928–32) in a military dictatorship. Chosen prime minister in 1932, he instituted a constitution establishing an authoritarian, corporate state in 1933. Salazar ruled as dictator for most of his life, remaining prime minister until a stroke incapacitated him in 1968. He was also minister of war (1936–44) and of foreign affairs (1936–47). He suppressed political opposition while stabilizing the country's finances and modernizing its infrastructure.

Salinger, J[erome] D[avid] (1919–) American writer. A famously reclusive author, he is known best for his novel of adolescent rebellion, *The Catcher in the Rye* (1951).

Salk, Jonas [Edward] (1914–95) American immunologist. Born in New York City, he received his M.D. from New York University in 1939. At the University of Michigan (1942–47), he helped develop the first influenza vaccine. Moving to the University of Pittsburgh (1947–63), he developed the world's first polio vaccine (1953). Salk was hailed as a savior, but, after 1960, his killed-virus polio vaccine was supplanted in most countries by **Albert Sabin's** live-virus vaccine. He founded the Salk Institute for Biological Studies in San Diego (1963). Books include *Man Unfolding* (1972).

Sandburg, Carl (1878–1967) American writer. He captured American history and popular sentiment in several genres, including poetry, biography, and prose. Works include the poetry collections *Chicago Poems* (1915), *Smoke and Steel* (1920), *The People, Yes* (1936), and *Complete Poems* (1950, Pulitzer Prize); the juvenile book *Rootabaga Stories* (1922); the biography *Abraham Lincoln—The War Years* (1939, Pulitzer Prize); and the song collection *The American Songbag* (1927).

Santayana, George (1863–1952) Spanish-born American philosopher. He immigrated to the U.S. in 1872 and studied at Harvard, where he taught (1889–1912) until retiring from teaching to live in Europe. His philosophy developed from a naturalistic one to a combination of materialism and Platonism. Works include *The Life of Reason* (1905–06), *Skepticism and Animal Faith* (1923), and *The Realms of Being* (four volumes, 1927–40). He also wrote poetry, criticism, and one novel, *The Last Puritan* (1935).

Sarnoff, David (1891–1971) Russian-born American broadcasting pioneer. After immigrating to the U.S. in 1900, he gained fame for his wireless reporting on the *Titanic* sinking in 1912. His 1915 proposal for a "radio music box" was the basis for present-day **radio** broadcasting. Working for the Radio Corporation of America (RCA), he founded the National Broadcasting Company (NBC), the first permanent broadcast network, in 1926. He was a pioneer in the development of black-and-white and color **television**. He led RCA from 1930 to 1970, first as president and then as chairman.

Sartre, Jean-Paul (1905–80) French philosopher and writer. Born in Paris, he graduated from the Ecole Normale Supérieure in 1929, the same year he met his lifelong companion, the writer **Simone de Beauvoir**. He published his first novel, *Nausea*, in 1938. During **World War II**, he worked for the French **resistance** and in 1943 expounded his existentialist philosophy in *Being and Nothingness*, in which he argued for the freedom and potentialities of human beings in a world without God or meaning. In 1945 he marked his heightened involvement as a left-wing political activist with the founding of the journal *Les Temps modernes* (in which he published his 1947 critical essay "*Qu'est-ce que la littérature?*"). Among his plays are *The Flies* (1943) and *No Exit* (1944). Other works include *Critique de la raison dialectique* (1960), which sets forth his political philosophy, and the autobiographical book *Words* (1963). In 1964 he refused the Nobel Prize for literature.

Sato Eisaku (1901–75) Japanese politician. He graduated in law from Tokyo Imperial University (1924). During the post–**World War II** period, he was a member of the Diet (from 1949) and held several ministerial posts, including construction and finance. As Liberal Democratic prime minister from 1964 to 1972, he presided over strong economic growth and the return of Okinawa from the U.S. to Japan (1972). For his policies against **nuclear weapons**, he was corecipient of the Nobel Peace Prize in 1974.

Saussure, Ferdinand de (1857–1913) Swiss linguist. Descended from a distinguished family of scientists, he was a professor of linguistics at the University of Geneva (1901–13). He broke away from his discipline's traditional focus on history of language to analyze structural features, such as the distinction between *langue,* or grammatical rules, and *parole,* or individual speech. His view of language as a system of signs influenced many disciplines, including anthropology and literary criticism. His most important work, *Course in General Linguistics* (1916), is a posthumous compilation of students' notes on his lectures.

Schiaparelli, Elsa (1896–1973) French fashion designer. Opening shops in Paris (c. 1927) and New York (1949), she established herself as a fashion innovator, popularizing the padded shoulder and use of zippers and synthetic fabrics in women's clothing. Her designs were known for their witty excess and bold colors, such as shocking pink.

Schleicher, Kurt von (1882–1934) German soldier and politician. Made lieutenant general in 1931, he was the last chancellor of the **Weimar Republic** (1932–33). His request to President **Paul von Hindenburg** for emergency powers and a ban on the Nazis was turned down. Upon Schleicher's resignation, Hindenburg appointed Hitler chancellor. Schleicher was murdered by the **SS** during the "night of the long knives."

Schlick, [Friedrich Albert] Moritz (1882–1936) German philosopher. He received his Ph.D. at the University of Berlin (1904), where he studied physics under **Max Planck**. A professor at the University of Vienna (1922–36), he directed a group of scientists and philosophers (such as **Rudolf Carnap**) called the Vienna Circle in discussions of science and positivism. He was murdered by one of his graduate students. Among his works is *General Theory of Knowledge* (1918).

Schmidt, Helmut (1918–) West German politician. A Social Democrat from 1946, he was active in federal government for decades, serving as minister of defense (1969–72) and finance (1972–74) before succeeding **Willy Brandt** as West German chancellor in 1974. His tenure was marked by attempts at more open communication with East Germany and sustained domestic economic stability. He was defeated in 1982 by German politician **Helmut Kohl**. He has been publisher of the newspaper *Die Zeit* since 1983.

Schoenberg, Arnold [Franz Walter] (1874–1951) Austrian-born American composer. Born in Vienna, he experimented with the techniques of Mahler and Wagner in his 1899 *Verklärte Nacht.* In 1908 he pioneered the use of atonal composition and in 1921 developed the 12-tone method for serial music that defined his work and influenced 20th-century composition. Following his 1933 dismissal from Berlin's Prussian Academy of Arts for his Jewish faith, he immigrated to the U.S. and taught at the University of California at Los Angeles (1936–41). Among his notable works are the operas *Von Heute auf Morgen* (1924) and *Moses und Aron* (1930–32, unfinished); the orchestral works *Pelleas und Melisande* (1902-3) and *2 Chamber Symphonies* (1906, 1939); concertos for violin and for piano; and songs and chamber music.

Schrödinger, Erwin (1887–1961) Austrian physicist. In 1926 he developed wave mechanics and the Schrödinger wave equation. With **Paul Dirac**, he shared the 1933 Nobel Prize for physics. He illustrated quantum indeterminacy with the "Schrödinger's cat" thought experiment (1935). Fleeing the Nazi **Anschluss** (1938), Schrödinger joined the Institute of Advanced Studies in Dublin (1939–56) before returning to Austria.

Schuman, Robert (1886–1963) French politician. Undersecretary of state for refugees in 1940 when he was imprisoned by Nazis, he escaped and fought with the French **resistance** in **World War II**. Postwar he served as finance minister (1946), prime minister (1947–48), foreign minister (1948–52), and minister of justice (1955–56). His Schuman Plan (1950) promoted European economic unity and reconciliation between France and Germany. It led to the formation of the European Coal and Steel Community (1952), an early part of the European Common Market.

Schuschnigg, Kurt von (1897–1977) Austrian politician. He entered parliament in 1927 and was minister of justice and education under **Engelbert Dollfuss**, upon whose assassination he became chancellor (1934–38). He tried unsuccessfully to prevent the Nazi takeover, an effort for which the Nazis imprisoned him (1938–45). He immigrated to the United States, where he taught political science at St. Louis University (1948–67). He returned to Austria in 1967.

Schwarzenegger, Arnold (1947–) Austrian-born American athlete and actor. As a bodybuilder whose charisma helped popularize the sport, he won three Mr. Universe titles and seven Mr. Olympia titles. He went on to become a Hollywood star, mostly of action films such as *The Terminator* (1984) and *True Lies* (1994). He was chairman of the President's Council on Physical Fitness and Sports (1990–94).

Schweitzer, Albert (1875–1965) French humanitarian. Born in **Alsace**, he devoted much of his early life to music, becoming an organist, writing a biography (1905), and coediting the work of German composer Johann Sebastian Bach (1685–1750). A theologian, he wrote *The Quest of the Historical Jesus* (1906) and other works. Pledging the rest of his life to humanity, he became a doctor and in 1913 founded the Lambaréené Hospital in Gabon (French Equatorial Africa), which became the center of his life's efforts. A philosopher, he centered his beliefs on the concept of "reverence for life," explicating them in *Philosophy for Civilization* (1923). The most respected humanitarian of his day, he was awarded the Nobel Peace Prize in 1952.

Scorsese, Martin (1942–) American film director. Born in Queens, N.Y., he was raised in Manhattan's Little Italy and graduated from New York University film school. With his early films *Mean Streets* (1973) and *Taxi Driver* (1976), he became known for tense dramas and innovative camera style. His films are often set in New York City and feature themes of violence and redemption. Later notable films include *Raging Bull* (1980), *The Last Temptation of Christ* (1988), *Goodfellas* (1990), and *The Age of Innocence* (1993).

Seaborg, Glenn Theodore (1912–) American nuclear chemist. He received his Ph.D. from the University of California at Berkeley (1937), where he later taught. He worked on development of the atomic bomb and was chairman of the Atomic Energy Commission (1961–71). He shared the 1951 Nobel Prize for chemistry for codiscovering a number of transuranic elements, including plutonium, americium, californium, einsteinium, and nobelium.

Segovia, Andrés (1893–1987) Spanish guitarist. Self-taught, he had toured several continents by the end of the 1920s, beginning a lifetime of popularizing the guitar. To broaden the repertoire of guitar works, he transcribed music and commissioned pieces from Spanish composer Manuel de Falla (1876–1946) and Brazilian composer **Heitor Villa-Lobos** (1887–1959), among others.

Sembène, Ousmane (1923–) African film director. Born in Senegal, he is the leading filmmaker in sub-Saharan Africa. Notable films—generally about cultural differences between Africa and Western society—include *Black Girl* (1966), *The Money Order* (1968), *The People* (1977), and *Camp de Thiaroye* (1988). In addition, he is a novelist and short-story writer (*The Last of the Empire*, 1981).

Senghor, Léopold [Sédar] (1906–) Senegalese poet and politician. He lived in Europe from 1928, studying and teaching in France and spending two years as a prisoner of war in Germany during **World War II**. With French West Indian poet Aimé Césaire (1913–), he developed the concept of *négritude* for the black African experience. In 1947 he cofound-ed the black cultural journal *Présence Africaine*. He represented his country in the French National Assembly in 1946; in 1948 he helped found the political party the Bloc Démocratique Sénégalais. He became independent Senegal's first president (1960–80). His volumes of poetry include *Chants d'ombre* (*Songs of Shadow*, 1945) and *Nocturnes* (1961). In 1984 he became the first black person elected to the French Academy.

Sennett, Mack (1880–1960) Canadian-born American film director and producer. Born Michael Sinott in Richmond, Quebec, he apprenticed with **D. W. Griffith** at Biograph Studios (1909–11). As owner of Keystone Studios (1911–15; part of Triangle Film Corporation from 1915 to 1917), he pioneered American slapstick comedy with his Keystone Kops comedies and produced films by **Frank Capra** and **Charlie Chaplin**. In 1917 he established Mack Sennett Comedies and launched the career of American come-dian Harry Langdon (1884–1944). Among his more than 1,000 films are *Tillie's Punctured Romance* (1914), the first American feature-length comedy, and *The Sheik of Araby* (1923). Throughout the silent era he was considered the "King of Comedy." He won a special Academy Award (1937).

Shamir, Yitzhak (1915–) Polish-born Israeli politician who emigrated to Palestine in 1935. A right-wing hard-liner, he led the **Likud Party** from 1983. As prime minister (1983–84, 1986–92), he resisted calls for a negotiated peace with the Palestinians.

Shaw, George Bernard (1856–1950) Irish playwright and critic. Born in Dublin, he moved to London in 1876. After five novels and many reviews, he focused on writing plays, including *Mrs. Warren's Profession* (1893), *Arms and the Man* (1894), *Caesar and Cleopatra* (1899), *Man and Superman* (1905), *Major Barbara* (1905), and *Saint Joan* (1923). His "dramas of ideas" revitalized British theater with their frank, witty exploration of social and politi-cal issues. His *Pygmalion* (1913) took on an extended life through its transformation into the stage musical (1956) and film (1964) *My Fair Lady*. Shaw is also esteemed as a critic of lit-erature, art, and music; his critical and political views were often expressed in prefaces to his plays. A Fabian socialist since 1884, he was an ardent spokesperson for the Fabian Society's vision of gradual social reform. Nonfiction works include *The Intelligent Woman's Guide to Socialism* (1928). He was awarded the Nobel Prize for literature in 1925.

Sholem Aleichem (1859–1916) Russian Yiddish writer. Pseudonym (meaning "Peace be with you" in Hebrew) of Sholem Yakov Rabinowitz. A rabbi, he left Russia in 1905, living in Europe before settling in New York in 1914. His warm, humorous tales influenced the acceptance of Yiddish as a literary language. His sketches in *Tevye's Daughters* (1894) were the basis for the 1964 musical *Fiddler on the Roof.*

Sholokhov, Mikhail Aleksandrovich (1905–84) Russian writer. His four-volume novel *And Quiet Flows the Don* (1928–40) describes **World War I** and the **Russian Revolution** from a Cossack point of view. Other works include *Virgin Soil Upturned* (1932–60). Elected to the Supreme Soviet in 1936, he received the Order of Lenin in 1939 and the Nobel Prize for literature in 1965. Although he supported the Soviet aesthetic doctrine of socialist realism, his work is considered more nuanced and complex than that doctrine demanded.

Shostakovich, Dmitry Dmitriyevich (1906–75) Russian composer. One of the century's most enduring musical figures, he wrote his first orchestral piece at age 13 and saw his first symphony performed in Leningrad in 1926. His 15 symphonies express wide purpose and range, including the political no. 2 and the satirical no. 3, with later creations more grave. From the 1930s until after **World War II**, his work often brought government denunciation; however, in 1956 and 1966 he was awarded the Order of Lenin. He has written 15 highly regarded string quartets (notably no. 2), operas (such as *The Nose*, 1930), and film scores, plus violin, cello, and piano concertos and other ensemble and solo works. His Russian-born American son Maxim Shostakovich (1938–) is a conductor and pianist.

Sibelius, Jean [Julius Christian] (1865–1957) Finnish composer. He gained national preeminence with his *Kullervo* Symphony (1892) and international fame by the end of the 19th century. His early works, influenced by romantic composers, embodied Finnish nationalism; later works are more personal. Among his compositions are seven symphonies (1899–1924), symphonic poems (including *Finlandia*, 1900), incidental music (including *Pelléas et Mélisande,* 1905, and *The Tempest,* 1925), chamber music, and songs. He ceased composing in 1926. Sibelius is considered the most accomplished Finnish composer in history.

Sihanouk, Norodom (1922–) Cambodian leader. As king of Cambodia (1941–55, 1993–), he cooperated with French authorities to help his nation achieve independence as a constitutional monarchy in 1953. He abdicated in favor of his father in 1955, becoming prime minister. Known as Prince Sihanouk, he later became president (1960–70, 1975–76, 1991–93). In the 1960s he suppressed political opposition and tried to remain neutral in the face of the **Vietnam War**. In 1970 he was deposed in a U.S.–backed coup by Prime Minister Lon Nol (1913–85). He returned to power in 1975, but only as nominal head of state under **Pol Pot**, who deposed him in 1976. The Vietnamese invasion of 1979 forced him into exile. Over the next decade, Sihanouk united the various opposing parties in a coalition. In 1991 he returned to power as interim president. He was proclaimed king in 1993.

Simpson, O[renthal] J[ames] (1947–) American athlete. He won the Heisman Trophy (1968) as a running back for the University of Southern California football team. As a professional player with the Buffalo Bills (1969–77) and San Francisco 49ers (1978–79), he set season records for most yards gained (2,003 in 1973) and most touchdowns (23 in 1975). After retiring from football in 1979, he became a popular sportscaster, advertising pitchman, and actor. In 1994 he was charged with murdering his ex-wife, Nicole Brown Simpson, and Ronald Goldman. In two highly publicized trials, he was acquitted of criminal charges (1995) but found liable for the deaths in a civil action (1997). The case aroused much discussion about race and the fairness of the judicial system.

Sinatra, Frank (1915–98) American singer. Born Francis Albert Sinatra in Hoboken, N.J., he reached stardom in the 1940s as "the Voice," a tender crooner with the Tommy Dorsey (1905–56) band, with hits including "I'll Never Smile Again." His career was rejuvenated in the 1950s, with his performance in *From Here to Eternity* (1953, best supporting actor Oscar) and a more mature, swinging song style ("Come Fly with Me," "I've Got You under My Skin") that earned him the moniker "Ol' Blue Eyes." Also during the 1950s, he and American arranger Nelson Riddle (1921–85) reimagined the long-playing (33 ⅓ r.p.m.) record albums through the development of "concept" album of songs linked by theme and treatment (*Songs for Swingin' Lovers!*, *In the Wee Small Hours*). By refocusing popular song as an intimate display of emotion, he elevated the popular singer to star, hastening the end of the big-band era and influencing generations of pop and rock singers afterward. He is considered by many critics the finest and most representative song stylist of the 20th century.

Sinclair, Upton [Beall] (1878–1968) American writer. Born in Baltimore, Md., he wrote several novels of social commentary, including *King Coal* (1917) and *Oil!* (1927), but is best known for his Socialist polemic set in the Chicago stockyards, *The Jungle* (1906). Its graphic descriptions hastened the passage of the Pure Food and Drug Act (1906) in the U.S. Congress. Sinclair was a Socialist candidate from California for the U.S. Congress (1920, 1922) and Democratic candidate for governor of California (1934), on a platform called EPIC (End Poverty in California). His novel *Dragon's Teeth* (1942) won the Pulitzer Prize.

Singer, Isaac Bashevis (1904–91) Polish-born American Yiddish writer. Born into generations of rabbis, he studied at the Warsaw Rabbinical Seminary but decided to become a writer. He immigrated to the U.S. in 1935, writing journalism in New York for the *Jewish Daily Forward*. His sharp, fabulous works, often about old age, estrangement, and lost Jewish worlds, include the novels *Satan in Goray* (1935) and *The Magician of Lublin* (1960) and the short-story collections *Gimpel the Fool* (1957), *The Spinoza of Market Street* (1961), and *Old Love* (1979). Memoirs include *My Father's Court* (1956) and *A Little Boy in Search of God* (1976). He was awarded the Nobel Prize for literature (1978). His brother Israel Joshua Singer (1873–1944) wrote popular novels, including the epic *The Brothers Ashkenazi* (1936).

Siqueiros, David Alfaro (1896–1974) Mexican painter. Jailed and exiled several times for left-wing revolutionary activities, he specialized in murals, including *March of Humanity*. His work is marked by striking colors, dynamic brushwork, and social protest. He produced landscapes, portraits, and other kinds of paintings.

Skinner, B[urrhus] F[rederic] (1904–90) American psychologist. He received his Ph.D. from Harvard in 1931, later teaching there and at the University of Minnesota, Indiana University, and Oxford. The leading American exponent of behaviorism, he coined the term "operant conditioning" and invented the Skinner box, in which a lab animal must learn to press a lever to get food. His works, some of which proposed techniques of social engineering, include *Walden Two* (1948) and *Beyond Freedom and Dignity* (1971).

Smith, Bessie [Elizabeth] (1894 or 1898–1937) American singer. Born in Chattanooga, Tenn., she was guided and influenced by American singer Gertrude "Ma" Rainey (1886–1939) before becoming a prominent jazz vocalist in the 1920s. Called the "Empress of the Blues" for her intensely emotional, classic presentation of song, she worked with such leading accompanists as the American musician **Louis Armstrong**.

Smith, Ian [Douglas] (1919–) Rhodesian politician. A white supremacist and leader of the Rhodesian Front Party, he became prime minister (1964) and unilaterally declared Rhodesia's independence from Britain (1965). Despite international economic sanctions and guerrilla war, his white-led government remained in power until 1980, when **Robert Mugabe** became prime minister under a new constitution.

Smuts, Jan Christian (1870–1950) South African soldier and politician. Educated in law at Cambridge, he gained national attention as an officer in the **Boer War** (1899–1902), during which he served as commander-in-chief of Republican forces in the Cape of Good Hope. After the war, he helped establish the Union of South Africa (1910), with its official policy of racial discrimination. While holding office in **Louis Botha**'s cabinet (1910–19), he organized South African forces during **World War I**. At the **Paris Peace Conference**, he supported the **League of Nations**. He went on to serve as prime minister (1919–24; 1939–48) and was elevated to field marshal (1941) during **World War II**. After the war, he wrote the preamble to the **United Nations** Charter.

Snead, Sam (1912–97) American athlete. Born Samuel Jackson Snead in Hot Springs, Va., he won more Professional Golfers' Association (PGA) tournament victories—84—than any golfer in history. Among his victories were three Masters tournaments (1949, 1952, 1954) and three PGA titles (1942, 1949, 1951). Nicknamed "Slammin' Sammy," he is considered one of the finest golfer in the game's history.

Snow, C[harles] P[ercy], baron (1905–80) British writer. A physicist and government administrator, he wrote *Strangers and Brothers* (1940–70), a series of 11 novels. In these novels and in essays, most notably *The Two Cultures and the Scientific Revolution* (1959), he explored the relations between science and society.

Solzhenitsyn, Aleksandr Isayevich (1918–) Russian writer. He served eight years in labor camps (1945–53) for criticizing **Joseph Stalin**. Though **Nikita Khrushchev** briefly permitted him to publish his work, Solzhenitsyn's writings were subsequently banned at home and published abroad. With official ire increasingly incited by his novels documenting Soviet oppression, he was deported to the West in 1974. He received the Nobel Prize for literature in 1970. Works include the short novel *One Day in the Life of Ivan Denisovich* (1962), the novel *The First Circle* (1968), and the three-volume nonfiction work *The Gulag Archipelago* (1973–75). In 1994, three years after the fall of the **Soviet Union** (1991), he returned to live in Russia.

Somoza [Garcia], Anastasio (1896–1956) Nicaraguan dictator. Educated in the United States, he used U.S. military aid to rule Nicaragua autocratically (1937–56) and establish a dynasty that lasted into the 1970s. His repressive, anti-Communist rule favored the landed elite and oppressed the poor. He was succeeded by his son Luis Anastasio Somoza Debayle (1922–67), who ruled, somewhat more liberally, from 1957 to 1963. Luis, in turn, was succeeded by his brother Anastasio Somoza Debayle (1925–80), the most ruthless of the dynasty. At times, the Somozas held the title of president; at other times, they granted the title to others answerable to them. Shortly after losing U.S. support, the younger Anastasio's regime (1963–79) fell to the Sandinista rebels. He was assassinated in exile.

Sondheim, Stephen [Joshua] (1930–) American composer. After contributing music to the Broadway musical *Girls of Summer* (1956), he became a major success in 1958 as the lyricist for *West Side Story* (music by **Leonard Bernstein**), which opened the door to a darker, more brooding Broadway musical. The next year saw another landmark collaboration: *Gypsy*, with music by British-born American composer Jule Styne (1905–94). His first solo effort was *A Funny Thing Happened on the Way to the Forum* (1962). Among his other musicals are *Company* (1970), *Follies* (1971), *A Little Night Music* (1973), *Sweeney Todd*

(1979), and *Into the Woods* (1987), all of which won Tony Awards for best musical. He is noted for the intricacy of his lyrics and his ability to convey cynicism and modern sensibilities.

Soong Qingling or **Ch'ing-ling** (1892–1981) Chinese politician. She married **Sun Yat-sen** in 1914 but after his death in 1925 broke with his **Guomindang**, or **Nationalist Party**, to join the Communist Party. After 1949 she was vice chairman of the People's Republic of China. Her brother T.V. Soong (1894–1971) served in the Guomindang government from the 1920s to the 1940s; her sister Soong Mei-ling (c. 1897–) married **Chiang Kai-shek** in 1927.

Sorel, Georges-Eugène (1847–1922) French philosopher. Retiring from a civil service job in 1892, he became a Marxist and supported revolutionary **syndicalism**. He developed a theory on the uses of myth and violence in history and wrote *Reflections on Violence* (1908), which advocated the use of the general strike as a weapon in class wars. In 1909 he left syndicalism and supported the monarchist movement. Other works include *Les Illusions du progrès* (1908).

Soyinka, Wole (1934–) Nigerian poet and playwright. Born Akinwande Oluwole Soyinka, he studied at the Universities of Ibadan and Leeds, England. He became known for attempts to develop native drama through his Masks and Orisun theater companies and his politically aware plays, including *A Dance of the Forests* (1960), *Death and the King's Horsemen* (1975), and *A Play of Giants* (1984). Poetic works include *Poems from Prison* (1969), *A Shuttle in the Crypt* (1972), and *Ogun Abibiman* (1976). Other works include the novel *The Interpreters* (1965) and autobiography *Aké: The Years of Childhood* (1981). A lifelong champion of individual rights, he was imprisoned by the government from 1967 to 1969. He won the Nobel Prize for literature in 1986.

Speer, Albert (1905–81) German architect. Head Nazi architect from 1934, he also served as minister of armaments during **World War II** (1942–45). At the **Nuremberg** tribunal he was convicted of war crimes and later served a 20-year sentence (1946–66). His memoir, *Inside the Third Reich* (1970), was a best seller.

Spengler, Oswald (1880–1936) German philosopher of history. In his major work *The Decline of the West* (1918–22), he proposed a cyclical, organic view of history, with Western civilization seen as being in its last stage. His views were popular with the Nazis, though he himself opposed **Adolf Hitler**'s rise to power.

Spielberg, Steven (1947–) Film director and producer. Born in Cincinnati, Ohio, he went from **television** directing to becoming one of the most commercially successful filmmakers of all time. His specialty is big-budget adventure or science fiction films notable for roller-coaster suspense and huge box-office returns; these include *Jaws* (1975), *Close Encounters of the Third Kind* (1977), *Raiders of the Lost Ark* (1981), *E.T.* (1982), and *Jurassic Park* (1993). He was acclaimed as a serious filmmaker for his **Holocaust** drama, *Schindler's List* (1993), which won Academy Awards for best picture and best director; he won the directing award a second time for *Saving Private Ryan* (1998). He has also produced many films directed by others, as founder (1984) of Amblin Entertainment and co-founder (1994) of the studio DreamWorks SKG.

Spock, Benjamin McLane (1903–98) American physician and writer. Born in New Haven, Conn., he wrote *The Common Sense Book of Baby and Child Care* (1946), a best-selling, highly influential child-care book for middle-class parents that advocated more open, permissive child rearing. Professor of child development at Case Western Reserve University from 1955, he resigned in 1967 to pursue peace and antinuclear activities (*Dr. Spock on Vietnam,* 1968).

Springsteen, Bruce (1949–) American singer and songwriter. Born in Freehold, N.J., he was touted as "the future of rock and roll" with his third album, *Born to Run* (1975), a collection of romantic rock anthems of longing and redemption. His album *Born in the U.S.A.* (1984) was an international success and made him a national icon, though the album's questioning lyrics were often misread. Other albums include *Nebraska* (1982) and *Tunnel of Love* (1988). An electric live performer, he has toured widely. He won a best-song Oscar for "Streets of Philadelphia" from *Philadelphia* (1993).

Stalin, Joseph Vissarionovich (1879–1953) Soviet dictator. Original surname Dzhugashvili; his assumed name *Stalin* means "man of steel." Born a cobbler's son in Gori, Georgia, he joined the Social Democratic Party in 1898, siding with **V. I. Lenin** and the **Bolsheviks** when the party split in 1903. Arrested six times for revolutionary activities, he was exiled to Siberia (1913–17). After the **Russian Revolution of November 1917,** he was appointed commissar of nationalities; he defended Tsaritsyn (later Stalingrad and now Volgograd) during the civil war. In 1922 he was made general secretary of the Communist Party. Upon Lenin's death in 1924, Stalin succeeded him as chairman of the Politburo. At first sharing power in a triumvirate with **Lev Kamenev** and **Grigory Zinoviev**, he was able to push them aside, along with archrival **Leon Trotsky**, by 1927. In 1928 Stalin launched the first of his five-year plans for agricultural collectivization and industrialization. The assassination of his aide **Sergey Kirov** gave him a pretext for the **Great Purges** (1934–38), in which he consolidated his power by using show trials to eliminate perceived enemies. Ruling by repression and terror, Stalin maintained absolute power over the **Soviet Union**; he accumulated titles, such as chairman of the Council of People's Commissars (prime minister) in 1941 and generalissimo in 1945. He formed a nonaggression pact with **Adolf Hitler** in 1939, but Hitler soon violated it by invading the Soviet Union (1941), prompting Stalin to enter **World War II** against Germany (1941–45). At Allied (see **Allied Powers**) conferences at Tehran (1943), **Yalta** (1945, see **Yalta Conference**), and **Potsdam** (1945, see **Potsdam Conference**), Stalin won Western recognition of Soviet hegemony over Eastern Europe. He died in office. Although he succeeded in building his nation into a superpower through industrialization and armament, he did so at great cost in lives. His successor, **Nikita Khrushchev**, denounced him in 1956, attempting to undo some of his excesses through de-Stalinization.

Stanislavsky, Konstantin (1863–1938) Russian theater director. Born Konstantin Sergeyevich Alekseyev, he cofounded, managed, and acted at the Moscow Art Theatre (1897), which showcased modern works by Russian playwright and short-story writer Anton Chekhov (1860–1904) and others. His "method" acting technique, relying on inner motivation, influenced actors for decades, particularly in the U.S. at the Actors Studio. Writings include his autobiography, *My Life in Art* (1924), and *An Actor Prepares* (1936).

Steffens, [Joseph] Lincoln (1866–1936) American writer. Managing editor of *McClure's Magazine* (1902–06), he wrote muckraking articles on city governmental corruption, notably those collected in the politically influential *The Shame of the Cities* (1904). Other books include *The Struggle for Self-Government* (1906), *Upbuilders* (1909), and *Autobiography* (1931). He was associate editor of *American Magazine* (1906–07) and *Everybody's Magazine* (1906–11). He supported the **Russian Revolution of November 1917** and revolutionary movements in other countries.

Stein, Gertrude (1874–1946) American writer. Born in Allegheny, Pa., she graduated from Radcliffe and studied at Johns Hopkins medical school before settling in Paris in 1903 and establishing a cultural salon in the 1920s. Frequented by leading writers and artists, including Americans **Ernest Hemingway** and **F. Scott Fitzgerald**, the salon often provided patronage and literary influence. A noted writer as well as impresario, her experimental works include short stories (*Three Lives,* 1909), poetry (*Tender Buttons,* 1914), and essays (*Lectures in America,* 1935). Her autobiography, *The Autobiography of Alice B. Toklas* (1933), was named for her companion, Toklas.

Steinbeck, John [Ernst] (1902–68) American writer. Born in Salinas, Calif., he became known for his novels of social justice, notably his politically influential study of a Depression-era Dust Bowl family, *The Grapes of Wrath* (1939, Pulitzer Prize). Other works include *Tortilla Flat* (1935), *Of Mice and Men* (1937), *East of Eden* (1952), and his picaresque nonfiction *Travels with Charley* (1962). He was awarded the Nobel Prize for literature (1962).

Steinem, Gloria (1934–) American feminist. As founder of the magazine *Ms.* in 1971, which she edited until 1987, she became a leading voice for the women's liberation movement.

Stevens, Wallace (1879–1955) American poet. Although he completed three years of course work (1893–96) as a "special student" at Harvard University, he left Harvard without a degree in 1900. Graduating from New York Law School, he was an insurance executive in Connecticut and author of several influential poetry collections, including *Harmonium* (1923), *The Man with the Blue Guitar* (1925), *Transport to Summer* (1947), and *Collected Poems* (1954, Pulitzer Prize). His works are noted for their vivid imagery and original use of language. Prose works include the essay collection *The Necessary Angel* (1951); he also wrote plays.

Stevenson, Adlai E[wing II] (1900–65) American politician. Grandson of Vice President Adlai E. Stevenson (1835–1914), he graduated from Princeton and Northwestern Law School and worked widely in government offices before being elected Democratic governor of Illinois (1949–53). In 1952 and 1956 he was the Democratic nominee for president, both times losing to Republican **Dwight D. Eisenhower**. Erudite and progressive, he was respected in the **Democratic Party**, serving as **United Nations** ambassador (1961–65) under President **John F. Kennedy**.

Stewart, James [Maitland] (1908–97) American actor. Born in Indiana, Pa., he graduated from Princeton and through classmates entered the theater group the University Players. In Hollywood from 1935, he established himself a star as the idealistic title character in *Mr. Smith Goes to Washington* (1939). The next year, he won an Academy Award for *The Philadelphia Story* (1940). Following service as an Army Air Corps bomber pilot during **World War II**, he turned to films that often explored darker aspects of human character. Among them are *It's a Wonderful Life* (1946), *Harvey* (1950), *Winchester 73* (1950), *Rear Window* (1954), and *Vertigo* (1958). He is remembered for embodying on screen the small-town virtues of honesty and steadfastness.

Strauss, Richard (1864–1949) German composer. Born in Munich, he became conductor of the Berlin Philharmonic (1894), Berlin Royal Opera (1898), and Vienna Opera (1919–24). His romantic, often highly orchestrated operas and symphonic poems are influenced by German composer Richard Wagner (1813–83). Notable symphonic poems include *Thus Spake Zarathustra* (1895); his frequently controversial operas include *Salomé* (1905), *Elektra* (1909) and *Ariadne auf Naxos* (1912), the latter two with Austrian poet and dramatist Hugo von Hofmannsthal (1874–1929). He also composed ballets, chamber music, and songs.

Stravinsky, Igor Feodorovich (1882–1971) Russian-born American composer. Through study with Russian composer Nikolay Androvich Rimsky-Korsakov (1844–1908), he gained public attention and was commissioned by **Sergey Diaghilev** to write a ballet for the Ballet Russes. His first work, *The Firebird* (1910), along with subsequent ones *Petrushka* (1911) and *The Rite of Spring* (1913), were noted for their originality and use of dissonance and irregular rhythms. Moving to Switzerland at the beginning of **World War I**, he wrote scores, dance scenes, ballets, and jazz-influenced works. In 1920 he moved to France, with works there including *Oedipus Rex* (1927), an opera-operetta with text by **Jean Cocteau**. In 1939 he immigrated to the U.S.; there he experimented with 12-tone music. Works of the period include *The Rake's Progress* (1951) and the ballet *Agon* (1957). He is considered the most versatile composer of the century.

Streep, Meryl (1949–) American actress. Born Mary Louise Streep, she is acclaimed for her thoughtful performances and skill with dialects. Her career began on the New York stage, but she was soon recruited by Hollywood for such films as *Kramer vs. Kramer* (1980), which won her an Oscar for best supporting actress, and *Silkwood* (1983), which won her an Oscar for best actress. Other films include *Sophie's Choice* (1982) and *The Bridges of Madison County* (1995).

Stresemann, Gustav (1878–1929) German politician. He founded the German People's Party in 1918, becoming chancellor (1923) and minister of foreign affairs (1923–29) in the **Weimar Republic**. He pursued conciliatory policies toward Germany's former foes and arranged Germany's entry into the **League of Nations**. He shared the 1926 Nobel Peace Prize with **Aristide Briand**.

Suharto (1921–) Indonesian soldier and politician. He cooperated with the Japanese during **World War II**, fighting afterward for independence from the Dutch. In 1963 he became major general and head of the Indonesian army under President **Achmed Sukarno**. In 1965 Suharto put down an attempted Communist coup, then led a violent purge of Communists. He deposed and arrested Sukarno (1967) and was elected president (1968–). Ruling in authoritarian fashion, Suharto built a growing economy and strong ties with the West. He invaded (1975) and annexed (1976) East Timor, killing more than 100,000 of its people. In 1998 Indonesia's currency collapsed; economic turmoil and antigovernment rioting followed. Faced with increasing opposition, Suharto resigned in 1998.

Sukarno, Achmed (1901–70) Indonesian politician. Beginning in the 1920s, he voiced nationalist opposition to Dutch colonial rule. After cooperating with Japanese occupation during **World War II**, he proclaimed Indonesian independence in 1945, winning recognition from the Netherlands and becoming his country's first president in 1949. He assumed dictatorial powers in 1959. He sought closer ties with Communist China but lost power after army leader **Suharto** put down an attempted Communist coup in 1965. In 1967 Sukarno was removed from office and spent his last years under arrest.

Sun Yat-sen or **Sun Chung-shan** (1866–1925) Chinese revolutionary. Known as the father of modern China, he was born Sun Wen near Canton, raised partly in Hawaii, and graduated from medical school in Hong Kong in 1892. After leading an unsuccessful revolt in China in 1895, he lived in exile for 16 years, building international support and developing his "Three People's Principles": nationalism, democracy, and the people's livelihood. In 1905 he organized a revolutionary alliance, the Tongmenghui (T'ung Meng Hui), committed to the establishment of a nationalist republic. Returning to China during the **Chinese Revolution** of 1911, he was elected president of the provisional government (1911–12) but resigned in favor of **Yuan Shikai**, who became increasingly dictatorial. As director of the **Guomindang** or **Nationalist Party**, Sun revolted, becoming president (1921) of a self-proclaimed government that succeeded in taking power in Canton in 1923. He began cooperating with the Chinese Communists and receiving help from the **Soviet Union**. Both Communists and Nationalists claimed to be his heirs after his death. He married **Soong Qingling** in 1914.

Sunday, Billy (1862–1935) American evangelist. Born William Ashley Sunday. After short careers in professional baseball (1883–91) and at the YMCA, he became a Presbyterian minister (1903) and gained fame for his showy preaching of fundamentalist evils, including liquor and science. His influence waned in the 1920s.

Synge, John Millington (1871–1909) Irish playwright. A literary critic, he was active in promoting the Celtic revival during the 1890s and later became known as a playwright with the Abbey Theatre in Dublin. Notable works include *The Well of the Saints* (1905), *The Playboy of the Western World* (1907), and the posthumously produced *Deidre of the Sorrows* (1910). Essay collections include *The Aran Islands* (1907) and *In Wicklow and in West Kerry* (1908).

Szilard, Leo (1898–1964) Hungarian-born American physicist. One of the first scientists to envision a nuclear chain reaction and grasp its potential use in weapons, he helped persuade the United States to develop the first atomic bomb. He helped develop the first self-sustaining nuclear fission reactor. After **World War II**, he was a vocal opponent of the nuclear arms race.

T

Taft, William Howard (1857–1930) Twenty-seventh U.S. president (1909–13). The son of former U.S. cabinet member Alphonso Taft, he attended Yale and the University of Cincinnati and practiced law from 1880. After serving as Ohio superior court judge (1887–90), U.S. solicitor general (1890–92), U.S. circuit court judge (1892–1900), first civil governor of the Philippine Islands (1901–04), and secretary of war (1904–08), he became the Republican candidate for president and was elected in 1908. He strongly backed antitrust legislation and established the Department of Labor. But his support of compromise tariff law the Payne-Aldrich Act (1909) cost the support of **Theodore Roosevelt** and the liberal wing of the **Republican Party** and led to his defeat and the election of Democratic candidate **Woodrow Wilson** in 1912. The next year Taft became professor of constitutional law at Yale, where he served until 1921, when he was appointed chief justice of the Supreme Court. His son was U.S. senator from Ohio Robert Alphonso Taft (1889–1953), notable for his sponsorship of the Taft-Hartley Labor–Management Relations Act (1947), afterwards known simply as the Taft-Hartley Act.

Tagore, Sir Rabindranath (1861–1941) Indian philosopher. The son of Indian mystic philosopher Debendranath Tagore (1817–1905), he was educated in England and became known for his prolific writings, including 15 books of philosophy (including *Sadhana: The*

Realization of Life, 1913), 50 plays (notably *Mukta Dhara,* 1922), 40 novels (such as *Gora,* 1910), and 100 works of verse (including *Naivedya,* 1901, and *Gitanjali,* 1912). He was awarded the Nobel Prize for literature in 1913. He was also an esteemed painter and composer. He founded the Bengali school Santiniketan (1901), which developed into Visva-Bharati University (1924). He was knighted in 1915 but resigned his peerage in 1919, protesting British repression of the Punjabs.

Tanizaki Jun'ichiro (1886–1965) Japanese writer. In novels such as *The Makioka Sisters* (1943–48), he explored the transition from old to new Japanese values. Some novels, such as *The Diary of a Mad Old Man* (1961–62), were notable for their eroticism. He also wrote plays and adapted the 11th-century classic *The Tale of Genji* into modern Japanese.

Tarbell, Ida Minerva (1857–1944) American writer. Born in Erie Co., Pa., she was a muckraking journalist on *McClure's Magazine* (1894–1906), specializing in exposés of large companies; her two-volume *History of the Standard Oil Company* was published in 1904. She wrote biographies of Abraham Lincoln (1900) and Owen D. Young (1932).

Taylor, Elizabeth [Roosevelt] (1932–) American actress. A child star in such Hollywood films as *National Velvet* (1944), she became a captivating adult star, winning two best actress Oscars for her performances in *Butterfield 8* (1960) and *Who's Afraid of Virginia Woolf?* (1966). For decades, her personal life was the stuff of gossip magazine headlines; her many marriages included two to **Richard Burton** (1964–70, 1975–76), her costar in several films, beginning with *Cleopatra* (1963). She has long been a prominent fund-raiser for **AIDS** research.

Teilhard de Chardin, [Marie-Joseph-]Pierre (1881–1955) French philosopher. Ordained a Jesuit priest in 1911, he was a paleontologist who helped discover Peking Man (1929). In works such as *The Phenomenon of Man* (1955), he presented a philosophy synthesizing biological and spiritual evolution.

Teller, Edward (1908–) Hungarian-born American physicist. He immigrated to the United States in 1935, becoming a citizen in 1941. During **World War II**, he worked on development of the atomic bomb; after the war, he helped develop the hydrogen bomb, first detonated in 1952. His institutional affiliations included George Washington University (1935–41), the University of Chicago (1946–52), and the University of California at Berkeley (1953–75). A longtime government adviser, he strongly advocated the development of nuclear weapons as a deterrent force.

Temple, Shirley (1928–) American actress. Appearing in short films before age four, she was a Hollywood star from 1934 to 1938 in films including *Bright Eyes* (1934), *The Little Colonel* (1935), *Curly Top* (1935), and *Rebecca of Sunnybrook Farm* (1938). An American icon in the Depression, she won a special Academy Award in 1934. Upon her 1950 marriage to American businessman Charles Black she became Shirley Temple Black. A Republican member of Congress from California in the 1960s, she later served as U.S. ambassador to Ghana (1974–76).

Teng Hsiao-p'ing See **Deng Xiaoping**.

Teresa, Mother (1910–97) Macedonian-born Indian missionary. Of Albanian descent, she was born Agnes Gonxha Bojaxhiv. She was a Roman Catholic nun in India when, in 1948, she began caring for the poor on the streets of Calcutta. She founded the Missionaries of Charity, which grew to operate food centers, schools, hospitals, and other charitable institutions around the world. Revered for her personal saintliness, she won the Nobel Peace Prize in 1979.

Thant, U (1909–74) Burmese diplomat. He was secretary of the ministry of information (1949–57) and permanent Burmese representative to the **UN** (1957–61). As secretary-general of the UN (1961–71), he helped negotiate peaceful resolutions of the **Cuban Missile Crisis** (1962), the **India-Pakistan War of 1965**, and conflicts in West New Guinea (1962), the Congo (1963), and Cyprus (1964).

Thatcher, Margaret [Hilda], baroness née Roberts (1925–) British politician. After graduating from Oxford (1947), she worked as a research chemist and tax lawyer; she married Denis Thatcher in 1951. She was elected as a Conservative M.P. in 1959. After serving as secretary of state for education and science (1970–74), she became party leader in 1975. In 1979 she became Britain's first female prime minister (1979–90). A right-winger, she adopted a monetarist policy of regulating the money supply by cutting social programs and maintaining high interest rates. Known as the "Iron Lady," she privatized state-owned industries, cut taxes, and curtailed trade-union power, notably by prevailing against organized labor in the miners' strike of 1984–85. Her policies reduced inflation but at first increased unemployment. In foreign affairs, she was a close ally of the United States, opposed European integration, and acted decisively to retrieve the Falkland Islands from Argentina during the **Falklands War** (1982). She faced growing **Irish Republican Army** terrorist activity, a recession in 1989, and popular disapproval of her imposition of a poll tax, or flat-rate tax. Forced to resign due to opposition from her own cabinet and party, she was succeeded by her chancellor of the exchequer, **John Major**. She was made a life peer in 1992.

Thomas, Dylan [Marlais] (1914–53) British writer. Born in Wales, he wrote powerful lyric poems with intricate imagery drawn from Christianity, the writings of **Sigmund Freud**, and Welsh legend. Volumes of poetry include *Eighteen Poems* (1934) and *Deaths and Entrances* (1946). He also wrote stories, sketches, and a radio play, *Under Milk Wood* (1954). His stormy private life ended with his death from alcoholism.

Thorpe, Jim (1888–1953) American athlete. One of the nation's finest all-around athletes, he was born James Francis Thorpe near Shawnee, Okla., and was an All-American halfback (1911–12) on the Carlisle (Pa.) Indian Industrial School football team. In the 1912 Olympics, he won gold medals in the pentathlon and decathlon but was forced to give them up when officials learned he played semiprofessional football (1909–10). He played major league baseball (1913–19) and professional football (1917–29), also serving as the first president of the National Football League (1920–21). In 1982 his Olympic medals were returned to his family. The town of Jim Thorpe, Pa., is named for him.

Thurber, James [Grover] (1894–1961) American writer. Staff member (1927–33) and longtime contributor to the *New Yorker,* he published whimsical, psychologically deft cartoons and stories like "The Secret Life of Walter Mitty" (1939). Collections include *My Life and Hard Times* (1933), *The Middle-Aged Man on the Flying Trapeze* (1935), and *The Thurber Carnival* (1945). With American writer E. B. White (1899–1985), he collaborated on the sex-manual satire *Is Sex Necessary?* (1929) and with American playwright Elliott Nugent (1899–1980), on the play *The Male Animal* (1940). Children's books include *The Thirteen Clocks* (1950).

Tillich, Paul Johannes (1886–1965) German-born American theologian and philosopher. A Lutheran, he taught theology at German universities but was dismissed in 1933 for his opposition to the Nazis. After coming to the United States, he taught at Union Theological Seminary (1933–55), Harvard University (1955–62), and the University of Chicago (1962–65). Viewing God as "the ground of being," he tried to correlate Christian revelation with existential philosophy. Works include *Systematic Theology* (1951–63) and *The Courage to Be* (1952).

Tito (1892–1980) Yugoslav politician. Born Josip Broz. A mechanic, he fought for the Red Army during the **Russian Civil War** and joined the Yugoslav Communist Party in the 1920s, becoming secretary-general in 1937. He led the Yugoslav partisans against German occupation in **World War II**, gaining the title marshal in 1943 and heading the government by war's end. In 1948 he broke with the **Soviet Union**, freeing himself to pursue relatively liberal policies, such as a decentralized system of workers' self-government. As first president of the republic of Yugoslavia (1953–80), he was a leader of the nonaligned nations.

Togo, Heihachiro (1846–1934) Japanese naval officer. Of samurai descent, he saw army service and studied at the Royal Naval College in England (1870–78). As naval commander-in-chief during the **Russo-Japanese War**, he defeated the Russian fleets at Port Arthur (1904) and Tsushima (1905). Considered Japan's greatest naval hero, he was made a count in 1907, admiral of the fleet in 1913, and a marquis in 1934.

Tojo, Hideki (1884–1948) Japanese politician. Chief of staff of the Kwantung Army in Manchuria in 1937–38, he went on to become vice minister of war (1938–39) and minister of war (1940–41). As prime minister (1941–44), he ordered the attack on U.S. forces at **Pearl Harbor** in 1941, bringing the U.S. into **World War II**. In 1944, after several military defeats, army opposition forced him to resign. Following Japan's surrender, he was hanged as a war criminal.

Tolkien, J[ohn] R[onald] R[euel] (1892–1973) South African–born British writer. A philologist and professor of medieval literature at Oxford (1925–59), he wrote scholarly works, including *Beowulf: The Monsters and the Critics* (1937), but he is best known for his fantasies set in Middle Earth, especially *The Hobbit* (1937) and the trilogy *The Lord of the Rings* (1954–55).

Toscanini, Arturo (1867–1957) Italian conductor. He is known for his interpretations of the music of Giuseppe Verdi, Ludwig van Beethoven, and Richard Wagner, among others. He conducted at La Scala in Milan (1898–1907; 1921–31), the Metropolitan Opera (1908–21), and the New York Philharmonic (1928–36), ending his long career as conductor of the National Broadcasting Company Orchestra (1937–54).

Toynbee, Arnold Joseph (1889–1975) British historian. Educated at Oxford, he taught there and at the University of London (1919–55). He presented a theory of the rise and fall of civilizations in the 12-volume *A Study of History* (1934–61). Other works include *The Western Question in Greece and Turkey* (1922).

Tracy, Spencer (1900–67) American actor. With his natural acting style, he embodied unpretentious integrity and wit in numerous films, two of which made him the first actor to win two consecutive best actor Academy Awards: *Captains Courageous* (1937) and *Boys Town* (1938). Married since 1923, he had an intimate relationship with **Katharine Hepburn** from 1942 to his death; Tracy and Hepburn became one of the screen's most famous teams in movies such as *Adam's Rib* (1949) and *Guess Who's Coming to Dinner* (1967). Other Tracy films included *San Francisco* (1936) and *Inherit the Wind* (1960).

Trotsky, Leon (1879–1940) Soviet revolutionary and politician. Born Lev Davidovich Bronstein in Yelisavetgrad (now Kirovograd), he became a Marxist in the 1890s. He was exiled to Siberia in 1900, escaping in 1902 to join **V. I. Lenin** in London and edit the journal *Iskra*. Returning to Russia during the **1905 Revolution**, he was exiled to Siberia and escaped again. With Lenin, he organized the **Russian Revolution of November 1917** and became the second most powerful man in the **Soviet Union**. As commissar for foreign affairs, he led the negotiations with Germany at the Brest-Litovsk Peace Conference (1918, see **Brest-Litovsk, Treaty of**) but resigned over differences with Lenin. Appointed commissar of war, he organized the Red Army, which won the **Russian Civil War** (1918–20). In the struggle for power after Lenin's death in 1924, he lost to his chief rival, **Joseph Stalin**, who opposed Trotsky's view that **socialism**'s success inside Russia depended on revolution in western Europe; Stalin believed "**socialism** in one country" could succeed. Under Stalin's influence, Trotsky was forced to resign as commissar of war (1925), expelled from the Communist Party (1927), and deported (1929). He settled in Mexico (1937), where he opposed Stalinism through works such as *The Revolution Betrayed* (1937). He was assassinated, probably by a Stalinist agent.

Trudeau, Pierre [Elliott] (1919–2000) Canadian politician. Receiving a law degree from Montreal University, he became parliamentary secretary and justice minister to Liberal Party leader **Lester Pearson**. As prime minister (1968–79, 1980–84) following Pearson's resignation, he worked to contain the Quebec separatist movement and to further the nation's economy. His efforts to revise the country's constitution led to the Constitution Act in 1982, which granted Canada full independence from England. His term was interrupted (1979–80) when the Liberal Party lost majority power.

Truffaut, François (1932–84) French film director. Immersed in movies from childhood, he was a film critic for the French journal *Cahiers du Cinéma* in his 20s and began directing films in 1954. With *The 400 Blows* (1959), he became a notable force of French New Wave. Renowned for their sensitivity and romance, his major works include *Shoot the Piano Player* (1960), *Jules and Jim* (1961), *Stolen Kisses* (1968), and *The Wild Child* (1970).

Truman, Harry S (1884–1972) Thirty-third U.S. president (1945–53). Born in Lamar, Mo., he served in **World War I** as an artillery officer and worked as a haberdasher before serving as a county court judge (1926–34) and U.S. senator (1935–45). In 1945 he was elected vice president under President **Franklin Roosevelt**, who had just been elected to his fourth term. Following Roosevelt's death on April 12, 1945, Truman became president. Aiming to hasten an end to **World War II**, he ordered the use of atomic weapons on the Japanese cities of **Hiroshima** on August 6, 1945, and on Nagasaki three days later. He baffled pollsters in 1948 when he defeated front-runner Republican Thomas Dewey (1902–) for the presidency. During his terms, he ordered or oversaw a number of foreign-policy initiatives, including the **Marshall Plan** (1948), the **Truman Doctrine** (1947), the development of the **Central Intelligence Agency** (1947), the **Berlin Airlift** (1949), and U.S. involvement in the **Korean War** (1950–53). He pursued a variety of social reforms, often without success, notably a national health insurance bill. In 1951 he relieved a publicly dissenting General **Douglas MacArthur** from command in the Korean War. Without the eloquence or pedigree of Roosevelt, Truman defined himself through decisiveness and plain speech.

Turing, Alan Mathison (1912–54) British mathematician. His 1937 paper "On Computable Numbers," which described a "Turing machine," or hypothetical computing device, influenced the development of digital **computers** in the 1940s. During **World War II**, when he worked on deciphering the German Enigma codes, and afterward at the National Physical Laboratory and the University of Manchester, he contributed to the invention of early **computers** and programming techniques. In 1950 he proposed the Turing Test for determining whether a machine thinks. He committed suicide after being charged with a homosexual offense.

Tutu, Desmond (1931–) South African cleric. Ordained in 1961, he became the first black African dean of Johannesburg in 1975. As general secretary of the South African Council of Churches (1978–84), he was an outspoken opponent of **apartheid**. His encouragement of nonviolent protest won him the Nobel Peace Prize in 1984. In 1986 he was elected the first black archbishop of Cape Town, becoming titular head of South Africa's Anglican Church.

U

Ulbricht, Walter (1893–1973) East German politician. Born in Leipzig, he cofounded the German Communist Party in 1919. He was elected to the Reichstag (1928) but fled to the **Soviet Union** when Hitler took power (1933). Returning to Germany in 1945, he helped found the Socialist Unity Party (1946), East Germany's Communist Party. He led the German Democratic Republic from its establishment in 1949, as deputy premier (1949), the party's secretary-general (1950–71), and chairman of the council of state (1960–71). He maintained close ties with the **Soviet Union** and ordered the construction of the **Berlin Wall** (1961).

Unamuno [y Jugo], Miguel de (1864–1936) Spanish philosopher. His philosophy anticipated **existentialism** in its emphasis on the absurdity of life and his faith in faith itself. His novels, poems, and plays reflected his philosophical views. A critic of the monarchy, he was exiled from Spain from 1924 to 1930. Works include the treatises *The Tragic Sense of Life* (1913) and *The Agony of Christianity* (1925), the novel *Mist* (1914), and the poetic work *The Christ of Velásquez* (1920).

Undset, Sigrid (1882–1949) Norwegian novelist. A prolific writer, she is best known for her trilogy of medieval Norwegian life, *Kristin Lavransdatter* (1920–22). Her works (including *Saga of Saints,* 1934) focused on religious concerns after her conversion to Roman Catholicism in 1924. During the Nazi occupation of Norway (1940–45) she lived in the U.S. She won the Nobel Prize for literature (1928).

Updike, John [Hoyer] (1932–) American writer. Born in Shillington, Pa., he graduated from Harvard, attended Oxford University, and in 1955 became a reporter for the *New Yorker.* He gained fame with the novel *Rabbit, Run* (1961), about middle-class disillusionment and realization as seen through protagonist Harry "Rabbit" Angstrom. Subsequent Rabbit titles include *Rabbit Redux* (1971), *Rabbit Is Rich* (1981, Pulitzer Prize), and *Rabbit at Rest* (1990). Other novels include *The Witches of Eastwick* (1984) and *S* (1988). Among essay collections are *Hugging the Shore: Essays and Criticism* (1983).

V

Valentino, Rudolph (1895–1926) Italian-born American actor. Born Rodolfo Guglielmi, he immigrated to the United States in 1913. He became a silent movie star in such films as *The Four Horsemen of the Apocalypse* (1921) and *The Sheik* (1921). His many female fans idolized him as a "Latin lover" and mourned his untimely death.

Varèse, Edgard (1883–1965) French-born American composer. After immigrating to the U.S. in 1915; he cofounded the International Composers' Guild (1921) for the advancement of experimental music. Pioneering the use of electronic and taped sound, he created innovative compositions that rejected traditional rhythm and tonality. Works include *Hyperprism* (1923), *Intégrales* (1925), *Ionisation* (1931), *Density 21.5* (1935), and *Poème électronique* (1958).

Vargas Llosa, [Jorge] Mario [Pedro] (1936–) Peruvian writer. His novels, which are structurally complex, examine and critique the society and politics of his native Peru. Novels include *The Green House* (1966), *Conversation in the Cathedral* (1969), and *The War of the End of the World* (1981). A centrist, he ran unsuccessfully for the Peruvian presidency in 1990.

Veblen, Thorstein [Bunde] (1857–1929) American economist. Born in Wisconsin and educated at Carleton College, Johns Hopkins, and Yale, he established himself with his first book, *The Theory of the Leisure Class* (1899). In it he outlined the class divisions of industrial societies, earmarking the pursuits of the leisure class as "conspicuous leisure and conspicuous consumption." Throughout the 20th century, his ideas carried weight for Western consumer societies. Veblen taught at several American universities throughout his career. Other works include *The Theory of Business Enterprise* (1904), *The Instinct of Workmanship* (1914), and *The State of the Industrial Arts* (1919).

Verwoerd, Hendrik Frensch (1901–66) South African politician. As a senator (1948–58) and minister of native affairs (1950–58), he was a principal architect of **apartheid**. As prime minister (1958–66), he instituted the policy of separate development by resettling black Africans in rural regions designated as "homelands." International controversy over his racial policies led him to withdraw South Africa from the British Commonwealth (1961). He was assassinated.

Villa, Pancho (1878–1923) Mexican revolutionary. Born Francisco Villa, he fought for the Madero revolution (1909–10). He opposed Presidents Victoriano Huerta and Venustiano Carranza. With **Emiliano Zapata**, Villa occupied Mexico City (1914–15) but was driven out. In 1916 he crossed onto U.S. soil and raided Columbus, N.M., killing 16 people. He was unsuccessfully pursued by U.S. troops led by General **J. J. Pershing**. He was assassinated.

Villa-Lobos, Heitor (1887–1959) Brazilian composer. Born in Rio de Janiero, he wrote more than 2,000 works, many integrating classical forms and Brazilian folk music. Among them are the series *Chôros* (1920–29), 12 symphonies (1920–59), symphonic poems *Uirapuru* (1917) and *Amazonas* (1929), operas, concertos, and chamber music. He was president of the Brazilian Academy of Music (1945–59).

W

Walcott, Derek [Anton] (1930–) West Indian writer. A poet and playwright from St. Lucia, he combins West Indian rhythms and imagery with English poetic forms. Works include the poetry collections *In a Green Night* (1962) and *The Star Apple Kingdom* (1979) and the plays *Henri Christophe* (1950) and *O Babylon!* (1978).

Waldheim, Kurt (1918–) Austrian politician. Having Entered diplomatic service in 1945, he was a member of the Austrian delegation to the **United Nations** from 1958 and its permanent representative from 1963 to 1968, chairing its outer space committee from

1965. Following an unsuccessful attempt at the Austrian presidency in 1971, he served as UN secretary-general from 1972 to 1981. Becoming president of Austria (1986–92), he generated controversy when documents related to his war record revealed possible knowledge of Nazi war crimes. He was cleared in court of charges.

Walesa, Lech (1943–) Polish labor leader and politician. An electrician in the Lenin Shipyard, Gdansk, he was dismissed from his job in 1976 for labor protests. In 1980 he took charge of the strike that persuaded the government to accept the right of workers to form independent unions and to strike. He was named chairman of the independent trade union **Solidarity**. In 1981 martial law was declared, Solidarity banned, and Walesa imprisoned for nearly a year. He received the 1983 Nobel Peace Prize. In 1989, as Poland's government began to lose power, Solidarity was legalized; the following year, Walesa was elected president (1990–95). As president, he encouraged free-market reforms but was criticized for trying to strengthen the presidency at the expense of parliament.

Walker, Alice [Malsenior] (1944–) American writer. Born in Eatonton, Ga., she established herself with her epistolary novel of injustice toward African-American women in the south, *The Color Purple* (1983, Pulitzer Prize). Other works exploring racial and "womanist" concerns include the story collection *You Can't Keep a Good Woman Down* (1981), the prose collection *In Search of Our Mother's Gardens* (1983), and the novel *The Temple of My Familiar* (1988).

Wallace, William Roy DeWitt (1889–1981) American publisher. Born in St. Paul, Minn., he married Lila Acheson in 1921 and in 1922 founded *Reader's Digest,* a magazine containing reprints of published articles of wide interest. Beginning in 1939 with the first British edition, dozens of foreign editions were published. In 1981 *Reader's Digest* became the largest-circulation magazine in the world (30.5 million copies, 16 languages). Throughout their lives, the Wallaces were noted philanthropists.

Warhol, Andy (1928–1987) American artist and filmmaker. The pioneer of the pop art movement was born Andrew Warhola in Pittsburgh, Pa., and attended the Carnegie Institute of Technology. In 1962 he exhibited his first paintings of household items (soup cans and Coca-Cola bottles) and sculpture of a Brillo pad box. In later works, he suggested mass production through his use of multiple images of one subject, such as **Marilyn Monroe**. Attracting a hip New York and international crowd, he meshed artistic accomplishment and celebrity. He founded *Interview* magazine; books include *The Philosophy of Andy Warhol* (1975). Among his films are *Eat* (1963), *The Chelsea Girls* (1966), and *Trash* (1970).

Warren, Earl (1891–1974) American jurist. Born in Los Angeles and educated at the University of California (1912), he was California's state attorney general (1939–43) and governor (1943–53). Though the vice presidency eluded him when he ran on the Republican ticket in 1948, President **Dwight D. Eisenhower** later appointed him the 14th chief justice of the U.S. Supreme Court (1953–69). Through several landmark decisions, he steered the court toward taking more liberal stands on issues of civil rights and individual liberties. Warren Court decisions included *Brown v. Board of Education* (1954), which made public school segregation unconstitutional, and *Miranda v. Arizona* (1966), which clarified the rights of police suspects. Warren headed the commission that investigated the assassination of President **John F. Kennedy**.

Washington, Booker T[aliaferro] (1856–1915) American educator and activist. Born a slave in Franklin County, Va., he founded (1881) and led the Tuskegee Institute in Alabama, an early institute for higher education, for African-Americans. His autobiography is *Up from Slavery* (1901). For decades he argued that economic independence for African-Americans was a necessary precondition for social equality.

Watson, James Dewey (1928–) American biochemist. In 1953, while at the Cavendish Laboratory, Cambridge, England, he and **Francis Crick** followed up on research by Irish biophysicist Maurice Wilkins (1916–) to codiscover the double helix structure of the DNA molecule. The feat earned the three men the 1962 Nobel for physiology or **medicine**. Watson later worked at the California Institute of Technology, Harvard, and the Cold Spring Harbor Laboratory. In 1989 he was named director of the National Center for Human Genome Research. Books include *The Double Helix* (1968).

Watson, John Broadus (1878–1958) American psychologist. Educated at the University of Chicago, he founded behaviorism, the school of psychology that describes behavior in terms of observable responses to stimuli. He taught at Johns Hopkins University (1908–20). Works include *Behaviorism* (1925).

Waugh, Evelyn [Arthur St. John] (1903–66) British writer. From his early success with *Decline and Fall* (1928), he was known as the era's finest satirical novelist. Other satires include *Vile Bodies* (1930) and *The Loved One* (1948). He also wrote biographies and travel books and gained lasting fame for his Catholic spiritual saga *Brideshead Revisited* (1945). His brother is British writer Alec Waugh (1898–1981).

Wayne, John (1907–79) American actor. Born Marion Michael Morrison in Winterset, Iowa, he attended the University of Southern California before turning to film in the 1920s. A moderately successful contract player for years, he established himself in director **John Ford**'s western *Stagecoach* (1939) as a quintessential American screen hero—strong, self-sufficient, ever searching. In his movies and westerns over the next four decades he radiated invincibility and, to many, represented America. Many memorable roles came in later Ford/Wayne collaborations, including *They Were Expendable* (1945), *Fort Apache* (1948), *She Wore a Yellow Ribbon* (1949), *Rio Grande* (1950), *The Quiet Man* (1952), *The Searchers* (1956), and *The Man Who Shot Liberty Valance* (1962). Other notable films include *Red River* (1948), *Sands of Iwo Jima* (1950), *The High and the Mighty* (1954), *The Longest Day* (1962), *True Grit* (1969, Academy Award), and *The Shootist* (1976), his final film.

Webb, Sidney James, first baron Passfield (1859–1947) and **[Martha] Beatrice Potter** (1858–1943) British reformers and social historians. Married in 1892, they were leaders of the Fabian Society (founded 1884), a socialist group that believed in gradual reform rather than revolution. The Webbs promoted their views through public discussion and writing; works include *The History of Trade Unionism* (1894), the multivolume *English Local Government* (1906–29), and *Soviet Communism: A New Civilization?* (1935). In 1895 they helped found the London School of Economics; in 1913 they founded the progressive periodical the *New Statesman*. They became influential in the **Labour Party** and championed much social legislation, such as the Educational Acts of 1902 and 1903. Both served on the royal poor-law commission (1905–09); their minority report in favor of the Poor Law (1909) prepared the way for the welfare state. As Labour M.P. (1922–29), Sidney Webb was president of the Board of Trade (1924) and colonial secretary (1929). He was made a peer in 1929.

Webber, Sir Andrew Lloyd See **Lloyd Webber, Sir Andrew**.

Weber, Max (1864–1920) German sociologist. He developed analytical sociological theory and influenced much of modern social science. His concept of "ideal types" proved significant to the study of cultures. He opposed the Marxist view of economic causation with studies of the role of religious and spiritual values in shaping societies. His best-known work is *The Protestant Ethic and the Spirit of Capitalism* (1905), which links the rise of **capitalism** to Calvinist tenets.

Weil, Simone (1909–43) French philosopher. A precocious student and independent scholar, she studied varieties of mysticism, exploring the religious dimensions of suffering. Of Jewish background, she became a Roman Catholic in 1938 and devoted her life and spiritual service to God. Most works were published posthumously, including *Gravity and Grace* (1947) and *Waiting for God* (1950). She committed suicide by starvation.

Weill, Kurt (1900–50) German-born American composer. Developing a forceful economical style, he established himself with the satirical operas *The Rise and Fall of the City of Mahoganny* (1927, rev. 1930) and *The Threepenny Opera* (1928), both with librettos by **Bertolt Brecht**. Following Nazi artistic condemnation and persecution for being a Jew, he immigrated to the U.S. in 1935. Works there include successful Broadway musicals *Knickerbocker Holiday* (1938), with M. Anderson; *Lady in the Dark* (1941); and *Street Scene* (1947). He was married to Austrian singer and actress Lotte Lenya (1900–81), who appeared in many of his works.

Weizmann, Chaim Azriel (1874–1952) Russian-born Israeli leader. As a chemist, he developed a synthetic acetone during **World War I**, useful for making explosives. Promoting Zionist causes, he was longtime president of the World Zionist Organization (1920–31) and was instrumental in generating the Balfour Convention (1917), which declared the need for a Jewish land in Palestine (see **Balfour Declaration**). He also helped gain U.S. support for Israel (1948). He was Israel's provisional (1948) and first president (1949–52).

Welles, Orson (1915–85) American film director. Born George Orson Welles in Kenosha, Wisc., he cofounded the Mercury Theatre in 1937. His 1938 Mercury Theatre of the Air's radio dramatization of H. G. Wells's *War of the Worlds* created national panic. His first film, *Citizen Kane* (1941), proved highly influential to filmmakers and made Welles an instant celebrity. Later films were often compromised by studio intervention or self-indulgence but were often noteworthy. They include *The Magnificent Ambersons* (1942), *The Lady from Shanghai* (1948), and *Touch of Evil* (1958).

Wells, H[erbert] G[eorge] (1866–1946) British writer. Upon graduation from London University (1890), he became a science teacher, but he soon switched to writing. With his first major novel, *The Time Machine* (1895), and such subsequent works as *The Invisible Man* (1897) and *The War of the Worlds* (1898), he helped found the genre of science fiction. He also wrote realistic novels, such as *Kipps* (1905), *Tono-Bungay* (1909), and *The History of Mr. Polly* (1910), and nonfiction works, such as *The Outline of History* (1920). A Fabian socialist, feminist, internationalist, and advocate of free love, he expressed his social and political views in his fiction as well as his nonfiction. Married twice, he had a liaison with writer **Rebecca West** from 1913 to 1923.

West, Mae (1892–1980) American actress and writer. She rose from vaudeville to appear on Broadway (1911–28) and in films (beginning in 1932). A master of comic sexual innuendo who parodied her image as a seductress, she wrote much of her own material. Plays she wrote and in which she starred include *Sex* (1926) and *Diamond Lil* (1928); her films, which she often scripted or coscripted, include *She Done Him Wrong* (1933), *I'm No Angel* (1933), and *My Little Chickadee* (1940). Her autobiography, *Goodness Had Nothing to Do with It* (1959), was named for one of her trademark one-liners.

West, Dame Rebecca (1892–1983) British writer. Rebecca West is the pen name of Cicily Isabel Fairfield. In her long career, she wrote criticism (*Henry James,* 1916), political journalism (*Black Lamb and Grey Falcon,* 1942; *The Meaning of Treason,* 1949), and novels (*The Judge,* 1922). She was a strong advocate of women's rights. She and her lover **H. G. Wells** had a son, the novelist and critic Anthony West (1914–).

Westmoreland, William C[hilds] (1914–) American soldier. A general since 1964, he commanded U.S. forces (1964–68) in the **Vietnam War**. Recalled when the Vietcong's Tet Offensive demonstrated the weakness of the U.S. war effort, he became army chief of staff (1968–72).

Wharton, Edith [Newbold Jones] (1862–1937) American writer. Born in New York City, she captured its society in subtle, ironic works including *The House of Mirth* (1905), *The Age of Innocence* (1920, Pulitzer Prize), and *Old New York* (1924). Perhaps best known is *Ethan Frome* (1911), a tragedy, uncharacteristically set in New England. From 1907 she lived in Europe; she was awarded the Cross of the Legion of Honor for **World War I** relief work in Paris. She maintained a long literary friendship with American novelist **Henry James**.

Whitehead, Alfred North (1861–1947) British mathematician and philosopher. He taught at Cambridge University (1885–1911), the University of London (1914–24), and Harvard University (1924–36). With **Bertrand Russell**, he wrote *Principia Mathematica* (1910–13), which attempted to deduce the laws of mathematics from purely logical principles. As a philosopher, he analyzed the structure of science and developed a metaphysical "philosophy of organism" based on the concept of becoming. Works include *Principles of Natural Knowledge* (1919), *Science and the Modern World* (1925), and *Process and Reality* (1929).

Wiesel, Elie (1928–) Romanian-born American writer. During **World War II**, he survived the Auschwitz and Buchenwald **concentration camps** but lost his parents and sister. His experiences and "survivor's guilt" led to his memoir-novel *Un di Velt hot geshvign* (1956) and its abbreviated edition, *Night* (1958). Through it and later works he has become an eloquent spokesperson of Jewish suffering during the **Holocaust**. Other novels include *The Accident* (1961) and *The Testament* (1980); nonfiction works include *One Generation After* (1970). Many works were originally written in French. He was awarded the Nobel Peace Prize in 1986.

Wilder, Billy (1906–) Austrian-born American film director. Born Samuel Wilder in Vienna, he abandoned pre-law studies at the University of Vienna to become a reporter and screenwriter. Fleeing Nazi persecution of Jews, he left Germany in 1933 for Paris and, later, Hollywood. From 1938 to 1950 he collaborated on screenplays (notably *Ninotchka,* 1939). From 1942 he also directed smart, sardonic comedies and dramas, including *Double Indemnity* (1944), *Sunset Boulevard* (1950), *Stalag 17* (1953), *Sabrina* (1954), and *Some Like It Hot* (1959). His *The Lost Weekend* (1945) and *The Apartment* (1960) won Oscars for best picture and best director.

Wilder, Thornton [Niven] (1897–1975) American writer. In novels and plays, he presented universal themes through the depiction of ordinary experience. He won the Pulitzer Prize for fiction for the novel *The Bridge of San Luis Rey* (1927) and two Pulitzers for drama for plays employing nontraditional theatrical techniques, *Our Town* (1938) and *The Skin of Our Teeth* (1942).

William II [Friedrich Wilhelm Viktor Albert] or **Wilhelm II** (1859–1941) Emperor (Kaiser) of Germany and king of Prussia (1888–1918). He was the son of Emperor Frederick III (Crown Prince Frederick of Prussia) and of Victoria, daughter of Great Britain's Queen Victoria. A headstrong, intemperate leader, William dismissed imperial chancellor Otto van Bismarck (1815–98) in 1890 and angered the U.S., Great Britain, France, and Russia with plans for German expansion. His support of Austria-Hungary in the 1914 crisis with Serbia hastened the start of **World War I**. During the war, his power eroded until he was forced to abdicate in 1918 and enter exile in Holland.

Williams, Tennessee (1911–83) American writer. Born Thomas Lanier Williams in Columbus, Miss., he gained immediate renown as a playwright in 1948 with his autobiographical memory play *The Glass Menagerie* (1945). The dominant voice on Broadway after **World War II**, he wrote several studies of human fragility and violence, including *A Streetcar Named Desire* (1947, Pulitzer Prize), *Summer and Smoke* (1947), *Cat on a Hot Tin Roof* (1955, Pulitzer Prize), *Suddenly Last Summer* (1958), and *The Night of the Iguana* (1961). He also wrote essays, short stories, and a novel.

Williams, William Carlos (1883–1963) American writer. A highly influential modern poet, he was born in Rutherford, N.J., and became a lifelong practicing physician. In such works as the five-volume *Paterson* (1946–58), he presents a sweeping view of America through its vernacular and the particulars of everyday life. Other works of poetry include *Collected Poems* (1934) and *Pictures from Brueghel and Other Poems* (1963, Pulitzer Prize); prose works include the essay collection *In the American Grain* (1925) plus plays, novels, and *Autobiography* (1951).

Wilson, Edmund (1895–1972) American critic. Born in Red Bank, N.J., he served in **World War I** and during the 1920s became an editor at *Vanity Fair* and the *New Republic*, where he was highly respected for his wide-ranging, erudite social criticism. He also wrote for the *New Yorker* (1944–48). Critical works include *To the Finland Station* (1940), *The Shores of Light* (1952), *The American Earthquake* (1958), and *Patriotic Gore* (1962). Other prose works include a literary analysis of symbolism, *Axel's Castle* (1931), and the short-story collection *Memoirs of Hecate County* (1946). He was married (1938–46) to the American writer **Mary McCarthy**.

Wilson, [James] Harold, baron (1916–95) British politician. An economist, he was elected a Labour M.P. in 1945. In 1963 he became party leader. As prime minister (1964–70, 1974–76) with a small majority, he tried to improve the British economy and form close links with Europe. Knighted in 1976, the year he retired, he was made a life peer in 1983.

Wilson, [Thomas] Woodrow (1856–1924). Twenty-eighth U.S. president (1913–21). Born in Staunton, Va., he attended Princeton and the University of Virginia and received a Ph.D. from Johns Hopkins in 1886. He was professor of jurisprudence and political economy at Princeton (1890–1902) and president of Princeton (1902–10). In 1910 he was elected governor of New Jersey on the Democratic ticket; his years in office (1911–13) were marked by reform. In 1912 he was elected president of the U.S., his victory due in part to a **Republican Party** split between incumbent president **William Howard Taft** and third-party candidate **Theodore Roosevelt**. In office, Wilson's New Freedom domestic program led to significant reforms, including the establishment of the **Federal Reserve System** (1913) and Federal Trade Commission (1914) and the passage of the Clayton Antitrust Act (1914). He attempted neutrality in the early years of **World War I** and won reelection in 1916 on the slogan, "He kept us out of war." But international tensions increased and on April 6, 1917, the U.S. declared war on Germany. Hoping to end the war, Wilson developed a peace program called the **Fourteen Points** and went to Europe in December 1918 to join in peace talks. His **League of Nations** came into being but never won U.S. ratification. Exhausted, he suffered a stroke in September 1919 and was largely incapacitated until his death. Wilson's wife, Edith, was instrumental in effecting presidential duties during the president's final months in office. He was awarded the Nobel Peace Prize in 1919.

Winfrey, Oprah [Gail] (1954–) American **television** entertainer. Born in Mississippi, she became a broadcasting phenomenon with her extraordinarily popular syndicated daytime talk show, the *Oprah Winfrey Show* (later called *Opera*) (1986–). She also won fame as an actress with her Oscar-nominated role in *The Color Purple* (1985) and is a film and television producer.

Witte, Sergey Yulyevich, count (1849–1915) Russian politician. From 1892 to 1903, he served as Russian minister of finance for **Nicholas II**, advocating rapid industrialization through the use of foreign capital. In 1905 he negotiated the Treaty of Portsmouth, ending the **Russo-Japanese War**. The same year, he was named the first constitutional Russian premier. He resigned in 1906.

Wittgenstein, Ludwig [Josef Johan] (1889–1951) Austrian-born British philosopher. Born in Vienna, he studied philosophy under **Bertrand Russell** at Cambridge, England, until **World War I** brought him back to Austria to fight for his country. Afterward, he published *Tractatus logico-philosophicus* (1921), in which he advanced a picture theory of meaning to account for the way language represents the world. Profoundly influencing the development of logical positivism, the book, for Wittgenstein, provided the solution to all philosophical problems. He therefore retired from philosophy to become a rural schoolteacher in Austria, until he began to think that some problems had not yet been solved. Returning to Cambridge in 1929 (as professor, 1939–47), he embarked on a second, different period of thought epitomized in the posthumously published *Philosophical Investigations* (1953). Proposing a theory of language games, this work emphasized close description of the uses of language in everyday activities. He became a naturalized British citizen in 1938. One of the greatest philosophers of the 20th century, Wittgenstein influenced not only his own field but also such others as linguistics and critical theory.

Wolfe, Thomas [Clayton] (1900–38) American writer. He is known for his epic, personal, lyrical studies of southern manhood, including *Look Homeward, Angel* (1929), *Of Time and the River* (1935), *The Web and the Rock* (1939), and *You Can't Go Home Again* (1940). American editor Maxwell Perkins (1884–1947) worked closely with Wolfe until the author left publisher Charles Scribner's Sons in 1937.

Woolf, [Adeline] Virginia (1882–1941) British novelist. Born Virginia Stephen, she married author and social reformer Leonard Woolf (1912), with whom she founded the Hogarth Press in 1917. Their home was the focus for the Bloomsbury group of writers, artists, and intellectuals. Her fiction—including the novels *Mrs. Dalloway* (1925), *To the Lighthouse* (1927), and *Orlando* (1928)—influenced other novelists with its attention to ordinary experience described through stream-of-consciousness techniques. As a critic and feminist, she is best known for the essay *A Room of One's Own* (1929). Plagued with mental illness, she drowned herself in 1941.

Wright, Frank Lloyd (1867–1959) American architect. Born in Richland Center, Wisc., he was assistant to American architect Louis Sullivan (1856–1924) but worked on his own from 1893. In early Chicago-area designs (such as Robie House, 1909), he introduced the elements of the Prairie school, which attempted to integrate architecture with its landscape. Other innovations such as open design have influenced architects for decades. Notable buildings include Oak Park Unity Temple, Oak Park, Ill. (1906); Wright's home, Talesin, in Spring Green, Ill. (1911, rebuilt twice); Fallingwater, Mill Run, Pa. (1936); and the Guggenheim Museum, New York City (1946–59).

Wright, Orville (1871–1948) and **Wilbur Wright** (1867–1912) American inventors. Originally bicycle mechanics based in Dayton, Ohio, they built the first successful, heavier-than-air, powered **airplane**. The first controlled, sustained flights of the machine were made at Kitty Hawk, N.C., on December 17, 1903. Afterward, the brothers improved their planes and publicized them through dramatic flights in Europe and the U.S. In 1909 they won the first contract to build planes for the U.S. Army.

Wright, Richard [Nathaniel] (1908–60) American writer. Born near Natchez, Miss., he moved to Chicago in 1934 and began writing. After publishing a collection of novellas (*Uncle Tom's Children*, 1938), he rose to prominence with the novel *Native Son* (1940), about the injustices wrought on U.S. blacks. Also influential was his autobiography *Black Boy* (1945), in part about the place of blacks and artists in society. Among other works are two that were posthumously published: the second part of his autobiography, *American Hunger* (1977), and the short-story collection *Eight Men* (1961).

Wyeth, Andrew Newell (1917–) American painter. Born in Chadds Ford, Pa., he was trained by his father, illustrator Newell Convers Wyeth (1882–1945). Following his first one-man show in 1937, he maintained critical and popular interest through his finely wrought, naturalistic style. His best-known works are *Christina's World* (1948), *The Trodden Weed* (1951), and *The Helga Pictures* (1971–85), an intimate portrait series.

X

Xian Xinghai (1905–45) Chinese composer. In the 1930s he wrote protest music against the Japanese occupation of Manchuria and, as a Communist supporter, served as director of music in the Lu Xun Academy. Combining Western and Chinese traditions, he wrote more than 500 songs and several orchestral pieces. Works include the *Yellow River Cantata,* which has been adapted for piano and orchestra as the *Yellow River Concerto.*

Xu Beihong (1895–1953) Chinese painter. Educated in Paris, he incorporated Western techniques in his paintings of horses and figures. He supported China's Communist Revolution and, as president of Beijing's Central Institute of Fine Arts, advanced the careers of many contemporary Chinese artists.

Y

Yamamoto Isoroku (1884–1943) Japanese naval officer. Original surname Takano. Of samurai descent, he served in the navy during the **Russo-Japanese War** (1904–05) and rose to the rank of admiral (1940) and commander of the combined fleet (1941). He directed the attack on **Pearl Harbor** (1941), which succeeded in devastating the U.S. fleet but drew the U.S. into **World War II**. He was killed when his plane was shot down.

Yeats, William Butler (1865–1939) Irish poet and playwright. The son of painter John Butler Yeats (1839–1922), he was born near Dublin and raised in Sligo and London. He turned from a painting career to become a poet with his first collection, *The Wanderings of Oisin* (1889). A leading figure in the Irish Renaissance, Yeats took his subject matter from Irish folklore, occult speculation, and contemporary and personal concerns, including nationalist politics and his unrequited love for Irish patriot Maud Gonne (1866–1953). He helped found the Irish Literary Theatre (1899; later the Abbey Theatre), which produced *The Countess Cathleen* (1899) and other poetic dramas of Yeats. Yeats's mature work, including *Michael Robartes and the Dancer* (1921), *The Tower* (1928), and *The Winding Stair* (1933), employed a rich system of symbols and a distinctive poetic language to explore philosophical and spiritual issues. Prose works include *Autobiographies* (1926) and the occult treatise *A Vision* (1925), written with his wife, medium Georgie Hyde-Lees. He was one of the first senators (1922–28) of the Irish Free State. One of the principal poets of the 20th century, he won the Nobel Prize for literature in 1923.

Yeltsin, Boris Nikolayevich (1931–) Russian politician. Born in Sverdlovsk (now Yekaterinburg) and educated as a construction engineer, he joined the Communist Party in 1961. As one of the liberal reformers favored by **Mikhail Gorbachev**, he was appointed first secretary of the Moscow City Party Committee in 1985, but soon proved too radical and was removed from the post (1987). Critical of Gorbachev and the Communist Party, Yeltsin was elected president of the Russian Soviet Socialist Republic (1990–91). His political power grew when he led the successful resistance to an attempted coup by Communist hard-liners in August 1991. In December 1991, when Gorbachev resigned and the **Soviet Union** ceased to exist, Yeltsin became president of independent Russia (1991–99). He directed the formation of the new, decentralized **Commonwealth of Independent States (CIS)**, made up of former Soviet republics. He advocated nuclear arms control, rapid privatization, and price deregulation. He courted Western aid and investment, but Russia's economic woes increased, diminishing his popularity. Yeltsin struggled for power with Communist-nationalist forces in parliament and his own vice president, Aleksandr Rutskoy. In 1993 Yeltsin tried to dissolve parliament, which responded by impeaching him and replacing him with Rutskoy, but when Rutskoy and many legislators occupied the parliament building Yeltsin used military force to drive them out. In 1994 Yeltsin began a bloody civil war with Chechnya, a republic attempting to secede from Russia; his harsh conduct of the war drew criticism at home and abroad. Despite these crises and his health problems, he won reelection in 1996. He resigned in 1999, naming prime minister Vladimir Putin (1952–) as his interim successor.

Yuan Shikai or **Yüan Shih-k'ai** (1859–1916) Chinese soldier and politician. He rose from the army to become governor of Shandong (1900), governor-general of Zhili Province (1901–07), and a grand councilor (1907). Forced to retire on the death of Empress Dowager Cixi (1908), he was recalled to command the northern forces and suppress the **Chinese Revolution** (1911). Instead he switched sides and persuaded Emperor P'u yi (1906–67) to resign (1912). **Sun Yat-sen**, first president of China, resigned to allow Yuan to become president (1912–16). He ruled in dictatorial fashion, dismissing parliament in 1914 and proclaiming himself emperor in 1915. Widespread revolt forced him to restore the republic just before his death.

Z

Zaharias, Babe Didrikson (1913–56) American athlete. Born Mildred Ella Didrikson in

Port Arthur, Tex., she was a member of the women's All-America basketball team, took eight events at the women's national track and field championships (both 1930–32), and won gold medals at the 1932 Olympics in javelin and the 80-meter hurdles. Turning to golf, she captured the U.S. amateur title in 1946 and the British in 1947 and then won the U.S. Open three times (1948, 1950, 1954). She is remembered as probably the foremost female athlete of the 20th century. In 1938, she married wrestler George Zaharias.

Zapata, Emiliano (1879–1919) Mexican revolutionary. An Indian tenant farmer, he raised a peasant army against a succession of federal governments to demand repossession of land (1910–19). He helped Francisco Madero (1873–1913) overthrow **Porfirio Diaz** (1911), but when Madero refused to redistribute land, Zapata broke with him, drafting the agrarian Plan of Ayala (1911). Zapata's army occupied Mexico City three times (1914–15). He was treacherously assassinated by an emissary of President Venustiano Carranza (1859–1920). Zapata has been honored since as a hero by peasants and rebel movements throughout the Americas.

Zhang Daqian (1899–1983) Chinese artist. He traveled widely in China, Japan, Europe, and the Americas and was a friend of **Pablo Picasso**. He is considered one of the greatest Chinese painters in history. His works include copies of the stone murals at the Dunhuang caves, ink paintings, scroll paintings, oil paintings, and calligraphy.

Zhou Enlai or **Chou En-lai** (1898–1976) Chinese politician. Born to wealth, he was a founding member of the Communist Party in the 1920s. He studied in Japan, France, and Germany. Back in China from 1924, he at first cooperated with the Nationalists and led Communist forces in the Northern Expedition (1927). After the Nationalists and Communists split, he became party leader **Mao Zedong**'s most important aide, participating in the **Long March** (1934–35) and heading negotiations with the Nationalists. When the People's Republic of China was founded in 1949, Zhou became its first premier (1949–76) and foreign minister (1949–58). In 1953 he helped bring an end to the **Korean War**; in 1971 he succeeded in having China admitted to the **UN**. A supporter of Mao in the **Cultural Revolution** (1966–69), he nevertheless led the reestablishment of China's contacts with the West in the 1970s.

Zhukov, Georgi Konstantinovich (1896–1974) Soviet soldier. In the Soviet army from 1915, he fought in the **Russian Revolution** (1917), led troops in Mongolia (1938–39), and became chief of staff in 1941. During **World War II** he led troops against German forces in sieges at Stalingrad and Leningrad (1942–43) and in a late attack on Berlin leading to German surrender (1945). Postwar he was commander of Soviet occupation forces (1945–46). Minister of defense from 1955, he was stripped of all duties in 1957 over his military views by Soviet leader **Nikita Khrushchev**.

Ziegfeld, Florenz (1869–1932) American theatrical producer. With the *Follies of 1907*, he introduced the lavish musical-comedy revue, rife with elaborate sets and beautiful women, to the New York stage. New editions of his Ziegfeld Follies appeared annually until 1931 (with a few interruptions in the 1920s), advancing the careers of such performers as American entertainers Fanny Brice (1891–1951), W. C. Fields (1880–1946), Eddie Cantor (1892–1964), and **Will Rogers**. He also produced such shows as *Show Boat* (1927). He was married to French actress Anna Held and American actress Billie Burke (1885–1970).

Zinoviev, Grigory Yevseyevich (1883–1936) Soviet politician. Born Ovsel Gershon Aronov Radomyslsky, he joined **V. I. Lenin** on the **Bolshevik** side when the Russian

Social Democratic Party split in 1903. In exile from 1908, he returned to Russia in 1917 to join the **Russian Revolution**. Afterward, he headed the **Comintern** (1919–26) and served on the Communist Party Politburo (1921–26). After Lenin's death in 1924, he joined in the triumvirate with **Joseph Stalin** and **Lev Kamenev**, but Stalin's growing power forced him and Kamenev into the Left Opposition. In 1927 he was expelled from the party; he was nominally readmitted in 1928. During Stalin's **Great Purge**, he was convicted and executed for treason and complicity in the assassination of **Sergey Kirov**.

CHAPTER FOUR

NATIONS OF THE WORLD

Afghanistan

Official name: Islamic State of Afghanistan

Location: South central Asia; landlocked; bordered by Turkmenistan (NW), Uzbekistan and Tajikistan (N), China (NE), Pakistan (E, S), Iran (W)

Capital: Kabul

Area: 250,000 sq. mi. (647,500 sq. km.)

Population (est. 1996): 22,664,136

Languages: Dari or Afghan Persian, Pushtu, other Turkic and minor languages

Government: Transitional

Religions: Sunni Muslim 84%, Shi'a Muslim 15%, other 1%

Monetary unit: Afghani

Main exports: Fruits and nuts, natural gas, hand-woven carpets, wool, cotton

This mountainous country, strategically located along trans–Asian trade routes, suffered wars of conquest from antiquity. In 1900 it was ruled by Emir Abdul Rahman Khan but, as a result of two Anglo–Afghan Wars (1838–42, 1878–80), it had become subject to British influence. The Anglo–Russian Entente of 1907 confirmed British interests in Afghanistan. In 1919 the new emir, Amanullah Khan, waged the Third Anglo–Afghan War, forcing Britain to sign the Treaty of Rawalpindi, recognizing Afghanistan's full independence.

Amanullah instituted Westernizing reforms, including the abolition of polygamy and universal education for both sexes. He proclaimed himself king in 1926. Considered too radical in his modernizing, he was forced to abdicate in 1929. His successors, Mohammed Nadir Shah and Nadir's son Mohammed Zahir Shah, were more conservative.

In 1964 Afghanistan became a constitutional monarchy. In 1973 the government fell to a military coup led by Mohammed Daud Khan, Zahir's cousin and former prime minister. Daud declared Afghanistan a republic, with himself as president. In 1978 he was deposed by a pro–Soviet Communist coup. The new leader, Nur Mohammad Taraki, tried to create a Marxist state but encountered widespread popular uprisings. In 1979 Taraki was overthrown; he was succeeded briefly by Hafizullah Amin and, by year's end, by Babrak Karmal, who called for Soviet military intervention. The Soviets invaded in December 1979, inaugurating a long civil war that caused an estimated one million deaths. Soviet forces contended with Islamic rebels called Mujahidin, or "holy warriors," who were aided by Pakistan, the U.S., and other nations. The Soviet Union withdrew its forces in 1988–89, but the pro–Soviet government fought on until its fall in 1992.

The rebel coalition formed an Islamic state but splintered into factions, reducing the country to anarchy. In 1995 the Taliban, a fundamentalist group, emerged as a major force. They gained control of much of the country, including the capital, Kabul, in 1996 and established a theo-cratic, military state. However, civil war continued, despite a 1999 agreement "in principle" to form a coalition government. The U.N. imposed sanctions on Afghanistan in November 1999 for refusing to surrender businessman Osama bin Laden to the U.S. for prosecution for alleged terrorist acts.

Afghanistan: 20th-Century Leaders

Emir

1880–1901: Abdul Rahman Khan (c. 1844–1901)

1901–19: Habibullah Khan

1919–26: Amanullah Khan (1892–1960)

King

1926–29: Amanullah Khan

1929–33: Mohammed Nadir Shah

1933–73: Mohammed Zahir Shah

President

1973–78: Mohammed Daud Khan (1909–78)

1978–79: Nur Mohammad Taraki (1917–79)

1979: Hafizullah Amin (1929–79)

1979–86: Babrak Karmal (1929–92)

1986–87: Haji Mohammad Chamkani (1947–)

1987–92: Sayid Mohammed Najib (Najibullah) (1947–96)

1992: Sibghatullah Mujaddidi (1926–)

1992–96: Burhanuddin Rabbani (1939–)

(Taliban leaders in power since 1996)

Prime Minister (since 1933)

1933–46: Sardar Mohammed Hashim Khan (1884–1953)

1946–53: Sardar Mahmud Shah Khan Ghazi (1888–1959)

1953–63: Mohammed Daud Khan

1963–65: Mohammed Yusuf

1965–67: Mohammed Hashim Maiwandwal (1921–73)

1967–71: Noor Ahmad Etamadi (1921–79)

1971–72: Abdul Zahir (1910–82)

1972–73: Mohammad Shafiq (1924–78)

1972–78: Mohammed Daud Khan

1978–79: Nur Mohammed Taraki

1979: Hafizullah Amin

1979–81: Babrak Karmal

1981–88: Sultan Ali Keshtamand (1937–)

1988–89: Mohammad Hassan Sharq (1926–)

1989–90: Sultan Ali Keshtamand

1990–92: Fazal Haq Khaliqyar (1934–)

1992: Abdul Sabur Farid Kuhestani

Albania

Official name: Republic of Albania

Location: Southeastern Europe; bordered by Yugoslavia (N and E), Macedonia (E), Greece (S), Adriatic and Ionian Seas (W)

Capital: Tiranë

Area: 11,100 sq. mi. (28,748 sq. km.)

Population (est. 1996): 3,249,136

Languages: Albanian (official dialect: Tosk), Greek

Government: Democracy

Religions: Muslim 70%, Albanian Orthodox 20%, Roman Catholic 10%

Monetary unit: Lek

Main exports: Asphalt, petroleum products, metals and metallic ores, electricity, crude oil, vegetables, fruits, tobacco

Albania began the 20th century as part of the Ottoman Empire, which had conquered the country in 1478. Popular uprisings against Turkish rule began in 1910, and independence was declared on November 28, 1912. Independence was recognized in 1913, following the First Balkan War (1912–13). The next few years were chaotic. William, prince of Wied, briefly held the post of mpret, or ruler, in 1914 but was overthrown by rebels led by Essad Pasha. During World War I, Essad Pasha ruled as president (1914–16), but civil disorders and foreign interventions during the war made his position untenable. Italy occupied southern Albania, and the country was declared an Italian protectorate in 1917.

Ahmed Zogu, a Muslim tribal chief, led resistance to plans to partition the country among Italy, Greece, and Yugoslavia. The country's independence was recognized in 1921. Zogu declared himself president in 1925 and king (as Zog I) in 1928.

On April 7, 1939, the invading army of Italian dictator Mussolini deposed Zog and forced him into exile. Italy's King Victor Emmannuel III was proclaimed Albania's ruler. During World War II, Albania fought on the Axis side. Communist partisans led by Enver Hoxha fought a guerrilla war, taking power in 1944 and proclaiming a Socialist republic in 1946.

Hoxha ruled the country until his death in 1985. A devoted Stalinist, he broke with the Soviet Union in 1961, instead forming an alliance with China that ended in 1978. Relying on brutal repression to stay in power, he made Albania one of the poorest, most totalitarian, and most isolated countries in the world.

After Hoxha's death, Ramiz Alia (who had officially been president since 1982) succeeded as ruler. A moderate reformist, he ended the country's isolation but tried to keep the Communist Party in control. Mass protests, a general strike, and heavy emigration forced Alia to democratize. His party won the 1991 elections but lost in 1992 and 1996 to the opposition Democratic Party. Sali Berisha, president from 1992, introduced economic and human rights reforms. But Albania remained Europe's poorest country, plagued by food riots and armed brigands. The government remained autocratic and prone to corruption. In 1997 Berisha's government was forced from power after the collapse of pyramid schemes that impoverished tens of thousands of families. Amid violence and looting, a multinational force was sent to Albania to try to restore order. Rexhep Mejdani succeed Berisha as president.

Elections in 1997 resulted in former Prime Minister Fatos Nano returning to power in a new government coalition led by the Socialist Party. However, the shooting in 1998 of opposition party politician Azem Hajdari prompted former President Berisha to blame Prime Minister Nano for the killings. Under mass riots, Nano and his cabinet fled the capital in September. The Socialist Party's General Secretary, Pandeli Majko, assumed power as Prime Minister.

The conflict in Kosovo, the Yugoslavian province that borders on Albania, in March 1999 led to hundreds of thousands of ethnic Albanian refugees fleeing across the border into Albania. Because Kosovo resistance fighters were stationed in northern Albania, Serbian forces shelled outposts in the area during the conflict. In April, Serb troops briefly invaded Albanian territory, attacking a border post in the town of Kamenica. An end to hostilities was announced on June 10, 1999. Most Kosovar refugees in Albania were repatriated by year's end.

Albania: 20th Century Leaders

Mpret (Ruler)

1914: William, prince of Wied (1876–1945)

President

1914–16: Essad Pasha (1863–1920)

1925–28: Ahmed Zogu (1895–1961)

King

1928–39: Zog I (formerly Ahmed Zogu)

First Secretary, Communist Party

1941–46: Enver Hoxha (1908–85)

1946–48: Koci Xoxe (1911–49)

1948–85: Enver Hoxha

1985–91: Ramiz Alia (1925–)

President

1945–46: Enver Hoxha

1946–53: Omer Nishani

1953–82: Hadji Lechi (1913–)

1982–92: Ramiz Alia

1992–97: Sali Berisha (1945–)

1997– : Rexhep Mejdani (1944–)

Prime Minister (since 1945)

1945–54: Enver Hoxha

1954–81: Mehmet Shehu (1954–81)

1982–91: Adil Çarçani (1922–)

1991: Fatos Nano (1952–)

1991: Ylli Bufi

1991–92: Vilson Ahmeti (1951–)

1992–97: Alexander Meksi (1939–)

1997–98: Fatos Nano

1998: Pandeli Majko

Algeria

Official name: Democratic and Popular Republic of Algeria

Location: North Africa; bordered by Mediterranean Sea (N), Tunisia and Libya (E), Mali and Niger (S), Morocco, Western Sahara, Mauritania (W)

Capital: Algiers

Area: 919,591 sq. mi. (2,381,740 sq. km.)

Population (est. 1996): 29,183,032

Languages: Arabic (official), French, Berber dialects

Government: Republic

Religions: Sunni Muslim 99% (state religion), Christian and Jewish 1%

Monetary unit: Algerian dinar

Main exports: Petroleum, natural gas

Once part of the Ottoman Empire, Algeria was invaded by France in 1830 and formally became part of France in 1848. The Arab-Berber Muslim population had no political or civil rights. During World War II, Algeria was administered by the Vichy government until the Allied liberation in 1942–43. Many Algerians joined the Free French, hoping that self-rule would follow the war. But France failed to honor its promise to grant political representation to Algerians, and the Algerian War of Independence (1954–62) began. Led by Ahmed Ben Bella, the Front de Libération Nationale (FLN) waged a fierce guerrilla campaign against the well-armed French and colonial forces. The French Fourth Republic nearly lost control of the military in Algeria; it took the return of Charles de Gaulle to power (1958) and the drafting of a new constitution to end the crisis. De Gaulle ordered negotiations that led to Algerian independence on July 3, 1962 (over the protests of the OAS, or Secret Army Organization, an underground colonists' group that attempted to assassinate de Gaulle rather than accept independence).

Ahmed Ben Bella was elected president in 1963. A Socialist, he nationalized foreign holdings and attempted to form a one-party state, but in 1965 he was ousted by a military coup led by his defense minister, Colonel Houari Boumédienne. Boumédienne suspended the constitution and headed a military government until his death in 1978. Under his rule, Algeria remained dependent on trade with France but in its culture shifted to an increasing emphasis on Arab and Muslim traditions, with a strong anti-Israel posture. In the 1980s, president Chadli Benjedid struggled with falling oil prices and growing foreign debt. He introduced market-oriented austerity measures that increased popular dissatisfaction.

In 1989 the constitution was revised to allow formation of political parties. Parliamentary elections were held in 1991, with victory going to the Islamic Salvation Front (FIS), a militant Islamic fundamentalist party. Apparently to prevent the fundamentalists from coming to power, army commanders secured Benjedid's resignation in 1992, instituting a state council in his place. The FIS was banned and the electoral process suspended. Violent civil strife broke out between security forces and Islamic fundamentalists. The latter were believed responsible for the assassination in June 1992 of President Mohammed Boudiaf. From 1992 to 1999, about 100,000 people died in the civil war. In 1994 Liamine Zeroual was appointed president; in 1995, he was voted into the same position, in an election boycotted by many opposition groups. Zeroual introduced several constitutional reforms in December 1996, but announced his retirement from office in 1998. At elections in 1999 former foreign minister Abdelaziz Bouteflika was voted the new president. Once again opposition candidates withdrew from what they considered a rigged election. Bouteflika made peace with the rebels and won popular approval for an amnesty plan.

Algeria: 20th-Century Leaders

President

1963–65: Ahmed Ben Bella

1965–78: Houari Boumédienne (c. 1927–78)

1978–79: Rabah Bitat (1925–)

1979–92: Chadli Benjedid

1992: Sid Ahmed Ghozali (1937–)

1992: Mohammed Boudiaf (1919–92)

1992–94: Ali Kafi (chairman of the High State Council)

1994–98: Liamine Zeroual

1999– : Abdelaziz Bouteflika (1937–)

Prime Minister

1958–61: Ferhat Abbas (1899–1985)

1961–62: Ben Yussef Ben Khedda

1962–65: Ahmed Ben Bella

1965–78: Houari Boumédienne

1979–84: Mohammed Ben Ahmed Abdelghani

1984–88: Abdelhamid Brahimi (1936–)

1988–89: Kasdi Merbah (1938–93)

1989–91: Mouloud Hamroche

1991–92: Sid Ahmed Ghozali

1992–93: Belaid Abdesalam (1928–)

1993–94: Redha Malek

1994–95: Mokdad Sifi

1995–98: Ahmed Ouyahia

1998–2000: Smail Hamdani

Andorra

Official name: Principality of Andorra

Location: Southwestern Europe; bordered by France (N and E), Spain (S and W)

Capital: Andorra la Vella

Area: 174 sq. mi. (450 sq. km.)

Population (est. 1996): 72,766

Languages: Catalan (official), French, Spanish

Government: Parliamentary democracy

Religions: Predominantly Roman Catholic

Monetary unit: French franc, Spanish peseta

Main exports: Petroleum and natural gas

Nestled in the Pyrenees between France and Spain, this tiny country has been under the joint suzerainty of the Spanish bishop of Urgel and the French state since 1278. The bishop and the president of France rule Andorra as coprinces. Traditionally, Andorra's major economic activity has been transshipment of goods between France and Spain.

Until 1982 Andorra's chief executive officer, selected by the country's General Council, was called the first syndic. In 1982 the post of first syndic was eliminated; in its place were created the posts of syndic general and president of government.

Andorra began to move toward the status of a modern nation–state in 1990, when it approved a customs union treaty with the European Union its first treaty in more than seven centuries. In March 1993 Andorra adopted its first formal constitution, which greatly reduced the power of the coprinces and established three branches of government, including a parliament with legislative powers. The constitution also extended the franchise and permitted political parties. Though still nominally headed by its coprinces, Andorra was now considered fully sovereign; it became a member of the UN in 1993. Andorra's first year of fully democratic government was 1994.

About 61 percent of Andorra's people are of Spanish ethnicity, 30 percent Andorran, and 6 percent French.

Andorra: 20th-Century Leaders

Head of Government

1989–94: Oscar Ribas Reig

1994– : Marc Forné Molné (1946–)

Angola

Official name: People's Republic of Angola

Location: Southwestern Africa; bordered by Zaire (N and E), Zambia (E), Namibia (S), South Atlantic Ocean (W); the Cabinda District is separated from the rest of Angola by Congo (N) and Zaire (S)

Capital: Luanda

Area: 481,350 sq. mi. (1,246,700 sq. km.)

Population (est. 1996): 10,342,899

Languages: Portuguese (official), Bantu

Government: Multiparty democracy

Religions: Indigenous beliefs 47%, Roman Catholic 38%, Protestant 15%

Monetary unit: New kwanza

Main exports: Oil, refined petroleum products, diamonds, gas, coffee, fish and fish products

Site of Portuguese settlements since the 16th century, Angola. Also known as Portugese West Africa, it did not draw large numbers of settlers from Portugal until after World War I. Following World War II, black Angolans called for independence. By the 1960s three nationalist factions had emerged: the MPLA (Popular Movement for the Liberation of Angola), FNLA (National Liberation Front of Angola), and UNITA (National Union for the Complete Independence of Angola). Guerrilla warfare began in 1961. Revolution (1974) against military rule in Portugal led quickly to independence for Angola (November 11, 1975).

The three factions now fell into civil war. The MPLA, supported by Soviet aid and Cuban troops, won the first round and proclaimed a socialist republic in 1975. But the government was dogged by insurrection from its former comrades. UNITA, led by Jonas Savimbi

(1934–), fought in the south, aided by the U.S. and South Africa; the FNLA fought in the north, aided by the U.S. and Congo. In addition, South Africa attacked southern bases of the South-West Africa People's Organization (SWAPO), a guerrilla group fighting for the independence of Namibia, the South African controlled territory south of Angola.

In 1987 President José Eduardo dos Santos, MPLA leader, instituted privatizing economic reforms to deal with Angola's failing economy. In 1988 South Africa, Angola, and Cuba signed a peace treaty providing for withdrawal of foreign forces and independence for Namibia. In 1991 MPLA and UNITA signed a treaty, but the peace fell apart in 1992 when UNITA refused to accept the outcome of that year's elections favoring MPLA. By 1993, 50,000 had been killed in the long civil war. In 1994 a new peace treaty was signed, but instability remained. Massacres attributed by the government to UNITA resulted in another outbreak of civil war in 1998; fighting continued in 1999.

Angola: 20th-Century Leaders

President

1975–79: Agostinho Neto (1922–79)

1979– : José Eduardo dos Santos (1942–)

Premier

1975–78: Lopo do Nascimento (1940–)

Prime Minister

1991–92: Fernando José de França van Dunem

1992–96: Marcolino Moco

1996– : Fernando van Dunem

Antigua and Barbuda

Official name: Antigua and Barbuda

Location: Eastern Caribbean Sea, SE of Puerto Rico

Capital: St. John's

Area: 170 sq. mi. (440 sq. km.)

Population (est. 1996): 65,647

Languages: English (official), local dialects

Government: Parliamentary democracy, recognizing Elizabeth II as head of state; member of Commonwealth of Nations

Religions: Anglican (predominant), other Protestant sects, Roman Catholic

Monetary unit: East Caribbean (EC) dollar

Main exports: Petroleum products, sugar cane, machinery and transportation equipment

Antigua is the largest of the islands that constitute this nation; Barbuda is smaller and

Redonda, an uninhabited rocky islet, smaller still. Colonized by Britain in 1632, the country did not achieve self-government until 1967, when it became an independent country in association with Britain. It gained full independence on November 1, 1981. The dominant political party from 1946 has been the Antigua Labour Party (ALP). Throughout most of that time, the government has been dominated by the Bird family. The 1980s and 1990s were marred by corruption scandals and dissension within the Bird family.

Most of the country's population is of African descent. The major industry is tourism. Many Barbuda residents favor severing relations with Antigua over cultural and political differences.

Antigua and Barbuda: 20th-Century Leaders

Governor-General

1981–93: Sir Wilfred E. Jacobs

1993– : Sir James Beethoven Carlisle

Prime Minister

1981–94: Vere Cornwall Bird

1994– : Lester B. Bird

Argentina

Official name: Argentine Republic

Location: Southern South America; bordered by Bolivia, Paraguay (N), Brazil (N, E), Uruguay (E), South Atlantic Ocean (E, S), Chile (S, W)

Capital: Buenos Aires

Area: (excluding Falkland Islands and Antarctic territory claimed by Argentina) 1,068,298 sq. mi. (2,766,890 sq. km.)

Population (est. 1996): 34,672,997

Languages: Spanish (official), English, Italian, German, French

Government: Federal republic

Religions: Roman Catholic 90%, Protestant 2%, Jewish 2%, other 6%

Monetary unit: Nuevo peso argentino

Main exports: Meat, wheat, corn, oilseed, manufactures

Independent from Spain since 1816, Argentina grew rapidly in population and stature from the mid 19th century. Partly as a result of heavy immigration from Europe (particularly Spain and Italy), Argentina's population increased eight-fold from 4 million in 1900 to 32 million in 1990. In the first decades of the 20th century, buoyed by growing exports of grain and beef, it established itself as a leading political and economic force in South America. Universal suffrage was granted in 1912. In 1914 Argentina helped to mediate a dispute between the U.S. and Mexico. Though neutral in World War I, it supplied foodstuffs to the Allies.

The Great Depression that began in 1929 caused severe economic hardship, which increased Argentina's chronic political instability. In 1930 the civilian government of the Radical Party, in power from 1916, was ousted by a military coup backed by the conservative elites. In the 1930s elections resumed, but Fascist organizations gained power, threatening the survival of democratic government. In 1943 the military took over direct rule of the country. Under military influence, Argentina refused to take a clear stand against the Axis Powers and even harbored German agents. On March 27, 1945, when Allied victory was certain, Argentina at last declared war on Germany and Japan.

After World War II, army officer Juan Domingo Perón won election as president (1946–55). As head of the Labor Party, he was supported by the poor and working class. During his tenure, he encouraged industrialization and nationalized key industries, such as the railways and telephone companies. His popular wife and unofficial copresident, Maria Eva Duarte de Perón, or "Evita," secured the vote for women, instituted social welfare programs, and was de facto minister of health and labor until her death in 1952. A 1955 coup deposed Perón and forced him into exile in Madrid. However, his Peróniste movement, which espoused economic nationalism, social justice, and support for labor, continued to enjoy a strong following despite military repression.

There ensued a long period in which weak civilian governments alternated with military rule while the economic outlook was bleak. From 1966 to 1973 violence from both left- and right-wing forces plagued the country, and the military permitted Perón's reelection as president in 1973. He died in office in 1974 and was succeeded by third wife and vice president, Isabel Perón (1930–). Regarding her as unable to restore order, the military deposed her in 1976.

The military junta, targeting leftist insurgents, now launched a "dirty war" in which tactics included state-sponsored abduction, torture, and murder of those deemed political opponents. Between 10,000 and 20,000 people disappeared between 1976 and 1983, attracting international outcries against human rights violations. In 1982 the government launched the Falklands War. This attempt to seize the Falkland/Malvinas Islands long held by Britain but claimed by Argentina ended in abject defeat, which led to the junta's resignation.

In 1983, as the country struggled with runaway inflation and heavy foreign debt, Raúl Alfonsín of the Radical Union Party was elected president. He strengthened the country's democratic institutions but failed to bring about economic reform. In 1989 Peronist candidate Carlos Saul Menem succeeded him as president. Menem cut the military, reduced social spending, and encouraged free enterprise and foreign investment. His austerity program resulted in high economic growth and the reduction of inflation to 4 percent by 1995. He was reelected in 1995, though rising unemployment threatened his position.

Most (85 percent) of Argentina's population is of European origin; ethnicities include Spanish, Italian, French, British, German, and Russian. Unlike other Latin American countries, Argentina has relatively few people of mixed and Native American heritage. Immigration from Europe is still officially encouraged.

Argentina is a thriving center of world culture. Its 20th-century authors include Julio Cortázar, Manuel Puig (1932–90), and Jorge Luis Borges. Artists and musicians of the 20th century include painter Cesareo Bernaldo de Quirós, classical composer Alberto Ginastera (1916–83), and tango composer Astor Piazzolla (1921–92).

Argentina: 20th-Century Leaders

President

1898–1904: Julio A. Roca (1835–1906)

1904–06: Manuel Quintana (1860–1931)

1906–10: José Figueroa Alcorta (1860–1931)

1910–14: Roque Sáenz Peña (1851–1914)

1914–16: Victorino de la Plaza (1840–1919)

1916–22: Hipólito Irigoyen (1852–1933)

1922–28: Marcelo Torcuato de Alvear (1868–1942)

1928–30: Hipólito Irigoyen

1930–32: José Felix Uriburu (1868–1932)

1932–38: Agustín P. Justo (1878–1943)

1938–41: Roberto M. Ortiz (1886–1942)

1941–43: Ramón S. Castillo (1873–1944)

1943–44: Pedro Ramírez (1884–1962)

1944–46: Edelmiro J. Farrell (1887–1980)

1946–55: Juan Domingo Perón (1895–1974)

1955: Eduardo Lonardi (1896–1956)

1955–58: Pedro Eugenio Aramburu (1903–70)

1958–62: Arturo Frondizi

1962–63: José Maria Guido (1910–75)

1963–66: Arturo Umberto Illia (1900–83)

1966–70: Juan Carlos Onganía

1970–71: Roberto Marcelo Levingston

1971–73: Alejandro Agustín Lanusse

1973: Hector J. Campora (1909–80)

1973: Rául Lastiri (1915–78) (interim president)

1973–74: Juan Domingo Perón

1975: Italo Luder (interim president)

1975–76: María Estela (Isabel) Martínez de Perón

1976–81: Jorge Rafael Videla

1981: Roberto Viola

1981: Horacio Tomás Liendo

1981–82: Leopoldo Galtieri

1982: Alfredo Oscar Saint-Jean

1982–83: Reynaldo Bignone

1983–89: Raúl Alfonsín

1989–99: Carlos Saul Menem (1930–)

1999– : Fernando de la Rúa (1937–)

Armenia

Official name: Republic of Armenia

Location: Southern Caucasus; landlocked; bordered by Georgia (N), Azerbaijan (E), Iran (S), Turkey (W)

Capital: Yerevan

Area: 11,506 sq. mi. (29,800 sq. km.)

Population (est. 1996): 3,463,574

Languages: Armenian (official), Russian

Government: Republic

Religions: Armenian Orthodox 94%

Monetary unit: Dram

Main exports: Machinery and transport equipment, gold and jewelry, aluminum, processed food

An ancient civilization dating to the sixth century B.C., Armenia occupies a strategically important location between the Black and Caspian Seas that was fought over by many empires. By the beginning of the 20th century, Armenia had been divided into two parts: the west, ruled by the Ottoman Turkish Empire, and the east, ruled by Russia. Beginning in 1894, the Turks used persecution and massacre to try to exterminate the Armenians in the western part. During World War I, the Turks accused the Armenians of aiding the Turk's Russian enemies. The charge was used to justify the 1915 deportation of Armenians to Syria and Iraq. During this deportation, about a million Armenians starved or were killed.

In 1918 the Treaty of Brest-Litovsk briefly created an independent Armenia. In 1920 Turkey reoccupied the western part, while the Soviets reoccupied the eastern part, proclaiming it a Soviet republic. In 1922 Armenia, Azerbaijan, and Georgia merged as the Transcaucasian Soviet Federated Socialist Republic. That entity was dissolved in 1936, with Armenia becoming a separate constituent republic of the Soviet Union.

By the late 1980s, as the Soviet Union weakened, long-standing ethnic tensions in the region began to boil over. Armenia claimed sovereignty over Nagorno-Karabakh, an Armenian enclave within neighboring Azerbaijan. In 1988 war broke out between the two republics; that same year, Armenia was devastated by massive earthquakes.

In 1991, with the war still raging, Armenia declared itself independent from the Soviet

Union. In October Levon Ter-Petrosyan was elected its first president. In December Armenia joined the Commonwealth of Independent States.

The war with Azerbaijan continued into the late 1990s. Armenia's economy suffered as a result, with production plummeting and inflation rising to more than 4,000 percent by 1994. A new constitution expanding presidential powers was approved by an allegedly corrupt referendum in 1995.

After President Ter-Petrosyan stated his readiness to discuss the Nagorno-Karabakh region with Azerbaijan, public protests and violent assaults on government members forced him to resign in February 1998. Prime Minister Robert Kocharyan, a strong nationalist, was elected president later that year. In 1999, armed men stormed Parliament, killing several, including Prime Minister Vazgen Sarkissian.

Armenia has been a Christian country since about A.D. 300, and its brand of Eastern Orthodoxy has helped define its national identity, as has its language, the sole member of a distinct Indo-European language group. Centuries of persecution have scattered Armenians around the world; many continue to communicate with and support their homeland.

Armenia: 20th-Century Leaders

President

1991–98: Levon Ter-Petrosyan (1945–)

1998– : Robert Kocharyan (1954–)

Premier

1918–20: R. I. Kachaznuni

(part of Soviet Union 1920–91)

1991–93: Gagic C. Arutyunyan

1993–96: Hrant Bagratyan

1996–97: Armen Sarkisyan

1997–98: Robert Kocharyan

1998– : Armen Darbinyan

1999– : Vazgen Sarkissian

Australia

Official name: Commonwealth of Australia

Location: Continent between Indian and Pacific Oceans; nearest neighbor is Papua New Guinea (N)

Capital: Canberra

Area: 2,967,897 sq. mi. (7,686,850 sq. km.)

Population (est. 1996): 18,260,863

Languages: English (official), native languages

Government: Federal parliamentary state recognizing **Queen Elizabeth II** as sovereign

Religions: Christian (Anglican 26.1%, Roman Catholic 24.3%, other Protestant 20%, Eastern Orthodox 4%), Jewish, Buddhist, Muslim

Monetary unit: Australian dollar

Main exports: Coal, gold, meat, wool

Explored by Captain James Cook in 1770, Australia was settled by the British in 1788 and maintained until the mid 19th century as a penal colony. Through the rest of the 19th century, Australia was settled as free colonies; the six colonies were united as a commonwealth in 1901. An additional region, the Northern Territory, was added to the commonwealth in 1911. As of 1907 Australia was recognized as a dominion: internally self-governing, but subject to British decisions on foreign policy and defense. In 1927 Australia's capital was moved from Melbourne to Canberra. In 1931 the Statute of Westminster effectively granted Australia full independence, though the country remains within the Commonwealth of Nations.

Australia consists of the continent Australia, the island state of Tasmania, and Australian external territories, including Norfolk Island, the Ashmore and Cartier Islands, the Australian Antarctic Territory, Heard Island and the McDonald Islands, Christmas Island, Coral Sea Islands, and Cocoa (Keeling) Islands. It also claims part of Antarctica.

Early in its existence as a commonwealth, Australia established a strong social welfare state that featured free compulsory education, trade union rights, women's suffrage, and old-age pensions. During World Wars I and II, the country fought on Britain's side. Although the Allied victory in the Coral Sea (1942) deterred Japanese invasion of the country, several sites were bombed by the Japanese, including Darwin, Port Jackson, and Newcastle. Australia provided troops for the U.S. during the Korean, Vietnam, and Persian Gulf Wars.

After World War II, the government was controlled (1949–66) largely by Robert Menzies and the Liberal Party. In 1975 the Liberal-Country Party, led by John Malcolm Fraser, was elected. His conservative changes included sizable cuts in government spending. In 1983 the Labour Party was elected the controlling party, with Robert Hawke becoming prime minister. In an unprecedented move, he was replaced in 1991 by another Labour Party member, Paul Keating. Labour Party control ended in 1996 with the election of a Liberal Party–National Party coalition led by John Howard. In a referendum in 1999, Australian voters rejected a proposal to make their country a republic.

Immigration has increased since the removal of discriminatory barriers in 1973, with most of the new population coming from Asia. Trade and economic ties to the entire Pacific Rim have also grown since that time.

Aborigines and Torres Strait Islanders, indigenous Australians who had long faced discrimination, received full citizenship in 1967.

Australia: 20th-Century Leaders

Governor-General (representing the British monarch)

1901–03: Lord Linlithgow, earl of Hopetoun (1860–1908)

1902–03 (Acting Governor–General): Hallam Tennyson, baron Tennyson (1852–1928)

1903–04: Hallam Tennyson, baron Tennyson

1904–08: Henry Stafford Northcote, baron Northcote (1846–1911)

1908–11: William Humble Ward, earl of Dudley (1867–1932)

1909–10: Viscount Chelmsford (1868–1933) (acting governor-general)

1911–14: Thomas Denman, Baron Denman (1874–1954)

1914–20: Viscount Novar of Raith (1860–1934)

1920–25: Varon Forster of Lepe (1866–1936)

1925–30: Baron John Lawrence Stonehaven (1874–1941)

1931–36: Sir Isaac Alfred Isaacs (1885–1948)

1936–45: Alexander Gore Arkwright Hore-Ruthven, Baron Gowrie (1872–1955)

1938: Baron Huntingfield (in absence of Lord Gowrie)

1944–45: Sir Winston J. Dugan (1877–1951) (in absence of Lord Gowrie)

1945–47: Prince Henry, duke of Gloucester (1900–74)

1947: Sir Winston J. Dugan

1947–53: Sir William John McKell (1891–1985)

1953–60: Viscount Slim (1891–1970)

1960–61: William Shepherd, Viscount Dunrossil (1893–1961)

1961–65: Viscount De L'Isle (1909–91)

1965–69: Lord Casey of Berwick (1890–1976)

1969–74: Sir Paul Hasluck (1905–93)

1974–77: Sir John Kerr (1914–91)

1977–82: Sir Zelman Cowan

1982–89: Sir Ninian Martin Stephen

1989–96: William "Bill" Hayden (1933–)

1996– : Sir William Deane (1931–)

Prime Minister

1901–03: Sir Edmund Batton (1849–1920)

1903–04: Alfred Deakin (1856–1919)

1904: J. C. Watson (1867–1941)

1904–05: Sir George Reid (1845–1918)

1905–08: Alfred Deakin

1908–09: Andrew Fisher (1862–1928)

1909–10: Alfred Deakin

1910–13: Andrew Fisher

1913–14: Sir Joseph Cook (1860–1947)

1914–15: Andrew Fisher

1915–23: Wiliam Morris Hughes (1864–1952)

1923–29: Stanley Melbourne, Viscount Bruce

1929–32: James Henry Scullin (1876–1953)

1932–39: Joseph Aloysius Lyons (1879–1939)

1939: Sir Earle Page (1880–1961)

1939–41: Sir Robert Gordon Menzies (1894–1978)

1941: Sir Arthur William Fadden

1941–45: John J. Curtin (1885–1945)

1945: Francis M. Forde (1890–1983)

1945–49: Joseph B. Chifley (1885–1951)

1949–66: Sir Robert Gordon Menzies

1966–67: Harold Holt (1908–67)

1967–68: Sir John McEwen (1900–80) (acting prime minister)

1968–71: John Grey Gorton

1971–72: William McMahon (1908–88)

1972–75: Edward Gough Whitlam

1975–83: John Malcolm Fraser

1983–91: Robert Hawke

1991–96: Paul Keating (1945–)

1996– : John Howard (1939–)

Austria

Official name: Republic of Austria

Location: Central Europe; landlocked; bordered by Germany and Czech Republic (N), Hungary and Slovak Republic (E), Slovenia and Italy (S), Switzerland and Liechtenstein (W)

Capital: Vienna

Area: 32,377 sq. mi. (83,855 sq. km.)

Population (est. 1997): 8,023,244

Languages: German

Government: Federal republic

Religions: Roman Catholic 85%, Protestant 6%, none or other 9%

Monetary unit: Austrian schilling

Main exports: Machinery, equipment, iron, steel, lumber

Part of Charlemagne's empire from 788, the landlocked territory now known as Austria was divided among feudal domains until the late 13th century, when it was brought under the control of Rudolph I of the House of Habsburg. By the 16th century the Habsburg empire increased its rule to encompass much of Europe, including the Holy Roman Empire, the Netherlands, and Spain. After centuries of decline and rebuilding, the Austrian empire was founded in 1804 and in 1867, the Dual Monarchy of Austria–Hungary was formed, granting autonomy to Hungary and allowing for end-of-century peace.

On June 28, 1914, World War I was instigated when Habsburg heir Archduke Franz Ferdinand was assassinated by a Serbian nationalist. The war destroyed the empire, and Austria became a small country, proclaimed the Republic of Austria in November 1918. A federal constitution was passed into law on October 1, 1920. Through the 1920s Austria faced chronic economic instability, leading to violence among political parties. The collapse of Austria's largest bank in 1931 further heightened national tensions, resulting in the 1932 election victory of the Austrian Nazi Party.

On March 12, 1938, German troops entered Austria, largely to Austrian favor. In what was called the Anschluss, Austria was annexed to Germany. In 1945 near the end of World War II, Allied forces occupied Austria; the Allies fostered its return to constitutional rule in November 1945. The combination of government reconstruction policies and Marshall Plan aid resulted in massive economic rebuilding during the 1950s. On May 15, 1955, Austria gained full sovereignty under the Austrian State Treaty. Signed by the the U.S., Britain, France, and the Soviet Union, the treaty recognized the second Austrian Republic and designated the removal of occupation forces. During the progressive rule of the 1970s, Austria enacted much social reform.

In the 1980s President Kurt Waldheim, a former UN secretary-general, was accused of war crimes as a German officer during World War II. In 1988 Chancellor Franz Vranitzky apologized for Austria's role in war crimes and attempted to quell international tension. Continuing his rule into the 1990s, Vranitzky was responsible for generating support for European Union membership, which was made effective January 1, 1995. In 1997 Vranitzky resigned and selected Finance Minister Viktor Klima as successor. The dominance of the Austrian Social Democratic Party was challenged late in the decade by the rightist, anti-immigrant Austrian Freedom Party.

Austria produced some of the 20th century's greatest thinkers, including Sigmund Freud, Ludwig Wittgenstein, Martin Buber, and Kurt Gödel.

Austria: 20th-Century Leaders

Emperor

1848–1916: Francis Joseph (1830–1916)

1916–18: Charles I (1887–1922)

President

1920–28: Michael Hainisch (1858–1940)

1928–38: Wilhelm Miklas (1872–1956)

1945–50: Karl Renner (1870–1950)

1951–57: Theodor Körner (1873–1957)

1957–65: Adolf Scharf (1890–1965)

1965–74: Franz Jonas (1899–1974)

1974–86: Rudolf Kirchschläger

1986–92: Kurt Waldheim (1918–)

1992– : Thomas Klestil (1932–)

German Governor–General

1938–39: Arthur Seyss–Inquart (1892–1946)

Chancellor

1919–20: Karl Renner (1870–1950)

1932–34: Engelbert Dollfuss (1892–1934)

1934–38: Kurt Elder von Schuschnigg

1945–53: Leopold Figl (1902–65)

1953–61: Julius Raab (1891–1964)

1961–64: Alfons Gorbach (1898–1962)

1964–70: Josef Klaus

1970–83: Bruno Kreisky (1911–90)

1983–86: Fred Sinowatz

1986–97: Franz Vranitzky (1937–)

1997– : Viktor Klima (1947–)

Azerbaijan

Official name: Republic of Azerbaijan

Location: Southern Caucasus; bordered by Georgia (NW), Russia (N), Caspian Sea (E), Iran (S), Armenia (SW). Nakhichevan Autonomous Republic, an Azerbaijan territory, is an enclave within Armenian territory.

Capital: Baku

Area: 33,436 sq. mi. (86,600 sq. km.)

Population (est. 1996): 7,676,953

Languages: Azerbaijani (official), Russian, Armenian

Government: Republic

Religions: Muslim 93.4%, Russian Orthodox 2.5%

Monetary unit: Manat

Main exports: Oil, gas, chemicals, oil field equipment, textiles, cotton

In the early 19th century, Russia acquired from Persia the territory of present–day Azerbaijan, inhabited by the Azeri, a Shi'ite Muslim people speaking a Turkic language. By the early 20th century, Azerbaijan's Caspian Sea port of Baku was an important hub of industry and trade, and a center of revolution. Following the Russian Revolution of 1917, Azerbaijan declared independence from Russia (1918). In 1920 the Soviet Red Army reconquered it and established the Azerbaijan Soviet Socialist Republic. In 1922 Azerbaijan merged with Armenia and Georgia in the Transcaucasian Soviet Federated Socialist Republic, but in 1936 it again became a separate republic of the Soviet Union.

In 1988 war broke out between Azerbaijan and the neighboring Soviet republic of Armenia. At issue was Armenia's claim of sovereignty over Nagorno-Karabakh, an Armenian enclave within Azerbaijan. In the midst of the war, Armenia declared itself independent from the Soviet Union (October 1991). In December, Azerbaijan joined the Commonwealth of Independent States.

By 1993 the war had turned against Azerbaijan and the country's economy was in a dire state. Armed rebels drove President Abulfaz Elchibey from office (1993). Heydar Aliyev, a former Communist Party leader, replaced him. Two coup attempts failed to topple him, and his New Azerbaijan Party handily won parliamentary elections in 1995, amid charges of electoral corruption. As the war with Armenia continued, Aliyev took steps to develop the country's extensive oil reserves for overseas export. Former president Elchibey attempted to oust Aliyev in December 1998 elections but eventually boycotted the elections, claiming the election laws were unfair.

Azerbaijan: 20th-Century Leaders

Chief of State

1918–19: Khan Khoiski (d. 1920)

1919–20: Nazim Beg Usubekov

President

1991–92: Ayaz N. Mutalibov (1938–)

1992: Yakub Mamedov

1992: Ayaz N. Mutalibov

1992: Isa Gambarov

1992–93: Abulfaz Ali Elchibey (1954–)

1993– : Heydar Aliyev (1923–)

Premier

1991–92: Hasan Hasanov

1992: Firuz Mustafayev

1992–93: Rakhim Guseynov

1993: Ali Masimov

1993: Panakh Guseynov

1993–94: Surat Husseynov

1994–96: Fuad Guliyev

1996– : Artur Rasizade

Bahamas

Official name: Commonwealth of the Bahamas

Location: Western Atlantic Ocean; nearly 700 islands in archipelago extending 590 mi. (950 km.) SE-NW between Florida and Haiti

Capital: Nassau

Area: 5,382 sq. mi. (13,939 sq. km.)

Population (est. 1996): 259,367

Languages: English, some Creole

Government: Independent commonwealth

Religions: Baptist 32%, Anglican 20%, Roman Catholic 19%, Protestant, Greek Orthodox, Jewish

Monetary unit: Bahamian dollar

Main exports: Pharmaceuticals, cement, rum, crawfish

Although discovered by Christopher Columbus in 1492, the Bahamas were settled by the British from the 1600s and became a British colony in 1717. Throughout the 20th century, tourism has been the primary industry of the Bahamas. The government was controlled by minority white leadership until the implementation of male suffrage (for minority property owners) in 1959 and woman suffrage in 1962. (About 85 percent of Bahamians are of African descent, 15 percent of European descent.) The Bahamas gained internal self-rule in 1964; in 1967 it held the first general election under universal suffrage, electing Progressive Liberal Party candidate Lynden Oscar Pindling as its first prime minister. On July 10, 1973, the Bahamas became an independent nation under the Commonwealth.

In the 1980s the government attempted to limit change by lowering Haitian immigration and curtailing the sale of property to foreigners. Prime Minister Pindling and other government officials were involved in corruption scandals during the 1980s, leading to his defeat in 1992 to Hubert Ingraham of the Free National Movement. Ingraham's conservative policies concentrated on increased economic diversification and plans to reduce the massive foreign deficit incurred during Pindling's tenure.

New Providence is the primary Bahamas island and the site of its capital. It is one of the 22 inhabited islands; others include Grand Bahama and San Salvador.

Bahamas: 20th-Century Leaders

Governor-General (representing the British monarch)

1973–79: Sir Milo B. Butler (1906–79)

1979–88: Sir Gerald C. Cash (1917–)

1988–92: Sir Henry Taylor (1903–)

1992–95: Sir Clifford Darling

1995– : Orville Turnquest (1929–)

Prime Minister

1964–67: Sir Roland Symonette (1898–1980)

1967–92: Lynden Oscar Pindling (1933–)

1992– : Hubert A. Ingraham (1947–)

Bahrain

Official name: State of Bahrain

Location: Archipelago in Persian Gulf; nearest neighbors Saudi Arabia (W), Qatar (SE)

Capital: Manama

Area: 239 sq. mi. (620 sq. km.)

Population (est. 1996): 590,042

Languages: Arabic (official), Farsi, Urdu, English

Government: Traditional monarchy

Religions: Shi'ite Muslim 70%, Sunni Muslim 30%

Monetary unit: Bahraini dinar

Main exports: Petroleum, aluminum, garments, jute and jute goods

An ancient center of trade, the island group of Bahrain has been ruled by the Al Khalifa dynasty since 1782. It became a British protectorate in 1861. Oil was discovered there in 1932, but the reserves were severely depleted by the mid-1970s. The country has since diversified: key industries now include oil refining, aluminum smelting, and international banking.

The UN rejected Iran's claims to Bahrain in 1970. In August 1971 Bahrain gained independence from Britain. The emir, Sheikh Isa ibn Sulman al-Khalifa, dissolved the country's first parliament in 1975, allegedly over its leftist leanings. Since then Bahrain's monarch has ruled absolutely; political parties are prohibited.

The Iranian Revolution of 1979 stoked revolutionary sentiment among the country's Shi'ite majority. In 1981 Iran supported an abortive coup, which led Bahrain to form a security pact with Saudi Arabia, a country now joined to Bahrain by a causeway. The U.S. also has an interest in Bahrain, represented by its military base there, which served as naval headquarters in the Persian Gulf War.

In 1995 and 1996, Bahraini Shi'ites protested against the government, voicing opposition to economic inequalities, high unemployment, and political repression. Violent clashes broke out and many dissidents were arrested.

Bahrain: 20th-Century Leaders

Emir

1961–99: Sheikh Isa ibn Sulman al-Khalifa (1933–99)

1999– : Khalifah ibn Sulman al-Khalifah (1935–)

Prime Minister

1970– : Khalifah ibn Sulman al-Khalifah (1935–)

Bangladesh

Official name: People's Republic of Bangladesh

Location: Southern Asia; bordered by India (W, N, E), Myanmar (SE), Bay of Bengal (S)

Capital: Dhaka

Area: 55,598 sq. mi. (144,000 sq. km.)

Population (est. 1996): 123,062,800

Languages: Bangla (official), English

Government: Republic

Religions: Muslim 83%, Hindu 16%, Buddhist, Christian, and other 1%

Monetary unit: Taka

Main exports: Garments, jute and jute goods, leather and leather goods, seafood

Bangladesh is the most densely populated nation in the world (excluding city-states such as Singapore) and one of the poorest. In 1996 it had a population density of 2,213.4 persons per square mile, compared to 74.9 in the U.S. and 774 in neighboring India. Most of the population is rural, living in flat, low-lying, alluvial areas subject to annual flooding.

Culturally, Bangladesh has much in common with West Bengal, the Indian state that borders it. Historically, it was known as East Bengal, and was part of British India from the 18th century. East Bengal was predominantly Muslim, unlike its largely Hindu western counterpart. In 1947 India achieved independence from Britain. The predominantly Muslim northwest portion of British India became West Pakistan, and East Bengal became East Pakistan. The two were joined in the Union of Pakistan.

East Pakistan soon found itself a poor cousin to the more powerful West Pakistan. Separated geographically by about a thousand miles, the two regions had little in common. Pakistan's government and military were dominated by West Pakistanis, who conducted official business in their native language of Urdu, which few of the Bangla-speaking easterners could even understand.

East Pakistan's Awami ("People's") League, founded in 1949, urged autonomy for the region. In Pakistan's first general elections in 1970, the Awami League, led by Sheikh Mujibur Rahman, won control of parliament but was not allowed to take its seats. In 1971 rioting broke out, which the military suppressed. Full-scale civil war developed, with East Pakistan declaring independence as Bangladesh. An estimated one million East Pakistanis were killed, with 10 million refugees fleeing into India. In the **India-Pakistan War** of December 1971, India invaded East Pakistan, capturing Dhaka and forcing Pakistan to acknowledge the independence of Bangladesh.

From its earliest years, the new nation suffered from political turmoil. As prime minister, Mujibur Rahman formed ties with the Soviet Union, introduced socialist practices, and nationalized industries. His attempt to form a one-party state led to his assassination in 1975. General Ziaur Rahman established military rule and was assassinated in 1981. Army chief of staff Hossain Mohammad Ershad took power in a coup in 1983. Amid opposition protests, he resigned from office in 1990.

Ziaur Rahman's widow, Begum Khaleda Zia, led the Bangladesh National Party to control of parliament in 1991. That year, the constitution was amended to make the president a figurehead and give real power to the prime minister. Zia promoted privatization and other free-market reforms, while opponents led strikes and protests against her rule. In 1996 she resigned and permitted elections, in which Sheikh Hasina Wazed, daughter of Mujibur Rahman, led the Awami League to victory for the first time since 1975.

Since independence, Bangladesh has been plagued not only by political upheaval but also by economic woes and natural disasters. A cyclone in 1991 killed more than 120,000 people and left millions homeless. Flooding in 1998 left almost 1,500 dead and displaced over 30 million.

Bangladesh: 20th-Century Leaders

President

1971–72: Sheikh Mujibur Rahman (1920–75); in prison with Syed Nazrul Islam (1925–75) as acting president of the government-in-exile

1972–73: Abu Sayeed Chowdhury (1921–87)

1973–75: Muhammadullah

1975: Sheikh Mujibur Rahman

1975– : Khandekar Mustaque Ahmed

1975–77: Abu Sadat Mohammed Sayem

1977–81: Ziaur Rahman (1936–81)

1981–82: Abdus Sattar (1906–85)

1982–83: Abul Fazal Mohammad Chowdhury

1983–90: Hossain Mohammad Ershad (1930–)

1990–91: Shahabuddin Ahmed

1991–96: Abdur Rahman Biswas (1926–)

1996– : Shahabuddin Ahmed (1930–)

Prime Minister

1971–72: Tajuddin Ahmed (1922–75)

1972–75: Sheikh Mujibur Rahman

1975: Mohammed Mansoor Ali (1919–75)

1975–77: Abu Sadat Mohammed Sayem

1977–79: Ziaur Rahman

1979–82: Shah Mohammad Azizur Rahman (1925–88)

1984–85: Ataur Rahman Khan (1905–85)

1986–88: Mizanur Rahman Chowdhury

1988–89: Moudud Ahmed (1940–)

1989–90: Kazi Zafar Ahmed (1940–)

1991–96: Begum Khaleda Zia (1944–)

1996: Mohammad Habibur Rahman

1996– : Sheikh Hasina Wazed (1947–)

Barbados

Location: Easternmost island in Caribbean Sea; neighbors include Trinidad (SW) and Venezuela (S)

Capital: Bridgetown

Area: 166 sq. mi. (430 sq. km.)

Population (est. 1996): 257,030

Languages: English

Government: Parliamentary democracy, recognizing Queen Elizabeth II as chief of state

Religions: Protestant 67% (including Anglican 40%, Pentecostal 8%, and Methodist 7%), Roman Catholic 4%, none or other 29%

Monetary unit: Barbados dollar

Main exports: Sugar and molasses, rum, chemicals, electrical components, clothing

A British colony since the 17th century, Barbados developed into a major sugar producer, relying on the labor of African slaves until they were emancipated in the 1830s. The country's ethnic composition is still 80 percent African, with 16 percent a mix of African and European and 4 percent European. Sugar and sugar products are still mainstays of the economy, though the tourist industry is the country's biggest employer.

Economic problems, resulting partly from the decline of the sugar industry, and tense race relations led to riots in 1937 and 1938. Greater diversity was then introduced into the economy, and universal suffrage was instituted in 1950. Grantley Herbert Adams (1898–1971), who cofounded the Barbados Labour Party in 1938, headed the government from 1946 to 1958 and urged full internal autonomy. This was granted in 1958.

In that year, Adams became prime minister of the Federation of the West Indies (1958–62), a federal union of 10 British colonies of the West Indies, comprising Trinidad and Tobago; Jamaica; Antigua and Barbuda; Barbados; Dominica; Grenada; Montserrat; Saint Kitts, Nevis, and Anguilla; Saint Lucia; and Saint Vincent and the Grenadines. The federation quickly broke apart when nationalist movements in Trinidad and Tobago and Jamaica won secession from the union.

In 1966 Barbados became independent as a member of the Commonwealth. The two dominant parties since then have been the Barbados Labour Party and the Democratic Labour Party. The latter, founded by Errol Walton Barrow, held power from 1961 to 1976 and 1986 to 1994. Since 1994 the Barbados Labour Party, which favored deficit spending to ease unemployment, has governed the country.

Barbados: 20th-Century Leaders

Governor-General (representing the British monarch)

1966–67: Sir John Montague Stow (1911–)

1967–76: Sir Winston Scott (1900–76)

1976–84: Sir Deighton Lisle Ward (1909–)

1984–90: Sir Hugh Springer (1913–)

1990–95: Dame Nita Barrow (1916–95)

1995–96: Sir Denys Williams (acting governor-general)

1996– : Sir Clifford Husbands (1926–)

Prime Minister

1966–76: Errol Walton Barrow (1920–87)

1976–85: J. M. G. "Tom" Adams (1931–85)

1985–86: Bernard St. John

1986–87: Errol Walton Barrow

1987–94: Erskine Sandiford (1937–)

1994– : Owen Arthur (1949–)

Belarus

Official name: Republic of Belarus

Location: Northeastern Europe; landlocked; bordered by Lithuania (N), Latvia (N), Russia (NE, E), Ukraine (S), Poland (W)

Capital: Minsk

Area: 80,154 sq. mi. (207,600 sq. km.)

Population (est. 1996): 10,415,973

Languages: Belarusian (official), Russian

Government: Republic

Religions: Eastern Orthodox 60%

Monetary unit: Belarusian ruble

Main exports: Machinery, transport equipment, chemicals, foodstuffs

Part of the Russian empire from the 18th century, this landlocked country was formerly called White Russia, Belorussia, or Byelorussia. It suffered from the ravages of battle during World War I. In 1918 it declared itself an independent republic, but by 1919 the Soviet Union had conquered it. In 1921, in the Treaty of Riga ending the Soviet-Polish War, western Belarus was ceded to Poland, while eastern Belarus went to the Soviet Union. Belarus was incorporated as the Belorussian Soviet Socialist Republic (S.S.R.) by the U.S.S.R. in 1922. In 1939 as a result of the Nazi-Soviet non-aggression pact, the Soviet Union annexed western Belarus, making it part of the Belorussian SSR.

During World War II Belorussia was occupied by German forces. About two million Belorussians were killed, including most of the republic's Jews. In 1945 the republic's western boundary was altered in favor of Poland.

In the postwar years, Belorussia's economy grew and prospered as a result of industrialization. Russians were encouraged to immigrate into the country. Despite the republic's relative prosperity, nationalism grew strong in the 1980s, focusing particularly on the survival of the Belarusian language. New political parties formed, and in July 1990 Belarus declared its sovereignty. Full independence was declared in August 1991. Stanislas Shushkevich, a free-market reformer, became the country's leader.

In 1994 Shushkevich was forced from office by a no-confidence vote in parliament, which still included many Communists. Aleksandr Lukashenko, who replaced him, became a virtual dictator. Under a new constitution in 1996, President Lukashenko was given the right to rule by decree and to appoint many members of the Constitutional Court and the Council of the Republic, the legislature's upper house.

Belarus has retained close ties to Russia. The young republic pushed for the formation of the Commonwealth of Independent States in December 1991. A customs union in 1995 and union treaties in 1996 and 1997 joined Belarus and Russia in a number of ways, including joint legal and tax systems and common defense, foreign, and economic policies.

In March 1998 the Belarusian ruble lost 30 percent of its value, throwing the country into economic panic. The government imposed price controls and suspended trading in hopes of stabilizing the economy.

Belarus: 20th-Century Leaders

President

1918–21: Piotra Kreuceuski

(part of Soviet Union 1921–91)

1991–94: Stanislas Shushkevich (1934–)

1994– : Aleksandr Lukashenko (1954–)

Prime Minister

1991–94: Vyacheslav Kebich (1936–)

1994–97: Mikhail Chyhir

1997– : Syargei Ling

Belgium

Official name: Kingdom of Belgium

Location: Northwestern Europe; bordered by Netherlands (N), Luxembourg and Germany (E), France (S), North Sea (W)

Capital: Bruxelles (Brussels)

Area: 11,780 sq. mi. (30,510 sq. km.)

Population (est. 1997): 10,170,241

Languages: Flemish (Dutch) 56%, French 32%, German 11% (legally bilingual)

Government: Constitutional monarchy

Religions: Roman Catholic 75%, Protestant or other 25%

Monetary unit: Belgian franc

Main exports: Iron, steel, transportation equipment, tractors, diamonds

Part of the Roman province of Belgica, named for the Belgae of Gaul, Belgium was conquered by Julius Caesar from 57 to 50 B.C. It formed part of various European empires before becoming an independent kingdom in 1830. Belgium entered the 20th century as a highly industrialized state and a colonial power: from 1885 it controlled the Congo Free State (later the Belgian Congo, the Democratic Republic of the Congo, and Zaire). It was also a country divided by ethnic conflict between the Dutch-speaking Flemings and French-speaking Walloons.

The German invasion of Belgium in 1914 effectively started World War I by triggering the entry of the British Empire into the war. Belgium remained a battleground throughout the war, with sites, including Ypres, sustaining heavy damage. Belgium's boundaries were reinstated by the Treaty of Versailles in 1919. During World War II, Belgium was occupied by Germany and was the site of much fighting. Central to Belgian involvement in World War II were the actions of King Leopold III, seen by many as collaborating with the enemy. After the war, though Belgium swiftly built a prosperous economy, it faced political strife over King Leopold. It was resolved only when he tried to return to Belgium in 1950 and was forced through internal protest to abdicate his position. His son Baudouin I became king on July 16, 1951.

After the war Belgium abandoned its neutral stance and became a member of NATO and the Benelux Union, actively becoming part of the European community. In 1960 Belgium saw it could no longer control its colonial holding, and the Belgian Congo gained independence.

During the 1960s tensions rose between the country's French-speaking and Flemish-speaking regions, both of which differed from the bilingual mix in Brussels. In an attempt to unite the regions and reduce tensions, Belgium adopted a new constitution in 1993 and became a federal state. Elections in 1995 gave parliamentary majority to a coalition Christian Democrat–Socialist government. In recent years the government has been rocked by a series of scandals that eventually led to the resignation of several members of the government and a reorganization of the police force.

Belgium: 20th-Century Leaders

King

1865–1909: Leopold II (1835–1909)

1909–34: Albert I (1875–1934)

1934–51: Leopold III (1901–83)

1951–93: Baudouin I (1930–93)

1993– : Albert II (1934–)

Regent

1944–50: Charles (1903–83)

Prime Minister

1939–45: Hubert Pierlot (1883–1963)

1945–46: Achille Van Acker (1898–1975)

1946: Paul-Henri Spaak (1899–1972)

1946: Achille Van Acker

1946–47: Camille Huysmans (1871–1968)

1947–49: Paul-Henri Spaak

1949–50: Gaston Eyskens (1905–88)

1950: Jean Duviesuart (1900–77)

1950–52: Joseph Pholien (1884–1968)

1952–54: Jean van Houtte (1907–c. 1990s)

1954–58: Achille Van Acker

1958–61: Gaston Eyskens

1961–65: Théodore Lefèvre

1965–66: Pierre C. J. M. Harmel

1966–68: Paul Vanden Boeynants

1968–73: Gaston Eyskens

1973–74: Edmond Leburton

1974–78: Léo Tindemans (1922–)

1978–79: Paul Vanden Boeynants

1979–81: Wilfried Martens

1981: Mark Eyskens

1981–92: Wilfried Martens

1992–99: Jean-Luc Dehaene (1940–)

1999– : Guy Verhofstadt (1950–)

Belize

Official name: Belize

Location: Northeastern coast of Central America; bordered by Mexico (N), Guatemala (S, W), and the Caribbean Sea

Capital: Belmopan

Area: 8,865 sq. mi. (22,960 sq. km.)

Population (est. 1996): 219,296

Languages: English (official), Spanish, Maya, Garifuna (Carib)

Government: Parliamentary democracy

Religions: Roman Catholic 62%, Protestant 30%

Monetary unit: Belizean dollar

Main exports: Sugar, citrus, bananas, clothing

Once part of the Mayan empire, Belize was explored by the Spanish and settled by the British, becoming in 1862 a colony (and in 1871 a Crown colony) known as British Honduras. The British granted it partial self-government in 1954, home rule in 1964, and full independence as a constitutional monarchy within the Commonwealth on September 21, 1981. Renamed Belize, it was the last British Crown colony on the American mainland to gain independence.

Guatemala immediately claimed long-disputed sovereign rights over Belize. In 1991 Guatemala recognized Belize's sovereignty but threatened it after British forces were removed from the country in 1994.

For three decades after 1954, politics in Belize was dominated by the social democratic People's United Party. In 1984 the conservative United Democratic Party won control of the government. Belize is a reputed center of illegal drug trafficking between Columbia and the U.S.

Belize: 20th-Century Leaders

Governor-General (representing the British monarch)

1981–93: Dame Minita Gordon

1993– : Sir Colville Norbert Young (1932–)

Prime Minister

1981–84: George Cadle Price

1984–89: Manuel Esquivel (1940–)

1989–93: George Cadle Price

1993–98: Manuel Esquivel

1998– : Said Musa (1944–)

Benin

Official name: Republic of Benin

Location: Western Africa; bordered by Burkina Faso (N), Niger (N), Nigeria (E), Gulf of Guinea (S), Togo (W)

Capital: Porto–Novo

Area: 43,483 sq. mi. (112,620 sq. km.)

Population (est. 1996): 5,709,529

Languages: French (official), Fon, Yoruba, tribal languages

Government: Multiparty democratic republic

Religions: Indigenous beliefs 70%, Muslim 15%, Christian 15%

Monetary unit: Franc CFA (Communauté Financiere Africaine)

Main exports: Cotton, crude oil, palm products, cocoa

From the 17th century, Benin was the site of a wealthy kingdom known as Dahomey, which profited from trade with Europeans. In the late 19th century, France grew more aggressive, annexing Dahomey in 1893 and incorporating it into French West Africa in 1904. After World War II Dahomey, like many African colonies, moved toward sovereign status, becoming autonomous in 1958 and winning full independence in 1960.

The new nation suffered through a decade of political instability. Five coups occurred as civilian governments gave way to military regimes and back again; tensions flared between the country's various ethnic groups, who varied widely in economic and educational background. In 1972 Mathieu Kérékou took power and soon reconstituted the government along Marxist lines. He banned opposition parties, nationalized businesses, and, in 1975, changed the country's name to Benin, that of a west African civilization that flourished from the 15th to 18th centuries.

By 1989 Benin's economy was in terrible shape and demonstrators urged Kérékou to resign. A new constitution allowing for a multiparty democracy was approved in 1990. In presidential elections held in 1991, opposition leader Nicéphore Soglo defeated Kérékou. Soglo was unable to make much economic progress and, in the 1996 election, lost the presidency to Kérékou.

Hot and humid, Benin is small but densely populated, with 131 persons per square mile in 1996.

Benin: 20th-Century Leaders

President

1960–63: Hubert Maga (1916–)

1963–64: Christophe Soglo (1912–83)

1964–65: Sorou-Migan Apithy (1913–89)

1965: Tairou Congacou (d. 1993)

1965–67: Christophe Soglo

1967: Maurice Kouandete (1939–)

1967–68: Alphonse Alley

1968–69: Emile Derlin Zinsou

1969–70: Maurice Kouandete

1970–72: Hubert Maga

1972: Justin Ahomadegbé

1972–91: Mathieu Kérékou (1933–)

1991–96: Nicéphore Soglo (1934–)

1996– : Mathieu Kérékou

Bhutan

Official name: Kingdom of Bhutan

Location: Southern Asia; landlocked; bordered by China (N, W), India (S, E)

Capital: Timphu

Area: 18,147 sq. mi. (47,000 sq. km.)

Population (est. 1996): 1,822,625

Languages: Dzongkha (official), Tibetan dialects, Nepalese dialects

Government: Monarchy

Religions: Lamaistic Buddhism 75%, Hinduism 25%

Monetary unit: Ngultrum, Indian rupee

Main exports: Cardamom, gypsum, timber, handicrafts

Landlocked in the Himalaya Mountains between Chinese-ruled Tibet and India, Bhutan has a history of Tibetan-style Lamaistic Buddhist theocracy dating from the 16th century. The British, ensconced in India, invaded Bhutan in 1865 and made it a protectorate in 1910. Bhutan became independent in 1949. India inherited from Britain a special treaty relationship with Bhutan, one in which India manages Bhutan's foreign affairs and subsidizes its government.

Though Bhutan is a constitutional monarchy in form, the National Assembly essentially confirms the king's decisions. The present ruling dynasty dates from 1907. In the 1960s the government introduced modernizing reforms, such as abolishing slavery and the caste system, emancipating women, and broadening education.

In the 1990s social tensions rose over treatment of the country's Nepalese minority. The government tried to expel Nepalese and restrict their immigration, creating more than 70,000 refugees since 1991. A pro-democracy movement was spearheaded by the Nepalese, with guerrillas conducting raids from bases in India and Nepal.

Bhutan is one of the world's poorest countries. Its population survives largely through subsistence farming.

Bhutan: 20th-Century Leaders

King

1926–52: Jigme Wangchuck (1902–52)

1952–72: Jigme Dorji Wangchuck (1929–72)

1972– : Jigme Singye Wangchuck (1955–)

Bolivia

Official name: Republic of Bolivia

Location: Central South America; landlocked; bordered by Brazil (N, E), Paraguay (S), Argentina (S), Chile (W), Peru (W)

Capital: Sucre (historic and judicial capital), La Paz (administrative capital)

Area: 424,162 sq. mi. (1,098,580 sq. km.)

Population (1996 est.): 7,165,257

Languages: Spanish, Quechua, Aymara (all official)

Government: Republic

Religions: Roman Catholic 85% percent–95%, Protestant

Monetary unit: Boliviano

Main exports: Tin and other metals, natural gas, soybeans, timber

Independent from its colonial ruler Spain since 1825, Bolivia lost much of its territory to neighboring nations; its access to the sea was lost in the War of the Pacific (1879–84). In 1903 Bolivia lost its Acre River region, a center of rubber production, to Brazil.

By the early 20th century, the government was dominated by a few wealthy tin-mining families. Many Bolivians were poor, with landlessness among Native Americans increasing as sharecropping agriculture spread. During the Chaco War (1932–35) 50,000 Bolivians lost their lives and Bolivia lost most of the disputed Gran Chaco region to Paraguay, though it did gain access to the River Paraguay and thereby to the Atlantic coast. The war combined with the Great Depression to wreak terrible damage to Bolivia's economy. The military broke into competing factions, as some members sided with the conservative land owners and others with middle-class reformers and intellectuals. In 1941 the National Revolutionary Movement (MNR) was founded by Victor Paz Estenssoro and others. Developing a mass following, it came to power in a revolt in 1943 but was forced to step down in 1946. In the 1952 Bolivian National Revolution, the MNR succeeded in establishing a more long-lasting regime. With Paz Estenssoro as president, the new government established universal suffrage, nationalized mines, and initiated land reform. The military overthrew the government in 1964, inaugurating nearly two decades of military rule.

In 1965 Che Guevara led a Cuban-backed guerrilla movement against Bolivia's military rulers. Aided by U.S. military advisers, Bolivia suppressed the guerrillas and captured and executed Guevara (1967). The military restored civilian control of the government in 1982, with left-leaning Hernán Siles Zuazo sworn in as president.

During Siles's presidency, the country was plagued by high inflation (nearly 3,000 percent) and the lowest per-capita income in South America. The collapse of world tin prices shook the country's economy. In 1985 Paz Estenssoro was reelected president. He implemented free-market policies, including privatization, and brought runaway inflation under control, but poverty remained great. In 1989 Jaime Paz Zamora, leader of the Movement of the Revolutionary Left, was elected president. In 1993 the MNR returned to power, with Gonzalo Sanchez de Lozada as president. He resumed free-market policies, causing distress among workers and prompting protests. In the face of a general strike in 1995, the government declared a state of siege and suspended civil liberties. In 1996 another general strike was held, this time stirring the government to enact some reforms, including raises for government employees. Lozada was driven from power in the 1997 elections by former dictator Hugo Banzer.

About 55 percent of Bolivians are American Indian, most of them either Quechua or Aymara. Another 30 percent are mestizo, and 15 percent are of pure European descent. More than 15 percent of Bolivian workers make their living from the cocaine-exporting industry, a continuing source of international tension.

Bolivia: 20th-Century Leaders

President

1899–1904: José Manuel Pando (c. 1848–1917)

1904–09: Ismael Montes (1861–1933)

1909–13: Eliodoro Villazón

1913–17: Ismael Montes

1917–20: José Gutiérrez Guerra (provisional junta, 1920–21)

1921–25: Bautista Saavedra (1870–1939)

1925–26: Felipe Guzmán (provisional president)

1926–30: Hernando Siles (1881–1942)

1930–31: Carlos Blanco Galindo (provisional president)

1931–34: Daniel Salamanca (1869–1935)

1934–36: José Luis Tejada Sorzano (1881–1938)

1936–37: José David Toro

1937–39: Germán Busch (d. 1939)

1939–40: Carlos Quintanilla (provisional president)

1940–43: Enrique Peñaranda

1943–46: Gualberto Villarroel (1908–46)

1946: Nester Guillen

1946–47: Tomás Monje Gutiérrez (1884–1954)

1947–49: Enrique Herzog

1949–51: Mamerto Urriolagoitia (1894–1974)

1951–52: Hugo Ballivián Rojas

1952– : Hernán Siles Zuazo

1952–56: Victor Paz Estenssoro

1956–60: Hernán Siles Zuazo

1960–64: Victor Paz Estenssoro

1964–65: René Barrientos Ortuña (1919–69)

1965–66: co-presidents: René Barrientos Ortuña; Alfredo Ovando Candía (1918-82)

1966–69: René Barrientos Ortuña

1969: Luis Adolfo Silas Salinas

1969–70: Alfredo Ovando Candía

1970–71: Juan José Torres (1921–76)

1971–78: Hugo Banzer Suárez (1926–)

1978: Juan Pereda Asbún

1978–79: David Padilla Arencibia

1979: Walter Guevara Arze

1979: Alberto Natusch Busch

1979–80: Lidia Gueiler Tejada

1980–81: Luis Garcia Meza Tejada

1981–82: Celso Torrelio Villa

1982: Guido Vildoso Calderón

1982–85: Hernán Siles Zuazo

1985–89: Victor Paz Estenssoro

1989–93: Jaime Paz Zamora

1993–97: Gonzalo Sanchez de Lozada

1997– : Hugo Banzer Suárez

Bosnia and Herzegovina

Official name: Republic of Bosnia and Herzegovina

Location: Southeastern Europe; bordered by Croatia (N, W), Yugoslavia (S, E, SE), Adriatic Sea (SW)

Capital: Sarajevo

Area: 19,776 sq. mi. (51,233 sq. km.)

Population (est. 1996): 2,656,240

Languages: Serbo-Croatian

Government: Emerging democracy

Religions: Muslim 40%, Orthodox 31%, Catholic 15%, Protestant 4%, other 10%

Monetary unit: Dinar

Main exports: Manufactured goods, machinery, raw materials

The two lands of Bosnia in the north and Hercegovina in the south were under Ottoman Turkish rule from the 15th to 19th centuries. Its Slavic people included Orthodox Serbs, Roman Catholic Croatians, and those whose ancestors had converted to Islam, the religion of the Ottomans. In 1878 Bosnia and Hercegovina came under the control of Austria-Hungary. By the early 20th century, it was a hotbed of nationalism. A Serb student from Bosnia, Gavrilo Princip, assassinated Archduke Francis Ferdinand the heir to the Austro-Hungarian throne in 1914, sparking World War I. After the war Bosnia and Hercegovina merged and became part of the independent Kingdom of the Serbs, Croats, and Slovenes (1918), which later became Yugoslavia (1929) and still later became a Communist state (1946). More heterogeneous than Serbia or Croatia, the two strongest components of Yugoslavia, Bosnia and Hercegovina had little influence in state affairs. In 1990 the Communist Party gave up power in Yugoslavia, and elections were held in Bosnia and Hercegovina. Alija Izetbegovic became president of a coalition government between Muslims, Serbs, and Croats.

The coalition soon broke apart over the issue of Bosnian independence. Izetbegovic and his Muslim Party of Democratic Action (PDA) wanted to secede from Serb-controlled Yugoslavia, while Bosnian Serbs wanted to retain ties. In March 1992 Bosnia and Hercegovina seceded. Bosnian Serb leader Radovan Karadzic, founder of the Serbian Democratic Party (SDP), countered by declaring the formation of the breakaway Serb Republic of Bosnia-Hercegovina, with its capital in Banja Luka, a suburb of Sarajevo. Supported by Yugoslavia, the Bosnian Serbs waged war against the Muslim-controlled Bosnian republic. In this Bosnian Civil War (1992–95), Bosnian Serbs took 70 percent of the country and kept Sarajevo under siege. Other countries condemned the Serbs for their policy of "ethnic cleansing": the expulsion, massacre, and rape of Muslims and Croats to drive them from areas considered Serb. A group of Croats also formed a breakaway state, called the Republic of Herzeg-Bosnia. Out of a prewar population of 4.36 million, about

100,000–250,000 people were killed and 200,000 wounded. More than two million refugees were displaced to areas inside and outside the country.

As a result of U.S pressure and UN mediation, the warring sides made peace in the Dayton Agreement (1995), which divided the country into two largely autonomous parts: a Muslim-Croat federation, with 51 percent of the territory, and the Serb Republic, with 49 percent. The reconstructed country depended for stability on 60,000 NATO peacekeeping troops led by the U.S. The UN international war crimes tribunal indicted more than 50 Bosnians, most of them Serbs, for war crimes; those indicted included Karadzic. Arrests began in 1997.

Bosnia's economy virtually collapsed during the war, with inflation rising to more than 1,000 percent and unemployment soaring as high as 75 percent. About 45 percent of industrial plants were damaged or destroyed. In 1990 its imports and exports were each valued at about $2 billion; by 1994 its exports ($32 million) were valued at just 5 percent of its imports ($588 million).

In 1996 Izetbegovic narrowly won reelection as president.

Bosnia and Hercegoviná: 20th-Century Leaders

President

1990– : Alija Izetbegovic (1925–1996, chairman of three-member collective presidency)

Botswana

Official name: Republic of Botswana

Location: Southern Africa; landlocked; bordered by Namibia (N, W), Zimbabwe (NE), South Africa (SE, S)

Capital: Gaborone

Area: 231,803 sq. mi. (600,370 sq. km.)

Population (est. 1996): 1,477,630

Languages: English (official), Setswana

Government: Parliamentary republic

Religions: Christian 50%, indigenous beliefs 50%

Monetary unit: Pula

Main exports: Diamonds, copper, nickel, meat

Occupied by the British in the 1880s, the semiarid region then known as Bechuanaland began the 20th century as a protectorate. It was named for its principal ethnic group, the Tswana. During the century, the protectorate evolved gradually toward self-government, with advisory councils established in 1920 to represent the interests of native and European inhabitants and a constitution framed in 1961 to provide for an elected legislature. South Africa's wishes to incorporate Bechuanaland were rebuffed, in part because of British disapproval of apartheid. In 1963–64, the British government accepted Botswanan proposals for self-rule. Now known as Botswana, the country became independent in 1966; its president was Seretse Khama, founder of the Bechuanaland (later Botswana) Democratic Party (BDP) in 1962.

Since independence, Botswana has been one of the most stable and prosperous democracies in Africa, enjoying genuine multiparty, multiracial rule. Its economy before independence relied largely on cattle-raising, but the discovery of large mineral deposits in the 1960s and 1970s brightened its economic outlook. It is now the world's largest supplier of gem-quality diamonds. Tourism is also an important industry, with visitors drawn by its game reserves; in addition, many Botswanans work in South Africa.

Entirely surrounded by Namibia, South Africa, and Zimbabwe, Botswana is heavily dependent on those countries for trade. During the period when its neighbors were controlled by white regimes, Botswana carefully expressed criticism of racist rule in those lands while retaining economic ties to them. To a limited extent, Botswana provided a sanctuary for South African and Zimbabwean guerrillas.

Droughts in the 1980s raised unemployment and increased the popularity of an opposition party called the Botswana National Front. Even so, the BDP, under Khama and his successor, Quett Ketumile Joni Masire, remained the party of government into the 1990s.

President Masire announced his retirement from his post in 1998. He was succeeded by his vice president, Festus Mogae.

Botswana: 20th-Century Leaders

President

1966–80: Sir Seretse Khama (1921–80)

1980–98: Quett Ketumile Joni Masire

1998– : Festus Mogae

Brazil

Official name: Federative Republic of Brazil

Location: Northeast and central South America; bordered by Colombia, Venezuela, Guyana, Suriname, French Guiana (all N), Atlantic Ocean (E), Uruguay, Argentina, Paraguay (all S), Peru (W), Bolivia (W)

Capital: Brasília

Area: 3,286,475 sq. mi. (8,511,965 sq. km.)

Population (est. 1996): 162,661,214

Languages: Portuguese (official), Spanish, English, French

Government: Federal republic

Religions: Roman Catholic 89%

Monetary unit: Real

Main exports: Iron ore, soybean bran, sugar, coffee, orange juice, footwear

Occupying nearly half the continent of South America, Brazil is the largest Latin American country; its largest city, São Paulo, is the biggest in South America. Most of the country is tropical, including large rain forests in the Amazon River basin. About 55 percent of Brazilians are of European origin, about 45 percent of mixed ethnicity (including European, African, and indigenous stock). Claimed by Portugal in 1500, Brazil grew into a large colony that declared its independence in 1822. At first ruled by an emperor, the new nation became a federal republic in 1889. Under this First Republic (1889–1930), state political elites came to dominate the central government. The state of São Paulo, which produced more than a third of Brazil's total economic output, enjoyed virtual autonomy. Presidents usually came from the states of São Paulo or Minas Gerais and only the literate (about 3 percent of the population before 1930) could vote.

Brazil's government proved ineffectual in dealing with the calamitous effects of the Great Depression that began in 1929. In 1930 the military overthrew the elected president, ending the First Republic. Getúlio Vargas became president (1930–45; 1951–54) and dedicated himself to centralizing political power and reducing states' rights. The state of São Paulo seceded, but Vargas persuaded it to return by restoring constitutional government (1934). In the face of civil unrest from Communists and Fascists (the latter organized as the pro–Nazi Integralists), Vargas declared a state of siege. In 1937, following Portuguese and Italian models of the day, he established the Estado Novo ("New State"), which gave him absolute power over a corporative state. His regime was repressive but, unlike those in Germany and Italy, did not promote a totalitarian ideology. He recruited technocrats to pursue economic modernization and industrialization. Despite his Fascist tendencies, he joined World War II on the Allied side and called for new elections in 1945. He won the 1945 election, but the military overthrew him that year, initiating the Second Republic.

Under the new constitution, guarantees of individual liberties were restored. Brazil's economy enjoyed a boost during and after World War II, but by the 1950s the country was suffering from growing foreign debt, inflation, and a worsening balance of trade. Traditionally dependent on agricultural exports, particularly coffee, the economy slumped whenever the price of its commodities fell. Vargas was reelected in 1950 but soon fell into disfavor, particularly when it was discovered that his guard has been involved in an assassination attempt on an opposition journalist. Facing demands for his resignation, he committed suicide in 1954.

Juscelino Kubitschek, who became president in 1956, tried to step up economic development. He oversaw the building of highways and dams and of a new capital, Brasília, located in central Brazil to encourage development there. Still inflation, debt, corruption, and poverty plagued the country. Kubitschek was succeeded by Jânio da Silva Quadros, who resigned in 1961 after only a few months in office. Vice president João Goulart became president. A populist, he supported the social justice demands of peasants and workers—a position that led the military to oust him in 1964.

The military governed Brazil until 1985. Guerrilla activity and opposition protests were brutally repressed, as death squads carried out torture and murder. Economically, Brazil's situation improved, though the gap between rich and poor remained wide. Under the military rule of the 1960s and 1970s, Brazil underwent rapid industrial growth, transforming itself from a largely agricultural economy to a diversified modern one. Even so, by 1982 Brazil was the world's largest debtor.

President João Baptista da Oliveira Figueiredo (1979–85), who had helped plan the 1964 military coup, oversaw the return to democracy in the mid-1980s. In 1985 Tancredo Neves was elected Brazil's first civilian president in 21 years, but he died before taking office. Instead, José Sarney, the vice presidential candidate, became president. Inflation continued to reach as high as 2,500 percent, but Sarney did succeed in promulgating a new, more democratic constitution in 1988.

In 1990 Fernando Collor de Mello became president. A conservative advocate of free-market policies, he privatized some companies and reduced military expenditures. Still, inflation and foreign debt seemed intractable. Collor strove to stop the destruction of the rain forest in the Amazon River basin. In 1992 Rio de Janeiro was the site of the UN Conference on Environment and Development, known as the "Earth Summit."

Charges of corruption forced Collor to resign in December 1992, though he was later cleared of all charges. He was succeeded by Vice President Itamar Franco, who continued to implement privatization but was hampered by new government corruption scandals, this time involving members of the legislature. Under Franco and his finance minister and successor, Fernando Henrique Cardoso, Brazil's economy improved, though the majority of the population remained malnourished. Cardoso, who became president in 1995, established federal control of state banks and redistributed land to peasants. In 1996 he was widely criticized for his decree allowing non-Native Americans to appeal land allocation decisions by Brazil's Indian Affairs Bureau. Although Cardoso won reelection in 1998, he faced a dramatic economic recession. In September 1998 the Brazilian stock index fell a record 15.8 percent. In January 1999, the real was intentionally devalued in hopes it would ease the recession.

An international cultural center, Brazil has been home to many noted authors, including fiction writer Joaquim Maria Machado de Assis (1839–1908), poet Olavo Bilac (1865–1918), and novelist Jorge Amado (1912–). Novelist and poet Mário de Andrade (1893–1945) was a leader of the Latin American literary movement called *modernismo* (see modernism). Brazilian artists have included painter Cândido Portinari (1903–62); musicians have included composer Heitor Villa-Lobos (1887–1959). Brazilian architect Oscar Niemeyer (1907–) designed the ultramodern public buildings in Brasília. The dance called the samba and the music called bossa nova, both of Brazilian origin, became internationally popular in the 20th century.

Brazil: 20th-Century Leaders

President

1898–1900: Manuel Ferraz de Campos Salles (1846–1913)

1900: Francisco de Assis Rosa e Silva

1900–02: Manuel Ferraz de Campos Salles

1902–06: Francisco de Paula Rodrigues Alves (1848–1919)

1906–09: Alfonso Augusto Moreira Penna (1847–1909)

1909–10: Nilo Peçanha (1867–1924)

1910–14: Hermes Rodrigues da Fonseca (1855–1923)

1914–17: Wenceslão Braz Pereira Gomes

1917: Urbano Santos da Costa Araujo

1917–18: Wencesláo Braz Pereira Gomes

1918–19: Delfim Moreira da Costa Ribeiro

1919–22: Epitácio da Silva Pessôa (1865–1942)

1922–26: Arthur da Silva Bernardes (1875–1955)

1926–30: Washington Luiz Pereira de Souza (1869–1957)

1930: Júlio Prestes de Albuquerque (president-elect; military revolt prevented him from taking office)

1930–45: Getúlio Dornelles Vargas (1883–1954)

1945–46: José Linhares

1946–51: Eurico Gaspar Dutra (1885–74)

1951–54: Getúlio Dornelles Vargas

1954–55: João Café Filho (1899–1970)

1955: Carlos Coimbra da Luz (1894–61)

1955: Nereu de Oliveira Ramos (1889–58)

1956–60: Juscelino Kubitschek de Oliveira (1902–76)

1960: Paschoal Ranieri Mazzilli (1910–75) (acting president)

1960–61: Juscelino Kubitschek de Oliveira

1961: Jânio da Silva Quadros (1917–92)

1961: Paschoal Ranieri Mazzilli (acting president)

1961–64: João Belchior Marques Goulart (1918–76)

1964: Paschoal Ranieri Mazzilli (acting president)

1964–67: Humberto de Alencar Castello Branco (1900–67)

1967–69: Arthur da Costa e Silva (1902–69)

1969–74: Emilio Garrastazú Médici (1905–85)

1974–79: Ernesto Geisel

1979–85: João Baptista da Oliveira Figueiredo

1985–90: José Sarnay

1990–92: Fernando Collor de Mello (1949–)

1992–95: Itamar Franco (1930–) (acting president)

1995– : Fernando Henrique Cardoso (1931–)

Prime Minister (position existed 1961–63)

1961–62: Tancredo de Almeida Neves (1910–85)

1962: Auro Soares de Moura Andrada

1962: Francisco Brochado da Rocha (1910–62)

1962–63: Hermes Lima (1902–)

Britain See United Kingdom.

Brunei

Official name: State of Brunei Darussalam

Location: Southeast Asia, on northwest coast of the island of Borneo, state of Sarawak, Malaysia (S), South China Sea (N)

Capital: Bandar Seri Begawan (formerly Brunei Town)

Area: 2,228 sq. mi. (5,770 sq. km.)

Population (est. 1996): 299,939

Languages: Malay (official), English, Chinese

Government: Constitutional sultanate

Religions: Muslim 63%, Buddhist 14%, Christian 8%

Monetary unit: Bruneian dollar

Main exports: Crude petroleum, liquefied natural gas, manufactured goods

Beginning in the 16th century, the Islamic sultanate of Brunei controlled a large part of northern Borneo, including the modern Malaysian states of Sarawak and Sabah. Over the centuries, Brunei declined into a tiny state that was placed under British protection in 1888. It became a British dependency in 1905. From the late 1920s, the sultanate became very rich from the discovery of oil fields in its territory and offshore waters. Brunei was occupied by Japan during World War II, then returned to British domination. In 1959 Sultan Omar Ali Saifuddin promulgated the first written constitution and regained control over internal affairs, though Britain retained control of defense and foreign policy matters. On January 1, 1984, Brunei became independent.

The country's economy depends on petroleum and international banking and finance. Its sultan is an absolute monarch whose royal palace in the capital is the world's largest. Islam is the state religion. About two-thirds of the population is Malay; minorities include Chinese, Indians, and indigenous peoples such as the Dayaks.

Brunei: 20th-Century Leaders

Sultan

1950–67: Omar Ali Saifuddin (1916–86)

1967– : Sir Hassanal Bolkiah (1946–)

Bulgaria

Official name: Republic of Bulgaria

Location: Southeastern Europe; bordered by Romania (N), Black Sea (E), Turkey (S), Greece (S), Macedonia (W), Yugoslavia (W)

Capital: Sofia

Area: 42,822 sq. mi. (110,910 sq. km.)

Population (est. 1996): 8,612,757

Languages: Bulgarian (official), Turkish

Government: Emerging democracy

Religions: Bulgarian Orthodox 85%, Muslim 13%, Jewish, Catholic, Protestant, Gregorian-Armenian (less than 1% each)

Monetary unit: Lev

Main exports: Agricultural products, metals and ores, chemicals, textiles and apparel, machinery and equipment

Part of the Ottoman Empire since the 14th century, Bulgaria gained autonomy in 1878. In 1908 Prince Ferdinand of Saxe-Coburg-Gotha declared Bulgaria independent and took the title czar (king). With Serbia, Montenegro, and Greece, Bulgaria joined in driving the Ottoman Empire from most of eastern Europe in the First Balkan War (1912–13). Having done much of the fighting, Bulgaria was dissatisfied with its territorial gains and, in the Second Balkan War (1913), turned against its former allies. Bulgaria lost the war and was forced to cede territory to the victors, including Macedonia and southern Dobrudja. Hoping to regain its lost lands, Bulgaria joined the Central Powers (1915) in World War I. Defeated, it was the first Central Power to conclude an armistice (September 29, 1918). In October, Czar Ferdinand abdicated in favor of his son, Boris III. In the peace that followed, Bulgaria was forced to give up most of its territorial gains from the Balkan Wars and World War I. Like the other defeated powers, it was required to reduce its armaments and pay reparations.

The 1920s were a time of political turmoil. Aleksandr Stambolisky (1879–1923), a populist who headed the Agrarian Party and became premier in 1919, created a virtual dictatorship under Boris III. Militant right-wing forces overthrew Stambolisky in 1923 and suppressed the country's left wing.

The Great Depression brought the center-left People's Bloc to power, but it was overthrown in a coup in 1934, after which Czar Boris assumed dictatorial powers (1935). In 1940 Germany won Bulgaria's favor by forcing Romania to restore southern Dobrudja to Bulgaria. Bulgaria joined the Axis Powers in December 1941, occupying parts of Yugoslavia and Greece. Boris died mysteriously in 1943. Simeon II, his underage son, acceded to nominal rule under a regency. In September 1944, the Soviet Union declared war on Bulgaria. As Soviet troops approached, Bulgaria switched sides against Germany. On September 9, a Communist-inspired coup created a new government and brought Bulgaria under Soviet domination.

In 1946 the Bulgarian People's Republic was established, with Georgi Dimitrov as its first premier. It soon put into effect Soviet-style economic policies and political repression. Of all Eastern European countries, Bulgaria was known as the most loyal and obedient to Moscow. Predominantly agricultural into the 1940s, the country was rapidly industrialized, a process that created large-scale environmental pollution. Its economy went into decline in the 1980s, as Bulgaria was internationally reviled for its repression of its Turkish minority and its role in trading illegal drugs and providing a harbor for terrorists.

In 1989 after 35 years in power, General Secretary and President Todor Zhivkov resigned. His successor, Petar Mladenov, put an end to the Communist one-party state, holding free elections in 1990. The Communists, reformed and renamed the Bulgarian Socialist Party, won. Mladenov resigned as president and the leader of the opposition Union of Democratic Forces (UDF) was named to the post.

The 1990s saw rising political instability, along with a still-sick economy and the spread of organized crime. Privatization measures were slow to produce economic improvement. In 1994 the Socialists regained control of the Assembly. After economic, agricultural, and political problems plagued the government, opposition UDF candidate Petar Stoyanov won winter 1996 elections for the presidency. The UDF also won April 1997 parliamentary elections after further economic problems, with Ivan Kostov assuming the post of prime minister.

Bulgaria has produced a significant share of writers and artists. The winner of the 1981 Nobel Prize in literature, Elias Canetti, was born in Bulgaria. Bulgarian-born American artist Christo (Christo Javacheff, 1935–) is known for his technique of wrapping buildings and landscape features.

Bulgaria: 20th-Century Leaders

Prince

1887–1908: Ferdinand of Saxe-Coburg-Gotha (1861–1948)

Czar (king)

1908–18: Ferdinand I (formerly Ferdinand of Saxe-Coburg-Gotha)

1918–43: Boris III (1894–1943)

1943–46: Simeon II (1937–); ruled 1943–44 under the regency of uncle Cyril (1895–1945)

President

1946–47: Vassil Kolarov (1877–1950)

1947–50: Mincho Neitsev (1888–56)

1950–58: Georgi Damianov (1892–58)

1959–64: Dimiter Ganev (1898–64)

1964–71: Georgi Traikov (1898–75)

1971–89: Todor Zhivkov

1989–90: Petar Mladenov (1936–)

1990–97: Zhelyu Zhelev (1935–)

1997– : Petar Stoyanov (1952–)

Premier (since 1944)

1944–46: Kimon Georgiev (1882–1969)

1946–49: Georgi Dimitrov (1882–1949)

1949–50: Vassil Kolarov

1950–56: Vulko Chervenkov (1900–80)

1956–62: Anton Yugov

1962–71: Todor Zhivkov

1971–81: Stanko Todorov

1981–86: Grisha Filipov

1986–90: Georgi Atanasov (1933–)

1990: Andrei Lukanov (1938–)

1990–91: Dimitar Popov (1927–)

1991–92: Filip Dimitrov (1955–)

1992–94: Lyuben Berov (1925–)

1994–97: Jan Videnov

1997– : Ivan Kostov (1949–)

General Secretary, Communist Party

1944–49: Georgi Dimitrov

1949–54: Vulko Chervenkov

1954–89: Todor Zhivkov

1989–90: Petar Mladenov

Burkina Faso

Official name: Burkina Faso

Location: Western Africa; landlocked; bordered by Mali (N, W), Niger (E), Benin, Togo, Ghana, Côte d'Ivoire (all S)

Capital: Ouagadougou

Area: 105,869 sq. mi. (274,200 sq. km.)

Population (est. 1996): 10,623,323

Languages: French (official), tribal languages

Government: Parliamentary democracy

Religions: Muslim 50%, indigenous beliefs 40%, Christian (mainly Roman Catholic) 10%

Monetary unit: Communauté Financière Africaine (CFA) franc

Main exports: Cotton, gold, animal products

Dominated by the Mossi Empire from as early as the 11th century, the region that is now Burkina Faso became a French protectorate in 1896. Known as Upper Volta, for the upper basin of the Volta River, it was integrated into French West Africa in 1919. In 1932 it was divided and parceled out among neighboring colonies. In 1947 it was reconstituted as one territory. In 1958 it became a self-governing state within the French Overseas Community. It won independence as Upper Volta on August 5, 1960.

The new country's politics were unstable, and a 1966 coup resulted in military rule. In 1977 General Lamizana established a new constitution, accepted by plebiscite, and was democratically elected president in 1978. In 1980 his government was overthrown and a military regime was established. In 1983 another coup occurred, this time leading to the foundation of a Libyan-style government. In 1984 the country's name was changed to Burkina Faso. President Thomas Sankara initiated social and economic reforms intended to aid peasants and women. He was killed in a 1987 coup.

Two attempted coups were suppressed in 1989. In 1992 President Blaise Compaoré permitted legislative elections, allowing a new prime minister to come to power. His party, however, was accused of electoral fraud in its parliamentary victory in 1992. As the decade continued, the country struggled to improve its impoverished economy. Mostly agricultural, with few natural resources, the country has a weak balance of trade and relies heavily on foreign loans.

Burkina Faso is known for its film industry. The Burkinabe filmmakers Idrissa Ouedraogo (1952–) and Gaston Kaboré (1951–) are internationally respected.

Burkina Faso/Upper Volta: 20th-Century Leaders

President

1959–66: Maurice Yaméogo

1966–80: Sangoulé Lamizana

1980–82: Sayé Zerbo

1982–83: Jean-Baptiste Ouedraogo

1983–87: Thomas Sankara (1949–)

1987– : Blaise Compaoré (1951–)

Prime Minister (position existed only intermittently)

1958–60: Maurice Yameogo

1971–74: Gérard Kango Ouedraoga (1925–)

1974–78: Sangoulé Lamizana

1978–80: Joseph Conombo

1980–82: Sayé Zerbo

1983: Thomas Sankara

1992–94: Youssouf Ouedraogo

1994–96: Marc-Christian Kaboré

1996– : Kadré Désiré Ouédraogo (1953–)

Burundi

Official name: Republic of Burundi

Location: Central Africa; landlocked; bordered by Rwanda (N), Tanzania (E, S), Zaire (W)

Capital: Bujumbura

Area: 10,745 sq. mi. (27,830 sq. km.)

Population (est. 1996): 5,943,057

Languages: Kirundi and French (both official), Swahili

Government: Republic

Religions: Roman Catholic 62%, indigenous beliefs 32%, Protestant 5%, Muslim 1%

Monetary unit: Burundi franc

Main exports: Coffee, tea, cotton, hides

Like its neighbor Rwanda, Burundi is populated by two principal ethnic groups: the agricultural majority Hutu (85 percent) and the cattle-raising minority Tutsi (14 percent). The latter traditionally held more political power, with a king (mwami) at the top of a feudal hierarchy. In 1899 Burundi, like Rwanda, was incorporated into German East Africa. Belgium occupied the region in 1916, during World War I; Burundi remained in Belgian control when it became part of the League of Nations mandate (1919) and, later, UN trust territory (1946) of Ruanda-Urundi. Under German and Belgian rule, the Tutsi kept their traditional dominance over the Hutu.

On July 1, 1962, Burundi became independent as a constitutional monarchy ruled by the mwami. It soon became enmeshed in political conflict, particularly between the Tutsi and Hutu. An attempted Hutu coup in 1965 failed, and many Hutu were killed in retaliation. In 1966 a coup led by Captain Michel Micombero, a Tutsi, overthrew the monarchy and established a republic. In 1972 a rebellion attempting to restore Mwami Ntare V to power failed, and Ntare was executed. Ten thousand Tutsi and 150,000 Hutu were killed during and soon after the rebellion. The Micombero government was ousted in a 1976 coup, with Jean-Baptiste Bagaza taking power. Bagaza persecuted the Catholic church, which was suspected of sympathizing with the Hutu; he was overthrown in 1987. The new leader, Pierre Buyoya, tried to improve relations with the West, end religious persecution, and bring about ethnic reconciliation. Even so, 1988 massacres drove many Hutus out of the country; most returned by 1989.

In 1993 Buyoya ushered in free presidential elections, in which he lost to Hutu Melchior Ndadaye. That president was quickly assassinated (1993), with Buyoya implicated. Civil war ensued, with the next president also assassinated (1994) and the one following overthrown in a coup (1996), which dissolved parliament and brought Buyoya back to power. The Tutsi remained the more powerful and wealthy of the two ethnic groups. Following peace talks that began in 1999, the warring parties signed a draft peace treaty in 2000.

One of the poorest African countries, Burundi also has one of the highest population densities, with 553 persons per square mile in 1996, compared with 79 persons per square mile in neighboring Tanzania.

Burundi: 20th-Century Leaders

Mwami (King)

1915–66: Mwambutsa IV (1912–77)

1966: Ntare V (1947–72)

President

1966–76: Michel Micombero (1940–83)

1976–87: Jean-Baptiste Bagaza (1946–)

1987–93: Pierre Buyoya (1949–)

1993: Melchior Ndadaye (1953–93)

1994: Cyprien Ntaryamira

1994–96: Sylvestre Ntibantunganya

1996– : Pierre Buyoya

Prime Minister

(position existed intermittently)

1961: Joseph Cimpaye (1932–72)

1961: Louis Rwagasore (1929–61)

1961–63: Andre Muhirwa

1963–64: Pierre Ngendamdumwe (1930–65)

1964–65: Albin Nyamoya

1965: Pierre Ngendamdumwe

1965: Pie Masumbuko (1931–) (acting prime minister)

1965: Joseph Bamina (1925–65)

1965–66: Léopold Biha

1966: Michel Micombero

1972–73: Albin Nyamoya

1976–78: Edouard Nzambimana (1946–)

1988–93: Adrien Sibomana

1993–94: Sylvie Kinigi

1994–95: Anatole Kanyenkiko

1995–96: Antoine Nduwayo

1996– : Pascal–Firmin Ndimira

Cambodia

Official name: Kingdom of Cambodia (Kampuchea)

Location: SE Asia, on Indochina Peninsula; bordered by Thailand (W, N), Laos (NE), Vietnam (E, S), Gulf of Thailand (W)

Capital: Phnom Penh

Area: 69,884 sq. mi. (181,000 sq. km.)

Population (est. 1997): 11,163,861

Languages: Khmer (official), French

Government: Constitutional monarchy

Religions: Theravada Buddhism 95%

Monetary unit: New riel

Main exports: Timber, rubber, rice, soybeans, sesame

Home of the Khmer people, Cambodia was once the heart of the Khmer Empire, which dominated Indochina from the ninth through the 13th centuries. In subsequent years, Vietnam and Thailand vied for control of Cambodia and took parts of its territory. In 1863 Cambodia became a French protectorate; it was incorporated into French Indochina in 1887, with the Cambodian monarchy retained.

In 1941 Norodom Sihanouk was made king. With the Vichy French colonial government, he cooperated with the Japanese occupation during World War II. After the war France remained in control of Cambodia, but pressure by Sihanouk and others led France to grant independence to Cambodia in 1953. In 1955 Sihanouk abdicated in favor of his father, becoming prime minister; he later served as head of state (1960–70, 1975–76, 1991–93). Beginning in the 1950s Sihanouk implemented moderately capitalist policies and repressed political opposition. He tried to remain neutral between the U.S. and Soviet Union, drawing on both for development aid. Cambodia's neutrality was threatened by the Vietnam War (1959–75), as both Vietminh and Vietcong forces used Cambodia as a supply route between North and South Vietnam, and the U.S. launched bombing raids on Cambodian territory. Encouraged by North Vietnam, the Khmer Rouge, a Communist guerrilla organization founded in the 1960s, initiated a rebellion. In 1970 a U.S.-backed coup by prime minister Lon Nol deposed Sihanouk. Lon Nol took the U.S. side in the Vietnam War, allowing ground combat to expand into Cambodia even as he waged the Cambodian Civil War (1970–75) against the Khmer Rouge. In 1975 Lon Nol was forced into exile by the victorious Khmer Rouge forces.

The Khmer Rouge installed Sihanouk as nominal head of state, but power was actually held by Pol Pot, leader of the Khmer Rouge, who established the Democratic Republic of Kampuchea. In 1976 Sihanouk was forced into exile and Pol Pot openly established his hold on power. His agrarian Marxist program, which required the entire population to work in agricultural communes, was carried out through genocide. The middle class was systematically eradicated, city dwellers were forced into rural labor camps, and 2 million –3 million people were killed.

In December 1978 Vietnam invaded, overthrowing Pol Pot in January 1979 and establishing a new government, headed by Heng Samrin. The new government attempted to restore Cambodia's pre-civil-war society and economy (though not the monarchy), but the Khmer Rouge, still powerful in the countryside, waged guerrilla war against it. In 1982 the exiled Sihanouk united the opponents of the Vietnam-backed regime, including the Khmer Rouge, in a coalition government recognized by the UN. In 1989, financially and militarily exhausted, Vietnam withdrew most of its troops from Cambodia; the warring parties signed a peace treaty in 1991. Sihanouk was named president (1991–93); elections for a constituent assembly were held in 1993 but boycotted by the Khmer Rouge. As of 1993 Cambodia again became a constitutional monarchy, with Sihanouk as king (1993–). Political tensions were high between the leading party, the royalist FUNCINPEC, which was headed by Sihanouk's son Norodom Ranariddh as first prime minister, and the Cambodia People's Party, headed by Hun Sen as second prime minister, who had formerly been prime minister in the Vietnam-backed government. In 1997 Hun Sen ousted Ranariddh and took control of Cambodia. The Khmer Rouge continued to oppose the coalition government with guerrilla warfare, though they turned against Pol Pot and imprisoned him a year before his 1998 death. Ranariddh and Sen put their differences aside after 1998 elections to form a coalition governement. The end of the year also saw the last remaining Khmer Rouge troops surrender to the government.

One of the world's poorest nations, Cambodia is still largely agricultural. As of the 1990s, economic production had not recovered from the years of civil war and turmoil, with the economy performing at only 40 percent–50 percent of its prewar capacity.

Cambodia: 20th-Century Leaders

King

1941–55: Norodom Sihanouk

1955–60: Norodom Suramarit (1896–60)

(no king until 1993)

1993– : Norodom Sihanouk

Head of State

1960–70: Norodom Sihanouk

1970–72: Cheng Heng

1972–75: Lon Nol (1913–85)

1975: Saukham Khoy

1975: Saksut Sakhan

1975–76: Norodom Sihanouk

1976–79: Khieu Samphan

1979–91: Heng Samrin (1934–)

1991–93: Norodom Sihanouk

Prime Minister

1952–53: Norodom Sihanouk

1953: Samdech Penn Nouth (1906–85)

1953: Chan Nak

1953–55: Samdech Penn Nouth

1955: Leng Ngeth

1955–56: Norodom Sihanouk

1956: Oum Chheang Sun

1956: Norodom Sihanouk

1956: Khim Tit

1956: Norodom Sihanouk

1956–57: San Yun

1957: Norodom Sihanouk

1957–58: Sim Var (1904–90)

1958: Samdech Penn Nouth

1958: Sim Var

1958–60: Norodom Sihanouk

1960–61: Pho Proeung

1961: Samdech Penn Nouth

1961–62: Norodom Sihanouk

1962: Chau Sen Cocsal Chhum

1962–66: Norodom Kantol

1966–67: Lon Nol

1967: Son Sann

1967–69: Samdech Penn Nouth

1969–72: Lon Nol

1972: Sisovath Sirik Matak (1914–75)

1972: Song Ngoc Thanh (1907–76)

1972–73: Hang Thun Hac

1973: In Tam (1922–75)

1973–75: Long Boret (1933–75)

1975–76: Samdech Penn Nouth

1976–79: Pol Pot

1981: Pen Sovan

1982–84: Chan Sy

1985–93: Hun Sen

1993–97: Norodom Ranariddh, first prime minister; Hun Sen, second prime minister

1997–98: Hun Sen and Ung Huot, co-prime ministers

1998– : Hun Sen

President

1998– : Norodom Ranariddh

Cameroon

Official name: Republic of Cameroon

Location: Western coast of central Africa; bordered by Nigeria (NW), Chad (NE), Central African Republic (E), Republic of the Congo (SE), Gabon, Equatorial Guinea (S), Gulf of Guinea (W)

Capital: Yaoundé

Area: 183,568 sq. mi. (475,440 sq. km.)

Population: 14,677,510 (est. 1997)

Languages: English and French (both official), 24 major African language groups

Government: Republic

Religions: Indigenous beliefs 51%, Christian 33%, Muslim 16%

Monetary unit: Communauté Financière Africaine (CFA) franc

Main exports: Crude oil and petroleum products, lumber, aluminum

Cameroon was a German protectorate from 1884. During World War I, British and French forces occupied Cameroon; afterward, the territory was divided, with the French assigned a League of Nations mandate in the east, the British in the west. In 1946 these became UN trust territories. In French Cameroon, guerrilla warfare in the 1950s hastened the coming of independence, which was granted in 1960. In 1961 a UN-supervised plebiscite was held in British Cameroon: the northern two-thirds elected to become part of Nigeria (independent since 1960), while the southern third united with the Republic of Cameroon. The latter, in 1961, became the Federal Republic of Cameroon, with two prime ministers and legislatures but only one president. At first the country had a multiparty system, but in 1966 all the parties joined to form the Cameroon National Union, which, under different names, has remained the dominant party since.

In 1972 a new constitution abolished the federal structure and created a unitary republic, the United Republic of Cameroon. In 1984 the nation returned to its original name, the Republic of Cameroon.

From independence in 1960 to 1982, Cameroon's president was Ahmadou Ahidjo (1924–89), the son of a Muslim Fulani chief. Reelected every five years, he acquired dictatorial powers and presided over a relatively stable and prosperous regime. Prime minister

Paul Biya replaced him when he retired in mid-term in 1982. During Biya's presidency, Cameroon suffered from economic woes related to falling commodity prices (e.g., oil, cocoa, coffee) and growing foreign debt. Required by the IMF to enact austerity measures as a condition of aid, Biya was met with public protests and demands for political liberalization. In 1992 Biya allowed multiparty elections, in which he was reelected president; some opposition parties boycotted the elections, and the results were disputed. A new constitution won the approval of Cameroon's legislature in 1995. Biya's party won legislative elections in 1997, amid charges of fraud.

Cameroon is a heterogeneous nation with more than 150 ethnic groups, including Cameroon Highlanders (31%), Equatorial Bantu (19%), Kirdi (11%), and Fulani (10%). Although oil is Cameroon's main export, Cameroon's economy is predominantly agricultural. Self-sufficient in food, the country exports cocoa, coffee, timber and rubber.

Cameroon: 20th-Century Leaders

President

1960–82: Ahmadou Ahidjo (1924–89)

1982– : Paul Biya (1933–)

Prime Minister

1960–61: Charles Assalé

1961–68: John Foncha (West Cameroon)

1961–65: Charles Assalé (East Cameroon)

1965: Vincent de Paul Ahanda (1918–75) (East Cameroon)

1965–72: Simon Tchoungi (East Cameroon)

1968–72: Solomon Tandeng Muna (West Camroon)

1975–82: Paul Biya

1982–83: Maigari Bello Bouba

1983–84: Luc Ayang

 (position abolished 1984–91)

1991–92: Sadou Hayatou

1992–96: Simon Achidi Achu

1996– : Peter Mufani Musonge (1942–)

Canada

Location: Northern North America; bordered by Arctic Ocean (N), Greenland (NE, across Baffin Bay), Atlantic Ocean (E), United States (S), Alaska (W)

Capital: Ottawa, Ontario

Area: 3,851,809 sq. mi. (9,976,186 sq. km.)

Population (est. 1997): 30,337,334

Languages: English, French

Government: Confederation with parliamentary democracy

Religions: Roman Catholic 45%, United Church 12%, Anglican 8%

Monetary unit: Canadian dollar

Main exports: Newsprint, wood pulp, timber, petroleum

In area the second-largest country in the world, Canada entered the 20th century as a popular site for immigration following the Klondike Gold Rush (1897-98). Immigrants from Europe and Asia settled largely in the western regions, where Alberta and Saskatchewan became provinces in 1905.

Over the first decades of the century, Canada was widely industrialized through use of its mineral reserves and electric and transportation building projects. Aiming to develop the economy, Liberal Party prime minister Wilfrid Laurier proposed free trade with the U.S.; the proposal was defeated, as was the prime minister, who was replaced in 1911 by Conservative Robert Borden.

During World War I Canada was represented first by volunteer and, after 1917, by conscripted troops. Its status as a dominion, in effect since 1907, gave Canada internal self-government but left foreign and defense policy in British hands. After the war, the Conservative-Liberal coalition leadership was replaced in 1921 by a Liberal government headed by William L. Mackenzie King. During his tenure (most of the period 1921–30) he brought national prosperity and increased commerce with the U.S. In 1931 Canada effectively gained independence through the passage of the Statute of Westminster, which created the Commonwealth of Nations.

Canada's agricultural and industrial sectors were overwhelmed during the worldwide economic depression of the 1930s. The federal government and local government efforts provided only partial assistance, and the economy began to be rebuilt only with Canada's entry into World War II in 1939. Their country strengthened by the war, Canadian voters reelected Mackenzie King as prime minister in 1945.

After the war the Canadian federal government expanded, developing social programs that included pensions, unemployment insurance, and medical care. In an attempt to lessen economic differences among provinces, the government also paid "equalization payments" to some regions.

In 1958 Newfoundland became a province of the Canadian federation. That year the Conservative Party took majority, electing John Diefenbaker prime minister. The Liberal Party regained power in 1963, but soon encountered increased political dissatisfaction and regionalism, particularly in the largely French-speaking province of Quebec. New political parties formed, such as the New Democratic Party (1961), and the Quebecois engaged in separatist terrorism, prompting Liberal Prime Minister Pierre Trudeau to send troops to Quebec in 1970. A 1980 referendum granting a separate "sovereignty-association" position for Quebec was rejected, but constitutional protection for Quebec was promised by Prime Minister Trudeau.

In 1982 the British Parliament passed the Canada Act, which made Canada a fully sovereign state with full constitutional autonomy. The bill, which went into effect on April 17, 1982, amended Canada's constitution, adding a Charter of Rights and Freedoms and recognizing native treaty rights. Quebec rejected the act, though it was legally binding on the federal government and all provinces.

In the 1980s a nationwide recession led to the election of a Conservative majority with Brian Mulroney as prime minister. Among his moves to stimulate economic growth was a free trade agreement with the U.S. in 1988–89.

To address continuing conflict with French-speaking Quebec, national and Quebec leaders created the Meech Lake Agreement in 1987, which granted additional self-governing powers to the provinces. However, antibilingual sentiment led Manitoba and Newfoundland to refuse to ratify the agreement, keeping it from becoming law. A national referendum to grant provinces more power was also defeated. A 1997 separatist referendum lost, but narrowly. In 1998, Canada's highest court ruled that Quebec cannot secede unilaterally.

Facing growing unpopularity, Prime Minister Mulroney resigned in February 1993 and was succeeded by Kim Campbell, who became the first female Canadian prime minister. In October 1993 the ruling Conservatives were defeated and Liberal leader Jean Chrétien became prime minister. He instituted cuts in social programs to reduce the budget deficit. In 1997 Liberals won by a slim majority.

In 1993 Canada became the first nation to ratify the North American Free Trade Agreement between Canada, the U.S., and Mexico. It went into effect on January 1, 1994. In 1998, Canada apologized to its native peoples for a history of mistreatment. This move was followed in 1999 with the establishment of Nunavut ("Our Lord") in the Northwest Territories as an Inuit homeland.

Canada: 20th-Century Leaders

Governor-General (representing the British monarch)

1898–1904: earl of Minto

1904–11: earl of Minto

1911–16: Duke of Connaught

1916–21: Duke of Devonshire

1921–26: baron Byng of Vimy

1926–31: Viscount Willingdon

1931–35: earl of Bessborough

1935–40: baron Tweedsmuir

1940–46: earl of Athlone (1874–1957)

1946–52: Viscount Alexander of Tunis (1891–1969)

1952–59: Vincent Massey (1887–1967)

1959–67: George P. Vanier (1888–1967)

1967–74: D. Roland Michener (1900–91)

1974–79: Jules Léger (1913–80)

1979–84: Edward R. Schreyer (1935–)

1984–90: Jeanne Sauvé

1990–95: Ramon John Hnatyshyn (1934–)

1995–99: Roméo LeBlanc (1927–)

1999– : Adrienne Clarkson (1939–)

Prime Minister

1896–1911: Sir Wilfrid Laurier

1911–17: Sir Robert L. Borden

1917–20: Sir Robert L. Borden

1920–21: Arthur Meighen

1921–26: W. L. Mackenzie King

1926: Arthur Meighen

1926–30: W. L. Mackenzie King

1930–35: Richard B. Bennett

1935–48: W. L. Mackenzie King (1874–1950)

1948–57: Louis S. St. Laurent (1882–1973)

1957–63: John G. Diefenbaker (1895–1979)

1963–68: Lester B. Pearson (1897–1972)

1968–79: Pierre Elliott Trudeau

1979–80: Charles Joseph Clark (1939–)

1980–84: Pierre Elliott Trudeau

1984: John Turner

1984–93: Brian Mulroney (1939–)

1993: Kim Campbell

1993– : Jean Chrétien (1934–)

Cape Verde

Official name: Republic of Cape Verde

Location: Atlantic Ocean; archipelago of 15 islands near northern Africa; neighbors include Senegal (about 300 mi./500 km. E)

Capital: Cidade de Praia

Area: 1,556 sq. mi. (4,030 sq. km.)

Population (est. 1997): 393,943

Languages: Portuguese and Crioulu (blend of Portuguese and West African)

Government: Republic

Religions: Roman Catholic mixed with indigenous beliefs

Monetary unit: Cape Verdean escudo

Main exports: Fish, bananas

Settled by the Portuguese in the 15th century, Cape Verde became a prosperous center for slave trade from Africa during the 16th century. The Portuguese colony was visited by U.S. whalers in the 19th century. U.S. interest in the country grew, and by the early 20th century Cape Verde had a U.S. consulate and was the site of U.S. Navy troop headquarters.

In 1953 Cape Verde became an overseas province and in 1959 it joined with Portuguese Guinea to form the African Party for the Independence of Guinea-Bissau and Cape Verde (PAIGC), which developed into an important social and political force for independence. Following the 1974 revolution in Portugal, the PAIGC helped to build a transitional government in Cape Verde that prefaced the country's independence on July 6, 1975. The PAIGC became the African Party for the Independence of Cape Verde (PAICV) in 1981 after a coup in Guinea-Bissau.

The PAIGC sustained its one-party political system until 1991, when Cape Verde held its first multiparty elections. The Movement for Democracy opposition party elected its first president, António Monteiro, and its first prime minister, Carlos Veiga. They introduced programs to privatize state-owned companies.

Cape Verde: 20th-Century Leaders

President

1975–91: Aristide Pereira (1923–)

1991– : António M. Monteiro (1944–)

Prime Minister

1975–1991: Pedro Pires

1991– : Carlos Alberto de Carvalho Veiga

Central African Republic

Official name: Central African Republic

Location: Central Africa; landlocked; bordered by Chad (N), Sudan (E), Democratic Republic of the Congo, Republic of the Congo (S), Cameroon (W)

Capital: Bangui

Area: 240,533 sq. mi. (622,980 sq. km.)

Population: (est. 1997) 3,342,051

Languages: French (official), Sangho (lingua franca and national language), Arabic, Hunsa, Swahili

Government: Republic

Religions: Protestant 25%, Roman Catholic 25%, indigenous beliefs 24%, Muslim 15%

Monetary unit: Communauté Financière Africaine (CFA) franc

Main exports: Diamonds, timber, cotton, coffee, tobacco

In 1894 France organized this tropical region as the colony of Ubangi-Shari. In 1910 it was incorporated into French Equatorial Africa, along with present-day Chad, the Republic of the Congo, and Gabon. As the Central African Republic, the country received internal self-government in 1958, and independence in 1960. The nation's founder is considered Berthélemy Bogonda (1910–59), the Central African prime minister who was killed in an airplane crash. David Dacko, the republic's first president after independence, was ousted in a 1966 coup led by army head Jean-Bedel Bokassa, who became president. His dictatorial reign was one of brutality and repression. In 1976 Bokassa declared himself emperor and changed the country's name to the Central African Empire. A 1979 coup aided by France, reinstated Dacko as president and restored the name Central African Republic. In 1981 a multiparty political system was instituted, prompting another army coup, this time led by André Kolingba; Dacko was overthrown and all political parties were banned. Opposition parties were made legal in 1991; after abortive elections in 1992, Ange-Félix Patassé was elected president in 1993. A new constitution became effective in 1995. Patassé's efforts to reduce the army's control of political life resulted in civil unrest. France intervened twice in 1996–97 to suppress army mutinies.

The Central African Republic is severely underdeveloped: it has no railroads, little manufacturing, and most of its people are subsistence farmers. The country relies heavily on foreign, especially French, aid.

Central African Republic: 20th-Century Leaders

President

1960–66: David Dacko (1930–)

1966–76: Jean-Bédel Bokassa

(position abolished 1976–79)

1979–81: David Dacko

1981–93: André Kolingba

1993– : Ange-Félix Patassé (1937–)

Emperor

1976–79 Bokassa I (formerly Jean-Bédel Bokassa)

Premier

1966–75: Jean-Bédel Bokassa

1975–76: Elisabeth Domitien

1976–78: Ange-Félix Patassé

1978–79: Henri Maïdou (1936–)

1979–80: Bernard Ayandho (1930–)

1980–81: Jean-Pierre Lebouder (1944–)

1981: Simon Narcisse Bozanga (1942–)

(position abolished 1981–91)

1991–92: Edouard Franck

1992–93: Timothée Malendoma (1935–)

1993: Enoch Lakoue

1993–95: Jean-Luc Mandaba

1995–96: Gabriel Koyambounou

1996–97: Jean-Paul Ngoupande

1997–99: Michel Gbezera-Bria

1999– : Anicet Georges Dologuele

Chad

Official name: Republic of Chad

Location: Central North Africa; landlocked; bordered by Libya (N), Niger, Nigeria, Cameroon (W), Central African Republic (S), Sudan (E)

Capital: N'Djamena

Area: 495,753 sq. mi. (1,284,000 sq. km.)

Population: 7,166,023

Languages: French, Arabic (both official), Sara, Sango, more than 100 other languages

Government: Republic

Religions: Muslim 50%, Christian 25%, indigenous beliefs 25%

Monetary unit: Communauté Financière Africaine (CFA) franc

Main exports: Cotton, cattle

From about 1400 this arid region was a meeting ground for the Muslim peoples of North Africa and the black African cultures of the interior. In the 1890s French troops striking from West Africa invaded Arab-ruled Chad; military conquest followed, and in 1910 it became part of French Equatorial Africa. The colonial authorities neglected it, allowing tensions to grow between the politically dominant Muslim peoples of the north and center and the more populous, non-Muslim ethnic groups of the south. (Chad has more than 200 distinct ethnic groups.) In 1958 Chad became autonomous. Independence was won in 1960, with the south providing the first president, Françoise Tombalbaye. The northern Muslims opposed his corrupt, nationalistic rule; local rebellions grew into a civil war (1966–68). French intervention in 1968 rescued the government temporarily, but Tombalbaye was deposed in a coup in 1975. Civil war resumed, lasting until 1979. Through international mediation, a coalition government headed by former northern rebel Goukouni Oueddai was installed in 1979, but civil war resumed in 1980. Despite the help of Libyan forces, Oueddai's government fell to southern rebel Hissen Habré in 1982. For the next few years French troops backing Habré in the south and Libyan forces backing Oueddai in the north vied for control of the country. Habré won a series of battles and succeeded in recapturing the north in 1987. A Libyan claim to the Aozou Strip on the border with Chad was dismissed by the World Court in 1994.

In 1990 Habré's repressive government was overthrown by General Idriss Déby. Déby partially liberalized the political system, permitting opposition parties but also allowing the army to use violence in support of his regime. In 1996 a new constitution was approved and Déby won election as president. Civil war continued, prompting the U.S. Peace Corps to withdraw in 1998.

Chad's economy is largely agricultural and pastoral, with most Chadians laboring at the subsistence level.

Chad: 20th-Century Leaders

President

1960–75: Françoise Tombalbaye (took name N'Garta Tombalbaye in the 1970s) (1918–75)

1975: Noël Odingar (acting president)

1975–79: Félix Malloum (1932–)

1979: Goukouni Oueddei (1944–)

1979: Lol Mohamed Shawa (1939–)

1979–82: Goukouni Oueddei

1982–90: Hissene Habré (1942–)

1990– : Idriss Déby (1952–)

Prime Minister

1991–92: Jean Alingué Bawoyea

1992–93: Joseph Yodoyman

1993: Fidèle Maungar

1993–95: Delwa Kassiré Coumakoye

1995–97: Koibla Djimasta

1997–99: Nassour Guelengdoussia Quaido

Chile

Official name: Republic of Chile

Location: Western South America; bordered by Peru (N), Bolivia (NE), Argentina (E), Pacific Ocean (W)

Capital: Santiago

Area: 292,259 sq. mi. (756,950 sq. km.)

Population: (est. 1997) 14,508,158

Languages: Spanish

Government: Republic

Religions: Roman Catholic 89%, Protestant 11%

Monetary unit: Chilean peso

Main exports: Copper, fish and fishmeal

Independent from 1818, Chile began the 20th century with strong economic growth as a result of mineral exports, particularly copper and nitrate. The industry profited Chilean elites, even though it was heavily controlled by U.S. and other foreign companies. The Chilean people enjoyed few of the benefits, and social strife increased: the cities mushroomed in population; workers and middle classes demanded political and economic change. Chile's parliamentary-style government was unresponsive to the popular outcry, and many workers turned to syndicalist and anarchist movements. Arturo Alessandri, elected president in 1920, appealed to workers by attempting to legalize trade unions and enact a social welfare program, but he was blocked by the Senate, which represented the conservative elites.

In 1924 the military deposed Alessandri, but he was recalled to office in 1925, at which time he introduced a new constitution, one that provided for universal male suffrage, separated church and state, and increased the power of the presidency. Soon after Alessandri stepped down in 1925, General Carlos Ibáñez took power as a dictator though he kept the title of president (1927–31). Despite Ibánez's use of political repression to maintain power, he was unable to cope with the economic ravages of the Great Depression and was forced to resign in 1931. Alessandri regained the presidency (1932–38), and his liberal economic reforms brought about some degree of recovery, but the condition of the working classes remained abominable and Fascist uprisings plagued the nation. Alessandri declined to run for reelection.

In 1939 the only Popular Front government outside of Europe was elected in Chile, as Radical candidate Pedro Aguirre Cerda became president at the head of a leftist coalition. The Radical Party stayed in power during and after World War II, in which Chile was at first neutral before siding with the Allies (1943). In 1948 Radical president Gabriel González Videla outlawed the Communist Party, his former colleagues in the Popular Front.

With the country buffeted by party divisions and growing inflation, former dictator Ibáñez was reelected president in 1952. Enacting austerity measures as a condition of IMF aid, he failed to make significant economic progress. Jorge Alessandri Rodríguez, Arturo's son, was president from 1958 to 1964: his liberal economic policies reduced inflation, but Chile's trade deficit grew and urban poverty worsened. President Eduardo Frei Montalva (1964–70), a Christian Democrat backed by conservatives, also failed to address the problems of workers and the poor.

In 1970 Salvador Allende became the first Marxist to win a presidential election in Latin America. As president, he nationalized industries, redistributed land, increased wages, and froze prices. Economic crisis and civil unrest followed, and, in 1973 General Augusto Pinochet Ugarte overthrew and killed Allende in a CIA-supported right-wing military coup. As head of a military junta and president of Chile, Pinochet ruled from 1973 to 1990, enforcing his power by imprisoning, killing, and torturing thousands. Many opponents "disappeared" and were presumed dead. His free-market reforms stabilized inflation, reduced foreign debt, and brought about an economic boom, but also widened the gap between rich and poor. The economy took a turn for the worse in 1982, with the gross national product falling 14 percent, a record for the nation. Pinochet's regime was confirmed by plebiscite in 1978 and 1980, but domestic and international pressure grew for him to step down, and a 1988 plebiscite voted against his continued rule. He accepted its verdict, resigning as president in 1990 but remaining commander-in-chief of the army until 1998. In England for surgery, Pinochet was put under house arrest at the request of Spanish prosecutors who wanted to extradite and try him for crimes against humanity. Pinochet declared diplomatic immunity as he was still a member of the Chilean Senate.

Pinochet's successors were Christian Democrats Patricio Aylwin Azócar (1990–94) and Eduardo Frei Ruiz-Tagle (1994–). Under their leadership, the economy improved and civil liberties were restored, though investigation of past human rights violations was hampered by the continued power of the military.

Chilean literature has an international following. Two Chilean poets, Gabriela Mistral (1889–1957) and Pablo Neruda, have won Nobel Prizes for literature.

Chile: 20th-Century Leaders

President

1896–1901: Federico Errázuriz Echaurren (1850–1901)

1901–06: Germán Riesco (1854–1916)

1906–10: Pedro Montt (1848–1910)

1910–15: Ramón Barros Luco (1835–1919)

1915–20: Juan Luis Sanfuentes (1858–1930)

1920–25: Arturo Alessandri Palma (1868–1951)

1925: Luis Altamarino

1925–27: Emiliano Figueroa Larrain

1927–31: Carlos Ibánez del Campo (1877–1960)

1931–32: Juan Estaban Montero (1879–1952)

1932: Carlos Dávila Espinoza

1932–38: Arturo Alessandri Palma

1938–42: Pedro Aguirre Cerda (1879–1946)

1942–46: Juan Antonio Ríos (1888–1946)

1946–52: Gabriel González Videla (1898–1980)

1952–58: Carlos Ibánez del Campo

1958–64: Jorge Alessandri Rodríguez (1896–1986)

1964–70: Eduardo Frei Montalva (1911–82)

1970–73: Salvador Allende (1908–73)

1973–90: Augusto Pinochet Ugarte (1915–)

1990–94: Patricio Aylwin Azócar (1918–)

1994–2000: Eduardo Frei Ruiz-Tagle

China

Official name: People's Republic of China

Location: Eastern Asia; bordered by Russia, Mongolia (N), North Korea (NE), Pacific Ocean (E), India, Nepal, Bhutan, Myanmar, Laos, Vietnam (S), Afghanistan, Pakistan (W), Kazakhstan, Kyrgyzstan, Tajikistan (NW)

Capital: Beijing

Area: 3,705,392 sq. mi. (9,596,960 sq. km.)

Population: 1,221,591,778 (est. 1997)

Languages: Mandarin (official), Yue (Cantonese), Wu, Hakka, Xiang, Gan, Minbei, Minnan, minority languages

Government: Communist state

Religions: Atheism (official), Buddhism, Taoism, Islam 2%–3%, Christianity 1%

Monetary unit: Yuan

Main exports: Garments, textiles, footwear, toys, machinery and equipment, weapon systems

With an area only slightly larger than the U.S. but nearly five times as many people, China is the most populous nation on earth. It has been inhabited by humans since prehistory, and its civilization dates back to 2000 B.C. From 1644 to 1911 it was ruled by the Qing (Manchu) imperial dynasty, which had gone into grave decline by the 19th century. By 1900 China was dominated by foreign powers (most notably Britain, France, Russia, Germany, and Japan), who had carved up its territory into spheres of influence. In 1899 and 1900 the United States negotiated the Open Door Policy, which guaranteed American trading rights in China. A Chinese secret society, with support from the dowager empress Cixi or Tz'u-Hsi (1835–1908), revolted against foreign domination in the Boxer Rebellion (1899–1900). The rebels went so far as to occupy Beijing but were suppressed in 1900 by an international force.

Facing public demands for modernization and liberalization, the Qing government tried, in 1902, to institute limited reforms. It was too late: revolutionary fervor was already growing. In 1905 Sun Yat-sen organized the revolutionary alliance the Tongmenghui, which aimed to establish a republic based on his "Three People's Principles" of nationalism, democracy, and the people's livelihood. In 1911 an army mutiny at Wuchang on October 10 grew into the Chinese Revolution, of which Sun Yat-sen took control. Yuan Shikai, commander of government forces in the north, switched sides and persuaded boy-emperor Pu'-i to abdicate (1912). China became a republic, and Sun, who had been provisional president (1911-12), stepped aside to allow Yuan to become president (1912–16) in return for his help in defeating the emperor.

Yuan's presidency was both dictatorial and ineffective. Following his death in 1916, warlords dominated the provinces, while the central government was weak. Cries for political reform grew heated. On May 4, 1919, students protesting anti-Chinese territorial provisions of the Versailles treaty launched the May Fourth Movement, in which intellectuals and activists resorted to demonstrations and boycotts to urge political renewal and social modernization. Sun revolted, becoming president (1917-25) of a self-proclaimed government that took power in Canton in 1923.

As leader of the Guomindang or Nationalist Party (founded in 1912), Sun cooperated with the Chinese Communist Party (founded in 1921), reorganizing his own party along Bolshevik lines and receiving aid from the Soviet Union. The cooperation between the parties was short-lived. Chiang Kai-shek, who became Guomindang leader and head of its army after Sun's death in 1925, expelled the Communists. In the Northern Expedition (1926–28), Chiang captured Beijing, reunified several provinces, and established a new capital at Nanjing (1928).

With China still not fully unified, the Guomindang vied for power with the Communists. The latter established a state called the Jiangxi Soviet Republic (1931), but it collapsed under attack from the Guomindang in 1934, forcing the Communists to escape in the Long March (1934–35), a 6,000-mile trek from Jiangxi Province to Shaanxi Province.

The seemingly endless civil turmoil put China in danger of attack from an expansionist Japan. Japan occupied the Chinese region of Manchuria in 1931, establishing the puppet state of Manchukuo. In the Sian Incident of 1936 Chiang was kidnapped by his own troops and forced to make a truce with the Communists so they could present a united front against the Japanese.

In 1937, the first year of the Sino-Japanese War (1937–45), Japan captured Beijing, Tientsin, Shanghai, and Nanjing. The Chinese moved their capital to Hankow and then to Chungking, fleeing Japanese expansion that finally stalled in 1939. For the rest of the war, the Guomindang engaged the Japanese in open combat while the Communists fought a guerrilla campaign in the north. After 1941 the war merged with World War II, with the U.S. giving air support to the Chinese.

The alliance between the Guomindang and the Communists ended soon after Japan's defeat in 1945. In the Chinese Civil War (1946–49) the Communists had the edge, having expanded their bases and influence among peasants in the north during the Sino-Japanese War. Despite aid from the U.S., the Guomindang was defeated and forced into exile in Taiwan in 1949. The victorious Communists, led by Chairman Mao Zedong, established the People's Republic of China on October 1, 1949. Though the Communists controlled China's vast mainland, the Taiwan-bound Guomindang established a rival government, the Republic of China (1950), which, until 1971 was the only Chinese government recognized by the UN. Until the early 1970s the U.S.–led West avoided contact with China, which was viewed as a cold war enemy. During the Korean War (1950–53) China became a battlefield enemy, as Chinese troops supporting North Korea clashed with UN forces, including those of the U.S.

With Soviet aid and advice, China's Communist leaders built a one-party state, reconstructing the country's social and economic life after decades of war. Land was redistributed to peasants working in rural cooperatives. Universal public education and health-care were instituted. Dissenters and "class enemies," such as landlords, were tried as criminals; religion was suppressed as the country became officially atheist. A first five-year plan for economic growth was announced in 1953. Though modeled on the Soviet Union, the country was not a carbon copy of that state. Mao adapted Marxism to Chinese conditions, emphasizing the peasantry rather than the urban proletariat.

Government repression abated in 1956–57, when Mao sponsored the Hundred Flowers campaign, in which he encouraged political and intellectual debate. However, the unexpected flood of criticism of the government triggered a new crackdown on dissenters.

In the Great Leap Forward (1958–60), Mao tried to transform the country into a major industrial power, organizing large agricultural communes to free laborers for industry. The program was a fiasco; it did not achieve its goal of instant industrialization and, coupled with natural disasters, it resulted in famines that killed about 20 million people. Blamed for the economic catastrophe, Mao was removed as chairman of the republic (1959); Liu Shao-ch'i took that position, though Mao remained party chairman.

The late 1950s and early 1960s were a period of increasing international conflict for China. Beginning in 1954 China bombarded the Taiwan-held offshore islands of Quemoy, Matsu, and the Tachens. The intervention of the U.S. Navy brought about a cease-fire in 1958, though China officially continued to assert its rights to Taiwan. In 1959 a rebellion in Tibet, which China had annexed in 1950, was brutally suppressed, as Tibet's temporal and spiritual leader, the Dalai Lama, fled to India. China and India disagreed over boundaries, resulting in the Sino-Indian Border War (1962), which China won. By the 1960s the Chinese alliance with the Soviet Union had deteriorated, with the Soviet Union withdrawing its advisers and financial assistance. Relations with the U.S. remained tense as China assisted insurgency movements in Vietnam and Laos. In 1964 China became a nuclear power as it exploded its first atomic bomb.

Domestically, China became more repressive during the Cultural Revolution (1966–69), a violent movement to purge the nation of bourgeois influences. The movement was led by Mao and carried out in large part by unofficial marauding bands of young "Red Guards." Party officials, intellectuals, and artists were among the targets: they were "purified" through imprisonment, execution, and "reeducation." About 500,000 people died in the Cultural Revolution. Liu was ousted from power and Mao was restored to full control of the purged Communist Party.

China's international isolation began to end in 1971, when it was admitted to the UN while Taiwan was expelled. In 1972 U.S. president Richard M. Nixon visited Beijing, further improving relations between China and the West. In 1979 China and the U.S. entered into formal diplomatic relations, with the U.S. rescinding its recognition of Taiwan's government as the legal government of China (while continuing to engage in nominally nongovernmental relations with Taiwan).

In the months prior to and following Mao's death on September 9, 1976, Deng Xiaoping, a moderate, struggled for power with a radical Maoist group known as the Gang of Four, which included Mao's widow, Jian Qing (1914–). The Gang of Four was arrested and convicted of treason. Political power passed to Deng Xiaoping, who held a number of posts and was the paramount Chinese leader of the late 1970s and 1980s.

Beginning with the policy of Four Modernizations (agriculture, industry, science and technology, and defense), announced in 1978, China transformed itself in the post-Mao period. Under Deng's direction, the government encouraged the development of a private sector in both rural and urban areas, promoted foreign investment, and decentralized management. The Chinese economy grew; tolerance for political dissent seemed, at times, to increase. Aside from a brief war with Vietnam in 1979, prompted in part by Vietnam's invasion of Chinese-supported Cambodia, China avoided military adventures.

Hopes for real democratization in China were dashed at Tiananmen Square in June 1989, when government troops violently halted a mass demonstration. Up to 3,000 people were killed and thousands were arrested. The Tiananmen Square massacre prompted international outrage and led the U.S. and other countries to institute economic sanctions. These sanctions were short-lived. By 1991 the U.S. and other Western nations had resumed full engagement with China, with the U.S. routinely renewing China's most-favored-nation trading status despite protest from human rights groups.

China's private-sector economy grew rapidly while political dissent remained stifled. Wages rose, as did income disparities and corruption. Despite a growing industrial sector, agriculture continued to employ about 60 percent of the work force. China enjoyed a foreign policy triumph with the return of Hong Kong from Britain to China (1997), a transfer that erased an old legacy of the country's weakness in the 19th century. Portugal returned Macao to China in 1999.

Following the Tiananmen Square massacre, Jiang Zemin, a protégé of Deng, was elected general secretary as a compromise candidate acceptable to the party's various factions. He also assumed the two other most powerful positions in the country, chairman of the Central Military Commission (1989) and president (1993). Upon Deng's death in 1997, Jiang became China's preeminent leader.

Relations with the U.S. temporarily worsened in 1999 over charges of Chinese nuclear spying in the U.S. and over the accidental NATO bombing of the Chinese embassy in Belgrade, Yugoslavia. But in 2000, ties between the two countries were strengthened when the U.S. Congress approved normalization of trade with China.

Chinese artists and writers of the 20th century have included philosopher Hu Shih, novelist and essayist Lin Yutang, actor Mei Lanfang, composer Xian Xinghai, painters Xu Beihong and Zhang Daqian, and film director Chen Kaige.

China: 20th-Century Leaders

Emperor

1875–1908: Tsai-tien, Kuang-hsü (1871–1908)

1908–12: P'u-i, Hsüang-t'ung (1906–67)

Empress

1898–1908: Tz'u-Hsi (1835–1908)

President

1912: Sun Yat-sen (provisional)

1912–13: Yuan Shikai (provisional)

1913–16: Yuan Shikai

1916–17: Li-Yüan-hung (1864–1928)

1917–18: Feng Kuo-chang

1917–25: Sun Yat-sen (president in Canton)

1918–22: Hsu Shih-chang

1922–23: Li-Yüan-hung

1923–24: Ts'ao K'un (1862–1938) (provisional)

1924–26: Tuan Ch'i-jui (1864–1936)

1928–49: Chiang Kai-shek

People's Republic of China

Chairman, Communist Party

1949–76: Mao Zedong

1976–81: Hua Guofeng

1981–87: Hu Yaobang (1915–89)

1987–89: Zhao Ziyang

1989– : Jiang Zemin (1926–)

Head of State

1949–59: Mao Zedong

1959–68: Liu Shao-ch'i

President

1983–88: Li Xiannian

1988–93: Yang Shungkun

1993– : Jiang Zemin

Paramount Leader

1980–97: Deng Xiaoping

Premier

1949–76: Zhou Enlai

1976–80: Hua Guo Feng

1980–88: Zhao Ziyang

1988–98: Li Peng

1998– : Zhu Rongji (1928 –)

Colombia

Official name: Republic of Colombia

Location: Northwestern South America; bordered by Caribbean Sea (N), Venezuela, Brazil (E), Peru, Ecuador (S), Panama, Pacific Ocean (W)

Capital: Bogotá

Area: 439,734 sq. mi. (1,138,910 sq. km.)

Population: (est. 1997) 37,418,290

Languages: Spanish

Government: Republic

Religions: Roman Catholic 95%

Monetary unit: Colombian peso

Main exports: Petroleum, coffee, coal, bananas, flowers

Colombia gained its independence from Spain in 1819–21 as part of the federation of Gran Colombia. The federation soon broke up, and what is now Colombia became a separate state in 1831 (originally as New Granada; renamed Colombia in 1886).

From 1899 to 1902 Liberal and Conservative elements in Colombia were engaged in a civil war, the War of a Thousand Days, which took 60,000 to 130,000 lives and ended in a Conservative victory. In 1903 Colombia refused to permit the U.S. to build a canal across the Isthmus of Panama, then part of Colombia. As a result, the U.S. instigated and gave military support to a revolt that year establishing Panama's independence.

The economic ravages of the Great Depression prompted voters to oust the Conservatives in the 1930 election, with the Liberals coming to power. (A new civil war was fought that year between followers of the two parties.) The Liberals brought socioeconomic reform and amended the Constitution (1936) to establish workers' right to strike, give government the power to regulate private property, and secularize public education. In 1944 a labor code provided for minimum wage scales and mandatory benefits for workers. Colombia sided with the Allies in World War II.

In the 1946 election Conservatives regained the presidency. In 1948 Liberal Party leader Jorge Eliécer was assassinated, sparking yet another civil war between Liberals and Conservatives. Known as "La Violencia" (1948–57), it killed more than 200,000, as guerrillas fought with Conservative government forces. A 1953 coup led by General Gustavo Rojas Pinilla brought about several years of dictatorship; another coup deposed Rojas Pinilla in 1957. That year, leaders of the two parties agreed, with the support of a plebiscite, to establish a power-sharing coalition known as the National Front. The agreement, which was to last 16 years, provided for regular alternation of the presidency between the parties and gave the parties a monopoly on political competition.

In the 1960s and 1970s the country was beset by guerrilla and paramilitary activity from left and right. The National Front coalition ended in 1974, and although the traditional two parties remained dominant, the political system was now open to other parties,. In the 1974 election the Liberals won control of the government. Leftist guerrillas grew bolder: in 1980 guerrillas held hostages inside the Dominican embassy for 61 days. In 1982 Conservative Belisario Betancur Cuartas was elected president; in 1984 he brought about a truce between government and rebel groups. The truce soon fell apart: in 1985 guerrillas seized the Palace of Justice in Bogotá. In the fighting that followed, 100 were killed, including the president of the supreme court and 10 other justices. By the mid-1990s the government had made peace with many of the guerrilla groups, though some continued their activity.

In the 1980s drug cartels that used murder and intimidation as weapons came to control large areas of Colombia, where narcotics such as coca and cannabis were grown for illegal export to other countries, principally the U.S. Under pressure from the U.S., Betancur tried to crack down on the growing drug trade, to little effect.

In 1989 the Liberal government of Virgilio Barco Vargas launched its own crackdown, arresting more than 10,000 people. In the 1990 election campaign the drug traffickers assassinated several presidential candidates. Liberal César Gaviria Trujillo was elected; with his support, a new constitution took effect (1991) that gave more power to the state in its battle with the drug cartels. Still, the drug trade continued; homicides rose until Colombia became the country with the world's highest murder rate, and government officials were widely viewed as corrupt. In 1996 Liberal president Ernesto Samper Pizano, accused of taking bribes from the drug barons, was indicted for corruption and coverup. Congress dismissed the charges. That same year, the U.S. "decertified" Colombia as a partner in the war on drugs, disqualifying it from most forms of U.S. economic aid.

Prior to 1998 congressional elections, rebel violence intensified, including a devastating attack on an army battalion that killed 62 government soldiers. At run-off elections for president that June, Conservative Andrés Pastrana Arango was declared the victor.

Colombia has faced serious natural disasters in recent decades, including a mudslide in 1985 and an earthquake in 1994. Its economy was relatively strong in the 1980s and 1990s: during the debt crisis of the late 1980s, Colombia was the only Latin American nation to maintain scheduled payments on loans.

Colombian writers of the 20th century include Gabriel García Márquez, who won the 1982 Nobel Prize for literature.

Colombia: 20th-Century Leaders

President

1898–1900: Manuel Antonio Sanclemente

1900–04: José Manuel Marroquín (1827–1908)

1904–08: Rafael Reyes (1850?–1921)

1908: Euclides de Angulo

1908–09: Rafael Reyes

1909: Jorge Holguín (acting)

1909–10: Ramón González Valencia

1910–14: Carlos E. Restrepo (1867–1937)

1914–18: José Vicente Concha

1918–21: Marco Fidel Suárez

1921–22: Jorge Holguín (acting)

1922–26: Pedro Nel Ospina

1926–30: Miguel Abadía Méndez (1867–1947)

1930–34: Enrique Olaya Herrera

1934–38: Alfonso López Pumarejo (1886–1959)

1938–42: Eduardo Santos

1942–45: Alfonso López Pumarejo

1945–46: Alberto Lleras Camargo (1906–90)

1946–50: Mariano Ospina Pérez (1891–1976)

1950–53: Laureano Gómez (1889–1965)

1951–53: Roberto Urdaneta Arbeláez (acting)

1953–57: Gustavo Rojas Pinilla (1900–75)

1957–58: Gabriel Paris (acting)

1958–62: Alberto Lleras Camargo

1960: Dario Echandía (acting)

1962–66: Guillermo-León Valencia (1909–71)

1966–70: Carlos Lleras Restrepo

1970–74: Misael Pastraña Borrero

1974–78: Alfonso López Michelsen

1978–82: Julio César Turbay Ayala

1982–86: Belisario Betancur Cuartas

1986–90: Virgilio Barco Vargas

1990–94: César Gaviria Trujillo

1994–98: Ernesto Samper Pizano

1998– : Andrés Pastrana Arango (1954–)

Comoros

Official name: Federal Islamic Republic of the Comoros

Location: Part of Comoros archipelago on Mozambique Channel, Indian Ocean, between Mozambique (W) and Madagascar (E); includes the islands Njazidja, Nzwami, and Mwali (formerly Grande-Comore, Anjouan, and Mohéli); another island, Mayotte, has voted to remain French territory

Capital: Moroni

Area: 838 sq. mi. (2,170 sq. km.)

Population (est. 1997): 528,893

Languages: Arabic and French (both official), Comoran

Government: Independent republic

Religions: Sunni Muslim 86%, Roman Catholic 14%

Monetary unit: Comoran franc

Main exports: Vanilla, ylang-ylang, cloves, perfume oils

Under French influence from the 1880s, the four islands of Comoros became a colony in

1912 and operated for years as a plantation economy. In 1946 it became a French Overseas Territory and gained political autonomy in 1961. It became an independent republic on July 6, 1975, electing Ahmed Abdallah Abderemane as president. He was overthrown that year and replaced by Ali Soilih, who set up a socialist economy. Abderemane returned to power in 1978 and developed its first constitution. He was assassinated in 1989 by a group of rebels and replaced by the half-brother of Ali Soilih, Mohamed Djohar.

The early 1990s were marked by charges of corruption against Djohar but also moves toward democratization, notably multiple parties and democratic elections. In 1995 Djohar was deposed in a coup and replaced, by 1996, with Mohamed Taki Abdoulkarim. In 1997 a rebel group seeking unification with France staged an insurrection, disrupting government. In November 1998 an interim government took control after Taki died of a heart attack. Before new elections could be held, the government was overthrown by a coup on April 30, 1999. It was the 18th coup the country had seen since independence. Colonel Assoumani Azzali proclaimed himself the new president of Comoros. Azzali declared he would rule only one year before running new elections.

Comoros: 20th-Century Leaders

President

1975: Ahmed Abdallah Abderemane (1919–89, assassinated)

1975: Ali Soilih (1937–78)

1975: Prince Sa'id Muhammad Jaffar (1918–75)

1976–78: Ali Soilih

1978: Said Attourmani

1978–89: Ahmed Abdallah Abderemane

1978: Mohammed Ahmed (1914–84) (co-president)

1989–95: Saïd Mohamed Djohar

1995–96: Caabi el Yachroutou Mohamed

1996–98: Mohammed Taki Abdoulkarim

1998–99: Tadjiddine Ben Saïd Massounde (interim)

1999– : Assumani Azzali (1951–)

Prime Minister

1972–73: Ahmad Abdallah

1975: Prince Sa'id Muhammad Jaffar

1976–78: Abdallah Mohammad

1978–82: Salim Ben Ali

1982–84: Ali Mroudjae

(position ceased to exist 1984–92)

1992: Mohamed Taki Abdoulkarim

1993: Ibrahim Abderamane Halidi

1993: Said Ali Mohamed

1993–94: Ahmed Ben Cheikh Attoumane

1994: Mohamed Abdou Madi

1994–95: Halifa Houmadi

1995–96: Caabi el Yachroutou Mohamed

1996: Tadjidine Ben Said Massounde

1997: Ahmed Abdou

1997–98: Nourdine Bourhane

1998–99: Abbas Djoussouf

1999– : Bianrifi Tarmid

Congo, Democratic Republic of the (formerly Zaire; also known as Congo-Kinshasa or Congo, as distinguished from its neighbor Congo-Brazzaville or Congo Republic)

Official name: Democratic Republic of the Congo

Location: Central Africa; bordered by Congo Republic (W), Central African Republic, Sudan (N), Uganda, Rwanda, Burundi, Tanzania (E), Zambia, Angola (S)

Capital: Kinshasa

Area: 905,564 sq. mi. (2,345,410 sq. km.)

Population: (est. 1996) 46,498,539

Languages: French (official), Bantu dialects, including Swahili, Lingala, Kingwana, and Kikongo

Government: Republic with strong presidency

Religions: Roman Catholic 50%, Protestant 20%, Muslim 10%, Kimbanguist 10%, syncretic sects and traditional beliefs 10%

Monetary unit: Congolese franc

Main exports: Copper, coffee, diamonds, cobalt, petroleum

In 1885 King Leopold of Belgium established the Congo Free State in this equatorial region named for the Congo River. The Congo Free State was not a Belgian colony but the king's personal possession run by a management corporation. Although that regime officially abolished slavery, it continued to practice it, requiring forced labor on rubber plantations and suppressing rebellion ruthlessly. Thousands died, and under international pressure, the Congo Free State was transformed into the colony of the Belgian Congo in 1908.

By the 1920s the Belgian Congo was a leading producer of copper, diamonds, gold, rubber, and other commodities, but most of the wealth from these enterprises went to the Europeans who controlled them. Native peoples did not participate in government except at the lowest levels. By the 1950s movements for independence had formed; the most important of these, the Congolese National Movement, was founded by Patrice Lumumba in 1958. Riots against Belgian rule took place in 1959; Lumumba survived arrest that year to become the first prime minister of the Republic of the Congo when it became independent on June 30, 1960.

With hundreds of ethnic groups and no developed tradition of governing elites, Congo soon fell into a state of near-anarchy known as the Congo Crisis (1960–65). Europeans fled the country, taking with them their technical and economic expertise. The prosperous province of Katanga declared its independence in July 1960, led by governor Moise Tshombe and supported by mercenaries hired by a Belgian mining company. In September President Joseph Kasavubu dismissed Prime Minister Lumumba, who was captured by supporters of Kasavubu and Colonel Joseph Mobutu and transported to Katanga, where he was murdered.

Due to the instability of its former colony, Belgium sent troops to the nation in 1961. The UN called on Belgium to withdraw its forces and sent its own peacekeeping force. The Katangan rebellion ended in 1963, and Tshombe was made prime minister of Congo in 1964, but soon faced another rebellion, this time of leftists who declared a "People's Republic" in Stanleyville. Tshombe suppressed the revolt but was overthrown in a coup led by Mobutu.

Mobutu established an authoritarian, one-party state, installing himself as prime minister (1966) and later president (1967–97). As part of a campaign of "national authenticity," he changed the Congo's name to Zaire (1971), drove away foreign investors, and ordered all Zairians with European names to replace them with African names (1972). The capital, Leopoldville, became Kinshasa, and he became Mobutu Sese Seko. His dictatorship was famously corrupt: Mobutu was believed to have amassed a fortune of $3 billion. Despite the country's great wealth of minerals and other natural resources, Mobutu allowed development to stagnate and the economy to decline. Opposition leaders were arrested or driven into exile.

In 1991 Mobutu agreed to allow multiparty elections, but he fired elected prime minister Étienne Tshisekedi in 1993. Despite international calls to transfer power to Tshisekedi, Mobutu held firm. With a flood of refugees from neighboring Rwanda destabilizing the country from 1994, a rebel army gained strength in eastern Zaire and began to move west. In 1997 rebel leader Laurent Kabila drove Mobutu from office and changed the country's name back to Congo.

New rebel forces began to form when Kabila showed signs of the same authoritarian excesses as his predecessor. Aided by Angola, Namibia and Zimbabwe, Kabila battled with rebels who were in turn aided by Rwanda and Uganda. A cease-fire agreement in 1999 failed to bring complete peace.

Congo is home to an indigenous religion called Kimbanguism, a nationalist, Christian separatist movement founded in 1921 by Simon Kimbangu, who was long imprisoned for sedition.

Democratic Republic of the Congo/Zaire: 20th-Century Leaders

President

1960–65: Joseph Kasavubu (c. 1913–69)

1965–97: Mobutu Sese Seko (1930–97)

1997– : Laurent Kabila

Prime Minister

1960: Patrice Lumumba (1925–61)

1961: Joseph Illeo (later called Ileo Songoamba)

1961–64: Cyrille Adoula (1921–78)

1964–65: Moise Tshombe (1919–69)

1965: Evariste Kimba (1926–66)

1965–66: Mulama Nyunyi Wa Kadima

1966–77: Mobutu Sese Seko

1977–79: Mpinga Kasenga (1937–)

1979–80: Bo-Boliko Lokonga (1934–)

1980–81: Nguza Karl-i-Bond (1938–)

1981–82: N'Singa Udjuu (1934–)

1982–86: Kengo wa Dondo (1935–)

1987–88: Mabi Mulumba

1988: Sambwa Pida Nbagui

1988–90: Kengo wa Dondo

1990–91: Lunda Bululu

1991: Mulumba Lukeji

1991: Etienne Tshisekedi wa Malumba

1991: Bernardin Mungul Diaka

1991–92: Nguza Karl-i-Bond

1992–93: Étienne Tshisekedi wa Malumba

1993–94: Faustin Birindwa

1994–97: Léon Kengo Wa Dondo

1997: Étienne Tshisekedi wa Malumba

1997– : Likulia Bolongo

Congo, Republic of the (also known as Congo; sometimes called Congo-Brazzaville or Congo Republic to distinguish it from its neighbor Congo-Kinshasa or Congo)

Official name: Republic of the Congo

Location: West Central Africa; bordered by Gabon (W), Cameroon (NW), Central African Republic (N), Congo (formerly Zaire) (E, S), Angola (SW), Gulf of Guinea (SW)

Capital: Brazzaville

Area: 132,046 sq. mi. (342,000 sq. km.)

Population: (est. 1997) 2,527,841

Languages: French (official); many African languages, including Lingala and Kikongo

Government: Republic

Religions: Christian 50%, indigenous beliefs 48%, Muslim 2%

Monetary unit: Communauté Financière Africaine (CFA) franc

Main exports: Petroleum, lumber, plywood

In 1883 France established a protectorate over this region's Teke Kingdom, which it renamed Middle Congo. In 1910 Middle Congo was incorporated into French Equatorial Africa, along with the present-day Central African Republic, Chad, and Gabon. After World War II, in which French Equatorial Africa was an important base for the Free French, the colony's inhabitants received political rights and greater autonomy (1946). In 1959 French Equatorial Africa was dissolved and Congo received full autonomy. On August 15, 1960, the Republic of the Congo became independent.

Poor economic conditions led to labor unrest and a 1963 coup that brought Alphonse Massamba-Débat to power. Thus began nearly three decades of coups, attempted coups, and new constitutions, with the country's leaders espousing Marxism but accepting help from the West, particularly France. In 1968 a coup led by Marien Ngouabi disposed Massamba-Débat; the presidency fell first to an interim leader, Alfred Raoul, then to Ngouabi himself, who proclaimed the country the People's Republic of the Congo (1970)." Ngouabi was assassinated in 1977; in 1979 Denis Sassou-Nguesso emerged as leader. In the 1980s he improved ties with the West, reduced state expenditures, and began to respond to calls for a liberalized political system. Marxism was renounced in 1990; in 1991 the name Republic of the Congo was restored and opposition parties were legalized. Pascal Lissouba was elected president in democratic elections in 1992. However, ethnic and regional tensions and personal rivalries continued to threaten stability. In 1997 Lissouba attempted to arrest his rival Sassou-Nguesso, prompting factional fighting in Brazzaville that eventually led to deposing of Lissouba's regime. Sassou-Nguesso became the nation's new president.

Republic of the Congo: 20th-Century Leaders

President

1960–63: Fulbert Youlou (1917–72)

1963–68: Alphonse Massamba-Débat (1963–68)

1968–69: Alfred Raoul (1938–)

1969–77: Marien Ngouabi (1938–77)

1977–79: Joachim Yhombi-Opango (1939–)

1979–92: Denis Sassou-Nguesso (1943–)

1992–97: Pascal Lissouba (1931–)

1997– : Denis Sassou–Nguesso (1943–)

Premier

1963–66: Pascal Lissouba

1966–68: Ambroise Noumazalay (1933–)

1968–69: Alfred Raoul

1969–73: Marien Ngouabi

1973–75: Henri Lopes (1937–)

1975–84: Louis Sylvain Ngoma (1941–)

1984–89: Ange-Edouard Poungui (1942–)

1989–90: Alphonse Poaty-Souchalaty

1990–91: Pierre Moussa

1991: Louis Sylvain Ngoma

1991–92: André Milongo

1992: Stéphane Maurice Bongho-Nouarra

1992–93: Antoine Dacosta

1993–96: Jacques Joachin Yhombi-Opango

1996–97: David Charles Ganao

1997– : Bernard Kolelas

Costa Rica

Official name: Republic of Costa Rica

Location: Central American isthmus; bordered by Nicaragua (N), Caribbean Sea (E), Panama (S), Pacific Ocean (W)

Capital: San José

Area: 19,730 sq. mi. (51,100 sq. km.)

Population (est. 1997): 3,534,174

Languages: Spanish (official), Jamaican dialect of English spoken around Puerto Limón

Government: Democratic republic

Religions: Roman Catholic 95%

Monetary unit: Costa Rican colón

Main exports: Raw materials, consumer goods, capital equipment

Independent from Spain since 1821 and holding democratic elections from 1889, the generally stable Costa Rica became a political dictatorship under the minister of war Federico Tinoco Granados in 1917. Following U.S. and internal protest, democracy was restored in 1918.

During World War II, Costa Rica was the only Central American country to maintain a democratic government. However, in 1948 the democracy was threatened by attempted election fraud, which generated a short civil war. Under leader "Don Pepe" Jose Figueres, democracy was preserved and a new constitution was effected in 1949. Other changes included universal suffrage and the abolishing of the Costa Rican army.

Since 1948 the country has largely been controlled by the social democratic Party of National Liberation (PLN). In the 1980s, during the Nicaragua–El Salvador conflict, it allowed U.S.—backed Contra forces to be stationed in the country. During that time Costa Rican president president Oscar Arias Sánchez developed a peace plan for the conflict, for which he received the 1987 Nobel Peace Prize.

During the 1980s, the conservative United Christian Social Party (PUSC) became a strong national opposition party, electing president Rafael Fournier (1990–94) and stressing economic development. The PLN regained power in 1994, electing José Maria Figueres Olsen, son of "Don Pepe." In 1995, with massive government overspending leading the IMF to withhold financing, the two opposing parties developed a program of long-term deficit reduction and economic growth.

Costa Rica: 20th-Century Leaders

President

1893–1902: Rafael Iglesias

1902–06: Ascensión Esquivel

1096–10: Cleto González Viquez

1910–14: Ricardo Jiménez Oreamuno (1859–1945)

1914–17: Alfredo González Flores

1917–19: Federico Tinoco Granados

1919–20: Francisco Aguilar Barquero (provisional)

1920–24: Julio Acosta

1924–28: Ricardo Jiménez Oreamuno

1928–32: Cleto González Viquez

1932–36: Ricardo Jiménez Oreamuno

1936–40: León Cortés Castro (1882–1946)

1940–44: Rafael Angel Calderón Guardia

1944–48: Teodoro Picado Michalski (1900–60)

1948: Santos León Herrera (1874–1950)

1948–49: José Figueres Ferrer (1906–90)

1949–53: Otilio Ulate Blanco (1892–1973)

1953–58: José Figueres Ferrer

1958–62: Mario Echandi Jiménez (1915–)

1962–66: Francisco J. Orlich Bolmarich (1907–69)

1966–70: José Joaquín Trejos Fernández

1970–74: José Figueres Ferrer

1974–78: Daniel Oduber Quirós

1978–82: Rodrigo Carazo Odio

1982–86: Luis Alberto Monge Alvarez

1986–90: Oscar Arias Sánchez (1941–)

1990–94: Rafael Calderón Fournier (1949–)

1994–98: José María Figueres Olsen

1998– : Miguel Angel Rodríguez Echeverría (1940–)

Côte d'Ivoire (Ivory Coast)

Official name: Republic of Côte d'Ivoire

Location: Western coast of Africa; bordered by Mali and Burkina Faso (N), Ghana (E), Gulf of Guinea (S), Liberia and Guinea (W)

Capital: Yamoussoukro (not recognized by U.S., which recognizes Abidjan)

Area: 124,502 sq. mi. (322,460 sq. km.)

Population: 14,986,218

Languages: French (official)

Government: Republic

Religions: Muslim 60%, indigenous beliefs 25%, Christian 12%

Monetary unit: Communauté Financière Africaine [CFA] franc

Main exports: Cocoa, coffee, tropical woods

Officially a French colony from 1893, Côte d'Ivoire began the 20th century by becoming a territory of French West Africa in 1910.

During World War II, French West Africa was held under Vichy rule. After the war several groups campaigned for independence. A West African group called the African Democratic Assembly joined with the French government and helped bring about such reforms as universal suffrage, and by 1956, self-rule. Côte d'Ivoire joined the French Community in 1958 and gained independence from France on August 4, 1960.

In the country's first elections African Democratic Assembly leader Félix Houphouët-Boigny was elected president. Over his 33 years in office he brought economic expansion through foreign investment and democratic practices including multiparty elections. He and his Democratic Party won the first election by a wide margin. Houphouet-Boigny died in 1993 and was succeeded by like-minded Democrat Henri Konan Bedie, who was reelected in 1995. A military coup overthrew him in 1999.

Côte d'Ivoire: 20th-Century Leaders

President

1960–93: Félix Houphouët-Boigny (1905–93)

1993–99 : Henri Konan Bédié (1934–)

1999– : Robert Guéi (1941–)

Prime Minister

(position existed intermittently)

1959–60: Félix Houphouët-Boigny

1990–93: Alassane Ouaattara (1942–)

1993–2000: Daniel Kablan Duncan (1943–)

Croatia

Official name: Republic of Croatia

Location: Southeastern Europe; bordered by Slovenia (W, N), Hungary (N), Yugoslavia, Bosnia and Herzegovina (E), Adriatic Sea (S)

Capital: Zagreb

Area: 21,824 sq. mi. (56,538 sq. km.)

Population: (est. 1997) 14,986,218

Languages: Croatian (official)

Government: Parliamentary democracy

Religions: Catholic 76.5%, Orthodox 11.1%, Slavic Muslim 1.2%

Monetary unit: Kuna

Main exports: Manufactures, chemicals, machinery, transport equipment

In existence since the 10th century as one of Europe's oldest states, Croatia began the 20th century as part of the Austro-Hungarian Empire. It enjoyed autonomy in local matters, but nonetheless resented Hungary's efforts to "Magyarize" the state, or make its culture more Hungarian.

With the collapse of the Austro-Hungarian Empire during World War I, Croatia became part of the Kingdom of Serbs, Croats, and Slovenes (later Yugoslavia) in 1918. Within that union, Croatians, largely Roman Catholic, were soon faced with unwelcome domination by the Serbs, who were Eastern Orthodox. In response to the repressive rule of Yugoslavian king Alexander I, who assumed dictatorial powers in 1929, Croatian politician Ante Pavelic (1889–1959) formed the Ustase, a paramilitary group fighting for the rights of Croatians. The Ustase, with Macedonian terrorists, arranged Alexander's assassination in 1934.

Croatia won autonomy within Yugoslavia in 1939, but that status was short-lived: Nazi Germany conquered and dismembered Yugoslavia in 1941. The Independent State of

Croatia, a puppet state under Italian and later German military control, was formed. Pavelic, whose Ustase movement collaborated with the Axis conquerors, became the country's Fascist dictator. His regime persecuted Serbs, Jews, and other minorities, killing about 100,000 people. As World War II ended in 1945, Pavelic's government fell and Tito's Communist partisans came to power, taking revenge through their own mass killings of Ustase members and suspected collaborators.

Croatia became part of the reconstituted Yugoslavia, again under Serb dominance, even though the country's leader, Tito, was from Croatia. Croatians protested in favor of greater freedom, prompting a government crackdown in 1971. Tito's death in 1980 increased Croatian demands for autonomy or secession, as did the election of a non-Communist president of Croatia, Franjo Tudjman, in 1990. Under Tudjman's leadership, Croatia seceded from Yugoslavia in June 1991. A civil war ensued against Croatian Serb militia forces, who, with military support from Yugoslavia, seized about a third of Croatia's territory. By 1995 Croatia had taken back most of this land, and 1996 saw the establishment of peaceful diplomatic relations between Yugoslavia and Croatia. President Tudjman won reelection in 1997, though many criticized his authoritarian rule. The country struggled to rebuild its economy, which had been devastated by the civil war. Tudjman died in 1999.

Croatia: 20th-Century Leaders

King

1941–43: Aimone of Spoleto

Dictator

1941–44: Ante Pavelic (1889–1959)

President

1990–99: Franjo Tudjman (1922–99)

Premier

1991–92: Franjo Greguric

1992–93: Hrvoje Sarinic

1993–95: Nikica Valentic

1995–2000: Zlatko Matesa (1949–)

Cuba

Official name: Republic of Cuba

Location: Island in Caribbean Sea; neighbors include Bahamas and U.S. (N), Mexico (W), Jamaica (S), Haiti (E)

Capital: Havana

Area: 42,803 sq. mi. (110,860 sq. km.)

Population (est. 1997): 10,999,041

Languages: Spanish (official)

Government: Communist state

Religions: Nonreligious 50%, Roman Catholic 33%, Protestant 1%

Monetary unit: Cuban peso

Main exports: Sugar, nickel, shellfish, tobacco

A Spanish possession since 1492, Cuba, the largest island in the West Indies, won its independence from Spain with U.S. military help in the Spanish-American War (1898). U.S. troops occupied Cuba until 1902. Afterward, Cuba was nominally a republic but virtually an American protectorate under the terms of the Platt Amendment. This 1901 legislation, named for U.S. senator Oliver Platt and not repealed until 1934, restricted Cuba's foreign policy, permitted U.S. naval bases on the island (including one still in operation, at Guantánamo Bay), and gave the U.S. the right to intervene militarily. The U.S. exercised that right to quell uprisings in 1906, 1912, and 1917. Even as popular discontent with the corrupt conservative government increased, U.S. business increased its investments and took control of Cuba's economy, dominating most industries, including sugar production.

President Gerardo Machado, who came to office in 1925, acquired dictatorial powers but was overthrown in an army-supported popular uprising in 1933. His successor, Carlos Manuel de Céspedes y Quesada, was overthrown later that year in an army revolt led by Fulgencio Batista y Zaldívar. Batista autocratically dominated Cuban politics until 1959, either as president (1940–44, 1952–59) or through puppet regimes. He ruled openly as a dictator from 1952. Though supported by Cuba's wealthy elite, his repressive and corrupt regime increasingly alienated the middle class as well as the poor.

On July 26, 1953, Fidel Castro launched his first revolutionary attack at the Moncada army base in Santiago. The attack failed, but in 1956 Castro returned from exile to begin a more successful campaign. In the Cuban Revolution (1956–59), Castro and his forces, who were known as the 26th of July Movement, waged guerrilla warfare against the Batista regime. In the early hours of January 1, 1959, Batista fled the country. A few days later, Castro took power.

Castro quickly moved to nationalize banks and businesses, mostly without compensating their owners. By 1961 the U.S. had cut off diplomatic relations and Castro had declared himself a Marxist-Leninist. Castro's socialist doctrines had great appeal for Cuba's rural poor, guaranteeing them access to medical care and education and improving their standard of living. But the wealthy and middle class fled by the thousands, most of them to the U.S., while critics of Castro were imprisoned or executed.

The U.S. viewed Castro's socialist government as an arm of its principal cold war enemy, the Soviet Union. The U.S. therefore backed an attempted invasion by Cuban exiles at the Bay of Pigs, Cuba, on April 17, 1961, but the attack failed. In October 1962 the Soviet Union's construction of nuclear missile sites in Cuba prompted U.S. president John F. Kennedy to order a naval blockade of the island leading to what was known as the Cuban Missile Crisis. The crisis was ended when Soviet premier Khrushchev agreed to dismantle the sites rather than commence a global thermonuclear war.

In the face of a U.S. economic embargo, Cuba became dependent on the Soviet Union and Eastern bloc countries for trade and assistance. With Soviet encouragement, Cuba financed and supported left-wing revolution in other countries, including Angola and Nicaragua. Cuban exiles continued to come to the U.S., notably in the controversial Mariel boatlift of

1980, when the 125,000 refugees included a small percentage of criminals and mentally ill patients.

Since the fall of its benefactor, the Soviet Union, in 1991, Cuba has struggled economically and permitted some private enterprise while remaining generally Communist. In 1996 Castro's government launched a crackdown on dissidents and shot down two private planes operating out of the U.S. The U.S. responded by tightening its economic embargo, adding penalties for foreigners investing in Cuba. Although committed to Communism, Castro gained favorable publicity when he permitted Pope John Paul II to visit Cuba in 1998. The U.S. eased restrictions on contact with Cuba in 1999, but relations between the two countries were tested in 2000 over custody of Elián González, a Cuban boy whose mother died in a shipwreck while trying to bring him to the U.S. The boy was returned to live with his father in Cuba, over the protests of his Miami relatives.

Cuba: 20th-Century Leaders

President

1902–06: Tomás Estrada Palma (1835–1908)

(occupied by U.S. 1906–09)

1909–13: José Miguel Gómez (1858–1921)

1913–21: Mario Garciá Menocal (1866–1941)

1921–25: Alfredo Zayas y Alfonso (1861–1934)

1925–33: Gerardo Machado y Morales (1871–1939)

1933: Carlos Manuel de Céspedes y Quesada (1871–1939) (provisional)

1933–34: Ramón Grau San Martín (1882–1969) (provisional)

1934–35: Carlos Mendieta (1873–1960)

1935–36: José A. Barnet y Vinageras

1936: Miguel Mariano Gómez y Arias

1936–40: Federico Laredo Bru (1875–1946)

1940–44: Fulgencio Batista y Zaldívar

1944–48: Ramón Grau San Martín

1948–52: Carlos Prío Socarrás (1903–77)

1952–59: Fulgencio Batista y Zaldívar

1959: Manuel Urrutía Lleo (1901–81) (provisional)

1959–76: Osvaldo Dórticos Torrado (1919–83)

1976– : Fidel Castro Ruz

Prime Minister

1959: José Miró Cardona (1902–74)

1959–76: Fidel Castro Ruz

(position abolished 1976)

Cyprus

Official name: Republic of Cyprus

Location: Island in eastern Mediterranean Sea; neighbors include Turkey (N), Syria (E)

Capital: Nicosia

Area: 3,571 sq. mi. (9,250 sq. km.)

Population (est. 1997): 752,808

Languages: Greek, Turkish (both official), English

Government: Republic

Religions: Greek Orthodox 78%, Muslim 18%

Monetary unit: Cypriot pound

Main exports: Citrus, potatoes, grapes, textiles

Inhabited for at least 10,000 years, the island of Cyprus was an Ottoman Turkish possession from the 16th to 19th centuries. In 1878 it came under British administration; Britain annexed Cyprus in 1914 and made it a colony in 1925. It was strategically important as a military base during World War II and the Suez Crisis (1956). From 1945 to 1948, it was a detention area for Jews immigrating illegally to Palestine.

In the 1950s in the context of post–World War II decolonization, Cypriots agitated for an end to British rule. The island's overwhelmingly Greek population, led by Archbishop Makarios III, head of the Cypriot Orthodox Church, favored union (enosis) with Greece, an option that the Turkish minority opposed. Under pressure from various groups, including the terrorist National Organization of Cypriot Fighters (EOKA), Britain granted independence to Cyprus in 1960. Britain retained sovereignty over two military bases, and Cyprus agreed not to unite with Greece or be partitioned. Cyprus entered the Commonwealth of Nations in 1961.

Communal fighting soon broke out between Cypriots of Greek and Turkish descent, prompting the UN to send a peacekeeping force in 1964. On July 15, 1974, a military coup by officers favoring enosis, a coup backed by Greece, deposed Makarios's government. Turkey responded by invading and occupying the northern 40 percent of Cyprus, ostensibly to protect the rights of ethnic Turks on the island. In 1975 Turkey announced a de facto partition of Cyprus, with the northern sector becoming the Turkish Federated State of Cyprus. Neither it nor its successor, the Turkish Republic of Northern Cyprus (so named in 1983), has been internationally recognized. About 200,000 Greek Cypriots were forced to move from the Turkish sector to the Greek, while many Turkish Cypriots fled in the opposite direction.

In the 1990s as Cyprus sought to enter the European Union, there was some movement toward uniting the two Cypriot republics in a federation.

Cyprus: 20th-Century Leaders

President

1960–74: Archbishop Makarios III (1913–77)

1974: Nikos Sampson (1935–)

1974: Glafkos Clerides

1974–77: Archbishop Makarios III

1977–88: Spyros Kyprianou (1932–)

1988–93: George Vassiliou (1931–)

1993– : Glafkos Clerides (1919–)

Turkish Republic of Northern Cyprus: 20th-Century Leaders (Only Turkey has recognized this country)

President

1983– : Rauf Dentkash(1924–)

Czech Republic

Location: Central Europe; bordered by Poland (N), Slovakia (E), Austria (S), Germany (W)

Capital: Prague

Area: 30,387 sq. mi. (78,703 sq. km.)

Population (est. 1997): 10,298,324

Languages: Czech (official), Slovak

Government: Parliamentary democracy

Religions: Atheist 39.8%, Roman Catholic 39.2%, Protestant 4.6%

Monetary unit: Koruna

Main exports: Machinery and equipment, manufactured goods, chemicals

Part of the Austrian empire and under Hapsburg rule from the early 17th century, Czechoslovakia gained independence only after the collapse of the Austrian-Hungarian Empire during World War I. The Czech lands and Slovakia were linked in the country of Czechoslovakia on November 14, 1918. The first president was Tomás Masaryk, who headed the revolutionary Czechoslovak National Council.

From March 1939 through World War II, Czechoslovakia was occupied by Germany. Its president and prime minister were forced into exile until April 1945. At the end of the war, Czech boundaries returned to their pre-1938 status.

Beginning in 1946 the Communist Party dominated Czech elections, and in 1948 it gained control of the government. After 42 years of existence as a Soviet state, Communist rule ended in 1989 with the election of Václav Havel as president. Promising democratic reform and economic development, he became a popular leader and was reelected in 1993.

The early 1990s were marked by the growth of a Slovakian independence movement. It culminated in the dissolution of the Czechoslovakian federation and the creation of two separate countries, the Czech Republic and Slovakia, on January 1, 1993. Economic instability plagued the nation in the mid-1990s. In 1999, the Czech Republic became a full member of NATO.

Czech Republic: 20th-Century Leaders

President

1918–1935: Tomás Garrigue Masaryk (1850–1937)

1935–38: Eduard Benes (1884–1948)

1938: Jan Syrovy (1885–)

1938–39: Emil Hácha (1872–1945)

1939: Annexed by Germany

1940–48: Eduard Benes (1940–45 in London)

1948–53: Klement Gottwald (1896–1953)

1953–57: Antonín Zápotocky (1884–1957)

1957–68: Antonín Novotny (1904–75)

1968–75: Ludvók Svoboda (1895–1979)

1975–89: Gustáv Husák (1913–91)

1989–92: Václav Havel (1936–)

1993– : Václev Havel

Prime Minister

1918–19: Karel Kramár (1860–1937)

1919–20: Vlasimil Tusar (1880–1924)

1920–21: Jan Cerny (1874–1959)

1921–22: Eduard Benes

1922–26: Andonín Svehla (1873–1933)

1926: Jan Cerny

1926–29: Antonín Svehla

1929–32: Frantisek Udrzal (1866–1938)

1932–35: Jan Malypetr (1873–1947)

1935–38: Milan Hodza (1878–1944)

1938: Jan Syrovy

1938–39: Rudolf Beran (1887–1954)

1940–45: Jan Srámek (1870–1956, in exile)

1945–46: Zdenek Fierlinger (1891–1976)

1946–48: Klement Gottwald

1948–53: Antonín Zápotocky

1953–63: Viliam Siroky (1902–71)

1963–68: Jozef Lenárt

1968–70: Oldrich Cerník

1970–88: Lubomír Strougal

1988–89: Ladislav Adamec

1989–92: Marián Calfa (1946–)

1992–93: Jan Strasky

1993–98: Václev Klaus

1998– : Milos Zeman (1944–)

Denmark

Official name: Kingdom of Denmark

Location: Northern Europe; bordered by Skagerrak Channel (N), Germany (S), Baltic Sea (E), North Sea (W)

Capital: Copenhagen

Area: 16,629 sq. mi. (43,070 sq. km.)

Population (est. 1997): 5,305,048

Languages: Danish, Faeroese, Greenlandic (an Inuit dialect), German (in a small minority)

Government: Constitutional monarchy

Religions: Evangelical Lutheran 91%, Protestant and Roman Catholic 7%, other

Monetary unit: Danish krone

Main exports: Meat and meat products, dairy products, transport equipment, fish

Although parts of Denmark may have been settled as early as c. 10,000 B.C., a history of this smallest of Scandinavian countries begins in the ninth century with Danish participation in the Viking raids of western Europe. Longstanding Danish territories include the Faeroe Islands in the North Atlantic (from 1383) and Greenland (from 1917). During the 19th century Denmark was transformed from a poor farming country to a wealthy agricultural power. Denmark began the 20th century with some instability following the the loss of duchies Schleswig and Holstein in a 1864 war with Prussia and Austria, and increasing national political conflict.

During World War I Denmark maintained neutrality. During World War II it was occupied by German troops from 1940 to 1945, when it was liberated by British forces. Although the occupation was sanctioned by Danish king Christian X, Danish resistance groups fought the Nazi presence throughout the war. In 1944 Iceland ended a centuries-old tie to Denmark and declared its independence.

After the war Denmark quickly rebuilt its economy and restored international ties, joining the United Nations in 1945 and NATO in 1949. In 1972 31-year-old Margrethe II took the throne, the first woman to head the Danish monarchy since the middle ages.

From 1982 and throughout the decade Denmark was led by Prime Minister Poul Schlüter of the Conservative Party. Dominant national concerns in the 1980s and 1990s included economic reform and international relations, notably NATO and European unification. Following allegations of misinformation to the government about Tamil refugees, Schlüter resigned, and a coalition led by the Social Democratic Party gained power in 1993 elections.

In a 1992 referendum Denmark voted against the Maastrict Treaty, which would have strengthened European affiliation and centralized economic and defense administration. After the EU granted concessions to Denmark, it approved the treaty in 1993. In 2000, Denmark voted not to join the euro currency zone.

Denmark: 20th-Century Leaders

King or Queen

1863–1906: Christian IX (1818–1906)

1906–12: Frederick VIII (1843–1912)

1912–47: Christian X (1870–1947)

1947–72: Frederick IX (1899–1972)

1972– : Margrethe II (1940–)

Prime Minister

1897–1900: Hugo Egmont Horring (1842–1909)

1900–01: Hannibal Sehested (1842–1924)

1901–05: Johan Henrik Deuntzer (1845–1918)

1905–08: Jens Christian Christensen (1856–1930)

1908–09: Niels T. Neergaard (1854–1936)

1909: Johan Ludvig Holstein (1839–1912)

1909–10: Carl Theodor Zahle (1866–1946)

1910–13: Klaus Berntsen (1844–1927)

1913–20: Carl Theodor Zahle

1920: C. J. Otto Liebe (1860–1929)

1920: Michael Petersen Friis (1857–1944)

1920–24: Niels T. Neergaard

1924–26: Thorvald A. M. Stauning (1873–1942)

1925–29: Thomas Madsen-Mygdal (1876–1943)

1929–42: Thorvald A. M. Stauning

1942: Vilhelm Buhl (1881–1954)

1942–45: Erik Scavenius (1877–1962)

1945:Vilhelm Buhl

1945–47: Knud Kristensen (1880–1962)

1947–50: Hans Hedtoft (1903–55)

1950–53: Erik Eriksen (1902–72)

1953–55: Hans Hedtoft

1955–60: Hans Christian Hansen (1906–60)

1960–62:Viggo Kampmann (1910–76)

1962–68: Jens Otto Krag (1914–78)

1968–71: Hilmar Baunsgaard (1920–89)

1971–72: Jens Otto Krag

1972–73: Anker Jórgensen (1922–)

1973–75: Poul Hartling

1975–82: Anker Jórgensen

1982–93: Poul Schlüter (1929–)

1993– : Poul Nyrup Rasmussen (1943–)

Djibouti

Official name: Republic of Djibouti

Location: Northeastern Africa; bordered by Red Sea (N), Gulf of Aden (E), Somalia (SE), Ethiopia (S, W, NW)

Capital: Djibouti

Area: 8,494 sq. mi. (22,000 sq. km.)

Population (est. 1997): 434,116

Languages: French and Arabic (both official)

Government: Republic

Religions: Muslim 94%, Christian 6%

Monetary unit: Djiboutian franc

Main exports: Hides and skins, transit of coffee

This small region (also known as Jibouti), located at the mouth of the Red Sea on the Horn of Africa, was under French control from 1859; it became French Somaliland, a protectorate, in the 1880s. Up to and particularly after the opening of the Suez Canal in 1869, it attracted the competing interests of Britain and France, both of which sought it for its strategic location. The colony entered the 20th century even more prized, with a new French-built railroad from Addis Ababa to Djibouti.

When Ethiopia was invaded by Italian forces in the 1930s, the colony was a focus of battles fought between French and Italian forces. During World War II it was first allied with the Vichy government. In 1942 it joined the Free French forces.

After the war in 1958 a referendum made the colony a French Overseas Territory. In 1967 it rejected unification with Somalia and took the name Territory of the Afars and Issas, for its primary ethnic groups. In the 1970s a growing nationalist movement led to the passage of another referendum calling for the colony's independence. As the Republic of Djibouti, it became independent on June 27, 1977, electing as its first president Hassan Gouled Aptidon (of the Issas). In 1981 he established a one-party state for his own Popular Union for Progress Party. Growing ethnic tensions led to a new constitution in 1992 and the formation of a multiparty democracy. In 1999 Aptidon announced he was stepping down as president due to his advanced age. Ismail Omar Guelleh, an associate of Aptidon, won the presidency in April 1999 elections. After the election, five landmines were set off in the north of the country by the Front for Union and Democracy, which supported Guelleh's opponent. The mines killed fifteen.

Despite its independence, Djibouti ended the century highly dependent on foreign aid.

Djibouti: 20th-Century Leaders

President

1977–99: Hassan Gouled Aptidon

1999– : Ismail Omar Guelleh (1947–)

Prime Minister

1977: Ahmed Dini Ahmed (1932–)

1978: Abdallah Mohamed Kamil (1936–)

1978– : Barkat Gourad Hamadou (1930–)

Dominica

Official name: Commonwealth of Dominica

Location: Eastern Caribbean Sea; neighbors include Guadeloupe (N), Martinique (S)

Capital: Roseau

Area: 290 sq. mi. (750 sq. km.)

Population (est. 1997): 66,633

Languages: English (official), French patois

Government: Parliamentary democracy

Religions: Roman Catholic 77%, Protestant 15%

Monetary unit: East Caribbean dollar

Main exports: Bananas, soap, bay oil

Inhabited by the Carib Indians from the 14th century, Dominica was explored by

Columbus in 1493 and settled by French missionaries during the 17th century. From the 18th century both France and England claimed control of the island, with England making it a sovereign state in 1805.

The 20th century for Dominica was marked by several moves toward independence. In 1951 it was granted universal suffrage. In 1967 it became a self-governing member of the West Indies Federation free association with Great Britain. Dominica became an independent republic within the Commonwealth on November 3, 1978.

In a landslide victory in 1980 Mary Eugenia Charles of the Freedom Party was elected prime minister. The Caribbean's first female prime minister, she enacted an economic reconstruction program after Hurricane David in 1979. Her conservative policies gradually lost favor, leading to victory in the 1995 elections by the opposition United Workers Party. Edison James was named prime minister.

Dominica: 20th-Century Leaders

President

1978: Sir Louis Cools-Lartique (1905–93)

1978–79: Frederick Degazon

1979: Sir Louis Cools-Lartique

1979–80: Jenner Armour

1980–83: Aurelius Marie

1983–93: Sir Clarence Augustus Seignoret

1993– : Sir Crispin Anselm Sorhaindo

1998– : Vernon Lorden Shaw (1930–)

Prime Minister

1974–79: Patrick Roland John (1937–)

1979–80: J. Oliver Seraphine (1943–)

1980–95: Mary Eugenia Charles (1919–)

1995– 2000: Edison C. James

Dominican Republic

Location: Eastern Hispaniola; bordered by north Atlantic Ocean (N), Mona Passage (E), Caribbean Sea (S), Haiti (W)

Capital: Santo Domingo

Area: 18,815 sq. mi. (48,730 sq. km.)

Population (est. 1997): 7,868,731

Languages: Spanish

Government: Republic

Religions: Roman Catholic 95%

Monetary unit: Dominican peso

Main exports: Ferronickel, sugar, gold, coffee

The Dominican Republic occupies the eastern two-thirds of the Caribbean island of Hispaniola; Haiti occupies the western third. Founded as a Spanish colony in the 15th century, the Dominican Republic has been independent since 1844, except for a brief period of Spanish rule in the 1860s. Perennially unstable and corrupt, the Dominican Republic was occupied by U.S. marines from 1916 to 1924. American investments grew during that period, with most sugar-growing land coming under American control. Not long after the departure of the marines, U.S.–trained Dominican military officer Rafael Trujillo established a dictatorship that he maintained for 31 years, from 1930 to 1961. Though not always president, Trujillo controlled whoever was president.

During his rule, Trujillo gained control of the army, police, and large portions of the labor force. He developed an industrial base and repaid national debts, while also amassing a personal fortune. His despotic practices included the killing of thousands of Haitians in the 1930s and the granting of exile to Latin American dictators.

By 1960 Trujillo's power (and U.S. support) had eroded. His rule ended with his assassination in 1961. Attempts to build a democracy followed, until broken by a coup against President Juan Bosch and an ensuing civil war. To reestablish order, the U.S. installed troops (1965–66); in 1966, U.S.–supported former Trujillo associate Joaquín Balaguer was elected president.

Balaguer's corrupt but economically effective rule ended in 1978, with the election of Antonio Guzmán, whose rule weakened the economy. In 1986 Balaguer was reelected and remained in office despite fraud charges until 1996. Balaguer was not involved in 1996 elections, which brought into office centrist-left Liberation Party candidate Leonel Fernández. The leftist candidate, Hipólito Mejía, was elected president in 2000.

Dominican Republic: 20th-Century Leaders

President

1899–1901: Horacio Vasquez

1901–03: Juan Isidro Jiménez

1903–04: Alejandro Woss y Gil

1904–05: Carlos Morales Lauguasco

1905–11: Ramón Cáceres

1911–12: Alfredo Victoria

1912–13: Adolfo A. Nouel

1913–14: José Bordas Valdés

1914–15: Ramón Báez

1915–16: Juan Isidro Jiménez

1916: Francisco Henríquez y Carvajal

(U.S. military government 1916–24)

1924–30: Horacio Vasquez

1930–38: Rafael Leonidas Trujillo (1891–1961)

1938–40: Jacinto Peynado

1940–42: Manuel de Jesus Troncoso

1942–52: Rafael Leonidas Trujillo

1952–60: Hector B. Trujillo

1960–2: Joaquín Balaguer

1962: Huberto Bogaert

1962–63: Rafael F. Bonnelly (1904–79)

1963: Juan Bosch

1963: Emilio de los Santos

1963–65: Donald Reid Cabral

1965: Jose Rafael Molina Urena

1965: Pedro Bartolome Benoit

1965: Antonio Imbert Berreras

1965–66: Héctor García Godoy

1966–78: Joaquín Balaguer

1978–82: Antonio Guzmán Fernández (1911–82)

1982: Jacobo Majluta Azar (1934–) (acting president)

1982–86: Salvador Jorge Blanco (1926–)

1986–96: Joaquín Balaguer

1996–2000: Leonel Fernández Reyna

Ecuador

Official name: Republic of Ecuador

Location: Northwestern South America; bordered by Colombia (N), Peru (E, S), Pacific Ocean (W)

Capital: Quito

Area: 109,483 sq. mi. (283,560 sq. km.)

Population (est. 1997): 12,105,124

Languages: Spanish (official), Quechua and other Native American languages

Government: Republic

Religions: Roman Catholic 95%

Monetary unit: Sucre

Main exports: Petroleum, bananas, shrimp

Independent from Spain since 1822, Ecuador was part of the Confederation of Gran Colombia until 1830, when it became a separate state. The major political rivals were the Conservatives, who supported the privileged elites and the Roman Catholic Church, and the Liberals, who sought social reform. From the Revolution of 1895 the Radical Liberal Party held power until 1944: it disestablished the Catholic Church; introduced freedom of religion, speech, and the press; and improved sanitation and public health.

Politically unstable since its birth, Ecuador in the 20th century suffered numerous coups, attempted coups, dictatorships, and periods of rule by military junta. In 1911 Eloy Alfaro, who had instituted many liberal reforms in his two terms as president, led a failed revolt, was imprisoned, and later was murdered by a lynch mob. José María Velasco Ibarra, a charismatic leader with strong appeal to voters, was made president five times but completed only one of his terms (1952–56), being overthrown by the army on the other four occasions (1934–35, 1944–47, 1960–61, 1968–72). A military attack by Peru in 1941 resulted in a loss of almost 40 percent of Ecuador's territory; the border dispute was revived, with new fighting, in 1950, 1960, 1981, and 1995. In 1998 the congresses of Peru and Ecuador agreed to accept international arbitration of the dispute. Popular resentment over loss of territory to Peru in 1941 contributed to the revolution that overthrew President Carlos Alberto Arroyo del Río (1940–44).

Ecuador's economy traditionally relied on agricultural exports: cocoa in the early part of the century, bananas from the 1950s. But in the 1960s large oil deposits were discovered, and by the 1970s Ecuador was Latin America's second-largest oil producer. Despite attempts at social reform by various administrations, the resulting economic boom did little to relieve the condition of Ecuador's many poor citizens, particularly the Indians. Political conditions remained unstable. A military junta ruled Ecuador from 1963 to 1966; the military briefly permitted elected government (1966–72) before again assuming direct control of the country (1972–79).

In 1979 the military at last allowed a stable form of democracy to come into being. Under a constitution enacted that year, Ecuador had a relatively peaceful succession of elected presidents. There were some disturbances: an attempted coup was foiled in 1986; austerity measures introduced by Conservative president Sixto Durán Ballén in 1994 led to mass protests; and Durán's vice president Alberto Dahik Garzoni resigned his post and fled arrest on charges of embezzlement. In 1997 Congress deposed President Abdala Bucaram, an eccentric and controversial leader, for "mental incapacity," replacing him with the leader of Congress, Fabian Alarcón, as interim president. Vice president Rosalía Arteaga protested, arguing from the constitution that the presidency should pass to her. Jamil Mahuad won presidential elections in 1998, but his tenure was also marked by turmoil as he grappled with ongoing economic crisis. In 2000, he was forced out of office and replaced by his vice president, Gustavo Novoa Bejarano.

Taking its name from the equator that runs through it, Ecuador is home to the highest peaks of the Andes and owns the Galápagos Islands, noted for their scientific value.

Ecuador: 20th-Century Leaders

President

1897–1901: Eloy Alfaro (1864–1912)

1901–05: Leonidas Plaza Gutiérrez

1905–06: Lizardo García

1907–11: Eloy Alfaro

1911: Emilio Estrada

1912–16: Leonidas Plaza Gutiérrez

1916–20: Alfredo Baquerizo Moreno (1859–1951)

1920–24: José Luis Tamayo

1924–25: Gonzalo S. Córdoba

(provisional junta, 1925–26)

1926–31: Isidro Ayora

1931: Luis A. Larrea Alba (provisional)

1931–32: Alfredo Baquerizo Moreno

1932: Alberto Guerrero Martínez (provisional)

1932–33: Juan de Dios Martínez Mera

1933–34: Abelardo Montalvo (provisional)

1934–35: José María Velasco Ibarra (1893–1979)

1935: Antonio Pons (provisional)

1935–37: Federico Páez

1937–38: G. Alberto Enríquez

1938: Manuel María Borrero

1938–39: Aurelio Mosquera Narvaez

1940: Andrés F. Cordova

1940–44: Carlos Alberto Arroyo del Río

1944–47: José María Velasco Ibarra

1947: Carlos Mancheno Cajas

1947: Mariano Suárez Vientimilla (acting)

1947–48: Carlos Julio Arosemena Tola (1894–1952)

1948–52: Galo Plaza Lasso (1906–87)

1952–56: José María Velasco Ibarra

1956–60: Camilo Ponce Enríquez (1912–76)

1960–61: José María Velasco Ibarra

1961–63: Carlos Julio Arosemena Monroy

1963–66: Ramón Castro Jijón

1966: Clemente Yerovi Indaburu

1966–68: Otto Arosemana Gómez (1925–84)

1968–72: José María Velasco Ibarra

1972–76: Guillermo Rodriguez Lara

1976–79: Alfredo Poveda Burbano (1926–90)

1979–81: Jaime Roldos Aguilera (1940–81)

1981–84: Oswaldo Hurtado Larrea (1940–)

1984–88: León Febres Cordero Rivadeneira (1931–)

1988–92: Rodrigo Borja Cevallos (1935–)

1992–96: Sixto Durán Ballén (1922–)

1996–97: Abdala Bucaram Ortiz

1997–98: Fabian Alarcón (1947–)

1998–2000: Jamil Mahuad Witt

Egypt

Official name: Arab Republic of Egypt

Location: Northeastern Africa and southwestern Asia; bordered by Mediterranean Sea (N), Israel (NE), Red Sea (E), Sudan (S), Libya (W)

Capital: Cairo

Area: 386,660 sq. mi. (1,001,450 sq. km.)

Population (est. 1997): 64,824,466

Languages: Arabic (official), English, French

Government: Republic

Religions: Muslim (mostly Sunni) 94%, Coptic Christian and other 6%

Monetary unit: Egyptian pound

Main exports: Crude and refined petroleum, cotton yarn, raw cotton, textiles

Egyptian civilization dates to 5000 B.C., but from the fourth century B.C. to the early 20th century A.D., Egypt was ruled by a series of conquerors: the Persians, Greeks, Romans, Byzantines, Arabs, and Ottoman Turks. In 1882 de facto rule of Egypt passed to the British, though the country was still nominally a part of the Ottoman Empire. In 1914 when the

Ottoman Empire joined the Central Powers in World War I, Britain declared Egypt a British protectorate and deposed the khedive, Abbas II.

After the war the nationalist Wafd Party, led by Zaghlul Pasha (c. 1850–1927), agitated for Egyptian independence and for social and economic reform. Egypt became a League of Nations mandate in 1922 and a constitutional monarchy in 1923. Though Egypt enjoyed internal autonomy, Britain maintained military forces there. The Anglo-Egyptian Treaty of 1936 officially ended British occupation of Egypt, but Britain still kept troops along the Suez Canal, was permitted to expand its forces in wartime, and refused to give up control of the Anglo-Egyptian Sudan (which did not become independent of both countries until 1956). Egypt's internal political life from the 1920s to the 1940s focused mainly on a struggle for power between the Wafd Party and the monarchy, represented by King Fu'ad I (1922–36) and King Farouk (1936–52).

During World War II British troops used Egypt as a base for their North African campaign. Their growing numbers fueled renewed nationalist sentiment in the postwar era against Britain and Farouk, who was regarded as weak and corrupt. Egypt's weakness was made vivid by the First Arab–Israeli War (1948), in which Egypt and other Arab countries failed in their attempt to resist the creation of Israel.

On July 23, 1952, the Free Officers, a secret army organization led by Gamal Abdel Nasser, overthrew Farouk. The monarchy was officially abolished the following year, with Egypt becoming a republic under the presidency of General Mohammed Naguib. In 1954 Nasser forced him out and became president, an office he retained until his death. Following a course he called Arab socialism, Nasser nationalized businesses, enacted land reform and social programs, promoted industrialization, built public works such as the Aswan Dam (completed 1968), and outlawed political opposition. In the Suez Crisis (1956) he nationalized the Suez Canal, prompting military intervention from Britain, France, and Israel until the UN upheld Egypt's claim. Though he accepted support from the Soviet Union, he was a co-founder of the non aligned movement, in which Third World countries sought to stay independent of Western and Eastern blocs.

In 1958 Egypt merged with Syria to form the United Arab Republic (UAR), with Nasser as president; Syria seceded in 1961, but Egypt retained the name UAR until 1971. Nasser tried to position Egypt as the leader of the Arab world, but the country's prestige was hurt in 1967 when Israel defeated Egypt and its allies in the Six-Day War. As a result of that war, Egypt lost the Sinai Peninsula to Israel and the Suez Canal was closed until 1975.

Nasser's successor, Anwar el-Sadat, rescinded many of Nasser's policies: he expelled Soviet advisers; improved relations with the U.S. and such conservative Arab states as Saudi Arabia, introduced free-market reforms, and invited foreign investment. He restored the confidence of Egyptians in their country's military prowess with the Yom Kippur War (1973), which Israel won only after heavy losses. Sadat took the dramatic step of opening peace negotiations with Israel. The resulting Camp David Accords (1978) led to a peace treaty with Israel (1979) and eventual restoration of the Sinai peninsula to Egypt. Sadat's peacemaking efforts earned the enmity of other Arab leaders, who suspended Egypt from the Arab League. Sadat was assassinated by Muslim fundamentalists in 1981.

Hosni Mubarak, Sadat's successor, largely continued his policies, maintaining peace with Israel while gradually restoring diplomatic contacts with the Arab world. In 1989 Egypt was readmitted to the Arab League. Under Mubarak, Egypt has struggled under heavy foreign debt and high population growth, while Muslim fundamentalists have resorted to bombings and assassinations to challenge the secular government's authority. Egypt sent troops to fight Iraq in the Persian Gulf War (1991), an act that was unpopular domestically but helped persuade the U.S. to forgive $7 billion in Egyptian debt. Mubarak was wounded by the knife of an attempted assassin in 1999.

Egypt is noted for its film industry and for its intellectual and literary culture. Egyptian writer Naguib Mahfouz won the 1988 Nobel Prize for Literature and was stabbed by Islamic fundamentalists in 1994.

Egypt: 20th-Century Leaders

King

1922–36: Fu'ad I

1936–52: Farouk I

1952–53: Fu'ad II (1952–)

President

1953–54: Mohammed Naguib (1901–84)

1954–70: Gamal Abdel Nasser

1970–81: Anwar el-Sadat

1981– : Hosni Mubarak

Prime Minister

(since institution of republic in 1953)

1952–54: Mohammed Naguib

1954: Gamal Abdel Nasser

1954: Mohammed Naguib

1954–62: Gamal Abdel Nasser

1962–65: Ali Sabry (1920–91)

1965–66: Zakaria Mohieddin

1966–67: Mohammad Sidky Soliman

1967–70: Gamal Abdel Nasser

1970–72: Mahmoud Fawzi (1900–81)

1972–73: Aziz Sidky

1973–74: Anwar el-Sadat

1974–75: Abdul Aziz Hegazy

1975–78: Mamdouh Salem (1918–88)

1978–80: Mustafa Khalil

1980–81: Anwar el-Sadat

1981–82: Hosni Mubarak

1982–84: Ahmad Fuad Mohieddin

1984–85: Kamal Hassan Ali

1985–86: Ali Lutfi

1986–97: Atef Sedki

1997–99: Kamal Ganzouri

1999– : Atef Obeid (1932–)

El Salvador

Official name: Republic of El Salvador

Location: Central America; bordered by Honduras (N, E), Pacific Ocean (S), Guatemala (W)

Capital: San Salvador

Area: 8,124 sq. mi. (21,040 sq. km.)

Population (est. 1997): 5,661,827

Languages: Spanish, Nahua

Government: Republic

Religions: Roman Catholic 97%

Monetary unit: Salvadoran colón

Main exports: Coffee, sugarcane, shrimp

Independent from Spain since 1821, El Salvador is the smallest and most densely populated (697 persons per square mile) Central American country. By the early 20th century its economy was largely based on coffee cultivation, with a few landowning families controlling most of the nation's wealth and political power. Widespread poverty made for chronic political turmoil. A peasants' uprising in 1931–32 was suppressed by the military. General Maximiliano Hernández Martínez, who was sympathetic to Fascism, took power in a coup in 1931 and ruled as dictator until 1944. Decades of civil unrest followed, punctuated by coups and junta rule. By the 1960s Salvadorans were immigrating heavily to Honduras; the resulting tensions exploded in a brief military conflict between the two countries known as the Soccer War (1969).

The political situation grew worse in the 1970s, with both left-wing and right-wing forces resorting increasingly to violence. In 1979 the military overthrew President Carlos Humberto Romero. In 1980 Archbishop Oscar Arnulfo Romero, an advocate for the country's poor, was assassinated by government agents. Responding to this and other acts of violence by government and pro-government paramilitary forces, several left-wing guerrilla groups merged to form the Farabundo Martí National Liberation Front (FMLN). Full-scale civil war (1980–92) broke out between the guerrillas and the government.

The U.S. withdrew military aid from El Salvador as a result of the 1980 rape and murder of four American churchwomen in El Salvador by government troops. The following year the U.S. resumed aid to El Salvador, fearing that the nation would become a Communist satellite of the Soviet Union if the rebels were successful. The U.S. poured money, arms, and advisers into El Salvador, despite evidence from international human rights groups that government forces and pro-government paramilitary groups called "death squads" were guilty of systematic murder and torture.

President José Napoleón Duarte's government introduced an agrarian reform program in 1980, but it was short-lived. Elections in 1982 were won by the rightist National Republican Alliance (ARENA) coalition. Its leader, Roberto D'Aubuisson, had ties to the death squads, and pressure from the U.S. prevented him from coming to power as president. After a new constitution went into effect in 1983, Duarte regained the presidency while the civil war dragged on. Salvadorans fled the country in droves, many entering the U.S. illegally.

In 1989 ARENA candidate Alfredo Cristiani became president. A major FMLN offensive was launched and repelled that year, but its temporary success demonstrated the continuing power of the rebels. Cristiani negotiated a peace treaty (1992) with the FMLN, ending the civil war, which had cost the lives of some 75,000 Salvadorans. The treaty called for disarmament on both sides, a general amnesty, the creation of a new police force, and a "truth" commission to investigate human rights violations. That commission has since determined that 85 percent of all human rights violations during the war could be attributed to government forces and the death squads.

The FMLN became a legitimate political party, and made a strong showing in the 1994 and 1997 elections, although the president elected in 1994, Armando Calderón Sol, was an ARENA candidate. As the decade ended, poverty remained high in El Salvador and crime was rampant.

El Salvador: 20th-Century Leaders

President

1899–1903: Tomás Regalado

1903–07: Pedro José Escalón

1907–11: Fernando Figueroa

1911–13: Manuel Enrique Araújo

1913–14: Carlos Meléndez (acting)

1914–15: Alfonso Quiñónez Molina (1873–1950) (provisional)

1915–19: Carlos Meléndez

1919–23: Jorge Meléndez

1923–27: Alfonso Quiñónez Molina

1927–31: Pio Romero Bosque

1931: Arturo Araújo

1931–34: Maximiliano Hernández Martínez

1934–35: Andrés Ignacio Menéndez (acting)

1935–44: Maximiliano Hernández Martínez

1944: Andrés Ignacio Menéndez (acting)

1944–45: Osmin Aguirre Salinas (1889–1977)

1945–48: Salvador Castañeda Castro (1888–1965)

1948–49: Manuel de Jesús Córdova

1949: Oscar Osorio

1949–50: Oscar Bolanos

1950–56: Oscar Osorio

1956–60: José María Lemus

1960–61: Miguel Castillo

1961–62: Aníbas Portillo

1962: Eusebio Rodolfo Cordon Cea (provisional)

1962–67: Julio Adalberto Rivera (1922–73)

1967–72: Fidel Sánchez Fernández

1972–77: Arturo Armando Molina Barraza

1977–79: Carlos Humberto Romero Mena

1979–80: Adolfo Majano Ramos, Jaime Abdul Gutierrez (copresidents)

1980–82: José Napoleón Duarte (1926–90)

1982–84: Alvaro Alfredo Magaña Borjo

1984–89: José Napoleón Duarte

1989–94: Alfredo Cristiani

1994–99: Armando Calderón Sol

1999– : Francisco Flores Perez (1959–)

Equatorial Guinea

Official name: Republic of Equatorial Guinea

Location: Bioko and other islands off West African coast, and Río Muni, mainland territory; bordered by Gabon (E, S), Cameroon (E, N), Gulf of Guinea (W)

Capital: Malabo

Area: 10,830 sq. mi. (28,050 sq. km.)

Population (est. 1997): 442,516

Languages: Spanish (official), pidgin English, Fang, Bubi

Government: Republic

Religions: Predominantly Roman Catholic, indigenous practices

Monetary unit: Communauté Financière Africaine (CFA) franc

Main exports: Coffee, cocoa beans, timber

Equatorial Guinea consists of Río Muni, the Mbini River basin on the West African coast, and five inhabited islands: Bioko (formerly Fernando Po); Pagalu (Annobón); Corisco; Elobey Grande; and Elobey Chico. About 75 precent of the population live in Río Muni, where the main ethnic group is the Fang; Bioko is largely populated by the Bubi. The country was a Portuguese colony from the 15th to 18th centuries, and Spanish from the 18th to 20th centuries. In the early 20th century Spain made efforts to develop the hitherto neglected colony, then known as Spanish Guinea. A plantation system, using workers from Nigeria, was put in place for the cultivation of cocoa and timber, chiefly in Bioko and Río Muni. In 1959 the colony was reorganized into two overseas Spanish provinces, each with its own governor. Nationalists opposed these steps toward assimilation, striving instead for independence. Local autonomy was granted in 1963 and independence in 1968.

Equatorial Guinea's first president, Francisco Macías Nguema, a Fang from Río Muni, declared a one-party state in 1970 and made himself president for life in 1972. His dictatorial regime brutally suppressed real or suspected opposition, outlawed the Roman Catholic Church, and drove 120,000 people into exile. With foreign investors fleeing and foreign workers forced to leave, the economy was gutted.

In 1979 Colonel Teodoro Obiang Nguema Mbasogo overthrew and executed his uncle Macías Nguema. Obiang lifted restrictions on the Roman Catholic Church, restored broken diplomatic ties, encouraged return of refugees and foreign investment, and freed political prisoners. But he continued the tradition of autocratic rule. A new constitution in 1991 called for multiparty democracy, but parliamentary elections in 1993 were boycotted by the opposition, which considered the system rigged in favor of the ruling party. Obiang's party won that election and Obiang won the presidential election of 1996.

The country received good economic news with the discovery of substantial oil reserves in the 1990s.

Equatorial Guinea: 20th-Century Leaders

President

1968–79: Francisco Macías Nguema (1924–79)

1979– : Teodoro Obiang Nguema Mbasogo (1942–)

Premier

(following adoption of 1982 constitution)

1982–92: Cristino Seriche Bioko

1992–96: Silvestre Siale Bileka

1996– : Angel Serafin Seriche Dougan (1946–)

Eritrea

Official name: State of Eritrea

Location: Horn of Africa (central-eastern Africa), bordered by Sudan (N, W), Red Sea (E), Djibouti and Ethiopia (S)

Capital: Asmara

Area: 46,842 sq. mi. (121,320 sq. km.)

Population (est.1997): 3,589,687

Languages: Tigrinya, Tigre, Kunama, other tribal languages

Government: Transitional

Religions: Muslim, Coptic Christian, Roman Catholic, Protestant

Monetary unit: Birr

Main exports: Livestock, sorghum, textiles

Occupied by Italy from 1889, Eritrea entered the 20th century a colony and base for Italian attacks on Ethiopia (1895–96, 1935–36). In 1941 during World War II, Eritrea came under British military control; in 1952 it was put under UN administration. That year the UN made it part of the Ethiopian empire. Ethiopia soon broke with UN aims for Eritrean freedom, fueling the Eritrean independence movement led by the Eritrean People's Liberation Front (EPLF). Ethiopian leader Mengistu Haile Marriam held off the Eritrean insurgency, but after he fell in 1991 the new government made peace with the rebels. In May 1993 Ethiopia adopted a transitional constitution; on May 27, 1993, Eritrea gained independence from Ethiopia. In 1995 the two countries set up a free-trade area. That year Eritrea also entered a dispute with Yemen over control of the Greater Hanish Island, which required UN mediation. Economic tension between Ethiopia and Eritrea helped lead to war in May 1998 over a border dispute. Fighting waged on and off into the summer of 1999–2000, when a cease-fire agreement was signed.

Eritrea: 20th-Century Leaders

President

1993– : Isaias Afwerki (1946–)

Estonia

Official name: Republic of Estonia

Location: Northeastern Europe; bordered by Gulf of Finland (N, NE), Russian Federation (SE), Latvia (SW), Baltic Sea (NW)

Capital: Talinn

Area: 17,413 sq. mi. (45,100 sq. km.)

Population (est. 1997): 1,436,558

Languages: Estonian (official), Latvian, Lithuanian, Russian

Government: Republic

Religions: Lutheran, Orthodox Christian

Monetary unit: Estonian kroon

Main exports: Textiles, food products, vehicles, metals

For much of the past millennium, Estonia was dominated by powerful countries of the age. During the 13th century it was overtaken and made serfs by the Teutonic Knights of Germany. In 1526 Sweden took power, ruling until the 18th century, when Estonia became a province of the Russian Empire.

After a War of Independence (1918–20) Estonia became an independent republic. Its independence lasted from 1918 to 1940, when it became a republic of the U.S.S.R. During much of World War II, from 1941 to 1944, it was occupied by Germany. In 1944 it became a Soviet republic.

In 1990 the Estonian congress removed the words "Soviet Socialist" from the country's name, reclaimed its 1918 coat of arms, and considered itself autonomous.

Following the failed Soviet coup to remove President Mikhail Gorbachev, Estonia declared independence from the Soviet Union on August 20, 1991. It joined the United Nations on September 17, 1991.

The 1992 elections were dominated by the right-wing Fatherland Party, bringing in President Lennart Meri and Prime Minister Mart Laar. Russian military presence in the country remained a point of conflict during the 1990s until the last Russian troops left in 1994. A far-left alliance led by former Communists won parliamentary elections in 1995, but in the 1999 elections, a coalition of three center-right parties wrested control from them.

Estonia: 20th-Century Leaders

Chief of State

1921–24: Konstantin Päts (1874–1956)

1927–28: Jaan Tonisson

1928–29: August Rei

1929–31: Otto Strandmann

1931–40: Konstantin Päts

(part of Soviet Union 1940–91)

President

1991–92: Arnold Rüütel (1928–)

1992– : Lennart Meri (1929–)

Prime Minister

1990–92: Edgar Savisaar

1992: Tiit Vähi (1947–)

1992–94: Mart Laar (1960–)

1994–95: Andres Tarand

1995–97: Tiit Vähi

1997–99: Maart Siiman

1999– : Mart Laar

Ethiopia

Official name: Federal Democratic Republic of Ethiopia

Location: Central eastern Africa; landlocked; bordered by Eritrea (N), Djibouti, Somalia (E), Kenya (S), Sudan (W)

Capital: Addis Ababa

Area: 435,184 sq. mi. (1,127,127 sq. km.)

Population (est. 1997): 58,732,577

Languages: Amharic (official), English, Tigrinya, Orominga, and about 70 other languages

Government: Federal republic

Religions: Muslim 45%–50%, Ethiopian Orthodox 35%–40%, animist 12%

Monetary unit: Birr

Main exports: Coffee, leather products, gold, petroleum products

One of the world's oldest independent states, Ethiopia (formerly known widely as Abyssinia) began the 20th century under Emperor Menelik II, who reigned from 1889 to 1911. Menelik thwarted an Italian invasion in 1896, expanded Ethiopia by conquest, and modernized the realm, making Addis Ababa his capital and promoting the building of the country's first railroad. Civil unrest followed Menelik's death in 1913: his heir and grandson, Lij Yasu, was overthrown in 1916, and Menelik II's daughter Zauditu came to power, with his cousin Ras Tafari Makonnen as regent and heir apparent. Upon Zauditu's death in 1930 Ras Tafari became emperor as Haile Selassie. In the Abyssinian War (1935–36), the forces of Italian dictator Benito Mussolini conquered Ethiopia and drove the emperor into exile. Joined with Eritrea and Italian Somaliland (now part of Somalia) as Italian East Africa, Ethiopia was occupied by Italy until 1941, when British and South African forces liberated it and restored Haile Selassie to the throne.

After World War II Haile Selassie worked assiduously to maintain Ethiopia's independence from Britain, which administered several provinces into the 1950s. Under a UN plan Eritrea was federated with Ethiopia in 1952, giving Ethiopia access to the sea; Ethiopia went further in 1962, making Eritrea a province with no distinct identity, a move that angered Eritreans and led to a guerrilla movement for secession.

Continuing his prewar focus on modernizing the country, Haile Selassie reformed Ethiopia's political system through a new constitution in 1955. But the country's economy remained underdeveloped, with most wealth in the hands of a few landowners and the Ethiopian church.

Haile Selassie foiled a coup attempt in 1960, but agitation for political liberalization and economic reform grew during the decade, as did guerrilla activity in Eritrea. A drought in 1973 exposed the government's corruption and inefficiency as it mishandled relief efforts. The military revolted in 1973, persuading Haile Selassie to appoint a liberal prime minister, Endalkatchew Makonnen, who drafted a more democratic constitution. But civil unrest continued, and on September 13, 1974, Haile Selassie was deposed in a coup; he died under house arrest a year later.

After the coup the constitution was suspended and parliament dissolved. The ruling

Provisional Military Administrative Council, known as the Derg, converted Ethiopia into a socialist state, nationalizing and redistributing land. In 1976 Ethiopia began accepting military aid from the Soviet Union, ending a previous alliance with the U.S. The country's leader, Mengistu Haile Marriam, head of state from 1977 to 1991, conducted the "red terror," a campaign of violence against opponents, in 1977.

Somalia invaded Ethiopia in 1977, seeking to take possession of disputed territory in the Ogaden region. With a large-scale infusion of Soviet arms and Cuban troops, Mengistu was able, in 1978, to repel the Somalis and retake land that had been lost to the Eritrean rebels. But the main Eritrean separatist group, the Eritrean People's Liberation Front (EPLF), continued to fight for secession, as did the Tigré People's Liberation Front (TPLF), which advocated independence for Tigré, another region of Ethiopia.

Drought, civil war, and the government's policies combined to bring about devastating famines in the 1980s. Mengistu continued to take a Marxist stance, renaming the country the People's Democratic Republic of Ethiopia in 1987, but the crumbling of Soviet power and the growth of internal opposition made that position difficult. By 1991 the EPLF had taken control of most of Eritrea. The Ethiopian People's Revolutionary Democratic Front (EPRDF), which included Tigré nationalists and other government opponents, launched a major offensive. Mengistu fled the country and the EPRDF captured Addis Ababa in May 1991.

Meles Zenawi, a Tigréan and head of the EPRDF, took power as president. Eritrean independence was swiftly acknowledged, and Zenawi initiated a process of democratization. A new constitution was enacted in 1994, establishing a parliamentary government over partially autonomous regions. Opposition parties boycotted the elections that followed in 1995, in which the EPRDF won and Zenawi became prime minister.

Economic tension between Ethiopia and Eritrea led to the outbreak of war between the two nations in 1998 over a disputed piece of border land. The fighting continued on and off into the summer of 2000, when a cease-fire agreement was signed.

Ethiopia: 20th-Century Leaders

Emperor

1889–1911: Menelik II (1844–1913)

1911–16: Lij Yasu (1896–1935)

1916–30: Zauditu (Waizero) (1876–1930) (empress, with Ras Tafari Makonnen, the future Haile Selassie, as regent)

1930–36: Haile Selassie

(Italian occupation, 1936–41)

1941–74: Haile Selassie

Head of State

1974: Aman Michael Andom (1924–74)

1974–77: Teferi Banti (1921–77)

1977–91: Mengistu Haile Marriam (1937–)

President

1991: Tesfaye Gebre Kidan (acting)

1991–95: Meles Zenawi (1955–)

1995– : Negasso Gidada (1943–)

Prime Minister

(since 1987)

1987–89: Fikre-Selassie Wogderess

1989–91: Haile Yemenu

1991: Tesfaye Dinka

1991–95: Tamirat Laynie

1995– : Meles Zenawi

Fiji

Official name: Republic of Fiji

Location: South Pacific Ocean; over 330 islands, 100 of them inhabited; largest islands include Viti Levu (4,109 sq. mi./10,642 sq. km.) and Vanua Levu (2,242 sq. mi./5,807 sq. km.)

Capital: Suva

Area: 7,054 sq. mi. (18,270 sq. km.)

Population (est. 1997): 792,441

Languages: English (official), Fijian, Hindustani

Government: Republic

Religions: Christian, Hindu, Muslim

Monetary unit: Fijian dollar

Main exports: Sugar, clothing, gold, processed fish

Following cession by the Fijian cheifs, Fiji became a British colony and possession of the British Crown in 1874. During World War II it served as a major air and naval station. It gained independence as a dominion within the Commonwealth on October 10, 1970, and joined the diplomatic group the South Pacific Forum in 1971.

After a military coup, leader Major General Sitiveni Rabuka declared Fiji a republic and removed it from the Commonwealth on October 6, 1987. A 1990 constitution guaranteed the political dominance of indigenous Fijians over the Indian minority, assuring Fijian control of the presidency, a majority of paraliamentary seats, and the prime ministership, among other positions. In 1992 and 1994 elections, Fijian Political Party leader Rabuka was elected prime minister. In May 1999 elections, Fijian Labor Party leader Mahendra Pal Chaudhry was elected prime minister. He became the first ethnic-Indian prime minister of the nation. In 2000 Chaudhry was taken hostage by indigenous Fijian gunmen; the hostage crisis led to a military takeover, followed by establishment of an interim civilian govenment.

Fiji: 20th-Century Leaders

Governor-General

1970–73: Sir Robert Foster

1973–83: Sir George Cakobau (1912–89)

1983–87: Sir Penaia Ganilau (1918–93)

Head of State

1987: Sitiveni Rabuka (1948–)

President

1987–93: Sir Penaia Ganilau

1993–2000: Sir Kamisese Mara

Prime Minister

1970–87: Ratu Sir Kamisese Mara

1987: Timoci Bavadra (1934–89)

1987–92: Ratu Sir Kamisese Mara

1992–99: Sitiveni Rabuka

1999–2000: Mahendra Pal Chaudray

Finland

Official name: Republic of Finland

Location: Northern Europe; bordered by Norway (N), Russian Federation (E), Gulf of Finland and Baltic Sea (S), Gulf of Bothnia, Sweden (W)

Capital: Helsinki

Area: 130,127 sq. mi. (337,030 sq. km.)

Population (est. 1997): 5,137,269

Languages: Finnish 93.5%, Swedish 6.3% (both official)

Government: Republic

Religions: Evangelical Lutheran 89%, Greek Orthodox 1%

Monetary unit: Markkaa

Main exports: Paper and pulp, machinery, chemicals

Conquered by Sweden in the 13th century and annexed by Russia in 1809, Finland entered the 20th century ruled by Russia as a semiautonomous province. In 1906 it established a parliament and in 1917 declared independence. In 1918 it erupted in a civil war involving the nationalist German-backed White Guard and the Russian-supported Red Guard. Victorious over the Red Guard, Finland established an independent republic in 1919, for the first time in its history.

After the start of World War II in 1939, the U.S.S.R. invaded Finland; after months of heroic defense, Finland capitulated in 1940. When Germany invaded the Soviet Union in 1941 Finland's forces joined the German assault on the U.S.S.R. in an attempt to recover lost territory, but surrendered to the Soviets in 1944. As a Soviet-occupied territory, Finnish troops were forced to battle German forces, sustaining severe damage.

A tough armistice (1947) between the Soviet Union and Finland required high reparations and granting of additional territory to the U.S.S.R. The U.S.S.R. forced the country to reject Marshall Plan aid.

From the 1950s Finnish leaders attempted peaceful Finnish-Soviet relations. The country gained economic stability through developing its industrial base. Politically it was controlled by the Social Democrat and Center Parties, both of which supported social programs and civil liberties. Finland joined the United Nations in 1955 and the European Free Trade Association in 1961 (as associate member) and 1985 (as full member).

The fall of the U.S.S.R. brought long-lived recession and unemployment to Finland, as well as a rightward political shift, marked by the election of a nonsocialist coalition led by the Center Party. In 1994 the Social Democratic Party regained power. In 1995 Finland became a member of the EU.

Finland: 20th-Century Leaders

Governor-General

1898–1904: Nikolaj Bobrikoff (1839–1904, assassinated)

1904–05: Ivan M. Obolenski (d. 1910)

1905–08: Nikolaj N. Gerard (d. 1929)

1908–09: Vladimir K. Boeckmann (d. 1923)

1909–17: Frans A. Seyn (d. 1918)

1917: Mikael Stahovich (d. 1923)

1917: Nikolai Nekrasov

President

1919–25: Kaarlo Juho Stählberg (1865–1952)

1925–31: Lauri Kristian Relander (1883–1942)

1931–37: Pehr Evind Svinhufvud

1937–40: Kyösti Kallio (1873–1940)

1940–44: Risto Heikki Ryti (1889–1956)

1944–46: Carl Gustaf Emil von Mannerheim (1867–1951)

1946–56: Juho Kusti Paasikivi (1870–1956)

1956–81: Urho Kekkonen (1900–86)

1981–94: Mauno Koivisto (1923–)

1994–2000: Martti Ahtisaari

Prime Minister

1891–1900: Sten Carl Tudeer (1840–1905)

1900–05: Constantin Linder (1836–1908)

1905: Emil Stren (1838–1911)

1905–08: Leo Mechelin (1839–1914)

1908–09: Edvard Hjelt (1855–1921)

1909: August Hjelt (1862–1919)

1909: Andrej Virenius

1909–13: Vladimir Markov (1859–1919)

1913–17: Michael Borovitinov

1917: Andrej Virenius

1917: Oskari Tokoi

1917: Emil Nestor Setälä (1864–1955)

1918: Juho Kusti Paasikivi

1918–19: Lauri Johannes Ingman (1868–1934)

1919: Kaarlo Castren (1860–)

1919–20: Juho Heikki Vennola (1872–1938)

1920–21: Rafeal Erich (1879–1946)

1921–22: Juho Heikki Vennola

1922: Aimo Kaarlo Cajander

1922–24: Kyösti Kallio

1924: Aimo Kaarlo Cajander

1924–25: Lauri Johannes Ingman

1925: Antti Agaton Tulenheimo (1879–1952)

1925–26: Kyösti Kallio

1926–27: Väinö Alfred Tanner

1927–28: Juho Emil Sunila (1875–1936)

1928–29: Oskari Mantere (1875–1942)

1929–30: Kyösti Kallio

1930–31: Pehr Evind Svinhufvud

1931–32: Juho Emil Sunila

1932–36: Toivo Mikael Kivimäki (1886–1968)

1936–37: Kyöosti Kallio

1937–39: Aimo Kaarlo Cajander

1939–40: Risto Heikki Ryti

1941–43: Johan Wilhelm Ranell

1943–44: Edwin Linkomies (1894–1963)

1944: Antti Hackzell (1881–1944)

1944: Urho Castren (1886–1965)

1944–46: Juho Kusti Paasikivi

1946–48: Mauno Pekkala (1890–1952)

1948–50: Karl-August Fagerholm

1950–53: Urho Kaleva Kekkonen

1953–54: Sakari Tuomioja (1911–64)

1954: Ralf Törngren (1900–61)

1954–56: Urho Kaleva Kekkonen

1956–57: Karl-August Fagerholm

1957: Vaino J. Sukselainen

1957–58: Rainer von Fieandt (1890–1972)

1958: Reino Kuuskoski (1907–65)

1961–62: Martti Miettunen (1907–)

1962–63: Ahti Karjalainen

1958–59: Karl-August Fagerholm

1959–61: Vaino J. Sukselainen

1963–64: Reino Lehto (1898–1966)

1964–66: Johannes Virolainen

1966–68: Rafael Paasio (1903–80)

1968–70: Mauno Koivisto (1923–)

1970: Teuvo Aura

1970–71: Ahti Karjalainen

1971–72: Teuvo Aura

1972: Rafael Paasio

1972–75: Kalevi Sorsa

1975: Keijo Liinamaa

1975–77: Martti Miettunen

1977–79: Kalevi Sursa

1979–82: Mauno Koivisto

1982–87: Kalevi Sursa

1987–91: Harri Holkeri (1937–)

1991–95: Esko Aho (1949–)

1995– : Paavo Tapio Lipponen (1941–)

France

Official name: French Republic

Location: Western Europe; bordered by English Channel (N), Belgium, Luxembourg, Germany, Switzerland, Italy (E), Mediterranean Sea, Spain (S), Atlantic Ocean (W)

Capital: Paris

Area: 176,460 sq. mi. (457,030 sq. km.)

Population (1997 est.) 58,609,285

Languages: French; limited use of regional dialects Provençal, Breton, Alsatian, Corsican, Catalan, Basque, Flemish

Government: Republic

Religions: Roman Catholic 90%, Protestant 2%, Muslim 1%, unaffiliated 6%

Monetary unit: French franc

Main exports: Machinery and transport equipment, chemicals, foodstuffs, agricultural products, chemicals, iron and steel products

Although it established itself as a cultural and colonial power in the 19th century, France suffered politically as the century closed. The collapse of the Second Republic during the Franco-Prussian War (1870) and the divisive effects of the Dreyfus affair (1894–96) led to political polarization in the Third Republic. Anti-Semitic rightists vied with strong Socialist and Radical Parties. The anticlerical Radical Party was instrumental in the passage of a 1904 law separating church and state.

Conscious of potential German aggression, France, Great Britain, and Russia formed the Triple Entente in 1907, which was meant to counter the Triple Alliance of Germany, Italy, and the Austro-Hungarian Empire and lessen chances for conflict. Nonetheless, France was a central force in World War I, and suffered severe losses—including millions of casualties—and much damage to its northern regions. Although active in the Versailles Conference of 1919, it was weakened as a world power. The Versailles Treaty, which detailed German reparations and loss of territory, left French-German relations unstable.

By the late 1930s France was further damaged by the worldwide economic depression, which effectively rendered the country unable to stand against Nazi Germany and Fascist Italy. Adding to the instability were conflicts among many political parties, including the leftist Popular Front and the appeasement policies of Prime Minister Edouard Daladier. In 1938 France signed the Munich Agreement in hopes of avoiding conflict; nonetheless, Germany attacked France in May 1940 and by June 1940 the country was occupied by

Nazi forces.

During World War II Germany occupied northern France, while southern French territory became known as *État Français,* or Vichy France, ruled by Marshal Philippe Pétain. The resistance, or Free French, forces operated from London under General Charles de Gaulle. Following the liberation of Paris on August 25, 1944, General de Gaulle headed a provisional government and on December 24, 1946, the Fourth Republic was formed. De Gaulle's ideas for strong executive powers were rejected and he left office. Fourth Republic leadership was unstable, though (initially with Marhsall Plan aid) it rebuilt its economy and fostered international relations, including becoming a founding member of NATO in 1949. French resistance to decolonization plunged it again into war. After losing the nine-year Indochina War, France granted independence to Indochina in 1954. In 1956 Morocco and Tunisia gained independence. Most traumatic during the 1950s was the long War of Algerian Independence between France and the Front de Liberation Nationale. Until the war Algeria was considered by the French a part of France. In 1958 General de Gaulle was named head of state and asked to resolve the war. In 1962 Algeria was granted independence.

Upon taking office in 1958, De Gaulle wrote a new constitution and established the Fifth Republic. Unlike past governments, the Gaullist state was marked by strong executive powers and popular support of presidential initiatives. In foreign policy he pushed for European integration and strengthened ties with Communist countries and the Third World. He also attempted renewed relations with Germany.

De Gaulle was reelected in a runoff in 1965, and despite the tumultuous 1968 student revolt, he was reelected that same year. On May 30, 1969, following continued demonstrations, De Gaulle resigned. Succeeding him was former premier Georges Pompidou; he continued Gaullist policy until his death in office from cancer in 1974.

Independent Republican Valéry Giscard d'Estaing succeeded Pompidou. Among other policies, he supported (as opposed to de Gaulle) British membership in the EEC, and worked for European unity. An economic recession and the increased liberalism of the era led to the 1981 election of the first Socialist president of France, François Mitterrand. His radical programs included dissolving the National Assembly and nationalizing banks and businesses. This led to economic instability and the election of Gaullist politician Jacques Chirac as prime minister. The two effectively divided duties, with Mitterrand handling foreign policy and Chirac handling domestic affairs. These included ending nationalization and cutting taxes and inflation.

In 1988 Mitterrand was reelected president, defeating Chirac, and a coalition of the Socialist and non-Communist Left took power. By the 1993 elections, the Socialists had only minority representation, with the rightist Rally for France gaining majority. In 1995 Mitterrand left office when Jacques Chirac was elected president. His efforts to continue dismantling state enterprises were hampered by record unemployment and a disruptive truckers' strike. In the 1997 assembly elections, a left coalition was elected, with Lionel Jospin becoming prime minister. In 1999, France contributed to the NATO security force in Kosovo.

Throughout the 20th century, France was a center for artistic and literary achievement. In the early century artists such as Henri Matisse, Georges Braque, and the Spanish-born Pablo Picasso helped to define modernism. For many expatriates like Picasso, France became a creative mecca. Among those drawn to Paris were the American writers who defined the

Lost Generation, including Ernest Hemingway and F. Scott Fitzgerald. In mid-century Jean-Paul Sartre and Albert Camus embodied the philosophy of existentialism. Other notable 20th-century French writers include Colette, Simone de Beauvoir, François Mauriac, and Jacques Maritain. French filmmakers, including Jean Cocteau and Jean Renoir, were central to the developing art of cinema. In the postwar years French directors Jean-Luc Godard, François Truffaut, and others introduced a more open filmmaking style known as the "Nouveau Vague" that influenced the form for decades.

France: 20th-Century Leaders

A. *Third Republic*

President

1899–1906: Émile Loubet (1838–29)

1906–13: Clément Armand Fallières (1841–1931)

1913–20: Raymond Poincaré (1860–1934)

1920: Paul Deschanel (1856–1922)

1920–24: Alexander Millerand (1859–1943)

1924–31: Gaston Doumergue (1863–1937)

1931–32: Paul Doumer (1857–1932, assassinated)

1932–40: Albert Lebrun (1871–1950)

Prime Minister

1906–09: Georges Clemenceau (1841–1929)

1909–11: Aristide Briand (1862–1932)

1912–13: Raymond Poincaré (1860–1934)

1913: Aristide Briand

1915–17: Aristide Briand (coalition head)

1917–20: Georges Clemenceau

1921–22: Aristide Briand (coalition head)

1922–24: Raymond Poincaré

1924–25: Edouard Herriot (1872–1957)

1925–26: Aristide Briand

1926–29: Raymond Poincaré

1929: Aristide Briand

1930: Camille Chautemps (1885–1963)

1931–32: Pierre Laval (1883–1945)

1932: Aristide Briand

1932: Edouard Herriot

1933: Eduard Daladier (1884–1970)

1933–34: Camille Chautemps

1934: Edouard Daladier (11 days)

1936–37: Léon Blum (1872–1950)

1937–38: Camille Chautemps

1938–40: Edouard Daladier

1940: Paul Reynard (1878–1966)

B. *Vichy Government*

Chief of State

1940–44: Henri Philippe Pétain (1856–1951)

Premier

1942–44: Pierre Laval (1883–1945, executed)

C. *Provisional Government*

Head of State

1944–46: Charles André Joseph Marie de Gaulle (1890–1970)

Premier

1946: Felix Gouin (1884–1977)

1946: Georges Augustin Bidault (1899–1983) (provisional president)

1946: Léon Blum

D. *Fourth Republic*

President

1947–54: Vincent Auriol (1884–1966)

1954–59: René Coty (1882–1962)

Premier

1946–47: Léon Blum

1947: Paul Ramadier (1888–1961)

1947–48: Robert Schuman (1886–1963)

1948: André Désiré Paul Marie (1897–1974)

1948: Robert Schuman

1948–49: Henri Queuille (1884–1970)

1949–50: Georges Augustin Bidault (1899–1983)

1950–51: René Pleven (1901–93)

1951: Henri Queuille (3 days)

1951–52: René Pleven

1952: Edgar Faure (1908–88)

1952–53: Antoine Pinay

1953: René Joël Simon Mayer (1895–1972)

1953–54: Joseph Laniel (1889–1975)

1954–55: Pierre Mendès-France (1907–82)

1955–56: Edgar Faure

1956–57: Guy Mollet (1905–75)

1957: Maurice Jean-Marie Bourgès-Maunoury (1914–93)

1957–58: Félix Gaillard (1919–70)

1958: Pierre Pflimlin

1958–59: Charles André Joseph Marie de Gaulle

E. *Fifth Republic*

President

1959–69: Charles André Joseph Marie de Gaulle

1969: Alain Poher

1969–74: Georges Jean Raymond Pompidou (1911–74)

1974: Alain Poher

1974–81: Valéry Giscard d'Estaing

1981–95: François Mitterrand

1995– : Jacques Chirac (1932–)

Prime Minister

1959–62: Michel Jean-Pierre Debré (1912–)

1962–68: Georges Jean Raymond Pompidou

1968–69: Maurice Couve de Murville (1907–)

1969–72: Jacques Chaban-Delmas (1915–)

1972–74: Pierre Messmer (1916–)

1974–76: Jacques Chirac (1932–)

1976–81: Raymond Barre

1981–84: Pierre Mauroy

1984–86: Laurent Fabius (1946–)

1986–88: Jacques Chirac

1988–91: Michel Rocard (1930–)

1991–92: Edith Cresson (1934–)

1992–93: Pierre Bérégovoy (1925–)

1993–95: Édouard Balladur

1995–97: Alain Juppé

1997– : Lionel Jospin (1937–)

Gabon

Official name: Gabonese Republic

Location: West central Africa; bordered by Equatorial Guinea and Cameroon (N), Congo (E, S), Atlantic Ocean (W)

Capital: Libreville

Area: 103,348 sq. mi. (267,670 sq. km.)

Population (est. 1997): 1,190,159

Languages: French (official), Bantu dialects

Government: Republic

Religions: Christian, Muslim, animist

Monetary unit: Communauté Financière Africaine (CFA) Franc

Main exports: Crude oil, wood, manganese

A country covered by rain forest and rich in mineral resources, Gabon has been inhabited by several cultures over the centuries, including Pygmies and the Fang. In the 15th century the Portuguese became Gabon's first European visitors; slave traders from France, Holland, and Britain followed in the 16th century. The territory was settled by the French in 1839 and became a French territory in 1888. In 1910 it became part of French Equatorial Africa.

During World War II Gabon was an important site for Free French activity. It was named an autonomous member of the French Union in 1958 and became an independent republic on August 17, 1960.

A stable but authoritarian government has dominated since independence. A 1967 military coup unseated first president Léon Mba and brought Omar Bongo into power; his government has been quietly supported by Western powers active in trade with the nation. International relations improved in recent years as Gabon moved to form a multiparty democracy. Bongo's 1998 reelection was marked by alleged voting irregularities.

Gabon: 20th-Century Leaders

President

1960–64: Léon Mba (1902–67)

1964: Jean Hilaire Aubaume

1964–67: Léon Mba

1967– : El Hadj Omar Bongo (1935–)

Prime Minister

1958–60: Léon Mba

1975–90: Léon Mebiame (1934–)

1990–94: Casimir Oye-Mba

1994–99: Paulin Obame Nguema

1999– : Jean-Francois Ntoutoume Emane (1919–)

Gambia, The

Official name: Republic of the Gambia

Location: Northwestern Africa; bordered by Senegal (N, E, S), Atlantic Ocean (W)

Capital: Banjul

Area: 4,363 sq. mi. (11,300 sq. km.)

Population (est. 1997): 1,248,085

Languages: English (official), Mandinka, Wolof, Fula

Government: Republic under military rule

Religions: Muslim 90%, Christian 9%, indigenous beliefs 1%

Monetary unit: Dalasi

Main exports: Peanuts and peanut products, fish, cotton

Settled by English merchants during the 17th century, Gambia was used as a source for slaves until the abolition of the British slave trade in 1807. It became a British colony and part of the Empire in 1843. It became an independent state within the British Commonwealth on February 18, 1965. Full independence was granted through a referendum in 1970. On April 24, 1970, Gambia proclaimed itself an independent republic. Its first president was Sir Dawda K. Jawara.

On July 23, 1994, a bloodless coup led by Yahya Jammeh overturned the Jawara government and instituted a military regime. The regime suspended the constitution and outlawed political parties. In response, the U.S., U.K., and European Union ended aid until Gambia reinstated democratic rule in 1996–97, though Jammeh remained in firm control.

The Gambia: 20th-Century Leaders

Governor-General

1965–66: Sir John Warburton Paul

1966–70: Alhaji Sir Farimang Singhateh

President

1970–94: Sir Dawda Jawara (1924–)

(military rule 1994–96)

1996– : Yahya Jammeh (1965–)

Prime Minister

1965–70: Sir Dawda Jawara

Georgia

Official name: Republic of Georgia

Location: Southwest Asia; bordered by Russia (N, NE), Turkey and Armenia (S), Azerbaijan (SE) Capital: Tbilisi

Area: 26,831 sq. mi.

Population: 5,174,642

Languages: Georgian (official), Russian

Government: Republic

Religions: Georgian Orthodox 65%, Muslim 11%, Russian Orthodox 11%

Monetary unit: Lari

Main exports: Citrus fruits, tea, other agricultural products, machinery, ferrous and nonferrous metals, textiles

The mountainous, varied area known as Georgia became a kingdom in about 4 B.C. It controlled a wide empire during the 12th century, was the site of conflict between Persia and Turkey during the 18th century, and became a protectorate of the Russian Empire in 1783. By the early 20th century it had engaged in several uprisings with Russia over Russian attempts to impose its language and culture on Georgia.

In 1918 Georgia proclaimed independence. It lasted until 1921, when the Red Army invaded Georgia and installed a Soviet government. In 1922 Georgia was merged with Armenia and Azerbaijan into the Transcaucasian Soviet Socialist Republic. In 1936, however, Georgia became a separate Soviet republic.

In April 1991 Georgia was declared an independent republic; in May 1991 democratic reformer Zviad Gamsakhurdia was elected president by a wide margin. Georgia became officially independent after the dissolution of the Soviet Union on December 26, 1991.

Shortly afterward, in January 1992, a two-week civil uprising took place, generated by charges against Gamsakhurdia of abuse of power and dictatorial practices. Gamsakhurdia fled to Armenia on January 6, 1992, but soon returned, calling for a civil war. In March 1992 Gamsakhurdia's government was overthrown in a military coup led by former political ally Tengiz Sigua, who became prime minister. Following failed attempts to restore power, Gamsakhurdia reportedly killed himself in December 1993. Eduard Shevardnadze became president in 1992.

After independence Georgia faced ongoing economic decline and required Russian support. To that end, Russia and Georgia signed a cooperation treaty in 1994 permitting Russia to maintain military bases in Georgia.

Georgia: 20th-Century Leaders

President

1991–92: Zviad Gamsakhurdia (1939–93)

1992– : Eduard Shevardnadze (1928–)

Prime Minister

1992–93: Tengiz Sigua (1939–)

1993– : Otar Patsatsia

Germany

Official name: Federal Republic of Germany

Location: Central Europe; bordered by Denmark, Baltic Sea (N), Poland, Czech Republic (E), Austria, Switzerland (S), France, Luxembourg, Belgium, Netherlands (W), North Sea (NW)

Capital: Berlin

Area: 137,803 sq. mi. (356,910 sq. km.)

Population (est. 1997): 82,071,765

Languages: German

Government: Federal republic

Religions: Protestant 45%, Roman Catholic 37%, unaffiliated or other 18%

Monetary unit: Deutsche mark

Main exports: Manufactures (including machines, machine tools, motor vehicles, chemicals, etc.), agricultural products, raw materials, fuels

Established in 1871, the German Empire under Kaiser William II was a rising industrial and military power at the start of the 20th century, with a growing colonial empire in Africa and the Pacific. Britain and France viewed German expansion as a threat to their own power; to oppose Germany, they formed the Triple Entente (1907) with Russia, which clashed with Germany in the century's early years over Germany's support of Austrian policy in the Balkans and its growing influence in the Ottoman Empire. The rivalry between the two power blocs led to the bloody global confrontation of World War I (1914–18), in which nearly 10 million combatants were killed, including 1.8 million Germans. Despite some initial successes, Germany was exhausted by the long stalemate into which the war settled. Its parliament became subservient to the quasi-dictatorial rule of military commanders Paul von Hindenburg and Erich Ludendorff (1916–18). In November 1918 revolution forced Emperor William II to abdicate, and on November 11 Germany signed an armistice that ended the war. The victorious Allied Powers imposed a harsh peace on Germany and the other Central Powers at the Paris Peace Conference (1919–20). In the Treaty of Versailles (1919) Germany was forced to acknowledge guilt for the war, surrender territory, and promise payment of reparations.

A new constitution adopted at Weimar, Germany, in 1919 established a parliamentary democracy known as the Weimar Republic, based on universal suffrage. Its first president, Friedrich Ebert (1919–25), put down the Kapp Putsch (1920), an attempted right-wing coup by followers of Wolfgang Kapp, but the government remained vulnerable to economic instability and political violence. Matthias Erzberger, finance minister from 1919 to 1920, was assassinated by right-wingers in 1921; Walther Rathenau, foreign secretary (1922), met the same fate in 1922. Widespread despair over high unemployment and inflation was manipulated by extreme nationalists, as was resentment over the humiliating conditions of the Versailles treaty.

Economic and political conditions improved in the later 1920s, as Gustav Stresemann, foreign minister from 1923 to 1929, succeeded in reducing reparations payments and getting Germany admitted into the League of Nations (1926). But in 1929 the Great Depression brought new devastation to Germany's economy. The Nazi Party, a far-right group that had launched a failed coup in Munich in the Beer Hall Putsch of 1923, attracted a mass following with its blend of anti-Semitism, anti-Communism, and fanatical nationalism. Unable to govern without Nazi support, Hindenburg, president from 1925 to 1934 appointed Adolf Hitler as chancellor on January 30, 1933. Preying on fears of Communists, who were blamed for the Reichstag fire of February 1933, Hitler persuaded Parliament in March to pass the Enabling Act, which gave him dictatorial powers. With Hindenburg's death the next year, the offices of president and chancellor were combined in Hitler, who called himself Führer, or leader.

As dictator over what he called the Third Reich, Hitler used propaganda and mass meetings to encourage a cult of adoration; he enforced his rule by terror, imprisoning or murdering opponents. Jews were regarded as racial enemies of the state and were systematically persecuted through legal disenfranchisement, ghettoization, and ultimately genocide in concentration camps. Six million Jews died, along with members of such other hated groups as gypsies and homosexuals, in the period of mass murder known as the Holocaust (1933–45).

Bent on expansion by conquest, Hitler rearmed the country, reoccupied the Rhineland (1936), and annexed Austria and the Sudetenland in 1938 and Czechoslovakia in 1939. His strategic position was buttressed by alliances with Italy and Japan (1936), with which it formed the core of the Axis Powers, and a nonaggression pact with the Soviet Union (1939).

Britain and France at first condoned German aggression through the appeasement policy, but Hitler's invasion of Poland on September 1, 1939, led them to declare war. In the worldwide conflagration that followed, World War II (1939–45), about 25 million troops died, including more than 3 million Germans. Germany initially seemed invincible, capturing Poland, France, Denmark, Norway, Belgium, the Netherlands, Luxembourg, Greece, and the Balkan states. But the tide of battle turned when Hitler's invasion of the Soviet Union led that country to side with the Allied Powers and resulted in the disastrous German defeat at Stalingrad (1943). Besieged from the west by U.S. and other Allied forces, and from the east by Soviet troops, Hitler committed suicide in April 1945 and Germany surrendered unconditionally that May.

Having been bombed into ruins, Germany was divided into four zones of occupation, governed by the Soviet Union in the east, France in the west, Britain in the north, and the U.S. in the south. Berlin, although inside the eastern zone, was also divided into four zones. With the cold war growing between the capitalist West and Communist East, the Soviet zone was administered separately from the other three, which coordinated their efforts. In 1948 the split became complete as the Soviets attempted to blockade West Berlin, but failed as a result of the Berlin airlift (1948–49), which kept the city supplied.

In 1949 Germany was divided into two countries—the Federal Republic of Germany (West Germany) and the German Democratic Republic (East Germany)—while Berlin remained a divided city.

The first chancellor of West Germany, a parliamentary democracy with its seat of government at Bonn, was Konrad Adenauer (1949–63), who helped the country achieve full independence (1955), guiding it into NATO (1955) and the European Economic Community (1957). West Germany's economy recovered spectacularly, benefiting from an infusion of U.S. aid via the Marshall Plan and from the policies of economics minister Ludwig Erhard (1949–63), who oversaw the creation of a flourishing "social market economy," a capitalist system with a strong state role in promoting social welfare.

Erhard succeeded Adenauer as chancellor (1963–66), and Kurt Kiesinger succeeded him (1966–69); all three were members of the Christian Democratic Union (CDU), a political party founded in 1945. The CDU lost its leading position in 1969, when the Social Democratic Party (SPD), a socialist group, took control under chancellor Willy Brandt (1969–74). Brandt improved ties with eastern Europe, including East Germany; that policy was continued by his Social Democrat successor Helmut Schmidt (1974–82) and Schmidt's Christian Democrat successor Helmut Kohl (1982–98).

In East Germany, Otto Grotewohl was the first prime minister (1949–64), but during his tenure Walter Ulbricht, secretary-general of the ruling Socialist Unity party (1950–71), was the country's most powerful leader. A satellite of the Soviet Union and a Warsaw Pact member from 1955, East Germany underwent the transformation of other Communist states: central economic planning, rapid industrialization, agricultural collectivization, and a secret police (the Stasi) to enforce loyalty to the regime. Economic conditions were hard at first, leading to a workers' uprising (1953) that was suppressed with the aid of Soviet forces. During the 1950s, each year saw the flight of hundreds of thousands of East Germans to West Berlin. To halt the exodus, Ulbricht ordered the construction of the Berlin Wall (August 1961), a barrier that became one of the most visible symbols of the cold war.

Erich Honecker, who succeeded Ulbricht as secretary-general (1971–89), was a staunch supporter of the Soviet Union but more willing than his predecessor to work for peaceful coexistence with the West. He oversaw the signing of a treaty with West Germany in 1973. During the 1970s East Germany enjoyed a high degree of prosperity compared to other eastern European nations, though a low degree compared to West Germany.

Honecker, an orthodox Communist to the last, resisted Soviet leader Mikhail Gorbachev's policies of *glasnost* and *perestroika*. In the face of mass pro-democracy demonstrations in October 1989, Honecker resigned his official posts and was replaced by Egon Krenz, who legalized the main opposition group, the New Forum. In November all border crossings to West Germany were opened, including the Berlin Wall, which began to be torn down.

Non-Communists were in power in East Germany from December 1989, but by then the country's days were numbered. West German chancellor Kohl swiftly proposed a plan for German unification, which was effected on October 3, 1990. The German Democratic

Republic ceased to exist, the unified Germany became a member of NATO, and the first all-German elections since 1933 were held in December 1990, with Kohl reconfirmed as chancellor.

Kohl now faced the daunting task of raising living standards in the former Communist state and integrating its economy into that of West Germany. Eastern Germany suffered from rising unemployment; taxes in western Germany increased to subsidize unification. The country faced a resurgence of far-right and neo-Nazi groups, particularly in eastern Germany; some of their members carried out violent attacks on foreign workers and immigrants. By 1996 Germany as a whole was suffering economic woes: unemployment was high and Kohl was forced to cut social spending to address a growing budget deficit. In 1998 Kohl and his Christian Democrats were voted out of power in favor of the Social Democrats for the first time since 1982.

Germany made many contributions to arts, letters, science, and scholarship in the 20th century. Among its cultural representatives have been scientist Albert Einstein (who emigrated to escape the rise of Nazism), writer Günter Grass, filmmaker Rainer Werner Fassbinder, and philosophers Martin Heidegger and Walter Benjamin.

Germany: 20th-Century Leaders

Emperor

1888–1918: William II

President

1919–25: Friedrich Ebert (1871–1925)

1925–34: Paul von Hindenburg

Chancellor

1894–1900: Prince Chlodwig Karl Viktor Hohenlohe-Schillingsfürst (1819–1901)

1900–09: Prince Bernhard von Bülow (1849–1929)

1909–17: Theobald von Bethmann-Hollweg (1856–1921)

1917: Georg Michaelis (1857–1936)

1917–18: Count Georg von Hertling (1843–1919)

1918: Maximilian (Prince Max of Baden) (1867–1929)

1918–19: Friedrich Ebert

1919: Philipp Scheidemann (1865–1939) (prime minister)

1919–20: Gustav Adolf Bauer (1870–1944) (prime minister)

1920: Hermann Müller (1876–1931)

1920–21: Konstantin Fehrenbach (1852–1926)

1921–22: Karl Joseph Wirth (1879–1956)

1922–23: Wilhelm Cuno (1876–1933)

1923: Gustav Stresemann

1923–25: Wilhelm Marx (1863–1946)

1925–26: Hans Luther (1879–1962)

1926–28: Wilhelm Marx

1928–30: Hermann Müller

1930–32: Heinrich Brüning (1885–1970)

1932: Franz von Papen

1932–33: Kurt von Schleicher

1933–45: Adolf Hitler

Führer (Leader)

1934–45: Adolf Hitler

Chancellor

1945: Karl Doenitz

Federal Republic of Germany (West Germany to 1990, reunified Germany afterward)

President

1949–59: Theodor Heuss (1884–1959)

1959–69: Heinrich Luebke (1894–1972)

1969–74: Gustav Heinemann (1899–1976)

1974–79: Walter Scheel (1919–)

1979–84: Karl Carstens (1914–92)

1984–94: Richard von Weizsäcker (1920–)

1994–99: Roman Herzog (1934–)

1999– : Johannes Rau (1931–)

Federal Chancellor

1949–63: Konrad Adenauer

1963–66: Ludwig Erhard (1897–1977)

1966–69: Kurt Georg Kiesinger (1904–88)

1969–74: Willy Brandt

1974–82: Helmut Schmidt

1982–98: Helmut Kohl

1998– : Gerhard Schröder (1944–)

German Democratic Republic (East Germany)

President

1949–60: Wilhelm Pieck (1876–1960)

1960–73: Walter Ulbricht

1973–76: Willi Stoph

1976–89: Erich Honecker (1912–)

1989: Egon Krenz (1937–)

1989–90: Manfred Gerlach (1928–)

1990: Sabine Bergmann-Pohl

(German Democratic Republic dissolved)

Premier

1949–64: Otto Grotewohl (1894–1964)

1964–73: Willi Stoph

1973–76: Horst Sindermann (1915–90)

1976–89: Willi Stoph

1989–90: Hans Modrow

1990: Lothar de Maiziere (1940)

Secretary-General

1950–71: Walter Ulbricht

1971–89: Erich Honecker

1989: Egon Krenz

1989–90: Gregor Gysi (1948–)

Ghana

Official name: Republic of Ghana

Location: Western Africa; bordered by Burkina Faso (N), Togo (E), Gulf of Guinea (S), Côte d'Ivoire (W)

Capital: Accra

Area: 92,100 sq. mi. (238,540 sq. km.)

Population (est. 1997): 18,100,703

Languages: English (official), Akan, Moshi-Dagomba, Ewe, Ga

Government: Republic

Religions: Indigenous beliefs 38%, Muslim 30%, Christian 24%, other 8%

Monetary unit: New cedi

Main exports: Cocoa, gold, timber, tuna

From the 1870s until independence in 1957, Ghana was known as the British colony of the

Gold Coast. Long-standing resistance by the Ashanti people was finally suppressed in 1901. Mining and cocoa-farming made the colony prosper, and education levels were high. A movement for home rule grew and, in 1946, Britain granted a new constitution that allowed Africans to hold a legislative majority. In general elections held in 1951, Kwame Nkrumah became the colony's prime minister at the head of the victorious Convention People's Party (CPP). In 1956 British Togoland, formerly a German colony, merged with the Gold Coast. On March 6, 1957, the Gold Coast became the independent Commonwealth nation of Ghana, named for a medieval West African empire. In 1960 Ghana became a republic with Nkrumah as president.

Nkrumah ruled autocratically, transforming the country into a socialist state, orienting it toward the Soviet Union and China and suppressing dissent. He built hospitals, schools, and other public works, but his period of rule was marred by corruption, growing debt, and economic decline. In 1966 he was overthrown in a coup and replaced by an anti-Socialist military regime. A series of other coups followed and the economy further deteriorated. Elections in 1969 brought the brief return of civilian government, only to be overthrown in a 1972 coup. In 1979 Flight Lieutenant Jerry Rawlings led another coup and briefly reintroduced civilian government, only to overthrow that administration in 1981. Rawlings has ruled Ghana ever since.

Economic conditions continued bleak, and many Ghanaians fled to Nigeria looking for work; Nigeria returned more than a million of these workers to Ghana in 1983. Rawlings introduced liberalizing economic reforms in 1983; with the help of the World Bank, these reforms produced a 6 percent economic growth rate in 1989, though at the cost of high unemployment and poverty.

In 1992 under a new multiparty constitution approved by referendum, Rawlings won the presidency, as he did again in 1996. In the early 1990s Ghana's resurgence was threatened by ethnic fighting in the north.

Ghana's international stature was raised in 1997, when Kofi Annan, a Ghanaian diplomat, became UN secretary-general.

Ghana: 20th-Century Leaders

Governor-General

1957: Sir Charles Arden-Clarke (1898–1962)

1957: Kobrina Arku Kosah (acting)

1957–60: William Francis Hare, earl of Listowel

President

1960–66: Kwame Nkrumah

1966–69: Joseph A. Ankrah

1969–70: Akwasi Afrifa

1970: Nii Amaa Ollennu (1906–86)

1970–72: Edward Akufo-Addo (1906–79)

1972–78: Ignatius K. Acheampong (1931–79)

1978–79: Fred W. K. Akuffo (1937–79)

1979: Jerry Rawlings (1947–)

1979–81: Hilal Limann (1934–)

1981– : Jerry Rawlings

Great Britain See United Kingdom.

Greece

Official name: Hellenic Republic

Location: Southeastern Europe; bordered by Albania, Macedonia, Bulgaria (N), Turkey (NE), Aegean Sea (E), Mediterranean Sea (S), Ionian Sea (W), includes many islands off the mainland

Capital: Athens

Area: 50,942 sq. mi. (131,940 sq. km.)

Population (est. 1997): 10,616,055

Languages: Greek (official), English, French

Government: Parliamentary republic

Religions: Greek Orthodox 98%, Muslim 1.3%, other 0.7%

Monetary unit: Drachma

Main exports: Manufactured goods, foodstuffs, fuels

Site of an ancient civilization famed for its contributions to world culture, Greece lost its independence to the Romans by the 2nd century B.C. It was ruled successively by the Romans, Byzantines, and Ottoman Turks until the early 19th century, when it gained its independence. At the beginning of the 20th century it was ruled by King George I (1863–1913), a Danish prince who introduced a democratic constitution (1864) and expanded the nation's territory. Greece acquired Crete in 1913 and, in the Balkan Wars (1912–13), added southeastern Macedonia and western Thrace to its domains.

George I was assassinated in 1913; Constantine I (1913–17; 1920–22), who succeeded him, initially kept his country neutral during World War I, despite the wishes of Prime Minister Eleutherios Venizelos (lived 1864–1936; prime minister 1910–15, 1917–20, 1924, 1928–32, 1933), whom he dismissed over the dispute. The Allies pressured Constantine into abdicating in favor of his younger son Alexander (1917–20); they also saw to it that Venizelos was reinstalled as prime minister. Greece entered World War I on the Allied side in 1917 and, at the Paris Peace Conference, was rewarded with yet more territory, in Thrace and Asia Minor; Turkey forced Greece to give back this land in the Treaty of Lausanne (1923).

The next decades were ones of political turmoil. On Alexander's death, Constantine was restored to the throne, but in 1923 his son George II (1922–24; 1935–47) was forced to abdicate. The republic that was established the following year was marked by coups and counter-coups; it ended with the restoration of the monarchy in accordance with a plebiscite in 1935. The power behind the throne was General Ioannis Metaxas, who established a right-wing dictatorship. Metaxas fought off invasion by Italy in 1940; Germany succeeded in occupying Greece (1941–44), though it faced a vigorous resistance movement. From 1946 to 1949 civil war raged between royalist forces and Communist rebels. In keeping with the newly articulated Truman Doctrine, the U.S. provided heavy economic and military aid to the royalists, who defeated the rebels.

After the war political instability remained high, with frequent changes of government, until a new constitution was ratified in 1951, the same year Greece joined NATO. Afterward strong prime ministers such as Constantine Karamanlis and Georgios Papandreou guided the state through a period of economic growth powered by an expanding industrial sector. Tensions persisted with Turkey over the status of Cyprus (independent from 1960). Internal tensions concerning the roles of the monarchy and the army came to the fore in 1967, when a military coup led by George Papadopoulos toppled King Constantine II. The monarchy was officially abolished in 1973. A military junta known as the Greek Colonels ruled Greece from 1967 to 1974; Papadopoulos was deposed as its head in 1973 and the junta itself collapsed in 1974 after a failed attempt to intervene in Cyprus.

Karamanlis oversaw the return of democracy in 1974; at the head of the New Democracy Party, he was chosen prime minister (1974–80). He led Greece into the European Economic Community, effective from 1981, but his party lost the 1981 election to the Panhellenic Socialist Movement (PASOK) led by Andreas Papandreou. Heading Greece's first Socialist government, Papandreou instituted Socialist reforms but his popularity faded in the late 1980s in the face of charges of corruption and misuse of power; he left office in 1989 and was acquitted of corruption charges in 1992. In 1993 he led his party back into power. Costas Simitis, who succeeded him as PASOK leader in 1996, resurrected privatization measures that had stalled under Papandreou.

Greece: 20th-Century Leaders

King

1863–1913: George I (1845–1913)

1913–17: Constantine I (1868–1923)

1917–20: Alexander (1893–1920)

1920–22: Constantine I

1922–24: George II (1890–1947)

(republic 1924–35)

1935–41: George II

(German occupation 1941–44)

1946–47: George II

1947–64: Paul I (1901–64)

1964–67: Constantine II (1941–)

Regent

1935: George Kondylis (1879–1936)

1944–46: Archbishop Damaskinos (1891–1949)

1967–73: George Zoetakis

(monarchy abolished 1973)

President

1924–26: Pavlos Konduriotis (1857–1935)

1926: Theodoros Pangalos (1878–1952)

1926–29: Pavlos Konduriotis (provisional)

1929–35: Alexandros Zaimis (1856–1936)

(republic abolished 1935–73)

1973: George Papadopoulos

1973–74: Phaedon Gizikis

1974–75: Michael Stassinopoulos

1975–80: Konstantinos Tsatsas (1899–1987)

1980–85: Constantine Karamanlis

1985–90: Christos Sartzetakis (1929–)

1990–95: Constantine Karamanlis

1995– : Konstantinos Stephanopoulos (1926–)

Prime Minister

(since 1936)

1936–41: Ioannis Metaxas

(German occupation 1941–44)

1944: Georgios Papandreou (1888–1968)

1945: Nikolas Plastiras (1883–1953)

1945: Petros Voulgaris (1884–1957)

1945: Archbishop Damaskinos

1945: Panayotis Kanellopoulos (1902–86)

1945–46: Themistocles Sophoulis (1861–1949)

1946: Panaghiotis Poulitsas (1881–1968)

1946–47: Constantine Tsaldaris (1884–1970)

1947: Demetrios Maximos (1873–1955)

1947: Constantine Tsaldaris

1947–49: Themistocles Sophoulis

1949–50: Alexandros Diomedes (1875–1950)

1950: Ioannis Theotokis (1880–1961)

1950: Sophocles Venizelos (1894–1964)

1950: Nikolas Plastiras

1950–51: Sophocles Venizelos

1951–52: Nikolas Plastiras

1952: Demetrios Kioussopoulos

1952–55: Alexandros Papagos (1883–1955)

1955: Stephen C. Stephanopoulos (1898–1982)

1955–58: Constantine Karamanlis

1958: Konstantine Georgacapoulos (1890–1973)

1958–61: Constantine Karamanlis

1961: Konstantine Dovas (1898–1973)

1961–63: Constantine Karamanlis

1963: Panayiotis Pipinelis (1899–1970)

1963: Stylianos Mavromihalis

1963: Georgios Papandreou

1963–64: Ioannis Paraskevopoulos

1964–65: Georgios Papandreou

1965: George Athanasiadis-Novas (1893–1987)

1965: Elias Tsirimokos (1907–68)

1965–66: Stephen C. Stephanopoulos

1966–67: Ioannis Paraskevopoulos

1967: Panayotis Kanellopoulos

1967: Constantine Kollias

1967–73: George Papadopoulos

1973: Spyridon Markezinis

1973–74: Adamantios Androutsopoulos

1974–80: Constantine Karamanlis

1980–81: George J. Rallis

1981–89: Andreas Papandreou

1989: Tzannis Tzannetakis

1989: Yiannis Grivas

1989–90: Xenophon Zolotas

1990–93: Constantine Mitsotakis

1993–96: Andreas Papandreou

1996– : Costas Simitis (1936–)

Grenada

Official name: Grenada

Location: Southeastern Caribbean Sea; bordered by Atlantic Ocean (NE, E, SE), Caribbean Sea (SW, W, NW), nearest neighbors include Trinidad (100 mi./160 km. N)

Capital: St. George's

Area: 131 sq. mi. (340 sq. km.)

Population (est. 1997): 95,537

Languages: English (official), French patois

Government: Parliamentary democracy recognizing British crown as chief of state

Religions: Roman Catholic, Anglican and other Protestant sects

Monetary unit: East Caribbean (EC) dollar

Main exports: Bananas, cocoa beans, nutmeg

Under British rule from 1783, Grenada operated on a sugar plantation economy using African slaves. It gained universal adult suffrage in 1951 and self-rule in 1967 and became fully independent on February 7, 1974. In 1979 the Labour government was overthrown by the leftist New Jewel Movement, establishing a Marxist government allied with Cuba; on October 19, 1983, its leader, Maurice Bishop, was assassinated. Following a request from members of the Organization of Eastern Caribbean States, the U.S. invaded the country on October 25, 1983. The hard-fought battle against the Cuban military led to the election of a centrist government in 1984. From 1990 to 1995 a coalition government ruled, formed by the National Democratic Congress Party; in 1995 the opposition New National Party gained control of the government.

Grenada: 20th-Century Leaders

Governor-General (representing the British monarch)

1974–78: Sir Leo de Gale (1921–86)

1978–92: Sir Paul Scoon (1935–)

1992–96: Sir Reginald Palmer

1996– : Sir Daniel C. Williams (1935–)

Prime Minister

1974–79: Eric M. Gairy

1979–83: Maurice Bishop (1944–83)

1983: Bernard Coard (1944–)

1983: Hudson Austin

1983–84: Nicholas Brathwaite

1984–89: Herbert A. Blaize (1918–89)

1989–90: Ben Jones (1924–)

1990–95: Nicholas Brathwaite

1995: George Brizan

1995– : Keith C. Mitchell (1946–)

Guatemala

Official name: Republic of Guatemala

Location: Central America; bordered by Mexico (N, W), Pacific Ocean (SW), El Salvador (S), Honduras, Caribbean Sea, Belize (E)

Capital: Guatemala City

Area: 42,042 sq. mi. (108,890 sq. km.)

Population (est. 1997): 11,685,695

Languages: Spanish (official), Native American languages

Government: Republic

Religions: Roman Catholic (predominant), Protestant, Mayan

Monetary unit: Quetzal

Main exports: Coffee, sugar, bananas

Home to the ancient Mayan civilization, which flourished from the fourth to the 10th centuries, Guatemala was conquered by Spain in the 16th century. Independence from Spain was achieved in 1821, and Guatemala became a distinct republic in 1839. From 1851 to 1944 the Liberal Party held power with the support of wealthy landowners and the U.S.–owned United Fruit Company. Dictatorial and repressive rule was common, though Guatemala's leaders did take steps to modernize the country: dictator Manuel Estrada Cabrera (1898–1920) oversaw progress in public health, education, and agriculture; dictator Jorge Ubico (1931–44) improved the country's finances. Both men were overthrown by revolution. After World War II the political system became more democratic; presidents Juan José Arevalo (1945–51) and Jacobo Arbenz Guzmán (1951–54) introduced labor and agrarian reforms to address the country's widespread poverty. Arbenz's nationalization of large estates, including those of the United Fruit Company, and his support by Communists prompted the U.S. to support a 1954 coup that deposed him.

After the coup the military ruled Guatemala, either directly or indirectly behind the facade of elected leaders. From 1960 to 1996 a seemingly endless civil war raged in which left-wing guerrillas, organized as the Guatemalan National Revolutionary Union (URNG), fought against the U.S.–backed army while right-wing death squads terrorized the population. About 100,000 people were killed, another 40,000 disappeared, and a million became refugees. Throughout the long war, most Guatemalans remained desperately poor.

From 1982 to 1986 a military junta ruled Guatemala. Democratic government was restored in 1986, but the military continued to wield strong influence. In 1993, with military support, President Jorgé Serrano Elías established a dictatorship, but it was short-lived. Within days, a domestic and international outcry prompted the army to oust Serrano and replace him with Ramiro de Leon Carpio.

In December 1996 the rebels and the government finally signed a peace accord ending the war. Álvaro Arzú Irigoyen, elected president that year, took steps to purge the military of corrupt members and to privatize the economy. In 1999, U.S. President Bill Clinton apologized for aid the U.S. had given to repressive forces. The rightist Guatemalan Republican Front won control of the government in 1999 elections.

Guatemala: 20th-Century Leaders

President

1898–1920: Manuel Estrada Cabrera (dictator)

1920–21: Carlos Herrera

1921–26: José María Orellana

1926–30: Lazaro Chacon

1930: Baudilio Palma

1930–31: Manuel Orellana

1931: José María Reina Andrade

1931–44: Jorge Ubico (dictator)

(military junta, 1944)

1944: Federico Ponce Vaides

(triumvirate, 1944–45)

1945–51: Juan José Arevalo

1951–54: Jacobo Arbenz Guzmán (1913–71)

1954: Carlos Enrique Díaz

(military junta, 1954)

1954–57: Carlos Castillo Armas (1914–57)

1957: Luis Arturo González López (1900–65)

(military junta, 1957)

1957–58: Guillermo Flores Avendaño

1958–63: Miguel Ydígoras Fuentes (1895–1982)

1963–66: Carlos Enrique Peralta Azurdia

1966–70: Julio César Méndez Montenegro

1970–74: Carlos Araña Osorio

1974–78: Kjell Eugenio Laugerud García (1930–)

1978–82: Fernando Romeo Lucas García

1982–83: Efraín Ríos Montt

1983–86: Oscar Humberto Mejía Víctores (1930–)

1986–91: Marco Vinicio Cerezo Arévalo (1942–)

1991–93: Jorge Serrano Elías (1945–)

1993–96: Ramiro de Leon Carpio

1996– 2000: Álvaro Arzú Irigoyen

Guinea

Official name: Republic of Guinea

Location: Western Africa; bordered by Guinea-Bissau (NW), Senegal (N), Mali (NE), Côte d'Ivoire (SE), Liberia, Sierra Leone (S), Atlantic Ocean (W)

Capital: Conakry

Area: 94,927 sq. mi. (245,860 sq. km.)

Population (est. 1997): 7,411,981

Languages: French (official), tribal languaes

Government: Republic

Religions: Muslim 85%, Christian 7%, indigenous beliefs

Monetary unit: Guinean franc

Main exports: Bauxite, alumina, diamonds, coffee, pineapple

A site of French interest since the 17th century, the territories that now compose Guinea became a separate colony in 1845 and were named French Guinea in 1893. Largely governed by Europeans until World War II, Guinea moved toward self-rule after the war by becoming part of the Federation of French West Africa in 1946. In 1958 the territories broke ties with France when they rejected a new French constitution and, on October 2, 1958, proclaimed independence. Promoting bauxite mining led to early postindependence economic growth.

Breaking diplomatic relations with France in 1965, President Ahmed Sékou Touré sought and received aid from the U.S.S.R., becoming Africa's first Marxist nation. Following Touré's death in 1984, General Lansana Conté instituted a military regime that promised to be less harsh than Touré's rule. In addition to surviving a 1995 coup attempt by former premier Diara Traoré, Conté promoted a market economy and reintroduced political relations with France. A new democratic constitution was approved on December 23, 1990. In June 1995 the country underwent its first multiparty elections, with Conté's Unity and Progress Party taking the majority of seats.

Guinea: 20th-Century Leaders

President

1958–84: Ahmed Sékou Touré (1922–84)

1984– : Lansana Conté (1935–)

Premier

1972–84: Louis Lansana Beavogui

1984: Diara Traoré

1984–96: Lansana Conté

1996–99: Sidya Touré

1999– : Lamine Sidimé (1944–)

Guinea-Bissau

Official name: Republic of Guinea-Bissau

Location: West Africa; bordered by Senegal (N), Guinea (E, S), Atlantic Ocean (W)

Capital: Bissau

Area: 13,948 sq. mi. (36,125 sq. km.)

Population (est. 1997): 1,178,584

Languages: Portuguese (official), Criolo, African languages

Government: Republic

Religions: Traditional 65%, Islam 30%, Christian 5%

Monetary unit: Guinea-Bissau peso

Main exports: Cashews, fish, peanuts, palm kernels

Discovered by Portuguese explorer Nuno Tristao, it was colonized in 1879 as Portuguese Guinea. By the end of the 19th century colonial resistance was growing, and Guinea-Bissau entered the 20th century a colony in change.

In 1952 Portuguese Guinea became an overseas territory of Portugal. Four years later the African Party for the Independence of Guinea-Bissau and Cape Verde was founded by Amilcar Cabral to free the territories from Portuguese rule. Guerrilla warfare began in 1961, and by 1972 rebel forces controlled the bulk of the country. The rebels soon established a civilian government that was broadly accepted. In 1973 Cabral was assassinated; in August 1974 Portugal agreed to grant independence to the province of Guinea-Bissau. It became an independent country on September 10, 1974.

Guinea-Bissau's first president, Luis Cabral, adopted Socialist policies with aid from Cuba and the U.S.S.R. In 1980 Cabral was deposed in a coup headed by Premier João Bernardo

Vieira, who placed himself and a Revolutionary Council in power. In 1984 he restored civilian rule; in 1991 the congress approved a multiparty system, later permitting opposition parties. In 1994 elections Vieira's party won the majority of seats; in a runoff, Vieira won reelection. In 1998 civil war broke out when, after being dismissed as army chief of staff, Brigadier General Ansumane Mane led rebels against the government and established himself as leader of a provisional military government. Government forces were augmented by troops from Senegal. Although a peace treaty was signed in November, hostilities resumed in early 1999 leading to a coup that ousted President Vieira. Elections in 1999 and 2000 restored civilian rule.

Guinea-Bissau: 20th-Century Leaders

President

1973–80: Luis de Almeda Cabral

1980–99: João Bernardo Vieira

1999– 2000: Malan Bacai Sanha

Premier

1973–78: Francisco Mendes (1939–)

1978: Constantino Teixeira (Acting Premier)

1978–80: João Bernardo Viera

1982–84: Víctor Saude Maria

1991–94: Carlos Correia

1995–97: Manuel Saturnino da Costa

1997–99: Carlos Correia

1999–2000: Francisco Fadul

Guyana

Official name: Co-operative Republic of Guyana

Location: Northeastern South America; bordered by Atlantic Ocean (N), Venezuela (W), Brazil (S), Suriname (E)

Capital: Georgetown

Area: 83,000 sq. mi. (214,970 sq. km.)

Population (est. 1997): 706,116

Languages: English, Native American languages

Government: Republic

Religions: Christian 57%, Hindu 33%, Muslim 9%, other 1%

Monetary unit: Guyanese dollar

Main exports: Bauxite, sugar, rice, shrimp, molasses

A Dutch possession from the 17th century, Guyana passed to the British in 1815 and became the colony of British Guiana in 1831. Descendants of African slaves, whether of mixed or unmixed race, form a large part of Guyana's present-day population (43 percent); an even larger segment (51 percent) are descendants of indentured servants imported from India to work the plantations following abolition of slavery in 1834.

After World War II Guyana moved gradually toward independence, which was delayed because of Britain's fear that a Communist government would be installed. Proportional representation was introduced in 1964, a system that favored the Socialist People's National Congress rather than the far-left People's Progressive Party. Guyana became independent on May 26, 1966, and was transformed into a "co-operative republic" in 1970. It was so named for the co-operative Socialism promoted by the People's National Congress, which remained in power until 1992. Under the leadership of Linden Forbes S. Burnham (prime minister 1964–80; president 1980–85), the government nationalized most large companies; its economic policies, coupled with declining sugar and bauxite prices, made for chronic poverty and high foreign debt. A new constitution providing for an executive presidency was adopted in 1980.

Since the 1960s Venezuela and Suriname disputed their borders with Guyana. Venezuela's claim to the western half of Guyana was suspended in 1970 but renewed in 1982; the two nations reached agreement on the dispute in 1989.

In 1978 Guyana made international headlines when more than 900 followers, mostly Americans, of the Reverend Jim Jones's (1931–78) People's Temple cult in Jonestown, Guyana, died in a mass suicide-execution.

In 1992 Cheddi Jagan of the People's Progressive Party was elected president, ending decades of rule by the People's National Congress. Unsuccessful attempts were made to privatize the sugar and bauxite industry. Upon Jagan's death in 1997, he was succeeded by Samuel Hinds, formerly prime minister; Jagan's widow, Janet Jagan, took over the post of prime minister. She later won election to the presidency, which she resigned for health reasons.

Guyana: 20th-Century Leaders

Governor-General

1966: Sir Richard E. Luyt (1915–94)

1966–69: Sir David J. E. Rose (1923–69)

President

1970–80: Arthur Chung

1980–85: Linden Forbes S. Burnham (1923–85)

1985–92: Desmond Hoyte

1992–97: Cheddi Jagan (1918–97)

1997–98: Samuel Hinds (1943–)

1998–99: Janet Jagan

1999– : Bharrat Jagdeo (1964–)

Prime Minister

1964–80: Linden Forbes S. Burnham

1980–84: Ptolemy Reid

1984–85: Desmond Hoyte

1985–92: Hamilton Green

1992–97: Samuel Hinds

1997–98: Janet Jagan

1998– : Samuel Hinds

Haiti

Official name: Republic of Haiti

Location: Western third of island of Hispaniola in Caribbean Sea; bordered by Atlantic Ocean (N), Dominican Republic (E), Caribbean Sea (S), Windward Passage (W)

Capital: Port-au-Prince

Area: 10,714 sq. mi. (27,750 sq. km.)

Population (est. 1997): 6,611,407

Languages: French (official), Creole

Government: Republic

Religions: Roman Catholic 80%, Protestant 16%, voodoo widely practiced

Monetary unit: Gourde

Main exports: Light manufactures, coffee, other agriculture

A French colony from 1697, Haiti became independent in 1804. By the beginning of the 20th century the republic's economy was dominated by U.S. investments. The political system was controlled by Haitians of mixed-race and European descent, who today constitute about 5 percent of the population, rather than those of mainly African descent, who constitute the remaining 95 percent. To protect American business interests from the country's chronic political instability and to ward off German influence, the U.S. occupied Haiti from 1915 to 1934. U.S. control over Haitian finances continued until 1947.

In 1957 François Duvalier was elected president with the support of black nationalist groups and the black business community. In a 1964 plebiscite he was confirmed as president for life. Known as "Papa Doc," he ruled as an absolute dictator, suppressing dissent with his much feared secret police, the *Tontons macoutes*, and curbing such traditional centers of power as the Roman Catholic Church and the business sector. Upon his death in 1971, his son Jean-Claude Duvalier, or "Baby Doc," succeeded him as dictator. The corruption and inequality of the two Duvalier regimes left Haiti the poorest country in the Western Hemisphere.

In 1986 the younger Duvalier was overthrown by the military and forced into exile. Attempts at democratization were repeatedly foiled by military coups. In 1990 Jean-Bertrand Aristide, a Roman Catholic priest, was elected president, but he was deposed in a coup in 1991 and driven into exile in the U.S. The U.S. and other countries imposed trade embargoes to try to pressure the ruling junta to permit Aristide to take office; the efforts failed. As conditions in Haiti worsened, Haitians fled the country in droves, many heading for the U.S. In September 1994 the U.S. was on the brink of invading Haiti when diplomatic efforts persuaded the junta leaders to step down. Backed by thousands of U.S. troops, Aristide was restored to power in October. U.S. troops were gradually withdrawn and replaced by an international peacekeeping force. Aristide disbanded the army and replaced it with a civilian police force.

In 1996 Aristide peacefully ceded power to his successor René Préval, elected in 1995. By this point, however, the government was paralyzed by internal dissension, and unable to address the country's urgent economic and political needs. The country was without a prime minister from 1997 to 1999, when Préval appointed one by decree.

Haiti: 20th-Century Leaders

President

1896–1902: Tiresias Simon Sam

1902: Boisrond Canal (provisional)

1902–08: Nord Alexis

1908–11: Antoine Simon

1911–13: Simon Cincinnatus Leconte

1913: Tancred Auguste

1913–14: Michel Oreste

1914: Oreste Zamor

1914: Davilmar Theodore

(occupied by U.S. 1915–34)

1915: Vilbrun Guillaume Sam

1915–22: Philippe Sudre Dariguenave

1922–30: Louis Borno (1865–1942)

1930–41: Sténio Joseph Vincent (1874–1959)

1941–46: Elie Lescot (1883–1974)

1946: Frank Lavaud

1946–50: Dumarsais Estimé

1950: Frank Lavaud

1950–56: Paul Magloire

1956–57: Joseph N. Pierre–Louis

1957: Frank Sylvain

1957: Léon Cantave (1910–68)

1957: Daniel Fignole (1914–86)

1957: Antoine T. Kebreau (1909–63)

1957–71: François Duvalier (1907–71)

1971–86: Jean-Claude Duvalier (1951–)

1986–88: Henri Namphy (1932–)

1988: Leslie Mangat (1930–)

1988: Henri Namphy

1988–90: Prosper Avril (1938–)

1990: Herard Abraham

1990–91: Ertha Pascal-Troillot (1943–)

1991: Jean-Bertrand Aristide (1953–)

1991–92: Joseph Nerette (military junta 1992–94)

1994–96: Jean-Bertrand Aristide

1996:René Préval

Prime Minister

1991: Réne Preval

1991–92: Jean-Jacques Honorat

1992–93: Marc Bazin

1993–96: Robert Malval

1996–97: Rosny Smarth

(position empty from 1997 to 1999)

1999– : Jacques-Edouard Alexis

Honduras

Official name: Republic of Honduras

Location: Central America; bordered by Caribbean Sea (N), Nicaragua (E), El Salvador, Nicaragua (S), Guatemala, El Salvador (W)

Capital: Tegucigalpa

Area: 43,278 sq. mi. (112,090 sq. km.)

Population (est. 1997): 5,571,384

Languages: Spanish, Indian dialects

Government: Republic

Religions: Roman Catholic 97%, Protestant

Monetary unit: Lempira

Main exports: Bananas, shrimp, coffee, lobster

An independent sovereign state from 1838, Honduras entered the 20th century under the economic and, to a great extent, political control of U.S. business interests. Exploitative businesses, particularly banana-growing, prompted Honduran protests and violence, leading to seven actions by the U.S. military between 1903 and 1937 to protect U.S. interests. With bananas accounting for 90 percent of Honduran exports during the 1920s, Honduras may have been the first country to be called by the disparaging term "banana republic."

A civil war in 1924 brought four presidents to office before the end of the 1920s. Beginning with the presidency of General Tiburcio Carías Andino (1932–49) and continuing with President Juan Manuel Gálvez (1949–54) and others into the early 1960s, Honduras was modernized economically and socially. Changes included the creation of a central bank and taxation of U.S. businesses.

In 1963 General Osvaldo López Arellano led a coup deposing the president and installing a military government. Despite charges of corruption, military rule lasted until 1982—two years after a new constitution was passed and a Constituent Assembly set up.

International conflicts included the 1969 Soccer War with El Salvador, which was prompted by the sudden Honduran deportation of thousands of established Salvadoran immigrants. During the 1980s Honduras was affected by civil wars in Nicaragua and El Salvador. The country was massively supported by U.S. military aid, with the U.S. nearly controlling its foreign policy. That policy included the harboring of the *contras*, rebels against the left-wing Sandinista government of Nicaragua. By the end of the 1980s, Honduras rejected U.S. control, supporting instead the Peace Plan of Arias Sánchez. In the 1990s reduced U.S. military aid and liberal presidential leadership decreased the power of the Honduran military. In 1999, the legistlature voted unanimously to put the military under civilian control.

Honduras was pounded by Hurricane Mitch in 1998. The devastating storm killed around 7,000 in Honduras while stranding 600,000.

Honduras: 20th-Century Leaders

President

1900–03: Terencio Sierra

1903–07: Manuel Bonilla (1849–1913)

1907–11: Miguel R. Dávila (d. 1927)

1911–12: Francisco Bertrand (d. 1927) (provisional)

1912–13: Manuel Bonilla

1913–19: Francisco Bertrand

1919–24: Rafael López Gutiérrez (d. 1924)

1924–25: Vicente Tosta (d. 1928) (provisional)

1925–29: Miguel Paz Baraona

1929–33: Vicente Mejía Colindres

1933–49: Tiburcio Carías Andino (1876–1969)

1949–53: Juan Manuel Gálvez (1887–1972)

1954–56: Julio Lozano Díaz (1885–1957) (chief of state)

1956–57: Roque I. Rodríguez

1957–63: José Ramón Villeda Morales (1909–71)

1963–71: Oswaldo López Arellano (1921–)

1971–72: Ramón Ernesto Cruz (1903–85)

1972–75: Osvaldo López Arellano

1975–78: Juan Alberto Melgar Castro (1938–87)

1978–82: Policarpio Paz García

1982–86: Roberto Suazo Córdova

1986–90: José Simeón Azcona Hoyo (1927–)

1990–94: Rafael Leonardo Callejas

1994–98: Carlos Roberto Reina Idiaquez

1998– : Carlos Roberto Flores Facusse (1950–)

Hungary

Official name: Republic of Hungary

Location: Eastern Europe; landlocked; bordered by Slovakia (N), Ukraine (NE), Romania (E), Yugoslavia (SE), Croatia (SW), Slovenia (W), Austria (NW)

Capital: Budapest

Area: 35,919 sq. mi. (93,030 sq. km.)

Population (est. 1997): 10,232,404

Languages: Hungarian 98.2%, other 1.8%

Government: Republic

Religions: Roman Catholic 67.5%, Protestant 25%, atheist and others 7.5%

Monetary unit: Forint

Main exports: Raw materials, chemicals, machinery, foods, consumer goods

Part of the Roman Empire 2,000 years ago, Hungary was invaded in 896 by the Asian tribe of Magyars, who established their first kingdom. In the 10th century it converted to Christianity under the rule of Stephen I (later St. Stephen) and was a powerful nation during the 14th century under Louis I (the Great). Beginning in 1389 it was at war with the Turks, with the decades of Turkish encroachment resulting in Hungary's submission to Habsburg rule after the Battle of Mohacs in 1526. In the 17th century, following a series of military losses, Hungary became part of the Habsburg empire. After a quelled 1848 revolt against the empire, the dual monarchy of Austria-Hungary was formed in 1867, with Hungary retaining much of its independence.

Following the defeat of the Central Powers in World War I, Ausria-Hungary was dissolved, with Hungary losing much of its territory. In 1918 a republic was established, replaced in 1919 by a Communist regime. However, the Communists were overthrown within months by Romanian troops, and in 1920 the legal concept of the monarchy was restored, with Admiral Miklós Horthy becoming regent. The Treaty of Trianon was also enacted in 1920, forcing Hungary to cede 68 percent of its land and 58 percent of its population.

During his rule Horthy orchestrated the return of Hungary's lost territories, and through links to Germany, gained land from Czechoslovakia and Romania in 1938 and 1940. As payment, Hungary allied with Germany during World War II and fought against the Soviet Union. In 1944 Hungary was occupied by Germany; near war's end, it was invaded and occupied by Soviet troops. In 1946 Hungary's National Assembly ended its monarchy and established a republic. The Treaty of Paris was enacted in 1947, which forced Hungary to pay reparations to the U.S.S.R.. and to relinquish the territory it acquired since 1937. In 1948 the Soviet government took control of Hungary, establishing a Soviet satellite People's Republic in 1949. After Stalin's death in 1953, moderate Imre Nagy was made prime minister, but he was pushed out in 1955.

In October 1956 a nation hoping for further reform staged an anti-Communist uprising. Former prime minister Nagy led the formation of a coaliton government that proclaimed neutrality, withdrew from the Warsaw Pact, and sought UN assistance. On November 4 Soviet troops invaded Hungary and quashed the rebellion, imprisoning many and forcing the exodus of 190,000 Hungarians. Prime Minister Nagy was removed from office and executed, replaced by the Soviet-backed János Kádár.

Beginning a period of some moderation, the Hungarian government granted amnesty in 1963 to participants in the 1956 uprising. Largely under Prime Minister Gyula Kallai relaxed economic policies were implemented, including the New Economic Mechanism (NEM), which permitted limited free enterprise and partially decentralized the economy.

In 1982 Hungary joined the World Bank and IMF. A supporter of Soviet prime minister Mikhail Gorbachev, Karoly Grosz, became president in 1988.

Free elections in 1990 were won by the Democratic Forum, which built a coalition government with the Smallholders and Christian Democratic Parties. Slowly attempting a transition to full free enterprise, it applied for membership in the European Union. In 1991 the last Soviet troops left Hungary, ending its 47-year presence within.

In 1994 economic problems including increased taxes and deficits led to the parliamentary election of a Socialist (formerly Communist) Party majority in 1994. In 1997, Hungary was admitted to NATO.

Hungary: 20th-Century Leaders

President

1919: Mihaly Karolyi (1875–1955)

1919: Bela Kun (1886–1939) (head of Bolshevik government)

1919: Joseph of Austria (regent)

1920–44: Admiral Miklós von Horthy of Nagybanya (1868–1957) (regent)

1944–45: Ferenc Szalasi (1897–1946) (regent)

1944–45: Bela Miklos (1896–1948) (regent, opposition party)

1946–48: Zoltán Tildy (1889–1961)

1948–50: Arpád Szakasits (1888–1965)

1950–52: Sándor Rónai (1892–1965)

1952–67: István Dobi (1898–1968)

1967–87: Pál Losonczy

1987–88: Károly Németh

1988–89: Bruno Ferenc Straub

1989–90: Mátyás Szürös (1933–)

1990–2000: Arpád Göncz (1921–)

Prime Minister

1903–05: Istvan Tisza (1861–1918)

1906–10: Alexander Wekerle (1848–1921)

1912–17: Istvan Tisza

1917–18: Alexander Wekerle

1918–19: Mihaly Karolyi

1919–20: Karoly Huszar

1920–21: Pal Teleki (1879–1941)

1921–31: Count Istvan Bethlen

1932–36: Gyula Gömbös (1886–1936)

1936–38: Kalman Daranyi (1886–1939)

1938–39: Béla Imrédy

1939–41: Pal Teleki

1942–44: Mikos Kallay

1945–46: Zoltán Tildy

1946–47: Ferenc Nagy (1903–79)

1947–48: Lajos Dinnyés (1901–61)

1948–52: István Dobi

1952–53: Máyás Rákosi (1892–1971)

1953–55: Imre Nagy (1895–1958)

1955–56: András Hegedüs

1956: Imre Nagy

1956–58: János Kádár (1912–89)

1958–61: Ferenc Muünnich (1886–1967)

1961–65: János Kádár

1965–67: Gyula Kállai

1967–75: Jenö Fock

1975–87: György Lázár

1987–88: Károly Grósz (1930–)

1988–90: Miklós Németh (1948–)

1990–93: József Antall (1932–93)

1993–94: Peter Boross

1994–98: Gyula Horn

1998– : Viktor Orbán

Iceland

Official name: Republic of Iceland

Location: North Atlantic Ocean, near Arctic Circle; neighbors include Greenland (190 mi./300 km. NW), Norway (about 620 mi./1,000 km E), U.K. (500 mi./800 km. S)

Capital: Reykjavík

Area: 39,768 sq. mi. (103,000 sq. km.)

Population (est. 1997): 269,697

Languages: Icelandic (official)

Government: Republic

Religions: Evangelical Lutheran 96%, other Protestant and Roman Catholic 3%, no affiliation 1%

Monetary unit: Icelandic króna

Main exports: Fish and fish products, animal products, aluminum, diatomite

Settled by the Vikings, Europe's second largest island was under Danish authority from 1380 until gaining effective independence in 1918. During World War II, Iceland's strategic location led it to be captured for use as a garrison by British (1940) and American (1941) troops. World War II also brought an end to Iceland's link to Denmark through shared King Christian X: the Nazi occupation of Denmark allowed Iceland to depose the king in 1944 and declare itself a republic.

Following full independence, Iceland's first president was Sveinn Björnsson (1945–52), who began the country's half-century of largely stable government marked by coalition ruling bodies and an effective but costly social welfare state. Fishing continued as Iceland's leading business, which has employed up to one in seven Icelanders. However, depletion of resources and foreign exploitation of the waters led Iceland to extend its territorial waters, prompting the "cod wars" with Great Britain in 1972. By the 1990s Iceland was establishing fishing quotas.

In 1946 Iceland became a member of the UN and in 1949 it became a member of NATO. It is also a member of the Nordic Council but has declined to join the EU, perceiving future restrictions on the fishing business.

In 1980 Iceland elected its first female president, Vigdís Finnbogadóttir.

Iceland 20th-Century Leaders

King

1918–44: Christian X (1870–1947)

Regent

1941–44: Sveinn Björnsson (1881–1952)

President

1945–52: Sveinn Björnsson (1881–1952)

1952–68: Asgeir Asgeirsson (1894–1972)

1968–80: Kristján Eldjárn (1917–82)

1980–96: Vigdis Finnbogadóttir (1930–)

1996– : Ólafur Ragnar Grímsson (1943–)

Prime Minister

1918–22: Jon Magnusson (1859–1926)

1922–24: Sigurdur Eggerz (1875–1945)

1924–26: Jon Magnusson

1926–27: Jon Thorlaksson (1877–1935)

1927–32: Tryggvi Thorhallsson (1889–1935)

1932–34: Asgeir Asgeirsson

1934–42: Hermann Jónasson

1942: Ólafur Thors (1892–1964)

1942–44: Björn Thordarson (1879–1963)

1944–47: Ólafur Thors (1892–1964)

1947–49: Stefán Jóhann Stafánsson (1894–)

1949–50: Ólafur Thors

1950–53: Steingrímur Steinthórsson (1893–1966)

1953–56: Ólafur Thors

1956–58: Hermann Jónasson (1896–1976)

1958–59: Emil Jónsson (1902–86)

1959–63: Iafur Thors

1963–70: Bjarni Benediktsson (1908–70)

1970–71: Johann Hafstein (1915–81)

1971–74: Ólafur Jóhannesson

1974–78: Geir Hallgrímssson

1978–79: Ólafur Jóhannesson

1979–80: Benedikt Gröndal

1980–83: Gunnar Thoroddsen (1910–83)

1983–87: Steingrímur Hermannsson

1987–88: Thorsteinn Pálsson (1947–)

1988–91: Steingrímur Hermannsson

1991– : Davíd Oddsson (1948–)

India

Official name: Republic of India

Location: Indian subcontinent in South Asia; bordered by Pakistan (NW), China, Nepal, Bhutan (N), Myanmar, Bangladesh (E), Bay of Bengal (E), Arabian Sea (W)

Capital: New Delhi

Area: 1,269,340 sq. mi. (3,287,590 sq. km.)

Population (est. 1997): 966,783,171

Languages: Hindi (official), English (associate official), 14 other languages recognized by the Constitution; more than 1,600 dialects

Government: Federal republic

Religions: Hindu 80%, Muslim 14%, Christian 2.4%, Sikh 2%

Monetary unit: Rupee

Main exports: Clothing, gems and jewelry, engineering goods, chemicals, leather manufactures, cotton yarn and fabric

Second in population only to China, India was home to one of the world's oldest civilizations, that of the Indus Valley, flourishing from about 2500 B.C. India began to come under British influence in the 17th century; by the 19th century it was a British crown colony, considered the jewel of Britain's empire. In 1885 the Indian National Congress (or Congress Party) was founded by Indians demanding greater participation in government. That demand grew more insistent with public outrage over the partition of Bengal in 1905, when Lord Curzon, the viceroy, divided Bengal into two sections, east and west, with the former predominantly Muslim, the latter Hindu; the partition was ended in 1911. In the Morley-Minto reforms of 1909, a small number of elected Indian representatives were allowed to participate in legislative councils; Muslims and Hindus were granted separate representation, a sign of divisions between the communities that would long persist. The Muslim League, founded in 1906, became the principal vehicle for the view that Muslim interests were different from those of the Hindu majority.

With the Government of India Act of 1919, Britain gave India a measure of self-rule, but a severely restricted one: it established provincial legislatures governed by a system known as dyarchy, in which elected Indian ministers shared power with appointed British governors. The act was too little to appease growing sentiment for self-rule, particularly in the light of the Rowlatt Act (1919), which suspended civil liberties, and the first Amritsar massacre (1919), in which troops under British command killed hundreds of nationalist demonstrators and wounded thousands more.

In 1920 the Indian National Congress, under the leadership of Mohandas Gandhi, began a policy of noncooperation with British rule. Indian opposition to British rule was made internationally visible in mass campaigns of *satyagraha*, or nonviolent resistance, a method developed by Gandhi that became a tool for protest movements around the world. Britain responded with a series of Round Table Conferences (1930, 1931, 1932) intended to move India closer to self-rule; these led to a second, more democratic Government of India Act (1935), providing for entirely Indian provincial governments and a federal legislature that was largely elected. However, Indian nationalists refused to stop short of full independence: during World War II, an Indian National Army under Subhas Bose aided the Japanese while many Congress leaders were imprisoned (1942–45) for their participation in the nonviolent "Quit India" campaign.

The quest for Indian independence was complicated by the insistence of the Muslim League, led by Muhammad Ali Jinnah, on a Muslim state separate from India, to be known as Pakistan. During postwar negotiations for independence, the Congress reluctantly agreed to that demand: on August 15, 1947, British India was divided into the dominions of India and Pakistan, both independent Commonwealth nations. India became a republic in 1950, Pakistan in 1956.

Upon independence, communal fighting broke out as Hindus in Pakistan and Muslims in India were attacked by the majority populations. The conflict was known in India as the Indian Civil War of 1947–48. Hundreds of thousands were killed; more than 12 million refugees streamed in both directions between Pakistan and India, seeking haven from persecution. Gandhi himself was assassinated in 1948 by a Hindu extremist who believed Gandhi was too sympathetic toward Muslims.

India and Pakistan settled into a state of chronic hostility and tension, marked by three India-Pakistan Wars: the first, known also as the Kashmir War (1947–49), and second (1965) over the disputed state of Kashmir; the third (1971) over Bangladesh's independence from Pakistan, secured with India's help as a result of the war. India has also experienced tension with its neighbor China, most notably in the Sino-Indian Border War (1962), which concerned disputed territory on the frontier between Tibet and India.

India's first prime minister, Congress Party leader Jawaharlal Nehru, remained in office from 1947 until his death in 1964. Abroad, Nehru pursued a foreign policy of nonalignment, playing one superpower off against the other. At home he developed India's industries through a series of five-year plans and instituted liberalizing social reforms. Indian unity was an overarching principle for Nehru: hundreds of semiautonomous princely states were brought into the federal system under his tenure, and he encouraged cultural and religious pluralism.

Soon after Nehru's death his daughter Indira Gandhi (1966–77; 1980–84) took up the mantle of prime minister. A split in the Congress Party followed (1969), with Indira's New Congress Party winning control of the government (1971) despite the efforts of her right-wing opponents in the Old Congress Party. Indira drew criticism for her autocratic style, notably exhibited in her coercive population control program. Found guilty in 1975 of illegal practices in the 1971 elections (a conviction later overruled by the Supreme Court), she refused to resign and declared a government emergency, jailing opponents and censoring the press. As a result, she fell out of public favor, and in the 1977 elections the Congress Party lost control of the government for the first time. The Janata coalition headed by Morarji Desai took power instead. Weaknesses in the coalition led to the Congress Party's return to power in 1979, and Indira again became prime minister the following year.

In the early 1980s militant Sikhs used terrorist tactics to press for an autonomous Sikh state in the Punjab. Indira responded with a crackdown, culminating in the June 1984 storming of the Golden Temple in Amritsar, Sikhdom's holiest shrine and a base for the independence movement. In retaliation, two Sikh members of Indira's personal guard assassinated her in October; Hindus retaliated for that act with anti-Sikh riots, known as the second Amritsar massacre. Indira's son Rajiv, who succeeded her as prime minister (1984–89), ended the rioting and strove for improved relations among India's ethnic and religious groups. But communal violence continued, and Rajiv's military intervention against Tamil separatists in Sri Lanka (1987–89) led to his assassination by Tamils in 1991. By then Rajiv's government had already fallen, replaced by the short-lived ministries of opposition parties.

From 1991 to 1996 the Congress Party was again in power, headed by P.V. Narasimha Rao. Rao accelerated Rajiv's efforts to liberalize the economy, moving away from the earlier tradition of central planning. Like Rajiv, Rao faced corruption scandals and lost the 1996 election. But the governments that followed were unstable, with one lasting only 12 days and the next only 10 months.

Tensions between India and Pakistan rose to a new level in 1998 when India conducted underground nuclear tests and declared itself a nuclear state (it had conducted its first, smaller-scale nuclear test in 1974). Pakistan swiftly responded with its own nuclear tests, leading to international concern about a nuclear arms race in South Asia. In 1999 Pakistani-backed separatists faced off with Indian forces in the continuing fight over Indian Kashmir.

Though self-sufficient in food production, with strong economic growth in the 1980s and 1990s, India has been troubled by widespread poverty and overpopulation. In 1984 India suffered a major disaster when a Union Carbide insecticide plant in Bhopal emitted toxic fumes, killing 2,500 people. Attempts since independence to dismantle the caste system, a system of social discrimination rooted in Hinduism, have proven difficult.

India has a thriving film industry, whose most acclaimed representative has been Satyajit Ray. Its writers of the 20th century have included Rabindranath Tagore.

India: 20th-Century Leaders

Governor-General

1947–48: Louis Mountbatten

1948–50: Chakravarti Rajagopalachari (1878–1972)

President

1950–62: Rajendra Prasad (1884–1963)

1962–67: Sarvepalli Radhkrishnan (1888–1975)

1967–69: Zakir Husain

1969–74: V. V. Giri (1894–1980)

1974–77: Fakhruddin Ali Ahmed (1905–77)

1977: Basappa D. Jatti

1977–82: Neelam Sanjiva Reddy

1982–87: Zail Singh

1987–92: Ramaswamy Venkataraman

1992–97: Shankar Dayal Sharma

1997– : K. R. Narayanan (1920–)

Prime Minister

1947–64: Jawaharlal Nehru

1964: Gulzarilal Nanda (acting)

1964–66: Lal Bahadur Shastri (1904–66)

1966: Gulzarilal Nanda (acting)

1966–77: Indira Gandhi (1917–84)

1977–79: Morarji Desai

1979–80: Chaudhury Charan Singh

1980–84: Indira Gandhi

1984–89: Rajiv Gandhi (1944–91)

1989–90: Vishwanath Pratap Singh (1931–)

1990–91: Chandra Shekhar (1927–)

1991–96: P. V. Narasimha Rao (1921–)

1996: Atal Bihari Vajpayee (1924–)

1996–97: H. D. Deve Gowda

1997–98: I. K. Gujral

1998– : Atal Bihari Vajpayee

Indonesia

Official name: Republic of Indonesia

Location: Archipelago southeast of Asian mainland; land borders with Malaysia (N), Papua

New Guinea (E)

Capital: Jakarta

Area: 741,097 sq mi. (1,919,317 sq. km.)

Population (est. 1997): 209,774,138

Languages: Bahasa Indonesian (form of Malay; official), English, Dutch, Javanese, local dialects

Government: Republic

Religions: Muslim 87%, Protestant 6%, Roman Catholic 3%, Hindu 2%

Monetary unit: Indonesian rupiah

Main exports: Manufactures, fuels

Under Dutch influence from the 17th century, Indonesia began the 20th century as the colony called the Dutch East Indies. Early in the century, nationalist groups arose, including Islamic ones such as the Sarekat Islam (founded 1912) and the Indonesian Communist Party (PKI, founded 1920). Sukarno rose to prominence as leader of the Indonesian Nationalist Party (PNI), which he founded in 1927. The Dutch colonial authorities suppressed all such groups, but during World War II they fell themselves to Japanese occupation (1942–45), with which Sukarno and other nationalists cooperated. After the war Sukarno declared Indonesia independent (1945) and resisted Dutch military attempts (1947–48) to reclaim the colony; the Netherlands acknowledged Indonesian independence in 1949.

As president (1949–68), Sukarno became increasingly authoritarian, ruling dictatorially from 1959. Though he claimed nonaligned status, he moved toward the left, courting Chinese aid, alienating the U.S., and allowing the Indonesian Communist Party to influence his government. He annexed Irian Jaya (western New Guinea), the last Dutch possession in the area, in 1963, and pursued an unpopular military conflict with Malaysia in the Confrontation (1963–66). In 1965 the Communists attempted a coup that was crushed by the army, led by Suharto; a violent purge of Communists followed, with Sukarno deposed and arrested (1967) and Suharto succeeding him as president (1968–98).

An authoritarian ruler, Suharto built strong ties with the West and a growing economy based heavily on oil revenues. He attempted, somewhat unsuccessfully, to relocate large numbers of people from crowded areas to sparsely inhabited ones, such as Sumatra, Borneo, and Irian Jaya. To international consternation he invaded (1975) and annexed (1976) East Timor, killing more than 100,000 of its people. In the 1980s Indonesia's economy faltered as oil prices declined. Austerity measures led to resumed growth, but poverty remained high. The government drew growing criticism at home and internationally for its undemocratic practices, corruption, and environmentally destructive policies. Guerrilla movements in East Timor and Irian Jaya and the rise of Islamic fundamentalist opposition contributed to instability. Following a catastrophic financial collapse, Suharto was forced to resign in 1998. In 1999 Suharto's successor, Bacharuddin Jusuf Habibie, permitted a referendum in which the East Timorese voted for independence, prompting pro-Indonesian militian groups to go on a rampage. UN troops entered the country to quell the violence.

Indonesia: 20th-Century Leaders

President

1949–68: Sukarno

1968–98: Suharto

1998–99: Bacharuddin Jusuf Habibie

1999– : Abdurrahman Wahid (1940–)

Prime Minister

1948–50: Mohammed Hatta (1902–80)

1950–51: Mohammed Natsir (1908–93)

1951–52: Sikiman Wirjosandjojo

1952–53: Wilopo

1953–55: Ali Sastroamidjojo (1903–75)

1955–56: Burhanuddin Harahap

1956–57: Ali Sastroamidjojo

1957–59: Kartawidjaja Djuanda (1911–63)

1959–66: Sukarno

1966–98: Suharto

Iran

Official name: Islamic Republic of Iran

Location: Western Asia; bordered by Armenia, Azerbaijan (N), Caspian Sea, Turkmenistan (NE), Pakistan, Afghanistan (E), Persian (Arabian) Gulf, Gulf of Oman (S), Turkey, Iraq (W)

Capital: Tehran

Area: 636,294 sq. mi. (1,648,000 sq. km.)

Population (est. 1997): 67,540,002

Languages: Persian (Farsi, official), Turkic, Kurdish, Luri

Government: Theocratic republic

Religions: Shi'a Muslim 89%, Sunni Muslim 10%, Zoroastrian, Jewish, Christian, and Baha'i 1%

Monetary unit: Iranian rial

Main exports: Petroleum, carpets, fruits, nuts, hides

Seat of a great empire in antiquity, the country was known as Persia until 1935, when the name Iran was formally adopted. Iran began the 20th century as a nominally independent country under the joint domination of Britain and Russia, who divided it into spheres of influence in 1907. Oil, discovered early in the century, drove the world's great powers to maintain interest in Iran. During World War I Britain and Russia occupied the country; afterward, it was virtually a British protectorate. In 1921 Reza Khan led a coup establishing a military dictatorship; in 1925 he deposed the reigning shah and took the position himself as Reza Shah Pahlavi. He made efforts to modernize the country's society and infrastructure, but his German sympathies during World War II led Britain and the Soviet Union to occupy Iran and force his abdication (1941) in favor of his son, Mohammad Reza

Pahlavi. Nationalists led by the shah's prime minister Mohammad Mosaddeq (1951–53), nationalized the oil industry and forced the shah into exile in 1953, but a royalist coup aided clandestinely by the U.S. and Britain allowed him to return to power later that year.

The shah pursued pro-Western, anti-Communist policies and a program of economic and social modernization called the "White Revolution." Though his regime won substantial military and economic aid from the U.S., it was unpopular with many Iranians; the shah's secret police force, Savak, suppressed dissent ruthlessly. In 1978–79, riots and strikes against his government grew to fever pitch until, on January 16, 1979, the shah was forced to flee to Egypt. In the Iranian Revolution Islamic fundamentalist leader Ayatollah Ruhollah Khomeini returned from exile in France to seize power in February from a weak regency council left by the shah and headed by Prime Minister Shahpur Bakhtiar (1916–91). Khomeini established a theocratic state based on Islamic law. He consolidated his power through a reign of terror, as thousands suspected of supporting the shah were arrested and executed. He broke relations with the West, showing his contempt for the U.S. by supporting the seizure of hostages at the U.S. embassy at Tehran (November 4, 1979). The hostage-taking militants demanded the return of the Shah and his assets to Iran; Algerian mediation and U.S. concessions brought about the release of the hostages on January 20, 1981.

Khomeini led a repressive, autocratic regime (1979–89) rooted in Shi'a Muslim fundamentalism and dedicated to reversing Westernization. Khomeini's government was accused of aiding international terrorism and was condemned by many countries for its 1989 death decree calling for the murder of British author Salman Rushdie for alleged blasphemy; the decree was not officially nullified until 1998.

From 1980 to 1988 Iran was locked in the Iran-Iraq War, in which it fought Iraq doggedly over possession of the Shatt-al-Arab waterway, Iraq's only access to the Persian Gulf. The war developed into one of attrition, in which neither country gained any territory; more than 500,000 people on both sides had died in the war by the time it ended with a cease-fire. Though the war allowed the government to strengthen its grip on the country by citing emergency conditions, the war also devastated Iran's economy, leaving the country nearly bankrupt. During the war the illegal sale of U.S. arms to Iran in return for Iranian influence in the freeing of American hostages in Lebanon was one of the underlying issues in the Iran-Contra Affair (1986), a scandal that weakened U.S. president Ronald Reagan.

Even before Khomeini's death in 1989, moderate and hard-line elements struggled to succeed him. Ali-Akbar Rafsanjani, who emerged as president (1989–97), proved to be a pragmatic leader who allowed some opening of the country's foreign and domestic policies while adhering to Islamic fundamentalist principles. The government felt pressure from popular discontent at home and isolating measures abroad, such as the trade sanctions imposed by the U.S. in 1996 against foreign companies investing in Iran. In the 1997 presidential election Rafsanjani lost to Mohammad Khatami, a moderate reformist. In 1999 mass protests were held by students who favored the reforms promoted by President Khatami, who had been battling against hard-liners in the government. As a result of the demonstrations, government security forces attacked the rallies, although these actions were latter condemned by Khomeini's successor as ayatollah, Sayyed Ali Khamenei.

Iran: 20th-Century Leaders

Shah

1896–1907: Muzaffar ad-Din (1853–1907)

1907–09: Mohammed Ali (1872–1930)

1909–25: Ahmed Mirza (1898–1930)

1925–41: Reza Shah Pahlavi

1941–79: Mohammad Reza Pahlavi

President

1980–81: Abolhassan Bani-Sadr (1933–)

1981: Mohammed Ali Raja'i (1933–81)

1981–89: Sayyed Ali Khamenei (1940–)

1989–97: Hashemi Rafsanjani (1934–)

1997– : Mohammad Khatami (1943–)

Prime Minister

(since the Islamic Revolution, 1979)

1979: Mehdi Bazargan

1980–81: Mohammed Ali Raja'i

1981: Mohammed Javad Bahonar (1934–81)

1981: Mohammed Reza Mahdavi-Kani

1981–89: Mir Hossein Moussavi

(position abolished 1989)

Grand Ayatollah

1979–89: Ayatollah Ruhollah Khomeini

1989– : Sayyed Ali Khamenei

Iraq

Official name: Republic of Iraq

Location: Western Asia; bordered by Jordan, Syria (W), Turkey (N), Iran (E), Kuwait, Saudi Arabia (S)

Capital: Baghdad

Area: 168,754 sq. mi. (437,072 sq. km.)

Population (est. 1997): 22,219,289

Languages: Arabic (official), Kurdish (official in Kurdish areas), Assyrian, Armenian

Government: Republic

Religions: Muslim 97% (Shi'a Muslim 60%–65%, Sunni Muslim 32%–37%), Christian and other 3%

Monetary unit: Iraqi dinar

Main exports: Crude oil and refined products, dates

Occupying most of the region called Mesopotamia in antiquity, Iraq was the site of one of the world's earliest civilizations, dating to before 3000 B.C. From the 16th to the early 20th centuries, Iraq was part of the Ottoman Turkish Empire. Britain occupied Iraq during World War I and, from 1920, governed it as a League of Nations mandate. In 1921 Iraq became a Hashemite monarchy, ruled by Faisal I under British protection. Independence was granted in 1932, but Britain, which wanted to guard its interests in Iraqi oil, retained close ties. Several anti-British coup attempts took place and, in 1941, one was briefly successful: Rashid Ali al-Gaylani, a pro-Axis minister who obtained Italian and German support, overthrew Emir Abd al-Ilah, regent for the child king Faisal II. British troops intervened to restore Abd al-Ilah and drive Rashid into exile in Germany. Iraq declared war against the Axis Powers in 1943.

As the cold war took shape following World War II, Iraq developed firm ties to the West. A 1952 agreement gave Britain more control over Iraqi oil; the two countries, with Turkey, Pakistan, and Iran, formed the Baghdad Pact, a security organization, in 1955. The U.S. gave Iraq technical aid and, from 1956, military assistance. Iraq broke diplomatic relations with the Soviet Union in 1955 over its support for Kurdish nationalism. Iraq opposed Israel's existence from its creation in 1948.

In February 1958 Iraq and Jordan were federated in an Arab Union. In July a left-wing, nationalist, pan-Arab coup overthrew the monarchy and established a republic under Abdul Karim Kassem. Kassem nationalized oil and other industries, dissolved the Arab Union, withdrew Iraq from the Baghdad Pact (1959), and restored relations with the Soviet Union (while pursuing a policy of nonalignment). He claimed sovereignty over Kuwait but his attempts to establish it were foiled by British military intervention. He was overthrown and killed in a 1963 coup.

The Kurds in northern Iraq (part of the region called Kurdistan) rebelled in 1962; fighting continued, with brief respites, throughout the decade, until Iraq promised in 1970 to grant autonomy. The breaking of the promise led to a renewal of fighting in 1974, with Iraq receiving international condemnation for its bombings of Kurdish villages later in the decade.

In 1968 the secular, nationalist, and Socialist Ba'ath Party took power in a revolution. The party took steps to modernize Iraq's economy and society while ruling by decree. Saddam Hussein, one of the Ba'ath Party leaders, quickly consolidated power. When he officially become president in 1979, he conducted a purge, killing leftist members of the party. Already threatened by the ongoing war with Kurdish rebels, he also faced resistance from the country's Shi'ite majority, who were inspired by the establishment of a Shi'ite theocracy in Iran in the Iranian Revolution (1979). Hussein kept control by ruthlessly suppressing dissent, with the help of secret police and elite republican guards.

From 1980 to 1988 Iraq fought Iran for possession of the Shatt-al-Arab waterway, Iraq's only access to the Persian Gulf. This Iran-Iraq War developed into one of attrition, in which neither country gained any territory and more than 500,000 people on both sides died. The war hurt Iraq's economy but strengthened Hussein's dictatorial control of the country. He developed chemical weapons capability, used against both the Kurdish rebels and Iranian forces, and attempted to develop biological and nuclear weapons. Attempting to slow down Iraq's nuclear program, Israel launched an air attack in 1981, destroying a nuclear reactor near Baghdad.

In August 1990 Iraq invaded, occupied, and annexed Kuwait. While Iraq ignored UN economic sanctions and resolutions to withdraw, the U.S. led the formation of an international coalition that deployed over 700,000 troops in the region. In the Gulf War (January–February 1991), massive air and ground attacks by the coalition swiftly liberated Kuwait. Iraq's infrastructure was devastated by air raids and hundreds of thousands of refugees fled to Turkey and Iran. Kurds in the north and Shi'ites in the south rebelled, but Iraq crushed the revolts militarily; to protect the populations from Iraqi force, the UN imposed "no-fly" zones over the areas of conflict.

Despite the havoc caused by the Gulf War, Hussein remained in power. UN sanctions remained in force as a result of Hussein's persistent refusal to comply with UN inspection requirements aimed at dismantling Iraq's chemical, biological, and nuclear weapons programs. Northern Iraq was declared a UN "safe haven" for Kurds, giving them de facto autonomy, with parliamentary elections held in 1992. Hussein soon reasserted some control over the region.

The U.S. bombed Iraq again in 1993, in retaliation for a 1992 Iraq-supported plot to assassinate President George Bush. In subsequent years, the U.S. threatened air strikes against Iraq unless it complied with UN inspection requirements; in the face of such ultimatums, Hussein repeatedly agreed to comply with the requirements, only to break the promise once the pressure was off. In late 1998 and afterwards, U.S. and British air strikes were launched against Iraq in response to failure to comply with UN inspection requirements.

Iraq: 20th-Century Leaders

King

1921–33: Faisal I

1933–39: Ghazi (1912–39)

1939–58: Faisal II (1935–58)

Regent

1939–53: Abd al–Ilah (1913–58)

President

1958–63: Najib al-Rubai

1963–66: Abdul Salam Mohammed Arif (1921–66)

1966–68: Abdul Rahman Arif

1968–79: Ahmed Hassan al-Bakr (1912–82)

1979– : Saddam Hussein

Prime Minister

(since overthrow of monarchy in 1958)

1958–63: Abdul Karim Kassem (1914–63)

1963: Ahmed Hassan al-Bakr

1963–65: Tahir Yahia (1913–86)

1965: Arif Abdel Razzak

1965–66: Abdul Rahman al-Bazzazz

1966–67: Naji Talib

1967: Abdul Rahman Arif

1967–68: Tahir Yahia

1968: Abdul Razak al-Naif (1933–78)

1968–79: Ahmed Hassan al-Bakr

1979–91: Saddam Hussein

1991: Sa'dun Hammadi

1991–93: Mohammed Hamzah al-Zubeidi

1993–94: Ahmad Husayn Khudayir as-Samarrai

1994– : Saddam Hussein

Ireland

Official name: Ireland

Location: Southern portion of island of Ireland in North Atlantic Ocean; bordered by Northern Ireland (part of United Kingdom) (N), nearby neighbor Great Britain (E)

Capital: Dublin

Area: 27,135 sq. mi. (70,280 sq. km.)

Population (est. 1998): 3,619,480

Languages: English predominates; Irish (Gaelic) is also spoken; both are official

Government: Republic

Religions: Roman Catholic 93%, Anglican 3%, other 4%

Monetary unit: Pound

Main exports: Chemicals, data processing equipment, industrial machinery

Ireland came under British rule in the 16th century and became part of the United Kingdom with the Act of Union in 1800. By the late 19th century, agitation for home rule was intense. The Irish nationalist party Sinn Féin, founded by Arthur Griffith in 1905, went further, seeking an independent Ireland. Poet William Butler Yeats was among those leading the Irish Renaissance, a nationalist movement to develop a distinctly Irish literature and culture.

The U.K. Parliament passed a Home Rule Act in 1914, but World War I intervened and the act was never put into effect. In 1916 the British military suppressed the Dublin rebellion called the Easter Rising and executed its leaders, making them martyrs and catalyzing resistance to British rule. Sinn Féin won a majority of the Irish seats in Parliament in 1918, but the newly elected members refused to take their seats, forming instead the Dáil Éireann (Irish Assembly) and proclaiming an Irish republic. A guerrilla war of independence followed (1919–21), with the Irish Republican Army (IRA), commanded by Michael Collins, opposing the regular British forces and their auxiliaries, the Black and Tans. The war ended with Britain agreeing to the establishment of the Irish Free State, which would have self-governing Dominion status; it would include all of Ireland save six northern counties with Protestant majorities (unlike the predominantly Catholic southern Ireland). The latter region, known as Ulster, remained in the United Kingdom as Northern Ireland. The Irish Free State came into being in 1922.

Although Dominion status, particularly as modified by the Statute of Westminster in 1931, gave Ireland de facto independence, it was not acceptable to everyone. In the Irish Civil War (1922–23), Eamon De Valera and an IRA faction fought the government in pursuit of a unified Ireland with no ties to Britain and were defeated. In 1926 De Valera founded the nationalist organization Fianna Fáil, which became Ireland's main political party. With De Valera as prime minister (1937–48, 1951–54, 1957–59), Ireland was established as a sovereign nation within the Commonwealth (1937) and, later, as a republic with no ties to Britain (1949).

During World War II Ireland was neutral, though sympathetic to the Allies. In the 1950s Ireland developed a moderate welfare state. The 1960s saw an emphasis on industrial development in what had formerly been a poor agricultural country. The 1960s also saw the beginning of the "troubles" in Northern Ireland, with Catholics and Protestants grappling violently for control of that region and the issue of unification revived in the Republic of Ireland. In the 1980s, Ireland gained a consultative role in the Northern Irish disputes; in the 1990s, Ireland participated in peace talks on the issue.

In 1973 Ireland joined the European Economic Community, a move that boosted its economy. The 1980s brought economic problems, including high inflation and unemployment, and a high degree of emigration by educated Irish. The political situation was volatile, with frequent changes of government between Fianna Fáil and Ireland's other major party, Fine Gael, often relying on coalitions with minor parties. In 1992 Irish voters approved the Maastricht Treaty, which advanced European economic and political integration. As the decade progressed, the economy rebounded strongly. There were signs of social change in this still deeply Catholic country, with Ireland's first female president, Mary Robinson, elected in 1990 and divorce legalized in 1994.

Good Friday, April 10, 1998, saw a historic peace agreement reached between the U.K. and Ireland over Northern Ireland. Despite hostility to the treaty by militant Irish nationals, voters in the Irish Republic and Northern Ireland gave it their overwhelming support. The peace treaty provided Northern Ireland with greater autonomy, including its own parliament.

Irish or Irish-born writers of the 20th century have included James Joyce, William Butler Yeats, George Bernard Shaw, John Synge, Rebecca West, and Iris Murdoch.

Ireland: 20th-Century Leaders

Irish Free State

Governor-General

1921–27: Timothy Michael Healy (1855–1931)

1928–32: James McNeill (1869–1938)

1932–37: Donal Buckley

Head of Government

1922: Arthur Griffith (1872–1922) (president)

1922: Michael Collins (head of provisional government)

1922–32: William Thomas Cosgrave (president of Executive Council)

1932–37: Eamon De Valera (president of Executive Council)

Republic of Ireland

President

1937–45: Douglas Hyde (1860–1949)

1945–59: Seán Thomas O'Kelly (1883–1966)

1959–73: Eamon De Valera

1973–74: Erskine Childers (1905–74)

1974–76: Cearbhall O'Dalaigh (1911–78)

1976–90: Patrick J. Hillary (1923–)

1990–97: Mary Robinson (1944–)

1997– : Mary McAleese (1951–)

Prime Minister

1937–48: Eamon de Valera

1948–51: John Aloysius Costello (1891–1976)

1951–54: Eamon De Valera

1954–57: John Aloysius Costello

1957–59: Eamon De Valera

1959–66: Seán F. Lemass (1899–1971)

1966–73: John Lynch

1973–77: Liam Cosgrave

1977–79: John Lynch

1979–81: Charles J. Haughey

1981–82: Garret Fitzgerald

1982: Charles J. Haughey

1982–87: Garret Fitzgerald

1987–92: Charles J. Haughey

1992–94: Albert Reynolds (1935–)

1994–97: John Bruton

1997– : Bertie Ahern (1951–)

Israel

Official name: State of Israel

Location: Western Asia; bordered by Lebanon (S), Syria (NE), Jordan (E), Egypt (SW), Mediterranean Sea (W), Gulf of Aqaba (S)

Capital: Jerusalem

Area: 8,019 sq. mi. (20,770 sq. km.)

Population (est. 1997): 5,534,672

Languages: Hebrew (official), Arab (official for Arab minority), English

Government: Republic

Religions: Jewish (82%), Muslim (mostly Sunni) 14%

Monetary unit: New shekel

Main exports: Machinery, cut diamonds, chemicals, textiles, clothing

Called Canaan in antiquity, the region was the site of the ancient kingdom of Eretz Israel, homeland to the Jewish people, founded about 1000 B.C. The area, later known as Palestine, passed through the hands of various conquerors, including Assyrians, Babylonians, Romans, Byzantines, Arabs, and Mongols, before becoming part of the Ottoman Empire in the 16th century. Jews were expelled in large numbers from Palestine beginning in 70 A.D., and settled throughout the world in what was called the Jewish Diaspora. In 1897 with the convening of the first World Zionist Congress, a movement called Zionism was founded, advocating the establishment of a Jewish national homeland in Palestine. In the early 20th century Jews immigrated to Palestine in growing numbers while Russian Zionist leader Chaim Weizmann urged the Ottoman Empire to approve a new state of Israel.

World War I brought the end of Ottoman rule of Palestine, which passed into British control in 1917 and became a distinct British League of Nations mandate in 1922. In 1917 Weizmann persuaded Britain to pledge its support for a Jewish homeland in Palestine with the Balfour Declaration. The pledge conflicted with British promises made to Arab leaders guaranteeing their right to rule Palestine. Palestinian Arabs voiced opposition to the increasing number of Jewish settlements and launched guerrilla attacks that were countered by the Jewish defense groups Haganah (founded 1920) and Irgun (founded 1931). Zionists impatient with lack of progress toward independence turned against Britain: the Irgun (from

1939) and Stern Gang (from 1940) carried out terrorist attacks on British individuals and installations. The genocide of Jews in the Holocaust gave renewed urgency to the Zionist cause.

In 1947 the UN voted to partition Palestine into a Jewish state, an Arab state, and an internationally administered zone around Jerusalem—an arrangement accepted by Jews but not Arabs. On May 14, 1948, the state of Israel came into existence. The following day, in the First Arab-Israeli War (1948–49), armies from Egypt, Syria, Transjordan (Jordan), Lebanon, and Iraq attacked Israel. Immediate hopes for a Palestinian Arab state evaporated as Egypt occupied the Gaza Strip and Jordan seized the West Bank and East Jerusalem. Israel successfully defended its existence, expanding its territory by about one-half. Armistices ended the conflict, though the Arab nations continued to refuse recognition to Israel, conducted an economic boycott of the new state, and sponsored guerrilla raids.

From 1949 to 1968 Mapai, a democratic Socialist organization, led coalition governments in Israel's unicameral legislature, the Knesset. In 1968 Mapai allied with two other like-minded parties to form the Labor Party, which remained in power until 1977.

Prime Minister David Ben-Gurion (1948–53, 1955–63) dominated the nation's early political life. According to the 1950 Law of the Return, all Jews who immigrated to Israel received automatic citizenship; the state provided jobs and housing as needed. Agriculture and industry developed rapidly; the spreading use of Hebrew, revived as a modern language by the Zionist movement and made official in 1948, united the polyglot population. In foreign affairs Israel became a staunch ally of the West but was chiefly concerned with defending itself against its Arab neighbors.

The Second Arab-Israeli War (1956) was prompted when Egypt nationalized the Suez Canal, in what was called the Suez Crisis. Britain and France encouraged Israel to invade Egypt, which had been sponsoring guerrilla raids against Israel. Israel captured the Gaza Strip and Sinai Peninsula but handed them over at war's end to a UN Emergency Force. In May 1967 a new war threatened when UN forces left the region at Egypt's request and Egypt massed its forces in the Sinai while blockading the Israeli port of Eilat. In the Six-Day War (Third Arab-Israeli War, June 5–10, 1967), Israel struck preemptively against Egypt and its allies Jordan and Syria. Israel captured the Gaza Strip and the Sinai Peninsula from Egypt; East Jerusalem and the West Bank from Jordan; and the Golan Heights from Syria. Israel's occupation of the captured lands became a new source of international tension, much of it focused on the situation of Palestinian Arabs living in the occupied territories and in exile in Arab countries.

Following the Six-Day War the Palestine Liberation Organization (PLO), founded in 1964, increasingly waged guerrilla warfare against Israel. Its chairman from 1969, Yasir Arafat, was viewed as a terrorist in many non-Arab countries but gradually gained international recognition as the leader of the Palestinian people.

In the Yom Kippur War (Fourth Arab-Israeli War, October 1973) an Arab alliance headed by Egypt and Syria launched a surprise attack that Israel repulsed at the price of heavy casualties. Israel's image of invincibility was tarnished, and Prime Minister Golda Meir (1969–74) resigned soon thereafter. In 1977 the Likud Party, a right-wing nationalist organization headed by Menachem Begin, took power, ending nearly three decades of Socialist government. Taking a generally hard line against Arab and Palestinian demands, Likud encouraged Jewish settlement in occupied lands and liberalized the economy, bringing strong economic growth in the 1980s and 1990s. Begin's period as prime minister (1977–83) saw the first peace agreement with an Arab nation: the Camp David Accords (1978) signed with Egyptian president Anwar Sadat. The accords, which were denounced by other Arab states, led to a 1979 peace treaty normalizing relations between the two countries and restoring the Sinai Peninsula to Egypt.

Following the Yom Kippur War, Israel restored some of its reputation for decisive military action with the 1976 raid on Entebbe, Uganda, in which more than 100 Jewish hostages were rescued, and the 1981 air strike against a nuclear reactor in Iraq, to prevent Iraqi acquisition of nuclear capability. Israel itself was believed to have developed nuclear weapons.

In June 1982 Israel invaded Lebanon, seeking to destroy PLO bases there. Encircling and bombing Beirut, Israel forced the PLO to evacuate to Tunisia. Facing international and domestic criticism for its occupation of southern Lebanon, Israel withdrew its forces in 1985.

Palestinians in the occupied territories soon began an uprising known as the Intifada (1987–94), in which Palestinians fought Israeli troops with stone-throwing and bombing. Israel also endured Scud missile attacks from Iraq during the Persian Gulf War (1991). Likud lost its hold on government in 1992, ceding power to Labor.

Unable to suppress the Intifada militarily, and facing persistent terrorist attacks by groups such as Hezbollah and Hamas, Prime Minister Yitzhak Rabin (1992–95) decided to negotiate peace with the PLO. In 1993 Israel signed peace accords with the PLO, in which the two sides mutually recognized each other's legitimacy and set a path for establishing Palestinian autonomy. Jericho and Gaza began to receive limited autonomy in 1994, the same year Jordan signed a peace agreement with Israel. In 1996 elections Arafat became president of the Palestinian government. For his efforts at promoting peace, Rabin was assassinated by an Israeli extremist in 1995.

A wave of suicide bombings and rocket attacks by Islamic terrorists in 1996 fueled Israeli distrust of Palestinians and led to the fall of the Labor government; Likud, under military hard-liner Benjamin Netanyahu, regained control. Peace negotiations slowed to a crawl, as Israel continued to build settlements on the West Bank and new Palestinian acts of terror were met with new Israeli restrictions. Netanyahu survived an influence-peddling investigation but his religious-nationalist coalition was embroiled in internal disputes. In 1998 a new agreement between Netanyahu and Arafat tentatively renewed progress toward peace. The election of liberal Ehud Barak as prime minister in 1999 temporarily provided new hope in the stalled peace process. Barak met with various Arab leaders soon after taking office, but failed to reach a new peace accord, a failure that led to a new wave of violence between Israelis and Palestinians in 2000.

Israel: 20th-Century Leaders

President

1948–52: Chaim Weizmann (1874–52)

1952–63: Isaac Ben-Zvi (1884–1963)

1963–73: Zalman Shazar (1889–1974)

1973–78: Ephraim Katzir

1978–83: Yitzhak Navon

1983–93: Chaim Herzog

1993–2000: Ezer Weizman

Prime Minister

1948–53: David Ben-Gurion

1953–55: Moshe Sharett (1894–1965)

1955–63: David Ben-Gurion

1963–69: Levi Eshkol (1895–1969)

1969: Yigal Allon (1918–80)

1969–74: Golda Meir

1974–77: Yitzhak Rabin

1977: Shimon Peres

1977–83: Menachem Begin

1983–84: Yitzhak Shamir

1984–86: Shimon Peres

1986–92: Yitzhak Shamir

1992–95: Yitzhak Rabin

1995–96: Shimon Peres

1996–99: Benjamin Netanyahu

1999–2001: Ehud Barak

Italy

Official name: Italian Republic

Location: Southern Europe; bordered by Switzerland and Austria (N), Slovenia (NE), Adriatic Sea (E), Ionian Sea (SE), Mediterranean Sea (W), France (NW)

Capital: Rome

Area: 116,305 sq. mi. (301,230 sq. km.)

Population: 56,830,508

Languages: Italian, German, French, Slovenian

Government: Republic

Religions: Roman Catholic

Monetary unit: Lira

Main exports: Textiles, clothing, metals, transport equipment, chemicals

The Italian capital of Rome was the seat of the ancient Roman Empire, which controlled much of the Mediterranean world from the second century B.C. until the fifth century A.D. In the Middle Ages and Renaissance, many of Italy's city-states developed into centers of high culture. Prevented from unification for decades by the intervention of various European countries, several city-states united to make Italy a kingdom in 1861.

At the start of World War I, Italy claimed neutrality, but joined Allied forces in 1915. After the war in 1919 former Socialist Benito Mussolini (also known as Il Duce) formed the Fascist Party, promising to fight Bolshevism in Italy. After a march in Rome, he was invited by the king to become premier on October 28, 1922. He soon assumed dictatorial powers, including making war on Ethiopia and annexing it in 1935, and sending troops to fight against the Republic of Spain in 1936.

From 1936 Mussolini allied Italy with Germany through the Rome-Berlin Axis, becoming part of the Axis Powers during World War II. In 1943 Fascism was overthrown in Italy and the dictatorship dissolved; Italy then joined Allied forces against Germany and Japan. Mussolini, who had been evacuated by Germans to head a puppet state in northern Italy, was executed by Italian partisans on April 28, 1945.

On May 9, 1946, King Victor Emmanuel III abdicated and went into exile. Succeeding him was his son, King Umberto II, who left the monarchy and also entered into exile on June 13.

Italy became a republic following a referendum on June 2–3, 1946. Through a peace treaty of September 15, 1947, Italy gave up claims to Greece and Ethiopia. Greece was granted the Dodecanese, five Alpine regions went to France, and part of the Istrian Peninsula to Yugoslavia.

The postwar years were marked by economic growth (in part through membership in the European Community) but economic instability due to corruption and organized crime. In 1978 former Prime Minister and Christian Democratic Party leader Aldo Moro was assassinated by Red Brigade members.

While violence continued into the 1980s, it was scandal that forced Prime Minister Arnaldo Forlani to resign on May 26, 1981, and end the postwar political control of the Christian Democrat Party. The widespread scandal linked party members and other officials to a secret Masonic lodge, "P-2." That year the Republican Party gained control of the government.

After regaining a majority in 1992, the Christian Democrats lost majority in 1994, replaced by a coalition government including the neo-Fascist National Alliance. Variously controlled governments continued until 1996, when a center-left coalition won parliamentary control.

Many Italians have made notable contributions to the arts. Among them are painter Amedeo Modigliani, postwar neorealist film directors Roberto Rossellini and Vittorio de Sica, film director Federico Fellini, and writers Carlo Levi, Primo Levi, and Dario Fo.

Italy: 20th-Century Leaders

King

1878–1900: Umberto I (1844–1900)

1900–46: Victor Emmanuel III (1869–1947)

1946: Umberto II (1904–83)

1946: Republic declared

President

1946–48: Enrico de Nicola (1877–1959)

1948–55: Luigi Einaudi (1874–1961)

1955–62: Giovanni Gronchi (1887–1978)

1961–64: Antonio Segni (1891–1972)

1964–71: Giuseppe Sarragat (1898–1988)

1971–78: Giovanni Leone

1978–85: Sandro Pertini (1896–1990)

1985–92: Francesco Cossica

1992–99: Oscar Luigi Scalfaro

1999– : Carlo Azeglio Ciampi (1920–)

Prime Minister

1903–05: Giovanni Giolitti (1842–1928)

1906–09: Giovanni Giolitti

1911–14: Giovanni Giolitti

1920–21: Giovanni Giolitti

1922–43: Benito Mussolini (1883–1945) (dictator)

1944–45: Ivanoe Bonomi (1873–1951)

1945: Ferruccio Parri (1890–1981)

1945–53: Alicide de Gasperi (1881–1954)

1953–54: Giuseppe Pella (1902–1981)

1954: Amintore Fanfani

1954–55: Mario Ccelba (1901–91)

1955–57: Antonio Segni

1957–58: Adone Zoli (1887–1960)

1958–59: Amintore Fanfani

1959–60: Antonio Segni

1960: Fernando Tambroni (1901–63)

1960–63: Amintore Fanfani

1963: Giovanni Leone

1963–68: Aldo Moro (1916–78)

1968: Giovanni Leone

1968–70: Mariano Rumor (1915–90)

1970–72: Emilio Colombo

1972–73: Giulio Andreotti

1973–74: Mariano Rumor

1974–76: Aldo Moro

1976–79: Giulio Andreotti

1979–80: Francesco Cossiga

1980–81: Arnaldo Forlani

1981–82: Giovanni Spadolini

1982–83: Amintore Fanfani

1983–87: Bettino Craxi

1987: Amintore Fanfani

1987–88: Giovanni Goria (1943–)

1988–89: Ciriaco De Mita

1989–92: Giulio Andreotti

1992–93: Giuliano Amato (1938–)

1993–94: Carlo Ciampi

1994–96: Silvio Berlusconi

1996–98: Romano Prodi (1939–)

1998–2000: Massimo D'Alema

Ivory Coast See **Côte d'Ivoire.**

Jamaica

Location: Northern Caribbean Sea; nearest neighbors include Cuba 87 mi. (145 km.) (N)

Capital: Kingston

Area: 4,243 sq. mi. (10,990 sq.km.)

Population (est. 1997): 2,595,275

Languages: English, Creole

Government: Parliamentary democracy

Religions: Protestant (including Anglican and Baptist), Roman Catholic, spiritualist cults

Monetary unit: Jamaican dollar

Main exports: Alumina, bauxite, sugar, bananas, rum

Originally inhabited by the Arawak Indians, Jamaica was explored by Christopher Columbus in 1494 and subsequently ruled by the Spanish until 1655. It then came under

British sovereignty and was a center for the slave trade until the abolition of slavery in 1833. In 1866 Jamaica became a British colony and by the early 20th century developed a flourishing banana plantation economy attracting foreign (largely U.S.) investors.

Long-present racial inequities increased with the Great Depression and brought about the formation of the People's National Party in 1938. An opposing conservative Jamaica Labor Party was founded in 1943. Political control shifted between the two parties during the 1940s and 1950s.

In an attempt to establish independence, Jamaica joined the Federation of the West Indies from 1958 to 1962, when it disbanded. Following a national referendum in 1961, Jamaica was granted independence from the United Kingdom on August 6, 1962. Socialist leadership under Prime Minister Michael Manley in the 1970s brought partial nationalization of industry and policies attempting to encourage internal self-reliance. Resulting economic chaos led to the election of Prime Minister Edward Seaga of the Labor Party in 1980s. Seaga's pro-investment policies improved tourism and agriculture development. However, increased poverty led to the reelection of Prime Minister Manley in 1989. Manley ruled until 1992, when he was replaced for health reasons by P. J. Patterson. Patterson's policies helped to decrease foreign debt and inflation.

Jamaica: 20th-Century Leaders

Governor–General

1962–73: Sir Clifford Campbell (1892–1991)

1973: Sir Herbert Duffus

1973–91: Sir Florizel A. Glastole

1991: Edward Zacca (acting governor-general)

1991– : Sir Howard F. H. Cooke (1915–)

Prime Minister

1959–62: Norman Washington Manley (1893–1969)

1962–67: Sir William Alexander Bustamante (1884–1977)

1967: Sir Donald Burns Sangster (1911–67)

1967–72: Hugh Lawson Shearer

1972–80: Michael Norman Manley

1980–89: Edward Seaga

1989–92: Michael Norman Manley

1992– : Percival James Patterson (1935–)

Japan

Location: Chain of over 3,000 islands extending 1,300 mi. (2,200 km.) NE to SW between Sea of Japan and western Pacific Ocean; neighbors include Sea of Okhotsk (N), Pacific Ocean (E), East China Sea (SW), Sea of Japan (W)

Capital: Tokyo

Area: 145,882 sq. mi. (377,835 sq. km.)

Population (est. 1997): 125,931,533

Languages: Japanese

Government: Constitutional monarchy

Religions: Shinto, Buddhist, others including Christian

Monetary unit: Yen

Main exports: Machinery, motor vehicles, consumer electronics

Long self-isolated, Japan was prohibited from trade with other countries from the mid-16th century until 1853, when relations were established through the entry of U.S. commodore Matthew Perry and a fleet into Tokyo Bay. By the end of the century, Japan became a modern trading and political power, with a parliamentary government established in 1889. Following a war with China in 1894–95, Japan gained Formosa (Taiwan), the Pescadores Islands, and a portion of southern Manchuria.

In 1904–05, Japan defeated Russia in the Russo-Japanese War and acquired part of southern Sakhalin (Karafuto) and Russian port and rail rights in Manchuria.

In 1910 Japan annexed Korea. During World War I Japan took Germany's Pacific Islands, which were granted to them by mandate after the war through the Treaty of Versailles. In the Washington Conference of 1921–22, Japan promised to honor China's boundaries. Japan breached its agreement with China in 1931 with the invasion of Manchuria. In 1932 Japan established there the puppet state of Manchukuo, which led to international denunciation and Japan's withdrawal from the League of Nations in 1933. In 1936 Japanese officers attempted to seize the government by assassinating the cabinet; this led to a consolidation of military leadership, with an aim of war against the West and gaining greater influence in Asia. In 1936 Japan signed the anti-Comintern pact, becoming part of Axis powers. In 1937 it invaded China, beginning the eight-year Sino-Japanese War (1937–1945). On December 7, 1941, it attacked U.S. forces at Pearl Harbor, Hawaii, prompting U.S. entry into World War II.

Early in the war Japan sustained several victorious campaigns in Burma, the Philippines, and much of the Pacific theater. But by mid-1945, Allied forces had gained the upper hand with control of Okinawa and Manchuria. On August 6, 1945, the city of Hiroshima was virtually destroyed by a U.S. nuclear attack; a second attack on Nagasaki occurred on August 9. A few days later Japan surrendered unconditionally, with formal surrender coming on September 2, 1945, aboard the battleship *Missouri* in Tokyo Bay. The Soviet Union regained control of Southern Sakhalin and the Kurile Islands; Formosa and Manchuria reverted to China.

From 1945 to 1952 Japan was under American occupation, with General Douglas MacArthur named supreme commander for the Allied Powers. While this military administration aimed to punish Japanese war criminals, it also meant to aid in a national rebuilding. To that end in 1947 Japan passed a new constitution promising social and political freedom. Japan regained complete sovereignty according to the Japanese Peace Treaty in 1951.

After occupation forces left in the early 1950s, a conservative Japanese government attempted to alter postwar reforms, including education and labor. This prompted mass public demonstrations, countered by police force.

From the 1950s through the 1970s, Japan experienced tremendous industrial expansion and economic growth. In part the "economic miracle" depended on new management techniques stressing equal involvement of workers and management in decision-making.

On May 15, 1972, following negotiations led by Prime Minister Eisaku Sato, the U.S. officially returned the Ryiukyu Islands (including Okinawa) to Japanese sovereignty. Surprised and potentially weakened internationally by the U.S. accord with China in 1974, Japan negotiated its own agreement with its former enemy.

From the late 1980s national politics was marked by a lack of focus. In 1989 elections Liberal Democratic Party president Toshiki Kaifu became prime minister, but the party saw its first major loss in four decades in parliamentary elections. Elected prime minister in 1991, Liberal Democrat Kiichi Miyazawa was criticized for political appointments and his government given a vote of no confidence in 1993; Miyazawa dissolved parliament. In 1994 elections a coalition of the Socialist and Liberal Democrat Parties saw Socialist Party leader Tomiichi Murayama elected prime minister. In 1996, Ryutaro Hashimoto of the Liberal Democratic Party became prime minister.

In 1995 the city of Kobe was struck by a huge earthquake, and the government criticized for insufficient aid.

While in the 1980s the Japanese economy was strengthened by its successful export industry, a massive correction in the early 1990s devalued the stock exchange by over 50 percent. During the 1990s scandals involving government and business precipitated economic turmoil, marked by lowered real estate values and widespread failures of banks and businesses. In 1998 the scandals and downturn brought about the resignation of Prime Minister Hashimoto and his replacement by Keizo Obuchi.

Japan: 20th-Century Leaders

Emperor

1867–1912: Meiji (1852–1912)

1912–26: Taisho (1879–1926)

1926–89: Hirohito (1901–89)

1989– : Akihito (1933–)

Prime Minister

1886–1901: Hirobumi Ito (1841–1909)

1913–14: Gombei Yamamoto (1852–1933)

1923–24: Gombei Yamamoto

1936–37: Koki Hirota (1878–1948)

1937–39: Fumimaro Konoye (1891–1945)

1940–41: Fumimaro Konoye

1945: Naruhiko Higashikuni (1887–1990)

1945–46: Kijuro Shidehara (1872–1951)

1945–54: American occupation

1946–47: Shigeru Yoshida (1878–1967)

1947–48: Tetsu Katayama (1887–1978)

1948: Hitoshi Ashida (1887–1959)

1948–54: Shigeru Yoshida

1954–56: Ichiro Hatoyama (1883–1959)

1956–57: Tanzan Ishibashi (1884–1973)

1957–60: Nobusuke Kishi (1896–1987)

1960–64: Hayato Ikeda (1899–1965)

1964–72: Eisaku Sato (1901–75)

1972–74: Kakuei Tanaka (1918–93)

1974–76: Takeo Miki (1907–88)

1976–78: Takeo Fukuda

1978–80: Masayoshi Ohira (1910–80)

1980: Masayoshi Ito (acting prime minister)

1980–82: Zenko Suzuki

1982–87: Yasuhiro Nakasone

1987–89: Noboru Takeshita

1989: Sousuke Uno

1989–91: Toshiki Kaifu (1931–)

1991–94: Kiichi Miyazawa

1994–96: Tomiichi Murayama

1996–98: Ryutaro Hashimoto

1998–2000: Keizo Obuchi

Allied Commander–in–Chief

1945–51: Douglas MacArthur (1878–1964)

1951–52: Matthew B. Ridgway (1895–1993)

Jordan

Official name: Hashemite Kingdom of Jordan

Location: Western Asia; bordered by Syria (N), Iraq (NE), Saudi Arabia (SE), Israel (W), Gulf of Aqaba (SW)

Capital: Amman

Area: 34,445 sq. mi. (89,213 sq. km.)

Population (est. 1996): 4,324,638

Languages: Arabic (official), English

Government: Constitutional monarchy

Religions: Sunni Muslim 92%, Christian 8%

Monetary unit: Jordanian dinar

Main exports: Fruits, vegetables, phosphates, fertilizers

In antiquity what is now Jordan encompassed the biblical lands of Edom, Moab, Ammon, and Bashan. The region became part of the Ottoman Empire in the 16th century. It was liberated by the Arab Revolt (1916–18) during World War I and came under the control of Faisal I, then king of Syria. French troops deposed Faisal in 1920; that year Jordan, then known as Transjordan, became part of the British-administered League of Nations mandate of Palestine. In 1921 the British made Jordan a separate mandate and instituted a Hashemite monarchy. With British help, Transjordan's first king, Abdullah ibn Hussein, founded political institutions and an army named the Arab Legion.

A 1928 treaty gave Britain the right to station troops in Transjordan. Transjordan joined the Allies in World War II and won full independence in 1946. In 1948 the country joined the Arab League and participated in the First Arab-Israeli War, in which it occupied East Jerusalem and the West Bank. The nation annexed the territories in 1950, changing its name to Jordan to reflect its holdings on both sides of the Jordan River. Palestinian Arab refugees flocked to Jordan, straining the economy and destabilizing the political system. King Abdullah was assassinated by a Palestinian in 1951. He was succeeded by his son Talal, who, on account of mental illness, was replaced in 1952 by his own son Hussein I. Hussein's generally moderate, pro-Western policies over more than four decades in power earned him the long-term support of Britain and the U.S.

Under Hussein, Jordan briefly federated with Iraq in an Arab Union (1958); that year Jordan faced down threats to its existence by Egypt and Syria, which were joined at the time in the United Arab Republic (U.A.R.). Jordan's relations with Syria remained rocky for decades, but Jordan and Egypt signed a mutual defense pact in 1967.

In the Six-Day War (1967), Jordan lost the West Bank and East Jerusalem to Israel and faced a new influx of Palestinian refugees. Tensions grew between Hussein's government and the Palestinian guerrilla organizations operating from Jordan, most notably the PLO. In a bloody civil war in 1970–71, Hussein defeated and expelled the Palestinian guerrillas. In retaliation Prime Minister Wasfi al-Tal was assassinated in 1971 by Black September, a Palestinian guerrilla group that took its name from the month in 1970 when the civil war began.

In 1974 Jordan joined the Arab world in recognizing the PLO as sole representative of the Palestinian people. Jordan also joined other Arab states in cutting off relations with Egypt in 1979 for its signing of a peace treaty with Israel. In 1988 Jordan renounced its claims to the West Bank and approved creation of an independent Palestinian state there.

Jordan supported Iraq in the Persian Gulf War (1991), straining relations with the U.S. The resulting loss of aid from the U.S., as well as from Saudi Arabia and Kuwait, weakened Jordan's economy, as did an influx of refugees from Iraq and Kuwait. Relations with the U.S. improved after Hussein agreed to join Middle East peace talks. The first multiparty elections since 1956 were held in 1993, confirming Hussein's loyalist base of support. In 1994 a formal peace agreement was signed between Jordan and Israel.

The discovery of oil in 1982 led to the foundation of a small oil industry, though the economy of this arid land is still largely agricultural.

After unsuccessful radiation treatments in the U.S., King Hussein died of cancer in 1999. He was succeeded by his son, Abdullah bin Hussein.

Jordan: 20th-Century Leaders

Emir

1921–46: Abdullah ibn Hussein (1882–1951)

King

1946–51: Abdullah ibn Hussein (Abdullah I)

1951–52: Talal ibn Abdullah (1909–72)

1952–99: Hussein ibn Talal (Hussein I)

1999– : Abdullah bin Hussein (Abdullah II) (1962–)

Prime Minister

(since full independence in 1946)

1946–47: Ibrahim Hashem (1878–1958)

1947–49: Samir el-Rifai (1901–65)

1949–50: Tewfik Abul-Huda (1895–1956)

1950: Said el-Mufti (1898–1989)

1950–51: Samir el-Rifai

1951–53: Tewfik Abul-Huda

1953–54: Fawzi el-Mulki (1910–62)

1954–55: Tewfik Abul-Huda

1955: Said el-Mufti

1955: Hazzaa Majali (1916–60)

1955–56: Ibrahim Hashem

1956: Samir el-Rifai

1956: Said el-Mufti

1956–57: Suleiman Nabulsi (1910–76)

1957: Hussein Khalidi (1895–1962)

1957–58: Ibrahim Hashem

1958–59: Samir el-Rifai

1959–60: Hazzaa Majali

1960–62: Bahjat al-Talhouni (1913–94)

1962–63: Wasfi al-Tal (1920–71)

1963: Samir el-Rifai

1963–64: Sherif Husain ibn Nasser

1964–65: Bahjat al-Talhouni

1965–67: Wasfi al-Tal

1967: Saad Jumaa (1916–79)

1967–69: Bahjat al-Talhouni

1969: Abdel Monem Rifai (1917–85)

1969–70: Bahjat al-Talhouni

1970: Abdel Monem Rifai

1970: Mohammed Daoud

1970: Ahmed Toukan

1970–71: Wasfi al-Tal

1971–73: Ahmed al-Lawzi

1973–76: Zaid al-Rifai

1976–79: Mudar Badran

1979–80: Sharif Abdul Hamid Sharaf

1980: Qassim el-Riwai (1918–82)

1980–84: Mudar Badran

1984–85: Ahmed Abdel Obeidat (1938–)

1985–89: Zaid al-Rifai

1989: Sharif Zeid ibn Shaker (1934–)

1989–91: Mudar Badran

1991: Taher al-Masri (1942–)

1991–93: Sharif Zeid ibn Shaker

1993–95: Abdel Salam al-Majali

1995–96: Sharif Zeid ibn Shaker

1996–97: Abdul Karim al-Kabariti

1997–98: Abdul Salem Majali (1925–)

1998–99: Fayez Tarawneh

1999–2000: Abdoul Raouf Al-Rawabdeh

Kazakhstan

Official name: Republic of Kazakhstan

Location: Central Asia; bordered by Russian (N), China (E), Kyrgyzstan and Uzbekistan (S), Caspian Sea and Turkmenistan (W)

Capital: Alma-Ata

Area: 1,049,000 sq. mi. (2,717,300 sq. km.)

Population (est. 1994): 17,100,000

Languages: Kazakh (official), Russian

Government: Constitutional republic

Religions: Muslim 47% , Russian Orthodox, Lutheran

Monetary unit: Tenge

Main exports: Oil, ferrous and nonferrous metals, chemicals, wool, grain, meat

Kazakh territory was originally inhabited by several disparate nomadic Turkic tribes. Lacking a united leadership, the tribes were overtaken by Mongols in the 13th century. They remained under the rule of Tartar Khanates until becoming a sovereign territory of the Russian Empire in 1831.

In 1922 it was incorporated into the Soviet Union as part of the Russian Socialist Soviet Republic, and in 1925 it became an Autonomous Soviet Socialist Republic. In 1936 Kazakhstan was named a Soviet constituent republic. During Stalin's years the country underwent forced collectivization and industrialization and served as the site of disparate groups of Soviet deportees.

Kazakhstan became a member of the Commonwealth of Independent States on December 21, 1991. It officially became the independent Republic of Kazakhstan following the dissolution of the Soviet Union on December 25, 1991. Nursultan Nazarbaev, chairman of the Supreme Soviet of the Kazakh S.S.R. in 1990, was named Kazakhstan's first president in 1991. Despite economic problems of high inflation and reduced industrial output, he was reelected in 1995 and 1999.

Kazakhstan: 20th-Century Leaders

President

1991– : Nursultan Nazarbaev (1940–)

Prime Minister

1991–97: Sergei A. Tereschenko (1961–)

1997–99: Nurlan Balgimbayev

1999– : Kasymzhomart Tokayev (1953–)

Kenya

Official name: Republic of Kenya

Location: Eastern Africa; bordered by Sudan (SW), Ethiopia (N), Somalia (E), Indian Ocean (SE), Tanzania (SW), Lake Victoria, Uganda (W)

Capital: Nairobi

Area: 224,962 sq. mi. (582,650 sq. km.)

Population: 28,803,085

Languages: English and Swahili (both official), indigenous languages

Government: Republic

Religions: Protestant 38%, Catholic 28%, indigenous beliefs 26%, Muslim 6%, other 2%

Monetary unit: Kenyan shilling

Main exports: Tea, coffee, petroleum and petroleum products

The ancient east African territory now known as Kenya was explored by British adventurers in the late 19th century. In 1885 East Africa was divided into two areas of influence, with its coastal region becoming a protectorate of Great Britain in 1890. The entire region became a British protectorate in 1895, a dependency in 1902, and a colony in 1920. British settlement began, with prime land being reserved for nonnatives. During World War I Kenya served as a major Allied post for the East African campaign. During World War II northern Kenya was occupied for a time by the Italian-controlled colony of Ethiopia. It was eventually reclaimed by Allied British forces.

After the war the dominant Kikiyu tribes led a fight for independence against British colonial rule called the MauMau rebellion. It put Kenya in a state of emergency from 1952 to 1956, and rebellion leader Jomo Kenyatta and other nationalists were sentenced to seven years in jail. In 1957 Britain granted Kenya greater participation in government, and several Africans were elected to the Legislative Council.

After years of civil unrest, Kenya became an independendent state on December 12, 1963. In 1964 it became a republic within the British Commonwealth. African nationalist pioneer Jomo Kenyatta, leader of the dominant political party Kenya African National Union (KANU), was elected Kenya's first president. Although Kenya was a one-party state, its moderate pro-Western government attracted international investors and maintained amity among tribes. In 1969 leftist opposition party the Kenya People's Union (KPU) was implicated in the assassination of political leader Tom Mboya, and the opposition party was dissolved.

Under President Daniel arap Moi in 1982, Kenya adopted a new constitution making it a one-party state. Although Moi was reelected twice in the 1980s, he was criticized internationally for human rights abuses. From the 1980s into the mid-1990s Kenya was marred by ethnic violence resulting in many deaths. In response to criticism by providers of aid, President Moi permitted opposition parties in 1991 and agreed to multiparty presidential elections in 1992. Due to divided opposition parties, Moi was reelected.

Pro-reform protests continued into the 1990s, in response to continued electoral restrictions and the 1995 arrest of two opposition leaders. After continued violence over election reform demonstrations, Moi agreed to reforms in July 1997.

An explosion at the U.S. embassy in Nairobi, later linked to Saudi millionaire Osama bin Laden, killed 247 and wounded 5,000 in August 1998.

Kenya: 20th-Century Leaders

Governor–General

1963–64: Malcolm MacDonald (1901–81)

President

1978– : Daniel T. arap Moi (1924–)

Prime Minister

1963–78: Jomo Kenyatta (1891–78)

Kiribati

Official name: Republic of Kiribati

Location: Mid-Pacific Ocean; 33 atolls in three main groups (E–W)—Line Islands, Phoenix Islands, Gilbert Islands; nearest neighbors are Nauru (W), Tuvalu and Tokelau (S)

Capital: Tarawa

Area: 277 sq. mi. (717 sq. km.)

Population (est. 1997): 82,449

Languages: English (official), Gilbertese

Government: Republic

Religions: Roman Catholic 52.6%, Protestant (Congregational) 40.9%, Seventh-Day Adventist, Baha'i

Monetary unit: Australian dollar

Main exports: Copra, seaweed

From 1892 to 1916, the Gilbert Islands was a British protectorate, inhabited mainly by Micronesians. In 1915–16 Britain made Gilbert and Ellice Islands a colony, later including Line and Phoenix Islands.

During World War II in 1942, Japanese forces occupied the Gilbert Islands; they were recaptured by the Allies in 1943 after costly battle in Tarawa. In 1957 Christmas Island (Kiritimati) was the site of a British hydrogen bomb test.

In 1971 Britain granted Kiribati self-rule, and on July 12, 1979, the Gilbert Islands separated to become Kiribati. In 1975 the Ellice Islands separated, forming Tuvalu in 1978. A 1979 friendship treaty granted portions of the Line and Phoenix Islands to the U.S.; during that year, the U.S. abandoned interest in several Kiribati islands, including Kanton and Enderbury. Largely a subsistence economy, Kiribati receives foreign support from England.

Kiribati: 20th-Century Leaders

President

1979–91: Ieremia Tabai (1950–)

1991–94: Teatao Teannaki

1994– : Teburoro Tito (1953–)

Korea, North

Official name: Democratic People's Republic of Korea

Location: Northern Korean peninsula in eastern Asia; bordered by China (NW), Sea of Japan (E), Republic of Korea, also known as South Korea (S), Yellow Sea (SW)

Capital: Pyongyang

Area: 46,541 sq. mi. (120,540 sq. km.)

Population (est. 1998): 21,234,387

Languages: Korean

Government: Communist state

Religions: Buddhism, Confucianism; virtually no religious activity

Monetary unit: Won

Main exports: Minerals, metallurgical products, agricultural products, manufactures

(For history prior to 1948, see **Korea, South**.)

Occupied by the Soviet Union at the close of World War II, the Korean peninsula north of the 38th parallel became the Democratic People's Republic of Korea in 1948. This Communist state was headed by Kim Il Sung from its inception until his death in 1994. He attempted to reunify Korea by launching an invasion of liberal-capitalist South Korea in 1950. In the Korean War (1950–53), U.S.–led UN forces thwarted the invasion, leaving Korea divided.

Kim led a staunchly Stalinist regime, even after Soviet leader Khrushchev began his destalinization campaign in the Soviet Union in 1956. Political, economic, and social life was strictly controlled; the country was rapidly industrialized; a personality cult began to take shape around Kim. With Soviet and Chinese aid the country prospered in the 1950s and 1960s, but stagnated in the 1970s. By the 1980s Kim's unwillingness to open the country to private enterprise, modern technology, or foreign investment was hurting the economy. So was his heavy military spending, tied to a persistently belligerent attitude toward South Korea. With the collapse of the Soviet Union in 1991 and the opening of diplomatic relations between China and South Korea in 1992, North Korea was increasingly isolated. Concern grew internationally over North Korea's support of terrorism and nuclear weapons development program.

Following Kim Il Sung's death in 1994, his son Kim Jong Il succeeded him as leader. Progress was made in resolving nuclear weapons issues and improving relations with South

Korea. In the meantime, chronic food shortages turned to famine in the mid–1990s, as North Korea suffered from floods, droughts, crop failures, and a virtually nonfunctioning food distribution system. In 1996 North Korea was even forced to accept emergency grants of rice from South Korea. In 1999, North Korea agreed to suspend long-range missile testing, prompting the U.S. to ease restrictions on travel and trade. Improvement of relations between North and South Korea and the U.S., continued in 2000.

North Korea: 20th-Century Leaders

Head of State

1948–72: Choi Yong Kun (1900–76)

1972–94: Kim Il Sung (1912–94)

1994– : Kim Jong Il (1942–)

Premier

1948–72: Kim Il Sung

1972–76: Kim Il (1911–84)

1976–77: Pak Sung Chul

1977–84: Li Jong Ok

1984–86: Kang Song San

1986–88: Li Gun Mo

1988–92: Yon Hyong Muk

1992–97: Kang Song San

1997– : Hong Song Nam

Korea, South

Official name: Republic of Korea

Location: Southern Korean peninsula in eastern Asia; bordered by China, Democratic People's Republic of Korea, also known as North Korea (N), Sea of Japan (E), East China Sea (S), Yellow Sea (SW) Capital: Seoul

Area: 38,023 sq. mi. (98,480 sq. km.)

Population (est. 1998): 21,234,387

Languages: Korean, English

Government: Republic

Religions: Christianity (mostly Protestant) 48.6%, Buddhism 47.4%, Confucianism 3%, folk religion

Monetary unit: Won

Main exports: Electronic and electrical equipment, electrical machinery, steel, automobiles

Long dominated by China, Korea came under Japanese influence in the late 19th century. Japan made it a protectorate in 1905 and annexed it in 1910. The Japanese ruled repressively, suppressing dissent harshly and denying civil and political rights. Independence movements arose; in 1919 Syngman Rhee established a provisional Korean government in exile in Shanghai, China. From 1934 Communist partisans supported by the Soviet Union and led by Kim Il Sung waged guerrilla war against Japan. In the late 1930s and during World War II (1939–45), Japanese rule became more brutal, as Japan deported Koreans to serve as forced laborers abroad and attempted to wipe out Korean language and culture.

Just before Japan's surrender to the Allies in 1945, Soviet forces occupied North Korea. The U.S. agreed to joint occupation of the country, with U.S. forces south of the 38th parallel and Soviet forces north of it. Efforts to unify the country failed, and in 1948, two separate states were created: the Republic of Korea (South Korea) and the Democratic People's Republic of Korea (North Korea). North Korea invaded the south in 1950, starting the Korean War (1950–53), in which U.S.–led UN forces held the line against the Soviet and Chinese-backed invasion. A truce was signed and a demilitarized zone was created along the 38th parallel, but peace was never formally settled between the two nations. Since the Korean War the demilitarized zone has been guarded by thousands of soldiers on both sides, with occasional shooting incidents. North Korean submarines have been captured and sunk off South Korean waters.

A poor agricultural country, South Korea relied on U.S. aid for its survival in the 1950s. Rhee, South Korea's first president (1948–60), ruled autocratically and with much government corruption. A student protest march over his apparently fraudulent victory in the 1960 election was violently suppressed, sparking a wave of uprisings. Rhee resigned and a Second Republic was instituted. This was overthrown in a 1961 coup led by General Park Chung, who proclaimed a Third Republic in 1963, with him as president. He, too, ruled autocratically, increasing his power through constitutional changes in 1972. He presided over an economic transformation, with South Korea becoming an exporter of manufactured goods, particularly for the consumer market. He was assassinated in 1979; the tradition of rule by military officers was continued under Choi Kyu Hah (1979–80) and Chun Doo Hwan (1980–88).

Despite a burgeoning economy, civil unrest grew during the 1970s and 1980s. Kim Dae-Jong, an opposition leader, was arrested several times. Thousands were killed in 1980 when the government massacred pro-democracy demonstrators in Kwangju. A new constitution in 1987 introduced some democratic reforms; President Roh Tae Woo (1988–93) introduced more. Former opposition leader Kim Yung Sam (1993–) succeeded him, becoming South Korea's first civilian president in more than 30 years. Roh Tae Woo and Chun Doo Hwan were convicted in 1996 on charges of corruption and other offenses, including responsibility for the 1980 Kwangju massacre. Kim himself faced mounting charges of corruption as the decade continued.

In the 1980s North Korea allegedly sponsored terrorist attacks on South Korea, including a 1983 bombing that killed several government officials and the 1987 destruction of a South Korean airliner over the border between Thailand and Burma (Myanmar). Peace talks aimed at reunification began in 1971; discussions continued in the 1980s and 1990s. In 2000, the first summit conference ever between North Korean and South Korean leaders took place in Pyongyang, North Korea.

South Korea: 20th-Century Leaders

President

1948–60: Syngman Rhee

1960: Ho Chong (1896–1988)

1960–62: Yun Po Sun (1897–1990)

1962–79: Chung Hee Park (1917–79)

1979–80: Choi Kyu Hah

1980: Park Choong Hoon

1980–88: Chun Doo Hwan (1931–)

1988–93: Roh Tae Woo (1932–)

1993–98: Kim Young Sam

1998– : Kim Dae Jung (1925–)

Premier

1948–50: Lee Bum Suk (1900–72)

1950: Shin Sung Mo (1891–1960)

1950–52: John Myun Chang (1899–1966)

1952: Lee Yun Yung (acting)

1952: Chang Taek-Sang (1893–1969)

1953–54: Paik Too Chin

1954–55: Pyun Yung Tai (1893–1969)

1960–61: John Myun Chang

1961: Chang Do Yong

1961–62: Chung Hee Park

1962: Song Yo Chan

1962: Chung Hee Park

1962–63: Kim Hyun Chul (1901–89)

1963–64: Choi Doo Sun (1894–1974)

1964–70: Chung Il Kwon (1917–94)

1970–71: Paik Too Chin

1971–75: Kim Jong Pil

1975–79: Cho Kyu Hah

1979–80: Shin Hyon Hwak

1980: Park Choong Hoon (acting)

1980–82: Nam Duck Woo

1982: Yoo Chang Soon

1982–83: Kim Sang Hyup

1983–85: Chin Iee Chong

1985–87: Lho Shin Yong

1987: Lee Han Key

1987–88: Kim Chung Yul (1917–92)

1988: Lee Hyun Jae

1988–90: Kanng Young Hoon

1990–91: Ro Jai Bong

1991–92: Chung Won Shik (1929–)

1992–93: Hyun Soong Jong

1993: Hwang In Sung

1993–94: Lee Hoi Chang

1994: Lee Yung Duk

1994–95: Lee Hong Koo

1995–97: Lee Soo Song

1997–98: Koh Kun

1998–2000: Kim Jong Pil

Kuwait

Official name: State of Kuwait

Location: Northeastern Arabian peninsula; bordered by Iraq (N, E); Saudi Arabia (S, E); Persian Gulf (E)

Capital: Kuwait City

Area: 6,880 sq. mi. (17,820 sq. km.)

Population (est. 1997): 1,834,269

Languages: Arabic (official), English

Government: Constitutional monarchy

Religions: Muslim 85% (Sunni 45%, Shi'a 30%, other 10%); Christian, Hindu, Parsi, and other 15%

Monetary unit: Kuwaiti dinar

Main exports: Oil

Kuwait became part of the Ottoman Empire in the 16th century. It became an autonomous emirate under Ottoman suzerainty, ruled by the al-Sabah dynasty, in the 18th century. From 1899 to 1961 the emirate was a British protectorate, with British control of foreign relations and defense. Full independence came in 1961.

Revenues from oil production, which began in 1946, made Kuwait one of the wealthiest Arab states. Besides enriching the ruling family, the wealth allowed Kuwaitis to enjoy free medical care, education, and social security without any taxation except customs duties. However, the majority of the population are not Kuwaitis but foreigners working in the oil industry, including Arabs from other nations and South Asians. The emirs ruled undemocratically, jailing opponents and, at one point, dissolving Parliament (1986–92).

In the early 1960s Iraq asserted a territorial claim to Kuwait but was foiled by British intervention; Iraq acknowledged Kuwaiti sovereignty in 1963. Kuwait sided with Iraq in the Iran-Iraq War (1980–88). In the face of Iranian attacks on Kuwaiti shipping during that conflict, the U.S. Navy escorted Kuwaiti tankers in the Persian Gulf from 1987 to 1989.

In August 1990 Iraq renewed its claim to Kuwait with a vengeance, invading, occupying, and annexing the country. The emir established a government-in-exile in Saudi Arabia. In the Gulf War (January–February 1991), a U.S.–led multinational coalition liberated Kuwait. Iraqi forces wreaked environmental havoc, setting fire to more than 500 Kuwaiti oil wells and destroying desalination plants. Kuwait later spent more than $5 billion to repair the damage to oil installations. Iraq formally recognized Kuwaiti sovereignty in 1994.

After the war Kuwait persecuted and expelled Palestinian residents for their suspected collaboration with the Iraqi occupiers. Bowing to international pressure to democratize the country, the emir permitted parliamentary elections in 1992.

Kuwait: 20th-Century Leaders

Emir

1950–65: Abdullah as-Salim as-Sabah (1895–1965)

1965–77: Sabah as-Salim as-Sabah (1913–77)

1977– : Jabir al-Ahmed al-Jabir as-Sabah (1926–)

Prime Minister

1963–65: Sabah as-Salim as-Sabah

1965–77: Jabir al-Ahmed al-Jabir as-Sabah

1978– : Saad Abdulla al-Salim as-Sabah (1930–)

Kyrgyzstan

Official name: The Kyrgyz Republic

Location: Central Asia; bordered by Kazakhstan (N, NW), Uzbekistan (SW), Tajikistan (S), China (SE)

Capital: Bishkek (Frunze)

Area: 76,000 sq. mi. (198,500 sq. km.)

Population (est. 1994): 4,500,000

Languages: Kyrgyz (official), Russian

Government: Constitutional republic

Religions: Sunni Muslim 70%, Russian Orthodox

Monetary unit: Som

Main exports: Fuel, metals, minerals, machinery, and transport equipment.

Formerly known as Kirghizia, this territory is almost entirely (95 percent) covered by the Tien Shen mountain range and originally inhabited by the Kyrgyz, a nomadic Turkish group. From 1864 it was part of the Russian empire. In the early 20th century Russia broadly colonized the area, which led to its participation in an unsuccessful revolt against the czar in 1916.

In 1918 after the Russian Revolution, it became part of the Turkestan Soviet Republic. In 1924 it was integrated into the Soviet Federated Socialist Republic, and was named a full member of the Union of Socialist Soviet Republics in 1936. Over decades the Soviet government forced industrialization on the nomadic native Kyrgyz people, causing disruption of their traditional way of life.

During the 1980s the country supported Mikail Gorbachev's reforms. It also developed an unstable nationalism, which manifested itself destructively with the 1990 massacre of its minority group, the Uzbek. On August 31, 1991, Kirghizia declared itself an independent state. It gained officialindependence after the breakup of the Soviet Union on December 25, 1991. As the Republic of Kyrgyzstan, it became part of the Commonwealth of Independent States in December 1991. In 1992 it joined the United Nations and the IMF, which demanded radical economic retooling. President Askar Akayev's strategies attracted foreign investment, and by the mid-1990s, the country was maintaining healthier economic markers (for example, lower inflation) than some other former Soviet republics.

Kyrgyzstan: 20th-Century Leaders

President

1990– : Askar Akayev (1944–)

Prime Minister

1991: Nasirindin Isanov

1991–93: Tursunbek Chyngyshev

1993–94: Apas Dzhumagulov (1934–)

1994–98: Kubanychbek Jumaliev

1998–99: Djumabek Ibrahimov

1999– : Armangeldi Muraliyev (1947–)

Laos

Official name: Lao People's Democratic Republic

Location: Southeast Asia; landlocked; bordered by China (N), Vietnam (E), Cambodia (S), Thailand (W), Myanmar (NW)

Capital: Vientiane

Area: 91,429 sq. mi. (236,800 sq. km.)

Population (est. 1998): 5,260,842

Languages: Lao (official), French, English, ethnic languages

Government: Communist state

Religions: Buddhist 60%, animist and other 40%

Monetary unit: New kip

Main exports: Electricity, wood products, coffee, tin

Historically dominated by Thailand and Vietnam, Laos became a French protectorate in 1893. Ruled by a puppet monarch, it formed part of the French-controlled Union of Indochina. France expanded Laos, adding territories from China and Thailand by 1917. Laos was ethnically heterogeneous, but nationalist awareness grew as France tried to impose European traditions.

During World War II Japan occupied Laos with the cooperation of the pro-Vichy colonial authorities. After the war, in 1946, France reestablished dominion over Laos; in 1949 Laos was granted local autonomy as a constitutional monarchy within the French Union. Laos became formally independent with France's withdrawal from Indochina (1954) following its defeat in Vietnam. Laos entered the UN in 1955.

During the 1950s a three-way civil war developed in Laos. The adversaries were the royalist government of King Sisavang Vong (reigned 1904–59); the neutralist movement of Prince Souvanna Phouma, which sought a neutral Laos free of foreign interference; and the Pathet Lao, a Communist movement led by Prince Souphanouvong and supported by North Vietnam. In 1962 an international conference seemed to settle the matter, guaranteeing Laotian neutrality while a provisional coalition government representing all factions was established, with neutralist leader Souvanna Phouma as premier. However, in 1964, the Communist Pathet Lao withdrew from the coalition and renewed the civil war. The civil war became linked to the Vietnam War (1959–75), as the Pathet Lao provided North Vietnam with supply lines along the Ho Chi Minh Trail through Laos. The U.S. bombed those supply lines and recruited Hmong tribesmen as irregular forces to attack the Pathet Lao.

The Pathet Lao steadily gained strength. Following a 1973 cease-fire, they dominated a coalition government formed under Souvanna Phouma in 1974. Encouraged by North Vietnam's victory in the Vietnam War, the Pathet Lao took control of the country in 1975, forcing the abdication of King Savang Vatthana (1959–75) and proclaiming the Democratic People's Republic of Laos.

Poor and devastated by years of war, Laos became a client state of Vietnam, dependent on that country for support and accepting the presence of Vietnamese troops. As Vietnam's economy became more liberalized in the late 1980s and early 1990s, that of Laos followed suit; foreign investment has been welcomed from 1989. A new constitution in 1991, approved by a Supreme People's Assembly elected in 1989, confirmed the Communist Party as the sole legal political party.

Laos: 20th-Century Leaders

King

1904–59: Sisavang Vong (1885–1959)

1959–75: Savang Vatthana (1907–81)

President

1975–86: Prince Souphanouvong (1912–)

1986–91: Phoumi Vongvichit

1991–92: Kaysone Phomvihan (1920–92)

1992–98: Nouhak Phounsavanh

1998– : Khamtai Siphandon

Prime Minister

(since full independence in 1954)

1954–55: Katay D. Sasorith (1904–59)

1956–58: Prince Souvanna Phouma (1901–84)

1958–59: Phui Sananikone (1903–83)

1959–60: Phoumi Nosavan (1920–85) (head of government)

1960: Kou Abhay Og Long

1960: Prince Somsanith

1960: Kong Le (1934–) (head of government)

1960: Prince Souvanna Phouma

1960: Sunthone Pattamavong (head of government)

1960: Quinim Pholsena (head of government)

1960–62: Prince Boun Oum

1962–75: Prince Souvanna Phouma

1975–91: Kaysone Phomvihan

1991–98: Khamtai Siphandon

1998– : Sisavat Keobounphan (1928–)

Latvia

Official name: Republic of Latvia

Location: Northeastern Europe; bordered by Baltic Sea (N), Estonia (NE), Russia, Belarus (S), Lithuania (W)

Capital: Riga

Area: 24,749 sq. mi. (64,100 sq. km.)

Population (est. 1997): 2,421,163

Languages: Latvian (official), Russian, ethnic languages, an Indo-European language written in Latin script

Government: Republic

Religions: Lutheran, Roman Catholic, Russian Orthodox

Monetary unit: Lats

Main exports: Timber, ferrous metals and products, electrical machinery and equipment, fish, furniture, pharmaceuticals, textiles, dairy

Although it had been subject to Russian rule since 1795, Latvia entered the 20th century rejuvenated by a 19th-century cultural revival highlighting folklore, language, and the arts. After the 1917 Russian Revolution, Latvia became a republic on November 18, 1918. For the first time in its history it gained political independence, with the Brest-Livosk World War I peace treaty between Germany and the Soviet Union.

In 1922 Latvia adopted a new constitution allowing for a single house of legislature with broad multiparty representation, but the lack of powerful central authority brought threats from extremist groups. In response, Prime Minister Karlis Ulmanis dissolved the Parliament in 1934, planning to rewrite the constitution to expand presidential powers and create another branch of government.

In 1939 Soviet troops occupied Latvia, and by 1940 Latvia was made a Soviet republic. From 1941 to 1944, during World War II, Latvia was occupied by German troops.

Communist leaders attempted to quash Latvian identity and impose severe Russianization. Deportations, particularly of educated or elite citizenry, were common: In 1945 alone Stalin-led deportations totaled about 100,000.

Beginning in the mid-1980s, the *glasnost* policies of Soviet premier Mikhail Gorbachev generated more dissident groups in Latvia. Changes in the leadership of the Latvian Communist Party led to its association with the Latvian Popular Front, and soon the entire political arena was being influenced by non-Communist groups.

In 1988 Latvia's official language changed from Russian to Latvian, and on May 5, 1990, Latvia announced its independence. Following the failed coup against Mikhail Gorbachev, Latvia declared independence on August 21, 1991. The Soviet Union recognized Latvia's independence on September 2, 1991. Latvia became a member of the UN in 1991 and gained associate status with the EU in 1995.

Since independence Latvia has faced ongoing problems of citizenship. In particular, it has struggled with whether to grant voting rights to its large minority of non-Latvian inhabitants. As of the mid-1990s, ethnic Latvians constitute just over 50 percent of the country's population. In a referendum in 1998, Latvian voters eased citizenship restrictions on ethnic Russians. In 1999, Latvia elected the first female president of a former Soviet republic, Vaira Vike-Freiberga.

Latvia: 20th Century Leaders

Chairman of Council

1918–20: Jan Chakste (d. 1927)

President of Assembly

1920–22: Jan Chakste

President

1922–27: Jan Chakste

1927–29: Gustav Zemgals

1930–36: Albert Kviesis

1936–40: Karlis Ulmanis

(Soviet republic 1940–91; occupied by Germany 1941–44)

1991–93: Anatolijs Gorbunovs (1942–)

1993–99: Guntis Ulmanis

1999– : Vaira Vike-Freiberga (1937–)

Prime Minister

1990–93: Ivars Godmanis

1993–94: Valdis Birkavs

1994–95: Maris Gailis

1995–97: Andris Skele

1997–98: Guntars Krasts

1998–98: Vilis Kristopans

1999–2000: Andris Skele

Lebanon

Official name: Republic of Lebanon

Location: Western Asia; bordered by Syria (N, E), Israel (S), Mediterranean Sea (W)

Capital: Beirut

Area: 4,015 sq. mi. (10,400 sq. km.)

Population (est. 1997): 3,449,578

Languages: Arabic and French (both official), Armenian, English

Government: Republic

Religions: Muslim 70%, Christian 30%

Monetary unit: Lebanese pound

Main exports: Agricultural products, chemicals, textiles, precious and semiprecious metals, jewelry

Site of the ancient Phoenician cities of Tripoli and Tyre, Lebanon came under Ottoman rule in the 16th century and French influence in the 18th century. After World War I Lebanon became a French League of Nations mandate (1920). Under a 1926 constitution, Lebanon became a self-governing republic; a 1943 National Covenant apportioned political representation among the country's frequently contentious religious groups. These included Maronite Christians, who held the presidency and dominated the government, Sunni Muslims, Shi'ite Muslims, and Druze. During World War II British and Free French forces took control from the Vichy government (1941). Full independence followed in stages, with the last French troops evacuated in 1946.

Until the early 1970s Lebanon flourished. Beirut became a center for Middle Eastern banking and trade; agriculture and industry grew. In 1958 a Syrian-backed Muslim rebellion, sparked by Arab nationalist anger against the government's close ties to the West, was foiled by U.S. military intervention. But instability increased as Lebanon's demographics changed. Muslims became the majority and resented the Maronite Christian control embedded in the constitution. Shi'ite Muslims resented the growth in economic inequality, as their group became poorer while Christians became wealthier. Tensions also grew over the increasing numbers of Palestinian refugees, particularly when the PLO, expelled from Jordan in 1970–71, made Lebanon its base for raids into Israel.

From 1975 to 1976 a bloody civil war raged among the various religious and ethnic groups, including the Palestinians, Lebanese Muslims supported by Syria, and Maronite Christians backed by Israel. About 60,000 people were killed and Syrian troops intervened before a 1976 cease-fire ended the fighting. Civil war among rival militias resumed in 1977.

In 1978 responding to PLO guerrilla attacks from Lebanon, Israel invaded and occupied what it called a security zone in southern Lebanon. On June 6, 1982, Israel launched a full-scale invasion. Israeli forces encircled and bombed Beirut, forcing the PLO to evacuate to Tunisia. Israeli and Syrian forces clashed in the Bekaa Valley. In August Bashir Gemayel of the Christian Phalangist Party was elected president but was killed in September by a bomb. Christian Phalangist forces retaliated with a massacre at Palestinian refugee camps at Sabra and Shatilla, killing nearly 900 civilians. Gemayel's brother Amin Gemayel was elected president soon thereafter.

A multinational force, including troops from the U.S., Britain, France, and Italy, attempted to enforce a cease-fire in 1983. In April of that year 50 people were killed when a bomb partially destroyed the U.S. embassy in Beirut. In October 241 U.S. Marines and 58 French soldiers were killed in separate suicide attacks by Muslims.

Throughout the 1980s Beirut remained a war zone, divided into opposing sectors and plagued by terrorist bombings and kidnappings of foreign nationals. By 1985 Israel had withdrawn from all but its six-mile-deep security zone in southern Lebanon.

Syria, which retained forces in Lebanon, attempted to bring an end to the civil war even as the rival factions splintered into smaller competing fragments. In October 1989 Christian and Muslim leaders agreed on the Taif Accord, a new national charter that would provide a basis for peace. But the prevailing chaos continued when Syrian-backed president René Moawad was assassinated that November.

In 1990 rival Shi'ite militias signed an agreement to end their fighting. By 1991 a Lebanese government dependent on Syrian support was functioning, and the civil war was at an end. Nearly 150,000 people had been killed and the economy and infrastructure had been devastated. Skirmishes continued in the security zone between Israel and Hezbollah Shi'ite guerrillas. The fighting escalated in 1996, when Israel launched air raids against suspected guerrilla bases in the south, killing more than 100 people at a UN refugee camp near Tyre. In 1998, Lebanon held its first municipal elections in more than three decades.

Lebanon: 20th-Century Leaders

President

1943–52: Bishara Khalil el–Khoury (1890–1964)

1952–58: Camille Chamoun (1900–87)

1958–64: Fuad Chehab (1902–73)

1964–70: Charles Hélou

1970–76: Suleiman Franjieh (1910–92)

1976–82: Elias Sarkis (1924–85)

1976-82: Elias Sarkis (1924-85)

1982-88: Amin Gemayel (1942-)

1989: René Moawad (1925-89)

1989-98: Elias Hrawi (1930-)

1998- : Emile Lahoud (1936-)

Prime Minister

1944-45: Riad es-Solh (1894–1951)

1945: Abdul Hamid Karami

1945-46: Sami es-Solh (1890–1968)

1946: Saadi Munla

1946-51: Riad es-Solh

1951: Hussein el-Oweini (1898–1971)

1951-52: Abdullah Ared al-Yafi

1952: Sami es-Solh

1952: Nazim Akkari

1952: Saab Salaam

1952: Fuad Chehab

1952–53: Khaled Chehab

1953: Saab Salaam

1953–54: Abdullah Yafi

1954–55: Sami es-Solh

1955–56: Rashid Karami (1921–87)

1956: Abdullah Yafi

1956–58: Sami es-Solh

1958–60: Rashid Karami

1960: Ahmed Daouk

1960–61: Saab Salaam

1961–64: Rashid Karami

1964–65: Hussein el-Oweini

1965–66: Rashid Karami

1966: Abdullah Yafi

1966–68: Rashid Karami

1968–69: Abdullah Yafi

1969–70: Rashid Karami

1970–73: Saab Salaam

1973: Amin Hafez

1973–74: Takieddin es-Solh (1909–88)

1974–75: Rashid es-Solh

1975–76: Rashid Karami

1976–80: Salim al-Hoss

1980–84: Shafiq al-Wazzan

1984–87: Rashid Karami

1987–90: Salim al-Hoss

1990–92: Omar Karami

1992: Rashid es-Solh

1992–98: Rafik al-Harari

1998– : Salim al-Hoss

Lesotho

Official name: Kingdom of Lesotho

Location: Central southern Africa; landlocked country bordered by South African territory

Capital: Maseru

Area: 11,718 sq. mi. (30,350 sq. km.)

Population (est. 1997): 2,007,814

Languages: Sesotho and English (official), Zulu, Xhosa

Government: Modified constitutional monarchy

Religions: Christian 80%, indigenous beliefs 20%

Monetary unit: Loti

Main exports: Clothing, furniture, footwear

The country now known as Lesotho was established as a native state under British protection in 1843 and became the British Protectorate of Basutoland in 1868 to provide shelter against the Boers.

It became the independent monarchy of Lesotho on October 4, 1966, under King Moshoeshoe. The first government was controlled by the pro–South African Basutoland National Party, electing Lebua Jonathan as prime minister. Jonathan suspended elections and the constitution after the 1970 elections, when Ntsu Mokhehle of the Socialist Basutoland Congress Party claimed victory. In 1986 Jonathan was deposed by a South African–supported coalition. Lesotho has long depended on surrounding neighbor South Africa for jobs, much of it in migrant labor. In January 1986 Lesotho was blockaded by South Africa for providing shelter to rebel troops aiming to overthrow the South African government. The blockade led to the installation of leaders who expelled the rebels.

The 1990s began with the exile of King Moshoeshoe by the military government in 1990 and his replacement by Letsie III. In 1991 a military regime replaced the coalition civilian government that had replaced Chief Jonathan in 1986. Elections in 1993 brought Ntsu Mokhele of the Basutoland Congress Party to power, the first civilian to hold the office in 23 years. In 1994 the Mokhele government was dismissed by the king. A military coup unseated the government in 1995. After constitutional rule was reinstated, King Letsie abdicated and King Moshoeshoe retook the throne in 1995. He died in a car accident in January 1996 and was replaced by Letsie.

An army mutiny in 1998 required armed assistance from South Africa. The mutiny was put down in a matter of days.

Lesotho: 20th-Century Leaders

King

1966–90: Motlotlehi Moshoeshoe II (1938–96)

1990–95: Letsie III (1963–)

1995–96: Motlotlehi Moshoeshoe II

1996– : Letsie III

Paramount Chief

1960–66: Motlotlehi Moshoeshoe II

Prime Minister

1965: Chief Sekhonyana Maseribane (1918–86)

1965–86: Chief Joseph Lebua Jonathan (1914–87)

1986–91: Justin Lekhanya (1938–)

1991–93: Elias Tutsoane Ramaema (1933–)

1993–98: Ntsu Mokhehle

1998– : Pakalitha Mosisili (1945–)

Liberia

Official name: Republic of Liberia

Location: Western Africa; bordered by Sierra Leone and Guinea (N), Côte d'Ivoire (E), Atlantic Ocean (S, W)

Capital: Monrovia

Area: 43,000 sq. mi. (111,370 sq. km.)

Population (est. 1997): 2,602,068

Languages: English (official), languages of Niger-Congo group

Government: Republic

Religions: Indigenous beliefs 70%, Muslim 20%, Christian 10%

Monetary unit: Liberian dollar

Main exports: Iron ore, rubber, timber

Liberia was founded by the American Colonization Society in 1822 in an effort to establish a homeland for freed American slaves. It declared independence on July 26, 1847, and was recognized as the Free and Independent Republic of Liberia. Its first president, American Joseph Jenkins Roberts (known as the "Father of Liberia") established a modern government and introduced Americo-Liberians or English-speaking U.S. blacks and their descendents as the nation's elite. Liberia entered the 20th century fending off attempts by France and England to encroach on its territory.

For several decades the government worked to open up the interior of Liberia. A landmark accomplishment was the building of the 43-mile railroad from Monrovia to the Bomi Hills. Leading Liberia through the postwar years of African decolonization was President William V. S. Tubman, who served from 1944 until his death in 1971.

Tubman's successor, William R. Tolbert Jr., was assassinated in a military coup on April 12, 1980, and replaced by coup leader Samuel K. Doe. Beginning in 1989 former Doe associate Charles Taylor led the antigovernment National Patriotic Forces of Liberia in a widespread rebellion that by 1990 had captured key areas of the country. A peacekeeping force of the Economic Community of West African States partitioned Liberia into two zones, one led by Doe, one by Taylor. Former Taylor associate Prince Johnson fought both Doe's and Taylor's forces and killed Doe in 1990.

The civil war continued into the 1990s, despite a short-lived cease-fire and peace agreement in 1993. An interim coalition government was established in 1994, with elections scheduled for November 1995. It was prevented by further civil war, which lasted until an

April 1996 cease-fire. In 1997 Liberia maintained some order through a Nigerian peace-keeping force. It allowed for the election of Charles Taylor as president.

Liberia: 20th-Century Leaders

President

1896–1900: William D. Coleman

1900–04: Garrett W. Gibson

1904–12: Arthur Barclay

1912–20: Daniel E. Howard

1920–30: Charles D. B. King

1930–44: Edwin Barclay

1944–71: William V. S. Tubman (1895–1971)

1971–80: William R. Tolbert Jr. (1913–80)

1980–90: Samuel K. Doe (1951–90)

1990–94: Amos Sawyer (1945–) (interim)

1994–95: David Kpormakor (chairman of the Council of State)

1995–96: Wilton Sankawulo (chairman of the Council of State)

1996–97: Ruth Perry (chairman of the Council of State)

1997– : Charles Taylor

Libya

Official name: Socialist People's Libyan Arab Jamahiriya

Location: North Africa; bordered by Mediterranean Sea (N), Egypt (E), Sudan (SE), Chad, Niger (S), Algeria (S, W), Tunisia (NW)

Capital: Tripoli (with Hun as administrative capital since 1987)

Area: 679,359 sq. mi. (1,759,540 sq. km.)

Population (est. 1997): 5,648,359

Languages: Arabic, Italian, English

Government: Jamahiriya, in theory a mass-state; in practice, a dictatorship

Religions: Sunni Muslim 97%

Monetary unit: Libyan dinar

Main exports: Petroleum

Part of the Ottoman Empire since the 16th century, this largely desert and semidesert country was invaded and conquered by Italy in a war that lasted from 1911 to 1912. After World War I Idris I, emir of Cyrenaica, Libya's largest region, led resistance to Italian colonial rule.

Italy made Libya a province in 1939, but lost control of Libya in World War II, when Libya became a focal point for the North African campaigns. The Allies occupied Libya in 1943; after the war the British and French shared control until December 24, 1951, when Libya became an independent constitutional monarchy, with Idris I as its first king. At first one of North Africa's poorest states, heavily dependent on Western aid, Libya became one of its wealthiest following the discovery of oil in the late 1950s. In 1963 a royal decree changed it from a federal to a unitary state.

In 1969 a military junta led by Colonel Muammar al-Qaddafi deposed Idris and established a republic. An Arab nationalist, Qaddafi nationalized foreign assets, closed foreign cultural centers, and ejected British and U.S. forces that had been stationed there. He instituted Islamic law and Socialist policies, including universal education and health care and a minimum wage. Under his political philosophy, Libya became a Jamahiriya or mass-state, ruled in theory by the people, through a General People's Congress, but in practice by him as dictator.

Libya, Egypt, and Syria formed an alliance called the Federation of Arab Republics in 1971, but plans for further unification were never realized. In 1977 Libya occupied Chad's northern region, with its rich uranium reserves; Libya was forced out by Chad forces in 1987. A vocal enemy of Israel, Libya aided Palestinian guerrilla groups and was accused of sponsoring international terrorism. In the 1980s the U.S. imposed economic sanctions on Libya and the two countries clashed in several military skirmishes. In April 1986 the U.S. accused Libya of responsibility for the bombing of a West Berlin nightclub in which two U.S. servicemen died. That month, in retaliation, the U.S. bombed Tripoli and Benghazi, Libya, apparently in an unsuccessful attempt to kill Qaddafi.

Despite some efforts since the 1980s to present a more moderate image, Qaddafi has remained the object of international disapprobation. In 1989 it was discovered that Libya had been acquiring equipment from a West German company to be used in construction of a chemical weapons plant. Libya refused to extradite two agents linked to the 1988 bombing of Pan Am Flight 103 over Lockerbie, Scotland. As punishment, the UN imposed limited economic sanctions in 1992. These were tightened in 1993, and in 1996 the U.S. authorized sanctions on foreign companies investing in Libya. In 1999 Libya handed over the suspects in the Pan Am bombing, ending UN sanctions, though U.S. anti-terrorism sanctions continued.

Libya: 20th-Century Leaders

King

1951–69: Idris I (1890–1983)

President

1969– : Muammar al-Qaddafi

Prime Minister

1951–54: Mahmoud Muntasser (1913–70)

1954: Mohammed al-Sakizly

1954–57: Mustafa bin Halim

1957–60: Abdul Majid Kubar

1960–63: Mohammed bin Othman es-Said

1963–64: Mohieddine al-Fekini

1964–65: Mahmoud Muntasser

1965–67: Hussain Mazik

1967: Abdel Kader el-Badry

1967–68: Abdul Hamid Bakkush

1968–69: Wanis al-Qaddafi

1969: Mahmoud Soliman al-Maghreby

1970–72: Muammar al-Qaddafi

1972–77: Abdul Salam Jalloud

(position abolished)

Liechtenstein

Official name: Principality of Liechtenstein

Location: Central Europe; landlocked; bordered by Austria (N, E), Switzerland (S, W)

Capital: Väduz

Area: 62 sq. mi. (160 sq. km.)

Population (est. 1997): 31,389

Languages: German (official), Alemannish dialect

Government: Hereditary constitutional monarchy

Religions: Roman Catholic 87.3%, Protestant 8.3%, other 4.4%

Monetary unit: Swiss franc

Main exports: Small specialty machinery, dental products, stamps, hardware, pottery

A relic of the Holy Roman Empire and member of the German Confederation (1815-66), Liechtenstein became an independent country in 1866 and was part of the Austro-Hungarian monarchy until 1918, when the monarchy was abolished. A constitution in 1921 provided for a unicameral legislature, the Landtag, the 25 members of which are elected to four-year terms. Since the early century, Liechtenstein has since been linked closely with Switzerland, its partner in a customs union and its director of foreign affairs. The country remained neutral during World Wars I and II.

The government is divided into three parts. The executive branch is led by a hereditary prince, the legislative branch is a single-chamber body, and the judiciary branch is independent.

The dynasty was led by Prince Franz Josef II from 1938 to 1984, when he granted executive authority to his son Hans-Adam. Prince Hans-Adam succeeded his father as head of government in 1989. From 1928 to 1970 the single-chamber government was led by the conservative Progressive Citizen's Party. From 1970 to 1974 and after 1978 it has been controlled by the centrist Fatherland Union. Presently the two parties rule in a coalition government. From 1993 the prime minister has been Dr. Mario Frick. Liechtenstein became a member of the United Nations in 1990 and full member of the European Free Trade Association in 1991. Women were granted the right to vote in 1984.

Until World War II Liechtenstein's economy depended largely on dairy farming. Over the ensuing decades it has become a highly industrialized service-oriented economy. Attractive to business for its low taxes, the country is the nominal headquarters for approximately 25,000 corporations.

Liechtenstein: 20th-Century Leaders

Prince

1858–1929: Johann II (1840–1929)

1929–38: Franz I (1853–1938)

1938–89: Franz Josef II (1906–89)

1989– : Hans-Adam II (1945–)

Prime Minister

1928–45: Franz Josef Hoop (1895–1959)

1945–62: Alexander Frick

1962–70: Gerard Batliner

1970–74: Alfred J. Hilbe

1974–78: Walter Kieber

1978–93: Hans Brunhart (1945–)

1993: Markus Büchel

1993– : Mario Frick (1965–)

Lithuania

Official name: Republic of Lithuania

Location: Northeastern Europe; bordered by Latvia (N), Belarus (E, SE), Poland (SW), Russian Federation (W), Baltic Sea (NW)

Capital: Vilnius

Area: 25,174 sq. mi. (65,200 sq. km.)

Population (est. 1997): 3,617,104

Languages: Lithuania (official), Russian, Polish, ethnic languages

Government: Republic

Religions: Roman Catholic, Lutheran

Monetary unit: Litas

Main exports: Electronics, petroleum products, food, chemicals

A province of the Russian Empire from 1795, Lithuania became an independent republic in 1918 through the Soviet-German Treaty of Brest-Litovsk. The republic was recognized by World War I allies in 1921. In 1926 Parliament was dissolved, replaced by the authoritarian regime of Antana Smetona. The secret 1939 Nazi-Soviet Pact led to the creation of the Lithuanian Soviet Socialist Republic in 1940. During much of World War II (1941–44) it was occupied by German troops. In 1944 it was retaken by the Soviet Union.

The Soviet *glasnost* policy of openness energized a Lithuanian nationalist movement during the 1980s. In 1988 the Lithuanian Movement for Reconstruction (Sajudis) was founded and became the country's central movement for independence from the Soviet Union. On February 24, 1990, Sajudis leader Vytautas Landsbergis was elected president. On March 11, 1990, Lithuania declared independence from the Soviet Union. In January 1991 the Soviet Union initiated an economic blockade and military presence in Lithuania; but after a compromise was negotiated, the Soviet Union recognized Lithuanian independence on September 6, 1991.

While Communist candidates (under the Democratic Labor Party banner) dominated 1992 elections, the non-Communist Homeland Union Party gained government control in 1996.

The final group of Soviet troops left Lithuania on August 31, 1993.

Lithuania: 20th-Century Leaders

President

1919–21: Antanas Smetona (1874–1944) (provisional president)

1922–26: Aleksandras Stulginskis (1885–1969)

1926: Dr. Kazys Grinius (1866–1950)

1926–40: Antanas Smetona (1874–1944)

1940–44: under German occupation

1944–90: Soviet republic

1990–92: Vytautas Landsbergis (1932–)

1992–98: Algirdas Mykolas Brazauskas

1998– : Valdus Adamkus

Prime Minister

1990–91: Kazimiera Prunskiené (1943–)

1991–92: Gediminas Vagnorius (1957–)

1992: Aleksandras Abisala

1992–93: Bronislovas Lubys (1938–)

1993–96: Adolfas Slezevicius

1996: Laurynas Mindaugas Stankevicius

1996–99: Gediminas Vagnorius

1999 : Rolandas Paksas

1999– : Andrius Kubilius (1956–)

Luxembourg

Official name: Grand Duchy of Luxembourg

Location: Western Europe; landlocked; bordered by Belgium (N, W), Germany (E), France (S)

Capital: Luxembourg

Area: 999 sq. mi. (2,586 sq. km.)

Population (est. 1997): 420,416

Languages: Luxembourgisch, French, German, English

Government: Unicameral legislature

Religions: Roman Catholic 97%, Protestant and Jewish 3%

Monetary unit: Luxembourg franc

Main exports: Steel and iron, chemicals, rubber products, glass, aluminum

Formerly a shared monarchy with the Netherlands, Luxembourg gained sovereignty in 1867, and became a single monarchy after the death of King William II in 1890. Luxembourg officially became independent when Grand Duke Adolf of Nassau took power.

For much of the century Luxembourg had an industrial and agriculturally based economy. To facilitate trade it entered into a customs union with Belgium in 1921, and entered the Benelux union of Belgium, Netherlands, and Luxembourg in the early 1940s. Currently the economy depends on international banking, which generates more than half of its gross national product. During World Wars I and II the country was overrun and occupied by Germany. Grand Duchess Charlotte fled to London in 1940; she returned when the country was liberated by Allied forces in 1944. Since World War II the constitutional monarchy has been stable, ruled largely by a coalition dominated by the Christian Social Party. In 1961 Prince Jean replaced his mother Grand Duchess Charlotte as head of state. When she abdicated in 1964, he became grand duke.

Luxembourg was a founding member of the United Nations in 1945 and became a member of NATO in 1949. It was also a founding member of the European Economic Commission. In 1992 Luxembourg's parliament approved the Maastricht Accord.

Luxembourg: 20th-Century Leaders

Grand Duke or Duchess

1890–1905: Adolphus (1817–1905)

1905–1912: William IV (1852–1912)

1912–19: Marie Adélaïde (1894–1924)

1919–64: Charlotte (1896–1985)

1964–2000: Jean (1921–)

Prime Minister

1937–53: Pierre Dupong (1885–1953)

1953–58: Joseph Bech (1887–1975)

1958–59: Pierre Frieden (1892–1959)

1959–74: Pierre Werner (1913–84)

1974–79: Gaston Thorn

1979–84: Pierre Werner

1984–95: Jacques Santer (1937–)

1995– : Jean–Claude Juncker (1954–)

Macedonia

Official name: Republic of Macedonia

Location: Southeast Europe on the Balkan peninsula; bordered by Serbia (N), Bulgaria (E), Greece (S), Albania (W), Yugoslavia (NE, N)

Capital: Skopje

Area: 9,781 sq. km. (25,333 sq. km.)

Population (est. 1997): 1,995,859

Languages: Macedonian, Albanian, Turkish, other

Government: Democratic republic

Religions: Eastern Orthodox 67%, Muslim 30%, other 3%

Monetary unit: Dinar

Main exports: Manufactured goods, machinery and transport equipment, raw materials, food and live animals

Throughout its history, Macedonia has had a variety of ethnic claims on it and has struggled to develop and maintain statehood and independence. Comprising the western region of the early Kingdom of Macedonia, the country was controlled from 1371 into the 20th century by the Ottoman Turks. Following the Balkan Wars (1912–13) Macedonia was placed largely into the hands of Serbia, with smaller portions divided between Greece and Bulgaria. World War I peace treaties distributed Macedonian land among Greece, Bulgaria, and Yugoslavia. During World War II (1941–44) Macedonia was dominated by Axis-friendly Bulgaria and occupied by Germany (though Macedonian resistance forces battled the occupation troops).

After World War II a reconstructed Yugoslavia under Communist president Josip Tito reclaimed Macedonia and in 1946 established the Macedonian People's Republic, part of a Communist federation of states. After Tito's death in 1980, Macedonia was part of a rotating "collegial rule" among the republics, lasting until it declared itself an independent republic in January 1992. In 1993 it was recognized by six European nations and by the United Nations; it was recognized by the U.S. in 1994. In September 1995 Macedonia was admitted into the Council of Europe.

In 1999 Serb ethnic cleansing of ethnic Kosovar Albanians during NATO bombing of Yugoslavia resulted in mass numbers of refugees fleeing over the border to Macedonia. Refugee camps were set up for the approximately 300,000 Kosovars near the Kosovo border. An end to the hostilities in June led to the return of the refugees.

Macedonia: 20th-Century Leaders

President

1990–99: Kiro Gligorov (1917–)

1999– : Boris Trajkovski (1956–)

Prime Minister

1990–92: Nikola Kljusev

1992–98: Branko Crvenkovski

1998– : Ljubco Georgievski (1966–)

Madagascar

Official name: Republic of Madagascar

Location: Island off coast of southeast Africa in Indian Ocean, opposite Mozambique.

Capital: Antananarivo

Area: 226,656 sq. mi. (587,041 sq. km)

Population (est. 1997): 14,061,627

Languages: Malagasy, French

Government: Republic

Religions: Indigenous beliefs 52%, Christian 41%, Muslim 7%

Monetary unit: Malagasy franc

Main exports: Coffee, cloves, vanilla, sugar, petroleum products

The world's fourth largest island became a French protectorate in 1885 and remained so until the French removed Queen Rànavàlona III (1894–95) and established a colony in 1896. In 1908 the Comoro Islands were attached to the territory.

During World War II the country was under Vichy forces until being occupied in 1942 by British and American forces. In 1943 it was brought under Free French rule.

In 1958 Madagascar became an autonomous republic within the French Community and gained independence from France on June 26, 1960. A military coup against President Philibert Tsiranana in 1973 led by Major General Gabriel Ramanantsoa instituted a largely anti-French government. In 1975 leftist Commander Didier Ratsiraka was named president and established Socialist rule, including the widespread nationalization of industries.

In 1991 an alternative government was formed, and in 1992 a new federal consitution was approved. Albert Zafy was elected prime minister in 1993; in 1997 Ratsiraka was reelected to the position. Currently 75 percent of the citizenry lives in poverty.

The low-lying country formerly contained a lush interior that now has been largely deforested. Nonetheless, its isolated geographic location generates wildlife of wide scientific interest.

Madagascar: 20th-Century Leaders

President

1959–72: Philibert Tsiranana (1910–78)

1972–75: Gabriel Ramanantsoa (1906–79)

1975: Richard Ratsimandrava (1931–75, assassinated)

1975: Gilles Andriamahazo (1919–89)

1975–93: Didier Ratsiraka (1936–)

1993–96: Albert Zafy

1996–97: Norbert Ratsirahonana (acting president)

1997– : Didier Ratsiraka

Prime Minister

1972–75: Gabriel Ramanantsoa

1976: Joel Rakotomalala (1929–76)

1976–77: Justin Rakatoniaini

1977–88: Désiré Rakotoarijoana (1934–)

1988–91: Victor Ramahatra (1945–)

1991–93: Guy Razanamasy

1993–95: Francisque Ravony

1995–96: Emmanuel Rakotovahiny

1996–97: Norbert Ratsirahonana

1997–98: Pascal Rakotomavo

1998– : Tantely Andranarivo (1954–)

Malawi

Official name: Republic of Malawi

Location: South central Africa; landlocked; bordered by Tanzania (N), Mozambique (E, S), Zambia (W), Lake Malawi (E)

Capital: Lilongwe

Area: 45,745 sq. mi. (118,480 sq. km.)

Population (est. 1997): 9,609,081

Languages: English and Chichewa

Government: Multiparty democracy

Religions: Protestant 55%, Roman Catholic 20%, Muslim and indigenous beliefs 20%

Monetary unit: Malawian kwacha

Main exports: Tobacco, tea, sugar, cotton

Following the explorations of Scottish missionary David Livingstone in the 1850s and 1860s, British forces annexed the Nyasaland territory in 1891 and established the Central African Protectorate in 1891. In 1907 it became known as Nyasaland. A main function of the territory was to provide labor for South African and Rhodesian mining and agriculture.

From 1953 Nyasaland became part of an independence movement with Northern and Southern Rhodesia, and in 1962 the country gained self-governing powers. In 1963 president of Nyasaland African Congress Dr. Hastings Kamuzu Banda was elected prime minister. Assuming the name Malawi, the territory gained full independence from the U.K. and became a member of the British Commonwealth in 1964. It became a republic within the Commonwealth of Nations in 1966.

Banda also became president, establishing one-party rule, prohibiting political dissent, and becoming the only African leader to recognize the apartheid rule of South Africa. In 1971 he became life president of the Republic of Malawi.

In 1992 following years of government corruption and oppression, citizens rebelled, staging several bloody strikes that resulted in over 35 deaths. Concurrently, in an attempt to spur democratic change in the Banda government, the U.S. and other industrial nations ceased foreign aid. In 1993 the country voted in a multiparty system and in May 1994 held its first free election, electing president Bakili Muluzi of the United Democratic Front. A new constitution was adopted in 1995, mandating a president, vice president, and National Assembly or parliament.

Malawi: 20th-Century Leaders

Governor–General

1964–66: Sir Glyn Smallwood Jones

President

1966–94: Hastings Kamuzu Banda

1994– : Elson Bakili Muluzi (1943–)

Prime Minister

1963–66: Hastings Kamuzu Banda

Malaysia

Official name: Malaysia

Location: 13 states in Southeast Asia, 11 in in Peninsular Malaysia, two (Sabah and Sarawak) about 400 mi. (640 km.) across South China Sea on northern coast of Borneo

Capital: Kuala Lumpur

Area: 127,317 sq. mi. (329,750 sq. km.)

Population (est. 1997): 20,491,303

Languages: Peninsular Malaysia—Malay (official), English, Chinese dialects, Tamil, Sabah—English, Malay, many tribal dialects, Mandarin and Hakka dialects (among Chinese), Sarawak—English, Malay, Mandarin, many tribal languages

Government: Constitutional monarchy

Religions: Peninsular Malaysia—Muslim (nearly all Malays), Buddhist (most Chinese), Hindu (most Indians); Sabah—Muslim 38%, Christian 17%, Other 45%; Sarawak—tribal religion 35%, Buddhist and Confucianist 24%, Muslim 20%, Christian 16%, Other 5%

Monetary unit: Malaysian ringgit

Main exports: Natural rubber, palm oil, timber, petroleum

From the 19th century, the British held several Malay states as protectorates, and after 1909 controlled its southern peninsula. Also since the 19th century, Great Britain held some control in northern Borneo, part of which belongs to Malaysia. Malay was overrun by Japan from 1942 to 1945.

On April 1, 1946, the Union of Malaya was formed from several of the Federated Malay States (Negri Sembilan, Pahang, Perak, and Selangor), Unfederated Malay States (Johore, Kedah, Kelantan, Perlis, and Trengganu), and Straits Settlements Malacca and Penang. On February 1, 1948, it became the Federation of Malaya and became independent in 1957. Following the suppression of Communist insurgency in the early 1950s, elections for home-rule government were held in 1955 and brought to power the Alliance Party. Its leader Tunku Abdul Rahman Putra became chief minister and minister for Home Affairs. The Federation of Malaya became independent in 1957, with Tunku Abdul Rahman Putra becoming its first prime minister.

On September 16, 1963, Malaysia was formed from a federation of Malaya, Singapore, Sabah (formerly North Borneo) and Sarawak, Tunku Abdul Rahman Putra oversaw the making of the federation and became prime minister. Singapore became an independent nation in 1965 and withdrew from the federation. Malaysia is a member of the Commonwealth of Nations.

The late 1960s in Malaysia were marked by ethnic rioting among Malays against the Chinese and Indians over the latter groups' disproportionate control of the nation's wealth. The prime minister's inability to reach suitable compromise among the groups led to his resignation in 1970.

Malaysia is a constitutional monarchy, with a bicameral legislature consisting of a 68-member Senate and 192-member House of Representatives, and a monarch chosen for five-year terms from among hereditary rulers in the nine Malay states. Since 1981 its government has been run by Mahathir Mohamad and his Barisan National Coalition, which moved the country from its agricultural base to a highly successful modern economy with an 8 percent growth rate during the 1980s. Among ambitious projects was the construction of the world's two tallest buildings.

Following an influx of Vietnamese refugees in the 1970s and 1980s, Malaysia moved to accept no further refugees after April 1989. However, in 1996 it announced that it had signed an international agreement to repatriate all Vietnamese seeking asylum.

The Asian financial crisis of 1997–98 severely hurt Malaysia's economy. In 1998, in the midst of recession, Prime Minister Mahathir fired his popular deputy prime minister, Anwar bin Ibrahim, and had him arrested; in 1999 and 2000, Amwar was convicted of corruption and sodomy.

Malaysia: 20th-Century Leaders

Paramount Ruler

1957–60: Tuanku Abdul Rahman (1895–1960)

1960: Tuanku Hisamuddin Alam Shah (1898–1960)

1960–65: Tuanku Syed, Putra Al-haj, raja of Perlis

1965–70: Tuanku Ismail Nasiruddin, shah of Trengganu

1970–75: Tuanku Abdul Halim Mu'azzam, shah of Kedah

1975–79: Tuanku Yahha Putra, shah of Kelantan

1979–84: Tuanku Sultan Haji Ahmad Shah Al-Musta'in Bilah Ibni Almarhum Sultan Abu Bakar Ri'ayatuddin Al-mu'adzam Shah (1930–)

1984–89: Tunku Mahmood Iskander Ibni Al-marhum Sultan Ismail (1932–)

1989–94: Tunku Azlan Muhibbudin Shah ibni al-Marhum Yusuff Ghafarullahu-Lahu Shah (1928–)

1994–99: Tuanka Ja'afar ibni al-Marhum Tuanku Abdul Rahman

1999– : Sultan Salahuddin Abdul Aziz Shah Alhaj (1926–)

Prime Minister

1957–59: Tunku Abdul Rahman (1903–90)

1959: Tun Abdul Razak (1922–76)

1959–70: Tunku Abdul Rahman

1970–76: Tun Abdul Razak

1976–81: Datuk Hussein bin Onn (1922–90)

1981– : Datuk Seri Mahathir bin Mohamad (1925–)

Maldives

Official name: Republic of Maldives

Loccation: Indian Ocean; chain of over 1,200 coral islands, of which nearly 1,000 are uninhabitable; bordered by Laccadive Sea (NE), Arabian Sea (N), Indian Ocean (S, W)

Capital: Malé

Area: 116 sq. mi. (300 sq. km.)

Population (est. 1997): 280,391

Languages: Divehi (dialect of Sinhala, script derived from Arabic), English

Government: Republic

Religions: Sunni Muslim

Monetary unit: Rufiyaa

Main exports: Fish, clothing

Originally known as the Maldive Islands, the Maldives was under the suzerainty of Ceylon before 1887, when the islands became a British protectorate. The country remained a dependency of the colony of Ceylon until 1948 and gained full independence from Britain on July 26, 1965.

For centuries a sultanate, the Maldives operated a republican government from 1953 until 1954, when a sultanate was reinstated. In 1968 a referendum reestablished the country as a republic, which as yet has no political parties. Its first president, Ibrahim Nasir, ruled until being removed by the 48-member Majlis (parliament) in 1978. The new president, Maumoon Abdul Gayoom, began his fourth five-year term in 1994, after surviving an attempted coup in 1988.

The citizenry of these low-lying islands is of Indian, Sinhalese, and Arab descent. Vulnerable to rising sea levels, the Maldives has warned against global warming since the 1980s.

Maldives: 20th-Century Leaders

President

1953: Amin Didi (1912–54)

1953–54: Ibrahim Mohamed Didi (co-president)

1953–54: Ibrahim Ali Didi (co-president)

1954–57: Ibrahim Mohamed Didi

(Sultanate restored 1954; presidency abolished 1957; sultanate abolished and presidency restored 1968)

1968–78: Ibrahim Nasir

1978– : Maumoon Abdul Gayoom (1937–)

Sultan

1954–68: Al Amir Mohamed Farid Didi (1901–)

Mali

Official name: Republic of Mali

Location: Northwest Africa; landlocked; bordered by Algeria (N), Niger (E), Burkina Faso,

Guinea, Côte d'Ivoire (S), Senegal, Mauritania (W)

Capital: Bamako

Area: 478,819 sq. mi. (1,240,142 sq. km.)

Population (est. 1997): 9,788,904

Languages: French (official), Bambara

Government: Republic

Religions: Muslim 90%, indigenous beliefs 9%, Christian 1%

Monetary unit: Communauté Financière Africaine (CFA) franc

Main exports: Machinery and equipment, foodstuffs, construction materials, petroleum, textiles

An important country in west African history for over 4,000 years, Mali was conquered by the French in the late 19th century and in 1898 became the colony French Sudan, part of French West Africa.

By the 1920s a Malian nationalist movement developed, led by Modibo Keita. In 1946 Mali gained partial self-rule and French citizenship when it became a member of the French Union. In 1958 Mali became autonomous within the French Overseas Community, and with Senegal in 1959 formed the Federation of Mali. On June 20, 1960, it became independent, and on September 22, after Senegal seceded from the federation, Mali became a republic. Its first elected president was nationalist leader Modibo Keita. Keita's harsh social and economic programs led to Mali's forced reaffiliation with the French in 1967 and to Keita's overthrow in 1968 by military forces led by Lieutenant Moussa Traoré. The military regime remained in force until 1979, when a new civilian constitution was enacted. Traoré was reelected; he controlled Mali until a 1991 coup installed a transitional government under civilian prime minister Soumana Sacko. In 1992 multiparty elections, Alpha Oumar Konaré became president and his Alliance for Democracy in Mali party gained a majority (76 of 116) of legislative seats. Following internal dissent, Sacko resigned, replaced by Younoussi Touré. Touré was replaced by Abdoulaye Sekow, who resigned in 1994 over conflicts with the majority party.

Under Konaré, the Mali economy improved, gaining commendation from the World Bank. In 1995 the government reached an agreement to end disputes with Tuareg nomads in northern Mali.

A 1970s drought destroyed much of the agrarian economy and caused thousands of deaths.

Mali: 20th-Century Leaders

President

1959–68: Modibo Keita (1915–77)

1968–91: Moussa Traoré (1936–)

1991–92: Amadou Toumani Traoré

1992– : Alpha Oumar Konaré

Head of Military Government

1968–69: Yoro Diakite (1932–73)

Prime Minister

(position did not exist until 1986)

1986–88: Mamadou Dembelé

1991–92: Soumana Sacko

1992–93: Younoussi Touré

1993–94: Abdoulaye Sekou Sow

1994–2000: Ihrahim Boubacar Kéita

Malta

Official name: Republic of Malta

Location: Archipelago in central Meditarranean; nearest neighbors include Sicily (N), Libya (S), Tunisia (W)

Capital: Valletta

Area: 124 sq. mi. (320 sq. km.)

Population (est. 1997): 377,177

Languages: Maltese and English (official)

Government: Parliamentary democracy

Religions: Roman Catholic 98%

Monetary unit: Maltese lira

Main exports: Machinery and transport equipment, clothing, printed matter

Malta is a country located on several islands, the largest of which include Malta, Gozo, and Comino.

Under British rule from 1800 and annexation in 1814, Malta gained limited self-rule in 1921 and 1939. During World War II it was bombed heavily by German and Italian forces, with the entire population of Malta receiving the George Cross for bravery.

On September 21, 1964, Malta became an independent state within the British Commonwealth; in 1974 it became a republic within the Commonwealth. In 1979 British forces left the island.

Political rule has vacillated between the leftist Labour and the pro-Western Nationalist Parties, with the Labour Party ruling from 1981 to 1987, the Nationalists from 1987 to 1996, Labour from 1996 to 1998, and the Nationalists since 1998.

Malta: 20th-Century Leaders

Governor–General

1964–71: Sir Maurice Henry Dorman (1912–93)

1971–74: Sir Anthony Mamo

President

1974–76: Sir Anthony Mamo

1976–82: Anton Buttigieg (1912–83)

1982–87: Agatha Barbara

1987–89: Paul Xuereb

1989–94: Censu Tabone

1994–99: Ugo Mifsud Bonnici (1932–)

1999– : Guido De Marco (1931–)

Prime Minister

1964–71: George Borg Olivier (1911–)

1971–84: Dominic Mintoff

1984–87: Carmelo Mifsud Bonnici

1987–96: Eddie Fenech Adami

1996–98: Alfred Sant (1948–)

1998– : Eddie Fenech Adami

Marshall Islands

Official name: Republic of the Marshall Islands (RMI)

Location: Western Pacific Ocean; nearest neighbors Guam (approx. 1,300 mi. NW), Hawaii (approx. 2,000 mi. NE)

Capital: Majuro

Area: 70 sq. mi. (181.3 sq. km.), including atolls of Bikini, Eniwetok, and Kwajalein

Population (est. 1997): 60,652

Languages: Marshallese and English (both official)

Government: Constitutional government in free association with U.S.

Religions: Predominantly Christian (largely Protestant)

Monetary unit: U.S. dollar

Main exports: Coconut oil, fish, live animals, trichus shells

The Marshall Islands comprise two chains of 31 coral-reef islands: the western (Ralik) group of atolls Jaluit, Kwajalein, Wotho, Bikini, and Eniwetak; and the eastern (Ratak) group of atolls Mili, Majuro, Maloelap, Wotje, and Likiep. They are part of the geographic region of Micronesia.

Under Japanese control from the beginning of World War I, the Marshall Islands were taken by Allied forces in 1944. In 1947 they were placed in U.S. hands as part of the UN Trust Territory of the Pacific. From 1946 to 1958 Bikini and Eniwetak were used by the U.S. as sites for nuclear testing; their residents were relocated beforehand. In 1994 the government considered the dumping of nuclear waste on the largely uninhabitable islands.

In 1986 the U.S. and Marshall Islands entered into a Compact of Free Association, effective October 21, 1986. As of November 3, 1986, the agreement terminated the U.S–administered UN Trusteeship Agreement between the two countries.

The Marshall Islands were admitted to the UN on September 17, 1991.

Marshall Islands: 20th-Century Leaders

President

1979–96: Amata Kabua (d. 1996)

1996–97: Kunio Lemari (acting president)

1997–2000: Imata Kabua (1943–)

Mauritania

Official name: Islamic Republic of Mauritania

Location: Northwest Africa; bordered by Morocco (N), Senegal (S), Algeria and Mali (E), Atlantic Ocean (W)

Capital: Nouakchott

Area: 297,953 sq. mi. (1,030,700 sq. km.)

Population (est. 1997): 2,411,317

Languages: Arabic (official) and French

Government: Republic

Religions: Muslim (almost 100%)

Monetary unit: Ouguyia

Main exports: Iron ore, fish, gum arabic, gypsum

Originally settled by the Berbers in the first millenium A.D., Mauritania entered the 20th century under French control, as a French protectorate in 1903 and a colony in 1920. Following an active post–World War II nationalist movement, it became a self-governing nation (as part of the French Overseas Community) in 1958. The next year, it elected its first president, Moktar Ould Daddah; it became an independent nation on November 28, 1960.

In 1961 Mauritania established itself as a Muslim state and adopted a new constitution mandating the presidency; that year it was also admitted to the UN.

In the 1960s facing conflict among its ethnic groups (Arabs and Berbers in the north, and black Africans in the south), the country aimed to make its primary culture Arab. These tensions, in addition to economic problems, led to an army coup in July 1978, in which President Moktar Ould Daddah was deposed and was replaced by Mohamed Khouna Ould Haidalla and a military government. A civilian government was set up in 1980, but it was overtaken by a military government under Maaouya Ould Sidi Ahmed Taya in 1981.

In 1991 the government announced a change to a multiparty system, with a change in the constitution approved in a referendum that year. Nonetheless, in 1991 Taya's party won 67 of 79 parliamentary seats, and conflict among political parties remains active.

From 1975 to 1979, Mauritania and Morocco waged war against an Algeria-backed independence group called the Polisaro Front over the control of the southern third of the Spanish Sahara. The war ended with a peace treaty in which Mauritania renounced claims to a 1975 agreement with Spain and Morocco granting control of the region to Mauritania.

Mauritania: 20th-Century Leaders

President

1960–78: Moktar Ould Daddah

1978–79: Mustapha Ould Mohamed Salek

1979–80: Mohamed Mahmoud Ould Ahmed Louly

1980–84: Mohamed Khouna Ould Haidalla (1940–)

1984– : Maaouya Ould Sidi Ahmed Taya

Prime Minister

1959–78: Moktar Ould Daddah

1979: Ahmed Ould Bouceif

1979: Ahmed Salem Ould Sidi (interim prime minister)

1979–80: Mohamed Khouna Ould Haidalla

1980–81: Sid Ahmed Ould Beneijara

1981–84: Maaouya Ould Sidi Ahmed Taya

1984: Mohamed Khouna Ould Haidalla

1984–92: Maaouya Ould Sidi Ahmed Taya

1992–96: Sidi Mohamed Ould Boubaca

1996– : Cheikh El Afia Ould Mohamed Khouna

Mauritius

Official name: Republic of Mauritius

Location: Southwestern Indian Ocean; two islands (Mauritius and Rodriguez) about 500 miles east of Madagascar, 2,400 miles southwest of India

Capital: Port Louis

Area: 718 sq. mi. (1,860 sq. km.)

Population (est. 1997): 1,154,272

Languages: English (official), Creole, French, Hindi, Urdu, Hakka, Bojpoori

Government: Parliamentary democracy

Religions: Hindu 52%, Christian (primarily Roman Catholic, small portion Anglican) 28.3%, Muslim 16.6%

Monetary unit: Mauritian rupee

Main exports: Textiles, sugar, light manufactures

Discovered by the Dutch in 1507, the island of Mauritius was settled by the Dutch in 1638 and later came under French rule (1721–1810). It was captured by the British in 1810 and became a colony. Following the British abolition of slavery in 1833, Indian immigrants were imported for plantation labor as the French had done with African workers. Indians were granted political rights in 1947.

The country became an independent parliamentary democracy within the British Commonwealth on March 12, 1968. Its pro-independence first leader, Sir Seewoosagur Ramgoolam, of the Mauritian Labor Party (MLP), ruled until 1982, when the leftist Mauritius Militant Movement (MMM) gained power, electing Anerood Jugnauth as prime minister. Following his ouster from the MMM, Jugnauth formed the Mauritian Socialist Movement (MSM) in 1983, winning elections in 1987 and 1991.

Mauritius officially broke with Britain on March 12, 1992, becoming a republic. In the 1995 elections a coalition government took all 60 seats and unseated Jugnauth for the first time since 1982.

Mauritius: 20th-Century Leaders

Governor–General (representing the British monarch)

1968: Sir John Rennie

1968–72: Sir Leonard Williams (1904–72)

1972–79: Sir Abdool Raman Muhammad Osman (1902–)

1979–83: Dayendranth Burrenchobay

1983–85: Sir Seewoosagur Ramgoolam (1900–85)

1986–92: Sir Veerasamy Ringadoo

President

1992– : Cassam Uteem (1941–)

Prime Minister

1961–82: Sir Seewoosagur Ramgoolam (chief minister 1961–64; prime minister 1964–82)

1982–95: Anerood Jugnauth (1930–)

1995–2000: Navin Chandra Ramgoolam (1947–)

Mexico

Official name: United Mexican States

Location: Southern North America; bordered by U.S. (N), Pacific Ocean (W), Guatemala, Belize (S), Gulf of Mexico (E)

Capital: Mexico City

Area: 761,603 sq. mi. (1,972,550 sq. km.)

Population (est. 1998): 98,552,776

Languages: Spanish (official), Native American languages

Government: Federal republic

Religions: Roman Catholic 89%, Protestant 6%

Monetary unit: Peso

Main exports: Crude oil, oil products, coffee, silver, engines, cotton

Mexico's indigenous Aztec civilization was conquered by Spain in the 16th century. Mexico won independence from Spain in 1821. Under the long, repressive dictatorship (1876–1911) of Porfirio Díaz, Mexico experienced an economic boom, but at the price of increasing dominance by foreign investors and a growing gap between rich and poor. Social and political tensions erupted in the Mexican Revolution (1910–40), which was sparked when opposition candidate Francisco Madero rejected Díaz's election in 1910 and called for armed rebellion. Peasants in northern Mexico rebelled under Pancho Villa, while Native Americans in the south rose under Emiliano Zapata. Díaz fled the country in 1911 and Madero was elected president.

Madero's failure to carry out land reform assured the continuation of the revolution. His chief of staff, Victoriano Huerta, overthrew him in a coup in 1913, but was himself forced from office in 1914 by the combined forces of Villa, Zapata, and Constitutionalist leader Venustiano Carranza. The overthrow was aided by the U.S., which seized the port of Veracruz, depriving Huerta of arms supplies. Carranza became president (1914–16), but was opposed by Villa and Zapata. In 1915 one of Carranza's generals, Alvaro Obregón, defeated Villa at the bloody battle of Celaya. By 1916 both Villa and Zapata were contained, respectively, in the north and south; Villa's 1916 raid in New Mexico brought U.S. forces under General John Pershing to Mexico in search of him. Carranza oversaw the framing of the Constitution of 1917, a progressive document that separated church and state, provided for nationalization of mineral resources, authorized land redistribution to benefit peasants and Native Americans, and granted workers' rights, including the right to strike. Though never fully implemented, the constitution became the enduring basis of Mexican government.

The revolution's most violent phase came to an end with the assassinations of Zapata (1919) and Carranza (1920); Villa was assassinated in 1923. President Obregón, who overthrew Carranza, oversaw a period of reconstruction, in which reforms were slowly begun and power was transferred peacefully to his elected successor, Plutarco Elías Calles. Calles, a dedicated supporter of the revolution, enacted anticlerical legislation, sparking the revolt of the Cristeros (Christers), Catholic militants opposed to the new secular state. The revolt was suppressed, in part through persecution of Catholics; from 1926 to 1929 no church services were held in Mexico. In 1929 Calles founded the National Revolutionary Party, which became the Institutional Revolutionary Party (PRI) in 1946 and has since remained Mexico's governing party.

Lázaro Cárdenas, president from 1934 to 1940, was the last leader to commit himself fully to the promises of the revolution. He redistributed 44 million acres of land and reorganized the ruling party to represent distinct constituencies—peasants, labor, the military, and the popular sector or middle class. Cárdenas nationalized foreign oil companies (with compensation), improved access to education and health-care, and reached a settlement with the Catholic Church.

In the first two decades (1910–30) of the Mexican Revolution, hundreds of thousands of Mexicans fled to the U.S., where many found work as migrant farm laborers. Some entered the country illegally, an issue that has plagued U.S.–Mexico relations throughout the century. Depending on the needs of the American agricultural industry, the U.S. has either encouraged or discouraged immigration. The U.S. repatriated 500,000 Mexican-Americans, sometimes forcibly, to Mexico during the Great Depression of the 1930s. In the 1940s, when Mexico joined the Allies in World War II and farm workers were needed to replace drafted citizens, the U.S. recruited Mexican laborers through the bracero program. During the postwar economic boom, the bracero program was kept alive; it ended in 1964. Since then, the U.S. has attempted, with varying strictness, to enforce immigration laws in the face of a continuing influx of workers from Mexico.

The 1940s saw a shift in Mexico away from revolutionary zeal and toward industrial and business development. President Miguel Alemán (1946–52) modernized the nation's infrastructure through public works and initiated a period of strong economic growth that continued into the 1970s. Economic inequality increased, with the condition of the poor becoming worse. Inflation and foreign debt rose in the 1970s, while declining oil prices in the 1980s damaged Mexico's ability to repay debt. The currency was devalued; capital moved out of the country. Mexico relied on a U.S. rescue loan in 1982 to bail out its economy.

Mexico tried to restore economic order in the 1980s by cutting government spending and adopting policies of economic liberalization and privatization. To reduce civil tensions, presidents Miguel de la Madrid and Carlos Salinas de Gortari instituted democratizing reforms that somewhat reduced the PRI's monopoly on power.

In 1994 the North American Free Trade Agreement (NAFTA) eliminated most trade barriers among Canada, the U.S., and Mexico. Mexico signed the agreement in hopes of attracting jobs and foreign investment, but it stoked fears that domestic industry and agriculture would lose needed state protection. Partly in response to NAFTA, the Chiapas Rebellion erupted in 1994, a guerrilla uprising of poor Native Americans who called themselves the Zapata Army of National Liberation. Later that year the PRI's presidential candidate Luis Donaldo Colosio Murrieta was assassinated. Newly elected president Ernesto Zedillo Ponce de Leon faced a currency crisis when the peso collapsed; the U.S. and the IMF provided a bail-out package.

The later 1990s saw increasing signs of change in Mexico. In 1996 peace talks with the Chiapas rebels, the government agreed to grant limited autonomy to indigenous Mexicans. In 1997, in an election widely considered more free than any other in Mexican history, the PRI lost control of the lower legislative house and the mayoralty of Mexico City. In 2000, the PRI lost the presidency to opposition candidate Vicente Fox Quesada.

Mexico: 20th-Century Leaders

President

1884–1911: Porfirio Díaz

1911: Francisco León De la Barra (1863–1939) (provisional)

1911–13: Francisco Indalecio Madero (1873–1913)

1913: Pedro Lascurain (provisional)

1913–14: Victoriano Huerta (1854–1916) (provisional)

1914: Francisco Carbajal (provisional)

1914: Venustiano Carranza (1859–1920)

1914–15: Eulalio Martín Gutiérrez

1915: Roque González Garza (provisional)

1915: Francisco Lagos Cházaro (provisional)

1915–17: Venustiano Carranza (provisional)

1917–20: Venustiano Carranza

1920: Adolfo de la Huerta (provisional)

1920–24: Alvaro Obregón (1880–1928)

1924–28: Plutarco Elías Calles (1877–1945)

1928–30: Emilio Portes Gil (provisional)

1930–32: Pascual Ortiz Rubio

1932–34: Abelardo L. Rodríguez (provisional)

1934–40: Lázaro Cárdenas

1940–46: Manuel Ávila Camacho (1897–1955)

1946–52: Miguel Alemán Valdés (1903–83)

1952–58: Adolfo Ruiz Cortines (1890–1973)

1958–64: Adolfo López Mateos (1910–69)

1964–70: Gustavo Díaz Ordaz (1911–79)

1970–76: Luís Echevarria Alvarez

1976–82: José López Portillo

1982–88: Miguel de la Mad'id Hurtado (1934–)

1988–94: Carlos Salinas de Gortari (1948–)

1994–2000: Ernesto Zedillo Ponce de Leon (1951–)

Micronesia

Official name: Federated States of Micronesia

Location: Group of 607 islands in the western Pacific Ocean; nearby neighbors include the Philippines (W), Guam (NW), the Marshall Islands (E), Papua New Guinea (S)

Capital: Palikir, on Pohnpei

Area: 271 sq. mi. (702 sq. mi.)

Population (est. 1998): 129,658

Languages: English (official), Trukese, Pohnpeian, Yapese, Kosrean

Government: Republic

Religions: Roman Catholic 50%, Protestant 47%

Monetary unit: U.S. dollar

Main exports: Fish, garments

As a regional name, Micronesia refers to a collection of western Pacific islands that today includes four independent nations: the Northern Mariana Islands, the Republic of the Marshall Islands, Palau, and the Federated States of Micronesia. The Federated States of Micronesia consists of hundreds of islands in the Caroline Islands archipelago; these are grouped into four states: Pohnpei (site of the capital), Truk, Yap, and Kosrae.

The territory that is now the Federated States of Micronesia was claimed by Spain in the 16th century and ceded to Germany in the 1890s. Japan occupied them (1914) during World War I and received them afterward (1920) as a League of Nations mandate. Japan developed agriculture, mining, and fishing there. During World War II U.S. forces captured the islands. In 1947 they became part of the U.S. Trust Territory of the Pacific Islands. They became self-governing in 1979 and independent in 1986, the year the new nation signed a compact of free association status with the U.S. Through that compact, the republic is defended by and receives economic aid from the U.S.

The Federated States of Micronesia was admitted to the UN in 1991. The compact of free association is scheduled to end in 2001.

Micronesia: 20th-Century Leaders

President

1986–87: Tosiwo Nakayama

1987–91: John R. Haglelgam

1991–97: Bailey Olter

1997–99: Jacob Nena

1999– : Leo Falcam (1935–)

Moldova

Official name: Republic of Moldova

Location: Southeastern Europe; landlocked; bordered by Ukraine (N,E,S), Romania (W)

Capital: Chisinau

Area: 13,000 sq. mi. (33,700 sq. km.)

Population (est. 1997): 4,457,206

Languages: Moldovan (official), based on Romanian but using Cyrillic alphabet, Russian, Gagauz

Government: Republic

Religions: Eastern Orthodox 98.5%, Jewish 1.5%

Monetary unit: Leu

Main exports: Foodstuffs, wine, tobacco, textiles, chemicals

Formerly known as Moldavia, Moldova consists of a small portion of the original country, the rest now part of Romania and Ukraine. Sixty-five percent of the inhabitants are of Moldavian and Romanian ethnicity, while 12 percent each are Ukrainian and Russian, among others. Controlled variously by Turkey, Romania, and the Russian empire during the 19th century, Moldavia became part of Russia in 1918. In 1924 the U.S.S.R. formed the Autonomous Soviet Socialist Republic (A.S.S.R.) of the Ukraine.

Following the Nazi-Soviet Nonagression Pact of 1939, Romania ceded Bessarabia and northern Bukovina to the Soviet Union in 1940. The Romanian-speaking districts of Bessarabia and the Moldavian A.S.S.R. were united to form the Moldavian Soviet Socialist Republic. German ally Romania occupied the area during World War II, but the Soviet Union reclaimed the region in 1944.

Over the next decades, the Soviet government officially differentiated Moldavians from Romanians by creating a Moldavian language and encouraging Russian and Ukrainian immigration to Moldavia. Public outcry led to the reestablishment of Romanian as the official language.

After the fall of the Soviet Union, Moldova offically declared its independence on August 27, 1991, and became an independent state upon the dissolution of the Soviet Union on December 26, 1991. Moldova elected its first president in December 1991. Moldova became a member of the Commonwealth of Independent States (CIS) in 1991 and the United Nations in 1992. Moldova forged links in the 1990s with other former Soviet republics.

A problem since independence has been conflict with ethnic separatist minorities (Gaugausian, ethnic Russian, and ethnic Ukrainian) in the Trans-Dniester region who oppose unification with Romania. Fighting broke out in that region in 1992 between separatists and Moldovan security forces. Independently, Dniester voters approved a separate constitution in 1995; in 1997 a peace accord was signed.

Moldova: 20th-Century Leaders

President

1991–97: Mircea Snegur (1940–)

1997– : Petro Lucinschi (1940–)

Prime Minister

1990–92: Valeriu Muravschi

1992–97: Andrei Sangheli

1997–99: Ian Ciubuc

1999 : Ion Sturza

1999– : Dumitru Braghis (1957–)

Monaco

Official name: Principality of Monaco

Location: Southwestern Europe; France (N, E, W), Mediterranean Sea (S)

Capital: Monaco

Area: 1.21 sq. mi. (1.95 sq. km.)

Population (est. 1997): 31,892

Languages: French (official), English, Italian, Monegasque

Government: Constitutional monarchy

Religions: Roman Catholic 95%

Monetary unit: French franc

Main exports: N/A; sizable revenues from value-added taxes

For over 300 years Monaco has been an independent principality, although in the 19th century it was under the protectorate of Sardinia (1815) and France (1861). The sovereign was considered the absolute ruler until 1911, when Prince Albert of Monaco granted Monaco a constitution and an 18-member National Council serving five-year terms.

Long aligned with France, Monaco was required in 1918 to adopt France's national concerns as its own. Additionally, a 1919 agreement between France and Monaco required that if a future male heir were not born or adopted by the ruling family, the country would become an autonomous state under a French protectorate. (The birth of son Albert in 1958 to Prince Rainier and American actress Grace Kelly obviated the problem for that generation.)

During Prince Rainier's rule, Monaco has been governed by one party, the National and Democratic Union, which has won all 18 seats in the National Council in elections from 1968 to 1988.

Economically, Monaco relies on light manufacturing and its famed tourism, which attracts up to 1.5 million visitors per year. About 50 percent of its revenues come from value-added taxes on hotels, banks, and industry. Gambling at the internationally known Monte Carlo casino now yields only 4 percent of Monaco's earnings, with Prince Rainier continuing efforts to broaden the economy.

In 1993 Monaco became a member of the United Nations.

Monaco: 20th-Century Leaders

Prince

1889–1922: Albert I

1922–49: Louis II (1870–1949)

1949– : Rainier III (1923–)

Minister of State (since 1994)

1994–97: Paul Dijoud

1997–2000: Michel Leveque

Mongolia

Official name: Mongolian People's Republic

Location: Central Asia; landlocked; bordered by Russia (N), China (S, E, W)

Capital: Ulan Bator

Area: 604,207 sq. mi. (1,565,000 sq. km.)

Population (1997 est.): 2,538,211

Languages: Khalkha Mongol, Turkic, Russian, Chinese

Government: Communist state

Religions: Tibetan Buddhist 96%, Muslim 4%

Monetary unit: Tughrik

Main exports: Copper, livestock, animal products, wool, hides, fluorospar, nonferrous metals

Known for its place of power through the 13th century under Kublai Khan, Mongolia (formerly Outer Mongolia) has been influenced during the 20th century by its powerful neighbors China and Russia. The country entered the 20th century under Manchu rule, but after the Chinese Revolution (1911) and fall of the Manchus (1912), it declared independence under Jebtson Damba Khutukhu, the Living Buddha of Urga, and became a monarchy.

Although the country was reoccupied by the Chinese in 1919, Mongolia, with assistance from the Russian Communist Party, gained independence from China on March 13, 1921. It sustained its monarchy until the death of the last living Buddha, when Soviet forces established the Communist Mongolian People's Republic in 1924. Communist rule brought rural collectivization and the oppression of religious freedom, demonstrated through the killing of thousands of monks in the late 1930s.

During World War II Mongolia was allied with Russia. Although China continued to claim Outer Mongolia for the next two decades, it relinquished the country in 1945 under the Chinese-Russian Treaty. Shortly thereafter Mongolia became a nominally independent country.

Afterward Mongolia aligned itself with the U.S.S.R.; this included the signing of a treaty of friendship and cooperation in 1966 that granted Mongolia the right to request military aid from the U.S.S.R. in the case of invasion. By the 1980s its reliance on the U.S.S.R. had extended to include over 75 percent of its exports and imports.

The fall of the Soviet Union brought slow change to Mongolian government. Although the Communist Party relinquished its constitutional powers in 1990 and a new 1992 constitution ended Mongolia's time as a People's Republic, former Communists, now the Mongolian People's Revolutionary party, won parliamentary elections in 1992.

A non-Communist Democratic Union Coalition won a majority of seats in 1996 parliamentary elections. But the former Communists surged back into power in 2000 parlimentary elections.

Mongolia: 20th-Century Leaders

Head of State/President

1946–53: Gonchigyiyin Bumatsenda (1881–1953)

1954–72: Zhamsaranghin Sambu (1895–1972)

1972–74: Sonomyn Luvsan (1924–) (acting head of state)

1974–84: Yunzhahiyun Tsedenbal (1916–91)

1984–90: Zhambyn Batmunkh (1926–)

1990–97: Punsalmaagiyn Ochirbat (1942–)

1997– : Natsagiin Bagabandi (1950–)

Premier

1939–52: Khorloghiyin Choibalsan (1895–1952)

1952–74: Yumzhaghiyun Tsedenbal

1974–84: Zhambyn Batmunkh

1984–90: Dumaagiyn Sodnom (1933–)

1990: Sharavym Gungaadorj (1935–)

1990–92: Dashlyn Byambasuren (1942–)

1992–96: Puntsagiyn Jasray

1996–98: Mendsaikhan Enkhsaikhan

1998: Tsakhiagiin Elbedgdorj

1998–2000: Janlaviin Narantsatsralt

Montenegro See **Yugoslavia.**

Morocco

Official name: Kingdom of Morocco

Location: Northwestern Africa; bordered by Atlantic Ocean (W, NW), Strait of Gibraltar

(N), Mediterranean Sea (NE), Algeria (E, SE), Western Sahara (SW)

Capital: Rabat

Area: 172,413 sq. mi. (446,550 sq. km.)

Population: 30,391,423

Languages: Arabic (official), Berber dialects, French

Government: Constitutional monarchy

Religions: Muslim 98.7%, Christian 1.1%, Jewish 0.2%

Monetary unit: Dirham

Main exports: Food and beverages, semiprocessed foods, consumer goods

Rich in mineral resources, Morocco was the home of the Berbers before the mid-eighth century and was controlled by various dynasties until the beginning of the 20th century, when European powers nearly came to war over the country's control. In 1904 Britain and France eased tensions over Morocco, as France acknowledged Britain's interest in Egypt, and Britain allowed French influence in Morocco. German interest in the area led to an international crisis in 1905 known as the First Moroccan Crisis, nearly culminating in war. In 1912 Morocco became a French protectorate, with its southern region put under Spanish control. Ongoing disputes led to the Tangier Statute in 1923, an agreement that established a demilitarized international zone at Tangier.

During World War II Morocco was the site of fighting between the Allied-supported Free French forces and the Axis-supported Vichy French government. Spain occupied the international zone until 1945.

In 1947 forces from the Moroccan independence movement that formed during the 1920s and 1930s began warfare against the French. Sultan Muhammad Ben Yusuf was deported to Madagascar by the French in 1953, but protest led to his return in 1955. After French forces left the country, Morocco became an independent sovereign state on March 2, 1956. That year France and Spain recognized Morocco's sovereignty. Upon Muhammad's death on February 26, 1961, his son Hassan was named king. In the early 1970s Hassan II survived two unsuccessful coup attempts.

The 1970s and early 1980s were marked by Morocco's claim to parts of Spanish Sahara. In 1975 thousands of Moroccans crossed the Spanish Sahara border to enforce the government's contention that the southern territory historically belonged to Morocco. In 1979 Morocco occupied and took administrative control of the Western Sahara. A referendum on the situation was promised but has not yet occurred.

In 1990 Morocco became the first Arab state to condemn the Iraqi invasion of Kuwait and briefly planned troop support for the U.S.–run military counterattack.

In 1993 elections Morocco moved toward democratization, but the king retained his position.

Morocco: 20th-Century Leaders

Sultan

1894–1908: Abd-ul-Aziz IV (1881–1943, deposed)

1908–12: Mulai Hafid (1875–1937)

1912–27: Mulai Yusef

1927–53: Muhammad V (1909–61)

1953–55: Sidi Muhammad Ben Moulay Arafa (1889–1976) (Muhammad V in exile)

1955–57: Muhammad V

King

1957–61: Muhammad V

1961–99 : Hassan II (1929–99)

1999– : Muhammad VI (1963–)

Prime Minister

1917–55: Muhammad al-Moqri (1841–1957) (grand vizier)

1955–58: M'Barek ben Mustafa el-Bekkai (1907–61)

1958: Ahmed Balafrej

1958–60: Mulay Abdullah Ibrahim

1960–61: Muhammad V

1961: Hassan II

1961–63: Ahmad Reda Guedira

1963–65: Ahmed Bahmini (1914–71)

1965–67: Hassan II

1967–69: Mohamed Benhima

1969–71: Ahmed Laraki

1971–72: Mohammed Karim Lamrani

1972–79: Ahmed Osman

1979–83: Maati Bouabid

1983–86: Mohammed Karim Lamrani

1986–92: Azzedine Laraki (1929–)

1992–94: Mohammed Karim Lamrani

1994–98: Abdellati Filali

1998– : Abderrahmane El Youssoufi (1924–)

Mozambique

Official name: Republic of Mozambique

Location: Eastern coast of Africa; bordered by Zambia (N), Indian Ocean (E, SE), South Africa and Swaziland (SW), Zimbabwe (W)

Capital: Maputo

Area: 309,494 sq. mi. (801,590 sq. km.)

Population: 18,165,476

Languages: Portuguese (official), indigenous languages

Government: Republic

Religions: Indigenous beliefs 50%, Christian 30%, Muslim 20%

Monetary unit: Metical

Main exports: Shrimp, cashews, cotton, sugar

From 1505 Mozambique was under Portuguese influence and for centuries served as an active trade station for gold, ivory, and slaves for South American plantations. In the late 19th century it was widely populated by the Portuguese, who organized a colony in 1885 also known as Portuguese East Africa. Mozambique remained under Portuguese economic control into the mid-20th century.

The post–World War II wave of decolonization in Africa led to the formation of Mozambique's resistance movement FRELIMO in 1964. After years of guerrilla warfare, Mozambique was granted independence from Portugal on June 25, 1975. Under the leadership of Samora Machel, it became a Marxist state, the Communist People's Republic of Mozambique.

Over the next decade Mozambique's economy foundered under widespread nationalization and the withdrawal of Portuguese resources and influence. In the late 1970s Rhodesia and Mozambique began fighting; conflict cooled when Rhodesia gained independence as Zimbabwe. But a rebel movement, RENAMO (Mozambique National Resistance), aimed at upturning the Communist government, intensified its fighting against Mozambique until the end of the 1980s.

After the 1986 death of Samora Michel, Joaquím Chissanó became president, instituting a more pragmatic rule. He softened Marxist policy and sought improved international relations, including an appeal to the IMF. In 1987 UN forces began a relief program.

In 1989 Mozambique formally ceased Marxist-Leninist rule, and in 1990 approved a new constitution widening democratic policy, such as multiparty elections and a free-market economy. Support for RENAMO (from Rhodesia, and later South Africa) declined, hastening a cease-fire to the civil war in 1992. In 1994 Mozambique's first free elections brought a slight majority for FRELIMO, over RENAMO.

In 1992 a severe drought brought much death and destruction, making much of the country dependent on foreign aid, including IMF relief. Floods in 1999 and 2000 also devastated the country.

Mozambique: 20th-Century Leaders

President

1975–86: Samora Machel (1933–86)

1986– : Joaquim Alberto Chissanó (1939–)

Prime Minister

1974–75: Joaquím Alberto Chissanó

1986–94: Marío de Graça Machungo

1994– : Pascoal Manuel Mocumbi (1941–)

Myanmar

Official name: Union of Myanmar

Location: Northwest Indochinese peninsula in SoutheastAsia; bordered by Bangladesh and India (NW), Thailand (SE), China (NE), Andaman Sea (S), Bay of Bengal (SW)

Capital: Yangon

Area: 261,969 sq. mi. (678,500 sq. km.)

Population (est. 1997): 46,821,943

Languages: Burmese, minority languages

Government: Military regime

Religions: Buddhist 89.1%, Christian 4.9%, Muslim 3.8%, Hindu 0.5%, Animist 1.3%

Monetary unit: Kyat

Main exports: Rice, teak, oilseeds, metals, rubber, gems

For centuries a desirable western trade site, Burma was annexed to British-controlled India over three wars (1824–26), 1852, 1885). It became self-governing under British protectorate in 1937. During World War II the country's Allied-built Burma Road provided an important supply line to Chinese Nationalist troops. When Burma was occupied by the Japanese in 1942, it became a major war theater.

On January 4, 1948, Burma became an independent state as the Union of Burma. In 1962 the democratic government was overthrown and replaced by a single-party state of the Burmese Socialist Program party led by General U Ne Win. The period was marked by decreased trade and international isolation. Under a new constitution in 1974, he resigned the military title for the position of president.

In 1988 General Saw Maung overthrew the civilian government and established a military regime consisting of the State Law and Order Restoration Council (SLORC), with himself as chairman and 20 members. In 1989 the government changed the name of Burma to Myanmar.

In 1990 SLORC nullified the first multiparty elections in three decades, which had brought to power the National League for Democracy. Its leader, Aung San Suu Kyi, was placed under house arrest from July 20, 1989 to July 10, 1995; while under arrest in 1991 she was awarded the Nobel Peace Prize. Although SLORC prohibited her appointment as leader of the National League for Democracy and her involvement in drafting a new Myanmar constitution, she remains an active pro-democracy leader for the country.

In November 1997 SLORC was replaced with a new military ruling body, the State Peace and Development Council (SPDC). Its chairman was Than Shwe, who had chaired SLORC since 1992.

Myanmar: 20th-Century Leaders

President

1948–52: Sao Shwe Thaik (1896–1962)

1952–57: Ba U (1887–1963)

1957–62: Mahn Win Maung (1916–89)

1962–81: General U Ne Win

1981–88: U San Yu

1988: U Sein Lwin

1988–92: Saw Maung

1992–97: Than Shwe (1933–)

Prime Minister

1946–47: U Aung San (1914–47, assassinated)

1947–56: U Nu (1907–)

1956–57: U Ba Swe (1915–)

1957–58: U Nu

1958–60: Ne Win

1960–62: U Nu

1962–74: Ne Win

1974–77: U Sein Win

1977–88: U Maung Maung Kha (1917–)

1988: U Tun Tin

1988–92: Saw Maung

1992– : Than Shwe

Chairman, State Law and Order Restoration Council (SLORC)

1988–92: Saw Maung

1992–97: Than Shwe

Chairman, State Peace and Development Council SPDC)

1997– : Than Shwe

Namibia

Official name: Republic of Namibia

Location: Southwest Africa; bordered by Angola (N), Botswana (E), South Africa (S), Atlantic Ocean (W)

Capital: Windhoek

Area: 318,259 sq. mi. (824,290 sq. km.)

Population (est. 1997): 1,727,183

Languages: Afrikaans common language, German, English, indigenous languages

Government: Republic

Religions: Christian 80%–90%, indigenous beliefs 10%–20%

Monetary unit: South African rand

Main exports: Diamonds, uranium, zinc, copper, meat, processed fish

The country now known as Namibia was established as the German colony of South-West Africa in 1884 and made a protectorate in 1890. It was overtaken by South African forces in 1915; the Treaty of Versailles made it a South African mandate in 1920.

The United Nations rejected South Africa's application for the incorporation of the territory in 1946. In 1949 the territory was granted representation in the South African government.

In the 1950s the growing independence movement in the country led to the founding of the Marxist South-West Africa People's Organization (SWAPO) in 1959. In 1966 SWAPO leader Sam Nujoma led the organization in an ongoing guerrilla war for the liberation of South-West Africa. In 1968 the UN General Assembly changed the name of South-West Africa to Namibia.

In 1969 South Africa broadened legislative control over Namibia, leading to a Security Council condemnation. In 1974 South Africa declined to follow the Security Council resolution to begin the transfer of power to Namibians, refusing to negotiate with SWAPO. Years of failed diplomacy and warfare continued until December 22, 1988, when an agreement for a cease-fire and end to South African administration of Namibia was signed. In 1989 South-West Africa held elections to set up a new government, with SWAPO leader Sam Nujoma elected president. Namibia gained independence from South Africa on March 21, 1990. SWAPO–supported leaders took majority in 1992 elections.

Namibia: 20th-Century Leaders

President

1990– : Sam Nujoma (1929–)

Prime Minister

1990– : Hage G. Geingob (1941–)

Nauru

Official name: Republic of Nauru

Location: Central Pacific Ocean south of equator, about 2,800 mi. (4,500 km.) southwest of Hawaii

Capital: Yaren

Area: 8.2 sq. mi. (21 sq. km.)

Population (est. 1997): 10,390

Languages: Nauruan (official), English

Government: Republic

Religions: Protestant 58%, Roman Catholic 24%, Confucian and Taoist 8%

Monetary unit: Australian dollar

Main exports: Phosphates

Formerly known as Pleasant Island, Nauru became a German protectorate in 1888 and was placed under a League of Nations mandate administered by Australia, New Zealand, and Britain after World War I. During World War II it was occupied by Japan. In 1947 it came under UN trusteeship, administered by Australia. The country became an independent republic on January 31, 1968.

Nauru is governed by a parliament of 18 members, from which a prime minister and cabinet are elected. Nauru was admitted to the UN in 1999.

The island contains large amounts of phosphate deposits, which fuel the country's economy. Australian interests control much of its mining and exports; most assets are controlled by the Nauru Cooperative Society and the state-operated Nauru Phosophate Corporation. Its specialized export allows for one of the world's highest per-capita incomes.

Nauru: 20th-Century Leaders

President

1968–76: Hammer DeRoburt (1922–92)

1976–78: Bernard Dowiyogo (1946–)

1978: Lagumot Harris

1978–86: Hammer DeRoburt

1986: Kennan Adeang

1986–89: Hammer DeRoburt

1989: Kenos Aroi

1989–95: Bernard Dowiyogo

1995–96: Lagumot Harris

1996: Bernard Dowiyogo

1996: Kennan Adeang

1996–97: Reuben Kun (interim president)

1997–99: Kinza Clodumar

1999–2000: Rene Harris

Nepal

Official name: Kingdom of Nepal

Location: Central Asia, in Himalayan mountain range; landlocked; bordered by China (N), India (E, S, W)

Capital: Kathmandu

Area: 54,363 sq. mi. (140,800 sq. km.)

Population (1997 est.): 23,107,464

Languages: Nepali (official); Newari, Bhutia, Maithali

Government: Parliamentary democracy

Religions: Hindu 90%, Buddhist 5%, Muslim

Monetary unit: Nepalese rupee

Main exports: Clothing, carpets, leather goods, grain

Unified in 1768 as the Kingdom of Nepal by King Prithwi Narayan Shah, Nepal entered the 20th century governed by the Rana family, which had overthrown the Shah dynasty in 1846. It was a protectorate of Great Britain from 1816 until granted independence in 1923.

Until 1951 Rana family members kept kings in protective custody and ruled as heredity prime ministers. Then King Tribhuyan overtook the Rana government and restored the monarchy to power. His son Mahendra Bir Bikram Shah became king in 1955, dissolved parliament in 1960, and proclaimed a new constitution in 1962.

In 1972 Birendra Bir Bikram Shah succeeded Mahendra as king, following his father's death. In a 1980 election (the first in 22 years), voters approved autocratic rule advised by a parliament unaffiliated by parties. In 1990 pro-democracy riots forced Birendra to have the constitution rewritten and to set up a multiparty democracy. Through the 1990s control of parliament alternated between the Nepal Congress Party and the United Marxist Left. In 1997 Birendra approved parliamentary control by a coalition of Marxist-Leninist and National Democratic Parties. Since 1996 a Maoist insurgency has rocked the country

Nepal: 20th-Century Leaders

King

1911–55: Tribhuyan (1906–55)

1955–72: Mahendra (1920–72)

1972– : Birendra (1945–)

Prime Minister

1900–32: Rana family

1932–45: Juddha Shumshere Rana (1875–1952)

1945–48: Padma Shumshere J. B. Rana (1882–1961)

1948–51: Mohan Shumshere J. B. Rana

1951–55: Matuika Prasada Koirala (1912–)

1955–56: Mahendra

1956–57: Tanka Prasad Acharya (1912–92)

1957: Kunvar Inderjih Singh (1906–82)

1959–60: Bishewar Prasad Koirala

1960–63: Mahendra

1963: Tulsi Giri

1963–64: Surya Bahadur Thapa

1964–65: Tulsi Giri

1965–69: Surya Bahadur Thapa

1969–70: Kirti Nidhi Bista

1970–71: Mahendra

1971–73: Kirti Nidhi Bista

1973–75: Nagendra Prasad Rijal

1975–77: Tulsi Giri

1977–79: Kirti Nidhi Bista

1979–83: Surya Bahadur Thapa

1983–86: Lokendra Bahadur Chand

1986: Nagendra Prasad Rijal

1986–90: Marish Man singh Shrestha (1942–)

1990: Lokendra Bahadur Chand

1990–91: Krishna Prasad Bhattarai (1924–)

1991–94: Girija Prasad Koirala

1994–95: Man Mohan Adhikari

1995–97: Sher Bahadur Deuba

1997: Lokendra Bahadur Chand

1997–98: Surya Bahadur Thapa

1998–99: Girija Prasad Koirala

1999–2000: Krishna Prasad Bhattarai

Netherlands, The

Official name: Kingdom of the Netherlands

Location: Western Europe; bordered by North Sea (N, W), Germany (E), Belgium (S)

Capital: Amsterdam

Area: 16,033 sq. mi. (41,526 sq. km.)

Population (est. 1997): 15,649,729

Languages: Dutch (official)

Government: Constitutional monarchy (includes Netherlands and former colony Netherlands Antilles)

Religions: Roman Catholic 34%, Protestant 25%, unaffiliated 36%, Muslim 3%

Monetary unit: Guilder

Main exports: Foodstuffs, natural gas, chemicals, metal products, textiles, tobacco

Independent from Spain since 1579, the Netherlands (also called Holland) established itself as a colonial sea power in the 17th century and became an important European trade and industrial power in the 19th and early 20th century.

Neutral in World War I, the Netherlands proclaimed neutrality during World War II but was nonetheless occupied from May 1940 to May 1945 by the Nazis, who widely deported Jews and other groups to concentration camps. Fleeing to England, Queen Wilhelmina and other Dutch leaders maintained a government-in-exile for the war's duration. The Netherlands sustained severe war damage. The end of the war brought the end of the Netherlands' centuries-long control of Asian territories, beginning with the East Indies (now Indonesia), which declared itself independent in 1945. Following a four-year battle between the two countries, the Netherlands recognized Indonesian independence in 1949. In 1963 it also yielded to Indonesia the western half of New Guinea. Suriname declared independence on November 25, 1975, making the Netherlands Antilles the Netherlands' only overseas territory. The island of Aruba was part of the Netherlands Antilles until separating in 1986 and being granted internal autonomy.

From the 1950s the Netherlands has rebuilt its economy through its association with the Benelux union of Belgium, Netherlands, and Luxembourg and participation in the Common Market. The relatively stable government was run by coalitions of the Catholic State and Labor (originally Social Democratic) Parties, followed after 1958 by a coalition of Christian or Liberal parties.

In the 1990s the parliament was governed by the Labor and Christian Democratic Parties, with the latter losing power over the decade. Dutch governments since the 1950s have been known for social liberalism, comprehensive social welfare programs, and free enterprise policies.

The Netherlands: 20th-Century Leaders

Queen

1890–1948: Queen Wilhelmina (1880–1962)

1948–80: Queen Juliana (1909–1980)

1980– : Queen Beatrix Wilhelmina Armgard (1938–)

German High Commissioner

1940–45: Artur von Seyss-Inquart (1892–1946, hanged)

Prime Minister

1940–45: Pieter Sjoerd Gerbrandy (1885–1961)

1945–46: Willem Schermerhorn (1894–1977)

1946–48: Louis Joseph Maria Beel (1902–77)

1948–58: Willem Drees (1886–1988)

1958–59: Louis Joseph Maria Beel

1959–63: Jan Edouard de Quay (1901–85)

1963–65: Victor Gerard Marie Marijnen (1917–75)

1965–66: Joseph Maria Laurens Theo Cals (1914–71)

1966–67: Jelle Zijlstra

1967–71: Pieter de Jong

1971–73: Barend W. Biesheuvel

1973–77: Joop M. Den Uyl (1919–87)

1977–82: Andreas Van Agt (1931–)

1982–94: Ruud Lubbers (1939–)

1994– : Wim Kok (1938–)

New Zealand

Location: South Pacific Ocean; bordered by South Pacific Ocean (N, E, S) and Tasman Sea (W)

Capital: Wellington

Area: 103,884 sq. mi. (270,534 sq. km.)

Population (est. 1997): 3,587,275

Languages: English and Maori (both official)

Government: Parliamentary democracy

Religions: Christian 81%, none or unspecified 18%, Hindu, Confucian, and other 1%

Monetary unit: New Zealand dollar

Main exports: Wool, lamb, mutton, beef, fruit, fish

A British colony from 1841, New Zealand became a Dominion in 1907, enjoying internal self-government though not control of foreign and defense matters. Effective independence came in 1931, when New Zealand became a member of the Commonwealth of Nations.

New Zealand fought with Allied forces during World Wars I and II, with UN forces during the Korean conflict, and on the U.S. side in the Vietnam War.

From the 19th century New Zealand pioneered in progressive social policy. In 1893 it became one of the first countries offering universal suffrage. Before the turn of the century it mandated old-age pensions (1898) and followed with a child welfare program (1907), unemployment and health insurance (1938), and other social welfare programs.

From the 1930s the government has been controlled by the National and Labour Parties. Significant programs include the 1984 effort begun by the newly elected Labour government to move New Zealand to a free-market economy. Since the 1996 elections the Nationalist Party has ruled in coalition with the New Zealand First Party.

Over the century the Maoris, the original settlers in New Zealand, have become a notable force. From a population low of 40,000 following 19th-century wars with European settlers, they have increased to over 400,000. They represent five percent of the House of Representatives.

New Zealand: 20th-Century Leaders

Governor–General (representing the British monarch)

1897–1904: Uchter John Mark, earl of Ranfurly (1856–1933) (governor)

1904–10: William Lee, baron Plunket (1864–1920) (governor)

1910–12: John Poynder Dickson-Poynder, baron Islington (governor)

1912–20: Arthur William de Brito Savile Foljambe, earl of Liverpool (1870–1941)

1920–24: John Rushworth, viscount Jellicoe of Scapa (1859–1935)

1924–30: Sir Charles Fergusson (1865–1951)

1930–35: Sir Charles Bathurst, viscount Bledisloe (1867–)

1935–41: George Vere Arundell Monckton-Arundell, viscount Galway (1882–1943)

1941–46: Sir Cyril Louis Norton, baron Newall (1886–1963)

1946–52: Sir Bernard Cyril Freyberg (1890–1963)

1952–57: Sir Charles Willoughby Moke Norrie (1893–1977)

1957–62: Charles John Lyttelton, viscount Cobham (1909–77)

1962–66: Sir Bernard Edward Fergusson (1911–80)

1967–72: Sir Arthur Porritt (1900–94)

1972–77: Sir Edward Denis Blundell (1907–84)

1977–80: Sir Keith Jacka Holyoake (1904–83)

1980–85: Sir David Stuart Beattie

1985–90: Sir Paul Reeves (1932–)

1990–96: Dame Catherine Tizard (1931–)

1996– : Sir Michael Hardie–Boys (1931–)

Prime Minister

1893–1906: Richard John Seddon (1845–1906)

1906: William Hall-Jones (1851–1936)

1906–12: Sir Joseph George Ward (1856–1930)

1912: Thomas Mackenzie (1854–1930)

1912–25: William Ferguson Massey (1856–1925)

1925: Sir Francis Henry Dillon Bell

1925–28: Joseph Gordon Coates (1878–1943)

1928–30: Sir Joseph George Ward (1856–1930)

1930–35: George William Forbes (1869–1947)

1935–40: Michael Joseph Savage (1872–1940)

1940–49: Peter Fraser (1884–1950)

1949–57: Sir Sidney George Holland (1893–1961)

1957: Sir Keith Jacka Holyoake

1957–60: Walter Nash (1882–1968)

1960–72: Sir. Keith Jacka Holyoake

1972: John Ross Marshall (1912–88)

1972–74: Norman Eric Kirk (1923–74)

1974–75: Wallace Edward Rowling (1927–90)

1975–84: Robert David Muldoon (1921–92)

1984–89: David R. Lange (1942–)

1989–90: Geoffrey Palmer (1942–)

1990: Mike Moore (1949–)

1990–97: James B. Bolger (1935–)

1997–99: Jennifer Shipley

1999– : Helen Clark (1950–)

Nicaragua

Official name: Republic of Nicaragua

Location: Central America; bordered by Honduras (N); Pacific Ocean (W), Costa Rica (S), Caribbean Sea (E)

Capital: Managua

Area: 49,998 sq. mi. (129,494 sq. km.)

Population (est. 1998): 4,583,379

Languages: Spanish (official)

Government: Republic

Religions: Roman Catholic 95%

Monetary unit: Córdoba

Main exports: Coffee, cotton, sugar, bananas, seafood, meat

The region that constitutes Nicaragua won independence from Spain in 1821. It joined the United Provinces of Central America, which was dissolved in 1838, making Nicaragua an independent republic. Liberal Party dictator José Santos Zelaya (1893–1909) earned the enmity of the U.S. for his independent policies, and the U.S. backed his overthrow in 1909. From 1912 to 1925 and from 1926 to 1933, U.S. marines occupied the country. Augusto César Sandino, a Liberal officer, led a guerrilla war against the occupation. The U.S. occupation ended in 1933, but Sandino continued to wage war against the Liberal regime left behind, which he viewed as a puppet of the U.S.; he was murdered in 1934 at the orders of the U.S.-trained National Guard leader Anastasio Somoza García.

In 1936 Somoza seized power in a coup; he assumed the presidency the following year. With U.S. assistance, he ran the country as a dictator until his assassination in 1956; when not occupying the presidency, he directed those who did. His son Luis Somoza Debayle succeeded him as dictator until his own death in 1967; Luis's brother Anastasio Somoza Debayle succeeded him, continuing the dictatorial dynasty until 1979. The three Somoza regimes were famous for their corruption and brutality, qualities that reached their worst under the younger Anastasio. The U.S. supported the dynasty for its staunch anti-Communism but began to withdraw support from the younger Anastasio. Following a 1978–79 revolution, a left-wing group called the Sandinista National Liberation Front (FSLN), named in memory of Sandino, took power.

The new regime redistributed land and improved social services. The U.S. initially aided the government, but President Ronald Reagan considered it Communist, withdrew support, and instituted a trade embargo. The U.S. funded and trained a right-wing counterrevolutionary force called the Contras, which waged guerrilla war (1983–90) against the Sandinistas. Part of the U.S. aid provided to the Contras came illegally from sale of arms to Iran, in what was called the Iran-Contra Affair.

The civil war and trade embargo severely damaged Nicaragua's economy, despite aid from the Soviet Union and Cuba. The Sandinista president, Daniel Ortega, agreed to a truce in 1988, and elections in 1990. The Sandinistas lost the elections and Violeta Barrios de Chamorro became president, leading a fragmented opposition coalition. For the most part, the Contras ended their war that year. The Sandinistas continued to exert influence over the military and government. Conservative candidate Arnoldo Aleman won the 1996 election, marking a shift toward free enterprise and closer relations with the U.S.

Nicaragua: 20th-Century Leaders

President

1893–1909: José Santos Zelaya (1853–1919)

1909–10: José Madriz (provisional)

1911: Juan J. Estrada

1911–16: Adolfo Díaz

1917–20: Emiliano Chamorro Vargas

1921–23: Diego Manuel Chamorro

1923–24: Bartolome Martínez (provisional)

1925–26: Carlos Solorzano

1926: Emiliano Chamorro Vargas

1926–28: Adolfo Díaz

1929–32: José María Moncada

1933–36: Juan Bautista Sacasa (1874–1946)

1936: Carlos Brenes Jarquin (provisional)

1937–47: Anastasio Somoza García

1947: Leonardo Arguello (1875–1947)

1947: Benjamin Lacayo-Sacasa (1884–1959)

1947–50: Victor M. Román y Reyes (1872–1950)

1950–56: Anastasio Somoza

1956–63: Luis Somoza Debayle Garcia (1922–67)

1963–66: René Schick Gutiérrez (1909–66)

1966–67: Lorenzo Guerrero Gutiérrez

1967–72: Anastasio Somoza Debayle (1925–80)

(rule by triumvirate 1972–74)

1974–79: Anastasio Somoza Debayle

1979: Francisco Urcoyo Maleaño

1979–90: Daniel Ortega Saavedra (1945–)

1990–97: Violeta Barrios de Chamorro (1929–)

1997– : Arnoldo Alemán (1946–)

Niger

Official name: Republic of Niger

Location: Landlocked country in western Africa; bordered by Algeria and Libya (N), Chad (E), Nigeria (S), Benin, Burkina Faso (SW), Mali (W)

Capital: Niamey

Area: 489,189 sq. mi. (1,267,000 sq. km.)

Population (est. 1997): 9,388,859

Languages: French (official), Hausa, Djerma

Government: Republic

Religions: Muslim 80%, Christian and indigenious beliefs 20%

Monetary unit: Communauté Financière Africaine (CFA) franc

Main exports: Uranium, livestock, cowpeas, onions

An active site of European explorers seeking the source of the Niger River in the 19th century, Niger came under French domination in the 1890s and was made part of French West Africa in 1896. Rebellions against the French followed for the next two decades, until a French colony was established in 1922.

After World War II (1946) citizens of Niger were granted French citizenship and limited self-rule. In 1956 Niger was made an autonomous state within the French Community, and in 1959 it approved a constitution. Niger gained full independence from France on August 3, 1960. Under a special agreement with France, the French controlled several governmental activities, including defense and economic policy.

Niger's first president, Hamani Diori, took office in 1960. He served until 1974, when his regime was overthrown for corruption and mishandling of drought relief funds. The coup's leader, Lieutenant Colonel Seyni Kountché, instituted a military regime, changed by referendum to civilian rule in 1987. Following Kountche's death in 1987, Colonel Ali Saibou took office. A new constitution was approved in 1992, and opposition candidate Mahame Ousmane was elected president in 1993. A 1996 military coup unseated Ousmane, bringing leader Lieutenant Colonel Ibrahim Baré Maïnassara to power as president. Maïnassara was himself overthrown and assassinated by a 1999 coup led by Major Daouda Mallam Wanke. Under a new constitution providing for return to civilian rule, elections were held in 1999.

Niger: 20th-Century Leaders

President

1960–74: Hamani Diori (1916–89)

1974–87: Lieutenant Colonel Seyni Kountché (1931–87)

1987–93: Col. Ali Saibou

1993–96: Mahame Ousmane

1996–99: Ibrahim Baré Maïnassara

1999 : Major Daouda Mallam Wanke

1999– : Tandja Mamadou

Prime Minister

1983: Mamane Oumarou

1983–88: Hamid Algabid

1988–89: Mamane Oumarou

1990–91: Aliou Mahamidou

1991–93: Amadou Cheiffou

1993–94: Mahamadou Issoufou

1994–95: Souley Abdoulaye

1995: Boubacar Cissé Amadou

1995–96: Hama Amadou

1996: Boukary Adji

1996–97: Boubacar Cissé Amadou

1997–2000: Ibrahim Hassane Mayaki

Nigeria

Official name: Federal Republic of Nigeria

Location: Western coast of Africa; bordered by Niger (N), Cameroon (E), Gulf of Guinea (S), Benin (W)

Capital: Abuja

Area: 356,668 sq. mi. (923,770 sq. km.)

Population: 107,129,469

Languages: English (official), Hausa, Yoruba, Ibo, Fulani, others

Government: Military government (since 1983)

Religions: Muslim 50%, Christian 40%, indigenous beliefs 10%

Monetary unit: Naira

Main exports: Oil, cocoa, rubber

Inhabited by native cultures from at least 700 B.C., the region now known as Nigeria became a slave source for the British and Portuguese from the 15th century. In the 19th century the slave trade ended, and Nigeria became a British colony in 1861. In 1914 the territory east of the Niger River, then known as the Protectorate of Southern Nigeria, was made administrative partner with the rest of Nigeria.

During World War I Nigeria formed part of West African forces fighting with French troops against Germany in the Cameroons. From the 1920s Britain began to grant Nigerian demands for local self-rule, and in 1954 the colony was reorganized as the Nigerian Federation.

On October 1, 1960, Nigeria was granted independence from Great Britain. From 1960 to 1963 it was a member of the British Commonwealth. In 1963 it became a republic, a federation of self-governing states.

The country's history has been marked by differences among Nigeria's 250 ethnic and linguistic groups. In 1966 many Ibos were massacred by Hausas, who had driven them from the north. The Ibos resettled in the eastern region, and in 1967 the eastern region of Nigeria seceded from the federation and declared independence under the name of Democratic Republic of Biafra. After 31 months of civil war, Biafra rejoined the federal government. Military rule prevailed from 1966 to 1979.

In 1979 civilian rule was reinstated with the election of Alhaji Shehu Shagari as president. A military regime was restored after a coup on December 31, 1983, bringing to power its leader, Major General Mohammed Buhari. He was overthrown in a bloodless coup on August 27, 1985. Its leader, Major General Ibrahim Babangida, became president.

A civilian government was attempted in the early 1990s; it was quashed when the military government anulled results of the June 1993 presidential election. Although Babangida resigned in August 1993, the military regime took power again in November, when Prime Minister Sani Abacha became president. After his death, General Abdulsalam Abubakar took power (1998), retaining military rule but vowing to leave office following civilian elections. Democratic hopes were undercut by the mysterious death of opposition leader Mashood Abiola in 1998. At elections in February 1999, former president Olusegun Obasanjo was declared the victor.

Obasanjo, the first popularly elected president of Nigeria in 16 years, had himself been military ruler of the country from 1976 to 1979, when he had previously restored it to civilian rule.

Nigeria: 20th-Century Leaders

Governor–General

1959–63: Nnamdi Azikiwe

President

1963–66: Nnamdi Azikiwe

1966: Johnson Aguiyi-Ironsi (1924–66) (head of Military Council)

1966–75: Yakubu Gowon (1934–) (head of Military Council)

1975–76: Murtala Ramat Mohammed (1938–76) (head of State)

1976–79: Olusegun Obasanjo (1937–)

1979–83   Alhaji Shehu Shagari

1983–85: Mohammed Buhari (1942–)

1985–93: Ibrahim Babangida (1941–)

1993–98: Sani Abacha

1998–99: Abdulsalam Abubakar

1999– : Olusegun Obasanjo

Norway

Official name: Kingdom of Norway

Location: Northern Europe; bordered by Norwegian Sea (N, W), Russian Federation, Finland (NE), Sweden (E), North Sea (S, W)

Capital: Oslo

Area: 125,182 sq. mi. (324,220 sq. km.)

Population (est. 1997): 4,399,993

Languages: Norwegian (official), Lapp, Finnish

Government: Constitutional monarchy

Religions: Evangelical Lutheran 87.8%, other Protestant and Roman Catholic 3%, other 8.7%

Monetary unit: Norwegian krone

Main exports: Petroleum and petroleum products, metals, foodstuffs

With a history dating to the sack of southwestern Europe by the Vikings during the 8th to 11th centuries, Norway spent its later centuries ruled by Denmark and Sweden. Since 1815 the socially diverse country was under uneasy imposed control by aristocratic Sweden, and was not granted independence until October 26, 1905. Universal male suffrage was granted in 1898; women's suffrage followed in 1913.

During World War I Norway maintained neutrality, aligning with Scandinavian neighbors Sweden and Denmark. The economic hardships of the 1920s and 1930s were marked in government by political conflict and fragmentation. From 1935, some stability was reached through the election and policies of the Social Democrat Party.

Early in World War II, on April 9,1940, Norway was invaded by German troops. In June it was fully occupied, forcing the king to flee to London to establish a government-in-exile. Nazi collaborator and Norwegian prime minister Vidkun Quisling encouraged German occupation and maintained Norway's wartime puppet government. He was executed by the Norwegians in October 1945, his name becoming a synonym for traitor.

After World War II Norway returned to Social Democrat rule under Einar Gerhardsen, quickly rebuilding its war-damaged country, extending the social welfare state, and strengthening international ties. Reflecting the country's commitment to international relations, it entered the North Atlantic Treaty Organization in 1949. Statesman Trygve Lie (1896–1968) served as secretary-general of the United Nations from 1946 to 1953. Social Democrat party control held into the 1970s.

In the mid-1980s, Norway returned to Labor Party control under Prime Minister Gro Harlem Brundtland, who remained in control (save for one year, 1989–90) well into the 1990s. She reinvigorated the country's international ties and commitment to underdeveloped countries. Her attempts to win national support for entry into the European Community failed, with Norway voting down membership in 1994. She resigned in 1996, replaced by Thorbjoern Jagland. In 1997 Kjell Magne Bondevik became prime minister.

Norway: 20th-Century Leaders

King

1872–1905: Oscar II (1829–1907) (king of Sweden and Norway)

1905–57: Haakon VII (1872–1957)

1940–45: German occupation

1957–91: Olav V (1903–91)

1991– : Harald V (1937–)

Prime Minister

1898–1902: Johannes Steen

1902–03: Otto Blehr (1847–1927)

1903–05: Georg Francis Hagerup

1905–07: Christian Michelsen (1857–1925)

1907–08: J. Lövland (1857–1925)

1908–10: Gunnar Knudsen (1848–1928)

1910–12: Wollert Konow (1848–1928)

1912–13: Jens Bratlie (1856–1939)

1913–20: Gunnar Knudsen

1920–21: Otto B. Halvorsen (1872–1923)

1921–23: Otto Blehr

1923: Otto B. Halvorsen

1923–24: Abraham Berge (1851–1936)

1924–26: Johan Ludwig Mowinckel (1870–1943)

1926–28: Ivar Lykke (1872–1949)

1928: Christopher Hornsrud (1859–1960)

1928–1931: Johan Ludwig Mowinckel

1931–32: Peder Kolstad (1878–1932)

1932–33: Jens Hundseid (1883–1965)

1933–35: Johan Ludwig Mowinckel

1935–45: Johan Nygaardsvold (1879–1952)

1942–45: Vidkun Quisling (1887–1945) (prime minister of German occupation government)

1945–51: Einar Gerhardsen (1897–1987)

1951–55: Oscar Torp (1893–1958)

1955–63: Einar Gerhardsen

1963: John Lyng (1905–1978)

1963–65: Einar Gerhardsen

1965–71: Per Borten

1971–72: Trygve Bratteli (1910–84)

1972–73: Lars Korvald

1973–76: Trygve Bratteli

1976–81: Odvar Nordli

1981: Gro Harlem Brundtland (1939–)

1981–86: Kare Isaachsen Willoch

1986–89: Gro Harlem Brundtland

1989–90: Jan Peder Syse (1930–)

1990–96: Gro Harlem Brundtland

1996–97: Thorbjoern Jagland

1997–2000: Kjell Magne Bondevik

Oman

Official name: Sultanate of Oman

Location: Southeastern Arabian peninsula; bordered by Gulf of Oman (N), Arabian Sea (E, S), Yemen (SW), Saudi Arabia (W), United Arab Emirates (NW), detached portion on Strait of Hormuz

Capital: Muscat

Area: 82,031 sq. mi. (212,460 sq. km.)

Population (est. 1997): 2,264,590

Languages: Arabic (official), English, Baluchi, Urdu, Indian dialects

Government: Monarchy

Religions: Ibadhi Muslim 75%, Sunni Muslim, Shi'a Muslim, Hindu 25%

Monetary unit: Omani rial

Main exports: Petroleum, reprocessed copper, agricultural goods

Oman (formerly known as Muscat) began the 19th century as Arabia's most powerful state but by century's end lost some of its territories and came into the realm of the British Empire. Once controlling areas stretching from eastern Africa to the coast of Iran, it relinquished in the 19th century Zanzibar and much of Baluchistan. It became a British protectorate in 1891 and entered the 20th century under the control of the British Empire.

From 1913 to 1920 Oman was weakened by a civil war between outlying tribes supporting imam and coastal troops supporting the sultan. Conflicts continued into the 1950s, when an uprising by imam and his followers (1955–57) was quelled with the aid of British troops. In 1958 Oman sold its last Baluchi possession, Gwadar, to Pakistan.

Oman gained independence from Britain in 1970, when Britain withdrew from the gulf and ended the protectorate. In 1970 Sultan Sa'id ibn Taymur was overthrown in a palace coup by his son Qabus ibn Sa'id. Attempting to modernize the isolated country, he joined the United Nations (1971) and instituted a long-term economic development program (1975). Part of the program focused on the development of avenues for oil export; by the 1990s petroleum accounted for 95 percent of Oman's exports. Limited moves toward social and political modernization have included the creation of a National Consultative Council in 1981.

In 1980 Oman granted the U.S. permission to build military bases in the country. In 1996 it became part of a consortium to build a pipeline feeding to the Black Sea.

Oman: 20th-Century Leaders

Sultan

1932–1970: Sa'id ibn Taymur (1910–72)

1970– : Qabus ibn Sa'id (1940–)

Pakistan

Official name: Islamic Republic of Pakistan

Location: Southern Asia; bordered by Afghanistan, China (N), India (E), Arabian Sea (S), Iran (W)

Capital: Islamabad

Area: 310,402 sq. mi. (803,940 sq. km.)

Population (est. 1998): 135,135,195

Languages: Urdu and English (both official), Punjabi, Sindhi, Pashtu, Balochi, Siraiki

Government: Republic

Religions: Sunni Muslim 77%, Shi'a Muslim 20%, Christian, Hindu, other

Monetary unit: Rupee

Main exports: Rice, cotton, textiles

This ethnically diverse, largely Muslim region came under British rule in the 19th century and was incorporated into British India; it included the provinces of Baluchistan, Sind, Punjab, and the North-West Frontier.

In the early 20th century, as nationalist resistance to British rule grew throughout India, Muslims were increasingly concerned about protecting their interests against those of India's Hindu majority. In 1940 the Muslim League under Muhammad Ali Jinnah proposed creation of a separate Muslim state, to be called Pakistan (from Urdu, "pure land"). In post–World War II negotiations for Indian independence from Britain, the Muslim League's demands prevailed. On August 15, 1947, both Pakistan and India came into being as independent states within the Commonwealth of Nations. Pakistan at that time included not only its present territory, then called West Pakistan, but the separate region of East Bengal or East Pakistan (now Bangladesh), which had a Muslim majority before independence. East and West Pakistan were separated from each other by about a thousand miles of Indian territory.

Upon independence, massive population movements ensued, accompanied by widespread violence, as Hindus in Pakistan fled to India and Muslims in India fled to Pakistan. Up to a million people were killed. In the midst of this strife, the first of three India-Pakistan Wars took place. Also known as the Kashmir War (1947–49), it concerned rival claims to Kashmir, an independent state bordering West Pakistan. A UN cease-fire (1948) and truce (1949) ended the war, with Kashmir informally partitioned along the battle front.

In its early years Pakistan was hampered by a lack of experience in self-government or administration, as well as a lack of national identity to unite its disparate ethnic groups. The early death of its first governor-general, Jinnah, in 1948, and the assassination of its first prime minister, Liaquat Ali Khan, in 1951 left a leadership vacuum. It took until 1956 before a constitution was adopted making Pakistan a republic. However, the country remained in economic and political turmoil.

In 1958 General Mohammad Ayub Khan took power in a military coup, abolished the constitution, and established a dictatorship. A new constitution went into effect in 1962, leaving Ayub Khan in power and establishing a federal Islamic republic.

Ayub Khan's prosecution of the second India-Pakistan War (1965) failed to resolve the Kashmir issue and ended in another UN cease-fire. Agitation for increased autonomy grew in East Pakistan, which was unhappy with West Pakistani dominance of the federal government. The instability was compounded by economic difficulties, leading Ayub Khan to resign in 1969 and hand over power to General Agha Mohammad Yahya Khan, head of the army.

In 1970 democratic elections were held to draft a new constitution, but Yahya Khan cancelled the results (1971) after the Awami League, an organization advocating full autonomy for East Pakistan, was declared the winner. East Pakistan thereupon declared independence as Bangladesh (1971). In the third India-Pakistan War (December 1971), India supported the Bangladeshi rebels and forced Pakistan to recognize the independence of its former eastern province.

Following the loss of East Pakistan, Pakistan People's Party (PPP) leader Zulfikar Ali Bhutto became president (1971–73) and prime minister (1973–77). He led a Socialist, nonaligned government that was unable to improve the economy or ease regional tensions. Overthrown in a 1977 coup by General Zia-ul Haq (1924–88), he was executed two years later, rousing international protests.

Zia-ul Haq ruled Pakistan under martial law until 1985, when he instituted a civilian government but remained in power as president. During his tenure, he emphasized his commitment to Islam and improved relations with the U.S., which offered aid in return for his support of Afghan rebels following the Soviet invasion of Afghanistan in 1979. He died in a plane crash in 1988.

In the 1988 elections that followed, Bhutto's daughter Benazir Bhutto (1953–) became prime minister. Hopes for a stable Pakistani democracy dimmed as Bhutto, unable to establish control over the country, was dismissed by President Ishaq Khan on charges of corruption. In 1993 she returned as prime minister but was arrested in 1996 and again dismissed from office on charges of corruption. In 1997 Nawaz Sharif's party won control of the government, and Parliament amended the constitution to prevent a president from dismissing a government.

In 1998 tensions between Pakistan and India rose when India conducted nuclear tests near the border with Pakistan. Pakistan promptly conducted nuclear tests of its own, raising fears of a nuclear arms race in south Asia. Tensions escalated in 1999 when Islamic separatist fighters clashed with Indian troops in Kashmir. India charged Pakistan with backing the rebels, a charge Pakistan denied. Internal dissension over the conflict led to a coup that unseated Sharif in 1999 and installed military rule.

Pakistan: 20th-Century Leaders

Governor–General

1947–48: Mohammed Ali Jinnah

1948–51: Khwaja Nazimuddin (1894–1964)

1951–55: Ghulam Mohammed (1895–1956)

1955–56: Iskander Mirza (1899–1969)

President

1956–58: Iskander Mirza

1958–69: Mohammad Ayub Khan (1907–74)

1969–71: Mohammad Yahya Khan (1917–80)

1971–73: Zulfikar Ali Bhutto

1973–78: Fazal Elahi Chaudhry (1904–82)

1978–88: Mohammad Zia ul-Haq (1924–88)

1988–93: Ghulam Ishaq Khan

1993: Wasim Sajjad

1993–97: Farooq Ahmed Leghari

1997–98: Wasim Sajjad (acting)

1998–: Mohammed Rafiq Tarar (1929–)

Prime Minister

1947–51: Liaquat Ali Khan (1895–1951)

1951–53: Khwaja Nazimuddin

1953–55: Mohammed Ali (1909–63)

1955–56: Chaudry Mohammed Ali (1905–80)

1956–57: Husain Shahid Suhrawardy (1893–1963)

1957: I. I. Chundrigar (1897–1960)

1957–58: Malik Firoz Khan Noon (1893–1970)

1958–69: Mohammad Ayub Khan

1969–71: Mohammad Yahya Khan

1971: Nurul Amin

1973–77: Zulfikar Ali Bhutto

1977–85: Mohammad Zia ul-Haq

1985–88: Mohammad Khan Junejo (1932–93)

1988: Mohammed Zia ul-Haq

1988–90: Benazir Bhutto (1953–)

1990: Ghulam Mustafa Jatoi

1990–93: Nawaz Sharif (1949–)

1993: Moeen Qureshi

1993–96: Benazir Bhutto

1996–97: Meraj Khalid (acting)

1997–99: Mohammed Nawaz Sharif

Head of Government (de facto)

1999– : General Pervez Musharraf (1943–)

Palau

Official name: Republic of Palau

Location: Western central Pacific Ocean; chain of over 200 islands (eight inhabited); neighbors include Guam (720 mi./1,160 km to NE), Federated States of Micronesia (to E), New Guinea (to S), Philippines (530 mi./850 km. to NW)

Capital: Koror (new capital in Babelthuap being built)

Area: 177 sq. mi. (458 sq. km.)

Population (est. 1997): 17,240

Languages: Palauan (official), English

Government: Republic

Religions: Christian (Roman Catholic, Seventh-day Adventists, Jehovah's Witnesses) 33%, Modeknegi (indegenous faith) 33%

Monetary unit: U.S. dollar

Main exports: Trochus (shellfish), tuna, copra, handicrafts

Officially under Spanish control from 1885, Palau (also known as Belau) entered the 20th century owned by Germany, after the islands were sold in 1899. The Germans introduced sanitary practices that controlled the devastating epidemics of dysentery and influenza.

In 1914 Japan occupied Palau and in 1920 received a League of Nations mandate over the country. During its occupation, Japan improved the country's agricultural, fishing, and mining capabilities. In 1938 Palau became a closed military area and during World War II was a prime Japanese naval base. Following a brutal battle, it was occupied by U.S. forces from 1944. On July 18, 1947, it (as part of the Trust Territory of the Pacific Islands) became a UN trusteeship under U.S. administration. In 1979 voters approved a new constitution, and in 1981 the country gained self-rule. Following the approval of the Compact of Free Association with the United States on October 1, 1994, Palau became an independent nation in association with the U.S.

Palau: 20th-Century Leaders

President

1993– : Kuniwo Nakamura (1943–)

Panama

Official name: Republic of Panama

Location: Central America; bordered by Caribbean Sea (N), Colombia (E), Pacific Ocean (S), Costa Rica (W)

Capital: Panama City

Area: 30,193 sq. mi. (78,200 sq. km.)

Population: 2,693,417

Languages: Spanish (official), English

Government: Constitutional republic

Religions: Roman Catholic 85%, Protestant 15%

Monetary unit: Balboa

Main exports: Bananas, shrimp, sugar

Explored by Columbus and Balboa in the 16th century, Panama was a shipping point for Spanish treasure and cargo in the 17th and 18th centuries. When Spain's American colonies won independence in the early 19th century, Panama became part of Columbia, but Panamanian nationalists soon agitated for independence. With support from the U.S., which wanted canal rights in Panama, Panama gained independence on November 3, 1903.

After purchasing ongoing canal rights for $10 million, the U.S. began construction on the Panama Canal in 1904. Completed in 1914 and built on U.S.-controlled territory, the 50.7-mile canal connecting the Atlantic and Pacific Oceans vastly increased commerce and assured U.S. influence in 20th-century Panamanian affairs.

In 1977 Panamanian leader Omar Torrijos Herrera and U.S. president Jimmy Carter signed two treaties on the canal—one transferring it to full Panamanian control on December 31, 1999, and one guaranteeing Panama's neutrality after the transfer. The treaties were approved by referendum by Panama, and after including changes permitting possible U.S. military intervention in the area, approved by the U.S. Senate in March–April 1978.

In 1968 President Arnulfo Arias was ousted by a National Guard junta, with its commander Omar Torrijos Herrera named Panama's leader in 1969. Over the next decade he brought social reform, including housing construction, a revision of labor laws, and increased taxes on foreign interests. In 1981 Torrijos died in an air accident; later a military official proclaimed the death an assassination and accused Panamanian general Manuel Noriega.

The country's military leader and virtual ruler by the late 1980s, Noriega was indicted by the U.S. on drug charges. He refused President Eric Arturo Delvalle's request for resignation and instead forced the National Assembly to appoint a new president, Manuel Solis Palma. Noriega annulled results of the 1989 presidential election and instead named himself dictator.

After an unsuccessful coup attempt, the U.S. invaded Panama in December 1989 and captured Noriega. He was brought to the U.S. and convicted on drug charges. The probable winner of the 1989 election, Guillermo Endara, was made president. In 1990 the U.S. suppressed a military revolt led by a former Noriega-linked police official.

After Endara left office under corruption charges in 1994, Panama completed its first democratic election in 26 years. Elected was left-center U.S.-educated businessman Ernesto Perez Balladares. His actions included talks with the U.S. to lengthen the period of American military presence at the Panama Canal after 1999.

Panama: 20th-Century Leaders

President

1904–08: Manuel Amador Guerrero (1833–1909)

1908–10: José Domingo de Obaldía

1910: Carlos Antonio Mendoza (acting)

1910–12: Pablo Arosemena (acting)

1912–16: Belisario Porras (1856–1942)

1916–18: Ramón Váldez

1918: Ciro Luis Urriola (acting)

1918–20: Belisario Porras (acting)

1920: Ernesto Lefevre

1920–24: Belisario Porras

1924–28: Rodolfo Chiari

1928–31: Florencio Harmodio Arosemena (1873–1945)

1931: Harmodio Arias (acting)

1931–32: Ricardo J. Alfaro

1932–36: Harmodio Arias

1936–39: Juan Demóstenes Arosemena (1879–1939)

1939–40: Augusto Samuel Boyd (1879–1957)(acting)

1940–41: Arnulfo Arias

1941–45: Ricardo de la Guardia (1899–1969)

1945–48: Enrique Adolfo Jiménez

National Guard Commander

1968–81: Omar Torrijos Herrera (1929–81)

1981–82: Florencio Floréz Aguilar (1931–)

1982–83: Rubén Darío Paaredes Del Rio (1931–)

1983–89: Manuel A. Noriega (1940–)

1948–49: Domingo Díaz Arosemena (1875–1949)

1949: Daniel Chanis Pinzón (1892–1961)

1949: Roberto F. Chiari

1949–51: Arnulfo Arias (1901–88)

1951–52: Alcibiades Arosemena (1883–1958)

1952–55: José Antonio Remón Cantera (1908–55, assassinated)

1955: José Ramón Guizado (1899–1964)

1955–56: Ricardo M. Arias Esponisa (1912–93)

1956–60: Ernesto de la Guardia Jr. (1904–83)

1960–64: Roberto F. Chiari

1964–68: Marco A. Robles (1905–90)

1968: Arnulfo Arias

1968–69: Jose M. Pinilla (1919–79)

1969–78: Demetrio Lakas Bahas (1925–78)

1978–82: Arístides Royo Sanchez

1982–84: Ricardo de la Espriella

1984: Jorge Illueca

1984–85: Nicolás Ardito Barletta (1938–)

1985–88: Eric Arturo Delvalle (1937–)

1988–89: Manuel Solis Palma

1989–94: Guillermo Endara Galimany

1994–99: Ernesto Pérez Balladares

1999– : Mireya Elisa Moscoso (1946–)

Papua New Guinea

Official name: Independent State of Papua New Guinea

Location: Eastern portion of the island of New Guine and approximately 600 smaller islands southeast of Asia; bordered by Bismarck Sea (N), Solomon Sea (E), Australia (S), Indonesia (W)

Capital: Port Moresby (administrative capital)

Area: 178,259 sq. mi. (461,690 sq. km.)

Population (est. 1997): 4,496,221

Languages: 715 indigenous languages, English 1%–2%, pidgin English, Moto (Papua region)

Government: Parliamentary democracy

Religions: Roman Catholic 22%, Lutheran 16%, other Christian 28%, indigenous beliefs 34%

Monetary unit: Kina

Main exports: Gold, copper ore, coffee, palm oil, timber, transport equipment, food, fuels, chemicals

The second largest island in the world, New Guinea was settled by the Papuan and Melanese thousands of years ago. From the 19th century the islands were divided among the Dutch, Germans, and British.

In 1905 Australia gained the southern half of eastern New Guinea from the British. During World War I Australia occupied the German-claimed northern sector of the country. After the war, the League of Nations mandated Australian administration for the islands.

In 1942, during World War II, Japanese forces took partial control of the island; Allies retook the island in 1944. In 1949 the United Nations granted Australia a trusteeship over the area.

On December 1, 1973, the territories gained self-rule; they gained full independence as Papua New Guinea on September 16, 1975. Secessionist groups among the country's many tribes fought the government in ongoing conflicts on Bougainville from 1988. Among the many deaths was that of Bougainville's chief minister, Theodore Miriung. In 1997, a truce ended the fighting.

Papua New Guinea maintains close political relations with Australia.

Papua New Guinea: 20th-Century Leaders

Governor–General (representing the British monarch)

1975–77: Sir John Guise (1914–91)

1977–83: Sir Tore Lokoloko

1983–90: Sir Kingsford Dibella (1932–)

1990–91: Sir Serei Eri (1936–93)

1991: Dennis Young

1991–97: Sir Wiwa Korowi (1948–)

1997– : Silas Atopare

Prime Minister

1975–80: Sir Michael T. Somare (1936–)

1980–82: Sir Julius Chan (1939–)

1982–85: Sir Michael T. Somare

1985–88: Paias Wingti (1951–)

1988–92: Rabbi Namaliu (1947–)

1992–94: Paias Wingti

1994–97: Sir Julius Chan

1997: John Giheno (acting prime minister)

1997: Sir Julius Chan

1997– : Bill Skate

1999– : Mekere Morauta (1946–)

Paraguay

Official name: Republic of Paraguay

Location: Central South America; landlocked; bordered by Bolivia (N), Brazil (E), Argentina (S. W.)

Capital: Asunción

Area: 157,046 sq. mi. (406,750 sq. km.)

Population (est. 1997): 5,651,634

Languages: Spanish (official), Guaraní

Government: Republic

Religions: Roman Catholic 90%, Mennonite and other Protestant denominations

Monetary unit: Guarani

Main exports: Cotton, soybeans, timber, vegetable oils, coffee, tung oil

Settled largely by Spain in the 16th century and in the 17th century (until their expulsion in 1767) by the Jesuits, Paraguay became an independent country in 1813. After decades of stable existence, the country became decimated from the Paraguayan War, or War of Triple Alliance (Uruguay, Brazil, Argentina). The war halved Paraguay's population, including 90 percent of its males, and cost 60,000 square miles of territory.

Throughout the 20th century Paraguay has been dominated largely by two political parties and has suffered from election tampering and authoritarian rule. From 1870 into the early 20th century, Paraguayan rule was dominated by the Brazil-backed Colorado Party. From 1904 to 1936, the country was ruled by the Argentina-backed Liberal (Azules) Party. In 1936 following a costly victory against Bolivia in the Chaco War (1932–35), the country came under military rule. That rule lasted until 1954, when General Alfredo Stroessner took over the presidency and joined political and military forces. In so doing he became head of the Colorado Party. Although he stabilized the economy in part through the huge Itaipú hydroelectric project (1973–82), he later brought economic downturn and was overthrown in 1989 by General Andrés Rodríguez. In 1993 democratic elections were held, with Colorado Party member Juan Carlos Wasmosy Monti becoming president. In 1997 General Lino Oviedo attempted a coup, but surrendered in December. New president Raul Cubas Grau released the general from prison in 1998, causing the Supreme Court to rule the act unconstitutional and bringing impeachment hearings against Cubas. Cubas was accused of arranging the assassination of his vice president, Luis María Argaño, in 1999. Violent demonstrations in 1999 led to the resignation of Cubas before the impeachment votes. He was replaced by Senate leader Luis Angel Gonzalez Macchi.

Paraguay: 20th-Century Leaders

President

1898–1902: Emilio Aceval

1902: Hector Carvallo

1902–04: Juan B. Escurra

1904–05: Juan Gaona (provisional)

1906: Cecilio Báez (1862–1941)

1906–08: Benigno Ferreira

1908–10: Emiliano González Navero (1861–1938)

1910–11: Manuel Gondra

1911: Albino Jara (provisional)

1911–12: Liberato Marcial Rojas (provisional)

1912: Pedro Peña

1912: Emiliano González Navero

1912–16: Eduardo Schaerer

1916–19: Manuel Franco (d. 1919)

1919–20: José Montero (acting)

1920–21: Manuel Gondra (1871–1927)

1921–23: Eusebio Ayala (1875–1942) (provisional)

1923–24: Eligio Ayala (provisional)

1924: Luis Riart (provisional)

1924–28: Eligio Ayala

1928–31: José Patricio Guggiari (1884–1957)

1931–32: Emiliano González Navero (provisional)

1932: José Patricio Guggiari

1932–36: Eusebio Ayala

1936–37: Rafael Franco (provisional)

1937–39: Félix Paiva

1939–40: José Félix Estigarribia (1888–1940)

1940–48: Higinio Moríñgo (1887–1985)

1948: Juan Manuel Frutos (provisional)

1948–49: Juan Naatalicio González (1897–1966)

1949: Raimundo Rolón

1949: Felipe Molas López (1901–54)

1949–54: Federico Chávez (1880–1978)

1954: Tomás Romero Pereira (1886–1954)

1954–89: Alfredo Stroessner

1989–93: Andrés Rodríguez

1993–97: Juan Carlos Wasmosy Monti (1938–)

1998–99: Raul Cubas Grau

1999– : Luis Angel Gonzalez Macchi (1947–)

Peru

Official name: Republic of Peru

Location: Western South America; bordered by Ecuador, Colombia (N), Brazil, Bolivia (E), Chile (S), Pacific Ocean (W)

Capital: Lima

Area: 496,224 sq. mi. (1,285,220 sq. km.)

Population (est. 1998): 26,111,110

Languages: Spanish and Quechua (both official), Aymara

Government: Republic

Religions: predominantly Roman Catholic

Monetary unit: Nuevo sol

Main exports: Fish meal, zinc, crude oil, copper

Peru was the site of the indigenous Inca civilization, which was conquered by Spain in the 16th century. Peru won independence in 1821. President Augusto B. Leguía (1908–12, 1919–30) dominated Peru in the first decades of the 20th century. For much of his time in office, he governed as a virtual dictator; aided by U.S. investment, he promoted economic development in the interests of the wealthy elite. Many Peruvians, including most Native Americans (a group that constitutes 45 percent of the total present population), remained poor, while the middle class felt disenfranchised. In 1924 Víctor Raúl Haya de la Torre founded the American Popular Revolutionary Alliance (APRA), which called for radical social and economic reform and attracted the poor and middle class. Leguía banned the party, as did his successor, Colonel Luis Sánchez Cerro, who overthrew Leguía in a coup in 1930.

Cerro inaugurated a decade of military rule, continued by General Oscar Benavides (1933–39) after Cerro's assassination. During the decade left-wing APRA supporters and the right-wing armed forces clashed violently several times. President Manuel Prado y Ugarteche (1939–45) restored civilian rule; he led Peru to conquer a large amount of territory in a war with Ecuador (1941) and sided with the Allies in World War II. His elected successor, José Luis Bustamante y Rivero (1945–48), was overthrown in a coup in 1948; the military regime that followed lasted until 1956. In 1962 the military seized power to prevent Haya de la Torre from being elected president. Civilian rule was restored the following year, only to be overthrown in 1968 by a reformist military regime (1968–75) that instituted land reform and nationalized the oil industry and other foreign-owned enterprises. A new junta, which came to power in 1975, ushered in the return of civilian government in 1980.

Like many Latin American nations in the 1980s, Peru struggled with a failing economy and foreign debt crisis. Fernando Belaúnde Terry (1980–85) instituted austerity measures that brought riots and strikes. Appealing to peasants sick of economic injustice, a Maoist, Andean-based guerrilla group called the Shining Path waged war against the government, as did the Tupac Amaru Revolutionary Movement. An illicit cocaine industry enriched drug barons whose corrupting influence further destabilized the country.

Alberto Fujimori, who headed a new movement called Cambio 90, won the 1990 presidential election. His privatization and liberalization policies promoted strong economic growth, though economic inequality remained high. In 1992 he dissolved the legislature and imposed martial law; a new constitution was adopted in 1993. He suppressed the Shining Path insurgency and, in 1997, mounted a commando raid that freed hostages held by Tupac Amaru rebels in the Japanese ambassador's residence; all the hostage-takers were killed. Despite praise for his decisiveness, many Peruvians increasingly criticized Fujimori for his authoritarian style. Fujimori resigned in 2000 amid changes of electoral fraud and other scandals.

Peru: 20th-Century Leaders

President

1899–1903: Eduardo López de Romaña

1903–04: Manuel Candamo (1842–1904)

1904: Serapio Calderón

1904–08: José Pardo (1864–1947)

1908–12: Augusto Bernadino Leguía (1863–1932)

1912–14: Guillermo Enrique Billinghurst (1851–1915)

1914: Oscar Raimundo Benavides (1876–1945)

1915–19: José Pardo

1919: Augusto Bernadino Leguía (provisional)

1919–29: Augusto Bernadino Leguía

(junta, 1930–31)

1931: Ricardo Leonicio Elías (provisional)

1931–33: Luis M. Sánchez Cerro (1889–1933)

1933–39: Oscar Raimundo Benavides

1939–45: Manuel Prado y Ugarteche (1889–1967)

1945–48: José Luis Bustamente y Rivero (1894–1988)

1948: Zenon Noriega

1948–50: Manuel A. Odría (1897–1974) (president, military junta)

1950: Zenon Noriega

1950–56: Manuel A. Odría

1956–62: Manuel Prado y Ugarteche

1962: Ricardo Pérez Godoy (president, military junta)

1962–63: Ricardo Pérez Godoy (president, military junta)

1963: Nicolás Lindley López

1963–68: Fernando Belaúnde Terry

1968–75: Juan Velasco Alvarado (1910–77)

1975–80: Francisco Morales Bermúdez

1980–85: Fernando Belaúnde Terry

1985–90: Alan García Pérez

1990–2000: Alberto Fujimori

Philippines, The

Official name: Republic of the Philippines

Location: About 500 mi. (800 km.) off southeastern Asia; bordered by Luzon Strait (N), Philippine Sea (E), Celebes Sea (S), Sulu Sea (SW), South China Sea (W)

Capital: Manila

Area: 115,830 sq. mi. (300,000 sq. km.)

Population: 76,103.564

Languages: Filipino and English (both official)

Government: Republic

Religions: Roman Catholic 83%, Protestant 9%, Muslim 5%, Buddhist 3%

Monetary unit: Peso

Main exports: Electrical equipment, textiles, coconut

The more than 7,000 islands constituting the Philippines were ruled from 1565 by Spain. The territory came under U.S. rule in 1898, during the Spanish-American War, and was ceded to the U.S. in 1899 through the Treaty of Paris at a cost of $20 million. An independence movement led by Emilio Aguinaldo proclaimed the country a republic and waged guerrilla attacks against the U.S. The fighting for independence continued from 1899 to 1905, when the U.S. gained victory.

Beginning with the Jones Law in 1916, which established an elective Senate and House of Representatives, the Philippines (with the help of U.S. foreign policy) moved toward self-rule. The 1934 Tydings-McDuffie Act set up a transitional period readying the Philippines to independence by 1946. In 1935 a new constitution mandated the establishment of the Commonwealth of the Philippines, with Manuel Quezon y Molina (1878–1944) as its first president.

In December 1941, during World War II, the Philippines were attacked by Japanese troops. Japanese forces destroyed U.S. bases and occupied the country. U.S. troops led by General Douglas MacArthur reinvaded the Philippines in October 1944 and liberated by 1945. For much of the Japanese occupation and until his 1944 death, President Quezon led a government in exile. Following the liberation of the Philippines, Sergio Osmeña became president.

The U.S. granted the Phillipines full independence on July 4, 1946. The U.S. established a special economic relationship with the Philippines and maintained military bases there. During the first decades of independence, the Philippine economy was fueled mainly by its large plantations, which generated economic growth but also inequality and social conflict, including a Communist insurgency.

From 1965 to 1986 the Philippines were under the rule of Ferdinand Marcos, who placed the country under martial law for eight years, from 1973 to 1981. In 1980 he freed popular national leader Senator Benigno Aquino Jr. Upon Aquino's return to Manila from self-exile in 1983, he was killed at Manila International Airport. The Marcos government was suspected of being responsible for his death.

Marcos was reelected president in 1986 against Aquino's widow, Corazon Aquino. The results were widely questioned and anti-Marcos sentiment continued. Upon the defection of Defense Minister Juan Enrile and Lieutenant General Fidel Ramos, Marcos went into exile in the U.S. on February 25, 1986. That year, Aquino assumed the presidency; she remained an internationally popular leader until leaving office in 1992, after deciding not to seek reelection. In 1992 elections General Fidel Ramos outpaced several opponents to be elected president.

The 1980s and 1990s were marked by the departure of U.S. military presence. In 1991 damage caused by volcanic eruptions at Mount Pinatubo, in addition to political differences between the U.S. and the Philippines, led to the closing of Clark Air Base. In September 1992 the U.S. Navy turned over its long-held Subic Air Base.

Having made national reconciliation a priority, Ramos oversaw a cease-fire with Muslim separatists in 1994, ending an ongoing conflict. He also announced amnesty for opposition groups. The country enjoyed economic growth throughout much of the late 1990s. A populist former movie actor, Joseph Estrada, won the 1998 presidential election. He was ousted in 2001 in the midst of a corruption scandal.

The Philippines: 20th-Century Leaders

President

1935–44: Manuel Luis Quezon y Molina (president of Commonwealth government) (1878–1944)

1942–45: Japanese occupation

1944–46: Sergio Osmeña (1878–1961)

1946–48: Manuel Roxas y Acuña (1892–1948) (first president of independent Philippines)

1948–53: Elpidio Quirino (1890–1955)

1954–57: Ramón Magsaysay (1907–57)

1957–61: Carlos P. García (1896–1971)

1961–65: Diosadado Macapagal

1965–86: Ferdinand E. Marcos (1917–89)

1986–92: Corazon Aquino (1933–)

1992–98: Fidel Ramos (1928–)

1998–2001: Joseph Ejercito Estrada (1937–)

Poland

Official name: Republic of Poland

Location: Eastern Europe; bordered by Baltic Sea (N), Russia and Lithuania (NE), Belarus and Ukraine (E), Czech Republic and Slovakia (S), Germany (W)

Capital: Warsaw

Area: 120,726 sq. mi. (312,680 sq. km.)

Population (est. 1997): 38,615,239

Languages: Polish

Government: Democratic state

Religions: Roman Catholic 90.7%, Eastern Orthodox and other 9.3%

Monetary unit: Zloty

Main exports: Intermediate goods, machinery and transport equipment

A major world power from the 14th to the 17th centuries, Poland weakened during the 18th century, allowing for partitions among three countries: Prussia, Russia, and Austria (1772, 1793, 1795). For over 100 years afterward Poland was not a state, though throughout the years it retained a strong interest in regaining its independence.

Empowered by Russia's loss of strength after World War I, Poland declared independence on November 11, 1918, naming Marshal Józef Pisudski as chief of state. Poland largely regained its borders following a war with Russia in 1921.

In 1926 Pisudski staged a coup, placing Poland under near-dictatorial rule until his death on May 12, 1935. In 1934 Poland and Germany signed a nonaggression pact, which was broken on September 1, 1939, when Nazi troops invaded Poland. On September 17, Russian troops invaded Poland, and on September 28 Poland was divided between the two invading countries. The division lasted until June 1941, when German troops attacked the U.S.S.R. and occupied Poland completely.

During World War II six million Poles were killed by the Nazis, including three million Jews. Up to that time Poland had the largest Jewish population in Europe. After the war in 1945 Poland and the U.S.S.R. signed a treaty outlining Polish–U.S.S.R. borders. In it Poland ceded 69,860 sq. mi. to Russia but gained 38,986 sq. mi. of German territory in return. In 1947 Communist candidates dominated Polish elections. In 1952 a new constitution established Poland as a "people's democracy" that followed Soviet domestic and foreign policy. Stalinist rule including collectivization, press censorship, and persecution of the Roman Catholic Church marked the next several years. Following a riot on June 28–29, 1956, a more liberal Politburo was established, permitting limited freedom of religion and the press, and ending collectivization of farms. Wladyslaw Gomulka was named first secretary of the party.

In 1970 a labor riot over price hikes and incentive wage rules resulted in Gomulka's resignation and the installation of Edward Gierek as party leader. The new labor changes were dropped.

In August 1980 a widespread strike that began in the shipyards was settled with historic concessions that included the right to strike and the right to form independent trade unions. The most notable of the unions was Solidarity, which was led by Lech Walesa and had membership of 9.5 million by 1981. Calling for freedom and improved working conditions, it led a five-day national strike that resulted in the removal of Premier Pinkowski. On December 13, 1981, the government imposed martial law and arrested Walesa and others. Martial law was formally ended in 1984.

Following several debilitating strikes in 1988, the Polish government made Solidarity legal again and permitted it to participate in elections. In the ensuing elections on June 4, Solidarity-supported candidates won all 169 seats. In 1990 Lech Walesa was elected president. A new temporary constitution was approved on October 17, 1992.

The Walesa-led government of free-market reform led to economic instability and the election of former Communist candidate Aleksander Kwasniewski as president in 1995. In 1997 a new constitution was approved; Solidarity candidates took a majority in 1997 parliamentary elections. Poland became a full member of NATO in 1999.

Poland: 20th-Century Leaders

President

1918–22: Józef Pisudski (Head of State) (1867–1935)

1922: Gabriel Narutowicz (1865–1922)

1922–26: Stanislaw Wojciechowski (1869–1953)

1926–39: Ignacy Móscicki (1867–1946)

1939–45: German occupation

1944–52: Boleslaw Beirut (1892–1956)

1952–64: Aleksander Zawadski (1899–1964)

1964–68: Edward Ochab (1906–89)

1968–70: Marian Spychalski (1906–80)

1970–72: Jósef Cyrankiewicz (1911–89)

1972–85: Henryk Jablónski

1985–90: Wojciech Jaruzelski

1990–95: Lech Walesa

1995– : Aleksander Kwasniewski (1954–)

Prime Minister

1923–25: Wladyslaw Grabski (1874–1938)

1935–39: Eugeniusz Kwiatskowski (1888–1974)

1945–47: Edward Osúbka-Morawski

1947–52: Jósef Cyrankiewicz

1952–54: Boleslaw Bierut

1954–70: Jósef Cyrankiewicz

1970–80: Piotr Jarosziewicz (1909–92)

1980–81: Józef Pinkowski

1981–85: Wojciech Jaruzelski

1985–88: Zbigniew Messner

1988–89: Mieczyslaw Rakowski

1989: Czeslaw Kiszczak

1989–91: Tadeusz Mazowiecki

1991: Jan Krzysztof Bielecki (1951–)

1991–92: Jan Olszewski (1930–)

1992: Wlademar Pawlak (1959–)

1992–93: Janna Suchocka (1946–)

1993–95: Wlademar Pawlak

1995–96: Jozef Oleksy

1996–97: Wlodzimierz Cimoszewicz (1950–)

1997– : Jerzy Buzek (1940–)

German Occupation

1939–45: Wladyslas Raczkiewicz (London Government) (1885–1947)

1939–43: Wladyslaw Sikorski (Premier and Commander-in-Chief) (1881–1943)

1944–47: Boleslaw Bierut (Chairman of National Home Council) (1892–1956)

Portugal

Official name: Republic of Portugal

Location: Iberian peninsula in southwest Europe, two archipelagos in Atlantic Ocean; bordered by Spain (N, E), Atlantic Ocean (S, W)

Capital: Lisbon (Lisboa)

Area: 35,552 sq. mi. (92,080 sq. km.)

Population: 9,931,045

Languages: Portuguese

Government: Republic

Religions: Roman Catholic 97%, Protestant 1%, other 2%

Monetary unit: Escudo

Main exports: Cotton textiles, machinery, cork and cork products

An independent kingdom from 1143 (except for brief rule by the Spanish Hapsburg dynasty from 1580 to 1640), Portugal entered the 20th century a diminished but still important trade and colonial power. Politically unstable and with a faltering monarchy, Portugal experienced a short-lived dictatorship in 1907 led by Prime Minister João Fernando Pinto Franco. In an attempt to build stability, a republic was declared on October 4, 1910, making Portugal the first kingdom to do so in the 20th century.

The change yielded political chaos, with eight presidents and 44 governments between 1911 and 1926. A military coup in 1926 led by António Oscar de Fragoso Carmona made António Salazar civilian dictator in 1928. Carmona became president and Salazar prime minister in 1932. Through tight economic control and a strict law-and-order program, Salazar and the Estado Novo dictatorship restored economic solvency and social stability but tightened military control and failed to develop the economy.

Portugal was little involved in World War II; it was able to be a neutral country while also an ally of Britain. After the war it received Marshall Plan aid and became a member of NATO in 1949. It joined the United Nations in 1955 and in 1959 was a founding member of the European Free Trade Association.

From the 1950s Portugal was part of the worldwide decolonization process. Premier Salazar rejected decolonization and engaged up to 200,000 Portuguese troops in protracted colonial wars that not only failed to preserve the territories but estranged the military from him. In 1968 ill health forced Salazar to retire. Among Portuguese colonies gaining independence in the 1970s were Angola, Guinea-Bissau, and Mozambique.

Salazar's successor, Marcelo Caetano, was overthrown in September 1974 in a bloodless coup led by António de Spínola. The latter was replaced that year by Costa Gomes and a Revolutionary Council, which in 1976 instituted a Socialist constitution. The government's wide-ranging nationalization contributed to economic recession during the decade. Portugal joined the European Community on January 1, 1986.

During the 1980s the newly elected Social Democrat–controlled government attempted to cease nationalization and promote free-market economics. Their programs led to a tripling of per capita income from 1985 to 1992, lifting Portugal from its status as the poorest EU country. However, the Socialist Party regained power during the 1990s, electing a prime minister in 1995 and president in 1996. Portugal returned Macao to China in 1999.

Portugal: 20th-Century Leaders

King

1889–1908: Carlos I (1863–1908, assassinated)

1908–10: Emanuel I (1889–1932)

President

1910–11: Teófilo Braga (1843–1919)

1911–15: Manoel José de Arriga (1840–1917)

1915: Teófilo Braga

1915–17: Bernardino Luiz Machado Guimares (1851–1944)

1917–18: Sidônio Bernadino Cardoso de Silva Paes (1872–1918)

1918–19: João de Canto e Castro Silva Antunes (1862–1934) (provisional)

1919–23: António José de Almeida (1866–1929)

1923–25: Manoel Teixwira Gomes (1860–1914)

1925–26: Bernardino Luiz Machado Guimares

1926–51: António Oscar de Fragoso Carmona (1869–1951)

1951–58: Francisco Higino Craveiro Lopes (1894–1964)

1958–74: Américo Deus Rodrigues Tomás (1894–1987)

1974: António de Spínola

1974–76: Francisco da Costa Gomes

1976–86: António Dos Santos Ramalho Eanes (1935–)

1986–96: Mário Soares (1924–)

1996– : Jorge Sampaio (1939–)

Premier

1932–68: António de Oliveira Salazar (1889–1970)

1968–74: Marcelo Caetano (1906–80)

1974: Adelino da Palma Carlos (1905–92)

1974–75: Vasco dos Santos Gonçalves

1975–76: José Pinheiro de Azevedo (1917–83)

1976–78: Mário Soares

1978: Alfredo Nobre da Costa

1978–79: Carlos da Mota Pinto (1936–85)

1979–80: Maria de Lourdes Pintasilgo (1930–)

1980–83: Francisco Sá Carneiro (1934–80)

1983–85: Mário Soares

1985–95: Aníbal António Cavaco Silva (1939–)

1995– : António Guterres (1949–)

Qatar

Official name: State of Qatar

Location: Peninsula extending northward from Arabian mainland into part of Persian (Arabian) Gulf; bordered by Persian Gulf (N,E,W), Saudia Arabia and United Arab Emirates (S)

Capital: Doha

Area: 4,247 sq. mi. (11,000 sq. km.)

Population (est. 1997): 547,761

Languages: Arabic (official), English commonly used as second language

Government: Traditional monarchy

Religions: Muslim 95%

Monetary unit: Qatari riyal

Main exports: Petroleum products, steel, fertilizers

Though it gained independence in 1868, Qatar entered the 20th century with claims held on it by Britain and the Ottoman Empire. In 1868 British forces set up an informal protectorate, and in 1872 the Ottoman Empire took authority over the sheiks of Qatar. When the Ottoman Empire granted authority over Qatar to the British in 1916, Qatar became a British protectorate, but with autonomy over internal affairs.

In 1971, when Britain removed itself from the Persian Gulf, Qatar declared independence (September 3, 1971). Sheikh Khalifah ibn Hamad ath-Thani, Qatar's ruler from 1972 to 1995, built a stable economy upon oil, natural gas, banking, and shipping services. In 1995 he was overthrown in a bloodless coup by his son, Sheikh Hamad ibn Khalifah ath-Thani, who has promoted democratic ideals, including woman suffrage and a free press. He has also supported trade diversification, concentrating more on exports of abundant natural gas over declining oil.

Qatar: 20th-Century Leaders

Emir

1960: Ali ibn Abdullah ibn Qasim (abdicated)

1960–72: Ahmad ibn Ali ibn Abdullah ath-Thani (1917–)

1972–95: Khalifah ibn Hamad ath-Thani

1995– : Hamad ibn Khalifah ath-Thani (1950–)

Romania

Official name: Romania

Location: Southeastern Europe; bordered by Ukraine (N), Moldova (NE), Black Sea (E), Bulgaria (S), Yugoslavia (SW), Hungary (NW)

Capital: Bucharest

Area: 91,699 sq. mi. (237,500 sq. km.)

Population (est. 1997): 22,395,848

Languages: Romanian, Hungarian, German

Government: Republic

Religions: Romanian Orthodox 70%, Roman Catholic 6%, Protestant 6%

Monetary unit: Leu

Main exports: Machinery, equipment, fuels, minerals, metals, manufactured consumer goods

Part of the Ottoman Empire from the 15th century, the states of Moldavia and Wallachia were unified in 1861 as Romania, which became independent in 1878. It was proclaimed a kingdom in 1881. Economic inequality between the wealthy landowners and poor peasants sparked a peasant revolt in 1907 that was harshly suppressed. As part of the coalition fighting Bulgaria in the Second Balkan War (1913), Romania acquired southern Dobrudja from Bulgaria. During World War I Romania fought on the Allied side, surrendered and made peace with the Central Powers, then reentered the war (November 1918) in time to participate in the spoils. It acquired several lands, including Transylvania, Bessarabia, and northern Bukovina, that more than doubled its territory, but the heterogeneous mix of peoples in those lands destabilized the country.

The 1920s and 1930s were a time of political and economic turbulence. The crown prince was exiled by the liberal government before being allowed to assume the throne as King Carol II (1930–40), once a conservative government had taken power. In 1937 Carol established a royal dictatorship. Despite close ties to Nazi Germany, which Romania supplied with oil, Germany and the Soviet Union forced Romania in 1940 to give up Bessarabia, northern Bukovina, northern Transylvania, and southern Dobrudja. Nationalist resentment over the land losses forced Carol to abdicate, and Ion Antonescu took power as dictator (1940–44). He was at first supported by the Fascist movement, the Iron Guards, which later attempted a coup and was crushed by Antonescu's military. Romania supported Germany during most of World War II and participated in the invasion of Russia. In 1944, in an effort to appease advancing Soviet troops, King Michael deposed Antonescu and switched sides against Germany.

The Soviets occupied Romania and in 1947 forced the abdication of King Michael and established a Communist republic.

Gheorghe Gheorghiu-Dej was its leader until his death in 1965. A dedicated Stalinist, he purged his enemies and nationalized the economy. In 1958 Soviet troops withdrew from Romania, and Gheorghiu-Dej set a somewhat independent path from the Soviet Union: he encouraged industrial development instead of complying with Soviet wishes to become a major food supplier and stayed neutral as the rift grew between the Soviet Union and China.

Gheorghiu-Dej was succeeded by his protegé Nicolae Ceausescu, who conducted his own purges and continued his predecessor's policy of distancing himself from the Soviet Union. Though he promoted closer ties with the West, he was a conservative Marxist who ruled tyrannically and repressively, staffing his government with relatives, including wife Elena. His economic reforms proved disastrous, particularly once Romania's oil industry began to suffer from shrinking reserves and declining oil prices in the 1980s. His drive to expand the country's population, in part by outlawing abortion, resulted in a vast increase of children raised in underfunded orphanages. In December 1989, as Soviet power in Eastern Europe faded, he was deposed by revolution. He and his wife were executed on Christmas Day 1989.

Ion Iliescu, a former Communist Party official, was named provisional president following Ceausescu's overthrow. His regime was dominated by former Communists and was hardly less repressive: In 1990 government troops and armed miners brought into Bucharest brutally suppressed student demonstrations. Attempts to move to a free-market economy brought food shortages and price increases, but Iliescu and his National Salvation Front won the 1992 elections. Many state-owned companies were privatized in 1996, the year that Iliescu and his party were voted out of power. A coalition government headed by Emil Constantinescu took office; it ended decades of official atheism by tying the government to the Romanian Orthodox Church.

Romania: 20th-Century Leaders

King

1881–1914: Carol I

1914–27: Ferdinand I (1865–1927)

1927–30: Michael

1930–40: Carol II (1893–1953)

1940–47: Michael

President

1948–52: Constantine I. Parhon (1874–1969)

1952–58: Petru Groza (1884–1958)

1958–61: Ion Gheorghe Maurer

1961–65: Gheorghe Gheorghiu-Dej (1901–65)

1965–67: Chivu Stoica (1908–75)

1967–89: Nicolae Ceausescu

1989–96: Ion Iliescu (1930–)

1996– : Emil Constantinescu

Prime Minister

1945–52: Petru Groza

1952–55: Gheorghe Gheorghiu-Dej

1955–61: Chivu Stoica

1961–74: Ion Gheorghe Maurer

1974–79: Manea Manescu

1979–82: Ilie Verdet

1982–89: Constantin Däscälescu

1989–91: Petre Roman (1946–)

1991–92: Theodor Stolojan (1943–)

1992–96: Nicolae Vacaroiu

1996–98: Victor Ciorbea

1998–99: Radu Vasile

1999– : Mugur Isarescu (1949–)

Russia

Official name: Russian Federation

Location: Northeastern Europe and northern Asia; bordered by Baltic Sea, Barents Sea, Kara Sea, East Siberian Sea (N), Bering Sea, Sea of Okhotsk, Sea of Japan (E), China, North Korea, Mongolia, Kazakhstan, Caspian Sea, Azerbaijan, Georgia, Black Sea (S), Ukraine, Belarus (W), Latvia, Estonia, Finland, Norway (NW)

Capital: Moscow

Area: 6,592,745 sq. mi. (17,075,200 sq. km.)

Population (est. 1998): 146,861,022

Languages: Russian (official), ethnic languages

Government: Federation

Religions: Russian Orthodox, Muslim, others

Monetary unit: Ruble

Main exports: Petroleum and petroleum products, natural gas, wood and wood products, coal, nonferrous metals, chemicals

Founded in the ninth century, Russia had, by the start of the 20th century, acquired many non-Russian areas to form a vast empire that stretched from present-day Poland to the Bering Straits. Despite rich natural resources and a steady pace of industrialization, the country had many weaknesses: autocratic rule by an incompetent czar who was largely deaf to the people's demands for political participation; government corruption and a high degree of economic inequality; a mix of over a hundred peoples, many of them resenting Russia's hold on their homelands; and a disorganized and inept military. The weaknesses of the military were showcased in the Russo–Japanese War (1904–05), in which Japan forced Russia, through a series of humiliating defeats, to give up its interests in Manchuria. The war helped spark the 1905 Russian Revolution, in which a series of uprisings by peasants, workers, the middle class, and the armed forces persuaded Czar Nicholas II to grant civil liberties and establish a representative Duma, or assembly.

In the following years protests continued but were suppressed by czarist forces. The Duma, particularly in the period 1907 to 1912, enacted mild reforms, but its powers were limited, and the outbreak of World War I in 1914 brought suspension of the body. Heavy military losses and war-related economic deterioration led to the two Russian Revolutions of 1917. In the February Revolution (January–March 1917), a wave of strikes, demonstrations, and mutinies forced Nicholas to abdicate. A provisional government took over, headed at first by Prince Georgy Lvov and later by Alexander Kerensky. V. I. Lenin, leader of the Bolshevik Party, a radical Marxist organization, took control of the Socialist workers' councils, or soviets, that were then being formed. Rallying popular anger over food shortages and continuing involvement in the war, the Bolsheviks led the *October Revolution* (November 1917), in which the government was overthrown and the world's first Communist state was proclaimed.

The Bolsheviks withdrew Russia from World War I and confirmed their authority in the Russian Civil War (1918–21). In this conflict, the Soviet or Red Army defeated counter-revolutionary armies known as the Whites, who were backed by troops from foreign countries, including the U.S., Britain, and Japan. At the same time, several regions, including Finland, Poland, Estonia, Latvia, and Lithuania, won independence from Russian rule. The Union of Soviet Socialist Republics (U.S.S.R., or Soviet Union) was constituted in 1922, placing Russia at the head of other constituent republics.

National legislative power resided in the Supreme Soviet, but in practice the Communist Party, headed by a general secretary, controlled government at all levels. Lenin established the tradition of dictatorial rule, which was enforced by a secret police force initially called the Cheka and later the NKVD and KGB. He instituted radical economic Socialism, which was modified by the New Economic Policy (1921) to include a degree of private initiative. Upon Lenin's death in 1924, a triumvirate consisting of Joseph Stalin, Lev Kamenev, and Grigoriy Zinoviev took power, but Stalin succeeded in pushing his partners aside, as well as another rival, Leon Trotsky. So began nearly three decades of dictatorial rule that ended only with Stalin's death in 1953.

During this period Stalinism came to mean a totalitarian form of Communism founded on ruthless terror and ideological rigidity. Stalin embodied these principles in his Great Purge (1934–38), in which he murdered millions of perceived enemies through show trials; the destruction of a whole class of kulaks, or landed peasants, through collectivization, deportation to labor camps, and execution; and the nearly complete nationalization of the economy, which was rapidly industrialized.

Stalin formed a nonaggression pact with German dictator Adolf Hitler in 1939 that allowed him to safely recover the Baltic republics (Estonia, Latvia, and Lithuania) lost to Russia two decades earlier. In 1941 Hitler soon violated the pact and attacked the Soviet Union, prompting Stalin to enter World War II (1939–45) against Germany. The Soviet Union suffered the worst civilian and military losses of the war, with about 20 million people killed, but its participation greatly contributed to Allied victory. Soviet wartime conquests in eastern Europe were recognized at Allied conferences at Tehran (1943) and Yalta (1945), and the Soviet Union was permitted to establish hegemony over the Socialist states in that region. After the war Germany itself was partitioned, with East Germany included in the Soviet bloc, formalized in 1955 as the Warsaw Pact.

World War II left the world polarized between two superpowers: the U.S. and the Soviet Union. With both nations possessing nuclear weapons by the end of the 1940s, both nations shied from direct military confrontation, engaging instead in a protracted struggle called the cold war. The Soviet Union supplied aid to Communist insurgents and governments around the world, assisting at various times China, Cuba, and Vietnam. The U.S. countered with economic and military aid to capitalist allies and proxies.

In 1956 Nikita Khrushchev won the power struggle that followed Stalin's death. Denouncing his predecessor, he embarked on a program of de-Stalinization that attempted to undo Stalin's worst excesses. Even so, the Soviet Union maintained a tight grip on its empire, as shown in the suppression of the Hungarian Revolution in 1956. Plagued by agricultural problems, a rift with Communist China, and his loss of face in backing down to the U.S. in the Cuban Missile Crisis (1962), Khrushchev was ousted in 1964.

Leonid Brezhnev, who succeeded Khrushchev as Soviet leader, promoted détente, or closer ties with the West (1972–74). But he was just as willing as his predecessors to enforce Soviet control of Eastern Europe, notably through the invasion of Czechoslovakia, to suppress a wave of reform (1968). In 1979 the Soviet invasion of Afghanistan renewed cold war tensions. At home the Communist regime grew more repressive while the centrally-planned economy stagnated, suffering in the 1980s from the burden of the stepped-up arms race with the U.S.

After the brief tenures of Yuri Andropov (1982–84) and Konstantin Chernenko (1984–85), Mikhail Gorbachev (1985–91) introduced sweeping liberal reforms intended to revitalize the nation's sluggish economy and boost morale. Adopting policies of *perestroika* (restructuring) and *glasnost* (openness), he relaxed censorship, eased travel restrictions, and encouraged limited forms of private enterprise. In 1989 Gorbachev founded a Congress of People's Deputies permitting dissident views. He withdrew Soviet forces from Afghanistan, allowed Communist regimes in Eastern Europe to fall (1989), and signed major new arms control agreements.

Though these changes effectively ended the cold war, they were not enough to save the Soviet Union. The economy worsened; food shortages multiplied. Ethnic tensions erupted in such constituent republics as Armenia, Azerbaijan, and Uzbekistan, while the Baltic republics campaigned for independence, which Gorbachev refused to grant. An attempted coup by Communist hardliners in August 1991 nearly toppled him. When he returned to power, his political base was severely weakened relative to that of Boris Yeltsin, president of the Russian republic, who had rallied opposition to the coup. On December 25, 1991, Gorbachev resigned. One week later the Soviet Union ceased to exist. Its constituent republics became independent nations. Russia itself became known as the Russian Federation, made up of 21 federated republics.

As president of independent Russia (1991–99), Yeltsin directed the formation of the new, decentralized Commonwealth of Independent States, made up of former Soviet republics; the Baltic republics chose not to join. Yeltsin signed the second Strategic Arms Reduction Treaty (START II) with the U.S. and pursued policies of rapid privatization and price deregulation. He courted Western aid and investment, but Russia's economic woes increased, with crime spreading and inflation reaching 930 percent in 1993. With his popularity waning, Yeltsin struggled for power with Communist-nationalist forces in parliament and his own vice president, Aleksandr Rutskoy. In 1993 Yeltsin tried to dissolve parliament, which responded by impeaching him and replacing him with Rutskoy. Rutskoy and many legislators occupied the parliament building; Yeltsin used military force to drive them out. In December 1993 a Yeltsin-supported constitution was adopted, centralizing power in the presidency and limiting the powers of the constituent republics.

In 1994 Yeltsin began a bloody civil war with Chechnya, a republic trying to secede from Russia; his harsh conduct of the war drew criticism at home and abroad. Despite these crises and his own mounting health problems, he won reelection in 1996. In 1997 a peace treaty ended the war with Chechnya. Yeltsin's efforts to speed up reform failed, and in 1998 Yeltsin dismissed his government, including Prime Minister Viktor Chernomyrdin, replacing him with Sergey Kiriyenko. In August Russia's stock market collapsed, causing economic downturn and political disorder. The Duma elected a new prime minister, Yevgeny Primakov. With Russia remaining unstable, other nations expressed concern about whether democracy would prevail there, and what the consequences would be for world peace and prosperity if it did not.

During the NATO bombing of Yugoslavia in 1999, Russia tried to find a diplomatic solution to the conflict, while at the same time denouncing NATO air strikes. At various times, Russia made vague references to the possibility of Russian forces getting involved in the conflict on the Serbian side, only to contradict itself shortly after.

In 1999 Yeltsin replaced Primakov with Sergey Stepashin, then replaced Stepashin with Vladimir Putin. Yeltsin avoided impeachment on five counts by the Duma that same year by a wide margin. Yeltsin resigned on December 31, 1999, appointing Putin as his interim successor. Putin went on to win election as president in 2000.

Russian artists and writers made many contributions to world culture in the 20th century—some after leaving Russia to escape the Bolshevik Revolution. In music, the century's greatest names include Igor Stravinsky; in painting, Marc Chagall; in dance, Sergey Diaghilev, Vaslav Nijinsky, and Anna Pavlova; and in literature, Vladimir Nabokov, Aleksander Solzhenitsyn, Boris Pasternak, and Isaac Babel.

Russia: 20th-Century Leaders

Czar

1894–1917: Nicholas II

Union of Soviet Socialist Republics (Soviet Union)

President

1919–46: Mikhail I. Kalinin (1875–1946)

1946–53: Nikolai M. Shvernik (1888–1970)

1953–60: Klimenti E.Voroshilov (1881–1969)

1960–64: Leonid I. Brezhnev

1964–65: Anastas I Mikoyan (1895–1978)

1965–77: Nikolai V. Podgorny (1903–83)

1977–82: Leonid I. Brezhnev

1982–83:Vasily V. Kuznetsov (1901–90)

1983–84:Yuri Andropov

1984–85: Konstantin Chernenko

1985–88: Andrei Gromyko (1909–89)

1988–91: Mikhail Gorbachev

Premier

1917–24:Vladimir Ilych Lenin

1924–30: Aleksei Ivanovich Rykov (1881–1938)

1930–41:Vyacheslav Mikhailovich Molotov (1890–1986)

1941–53: Joseph Stalin

1953–55: Georgi M. Malenkov (1902–88)

1955–58: Nikolai A. Bulganin (1895–1975)

1958–64: Nikita Khrushchev

1964–80: Aleksei N. Kosygin (1904–80)

1980–85: Nikolai A. Tikhonov

1985–91: Nikolai A. Ryzhkov (1929–)

1991:Valentin S. Pavlov (1937–)

1991: Ivan Silayev (1930–)

General Secretary, Communist Party

1922–53: Joseph Stalin

1953–64: Nikita Khrushchev

1964–82: Leonid I. Brezhnev

1982–84:Yuri Andropov

1984–85: Konstantin Chernenko

1985–91: Mikhail Gorbachev

Russian Federation

President

1991–99: Boris Yeltsin

1999– : Vladimir Putin

Prime Minister

1991–92: Boris Yeltsin

1992: Yegor Timurovich Gaidar

1992–98: Viktor Chernomyrdin

1998: Sergey Kiriyenko

1998–99: Yevgeny Primakov

1999: Sergey Stepashin

1999: Vladimir Putin (1952–)

1999–2000: Mikhail Kasyanov (1957–)

2000– : Mikhail Kasyanov (1957–)

Rwanda

Official name: Republic of Rwanda

Location: East central Africa; bordered by Congo (W), Uganda (N), Tanzania (E), Burundi (S)

Capital: Kigali

Area: 10,169 sq. mi. (26,338 sq. km.)

Population (est. 1996): 6,853,359

Languages: Kinyarwanda, French (both official)

Government: Republic

Religions: Christian 74% (Roman Catholic 56%, Protestant 18%), animist 25%, Muslim 1%

Monetary unit: Rwanda franc

Main exports: Coffee, tea, tungsten, tin, pyrethrum

Prior to becoming a German colony in 1899, the region now called Rwanda was ruled by a mwami (king) at the head of a feudal social system. The cattle-owning Tutsi, traditionally representing about 14 percent of the population, ruled over the agricultural Hutu, representing about 85 percent. Germany took over the region without resistance in 1899, administering it as part of German East Africa until Belgium occupied it in 1916, during World War I. The region remained under Belgian control as part of the League of Nations mandate of Ruanda-Urundi in 1919 and as a UN trust territory in 1946. Under German and Belgian regimes, the Tutsi retained their traditional dominance over the Hutu.

The Hutu began a revolution against Tutsi power in 1959, resulting in abolition of the monarchy and installation of a republic in 1961; revolutionary leader Grégoire Kayibanda was elected president. On July 1, 1962, Rwanda became independent. Many Tutsi were killed or forced into exile: from 1959 to 1964, 150,000 Tutsi fled to neighboring countries.

In July 1973 a military coup overthrew the government; Major General Juvénal Habyarimana became president. In 1978 a new constitution legitimizing his one-party rule was adopted. In 1990 the regime began to permit opposition parties while battling a military invasion of Tutsi refugees calling themselves the Rwandan Patriotic Front (RPF). Years of civil war and frail international peace efforts followed.

On April 6, 1994, President Habyarimana and Burundi's President Cyprien Ntaryamira were killed when a rocket downed their airplane. Groups of Hutu, including some Rwandan army members, responded with genocide, massacring about 500,000 Tutsi.

The RPF succeeded in installing a Tutsi-dominated government on July 19, headed by President Pasteur Bizimingu. As civil war continued, both Tutsi and Hutu refugees fled in droves to nearby countries, creating humanitarian relief crises. In 1996, about one million refugees returned to Rwanda. In 1998, trials for genocide led to a wave of executions and to a life sentence for former prime minister Kambanda.

Africa's most densely populated country (673 persons per square mile in 1996), Rwanda has historically been poor, with over 90 percent of the population dependent on farming and prey to famine. As a home to rare wildlife, including the mountain gorilla, Rwanda has attracted scientists and tourists.

Rwanda: 20th-Century Leaders

President

1961–73: Grégoire Kayibanda (1924–76)

1973–94: Juvénal Habyarimana (1937–94)

1994: Theodore Sindikubwabo

1994–2000: Pasteur Bizimingu

Prime Minister

1991–92: Sylvestre Nsanzimana

1992–93: Dismas Nsengiyaremye

1993–94: Agathe Kwilingiyimana

1994: Jean Kambanda

1994–95: Faustin Twagiramungu

1995–2000: Pierre-Céléstin Rwigema

Saint Kitts and Nevis

Official name: Federation of Saint Kitts and Nevis

Location: Two islands in eastern Caribbean Sea; nearest neighbor is Antigua, about 45 mi. (72 km.) SE

Capital: Basseterre

Area: 99 sq. mi. (262 sq. km.); Saint Kitts 65 sq. mi. (169 sq. km.), Nevis 34 sq. mi. (93 sq. km.)

Population (est. 1997): 41,803

Languages: English

Government: Parliamentary democracy

Religions: Anglican, other Protestant sects, Roman Catholic

Monetary unit: East Caribbean dollar

Main exports: Foods, manufactures, postage stamps

British possessions from 1783, the two islands were united in 1882 and entered the 20th century known as Saint Christopher-Nevis. From 1967 it was part of the West Indies Associated States (Antigua, Saint Kitts–Nevis–Anguilla of the Leeward Islands, and Dominica, Grenada, Saint Lucia, and Saint Vincent of the Windward Islands). It gained independence from the British on September 19, 1983, becoming known as Saint Kitts and Nevis.

From 1983 it was ruled by Kennedy Alphonse Simmonds of the People's Action Movement. In 1995 Denzil Douglas of the opposition Labour party was elected in parliamentary elections. In 1990 Hurricane Hugo nearly destroyed the islands' sugar crop, which provides their primary income source. In 1998, a referendum on secession of Nevis failed to carry.

Saint Kitts and Nevis: 20th-Century Leaders

Governor–General (representing the British monarch)

1983–95: Sir Clement Athelston Arrindell (1932–)

1996– : Cuthbert Sebastian (1921–)

Prime Minister

1980–95: Kennedy Alphonse Simmonds (1936–)

1995– : Denzil Douglas (1953–)

Saint Lucia

Official name: Saint Lucia

Location: Southeastern Caribbean Sea; nearest neighbors include Martinique (N), Saint Vincent (SW)

Capital: Castries

Area: 239 sq. mi. (620 sq. km.)

Population (est. 1997): 150,630

Languages: English (official), French patois

Government: Parliamentary democracy

Religions: Roman Catholic 90%, Protestant 7%, Church of England 3%

Monetary unit: East Caribbean (EC) dollar

Main exports: Bananas, clothing, cocoa, vegetables, fruits

Under British control from 1814, Saint Lucia was a member of the Federation of the West Indies from 1958 until the group's collapse in 1962. It returned to British control until gaining home rule in 1967 as a member of the West Indies Associated States. It became an independent member of the Commonwealth on February 22, 1979.

From the 1960s the government has been controlled by the United Workers Party, with its prime minister John Compton. In 1979 civil unrest led to elections that gave the Labour Party majority rule. Compton and his party regained power in 1982 but faced years of economic decline because of the destruction of much of the country's banana plantations two years earlier. Compton attempted economic rebuilding through agrarian reform and legalized gambling, to limited success. A public-sector strike unsettled the economy in 1995; two years later, Compton was replaced by Labour Party prime minister Kenny B. Anthony.

Saint Lucia: 20th-Century Leaders

Governor–General (representing the British monarch)

1979–80: Allen Montgomery Lewis (1909–93)

1980–82: Boswell Williams

1982–87: Allen Montgomery Lewis

1987–88: Sir Vincent Floissac

1988–96: Sir Stanislaus A. James (1919–)

1996–97: William George Mallet

1997– : Perlette Louisy (1946–)

Prime Minister

1964–79: John G. M. Compton

1979–81: Allan Louisy

1981–82: Winston F. Cenac

1982: Michael Pilgrim

1982–96: John G. M. Compton

1996–97: Vaughan Lewis

1997– : Kenny B. Anthony

Saint Vincent and the Grenadines

Official name: Saint Vincent and the Grenadines

Location: Southeastern Caribbean Sea; large island (Saint Vincent) and about 50 smaller islands; islands lie abut 21 mi. (34 km.) SW of Saint Lucia and 100 mi. (160 km.) W of

Barbados.

Capital: Kingstown

Area: 131 sq. mi. (340 sq. km.)

Population (est. 1997): 119,092

Languages: English, French, Carib Indian

Government: Independent state within Commonwealth

Religions: Anglican, Methodist, Roman Catholic, Seventh-Day Adventist

Monetary unit: East Caribbean (EC) dollar

Main exports: Bananas, eddoes and dasheen (taro), arrowroot, tennis rackets

A British colony from 1763, Saint Vincent and the Grenadines became a member of the Federation of the West Indies (1958–62) and a self-governing state in association with Great Britain in 1969. It was named an independent state within the Commonwealth on October 27, 1979.

A poor country, it has been damaged throughout the century by natural disasters. In 1902 the volcano La Soufrière erupted, killing 2,000. Its 1979 eruption caused severe agricultural destruction. Two hurricanes (1980, 1986) also caused great damage.

Since 1984 the country has been governed by Prime Minister James Fitz-allen Mitchell and the New Democratic Party, despite corruption charges raised during the 1989 and 1994 elections.

Saint Vincent and the Grenadines: 20th-Century Leaders

Governor–General (representing the British monarch)

1979–85: Sir Sydney Gun-Munro (1916–)

1985–88: Sir Joseph Lambert Eustace (1908–)

1988–89: Henry Harvey Williams

1989–97: Sir David Jack

1997– : Sir Charles James Antrolous (1933–)

Prime Minister

1979–84: Milton Cato

1984– : Sir James Fitz-Allen Mitchell (1931–)

Samoa

Official name: Independent State of Samoa

Location: Nine islands in the South Pacific Ocean; 1,500 mi. (2,400 km.) NE of New Zealand, 2,200 mi. (3,540 km.) S of Hawaii

Capital: Apia

Area: 1,093 sq. mi. (2,831 sq. km.)

Population (est. 1997): 219,504

Languages: Samoan, English (official)

Government: Constitutional monarchy under native chief

Religions: Christian 99.7%

Monetary unit: Tala

Main exports: Copra, cocoa, coconut oil and cream, timber

Discovered in the 18th century, the tropical Samoa Islands were of interest to the Dutch and English and were eventually divided by treaty in 1899: the eastern portion was given to the U.S. (American Samoa), and the western portion was given to Germany (Western Samoa). The latter developed into what is today the independent country of Samoa.

In 1914 New Zealand troops occupied Western Samoa. New Zealand governed the territory under a League of Nations mandate from 1920. Samoans protested racist governing practices and, beginning in 1935, persuaded the New Zealand Labour government to enact reforms. In 1947 the island group became a UN trust territory administered by New Zealand. Home rule was established in 1959, and the island group was granted independence as Western Samoa on January 1, 1962. Its government consists of a 49-seat legislative assembly and combines traditional Western and Samoan tribal governmental practices. Most women were granted the right to vote in 1990.

In Western Samoa's first free election in 1991, the Human Rights Protection Party won majority rule. In July 1997 the legislative assembly voted to change the country's name to Samoa.

Samoa/Western Samoa: 20th-Century Leaders

President

1962–63: Malietoa Tanumafili II (1913–) (co-president)

1962–63: Tupua Tamasese Mea'ole (d. 1963) (co-president)

Head of State

1963– : Malietoa Tanumafili II

Prime Minister

1962–70: Fiame Mata'afa Faumuina Mulinu'u II (1921–83)

1970–73: Tupua Tamasese Lealofi IV (1922–83)

1973–75: Fiami Mata'afa Faumuina

1975–76: Tupua Tamasese Lealofi VI

1976–82: Taisi Tupuola Efi (1938–)

1982: Va'ai Kolone

1982: Taisi Tupuola Efi

1982–85: Tofilau Eti Alesana (1924–)

1986–88: Va'ai Kolone

1988–98: Tofilau Eti Alesana

1998– : Tuila'epa Sailele Malielegaoi (1945–)

San Marino

Official name: Most Serene Republic of San Marino

Location: On Mt. Titano in Apennines, inland from the Adriatic Sea; surrounded by Italy

Capital: San Marino

Area: 23 sq. mi. (60 sq. km.)

Population (est. 1997): 24,714

Languages: Italian

Government: Republic

Religions: Roman Catholic

Monetary unit: Italian lira

Main exports: Wine, wheat, woolen goods, furniture, wood, and dairy products.

Founded around A.D. 301, the Most Serene Republic of San Marino is the oldest (and smallest) republic in the world. It maintained independence throughout history despite many battles along the Italian peninsula, notably during the 19th century.

In the 20th century, San Marino was neutral during World War I and maintained neutrality in World War II until being occupied by German forces in September 1944. During this century, the country has balanced agriculture and industry to maintain an overall prosperity. Postwar it has been governed by a coalition of Socialists and Christian Democrats.

San Marino is ruled by a body called the Grand and General Council. It is headed by two governing captains or coregents who are chosen by a popularly elected Great and General Council every six months. San Marino joined the United Nations in 1992.

São Tomé and Príncipe

Official name: Democratic Republic of São Tomé and Príncipe

Location: Two islands in Gulf of Guinea; about 150 mi. (240 km.) from West Africa

Capital: São Tomé

Area: 386 sq. mi. (1,001 sq. km.); São Tomé 332 sq. mi; 859 sq. km.); Príncipe 40 sq. mi.; 142 sq. km.

Population (est. 1997): 147,865

Languages: Portuguese (official)

Government: Republic

Religions: Roman Catholic, evangelical Protestant, Seventh-Day Adventist

Monetary unit: Dobra

Main exports: Cocoa, coffee, copra, palm oil

Discovered by Portuguese navigators in 1471, these volcanic islands became (through slave labor from the mainland) important producers of sugar, coffee, and cacao over the next centuries, with São Tomé becoming by 1908 the world's largest provider of cacao. Although Portugal abolished slavery in 1876, brutal treatment of labor continued well into the 20th century.

In 1953, following bloody clashes with the Portuguese in which hundreds of workers were killed, an exile liberation group was built—the Movement for the Liberation of São Tomé and Príncipe (MLSTP). Continued protest led to the end of Portuguese rule in 1974 and the granting of power to the liberation forces in July 12, 1975. Originally setting up a one-party Socialist state, the government instituted a multiparty democracy in 1991. It has also sought foreign investment and internal economic reform to stimulate the economy. A military coup was thwarted by government forces in 1995.

São Tomé and Príncipe: 20th-Century Leaders

President

1975–91: Manuel Pinto da Costa (1937–)

1991– : Miguel Trovoada

Premier

1975–79: Miguel Trovoada

1988–91: Celestino Rocha Da Costa

1991–92: Daniel Lima Dos Santos

1992–94: Norberto José D'Alva Costa Alegre

1994: Evaristo Carvalho

1994–95: Carlos da Graça

1995–96: Armindo Vaz d'Almeida

1996–99: Raul Bragança Neto

1999– : Guilherme Posser da Costa (1945–)

Saudi Arabia

Official name: Kingdom of Saudi Arabia

Location: Arabian peninsula, southwestern Asia; bordered by Jordan, Iraq, Kuwait (N), Persian Gulf, Qatar, United Arab Emirates (E), Oman (SE), Yemen (S, E), Red Sea (W)

Capital: Riyadh

Area: 756,982 sq. mi. (1,960,582 sq. km.)

Population: (est. 1997) 20,087,965

Languages: Arabic

Government: Monarchy

Religions: Muslim 100%, predominantly Sunni Muslim

Monetary unit: Saudi riyal

Main exports: Petroleum and petroleum products

Though Arabia was nominally under Ottoman rule from the 16th century, its central region, Nejd, was claimed by the Saud royal family. Beginning in 1902, Ibn Saud reconquered the lands to which he laid ancestral claim. He proclaimed himself leader of the Wahabi, a puritanical Islamic sect, and led a revolt against the Ottoman Turks (1912–13). During World War I Britain aided him and his rival Hussein ibn Ali in their struggle with the Turks. As a result Britain established hegemony in Arabia, with a protectorate instituted in 1915.

After World War I Ibn Saud conquered the Hejaz (1924–26), a region that had been dominated by Hussein ibn Ali. The British recognized Ibn Saud as king of Nejd and Hejaz in 1927. In 1929 he defeated the Ikhwan, an ascetic warrior group he had founded but that had gotten out of his control. In 1932 he unified Nejd and Hejaz as Saudi Arabia. He instituted a stable, nationalistic form of government based on the *sharia*, or Islamic law. Then as now, the country was an absolute monarchy with no written constitution or parliament. The king does consult a Council of Ministers, and a consultative assembly with no powers of decision was established in 1993.

A U.S.-chartered corporation, later known as the Arabian-American Oil Company (ARAMCO), was granted an exclusive oil prospecting concession in 1933. By 1938 oil from Saudi Arabia's huge reserves was being exported. The discovery transformed the country from a poor desert state to one of the world's wealthiest. At first the wealth principally enriched the ruling clan and supported a growing population of foreign oil workers. From the 1960s, with the reforms of King Faisal, it produced a greater number of material benefits for the Saudi Arabian people, including an extensive health-care system. ARAMCO was fully nationalized in the 1970s.

Saudi Arabia was neutral during most of World War II but declared war against the Axis Powers in March 1945. A founding member of both the UN and the Arab League, Saudi Arabia opposed Israel since its creation: Saudi troops fought in both the 1948 and 1973 Arab-Israeli Wars. Saudi funds have aided Egypt and other Arab League states since the 1967 Arab-Israeli War. The country's international influence was magnified in 1973, when, as a leader of the Organization of Petroleum Exporting Countries (OPEC), it helped organize the oil embargo to protest U.S. and Western support for Israel in the Yom Kippur War. The embargo and the worldwide recession it triggered drew attention to the power of the Arab oil-producing countries. Since then Saudi Arabia has generally argued for stable production and prices.

Ibn Saud reigned until his death in 1953. His eldest son, Saud ibn Abd (1902–69; reigned 1953–64), succeeded him as king, but was considered incompetent. Saud's brother Faisal ibn Abd al–Aziz, who served his brother as prime minister (1953–60) and defense minister (1958–64), concentrated power during his reign and deposed him, becoming king in his place (1964–75). Faisal promoted economic and educational progress while remaining conservative culturally and politically. Faisal was assassinated by a nephew and succeeded by his brother Khalid (1913–82; reigned 1975–82). Khalid, in turn, was succeeded by yet another brother, Fahd ibn Abd al-Aziz (1921–).

Under Ibn Saud and his successors, Saudi Arabia was an ally of the U.S., which built military bases there, sold arms to the country, and relied on its staunch anti-Communism during the cold war. In the 1980s during Fahd's reign, Saudi Arabia became important to the U.S. as a moderating influence in the face of threats to stability, notably the Islamic fundamentalism of Iran and the growing belligerence of Iraq. Iraq's 1990 invasion of Kuwait menaced Saudi Arabia, which provided bases, troops, and financing for the U.S.-led military response in the Persian Gulf War (1991). Since the Gulf War, Saudi Arabia has cooperated in attempts to achieve peace between the Arab world and Israel. Several Americans were killed in terrorist incidents in Saudi Arabia in 1995 and 1996.

Saudi Arabia is the site of the holy cities of Mecca and Medina, and the Saudi kings administer the annual Muslim pilgrimages there, giving them great authority in the Islamic world. In the 1990s the pilgrimage to Mecca was plagued by highly publicized disasters, notably pedestrian stampedes in 1990 and 1994 and a tent fire in 1997, each of which killed hundreds.

Islamic law is strictly enforced in Saudi Arabia: alcohol is forbidden and women's public activities are restricted. Eighty-five percent of Saudi exports are related to the oil industry, though the agricultural sector has grown with the expansion of irrigation projects to reclaim desert. Bedouin nomads continue to raise camels and sheep in the desert interior, as they have for centuries.

Saudi Arabia: 20th-Century Leaders

King

1932–53: Ibn Saud

1953–64: Saud ibn Abd (1902–69)

1964–75: Faisal ibn Abd al-Aziz

1975–82: Khalid ibn Abd al-Aziz (1913–82)

1982– : Fahd ibn Abd al-Aziz (1921–)

Senegal

Official name: Republic of Senegal

Location: Northwestern Africa; bordered by Mauritania (N), Mali (E), Guinea and Guinea-Bissau (S), Atlantic Ocean (W)

Capital: Dakar

Area: 75,749 sq. mi. (196,190 sq. km.)

Population (est. 1997): 9,403,546

Languages: French (official), Wolof, Pulaar, Diola, Mandingo

Government: Republic under multiparty democratic rule

Religions: Muslim 92%, indigenous beliefs 6%, Christian 2%

Monetary unit: Communauté Financière Africaine (CFA) franc

Main exports: Fish producs, peanuts, petroleum products, phosphates

Although pursued by the British, Dutch, French, and Portuguese from the 16th century, Senegal was largely dominated by the French from the 17th century and came under its complete control in 1893. In 1920 it became a French colony, with Dakar the capital of French West Africa.

In 1946 Senegal established a territorial assembly, and it gained further self-governing power over the years, becoming part of the French Community of Nations in 1958. With French cooperation, Senegal and French Sudan (later Mali) became independent in the Mali Federation on June 20, 1960. That year Senegal withdrew from the Federation (which was dissolved that year) and established itself as an independent nation.

Its first president was Léopold Sédar Senghor, a French-trained statesman, poet, and scholar who had engineered the creation of the Mali Federation in 1959. Upon his retirement in 1981, he was replaced by Prime Minister Abdou Diouf. Attempting more democratic rule, Diouf was reelected several times, the last in 1993. From the 1980s the country has faced ongoing internal conflict with the separatist group Movement of Democratic Forces of Casamance.

Senegal: 20th-Century Leaders

President

1960–80: Léopold Sédar Senghor (1906–)

1981–2000: Abdou Diouf (1935–)

Prime Minister

1958–62: Mamadou Dia

1970–80: Abdou Diouf

1983: Moustapha Niasse (1939–)

1991–98: Habib Thiam (1933–)

1998–2000: Mamadou Lamine Loum

Serbia See Yugoslavia.

Seychelles

Official name: Republic of Seychelles

Location: Western Indian Ocean; 82 islands located about 1,000 mi. (1,600 km) E of Kenya and Tanzania; bordered by Madagascar (about 130 mi./210 km. S of southern islands)

Capital: Victoria

Area: 176 sq. mi. (455 sq. km.)

Population (est. 1997): 78,107

Languages: English and French (both official), Creole

Government: Republic

Religions: Roman Catholic 90%, Anglican 8%, other 2%

Monetary unit: Seychelles rupee

Main exports: Fish, copra, cinnamon bark

Part of the British Empire from 1814, the Seychelles were governed from Mauritius until becoming a separate British colony in 1903. They maintained a successful economy of coconut and spice and guano mining, using imported African and Indian labor.

After World War II the home rule government, under the Seychelles Democratic Party, rejected independence, but by the mid-1960s, the Seychelles People's United Party led by France Albert René actively moved for independence. Following the encouragement of the Organization of African Unity, the UN, and Britain itself, the Seychelles announced independence on June 19, 1976.

In 1977 Socialist forces led by Prime Minister René under the Seychelles People's Progressive Front (SPPF, formerly the Seychelles People's United Party) cited rash spending practices and ousted the government. By 1979 the SPPF was made the only legal party. A 1981 attempted coup against René was unsuccessful; attempts in 1992 to revise the constitution were defeated in a referendum. In 1993 elections, René and the SPPF retained parliamentary power; however, a constitution mandating a multiparty system was approved.

The Seychelles' largest island is Mahé, site of its capital; other large islands include Praslin and La Digue. Since the 1970s, the government has made tourism its dominant and most lucrative industry, generating over three-fourths of revenue.

Seychelles: 20th-Century Leaders

President

1976–77: James Mancham (1940–)

1977– : France Albert René (1935–)

Prime Minister

1975–76: James Mancham

1976–77: France Albert René

Sierra Leone

Official name: Republic of Sierra Leone

Location: West central Africa: bordered by Guinea (N, E), Liberia (S), Atlantic Ocean (W)

Capital: Freetown

Area: 27,699 sq. mi. (71,740 sq. km.)

Population (1997 est.): 4,891,546

Languages: English (official), Mende, Temne, Krio

Government: Constitutional democracy

Religions: Muslim 60%, indigenous beliefs 30%, Christian 10%

Monetary unit: Leone

Main exports: Rutile, bauxite, cocoa, diamonds

Sierra Leone was a British colony from 1808. Freetown, now the capital of Sierra Leone, was a safe haven for freed and escaped slaves, largely from the Americas. It became a British protectorate in 1896 and soon erupted in a war with the indigenous population over a hut tax. A decolonization program began in 1953. Sierra Leone became an independent nation on April 27, 1961, and a republic on April 19, 1971. Since the country's independence, its government has been marked by military coups, internal corruption, and civil war.

Sir Milton Margai, head of the Sierra Leone People's Party, held power until 1967, when he was replaced by Siaka P. Stevens of the All People's Party. In 1978 Stevens installed a one-party system, in which he was the first president. Upon Stevens's 1985 retirement, Prime Minister Joseph Saidu Momoh was elected without opponents. In 1992 Momoh was deposed by a coup led by Captain Valentine Strasser; he was overthrown by rebel army forces in 1996. The government attempted to appease the rebels by holding multiparty elections in 1996. Sierra Leone People's Party candidate Ahmad Tejan Kabbah was elected; he and his government were overthrown by the military in 1997. African peacekeeping troops restored him to power in 1998.

During the 1990s Sierra Leone suffered a civil war between the government and rebel military forces. Rebel groups were internationally condemned for killing and mutilating civilians suspected of supporting the government; 300,000 citizens were uprooted, 150,000 killed or maimed. On July 7, 1999, a peace accord was signed between the warring parties, but the accord collapsed in 2000.

Sierra Leone: 20th-Century Leaders

Head of State

1961–62: Sir Maurice Dorman (1912–93) (governor-general)

1962–67: Sir Henry Lightfoot Boston (1898–1969) (governor-general)

1967: David Lansana (1922–75) (head of state)

1967: Ambrose Genda (chairman, National Reformation Council)

1967–68: Andrew Juxon-Smith (chairman, National Reformation Council)

1968: Patrick Conteh (chairman, National Interim Council)

1968–71: Banja Tejan-Sie (governor-general)

1971: Christopher Okoro Cole (governor-general; president)

1971–85: Siaka Stevens (1905–88) (president)

1985–92: Joseph Saidu Momoh (1937–) (president)

1992–96: Valentine Strasser (president; chairman, Supreme Council of State)

1996: Julius Maada Bio (chairman, Supreme Council of State)

1996–97: Ahmad Tejan Kabbah (1932–) (president)

1997–98: Johnny Paul Koroma (president)

1998– : Ahmad Tejan Kabbah (president)

Singapore

Official name: Republic of Singapore

Location: Southern Malay peninsula; Singapore Island and about 57 islets linked by causeway to peninsula

Capital: Singapore

Area: 244 sq. mi. (633 sq. km.)

Population (est. 1997): 3,440,693

Languages: English (official), Chinese, Malay, Tamil

Government: Republic

Religions: Chinese—primarily Buddhist or atheist; Malays—almost exclusively Muslim; others—Christian, Hindu, Sikh, Tao, Confucianist

Monetary unit: Singapore dollar

Main exports: Petroleum products, rubber, electronics, manufactured goods

Founded by the British East Asia Company in 1819 and granted to Britain in 1824, Singapore became part of the British Straits Settlement colony in 1826 and entered the 20th century as a central port for international trade. Throughout the century its population has been primarily Chinese, with a mix of Malays, Indians, and several minorities.

During World War II Singapore was a major British naval base for Asia and Australia before being taken by the Japanese in 1942. It was reoccupied by the British in 1945 and became a British colony in 1946. In 1959 it became a self-governing parliamentary democracy in the British Commonwealth, with Lee Kuan Yew as its first prime minister. On September 16, 1963, it joined Malaya, Sarawak, and Sabah to form the Malaysian Federation. Facing Chinese persecution by the Malay majority, Singapore left the federation to become an independent nation on August 9, 1965.

Since its independence, Singapore's government has faced charges of corruption, yet has maintained a strong economy built on trade, finance, high technology, and communication.

Singapore: 20th-Century Leaders (See also Malaysia)

President

1959–70: Yusof bin Ishak (1910–70)

1970–71: Yeoh Ghim Seng (1918–)

1971–81: Benjamin H. Sheares (1907–81)

1981: Yeoh Ghim Seng

1981–85: Chengara Veetil Devan Nair (1923–)

1985: Yeoh Ghim Seng

1985–93: Wee Kim Wee

1993–99: Ong Teng Cheong

1999– : S. R. Nathan (1924–)

Prime Minister

1959–90: Lee Kwan Yew (1923–)

1990– : Goh Chok Tong (1941–)

Slovakia

Official name: Slovak Republic

Location: Central Europe; bordered by Czech Republic and Poland (N), Ukraine (E), Hungary (S), Austria (W)

Capital: Bratislava

Area: 18,859 sq. mi. (48,845 sq. km.)

Population (est. 1997): 5,387,665

Languages: Slovak (official), Hungarian

Government: Parliamentary democracy

Religions: Roman Catholic 60.3%, atheist 9.7%, Protestant 8.4%, Orthodox 4.1%

Monetary unit: Koruna

Main exports: Machinery and transport equipment, chemicals, manufactured goods

Almost exclusively under Hungarian rule since the 10th century, Slovakia entered the 20th century with strongly nationalist interests aimed at preserving its identity as a country of farming, small business, and a strong Catholic presence. In particular it feared political and cultural encroachment from its neighbor, the Czech Republic.

When the Austro-Hungarian Empire collapsed after World War I, Slovakia disassociated itself from Hungary for the first time in centuries. With Slovak support, Czech politicians combined the Czech Republic and Slovakia into the Republic of Czechoslovakia in 1918. The Slovak Populist Party's attempts at an opposition movement over the next several years proved fruitless.

In 1939 German chancellor Adolf Hitler dissolved Czechoslovakia and granted Slovakia partial autonomy; in 1940 it was granted full independence. To maintain independence, Slovakia was required to follow Nazi policy. This included declaring war on Poland (1939) and the U.S.S.R., U.S., and Great Britain (1940) and expelling Jewish citizens.

In 1945 Czechoslovakia was restored and in 1948 it came under Communist rule. It remained a Communist country until 1989. In July 1992 the Slovak National Council approved a declaration of sovereignty, and in September 1992 the Slovak and Czech parliaments approved the split. The nation of Czechoslovakia was officially divided into the Czech Republic and Slovakia on January 1, 1993. That year Michal Kováč was elected Slovakia's first president. An unstable economy and charges of corruption marked the

Slovak government's early years.

In 1995 Slovakia applied for membership in the European Union. In 1999 elections, the first in Slovakia decided by popular vote, Rudolf Schuster was elected president. The nation had gone a year without a head of state prior to the election.

Slovakia: 20th-Century Leaders

President

1993–98: Michal Kovác

1999– : Rudolf Schuster (1934–)

Prime Minister

1994–98: Vladimir Meciar

1998– : Mikulas Dzurinda (1955–)

Slovenia

Official name: Republic of Slovenia

Location: Southeastern Europe; bordered by Austria (N), Hungary (NE), Croatia (E, S), Adriatic Sea and Italy (W)

Capital: Ljubljana

Area: 7,836 sq. mi. (20,296 sq. km.)

Population (1997 est.): 1,973,096

Languages: Slovenian 91%, Serbo-Croatian 6%

Government: Emerging democracy

Religions: Catholic 70.8%, Lutheran 1%, Muslim 1%, other 27.2%

Monetary unit: Tolar (SLT)

Main exports: Machinery and transport equipment, other manufactured goods, chemicals, fuels, and lubricants

Part of Austria since 1282, Slovenia entered the 20th century a member (from 1867) of the Austrian arm of the dual Austrian/Hungarian monarchy, the Ausgleich. After the monarchy collapsed during World War I, Slovenia became part of the Kingdom of Serbs, Croats, and Slovenes, which became Yugoslavia in 1929. During World War II, Slovenia was split and annexed, with the northern portion going to Austria and the southern portion to Italy. The country was reconstituted after the war, reclaiming portions on the Istrian peninsula that had been lost earlier in the century. In 1946 Slovenia became part of Federal Yugoslavia and was under the Communist rule of Josip Tito until 1980, as Communist rule was falling apart in Eastern Europe. Slovenia, along with Croatia, declared independence on June 25, 1991.

A short civil war with Yugoslavia (Serbia) followed, its brevity caused by Yugoslavia's involvement in conflicts with Bosnia and Croatia, and its distance from Slovenia. Following the war, Slovenia evolved to a successful capitalist state governed from 1990 by a multiparty coalition.

Slovenia: 20th-Century Leaders

President

1990– : Milan Kuçan (1941–)

Premier

1990–92: Lujze Peterle

1992– : Janez Drnovsek (1950–)

Solomon Islands

Official name: Solomon Islands

Location: Archipelago in South Pacific, east of Papua New Guinea; bordered by South Pacific Ocean (N, E, S), Solomon Sea (W)

Capital: Honiara

Area: 10,985 sq. mi. (28,450 sq. km.)

Population (est. 1998): 441,039

Languages: English (official), Melanesian (pidgin), Papuan, Polynesian languages

Government: Parliamentary democracy within Commonwealth

Religions: Anglican 34%, Roman Catholic 19%, Baptist 17%, other Christian 26%, traditional beliefs 4%

Monetary unit: Dollar

Main exports: Fish, timber, copra, palm oil

The sovereign nation of the Solomon Islands includes only the portion of the archipelago formerly governed by Britain. Two northern Solomon Islands formerly held by Germany, Bougainville and Buka, are now part of Papua New Guinea.

The British established a protectorate over the southern Solomon Islands, including Guadalcanal, San Cristobal, and Malata, in 1893. The protectorate was enlarged with the addition of the eastern islands in 1893 and several German possessions in the North Solomons, including Choiseul and Santa Isabel, in 1898 and 1900. Japan occupied the major islands in 1942; the Allies recaptured them in fierce fighting, notably on Guadalcanal, in 1943.

An independence movement called Marching Rule developed in the late 1940s. Britain began to introduce parliamentary government in the 1950s. The islands gained self-government in 1976 and independence within the Commonwealth of Nations, on July 7, 1978.

The border between the Solomon Islands and Papua New Guinea has been tense in recent years, with the former protesting military incursions by the latter in 1997. Papua New Guinea is concerned about a secessionist movement in Bougainville.

Violence erupted on Guadalcanal in June 1999, when militant islanders revolted against squatters taking land on the island. A peace treaty was signed later that month.

Solomon Islands: 20th-Century Leaders

Governor–General

1978–88: Sir Baddely Devesi (1941–)

1988–94: Sir George Lepping (1947–)

1994–99: Sir Moses Pitakaka

1999– : Rev. John Lapli

Prime Minister

1978–81: Peter Kenilorea (1943–)

1981–84: Solomon Mamaloni

1984–86: Peter Kenilorea

1986–89: Ezekial Alebua

1989–93: Solomon Mamaloni

1993–94: Francis Billy Hilly

1994–97: Solomon Mamaloni

1997–2000: Bartholomew Ulufa'alu

Somalia

Official name: Somalia

Location: Eastern Africa; bordered by Gulf of Aden (N), Indian Ocean (E), Kenya (SW), Ethiopia (W), Djibouti (NW)

Capital: Mogadishu

Area: 246,201 sq. mi. (637,660 sq. km.)

Population (est. 1998): 6,841,695

Languages: Somali (official), Arabic, Italian, English

Government: None

Religions: Sunni Muslim

Monetary unit: Somali shilling

Main exports: Bananas, live animals, fish, hides

Located strategically on the Horn of Africa, the territory that is now Somalia was split up between a British protectorate and an Italian colony in the 1880s. Britain ceded portion, Jubaland, to Italy in 1925. During and after World War II Britain occupied Italian Somaliland (1941–49). A 1949 UN pact gave Italy a trusteeship in the southern part of the colony. Legislative elections were held in the Italian region in 1956 and in the British region in 1958. Both regions became independent in 1960; they were unified as the Somali Republic on July 1, 1960.

In 1969 a coup led by General Mohammed Siad Barre took power, abolished the national assembly, and established rule by military junta. Barre instituted a Socialist regime and received military assistance from the Soviet Union. Somalia had always claimed the Ogaden region of Ethiopia, which had a large ethnic Somali population, and in a 1977–78 war, Somalia tried to annex it. The Soviet Union switched sides and aided Ethiopia, allowing it to win the war. After the war Barre switched sides and courted and received military assistance from the U.S.

Barre's central-planning policies contributed to a sharp economic decline in the 1980s. Various groups engaged in guerrilla warfare against the government, including the Patriotic Front in the south and the Somali National Movement in the northwest. In 1991 Barre was overthrown. The country descended into civil war and anarchy, with a multitude of clan-based guerrilla factions vying over territory. Drought and civil war brought about a devastating famine, killing 50,000 people by 1992 and driving more than a million refugees out of the country. The civil war made famine relief efforts virtually impossible. In cooperation with the UN, U.S. president George Bush sent ground troops in December 1992 to attempt to restore order and secure distribution of food. Peace talks began but collapsed by 1994. Hostility from the warring factions and Somali civilians led the U.S. to withdraw in 1994, transferring control to UN forces that withdrew in 1995. Somalia was left with no recognized government and continuing factional warfare.

One factional leader, General Mohammed Farah Aidid, declared himself president for life in 1995 but was not recognized internationally and was shot dead the following year. Various warlords set up mini-states, including Puntland and Jubaland.

Somalia: 20th-Century Leaders

President

1960–67: Aden Abdullah Osman Daar

1967–69: Abdirashid Ali Shermarke (1919–69)

1969–91: Mohammed Siad Barre (1912–)

(no functioning government from 1991)

Prime Minister

1960: Mohammed Ibrahim Egal (1928–)

1960–64: Abdirashid Ali Shermarke

1964–67: Abdirizak Haji Husain

1967–69: Mohammed Ibrahim Egal

1969–87: Mohammed Siad Barre

1987–90: Muhammad Ali Samatar (1931–)

1990–91: Muhammad Hawadie Madar

South Africa

Official name: Republic of South Africa

Location: Southern Africa; bordered by Namibia (NW), Botswana, Zimbabwe (N), Mozambique (NE), Swaziland, Indian Ocean (E), Atlantic Ocean (W); entirely surrounds Lesotho

Capital: Cape Town (legislative), Pretoria (executive), Bloemfontein (judicial)

Area: 471,444 sq. mi. (1,221,040 sq. km.)

Population (est. 1998): 42,834,520

Languages: Afrikaans, English, Zulu, Xhosa, Sotho, Ndebele, Pedi, Swazi, Tsonga, Venda, Tswana (all official)

Government: Republic

Religions: Predominantly Christian, some Hindu, Muslim, and traditional beliefs

Monetary unit: Rand

Main exports: Gold, minerals, metals, food, chemicals

San and related peoples were South Africa's first inhabitants. In the 15th century, Bantu peoples, including the Zulu and Xhosa, began to arrive and establish kingdoms; Dutch settlers arrived in the 17th century. Descendants of the Dutch, the Afrikaners or Boers, came into conflict with the British, who established Cape Colony and annexed Natal in the 1840s. In the South African or Boer War (1899–1902) Britain annexed the Afrikaner republics of the Orange Free State and the Transvaal. Self-government came to the region in 1907, which, in 1910, was united as the Union of South Africa, with Louis Botha (1910–19) as its first prime minister. In 1931 South Africa gained effective independence as a founding member of the Commonwealth of Nations.

During World War I South Africa fought on the Allied side and occupied South-West Africa (now Namibia). South Africa retained Namibia afterward as a League of Nations mandate.

Botha's South African Party favored close ties between Britain and South Africa, but the National Party, founded by James Hertzog in 1913, represented Afrikaner opposition to that policy. The National Party won the 1924 elections and Hertzog became prime minister (1924–39). During his tenure, Afrikaans, the Afrikaner language, gained the status of an official language (1925). The National Party splintered in 1934, when Hertzog reunited with the South African Party (led by Jan Christian Smuts from 1919) to form the United South African National Party, while fusion opponent Daniel François Malan formed the Purified National Party.

Hertzog was forced to resign in 1939 for his opposition to South African entry into World War II; Smuts, as head of the United Party, led the country as it fought on the Allied side. After the war Malan's reunified National Party won the 1948 elections, beginning more than four decades of National Party domination, during which racial politics was the government's predominant concern. Responding to white fear of the country's nonwhite majority, the party strengthened the country's existing racial laws, which had emerged from segregationist policies that predated South Africa's formation, and formally named the policy apartheid (Afrikaans for "apartness").

Under apartheid all South Africans were classified as either white, black African (Bantu), mixed (colored), or Asian. Laws passed in the 1950s reserved 80 percent of the land for whites, banned nonwhites from living or doing business in certain areas, prohibited social relations between races, and forced nonwhites to carry identification documents. Nonwhites were denied most political and civil rights. From 1951 the government instituted a policy of "separate development" that relegated blacks to bantustans or "homelands" within South Africa. These homelands were given nominal independence in the 1970s and 1980s; this was generally regarded as a cover for continuing apartheid.

The African National Congress (ANC) had been founded in 1912 to oppose racial discrimination. Until the 1940s it relied on peaceful lobbying, but leaders Nelson Mandela and Oliver Tambo (1917–93), who founded the ANC Youth League in 1944, turned the group in a more militant direction. In the 1950s the ANC conducted nonviolent resistance campaigns against apartheid. Police killings of black demonstrators in the Sharpeville massacre (1960) led the government to ban the ANC, which moved into exile in Mozambique and adopted guerrilla warfare as one of its tactics. For his guerrilla activities, Mandela was imprisoned from 1962 to 1990; during that time, Tambo became president-general of the ANC (1977–90) and made it the nucleus of an international anti-apartheid campaign.

South Africa severed all ties with Great Britain and became a republic in 1961. South Africa's economy boomed from 1965 to 1975, benefiting the white minority but leaving most black Africans in poverty. In 1976 the violent crushing of the Soweto uprising against apartheid focused world attention on the injustice of the regime. The continuing imprisonment of Mandela also became a focus of international disfavor, as did South African military interventions in such countries as Angola and Mozambique and its refusal to grant independence to Namibia.

The government modified some apartheid laws in the 1970s and 1980s, but not enough to satisfy opponents. Continuing unrest, international economic sanctions, and isolation in the world community took their toll on the government's resolve. In 1990 South African president F. W. de Klerk granted independence to Namibia, released Mandela, and legalized the ANC. Apartheid was dismantled and a transitional constitution approved in 1993. In 1994 the ANC won victory in the country's first multiracial national elections. It formed a Coalition Government of National Unity with the National Party and the Inkatha Freedom Party. The latter was led by Gatsha Buthelezi (1928–), a Zulu leader who had criticized the ANC and supported the South African government during the 1980s.

A permanent constitution was approved in 1996, establishing the country as one with a strong central government, universal suffrage, and a broad bill of rights. The National Party left the governing coalition in 1996 to become an opposition party. Under Mandela the government emphasized racial harmony and modified the ANC's earlier Socialism to embrace capitalism.

Elections in 1999 brought Mandela associate Thabo Mvuyelwa Mbeki to the presidency. However, racial tensions remain; the continuing poverty of many black South Africans is a concern, as is the legacy of the human rights offenses perpetrated during apartheid. In 1997 the Truth and Reconciliation Commission began hearings regarding such crimes, offering amnesty to any who confessed.

South Africa: 20th-Century Leaders

Governor–General

1910–14: Herbert John Gladstone, viscount Gladstone (1854–1930)

1914–20: Sydney Charles Buxton, earl Buxton (1853–1934)

1920–24: Prince Arthur Frederick Patrick Albert of Connaught (1883–1938)

1924–31: Alexander Augustus Frederick William Alfred George, earl of Athlone (1874–1957)

1931–37: George Herbert Hyde Villiers, earl of Clarendon (1877–1955)

1937–43: Sir Patrick Duncan (1870–1943)

1943–45: Nicolas Jacobus De Wet (1873–1960) (acting)

1946–50: Gideon Brand van Zyl (1873–1956)

1951–59: Ernest George Jansen (1881–1959)

1959–61: Charles Robberts Swart (1894–1982)

President

1961–67: Charles Robberts Swart

1967–68: Jozua Naude (1889–1969) (acting)

1968–75: Jacobus Johannes Fouché (1898–1980)

1975–78: Nicolaas Diederich (1903–78)

1978–79: John Vorster (1915–83)

1979–84: Marais Viljoen

1984–89: Pieter Botha

1989: J. Christian Heunis

1989: Pieter Botha

1989–94: F. W. de Klerk

1994–99: Nelson Mandela

1999– : Thabo Mvuyelwa Mbeki (1942–)

Prime Minister

1910–19: Louis Botha

1919–24: Jan Christian Smuts

1924–39: James Barry Munnik Hertzog (1866–1942)

1939–48: Jan Christian Smuts

1948–54: Daniel François Malan (1874–1959)

1954–58: Johannes Gerhardus Strijdom (1873–1958)

1958: Charles Robberts Swart (acting)

1958–66: Hendrik Frensch Verwoerd (1901–66)

1966: Theophilius Eben Donges (1898–1968) (acting)

1966–78: John Vorster

1978–84: Pieter Botha

(position abolished)

Soviet Union See Russia.

Spain

Official name: Kingdom of Spain

Location: Iberian Peninsula in southwest Europe; bordered by Portugal, Atlantic Ocean (W), Bay of Biscay, France (N), Mediterranean Sea (E, S), Strait of Gibraltar, separating it from Morocco (S)

Capital: Madrid

Area: 194,884 sq. mi. (504,750 sq. km.)

Population (est. 1998): 39,133,996

Languages: Castilian Spanish (official), Catalán, Galician, Basque

Government: Parliamentary monarchy

Religions: Roman Catholic 99%

Monetary unit: Peseta

Main exports: Cars and trucks, manufactures, foodstuffs, machinery

In the 16th century Spain built a vast colonial empire and became one of the world's great powers. By the late 19th century Spanish power had severely declined; in the Spanish-American War of 1898, it lost most of the last remnants of its empire, including Cuba, Puerto Rico, and the Philippines. Still, under King Alfonso XIII (1886–1931), Spain clung to imperial pretensions, establishing a protectorate over part of Morocco in 1912. Spanish control of this region was nearly overthrown in the Rif War (1921–26), which Spain won only with French help.

Spain stayed neutral in World War I. Wartime profits from increased trade gave way to post-war economic turmoil and labor unrest. Anarcho-syndicalists, socialists, and other protesters mounted strikes, demonstrations, terrorist attacks, and uprisings. In a 1923 coup Miguel Primo de Rivera, with Alfonso's support, established a military dictatorship. He instituted progressive social reforms and improved labor relations, but antagonized landowners and the military. He was forced to resign in 1930. Bowing to an electoral victory for Republican parties in 1931, Alfonso also resigned and the Second Republic was established (the first had been in the 19th century).

Under the republic's first prime minister, Manuel Azaña y Díaz (1931–33), the government took steps to secularize and modernize the country, such as instituting Catalan autonomy, curbing Church influence, and expanding the educational system. These reforms were opposed by the right wing, which took power in the 1933 elections and was in turn opposed through strikes and demonstrations. A miners' strike in the Asturias was violently suppressed in 1934. The country grew more polarized, with the Falange, a Fascist organization, attracting followers.

In 1936 the election of a leftist "Popular Front" government coalesced right-wing Nationalist opposition to the republic. In July, right-wing military officers in Morocco and Spain staged revolts. The Spanish Civil War (1936–39) broke out, with Nationalist forces headed by Francisco Franco and aided by Germany and Italy emerging victorious against Republican forces aided by the Soviet Union. Franco reorganized the Falange in 1937, making it the rebel government's official political movement. He ruled dictatorially (1939–75) until his death.

Though sympathetic to Hitler, Franco kept Spain neutral during World War II. In 1947 he arranged for succession by proclaiming Spain a monarchy, with himself as a dictatorial regent for life. His staunch anti-Communism attracted U.S. economic and military aid during the cold war. His technocratic ministers, most of them from the Catholic organization Opus Dei, stepped up the pace of industrialization and foreign investment after 1958, causing Spain's formerly sluggish economy to grow. Despite Franco's encouragement of Catholic traditionalism, the country grew increasingly secular. In 1967 Franco partially liberalized his regime, allowing some independence in the Cortes, or legislature, and relaxing censorship. In 1969 Franco named Juan Carlos, grandson of Alfonso XIII, as his successor; Juan Carlos took the throne upon Franco's death in 1975.

King Juan Carlos and his prime minister Adolfo Suárez González presided over Spain's swift transition from dictatorship to democracy. Political parties were made legal; the Cortes were transformed into a bicameral legislature whose members were elected by universal suffrage. A new constitution was adopted in 1978. Catalonia and the Basque country received home rule in 1980, but a terrorist campaign for complete Basque independence continued, despite a truce from 1998 to 1999.

An attempted military coup in 1981 was foiled, in part by the defiance of Juan Carlos. In the 1980s Spain was integrated into Western Europe, joining NATO in 1982 and the European Community in 1986. Under the social democratic policies of the Socialist Party (1982–96), led by Felipe González Márquez, Spain's economy and the pace of foreign investment grew impressively. From 1992 economic growth slowed and unemployment rose, as did tensions in the Catalan and Basque regions. A scandal over alleged government involvement in the assassination of Basque separatists led the party to lose the 1996 elections. The moderate right-wing Popular Party, led by José María Aznar, came to power and improved economic growth.

Spain: 20th-Century Leaders

King

1886–1931: Alphonso XIII

(no king 1931–75)

1975– : Juan Carlos I

President

1931–36: Niceto Alcalá Zamora (1877–1949)

1936: Manuel Azáña y Díaz

(civil war 1936–39)

Head of State

1939–75: Francisco Franco

Regent

1885–1902: María Cristina (1858–1929)

Premier

1931–33, 1936: Manuel Azáña y Díaz

1939–73: Francisco Franco

1973: Luis Carrero Blanco (1903–73)

1973–76: Carlos Arias Navarro (1908–89)

1976–81: Adolfo Suárez González (1932–)

1981–82: Leopoldo Calvo Sotelo y Bustelo (1926–)

1982–96: Felipe González Márquez (1942–)

1996– : José María Aznar López (1953–)

Sri Lanka

Official name: Democratic Socialist Republic of Sri Lanka

Location: Indian Ocean; island about 50 mi. (80 km) SE of India

Capital: Colombo

Area: 25,332 sq. mi. (65,610 sq. km.)

Population (est. 1997): 18,721,178

Languages: Sinhala (official), Tamil, English

Government: Republic

Religions: Buddhist 68%, Hindu 15%, Christian 8%, Muslim 8%

Monetary unit: Sri Lankan rupee

Main exports: Tea, textiles and garments, petroleum products, gems, rubber

The country now known as Sri Lanka is an island nation off the southeast coast of India in the Indian Ocean. Occupied by the Portuguese in the 16th century and by the Dutch in the 17th century, it became a British colony in 1797. In the 19th century Sri Lanka (then known as Ceylon) developed into a lucrative plantation economy for the Empire. It entered the 20th century ready to move toward independence.

During the 1930s and 1940s, under the leadership of President Senanayake, Ceylon enjoyed social and agricultural reform, including improved irrigation programs and increased education spending. It became an independent member of the British Commonwealth on February 4, 1948, as Ceylon.

In 1952 the early death of Prime Minister Don Stephen Senanayake resulted in his replacement by his son, Dudley Senanayake, who lacked the political skills and national admiration of his father. In 1956 elections Solomon Bandaranaike took power, pursuing more anti-Western, pro-Buddhist, and Sinhalese majority interests. Complicating the political scene was the assassination of Prime Minister W. R. D. Bandaranaike on September 25, 1959. The prime minister's widow, Mrs. Sirimavo Bandaranaike, was elected to replace him and was reelected in 1970.

In 1972 Ceylon severed ties with the Commonwealth and, under a new Socialist constitution, was renamed the Republic of Sri Lanka.

The 1970s in Sri Lanka were marked by the nationalization of plantations but reduced private investment. The resulting economic instability led to the collapse of the Bandaranaike government in 1977 and the election of Junius R. Jayawardene in the elections that year. Jayawardene instituted economic reforms and a new constitution. The 1980s were marked by the eruption of ethnic tensions simmering for decades, with a civil war between Tamil and Sinhalese separatist groups starting in 1983 and continuing into the 1990s. In 1993 President Ranasinghe Premadasa was assassinated by a Tamil separatist.

The government moved leftward in 1994, with the election of Chandrika Bandaranaike Kumaratunga as president. She named her mother, Sirimavo Bandaranaike, as prime minister.

Sri Lanka: 20th-Century Leaders

Governor–General

1948–49: Sir Henry Monck-Mason Moore (1887–1964)

1949–54: Herwald Ramsbotham, viscount Soulbury (1887–1971)

1954–62: Sir Oliver Ernest Goonetilleke

1962–72: Sir William Gopallawa (1897–1981)

President

1972–78: Sir William Gopallawa

1978–89: Junius R. Jayawardene

1989–93: Ranasinghe Premadasa (1924-93)

1993–94: Dingiri Banda Wijetunga (1922–)

1994– : Chandrika Bandaranaike Kumaratunga

Prime Minister

1947–52: Don Stephen Senanayake (1884–1952)

1952–53: Dudley Senanayake (1911–73)

1953–56: Sir John Kotelawala (1897–1980)

1956–59: Solomon West Ridgeway Dias Bandaranaike (1899–1959)

1959–60: Wijeyananda Dahanayake

1960: Dudley Senanayake

1960–65: Sirimavo R. D. Bandaranaike (1916–2000)

1965–70: Dudley Senanayake

1970–77: Sirimavo R. D. Bandaranaike

1977–78: Junius R. Jayawardene

1978–89: Ranasinghe Premadasea

1989–93: Dingiri Banda Wijetunge

1993–1994: Ranil Wickremasinghe

1994: Chandrika Bandaranaike Kumaratunga

1994–2000: Sirimavo R. D. Bandaranaike

Sudan

Official name: Republic of the Sudan

Location: Northeastern Africa; bordered by Egypt (N), Red Sea, Eritrea, Ethiopia (E), Kenya, Uganda, Zaire (S), Central African Republic, Chad, Libya (W)

Capital: Khartoum

Area: 967,495 sq. mi. (2,505,810 sq. km.)

Population (est. 1997): 32,594,128

Languages: Arabic (official), Nubian, Ta Bedawie, many dialects of Nilotic, Nilo–Hamitic, and Sudanic languages, English

Government: Military junta

Religions: Sunni Muslim 70%, indigenous beliefs 25%, Christian 5%

Monetary unit: Sudanese pound

Main exports: Cotton, meat, gum arabic, sesame

Known as Nubia in antiquity, Sudan was conquered by Egypt and in the 19th century was under the control of the Ottoman Empire. A revolt by the mahdi, a religious leader, was crushed by British and Egyptian troops in 1898; Anglo-Egyptian joint rule, or condominium, followed from 1899.

In 1953 Britain and Egypt granted self-government and self-determination to Sudan. Full independence as a parliamentary republic came in 1956, with the central government dominated by the predominantly Muslim and Arab north. In the Christian and animist south, which was populated largely by black Africans, a revolt had already begun (1955–72) against northern Muslim dominance.

From 1958 to 1964 a military government established by coup held power in Sudan. Civilian rule was restored in 1964, but a new coup in 1969 established the Socialist military regime of General Mohamed Nimeiri. Nimeiri ended the civil war, in which about 1.5 million southerners had died through battle, starvation, and disease, by granting autonomy to the southern provinces (1972). Nimeiri's economic policies contributed to a worsening of Sudan's economy and much civil unrest. Nimeiri ended southern autonomy and, in 1983, seeking to win the support of Islamic fundamentalists, instituted Islamic law. These changes brought about a new civil war (1983–), with the Southern Sudan Independence Army (SSIA) and the Sudan People's Liberation Army (SPLA) emerging as the main rebel groups.

Nimeiri was overthrown in a 1985 coup; short-lived civilian government (1986–89) ended with yet another military coup, this one bringing to power a junta that reaffirmed the supremacy of Islamic law. International human rights groups, including Amnesty International, condemned Sudan's government for atrocities and genocidal crimes against southerners. Since 1983 about 1.9 million people have died from the war and from related famine and 4.5 million southerners have been displaced. Sudan has also been accused of sponsoring terrorism, including the attempted assassination of Egyptian president Hosni Mubarak in Ethiopia in 1995. In 1998, U.S. missiles attacked Sudan for alleged terrorist activities. In 1999, President Omar al-Bashir dissolved parliament and declared a state of emergency.

Sudan: 20th-Century Leaders

President

1958–64: Ibrahim Abboud (1900–83)

1965–69: Ismail al-Azhari (1900–69)

1969–85: Gaafar el-Nimeiri (1930–85)

1985–86: 'Abd ar-Rahman Siwar ad-Dahab

1986–89: Ahmad al-Mirghani

1989– : Omar al-Bashir (1944–)

Prime Minister

1956–58: Abdullah Khalil (1892–1970)

1958–64: Ibrahim Abboud

1964–65: Sirr al-Khatim al-Khalifa

1965–66: Muhammad Ahmad Mahjub

1966–67: Sadiq al-Mahdi (1936–)

1967–69: Muhammad Ahmad Mahjub

1969: Abubakr Awadallah

1969–76: Gaafar el-Nimeiri

1976–77: Rashid Bakr (1931–)

1977–85: Gaafar el-Nimeiri

1985–86: Al-Jazuli Daf'allah (1935–)

1986–89: Sadiq al-Mahdi

1989– : Omar al-Bashir

Suriname

Official name: Republic of Suriname

Location: Northwestern coast of South America; bordered by the Atlantic Ocean (N), French Guiana (E), Brazil (S), Guyana (W)

Capital: Paramaribo

Area: 63,039 sq. mi. (163,270 sq. km.)

Population (est. 1997): 424,569

Languages: Dutch (official), English, Sranan Tongo (a.k.a. Taki-Taki)

Government: Republic

Religions: Hindu 27.4%, Protestant 22.8%, Roman Catholic 19.6%, Muslim

Monetary unit: Suriname guilder

Main exports: Alumina, bauxite, aluminum, agricultural products, wood and wood products

Settled by Dutch and English explorers in the 17th century, Suriname became known as Dutch Guiana. It remained a Dutch colony (except for a short period of British control) into the 20th century. It was known for its plantation economy, fueled by slaves until the abolition of slavery (1863), and afterward by imported laborers.

In 1948 the colony became part of the Kingdom of the Netherlands; in 1954 it was granted full autonomy as part of the Netherlands. Suriname was granted independence on November 25, 1975. Although Suriname received Dutch aid, it suffered initially with the emigration of over 100,000 Surinamese.

Suriname moved quickly to military rule, which was established in 1980 following a bloodless coup led by army commander Dési Bouterse. Bouterse took over direct rule as head of state in 1982, though he named Lachmipersad F. Ramdutmisier to serve as nominal president. Military rule ended with the 1988 election of Ramsewak Shankar, who was overthrown in a bloodless coup in 1990. Civilian rule was reinstated in 1991.

Suriname: 20th-Century Leaders

President

1975–80: Johann Henri Ferrier (1910–)

1980–82: Hendrick R. Chin A Sen (1934–)

1982: Dési Bouterse (1946–) (head of state)

1982–88: Lachmipersad F. Ramdutmisier

1988–90: Ramsewak Shankar

1991–96: Ronald Venetiaan

1996– : Jules Wijdenbosch (1941–)

Prime Minister

1975–80: Henck Arron (1936–)

1980–82: Hendrick R. Chin A Sen

1982: Henry Neyhorst

1982: Notwen Nosredna (1953–)

1983–84: Errol Alibux

1984–86: Wim Udenhout

1986–87: Pretaapnarian Radhakishun

1987–88: Jules Wijdenbosch

1988–90: Henck Arron

1990–91: Jules Wijdenbosch

1991: Jules R. Adjodhia

Swaziland

Official name: Kingdom of Swaziland

Location: Southern Africa; landlocked; bordered by South Africa (N, SE, W), Mozambique (E)

Capital: Mbabane

Area: 6,703 sq. mi. (17,360 sq. km.)

Population (est. 1997): 1,031,600

Languages: English and siSwati (both official)

Government: Monarchy; independent member of Commonwealth

Religions: Christian 60%, indigenous beliefs 40%

Monetary unit: Lilangeni

Main exports: Soft drink concentrates, sugar, wood, and forest products

Explored by British and Boer traders beginning in the 1830s, Swaziland became highly desirable to Europeans in the 1880s after the discovery of gold. European settlers tricked native Swazi leaders into transferring their rights to the land. In 1894 the land came under Boer control; in 1902, after the Boer War, rights reverted to the British.

During World War II, Swaziland supported the Allied war effort.

Beginning in the 1920s, King Sobhuza II appealed to Britain for Swaziland's independence, and in 1967 Swaziland was granted internal self-rule from the British. It gained independence as a constitutional monarchy on September 6, 1968. In 1973 King Sobhuza replaced the British-designed constitution with one that incorporated Swazi traditions and that allowed him to act as an absolute monarch. Throughout his rule he attempted to maintain economic stability and encourage foreign investment.

King Sobhuza died in 1982 and was replaced in 1986 by his 18-year-old son, who became King Mswati III. During the 1990s his rule was marked by student protests and calls for multiparty elections.

Swaziland: 20th-Century Leaders

King

1899–1982: Sobhuza II

1982–83: Dzeliwe Shongwe (queen regent)

1983–86: Ntombe Thwala

1986– : Mswati III (1968–)

Prime Minister

1967–76: Makhosini Dlamini (1914–78)

1976–79: Maphevu Dlamini (1914–79)

1979–83: Mandabala Fred Dlamini

1983–85: Bhekimpi Dlamini

1985–89: Sotsha Dlamini

1989–93: Obed Dlamini

1993: Andreas Fakudze (acting prime minister)

1993–96: Prince Jameson Mbilini Dlamini

1996– : Sibusiso Barnabas Dlamini (1942–)

Sweden

Official name: Kingdom of Sweden

Location: Northwest Europe, Scandinavian peninsula; bordered by Norway (NE, W), Finland (NE), Gulf of Bothnia (E), Baltic Sea (E, S), Skagerrak Channel (SW)

Capital: Stockholm

Area: 173,731 sq. mi. (449,964 sq. km.)

Population: 8,865,051

Languages: Swedish, Lapp- and Finnish-speaking minorities

Government: Constitutional monarchy

Religions: Evangelical Lutheran 94%, Roman Catholic 1.5%, other 4.5%

Monetary unit: Swedish krona

Main exports: Machinery, motor vehicles, paper products, pulp and wood, iron and steel products

A great European power from the 17th century until its defeat in the Napoleonic Wars, Sweden entered the 20th century rebuilding its economy through industrialization, yet facing high emigration to the U.S. In 1905 it granted independence to its neighbor Norway, which it had incorporated after gaining it from Russia (1814) in return for Finland (1809). Through its industrial and agrarian strengths, and shared social and political goals during the Great Depression, Sweden sustained economic stability throughout the 20th century.

Sweden's general stability also grew from its neutral stance during World Wars I and II. It was the only Scandinavian country during World War II to maintain such a position. Sweden's neutrality continued postwar with its refusal to join NATO and the Common

Market. However, it accepted aid from the Marshall Plan and was a charter member of the UN. It also joined the Council of Europe in 1948 and helped to form the Nordic Council in 1952 and 1953 to provide economic and political support among neighboring countries (Sweden, Norway, Denmark, Iceland; Norway from 1956).

From 1936 until the beginning of World War II (when a national coalition government was instated), the country was run by the Social Democratic Party. That party resumed control after the war, led by Prime Minister Tage Erlander who promoted a program of economic growth and social services. After Erlander resigned in 1969, Olof Palme gained power, adopting a more Socialist government, divesting the sovereign of rights as commander-in-chief, and appointing prime ministers.

Sweden faced economic stagnation and labor unrest during the 1970s, leading to the election of a conservative government in 1976. Palme was assassinated in 1986 and replaced by Ingvar Carlsson, whose Social Democratic program aimed to tax business profits to fund labor unions and promote labor ownership of private companies. Carlsson was unseated in 1991 and replaced by a conservative coalition government that lasted until 1994, when he was reelected in response to growing debt and inflation; the Social Democrat and Liberal Parties formed a coalition parliament when no party gained majority. In January 1995 Sweden joined the European Union. In 1996 Prime Minister Carlsson resigned for personal reasons and was succeeded by Göran Persson.

Sweden: 20th-Century Leaders

King

1872–1907: Oscar II (1829–1907)

1907–50: Gustav V (1858–1950)

1950–73: Gustav VI Adolf (1882–1973)

1973– : Carl XVI Gustav (1946–)

Prime Minister

1891–1900: Erik Gustav Boström (1842–1907)

1900–02: Fredrik Wilhelm von Otter (d. 1910)

1902–05: Erik Gustav Boström

1905: Johan Olof Ramstedt (1852–1935)

1905: Christian Lundeberg (1842–1911)

1905–06: Karl Albert Staaff (1860–1915)

1906–11: Salomon Arvid Achates Lindman

1911–14: Karl Albert Staaff

1914–17: Knut Hjalmar Hammerskjöld (1862–1953)

1917: Carl Johan Gustav Swartz (1858–1926)

1917–20: Nils Eden (1871–1945)

1920: Karl Hjalmar Branting (1860–1925)

1920–21: Louis de Geer (1854–1935)

1921: Oskar Fredrik von Sydow (1873–1936)

1921–23: Karl Hjalmar Branting

1923–24: Ernst Trygger

1924–25: Karl Hjalmar Branting

1925–26: Richard Johannes Sandler (1884–1965)

1926–28: Carl Gustav Ekman (1872–1945)

1928–30: Salomon Arvid Achates Lindman (1862–1936)

1930–32: Carl Gustav Ekman

1932: Felix Teodor Hamrin (1875–1937)

1932–36: Per Albin Hansson

1936: Axel Alarik Pehrsson-Bramstorp (1883–1954)

1936–46: Per Albin Hansson

1946–69: Tage Erlander (1901–85)

1969–76: Olof Palme (1927–86, assassinated)

1976–78: Thorbjorn Falldin

1978–79: Ola Ullsten

1979–82: Thorbjorn Falldin

1982–86: Olof Palme

1986–91: Ingvar Carlsson (1934–)

1991–94: Carl Bildt (1949–)

1994–96: Ingvar Carlsson

1996– : Göran Persson (1949–)

Switzerland

Official name: Swiss Confederation

Location: Central Europe; bordered by Germany (N), Austria (E), Italy (S), France (W)

Capital: Berne (Bern)

Area: 15,942 sq. mi. (41,290 sq. km.)

Population (est. 1997): 7,240,463

Languages: German 63.7%, French 19.2%, Italian 7.6%, Romansch 0.6%, others 8.9%

Government: Federal republic

Religions: Roman Catholic 46.7%, Protestant 40%

Monetary unit: Swiss franc

Main exports: Machinery and equipment, precision instruments, textiles, foodstuffs, metal products

Officially known as the Swiss Confederation, Switzerland comprises 23 sovereign cantons; three are half-cantons. Through the 18th century, Switzerland was one of Europe's poorest countries, occupied by French revolutionary troops. It became independent and was defined by the Congress of Vienna as a country of "permanent neutrality" in 1815; in 1874 it established a federal constitution with a strong central government and autonomy among the cantons. Switzerland entered the 20th century a unified, neutral country.

Although tourism, alpine skiing, and banking invigorated the Swiss economy in the 19th century, Switzerland established its long-lived economic stability early in the 20th century by developing areas of specialty—notably high-quality manufacturing (watches, textiles, electrical machinery) and international banking that became prized for its secrecy. Switzerland was neutral during World War I; after the war, Geneva became the seat of the League of Nations.

Switzerland also maintained neutrality during World War II, thus requiring no postwar rebuilding. Instead it concentrated efforts on developing the economy's service sector, which eventually supplanted manufacturing as the country's primary employment source. Through the 1980s it maintained at least acceptable rates of growth, establishing itself as a stable economic power.

Maintaining its independence, Switzerland has consistently rejected membership in the UN, though it maintains observer status. It maintains ties to the EU but as of 1995 was not a member. It is a member of the European Free Trade Association.

In 1971 Switzerland became the last major European country to grant women the right to vote. Still a highly militarized government, it devotes 30 percent of its federal budget to defense spending, though a sizable minority (one-third) voted in a 1989 referendum to end the Swiss army.

Switzerland's actions during World War II remain a subject of international controversy, as Holocaust survivors and their families worldwide seek banks' reimbursement of monies deposited in the 1930s and 1940s. Switzerland has been criticized for inadequate accounting of Holocaust-related funds. In 1998, Swiss banks agreed to pay $1.25 billion in reporations for Holocaust survivors.

Switzerland: 20th-Century Leaders

President

1900: Walter Hauser

1901: Ernst Brenner (1856–1911)

1902: Joseph Zemp (1834–1908)

1903: Adolf Deucher

1904: Robert Comtesse (1847–1922)

1905: Marc-Emile Ruchet (1853–1912)

1906: Ludwig Forrer (1845–1921)

1907: Eduard Müller

1908: Ernst Brenner

1909: Adolf Deucher

1910: Robert Comtesse

1911: Marc-Emile Ruchet

1912: Ludwig Forrer

1913: Eduard Müller

1914: Arthur Hoffmann (1857–1927)

1915: Giuseppe Motta (1871–1940)

1916: Camille Decoppet (1862–1925)

1917: Edmund Schulthess (1868–1944)

1918: Felix Ludwig Calonder (1863–1952)

1919: Gustave Ador (1845–1928)

1920: Giuseppe Motta

1921: Edmund Schulthess

1922: Robert Haab (1865–1959)

1923: Karl Scheurer (1872–1929)

1924: Ernest Chuard (1857–1942)

1925: Jean-Marie Musy (1876–1952)

1926: Heinrich Häberlin (1868–1947)

1927: Giuseppe Motta

1928: Edmund Schulthess

1929: Robert Haab

1930: Jean-Marie Musy

1931: Heinrich Häberlin (1868–1947)

1932: Giuseppe Motta

1933: Edmund Schulthess

1934: Marcel Pilet-Golaz (1889–1958)

1935: Rudolf Minger (1881–1955)

1936: Albert Meyer (1870–1953)

1937: Giuseppe Motta

1938: Johannes Baumann (1874–1953)

1939: Philipp Etter (1891–1977)

1940: 1940: Marcel Pilet-Golaz

1941: Ernst Wetter (1877–)

1942: Philipp Etter

1943: Enrico Celio (1889–1980)

1944: Walter Stämpfli (1884–)

1945: Eduard von Steiger (1881–1962)

1946: Karl Kobelt (1891–1968)

1947: Philipp Etter (1891–1977)

1948: Enrico Celio (1889–1980)

1949: Ernst Nobs (1887–1957)

1950: Max Petitpierre (1899–1994)

1951: Eduard von Steiger

1952: Karl Kobelt

1953: Philipp Etter

1954: Rodolphe Rubattel (1896–1961)

1955: Max Petitpierre

1956: Markus Feldmann (1897–1958)

1957: Hans Streuli (1892–1970)

1958: Thomas Holenstein (1896–1962)

1959: Paul Chaudet (1904–1977)

1960: Max Petitpierre

1961: Friedrich Wahlen (1899–1985)

1962: Paul Chaudet

1963: Willy Spühler (1902–1990)

1964: Ludwi von Moos (1910–1990)

1965: Hans-Peter Tschudi (1913–)

1966: Hans Schaffner (1908–)

1967: Roger Bonvin (1907–82)

1968: Willy Spühler

1969: Ludwig von Moos

1970: Hans-Peter Tschudi

1971: Rudolf Gnägi (1917–85)

1972: Nello Celio (1914–)

1973: Roger Bonvin

1974: Ernst Brugger (1914–)

1975: Pierre Graber (1908–)

1976: Rudolf Gnägi

1977: Kurt Furgler (1924–)

1978: Willi Ritzchard (1918–83)

1979: Hans Hürlimann (1918–)

1980: Georges-André Chevallaz (1915–)

1981: Kurt Furgler

1982: Fritz Furgler

1983: Pierre Aubert (1927–)

1984: Leon Schlumpf (1925–)

1985: Kurt Furgler

1986: Alphons Egli (1924–)

1987: Pierre Aubert

1988: Otto Stich

1989: Jean-Pascal Delamurraz (1936–)

1990: Arnold Koller (1933–)

1991: Flavio Cotti (1939–)

1992: Rene Felber (1933–)

1993: Adolf Ogi

1994: Otto Stich

1995: Kaspar Villiger

1996: Jean-Pascal Delamurraz

1997: Arnold Koller

1998: Flavio Cotti

1999: Ruth Dreifuss

Syria

Official name: Syrian Arab Republic

Location: Western Asia; bordered by Turkey (N), Iraq (E), Jordan (S), Lebanon, Israel (SW), Mediterranean Sea (W)

Capital: Damascus

Area: 71,498 sq. mi. (185,180 sq. km.)

Population (est. 1997): 16,137,899

Languages: Arabic (official), Kurdish, Armenian, Aramaic, Circassian, French

Government: Republic, under military regime

Religions: Sunni Muslim 74%, Alawite, Druze, and other Muslim sects 16%, Christian 10%

Monetary unit: Syrian pound

Main exports: Petroleum, textiles, food, and live animals

An ancient center of civilization, Syria became part of the Ottoman Empire in the 16th century. During World War I British and Arab forces ended Ottoman rule. In 1920 Faisal I was briefly proclaimed king of Syria, but French troops deposed him later that year and Syria and Lebanon became a French League of Nations mandate. French rule was unpopular and opposed in several uprisings; considerable autonomy was granted to Syria in the 1930s. During World War II the mandate administration declared loyalty to the Vichy regime in France, prompting invasion and occupation by British and Free French forces in 1941. An independent Syrian republic was declared that year, though effective full independence did not come until the withdrawal of all foreign troops in 1946.

Syria's first years were politically unstable, with frequent coups. In 1958 Syria joined with Egypt to form the United Arab Republic (U.A.R.); following a 1961 military coup, Syria withdrew over Egyptian dominance of the partnership. In 1963 the Socialist, pan-Arab Ba'ath Party came to power in another coup. Other political parties were abolished as the Ba'ath Party moved the country to the left, nationalizing industries and redistributing land. The party leadership was dominated by the country's minority Alawite community. In a 1970 coup, Hafiz al-Assad, a prominent Ba'ath Party member, came to power as the country's leader. He has been president since 1971.

Under Assad's rule dissent was repressed, oil revenues (based on oil reserves discovered in 1966) brought economic growth, and Syria strengthened ties to the Soviet Union. In 1976 Syria intervened in a civil war in Lebanon and has since retained strong influence and a military presence in that country.

Syria was a staunch foe of Israel in all the Arab-Israeli Wars. In the Six-Day War (1967) Israel captured Syria's Golan Heights, from which Syria had long bombarded Israeli settlements. Syrian and Israeli troops clashed directly in 1982 in Lebanon, following the Israeli invasion of that country. Syria supported radical elements within the PLO and aided them in driving Yasir Arafat's centrist faction from its headquarters in Tripoli, Lebanon, in 1983.

Syria under Assad has long been accused of sponsoring international terrorism, notably in support of Palestinian, Libyan, and Iranian causes. Relations with the West improved during the Gulf War (1991), when Syria sided with U.S.–led coalition forces against Iraq. The collapse of the Soviet Union (1991) forced Assad to accept a greater degree of Western influence. Syria's heavy military expenditures contributed to growing economic troubles in the 1990s.

In 1991 Syria joined in peace negotiations with Israel, but progress was slow, and peace talks were suspended in 1995. Syria has insisted on return of the Golan Heights as a condition for peace with Israel. In 2000, Assad died and was succeeded by his son Bashar al-Assad.

Syria: 20th-Century Leaders

President

1944–49: Shukri el-Kuwatli (1891–1967)

1949: Husni Zaim (1897–1949)

1949: Sami Hinnawi (1898–1950)

1949–51: Hashim el-Atassi (1875–1960)

1951–53: Fawzi Silo

1953–54: Abid es-Shishakli (1909–64)

1954–55: Hashim el-Atassi

1955–58: Shukri el-Kuwatli

(Syria part of United Arab Republic 1958–61)

1961–62: Nazim el-Kudsi

1962: Abdul Karim Zahreddin

1962-63: Nazim el-Kudsi

1963: Louai Atassi

1963-66: Amin al-Hafiz

1966–70: Nureddin el-Atassi (1929–92)

1970–71: Ahmed al-Khatib

1971–2000: Hafiz al-Assad (1928–2000)

Prime Minister

1943–46: Saadullah el-Jabri (1893–1947)

1946–48: Jamil Mardam (1888–1960)

1948–49: Khaled el-Azam (1903–65)

1949: Mushin Barazi (1893–1949)

1949: Hashim el-Atassi

1949: Nazim el-Kudsi

1949–50: Khaled el-Azam

1950–51: Nazim el-Kudsi

1951: Khaled el-Azam

1951: Hassan Hakin

1951: Maruf ed-Dawalibi

1951–53: Fawzi Silo

1953–54: Abid es-Shishakli

1954: Sabri el-Assali

1954: Said el-Ghazzi

1954–55: Faris el-Khouri

1955: Sabri el-Assali

1955–56: Said el-Ghazzi

1956–58: Sabri el-Assali

1961: Mahmoun el-Kuzbari

1961: Izzat al-Nus

1961–62: Maruf ed-Dawalibi

1962: Abdul Karim Zahreddin

1962: Bashir al-Azmah

1962–63: Khaled el-Azam

1963: Salah al-Din Bitar (1912–80)

1963–64: Amin al-Hafiz

1964: Salah al-Din Bitar

1964-65: Amin al-Hafiz

1965: Youssef Zouayen

1965-66: Salah al-Din Bitar

1966-68: Youssef Zouayen

1968-70: Nureddin el-Atassi

1970-71: Hafiz al-Assad

1971-72: Abdul Rahman Khleyfawi

1972-76: Mahmoud Ayoubi

1976-78: Abdul Rahman Khleyfawi

1978–80: Mohammed Ali al-Halabi (1937–)

1980–87: Abdul Rauf al-Kassem (1937–)

1987– : Mahmoud Zoubi (1938–)

Taiwan

Official name: Republic of China

Location: Island of Taiwan and several small islands in Pacific Ocean off Asian mainland; Formose Strait (W) separates it from China

Capital: Taipei

Area: 13, 892 sq. mi. (35,980 sq. km.)

Population: (est. 1998): 21,908,135

Languages: Mandarin Chinese (official), Taiwanese and Hakka dialects

Government: Republic

Religions: Buddhist, Taoist, Confucian (total 93%), Christian 4.5%

Monetary unit: New Taiwan dollar

Main exports: Electrical equipment and machinery, textiles, basic metals and metal products

Taiwan, or Formosa, was inhabited by aborigines of Malayan descent until the 17th century, when China took possession of the island and large-scale Chinese immigration began. After the Sino-Japanese War (1894–95) Taiwan was ceded to Japan, which developed the island's economy and infrastructure. Japan suppressed the island's Chinese customs and ended fighting among factional warlords. At the end of the World War II Taiwan was returned to China. In December 1949, when Chiang Kai-shek's Guomindang (Nationalist) government was overthrown by the Communists in the Chinese Civil War, Chiang and about two million followers fled to Taiwan. There they reestablished the Republic of China, which purported to be the legitimate government of all China. On the mainland, the People's Republic of China regarded Taiwan as a breakaway province. Chiang hoped for the reconquest of China, but the U.S. made clear that it would not assist him in that venture, though it would defend Taiwan against Communist attack. On several occasions U.S. forces intervened to protect the Taiwanese islands of Quemoy and Matsu from assault by mainland China.

As president and head of the Guomindang Party until his death in 1975, Chiang ruled autocratically. With foreign investment and U.S. military and economic assistance, Chiang industrialized the country and developed a strong economy based on export of manufactured goods. In 1971 Taiwan lost its UN seat representing all of China; the People's Republic took the seat instead. In 1979 the U.S. opened diplomatic relations with the People's Republic, though nominally nongovernmental relations were maintained with Taiwan.

Economic growth continued under Chiang's son Chiang Ching-kuo (premier 1972–78, president 1978–88). Chiang liberalized the government somewhat, introducing more ethnic Taiwanese, who constitute 84 percent of the population, to positions of authority and attacking corruption. Competitive national elections were introduced in 1980 and 1983. In the 1990s a two-party system emerged: the opposition Democratic Progressive Party won the 1994 local elections.

In 1996 Taiwan held its first free presidential election, despite military intimidation from the People's Republic. Incumbent Guomindang president Lee Teng-hui was reelected. With Taiwan advocating a separate UN seat for itself, while the People's Republic advocates reunification, the question of Taiwan's future status remains open. In 1999 President Lee Teng-hui stated that he advocated state-to-state relations with mainland China, a move that produced open hostility from the People's Republic.

Taiwan: 20th-Century Leaders

President

1949–50: Li Tsung-jen (1890–1969)

1950–75: Chiang Kai-shek

1975–78: Yen Chia-kan (1905–93)

1978–88: Chiang Ching-kuo (1910–88)

1988–2000: Lee Teng-hui (1923–)

Premier

1949–50:Yen Hsi-shan (1883–1960)

1950–54: Chen Cheng (1898–1964)

1954–58: O. K.Yui (1896–1960)

1958–63: Chen Cheng

1963–72:Yen Chia-kan

1972–78: Chiang Ching-kuo

1978–84: SunYun-suan

1984–89:Yu Kuo-hwa

1989–90: Lee Huan

1990–93: Hau Pei-Tsun

1993–97: Lien Chan

1997–2000:Vincent Siew

Tajikistan

Official name: Republic of Tajikistan

Location: Southeast central Asia; bordered by Kyrgystan (NE), China (E), Afghanistan (S, SW), Uzbekistan (NW, N)

Capital: Dushanbe (formerly Stalinabad, 1929–61)

Area: 55,251 sq. mi. (143,100 sq. km.)

Population (est. 1997): 5,945,903

Languages:Tajik (official), Russian

Government: Republic

Religions: Sunni Muslim 80%, Shi'a Muslim 5%

Monetary unit:Tajikistani ruble

Main exports: Aluminum, cotton, fruits, vegetable oils, textiles

The mountainous, earthquake-prone region now known as Tajikistan was originally inhabited by the Tajiks, a non-nomadic Persian-speaking people. It became a sovereign of the Russian Empire in 1868 and was incorporated into the Turkestan Autonomous Soviet Socialist Republic in 1918. It was named Tadzhikistan in the 1920s, and as the Tajik A.S.S.R., it became part of the Uzbek Soviet Socialist Republic in 1924. In 1929 it was named a discrete Soviet Republic, the Tajik S.S.R.

In the 1930s Soviet rule brought bitterly fought attempts at collectivization. Economic progress was limited, and Tajikistan continues to maintain one of the region's lowest standards of living. Ethnic tensions between Tajikistan and Uzbekistan continued, including a border conflict in 1989.

Tajikistan declared itself a sovereign state in August 1990. In 1991, after the failure of the government-supported coup against Mikhail Gorbachev, pro-democracy groups forced the resignation of President Kadreddin A. Aslonov. Tajikistan became an independent republic after the breakup of the Soviet Union on December 25, 1991. Its first president was former Soviet Central Committee Chairman Rakhman Nabiyev. Tajikistan joined the Commonwealth of Independent States in December 1991.

In 1992 following a near civil war, Nabiyev ceded partial governmental power to Islamic fundamentalist and anti-Communist groups. In September Nabiyev resigned the presidency. Imomali Rakhmonov was elected president in November 1992; seven days afterward, presidential rule was abolished (November 20, 1992). Rakhmonov continued to head the country as chairman of the National Assembly and acting president.

In 1994 a new constitution was approved and Rakhmonov was elected president. Civil wars between Islamic rebels and the ex-Communist government have continued since 1994. In a referendum in 1999, voters approved constitutional changes, including legalization of Islamic political parties.

Tajikistan: 20th-Century Leaders

President

1991–92: Rakhman Nabiyev (1930–93)

1992: Akbar Shah Iskandrov

1992– : Imomali Rakhmonov (1952–)

Prime Minister

1993–94: Abdujhalil Samadov

1994–96: Jamshed Karimov

1996–99: Yakhyo Azimov

1999– : Akil Akilov (1944–)

Tanganyika See Tanzania.

Tanzania

Official name: United Republic of Tanzania

Location: East Africa; country of Tanganyika on eastern coast of Africa, islands of Zanzibar and Pemba in Indian Ocean 23 mi. (38 km.) from Tanganyika coast

Capital: Dar es Salaam

Area: 364,900 sq. mi. (942,799 sq. km.)

Population (est. 1997): 29,460,753

Languages: Swahili and English (both official)

Government: Republic

Religions: Tanganyika—Christian 45%, Muslim 35%, indigenous beliefs 20%; Zanzibar—almost completely Muslim

Monetary unit: Tanzanian shilling

Main exports: Coffee, cotton, sisal, cashew nuts, tobacco, cloves

Tanzania comprises the African mainland region of Tanganyika and the island of Zanzibar. It includes three of Africa's greatest lakes—Lakes Nyasa, Tanganyika, and Victoria—and its tallest mountain, Mount Kilimanjaro. Tanganyika was under the control of the sultan of Oman until 1885, when it (along with modern-day Burundi and Rwanda) became part of the colony of German East Africa. After World War I it became a British trusteeship under the United Nations and British mandate under the League of Nations. Zanzibar was controlled by Oman until 1861 and became a British protectorate in 1890.

On December 19, 1961, Tanzania gained independence from Great Britain. Zanzibar gained independence from Great Britain on December 19, 1963, and became a republic in 1964. The union of the two countries created the United Republic of Tanganyika on April 26, 1964. It was renamed Tanzania within the year.

In late 1978 Tanzania was invaded by Ugandan troops, prompting a war that lasted until 1980. The 1980s were marked by the continued rule of the Tanganyika African National Union under Presidents Julius Nyerere until 1985, and Ali Hassan Mwinyi afterward. Mwinyi's tenure was marked by his plans to move the country to a multiparty democracy. He ruled until 1995, when he was replaced by Benjamin Mkapa, who had won that year's first-ever multiparty elections.

In 1998 a bomb at the U.S. Embassy in Dar es Salaam killed 11 people and injured at least 70.

Tanzania: 20th-Century Leaders

Governor–General

1961–62: Sir Richard Turnbull

President

1964–85: Julius Kambarage Nyerere (1922–99)

1985–95: Ali Hassan Mwinyi

1995– : Benjamin William Mkapa (1938–)

Prime Minister

1960–61: Julius Nyerere (chief minister)

1962: Rashidi Kawawa

1972–77: Rashidi Kawawa

1977–80: Edward Sokoine (1938–84)

1980–83: Cleopa David Msuya

1983–84: Edward Sokoine

1984–85: Salim Ahmed Salim (1942–)

1985–90: Joseph Sinde Warioba (1940–)

1990–94: John Malecela (1934–)

1994–95: Cleopa Msuya

1995– : Frederick Tluway Sumaye (1950–)

Tanganyika: 20th-Century Leaders

President

1962–64: Julius Kambarage Nyerere

Zanzibar: 20th-Century Leaders

Sultan

1963–64: Seyyid Jamshid bin Abdullah bin Khalifa (deposed)

President

1964: Abeid Amani Karume

Thailand

Official name: Kingdom of Thailand

Location: Southeast Asia; bordered by Myanmar (W, N), Laos (NE), Cambodia and Gulf of Thailand (E), Malaysia (S), Andaman Sea (SW)

Capital: Bangkok

Area: 198,456 sq. mi (524,000 sq. km.)

Population (est. 1997): 59,450,818

Languages: Thai, English, ethnic and regional dialects

Government: Constitutional monarchy

Religions: Buddhist 95.5%, Muslim 4%, other 0.5%

Monetary unit: Baht

Main exports: Manufactured goods, agricultural and fishery products, raw materials

Thailand, formerly known as Siam, was settled by emigrants from southern China beginning in the sixth century. Unlike other Southeast Asian countries in the 19th century, it was never made a European colony but remained independent under an agreement with Britain and France in 1894. The agreement and other modernizing social policy resulted from the 60-year reign (1851–1910) of King Mongkut and his son King Chulalongkorn.

The absolute monarchy of Siam ceased in 1932, when a coup resulted in the establishment of a representative government with universal suffrage. Siam was renamed the Kingdom of Thailand in 1939.

From 1941 to 1944 Japanese troops occupied the country, making it a center for its Malaya campaign. After the Japanese surrender, Thailand rescinded its declaration of war against Britain and the U.S.

During the 1960s Thailand fought guerrilla Communist invaders from the north, its military supported in part by the U.S. The U.S. also funded Thai troops sent to Vietnam during the Vietnam War. After the war Thailand requested that the U.S. remove its long-lived military presence, which it did in the mid-1970s.

A bloody coup in 1976 ended Thai civilian government and instated military rule. By 1980 limited political freedom was granted, and by 1986 a coalition government was brought to power. The early 1980s were marked by battles with invading Vietnamese forces loyal to former Cambodian Prime Minister Pol Pot and the growing presence of hundreds of thousands of refugees from Laos, Cambodia, and Vietnam.

Military coups in 1981 and 1985 failed to unseat Prime Minister Prem Tinsulanonda. Another military coup in 1991 succeeded in ousting the democratically chosen prime minister, General Chatichai Choonhavan, and declaring martial law. Following public demonstration and the intervention of the king, a reform democratic government led by Chuan Leekpai was elected in 1992. Over the next three years, the government helped foster economic growth and approved pro-democracy constitutional changes. In 1995 elections Banharn Silpaarcha became prime minister of another coalition government. In elections the following year, General Chavalit Yongchaiyudh led a multiparty coalition, becoming prime minister. In 1997 economic instability forced Thailand to seek international loans from the U.S. and IMF. A new constitution received legislative approval in 1997.

Since the 1990s Thailand has faced a major health threat with serious growth in AIDS cases.

Thailand: 20th-Century Leaders

King

1868–1910: Chulaongkorn (1853–1910)

1910–25: Mongkut Klao (1881–1925)

1925–35: Prajadhipok (1893–1941)

1935–46: Ananda Mahidol (1925–46)

1946– : Bhumibol Adulyadej

Prime Minister

1944–45: Khuang Aphaiwong (1902–68)

1945: Thawi Bunyaket

1945–46: Seni Pramoij

1946: Khuang Aphaiwong

1946: Pridi Phanomyong (1900–83)

1946–47: Luang Dhamrong Nawasawat

1947–48: Khuang Aphaiwong

1948–57: Luang Pibul Songgram

1957: Pote Sarasin

1957–58: Thanon Kittakachorn

1958–63: Sarit Thanarat (1908–63)

1963–73: Thanon Kittakachorn

1973–75: Sanya Dharmasakti

1975: Seni Pramoj

1975–76: Kukrit Pramoj

1976: Seni Pramoj

1976–80: Sangad Chaloryu (1915–80)

1976–77: Thanin Kraivichien

1977–80: Kriangsak Chomanand

1980–88: Prem Tinsulanonda

1988–91: Chatichai Choonhavan

1991–92: Anand Punyarachun (1932–)

1992: Suchinda Kraprayoon (1938–)

1992: Anand Punyarachun

1992–95: Chuan Leekpai (1938–)

1995–96: Banharn Silpa–archa

1996–97: Chavalit Yongchaiyudh

1997– : Chuan Leekpai

Togo

Official name: Republic of Togo

Location: Western Africa; bordered by Burkina Faso (N), Benin (E), Gulf of Guinea (S), Ghana (W)

Capital: Lomé

Area: 21,927 sq. mi. (56,790 sq. km.)

Population (est. 1997): 4,735,610

Languages: French (official), Ewe, Mina, Dagomba, Kabyé

Government: Republic under transition to multiparty democratic rule

Religions: Indigenous beliefs 70%, Christian 20%, Muslim 10%

Monetary unit: Communauté Financère Africane (CFA) franc

Main exports: Phosphates, cotton, cocoa, coffee

Peopled by Ewe-speaking immigrants in the 14th century, Togo was explored by the

Portuguese, who developed it into a port of slave trade from the 16th to the 18th century. In 1884 Germans declared it a protectorate, Togoland.

Under a United Nations mandate after World War I, Togo was divided among England and France, with England administering the western third from Ghana and France the eastern two-thirds. After World War II, in 1946, Togo was named a United Nations trusteeship. In 1956 British Togoland was incorporated into Ghana. That year France named French Togo an autonomous republic, but with government functions remaining under French control. Following the election of self-rule proponents in Togo's 1958 elections, the country was granted independence as the Republic of Togo on April 27, 1960.

External friction with Ghana and internal conflict among more prosperous groups in the south and poorer ones in the north marked much of the republic's tumultuous first decade. Togo's first president, Sylvanus Olympio, was assassinated in 1963. A coup brought in successor Nicolas Grunitzky, who effected a new constitution granting more political freedom. But in 1967 another coup brought in Lieutenant Colonel Gnassingbe Eyadema, whose self-serving, unrealistic public spending led to massive public debt. In the 1990s Eyadema bowed to popular pressure for democratization and accepted reduced powers as president; multiparty elections were held to select a prime minister with executive powers. In 1994 parliamentary elections unseated Eyadema's ruling party, the Rassemblement du Peuple Togolais, replacing them with opposition party Union Togolais representatives, and a new prime minister.

Togo: 20th-Century Leaders

President

1960–63: Sylvanus Olympio (1902–63)

1963–67: Nicolas Grunitzky (1913–69)

1967: Kléber Dadjo

1967– : Gnassingbé Eyadéma (1937–)

Prime Minister

1991–94: Joseph Kokou Koffigoh (1948–)

1994–96: Edem Kodjo

1996–99: Kwassi Klutse

1999–2000: Eugene Koffi Adoboli

Tonga

Official name: Kingdom of Tonga

Location: South Pacific Ocean; group of 150 islands, of which 36 are inhabited; neighbors include Fiji Islands (W)

Capital: Nuku'alofa

Area: 290 sq. mi. (751 sq. km.)

Population (est. 1996): 106,466

Languages: Tongan, English

Government: Constitutional monarchy

Religions: Christian (including Free Wesleyan Church)

Monetary unit: Pa'anga

Main exports: Corn, coconut products, bananas, other fruits, vegetables, fish, vanilla

Also called the Friendly Islands, Tonga was founded in 1831 by Taufa'ahau Tupou (a.k.a. George I) and entered the 20th century governed by his great grandson George II. A friendship agreement with Great Britain in 1900 made it a British-protected state. Tonga gained independence on June 4, 1970.

In 1992 factions worked to form a political party not aligned with the hereditary nobility, and in 1995 elections six parliamentary seats went to pro-democracy candidates. Issues of democratization and the power of the monarchy dominated political discourse during the 1990s.

Tonga: 20th-Century Leaders

King or Queen

1893–1918: George Tupou II (d. 1918)

1918–65: Queen Salote Tupou III (1900–65)

1965– : Taufa'ahau Tupou IV (1918–)

Prime Minister

1970–91: Prince Fatafehi Tu'ipelchake (1922–)

1991–2000: baron Vaea

Trinidad and Tobago

Official name: Republic of Trinidad and Tobago

Location: Two islands in southwestern Caribbean Sea; off the coast of Venezuela

Capital: Port of Spain

Area: 1,981 sq. mi. (5,130 sq. km.)

Population: 1,130,337

Languages: English (official)

Government: Parliamentary democracy

Religions: Roman Catholic 32.2%, Hindu 24.3%, Anglican 14.4%, other Protestant 14%, Muslim 6%, unknown 9.1%

Monetary unit: Trinidad and Tobago dollar

Main exports: Petroleum and petroleum products, chemicals, steel products, fertilizer, sugar, cocoa

Trinidad was discovered by Christopher Columbus in 1498 and became a Spanish possession until 1797, when it was granted to Britain. The British claimed possession of nearby island Tobago in 1802, and since 1888 Trinidad and Tobago have been administered jointly as a colony.

In the 20th century the island state worked toward independence from the British. From 1958 to 1962 Trinidad and Tobago was a member of the West Indian Federation. It became an independent state and part of the British Commonwealth on August 31, 1962. Elected Trinidad's first prime minister was then-Chief Minister Eric Williams, who also developed the country's first political party. On August 31, 1976, Trinidad and Tobago became a republic, under the leadership of a president.

For 25 years (1956–81) the social democratic People's National Movement controlled the government. After a short period of control by the National Alliance for Reconstruction, it regained power in the 1991 elections, naming Patrick Manning as prime minister. The decade marked by government decontrol, the freeing of industry and currency in the marketplace, and the growing political presence of Islamic fundamentalist groups.

Trinidad and Tobago: 20th-Century Leaders

Governor–General

1962–72: Sir Solomon Hochoy (1905–83)

1972–87: Sir Ellis Emmanuel Innocent Clarke (1917–)

President

1987–97: Noor Mohammad Hassanali

1997– : Arthur Napoleon Robinson (1926–)

Chief Minister

1956–62: Eric Eustace Williams (1911–81)

Prime Minister

1962–81: Eric Eustace Williams

1981–86: George Chambers

1986–91: Arthur Napoleon Robinson

1991–95: Patrick Manning (1946–)

1995– : Basdeo Panday (1933–)

Tunisia

Official name: Republic of Tunisia

Location: North Africa; bordered by Mediterranean Sea (N, E), Libya (S), Algeria (W)

Capital: Tunis

Area: 63,170 sq. mi. (163,610 sq. km.)

Population (est. 1996): 9,019,687

Languages: Arabic, French

Government: Republic

Religions: Muslim 98%, Christian 1%, Jewish less than 1%

Monetary unit: Tunisian dinar

Main exports: Textiles, crude oil, olive oil, phosphoric acid, chemical fertilizers. triple super-phosphate, fish, dates

Settled by the Phoenicians around 1000 B.C., Tunisia became an Islamic cultural center in the early Middle Ages and was part of the Ottoman Empire from 1574. By the late 19th century (1881) it was under French occupation, and entered the 20th century a French protectorate. During World War II, Tunisia was under Vichy rule and became an important battle site in 1942 and 1943. After the war France reclaimed power over Tunisia. However, the nationalist movement originating in the early 20th-Century gained strength, generated national unrest, and by 1955 forced the French to grant self-rule. In 1957 Tunisia gained independence and sovereignty. That year the Constituent Assembly unseated the bey and the Neo-Destour, or New Constitution Party, took power, electing Habib Bourguiba as president.

Throughout Bourguiba's 30-year rule he maintained strong pro-Western ties. His foreign policy generated some internal opposition, which was in part responsible for his removal by Prime Minister General Zine Ben Ali in 1987. Employing stringent voter qualifications that prohibited multiple-party listings, he ran unopposed in 1994 elections. His political dominance has been threatened by Muslim fundamentalist groups, which the government has attempted to control through repression and censorship.

In 1995 Tunisia signed an Association Agreement with the EU, making Tunisia part of a free-trade area called the European Economic Area.

Tunisia: 20th-Century Leaders

President

1943–57: Muhammad VIII El-Amin (1881–1962) (bey)

1957–87: Habib Ben Ali Bourguiba

1987– : Zine al-Abidine Ben Ali (1936–)

Prime Minister

1954–56: Tahar Ben Ammar

1956–57: Habib Ben Ali Bourguiba

1969–70: Bahi Ladgham

1970–80: Hedi Nouira (1911–93)

1980–86: Mohammed Mzali

1986–87: Rachid Sfar

1987: Zine al-Abidine Ben Ali

1987–89: Hedi Baccouchi

1989–99 : Hamed Karoui

1999– : Mohammed Ghannouchi (1941–)

Turkey

Official name: Republic of Turkey

Location: Southeastern Europe and western Asia; bordered by Black Sea (N), Georgia, Armenia (NE), Iran (E), Iraq, Syria, Mediterranean Sea (S), Aegean Sea, Greece (W), Bulgaria (NW)

Capital: Ankara

Area: 301,382 sq. mi. (780,580 sq. km.)

Population (est. 1997): 64,566,511

Languages: Turkish (official), Kurdish, Arabic

Government: Republic

Religions: Muslim (mostly Sunni) 99.8%

Monetary unit: Lira

Main exports: Textiles and apparel, steel products, foodstuffs

The predecessor of modern Turkey was the Ottoman Empire, an Islamic state that acquired vast territories in southeastern Europe, the Middle East, and North Africa from the 14th to 16th centuries. By the beginning of the 20th century, the Ottoman Empire had long been in decline; with much of its empire dismantled or weakened, it was known as the "Sick Man of Europe." The autocratic rule of Sultan Abdulhamid II (reigned 1876–1909) was opposed by the Young Turks, who forced him, in a 1908 revolt, to recognize constitutional limits on his power and ousted him in 1909, replacing him with Sultan Muhammad V. After the Balkan Wars (1912–13), in which the empire lost most of its European possessions, Young Turk leader Enver Pasha seized power in a coup. He led the empire into World War I (1914–18), which it lost as one of the Central Powers. In the Treaty of Sèvres (1920) the Ottoman Empire's non-Turkish possessions were stripped away, including what are now the Arab countries of the Middle East, and the Ottoman state was reduced to a small piece of northern Anatolia. An independent republic of Armenia was created and Kurdistan gained autonomy.

Mustafa Kemal (later known as Kemal Atatürk), a former Young Turk, rallied opposition to the Treaty of Sèvres, which was never ratified by the Ottoman Parliament. In the Greco-Turkish War (1921–22) he successfully drove back Greek occupation forces. As head of the Grand National Assembly (from 1920), he abolished the sultanate (1922) and negotiated the Lausanne Treaty of 1923, which established Turkey's borders approximately as they exist today. Kurdish autonomy and Armenian independence ended as those regions were incorporated into Turkey. Other regions, including Cyprus and what are now the Arab countries, were conceded to be lost. The Dardanelles and Bosporus were demilitarized and placed under international control until 1936, when Turkey regained control.

From its creation in 1923 to his death in 1938, Kemal was president of the Republic of Turkey. He expelled the last caliph, titular head of Islam, in 1924, making Turkey a secular state. He established a parliamentary government, though with one party that supported his authoritarian tendencies. He strove to Westernize the country, introducing European-style law codes, state schools, woman suffrage (1934), and a ban on the veil and fez, two symbols of Ottoman rule. He developed the country's industrial base, largely through state-owned industries, and developed friendly relations with neighbors.

Turkey was neutral during most of World War II, but declared war on the Axis Powers in 1945, and was a founding member of the UN. As the cold war developed, Turkey aligned itself with the West, receiving substantial U.S. aid, joining NATO, and allowing the establishment of U.S. military bases in Turkey. Kemal's successor as president, Ismet Inönü (1938–50), established a multiparty system; his own party, the Republican People's Party, lost the 1950 elections to the right-wing Democratic Party. As Democratic prime minister, Adnan Menderes (1950–60) liberalized the economy; an economic crisis and discontent with his repressive rule led to a military coup in 1960. A junta took power and tried and executed Menderes.

A new constitution, approved in 1961, established a second Turkish republic. In the 1960s politics became increasingly polarized between left and right, with Islamic fundamentalist and Kurdish separatist movements emerging. Military rule was instituted from 1971 to 1973. In 1974 Turkey invaded and occupied the northern 40 percent of Cyprus in response to a coup that increased Greek influence there. Though Turkey's action strained relations with the U.S., the northern sector of Cyprus, organized as a state in 1975, has remained under Turkish control.

Neither the Republican People's Party or the Justice Party (successor to the Democratic Party) were able to establish majority governments in the late 1970s, and economic conditions and civil unrest worsened. Following another coup in 1980, Turkey was under repressive military rule until 1987. Turkey was a member of the anti-Iraq coalition in the Gulf War (1991) and allowed the U.S. to use Turkish bases in that conflict.

In the 1980s and 1990s a Kurdish insurgency grew in strength. In 1995 Turkey invaded Iraq, seeking to end guerrilla raids by Kurds from Iraqi territory. In 1999, Turkey captured Kurdish rebel leader Abdullah Öcalan and sentenced him to death. His organization announced that it would end its insurgency.

In the early 1990s the conservative True Path Party, the successor to the Justice Party, dominated government. Turkey's first woman prime minister, Tansu Ciller (1993–95), came from that party. Corruption scandals brought her government down; in the 1995 elections that followed, the pro-Islamic Welfare Party won the largest share of the vote. Several short-lived coalition governments followed; other parties, committed to Turkish secularism, were loath to form a government with an Islamic party. In 1996 Welfare leader Necmettim Erbakan became prime minister, heading Turkey's first openly pro-Islamic government. In 1997 he was forced from office under pressure from the military and succeeded by Mesut Yilmaz. Yilmaz sought to outlaw the Islamic Refah Party on the grounds that it was unconstitutional; the Constitutional Court ruled in favor of the government in 1998.

Turkey: 20th-Century Leaders

Ottoman Empire

Sultan

1876–1909: Abdulhamid II (1842–1918)

1909–18: Muhammad V (1844–1918)

1918–22: Muhammad VI (1861–1926)

(sultanate abolished)

Republic of Turkey

President

1923–38: Kemal Atatürk

1938–50: Ismet Inönü (1884–1973)

1950–60: Celal Bayar (1884–1986)

1960–66: Cemal Gürsel (1895–1966)

1966–73: Cevdet Sunay (1900–82)

1973–80: Fahri Korutürk (1903–87)

1980: Ihsan Sabri Caglayangil (acting)

1980–89: Kenan Evren

1989–93: Turgut Ozal (1927–93)

1993: Husamettin Cindoruk (acting)

1993–2000: Süleyman Demirel (1924–)

Prime Minister

(since new constitution in 1982)

1980–83: Bülent Ulusu

1983–89: Turgut Ozal

1989–91: Yildirim Akbulut (1935–)

1991: Mesut Yilmaz (1947–)

1991–93: Süleyman Demirel

1993: Erdal Inonu (acting)

1993–95: Tansu Ciller

1996: Mesut Yilmaz

1996–97: Necmettin Erbakan

1997–98: Mesut Yilmaz

1998– : Bülent Ecevit

Turkmenistan

Official name: Republic of Turkmenistan

Location: Central Asia; bordered by Kazakhstan (N), Uzbekistan (N, E), Iran (S), Afghanistan (SE), Caspian Sea (W)

Capital: Ashkhabad

Area: 188,456 sq. mi. (488,100 sq. km.)

Population (est. 1994): 4,229,249

Languages: Turkmen (official), Russian, Uzbek

Government: Republic

Religions: Muslim 89%, Eastern Orthodox 9%, unknown 2%

Monetary unit: Turkmen manat

Main exports: Natural gas, petroleum products, cotton, textiles

This remote and rugged territory, 90 percent blanketed by the Black Sand (or Kara Kum) desert, was inhabited by Turkic tribes since the 10th century. During the 17th and 18th centuries the region was ruled by the Uzbek in the northern Turkmen territory and Persians in the south. After the battle of Gok Tepe with Russia in 1881, it became part of the Russian empire, and was incorporated into Russian Turkestan.

In 1918 the U.S.S.R. established the Turkestan Autonomous Soviet Socialist Republic (A.S.S.R.). Although a nationalist (and British-backed) attack overthrew the A.S.S.R., it was returned to Soviet power, becoming the Turkmen Soviet Socialist Republic in 1924.

For years thereafter, the U.S.S.R. forced collectivization on the nomadic Turkmen people, damaging their way of life. Purges removed intellectuals and scholars.

In 1990 the Turkmen language replaced Russian as the official language. Turkmenistan declared its independence on October 27, 1991, and officially became an independent republic after the disbanding of the Soviet Union on December 25, 1991. In December 1991 it joined the Commonwealth of Independent States. Saparmurad A. Niyazov, who served as president of the Supreme Soviet from 1990, became Turkmenistan's first president.

His ties to the Communist Party assured the party's dominance in politics. National sentiment to democratize has been much more limited than in other former U.S.S.R. republics. In fact Niyazov's popularity has grown, with the leader receiving at least 95 percent of the vote in popular elections through the 1990s.

With plentiful oil and gas resources, Turkmenistan has been able to effect beneficial international ties, such as a 1996 rail link with Iran, and ongoing relations with Turkey.

Turkmenistan: 20th-Century Leaders

President

1990– : Saparmurad A. Niyazov (1940–)

Tuvalu

Location: South Pacific Ocean; group of nine atolls; neighbors include Kiribati (N), Fiji (S), Solomon Islands (W)

Capital: Funafuti

Area: 10 sq. mi. (26 sq. km.), scattered over 500,000 sq. mi.

Population (est. 1997): 10,297

Languages: Tuvaluan, English

Government: Independent state, special member of Commonwealth

Religions: Christian, mainly Protestant

Monetary unit: Tuvaluan dollar or Australian dollar

Main exports: Copra

The nine Polynesian islands now known as Tuvalu entered the 20th century a British protectorate (1892) and soon became part of the British Crown Colony of the Gilbert and Ellice Islands (1915). During World War II, some of the Ellice Islands were used as Allied bases in the Pacific theater.

In 1971 the Gilbert and Ellice Islands were granted self-rule. Acting on long-existing differences with the Gilbert Islanders, the Ellice Islands seceded from the colony in 1975. They were granted full independence as Tuvalu on September 30, 1978 (with the Gilbert Islands becoming Kiribati in 1979).

In 1979 the U.S. and Tuvalu signed a friendship agreement, permitting the U.S. to use their military airfields and removing U.S. claims on four Tuvalu islands.

Tuvalu: 20th-Century Leaders

Governor–General (representing the British monarch)

1978–86: Penitala Fiatau Teo

1986–90: Sir Tupua Leupena

1990–93: Sir Toaripi Lautti

1994: Tomu Sione

1994–98: Tulaga Manuella

1998– : Tomasi Puapua (1938–)

Prime Minister

1975–76: Toaripi Lautti (chief minister)

1976–81: Toaripi Lautti

1981–89: Tomasi Puapua

1989–93: Bikenibeu Paeniu (1956–)

1993–96: Kamuta Laatasi

1996–99: Bikenibeu Paeniu

1999– : Ionatana Ionatana

U.A.R. See **Egypt, Syria.**

U.K. See **United Kingdom.**

U.S. See **United States.**

U.S.S.R. See **Russia.**

Uganda

Official name: Republic of Uganda

Location: Eastern Africa; landlocked; bordered by Sudan (N), Kenya (E), Lake Victoria (SE), Tanzania (S), Rwanda (SW), Zaire (W)

Capital: Kampala

Area: 91,135 sq. mi. (236,040 sq. km.)

Population (est. 1997): 20,604,874

Languages: English (official), Luganda, Swahili, other Bantu and Nilotic languages

Government: Republic

Religions: Roman Catholic 33%, Protestant 33%, Muslim 16%, indigenous beliefs 18%

Monetary unit: Ugandan shilling

Main exports: Coffee, cotton, tea

The region of present-day Uganda became a British protectorate in 1894. British and Indian immigrants developed the colony's agriculture. During World War I Lake Victoria was the site of battles between Britain and Germany, which controlled Tanganyika (present-day Tanzania).

In 1955 the British established a local parliamentary government with some African ministers. Independence within the Commonwealth came on October 9, 1962. The new nation's traditional kingdoms at first retained local autonomy, but constitutional changes in the 1960s ended that system and made Uganda a republic (1967). Power instead was concentrated in the presidency, which was occupied from 1966 to 1971 and from 1980 to 1985 by Milton Obote, head of the Uganda People's Congress. Previously prime minister, Obote became president by deposing his predecessor Mutesa II, leader of the Buganda, Uganda's largest ethnic group.

Obote's Socialist regime was weakened by scandal, ethnic conflict, and economic difficulties. His army commander Idi Amin Dada overthrew him in a 1971 coup and ruled as dictator while Obote lived in exile in Tanzania. Though supported by the U.S. and Britain for his rejection of Socialism, Amin proved to be a cruel and corrupt despot who ruled by terror, devastated the economy, and incited anarchic violence. About 300,000 Ugandans are believed to have been tortured and killed during his presidency. He expelled Uganda's indigenous population and encouraged hatred of Jews and Asians. An Israeli commando raid at Entebbe in 1976 rescued more than 100 Jewish hostages captured in a skyjacking by Palestinian and German terrorists.

Seeking to establish a "Greater Uganda," Amin, with Libyan help, attacked Tanzania in 1978. The following year, Tanzanian forces invaded Uganda and captured Kampala, driving Amin into exile. In corrupt elections in 1980, Obote was restored to the presidency.

Obote turned away from Socialism, earning the support of the U.S. and Britain despite reported human rights offenses. Yoweri Kaguta Museveni waged civil war against Obote, who was deposed in 1985. After a period of near anarchy, Museveni took power as president the following year. In some regions of the country civil war continued, but Museveni succeeded in stirring economic growth and rising in popularity. A new constitution was enacted in 1995, continuing the existing ban on political parties until 2000. Museveni was confirmed as president in the 1996 elections.

Uganda: 20th-Century Leaders

President

1962–63: Sir Walter Coutts (1912–88)

1963–66: Sir Edward Mutesa II (1924–69)

1966–71: Apollo Milton Obote

1971–79: Idi Amin Dada

1979: Yusufu K. Lule (1912–85)

1979–80: Godfrey Binaisa

1980: Paulo Muwanga

1980–85: Apollo Milton Obote

1985–86: Tito Okello

1986– : Yoweri Museveni (1944–)

Prime Minister

1962–71: Apollo Milton Obote

(position abolished 1971–80)

1980–85: Erifasi Otemi Allimadi (1929–)

1985: Paulo Muwanga

1985–86: Abraham Waligo

1986–91: Samson Kisekka

1991–94: George Cosmas Adyebo (1947–)

1994–99: Kintu Musoke

1999– : Apollo Nsibambi (1938–)

Ukraine

Official name: Ukraine

Location: Southeastern Europe; bordered by Belarus (N), Russian Federation (E, NE), Hungary, Slovakia, and Poland (W), Romania and Moldova (SW), Baltic Sea and Sea of Azov (S)

Capital: Kyiv (Kiev)

Area: 233,000 sq. mi. (603,700 sq. km.)

Population (est. 1996): 50,864,009

Languages: Ukrainian

Government: Constitutional republic

Religions: Orthodox 76%, Ukrainian Catholic 13.5%, Jewish 2.3%, Baptist, Mennonite, Protestant, and Muslim 8.2%

Monetary unit: Karbovanets

Main exports: Coal, electric power, ferrous and nonferrous metals, chemicals, machinery and transportation equipment, grain and meat

Part of the Russian empire from the late 18th century, Ukraine declared independence on January 28, 1918, after the 1917 Russian Revolution. It was reoccupied by the Red Army, and after years of warfare, the Ukraine was recaptured and made a founding country of the United Soviet Socialist Republics in 1922. Famine and Soviet neglect and deportation resulted in the agricultural country's decimation. During two decades of Soviet rule in the 1920s and 1930s, seven million Ukrainians died.

In World War II Ukraine sustained severe damage. Millions of deaths occurred under the German occupation from 1941 to 1944. After the war it regained old territories and increased its size, adding Transcarpathia in 1946 and Crimea in 1954.

In 1986 the world's worst nuclear accident to date occurred at the nuclear power plant at Chernobyl. The attempted Soviet cover-up sparked the formation of a strong opposition movement, the Ukrainian People's Movement for Restructuring (Rukh). The accident, along with Soviet policies of *glasnost,* fueled Ukrainian nationalism, and on July 16, 1990, Ukraine declared sovereignty. On August 24, 1991, Ukraine announced its independence. In December 1991 Ukraine and 10 other former Soviet republics signed the Alma-Ata Declaration, making them part of the Commonwealth of Independent States.

In 1996 Ukraine approved a new constitution as well as provisions legalizing the ownership of private property and the establishment of Ukrainian as the country's sole official language. Following years of dispute over the Black Sea fleet and other matters, Ukraine and Russia signed a treaty of cooperation in 1997.

Ukraine: 20th-Century Leaders

President

1991–94: Leonid Kravchuk (1934–)

1994– : Leonid D. Kuchma (1938–)

Premier

1990–92: Vitold Fokin

1992: Valentyn Symonenko

1992–93: Leonid D. Kuchma

1993–94: Yukhim Zvyahilsky

1994–95: Vitaly Masol

1995–96: Yevhen Marchuk

1996–97: Pavlo Lazarenko

1997–99: Valery Pustovoytenko

1999– : Viktor Yushchenko (1954–)

Union of Soviet Socialist Republics See Russia.

United Arab Emirates

Location: Eastern Arabian peninsula; bordered by Persian Gulf (N), Gulf of Oman (NE), Oman (E), Saudi Arabia (S, W)

Capital: Abu Dhabi

Area: 29,182 sq. mi. (75,581 sq. km.)

Population (est. 1997): 2,262,309

Languages: Arabic (official), Hindi, Urdu, Farsi

Government: Federation with specified powers delegated to U.A.E. central government and other powers reserved to member emirates

Religions: Muslim 96%, Christian, Hindu, and others 4%

Monetary unit: Emirian dirham

Main exports: Crude oil, natural gas, re-exports, dried fish, dates

The seven sheikdoms on the Persian Gulf that now constitute the United Arab Emirates (Abu Dhabi, Ajman, Dubai, Fujairah, Ras al Khaimah, Sharjah, and Umm al Qaiwain) became British protectorates in the 1820s. The region was formerly known as the Pirate Coast and later the Trucial Oman, the Trucial Coast, or the Trucial Sheikdoms for its truce with Great Britain in the 19th century. From 1893 it received military protection from Great Britain.

In 1971 Great Britain removed military forces from the Persian Gulf. The seven sheikdoms then formed a federation and gained independence from the United Kingdom as the United Arab Emirates on December 2, 1971.

As the world's eighth largest oil producer, the United Arab Emirates enjoys one of the world's highest per capita incomes. Its economy is centered on petroleum. Threatened by Saddam Hussein in 1990, it was part of the anti-Iraq coalition during the Gulf War.

United Arab Emirates: 20th-Century Leaders

President

1971– : Sheikh Zayed bin Sultan al-Nahyan of Abu Dhabi (1918–)

Prime Minister

1971–79: Sheikh Maktum ibn Rashid al-Maktum (1943–)

1979–90: Sheikh Rashid ibn Said al-Maktum (1914–90)

1990– : Sheikh Maktum ibn Rashid al-Maktum

United Arab Republic See Egypt, Syria.

United Kingdom

Official name: United Kingdom of Great Britain and Northern Ireland

Location: northwestern Europe, occupying the major part of the British Isles; comprising Great Britain (England, Scotland, and Wales) and Northern Ireland; bordered by Atlantic Ocean (W, NW), North Sea (E), English Channel, separating it from France (S)

Capital: London

Area: 94,525 sq. mi. (244,820 sq. km.)

Population (est. 1998): 58,970,119

Languages: English, Welsh, Scottish form of Gaelic

Government: Constitutional monarchy

Religions: Anglican 47%, Roman Catholic 9%, other Christian (including Presbyterian and Methodist), Jewish, Muslim, Hindu

Monetary unit: British pound or pound sterling

Main exports: manufactured goods, machinery, fuels, chemicals, semifinished goods, transport equipment

Great Britain began the 20th century as the most powerful nation on earth, with an empire that encompassed about a quarter of the earth's territory and population. A constitutional monarchy whose royal line of succession could be traced to the ninth century, it was, by the late 19th century, preeminent in industry, commerce, finance, and naval strength. However, the seeds of British decline were already evident by 1900, with the U.S. and Germany both rising as industrial and military powers and nationalism dawning or growing in many of Britain's colonies. By century's end, two World Wars and an inexorable process of decolonization left Great Britain as a small, powerful, but no longer dominant nation.

As the 20th century began, Britain was engaged in the South African War (1899–1902), which it won only with heavy losses. The war extended British control over all of present-day South Africa, but the imperial gain proved short-lived: in 1907, South Africa, Australia, Canada, Newfoundland, and New Zealand were transformed into self-governing Dominions. Ireland, except for six northern provinces (Northern Ireland or Ulster), won the same status in 1922, following the Irish War of Independence or Anglo-Irish War (1919–21). Thereafter, the entity that had been the United Kingdom of Great Britain and Ireland became the United Kingdom of Great Britain and Northern Ireland. The Dominions gained effective independence as members of the Commonwealth of Nations in 1931.

In domestic politics in 1900, the Conservative Party was nearing the end of nearly two decades in power. Robert Gascoigne-Cecil, 3rd marquess of Salisbury (1830–1903), who served several times as prime minister (1885–86, 1886–92, 1895–1902), was succeeded in 1902 by his nephew and fellow Conservative Arthur James Balfour (1902–05). A split in the party over tariff reform, which would have given trade preference to British colonies and dominions, led to Balfour's resignation. The Liberal Party took power under Henry Campbell-Bannerman (1905–08) and Herbert Henry Asquith (1908–16). Asquith's government enacted social welfare legislation, including old-age pensions (1908) and unemployment insurance (1911), and abolished the veto power of the House of Lords through the Parliament Act of 1911.

Fearing the growth of German power, Britain formed the Triple Entente, an alliance with France and Russia, in 1907. As World War I began in 1914, Britain felt compelled to enter the war to defend France and Russia against Germany. British and other Allied forces engaged the Central Powers in Europe, the Middle East, Africa, and at sea. Early military setbacks led to Asquith's resignation in 1916; David Lloyd George, a Liberal leading a coalition cabinet (1916–22), helped turn the tide toward Allied victory. More than 900,000 British subjects throughout the empire lost their lives in the war and more than 2 million were wounded.

Lloyd George participated in the Paris Peace Conference (1919–20), where he served to moderate French demands for punitive measures against Germany. After the war, the British Empire reached its greatest extent, with Britain obtaining several German and Ottoman possessions as League of Nations mandates, including Tanganyika (Tanzania), Palestine, Transjordan (Jordan), and Iraq. But the war left Britain economically weak, and nationalist unrest was growing throughout its empire, particularly in India, where Mohandas Gandhi began leading *satyagraha*, or nonviolent resistance, campaigns against British rule in 1920.

In the 1920s the Liberal Party faded in importance relative to the more left-leaning Labour Party, which had been founded as the Labour Representation Committee in 1900. Emphasizing social welfare and workers' interests, the Labour Party became the principal opposition to the Conservative Party in the 1920s. Conservatives dominated Parliament for much of the 1920s and 1930s. Stanley Baldwin, prime minister three times (1923–24, 1924–29, 1935–37), broke a general strike in 1926 and won passage of the Trade Disputes Act (1927) limiting union power. His government extended suffrage to women over 21 (1928); women over 30 had already received it (1918). Baldwin remained influential in the coalition National government headed by James Ramsay MacDonald (1931–35). In 1936 Baldwin secured the abdication of King Edward VIII over his decision to marry a divorced American; Edward's brother succeeded him as George VI.

The worldwide Great Depression wracked the economy of Britain, which raised tariffs and abandoned the gold standard in 1935 in an effort to cope financially. In foreign affairs Conservative prime minister Neville Chamberlain (1937–40) hoped to avert war by pursuing a policy of appeasement toward the increasingly aggressive Fascist governments of

Germany and Italy. In 1939 German leader Adolf Hitler's invasion of Poland marked the start of World War II (1939–45) and brought an end to appeasement. Britain declared war on Germany and soon found itself under attack; German and British planes fought in the aerial Battle of Britain (1940), and Germany bombed British cities in the Blitz (1940–41). Prime Minister Winston Churchill (1940–45, 1951–55), a Conservative heading a wartime coalition government, rallied the British to fight doggedly. He forged an alliance with the U.S., embodied in the statement of war aims called the Atlantic Charter (1941), and participated in the Allied conferences at Tehran (1943), Yalta (1945), and Potsdam (1945). Under Churchill's leadership, Britain resisted a threatened (but never realized) German invasion and joined with other Allied forces in engaging the Axis Powers in North Africa, Europe, and the Pacific.

The war ended in Allied victory, but Britain suffered serious losses. More than 350,000 British troops died in battle; British cities lay in ruins; and Britain ceded its one–time status as preeminent world power to the U.S. and the Soviet Union, which emerged from the conflagration with the world's most powerful military. Britain accepted reconstruction aid from the U.S. through the Marshall Plan and accepted U.S. leadership of NATO, the Western military alliance founded in 1949.

Britain's overseas empire was quickly dismantled, with India and Pakistan becoming independent in 1947, followed in 1948 by Israel (formerly part of Palestine), Burma (Myanmar), and Sri Lanka. The 1956 Suez Crisis in Egypt demonstrated Britain's inability to impose its will on regions formerly under its hegemony. The 1960s saw many other British colonies gaining independence, among them Nigeria, Malaysia, and Jamaica, though a few—Zimbabwe, Belize, and Brunei—did not gain independence until the 1980s.

In domestic politics, the Labour government of Clement Attlee (1945–51) instituted a Socialist welfare state, with key industries nationalized and citizens entitled to free healthcare and comprehensive "national insurance." The Conservative governments that followed from 1951 to 1964—those of Churchill, Anthony Eden, Harold Macmillan, and Alexander Douglas-Home—accepted most of these changes. In 1964 Labour regained control of Parliament under Harold Wilson (1964–70, 1974–76); he and his Conservative successor Edward Heath (1970–74) struggled with high inflation and a powerful labor movement. Britain resisted European economic integration in the 1950s but finally joined the European Community in 1973.

The government of Labour prime minister Leonard James Callaghan (1976–79) was crippled by economic recession and an inability to overcome trade-union opposition to his austerity measures. His government fell to Margaret Thatcher, Britain's first woman prime minister (1979–90), who inaugurated 18 years of Conservative rule. Staunchly right-wing and determined to reduce inflation, she privatized state-owned industries, cut social programs, cut taxes, maintained high interest rates, and curtailed trade-union power. Though unemployment rose at first, inflation went down, and her decisive action to retrieve the Falkland Islands from Argentina in the Falklands War (1982) boosted her popularity. Her imposition of a poll tax, or flat-rate tax, was unpopular; in the midst of economic recession, she was replaced as prime minister by John Major (1990–97), who abolished the tax.

A revitalized Labour Party under centrist Tony Blair took back control of Parliament in 1997. Blair convinced his party to give up its commitment to nationalization and emphasize personal responsibility and law and order. Blair moved to reform the constitution to permit decentralization; Scotland and Wales elected in 1997 to form their own parliaments, for which elections were held in 1999. Blair also shepherded a 1998 peace agreement for Northern Ireland, though violence on both sides of that conflict has continued. Britain was a leader in the NATO air war against Yugoslavia in 1999.

Britain's queen since 1952 has been Elizabeth II. The personal lives of her family became tabloid fodder in the 1980s and 1990s, particularly the marriage and divorce of her son and heir apparent, Prince Charles, to Lady Diana Spencer, whose death in 1997 provoked a worldwide outpouring of grief.

A 99-year British lease of Hong Kong that began in 1898, when Britain was still at its height of imperial power, expired in 1997, at which time Hong Kong reverted from British to Chinese control. Britain's remaining dependencies are Anguilla, Bermuda, British Antarctic Territory, British Indian Ocean Territory, British Virgin Islands, Cayman Islands, Channel Islands, Falkland Islands and Dependencies, Gibraltar, Isle of Man, Montserrat, Pitcairn Island, Saint Helena, and Turks and Caicos Islands.

With a literary tradition that dates back to Shakespeare and Chaucer, Britain continued to produce esteemed works of literature in the 20th century. British writers of the century included Joseph Conrad, E. M. Forster, Virginia Woolf, Ford Madox Ford, H. G. Wells, W. H. Auden, and Kingsley Amis.

United Kingdom: 20th-Century Leaders

King or Queen

1837–1901: Victoria (1819–1901)

1901–10: Edward VII

1910–36: George V

1936: Edward VIII

1936–52: George VI

1952– : Elizabeth II

Prime Minister

1895–1902: Robert Gascoigne-Cecil, 3rd marquess of Salisbury (1830–1903)

1902–05: Arthur James Balfour

1905–08: Henry Campbell-Bannerman

1908–16: Herbert Henry Asquith

1916–22: David Lloyd George

1922–23: Andrew Bonar Law

1923–24: Stanley Baldwin

1924: Ramsay MacDonald

1924–29: Stanley Baldwin

1929–35: Ramsay MacDonald

1935–37: Stanley Baldwin

1937–40: Neville Chamberlain

1940–45: Winston Churchill

1945–51: Clement Attlee

1951–55: Winston Churchill

1955–57: Anthony Eden

1957–63: Harold Macmillan

1963–64: Alec Douglas–Home

1964–70: Harold Wilson

1970–74: Edward Heath

1974–76: Harold Wilson

1976–79: Leonard James Callaghan

1979–90: Margaret Thatcher

1990–97: John Major

1997– : Tony Blair

United States

Official name: United States of America

Location: North America; bordered by Canada (N), Atlantic Ocean (E), Mexico (S), Pacific Ocean (W)

Capital: Washington, D.C.

Area: 3,675,031 sq. mi. (9,372,610 sq. km.)

Population (est. 1998): 269,816,000

Languages: English (predominant), Spanish-speaking minority

Government: Federal republic

Religions: Protestant 61%, Roman Catholic 25%, Jewish 2%, other 5%, none 7%

Monetary unit: Dollar

Main exports: Machinery, chemicals, aircraft, military equipment, cereals, motor vehicles, grains

The country that would end the 20th century as the most powerful nation on earth began its history as a collection of 13 American colonies founded by Great Britain in the 17th and 18th centuries. The United States declared independence in 1776; Britain accepted independence in 1783, at the conclusion of the American Revolution. The Constitution that defines the nation's republican, federal system of government was adopted in 1789.

Despite a bloody Civil War (1861–65), the 19th century saw a rapid expansion in territory and population. The four decades that followed the Civil War were marked by internal rebuilding, western frontier settlement, and increasing immigration. As a consequence, the U.S. entered the 20th century growing in size, international stature, and social diversity.

In the Spanish-American War (1898), the U.S. acquired Guam, Puerto Rico, and the Philippines and won oversight of Cuba (Cuba and the Philippines later gained full independence, while Guam and Puerto Rico remain U.S. possessions.). In 1900 the U.S. was already an industrial power, producing 30 percent of the world's manufactured goods. By the mid-20th century, the U.S. would be considered the world's dominant democratic power, and by century's end the world's only superpower.

In September 1901 Republican president William McKinley was assassinated by anarchist Leon Czolgosz. McKinley was replaced by his vice president, Theodore Roosevelt, who moved the country into the Progressive era.

Considering the presidency a "bully pulpit," President Roosevelt introduced wide-ranging reforms concerning food and drug safety (the Pure Food and Drug Act, 1906); federal regulation of business (Hepburn Act); and conservation. He supported legislation to preserve national lands and create national parks. His trust-busting efforts included the Northern Securities Case, which led to the breakup of a dominant railroad trust held by American businessmen J. Pierpont Morgan and James Hill. His efforts reflected a national movement known as progressivism, which advocated public and private acts to improve society. After leaving office in 1909, Roosevelt ran for president on the Progressive Party ticket in 1912, but was defeated by Democrat Woodrow Wilson.

Internationally, the opening of the U.S.–built Panama Canal in 1914 allowed trade passage between the Atlantic and Pacific Oceans and ensured control of the region. (A 1978 U.S.–Panama agreement assigned control of the Canal to Panama in 2000.)

The U.S. was slow to enter World War I. President Wilson was reelected in 1916 (over Republican candidate Charles Evans Hughes) on a campaign reminder that he "kept us out of war," but massive German submarine warfare led him to request a declaration of war against the Central Powers in April 1917. After the war, in which the U.S. helped to lead the Allies to victory, the country returned to its pre-war isolationism, with Congress refusing to join the League of Nations, the international peacekeeping organization largely created by President Wilson.

Between 1900 and 1920 the U.S. admitted two states to its union: New Mexico and Arizona (1912). Women in the U.S. gained the right to vote in 1920, with the approval of the 19th Amendment to the Constitution.

The 18th Amendment to the Constitution, which prohibited the sale, manufacture, and transportation of alcoholic beverages, and the Volstead Act (1919), which was passed to enforce it, attempted public moral reform. Instead it spawned a criminal underground market for liquor, often controlled by gangsters such as Al Capone, who gained public notoriety and celebrity.

Republican Warren Harding was elected President in 1920, ushering in a decade of conservative leadership. Under Presidents Harding and Calvin Coolidge (1923–29) the country maintained an economic boom, based largely on stock speculation and consumer credit spending. It ended in October 1929, when the stock market collapsed, losing much of its value and triggering the Great Depression, a worldwide slide into unemployment, falling demand for goods, and decreased production. The U.S. experienced massive corporate bankruptcies and individual poverty; by 1930 the unemployment rate was 25 percent. Elected in 1928, Republican president Herbert Hoover claimed the economy would correct itself.

Promising a "New Deal for the American people," Democratic candidate Franklin Delano Roosevelt defeated Hoover and was elected president in 1932. Beginning in his first hundred days, he implemented major legislation (including a bank holiday and an end to Prohibition) and created dozens of federal agencies and programs to create hundreds of thousands of jobs and rebuild the economy (e.g., the National Recovery Administration, Works Progress Administration, Civilian Conservation Corps, and Public Works Administration). Social welfare programs included the national old-age payment program Social Security. His activism, combined with his skill at communicating, helped to revive national morale. He was reelected in 1936 (against Republican Alfred M. Landon), 1940 (against Republican Wendell Willkie), and 1944 (against Republican Thomas E. Dewey). In reaction to his election to an unprecedented four terms, a Constitutional amendment was later adopted limiting future U.S. presidents to two consecutive terms.

The effects of the Depression still lingered when the U.S. was attacked by Japanese troops at Pearl Harbor, Hawaii, on December 7, 1941. The U.S. declared war, joining Allied forces in the European and Pacific theaters. The immediate need for war material created a boom economy, finally ending the long economic downturn.

After multiple Axis victories in 1941 and 1942, U.S. forces in the Pacific won decisive naval battles in the Coral Sea and Midway that shifted dominance in the Pacific theater to the Allies. On June 6, 1944, Allied commander in chief General Dwight D. Eisenhower led forces in the Allied invasion of Normandy. By late 1944, Belgium and France were liberated, and after months of fighting in Germany, the Germans tendered unconditional surrender on May 7, 1945. In declining health for months, President Roosevelt died on April 12, 1945. Roosevelt was replaced by Vice President Harry S Truman.

Beginning in 1941 American scientists began the secret Manhattan Project to develop an atomic bomb. On August 6, 1945, President Truman authorized the release of the atomic bomb on Hiroshima, Japan. Another attack followed on August 9, 1945, in Nagasaki. Japan issued unconditional surrender on August 14, 1945.

The lasting effect of World War II was to establish the U.S. as the world's dominant democratic-capitalist power. Its power was reinforced by the U.S. postwar foreign aid program, the European Recovery Program (or Marshall Plan), which from 1948 to 1951 provided over $12 billion in reconstruction funds to war-damaged countries. At the same time, the U.S. maintained its military arsenal in cold war preparedness and followed the Truman Doctrine of support to countries resisting Communism.

Following this foreign policy of Communist containment, U.S. troops joined UN and South Korean forces in 1950 to fight Communist North Korean invaders. U.S. involvement in the conflict, known as the Korean War, lasted until 1953 when newly elected Republican president and former army chief of staff Dwight D. ("Ike") Eisenhower fulfilled a campaign promise to end the conflict and directed the completion of a cease-fire agreement in July 1953.

From the late 1940s through the early 1950s, domestic politics was dominated by the search for Communists within U.S. borders. Prominent examples were Americans Julius and Ethel Rosenberg, who were convicted of spying for and delivering nuclear secrets to the Soviet Union; they were executed on July 19, 1953. A more broad-based hunt for Communists began in the late 1940s with the public investigations of the House Un-American Activities Committee (HUAC), which led to widespread blacklisting of suspected subversives. U.S. senator Joseph McCarthy initiated public support for anti-Communist investigations when in 1950 he claimed proof of 205 State Department Communists or Communist sympathizers.

Judicial activism in the Supreme Court, along with the civil rights movement and presidential involvement, led to advances in civil rights, notably in ending legal racial segregation in the South. Under presidential orders, troops were sent to Little Rock, Arkansas, to effect a public school desegregation decision, *Brown v. Board of Education*, in 1957.

The U.S. enjoyed a strong economy throughout most of the 1950s and into the 1960s. The government-sponsored G.I. Bill and G.I. Loan programs permitted low-cost higher education and home purchases, resulting in a better educated, better paid populace. The 49th and 50th states were added to the union in 1959: Alaska and Hawaii.

In 1956 President Eisenhower was reelected easily (again over Democratic candidate Senator Adlai Stevenson). His vice president, Richard Nixon, was defeated in 1960 presidential elections by Democratic senator John Fitzgerald Kennedy, who at 43 became the youngest man to be elected U.S. president.

His platform, the "New Frontier," stressed federal involvement to effect tax reform, education funding, and civil rights. Citing the need for civic duty, he founded the Peace Corps in 1962. Yet the early 1960s in the U.S. were marked by international crises related to cold war U.S.–Communist tensions. They included the attempted Bay of Pigs Invasion of Cuba in 1961 and the Cuban Missile Crisis in 1962, in which he imposed a naval blockade on Cuba to force the removal of Soviet-built missiles. President Kennedy was assassinated on November 22, 1963, in Dallas, Texas. Suspected killer Lee Harvey Oswald was killed by U.S. businessman Jack Ruby on November 24, 1963. Sworn in as president was Vice President Lyndon Baines Johnson. Beginning in 1963 and continuing after his landslide reelection in 1964, he enacted a domestic policy known as the "Great Society," fulfilling many social reforms begun in the Kennedy years. Among them were a Medicare (health insurance) bill, the Civil Rights Act, and the Voting Rights Act of 1965.

In 1961 the U.S. sent its first troops to support the South Vietnamese government against Communist-led North Vietnamese guerrillas. U.S. troop involvement rose massively through the 1960s under President Johnson (reaching over 500,000 by 1969) as national support dwindled and debate about the ethics of U.S. involvement divided the country. War divisions split the Democratic Party, fostered a growing protest movement, and led President Johnson to decline to seek a second term. Compounding the domestic turmoil was the rise of a youth counterculture with radically different morals and beliefs from those of older Americans. The assassinations of civil rights leader Martin Luther King Jr., and leading Democratic candidate Robert Kennedy in 1968 fed the sense of growing chaos.

On a law-and-order platform, Republican candidate Richard Nixon was elected president in November 1968. As president, Nixon increased bombing of Vietnam and began a process of troop withdrawal. Promising "Peace with Honor," he was soundly reelected for a second term in 1972 against Democrat George McGovern. Following a cease-fire agreement in

1973, U.S. troops withdrew from Vietnam.

In 1972, the U.S. and China reestablished diplomatic relations, marked by President Nixon's groundbreaking visit to the country. Yet in July 1972 a break-in at Democratic Party headquarters in Washington, D.C., by operatives for the Nixon re-election campaign overshadowed and eventually ended Nixon's presidency. The Watergate Affair resulted in Senate hearings revealing a massive cover-up and political espionage. After three articles of impeachment were drawn against him, President Nixon resigned from office on August 9, 1974. Vice President Gerald Ford assumed the presidency and in September 1974 pardoned the former president.

The pardon, along with rising inflation and a recession brought about Ford's loss in the 1976 presidential elections. Democrat Jimmy Carter was meant to signal a clean slate for the presidency. Yet the prevailing national mood remained unsettled, eventually characterized by Carter as a "malaise." Compounding the unease domestically was high inflation of up to 16 percent per year, rising oil prices, and unsteady relations with oil-producing countries. The situation was crystallized by the November 4, 1979, invasion by Iranian militants of the U.S. Embassy and taking of 52 hostages. President Carter's inability to broker a release led in part to his defeat to former governor and Republican candidate Ronald Reagan in 1980. The hostages were released on January 20, 1981, coincident with President-elect Reagan's inauguration. In March 1981 Reagan was wounded in an assassination attempt but recovered fully.

Domestically, Reagan acted on promises of conservative reform by reducing taxes and social spending. Yet his commitment to countering the Soviet Union through a strong defense, hallmarked by the Strategic Defense Initiative, led to a massive increase in the federal deficit. An adept, direct communicator and welcome voice of national optimism, he was reelected by landslide in 1984.

His second term was marked by Congressional investigations of his involvement in the sale of U.S. arms to Iran and the transfer of profits to Nicaraguan "Contra" rebels. Transcending that scandal was his contribution to improved relations with Russia; the break-up of the Soviet Union that followed his presidency ended the decades-long cold war and left the U.S. the world's sole superpower. In 1988 Republican vice president George Bush was elected president. His acts of foreign policy, including the 1989 removal of Panamanian dictator Manuel Noriega and the 1991 U.S. role in the Gulf War liberation of Kuwait from Iraqi control, assured continued U.S. dominance. But domestically, he failed to reduce the U.S. deficit and raised taxes. The boom of the 1980s ended.

In November 1992 elections, the Democratic Party regained control of the White House when William Clinton defeated President Bush. During his first term, he pledged to "Put People First," with ambitious plans that included restructuring the health-care system. Deemed too complicated, they were aborted in a Republican-controlled Congress. Despite ongoing investigations of a real-estate deal, White House office dealings, and a sexual harassment claim, Clinton was reelected to a second term in 1996.

For much of his tenure, the country enjoyed a strong economy, bolstering his popularity. His policies included reducing the federal spending, which resulted in elimination of the deficit. He helped broker limited Mideast peace agreements between Israel and Palestine. Nonetheless, continuing investigations and Republican opposition weakened the Clinton presidency. In late 1998, following initial denial and eventual public disclosure of an "inappropriate" relationship with a White House intern, Monica Lewinsky, President Clinton was charged with four counts of impeachment. The Senate acquitted Clinton on all counts in 1999. His vice president, Al Gore, failed to prevail in a closely contested presidential election against Republican candidate George W. Bush in 2000. But Clinton's wife, Hillary Rodham Clinton, made headlines that year when she was elected to serve as U.S. Senator from New York, becoming the first First Lady to be elected to political office.

Throughout the century, the U.S. has been highly influential in the arts, particularly the popular arts. Notables include artists and photographers Georgia O'Keefe, Jackson Pollock, Walker Evans, and Robert Frank; writers Ernest Hemingway, F. Scott Fitzgerald, William Faulkner, Edith Wharton, Norman Mailer, and Toni Morrison; filmmakers John Ford, Orson Welles, and Steven Spielberg; composers Irving Berlin, Cole Porter, Richard Rodgers and Oscar Hammerstein, and Duke Ellington; musicians Louis Armstrong, Miles Davis, and Charlie Parker; and singers Billie Holiday, Bing Crosby, and Frank Sinatra.

In addition to Guam and Puerto Rico, U.S. territories and outlying areas include the U.S. Virgin Islands; American Samoa; the Northern Mariana Islands; Midway Islands; Wake Island; Johnston Atoll; Baker, Howland, and Jarvis Islands; Kingman Reef; Navassa Island; and Palmyra Atoll.

United States: 20th-Century Leaders

President

1897–1901: William McKinley

1901–09: Theodore Roosevelt

1909–13: William Howard Taft

1913–21: Thomas Woodrow Wilson

1921–23: Warren Gamaliel Harding

1923–29: Calvin Coolidge

1929–33: Herbert Clark Hoover

1933–45: Franklin Delano Roosevelt

1945–53: Harry S Truman

1953–61: Dwight David Eisenhower

1961–63: John Fitzgerald Kennedy

1963–69: Lyndon Baines Johnson

1969–74: Richard Milhous Nixon

1974–77: Gerald Rudolph Ford

1977–81: Jimmy [James Earl] Carter

1981–89: Ronald Wilson Reagan

1989–93: George Herbert Walker Bush

1993–2001: Bill [William Jefferson] Clinton

Uruguay

Official name: Oriental Republic of Uruguay

Location: Southeastern South America; bordered by Brazil (N), Atlantic Ocean (E, S), Argentina (W)

Capital: Montevideo

Area: 68,039 sq. mi. (176,220 sq. km.)

Population (est. 1998): 3,284,841

Languages: Spanish

Government: Republic

Religions: Roman Catholic 66%, Protestant 2%, Jewish 2%, nonprofessing or other 30%

Monetary unit: Peso

Main exports: Hides and leather goods, beef, wool, rice

Claimed by both Argentina and the Portuguese colony of Brazil, Uruguay established itself as an independent country in 1828. The Colorados, or Liberals, dominated the government from 1865 until 1958, despite opposition from the Blancos, or Conservatives. President José Batlle y Ordóñez (1903–07, 1911–15), a progressive Colorado, was the major political figure of the early 20th century. Presiding over a period of economic prosperity, he instituted social welfare programs, including minimum wages, pensions, and Latin America's first eight-hour workday. He nationalized foreign-owned companies and built public works that lowered unemployment. A new constitution in 1919 embodied his idea of a plural executive in which the president shared power with a collegial National Council of Administration.

The Great Depression brought political turmoil. President Gabriel Terra staged a coup in 1933 which abolished the constitution and made Terra a dictator. A new constitution in 1934 reestablished the president as sole executive. This was overturned by a 1951 plebiscite that approved restoration of the plural executive; another people's vote in 1966 reestablished the single executive.

Democracy was restored in 1942. By the 1950s the economy was in decline, strained by a bloated state administration linked to the country's social welfare programs. In 1958 the Colorados were voted out of power and the Blancos became the party of government until 1967. By that time, civil unrest driven by economic difficulties had begun to shake the country. The leftist Tupamaros, or National Liberation Movement, formed in 1967, began a guerrilla war. In 1973 Congress was dissolved and military rule instituted. The military regime was brutally repressive and carried out many human rights abuses. It liberalized and privatized the economy, though living standards continued to plummet. The regime's proposed new constitution was rejected in a 1980 plebiscite.

In 1985 civilian government was restored, following Colorado candidate Julio María Sanguinetti Cairolo's victory in the 1984 presidential election. He attracted foreign investment and improved economic conditions but was voted out of office in favor of National Party candidate Luis Alberto Lacalle in 1989. Sanguinetti returned to the presidency in the 1994 elections. He tried to grapple with high inflation and foreign debt through further privatization and tax increases.

Uruguay: 20th-Century Leaders

President

1897–1903: Juan Lindolfo Cuestas (1837–1905)

1903–07: José Batlle y Ordóñez (1856–1929)

1907–11: Claudio Williman (1863–1934)

1911–15: José Batlle y Ordóñez

1915–19: Feliciano Viera (1870–1929)

1919–23: Baltasar Brum (1883–1933)

1923–27: José Serrato

1927–31: Juan Campisteguy (1859–1937)

1931–38: Gabriel Terra

1938–43: Alfredo Baldomir (1884–1948)

1943–47: Juan José Amézaga (1881–1956)

1947: Tomas Berreta (1875–1947)

1947–51: Luis Batlle Berres (1897–1964)

1951–54: Andrés Martínez Trueba (1884–1959)

1954–56: Luis Batlle Berres

1956–57: Alberto Zubiria (1901–71)

1957–58: Arturo Lezama

1958–59: Carlos Z. Fisher

1959–60: Martín R. Echegoyen

1960–61: Benito Nardone (1907–64)

1961–62: Eduardo Victor Haedo

1962–63: Faustino Harrison (1900–63)

1963–64: Daniel Fernández Crespo (1901–64)

1964–65: Luis Giannattasio (1895–1965)

1965–66: Washington Beltrán

1966–67: Alberto Héber Usher

1967: Oscar Gestido (1901–67)

1967–72: Jorge Pacheco Areco

1972–76: Juan María Bordaberry

1976: Alberto Demicheli (1894–1980)

1976–81: Aparacio Méndez Manfredini (1904–88)

1981–85: Gregorio Conrado Alvarez Armelino

1985–90: Julio María Sanguinetti Cairolo (1936–)

1990–95: Luis Alberto Lacalle (1941–)

1995–2000: Julio María Sanguinetti Cairolo

Uzbekistan

Official name: Republic of Uzbekistan

Location: Central Asia; bordered by Kazakhstan (N, NE, NW), Kyrgystan (E), Tajikistan (SE)

Capital: Tashkent

Area: 172,741 sq. mi. (447,400 sq. km.)

Population (est. 1997): 23,467,724

Languages: Uzbek (official; member of Eastern Turk language group written in Cyrillic script since 1940) 74%, Russian 14.2%, Tajik 7.1%, other languages

Government: Republic

Religions: Sunni Muslim 88%, Orthodox 9%, other 3%

Monetary unit: Som

Main exports: Cotton, gold, natural gas, mineral fertilizers, textiles

Under Russian control from 1876, Uzbekistan entered the 20th century an important Russian transit site with the building of the Transcaucasian Railway. After the Russian Revolution of 1917, Uzbekistan became part of the Russian state as the Turkestan Autonomous Soviet Socialist Republic (A.S.S.R.) in 1918. In 1924 it became the Uzbek Republic, and in 1925 the independent Uzbek Soviet Socialist Republic.

During the 1920s the Soviet Union attempted to develop a new literary language through a program called the National Delimitation of the Central Asian Republics. Simultaneously the Soviet government pursued active programs against Islam and its believers. In World War II Uzbekistan it was a major site of Soviet munitions production.

Under the *glasnost* policy of Soviet premier Mikhail Gorbachev in the 1980s, Uzbeks became more politically vocal—in particular lobbying to change the official language from Russian to Uzbek. Following the failed 1991 Moscow coup, Uzbekistan announced its independence on August 31, 1991. It signed the Alma-Alta Declaration and became a member of the Commonwealth of Independent States. Uzbekistan gained formal independence with the dissolution of the Soviet Union on December 26, 1991.

In 1991 former Communist leader Islam Karimov was elected president. Upon taking office, he banned nearly all political opposition and instituted a limited program of economic development. Opposition groups formed in 1993 but were challenged by the government. Elections in 1994 and 1995 generated strong wins for the ruling party.

Uzbekistan: 20th-Century Leaders

President

1990– : Islam A. Karimov (1938–)

Prime Minister

1991–95: Abdulhashim Mutalov

1995– : Uktir Sultanov (1939–)

Vanuatu

Official name: Republic of Vanuatu

Location: South Pacific Ocean; chain of 82 islands; nearest neighbor is Santa Cruz Islands (N), other neighbors include Fiji (about 500 mi./800 km. E), Australia (about 1,100 mi./2,800 km. W)

Capital: Port Vila

Area: 5,699 sq. mi. (14,760 sq. km.)

Population (est. 1997): 181,358

Languages: English and French (official), pidgin (known as Bislama or Bichelam), in over 100 dialects

Government: Republic

Religions: Presbyterian 36.7%, Roman Catholic 15%, Anglican 15%, other Christian religions 10%

Monetary unit: Vatu

Main exports: Copra, cocoa, meat, timber

Vanuatu, then known as New Hebrides, was under Anglo-French naval administration from 1887 until it became an Anglo-French colony, or condominium government, in 1906. For several decades before 1906, approximately 35,000 island residents were used to work on Queensland, Australia, sugar plantations. New Hebrides itself operated a successful plantation economy into the 1920s using imported Vietnamese labor.

During World War II New Hebrides escaped Japanese occupation; the French population supported Free French forces, and the islands were used as Allied bases. Despite a minor rebellion among the French settlers and imported workers (put down with the aid of New Guinea forces), the islands gained independence within the British Commonwealth on July 30, 1980, under the name Vanuatu.

The government consists of a parliamentary system and a National Council of Chiefs to decide on matters of custom and tradition. The educational system is divided between French and English schools. Espiritu Sante and Efâte are the chain's largest islands.

Vanuatu: 20th-Century Leaders

President

1980–89: Ati George Sokomanu (1938–)

1989: Onneyn Tahi

1989–94: Fred Timakata (1936–)

1994–99: Jean-Marie Leye

1999– : Father John Bani

Prime Minister

1980–91: Reverend Walter Lini (1942–)

1991: Donald Kalpokas

1991–95: Maxime Carlot Korman

1995–96: Serge Vohor

1996: Maxime Carlot Korman

1996–98: Serge Vohor

1998–99 : Donald Kalpokas

1999– : Barak Sopé

Vatican City

Official name: Vatican City (Holy See)

Location: On Vatican Hill within the city of Rome, Italy; 13 buildings in Rome and Castel Gandolfo, the pope's summer residence, have extraterritorial rights; entirely surrounded by Italy

Capital: Vatican City

Area: 0.17 sq. mi. (0.44 sq. km.)

Population (est. 1997): 850

Languages: Italian, Latin

Government: Monarchical-sacerdotal state

Religion: Roman Catholic

Monetary unit: Vatican lira, interchangeable with Italian lira

Main exports: N.A.

Vatican City is the last remnant of the Papal States, which comprised about 17,000 sq. mi. (44,030 sq. km.) until incorporated into the new Kingdom of Italy in the 19th century. The popes refused to recognize Italian limits on their sovereignty until 1929, when the Lateran Treaties were signed between Benito Mussolini and Pope Pius XI. Under these agreements, the independent state of Vatican City was established. Many churches and the papal summer residence were restored to the papacy. The papacy pledged itself to perpetual neutrality, while Italy agreed to compensate the papacy for the loss of the Papal States and declared Roman Catholicism the state religion.

After World War II the Lateran Treaties became part of the Italian constitution (1947). The Concordat of 1984 revised the agreements to allow for Italian separation of church and state.

The spiritual head of the Roman Catholic Church, the pope is absolute sovereign of Vatican City. The number of diplomatic contacts between the Holy See and other nations has grown in recent years: the Vatican opened diplomatic relations with the U.S. in 1984 and with Israel and Jordan in 1994; diplomatic relations with Eastern Europe grew after the fall of Communism there. The popes have often sought to exert a moral influence on international politics, though the effects of that influence are hard to assess. Pope John Paul II has traveled widely, visiting Roman Catholic congregations and reflecting on the relation of the Gospel to social and political issues, notably in Cuba in 1998.

Vatican City: 20th-Century Leaders

Pope

1922–39: Pius XI

1939–58: Pius XII

1958–63: John XXIII

1963–78: Paul VI

1978: John Paul I

1978– : John Paul II

Venezuela

Official name: Republic of Venezuela

Location: Northern South America; bordered by Caribbean Sea (N), Guyana (E), Brazil (S), Colombia (W)

Capital: Caracas

Area: 352,144 sq. mi. (912,050 sq. km.)

Population (est. 1998): 22,803,409

Languages: Spanish (official), Native American dialects

Government: Republic

Religions: Roman Catholic 96%, Protestant 2%

Monetary unit: Bolívar

Main exports: Petroleum, bauxite, aluminum, iron ore, agricultural products

Venezuela gained independence from Spain as part of Gran Colombia in 1821 and became an independent republic in 1830. For most of the first six decades of the 20th century, it was governed by military dictators: from 1899 to 1908 by General Cipriano Castro; from 1908 to 1935 by Juan Vicente Gómez; and then by Eleazar López Conteras (1935-41) and Isaías Medina Angarita (1941–45).

In 1928 a leftist student named Rómulo Betancourt led a failed rebellion against Gómez; the student movement the Generation of 28 developed, which grew into the political party Democratic Action, founded by Betancourt in 1941. Betancourt enlisted army support in ousting Medina Angarita and framing a new democratic constitution. Democratic Action's presidential nominee Rómulo Gallegos Freire won the 1947 elections but was overthrown in 1948 and replaced by another military regime, led by Marcos Pérez Jiménez (1952–58). In 1958 a civilian-military coalition overthrew him. Betancourt returned from exile to be elected president that year. One of Latin America's most stable multiparty democracies was soon established; based on the new constitution of 1961, it has lasted to the present day.

The stability of the government was aided by petroleum revenues that brought economic growth and permitted industrial development and agrarian reform. In the 1980s declining oil prices brought recession and struggle with a huge burden of foreign debt. The government instituted tight economic controls and reduced social spending. The austerity measures of President Carlos Andrés Pérez (1989–93) sparked bloody riots and, in 1992, two attempted coups. In 1993 Pérez was impeached for corruption and forced to step down.

In 1994 Rafael Caldera Rodriguez was elected president. He faced continuing economic difficulties, most notably a sharp currency depreciation in 1994 resulting from the collapse of Banco Latino, the country's second largest bank. In the face of continuing antigovernment demonstrations and rising crime, he suspended some civil rights, though these were restored in most of the country in 1995. Continuing austerity measures and an IMF loan helped bring inflation under control by 1997. A leader in the 1992 coup attempts, Hugo Chávez Frías, won election to the presidency as a populist in 1998 and took office in 1999. He spearheaded a new constitution, approved in 1999, that increased presidential power.

Venezuela: 20th-Century Leaders

President

1899–1908: Cipriano Castro (1858?–1924)

1908–14: Juan Vicente Gómez (1857?–1935)

1915–22: Victorio Marquez Bustillos (provisional)

1922–29: Juan Vicente Gómez

1929–31: Juan Bautista Pérez (provisional)

1931–35: Juan Vicente Gómez

1935–41: Eleazar López Conteras

1941–45: Isaías Medina Angarita (1897–1945)

1945–48: Rómulo Betancourt (1908–81)

1948: Rómulo Gallegos Freire (1884–1969)

1948–50: Carlos Delgado Chalbaud (1909–50)

1950–52: German Suarez Flamerich

1952–58: Marcos Pérez Jiménez

1958: Wolfgang Larrazabál Ugueto

1958–59: Edgard Sanabria

1959–63: Rómulo Betancourt

1963–69: Raúl Leoni (1905–72)

1969–74: Rafael Caldera Rodriguez

1974–79: Carlos Andrés Pérez

1979–84: Luis Herrera Campíns

1984–89: Jaime Lusinchi

1989–93: Carlos Andrés Pérez

1993: Octavio Lepage

1993–94: Ramón José Velásquez (interim)

1994–99: Rafael Caldera Rodriquez

1999– : Hugo Chávez Frías (1954–)

Vietnam

Official name: Socialist Republic of Vietnam

Location: Southeast Asia; bordered by China (N), Gulf of Tonkin (NE), South China Sea (E), Laos, Cambodia (W)

Capital: Hanoi

Area: 127,243 sq. mi. (329,560 sq. km.)

Population (est. 1998): 76,236,259

Languages: Vietnamese (official), French, English, Khmer, Chinese

Government: Communist state

Religions: Buddhist, Roman Catholic, Muslim, Taoist, Confucian, Animist

Monetary unit: New dong

Main exports: Crude oil, rice, marine products, coffee

Occupying the eastern and southern parts of the Indochinese peninsula, Vietnam was an independent empire when it came under French control in the 19th century. In 1887 France united its Vietnamese protectorates with Cambodia in the Union of Indochina; Laos joined the union in 1893. Vietnam retained its emperor as a puppet of the French.

Nationalist resistance to French rule grew in the 1920s. Ho Chi Minh emerged as a powerful revolutionary leader, founding the Indochinese Communist Party in 1930. During World War II Japan occupied French Indochina (1940), with the collaboration of a pro–Vichy colonial government. Ho's Viet Minh, an independence movement, waged guerrilla war against the Japanese occupiers. In 1945 the Viet Minh captured Hanoi and declared Vietnam independent as the Democratic Republic of Vietnam; Emperor Bao Dai was deposed and Ho became president. In the Indochina War (1946–54) France tried to reassert control and oust Ho's government. Establishing control of the south, France reinstalled Bao Dai as chief of state there in 1949. After heavy losses at Dien Bien Phu (1954), France recognized it would not be able to conquer the north.

An international conference called for a temporary division of Vietnam along the 17th parallel, which would divide Communist North Vietnam from South Vietnam. Elections to reunite the country were planned for 1956 but South Vietnam refused to participate. By that time Bao Dai had been overthrown by his prime minister, Ngo Dinh Diem, who, in 1955 established the Republic of Vietnam with himself as president. The U.S. took France's place as the protector of anti-Communist South Vietnam, while the Soviet Union and China aided North Vietnam. The Vietnam War followed (1959–75).

Aiming to overthrow Ngo's government and unify the country under Communist rule, North Vietnam sponsored formation of a South Vietnamese resistance movement, the National Liberation Front, with the Vietcong as its military arm (1960). Supplied by North Vietnam, these forces waged guerrilla warfare and eventually open combat with South Vietnamese forces. U.S troops were sent to support South Vietnam, at first in small numbers, but by the hundreds of thousands after 1964. Despite superior weaponry and command of the air, the U.S. could not defeat the enemy, which was shielded by the civilian population. Diem's repressive regime was unpopular, as was the corrupt government of Nguyen Van Thieu (president 1967–75), who led a 1963 coup overthrowing Diem.

In the Paris Peace Accords (1973), all parties agreed to a cease-fire; by 1975 the U.S. had withdrawn all its forces. In April 1975 North Vietnam toppled the South Vietnamese government and captured the capital, Saigon (renamed Ho Chi Minh City). The two countries were united as the Socialist Republic of Vietnam in 1976. Hundreds of thousands of refugees fled as businesses were nationalized and agriculture collectivized.

General Secretary Le Duan (1976–86; lived 1908–86) tried to expand Vietnam by invading Cambodia (then called Kampuchea) in 1978 and installing a new government. Relations with China deteriorated over this and other issues, and the two countries fought a brief war in 1979. Vietnam's weak economy was propped up by the Soviet Union, but the decline of Soviet power in the 1980s forced Vietnam to reconsider its policies. In 1989 it withdrew its troops from Cambodia. By 1992 the government was encouraging private enterprise and foreign investment Contacts with the U.S. were restored, with the U.S. trade embargo ended in 1994 and full diplomatic relations established in 1995. Despite economic restructuring, Vietnam's one-party political structure remained intact.

Vietnam: 20th-Century Leaders

South Vietnam

Head of State

1949–55: Bao Dai

President

1955–63: Ngo Dinh Diem

1963–64: Duong Van Minh

1964: Nguyen Khanh

1964: Duong Van Minh

1964: Nguyen Khanh

1964: Duong Van Minh

1964–65: Phan Khac Suu (1905–70)

1967–75: Nguyen Van Thieu

1975: Tran Van Huong

1975: Duong Van Minh

1975–76: Huynh Tan Phat (1913–89)

Premier

1949–50: Bao Dai

1950: Nguyen Phan Long (1889–1960)

1950–52: Tran Van Huu (1896–1984)

1952–53: Nguyen Van Tam (1895–1990)

1954: Prince Buu Loc

1954–63: Ngo Dinh Diem

1963–64: Nguyen Ngoc Tho

1964: Nguyen Khanh

1964: Nguyen Xuan Oanh

1964: Nguyen Khanh

1964–65: Tran Van Huong

1965: Nguyen Xuan Oanh

1965: Phuy Huy Quat (1909–79)

1965–67: Nguyen Cao Ky

1967–68: Nguyen Van Loc

1968–69: Tran Van Huong

1969–75: Tran Thien Khiem

1975: Nguyen Ba Can

1975: Vu Van Mau

Socialist Republic of Vietnam

(known as the Democratic Republic of Vietnam or North Vietnam prior to 1976)

President

1945–69: Ho Chi Minh

1969–80: Ton Duc Thang (1888–1980)

1980–81: Nguyen Huu Tho

1981–87: Truong Chinh (1907–88)

1987–92: Vo Chi Cong

1992–97: Le Duc Anh

1997– : Tran Duc Luong (1937–)

Premier

1955–87: Pham Van Dong

1987–88: Pham Hung (1912–88)

1988: Vo Van Kiet

1988–91: Do Muoi

1991–97: Vo Van Kiet

1997– : Phan Van Khai (1933–)

Yemen

Official name: Republic of Yemen

Location: Southern coast of the Arabian Peninsula; bordered by Saudi Arabia (N), Oman (E), Gulf of Aden (S), Red Sea (W)

Capital: San'a

Area: 203,850 sq. mi. (527,970 sq. km.)

Population (est. 1997): 13,972,477

Languages: Arabic

Government: Republic

Religions: Predominantly Muslim (Sunni and Shi'a), some Christian and Hindu

Monetary unit: Yemeni rial

Main exports: Oil, cotton, coffee, hides

Since antiquity, when it was part of the kingdom of Sheba or Saba, Yemen has been of strategic importance as a center of trade among India, Africa, and the Middle East. It became part of the Ottoman Empire in the 16th century. Southern Yemen came under British control in 1839, when Britain made a colony of its most important city, Aden; the region became the Aden Protectorate in 1937. Northern Yemen remained under Ottoman rule until 1918, when it became independent under the Zaidi imams, a centuries-old dynasty of theocratic rulers who had previously governed with Ottoman consent.

Northern Yemen remained economically underdeveloped under the Zaidi imams' rule. The Imam Yahya was assassinated in a palace revolt in 1948 and was succeeded by his son Ahmad. His son Muhammad al-Badr, the last imam, was overthrown in 1962 by General Abdullah al-Sallah, who established the Yemen Arab Republic (known also as North

Yemen). Civil war between republicans and royalists lasted until 1970, when a coalition republican government was formed. A military coup brought Colonel Ibrahim al-Hamidi to power in 1974; he was assassinated in 1977. After further turmoil, Ali Abdullah Saleh took power as president in 1978.

In the Aden Protectorate Britain permitted the formation of the South Arabian Federation of Arab Emirates in 1959; the British colony of Aden joined it in 1963. Nationalist and republican elements formed a National Liberation Front (NLF) and launched a civil war against the British-backed Federation. The NLF defeated a rival nationalist group, the Front for the Liberation of Occupied South Yemen (FLOSY), and won independence for South Yemen in 1967. A new constitution in 1970 made the country the Democratic People's Republic of Yemen, a Socialist state that received Soviet aid in support of such measures as nationalization and collectivization.

Disputing their borders, South Yemen and North Yemen fought each other in 1972–73 and again in 1979. In the 1980s relations improved. After a 1986 civil war brought a new government to power in South Yemen, the countries made progress toward unification, which was achieved in 1990, as the two became the Republic of Yemen. North Yemen's president, Ali Abdullah Saleh, became the united nation's president, while Bakr al-Attas, former president of South Yemen, became prime minister. Internal conflict soon rocked the new government, and South Yemen declared itself independent again in 1994. North Yemenite forces occupied Aden, reestablishing unity, though it now became clear that the North would dominate the South. A 1994 constitution established Islamic law, the *sharia*, as the nation's legal basis.

Yemen's economy was largely agricultural and dependent on cotton until the discovery of oil in the 1980s. The border between Saudi Arabia and southern Yemen has long been disputed, the more so since oil was discovered in that region. In 2000, Yemen was the site of a terrorist attack on the U.S.S. *Cole*, in which 17 Americans died.

Yemen: 20th-Century Leaders

North Yemen

Imam

1904–48: Yahya Hamied Alddien (1871–1948)

1948: Sayf Abdullah (1912–48)

1948–62: Ahmed (1898–1962)

1962: Muhammad al-Badr

President

1962–67: Abdullah al-Sallal

1967–74: Abdul Rahman al-Iryani

1974–77: Ibrahim al-Hamdi (1943–77)

1977–78: Ahmed Hussein al-Ghashmi

1978–90: Ali Abdullah Saleh (1942–)

South Yemen

President

1967–69: Qahtan Muhammad al-Shaabi (1925–81)

1969–78: Salem Ali Rubayyi (1934–78)

1978: Ali Nassir Muhammad Hussani (1939–)

1978–80: Abd-al Fattah Ismail (1939–86)

1980–86: Ali Nassir Muhammad Hussani

1986–90: Haidar Abu Bakr al-Attas

Republic of Yemen

(formed from union of South Yemen and North Yemen in 1990)

President

1990– : Ali Abdallah Salih

Prime Minister

1990–94: Haidar Abu Bakr al-Attas

1994: Muhammad Said al-Attar (acting)

1994–97: 'Abd al-Aziz 'Abd al-Ghani

1997–98: Faraj Said ibn Ghanem

1998– : Abdul Karim al-Iryani (1934–)

Yugoslavia

Official name: Federal Republic of Yugoslavia

Location: On Balkan peninsula in southeastern Europe; bordered by Hungary (N), Romania (NE), Bulgaria (E), Macedonia, Albania (S), Adriatic Sea, Bosnia and Herzegovina (W), Croatia (NW)

Capital: Belgrade

Area: 39,424 sq. mi. (102,136 sq. km.)

Population (est. 1998): 10,526,135

Languages: Serbo-Croatian (official), Albanian

Government: Republic

Religions: Orthodox Christian 65%, Muslim 19%, Catholic 4%, Protestant 1%, other 11%

Monetary unit: New dinar

Main exports: Manufactured goods, food and live animals, raw materials

Present-day Yugoslavia consists of Serbia and Montenegro, states that came under Ottoman control from the 14th to 16th centuries. They gained independence from the Ottoman

Empire in 1878. Both won territory in the Balkan Wars (1912, 1913), which left Serbia, a thriving constitutional monarchy ruled by King Peter I (1903-08), as the foremost Slavic power in the Balkans.

Serbia hoped to annex Bosnia and Herzegovina, which was part of the Austro-Hungarian Empire but had a sizable Serb population favoring union with Serbia. On June 28, 1914, a Serb nationalist in Bosnia assassinated the Austrian heir apparent, Archduke Francis Ferdinand (1863–1914). The event prompted Austria to declare war on Serbia, an act that brought a tangled web of prewar alliances into play. The result was the global carnage and devastation of World War I (1914–18).

During the war, Serbia and Montenegro were overrun by the Central Powers (1915), but the Serbian government retreated to Corfu. There, in July 1917, representatives of the South Slavic peoples agreed that after the war, Peter I would rule a unified Kingdom of the Serbs, Croats, and Slovenes. This state was established on December 1, 1918, and included not only present-day Serbia and Montenegro, but what are now the independent countries of Macedonia (then part of Serbia), Slovenia, Croatia, and Bosnia and Herzegovina.

Serbia dominated the new state despite the wishes of its constituent peoples for autonomy within a federal system. A 1921 constitution established a strong central government. Political disputes between regional representatives in Parliament gave way to violence and civil disorder. In 1929 King Alexander I (reigned 1921–34) declared a dictatorship, dissolved Parliament, and renamed the country Yugoslavia ("Land of the Southern Slavs"). The dictatorship officially ended in 1931, but Serbians continued to dominate the government, and Alexander was assassinated by Macedonian terrorists and the Ustase, a Croatian paramilitary group, in 1934. His son Peter II (1934–45) succeeded under the regency of his cousin Prince Paul, who oversaw establishment of Croatian autonomy in 1939.

During World War II Prince Paul aligned Yugoslavia with the Axis Powers, prompting the military and people to overthrow him (1941). Germany invaded and occupied Yugoslavia, forcing Peter II into exile. The Germans divided up Yugoslavia, establishing Serbia and Croatia as puppet states while committing atrocities. Two main guerrilla resistance movements emerged, the Serbian royalist Chetniks and the Communist partisans. The latter, led by Marshall Tito and supported by the Soviet Union, established dominance over the former. In 1944 the Germans were forced to leave Yugoslavia; by war's end in 1945, two million Yugoslavs had died. In 1945 the monarchy was abolished and a republic proclaimed, with Tito as its leader. As prime minister (1945–63) and president (1953–80) of the Federal People's Republic of Yugoslavia, he headed the country until his death. It consisted of six republics and two nominally autonomous areas in Serbia, Vojvodina and Kosovo.

Tito rebuilt the country on the Communist model, collectivizing agriculture and developing state-run industries. At first aided by the Soviet Union, he broke with that country in 1948, accepting U.S. aid instead and eventually becoming a leader of the nonaligned movement. (Relations with the Soviet Union improved in the mid-1950s.) Yugoslavia remained Communist, but in a decentralized fashion that allowed for self-management in agriculture and industry, producing impressive economic growth. Ruling in authoritarian fashion, Tito suppressed nationalist strivings in Yugoslavia's different regions, but these reemerged in the 1970s. A 1974 constitution gave more autonomy to the constituent republics and autonomous provinces, but nationalism continued to grow. After Tito's death, riots in Kosovo, a Serbian province with an ethnic Albanian majority, were violently suppressed

(1981); its autonomy was curtailed and, after more violence, abolished (1989).

In 1989–90 as Communist power waned in Eastern Europe, elections were held across Yugoslavia in which only Serbia and Montenegro held onto their old Communist leadership. In Serbia, Slobodan Milosevic, general secretary of the Serbian Communist Party, was elected president in 1989. Serbian attempts to impose its authority on the rest of the country failed, and Yugoslavia fell to pieces. Beginning in June 1991, Slovenia, Croatia, Macedonia, and Bosnia and Herzegovina all seceded. In 1992 Serbia and Montenegro, the sole remnants of Yugoslavia, declared themselves the Federal Republic of Yugoslavia. Dominated by Serbia and its leader Milosevic (president of Serbia 1989–97; president of Yugoslavia 1997–2000), the new government gave military aid to ethnic Serbian rebels in Croatia and in the bloody Bosnian Civil War (1992–95). The UN imposed economic sanctions on Yugoslavia for its support of the insurgents; this and other forms of international pressure persuaded Milosevic to join in negotiating peace in the Dayton Agreement (1995).

Small as it now was, Yugoslavia underwent still more secessionist activity in Montenegro and Kosovo in 1997 and 1998. In Kosovo, Serbian repression of ethnic Albanian resistance brought world condemnation. The unwillingness of the Serbian government to sign a treaty with Kosovar Albanian leaders led to NATO air strikes in Yugoslavia in March 1999. Hundreds of thousands of ethnic Albanians fled or were forced out of Kosovo A new treaty was signed in June, which called for a withdrawal of Serb forces and greater autonomy for Kosovo. Meanwhile, Yugoslavia's economy was left chronically weak by years of war, sanctions, and turmoil. In 2000 Milosevic was finally forced out of office by demonstrations over his refusal to accept his election defeat to Vojislav Kostunica.

Yugoslavia: 20th-Century Leaders

(known as the Kingdom of the Serbs, Croats, and Slovenes prior to 1929)

King

1918–21: Peter I (1844–1921)

1921–34: Alexander I (1888–1934)

1934–45: Peter II (1923–70)

Regent

1918–21: Prince Alexander (later King Alexander I)

1934–41: Prince Paul (1893–1976)

President

1945–53: Ivan Ribar (1881–1968)

1953–80: Tito

1980: Lazar Kolisevski

1980–81: Cvijetin Mijatoviç

1981–82: Sergej Kraigher

1982–83: Peter Stamboliç

1983–84: Mika Spiljac

1984–85: Veselin Djuranovic

1985–86: Radovan Vlajkovic

1986–87: Sinan Hasani

1987–88: Lazar Mojsov

1988–89: Raif Dizareviç

1989–90: Janez Drnovsek (1950–)

1990–91: Borisav Joviç

1991: Stipe Mesic

1991–92: Branko Kostic

1992–93: Dobrica Cosiç

1993–97: Zoran Lilic

1997: Srdja Bozovic (acting)

1997–2000: Slobodan Milosevic (1941–)

Prime Minister

(since establishment of republic in 1945)

1945–63: Tito

1963–67: Peter Stamboliç

1967–69: Mika Spiljac

1969–71: Mitja Ribicic

1971–77: Dzemal Bijediç

1977–82: Veselin Djuranovic

1982–86: Milka Planinc

1986–89: Branko Mikulic

1989–91: Ante Markovic

1992: Milan Panic

1992–98: Radoje Kontic

1998– : Momir Bulatovic (1956–)

Zambia

Official name: Republic of Zambia

Location: Landlocked country in southern central Africa; bordered by Zaire (N), Tanzania (E), Botswana, Zimbabwe, Mozambique (S), Namibia (SW), Angola (W)

Capital: Lusaka

Area: 290,583 sq. mi. (752,610 sq. km.)

Population (est. 1997): 9,349,975

Languages: English (official), about 70 indigenous languages

Government: Republic

Religions: Christian 50%–75%, Muslim and Hindu 24%–49%, indigenous beliefs 1%

Monetary unit: Kwacha

Main exports: Copper, zinc, cobalt, lead, tobacco

Inhabited by Bantu tribes from the 15th century, the country now known as Zambia was widely explored in the 19th century by British voyagers such as David Livingstone and Cecil Rhodes, who discovered its rich copper and mineral resources. In 1891 Northern Rhodesia became a British protectorate. early in the 20th century (1911) its borders were established, and from 1924 it was under British colonial rule.

After World War II nationalist movements grew in strength. In 1953 the Federation of Rhodesia and Nyasaland was formed by Nyasaland and Northern and Southern Rhodesia; it was dissolved in 1963. On October 24, 1964, Northern Rhodesia gained independence from Great Britain and was renamed the Republic of Zambia. Its first president was long-time movement leader Kenneth Kaunda, a moderate. In 1973 his United National Independence Party was named Zambia's only official party.

From the 1970s economic instability brought on by plummeting copper prices led to massive foreign debt and internal unease. To gain IMF aid in the 1980s, President Kuanda attempted an economic restructuring program. In 1990 opposition parties were permitted, and in 1991 the opposition Labor Party gained power, with Frederick Chiluba becoming president. His economic programs substantially reduced the country's debt. Political conflict between Chiluba and Kaunda continued, with Kaunda remaining highly critical of the government.

On August 31, 1991, the office of prime minister was abolished. A coup attempt was defeated in 1997.

Zambia: 20th-Century Leaders

President

1964–91: Kennneth David Kaunda (1924–)

1991– : Frederick Chiluba (1943)

Prime Minister

1964–73: Kenneth David Kaunda

1973–75: Mathias Mainza Chona (1930–)

1975–77: Elijah Mudenda (1927–)

1977–78: Mathias Mainza Chona

1978–81: Daniel Lisulo (1930–)

1981–85: Nalumino Mundia (1926–88)

1985–89: Kebby Musokotwane (1946–)

1989–91: Malimba Masheke

(position abolished 1991)

Zanzibar See Tanzania.

Zimbabwe

Official name: Republic of Zimbabwe

Location: Southern Africa; landlocked; bordered by Zambia (NW), Mozambique (E), South Africa (S), Botswana (SW)

Capital: Harare (formerly Salisbury)

Area: 150,803 sq. mi. (390,580 sq. km.)

Population (est. 1998): 11,044,147

Languages: English (official), ChiShona, Si Ndebele

Government: Republic

Religions: Syncretic (Christian and indigenous beliefs) 50%, Christian 25%, indigenous beliefs 24%, Muslim 1%

Monetary unit: Dollar

Main exports: Tobacco and other agricultural goods, manufactures, gold

Zimbabwe is named for Great Zimbabwe, a ruined city built by a society that flourished in the ninth to 13th centuries. Two Bantu-speaking peoples, the Shona (Mashona) and Matabele (Ndebele), came to dominate the region, with the latter assuming rule in the early 19th century. In the 1880s and 1890s British industrialist Cecil Rhodes (1853–1902) transformed it into the protectorate of Rhodesia, which suppressed native African opposition and attracted European settlement and investment. Rhodes's British South African Company administered Rhodesia until 1923, when it was partitioned into Northern Rhodesia (now Zambia) and Southern Rhodesia (now Zimbabwe). That year white settlers in Southern Rhodesia voted against union with South Africa, becoming instead a self-governing state within the British Empire.

The economy bloomed, based on rich agricultural and mineral resources, but the benefits went to the white minority, while blacks remained poor and disenfranchised. In 1953 Southern Rhodesia became a member of the Federation of Rhodesia and Nyasaland, which also included Northern Rhodesia and Nyasaland (now Malawi). The federation crumbled in 1963 due to growing agitation for black participation in government, particularly in Northern Rhodesia and Nyasaland. Southern Rhodesia's racist Rhodesian Front government, led by Ian Smith (prime minister 1964–79), pressed for independence from Britain, which refused to grant it unless the black majority received appropriate political representation. In 1965 Southern Rhodesia unilaterally declared its independence from Britain under a constitution that guaranteed white rule.

Britain and the UN refused to recognize the new republic of Rhodesia and imposed economic sanctions. South Africa and Mozambique (until the latter's independence in 1975) supported Rhodesia. Internally, the Rhodesian government faced guerrilla resistance from the Zimbabwe African People's Union (ZAPU) and the Zimbabwe African National Union (ZANU), two organizations founded in the 1960s to oppose white rule. The two parties joined to form the Patriotic Front coalition in 1976. Over 30,000 people died in the civil war between the government and rebels.

Unable to defeat the rebels, the government entered peace negotiations. A 1978 settlement between the government and some nationalist leaders, an arrangement that kept whites in a privileged position in a country renamed Zimbabwe-Rhodesia, was rejected by the Patriotic Front (PF). In 1979 a peace settlement acceptable to all parties was reached. Transitional British rule was reinstituted, and on April 18, 1980, Zimbabwe, as the country was now called, became independent. Its first prime minister (1980–87) was Robert Mugabe, head of ZANU and a member of the majority Shona. ZAPU, which represented the minority Matabele, split from ZANU and fought a sporadic guerrilla war against the government until 1987, when it merged with ZANU in the ZANU-PF, making Zimbabwe a de facto one-party state.

As prime minister and later president (1987–), Mugabe was a moderate, pragmatic leader who improved health care and education for the black majority while reconciling whites to the new multiracial regime. During an agreed-upon transitional period, whites continued to hold a disproportionate number of seats in Parliament, but Parliament voted in 1987 to end that arrangement through a new constitution establishing an executive presidency. Mugabe instituted multiparty elections in 1990 and repudiated his party's previous commitment to Marxism in 1991. In 1996 Mugabe won reelection as president.

Zimbabwe: 20th-Century Leaders

Rhodesia

(called Zimbabwe-Rhodesia from 1978)

Governor

1959–69: Sir Humphrey V. Gibbs (1902–90)

(position abolished 1969–70)

1979–80: Christopher Soames, baron of Fletching (1920–87)

President

1970–76: Clifford W. DuPont (1905–78)

1976–78: John J. Wrathall (1913–78)

1978– : Henry Everard (acting)

1978–79: Jack Pithey

1979: Josiah Zion Gumede

Prime Minister

1964–79: Ian Smith

1979: Abel Muzorewa

Zimbabwe

President

1987– : Robert Mugabe

Prime Minister

1980–87: Robert Mugabe

(position abolished 1987)

Gross Domestic Product (GDP)
of the World's Independent Nations 1976–96
(in billions of dollars)

Nations not independent in a given year are listed as "n.a."; "—" indicates no definite figures available. Year 1996 data is based on purchasing power parity calculations. Dollar values are uncorrected for inflation. For reference, a dollar in 1976 was the equivalent of $2.76 in 1996 dollars.

Nation	1976	1996
Afghanistan	2.20	18.100
Albania	1.300	4.400
Algeria	14.840	115.900
Andorra	n.a.	1.200
Angola	3.150 (1975)	8.300
Antigua and Barbuda	n.a.	0.446
Argentina	36.750 (1975)	296.900
Armenia	n.a.	9.700
Australia	86.100	430.500
Austria	48.150	157.600
Azerbaijan	n.a.	11.900
Bahamas	0.500 (1975)	4.800
Bahrain	1.100 (1974)	7.700
Bangladesh	7.290 (1977)	155.100
Barbados	0.508 (1978)	2.65
Belarus	n.a.	51.900
Belgium	68.480	204.8
Belize	n.a.	0.649
Benin	0.500	8.200
Bhutan	0.090	1.3 (1995)
Bolivia	2.950	21.500
Bosnia and Herzegovina	n.a.	1.9 (1995)
Botswana	01.000 (1974)	4.600
Brazil	144.920 (1977)	1,022.0 (1995)
Brunei	n.a.	4.600
Bulgaria	15.000 (1974)	39.900
Burkina Faso (Upper Volta in 1976)	0.420 (1974)	8.000
Burundi	0.340 (1974)	4.000
Cambodia (Kampuchea in 1976)	—	7.700
Cameroon	2.18	17.500
Canada	193.870 (1977)	721.000
Cape Verde	0.130	0.472 (1995)
Central African Republic (Central African Empire in 1976)	0.310 (1974)	
Chad	0.54	3.3 (1995)
Chile	14.920 (1977)	120.600
China	340.000	3,390.0 (1995)
Columbia	12.660 (1975)	201.400

Nation	1976	1996
Comoros	0.070 (1975)	0.37 (1995)
Congo, Dem. Rep. of the/Zaire	3.380	16.5 (1995)
Congo, Republic of the	0.670	4.9 (1995)
Costa Rica	2.350 (1975)	19.000
Côte d'Ivoire (Ivory Coast in 1976)	6.320 (1977)	23.900
Croatia	n.a.	21.400
Cuba	5.800 (1974)	16.200
Cyprus (1996 figure does not include Turkish held northern Cyprus)	0.753	8.800
Czech Republic (Czechoslovakia in 1976)	47.000 (1974)	114.300
Denmark	40.240	118.200
Djibouti	—	0.5 (1995)
Dominica	n.a.	0.208 (1995)
Dominican Republic	3.910	29.800
Ecuador	4.950	47.000
Egypt	18.760 (1977)	183.900
El Salvador	2.180	12.200
Equatorial Guinea	0.120 (1974)	0.328
Estonia	n.a.	8.100
Ethiopia	2.890	24.800
Fiji	0.663	5.100
Finland	8.500	97.100
France	347.000	1,220.000
Gabon	1.660 (1975)	6.300
Gambia	89.670	1.1 (1995)
Georgia	n.a.	7.100
Germany	—	1,700.000
in 1976:		
East Germany	59.000 (1974)	—
West Germany	398.700 (1975)	—
Ghana	5.26 (1975)	27.000
Greece	21.800	106.900
Grenada	0.044 (1974)	0.300
Guatemala	4.290	39.000
Guinea	0.590 (1974)	7.100
Guinea-Bissau	0.160 (1974)	1.100
Guyana	0.464 (1975)	1.800
Haiti	0.922 (1975)	6.800
Honduras	1.200	11.500
Hungary	24.600 (1974)	74.700
Iceland	1.400	5.300
India	80.630	1,538.000
Indonesia	37.270	779.700
Iran	66.400	343.500
Iraq	13.6200 (1975)	42.000
Ireland	7.970	59.900

Nation	1976	1996
Israel	12.450	85.700
Italy	162.430	1,120.000
Jamaica	3.040	8.400
Japan	562.170	2,850.000
Jordan	1.490 (1977)	20.900
Kazakhstan	n.a.	48.600
Kenya	3.430	39.200
Kiribati	n.a.	0.062
Korea, North	7.600	20.900
Korea, South	25.300	647.000
Kuwait	12.800	32.500
Kyrgyzstan	n.a.	5.800
Laos	0.300	5.700
Latvia	n.a.	9.400
Lebanon	2.090 (1972)	13.000
Lesotho	0.200	3.700
Liberia	0.855 (1975)	2.4 (1995)
Libya	13.160 (1975)	34.500
Liechtenstein	—	0.713
Lithuania	n.a.	14.100
Luxembourg	2.040 (1975)	10.0 (1995)
Macedonia	n.a.	2.000
Madagascar	1.690	12.100
Malawi	0.875 (1977)	7.500
Malaysia	11.05	214.700
Maldives	0.020	0.423 (1995)
Mali	0.423 (1974)	5.8 (1995)
Malta	0.603 (1977)	4.700
Marshall Islands	n.a.	0.094 (1995)
Mauritania	0.277 (1973)	2.8 (1995)
Mauritius	0.518 (1975)	11.700
Mexico	61.190	777.300
Micronesia	n.a.	0.205
Moldova	n.a.	10.800
Monaco	—	0.800
Mongolia	1.200	5.100
Morocco	7.970	97.600
Mozambique	3.000 (1974)	12.2 (1995)
Myanmar (Burma in 1976)	3.950	51.500
Namibia	n.a.	6.200
Nauru	0.100	0.1 (1993)
Nepal	1.18 (1975)	26.500
Netherlands	88.300	317.800
New Zealand	12.636	65.600
Nicaragua	1.840	7.700
Niger	0.650	5.900

Nation	1976	1996
Nigeria	32.260 (1977)	143.400
Norway	31.300	114.100
Oman	2.530 (1977)	20.800
Pakistan	13.220	296.500
Palau	n.a.	0.082 (1994)
Panama	2.030	14.000
Papua New Guinea	1.880 (1978)	10.700
Paraguay	1.690	17.700
Peru	11.080	92.000
Philippines	17.470	194.200
Poland	71.000 (1974)	246.300
Portugal	13.710 (1975)	122.100
Qatar	2.200 (1974)	11.700
Romania	40.000	113.200
Russia (Soviet Union in 1976)	560.000 (1974)	767.000
Rwanda	0.771 (1971)	3.8 (1995)
St. Kitts and Nevis	n.a.	0.235
Saint Lucia	n.a.	0.695
Saint Vincent and the Grenadines	n.a.	0.259
Samoa	0.050	0.415
San Marino	—	0.408
Sao Tome and Principe	0.040	0.149
Saudi Arabia	55.100 (1977)	205.6
Senegal	1.570 (1975)	15.600
Seychelles	0.027	0.450 (1995)
Sierra Leone	0.522	4.700
Singapore	5.970	72.200
Slovakia	n.a.	42.800
Slovenia	n.a.	24.000
Solomon Islands	n.a.	1.200
Somalia	0.370 (1974)	3.600 (1995)
South Africa	33.400	227.000
Spain	102.490	593.000
Sri Lanka	2.990	69.700
Sudan	5.100	26.600
Suriname	0.501 (1975)	1.400
Swaziland	0.313 (1977)	3.800
Sweden	74.100	184.300
Switzerland	57.200	161.300
Syria	5.810	98.300
Taiwan	17.300	315.000
Tajikistan	n.a.	5.400
Tanzania	2.250 (1975)	18.900 (1995)
Thailand	15.940	455.700
Togo	0.560	4.450
Tonga	0.040	0.228

Nation	1976	1996
Trinidad and Tobago	2.720	17.100
Tunisia	4.440	43.300
Turkey	39.800	379.100
Turkmenistan	n.a.	11.800
Tuvalu	n.a.	0.008 (1995)
Uganda	3.100	16.800 (1995)
Ukraine	n.a.	161.100
United Arab Emirates	6.000	72.900
United Kingdom	218.400	1,190.000
United States	1,872.500 (1977)	7,610.000
Uruguay	3.130	26.000
Uzbekistan	n.a.	57.000
Vanuatu	n.a.	0.219 (1995)
Venezuela	31.000	197.000
Vietnam	—	108.700
Yemen	—	39.100
in 1976:		
North Yemen	1.650	—
South Yemen	0.430	—
Yugoslavia	27.950 (1975)	21.000 (1995)
Zambia	2.020	9.700
Zimbabwe (Rhodesia in 1976)	3.250	26.400

Sources: World Almanac and Book of Facts 1978, 1979, 1981; Time Almanac 1999

Infant Mortality (per 1,000 live births) in the
World's Independent Nations 1975–98

Nations not independent in a given year are listed as "n.a."; "—" indicates no definite figures available. Data reported for some countries in the 1975 column are for years other than 1975; if more than three years distant, year of data is specified.

Nation	1975	1998
Afghanistan	189	144
Albania	86.8 (1971)	45
Algeria	86.3	45
Andorra	n.a.	4
Angola	24.1	132
Antigua and Barbuda	n.a.	21
Argentina	58.9	19
Armenia	n.a.	41
Australia	16.5	5
Austria	20.6	5
Azerbaijan	n.a.	82
Bahamas	24.7	19
Bahrain	—	16
Bangladesh	140	98
Barbados	28.3	17
Belarus	n.a.	14
Belgium	17.4	6
Belize	n.a.	32
Benin	109.6	100
Bhutan	—	112
Bolivia	77.3	64
Bosnia and Herzegovina	n.a.	31
Botswana	97	59
Brazil	94	37
Brunei	n.a.	23
Bulgaria	21.8	13
Burkina Faso (Upper Volta in 1975)	182	109
Burundi	150 (1971)	101
Cambodia (Kampuchea in 1975)	127	107
Cameroon	137	77
Canada	12.4	6
Cape Verde	104.9	48
Central African Republic (Central African Empire in 1975)	190	106
Chad	160	117
Chile	54.7	10
China	55	45
Colombia	46.6	25
Comoros	51.7	85
Congo, Dem. Rep. of the/Zaire	104	102

Nation	1975	1998
Congo, Republic of the	180	103
Costa Rica	27.8	13
Côte d'Ivoire (Ivory Coast in 1975)	138	96
Croatia	n.a.	8
Cuba	24.8	8
Cyprus	17.5	8
Czech Republic (Czechoslovakia in 1975)	18.7	7
Denmark	8.9	5
Djibouti	—	102
Dominica	n.a.	9
Dominican Republic	37.2	44
Ecuador	65.8	32
Egypt	89.2	69
El Salvador	59.5	29
Equatorial Guinea	53.2	93
Eritrea	n.a.	79
Estonia	n.a.	14
Ethiopia	84.2	126
Fiji	14.5	17
Finland	12	4
France	11.4	6
Gabon	229	85
Gambia	165	77
Georgia	n.a.	51
Germany		5
in 1975:		
East Germany	13.2	
West Germany	15.5	
Ghana	156	78
Greece	20.3	7
Grenada	23.5	11
Guatemala	76.5	48
Guinea	216	128.9
Guinea-Bissau	47.1 (1969)	112
Guyana	50.5 (1972)	49
Haiti	150	99
Honduras	31.4	42
Hungary	24.3	10
Iceland	10.8	5
India	122	63
Indonesia	125	59
Iran	108.1	49
Iraq	33.1	62
Ireland	15.7	6
Israel	17.8	8
Italy	17.6	6

Nation	1975	1998
Jamaica	20.4	14
Japan	8.9	4
Jordan	14.9	33
Kazakhstan	n.a.	58
Kenya	51.4	59
Kiribati	n.a.	50
Korea, North	110	88
Korea, South	35	8
Kuwait	39.1	11
Kyrgyzstan	n.a.	75
Laos	123	92
Latvia	n.a.	17
Lebanon	13.6	32
Lesotho	114.4 (1971)	78
Liberia	159.2 (1971)	103
Libya	130	56
Liechtenstein	6.5	5
Lithuania	n.a.	15
Luxembourg	10.6	5
Macedonia	n.a.	19
Madagascar	102 (1966)	91
Malawi	142.1 (1972)	134
Malaysia	31.8	22
Maldives	118.8	41
Mali	120	122
Malta	14.4	8
Marshall Islands	n.a.	45
Mauritania	187	78
Mauritius	33.8	17
Mexico	54.7	26
Micronesia	n.a.	35
Moldova	n.a.	44
Monaco	9.3	7
Mongolia	75	66
Morocco	149	53
Mozambique	19.1	120
Myanmar	63.9 (1967)	78
Namibia	n.a.	67
Nauru	19	41
Nepal	169	76
Netherlands	9.5	5
New Zealand	14.2	6
Nicaragua	37	42
Niger	200	114
Nigeria	62	71
Norway	9.2	5

Nation	1975	1998
Oman	—	26
Pakistan	124	93
Palau	n.a.	19
Panama	22.7	24
Papua New Guinea	—	57
Paraguay	38.6	37
Peru	70.3 (1972)	43
Philippines	47.6	35
Poland	22.4	13
Portugal	38.9	7
Qatar	—	18
Romania	31.2	19
Russia (Soviet Union in 1975)	27.7	23
Rwanda	127 (1970)	113
St. Kitts and Nevis	n.a.	18
Saint Lucia	n.a.	17
Saint Vincent and the Grenadines	n.a.	16
Samoa	10.4	32
San Marino	24.1	5
São Tomé and Príncipe	64.3	55
Saudi Arabia	152	41
Senegal	92.9 (1960-61)	61
Seychelles	n.a.	17
Sierra Leone	136	129
Singapore	12.5	4
Slovakia	n.a.	10
Slovenia	n.a.	5
Solomon Islands	n.a.	24
Somalia	177	126
South Africa	117	52
Spain	15.6	7
Sri Lanka	45.1	16
Sudan	93.6	73
Suriname	30.4	27
Swaziland	149	103
Sweden	7.7	4
Switzerland	9.8	5
Syria	15.3	38
Taiwan	18	6
Tajikistan	n.a.	112
Tanzania	160–165 (1967)	97
Thailand	25.5	31
Togo	127	80
Tonga	20.5	39
Trinidad and Tobago	28.6	19
Tunisia	125	33

Nation	1975	1998
Turkey	153 (1967)	38
Turkmenistan	n.a.	73
Tuvalu	n.a.	26
Uganda	160	93
Ukraine	n.a.	22
United Arab Emirates	—	15
United Kingdom	14	6
United States	14	6
Uruguay	45.9	14
Uzbekistan	n.a.	71
Vanuatu	n.a.	61
Venezuela	40.4	28
Vietnam	150	36
Yemen		72
in 1975:		
North Yemen	152	
South Yemen	152	
Yugoslavia	33.6	14
Zambia	259	93
Zimbabwe (Rhodesia in 1975)	122	62

Sources: World Almanac and Book of Facts 1979, 1981, 1999; Information Please Almanac 1980; Time Almanac 1999

Literacy in the World's Independent Nations 1975–98
(percentage of adult population)

Nations not independent in a given year are listed as "n.a.";"—" indicates no definite figures available.

Nation	1975	1998
Afghanistan	8	29
Albania	75	72
Algeria	26	57
Andorra	n.a.	100
Angola	12	42
Antigua and Barbuda	n.a.	90
Argentina	93 (1973)	96 (1990)
Armenia	n.a.	99 (1989)
Australia	98 (1973)	100
Austria	75	99
Azerbaijan	n.a.	100 (1995)
Bahamas	—	95
Bahrain	50	77
Bangladesh	25	35
Barbados	97	99
Belarus	n.a.	100
Belgium	98	99
Belize	n.a.	91
Benin	20	23
Bhutan	—	42
Bolivia	40	82
Bosnia and Herzegovina	n.a.	86 (1991)
Botswana	20	74
Brazil	68	81
Brunei	n.a.	80
Bulgaria	95	98
Burkina Faso (Upper Volta in 1975)	7	18
Burundi	10	41
Cambodia (Kampuchea in 1975)	50	69
Cameroon	12	54
Canada	95	99
Cape Verde	—	67
Central African Republic (Central African Empire in 1975)	12	38
Chad	7	30
Chile	90	95
China	95	84
Colombia	78	87
Comoros	—	48
Congo, Dem. Rep. of the/Zaire	13	72

Nation	1975	1998
Congo, Republic of the	20	57
Costa Rica	89	93
Côte d'Ivoire	20	54
Croatia	n.a.	97
Cuba	83	94
Cyprus	80	94
Czech Republic (Czechoslovakia in 1975)	99	99
Denmark	99	99
Djibouti	—	48
Dominica	—	94
Dominican Republic	68	84
Ecuador	75	90
Egypt	40	48
El Salvador	58	73
Equatorial Guinea	20	50
Eritrea	n.a.	20
Estonia	n.a.	100
Ethiopia	7	28
Fiji	64	79
Finland	99	100
France	99	99
Gabon	12	61
Gambia	10	27
Georgia	n.a.	99 (1995)
Germany		99
in 1975:		
East Germany	99	
West Germany	99	
Ghana	25	60
Greece	84	93
Grenada	—	98
Guatemala	46	55
Guinea	10	24 in French; 48 in local langs.
Guinea-Bissau	—	37
Guyana	85	96
Haiti	10	53
Honduras	50	73
Hungary	98	98
Iceland	99	100
India	36	52
Indonesia	60	84
Iran	37	54
Iraq	26	60
Ireland	99	98
Israel	88	92

Nation	1975	1998
Italy	94	97
Jamaica	86	98
Japan	99	99
Jordan	32	80
Kazakhstan	n.a.	98
Kenya	25	69
Kiribati	n.a.	90
Korea, North	85	100
Korea, South	88	98
Kuwait	55	73
Kyrgyzstan	n.a.	100
Laos	22	45
Latvia	n.a.	100
Lebanon	86	80
Lesotho	50	56 (1989)
Liberia	10	40
Libya	30	64
Liechtenstein	—	100
Lithuania	n.a.	98
Luxembourg	98	100
Macedonia	n.a.	89 (1996)
Madagascar	39	80
Malawi	22	49
Malaysia	61	78
Maldives	36	91
Mali	10	32
Malta	80	88
Marshall Islands	n.a.	91
Mauritania	5	34
Mauritius	62	81
Mexico	82	87
Micronesia	n.a.	85
Moldova	n.a.	96 (1995)
Monaco	—	99
Mongolia	95	97
Morocco	20	50
Mozambique	7	33
Myanmar (Burma in 1975)	76	81
Namibia	n.a.	38
Nauru	—	99
Nepal	36	26
Netherlands	98	99
New Zealand	64	99
Nicaragua	57	57
Niger	5	28
Nigeria	25	51
Norway	99	99

Nation	1975	1998
Oman	50	65.8
Pakistan	25	35
Palau	n.a.	86
Panama	79	89
Papua New Guinea	29	50
Paraguay	74	90
Peru	72	85
Philippines	80	94
Poland	98	98
Portugal	65	85
Qatar	10	76
Romania	98	96
Russia (Soviet Union in 1975)	99	98
Rwanda	23	50
Saint Kitts and Nevis	n.a.	98
Saint Lucia	n.a.	67
Saint Vincent and the Grenadines	n.a.	96
Samoa	—	98.3
San Marino	—	96
São Tomé and Príncipe	—	57
Saudi Arabia	15	62
Senegal	10	38
Seychelles	n.a.	58
Sierra Leone	15	21
Singapore	76	90
Slovakia	n.a.	99
Slovenia	n.a.	99
Solomon Islands	n.a.	30
Somalia	5	24
South Africa	35	76
Spain	92	95
Sri Lanka	84	88
Sudan	19	27
Suriname	—	95
Swaziland	36	70
Sweden	99	99
Switzerland	99	99
Syria	40	65
Taiwan	88	92
Tajikistan	n.a.	98 (1989)
Tanzania	18	52
Thailand	82	93
Togo	10	43
Tonga	—	47
Trinidad and Tobago	90	95
Tunisia	32	65
Turkey	55	81

Nation	1975	1998
Turkmenistan	n.a.	98
Tuvalu	n.a.	under 50
Uganda	20	54
Ukraine	n.a.	100
United Arab Emirates	20	68
United Kingdom	98	99
United States	99	97
Uruguay	91	96
Uzbekistan	n.a.	97
Vanuatu	n.a.	55
Venezuela	82	91.1
Vietnam	65	94
Yemen		39
in 1975:		
North Yemen	10	
South Yemen	15	
Yugoslavia	86	90.5
Zambia	40	73
Zimbabwe (Rhodesia in 1975)	27	85

Sources: World Almanac and Book of Facts 1981; U.S. Census Bureau, reported in Time Almanac 1999

Population of the World's Independent Nations *at 30-year Intervals,*
1900–90

Includes only independent nations. Nations not independent in a given year are listed as "n.a." Figures are from contemporary censuses or estimates. "—" indicates no definite figures available.

Nation	1900	1930	1960	1990
Afghanistan	4,000,000	6,330,500	13,000,000	15,592,000
Albania	n.a.	1,003,068	1,607,000	3,268,000
Algeria	n.a.	n.a.	n.a.	25,714,000
Angola	n.a.	n.a.	n.a.	8,802,000
Antigua and Barbuda	n.a.	n.a.	n.a.	64,000
Argentina	4,044,911	10,904,022	20,009,000	32,291,000
Australia	n.a.	6,429,209	10,166,173	16,646,000
Austria	41,827,700	6,675,283	7,067,000	7,595,000
Bahamas	n.a.	n.a.	n.a.	251,000
Bahrain	n.a.	n.a.	n.a.	512,000
Bangladesh	n.a.	n.a.	n.a.	117,976,000
Barbados	n.a.	n.a.	n.a.	260,000
Belgium	6,030,043	7,995,558	9,153,000	9,895,000
Belize	n.a.	n.a.	n.a.	180,400
Benin	n.a.	n.a.	1,720,000	4,840,000
Bhutan	n.a.	n.a.	700,000	1,566,000
Bolivia	2,500,000	2,952,139	3,462,000	6,730,000
Botswana	n.a.	n.a.	n.a.	1,218,000
Brazil	18,000,000	40,272,650	70,799,000	153,771,000
Brunei	n.a.	n.a.	n.a.	372,000
Bulgaria	n.a.	5,596,800	7,867,000	8,978,000
Burkina Faso	n.a.	n.a.	3,500,000	8,941,000
Burundi	n.a.	n.a.	n.a.	5,647,000
Cambodia	n.a.	n.a.	4,952,000	6,592,000
Cameroon	n.a.	n.a.	3,225,000	11,900,000
Canada	n.a.	9,934,500	18,238,247	26,620,500
Cape Verde	n.a.	n.a.	n.a.	339,000
Central African Republic	n.a.	n.a.	1,180,000	2,879,000
Chad	n.a.	n.a.	2,580,000	5,064,000
Chile	3,110,085	4,364,395	7,627,000	13,000,000
China	402,680,000	400,800,000	669,000,000	1,130,065,000
Colombia	4,600,000	7,967,788	14,132,000	32,598,000
Comoros	n.a.	n.a.	n.a.	459,000
Congo, Dem. Rep. of the/Zaire	8,000,000	n.a.	14,150,000	35,330,000
Congo, Republic of the	n.a.	n.a.	790,000	2,305,000

Nation	1900	1930	1960	1990
Costa Rica	309,683	471,521	1,171,000	3,032,000
Cuba	1,600,000	3,607,919	6,743,000	10,582,000
Cyprus	n.a.	n.a.	563,000	708,000
Czechoslovakia	n.a.	14,523,186	13,649,000	15,695,000
Denmark	2,172,205	3,434,555	4,581,000	5,134,000
Djibouti	n.a.	n.a.	n.a.	530,000
Dominica	n.a.	n.a.	n.a.	85,000
Dominican Republic	600,000	897,405	3,014,000	7,253,000
Ecuador	1,300,000	1,500,000	4,298,000	10,506,000
Egypt	n.a.	14,168,756	26,080,000	54,139,000
El Salvador	800,500	1,610,000	2,612,000	5,221,000
Equatorial Guinea	n.a.	n.a.	n.a.	360,000
Estonia	n.a.	1,110,538	n.a.	n.a.
Ethiopia	4,500,000	10,000,000	22,000,000	51,375,000
Fiji	n.a.	n.a.	n.a.	772,000
Finland	n.a.	3,582,406	4,477,300	4,977,000
France	38,517,975	40,745,874	45,355,000	56,184,000
Gabon	n.a.	n.a.	410,000	1,069,000
Gambia	n.a.	n.a.	n.a.	860,000
Germany	46,329,901	62,348,782	72,875,000	79,070,000
Ghana	n.a.	n.a.	6,691,000	15,310,000
Greece	2,433,806	6,204,468	8,327,000	10,066,000
Grenada	n.a.	n.a.	n.a.	84,000
Guatemala	1,535,632	2,119,165	3,759,000	9,340,000
Guinea	n.a.	n.a.	3,000,000	7,269,000
Guinea-Bissau	n.a.	n.a.	n.a.	998,000
Guyana	n.a.	n.a.	n.a.	765,000
Haiti	1,211,625	2,300,200	3,505,000	5,862,000
Honduras	420,000	773,408	1,950,000	5,261,000
Hungary	n.a.	8,603,922	10,002,000	10,546,000
Iceland	n.a.	103,317	176,000	251,000
India	n.a.	n.a.	440,316,000	844,000,000
Indonesia	n.a.	n.a.	92,600,000	191,266,000
Iran	7,653,600	10,000,000	20,633,000	55,647,000
Iraq	n.a.	3,000,000	7,085,000	18,782,000
Ireland	n.a.	2,972,802	2,834,000	3,557,000
Israel	n.a.	n.a.	2,105,530	4,371,000
Italy	20,699,785	41,168,000	50,763,000	57,657,000
Ivory Coast	n.a.	n.a.	3,200,000	12,070,000
Jamaica	n.a.	n.a.	n.a.	2,513,000
Japan	41,089,940	62,938,200	93,600,000	123,778,000
Jordan	n.a.	n.a.	1,695,000	3,065,000
Kenya	n.a.	n.a.	n.a.	25,393,000
Kiribati	n.a.	n.a.	n.a.	65,000
Korea, North	n.a.	n.a.	8,250,000	23,059,000
Korea, South	10,519,000	n.a.	24,994,117	43,919,000

Nation	1900	1930	1960	1990
Kuwait	n.a.	n.a.	n.a.	2,080,000
Laos	n.a.	n.a.	3,000,000	4,024,000
Latvia	n.a.	1,895,016	n.a.	n.a.
Lebanon	n.a.	n.a.	1,646,000	3,340,000
Lesotho	n.a.	n.a.	n.a.	1,757,000
Liberia	1,050,000	1,500,000	2,750,000	2,644,000
Libya	n.a.	n.a.	1,195,000	4,280,000
Liechtenstein	n.a.	11,500	16,495	28,000
Lithuania	n.a.	2,316,615	n.a.	n.a.
Luxembourg	—	285,524	314,000	369,000
Madagascar	n.a.	n.a.	5,200,000	11,802,000
Malawi	n.a.	n.a.	n.a.	9,080,000
Malaysia	n.a.	n.a.	6,909,000	17,053,000
Maldives	n.a.	n.a.	n.a.	219,000
Mali	n.a.	n.a.	3,708,000	9,182,000
Malta	n.a.	n.a.	n.a.	354,900
Mauritania	n.a.	n.a.	650,000	2,038,000
Mauritius	n.a.	n.a.	n.a.	1,141,900
Mexico	12,619,949	16,404,030	34,625,903	88,335,000
Monaco	—	24,927	22,500	29,000
Mongolia	n.a.	1,800,000	1,000,000	2,185,000
Morocco	6,500,000	n.a.	10,780,000	26,249,000
Mozambique	n.a.	n.a.	n.a.	14,718,000
Myanmar	n.a.	n.a.	20,662,000	41,279,000
Namibia	n.a.	n.a.	n.a.	1,372,000
Nauru	n.a.	n.a.	n.a.	8,100
Nepal	2,000,000	5,639,092	9,180,000	19,158,000
Netherlands	4,450,870	7,625,938	11,417,254	14,864,000
New Zealand	n.a.	1,407,165	2,403,488	3,397,000
Nicaragua	420,000	638,119	1,475,000	3,606,000
Niger	n.a.	n.a.	2,600,000	7,691,000
Nigeria	n.a.	n.a.	34,296,000	118,865,000
Norway	n.a.	2,649,775	3,587,000	4,214,000
Oman	n.a.	n.a.	n.a.	1,305,000
Pakistan	n.a.	n.a.	88,211,000	113,163,000
Panama	n.a.	467,459	1,053,000	2,423,000
Papua New Guinea	n.a.	n.a.	n.a.	3,613,000
Paraguay	600,000	791,469	1,760,000	4,660,000
Peru	3,000,000	5,500,000	10,857,000	21,904,000
Philippines	n.a.	n.a.	27,456,000	66,647,000
Poland	n.a.	30,212,962	29,731,000	38,363,000
Portugal	4,708,178	5,628,610	9,124,000	10,528,000
Qatar	n.a.	n.a.	n.a.	498,000
Romania	5,376,000	17,393,149	18,403,000	23,269,000
Russian Empire/ Soviet Union	136,000,000	158,500,000	214,400,000	290,939,000

Nation	1900	1930	1960	1990
Rwanda	n.a.	n.a.	n.a.	7,603,000
St. Kitts and Nevis	n.a.	n.a.	n.a.	40,000
Saint Lucia	n.a.	n.a.	n.a.	153,000
Saint Vincent and the Grenadines	n.a.	n.a.	n.a.	106,000
Samoa	n.a.	n.a.	n.a.	169,000
San Marino	—	12,027	15,000	23,000
São Tomé and Príncipe	n.a.	n.a.	n.a.	125,000
Saudi Arabia	n.a.	7,000,000	6,500,000	16,758,000
Senegal	n.a.	n.a.	2,260,000	7,740,000
Seychelles	n.a.	n.a.	n.a.	71,000
Sierra Leone	n.a.	n.a.	n.a.	4,168,000
Singapore	n.a.	n.a.	n.a.	2,703,000
Solomon Islands	n.a.	n.a.	n.a.	314,000
Somalia	n.a.	n.a.	2,500,000	8,415,000
South Africa	n.a.	6,928,580	15,841,128	39,550,000
Spain	17,550,216	22,760,854	30,128,000	39,623,000
Sri Lanka	n.a.	n.a.	10,167,000	17,135,000
Sudan	n.a.	n.a.	10,262,674	25,164,000
Suriname	n.a.	n.a.	n.a.	408,000
Swaziland	n.a.	n.a.	n.a.	779,000
Sweden	4,784,981	6,120,080	7,450,000	8,407,000
Switzerland	2,933,334	4,018,500	4,561,000	6,628,000
Syria	n.a.	n.a.	n.a.	12,471,000
Taiwan	n.a.	n.a.	10,611,000	20,454,000
Tanzania	n.a.	n.a.	n.a.	26,070,000
Thailand	5,700,000	11,506,200	25,520,000	54,890,000
Togo	n.a.	n.a.	1,440,000	3,566,000
Tonga	n.a.	n.a.	n.a.	108,000
Trinidad and Tobago	n.a.	n.a.	n.a.	1,270,000
Tunisia	n.a.	n.a.	4,060,000	8,094,000
Turkey	20,923,900	13,640,810	27,829,000	56,549,000
Tuvalu	n.a.	n.a.	n.a.	9,000
Uganda	n.a.	n.a.	n.a.	17,593,000
United Arab Emirates	n.a.	n.a.	n.a.	2,250,000
United Kingdom	37,888,439	44,173,704	52,675,094	57,121,000
United States	75,994,575	122,775,046	179,323,175	248,709,873
Uruguay	840,725	1,850,129	2,827,000	3,002,000
Vanuatu	n.a.	n.a.	n.a.	150,000
Vatican City	n.a.	565	1,000	750
Venezuela	2,444,816	3,026,818	6,709,000	19,753,000
Vietnam	n.a.	n.a.	29,000,000	68,488,000
Yemen	n.a.	2,500,000	5,000,000	11,500,000
Yugoslavia	2,096,043	13,290,000	18,667,000	23,864,000

Nation	1900	1930	1960	1990
Zambia	n.a.	n.a.	n.a.	8,119,000
Zimbabwe	n.a.	n.a.	n.a.	10,205,000

Sources: World Almanac and Book of Facts 1901, 1931, 1961, 1962, 1963, 1991, 1992; *Britannica Book of the Year* 1962.

Notes:

Australia—Like Canada, New Zealand, and South Africa, Australia was recognized as a a self-governing dominion of the British Empire as of 1907, though complete independence did not come until 1931.

Austria—1900 figure is for the Austro-Hungarian Empire; later figures are for Austria only.

Benin—Called Dahomey in 1960.

Burkina Faso—Called Upper Volta in 1960.

Canada—Dominion as of 1907 (see Australia); 1960 figure is from 1961 census.

Congo, Democratic Republic of the—1900 figure is for Congo Free State; no figure for 1930, because the region was then a colony, the Belgian Congo; called Congo in 1960; called Zaire in 1990. In 1997, the country regained the name Congo.

Czechoslovakia—Divided into Czech Republic and Slovakia in 1993.

Egypt—1960 figure is for Egypt as a component of the United Arab Republic, which consisted of both Egypt and Syria. Total 1960 population of Egypt and Syria combined: 30,641,000.

Germany—1900 figure is for the German Empire, exclusive of German Africa; 1960 figure is combined total of 55,577,000 in West Germany (Federal Republic of Germany) and 17,298,000 in East Germany (German Democratic Republic).

India—1960 figure is from 1961 UN estimate.

Iran—Called Persia in 1900.

Ireland—1930 figure is for Irish Free State.

Korea, North—In 1900 and 1930, North Korea was not a separate state; its population is included under heading South Korea.

Korea, South—1900 figure is for Korea, comprising the regions that would become South and North Korea; the no figure for 1930, because Korea was then a Chinese colony.

Madagascar—1960 figure is for Malagasy Republic.

Malaysia—1960 figure is for Federation of Malaya; 1990 figure is for Malaysia.

Myanmar—Called Burma in 1960.

New Zealand—Dominion as of 1907 (see Australia).

Russia—1900 figure is for the Russian Empire; 1930, 1960, and 1990 figures are for the Soviet Union. The Soviet Union ceased to exist in 1991.

Samoa—Called Western Samoa in 1990.

Saudi Arabia—Called Arabia in 1930.

South Africa—Dominion as of 1907 (see Australia).

Sri Lanka—Called Ceylon in 1960; 1960 figure is from 1961 census.

Sweden—1900 figure is for Sweden only, excluding Norway, which was then united to it.

Syria—1960 figure is for Syria as a component of the United Arab Republic. See note on Egypt.

Thailand—Called Siam in 1900 and 1930.

Turkey—1900 figure is for European Turkey and Asiatic Turkey, components of Turkish (Ottoman) Empire; later figures are for modern Turkey only.

United Kingdom—1900 figure is for Great Britain and Ireland; 1930 and later figures are for Great Britain and Northern Ireland; 1960 figure comes from 1961 census.

Vietnam—1960 figure is total of 16,000,000 in North Vietnam (Democratic Republic of Vietnam) and 13,000,000 in South Vietnam (Republic of Vietnam).

Yugoslavia—1900 figure is for Serbia only. Montenegro, also independent at that time, had a population of 245,380; with Serbia and other regions, it became part of Yugoslavia in 1928.

Historical Gazetteer:
Geographic Changes 1900–present

This section shows at a glance how the world of 1900 was transformed into the world of 2000. It is a convenient place to look up 20th-century geographical terms no longer in use, such as "Ceylon" and "German East Africa," and to see how they relate to places that still exist.

The **bolded** headword at left indicates a territorial division in 1900; the parenthetical statement next to the headword gives its status in 1900 and its location. Each arrow → indicates a major change in that region's geographic identity, such as name change; gain or loss of independence; fragmentation; or union. **Bolded** words within an entry refer to other entries in this section. This section does not include all internal changes in government, such as that from monarchy to republic; all boundary alterations; or all periods of military occupation.

Abyssinia Common name for **Ethiopia** in early 20th century.

Aden (British colony, Asia) → 1937, surrounding region organized as Aden Protectorate (British-ruled) → 1959, Aden Protectorate became South Arabian Federation of Arab Emirates (British-ruled) → 1963, the colony of Aden itself joined the federation → 1967, the federation became the People's Republic of Southern Yemen, independent (also known as South Yemen) → 1970, Democratic People's Republic of Yemen → 1990, merged with North Yemen to form the Republic of Yemen.

Afghanistan (independent country, Asia) Status unchanged.

Albania (part of Ottoman Empire, Europe) → 1912, independent.

Algeria (French colony, Africa) → 1962, independent.

Andorra (co-ruled by France and Spanish bishop of Urgel, Europe) → 1993, effectively independent.

Anglo-Egyptian Sudan See **Sudan**.

Annam See **French Indochina**.

Angola (Portuguese colony, Africa; also known as Portuguese West Africa) → 1975, Angola, independent.

Antigua and Barbuda (British colony, West Indies) → 1981, independent.

Arabia (part of Ottoman Empire, Asia) → 1915, British protectorate → 1927, Kingdom of Hejaz and Nejd, independent → 1932, Saudi Arabia.

Argentina (independent country, South America) Status unchanged.

Armenia (part of Ottoman Empire, Asia) → 1918, independent → 1920, annexed by Soviet Union → 1922, became part of the **Transcaucasian** Soviet Federated Socialist Republic → 1936, Armenia became separate constituent republic of Soviet Union → 1991, independent.

Australia (British possession, between Indian and Pacific Oceans) → 1901, six colonies (New South Wales, Victoria, Tasmania or Van Diemen's Land, South Australia, Queensland, Western Australia) federated as states in the Commonwealth of Australia → 1931, independent.

Austria See **Austro-Hungarian Empire**.

Austro-Hungarian Empire (independent empire, Europe) → 1918, empire collapsed, giving rise to the following independent countries: Austria; Hungary; Czechoslovakia; Kingdom of the Serbs,

Croats, and Slovenes (later Yugoslavia). Austria and Hungary remained independent throughout the century, except for occupation by Nazi Germany during World War II (1938–45 in Austria's case, 1944–45 in Hungary's case) and by Allied troops briefly after the war. For Yugoslavia, see **Serbia**; for Czechoslovakia, see **Czech lands and Slovakia**.

Azerbaijan (part of Russian Empire, Asia) → 1918, independent → 1920, annexed by Soviet Union → 1922, became part of the **Transcaucasian** Soviet Federated Socialist Republic → 1936, Azerbaijan became separate constituent republic of Soviet Union → 1991, independent.

Bahamas (British colony, West Indies) → 1973, independent.

Bahrain (British protectorate, Persian Gulf) → 1971, independent.

Bangladesh See **East Bengal, British India**.

Barbados (British colony, West Indies) → 1966, independent.

Basutoland (British protectorate, Africa) → 1966, independent as Lesotho.

Bechuanaland (British protectorate, Africa) → 1966, independent as Botswana.

Belarus See **Belorussia**.

Belgium (independent country, Europe) Status unchanged.

Belorussia (part of Russian Empire, Europe) → 1918, independent → 1919, annexed by Soviet Union → 1921, western portion ceded to Poland → 1939, western portion reannexed by Soviet Union → 1991, independent as Belarus.

Belize See **British Honduras**.

Benin See **Dahomey**.

Bhutan (British possession, Asia) → 1910, British protectorate → 1949, independent.

Bismarck Archipelago (German protectorate, Pacific Ocean) → 1920, League of Nations mandate to Australia → 1947, UN trust territory to Australia → 1973, incorporated into self-governing Papua New Guinea, under Australian administration → 1975, Papua New Guinea independent.

Bokhara See **Bukhara**.

Bolivia (independent country, South America) Status unchanged.

Borneo Island that includes **Brunei** and parts of Malaysia (former **British Malaya**) and Indonesia (former **Dutch East Indies**).

Bosnia and Hercegovina (part of Austro-Hungarian Empire, Europe) → 1918, became part of the Kingdom of the Serbs, Croats, and Slovenes → 1929, that state renamed Yugoslavia → 1992, Bosnia and Hercegovina independent.

Botswana See **Bechuanaland**.

Brazil (independent country, South America) Status unchanged.

Britain See **United Kingdom**.

British Central African Protectorate (British protectorate, Africa; also called Nyasaland or North-East Rhodesia) → 1907, Nyasaland, British protectorate → 1953, became part of British-ruled Federation of **Rhodesia** and Nyasaland → 1963, federation dissolved; Nyasaland independent as Malawi.

British East Africa Former name for the British dependencies that became **Kenya, Uganda,** and Tanzania (see **German East Africa**).

British Guiana (British colony, South America) → 1966, independent as Guyana.

British Honduras (British colony, Central America) → 1981, independent as Belize.

British India (British colony, Asia) → 1937, Burma, formerly part of British India, made a separate protectorate (see **Burma**) → 1947, remainder of British India independent as India and Pakistan → 1950, India transformed into republic → 1956, Pakistan transformed into republic → 1971, East Pakistan (the part of Pakistan that had been called East Bengal under British rule) independent as Bangladesh.

British Malaya (British colony, Asia) → 1957, a portion of this territory independent as the Federation of Malaya → 1963, Malaysia formed from a union of the Federation of Malaya with other parts of British Malaya: Singapore, Sabah (formerly known as North Borneo or British North Borneo), and Sarawak → 1965, Singapore withdrew from Malaysia, becoming independent.

British North Borneo See **British Malaya**.

British Somaliland See **Somaliland**.

Brunei (British protectorate on island of Borneo, Asia) → 1905, British dependency → 1984, independent.

Bukhara (part of Russian Empire; also known as Bokhara) → 1918, merged with Khiva and Kokand, nearby states that shared its Uzbek ethnicity, to form part of the **Turkestan** Autonomous Soviet Socialist Republic of the Soviet Union → 1924, reorganized as Uzbek Soviet Socialist Republic → 1991, independent as Uzbekistan.

Bulgaria (part of Ottoman Empire, Europe) → 1908, independent.

Burkina Faso See **Upper Volta**.

Burma (part of British India, Asia) → 1937, separated from British India as self-governing colony under British protectorate → 1948, independent → 1989, name changed to Myanmar.

Burundi See **German East Africa**.

Cambodia (part of French Indochina, Asia) → 1953, independent. Also known as Kampuchea, particularly 1976–79.

Cameroon (German protectorate, Africa) → 1919, divided between Britain and France as League of Nations mandates: western part, known as British Cameroon, incorporated into British colony of **Nigeria**; eastern part, known as French Cameroon, treated as a discrete colony → 1946, both parts, known collectively as the Cameroons, became UN trust territories → 1960, French Cameroon independent as Cameroon; Nigeria, including British Cameroon, also became independent → 1961, southern third of British Cameroon was united with independent Cameroon; northern two-thirds remained part of Nigeria.

Cameroons Former term for the region comprising British Cameroon and French Cameroon (see **Cameroon**).

Canada (British dominion, North America) → 1931, independent → 1949, added Newfoundland as a province (previously a separate British dominion).

Cape Colony (British colony, Africa; nearby Natal was also a British colony) → 1902, British territory near Cape Colony expanded with addition of Transvaal, which was formerly the independent South African Republic, and the formerly independent Orange Free State → 1910, Cape Colony (renamed Cape of Good Hope), Natal, Transvaal, and Orange Free State united as Union of South Africa, a self-governing British dominion → 1931, South Africa effectively independent → 1961, renamed Republic of South Africa.

Cape Verde (Portuguese colony, Atlantic Ocean, near Africa) → 1953, overseas province of Portugal → 1975, independent as Cape Verde.

Caroline Islands (German possession, Pacific Ocean) → 1920, League of Nations mandate, Japan → 1947, part of U.S.-administered UN Trust Territory of the Pacific Islands → 1986, some islands independent as Micronesia → 1994, other islands independent as Palau.

Central African Protectorate See **British Central African Protectorate**.

Central African Republic See **Ubangi-Shari**.

Ceylon (British colony, Indian Ocean) → 1948, independent → 1972, renamed Sri Lanka.

Chad (French colony, Africa) —> 1910, incorporated into French Equatorial Africa → 1960, independent.

Chile (independent country, South America) Status unchanged.

China (independent empire, Asia) → 1912, became Republic of China; region of **Tibet** became independent → 1949, People's Republic of China established on mainland; rival Republic of China government installed in **Taiwan** → 1951, annexed Tibet.

Cochin China See **French Indochina**.

Colombia (independent country, South and Central America) → 1903, Central American region gained independence as Panama.

Comoros (French possession, Indian Ocean) → 1912, colony → 1946, French overseas territory → 1975, independent.

Congo Common name of two African countries. For country formerly known as Zaire with capital at Kinshasa, see **Congo Free State**. For country with capital at Brazzaville, see **Middle Congo**.

Congo Free State (Belgian king's possession, Africa) → 1908, reorganized as Belgian Congo, a colony of Belgium → 1960, independent as Republic of the Congo → 1966, renamed Democratic Republic of the Congo → 1971, renamed Republic of Zaire → 1997, renamed Democratic Republic of the Congo. Sometimes called Congo-Kinshasa, for its capital at Kinshasa, to distinguish it from Congo-Brazzaville (see **Middle Congo**).

Costa Rica (independent country, Central America). Status unchanged.

Côte d'Ivoire (French colony, Africa; also called Ivory Coast) → 1960, independent.

Croatia (part of Austro-Hungarian Empire, Europe) → 1918, part of the Kingdom of the Serbs, Croats, and Slovenes → 1929, that state renamed Yugoslavia → 1991, Croatia independent.

Cuba (under U.S. occupation, West Indies) → 1902, independent.

Cyprus (part of Ottoman Empire under British administration, Mediterranean Sea) → 1914, annexed by Britain → 1925, colony of Britain → 1960, independent → 1975, de facto partition between the Republic of Cyprus in south and the Turkish Federated State of Cyprus (controlled by Turkey) in north → 1983, Turkish Federated State of Cyprus renamed the Turkish Republic of

Northern Cyprus, nominally independent though not internationally recognized.

Czech lands and Slovakia (parts of Austro-Hungarian empire, Europe; the Czech lands consisted of Bohemia, Moravia, and Czech parts of Silesia) → 1918, united as Czechoslovakia following collapse that year of Austro-Hungarian empire → 1993, divided into two countries, the Czech Republic and Slovakia.

Dahomey (French colony, Africa) → 1904, incorporated into French West Africa → 1960, independent as Dahomey → 1975, name changed to Benin.

Denmark (independent country, Europe) Status unchanged.

Djibouti See **Somaliland.**

Dominica (British colony, West Indies) → 1978, independent.

Dominican Republic (independent country, West Indies) Status unchanged.

Dutch East Indies (Dutch colony, Asia; also called Netherlands East Indies) → 1945, independent as Indonesia → 1963, annexed Irian Jaya or West Irian, previously a Dutch possession on island of New Guinea → 1976, annexed East Timor, previously a Portuguese colony.

Dutch Guiana (Dutch colony, South America) → 1975, independent as Suriname (also spelled Surinam).

East Bengal (part of British India, Asia) → 1947, part of independent Pakistan, known as East Pakistan → 1971, independent as Bangladesh.

Ecuador (independent country, South America) Status unchanged.

Egypt (part of Ottoman Empire under British administration, Africa) → 1914, British protectorate → 1922, independent → 1958, merged with Syria to form United Arab Republic → 1961, Syria seceded; Egypt retained name United Arab Republic → 1971, name changed back to Egypt.

El Salvador (independent country, Central America; also known as Salvador) Status unchanged.

Ellice Islands See **Gilbert and Ellice Islands.**

Equatorial Guinea See **Spanish Guinea.**

Eritrea (Italian colony, Africa) → 1941, occupied by Britain → 1952, became part of Ethiopia → 1991, independent.

Fernando Po See **Spanish Guinea.**

Fiji (British colony, Pacific Ocean) → 1970, independent.

Finland (part of Russian Empire, Europe) → 1917, independent.

Formosa See **Taiwan.**

France (independent country, Europe) Status unchanged.

French Equatorial Africa (French colony, also called French Congo) Created in 1910, comprising a federation of **Chad, Gabon, Middle Congo** (modern Republic of Congo), and **Ubangi-Shari** (modern Central African Republic) → 1958, dissolved. See also individual entries.

French Guinea (French colony, Africa) → 1958, independent as Guinea.

French Indochina (French-ruled federation, Asia; also known as Union of Indochina) Federation comprising French colony of Cochin China and French protectorates of Tonkin, Annam, Laos, and Cambodia → 1945, Vietnam (former Tonkin, Annam, and Cochin China) independent → 1954, Vietnam divided into Democratic Republic of Vietnam or North Vietnam (former Tonkin and part of Annam) and Republic of Vietnam or South Vietnam (former Cochin China and part of Annam) → 1975, North Vietnam conquered South Vietnam → 1976, North and South Vietnam united as Socialist Republic of Vietnam. For **Cambodia** and **Laos**, see separate entries.

French Somaliland See **Somaliland.**

French Sudan (French colony, Africa) → 1960, independent as part of Mali Federation (comprising itself and Senegal) → 1960, with dissolution of federation, independent as Mali.

French West Africa (federation of French territories, Africa) Created in 1895, the federation came to comprise **Dahomey** (now Benin), **French Guinea** (now Guinea), **French Sudan** (now Mali), **Côte d'Ivoire, Mauritania, Niger, Senegal**, and **Upper Volta** (now Burkina Faso) → 1959, federation dissolved. See also individual entries.

Friendly Islands See **Tonga.**

Gabon (French colony, Africa) → 1910, French Equatorial Africa → 1960, independent.

Gambia (British colony, Africa) → 1965, independent.

Georgia (part of Russian Empire, Asia) → 1918, independent → 1921, annexed by Soviet Union → 1922, became part of the **Transcaucasian** Soviet Federated Socialist Republic → 1936, Georgia became separate constituent republic of Soviet Union → 1991, independent.

German East Africa (German colony, Africa) → 1919, divided into Ruanda-Urundi (League of Nations mandate, Belgium) and Tanganyika (League of Nations mandate, Britain; considered part of **British East Africa**) → 1946, Ruanda-Urundi (UN trust territory, Belgium), Tanganyika (UN trust territory, Britain) → 1961, Tanganyika independent → 1962, Ruanda independent as Rwanda; Urundi independent as Burundi → 1964, Tanganyika united with **Zanzibar** as Tanzania.

German Empire (independent empire, Europe) → 1918, empire collapsed → 1919, Germany formed as a republic → 1949, Germany divided into the Federal Republic of Germany (West Germany) and the German Democratic Republic (East Germany) → 1990, German Democratic Republic (East Germany) dissolved; Germany reunified as Federal Republic of Germany.

German South-West Africa (German protectorate, Africa) → 1915, conquered by South Africa → 1920, League of Nations mandate assigned to South Africa and known as South-West Africa → 1949, incorporated into South Africa → 1990, independent as Namibia.

Germany See **German Empire.**

Ghana See **Gold Coast.**

Gilbert and Ellice Islands (British protectorate, Pacific Ocean) → 1915-16, British colony → 1975, Gilbert Islands separated from Ellice Islands → 1978, Ellice Islands became independent Tuvalu → 1979, Gilbert Islands became independent Kiribati.

Gold Coast (British colony, Africa) → 1956, British Togoland added → 1957, independent as Ghana.

Great Britain See **United Kingdom.**

Greece (independent country, Europe) Status unchanged.

Grenada (British colony, West Indies) → 1974, independent.

Guatemala (independent country, Central America) Status unchanged.

Guinea Present-day name of former **French Guinea**. See also **Portuguese Guinea** and **Spanish Guinea**.

Guinea-Bissau See **Portuguese Guinea**.

Guyana See **British Guiana**.

Haiti (independent country, West Indies) Status unchanged.

Honduras (independent country, Central America) Status unchanged.

Hungary See **Austro-Hungarian Empire**.

Iceland (Danish possession, Atlantic Ocean) → 1918, independent but shared king with Denmark → 1944, independent republic.

Ifni See **Morocco**.

India See **British India**.

Indochina See **French Indochina**.

Indonesia See **Dutch East Indies**.

Iran See **Persia**.

Iraq (part of Ottoman Empire, Asia; also known as Mesopotamia) → 1920, League of Nations mandate assigned to Britain → 1932, independent.

Ireland (part of **United Kingdom of Britain and Ireland**, Europe) → 1922, self-governing Irish Free State in all but the northern part of Ireland → 1931, effectively independent as dominion → 1937, independent republic.

Irian Jaya See **New Guinea**.

Israel See **Palestine**.

Italian Somaliland (or Somal Coast) See **Somaliland**.

Italy (independent country, Europe) Status unchanged.

Ivory Coast See **Côte d'Ivoire**.

Jamaica (British colony, West Indies) → 1962, independent.

Japan (independent empire, Pacific Ocean) Status unchanged.

Jibouti See **Somaliland**.

Jordan See **Transjordan**.

Kampuchea Alternate name for **Cambodia**.

Katar See **Qatar**.

Kazakhstan (part of Russian Empire, Asia) → 1920, part of Soviet Union → 1991, independent.

Kenya (British protectorate, Africa) → 1902, British dependency → 1920, colony (part of **British East Africa**) → 1963, independent.

Khiva See **Bukhara**.

Khorezm (or Khwarazm) Alternate name for Khiva. See **Bukhara**.

Kingdom of the Serbs, Croats, and Slovenes See **Serbia**.

Kirghizia (part of Russian Empire, Asia) → 1918, incorporated into Soviet Union as part of the **Turkestan** Autonomous Soviet Socialist Republic → 1936, as Kyrgyzstan, became constituent republic of the Soviet Union → 1991, independent.

Kiribati See **Gilbert and Ellice Islands**.

Kokand See **Bukhara**.

Korea (independent country, Asia) → 1905, Japanese protectorate → 1910, annexed by Japan → 1945, occupied by Allied forces → 1948, divided into two independent countries, the Republic of Korea (South Korea) and the Democratic People's Republic of Korea (North Korea).

Kuwait (British protectorate, Asia) → 1961, independent.

Kyrgyzstan See **Kirghizia**.

Lagos See **Nigeria**.

Laos (part of French Indochina, Asia) → 1954, independent.

Latvia (part of Russian Empire, Europe) → 1918, independent → 1940, incorporated into Soviet Union → 1991, independent.

Lebanon (part of Ottoman Empire, Asia) → 1920, League of Nations mandate, France → 1941, independent.

Lesotho See **Basutoland**.

Liechtenstein (independent country, Europe) Status unchanged.

Liberia (independent country, Africa) Status unchanged.

Libya See **Tripoli**.

Lithuania (part of Russian Empire, Europe) → 1918, independent → 1940, incorporated into Soviet Union → 1991, independent.

Luxembourg (independent country, Europe) Status unchanged.

Macedonia (part of Ottoman Empire, Europe) → 1913, divided among Serbia, Greece, and Bulgaria, with Serbia receiving the largest share → 1918, Serbian portion of Macedonia became part of the Kingdom of the Serbs, Croats, and Slovenes → 1929, that state renamed Yugoslavia → 1991, Macedonia independent.

Madagascar (French colony, Indian Ocean) → 1960, independent.

Malawi See **British Central African Protectorate**.

Malaya See **British Malaya**.

Malaysia See **British Malaya**.

Maldives (British protectorate, Indian Ocean) → 1965, independent.

Mali See **French Sudan**.

Malta (British possession, Mediterranean Sea) → 1964, independent.

Marshall Islands (German possession, Pacific Ocean) → 1920, League of Nations mandate, Japan → 1947, part of U.S.-administered UN Trust Territory of the Pacific Islands → 1986, independent.

Mauritania (region under French influence, Africa) → 1903, protectorate → 1920, colony, part of French West Africa → 1960, independent.

Mauritius (British colony, Indian Ocean) → 1968, independent.

Mesopotamia See **Iraq**.

Mexico (independent country, North America) Status unchanged.

Micronesia See **Caroline Islands**.

Middle Congo (French colony, Africa) → 1910, incorporated into French Equatorial Africa → 1960, independent as Republic of the Congo → 1970, renamed People's Republic of the Congo → 1991, renamed Republic of the Congo. Sometimes called Congo-Brazzaville, for its capital at Brazzaville, to distinguish it from Congo-Kinshasa (see **Congo Free State**).

Moldova See **Moldovia**.

Moldovia (region divided between the Russian empire and the Ottoman Empire, Europe) → 1918, Russian portion passed on to Soviet Union; Ottoman portion ceded to Romania → 1940, Romania ceded its portion to the Soviet Union; region united as the Moldovan Soviet Socialist Republic, a constituent republic of the Soviet Union → 1991, independent.

Monaco (independent country, Europe) Status unchanged.

Mongolia See **Outer Mongolia**.

Montenegro (independent country, Europe) → 1918, became part of the Kingdom of the Serbs, Croats, and Slovenes → 1929, that state renamed Yugoslavia.

Morocco (independent country, Africa) → 1912, divided between French and Spanish protectorates → 1956, most of the region independent as Morocco; Spain retained portions called the Southern Protectorate and Ifni → 1958, Southern Protectorate ceded to Morocco → 1969, Ifni ceded to Morocco.

Mozambique See **Portuguese East Africa**.

Myanmar See **Burma**.

Namibia See **German South-West Africa**.

Natal See **Cape Colony**.

Nauru (German protectorate, Pacific Ocean; also known as Pleasant Island) → 1920, League of Nations mandate, Australia → 1947, UN trust territory, Australia → 1968, independent.

Nepal (British protectorate, Asia; also spelled Nepaul) → 1923, independent.

Netherlands (independent country, Europe) Status unchanged.

Netherlands East Indies See **Dutch East Indies**.

New Guinea (island divided into Dutch section, known as Netherlands New Guinea, West New Guinea, West Irian, or Irian Jaya; British section, known as British New Guinea or Papua; and German section known as German New Guinea or Kaiser Wilhelm's Land) → 1905, British New Guinea ceded to Australia as Territory of Papua → 1920, Kaiser Wilhelm's Land became Australia-administered League of Nations mandate, known as territory of New Guinea → 1947, territory of New Guinea became UN trust territory, Australia → 1949, territories of Papua and New Guinea merged under Australian administration; came to be known as Papua New Guinea → 1963, Irian Jaya annexed by Indonesia → 1973, Papua New Guinea became self-governing; incorporated nearby **Bismarck Archipelago**, formerly an Australia-administered UN trust territory → 1975, Papua New Guinea independent.

New Hebrides (islands under Anglo-French naval administration, Pacific Ocean) → 1906, Anglo-French condominium → 1980, independent as Vanuatu.

New Zealand (British colony, Pacific Ocean) → 1907, self-governing dominion → 1931, independent.

Newfoundland See **Canada**.

Nicaragua (independent country, Central America) Status unchanged.

Niger (French colony, part of French West Africa) → 1960, independent.

Nigeria (British posession, Africa, divided into the Colony and Protectorate of Southern Nigeria and the Protectorate of Northern Nigeria; colony of Lagos was core of Southern Nigeria) → 1914, two regions united as the Colony and Protectorate of Nigeria → 1919, British **Cameroon** added to Nigeria → 1960, Nigeria independent → 1961, southern third of former British Cameroon ceded to Cameroon.

North Borneo See **British Malaya**.

Northern Rhodesia (British protectorate, Africa; also called North-West Rhodesia to distinguish it from North-East Rhodesia, better known as the British Central African Protectorate or Nyasaland, now Malawi) → 1953, became part of British-ruled Federation of Rhodesia and Nyasaland → 1963, federation dissolved → 1964, Northern Rhodesia independent as Zambia.

Norway (region united with Sweden, Europe) → 1905, independent.

Nyasaland See **British Central African Protectorate**.

Oman (British protectorate, Asia) → 1970, independent.

Orange Free State See **Cape Colony**.

Ottoman Empire (empire, Asia, Europe, and Africa; also known as Turkish Empire) → 1908-20, lost much of its empire, including **Albania, Arabia, Armenia, Bulgaria, Cyprus, Egypt, Iraq, Lebanon, Macedonia, Moldovia, Palestine, Qatar, Syria, Transjordan, Tripoli,** and **Yemen**; see individual entries → 1923, remnant of Ottoman Empire became Republic of Turkey.

Outer Mongolia (part of China, Asia) → 1921, independent as Mongolia.

Pakistan See **British India**.

Palau See **Caroline Islands**.

Palestine (part of Ottoman Empire, Asia) → 1922, League of Nations mandate assigned to Britain → 1948, part of Palestine independent as Israel; Gaza Strip occupied by Egypt; West Bank occupied by Transjordan (Jordan) → 1967, Israel occupied Gaza Strip and West Bank → 1994, limited autonomy began in Gaza Strip and West Bank.

Panama (part of Colombia, Central America) → 1903, independent.

Papua New Guinea See **New Guinea**.

Paraguay (independent country, South America) Status unchanged.

Persia (independent country, Asia) → 1935, name changed to Iran.

Peru (independent country, South America) Status unchanged.

Philippines (American colony, off Asian coast) → 1946, independent.

Pleasant Island See **Nauru**.

Poland (part of Russian Empire, Europe) → 1918, independent.

Portugal (independent country, Europe) Status unchanged.

Portuguese East Africa (Portuguese colony, Africa; also known as Mozambique) → 1975, independent as Mozambique.

Portuguese Guinea (Portuguese colony, Africa) → 1974, independent as Guinea-Bissau.

Portuguese West Africa See **Angola**.

Qatar (part of Ottoman empire, Asia; also spelled Katar) → 1916, British protectorate → 1971, independent.

Rhodesia (British protectorate, Africa; the core of it was Southern Rhodesia, now Zimbabwe; the term also encompassed North-West or Northern Rhodesia, now Zambia, and North-East Rhodesia, better known as the British Central African Protectorate or Nyasaland, now Malawi) → 1923, the entire region except Nyasaland partitioned into Northern Rhodesia and Southern Rhodesia → 1953, the region united as the British-ruled Federation of Rhodesia and Nyasaland → 1963, federation dissolved → 1965, Southern Rhodesia unilaterally declared independence as Rhodesia; not recognized by most countries → 1978, renamed Zimbabwe-Rhodesia → 1980, renamed Zimbabwe, with international recognition of independence. For **Northern Rhodesia** and **British Central African Protectorate**, see separate entries.

Río de Oro (Spanish protectorate, Africa) → 1958, united with adjoining Spanish possession of Saguia el Hamra to form Spanish Sahara → 1976, region renamed Western Sahara and divided between Morocco and Mauritania → 1979, Mauritanian portion of Western Sahara ceded to Morocco.

Río Muni See **Spanish Guinea**.

Romania (independent, Europe; also spelled Roumania and Rumania) Status unchanged.

Ruanda-Urundi See **German East Africa**.

Russian Empire (empire, Europe and Asia) → 1917, czar (emperor) overthrown; Russia, the core of the Russian Empire, became the Russian Soviet Federated Socialist Republic → 1917-22, Russia reunited with much of the old Russian Empire as the Union of Soviet Socialist Republics (U.S.S.R.), or Soviet Union (formally constituted 1922) → 1991, Soviet Union dissolved; Russia reconstituted as Russian Federation; other Soviet republics gained independence, though many continued to be associated with Russia in the Commonwealth of Independent States. See also individual entries on former parts of Russian Empire and/or Soviet Union, including **Armenia, Azerbaijan, Belorussia, Bukhara, Finland, Georgia, Kazakhstan, Kirghizia, Latvia, Lithuania, Moldovia, Poland, Tajikistan, Transcaspian Region, Transcaucasia, Turkestan,** and **Ukraine**.

Rwanda See **German East Africa**.

Sabah See **British Malaya**.

Saguia el Hamra See **Río de Oro**.

Saint Kitts and Nevis (British colony, West Indies; also called Saint Christopher and Nevis) → 1983, independent.

Saint Lucia (British colony, West Indies) → 1979, independent.

Saint Vincent and the Grenadines (British colony, West Indies) → 1979, independent.

Samoa (islands divided between American possession called American Samoa and German possession called Western Samoa) → 1920, Western Samoa became a League of Nations mandate administered by New Zealand → 1947, UN trust territory administered by New Zealand → 1962, independent as Western Samoa → 1997, renamed Samoa.

San Marino (independent, Europe) Status unchanged.

São Tomé and Príncipe (Portuguese colony, off African coast) → 1975, independent.

Sarawak See **British Malaya**.

Saudi Arabia See **Arabia**.

Senegal (French colony, part of French West Africa) → 1960, independent as part of the Mali Federation (comprising former **French Sudan** and Senegal) → 1960, withdrew from federation to become independent Senegal.

Serbia (independent country, Europe; also spelled Servia) → 1912-1913, expanded its territory, gaining present-day Macedonia → 1918, became dominant part of the Kingdom of the Serbs, Croats, and Slovenes, which also included present-day Bosnia and Hercegovina, Croatia, Montenegro, and Slovenia → 1929, Kingdom of the Serbs, Croats, and Slovenes renamed Yugoslavia → 1991, Croatia, Macedonia, and Slovenia became independent from Yugoslavia → 1992, Bosnia and Hercegovina became independent from Yugoslavia; only Serbia and Montenegro remained as Yugoslavia.

Serbs, Croats, and Slovenes, Kingdom of the See **Serbia**.

Seychelles (British possession governed from Mauritius, Indian Ocean) → 1903, became separate colony → 1976, independent.

Siam (independent country, Asia) → 1939, renamed **Thailand**.

Sierra Leone (British protectorate, Africa) → 1961, independent.

Singapore (British colony, Asia) → 1963, became part of independent country of Malaysia → 1965, withdrew from Malaysia, becoming independent.

Slovakia See **Czech lands and Slovakia**.

Slovenia (part of the Austro-Hungarian Empire, Europe) → 1918, part of the Kingdom of the Serbs, Croats, and Slovenes → 1929, that state renamed Yugoslavia → 1991, Slovenia independent.

Solomon Islands (British protectorate, Pacific Ocean) → 1978, independent.

Somalia See **Somaliland**.

Somaliland (region, Africa; divided among British protectorate of British Somaliland; Italian colony of Italian Somaliland; and French protectorate of French Somaliland or Jibouti) → 1941, Italian

Somaliland occupied by Britain → 1950, Italian Somaliland became a UN trust territory administered by Italy → 1960, British and Italian Somaliland united and made independent as Somalia → 1967, French Somaliland (a French overseas territory since the 1940s) renamed the Territory of the Afars and Issas → 1977, Territory of the Afars and Issas independent as Djibouti.

South Africa See **Cape Colony**.

South-West Africa See **German South-West Africa**.

Southern Rhodesia See **Rhodesia**.

Soviet Union See **Russian Empire**.

Spain (independent country, Europe) Status unchanged.

Spanish Guinea (Spanish colony, Africa) → 1959, reorganized as Spanish overseas provinces of Río Muni and Fernando Po (the latter today called Bioko) → 1968, independent as Equatorial Guinea.

Spanish Sahara See **Río de Oro**.

Sri Lanka See **Ceylon**.

Sudan (Anglo-Egyptian condominium, or jointly ruled possession of Britain and Egypt; also known as Anglo-Egyptian Sudan) → 1956, Sudan, independent.

Suriname See **Dutch Guiana**.

Swaziland (protectorate of the Transvaal, Africa) → 1902, became British protectorate → 1968, independent.

Sweden (independent country, Europe) → 1905, granted independence to Norway, formerly united with Sweden.

Switzerland (independent country, Europe) Status unchanged.

Syria (part of Ottoman Empire, Asia) → 1920, independent → 1920, League of Nations mandate, France → 1946, independent.

Taiwan (Japanese possession, Pacific Ocean) → 1945, ceded to Republic of China → 1949, became seat of Republic of China following that government's expulsion from the mainland (see **China**).

Tajikistan (part of Russian Empire) → 1918, incorporated into Soviet Union as part of **Turkestan** Autonomous Soviet Socialist Republic → 1924, became part of Uzbek Soviet Socialist Republic → 1929, became the Tajik Soviet Socialist Republic → 1991, independent.

Tanganyika See **German East Africa**.

Tanzania See **German East Africa**.

Thailand See **Siam**.

Tibet (region under Chinese suzerainty, Asia; also called Xizang) → 1912, independent → 1950, invaded by China → 1951, annexed by China, though formally autonomous.

Timor (island divided between Netherlands and Portugal, located between Indian and Pacific Oceans; Dutch Timor part of Dutch East Indies) → 1946, Dutch Timor became part of Indonesia (former Dutch East Indies) → 1975, Portuguese Timor independent as East Timor; invaded by Indonesia → 1976, Indonesia annexed East Timor.

Togo See **Togoland**.

Togoland (German protectorate, Africa) → 1920, League of Nations mandate, divided between Britain (British Togoland) and France (French Togoland) → 1946, UN trusteeship assigned to Britain and France → 1956, British Togoland incorporated into British colony of **Gold Coast** → 1957, Gold Coast independent as Ghana → 1960, French Togoland independent as Togo.

Tonga (British protectorate, Pacific Ocean; also known as the Friendly Islands) → 1970, independent.

Tonkin See **French Indochina**.

Transcaucasia (part of Russian Empire, Asia)   Region comprising present-day **Armenia**, **Azerbaijan**, and **Georgia**. These three republics were united in the Transcaucasian Soviet Federated Socialist Republic, a constituent republic of the Soviet Union, from 1922 to 1936. See also individual entries.

Transcaspian Region (part of Russian Empire, Asia; also called Turkmenia or Turkmenistan) → 1919-20, conquered by Red Army in civil war → 1921, renamed Turkmen Region → 1922, incorporated into Soviet Union as part of the **Turkestan** Autonomous Soviet Socialist Republic → 1925, as Turkmenistan, became a distinct constituent republic of Soviet Union → 1991, independent.

Transjordan (part of Ottoman Empire, Asia) → 1920, part of British-administered League of Nations mandate of Palestine → 1921, became separate British-administered mandate of Transjordan → 1946, independent as Transjordan → 1948, occupied the West Bank region of **Palestine** → 1949, name changed to Jordan → 1967, lost the West Bank to Israel.

Transvaal See **Cape Colony**.

Trinidad and Tobago (British colony, West Indies) → 1962, independent.

Tripoli (part of Ottoman Empire, Africa) → 1912, conquered by Italy → 1939, as Libya, became province of Italy → 1951, independent.

Trucial Oman (British protectorate, Asia: also known as Trucial States, Trucial Coast, or Trucial Sheikdoms) → 1971, independent as United Arab Emirates.

Tunisia (French protectorate, Africa; also called Tunis) → 1956, independent as Tunisia.

Turkestan (part of Russian Empire, Asia; also spelled Turkistan)   Region comprising present-day Turkmenistan (see **Transcaspian Region**), Uzbekistan (see **Bukhara**), Tajikistan, Kyrgyzstan (see **Kirghizia**), and southern Kazakhstan. The Turkestan Autonomous Soviet Socialist Republic was a part of the Soviet Union from 1918 to 1924. See also individual entries.

Turkey See **Ottoman Empire**.

Turkish Empire See **Ottoman Empire**.

Turkmenistan See **Transcaspian Region**.

Tuvalu See **Gilbert and Ellice Islands**.

U.K. See **United Kingdom of Great Britain and Ireland**.

U.S.A. See **United States of America**.

U.S.S.R. See **Russian Empire**.

Ubangi-Shari (French colony, Africa) → 1910, incorporated into French Equatorial Africa → 1960, independent as Central African Republic → 1976, name changed to Central African Empire →

1979, name restored to Central African Republic.

Uganda (British protectorate, Africa; considered part of British East Africa) → 1962, independent.

Ukraine (part of Russian Empire, Europe) → 1918, independent → 1922, became part of the Soviet Union → 1991, independent.

Union of Indochina See **French Indochina**.

Union of Soviet Socialist Republics See **Russian Empire**.

United Arab Emirates See **Trucial Oman**.

United Kingdom of Great Britain and Ireland (independent country, Europe) → 1922, became United Kingdom of Great Britain and Northern Ireland; southern **Ireland** became self-governing.

United States of America (independent country, North America) → 1907, added Oklahoma, 46th state → 1912, added New Mexico, 47th state, and Arizona, 48th state → 1959, added Alaska, 49th state, and Hawaii, 50th state (all had been U.S. territories in 1900).

Upper Volta (French protectorate, Africa) → 1919, integrated into French West Africa → 1932, divided up and parceled out among neighboring colonies → 1947, reconstituted as one territory → 1960, independent as Upper Volta → 1984, name changed to Burkina Faso.

Uruguay (independent country, South America) Status unchanged.

Uzbekistan See **Bukhara**.

Vanuatu See **New Hebrides**.

Vatican (part of Italy, Europe) → 1929, independent as Vatican City, which included the Vatican and other buildings in Rome and environs.

Venezuela (independent country, South America) Status unchanged.

Vietnam See **French Indochina**.

West Irian See **New Guinea**.

Western Sahara See **Río de Oro**.

Yemen (part of Ottoman Empire, Asia) → 1918, independent → 1967, became commonly known as North Yemen, to distinguish it from South Yemen (former **Aden** Colony and Protectorate), founded this year → 1990, North Yemen and South Yemen merged to form the Republic of Yemen.

Yugoslavia See **Serbia**.

Zambia See **Northern Rhodesia**.

Zanzibar (British protectorate, Africa) → 1963, independent → 1964, merged with Tanganyika to form Tanzania; see **German East Africa**.

Zimbabwe See **Rhodesia**.

BIBLIOGRAPHY

Appiah, Kwame Anthony, and Henry Louis Gates, Jr., eds. *The Dictionary of Global Culture*. New York: Alfred A. Knopf, 1997.

Ash, Russell. *The Top Ten of Everything*. London: Dorling Kindersley, 1994.

Associated Press. *The Wire*. http://wire.ap.org.

Axelrod, Alan, and Charles Phillips. *What Everyone Should Know about the 20th Century: 200 Events that Shaped the World*. Holbrook, Mass.: Adams Media Corporation, 1995.

Benét's Reader's Encyclopedia. 3d ed. New York: Harper & Row, Publishers, 1987.

Blackburn, Simon. *The Oxford Dictionary of Philosophy*. Oxford: Oxford University Press, 1994.

Bowman, John S., ed. *The Cambridge Dictionary of American Biography*. Cambridge: Cambridge University Press, 1995.

Briggs, Asa, ed. *Dictionary of Twentieth-Century World Biography*. Oxford: Oxford University Press, 1993.

Britannica Online. http://www.eb.com.

Brooks, Tim, and Earle Marsh. *The Complete Directory to Prime Time Network TV Shows 1946–Present*. 3d ed. New York: Ballantine Books, 1985.

Brownstone, David, and Irene Franck. *Dictionary of 20th-Century History*. New York: Prentice Hall, 1990.

————. *Timelines of the 20th Century*. Boston: Little, Brown and Company, 1996.

Brunner, Borgna, ed. *The Time Almanac 1999*. Boston: Information Please LLC, 1998.

Carruth, Gorton. *A Chronology of Life and Events in America*. New York: Signet, 1989.

Castleman, Harry, and Walter J. Podrazik. *Harry and Wally's Favorite TV Shows*. New York: Prentice Hall Press, 1989.

Central Intelligence Agency. *The World Factbook 1998*. http://www.odci.gov/cia/publications/factbook.

Chernow, Barbara A., and George A. Vallasi, eds. *The Columbia Encyclopedia*. 5th ed. New York: Columbia University Press, 1993.

Chilvers, Ian, and Harold Osborne, eds. *The Oxford Dictionary of Art*. Oxford: Oxford University Press, 1988.

Cottrell, Philip L., ed. *Events: A Chronicle of the Twentieth Century*. Oxford: Oxford University Press, 1992.

Current Biography 1940–Present (electronic). New York: H. W. Wilson.

Dawidowicz, Lucy S. *The War against the Jews 1933–1945*. New York: Bantam Books, 1976.

Dictionary of 20th-Century World History. Lincolnwood, Ill.: NTC Publishing Group, 1997.

Dolmatch, Theodore B., ed. *Information Please Almanac 1980*. New York: Simon and Schuster, 1979.

Egan, Edward W., et al., eds. *Kings, Rulers and Statesmen*. Rev. ed. New York: Sterling Publishing Company, 1976.

Facts on File Weekly World News Digest. New York: Facts on File News Services.

Fink, Gary M. *Labor Unions*. Westport, Conn: Greenwood Press, 1977.

Foner, Eric, and John A. Garraty, eds. *The Reader's Companion to American History*. Boston: Houghton Mifflin Company, 1991.

Goldstein, Erik. *Wars and Peace Treaties 1816–1991*. London: Routledge, 1992.

Grun, Bernard. *The Timetables of History*. Updated ed. New York: Touchstone, 1979.

Hardy, Phil, and Dave Laing. *The Faber Companion to 20th-Century Popular Music*. London: Faber and Faber, 1992.

Hartnoll, Phyllis, ed. *The Oxford Companion to the Theatre*. 4th ed. Oxford: Oxford University Press, 1993.

Information Please Almanac Atlas & Yearbook 1990. 43d ed. Boston: Houghton Mifflin Company, 1990.

Information Please Almanac Atlas & Yearbook 1993. 46th ed. Boston: Houghton Mifflin Company, 1993.

Information Please Almanac Atlas & Yearbook 1995. 48th ed. Boston: Houghton Mifflin Company, 1995.

Internet Movie Database. http://www.imdb.com.

Johnson, Otto, ed., *Information Please Almanac Atlas & Yearbook 1997*. 50th ed. Boston: Houghton Mifflin Company, 1997.

Kane, Joseph Nathan. *Facts About the Presidents*. 6th ed. New York: H.W. Wilson Company, 1993.

Katz, Ephraim. *The Film Encyclopedia*. 3d ed. New York: HarperPerennial, 1998.

Kennedy, Paul. *The Rise and Fall of the Great Powers*. New York: Random House, 1987.

Kohn, George C. *Dictionary of Wars*. New York: Anchor Books, 1986.

Lentz, Harris M., III. *Heads of States and Governments*. Jefferson, N.C.: McFarland & Company, 1994.

Levy, Judith S., and Agnes Greenhall with the Reference Staff of Columbia University Press. *The Concise Columbia Encyclopedia*. New York: Avon Books, 1983.

Mabunda, L. Mpho, ed. *The African-American Almanac*. 7th ed. Detroit: Gale, 1997

Maltin, Leonard, ed. *Leonard Maltin's Movie and Video Guide, 1996 Edition*. New York: Signet, 1995.

Microsoft Encarta 97 Encyclopedia (electronic). Microsoft Corporation, 1993–96.

The New York Public Library Desk Reference. 3d ed. New York: Macmillan, 1998.

The New York Times. Print and Internet versions. http://www.nyt.com.

Ochoa, George, and Melinda Corey. *The Wilson Chronology of the Arts*. New York: H.W. Wilson Company, 1998.

———. *The Wilson Chronology of Ideas*. New York: H.W. Wilson Company, 1998.

———. *The Wilson Chronology of Science and Technology*. New York: H.W. Wilson Company, 1997.

Ousby, Ian, ed. *The Cambridge Guide to Literature in English*. Cambridge: Cambridge University Press, 1991.

Overy, Richard, ed. *The Times Atlas of the 20th Century*. London: Times Books, 1996.

Palmowski, Jan. *A Dictionary of Twentieth-Century World History*. Oxford: Oxford University Press, 1997.

Perkins, George, Barbara Perkins, and Phillip Leininger, eds. *Benét's Reader's Encyclopedia of American Literature*. New York: Harper Collins Publishers, 1991.

Rand McNally World Atlas. 1970 ed. Chicago: Rand McNally & Company, 1968.

Roberts, J. M. *The Penguin History of the World*. New ed. London: Penguin Books, 1995.

Seager, Joni, and Ann Olson. *Women in the World: An International Atlas*. New York: Touchstone Books, 1986.

Stern, Jane, and Michael Stern. *Jane and Michael Stern's Encyclopedia of Pop Culture*. New York: HarperPerennial, 1992.

Townson, Duncan. *The New Penguin Dictionary of Modern History 1789–1945*. London: Penguin Books, 1994.

Trager, James. *The People's Chronology*. New York: Henry Holt and Company, 1992.

Tuleja, Tad. *The New York Public Library Book of Popular Americana*. New York: Macmillan, 1994.

Variety.com. http://www.variety.com.

Webster's New Biographical Dictionary. Springfield, Mass.: Merriam-Webster Inc., 1988.

Wetterau, Bruce. *Macmillan Concise Dictionary of World History*. New York: Macmillan, 1983.

The World Almanac and Book of Facts 1931. New York: New York World, 1931.

The World Almanac and Book of Facts 1961. New York: New York World-Telegram, 1961.

The World Almanac and Book of Facts 1962-1963. New York: New York World-Telegram and The Sun, 1962–63.

The World Almanac and Book of Facts 1976-1981. New York: Newspaper Enterprise Association, 1976–81.

The World Almanac and Book of Facts 1979. New York: Newspaper Enterprise Association, 1978.

The World Almanac and Book of Facts 1981. New York: Newspaper Enterprise Association, 1980.

The World Almanac and Book of Facts 1992. New York: World Almanac, 1991.

The World Almanac and Book of Facts 1998. New York: World Almanac Books, 1997.

The World Almanac and Book of Facts 2001. New York: World Almanac Books, 2001.

The World Almanac and Encyclopedia 1900–1902. New York: Press Publishing Company/New York World., 1900–1902.

Wright, John W., ed., with editors and reporters of *The New York Times*. *The New York Times 1998 Almanac*. New York: Penguin Reference Books, 1997.

———. *The New York Times 2000 Almanac*. New York: Penguin Reference Books, 1999.

INDEX

Allen, Woody, 190, 195, 213, **371**
Allenby, Edmund, 38
Allende Gossens, Salvador, **371,**
    474
Allende, Isabel, 211
Allende, Salvador, 173,180, 575,
    576
Allers, Roger, 246
Alley, Alphonse, 546
Allied Powers (Allies), **268–69,**
    273, 275, 278, 283, 287, 311,
    329, 330–31, 334, 336, 343,
    348, 350, 357, 359–66, 374,
    382, 393, 395, 406, 410, 423,
    424, 434, 449, 456, 459, 460,
    462, 473, 474, 483, 484, 495
Allimadi, Erifasi Otemi, 838
All-India Congress Party, 78, 413
All-India Muslim League, 15
All-Military Revolutionary Coun-
    cil, 157
Allon, Yigal, 676
All-Star Game (baseball), 79
Ally McBeal, 243
Almaden to Zem Zem, 112
Almayer's Folly, 395
Almodóvar, Pedro, 224, 249
Along This Way, 434
Alpha Beta Food Market, 29
alpha particles, 16
Alphaville, 161
Alphonso XIII, King of Spain,
    803, 804
ALS, 101
Alsace-Lorraine, **269**
Altair, 186
Altamarino, Luis, 576
alternative medicine, 316
Alternative Rock, 226
Alternative Service Book, 200
Althusser, Louis, 161
Altman, Robert, 173, 184, 229,
    319
aluminum cans, 151, 156
Alvarez, Luis W., 150, 230
Alvear, Marcelo Torcuato de, 526
Alvin, 191
"Always," 380
Alzheimer, Alois, 27
Alzheimer's Disease, 242
"Am I Blue," 388
Amadeus, 195, 208
Amado, Jorge, 163, 312, 554
Amadou, Boubacar Cissé, 749
Amadou, Hama, 749
Amahl and the Night Visitors, 456
Amana Refrigeration Company,
    168
Amarcord, 181
Amaru II, Tupac, 349
Amato, Giuliano, 679

Amazonas, 504
Ambassadors, The, 8, 433
Ambedkar, Bhimrao Ramji, 57
Amblin Entertainment, 494
Ambulocetus natans, 235
Amédée, 432
Amen Corner, The, 376
amendments, 31, 43, 46, 50, 78,
    88, 119, 125, 160, 167, 176
America's Cup (yachting), 82, 208
American Ballet Theatre, 287,
    376, 377
American Beauty, 71, 249
American Buffalo, 190
"American Century," 99
American Civil Liberties Union,
    370, 554
American Dance Theater, 287
American Daughter, An, 243
American Earthquake, 509
American Expeditionary Force,
    269, 473
American Federation of Labor
    (AFL), 137, 265–66, 310, 418
American Foundation for the
    Blind, 437
American Gothic, 69
American Graffiti, 448
American Hunger, 511
American in Paris, An, 124, 416,
    437
American Institute of Public
    Opinion, 413
American Interior, 79
American Language, The, 42, 455
American Magazine, 495
American Mercury, 455, 455
American Museum of Natural
    History, 455
American Muslim Mission, 276
American Neutrality Act, The, 83
American Pastoral, 485
American Photographs, 408
*American Power and the New
    Mandarins,* 392
American Psychiatric Association,
    128
American Red Cross, The, 101
American Renaissance, 135
American School of Design, 458
American Society of Composers,
    Authors, and Publishers
    (ASCAP), 34
American Songbag, The, 487
See American Telephone and
    Telegraph, 57, 205, 206
American Tragedy, An, 58, 403
American Way of Death, The, 157
Americans, The, 144
Amerika, 63
Ames, Rosario, 236

Amézaga, Juan José, 852
Amin Dada, Idi, 176, 196, **371,**
    466–67, 837, 838
Amin, Hafizullah, 515, 516, 517
Amin, Muhammad VIII El-, 831
Amin, Nurul, 757
amino acids, 123, 174
Amis, Martin, 213, 243, 371
Amis, Sir Kingsley, 131, 213, 312,
    371, 844
Amityville, 175
Ammar, Tahar Ben, 831
Amnesty International, 153
Amoco Cadiz, 194
Amores, 443
ampere, 21
Ampex Corporation, The, 139
Amritsar massacre, 414
Amtrak, 176
Amundsen, Roald, 9, 27
Amy and Isabelle, 249
amyotrophic lateral sclerosis, 233
An Unfinished Woman, 425
An Wang, 118, 126
Anaconda, 478
Analysis of Mind, The, 47
analytical psychology, 436
Analyze This, 249
Ananda Mahidol, 826
anaphylaxis, 7
anarchism, **269,** 343
Anarchy, State, and Utopia, 182
Anastasia, 379
Anatomy of Criticism, 413
anatomy, 121
Anchluss, The, 90
And I Still Rise, 372
And Quiet Flows the Don, 65, 79,
    491
Anders, William A., 170
Anderson, Carl D., 75, 89
Anderson, Gil, 36
Anderson, Laurie, 198
Anderson, Marian, **371**
Anderson, Maxwell, 82, 194, 507
Anderson, Sherwood, 42, 74, 77,
    371–72, 409
Andersonville, 135
Andino, Tiburcio Carías, 654
Andom, Aman Michael, 619
Andorra, **521–22**
Andrada, Auro Soares de Moura,
    556
Andrade, José María Reina, 646
Andranarivo, Tantely, 714
Andreotti, Giulio, 679
Andretti, Mario, **372**
Andrew, Prince, 407
Andrewes, C., 78
Andrews, Julie, **372**
Andrews, Roy Chapman, 51–52

E

Eagle or Sun, 471
Eagles, The, 177
Eagleton, Terry, 206
Eanes, António Dos Santos
    Ramalho, 772
Earhart, Amelia, 66, 76, **405**
Early Spring, 469
Early Sunday, 69
Early Sunday Morning, 429
Earrings of Madame De, The, 468
Earth, The, 69
Earth Day, 174, 292
Earth Summit, 230
earthquake, 9, 13, 16, 21, 46, 54,
    76, 121, 128, 156, 158, 165,
    174, 178, 186, 189, 212, 220,
    223, 225, 233, 236, 239, 252
East Germany, 275
    military, 331
    politics, 130, 152, 178, 222,
        340, 353
    See also Germany
East of Eden, 126, 399, 496
East Pakistan, 175, 303. *See also*
    Bangladesh
"Easter 1916," 47
Easter Parade, 374, 415
Easter Rebellion, 337, 395, 401
Easter Rising, **291**
Easter Uprising, 36
Eastern Orthodox Church, 163
Easthope, Anthony, 226
Eastman Kodak Co., 2, 109
Easton, David, 129
Eastwood, Clint, 229, **405**
Easy Rider, 171, 410
Eat, 505
Eat Drink Man Woman, 234
Ebert, Friedrich, 634, 636
Ebola, 189, 239
Ecce Homo, 89
Ecevit, Bulent, 193, 834
Echandi Jiménez, Mario, 591
Echandía, Dario, 584
Echaurren, Federico Errázuriz,
    576
Echegoyen, Martín R., 852
Echevarría, Miguel Angel
    Rodríguez, 592
Echevarria Alvarez, Luís, 188,
    727
Echo, the, 128
echolocation, 150
Eckert, J. Presper, Jr., 111
Eco, Umberto, 169, 198
ecological niche, concept of, 141
*Economic Consequences of the
    Peace, The,* 43, 438
economic sanctions, 227

economics, 26, 31, 40, 43, 53, 71,
    77, 83, 107, 111, 117, 129, 143,
    149, 201, 217, 224, 234, 238,
    240, 241, 314–15
*Economics of Imperfect Competi-
    tion, The,* 77
Economy Act, 323
ecosystem, 197
Écrits, 164
Ecuador, 4, **606–9**
    military, 109, 359–66
    politics, 83, 127, 196, 327
    society, 121
Ed Sullivan Show, 117
Eddington, Arthur, 33, 46, 54, 93
Eden, Anthony, 91, 136
Eden, Nils, 812
Eden, Sir Anthony, first earl of
    Avon, **405,** 843, 845
Ederle, Gertrude, 62
Edin, Kathryn, 243
Education of Henry Adams, The,
    40
education, **17,** 36, 58, 62, 80, 90,
    93, 109, 169, 207, 232, 293
Educational Acts of 1902 and
    1903, 506
Edward VII, King of England, 4,
    24, 86, **405,** 416, 844
Edward VIII, King of England,
    265, 376, **405,** 416, 842, 844
Edward, Prince, 407
Edwards, Blake, 159
Edwards, Robert, 194
EEC. *See* European Economic
    Community
Effi Briest, 181
Efi, Taisi Tupuola, 786
Egal, Mohammed Ibrahim, 799
Eggerz, Sigurdur, 659
Ego and the Id, The, 53
Egoyan, Atom, 234
Egypt, 273, 486, **609–12**
    military, 36, 99, 112, 138,
        270, 299–300, 338, 342,
        359–67
    politics, 10, 51, 53, 65, 72,
        83, 105, 110, 127, 132,
        135, 143, 185, 191, 193,
        196, 202, 238, 270, 279,
        296, 321, 321, 328
    science and technology, 52,
        133
    society, 245, 252
Ehrenburg, Ilya, 99
Ehrlich, Paul, 25
Eichmann, Adolf, 150, **406**
*Eichmann in Jerusalem: A Report
    on the Banality of Evil,* 157,
    373
Eiffel Tower, The, 23

Eight Men, 511
Eighteen Poems, 500
Eightfold Way, 153
Einaudi, Luigi, 678
Einstein, Albert, 13, 18, 21, 37,
    56, 59, 68, 78, 80, 314, 332,
    333–34, **406,** 636, 637.
Einstein on the Beach, 187, 417
Einstein's Monsters, 213
Eisenhower, Dwight D., 103,
    107, 127, 128, 130, 133, 136,
    138, 141, 287, 289, 290, 334,
    349, 404, **406,** 439, 465, 496,
    505, 847, 850
Eisenhower Doctrine, 141, 404
Eisenstein, Sergey Mikhailovich,
    57, 65, 67, 90, 105, 318, **406**
Ekman, Carl Gustav, 813
El Aleph, 382
El Cid, 151
El Mar y tú: Otros poemas, 386
El Salón México, 396
El Salvador, **612–14**
    military, 14, 195, 199, 338,
        359–66
    politics, 150, 199, 327
Elastica, 237
Elbedgdorj, Tsakhiagiin, 732
Elchibey, Abulfaz Ali, 534
Eldjárn, Kristján, 659
Eldredge, Niles, 178
electric power, 87
electrical engineer, 10
electricity, 125
electromagnetic radiation, 66
electron microscope, 88, 97, 111
Electronic Data Systems, 472
electronic mail, 178, 306
electroshock therapy, 88
electroweak theory, 170
Elektra, 22, 497
*Elementary Forms of Religious
    Life,* 28, 404
*Elementary Structures of Kin-
    ship,* 120, 445
Elements IV, 206
Elephant Célébes, The, 47
Elephant Man, The, 429
elephant, African, 223
Elgar, Edward, 1, 4, 14, 36, **406–
    7**
Eli Lilly, 205
Eliade, Mircea, **407**
Elías, Jorge Serrano, 646, 647
Elias, Ricardo Leonicio, 766
Eliécer, Jorge, 582
Eliot, Charles William, **407**
Eliot, T. S., 37, 51, 69, 77, 82,
    85, 101, 104, 312, 317, **407,**
    477
Elizabeth, 246